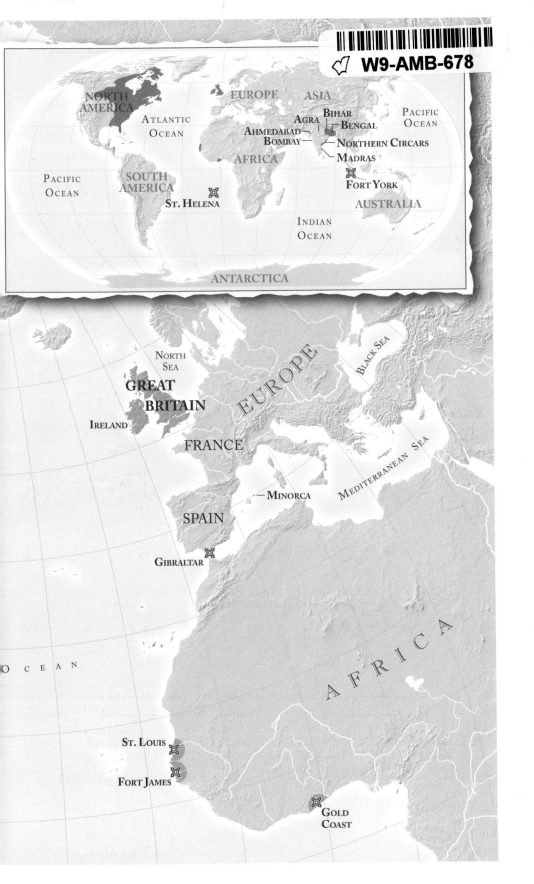

NORTH
AMERICA

EUROPE   ASIA

ATLANTIC
OCEAN

PACIFIC
OCEAN

BIHAR
AGRA
AHMEDABAD — BENGAL
BOMBAY
NORTHERN CIRCARS
MADRAS

AFRICA

PACIFIC
OCEAN

SOUTH
AMERICA

ST. HELENA

FORT YORK

AUSTRALIA

INDIAN
OCEAN

ANTARCTICA

NORTH
SEA

EUROPE

BLACK SEA

GREAT
BRITAIN

IRELAND

FRANCE

MEDITERRANEAN SEA

MINORCA

SPAIN

GIBRALTAR

AFRICA

OCEAN

ST. LOUIS

FORT JAMES

GOLD
COAST

The British
Are Coming

ALSO BY RICK ATKINSON

The Long Gray Line

Crusade

An Army at Dawn

In the Company of Soldiers

The Day of Battle

The Guns at Last Light

The British Are Coming

The British Are Coming

THE WAR FOR AMERICA, LEXINGTON TO PRINCETON, 1775–1777

VOLUME ONE
OF THE REVOLUTION TRILOGY

Rick Atkinson

HENRY HOLT AND COMPANY

NEW YORK

Henry Holt and Company
Publishers since 1866
175 Fifth Avenue
New York, New York 10010
www.henryholt.com

Henry Holt® and ⬚® are registered trademarks of Macmillan Publishing Group, LLC.

Library of Congress Cataloging-in-Publication Data

Names: Atkinson, Rick, author.
Title: The British are coming : the war for America, Lexington to Princeton,
1775–1777 / Rick Atkinson.
Description: First edition. | New York : Henry Holt and Company, [2019] | Series: Revolution trilogy ;
volume 1 | Includes bibliographical references and index.
Identifiers: LCCN 2018029510 | ISBN 9781627790437 (hardcover)
Subjects: LCSH: United States—History—Revolution, 1775–1783—Campaigns.
Classification: LCC E230 .A84 2018 | DDC 973.3—dc23
LC record available at https://lccn.loc.gov/2018029510

Our books may be purchased in bulk for promotional, educational, or business use. Please contact
your local bookseller or the Macmillan Corporate and Premium Sales Department at (800) 221-7945,
extension 5442, or by e-mail at MacmillanSpecialMarkets@macmillan.com.

First Edition 2019

Maps © Gene Thorp

Designed by Meryl Sussman Levavi

Printed in the United States of America

1   3   5   7   9   10   8   6   4   2

To Jane, for forty years

The hour is fast approaching on which the honor and success of this army and the safety of our bleeding country depend. Remember, officers and soldiers, that you are freemen, fighting for the blessings of liberty.

—George Washington, General Orders, August 23, 1776

Contents

LIST OF MAPS   xiii

MAP LEGEND   xiv

LIST OF ILLUSTRATIONS   xv

PROLOGUE, *England, June 1773–March 1775*   1
    1. Inspecting the Fleet
    2. Avenging the Tea
    3. Preparing for War

Part One

1. GOD HIMSELF OUR CAPTAIN   35
    Boston, March 6–April 17, 1775

2. MEN CAME DOWN FROM THE CLOUDS   55
    Lexington and Concord, April 18–19, 1775

3. I WISH THIS CURSED PLACE WAS BURNED   83
    Boston and Charlestown, May–June 1775

4. WHAT SHALL WE SAY OF HUMAN NATURE?   116
    Cambridge Camp, July–October 1775

5. I SHALL TRY TO RETARD THE EVIL HOUR   141
    Into Canada, October–November 1775

6. AMERICA IS AN UGLY JOB   164
    London, October–November 1775

7. THEY FOUGHT, BLED, AND DIED LIKE ENGLISHMEN   182
    Norfolk, Virginia, December 1775

8. THE PATHS OF GLORY   195
    Quebec, December 3, 1775–January 1, 1776

Part Two

9. THE WAYS OF HEAVEN ARE DARK AND INTRICATE   219
    Boston, January–February 1776

10. THE WHIPPING SNAKE   241
    *Cork, Ireland, and Moore's Creek, North Carolina,
    January–March 1776*

11. CITY OF OUR SOLEMNITIES   257
    Boston, March 1776

12. A STRANGE REVERSE OF FORTUNE   273
    Quebec, April–June 1776

13. SURROUNDED BY ENEMIES, OPEN AND CONCEALED   297
    New York, June 1776

14. A DOG IN A DANCING SCHOOL   323
    Charleston, South Carolina, June 1776

15. A FIGHT AMONG WOLVES   348
    New York, July–August 1776

16. A SENTIMENTAL MANNER OF MAKING WAR   380
    New York, September 1776

Part Three

17. MASTER OF THE LAKES   405
    Lake Champlain, October 1776

18. THE RETROGRADE MOTION OF THINGS   431
    New York, October–November 1776

19. A QUAKER IN PARIS   465
    France, November–December 1776

20. FIRE-AND-SWORD MEN   485
    New Jersey, December 1776

21. THE SMILES OF PROVIDENCE   511
    Trenton, December 24–26, 1776

22. THE DAY IS OUR OWN   530
    Trenton and Princeton, January 1777

EPILOGUE, *England and America, 1777*   555

AUTHOR'S NOTE   565

NOTES   567

SOURCES   703

ACKNOWLEDGMENTS   747

INDEX   753

Maps

1. The British Empire, *1775*   ENDPAPERS

2. The North American Theater, *April 1775–January 1777*   32

3. Boston, *Spring 1775*   41

4. March to Concord, *April 18–19, 1775*   56

5. British Retreat from Concord, *April 19, 1775*   65

6. Bunker Hill, *June 17, 1775*   91

7. Invasion of Canada, *September–November 1775*   140

8. Great Bridge and the Burning of Norfolk,
   December 1775–January 1776   187

9. Disaster at Quebec, *December 31, 1775*   201

10. Siege of Boston, *Winter 1775–1776*   218

11. Skirmish at Moore's Creek Bridge, *February 27, 1776*   249

12. Retreat from Canada, *May–June 1776*   272

13. Greater New York, *Summer 1776*   298

14. New York City, *Summer 1776*   303

15. Battle of Sullivan's Island, *June 28, 1776*   322

16. Battle of Long Island, *August 22–30, 1776*   353

17. Battle of Kip's Bay and Harlem Heights, *September 15–16, 1776*   391

18. Battle for Lake Champlain, *October 1776*   404

19. Battle for Westchester County, *October 1776*   430

20. Attacks on Fort Washington and Fort Lee,
    November 16–20, 1776   449

21. Franklin in France, *December 1776*   464

22. Retreat Across New Jersey, *November–December 1776*   484

23. First Battle of Trenton, *December 25–26, 1776*   515

24. Second Battle of Trenton and Battle of Princeton,
    January 2–3, 1777   535

Legend

	AMERICAN		BRITISH
	➡️	Movement	⬅️
	➡️	Advance	⬅️
	⇢	Retreat	⇠
	▬▬	Infantry	▬▬
	••••••	Skirmish line	••••••
	═══	Earthworks/ fortifications	───
	⚜	Artillery	⚜
	🚢	Transport ships	🚢
	⛵	Warships	⛵

FEATURES

○	City/Town	═══	Road
◉	Capital	───	River
🏠	House	─ ─ ─	Boundary
🏚	Tavern	─ ─ ─	Fence
⛪	Church	×—×—	Rail fence
🏛	Hall/Meeting house/ Prison/Theater/ College	▧▧▧	Stone wall
🏭	Mill		Body of water
🏰	Fort		Woods
† ✡	Cemetery		Marsh
⊔	Bridge		Mudflat
⌣	Pass		Beach
▢	Other feature		Terrain
✳	Clash	⛰	Highlighted terrain
✕	Previous engagement		
ꙮ	Burned		

A Union Jack appears on some maps to signify British positions; no comparable American national flag was yet in wide use early in the war.

Boundaries and geographic labels generally reflect British cartographic surveys from the mid-eighteenth-century. Borders often were disputed.

Illustrations

FIRST INSERT

1. Johan Joseph Zoffany, *George III*, oil on canvas, 1771. (Royal Collection Trust / © Her Majesty Queen Elizabeth II 2018)
2. John Clevely, *George III Reviewing the Fleet at Spithead, 22 June 1773*, watercolor, 1773. (© National Maritime Museum, Greenwich, London)
3. John Russell, *Frederick North, 2nd Earl of Guilford*, oil on canvas, c. 1765-68. (Private collection/Bridgeman Images)
4. Nathaniel Hone I, *William Legge (1731–1801), Second Earl of Dartmouth*, oil on canvas, 1777. (Courtesy of Hood Museum of Art, Dartmouth College. Gift of Earle W. Newton, P.960.100)
5. Jan Josef Horemans II, *Tea Time*, oil on canvas, second half of eighteenth century.
6. John Collet, *Scene in a London Street*, oil on canvas, 1770. (Courtesy Yale Center for British Art, Paul Mellon Collection)
7. Christian Schussele, *Franklin before the Lords' Council, Whitehall Chapel, London, 1774*, engraved by Robert Whitechurch, c. 1859. (Courtesy Library of Congress)
8. Rudolf Ackermann et al, House of Commons from *Microcosm of London*, 1808–10. (Courtesy British Library)
9. Johan Joseph Zoffany, *George III, Queen Charlotte, and Their Six Eldest Children*, oil on canvas, 1770. (Royal Collection Trust / © Her Majesty Queen Elizabeth II 2018)
10. Gold State Coach, gilded and painted wood, leather, 1762. (Photograph, Royal Collection Trust / © Her Majesty Queen Elizabeth II 2018)
11. Thomas Bowles, *A View of St. James's Palace Pall Mall*, engraving, 1771. (Courtesy Yale Center for British Art, Paul Mellon Collection)
12. John Singleton Copley, *General Thomas Gage*, oil on canvas, c. 1768. (Courtesy Yale Center for British Art, Paul Mellon Collection)
13. John Singleton Copley, *Mrs. Thomas Gage*, oil on canvas, 1771. (Putnam Foundation, Timken Museum of Art)
14. John Trumbull, *Benjamin Franklin*, oil on wood, 1778. (Courtesy Yale University Art Gallery)
15. John Singleton Copley, *Paul Revere*, oil on canvas, 1768. (Photograph © Museum of Fine Arts, Boston)
16. John Singleton Copley, *Joseph Warren*, (unfinished), oil on canvas, c. 1772. (Courtesy National Park Service, Adams National Historical Park)
17. Thomas Sully, after Charles Willson Peale. *Major General Artemas Ward*, oil on canvas, c. 1830-40. (Collection of the Massachusetts Historical Society)
18. Dominique C. Fabronius, *Maj. Gen. Israel Putnam. "He dared to lead where any dared to follow,"* lithograph, c. 1864. (Courtesy Library of Congress)

19. *John Stark*, date unknown. (Courtesy Print Collection, New York Public Library)

20. Gilbert Stuart, *Hugh Percy, Second Duke of Northumberland*, oil on canvas, c. 1788. (Courtesy High Museum of Art, Atlanta)

21. Amos Doolittle, *A View of the Town of Concord*, plate II, engraving, Dec. 1775, reprint by Charles E. Goodspeed, 1903.

22. Henry A. Thomas, *The Battle at Bunker's Hill*, lithograph, c. 1875. (Courtesy Library of Congress)

23. Charles Willson Peale, *George Washington*, oil on canvas, 1776. (Courtesy Brooklyn Museum, Dick S. Ramsay Fund)

24. Charles Peale Polk, copy after Charles Willson Peale, *Henry Knox*, oil on canvas, after 1783. (Courtesy National Portrait Gallery, Smithsonian Institution)

25. *Washington's Headquarters, Cambridge*, date unknown. (Courtesy Print Collection, New York Public Library)

26. Nathaniel Hone, *George Sackville Germain, 1st Viscount Sackville*, oval portrait, 1760. (© National Portrait Gallery, London)

27. Joshua Reynolds, *John Murray, 4th Earl of Dunmore*, oil on canvas, 1765. (National Galleries Scotland)

28. H. B. Hall after John Trumbull, *Benedict Arnold*, engraving, published after 1879. (Courtesy National Archives, 532921)

29. *Ph. Schuyler*, date unknown. (Courtesy Print Collection, New York Public Library)

30. Alonzo Chappel, *Richd. Montgomery*, engraving by George R. Hall, 1881. (Courtesy Print Collection, New York Public Library)

31. Eyving H. de Dirkine Holmfield, *Guy Carleton*, oil on canvas, c. 1895. (© Château Ramezay, Historic Site and Museum of Montréal)

32. *Quebec in 1775*, date unknown. (Courtesy Print Collection, New York Public Library)

33. John Trumbull, *The Death of General Montgomery in the Attack on Quebec, December 31, 1775*, oil on canvas, 1786. (Courtesy Yale University Art Gallery)

34. *Château Ramezay*, artist and date unknown. (© Château Ramezay, Historic Site and Museum of Montréal)

35. James Peale, *Horatio Gates*, oil on canvas, copy after Charles Willson Peale, 1782. (Courtesy National Portrait Gallery, Smithsonian Institution)

36. *Gen. Sir William Howe*, date unknown. (Courtesy Print Collection, New York Public Library)

37. *John Burgoyne*, date unknown. (Courtesy National Archives, 532920)

38. Michael Angelo Wageman, *Genl. Howe Evacuating Boston*, engraving by John Godfrey, 1861. (Courtesy Anne S. K. Brown Military Collection, Brown University Library)

SECOND INSERT

39. John Singleton Copley, *Admiral Richard Howe, 1st Earl Howe*, oil on canvas, 1794. (© National Maritime Museum, Greenwich, London, Caird Collection)

40. Archibald Robertson, *View of the Narrows between Long Island & Staten Island with our fleet at anchor, etc.*, ink and wash on paper, 1776. (Courtesy New York Public Library, Spencer Collection)

41. Allan Ramsay, *Flora Macdonald*, oil on canvas, 1749. (Ashmolean Museum of Art and Archeology, University of Oxford)

42. *Sir Henry Clinton*, date unknown. (Courtesy Print Collection, New York Public Library)

43. *Gen. Lord Cornwallis*, date unknown. (Courtesy Print Collection, New York Public Library)

44. *Major Gen.l Charles Lee*, date unknown. (Courtesy Print Collection, New York Public Library)

45. Charles Willson Peale, *William Moultrie*, oil on canvas, 1782. (National Portrait Gallery, Smithsonian Institution. Transfer from the National Gallery of Art, gift of the A. W. Mellon Educational and Charitable Trust, 1942)

46. Slave auction notice, 1760. ("The Atlantic Slave Trade and Slave Life in the Americas," website for Virginia Foundation for the Humanities. Original source: Library of Congress, Prints and Photographs Division, LC-USZ62-10293)

47. Thomas Leitch, *A view of Charles-Town, the capital of South Carolina*, engraved by Samuel Smith, 1776. (Courtesy Library of Congress)

48. Nicholas Pocock, *A View of the Attack Made by the British Fleet under the Command of Sir Peter Parker*, etc., oil on canvas, 1783. (South Caroliniana Library, University of South Carolina)

49. Charles Édouard Armand-Dumaresq, *The Declaration of Independence of the United States of America, July 4, 1776*, oil on canvas, c. 1873.

50. Laurent Dabos, *Thomas Paine*, oil on canvas, c. 1792. (Courtesy National Portrait Gallery, Smithsonian Institution)

51. James Wallace and Dominic Serres, *The* Phoenix *and the* Rose *engaged by the enemy's fire ships and galleys on the 16 Augst. 1776*, engraving, 1778. (Courtesy Print Collection, New York Public Library)

52. Alonzo Chappel, *Battle of Long Island*, oil on canvas, 1858. (Brooklyn Historical Society)

53. *Bushnell's American Turtle*, engraving, 1881. (Courtesy Library of Congress)

54. Thomas Mitchell, *Forcing a passage of the Hudson River, 9 October 1776*, oil on canvas, date unknown, copy of original by Dominic Serres the Elder. (© National Maritime Museum, Greenwich, London)

55. Robert Cleveley, *The British landing at Kip's Bay, New York Island, 15 September 1776*, pen and ink, black and watercolor, 1777. (© National Maritime Museum, Greenwich, London)

56. *The Battle of Harlem Heights, September 16, 1776*, date unknown. (Courtesy Print Collection, New York Public Library)

57. Charles Willson Peale, *Nathanael Greene*, watercolor on ivory, 1778. (Courtesy Metropolitan Museum of Art, bequest of Charles Allen Munn, 1924)

58. Luther G. Hayward, *Colonel Roger Morris' House*, 1854. (© The Morris-Jumel Mansion, gift of Lydia Malbin)

59. John Trumbull, *General John Glover*, graphite, 1794. (Courtesy Yale University Art Gallery)

60. *William Glanville Evelyn*, frontispiece portrait, artist unknown, 1775. (From G. D. Scull, ed., *Memoirs and Letters of Captain W. Glanville Evelyn*, 1879)

61. Thomas Davies, *The landing of the British forces in the Jerseys on the 20th of November 1776*, etc., watercolor, 1776. (Courtesy Print Collection, New York Public Library)

62. Jean-Marc Nattier, *Portrait of Pierre-Augustin Caron de Beaumarchais*, oil on canvas, 1755. (ART Collection/ Alamy Stock Photo)

63. Jean-Baptiste Raguenet, *A View of Paris from the Pont Neuf*, oil on canvas, 1763. (Courtesy Getty Center, Open Content Program, J. Paul Getty Museum)

64. *Silas Deane*, date unknown. (Courtesy Print Collection, New York Public Library)

65. Joseph Duplessis, *Portrait of Louis XVI, King of France and Navarre*, oil on canvas, c. 1776-78.

66. Antoine-François Callet, *Charles Gravier Comte de Vergennes*, engraving by Vincenzio Vangelisti, c. 1774–89. (Courtesy Library of Congress)

67. Charles Willson Peale, *Dr. Benjamin Rush*, oil on canvas, 1783–86. (Winterthur Museum, gift of Mrs. Julia B. Henry)

68. Thomas Sully, *The Passage of the Delaware*, oil on canvas, 1819. (Photograph © Museum of Fine Arts, Boston; gift of the Owners of the Old Boston Museum)

69. *John Sullivan*, wood engraving, date unknown. (Courtesy Print Collection, New York Public Library)

70. *Brig. Gen. Joseph Reed*, date unknown. (Courtesy Print Collection, New York Public Library)

71. John Trumbull, *The Capture of the Hessians at Trenton, December 26, 1776*, oil on canvas, 1786–1828. (Courtesy Yale University Art Gallery)

72. "Plan of Princeton, Dec. 31, 1776," manuscript map, pen and ink. (Courtesy Library of Congress)

73. *Major Gen. James Grant, Colonel of the 55th Foot*, date unknown. (Courtesy Print Collection, New York Public Library)

74. John Trumbull, *Gen. Hugh Mercer*, copy of an original pencil sketch created in 1791. (Courtesy Print Collection, New York Public Library)

75. John Trumbull, *Death of General Mercer at the Battle of Princeton*, sketch for *The Battle of Princeton*, pen and ink wash, 1786. (Courtesy Battle of Princeton Prints Collection, GC047, Graphic Arts Collection, Department of Rare Books and Special Collections, Princeton University Library)

76. James Peale, *The Battle of Princeton*, oil on canvas, c. 1782. (Princeton University Art Museum/Art Resource, NY)

The British
Are Coming

Prologue

Inspecting the Fleet

At three-thirty a.m. on June 22, 1773, fifteen minutes before sunrise, a royal chaise pulled by four matched horses burst from the gates of Kew Palace, escorted by cavalry outriders in scarlet coats. South they rode, skirting the Thames valley west of London before rattling onto the Surrey downs. Pearly light seeped into the landscape, and the brilliant green of an English summer day—the first full day following the solstice—emerged from the fens and fields. Even at this early hour the roads were crowded, for all England knew that a great review was planned at the royal dockyards in Portsmouth, a four-day celebration of the fleet that a decade before had crushed France and Spain in the Seven Years' War to give rise to the British Empire. An exasperated message to the Admiralty headquarters in London earlier this week had warned of "it being almost impossible to get horses on the road owing to the multitude of people going to Portsmouth." That throng, according to a newspaper account, included "admirals, captains, and honest Jack Tars in abundance . . . courtiers and parasites, placemen and pensioners, pimps and prostitutes, gamblers and pickpockets." Innkeepers on the south coast were said to demand ten guineas a night for a bed.

The king himself, a demon for details, had choreographed this seven-hour journey from Kew, arranging the postilions, footmen, and grooms like chess pieces. He had calculated the distance and duration of each leg along the sixty-three-mile route, writing memoranda in his looping, legible hand, adorned only with a delicate filigree of ink that rose from each final lowercase *d*—as in "God"—to snake back across the paper like a fly fisherman's line. Nine relays of horses waited along the route in places called Ripley and Godalming, but none at Lotheby Manor on the Portsmouth road, perhaps because an ancient English custom required that if a monarch visited Lotheby, the lord of the manor was "to present His Majesty with three whores." Or so the *London Chronicle* claimed.

Bells pealed in welcome as the cavalcade rolled into Hampshire. Country folk stood before their rude cottages, some in farm frocks and red cloaks, some in their Sunday finery, though it was Tuesday. All strained for a glimpse of the man who sat alone with his thoughts in the chaise: George William Frederick, or, as he had been proclaimed officially upon ascending the throne in 1760, "George III, by the grace of God, king of Great Britain, France, and Ireland, defender of the faith, and so forth." (The claim to France was a bit of nostalgia dating to the fourteenth century.) Below Petersfield, the crowds thickened, spilling along the chalky ridges above the roadbed, and when George emerged from his carriage for a five-minute pause at Portsdown Hill, five thousand people bayed their approval while he admired the vista of the harbor below and the sapphire anchorage that stretched across to the Isle of Wight.

Half an hour later, a royal salute of twenty-one guns sounded from Portsea Bridge. Just after ten a.m. the White Boys, local burghers dressed entirely in white, cleared a lane for the king's chaise through the throng at Landport Gate. More salutes greeted him, including a triple discharge from 232 guns on Portsmouth's ramparts in a mighty cannonade heard sixty miles away. When the jubilant crowd pressed close, soldiers from the 20th Regiment prodded them back with bayonets until George urged caution. "My people," he said, "will not hurt me."

Most of his cabinet ministers had traveled from London, along with Privy Council members and a royal household contingent of physicians, surgeons, and apothecaries, who had been advised to bring ample spirits of lavender to calm the jittery. Dense ranks of army and navy officers, along with Portsmouth's better sort, jammed a public levee at the Governor's House in hopes of kissing the king's hand. A prayer that "the fleet may ever prove victorious" was followed by a recitation of "The Wooden Walls of England," a new, four-stanza tribute to the navy: "Hail, happy isle! . . . Spread then thy sails where naval glory calls, / Britain's best bulwarks are her wooden walls."

Then it was off to see those wooden walls. At one-thirty p.m., draped in a crimson boat cloak adorned with an enormous star of the Order of the Garter, George stepped aboard his ten-oar barge for the three-mile trip to Spithead anchorage. A flotilla trailed in his wake, filled to the gunwales with nobility, gentry, and sea dogs in blue and braid; the procession included the venerable *Fubbs*—the word was slang for chubby—a yacht named for a favorite mistress of Charles II's. A gentle June breeze riffled the sea, and in the clear sunshine five hundred vessels large and small could be seen all around: brigs, corvettes, wherries, schooners, frigates, sloops.

Most imposing were twenty ships of the line moored in two facing ranks along five miles of roadstead. Each wore new paint, their bowsprits steeved at a pugnacious tilt of thirty-six degrees above the horizon, their sterns boasting names like *Royal Oak, Centaur, Terrible*, and *Triumph*. Some six thousand crewmen crowded their decks, and as the king drew near, fourteen hundred guns opened in another thunderous salute, salvo upon salvo. At last the cannonade stopped, the great gouts of smoke drifted off, and each vessel hoisted its colors, a bright riot of pendants and banners; four hundred flags fluttered from *Kent* alone. Spectators lined the walls in Portsmouth and along the promenade in adjacent Gosport, where alehouse keepers had erected canvas booths to sell fried sausages and shilling lumps of veal and ham. Now the crowds pressed to the water's edge, delirious with pride, and their roar carried to the king's ear, still ringing from all those guns.

As he braced himself in the rocking barge, he looked the part, this king, all silk and fine brocade, "tall and full of dignity," as one observer recorded, "his countenance florid and good-natured." At thirty-five, George had the round chin and long nose of his German forebears, with fine white teeth and blue eyes that bulged from their orbits. He had been a sickly baby, not expected to survive infancy; now he incessantly touted "air, moderate exercise, and diet," and he could often be found on horseback in pursuit of stag or hare. Not for another fifteen years would he be stricken with the first extended symptoms—perhaps caused by porphyria, a hereditary affliction—that included abdominal pain, neuritis, incoherence, paranoia, and delirium. More attacks followed later in his life, along with the madness that wrecked his old age.

Unkind and untrue things often were said of him, such as the claim that he could not read until age eleven; in fact, at a much younger age he could read and write in both English and German. There was no denying that he was an awkwardly shy boy, "silent, modest, and easily abashed," as a courtier observed. In 1758 a tutor described the prince at twenty, noting traits that would bear more than a passing resemblance to the adult king: "He has rather too much attention to the sins of his neighbor. . . . He has great command of his passions, and will seldom do wrong except when he mistakes wrong for right." Still, in the past decade or so he had grown into an admirable man of parts—diligent, dutiful, habitually moderate, peevish but rarely bellicose. Not easily duped, he had what one duchess called "a wonderful way of knowing what is going forward." He was frugal in an age of excess, pious at a time of impiety. His interests ranged from physics and theology to horticulture and astronomy—he had built the Royal Observatory at Richmond to view the transit of Venus in 1769—and his tastes ran from high to low: Handel, Shakespeare, silly farces that brought his hearty guffaw ringing from the royal box. His sixty-five thousand books would stock the British national library.

Even his idiosyncrasies could be endearing. Until blindness overtook him in the early 1800s, George served as his own secretary, meticulously dating his correspondence with both the day of the month and the precise time, to the very minute. He copied out his own recipes for cough syrup (rosemary, rice, vinegar, brown sugar, all "boiled in silver") and insecticide (wormwood, vinegar, lime, swine's fat, quicksilver). He kept critical notes on dramatic actors—"had a formal gravity in his mien, and a piercing eye" or "more manly than elegant, of the middle stature, inclining to corpulency." He would personally decide which English worthies should get the pairs of kangaroos brought home by an expedition to Australia. Increasingly his conversational style inclined to repetitive exclamation: "What! What! What!" or "Sad accident! Sad accident!" His compulsion for detail drew him into debates on the proper placement of straps on Foot Guards uniforms.

Unlike the two German-born Georges who preceded him—the House of Hanover had been tendered the throne at Westminster in 1714, when Britain was desperate for a Protestant monarch—this George was thoroughly English. "Born and educated in this country," he proclaimed, "I glory in the name of Britain." The three requirements of a British king came easily to him: to shun Roman Catholicism, to obey the law, and to acknowledge Parliament, which gave him both an annual income of £800,000 and an army. Under reforms of the last century, he could not rule by edict but, rather, needed the cooperation of his ministers and both houses of Parliament. He saw himself as John Bull, the frock-coated, commonsensical embodiment of this sceptered isle, while acknowledging that "I am apt to despise what I am not accustomed to."

There was the rub. Unkind things were sometimes said of him, and not all were untrue. George disliked disorder, and he loathed disobedience. He had an inflexible attachment to his own prejudices, with, one biographer later wrote, "the pertinacity that marks little minds of all ranks." His "unforgiving piety," in the phrase of a contemporary, caused him to resist political concession and to impute moral deficiencies to his opponents. He bore grudges.

He saw himself as both a moral exemplar and the guardian of British interests—a thankless task, given his belief that he lived in "the wickedest age that ever was seen." Royal duty required that he help the nation avoid profligacy and error. He was no autocrat, but his was the last word; absent strong, countervailing voices from his ministers, his influence would be paramount, particularly with respect to, say, colonial policy.

His obstinacy derived not only from a mulish disposition but from sincere conviction: the empire, so newly congealed, must not melt away. George had long intended to rule as well as reign, and as captain general of Britain's armed forces, he took great pride in reciting the capital ships in his navy, in scribbling endless lists of regiments and army generals, in knowing the strong points of Europe's fortified towns and the soundings of naval ports and how many guns the Royal Artillery deployed in America. He was, after all, defender not only of the faith but of the realm. In recent sittings for portrait painters, he had begun to wear a uniform.

And if his subjects cheered him to the echo, why should they not? Theirs was the greatest, richest empire since Rome. Britain was ascendant, with mighty revolutions—agrarian and industrial—well under way. A majority of all European urban growth in the first half of the century had occurred in England; that proportion was now expanding to nearly three-quarters, with the steam engine patented in 1769 and the spinning jenny a year later. Canals were cut, roads built, highwaymen hanged, coal mined, iron forged. Sheep would double in weight during the century; calf weights tripled. England and Wales now boasted over 140,000 retail shops. A nation of shopkeepers had been born.

War had played no small role. Since the end of the last century, Britain had fought from Flanders and Germany to Iberia and south Asia. Three dynastic, coalition wars against France and her allies, beginning in 1689, ended indecisively. A fourth—the Seven Years' War—began so badly that the sternest measures had been taken aboard the *Monarch* in these very waters. Here on March 14, 1757, Admiral John Byng, convicted by courtmartial of "failing to do his utmost" during a French attack on Minorca, had been escorted in a howling gale to a quarterdeck sprinkled with sawdust to absorb his blood. Sailors hoisted aboard a coffin already inscribed with his name. Dressed in a light gray coat, white breeches, and a white wig, Byng knelt on a cushion and removed his hat. After a pardonable pause, he dropped a handkerchief from his right hand to signal two ranks of marines with raised muskets. They fired. Voltaire famously observed that he died *"pour encourager les autres."*

The others had indeed been encouraged. The nation's fortunes soon reversed. Triumphant Britain massed firepower in her blue-water fleet and organized enough maritime mobility to transport assault troops vast distances, capturing strongholds from Quebec and Havana to Manila in what would also be called the Great War for the Empire. British forces routed the French in the Caribbean, Africa, India, and especially North America, with help from American colonists. "Our bells are worn threadbare with ringing for victories," one happy Briton reported.

Spoils under the Treaty of Paris in 1763 were among the greatest ever won by force of arms. From France, Britain took Canada and half a billion fertile acres between the Appalachian Mountains and the Mississippi River, plus several rich islands in the West Indies and other prizes. Spain ceded Florida and the Gulf Coast. Britain emerged with the most powerful navy in history and the world's largest merchant fleet, some eight thousand sail. The royal dockyards, of which Portsmouth was preeminent, had become both the nation's largest employer and its most sophisticated industrial enterprise.

"There shall be a Christian, universal, and perpetual peace," the treaty had declared, "as well by sea as by land." In time, none of that would hold true. Yet for now, Britain cowed her rivals and dominated Europe's trade with Asia, Africa, and North America. "I felt a completion of happiness," the Scottish diarist James Boswell had recently exclaimed. "I just sat and hugged myself in my own mind." This year another writer, George Macartney, would coin a more dignified phrase, a paean to "this vast empire, on which the sun never sets."

The king had agreed to dine that June afternoon aboard the ninety-gun *Barfleur*, and as he clambered to the weather deck, sailors hoisted his royal standard to the main topmast head. A boatswain tweeted a silver whistle, kettledrums rumbled, the marine guard snapped to attention, and every ship in the fleet loosed another twenty-one-gun salute. George adored his navy, over three hundred warships scattered across the seven seas, and with *Barfleur* cleared for action, he took time to poke about.

More than two thousand mature oaks had been felled to build a ship like this, the biggest, most complex machine in the eighteenth-century world, the steam engine and spinning jenny be damned. The king admired the massive oak balks, the knees chopped from tree forks, the thick planks wider than a big man's handspan, the gun decks painted bright red to lessen the psychological shock of blood spilled in battle. Twenty or more miles of rope had been rigged in a loom of shrouds, ratlines, stays, braces, and halyards. Masts, yards, spars, tops, and crosstrees rose overhead in geometric elegance. Even at anchor this wooden world sang, as timbers pegged and jointed, dovetailed and mortised, emitted creaks, groans, and squeals. Belowdecks, where each sailor got twenty-eight inches of sleeping width for his hammock, the powder monkeys wore felt slippers to avoid creating sparks in the magazine. The smells of tar, hemp, pine pitch, and varnish mingled with the brine of bilgewater and vinegar fumigant and the hog-lard pomade sailors used to grease their queues. All in all, it was the precise odor of empire.

Thirty dining companions joined George around a horseshoe table. The royal cook had lugged the king's plate and silver from St. James's Palace, along with seemingly enough linen to give *Barfleur* a new suit of sails. For nearly three hours they feasted on thirty-one covers, billed as "soups, removes of fish, removes of roasts, pies," then more "roasts, pastry, aspics, blancmanges, and jellies," followed by fruit, ices, and compotes. The libations carted to Portsmouth were no less prodigious: 5,580 bottles of wine and 1,140 bottles of rum, arrack, brandy, beer, and cider.

At six p.m., the assembled guests toasted Queen Charlotte's health, and by custom, after the king left the table, they drank to his health, too. Again aboard his barge, he passed down the double line of ships. Each company gave three cheers and separate gun salutes. When his oarsmen pulled for Portsmouth, the dockyard cannons barked again, joined by ringing bells. Farthing candles stuck in saucers and gallipots illuminated every window in town. George would later declare that he had never had a finer day.

The king was quartered in a quiet, well-aired house within the dock-yards, his bedstead, sheets, and a few sticks of furniture sent from London. That evening he was again alone with his thoughts, except for three aides in adjacent rooms, servants in the garret, and a hundred soldiers of the Foot Guards patrolling outside. An elegant model of the 104-gun *Victory* had been placed in the sitting room for his pleasure.

James Boswell might hug himself in happiness, but uneasy lies the head that wears a crown. George knew very well that victory in war and a decade of empire building brought complications. New territories had to be absorbed and organized, both for defense and for the profit of the mother country. Did London have the wit to manage these vast holdings, scattered across five continents? Britain now owned thirty separate colonies in the New World alone, with almost two thousand slave plantations growing sugarcane in the West Indies. Emigration from the British Isles, higher this year than ever, had become "epidemical amongst the most useful of our people," an official warned; in just fifteen years, 3 percent of Scotland's population and almost as many Irish had bolted for the New World in what one Scot called "America madness." The empire was both a political construct and a business enterprise—colonies existed to enhance imperial grandeur by providing raw materials and buying British goods—so the "disease of wandering," as Dr. Samuel Johnson dubbed this migration, was unnerving. And, of course, the Treaty of Paris had left various European powers aggrieved if not humiliated, with smoldering resentments among the Prussians, the Spanish, the Dutch, and, most of all, the French. After the treaty was signed, Britain would remain bereft of European allies for a quarter century.

Then there was debt: the Great War for the Empire had cost £100 million, much of it borrowed, and the country was still strapped for money. There had been fearful, if exaggerated, whispers of national bankruptcy. With the British debt now approaching a quarter billion pounds, interest payments devoured roughly half of the £12 million collected in yearly tax revenue. Britons were already among Europe's most heavily taxed citizens, with ever-larger excise fees on soap, salt, candles, paper, carriages, male servants, racehorses—often 25 percent or more of an item's value. The cost of this week's extravaganza in Portsmouth—estimated at £22,000—would not help balance the books.

It had seemed only fair that the colonists should help shoulder the burden. A typical American, by Treasury Board calculations, paid no more than sixpence a year in Crown taxes, compared to the average Englishman's twenty-five shillings—a ratio of one to fifty—even as Americans benefited from eradication of the French and Spanish threats, from the protection of trade by the Royal Navy, and from British regiments keeping peace along the Indian frontier at a cost that soon exceeded £400,000 a year. Yet things had gone badly. The Stamp Act, adopted in 1765, taxed paper in the colonies, from playing cards and pamphlets to wills, newspapers, and tax receipts. Americans reacted by terrorizing British revenue officers—stamp agents in the thirteen colonies reportedly collected a total of £45, all of it in Georgia—and by boycotting imports so ferociously that some British factories closed, idling thousands. Repeal of the act in March 1766 triggered drunken revels from Boston to Savannah, with fireworks, much bad celebratory verse, and, in New York, the commissioning of a huge equestrian statue of George III, the "best of kings," tricked up as Marcus Aurelius.

English workers in places like Sheffield and Birmingham also cheered, but the best of kings had doubts. "I am more and more grieved at the accounts in America," he had grumbled in December 1765. "Where this spirit will end is not to be said." Two years later, the government tried again with the Townshend Acts, named for a witty, rambunctious chancellor of the exchequer known as "Champagne Charlie." Import duties on lead, glass, paint, and other commodities provoked another violent American reaction, with British exports to the colonies plummeting by half. To maintain order, in 1768 the government dispatched four regiments to fractious Boston; that, too, turned sour in March 1770, when skittish troops fired into a street mob, killing five. Two soldiers were convicted of manslaughter—their thumbs so branded—and the regiments discreetly decamped from town, including "the Vein Openers," as Bostonians called the 29th Regiment troops involved in "the Massacre." That spring, Britain repealed all Townshend duties except for the trifling tax on tea, left intact to affirm Parliament's fiscal authority.

An edgy calm returned to the colonies, but British moral and political authority had sloughed away, bit by bit. Many Britons now viewed Americans as unruly, ungrateful children in need of caning. Many Americans nurtured an inflated sense of their economic leverage and pined for the traditional policy of "salutary neglect," which for generations had permitted self-sufficiency and autonomy, including governance through local councils and colonial assemblies that had long controlled fiscal matters. Colonists also resented British laws that prohibited them from making hats, woolens, cloth, and other goods that might compete with manufacturers in the mother country. Almost imperceptibly, a quarrel over taxes and filial duty metastasized into a struggle over sovereignty. With no elected delegates in Parliament, the Americans had adopted a phrase heard in Ireland for decades: "no taxation without representation."

George had never traveled beyond England, and in his long life he never would, not to Ireland, to the Continent, not even to Scotland, and certainly not to America. None of his ministers had been to the New World, either. There was much they did not know or understood imperfectly: that the American population, now 2.5 million, was more than doubling every quarter century, an explosive growth unseen in recorded European history and fourfold England's rate; that two-thirds of white colonial men owned land, compared to one-fifth in England; that two-thirds were literate, more than in England; that in most colonies two-thirds could vote, compared to one Englishman in six; that provincial America glowed with Enlightenment aspiration, so that a city like Philadelphia now rivaled Edinburgh for medical education and boasted almost as many booksellers—seventy-seven—as England's top ten provincial towns combined.

Also: that eradication of those French and Spanish threats had liberated Americans from the need for British muscle; that America now made almost 15 percent of the world's crude iron, foreshadowing an industrial strength that would someday dwarf Britain's; that, if lacking ships like

Barfleur, the Americans were fearless seafarers and masters of windship construction, with an intimate knowledge of every inlet, estuary, and shoal from Nova Scotia to Barbados; that nearly a thousand American vessels traded in Britain alone.

And: that unlike the Irish and other subjugated peoples, the Americans were heavily armed. Not only were they nimble with firelocks, which were as common as kettles; they also deployed in robust militias experienced in combat against Europeans, Indians, and insurrectionist slaves.

Sensing its own ignorance, the government had drafted a rudimentary questionnaire that would soon be sent to colonial governors. The twenty-two questions ranged from No. 3, "What is the size and extent of the province, the number of acres supposed to be contained therein?" and No. 4, "What rivers are there?" to No. 10, "What methods are used to prevent illegal trade, and are the same effectual?" and No. 21, "What are the ordinary & extraordinary experiences of your government?" No doubt some helpful answers would emerge.

The remainder of the king's stay in Portsmouth flew past. George once asserted that seven hours of sleep sufficed for a man, eight for a woman, and nine for a fool. No fool, he was up early each morning to stick his nose into every corner of the dockyard, asking questions and pondering the nuances of ship ballast and the proper season for felling compass timber. As he examined the new ninety-gun *Princess Royal*, soon to be launched, a master shipwright bellowed for silence; thirty comrades then shouldered their adzes and sang, "Tell Rome and France and Spain, / Britannia scorns their chain, / Great George is king." Later he watched intently as workmen caulked the *Ajax*, set the mainmast on *Valiant*, and swung the ribs into position on *Lyon* and *Berwick*. He toured the new oar maker's shop, the hemp house, the brewery, the cooperage, sail lofts, and mast sheds. Smiths in the forge repaired a four-ton anchor under his eye, and in the ropewalk he watched as three thousand strands were woven into a single twenty-four-inch cable intended for the largest ships of the line. Each afternoon he returned to the *Barfleur* for dinner, trailed by the usual squadron of yachts and yawls. On Friday night, soldiers, sailors, and townsfolk lined Portsmouth's ramparts and huzzahed themselves hoarse during a final *feu de joie*, with another triple discharge of cannons and muskets.

Even a landlubber king recognized that just as his empire was under stress, so too his fleet. Sea power was fragile. A half dozen obsolete ships had been broken up for scrap in the past year, and no new ones launched. The *Princess Royal*, headed for sea in October, had taken six years to build.

Although some wooden warships gave service for decades, many lasted only eight to fifteen years, depending on the seas they plied. Each required incessant, costly repairs in jammed yards like this one. Ships built with green timber—seasoned for less than three years—sometimes had only half the life span, or even a third. The urgent naval demands of the Seven Years' War had devoured England's reserves of seasoned oak; many warships during and after the war were built green, which left them vulnerable to dry rot and other ills. New seasoning sheds were under construction to replenish timber supplies, but much of the British fleet was nearing the end of its life. Simply making a new eighteen-ton mainmast for a one-hundred-gun ship—a white pine stick forty yards long and forty inches in diameter—took a dozen shipwrights two months. Portsmouth and other royal yards needed more skilled shipwrights, many more. It did not help recruitment that they earned the same two shillings and one penny per day paid in 1699.

Uneasy lay the head, but at six forty-five a.m. on Saturday, June 26, after pardoning debtors in the Portsmouth jail and dispensing a few royal favors—including £250 for the local poor and £1,500 to be divided among the dockyard workforce—the king climbed into his chaise for the return to Kew. A few final gun salvos boomed, and happy subjects ran after his cavalcade as it rolled beyond Portsea Bridge. In Godalming he emerged from the cab to stand in flowers piled to his knees. A band crashed through "God Save the King," sung with such fervor by the locals that George wept, then joined the chorus.

"The king is exceeding delighted with his reception at Portsmouth," wrote the painter Joshua Reynolds, president of the Royal Academy of Arts. "He was convinced he was not so unpopular as the newspapers would represent him to be." Foreign ambassadors in London who had been invited guests in Portsmouth sent reports to their capitals with admiring descriptions of Britain's might, just as the government had intended. Particular note was taken of the courier who set out for Versailles from the French envoy's house in Great George Street; that dispatch reportedly described the review as "most noble."

Later in the year, the Portsmouth spectacle would be mounted as a stage production by the celebrated actor David Garrick, who hired a Parisian set designer to convert the Theatre Royal in Drury Lane into a dockyard and anchorage. Toy cannons popped, model ships sailed on billowing fabric that simulated a rolling sea, and the cast pressed toward the footlights. "Rule, Britannia!" they sang. "Britannia, rule the waves."

Avenging the Tea

The celebratory mood soon faded: the next eighteen months proved bleak. An American woman the king would never meet, a New Jersey Presbyterian named Jemima Condict, captured the prevailing distemper in the colonies when she wrote, "We have troublesome times a-coming for there is a great disturbance abroad in the earth & they say it is tea that caused it."

Seventeen million pounds of troublesome tea, more than England consumed in a year, had accumulated mostly in warehouses along Lime and Fenchurch Streets, a short walk from the Tower of London. The East India Company, Britain's largest mercantile enterprise, tottered toward bankruptcy, in part because too many Britons preferred cheaper tea provided by European smugglers. Even a new East India monopoly on Indian opium, to be peddled in China, could not compensate for the firm's mismanagement, plus a depressed international market for tea. The company's dire financial plight jeopardized the broader British economy.

Just before the king's excursion to Portsmouth, an ingenious, ill-advised rescue plan had passed Parliament, hardly noticed by the London press. The Tea Act restructured the East India Company and gave it a monopoly on tea sold in America. The company could appoint its own American agents, eliminating the expense of British wholesalers; the tax of three pence per pound imposed under the Townshend Acts would be retained to again affirm Parliament's authority, but other export duties were eliminated. The price of tea in America would drop by more than a third, selling for less than the smuggled Dutch, Danish, and Portuguese tea popular in the American market. Pleased by this windfall, the East India Company prepared two thousand lead-lined tea chests for shipment to New World ports.

Too clever by half, the plan infuriated both smugglers and American merchants now superseded by favored East India agents. It implied Parliament's authority to create monopolies for other commodities and reawakened the fraught issue of taxation without representation. The cynical manipulation of colonial markets on behalf of British mercantile interests nudged American moderates toward common cause with radicals who deplored all British meddling in American affairs. In an attempt to stigmatize the beverage, one writer asserted that tea turned those who drank it into "weak, effeminate, and creeping valetudinarians." English tea supposedly attracted insects, aggravated smallpox, and, a Boston physician insisted, caused "spasms, vapors, hypochondrias, apoplexies of the serious kind, palsies, and dropsies."

Others took bolder measures. On the evening of December 16, 1773, a few dozen men said to be "dressed in the Indian manner," their faces darkened by lampblack or charcoal, descended with war whoops down Milk Street in Boston to board three merchant ships moored at Griffin's Wharf. Prying open the hatches, they used block and tackle to hoist from the holds hundreds of heavy chests containing forty-five tons of Bohea, Congou, Singlo, Souchong, and Hyson tea. For three hours they methodically smashed the lids and scooped the leaves into the harbor. Confederates in small boats used rakes and oars to scatter the floating piles, and by morning almost £10,000 worth of soggy brown flakes drifted in windrows from the wharf to Castle Island and the Dorchester shore. "The devil is in these people," a British naval officer wrote after surveying the damage. But a local lawyer exulted. "This destruction of the tea," John Adams declared, "is so bold, so daring, so firm, intrepid, & inflexible." An equestrian silversmith named Paul Revere carried a detailed account of the event to New York and Philadelphia in the first of his famous gallops. The tea party, as this episode later was called, inspired the kind of doggerel that always annoyed the British: "Rally, Mohawks, bring out your axes, / And tell King George we'll pay no taxes / On his foreign tea."

"I am much hurt," King George confessed when news of this outrage reached him in mid-January 1774. Sorrow soon yielded to anger. An American in London described "a great wrath" sweeping Britain, not least because although thousands had watched or participated at Griffin's Wharf on the night of December 16, only one witness agreed to testify in court, and then only if the trial convened in London. Demands mounted for vengeance against Boston, "the metropolis of sedition," including proposals that the town be reduced to salted ruins, like Carthage. The essayist and lexicographer Samuel Johnson, known without affection as Dictionary Johnson, had already denounced the Americans as "a race of convicts, [who] ought to be thankful for anything we allow them short of hanging." Now Dr. Johnson "breathed out threatenings and slaughter, calling them rascals, robbers, pirates, and exclaiming that he'd burn and destroy them," his companion James Boswell recorded.

What should be done? Some merchants—potters and shoemakers in Staffordshire, the makers of fishing nets and lines in Bridport—signed petitions urging caution, for fear that the loss of American markets would cripple their businesses. The colonists bought up to 20 percent of British manufactured goods, but the market for certain commodities was much bigger—a quarter of British white salt and wrought brass, a third of refined sugar, tin, and worsted socks, half of wrought copper, glassware, and silk goods, and two-thirds to three-quarters of iron nails, English cordage, and beaver hats. The Scottish philosopher Adam Smith, at work on a sweeping study of political economy titled *The Wealth of Nations*, to be published in

1776, argued that Britain would be better off jettisoning her colonies. The New World was "not an empire, but the project of an empire; not a gold mine, but the project of a gold mine . . . mere loss instead of profit." Confusion and uncertainty plagued the government, beset with conflicting reports and opinions. Was this challenge to British authority widespread or limited to a few scoundrels in New England? Was conciliation possible? Appeasement had failed after the Stamp and Townshend Acts—would violence now be necessary?

The king's heart hardened. Spurning petitions and appeals from those pleading for moderation, he vowed in March 1774 to "stop the present disorders." To Parliament he denounced "a dangerous spirit of resistance" in America among "my deluded subjects," who, according to a new legal opinion by the British attorney general, were committing "the crime of high treason." The troubles in Boston threatened "anarchy, the most terrible of all evils."

George's resolve helped his ministers rally around three critical assumptions, each of which proved false: that most colonists remained loyal to the Crown, notwithstanding troublemakers in Massachusetts capable of inciting a rabble; that firmness, including military firepower if necessary, would intimidate the obstreperous and restore harmony; and that failure to reassert London's authority would eventually unstitch the empire, causing Britain to "revert to her primitive insignificancy in the map of the world," as a member of the House of Commons warned.

Here, then, was the crux. The king and his men believed that British wealth and status derived from the colonies. The erosion of authority in America, followed by a loss of sovereignty, would encourage rebellions in Canada, Ireland, the Caribbean, India. Dominoes would topple. "Destruction must follow disunion," the colonial secretary, Lord Dartmouth, warned. With the empire dismembered, an impoverished Great Britain, no longer great, would invite "the scorn of Europe" and exploitation by enemies in France, Spain, and elsewhere. Those windrows of wet tea leaves foretold political and economic ruin.

From late March through June 1774, Parliament adopted four laws known collectively in Britain as the Coercive Acts (and later in America as the Intolerable Acts). The first was punitive: Boston's port must close until the cost of the ruined tea was paid to the East India Company. The other laws tightened British control over Massachusetts by converting an elected council into one appointed by the governor, by restricting town meetings and jury selection, and by permitting royal officials accused of serious crimes to be tried in England or another colony. British troops would return to Boston under a commander in chief who would also serve as the royal governor.

With exquisitely bad timing, in June Parliament passed another sweeping law, one that colonists assumed was part of the tea party retaliation but that in fact had taken years to craft. The Quebec Act replaced military rule in newly acquired Canada with an autocratic civilian government, while legitimizing the Catholic Church's authority and vastly extending the provincial boundaries west and south, to the rich territory between the Mississippi and Ohio Rivers. The empowerment of popery enraged Protestant New Englanders, who for more than a century had battled French Catholics and their Indian allies; colonists from New York through the Carolinas, keen to expand west of the Appalachians, were likewise infuriated at being confined to the Atlantic seaboard.

"The die is now cast," George wrote. "The colonies must either submit or triumph. We must not retreat."

The die was indeed cast. Despite London's hope of isolating Boston as a pariah, indignation and resentment swept the colonies. The Coercive Acts and the Quebec Act galvanized American resistance, empowering the radicals and further converting neutrals and moderates to a cause now touched with fire. Rather than shun those who staged the tea party, towns in New England and as far south as Charleston sent food, firewood, and money to sustain Boston when the port closed in June.

In September, fifty-five delegates from a dozen colonies—Georgia remained ambivalent—gathered in Philadelphia, emboldened enough to call themselves the Continental Congress. Not only did they endorse resistance to the Coercive Acts, the delegates also agreed to halt trade with the British Empire over the coming months. Imports and exports would be forbidden in an escalating economic campaign intended to pressure London by hurting British merchants, manufacturers, and consumers. Elected committees of safety and inspection "in every county, city, and town" were to enforce this agreement on retaliatory trade restrictions, known as the Association. Civic virtue would be measured by a colonist's refusal to consume British goods or trade with the mother country; transgressors were to be publicly shamed, or worse. The Association committees—revolutionary and robust—drew an estimated seven thousand Americans into political office for the first time. At the same time, American militia leaders had begun stockpiling gunpowder and other munitions.

"A most daring spirit of resistance and disobedience" had infected the colonies, George told Parliament that November, with "fresh violences of a very criminal nature." As captain general and first soldier of the empire, the king would do what was necessary to compel obedience from over two million recalcitrant subjects, even if they lived three thousand miles away in a country six times larger than England. What he would call his "great lenity" toward the Americans had been a mistake; he would not make it again. "I am not sorry that the line of conduct seems now chalked out," he wrote his chief minister, Lord North, in a note dated "48 minutes past midnight" on November 18. "Blows must decide."

London on the march toward war was much like London at peace—aggressive, vivid, and alive with animal spirits. Cockfights and bearbaiting remained popular, especially on Mondays and Tuesdays. Raucous crowds assembled on January 10, 1775, to see six criminals—four burglars and two thieves—trundled in carts down Oxford Street to the Tyburn gallows. Another eight were condemned to death that week in an Old Bailey courtroom, among them a defendant who stole sixpence from a farm boy. The British penal code listed nearly two hundred capital crimes, including such heinous offenses as demolishing fishponds and wandering at night with one's face blackened, not unlike the tea party hooligans in Boston. Tyburn's hangman would rarely be idle.

The largest city in the Western world now held three-quarters of a million souls, and what a din they made: the bawl of balladmongers, knife grinders, itinerant musicians, and pleading beggars, some with rented babies on their hips; the clop and clatter of hooves and iron-wheeled carts on paving stones; the tinkling bells of scavenger drays; the cries of Thames ferrymen and higglers selling flowers, or apples, or jellied eels, or quack potions. Watchmen known as Charlies—the office dated to Charles II's reign—called out the hour when clocks struck, proclaiming good weather or bad. With noise came the stink of sea coal and wood smoke and thick effusions from smithies, dyers' yards, and earthenware kilns. Pigs, chickens, and cows lived in cellars with their owners, and streets served as open sewers for tripe dressers, sausage makers, and the offal of catgut spinners.

The city had 42 markets and countless public houses, including, by one later tally, 55 Swans, 90 King's Heads, 120 Lions, but only 1 Good Man; the author Tobias Smollett claimed a man could get drunk for a penny and dead drunk for tuppence. Among the estimated ten thousand prostitutes, streetwalkers worked the Strand or the alleys near Covent Garden, where higher-priced courtesans preened in bay windows on the piazza and men paid to be flogged by women known as "posture molls." Freaks and frauds peopled the metropolis: a certain Mary Tofts who supposedly gave birth to rabbits, an armless man who shaved with his foot, a Scot who broke glasses with a mighty shout, and shopkeepers who sold donkey as mutton and white bread kneaded with chalk or bone ash. But mostly it was a city that toiled hard: clerks and barbers, merchants and printers, coal heavers and coppersmiths with their beards stained green. If not already the world's greatest metropolis, London was working to earn that laurel.

For those whose carriages and sedan chairs kept them above such hurly-burly, the queen's birthday, on January 18, marked the traditional opening of London's social season, with Parliament scheduled to convene the following day. Charlotte had been an obscure, drab German princess in 1761 when George chose her sight unseen to be his queen. During the voyage across the North Sea to Britain she took English lessons and learned to play "God Save the King" on the harpsichord; they were wed in St. James's Palace six hours after her arrival. At his instruction, the marriage bedroom decor included seven hundred yards of blue damask, a mahogany four-poster with five mattresses, and large glass basins of goldfish. The happy union proved fecund—she produced children with lunar regularity, eventually to number fifteen—and her birthday was always cause for carefully orchestrated jubilation at St. James's.

A peal of bells marked the day, with an oration by the archbishop of Canterbury and an ode by a royal chorus. The poet laureate scribbled verse to fill up strophes, antistrophes, and various declamations on Charlotte's virtues. The Tower guns fired at one p.m., and illuminations brightened Westminster; those at the French ambassador's house were exceptionally radiant, a tribute, it was said, from Queen Marie Antoinette as a gesture of royal sisterhood. But it was the birthday ball that had kept West End milliners, mantua makers, and bespoke shoe cobblers in a stitching frenzy for weeks.

The evening began badly. A fine day turned wet, and churning fog limited the visibility around St. James's to five yards. Even footmen wielding white wands could not prevent the collision of several coaches, with bones broken and horses entangled. Constables spotted seven suspected pickpockets sidling through the pandemonium, and marched them off to Bridewell Prison. The guests soldiered on, rescuing the night through determined elegance. Pigmented ceruse rouged the cheeks, and wigs were powdered to make the eyes appear brighter, an effect enhanced by false eyebrows made from mouse skins, which were applied with gum. "The dresses were splendid and magnificent, much beyond anything I had ever before seen," one foreign visitor wrote. "The queen appears amiable." Of 177 peers of the realm, including 23 dukes and 77 earls, a gratifying number strode through the fog to attend their amiable queen, who wore a new diamond stomacher over her brocaded gown, with matching necklace and earrings. The minuets began at nine p.m. and continued for two hours, followed by country dances. The *Morning Chronicle* would assure its readers that "more brilliants were never there at one time than was seen last night."

The king, regal in a suit of blue velvet trimmed in silver, appeared to be a happy man. Few knew that George's good spirits derived not only from a successful fête for his queen, but from hopes that a decisive strategy had emerged to crush the American insurgency once and for all. During secret meetings this week at offices in Cleveland Row, a narrow street behind St. James's, cabinet ministers—heeding their monarch's sensible request for "a general plan"—drafted a scheme to send more regiments, warships, cash, and marines to Boston, along with instructions for hunting down insurgent leaders. But first, Parliament would have to agree.

For more than two hundred years, the House of Commons had met in St. Stephen's Chapel, built within the palace of Westminster in the twelfth century for the monarch's private worship. Window glass depicted biblical stories. Peacock feathers and squirrels' tails had been used to paint angels on the walls and saints around the altar; white down plucked from the breasts of royal swans was daubed in paint to inflect the high blue ceiling with thousands of gold stars. When Henry VIII shifted to a new palace at Whitehall, old choir stalls became members' benches, a Speaker's chair replaced the altar, whitewash covered the wall paintings, and the spangled ceiling was lowered to improve the acoustics. Architect Christopher Wren added galleries above the debating chamber, which was smaller than a tennis court. The hall retained an ecclesiastical air, even as parliamentarians cracked nuts, peeled oranges, or wandered out through the lobby for a game of whist and a glass of Madeira.

On January 19, when the Commons reconvened after the Christmas holiday, members as usual were packed like sprats in a tin. With a thud, a clerk dropped 149 documents on a central table, announced that they were "papers relating to the disturbances in North America," and in a somber tone began to read the titles of each: Royal Navy dispatches from American waters; seditious extracts from the Continental Congress; reports written by royal officials from New Hampshire to Georgia; official correspondence from London to colonial governors.

Slouched on the Treasury bench to the right of the Speaker's chair, a corpulent, round-shouldered figure listened as the recitation droned on, his eyelids so heavy that he appeared to be dozing. Thick-lipped, with both brow and chin receding, he was said to have a tongue "too large for his mouth" and "prominent eyes that rolled about to no purpose." No matter: Lord Frederick North, a man without vanity who referred to himself as "an old hulk," was always pleased to be underestimated.

In the first decade of George III's reign, six men held the office of prime minister, better known at the time as chief or first minister. They had little in common other than slender competency and an unsteady handling of Parliament. In 1770 the king turned to a childhood playmate—he and North had acted together in a schoolboy production of Joseph Addison's *Cato*—and a political partnership began that would endure through a dozen difficult years. George knew he had his man when he wrote North just a few months into his new chief minister's tenure, pleading for £13,000 in cash by day's end because of "a most private and delicate" need—the Duke of Cumberland had successfully sued the king's younger brother after catching him in flagrante delicto with his wife. North replied within hours that he had "no doubt of being able to procure the sum desired . . . in such a manner to keep it as much out of sight as possible." George answered, "This takes a heavy load off of me."

Even his adversaries adored North, a man "of infinite wit and pleasantry," as one admitted. A diplomat added, "It was impossible to experience dullness in his society." Now forty-two, the son of an earl, he was a gifted Greek and Latin scholar, adept in French, German, and Italian, with an adhesive memory, a youthful delight in the absurd, and "a temperament completely free from irascibility," as one admirer observed. A happy husband and a doting father to six children, he was generous, companionable, and honest. "He kept his hands clean and empty," a colleague wrote, while another noted, "What he did, he did without a mask." North held a constituency in Banbury with fewer than two dozen eligible voters, who routinely reelected him after being plied with punch and cheese, and who were then rewarded with a haunch of venison.

Capable of reciting budget statistics for hours without consulting a note, he supervised national finance as head of the Treasury Board. Deft in debate, North was the principal defender of government policy in the Commons. In the past year he had delivered more than a hundred speeches on various measures, most of them harsh, relating to America. Many more such speeches lay ahead.

Ahead, too, lay calamity. By his own recent acknowledgment, North was "fond of indolence and a retired life." Averse to confrontation and an instinctive conciliator, he was given to melancholy and indecision. Now he was fated to be a war minister, with his king's empire in the balance. He could talk tough, as in his claim that "America must fear you before they will love you" or his assurance to the Commons that "four or five frigates" could close Boston Harbor because "the militia of Boston were no match for the force of this country." Yet colleagues sensed that his heart was not in it; he lacked, one said, the requisite "despotism and violence of temper." His confession that "upon military matters I speak ignorantly, and therefore without effect" revealed his ambivalence.

Devoted to George, he would stay the course set by his monarch, a vessel for the king's obstinacy. A loyal friend though perhaps not a good one, he reinforced His Majesty's narrow attitudes rather than gently widening his vision. It was North, after all, who in 1770 had said, "I can never acquiesce in the absurd notion that all men are equal." Now, with his stack of 149 documents as proof of American perfidy, he would seek Parliament's agreement to force submission.

The first obstacle arose in the other chamber, the House of Lords, which met nearby in a medieval hall at the south end of the Westminster warren. On January 20, William Pitt, the Earl of Chatham, the venerable statesman and strategist who had engineered Britain's victory in the Seven Years' War, rose to his feet to denounce the government's folly and to demand withdrawal of British troops from Boston. "He seemed like an old Roman senator," a witness in the gallery reported, "rising with the dignity of age, yet speaking with the fire of youth." Chatham's long decline, physical and mental, was well advanced—he called himself "the scarecrow of violence"— but he knew his mind in urging reconciliation with the Americans. "All attempts to impose servitude upon such men, to establish despotism over such a mighty continental nation must be in vain," he warned. "We shall be forced, ultimately, to retract. Let us retract while we can, not when we must." France and Spain, he told the peers, "are watching your conduct, and waiting for the maturity of your errors." He continued:

> My lords, there is no time to be lost. Every moment is big with dangers. . . . The very first drop of blood will make a wound that will not easily be skinned over.

The old lion's eloquence changed few minds; his motion lost 68 to 18. Ten days later, Chatham would try again with a proposal to designate Congress as a lawful entity and to suspend the Coercive Acts, with complete repeal to follow upon American acknowledgment of Parliament's authority. Once again a heavy majority defeated the bill. Chatham wrote his wife that the government seemed "violent beyond expectation, almost to madness."

To Lord North's satisfaction, the House of Commons proved no less bellicose. American insurgents were "an enemy in the bowels of the kingdom," one member insisted. Another who had seen military service in America during the last war assured his colleagues that five thousand

British regulars could march through the colonies unhindered; Americans, "of a pusillanimous disposition, and utterly incapable of any sort of order or discipline," would "never dare to face an English army." It helped the government's cause that roughly a hundred members of the Commons were past or current military officers, reliably loyal. It also helped that North had spent £50,000 from a Treasury slush fund in the 1774 election to buy a couple dozen seats for other pliant candidates. Further, the king had purchased additional loyalty by sprinkling lucrative sinecures and patronage appointments among members of both houses, including eleven grooms of the bedchamber, a master of the jewel office, a master falconer, an usher of the exchequer, rangers of the royal forests, seven equerries, and various masters of the harriers, buckhounds, and staghounds. "This Parliament," observed the writer Horace Walpole, the son of a former prime minister, "appeared to be even more corrupt and servile than the two last."

At two-thirty a.m. on February 7, the Commons by a vote of 288 to 105 supported North's proposal to ask the king to declare Massachusetts in rebellion, and to take all measures needed to bring American insurgents to heel. "If they would submit and leave us the constitutional right of supremacy," North said, "the quarrel would be at an end." The Lords followed suit, 104 to 29, at one-forty a.m. the following morning. Among new members voting with the Commons majority was an elfin man with a double chin and a squat nose who in his study on Bentinck Street was writing a great saga, the first volume of which would soon be published as *The History of the Decline and Fall of the Roman Empire*. Few parliamentarians would be as steadfast for the Crown as Edward Gibbon. "We have both the right and the power on our side," he had told a friend a week earlier. "We are now arrived at the decisive moment of preserving, or of losing forever, both our trade and empire." Yet few would be as reflective, as when he later conceded, "I took my seat at the beginning of the memorable contest between Great Britain and America, and supported with many a sincere and silent vote, the rights, though not perhaps the interest, of the mother country." For now, a few hours after casting his vote, Gibbon wrote, "With firmness, all may go well. Yet I sometimes doubt."

The king had *no* doubts. Parliament's resolve "ought to open the eyes of the deluded Americans," he wrote North on the morning of Wednesday, February 8. "But if it does not, it must set every delicate man at liberty to avow the propriety of the most coercive measures." Beyond majority votes in both houses, George wanted a theatrical, public display of support. A few hours later, he again wrote North to propose "a large attendance" at

St. James's the next day. Hundreds from the Commons and the Lords were to make the short journey to the palace, as a group, to demonstrate unity. "I therefore hope," he added, "you will insinuate the propriety of this."

Shortly before three p.m. on Thursday, braving a blustery wind from the southwest, Parliament picked a path through the willows and poplars of St. James's Park to the red brick octagonal towers of that "irregular pile," as one critic described the palace. The *London Gazette* would report that "there never was known so many of the bishops and peers to attend an address to His Majesty. . . . There was also the greatest number of commoners ever known on a like occasion." Not far from the hearth inscribed with the initials of Henry VIII and his doomed queen Anne Boleyn, the king listened as Parliament's petition was read aloud:

> We find that a part of your Majesty's subjects in the province of the Massachusetts Bay have proceeded so far to resist the authority of the supreme legislature, that a rebellion at this time actually exists. . . . We consider it as our indispensable duty, humbly to beseech your Majesty that you will take the most effectual measures to enforce due obedience to the laws and authority of the supreme legislature.

George was nearsighted, and some faces around the room were blurry as he read his brief reply, composed with North's help:

> You may depend on my taking the most speedy and effectual measures for enforcing due obedience to the laws. . . . It is my ardent wish that this disposition may have a happy effect on the temper and conduct of my subjects in America.

Events now moved swiftly. That very day the king ordered several regiments in Ireland to prepare for "foreign service." On Friday, North introduced another bill, this one to prevent all New England colonies from trading with any foreign nations and to exclude them from the world's richest fishing grounds, in the North Atlantic. That measure would again muster large majorities. A few days later, Parliament approved hiring another two thousand sailors for the navy; the government also requested money for an extra 4,400 soldiers, with the intention of expanding the army in America to almost 11,000. In recent weeks, the king had considered ousting the military commander there, Lieutenant General Thomas Gage, on suspicion of insufficient grit; instead he chose to send three young major generals to stiffen Gage's spine. He told North to give each an extra £500 before they sailed—"they have behaved so very properly and are so poor." Whatever Gage's shortcomings, North knew that nearly all of the forty-five generals senior to him, some in their eighties, lacked the vigor, the experience, or the bloody-mindedness to take command in Boston. "I do not know whether our generals will frighten the enemy," he supposedly quipped, "but I know that they frighten me."

Still, the king felt sure of his course. To North he wrote on February 15, at precisely 10:06 a.m.: "I entirely place my security in the protection of the Divine Disposer of All Things, and shall never look to the right or left but steadily pursue the track which my conscience dictates to be the right one."

Preparing for War

For more than three centuries, the Tower of London had issued departing armies the ordnance needed to fight Britain's expeditionary battles, from field guns and shoulder arms to bullet molds, powder flasks, and musket flints. In the early spring of 1775, the place grew busy again. "Many thousand firearms sent out of the Tower and shipped on board the transports," a visiting American artist wrote. "Kegs of flints marked 'Boston' on each keg, with all the implements of war." A Tower armory reportedly held eighty thousand stand of arms, "bright and shining." Visitors could pay four pence to view the "Royal Train of Artillery," from 6-pounders to 24-pounders, some with new leveling screws for quicker aim and greater accuracy. The train also included 13-inch mortars and "carcass" shells packed with combustibles designed to incinerate enemy towns. New brass cannons filled an adjacent storehouse more than a hundred yards long, with sponges, rammers, handspikes, drag ropes, and other gunnery tools, plus four thousand harnesses for pull teams. Obsolete weapons decorated Tower walls in fantastic sculptures, like the seven-headed hydra constructed from old pistols. Stacked bayonets and ancient firelocks formed a corkscrew pillar twenty-two feet high. The place was a tabernacle of firepower.

Gun shops clustered along the Thames below the Tower walls assembled the flintlock musket known as the Brown Bess. Smiths fitted the barrels and locks, mostly forged in the Midlands from imported Swedish iron, to walnut stocks; they then attached the "furniture"—brass and iron mounts, including triggers and butt plates. Each musket cost one pound, thirteen shillings, plus four pence to prove the barrel and fit a bayonet. Tower officials also tested the potency of gunpowder made in government and private mills. The British appetite for powder was voracious: each foot regiment typically received 42,000 powder charges a year, enough for every soldier to fire 60 to 120 lead balls. That allotment would increase in heavy combat. A single warship of 100 guns might carry 535 barrels, nearly 27 tons; even a small naval sloop could carry 6 tons, more powder than would be found in all the rebel magazines around Boston a few months hence. "Incredible quantities of ammunition and stores shipped and shipping from Tower Wharf for America," another correspondent reported.

Precisely how this formidable strength should be wielded against America remained in dispute among the king's men. "A conquest by land is unnecessary," the secretary at war, Lord William Barrington, had advised in December, "when the country can be reduced first to distress, and then to obedience, by our marine." That marine—the Royal Navy—might have its own woes, but General Edward Harvey, the adjutant general and the highest army official in Britain, agreed that "attempting to conquer America internally with our land force is as evil an idea as ever controverted common sense." He added bluntly: "It is impossible."

The army's small size fueled this consternation. In 1760, at the height of the Seven Years' War, Britain had mustered more than 200,000 men, including mercenaries. Now the army's paper strength had dipped below 50,000—less than a third the size of France's army—and no more than 36,000 soldiers actually filled the ranks, of whom thousands kept the restive Irish in check. Recruiting was difficult, and although many of the army's 3,500 officers had combat experience, the force had fought few major battles since Quebec and Minden, sixteen years earlier. A few prominent commanders refused to fight the Americans, among them Sir Jeffrey Amherst, who had led North American forces against the French from 1758 to 1763. While some junior officers were keen to earn their spurs in New England, enough were leaving the service that in February the king declared he would "not listen to any further requests" from those hoping to sell their commissions rather than embark for America; he deemed such behavior a "great impropriety." Lord North, as early as September 1774, had suggested that "Hessians and Hanoverians could be employed if necessary." During the winter, secret negotiations had begun in Kassel to retain German hirelings, should war erupt in America.

A fateful momentum swept the government along. Something must be done; even those wary of war agreed that American rebellion could not be condoned. Much of the particular planning fell to slender, rigorous William Legge, the Earl of Dartmouth and the colonial secretary, who was so pious a Christian that he was known as the "Psalm Singer"; his country home near Birmingham had provided a refuge for evangelical preachers and for revival meetings of sobbing, hysterical worshippers. Raised in the same household as North, his stepbrother, Lord Dartmouth was hardly a warmonger. But he believed that prideful rebels disobeyed both their British masters and their God. Obedience and Christ's redemption were needed to set things right, along with a few regiments. After a decade of fitful, indecisive political skirmishing, a short, sharp contest of arms offered an appealing clarity.

And so war stuffs spilled from the Tower and other depots to be loaded onto westbound ships: canteens, leather cartridge boxes, watch coats, tents, five-ton wagons by the dozen, muskets by the hundreds, powder by the ton. There was a run on New World maps, although one London skeptic later wrote, "The small scale of our maps deceived us, and as the word 'America' takes up no more room than the word 'Yorkshire,' we seemed to think the territories they represent are much the same bigness, though Charleston is as far from Boston as London from Venice."

Troops tramped toward the ports. A London newspaper reported that a light cavalry regiment preparing to deploy had inscribed "DEATH OR GLORY" on its caps, with an embroidered skull. Seven regiments of foot bound for America were brought to strength by drafting soldiers from units left behind. Each regiment was also permitted to take sixty women, twelve servants, and eighty-six tons of baggage. On the southern coast of Ireland, Cork grew so crowded that officers waiting to embark on transport ships complained of difficulty in finding lodging. Soldiers living in hovels on Blarney Lane or Brogue Market Street practiced the manual of arms, though some lacked muskets. Each would be issued a bunk, a bolster, a blanket, and a spoon for the voyage. The usual drunken sprees and fistfights between soldiers and sailors kept officers alert; dragoons preparing to sail from Cork found the ships' holds stacked with so many casks of porter being smuggled for sale in Boston that they could not reach the stalls to feed their horses.

As the squadrons awaited a fair wind, a vague unease drifted through the kingdom. "Our stake is deep," wrote Horace Walpole. "It is that kind of war in which even victory may ruin us." But the man who reigned over that kingdom remained constant, as ever. "When once these rebels have felt a smart blow," George told his Admiralty, "they will submit."

Blows would decide, as the king had predicted. Yet no one could foresee that the American War of Independence would last 3,059 days. Or that the struggle would be marked by more than 1,300 actions, mostly small and bloody, with a few large and bloody, plus 241 naval engagements in a theater initially bounded by the Atlantic seaboard, the St. Lawrence and Mississippi

Rivers, and the Gulf of Mexico, before expanding to other lands and other waters.

Roughly a quarter million Americans would serve the cause in some military capacity. At least one in ten of them would die for that cause—25,674 deaths by one tally, as many as 35,800 by another. Those deaths were divided with rough parity among battle, disease, and British prisons, a larger proportion of the American population to perish in any conflict other than the Civil War. If many considered the war providential—ordained by God's will and shaped by divine grace—certainly the outcome would also be determined by gutful soldiering, endurance, hard decisions (good and bad), and luck (good and bad). The odds were heavily stacked against the Americans: no colonial rebellion had ever succeeded in casting off imperial shackles. But, as Voltaire had observed, history is filled with the sound of silken slippers going downstairs and wooden shoes coming up.

This would not be a war between regimes or dynasties, fought for territory or the usual commercial advantages. Instead, what became known as the American Revolution was an improvised struggle between two peoples of a common heritage, now sundered by divergent values and conflicting visions of a world to come. Unlike most European wars of the eighteenth century, this one would not be fought by professional armies on flat, open terrain with reasonable roads, in daylight and good weather. And though it was fought in the age of reason, infused with Enlightenment ideals, this war, this civil war, would spiral into savagery, with sanguinary cruelty, casual killing, and atrocity.

Those 3,059 hard days would yield two tectonic results. The first was in the United Kingdom, where the reduction of the empire by about one-third, including the demolition of the new dominions in North America, proved to be as divisive as any misfortune to befall the nation in the eighteenth century, at a cost of £128 million and thousands of British lives. The broader conflict that began in 1778, with the intervention of European powers on America's behalf, led to the only British defeat in the seven Anglo-French wars fought between 1689 and 1815. Of course, what was lost by force of arms could be regained, and a second British Empire, in different garb, would flourish in the next century.

The second consequence was epochal and enduring: the creation of the American republic. Surely among mankind's most remarkable achievements, this majestic construct also inspired a creation myth that sometimes resembled a garish cartoon, a melodramatic tale of doughty yeomen resisting moronic, brutal lobsterbacks. The civil war that unspooled over those eight years would be both grander and more nuanced, a tale of heroes and knaves, of sacrifice and blunder, of redemption and profound suffering. Beyond the battlefield, then and forever, stood a shining city on a hill.

An unusual bustle disturbed placid Craven Street on Monday morning, March 20, 1775. At No. 27, a looming town house with fourteen fireplaces, crates and trunks had been packed and prepared for shipment. Visitors in fine carriages had recently been seen wheeling up and wheeling off, bidding good-bye, adieu, bon voyage. Among the neighbors it was rumored that after almost two decades in London, Dr. Franklin was going home.

He was famous in Craven Street, as he was famous everywhere, though he still referred to himself as "B. Franklin, printer." Except for a brief return visit to Philadelphia in 1763–64, and a temporary move a few years later to a different house on the street, he had lived at No. 27 since arriving in England as a colonial agent in 1757. Because he was widely deemed a "universal genius"—the accolade did not displease him—his eccentricities were forgiven: chuffing up and down the nineteen oak stairs, dumbbells in hand, for exercise; sitting nude in the open window above the street, regardless of the season, for his morning "air bath"; playing his "harmonica," an improbable contraption constructed of thirty-seven glass hemispheres mounted on an iron spindle and rotated with a foot treadle so that he could elicit three ghostly octaves by touching the moving edges with his moistened fingers. (Mozart and Beethoven, among others, would compose for the instrument.) And Craven Street had also been his laboratory, the site where he had launched inquiries into sunspots, magnetism, lead poisoning, the organic origins of coal, carriage wheel construction, and ocean salinity. At the foot of the street, on the Thames, he had repeated his celebrated kite-and-key demonstration; St. Paul's Cathedral, nearby, was Britain's first structure to install his lightning rod.

The tall man who emerged onto the front stoop that morning was now sixty-nine, with thin, graying hair and sensual lips that made him look younger. He retained the broad shoulders of the leather-apron tradesman who'd once carried lead type for a living, though he had grown plump enough to call himself "a fat old fellow." Furrows creased the prominent dome of his forehead, and the hooded blue eyes sagged. "Anxiety begins to disturb my rest," he had written a friend in America a few weeks earlier, "and whatever robs an old man of his sleep soon demolishes him."

He had chosen to spend this final day in London in semi-seclusion with Joseph Priestley, a fellow natural philosopher who lived a mile distant. As Franklin made his way across the city he had once loved, those anxieties weighed on him. How far he had traveled, this fifteenth child of an impoverished Boston candlemaker! With only two years of formal school-ing, he had become not only a prosperous printer but the largest bookseller in Philadelphia and the most prominent paper merchant in America. At forty-two, self-made, he retired from the trades to devote himself to good causes—smallpox inoculations, paper money, and streets made safer by night watchmen paid through public taxes. He also threw him-self into practical science, with inventions ranging from bifocals to effi-cient stoves. He had once told his mother that for his epitaph, "I would rather have it said, 'He died usefully,' than, 'He died rich.'" His 1751 trea-tise *Experiments and Observations on Electricity* brought international fame for discoveries lauded by a contemporary as "the greatest, perhaps, since the time of Sir Isaac Newton." He not only invented the first device for storing electrical charges, he also named it—the battery—as he named other things in this new field: conductor, charge, discharge, armature. Electrical experimenters in France were known as *franklinistes*. The Ger-man philosopher Immanuel Kant called him "the new Prometheus," a man who had captured heaven's fire.

He was proud, perhaps prideful. The ink-stained printer became Dr. Franklin, thanks to the honorary degrees from Oxford and St. Andrews, and he was not above snickering at American provincialism. "Learned and ingenious foreigners that come to England almost all make a point of visiting me," he had written in 1772 to his son William, who, thanks to Franklin's influence, was the royal governor of New Jersey. "The K[ing] too has lately been heard to speak of me with great regard." If esteemed and club-bable, he still at times seemed opaque. A man of masks and personas, he was Poor Richard, after the pseudonym adopted for the almanac he'd first pub-lished in 1732; he was also, thanks to his many whimsical pen names, Silence Dogood, Cecilia Shortface, and Obadiah Plainman. Since moving to London at age fifty-one to represent Pennsylvania, and then other colonies, he had used forty-two different signatures on his published articles.

So, too, was he a creature of contradiction. An advocate for the rights of man, he had owned slaves for thirty years, complaining that most of them were thieves. A man of temperance and discretion, he enjoyed "intrigues with low women that fell in my way" and took a common-law wife in 1730. Perhaps most confounding, he had been a zealous citizen of the empire, so exuberant in his Anglophilia that in September 1761 he curtailed a trip to the Continent to attend George III's coronation. He had long favored excluding Germans and other non-English émigrés from the colonies. Americans "love and honor the name of Englishman," Franklin had writ-ten in the *London Chronicle* in 1770; aping "English manners, fashions, and manufacturers, they have no desire of breaking the connections between the two countries." Yet in the past year he had become so hostile to Britain that now he could fulminate like a Boston radical, his face white with rage. Franklin, these days, was a few steps ahead of an arrest warrant.

His good friend Priestley, beak-nosed and thin-lipped, offered a sympathetic ear. As librarian and companion to the Earl of Shelburne, Priestley lived in the earl's sprawling mansion just off Berkeley Square. The son of a Calvinist cloth dresser, he, too, was a universal genius, one who, it was said, wrote books faster than people could read them. The previous August he had discovered the gas called oxygen, and he would be credited with identifying nitrogen, ammonia, carbon monoxide, and other gases, as well as photosynthesis, the principles of combustion, and the recipe for soda water. On this Monday he and Franklin pondered electricity and sundry scientific mysteries, as they had for years. Then the conversation turned to politics and what Franklin called "the impending calamities." "Much of the time was employed in reading American newspapers," Priestley later wrote of that day with Franklin, "especially accounts of the reception which the Boston Port Bill met with in America. And as he read . . . the tears trickled down his cheeks." The coming war would likely last ten years, Franklin predicted, and he would "not live to see the end of it."

He wept, not least, for his own shortcomings. For decades he had championed a greater Great Britain, an Anglo-American union of "mutual strength and mutual advantage." As political upheaval strained those blood ties, he sought "to palliate matters" with various compromises, including an offer to pay for Boston's drowned tea from his own pocket. Even now he considered the schism to be "a matter of punctilio, which two or three reasonable people might settle in half an hour." But by degree he had grown vexed, then angry at what he called the "insolence, contempt, and abuse" of arrogant British officials toward his countrymen; the condescending reference to Americans as "foreigners" infuriated him. His writings turned acerbic: he proposed to answer the British practice of shipping convicts to America by exporting rattlesnakes to England, and his Swiftian essay, "Rules by Which a Great Empire May Be Reduced to a Small One," postulated that "a great empire, like a great cake, is most easily diminished at the edge."

Then, two years ago, disaster had struck when a wise man did a foolish thing. Someone whose identity remained obscure gave Franklin a sheaf of private letters written by a Crown official in Massachusetts to a British undersecretary, urging stern measures by the government against New England troublemakers. One passage even advocated "an abridgement of what are called English liberties." In December 1772, Franklin sent the letters to Boston as confidential intelligence for patriot leaders, but six months later they were published, causing an uproar in New England, and then in Britain. Franklin eventually placed a notice in the *London Chronicle*, disclosing his responsibility. British newspapers vilified him as "this old snake," "old Doubleface," and a "base, ungrateful, cunning, upstart thing."

On January 29, 1774, he appeared before the king's council in the Cockpit, a Whitehall amphitheater once used for cockfights. For more than an hour, Franklin was pelted with invective, denounced as a "man without honor" and a "hoary-headed traitor" who had "forfeited all the respect of societies and men." The packed gallery jeered while he stood as still as statuary, wearing a fine blue suit of spotted Manchester velvet. It was the greatest humiliation of his life, and a day later he was sacked as deputy postmaster general for North America. He had made a serious error of judgment, but so had Britain, by demeaning the Crown's best American ally in promoting imperial harmony.

In the months since that wretched day, he had shrugged off the ordeal to continue mediating between Crown and colonies. He took meetings, public and private, enduring endless palaver with men of influence and no influence, men of goodwill and ill will, men with potential remedies and men spouting nonsense. Franklin admitted to growing "irritated and heated"; he insisted on repealing the Coercive Acts, withdrawing the fleet from Boston, and removing British soldiers to Quebec or Florida. "The true art of governing the colonies," he believed, "lies in . . . only letting them alone." The government secretly intercepted and read his mail, carefully repairing the seals and making copies with a cover note that labeled him "this arch traitor." Public hopes for reconciliation ascended, then subsided, only to rise again. The stock market jumped in late December on false news that he and Lord North had reached a peace deal.

But there would be no peace. These febrile efforts, he wrote, "availed no more than the whistling of the winds." While government officials considered him the "great director" of New England radicals, the radicals themselves wondered if he was "too much of an Englishman." He felt "like a thing out of its place, and useless because it is out of its place." Like many Americans, he found that the middle ground was narrow and perilous; he, too, gradually chose insurrection. Britain, he concluded, had become "this old rotten state." He was reduced to quoting from Horace's *Odes*: "What is bad now may not always be."

Franklin spent his final night on Craven Street. The last of his books, papers, and scientific instruments packed, he caught the post coach for Portsmouth on March 21. Beyond the political turmoil, two personal matters gnawed at him as he rolled through Surrey on a route similar to that taken by the king to the dockyards twenty-one months earlier. In New

Jersey, Governor William Franklin, the great man's son, seemed intent on remaining loyal to the Crown. "You, who are a thorough courtier," Franklin wrote in a letter, "see everything with government eyes." And in Philadelphia, his common-law wife of forty-four years, Deborah, had died in December after a long decline. Although a faithful correspondent, Franklin had not seen her in a decade. Regret and perhaps guilt dogged him up the gangplank onto the *Pennsylvania Packet*, moored along the Portsmouth waterfront.

Franklin never went to sea without vowing never to go again. Yet here he was in his seventieth year, a large man in a small cabin on a small ship. He had resolved to stay busy during the passage, scrutinizing the heavens with his telescope and frequently measuring ocean temperatures with a thermometer suspended on a long rope, as part of his perpetual study of the Gulf Stream. He promptly started a letter to William, which began, "Dear Son" and grew to twenty thousand words on 250 foolscap pages, as it became a detailed account of his failed diplomacy in Britain. That failure had taught him lessons in patience, tact, intrigue, and power—lessons that would prove useful, since his best days as a diplomat, perhaps the greatest America ever produced, still lay ahead of him.

The bells of Philadelphia would ring for joy upon his arrival six weeks hence. The man who had felt "like a thing out of place" would find his rightful place. Among the slurs hurled at him in the Cockpit was the accusation of being a "true incendiary." That much was certain, as befitted the American Prometheus. He was the best of his breed, this kite flier, this almanac maker, this lightning tamer. The *Pennsylvania Packet* shrugged off her moorings and crowded on sail, bearing him home, where he belonged.

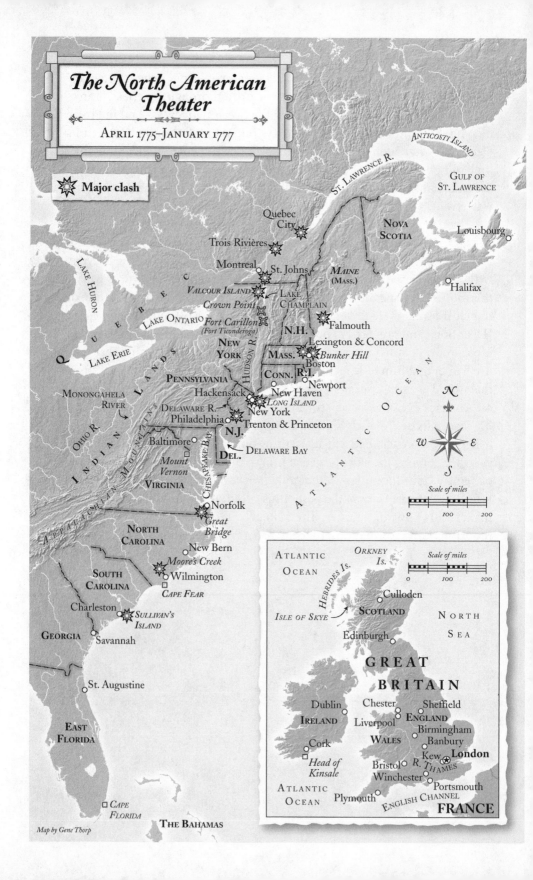

The North American Theater

APRIL 1775–JANUARY 1777

✴ Major clash

ANTICOSTI ISLAND

GULF OF ST. LAWRENCE

ST. LAWRENCE R.

Quebec City

NOVA SCOTIA

Louisbourg

Trois Rivières

Montreal   St. Johns

MAINE (MASS.)

Halifax

LAKE HURON

VALCOUR ISLAND
Crown Point
Fort Carillon
(Fort Ticonderoga)

LAKE CHAMPLAIN

QUEBEC

LAKE ONTARIO

LAKE ERIE

NEW YORK

N.H.

Falmouth

Lexington & Concord

Bunker Hill
Boston

MASS.

CONN.   R.I.

Newport

HUDSON R.

PENNSYLVANIA

Hackensack

New Haven

MONONGAHELA RIVER

DELAWARE R.

Philadelphia

Long Island

New York

Trenton & Princeton

OHIO R.

Baltimore

N.J.

DEL.

Delaware Bay

INDIAN LANDS

Mount Vernon

VIRGINIA

CHESAPEAKE BAY

ATLANTIC OCEAN

N
W   E
S

Scale of miles
0   100   200

Norfolk
Great Bridge

APPALACHIAN MOUNTAINS

NORTH CAROLINA

New Bern

Moore's Creek

SOUTH CAROLINA

Wilmington

CAPE FEAR

Charleston

SULLIVAN'S ISLAND

GEORGIA   Savannah

St. Augustine

EAST FLORIDA

CAPE FLORIDA

THE BAHAMAS

Map by Gene Thorp

Inset map:

ATLANTIC OCEAN

ORKNEY Is.

Scale of miles
0   100   200

HEBRIDES IS.

ISLE OF SKYE

Culloden

SCOTLAND

NORTH SEA

Edinburgh

GREAT BRITAIN

Dublin

Chester

Sheffield

IRELAND

ENGLAND

Liverpool

Birmingham

Cork

WALES

Banbury

Kew   London

Head of Kinsale

Bristol   R. THAMES

Winchester   Portsmouth

ATLANTIC OCEAN

Plymouth   ENGLISH CHANNEL   FRANCE

Part One

1.

———

God Himself Our Captain

The mildest winter in living memory had yielded to an early spring. Not once had the Charles River iced over, and even now whispers of green could be seen on the Common sward and across the tumbling hills to the north. By reducing the need for firewood, this "extraordinary weather for warlike preparations," as one pugnacious clergyman called it, had preserved Boston from even greater suffering in the nine months since British warships had closed the port. Still, warehouses stood vacant, shipyards idle, wharves deserted, shop shelves barren. The only topsail vessels in view were the eight Royal Navy men-of-war plugging the harbor approaches. "It is now a very gloomy place, the streets almost empty," a woman wrote an English friend in early March 1775. "Many families have removed from it, & the inhabitants are divided. . . . Some appear desponding, others full of rage."

Only a bountiful local crop of lambs and charity from other colonies preserved Boston from hunger: fish and flour from elsewhere in New England, rice from the Carolinas, rye from Baltimore, a thousand bushels of wheat from Quebec, cash from Delaware and Montreal. By British decree, provisions arriving by sea were unloaded in Marblehead and carted twenty miles to Boston, an expensive, tedious detour. Town selectmen launched projects to employ the unemployed—street paving, well digging, building a new brickyard. But gangs of idle sailors, longshoremen, ropemakers, riggers, and carpenters could often be found loitering by the docks or in the town's ninety taverns.

Even in better days, Boston had known ample misery—smallpox and measles epidemics, Quaker and witch hangings. For the past three decades the population had stagnated at fifteen thousand people, all of them wedged into a pear-shaped, thousand-acre peninsula with seventeen churches, no banks, no theaters, and a single concert hall, in a room above a shop. Puritan severity was not far removed. A generation earlier, both actors and theatergoers could be fined for "immorality, impiety, and a contempt for religion"; other miscreants were branded alphabetically—"A" for adulterers, "B" for burglars, "F" for forgers. Counterfeiters who escaped a scorching "C" might be nailed to the pillory by their ears. But never had the town seemed more abject or more menacing; these days there were as many British soldiers in Boston as adult male civilians. One resident watching the regiments at drill lamented that the Common "glows with warlike red."

On Monday morning, March 6, the "gloomy place" abruptly sprang to life. Hundreds and then thousands filled the streets, most of them walking, since by ordinance no carriage or wagon could be driven at speeds faster than "foot pace" without risk of a ten-shilling fine. The annual commemoration of the 1770 Boston Massacre would be held a day late this year to avoid profaning the Sabbath, and Dr. Joseph Warren, a prominent local physician, intended to deliver a speech titled "The Baleful Influence of Standing Armies in Time of Peace." An "immense concourse of people," as one witness described it, made for Milk and Marlborough Streets, where an octagonal steeple rose 180 feet above the Old South Meeting House, with its distinctive Flemish-bond brick walls, enormous clock, and split-banner weathervane. By eleven a.m., five thousand packed the place to the double rafters and cambered tie beams. More than a hundred box pews filled Old South's floor, with high paneled sides to block chilly drafts and wooden writing arms for those inclined to take notes on the day's sermon. An upper gallery with benches wrapped around the second floor. Between the arched compass-headed windows rose a high pulpit, now draped in black and crowned with a sounding board.

"People's expectations are alive for the oration," the lawyer John Adams had recently written. An uneasy murmur rose from the congregants, along with the smell of damp wool, perspiration, and badly tanned shoe leather. It was rumored that mass arrests were likely this morning, and that British officers had agreed that if the king were insulted they would draw swords and slaughter the offenders. "We may possibly be attacked in our trenches," Samuel Adams had warned, and a witness reported that almost every man in attendance "had a short stick, or bludgeon in his hand." The murmur in Old South grew louder when several dozen red-coated officers clumped through the door and stood in the aisles.

Samuel Adams was ready for them. An undistinguished petty official who had squandered a family malthouse fortune, Adams ran an impressive political organization, deftly shaping public opinion through a newspaper syndicate that for years had told other colonies—often with lurid hyperbole—what life was like in a free town occupied by combat troops.

"He eats little, drinks little, sleeps little, thinks much," an adversary later wrote, "and is most decisive and indefatigable." Now fifty-two and afflicted with a pronounced tremor in his head and hands, he often stood on his toes when excited, and surely he was on his toes now. He quickly cleared the front pews and beckoned the officers so that, as he later explained, they "might have no pretense to behave ill." About forty eventually took seats on the forward benches or the pulpit stairs, while Adams settled into a deacon's chair, within sword thrust.

The crowd hushed when Dr. Warren appeared at the pulpit after sidling through the congested aisles. He was handsome and young, just thirty-three, pitied for having recently lost his wife, who'd left him four young children, yet much admired for his kindness, grace, and medical skill; more than a few of those in the audience had been inoculated by him during the smallpox outbreak a decade before. He was also a ringleader. As chairman of the extralegal Committee of Safety, he proved to be a capable organizer and insurgent strategist. John Adams, the previous day, had praised his "undaunted spirit and fire."

Later accounts would depict Warren wearing a white toga over his breeches, symbolic of antique virtues—simplicity, industry, probity, civic good over private interest. Although the doctor was likely dressed more conventionally, he did affect what was described as a "Demosthenian posture," with a handkerchief in his right hand, as he addressed "my ever honored fellow citizens":

> Unhappily for us, unhappily for Britain, the madness of an avaricious minister . . . has brought upon the stage discord, envy, hatred, and revenge, with civil war close in their rear. . . . Our streets are again filled with armed men. Our harbor is crowded with ships of war. But these cannot intimidate us. Our liberty must be preserved. It is far dearer than life.

Warren invoked the long struggle to carve a country from the New England wilderness. He described Britain's recent efforts to assert hegemony over that country, and the shootings five years before that left "the stones bespattered with your father's brains." Then came the Coercive Acts, insult upon injury. "Our wish is that Britain and the colonies may, like the oak and the ivy, grow and increase in strength together," Warren said. "But if these pacific measures are ineffectual, and it appears that the only way to safety is through fields of blood, I know you will not turn your faces from your foes."

Several British officers hissed and rapped their sticks on the floor in disapproval. A captain sitting on the pulpit steps allegedly held up several lead bullets in his open palm, a menacing gesture.

Although one skeptic would describe the oration as "true puritanical whine," Dr. Warren knew his audience: farmers and merchants, seamen and artisans, with their queued hair, knee buckles, and linen shirts ruffled at the cuff, their pale, upturned faces watching him intently. They were a borderland people, living on the far rim of empire, where in six or seven generations the American clay had grown sturdy and tall. They were patriots—if that term implied political affiliation rather than a moral state of grace—who were disputatious and litigious, given to violence on the frontier and in the street: a gentle people they were not. Their disgruntlement now approached despair, with seething resentments and a conviction that designing, corrupt men in London—the king's men, if not the king himself—conspired to deprive them of what they and their ancestors had wrenched from this hard land. They were, a Boston writer concluded, "panting for an explosion."

Reasonably democratic, reasonably egalitarian, wary of privilege and outsiders, they were accustomed to tending their own affairs, choosing their own ministers, militia officers, and political leaders. Convinced that their elected assemblies were equal in stature and authority to Parliament, they believed that governance by consent was paramount. They had *not* consented to being taxed, to being occupied, to seeing their councils dismissed and their port sealed like a graveyard crypt. They were godly, of course, placed here by the Almighty to do His will. Sometimes political strife was also a moral contest between right and wrong, good and evil. This struggle, as the historian Gordon S. Wood later wrote, would prove their blessedness.

Warren circled round to that very point:

> Our country is in danger, but not to be despaired of. Our enemies are numerous and powerful, but we have many friends, determining to be free. . . . On you depend the fortunes of America. You are to decide the important question, on which rest the happiness and liberty of millions yet unborn. Act worthy of yourselves.

Applause rocked Old South. One British lieutenant would denounce "a most seditious, inflammatory harangue," although another concluded that the speech "contained nothing so violent as was expected." Swords remained sheathed. But when Samuel Adams heaved himself from his chair to move that "the thanks of the town should be presented to Dr. Warren for his elegant and spirited oration," the officers answered with more hisses, more stick rapping, and shouts of "Oh, fie! Fie!"

That was but a consonant removed from "fire." Panic swept the meeting-house, "a scene of the greatest confusion imaginable," Lieutenant Frederick Mackenzie told his diary. Women shrieked, men shouted, "Fire!," sniffing for smoke. Others thought a command to shoot had been issued, an error compounded by the trill and rap of fifes and drums from the 43rd Regiment, which happened to be passing in the street outside. Five thousand people tried "getting out as fast as they could by the doors and windows," wrote Lieutenant John Barker of the 4th Regiment of Foot. The nimbler congregants in the galleries "swarmed down gutters like rats," then hied through Coopers Alley, Cow Lane, and Queen Street.

A tense calm finally returned to a tense town. "To be sure," Ensign Jeremy Lister of the 10th Foot later wrote, "the scene was quite laughable."

Across the street from Old South, in the three-story brick mansion called Province House, Lieutenant General Gage was not laughing. Worried that the morning's oration would turn violent, he had placed his regiments under arms and on alert. The risible stampede came as a relief.

Thomas Gage was a mild, sensible man with a mild, sensible countenance; only a slight protrusion of his lower lip suggested truculence. Now in his mid-fifties, with thinning gray hair and a fixed gaze, he was the most powerful authority in North America as both military commander in chief and the royal governor of the Province of Massachusetts Bay. Comrades knew him as "Honest Tom," and even an adversary conceded that he was "a good and wise man surrounded with difficulties." As a young officer he had seen ghastly combat in the British defeat by the French at Fontenoy in 1745 and in the British victory over rebellious Highlanders at Culloden a year later. In 1755, he led the vanguard of General Edward Braddock's expedition against the French in western Pennsylvania, where a disastrous ambush at the Monongahela River killed his commander and several hundred comrades; swarming bullets grazed Gage's belly and eyebrow, ventilated his coat, and twice wounded his horse. Three years later, Gage was a senior commander when the French battered a British expedition in New York at Fort Carillon, subsequently renamed Ticonderoga. These actions revealed a soldier without conspicuous gifts as a combat leader, a man perhaps meant to administer rather than command. It was Gage's misfortune to live in turbulent times.

Even so, twenty years of American service had been good to him, providing Gage with high rank, a comely American wife—the New Jersey heiress Margaret Kemble—and vast tracts of land in New York, Canada, and the West Indies. He evinced little sympathy for American political experiments. "Democracy is too prevalent in America," he had declared in 1772, when his headquarters was in New York.

The tea party had pushed his lower lip out a bit more. In an uncharacteristic fit of bravado during a return visit to London in February 1774, he assured King George that four regiments in Boston should suffice—perhaps two thousand men—since the Americans would be "lions whilst we are lambs" but would turn "very meek" in the face of British resolve. Other colonies were unlikely to support Massachusetts; southerners especially "talk very high," but the fear of slave rebellions and Indian attacks "will always keep them quiet." The thirteen colonies seemed too geographically scattered and too riven by diverse interests to collaborate effectively. Promises of suppression on the cheap appealed to the shilling pinchers in Lord North's government. Gage's views had also helped shape the Coercive Acts by feeding the pleasant delusion in Britain that insurrection was mostly a Boston phenomenon, organized by a small cabal of ambitious cynics able to gull the masses.

Gage's report so encouraged the king and his court that the general was dispatched to Massachusetts as both governor of the colony and military chief of the continent. Respectful Bostonians had greeted him with an honor guard, banners, and toasts in Faneuil Hall, although two weeks later he shifted his headquarters to Salem, upon closing Boston Harbor at noon on June 1, 1774. His marching orders from the government urged him "to quiet the minds of the people, to remove their prejudices, and, by mild and gentle persuasion to induce . . . submission on their part." He imposed neither martial law nor press censorship. Troublemakers were permitted to assemble, to travel, to drill their militias, to fling bellicose insults at the king's regulars.

Gage had evidently learned little on the Monongahela or at Fort Carillon about the hazard of underestimating his adversaries; precisely what he had absorbed from two decades in America was unclear. But within weeks of planting his flag in Salem, he recognized that he had misjudged both the depth and the breadth of rebellion. The Coercive Acts, including the abrogation of colonial government in Massachusetts, had inflamed the insurrection. One ugly incident followed another. In mid-August, fifteen hundred insurgents prevented royal judges and magistrates from taking the bench in Berkshire County in western Massachusetts. Two weeks later, Gage sent foot troops to seize munitions from the provincial powder house, six miles northwest of Boston; rumors spread that the king's soldiers and sailors were butchering Bostonians. At least twenty thousand rebels

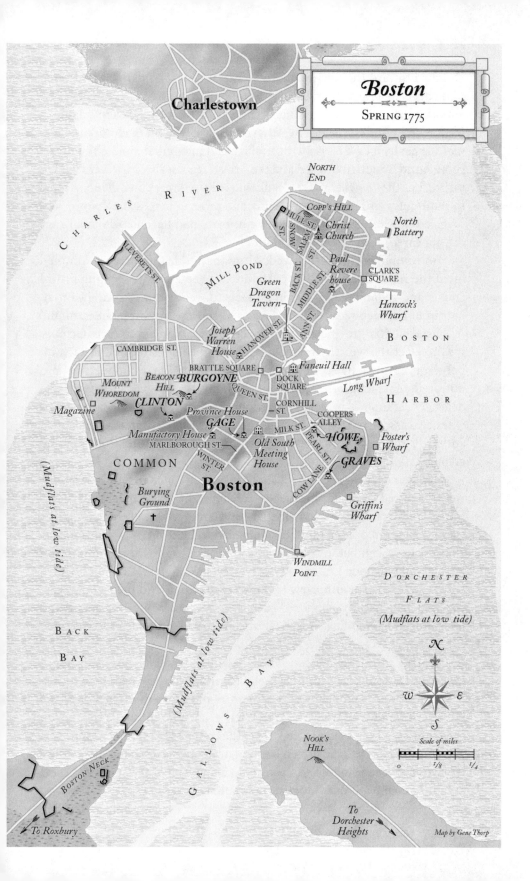

marched toward the town with firelocks, cudgels, and plowshares beaten into edged weapons. "For about fifty miles each way round, there was an almost universal ferment, rising, seizing arms," wrote one clergyman. An Irish merchant described how "at every house women & children [were] making cartridges" and pouring molten lead into bullet molds. The insurgents found Boston unbruised and the British regulars back in their fortified camps, but the "Powder Alarm" emboldened the Americans, demonstrated the militancy of bumpkins in farms and villages across the colony, and revealed how crippled the Crown's authority had become. "Popular rage has appeared," Gage advised London.

Additional episodes followed. More than four thousand militiamen lined the main street in Worcester in early September, closing the royal courts and requiring two dozen officials to walk a quarter-mile gantlet, hats in hand, each recanting his loyalty to the Crown thirty times, aloud. A Massachusetts Provincial Congress convened in Salem in early October 1774 to elect the wealthy merchant John Hancock as president—a vain, petulant "empty barrel," in John Adams's estimation. Of more than two hundred Massachusetts communities, only twenty-one failed to send delegates. Like similar congresses soon established in other colonies, this extralegal assembly acted as a provisional government to circumvent British authority by passing resolutions, collecting revenue, and coordinating colonial affairs with the Continental Congress in Philadelphia.

Amassing military supplies and making other martial preparations were entrusted to the Committee of Safety, led by Dr. Warren. Such committees in Massachusetts and other colonies enforced loyalty oaths, stigmatized ideological opponents, and compelled fence straddlers to make hard choices. In December, rebel raiders seized forty-four British cannons on Fort Island in Rhode Island. Two days later, several hundred men stormed a fortress in Portsmouth, New Hampshire, overpowered the six-man garrison, snatched nearly a hundred barrels of powder from the magazine, and lowered the British flag. A day later they returned to haul away sixteen cannons and sixty muskets.

Fearing for his own safety, Gage had abandoned Salem for Province House in Boston in late summer. Set back from Marlborough Street, with broad stone steps and the royal coat of arms affixed over the front door, the house featured wall tapestries, an iron fence, and ancient shade trees. Atop the eight-sided cupola swiveled a weathervane of hammered copper—a glass-eyed Indian in a feathered bonnet, drawing his bow and "bedazzling the eyes of those who looked upward, like an angel of the sun," as a local author named Nathaniel Hawthorne would later write.

From his high-ceilinged study, Gage had sent a volley of gloomy dispatches to London that fall. "Civil government is near its end," he warned in September, revoking his earlier optimism. "Conciliating, moderation, reasoning is over. Nothing can be done but by forcible means." To Lord Dartmouth, the colonial secretary, he expressed shock "that the country people could have been raised to such a pitch of phrenzy." American farmers for the past decade had generally been more restrained than their urban brethren in protesting British rule, but they now seemed just as bellicose; the imperial insult of closing the Boston port had proved especially offensive to them. Militia companies were training intensely; some had formed quick-reaction units called "minute men," who reportedly carried their muskets even to church. The "disease" of insurrection, Gage wrote, had become "so universal there is no knowing where to apply a remedy." Connecticut had ordered six militia regiments equipped for active service. Companies were drilling in New Hampshire and Rhode Island, and every county in Virginia was said to be arming soldiers. In obedience to the Continental Congress's declared boycott of British goods, thousands of provincials would soon serve on local committees throughout the colonies, enforcing the ban and rooting out "enemies of American liberty" with threats, public scoldings, and violence. As local assemblies and committees of safety grew stronger, royal governors grew weaker. To Barrington, the secretary at war, Gage pleaded in November, "If you think ten thousand men sufficient, send twenty. If one million is thought enough, give two. You will save both blood and treasure in the end."

Perhaps, he advised London, the Coercive Acts should be lifted as a conciliatory gesture. The king, appalled, replied that the "idea of suspending the acts appears to me the most absurd that can be suggested." Lord North insisted that "the acts must and should be carried into execution." While the government assembled reinforcements for Boston, including more generals, Gage's reputation sagged. There was muttering in England about the "lukewarm coward" in Massachusetts. His king referred to him as "the mild general," and his own soldiers now called him "Old Woman" behind his back. A senior officer concluded that "his disposition and manners are too gentle for the rough, republican fanatic people." Certainly there would be no more toasts and honor guards from those rough Americans. Instead, Gage effigies burned in bonfires. He was accused of papism, drunkenness, and even pederasty, as in a lewd verse that ended, "I'm informed by the innkeepers, / He'll bung with shoeboys, chimney sweepers." On the last day of 1774, Barrington wrote, "I pity, dear sir, the situation you are in."

The new year brought only new troubles. "Every day, every hour, widens the breach," Dr. Warren warned. On Sunday, February 26, barely a week before the Old South oration, Gage sent 240 regulars by naval transport from Boston across Massachusetts Bay to Marblehead, where they marched in a red column four miles northwest to Salem in search of rebel cannons while most local citizens were in church. A militia colonel burst into the North Meeting House, shouting, "The regulars are coming!" A raised drawbridge over the North River delayed the column; insurgents perched on the uptilted span like roosting chickens as "a vast multitude" soon assembled to heckle the troops as "lobstercoats" and to vow that "if you fire you will all be dead men." After ninety minutes, a compromise ended the standoff: the bridge was lowered, the troops tramped across, and after precisely 30 rods—165 yards—they made a smart about-face, as agreed, and returned to Boston empty-handed. "Go home," a young nurse named Sarah Tarrant barked from an open window, and "tell your master he has sent you on a fool's errand."

Gage could only agree. His governance reached no farther than could be seen through the glass eyes of the weathervane Indian above him, and his command was limited to the troops assembled within the sound of his voice on the Common. He expected imminent orders from London "to act offensively" since, as he readily acknowledged, "to keep quiet in the town of Boston only will not terminate affairs. The troops must march into the country." But in a dispatch written in early March, he warned the government of insurgent legions "actuated by an enthusiasm wild and ungovernable." American "bushmen," he added, had demonstrated "their patience and cunning in forming ambushments."

London promised to send him a hospital, "on a large scale."

The six weeks following Dr. Warren's oration were suffused with "dread suspense," as the Reverend William Emerson of Concord later wrote. Yet daily life plodded on. Goods smuggled or stockpiled before the port closing could be found for a price, including candles for five shillings a pound in the Faneuil Hall market, along with indigo and a few hogsheads of sugar. Greenleaf's Auction Room sold German serges, Irish linens, and Kippen's snuff by the cask. Harbottle Dorr's shop in Union Street advertised spades, Smith's anvils, and brass kettles, "none of which have been imported since the port was shut up." A vendor near Swing Bridge offered fish hooks, cod lines, and "nails of all sorts." With spring coming on fast, W. P. Bartlett's shop in Salem sold seeds for crimson radishes, yellow Spanish onions, tennisball lettuce, and several kinds of peas, including black-eyed, sugar, blue union, and speckled. "Choice cayenne cocoa" could be found on Hancock's Wharf, and pearl dentifrice—reputedly invented by the queen's dentist "for the preservation of the teeth"—was peddled in a shop on Ann Street. The London Book-Store in Cornhill, owned by gregarious young Henry Knox, offered lottery tickets and globes showing the reach of that empire on which the sun never set. For four pence on Marlborough Street, those desperate to glimpse a brighter tomorrow could buy a calculator that displayed the projected annual increase of colonial populations in America.

Auction houses sold the furniture of distraught residents determined to move—to England, to Halifax, deeper into New England, or just *away*. Mahogany tables, featherbeds, and looking glasses went for a song. For those who preferred to dance away their troubles, an unlikely new school in Boston offered lessons in minuets, hornpipes, and English country steps "in the most improved taste." The *Boston Gazette*, known to loyalists as "the Weekly Dung Barge," reminded readers that lofty talk of freedom had limits: a March 6 advertisement touted "a healthy Negro girl, about 20 years of age. . . . She is remarkably good-natured and fond of children. . . . Her price is £40." Another ad offered a reward for a runaway "servant for life," using the Massachusetts euphemism for a slave; this one, named Caesar, "is supposed to be strolling about in some of the neighboring towns. Walks lame and talks much of being free. . . . Had on when he went away a blue jacket." A Boston ordinance required the night watch "to take up all Negroes, Indians, and mulatto slaves that may be absent from their master's house after nine o'clock at night," unless they carried a lighted lantern and could account for themselves.

Freeholders gathered for meetings, as usual, in Faneuil Hall. The town agreed to borrow £600 to buy grain for the almshouse poor. A report in late March noted that thirty-eight smallpox patients were quarantined on a hospital scow in the Charles River, "some distance from the wharf." Freeholders voted to continue a recent ban on inoculation; many now feared that it posed a greater risk of epidemic than natural infection. Any household with sick inhabitants was required to display a large red flag on a six-foot pole or incur a £50 fine. For those intent on inoculation, newspapers advertised the services of a private hospital in New York.

Friction between patriots and loyalists intensified. Hundreds of Tories, as they often were called with a sneer, arrived from the provinces to seek the king's protection in Boston. The "once happy town" was now "a cage for every unclean bird," in Mrs. Samuel Adams's estimation. "Humbling the Tories" had become a blood sport in Massachusetts Bay, with excrement smeared on houses or dumped through open windows, with severed sheep's heads tossed into open chaises, or with loyalists locked in smokehouses—the chimney flues obstructed—until they renounced the Crown. A tavern keeper in South Danvers was forced to recite in public, "I, Isaac Wilson, a Tory I be, / I, Isaac Wilson, I sells tea." A radical Presbyterian cleric thanked God from the pulpit for "sufficient hemp in the colonies to hang all the Tories," while a loyalist woman hoped someday soon to be riding through rebel blood to the hubs of her carriage wheels. Small wonder that a Falmouth minister believed the colony was suffering "a discontent bordering on madness."

A Calvinist people marinated in the doctrine of predestination braced for the inevitable, and preparations for war continued apace. Clandestine military cargo had arrived all winter from Hamburg, Holland, even London, smuggled through a hundred coves and stored in a thousand barns. The Simsbury Iron Works in Connecticut cast cannonballs. Salem women secretly cut and stitched five thousand flannel powder cartridges for field guns. The provincial congress, meeting first in Cambridge and then in Concord, ordered enough military stores amassed for fifteen thousand militiamen: canteens, bell tents, field tents, Russian linen, wooden spoons. By April, the provincial stockpile included 21,549 firelocks, nine tons of gunpowder, eleven tons of cannonballs, ten thousand bayonets, 145,000 flints. Fifteen medicine chests, purchased for £500 from Boston apothecaries, contained opium, liquid laudanum, emetics, mercurial ointments, tourniquets, and a trepan for boring holes in a skull to relieve pressure from an injured brain. Dr. Warren would distribute the chests among seven towns by mid-April, including two sent to Concord.

Farm carts hauled ammunition and powder kegs down country lanes, to be hidden in attics or buried in new-plowed furrows, along with those radish and onion seeds. British soldiers searching a countryman's wagon in mid-March seized more than a ton of musket balls and over thirteen thousand musket cartridges stacked in candle boxes; the teamster insisted that the munitions were for his private use. But most shipments went undiscovered. In Concord a militia colonel, James Barrett, listed more than three dozen caches in his notebooks—including rice, ammunition, axes, oatmeal, and wood-bladed shovels rimmed with iron shoes. As ordered by the provincial Committee of Supply, he appointed "faithful men" to guard the stocks, with teams ready "by day and night, on the shortest notice" to haul the matériel away as required.

The provincial congress also chose five militia generals and approved a system for alerting the colony with mounted couriers in moments of peril. Several dozen articles of war were adopted; the first two required soldiers to attend church and to avoid profane oaths, with a fine of four shillings per cuss for officers, less for privates. Virtually every white male from sixteen to sixty in Massachusetts was required to serve under arms. "The parson as well as the squire stands in the ranks with a firelock," a Boston merchant wrote. Instead of exercising once every three months, many companies now met three times a week. An Essex County militia colonel, Timothy Pickering, simplified the manual of arms with his *Easy Plan of Discipline for a Militia*, which would be widely adopted. Muskets could be primed and loaded with one order and ten motions. "Lean the cheek against the butt of the firelock," the *Easy Plan* instructed. "Shut the left eye, and look with the right along the barrel."

Each company elected its own officers, but at a militia gathering in March, Reverend Emerson drew from the Second Book of Chronicles to remind the men of Concord who really led them: "Behold, God himself is with us for our captain."

Boston's natural beauty had once beguiled British soldiers. "The entrance to the harbor, and the view of the town of Boston from it, is the most charming thing I ever saw," an officer wrote home in 1774. That enchantment had faded by the spring of 1775. "No such thing as a play house," a lieutenant in the 23rd Foot complained. "They [are] too puritanical to admit such lewd diversions, though there's perhaps no town of its size could turn out more whores than this could." A captain in the 38th Foot told his brother in Ireland, "The people here and we are on bad terms, ready to cut one another's throats." Small insults bred seething resentments. All it took was an overbearing British customs official, mud flung at a fusilier on the street, or a fistfight over a girl between a "Jonathan"—a rebellious American, in British slang—and a lobstercoat.

A Royal Navy officer described seeing miniature effigies of British soldiers hanging by nooses from roadside trees, each wearing a tiny red coat. In March, a marine lieutenant reported how passing Bostonians made coarse gestures with their hands on their backsides. For their part, devout colonists resented regulars dishonoring the Sabbath by ice-skating across a Roxbury pond; they also loathed British Army profanity, which dated at least to the Hundred Years' War, when English bowmen were known as "Goddams." Major John Pitcairn, the marine commander in Boston, advised the Admiralty in March, "One active campaign, a smart action, and burning two or three of their towns, will set everything to rights. Nothing now, I am convinced, but this will ever convince these foolish bad people that England is in earnest."

The British garrison now exceeded five thousand, of whom more than four-fifths were soldiers, gunners, and marines in thirteen regiments. They crowded every corner of the town: artillerymen billeted in warehouses on Griffin's Wharf, the 4th Regiment of Foot—known as the King's Own—in a vacant distillery in West Boston, the 64th Foot in Castle William on a harbor island, the 43rd Foot on Back Street. Troops drilled in Brattle Square and on the Common, throwing stones to drive away the cows and avoiding the burial ground that held the graves of a hundred comrades dead from disease and mischance. Regiments took target practice on the wharves, six to ten rounds for each soldier, firing at river flotsam or at man-size figures cut from thin boards. A physician visiting from Virginia told his diary of watching light infantry exercises in late March, "young active fellows" who loaded firelocks while lying on their backs, then flipped over to fire from their bellies. "They run out in parties on the wings of the regiment," he added. "They secure their retreat & defend their front while they are forming."

Ugly encounters between Jonathans and lobstercoats multiplied. Officers mocked the Old South oration with a parody delivered from a coffee-house balcony in "the most vile, profane, blackguard language," a witness reported. In mid-March, soldiers from the King's Own pitched tents within ten yards of a meetinghouse and played drums and fifes throughout the worship service; troops later vandalized John Hancock's elegant house facing the Common. A peddler from Billerica named Thomas Ditson, Jr., who was accused by British soldiers of trying to buy old uniforms and a musket from the 47th Regiment, was stripped, tarred, feathered, and paraded from Foster's Wharf through King Street while a fifer played "The Rogue's March." A placard labeled "AMERICAN LIBERTY" was draped around his neck. "It gave great offense to the people of the town," a British officer wrote, "and was much disapproved of by General Gage."

The indiscipline of a bored, anxious army weighed on Gage. Gambling had become so pernicious that he imposed wager limits and established the Anti-Gambling Club. Worse still was inebriation in a town awash with cheap liquor. Regulars preferred West Indies rum, although it was often contaminated with lead, but 140 American distilleries also produced almost five million gallons a year, which sold for less than two shillings a gallon. "The rum is so cheap that it debauches both navy and army, and kills many of them," Major Pitcairn, the marine, warned the Admiralty in March. "It will destroy more of us than the Yankees will." A soldier caught trading his musket for a jug of New England Kill-Devil could draw five hundred lashes with a nine-cord cat, enough to lay bare the ribs and kidneys. Lieutenant Frederick Mackenzie of the 23rd Foot—the Royal Welch Fusiliers—recorded in his diary that many men "are intoxicated daily" and that two had died of alcohol poisoning in a single night. "When the soldiers are in a state of intoxication," he added, "they are frequently induced to desert."

And desert they did. Drunk or sober, redcoats were lured by Americans who offered farm-smock disguises, escape horses, and three hundred acres to any absconding regular. Estimates of British Army desertions over the past year ranged from 120 to more than 200. Five-guinea rewards were advertised by company officers in the *Boston Post-Boy* for the likes of Private Will Gibbs, "about 5 feet 7 inches high, and of a fair complexion," last seen wearing a round hat and a brown coat trimmed in blue. The problem was even worse for naval captains: more than twenty thousand British seamen had jumped ship in American ports since early in the century, and nearly another eighty thousand—almost 14 percent of all jack-tars who served—would abscond during the coming war, including those who deserted in home waters. Many had been forced into service by press gangs, while some detested the harsh life at sea; all resented the paltry nineteen shillings a month paid seamen since the reign of Charles II. Boston was particularly notorious for desertion, and the Royal Navy ships now blockading the harbor had remained at anchor through the winter with their gunports caulked and their topmasts housed against the weather, unable to berth for fear of mass defections.

Floggings, and worse, had limited deterrence. Private Valentine Duckett, barely twenty-one, had been sentenced to die after a three-day trial for desertion in the fall. "I am now to finish a life, which by the equitable law of my country, I just forfeited," he told his comrades while being lashed to a stake on the beach below the Common. A six-man firing squad botched the job even at eight yards' range, but after a coup de grâce to the head, the entire army was ordered to march "in a slow, solemn step" to view Private Duckett in his coffin. Private William Ferguson of the 10th Foot, a former tailor now dressed in a white shroud, suffered a similar fate on December 24. The execution, a lieutenant observed, was "the only thing done in remembrance of Christmas." On March 13, Gage commuted the death sentence of Private Robert Vaughan, but after more soldiers deserted the next day, the high command announced that this would be "the last man he will pardon." Vaughan took advantage of his reprieve to flee again a month later, this time without getting caught.

By contrast, many young British officers hankered for action. Among them was a tall, dark-eyed captain in the King's Own, the eldest son of a vicar from County Antrim. William Glanville Evelyn, now thirty-three and still unmarried, had a shark-fin nose, a dimpled chin, and the faint spatter of smallpox scars across his cheeks. He had soldiered for the king since the age of eighteen and was ever alert for the patron and cash needed to secure his next promotion; most army commissions came with a price tag, ensuring that only the better sort filled the officer ranks. (A lieutenant colonelcy in a foot regiment might cost £3,500.) In one of the sixteen surviving letters he would write from America, Evelyn assured his father that he was "pretty well known" to General Gage and that other senior officers in Boston had been "very civil to me." The 4th Foot—raised a century earlier and designated the King's Own to honor George I in 1714—was serving the empire at a critical moment in a vital place. To properly dress the part, Evelyn had asked that a Bedford Street cloth merchant in London send out scarlet, white, and blue material for two new uniforms, plus "the proper quantity of regimental buttons," a pair of epaulettes, and two hats "with silver buttons."

Nine months of duty in Boston had showed young Glanville Evelyn that a New England posting was not all hardship and tedium. "We get plenty of turtle, pineapple, and Madeira," he wrote. "The weather is delightful beyond description." Yet his contempt for the Americans had increased week by week. "There does not exist so great a set of rascals and poltroons," he told his father a month after arriving in Boston. By October 1774, he had concluded that "a civil war must inevitably happen in the course of a few months, or Great Britain might forever give up America." By December he fully shared his government's conviction that "a few enterprising, ambitious demagogues" had incited the insurrection; moreover, he believed that many thousands of loyalists were "inclined to our side," though they would not "openly declare themselves" until the Crown asserted its full authority. "Never," he wrote, "did any nation so much deserve to be made an example of to future ages." As his soldiers practiced their sharpshooting and beat their drums to annoy the Jonathans, Evelyn's greatest worry was that "unsteadiness" in Lord North's ministry might lead to a political settlement that spared the Americans from imperial wrath. "We only fear they will avail themselves of the clemency and generosity of the English," he wrote a cousin in London, "and evade the chastisement due to unexampled villainy, and which we are so impatiently waiting to inflict."

With the early arrival of spring, the chances of a pernicious peace faded. Captain Evelyn was glad. Blood had risen in his gorge. "The hour is now very nigh in which this affair will be brought to a crisis," he told his father. "The resolutions we expect are by this time upon the water, which are to determine the fate of Great Britain and America. . . . We shall shortly receive such orders as will authorize us to scourge the rebellion with rods of iron." As usual, he signed his letter, "Yours ever affectionate, W.G.E."

The expected orders arrived on Friday, April 14, when a burly, flush-faced dragoon captain bounded into Boston from the *Nautilus*. He had been sent ahead to Massachusetts to buy mounts for his regiment, now following on the high seas from Ireland, but his first task was to deliver a sealed dispatch marked "SECRET" to Province House. Striding past the budding elms and up the broad front steps beneath the gaze of the copper Indian on the roof, the captain handed over the document, saluted, and wandered off to look at horseflesh.

Upon breaking the seal, Gage found a twenty-four-paragraph letter from Lord Dartmouth, the Psalm Singer, written with the cocksure clarity of a man who slept in his own bed every night three thousand miles from trouble. Drafted on January 27, in consultation with the king and North's cabinet, the order had remained in Dartmouth's desk for weeks while events played out in London, including those futile conversations with Dr. Franklin, Parliament's minuet with the monarch at St. James's Palace, and the introduction of more punitive legislation. Further weeks passed while ill-tempered westerly gales kept *Nautilus* and her companion sloop *Falcon* pinned to the south coast of England. But at last the fatal command had arrived:

> The violences committed by those who have taken up arms in Massachusetts have appeared to me as the acts of a rude rabble, without concert, without conduct; and therefore I think that a small force now, if put to the test, would be able to conquer them. . . . It is the opinion of the King's servants, in which His Majesty concurs, that the essential step to be taken toward reestablishing government would be to arrest and imprison the principal actors and abettors in the provincial congress, whose proceedings appear in every light to be acts of treason and rebellion.

There was more: reinforcements were en route, though hardly the twenty thousand that Gage thought necessary. Twice Dartmouth conceded that "your own judgment and discretion" must shape any operation; yet, with proper preparation and secrecy, "it can hardly fail of success, and will perhaps be accomplished without bloodshed. . . . Any efforts on their part to encounter a regular force cannot be very formidable." It was agreed in

London that Gage had demonstrated restraint to the point of lamentable indulgence; now he must be firm, come what may. "The king's dignity and the honor and safety of the empire require that in such a situation, force should be repelled by force."

Although clear enough, this dispatch from Dartmouth was actually a duplicate. The original, with appended documents, was aboard the *Falcon*, and Gage, ever scrupulous, ever cautious, would await that vessel's arrival in Boston before striking. Meanwhile, there was plenty to do, and orders flew from Province House. Newly repaired navy longboats were to be lashed to the sterns of the *Somerset*, *Boyne*, and *Asia* for quick repositioning. The fortifications at Boston Neck, the slender isthmus leading into the town from Roxbury, would be double-checked for strength and security. Rumors were afoot that insurgents intended to burn Boston before British reinforcements arrived. A moat now stretched across the Neck, filled by each rising tide, and the defenses included a drawbridge, mud breastworks with walls twelve feet thick, wooden blockhouses, and more than twenty cannons.

Gage had no cavalry for a quick, bold strike into the countryside. Few enlisted regulars had ever heard a shot fired in anger, although a substantial number had been in uniform for five to ten years, or longer. The most agile and many of the strongest were grouped into elite light infantry and grenadier companies; regiments usually had one of each, typically with three dozen soldiers apiece. Forced to rely on infantry plodders, Gage ordered these elite troops relieved of their regular duties on Saturday, April 15, and formed into a makeshift brigade with twenty-one companies—eleven of grenadiers and ten of light infantry, some eight hundred men altogether. Gage, the man who had formed the Anti-Gambling Club, was betting that the advantage of concentrating these companies—with their skirmishing skills, marksmanship, and ferocity—would outweigh the disadvantage of severing them from their accustomed regiments and senior officers. Word of this improvisation quickly spread through Boston. "I dare say they have something for them to do," Lieutenant Barker told his diary.

But what, and where? Small, daylong expeditions had marched beyond Boston repeatedly in recent weeks—five regiments here, two there, trampling grain fields, toppling fences, gathering intelligence, and, not least, spooking the Jonathans. Gage also had dispatched officers "capable of taking sketches of a country." Dressed in country clothes—the disguises fooled no one—British scouts wandered into Suffolk and Middlesex Counties with instructions to "mark out the roads and distances from town to town." They also were to note the depth and breadth of rivers, to determine the steepness of creek banks, and to assess whether various churchyards "are advantageous spots to take post in, and capable of being made defensible."

Gage also had a clandestine espionage network. Through American spies on the British payroll, he knew that militia generals had been appointed. He knew that several dozen men, mostly artisans and mechanics, routinely met at the Green Dragon Tavern, a two-story brick building with symmetrical chimneys, to coordinate surveillance of British troop movements; at each meeting they swore themselves to secrecy on a Bible. Further, Gage had been told that mounted rebel couriers could quickly rouse 7,500 minutemen, and that caches of military stores were hidden in Worcester, Watertown, and other settlements. Even so, he doubted the Americans had a field marshal "capable of taking the command or directing the motions of an army."

That steady gaze of his had fixed on Concord, said to be the first village founded in Massachusetts Bay "beyond the sight and sound of the sea." Eighteen miles from Boston and now home to 265 families, it was a place where church attendance was compulsory, where the provincial congress sometimes met, and where, according to Gage's spies, munitions and other war supplies had been secreted in bulk. He even had a hand-drawn map, crude but detailed, showing the houses, outbuildings, and other hiding places where caches could be found.

The Americans, too, had informants. Gage would complain that the rebels collected "good, full, and expeditious intelligence on all matters transacting in England." Reports sent from London to patriot leaders warned of regiments preparing for deployment and of the blunt new instructions sent Gage. Since early April, many families had fled Boston for country refuges. Among the most prominent patriot leaders, only Dr. Warren remained in town. Samuel Adams and John Hancock had retired to Lexington, east of Concord. The provincial congress adjourned on April 15 for three weeks—entrusting the Committee of Safety to oversee military matters—and various false alarms kept the province on edge. Gage's concentration of longboats, grenadiers, and light infantry companies hardly passed unremarked. "Some secret expedition," one merchant noted, was no doubt afoot.

On Sunday, April 16, the *Falcon* glided into Boston Harbor. "In want of many men and stores, and very leaky" after her rough passage, as the Royal Navy reported, the sloop nonetheless carried Dartmouth's original orders. Now Gage could complete his preparations. Using the discretion permitted him, he chose to ignore Dartmouth's proposal of targeting "actors and abettors" like Hancock and Adams; chasing such scoundrels across the province seemed futile, if not capricious. A hard strike against the depot in Concord would be more fruitful, although disappointing late intelligence indicated that the cagey rebels had evacuated at least some military stocks to other sites. Opposition seemed unlikely except perhaps from scattered "parties of bushmen."

Gage drafted a 319-word order for Lieutenant Colonel Francis Smith of the 10th Foot, appointed to lead the strike brigade. If corpulent and edging toward retirement, Smith was mature, experienced, and prudent. He was to march "with the utmost expedition and secrecy to Concord," Gage noted, adding,

> You will seize and destroy all artillery, ammunition, provisions, tents, small arms, and all military stores whatever. But you will take care that the soldiers do not plunder the inhabitants, or hurt private property.

The map enclosed with the order illustrated Gage's demand that two bridges over the Concord River be secured by an advance "party of the best marchers." Captured gunpowder and flour were to be dumped into the river, tents burned, salt pork and beef supplies destroyed. Enemy field guns should be spiked or ruined with sledgehammers. The expedition would carry a single day's rations and no artillery; speed and surprise were essential. Sentries on horseback would be positioned to prevent rebel couriers from sounding an alarm.

Gage concluded his order without sentiment: "You will open your business and return with the troops as soon as possible."

And now, as one loyalist wrote, "The war began to redden. . . . The iron was quite hot enough to be hammered."

2.

———✦———

Men Came Down from the Clouds

LEXINGTON AND CONCORD, APRIL 18–19, 1775

S hadows scuttled beneath the elm and linden trees along Boston Common. Hoarse whispers carried on the night air, along with the creak of leather and the clatter of a stone kicked down a lane. It would later be reported that a barking dog was bayoneted to enforce the silence. Not until the moon rose at ten p.m. on Tuesday, April 18, three nights past full but still radiant, did shape and color emerge from the hurrying gray figures to reveal hundreds of men in blood-red coats congregating on the beach near the town magazine, close to where Privates Duckett and Ferguson had been shot for desertion. Moonglow glinted off metal buttons and silvered the tall bearskin caps of the grenadiers. The soldiers reeked of damp wool and sweat, mingled with the tang of the brick dust and pipe clay used to scour brass and leather. Their hair had been greased, powdered, and clubbed into queues held with leather straps. The moon also gave tint to the facings on their uniform coats—purple or green, buff or royal blue, depending on the regiment from which each man had been plucked for the march to Concord.

The navy had collected only twenty longboats, and two lifts would be needed to shuttle all eight hundred men to marshy Lechmere Point, a mile distant across Back Bay. Sailors bent to their ash oars against the tide, and the standing soldiers swayed with every stroke. Each man's kit included the eleven-pound Brown Bess, three dozen rounds of ammunition in a cartridge box, and a haversack to carry bread and salt pork. Beneath the heavy coats and crossbelts they wore wool waistcoats, white linen shirts, breeches buckled at the knee, and canvas or linen gaiters to keep pebbles from their low-topped brogans. Most wore black leather caps or felt hats with the brim stitched up to give a forepeak and two corners. Gorgets hung by neck cords at the officers' throats—small silver or gilt crescents worn as an emblem of rank, a last remnant of medieval armor.

Loading was haphazard, and as the soldiers clambered from the boats to wade through the reeds on the far shore, sergeants hissed and clucked

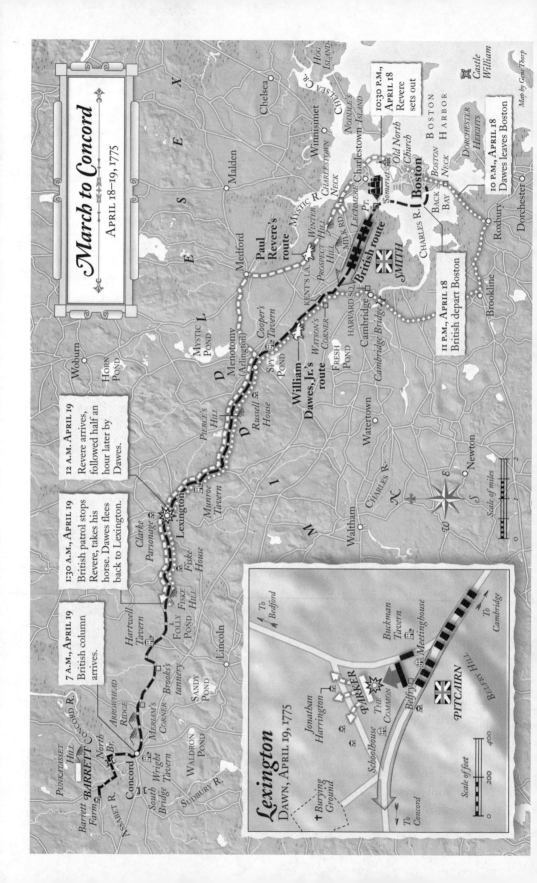

March to Concord
APRIL 18–19, 1775

10:30 P.M., APRIL 18 Revere sets out

10 P.M., APRIL 18 Dawes leaves Boston

11 P.M., APRIL 18 British depart Boston

12 A.M., APRIL 19 Revere arrives, followed half an hour later by Dawes.

1:30 A.M., APRIL 19 British patrol stops Revere, takes his horse. Dawes flees back to Lexington.

7 A.M., APRIL 19 British column arrives.

Paul Revere's route

William Dawes, Jr.'s route

British route

Scale of miles

Map by Gene Thorp

Lexington
DAWN, APRIL 19, 1775

Scale of feet

to reassemble the ten discomposed companies of light infantry and eleven of grenadiers. "We were wet up to the knees," Lieutenant Barker later reported. Midnight had passed by the time the second lift arrived, and further delays followed as navy provisions in the boats were handed out—supplies that, Barker added, "most of the men threw away." Fording a shallow inlet on the edge of Cambridge further wetted each shivering man to his waistcoat, but at last they reached the wide road leading west, unpaved except for napped stones and gravel shoveled into mud holes.

Few knew their destination. Two a.m. had come and gone as they put on speed. With their wet shoes squelching at more than a hundred steps per minute, their pace approached four miles an hour. Past apple and plum orchards they tramped, past smokehouses and cider mills and oblique driftways that led into cow pastures. The heavy footfall rattled pewter dishes on dressers and in cupboards, and an eight-year-old boy, awake when he should have been sleeping, later recalled a wondrous sight on the road outside his window: a long bobbing column of red, "like a flowing river," sweeping northwest beneath the gibbous moon.

A brigade of armed men tiptoeing through Boston in the middle of the night had not gone unnoticed. "The town," a British fusilier acknowledged, "was a good deal agitated." Joseph Warren may have watched the mustering troops himself; he lived in a rented house on Hanover Street, barely a mile from the foot of the Common, and several companies had made for the boats from his North End neighborhood. Regardless, he was soon well informed. Two weeks earlier, the provincial congress had agreed that an enemy force greater than five hundred men leaving town with baggage and artillery ought to be considered a threat to the province and met by an assembled "army of observation . . . to act solely on the defensive so long as it can be justified." This British force, even without heavy guns, was threatening enough for Dr. Warren. Before the first boats pulled off the Boston beach, he had summoned two couriers to carry the alarm to Samuel Adams and John Hancock, holed up in a Lexington parsonage, and to alert the wider countryside.

The first herald was a beefy, slab-jawed tanner in a slouched hat. William Dawes, Jr., barely thirty, still lived in Ann Street, where he had been raised by Puritan stock so strict that children were forbidden to look outside the window on Sundays and the instructive *School of Good Manners* advised, "Let thy recreations be lawful, brief, and seldom." Dawes had overcome such constrictions to become an adept smuggler, a patriot messenger, a militia adjutant, and an intelligence agent; while surveilling British officers, he supposedly sometimes posed as a vegetable peddler, sometimes as a miller, sometimes as a drunk. At Warren's instruction, he would now ride through the Boston Neck gate on a "slow-jogging horse," then loop northwest through Cambridge, rousing households on the way to Lexington.

The second herald had already proved his value as a trusted courier in nearly a dozen rides to New York, Philadelphia, New Hampshire, and, twice so far this month, Lexington and Concord. Paul Revere had often been mentioned in various newspapers over the past year because of the dispatches he carried hither and yon from Boston; he had, as the historian David Hackett Fischer would write, "a genius for being at the center of great events." Now forty, with the brown eyes of his French Huguenot forebears, a broad, ruddy face, and the sinewy arms of a metalworker, he had run his own business as a silver- and goldsmith for more than twenty years—making teapots, mending spoons, inventing alloys, and setting false teeth, including two for Dr. Warren. He had become a skilled copperplate engraver, a concocter of allegory and caricature, who also made plates for playing cards, broadside illustrations, and paper money. For all his legendary bravura, Revere's life was stained with tragedy: he would father sixteen children, his "little lambs," and most would die before their time.

This was *his* time. After a brief consultation with Warren, he hurried to his nearby house in Clark's Square, snatched up his riding boots and a long surtout, then picked his way through the twisting North End alleys to the waterfront. Two confederates waited with a dinghy. Softly they rowed from the wharf, against the young flood and under that old moon, with a temperate breeze stirring out of the southwest. Ahead loomed the *Somerset*, a seventy-gun warship anchored as a sentinel in the ferryway between Boston and Charlestown, in water so shallow she could barely swing at anchor. Some of *Somerset*'s crewmen were either manning the longboats at Lechmere Point or working her pumps; an inspection this week had showed the man-of-war to be in desperately poor repair—seams rotten, butt ends open, and long overdue for caulking and sheathing in Halifax. Whether distracted or sightless, the watch failed to spot the small boat that scooted past her stern and on to the Charlestown shore.

In 1775, America had more than three thousand churches, representing eighteen denominations, but none was more important on this April night than Christ Church in Boston's Salem Street. Known as Old North, the church featured eight great bells cast in England, a magnificent quartet of hand-carved wooden angels perched above the nave, and a towering steeple, long used as a landmark by navigators entering the harbor and featured in a Boston panorama engraved by Revere the previous year. As carefully planned earlier in the week, another confederate—Revere identified him only as "a friend"—climbed 154 stairs and then a rickety ladder to a window in the steeple's north face, lugging two lanterns of tinned steel with glass panels, pewter finials, and metal rings for hanging or carrying. For plainspun Boston, the lanterns—or at least the one that has survived— were fancy artifacts: fourteen inches high, six inches wide and deep, with two hundred perforations in the top, arranged to throw exquisite shadows shaped as circles, diamonds, and Maltese crosses. Flint and steel soon lighted the candles, and twin gleams could be seen across the harbor. As Revere intended, rebel leaders beyond the Charles now knew that British troops were on the move via Back Bay—two if by sea—rather than taking the more circuitous, one-if-by-land route through Roxbury.

Dramatic as the signal was, and as enduring in American iconography, it proved to be superfluous, since both Dawes and Revere successfully eluded British patrols to spread the word themselves. Handed the reins to a big brown New England mare, Revere swung into the saddle and took off at a canter across Charlestown Neck, hooves striking sparks, rider and steed merged into a single elegant creature, bound for glory.

Two hours later, Revere trotted into Lexington, his mount thoroughly lathered after outgalloping a pair of Gage's equestrian sentinels near Charlestown. Veering north toward the Mystic River to avoid further trouble, Revere had alerted almost every farmstead and minute captain within shouting distance. Popular lore later credited him with a stirring battle cry—"The British are coming!"—but a witness quoted him as warning, more prosaically, "The regulars are coming out." Now he carried the alarm to the Reverend Jonas Clarke's parsonage, just up the road from Lexington Common. Here Clarke had written three thousand sermons in twenty years; here he called up the stairs each morning to rouse his ten children—"Polly, Betsey, Lucy, Liddy, Patty, Sally, Thomas, Jonas, William, Peter, get up!" And here he had given sanctuary, in a bedroom to the left of the front door, to the renegades Hancock and Samuel Adams.

A squad of militiamen stood guard at the house as Revere dismounted, spurs clanking. Two warnings had already come from the east: as many as nine mounted British officers had been seen patrolling the Middlesex roads, perhaps "upon some evil design." At the door, a suspicious orderly sergeant challenged Revere, and Clarke blocked his path until Hancock reportedly called out, "Come in, Revere, we're not afraid of *you*." The herald delivered his message: British regulars by the hundreds were coming out, first by boat, then on foot. There was not a moment to lose.

Thirty minutes later, Dawes arrived with the same warning, and the two riders soon swung toward Concord. As Adams packed up to move deeper into the countryside, Hancock lumbered about the parsonage with his sword and pistol, prattling on about making a desperate stand until he, too, was persuaded to bolt for safety in his fine carriage.

Now the Lexington bell began to clang in the wooden tower, hard by the meetinghouse. More gallopers rode off to rouse half a hundred villages. Warning gunshots echoed from farm to farm. Bonfires flared. Drums beat. Across the colony, in an image that would endure for centuries, solemn men grabbed their firelocks and stalked off in search of danger, leaving the plow in the furrow, the hoe in the garden, the hammer on the anvil, the bucket at the well sweep. This day would be famous before it dawned.

Lexington spread across ten thousand acres, occupied by 750 people and 400 cows. Hardwood copses separated fields and pastures, and many small creeks snaked toward the distant Charles and Mystic Rivers. Two cleared acres had been given over to the Common, where the eleven-mile road from Charlestown approached straight and level for the final five hundred yards, then forked at the three-story meetinghouse, big and homely as a barn, before continuing to cover the six miles to Concord. On these two acres some 130 militiamen, summoned by that insistent pealing, milled about, stamping their feet against the nighttime chill. They awaited orders from their captain, John Parker, described as "a great tall man . . . with a high, wide brow." Now forty-five, a farmer, father of seven, and sometime town assessor, he had fought as a sergeant in the French and Indian War at Louisbourg and Quebec. Shadows falling across the Common deepened the dark sockets around Parker's eyes, symptomatic of the pulmonary tuberculosis that would kill him five months later.

Massachusetts Bay had been the first colony to form its militia into regiments, one per county in 1636, in an effort to fashion a military organization suitable for more than haphazard local defense. Each generation since had gone to war at least once; an estimated one in four able-bodied Massachusetts men had served in the last French war. Some militia units were little more than armed rabble, saluting unsuspecting officers by firing blank charges at their feet or sneaking up on young women before shooting into the air in a weird courtship ritual. Lexington's troops, ranging in age from sixteen to sixty-six, were more disciplined; under militia rules, any man interrupting the clerk while he called the roll was fined two shillings. The town had no minute company but had voted money for drums, a carriage to bury the dead, and gunpowder, now stored in the meetinghouse.

A scout dispatched in search of redcoats returned around three a.m. to advise Parker that none could be found. Perhaps this was another false alarm, or a British feint. Rather than keep his men out in the cold to no purpose, the captain dismissed the company with orders to reassemble at the sound of a drum. Some men ambled home. Most headed to the red-doored Buckman Tavern, an ancient "public house of entertainment" with a double hip roof on the edge of the Common. Here they could find a crackling fire and a mug of warm flip, heated at the hearth with a hot iron.

Parker's scout had not ventured far enough east. The British were coming on hard, spurred by the distant pop of warning shots and the gleam of alarm fires flaring on the horizon. Lieutenant Colonel Smith, the expedition commander, had heeded Gage's order to lunge for the Concord River bridges with a "party of the best marchers"; six light infantry companies now hurried ahead of the main column. Assured by a passing teamster that a thousand rebels were in arms, Smith also sent a courier to Boston to plead for reinforcements, a wise impulse.

The vanguard making for Concord was led by John Pitcairn. Not only was Major Pitcairn, the marine, now on horseback and far from the sea to which he was accustomed; he was commanding more than two hundred men from a half dozen army regiments to whom he was a stranger. The Scottish son of a Fifeshire minister, portly and affable with heavy brows and full lips, Pitcairn could usually be found in Old North Church on Sundays, although his weekday profanity was described as "a Boston legend." Now in his mid-fifties, he did not extend his geniality to rebels, who deserved only "severe chastisement." "If I draw my sword but half out of my scabbard," he had asserted, "the whole banditti of Massachusetts will run away." The major, an American clergyman later suggested, was "a good man in a bad cause."

As an apricot glow began to brighten the eastern sky soon after four a.m., the sounds of a country folk alert and alarmed intensified—bells, shots, distant hoofbeats. Pitcairn ordered his troops to halt and load their weapons, a portentous command. With practiced motions, each soldier plucked a paper cartridge from his waist pouch, bit open the end with his teeth, dribbled some powder grains into the musket flash pan, then poured the rest—close to half an ounce—down the muzzle, followed by the bullet and the cartridge wadding, which were tamped home with a steel ramrod. There was nothing precise about the Brown Bess—that "outspoken, flinty-lipped, brazen-faced jade," in Rudyard Kipling's description. Imperfect barrels, imperfect balls, a lack of sights, variable powder, and windage between ball and barrel meant the musket was marginally accurate at fifty yards, hopeless beyond a hundred. But that hardly mattered when bullets were fired in swarms at close range. The enormous lead slug, nearly three-quarters of an inch in diameter and an ounce in heft, could stop a charging bull.

At Pitcairn's command, the men seated their ramrods and surged forward, breathing hard, pulses pounding. The fourteen-inch bayonets on their muskets protruded above their heads like a picket fence. Scraps of cartridge paper, spat out, littered the road behind them.

The British were less than two miles from Lexington when another scout brought word to Parker of their approach. A drum beat to arms, and that infernal bell tolled again. Men in Buckman Tavern set their tankards next to the guttering candles and scrambled out to the Common. Other men, filling their powder horns in an upper gallery of the meetinghouse that served as the village armory, clattered down the stairs and through the door. But only half the company answered this second call, fewer than eighty men in two ranks, anxiously peering east for redcoats. "Don't molest them," Parker said, "without they being first." Precisely why he chose to confront a superior force from the exposed expanse of the village lawn rather than from a nearby thicket or stone wall would never be clear. Perhaps, dying himself, he had lost all impulse to seek shelter. Certainly he seemed fixed on something larger than this life. When an anxious militiaman said, "There are so few of us. It is folly to stand here," the captain replied, "The first man who offers to run shall be shot down."

Full dawn brought the loamy smell of plowed fields and another mild, pleasant morning. The British vanguard swung into view. The tramp of heavy brogans broke the quiet as three companies veered to the right of the meetinghouse at double-quick time. Pitcairn, on his horse, led the rest of the column to the left, following the curve of the Concord road before cantering onto the Common. A guttural roar began to build in the ranks, more growl than cheer. "Soldiers, don't fire," Pitcairn yelled, according to a British lieutenant. "Keep your ranks. Form and surround them." Spectators gawking from the road heard other officers yell, "Throw down your arms, ye villains, ye rebels!" and "Disperse, you rebels, immediately!" When regulars closed to within fifty yards, Parker apparently took the command to heart. As he swore in a deposition a week later, "Upon their sudden approach, I immediately ordered our militia to disperse and not to fire."

A single gunshot sounded above the clamor, possibly a warning shot or a sniper at Buckman Tavern. Whoever fired first on the Common would remain forever uncertain, but muskets quickly barked along the British line, promiscuous shooting from agitated soldiers in a makeshift command, led by a stranger. "Without any order or regularity," as Pitcairn later acknowledged, "the light infantry began a scattered fire . . . contrary to the repeated orders both of me and the officers that were present." With each trigger pulled, flint in the falling hammer struck a glancing blow against the steel frizzen, sprinkling sparks to ignite powder in the pan, which, in turn, set off the main charge through a touchhole in the side of the breech. Brilliant yellow flame erupted from each muzzle, along with a flat boom, a belch of smoke, and that heavy lead slug moving at a thousand feet per second. Those who outlived the day would remember the acrid smell of burning powder, the rattle of ramrods shoving home another volley, the whiz of balls that missed and the terrible thud of balls hitting home, the shouts, the screams, the puffs of dust from bullets smacking a wall, as if the stone were breathing. Billowing smoke grew so dense that soon only the upper torsos of officers on horseback could be seen clearly. One lieutenant from the 38th Foot lost control of his spooked mount, which bolted six hundred yards through the village until the rider finally reined in.

Few of Parker's men managed to fire more than once, if that. Nothing was right, except the courage. Militiaman John Munroe, grazed across the cheek and with a scorch mark on his jacket where another bullet had passed between his arm and his waist, fired, retreated a short distance, then loaded his musket with a double charge, which blew off a foot of the barrel. Jonas Parker, a cousin of the captain's, neatly placed his bullets and spare flints in a hat at his feet. A British ball knocked him to his knees, and as he fumbled to reload, British bayonets tore him dead. Pitcairn slashed at the air with his sword in a futile signal to cease fire. "Our men without any orders rushed in upon them," Lieutenant Barker of the King's Own told his diary. "The men were so wild they could hear no orders."

Only when Colonel Smith cantered into the village with his grenadier companies and ordered a drummer to beat to arms did the carnage end. "I was desirous," Smith later wrote, "of putting a stop to all further slaughter of those deluded people." After a final sputter of gunfire, gray smoke drifted off, revealing dying lumps on the greening grass, blood and so much more leaking away.

Lexington had been not a battle, or even a skirmish, but an execution. The only British casualties were two privates, lightly wounded by gunshots, and Pitcairn's horse, nicked twice in the flank. The American tally was far worse. Eight rebels were dead, nine wounded. Of those slain, only two bodies lay on the original American line. Several had taken bullets in the back while dispersing, including one man captured earlier in the morning and killed while ostensibly trying to escape a hundred yards to the east. Jonathan Harrington was shot close to his house on the western lip of the Common and reportedly died on his doorstep, within view of his wife and son.

Samuel Adams, upon hearing of the gunplay, exclaimed, "Oh, what a glorious morning is this!" But Adams had not been there to see the divine clay smeared on Lexington's green, along with the litter of hundreds of torn paper cartridges. Reverend Clarke was there, watching from several hundred yards' distance as Smith, who had prevented his men from pillaging the nearby houses, agreed to allow them a celebratory salute. The redcoats "drew up and formed in a body on the Common," Clarke reported, "fired a volley and gave three huzzahs by way of triumph." Then, forming again by companies, they turned and marched west, toward Concord.

Concord was ready for them. Paul Revere had been captured by a British mounted patrol at a bend in the road near Folly Pond, but William Dawes managed to escape at a gallop. Continuing his charmed morning, Revere—saucy and unrepentant, even with a pistol clapped to his head—was soon released, though without his brown mare, to make his way on foot back to the Clarke parsonage. But others had carried warnings into Concord, where a sentinel at the courthouse fired his musket and heaved on the bell rope. The clanging, said to have "the earnestness of speech" and pitched to wake the dead, soon drove all fifteen hundred living souls from their beds.

Reports of shooting in Lexington "spread like electric fire," by one account, though some insisted that the British would only load powder charges without bullets. Many families fled west or north, or into a secluded copse called Oaky Bottom, clutching the family Bible and a few place settings of silver while peering back to see if their houses were burning. Others buried their treasures in garden plots or lowered them down a well. Boys herded oxen and milk cows into the swamps, flicking at haunches with their switches.

Militiamen, alone or in clusters or in entire companies with fife and drum, rambled toward Concord, carrying pine torches and bullet pouches, their pockets stuffed with rye bread and cheese. They toted muskets, of course—some dating to the French war, or earlier—but also ancient fowling pieces, dirks, rapiers, sabers hammered from farm tools, and powder in cow horns delicately carved with designs or calligraphic inscriptions, an art form that had begun in Concord decades earlier and spread through the colonies. Some wore "long stockings with cowhide shoes," a witness wrote. "The coats and waistcoats were loose and of huge dimensions, with colors as various as the barks of oak, sumac, and other trees of our hills and swamps could make them." In Acton, six miles to the northwest,

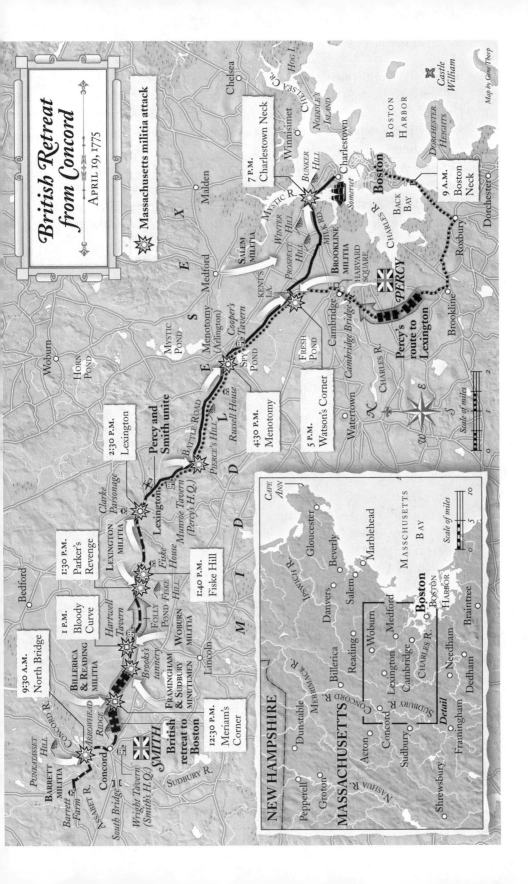

British Retreat from Concord
APRIL 19, 1775

✵ Massachusetts militia attack

Map by Gene Thorp

7 P.M. Charlestown Neck

9 A.M. Boston Neck

Percy's route to Lexington

2:30 P.M. Lexington
Percy and Smith unite

4:30 P.M. Menotomy

5 P.M. Watson's Corner

1:30 P.M. Parker's Revenge

1 P.M. Bloody Curve

1:40 P.M. Fiske Hill

9:30 A.M. North Bridge

12:30 P.M. Meriam's Corner
British retreat to Boston

Scale of miles

NEW HAMPSHIRE

MASSACHUSETTS

MASSACHUSETTS BAY

Detail

Scale of miles

nearly forty minutemen gathered at Captain Isaac Davis's house, polishing bayonets, replacing gunlock flints, and powdering their hair with flour. Davis, a thirty-year-old gunsmith with a beautiful musket, bade good-bye to his wife and four youngsters with a simple, "Hannah, take good care of the children."

"It seemed as if men came down from the clouds," another witness recalled. Some took posts on the two bridges spanning the Concord River, which looped west and north of town. Most made for the village green or Wright Tavern, swapping rumors and awaiting orders from Colonel James Barrett, the militia commander, a sixty-four-year-old miller and veteran of the French war who lived west of town. Dressed in an old coat and a leather apron, Barrett carried a naval cutlass with a plain grip and a straight, heavy blade forged a generation earlier in Birmingham. His men were tailors, shoemakers, smiths, farmers, and keepers from Concord's nine inns. But the appearance of tidy prosperity was deceiving: Concord was suffering a protracted decline from spent land, declining property values, and an exodus of young people, who had scattered to the frontier in Maine or New Hampshire rather than endure lower living standards than their elders had enjoyed. This economic decay, compounded by the Coercive Acts and British political repression, made these colonial Americans anxious for the future, nostalgic for the past, and, in the moment, angry.

Sometime before eight a.m., perhaps two hundred impatient militiamen headed for Lexington to the rap of drums and the trill of fifes. Twenty minutes later, eight hundred British soldiers hove into view barely a quarter mile away, like a scarlet dragon on the road near the junction known as Meriam's Corner. "The sun shined on their arms & they made a noble appearance in their red coats," Thaddeus Blood, a nineteen-year-old minuteman, later testified. "We retreated."

They fell back in an orderly column, as if leading an enemy parade into Concord, the air vibrant with competing drumbeats. "We marched before them with our drums and fifes going and also the British drums and fifes," militiaman Amos Barrett recalled. "We had grand music." Past the meetinghouse the militia marched, past the liberty pole that had been raised as an earnest of their beliefs. A brief argument erupted over whether to make a stand in the village—"If we die, let us die here," urged the militant minister William Emerson—but most favored better ground on the ridgeline a mile north, across the river. Colonel Barrett agreed, and ordered them to make for North Bridge. Concord was given over to the enemy.

The British brigade wound past Abner Wheeler's farm, and the farms of the widow Keturah Durant and the spinster seamstress Mary Burbeen and then the widow Olive Stow, who had sold much of her land, along with a horse, cows, swine, and salt pork, to pay her husband's debts when he'd died, three years earlier. They strode past the farms of Olive's brother, Farwell Jones, and the widow Rebecca Fletcher, whose husband also had died three years before, and the widower George Minot, a teacher with three motherless daughters, who was not presently at home because he was the captain of a Concord minute company. Into largely deserted Concord the regulars marched, in search of feed for the officers' horses and water for the parched men. From Burial Ground Hill, Smith and Pitcairn studied their hand-drawn map and scanned the terrain with a spyglass.

Gage's late intelligence was accurate: in recent weeks, most military stores in Concord had been dispersed to nine other villages or into deeper burrows of mud and manure. Regulars seized sixty barrels of flour found in a gristmill and a malt house, smashing them open and powdering the streets. They tossed five hundred pounds of musket balls into a millpond, knocked the trunnions from several iron cannons found in the jail yard, chopped down the liberty pole, and eventually made a bonfire of gun carriages, spare wheels, tent pegs, and a cache of wooden spoons. The blaze briefly spread to the town hall, until extinguished by a bucket brigade of regulars and villagers.

With the pickings slim in Concord, Colonel Smith ordered more than two hundred men under Captain Lawrence Parsons to march west toward Colonel Barrett's farm, two miles across the river. Perhaps they would have better hunting there.

Since 1654, a bridge had spanned the Concord River just north of the village. The current structure, sixteen feet wide and a hundred feet long, had been built for less than £65 in 1760 by twenty-six freemen and two slaves, using blasting powder and five teams of oxen. The timber frame featured eight bents to support the gracefully arcing deck, each with three stout piles wedged into the river bottom. Damage from seasonal floods required frequent repairs, and prudent wagon drivers carefully inspected the planks before crossing. A cobbled causeway traversed the marshy ground west of the river.

Seven British companies crossed the bridge around nine that Wednesday morning, stumping past stands of black ash, beech, and blossoming cherry. Dandelions brightened the roadside, and the soldiers' faces glistened with sweat. Three companies remained to guard the span, while the other four continued with Captain Parsons to the Barrett farm, where they would again be disappointed: "We did not find so much as we expected," an ensign acknowledged. A few old gun carriages were dragged from the barn, but searchers failed to spot stores hidden under pine boughs in Spruce Gutter or in garden furrows near the farm's sawmill.

The five Concord militia companies had taken post on Punkatasset Hill, a gentle but insistent slope half a mile north of the bridge. Two Lincoln companies and two more from Bedford joined them, along with Captain Davis's minute company from Acton, bringing their numbers to perhaps 450, a preponderance evident to the hundred or so redcoats peering up from the causeway; one uneasy British officer estimated the rebel force at fifteen hundred. On order, the Americans loaded their muskets and rambled downhill to within three hundred yards of the enemy. A militia captain admitted feeling "as solemn as if I was going to church."

Solemnity turned to fury at the sight of black smoke spiraling above the village: the small pyre of confiscated military supplies was mistaken for British arson. Lieutenant Joseph Hosmer, a hog reeve and furniture maker, was described as "the most dangerous man in Concord" because young men would follow wherever he led. Now Hosmer was ready to lead them back across the bridge. "Will you let them burn the town down?" he cried.

Colonel Barrett agreed. They had waited long enough. Captain Davis was ordered to move his Acton minutemen to the head of the column—"I haven't a man who's afraid to go," Davis replied—followed by the two Concord minute companies; their bayonets would help repel any British counterattack. The column surged forward in two files. Some later claimed that fifers tootled "The White Cockade," a Scottish dance air celebrating the Jacobite uprising of 1745. Others recalled only silence but for footfall and Barrett's command "not to fire first." The militia, a British soldier reported, advanced "with the greatest regularity."

Captain Walter Laurie, commanding the three light infantry companies, ordered his men to scramble back to the east side of the bridge and into "street-firing" positions, a complex formation designed for a constricted field of fire. Confusion followed, as a stranger again commanded strangers. Some redcoats braced themselves near the abutments. Others spilled into an adjacent field or tried to pull up planks from the bridge deck.

Without orders, a British soldier fired into the river. The white splash rose as if from a thrown stone. More shots followed, a spatter of musketry that built into a ragged volley. Much of the British fire flew high—common among nervous or ill-trained troops—but not all. Captain Davis of Acton pitched over dead, blood from a gaping chest wound spattering the men next to him. Private Abner Hosmer also fell dead, killed by a ball that hit below his left eye and blew through the back of his neck. Three others were wounded, including a young fifer and Private Joshua Brooks of Lincoln, grazed in the forehead so cleanly that another private concluded that the

British, improbably, were "firing jackknives." Others knew better. Captain David Brown, who lived with his wife, Abigail, and ten children two hundred yards uphill from the bridge, shouted, "God damn them, they are firing balls! Fire, men, fire!" The cry became an echo, sweeping the ranks: "Fire! For God's sake, fire!" The crash of muskets rose to a roar.

"A general popping from them ensued," Captain Laurie later told General Gage. One of his lieutenants had reloaded when a bullet slammed into his chest, spinning him around. Three other lieutenants were wounded in quick succession, making casualties of half the British officers at the bridge and ending Laurie's fragile control over his detachment. Redcoats began leaking to the rear, and soon all three companies broke toward Concord, abandoning some of their wounded. "We was obliged to give way," an ensign acknowledged, "then run with the greatest precipitance." Amos Barrett reported that the British were "running and hobbling about, looking back to see if we was after them."

Battle smoke draped the river. Three minutes of gunplay had cost five American casualties, including two dead. For the British, eight were wounded and two killed, but another badly hurt soldier, trying to regain his feet, was mortally insulted by minuteman Ammi White, who crushed his skull with a hatchet.

A peculiar quiet descended over what the poet James Russell Lowell would call "that era-parting bridge," across which the old world passed into the new. Some militiamen began to pursue the fleeing British into Concord, but then veered from the road to shelter behind a stone wall. Most wandered back toward Punkatasset Hill, bearing the corpses of Davis and Abner Hosmer. "After the fire," a private recalled, "everyone appeared to be his own commander."

Colonel Smith had started toward the river with grenadier reinforcements, then thought better of it and trooped back into Concord. The four companies previously sent with Captain Parsons to Barrett's farm now trotted unhindered across the bridge, only to find the dying comrade mutilated by White's ax, his brains uncapped. The atrocity grew in the retelling: soon enraged British soldiers claimed that he and others had been scalped, their noses and ears sliced off, their eyes gouged out.

As Noah Parkhurst from Lincoln observed moments after the shooting stopped, "Now the war has begun and no one knows when it will end."

No fifes and drums would play the British back to Boston. From his command post in Wright Tavern, Smith, described by one of his lieutenants as "a very fat heavy man," moved with unwonted agility in organizing the retreat. Badly wounded privates would be left to rebel mercy, but horse-drawn chaises for injured officers were wheeled out from Concord's barns and stables. Troops filled their canteens, companies again arranged themselves in march order, and a final round of food and brandy was tossed back. Before noon the red procession headed east, silent and somber, every man aware that eighteen miles of danger lay ahead.

The first mile proved almost tranquil. The road here was wide enough—four rods, or sixty-six feet—for the troops to march eight abreast, in a column stretching three hundred yards or more. Using tactics honed during years of combat in North American woodlands, scores of light infantry flankers swept through the tilled fields and apple orchards, stumbling over frost-heaved rocks while searching for rebel ambushers. "The country was an amazing strong one, full of hills, woods, stone walls, &c.," Lieutenant Barker of the King's Own would tell his diary. "They were so concealed there was hardly any seeing them."

But the rebels were there. Arrowhead Ridge loomed above the north side of the road, offering a sheltered corridor through the Great Fields for hundreds of militiamen hurrying from North Bridge to Meriam's Corner. Here the road narrowed to a causeway across boggy ground, canalizing and slowing the column. Skirmishers in slouch hats could be seen loping behind outbuildings and across the pastures and meadows. British soldiers wheeled and fired, but again threw their shot high. "This ineffectual fire gave the rebels more confidence," one officer observed. A return volley killed two redcoats and wounded several more. Some officers dismounted to be less conspicuous; the morning had demonstrated how American marksmen—"with the most unmanly barbarity," a redcoat complained—already had begun targeting those with shiny gorgets at their necks and the bright vermilion coats commonly worn by the higher ranks.

Now the running gun battle began in earnest, with crackling musketry and spurts of smoke and flame. The provincial ranks swelled to a thousand, twelve hundred, fifteen hundred, more by the hour—"monstrous numerous," a British soldier would write to his mother. The road—Battle Road, as it would be remembered—angled past Joshua Brooks's tannery; the smell of tannins rose from the pits, drying racks, and currier shop, and a sharper odor wafted from the nearby slaughterhouse that sluiced offal into Elm Brook. Just to the east, past where the wetlands had been ditched and drained to create a hay meadow, the road began to climb through a cut made in the brow of a wooded hill, then nearly doubled back on itself in a hairpin loop soon known as the Bloody Curve. Here was "a young growth of wood well-filled with Americans," a minuteman wrote. "The enemy was now completely between two fires."

Plunging fire gashed the column; grazing fire raked it. Men primed, loaded, and shot as fast as their fumbling hands allowed. A great nimbus of smoke rolled across the crest of the hill. Bullets nickered and pinged, and some hit flesh with the dull thump of a club beating a heavy rug. Militiamen darted from behind stone walls to snatch muskets and cartridge boxes from eight dead redcoats and several wounded who lay writhing in the Bloody Curve. One regular later acknowledged in a letter home that the rebels "fought like bears." An American private reported seeing a wounded grenadier stabbed repeatedly by passing militiamen so that "blood was flowing from many holes in his waistcoat." He later reflected, "Our men seemed maddened with the sight of British blood, and infuriated to wreak vengeance on the wounded and helpless."

More vengeance lurked a mile and a half ahead. Captain John Parker's company had suffered seventeen casualties in Lexington eight hours earlier, but Parker and his men—perhaps a hundred or more—were keen to fight again. Two miles west of the Common, they dispersed above a granite outcrop in a five-acre woodlot thick with hardwood—hickory, beech, chestnut, red and white oak—and huckleberry bushes. Battle noise drifted from the west, and around two p.m. the thin red line came into view six hundred yards down Battle Road, moving briskly despite more than sixty wounded, not to mention the two dozen dead already left behind. A small bridge at a sharp bend in the road again constricted the column, and as the British vanguard approached within forty yards, the rebels fired. Bullets struck Colonel Smith in the thigh and Captain Parsons in the arm. Major Pitcairn galloped forward to take command as redcoats sprayed the woodlot with lead slugs. When enemy soldiers began to bound up both flanks, Parker and his men turned and scampered through the trees, drifting toward Lexington to join other lurking ambuscades.

The "plaguey fire," as one British captain called it, now threatened the column with annihilation. "I had my hat shot off my head three times," a soldier later reported. "Two balls went through my coat, and carried away my bayonet from my side." Gunfire seemed to swarm from all compass points at Bloody Bluff and, five hundred yards farther on, at Fiske Hill. Pitcairn's horse threw him to the ground, then cleared a wall and fled into the rebel lines. The major wrapped up his injured arm and pressed on. Ensign Jeremy Lister was shot through the right elbow; a surgeon's mate extracted the ball from under his skin, but a half dozen bone fragments would later be removed, some the size of hazelnuts.

The combat grew even more ferocious and intimate at Ebenezer Fiske's house, still thirteen miles from Boston Harbor. James Hayward, a twenty-five-year-old teacher, had left his father's farm in Acton that morning with a pound of powder and forty balls. At Fiske's well, he abruptly encountered a British soldier. Both fired. The redcoat died on the spot; Hayward would linger for eight hours before passing, shards of powder horn driven into his hip by the enemy bullet. Several wounded British soldiers were left by their comrades in the Fiske parlor, and there they died.

"Our ammunition began to fail, and the light companies were so fatigued with flanking they were scarce able to act," Ensign Henry De Berniere later wrote. "We began to run rather than retreat." Officers tried to force the men back into formation, but "the confusion increased rather than lessened." Hands and faces were smeared black from the greasy powder residue on ramrods; tiny powder burns from firelock touchholes flecked collars. The ragged procession entered Lexington, with the blood-streaked Common on the left. Officers again strode to the front of the column, brandished their weapons, and "told the men if they advanced they should die," De Berniere added.

And then, like a crimson apparition, more than a thousand redcoats appeared on rising ground half a mile east of the village: three infantry regiments of the 1st Brigade and a marine battalion, sent from Boston as reinforcements. Smith's beleaguered men gave a hoarse shout and pelted forward into the new British line, "their tongues hanging out of their mouths, like those of dogs after a chase," as a later account described them. Wounded men collapsed under the elm trees or crowded into Munroe Tavern, sprawling across the second-floor dance hall or in bunks normally rented by passing drovers. To the delight of those rescued, and the dismay of the insurgents close on their heels, two Royal Artillery guns began to boom near the tavern, shearing tree limbs around the Common and punching a hole in Reverend Clarke's meetinghouse. Gunners in white breeches with black spatterdashes swabbed each bore with a sponge, then rammed home another propellant charge and 6-pound ball. Sputtering portfire touched the firing vents and the guns boomed again with great belches of white smoke. Cast-iron shot skipped across the ground a thousand yards or so downrange, then skipped again with enough terrifying velocity to send every militiaman—under British artillery fire for the first time ever—diving for cover.

Overseeing this spectacle from atop his white charger, splendidly uniformed in scarlet, royal blue, and gold trim, Brigadier Hugh Earl Percy could only feel pleased with his brigade and with himself. "I had the happiness," he would write his father, the Duke of Northumberland, on the following day, "of saving them from inevitable destruction." Heir to one of the empire's greatest fortunes and a former aide-de-camp to George III, Lord Percy at thirty-two was spindly and handsome, with high cheekbones, alert eyes, and a nose like a harpoon blade. As a member of Parliament, he at times had opposed the government's policies, including the coercive measures against Massachusetts. As a professional soldier, he was capable, popular—the £700 spent from his own pocket to transport his soldiers' families to Boston helped—and a diligent student of war, sometimes citing Frederick the Great, whose maxim on artillery was proved here in Lexington: "Cannon lends dignity to what might otherwise be a vulgar brawl."

A year in New England had expunged whatever theoretical affection Percy held for the colonists, whom he now considered "extremely violent & wrong-headed," if not "the most designing, artful villains in the world." To a friend in England he wrote, "This is the most beautiful country I ever saw in my life, & if the people were only like it, we should do very well. . . . I cannot but despise them completely." Now he was killing them.

Two blunders early in the day had already marred the rescue mission. Gage's letter directing the 1st Brigade to muster at four a.m. on the Common was carelessly mislaid for several hours. Then the marines failed to get word—the order was addressed to Major Pitcairn, who had long departed Boston—causing further delays. At nine a.m., five hours late, Percy's column had surged across Boston Neck. "Not a smiling face was among them," a clergyman reported. "Their countenances were sad." To lift spirits, fifers played a ditty first heard in a Philadelphia comic opera in 1767, with lyrics since improvised by British soldiers:

> *Yankee Doodle came to town*
> *For to buy a firelock;*
> *We will tar and feather him*
> *And so we will John Hancock.*

Not until one p.m., after passing the village of Menotomy, five miles from Lexington, did Percy first get word that Smith's beleaguered expedition was retreating in mortal peril. By that time, a third mishap was playing out behind him. Desperate to make speed from Boston, Percy had declined to take a heavy wagon loaded with 140 extra artillery rounds; until reprovisioned, his gunners would make do with the twenty-four rounds carried for each 6-pounder in their side boxes, just as each infantryman would make do with his thirty-six musket cartridges. Two supply wagons had eventually followed the column only to be ambushed by a dozen "exempts"—men too old for militia duty—at an old cider mill across from the Menotomy meetinghouse. Two soldiers and four horses were killed, and several other redcoats were captured after reportedly tossing their muskets into Spy Pond. Rebels dragged the carcasses into a field, hid the wagons in a hollow, and swept dust over bloodstains on the road.

At three-fifteen p.m., Percy ordered his troops, now eighteen hundred strong, back to Boston. The Royal Welch Fusiliers formed a rear guard, and Smith's exhausted men tucked in among their fresher comrades. The wounded hobbled as best they could or rode on gun barrels or the side boxes, spilling off whenever gunners unlimbered to hurl more iron shot. Percy was unaware that his supply train had been bushwhacked and that rebel numbers were approaching four thousand as companies from the outer counties arrived. Despite those dignified cannons, he was in for a vulgar brawl.

Looting began even before the column cleared Lexington. In light infantry slang, "lob" meant plunder taken without opposition; "grab" was booty taken by force. "There never was a more expert set than the light infantry at either grab, lob, or gutting a house," a British officer later acknowledged. Lieutenant Barker complained in his diary that soldiers on the return march "were so wild and irregular that there was no keeping 'em in any order. . . . The plundering was shameful." Sheets snatched from beds served as peddler's packs to carry beaver hats, spinning wheels, mirrors, goatskin breeches, an eight-day clock, delftware, earrings, a Bible with silver clasps, a dung fork. "Many houses were plundered," Lieutenant Mackenzie wrote. "I have no doubt this enflamed the rebels. . . . Some soldiers who stayed too long in the houses were killed in the very act of plundering."

Every mile brought heavier fire. "We were attacked on all sides," wrote Captain Glanville Evelyn, whose King's Own company accompanied Percy, "from woods and orchards and stone walls, and from every house on the road. . . . They are the most absolute cowards on the face of the earth." The day's bloodiest fighting erupted in Menotomy—street to street, house to house, room to room. Here twenty-five Americans and forty British would die, with scores more wounded. "All that were found in the houses," Lieutenant Barker wrote, "were put to death."

Over a hundred British bullets perforated Cooper's Tavern while the innkeeper and his wife cowered in the cellar. Two unarmed patrons were killed upstairs, according to a deposition, "their brains dashed across the floor and walls." At the Jason Russell house, Danvers militiamen piled up shingles as a breastwork in the yard only to be outflanked and caught in a British cross fire. Some fled into the house as balls poured through the windows, "making havoc of glass." Russell was shot on his doorstep and bayoneted nearly a dozen times; Timothy Munroe ran for his life and escaped, despite a bullet in the leg and buttons on his waistcoat shot away. Eight militiamen who barricaded themselves in the cellar survived after shooting a regular who ventured down the stairs, but others upstairs were killed, perhaps executed. A dozen bodies later were laid side by side in the south room, their blood soaking the plank floor.

"We retired for 15 miles under an incessant fire, which like a moving circle, surrounded and followed us wherever we went," Percy would write the following day. "It was impossible not to lose a good many men." He would have lost a good many more had he not made the best British tactical decision of the day. As his vanguard approached Cambridge around five p.m., Percy studied two paper sheets pinned together as a sketch map of the road ahead. Rather than returning via the only bridge over the Charles River to reach Roxbury and Boston Neck, he ordered the column to pivot left into Kent's Lane and head for Charlestown. The route would require ferrying his men into Boston, but *Somerset* and other warships would offer protection. As he suspected and later confirmed, a large rebel force had tossed the bridge planks into the Charles and militiamen waited in ambush behind barricades. Had the column not veered away, a senior British general later concluded, "there would have been an end that day of British government in America."

The final miles to Charlestown were harrowing enough—casualties climbing, ammunition dwindling, sun sinking, men at the last pitch of exhaustion. The column avoided an ambush at Harvard Square, but several soldiers died in another gunfight near the future Beech and Elm Streets while three rebels who had built a redoubt at Watson's Corner were encircled and bayoneted. William Marcy, described as "a simple-minded youth" who thought he was watching a parade, was shot dead while sitting on a wall, cheering. Percy's white charger was also hit; he found another, nonplussed to see American gunmen who, he wrote, "advanced within ten yards to fire at me & other officers." Ensign Jeremy Lister, slumped on a horse and faint with blood loss from his shattered elbow, "found the balls whistled so smartly about my ears I thought it more prudent to dismount." It was said that footsore soldiers flung themselves onto low ground near the Charles and "drank like dogs from an old pond." Now everyone's tongue was hanging out. "Taking the whole together," a militiaman wrote, "it was the most fatiguing day's work I ever heard of."

Of Cambridge's eight hundred residents, many hid a mile west at Fresh Pond. Hannah Winthrop, the wife of a Harvard mathematics professor, wrote that a remote house there was "filled with women whose husbands had gone forth to meet the assailants, seventy or eighty of these, with numbers of infant children, weeping and agonizing for the fate of their husbands." In Charlestown, the chatter of musketry and an occasional cannon boom carried from Milk Road on the approach to Charlestown Neck.

Dusk brightened each muzzle flash, and scarlet bursts limned the line of retreat. Some Charlestown residents fled across the Mystic River at Penny Ferry or scurried along the marshes toward Medford. Others hid in clay quarries below the high pasture that would soon be known as Breed's Hill. Terrified women and children huddled in the local Pest House, usually reserved for the infectious. Returning British officers crowded a tavern near the town hall. "All was tumult and confusion," a witness reported, "nothing but drink called for everywhere." Edward Barber, the fourteen-year-old son of a sea captain, was shot dead while watching the column from his front window. Rumors spread quickly that the British were massacring children.

The shooting ebbed and finally faded away, along with this very long day. Percy ordered the grenadiers and light infantry to the Charlestown wharves, where boat crews waited to row them the half mile to Boston. Five hundred fresh regulars arrived to garrison the heights below Charlestown Neck, including Bunker Hill. Militiamen scraped beds from the hillsides north of the Neck or stumbled back into Cambridge to sleep on their arms. "The civil war was begun at Concord this morning," a parson told his diary. "Lord direct all things for His glory." A Roxbury physician said simply, "Well, the nail is driven."

The great spire atop Old North loomed above the river. Keening carried from the homes of the dead. The moon rose, a bit later than the previous night, and found the world changed, changed utterly.

A thousand campfires glittered from the high ground in a semicircle around Boston, tracing the contours of the siege that would last for almost a year. Rebel sentinels posted the Neck at Roxbury, and patrols scuffed through the night. "We had as much liquor as we wanted," Private Samuel Haws wrote in his journal, "and every man drawed three biscuit which were taken from the Regulars the day before, which were hard enough for flints." British ships remained cleared for action, with guard boats doubled and the Charlestown ferry lane closed but for the steady shuttling of soldiers back to their barracks. In a tense conference with General Gage late Wednesday night, the Royal Navy urged "burning and laying waste the whole country" before insurgents could attack the garrison. Gage rejected the proposal as "too rash and sanguinary," and soon pulled his exposed troops from the Charlestown peninsula. British rule in New England now ended at Boston's town limits.

The countryside hardly slept. Horses, cattle, pigs, and men lay dead across a twenty-mile corridor from the Charles to the Concord River. A rumor that redcoats were on the march northeast of Boston sent civilians fleeing into the woods, the village streets behind them strewn with bedding and cookware that had tumbled from farm carts. "Men and horses driving post up and down the roads," a deacon in Brighton noted in his diary. "People were in great perplexity." More family silver was lowered down wells or tucked into tree hollows. Horses were saddled and unsaddled, oxen yoked and unyoked. Some farmers armed themselves with pikes, whittled sharp and fire-hardened.

Women in Framingham clutched axes and pitchforks, convinced that black servants incited by the British were intent on murder. A similar report in Menotomy prompted a woman to ask her approaching slave, "Are you going to kill us, Ishmael?" The Anglican church in Cambridge became a field hospital, and wounded men jammed private homes. Nathaniel Cleaves of Beverly would receive a three-shilling bill from a surgeon for "amputating finger, sutures, &c.," and Israel Everett was also charged three shillings, for "extracting a bullet from the cubitus," the forearm. Samuel Whittemore, said to be eighty-one when he fought with musket, pistols, and sword behind a stone wall west of Cambridge, was treated for bayonet wounds and a gunshot that carried away part of his cheek; he would live to see his great-great-grandchildren, according to the obituary published when he died at ninety-eight in 1793. Young John Tolman, shot between the shoulder blades and left for dead, also recovered to write, in his old age, "Freedom or independence was the hobby I mounted, sword in hand, neck or nothing, life or death."

In Boston, surgeons toiled in the barracks and wherever wounded regulars had collapsed, snipping off bloody uniforms, lopping away ruined arms and legs, dosing their patients with Jesuit's bark in an effort, often vain, to prevent mortification. Officer casualty rolls listed the wounds with anatomical simplicity: "thigh," "breast," "throat." One British doctor complained in a letter home that American balls were deliberately scored to shatter on impact and inflict greater damage. Perhaps, but more typically hand-cast bullets often had a ridged seam that left hideous, ragged wounds. The butcher's bill was grim indeed. British casualties totaled 273, nearly 15 percent of the total force that marched into Middlesex on April 19; of those, 73 men were killed or would die of their wounds. American casualties numbered 95, over half of them—49—dead.

Collecting bodies began promptly. A Dedham militia company was ordered to search the battlefield and to bury the unburied. Reverend David McClure rode from Roxbury toward Lexington in the drizzle that fell on Thursday, April 20. "I saw several dead bodies, principally British, on & near the road," he wrote. "They were all naked, having been stripped. . . . They lay on their faces." As a gesture to British widows and orphans she would never know but could not ignore, Mary Hartwell of Lincoln took her children by the hand and followed an ox-cart hearse to a large trench in the town burial ground where the dead regulars were interred. "There was one in a brilliant uniform, whom I supposed to have been an officer," she recalled. "His hair was tied up in a queue."

The fourteen-year-old son of John Hicks found his father's body on the roadside near the Watson's Corner barricade; the boy took him home in a wagon. The corpse of Isaac Davis, killed in the first volley at North Bridge, was laid out in his bedroom before interment with some of his other comrades from Acton. "His countenance was pleasant, and seemed little altered," his widow, Hannah, would recall in 1835 when she was eighty-nine. Davis's epitaph deemed him "a loving husband, a tender father, a kind neighbor, an ingenious craftsman, and serviceable to mankind."

In Danvers, a young girl noted that the seven dead men stacked on a cart all wore gray homespun stockings; two minute companies with reversed arms and muffled drums escorted them to their common grave. A dozen corpses in Menotomy were hauled to a burial trench on an ox-drawn sled, legs and arms splayed and rubbery; they were buried, a witness reported, "head to point, with their clothes on just as they fell." The eight dead from Lexington were laid in rude coffins, described as "four large boards nailed up." Villagers dug a trench close to the tree line in the cemetery. "I saw them let down into the ground," a daughter of Reverend Clarke recalled. "It was a little rainy, but we waited to see them covered up with clods." Using pine and oak boughs, the parson himself helped hide the raw gash in case the British should return in a mood of desecration.

The British would never return, not here. The first of the war's thirteen hundred actions had been fought, the first battle deaths mourned. Fifty-eight towns and villages, from Acton to Woburn, had sent men into the fight; fourteen thousand had marched against the regulars, of whom about four thousand actually heaved themselves at the British column. For all the chaos of the day, the Americans had demonstrated impressive organizational skills, although combat leadership above the grade of captain had been erratic and sometimes nonexistent. Each militia company had essentially fought alone, improvising without tactical orchestration from higher command. A Massachusetts general—the tubby, sensible William Heath of Roxbury—had trundled out to Menotomy on Wednesday afternoon, perhaps inspiriting young musketmen but hardly imposing his will on what was the first battle he had ever seen. On Thursday he would be supplanted by Major General Artemas Ward, who shrugged off an excruciating attack of kidney stones to ride forty miles from his Shrewsbury farm to Cambridge.

The limits of the musket even in close combat were clear enough after the daylong battle. Later scholars calculated that at least seventy-five thousand American rounds had been fired, using well over a ton of powder, but only one bullet in almost three hundred had hit home. The shot heard round the world likely missed. Fewer than one militiaman in every ten who engaged the column drew British blood, despite the broad target of massed redcoats. A combat bromide held that it took a man's weight in bullets to kill him, and on Battle Road that equation was not far exaggerated.

Still, British survivors emerged from the maelstrom with a new respect for American fighters. "Whoever looks upon them as an irregular mob will find himself very much mistaken," Percy wrote General Harvey, the adjutant general in London, a few hours after returning to Boston. "They have men amongst them who know very well what they are about." Lieutenant Mackenzie acknowledged his foe's "violent and determined spirit."

The British combat performance, if often courageous in the ranks, had been troubling, with miserable staff work and inert commanders, Percy excepted. The day's action included looting, arson, and various atrocities, suggesting that the usual decorum of eighteenth-century warfare would be adapted to an American setting. On April 21, Gage publicly rebuked his men for "great inattention and neglect to the commands of their officers"; he demanded that they "behave with more discipline and in a more soldier-like manner." General Harvey, upon reading accounts of April 19, later wrote, "I am much concerned at the wild behavior of the men." To Percy he added, "It was an unlucky day."

Like a burning fuse, accounts of that day raced across New England and down the seaboard, carried in some instances by Paul Revere for a four-shilling per diem plus "expenses for self and horse." "To arms!" criers cried. "Gage has fired upon the people!" A rider appeared on a Providence wharf where deckhands were unloading salt. "War, war, boys," he called. "There is war." Newspapers printed stories of variable accuracy, beginning with a twenty-six-line account in the loyalist *Boston News-Letter* on April 20, deploring "this shocking introduction to all the miseries of a civil war." The *New-Hampshire Gazette*'s headline read, "Bloody News."

In barely three weeks, the first reports of the day's action would reach Charleston and Savannah. Lurid rumors spread quickly: of grandfathers shot in their beds, of families burned alive, of pregnant women bayoneted.

Americans in thirteen colonies were alarmed, aroused, angry. "The times are very affecting," Reverend Ezra Stiles told his diary in Rhode Island on April 23. Freeholders in Hackensack authorized payment of a shilling and sixpence to a local gunsmith for each musket cleaned. Eight thousand citizens rallied for a town meeting in Philadelphia, where an observer noted that "the *rage militaire*, as the French call a passion for arms, has taken possession of the whole continent." A New Yorker wrote a friend in London, "There is no such thing as being a looker on." Militia companies in Pennsylvania rushed to order drums and colors; soon men in uniform, said to be "as thick as bees," were exercising twice daily under arms, including many "Broadbrims," as John Adams called the pacifist Quakers.

Meeting in Concord on April 22, the Massachusetts Provincial Congress appointed a committee to take sworn statements from nearly a hundred eyewitnesses, to be published promptly in colonial newspapers. Joseph Warren appended a cover letter to these accounts, lamenting that "we are at last plunged into the horrors of a most unnatural war." The myth of violated innocence meant that the rebel stockpiling of war supplies in recent months must remain obscure, along with details about the colony's deft, robust call to arms. A narrative congealed, and with it a brilliant propaganda stratagem: Gage was the aggressor; redcoats fired first; helpless civilians had been slaughtered.

A swift American schooner, the *Quero*, sailed from Salem for England on April 29 carrying recent copies of the *Essex Gazette*, with an article that began, "Last Wednesday, the 19th of April, the Troops of his Britannick Majesty commenced Hostilities upon the People of this Province." The cargo also included eyewitness depositions and a corroborative statement from a captured British officer. Warren admonished the skipper, Captain John Derby, to keep the voyage "a profound secret from every person on earth." After an unmolested crossing in just twenty-nine days, Derby delivered his packet in London, where the accounts appeared in the threepenny *Evening Post* to be read by, among others, George III and Lord North.

The king's resolve was unshaken. He still believed that "with firmness and perseverance America will be brought to submission." Others in England were less sanguine. The government was unable to offer a coherent rejoinder to the American claims except to plead for "a suspension of belief." "This looks serious," Edward Gibbon wrote, "and is indeed so."

The news of Concord "flew like wildfire and threw the whole Continent into a flame," Horace Walpole told his journal. "Bitter invectives were published every day against the governing party." The guard at St. James's Palace reportedly was doubled. Even staunch supporters of North's regime felt bewildered. "All my prejudices are against the Americans," the theologian John Wesley wrote Lord Dartmouth, but "waiving all considerations of right and wrong, I ask is it common sense to use force toward the Americans?" Gage's laconic, tardy version of events, sent aboard the sluggish brig *Sukey*, did not arrive in England until June 9; the commander in chief's dispatch, only four paragraphs long, hardly reassured his monarch, his government, or his fellow Englishmen, particularly since he closed by noting, "Several thousand are now assembled about this town, threatening an attack and getting up artillery, and we are very busy making preparations to oppose them."

Preparations also continued in the American camp. Citizens in Concord retrieved cannons and musket balls from millponds, thickets, and various hiding places. A seven-year-old in Braintree named John Quincy Adams later recalled how militiamen "took the pewter spoons out of our kitchen to melt them into bullets." Men in Menotomy pried the shoes from the four horses killed while pulling Percy's ill-fated supply wagons. A scavenged red coat was draped across a brace of sticks in a greening field as both a scarecrow and a warning. On the Sunday following the battle, and for many Sundays to come, preachers drew from Lamentations to remind parishioners that their suffering reflected divine judgment on their own imperfections: "The joy of our heart is ceased. Our dance is turned into mourning."

Yet many also felt vibrant, even exhilarated, and aware that "something clear and fine" had transpired, as the historian Allen French would write a century and a half later. They were now swept up in events grander than themselves, in "the meeting of strong men, at the beginning of great things."

True enough. But something opaque and awful also had happened, a fraternal bloodletting. The enmity of recent years had curdled into hatred. Young men had died in agony, as befell young men in war, and many, many more were still to die. One of them was Lieutenant Edward Hull of the 43rd Foot. Shot at North Bridge, then shot again in a chaise ambulance during the retreat through Menotomy, Hull had been left behind in rebel care. A day after the battle, Reverend McClure found the young Scot in obvious anguish from three bullet wounds, yet still "of a youthful, fair, and delicate countenance." Sprawled across a feather bed in Samuel and Elizabeth Butterfield's house near Cooper's Tavern, he wore a greatcoat and fur hat provided by his captors, since his own men had stripped him of his tunic, waistcoat, and shirt before the militia snatched his shoes and buckles. His bloody breeches lay beside him on the bed, and he sucked on an orange donated by a neighbor. "I asked him if he was dangerously wounded," McClure wrote. "He replied, 'Yes, mortally.'" Lieutenant Hull would linger for nearly two weeks in a twilight of pain and remorse; then, on May 2, he "took heaven by the way," as the expression went. Six rebel officers escorted his coffin to the Charlestown ferryway, where British bargemen rowed him to Boston for burial.

He, at least, would be drummed into the next world. The graves of many others remained unmarked and unremembered, except for the long bones and the ribs and the skulls that over the years pushed to the surface in Middlesex meadows and woodlands, memento mori from one raving afternoon on Battle Road.

3.

I Wish This Cursed Place Was Burned

An army of sorts soon bivouacked along a ten-mile crescent from Roxbury to Chelsea, determined to serve the god of battle by driving the British into the sea. In late April, the provincial congress called for thirty thousand American troops to turn out, and legions left farm, shop, and hearth, including one patriot and his three sons who hurried from their sawmill without even bothering to shut the gate. Two thousand were said to march from New Hampshire. Forty-six of Connecticut's seventy-two towns sent men, and classes at Yale College were canceled for lack of students. "The ardor of our people is such that they can't be kept back," a committee in New Haven informed John Hancock. A woman in Philadelphia wrote, "My only brother I have sent to the camp. . . . Had I twenty sons and brothers, they should go."

The *Essex Gazette* would name this host the Grand American Army, though William Tudor, a protégé of John Adams's who soon would serve as judge advocate, called it "little better than an armed mob." Houses abandoned by loyalist families in Cambridge were confiscated for barracks and officers' billets. Eleven hundred tents accumulated by the Committee of Supply sprouted along the Charles, and a request went out to sailmakers and ship masters for more. "We have stripped the seaports of canvas to make tents," a member of the provincial congress reported. Any man who enlisted fifty-nine others into a company qualified for a captaincy; any captain who organized ten companies might be designated a regimental colonel.

Drums beat reveille daily at four a.m., and after roll call the men marched to morning prayers. "The camp abounds with clergymen," one soldier wrote, and more than a dozen local divines volunteered their services for regiments without chaplains. Officers were empowered to suppress "tumults" in the ranks, to confine men to their tents after evening tattoo, and to shutter grogshops selling liquor to the troops. The smells of encampment grew ripe—wood smoke, roasting meat, imperfectly dug latrines.

Soldiers cast new bullets with molding tools, fashioning cartridges from paper scraps and thimbles of powder. A homesick soldier hanged himself in a barn. "I went down & saw him," a private noted in his journal, then added, "I went home & took a nap." More rumors flew, including a pastor's warning in early May to beware "lest General Gage should spread the small-pox in your army."

No sooner did the Grand American Army muster than it began to melt away. Farmers left to tend their spring fields, shopkeepers to tend their counters. Most Connecticut troops soon wandered home, discouraged by the shortage of provisions around Boston. The force would dwindle to six-teen thousand or so within a month after the shots at Lexington, although no one was sure of the number. "As to the army, it is in such a shifting, fluc-tuating state," a Committee of Safety member wrote. "They are continu-ally going and coming." To deceive the British in mid-May, a brigade of seven hundred men in Roxbury marched round and round a hill to feign preponderance; a mile-long column of more than two thousand marched from Cambridge to the Charlestown fish market, bared their fangs across the Charles, then marched back.

Shortages extended beyond canvas and rations. "We are in want of almost everything, but of nothing so much as arms and ammunition," Joseph Warren wrote on May 15 to Philadelphia, where the Second Conti-nental Congress had just convened. Massachusetts counted thirty-eight cannons, mostly inferior iron guns. Rhode Island sent a few brass field-pieces to the siege line, but they hardly sufficed to confront the British Empire. In mid-month, welcome news arrived from Lake Champlain in New York, more than two hundred miles northwest: at three-thirty a.m. on May 10, eighty-five whooping New England roughnecks, later described as "tatterdemalions in linsey-woolsey who call themselves Green Moun-tain Boys," had swarmed from a scow-rigged bateau to overrun the British garrison at Fort Ticonderoga.

Almost fifty sleepy redcoats had surrendered without a fight, as had a smaller detachment at nearby Crown Point. The captured booty included some two hundred iron cannons, ten tons of musket balls, thirty thousand flints, and forty-nine gallons of rum, much of it consumed by those tatter-demalions to celebrate their victory. Two men led the raid in an unsteady collaboration: a strapping, profane, sometime farmer, lead miner, and tosspot philosopher named Ethan Allen and a short, gifted Connecticut apothecary, merchant prince, and hothead named Benedict Arnold, who had been given a colonel's commission by Joseph Warren and whose long nose and dark hair caused him to resemble a raven in human form. How the captured munitions would be transported from the remote fortress remained to be seen, but no one who knew Allen and Arnold, or knew of them, doubted that both would be heard from again. For now, the "acts of burglarious enterprise," in one British writer's description, gave the Americans control not only of Ticonderoga—the most strategic inland position on the continent—but also of the long blue teardrop of Lake Champlain, the traditional invasion route into, or out of, Canada.

Life in besieged Boston grew grimmer by the day. Soon after the fighting began, General Gage agreed to issue exit permits to those who wanted to leave town if all citizens surrendered their weapons at Faneuil Hall. By late April, some 1,778 firelocks had been handed over, plus 634 pistols, 973 bayonets, and 38 ancient blunderbusses. Gage insisted that swords also be added to the pile. "Nearly half the inhabitants have left the town already," the merchant John Andrews wrote a friend on May 6. "You see parents that are lucky enough to procure papers, with bundles in one hand and a string of children in the other, wandering out of town . . . not knowing where they'll go." Provisions grew short, prices soared, fresh food vanished. "Pork and beans one day," Andrews wrote, "and beans and pork another."

Loyalists from the countryside slipped into Boston for Crown protection, then complained bitterly to Gage that allowing all rebel sympathizers to leave would invite bombardment of the town; hostages must be kept to discourage attack. Gage saw the point, and the exodus largely stopped except for those able to sneak out by boat. "It is inconceivable the distress and ruin this unnatural dispute has caused to this town and its inhabitants," the surveyor Henry Pelham wrote on May 16. "Almost every shop and store is shut. No business of any kind is going on." A British lieutenant observed after taking a stroll, "I can't help looking on it as a ruined town. I think I see the grass growing in every street." More grass was needed: provender for British horses by late May was short by three thousand tons. Warming weather and a diet of salt meat brought widespread illness. Reverend Henry Caner, a loyalist, would write to London, "It is not uncommon to bury 20 to 30 a week among the troops and inhabitants. . . . If our lives must pay for our loyalty, God's will be done." Another loyalist clergyman, Reverend John Wiswall, who took refuge with his family in Boston from Cape Cod, noted in his journal, "My daughter died the 23rd and my wife the 26th. Buried in family tomb the 28th."

From his Province House headquarters, Gage awaited reinforcements and braced against a rebel assault. Regiments built several small batteries on the Common and a larger redoubt on Beacon Hill. Gunners at Boston Neck were ordered to keep lighted matches by their cannons at all times.

Regulars patrolled the wharves every half hour. Loyalist volunteers with white cockades in their hats kept vigil in the streets at night. "We are threatened with great multitudes," Gage wrote Lord Dartmouth in mid-May. "The people called friends of government are few." News from the other provinces was bleak. Connecticut, Rhode Island, and New Hampshire were "in open rebellion," he told London. "They are arming at New York and, as we are told, in Philadelphia and all the southern provinces." The royal mail was no longer secure; a postal rider with official correspondence from New York had been detained, his locked bag jimmied open with hammer and pliers.

Guard boat crews patrolled the harbor with 6-pounders, alert for fire rafts and often ducking sniper rounds from the far shore. Ships from England no sooner dropped anchor than potshots rang out. "The country is all in arms, and we are absolutely invested with many thousand men, some of them so daring as to come very near our outposts," Captain Glanville Evelyn wrote his father in Scotland. Morale sank in the regular ranks. A Royal Navy surgeon permitted to treat wounded British captives in Cambridge wrote in May that the rebel army "is truly nothing but a drunken, canting, lying, praying, hypocritical rabble, without order, subjection, discipline, or cleanliness." A new British drinking song warned:

> *Boston we shall in ashes lay,*
> *It is a nest of knaves,*
> *We'll make them soon for mercy pray,*
> *Or send them to their graves.*

There would be ashes on May 17. That night, a sergeant in the 65th Regiment reportedly delivered musket cartridges by candlelight to the barracks on Treat's Wharf; soon after his arrival, a small, accidental blaze grew into a conflagration that burned until three a.m. Gage had placed the town's fire engines under military control, and inept redcoats, one merchant complained, operated the apparatus "with such stupidity that the flames raged with incredible fury & destroyed 30 stores." The losses at Dock Square also included regimental uniforms, weapons, and donations collected for Boston's poor.

Fresh meat for British larders and forage for British horses could be found within a mile or two of Province House, but trouble could be found there as well. In Boston Harbor, more than thirty islands—used for over a century as livestock pastures and hay fields—stippled the narrow, twisting approaches from open water. Shoals, mudflats, salt creeks, and sandbars changed shape with each new tide. Much of the harbor at low water was no deeper than three fathoms—eighteen feet—while the three largest Royal Navy ships on station drew twenty feet or more. American mariners skittered through this watery terrain in smacks, canoes, and whaleboats, trading shots at long range with British foraging parties. On May 21, Gage sent several sloops to Grape Island, but they scavenged only eight tons of hay before rebels burned eighty more.

On Saturday morning, May 27, six hundred Massachusetts and New Hampshire militiamen scuffed from the Chelsea meetinghouse down Beach Road to the shoreline. By eleven a.m., the ebbing tide had fallen enough to let them slosh knee-deep across narrow Belle Isle Creek to Hog Island, where, as ordered by the Committee of Safety, they rounded up 411 sheep, 27 cows, and 6 horses, shooting those that would not be herded. The British were to get none. Thirty men waded across Crooked Creek to adjacent Noddle's Island, at the confluence of the Charles and Mystic Rivers. At seven hundred acres, Noddle's was the largest of the harbor isles, once a refuge for Baptist apostates driven from Boston by Puritans, and long a favorite dueling ground for aggrieved parties of all denominations. Here the rebels set fire to a barn piled high with salt hay.

Aboard the fifty-gun *Preston* in the Boston anchorage, the sight of thick smoke to the east caught the squinting eye of Samuel Graves, commander of the North American station. Graves this very week had received news from London of his promotion to vice admiral of the white; he celebrated with a thirteen-gun salute from his squadron and colors appropriate to his new rank hoisted above *Preston*'s deck. A sixty-two-year-old sea dog who had never held high command before arriving in America a year earlier, Graves was a harbor admiral; recovering from a small stroke, he had shuttled between his flagship and a comfortable house on Pearl Street without once in nineteen months venturing out past the Boston lighthouse. His talents were modest—the new promotion notwithstanding—and his grievances many. With thirty vessels in his squadron, but only four substantial ships of force, he was to ensure that Britannia ruled the waves along an eighteen-hundred-mile littoral, from the Gulf of St. Lawrence to Cape Florida. Despite a stupendous increase in smuggling by American insurgents, he admitted that during this past winter "no seizures of any consequence have been made."

Graves badgered the Admiralty with legitimate complaints about "properly guarding this extensive coast with the few vessels I have"; about the poor condition of those vessels—*Hope* was "very leaky," and so were *Halifax*, *Somerset*, and others; about the difficulty of getting guns, pilots, provisions, and proper sailors; and about idiotic orders from home, including a directive to search the ballast of every ship arriving in North America for smuggled musket flints, as if ample flint could not be found in American rock. He also complained about General Gage, whom he detested and who detested him in return. With four nephews at sea in the king's service, Graves was a master of nepotism; Lord North's undersecretary, William Eden, would describe him this year as "a corrupt admiral without any shadow of capacity." He was suspected, among other indiscretions, of selling stringy mutton on the Boston black market. Captain Evelyn spoke for many in asserting that "every man both in the army and navy wishes him recalled."

Graves loathed "rebellious fanatics," and in that smoke billowing from Noddle's Island he spied a chance to show General Gage how they should be fought. At three p.m., a detachment of 170 marines from *Glasgow, Cerberus,* and *Somerset* landed on the island's western flank. At the same time, the *Diana,* a new 120-ton armed schooner just that morning back from chasing gunrunners in Maine under the command of Lieutenant Thomas Graves—from the quartet of nephews—worked her way into Chelsea Creek, which separated the mainland from Noddle's and Hog Islands. More marines followed *Diana* in a dozen longboats to cut off the rebel retreat. The pop of militia muskets now sounded from behind stone walls around the Winnisimet ferry landing. *Diana* answered with grapeshot and bore down on rebel drovers herding livestock through the shallows and onto Beach Road. Fifteen militiamen squatted in a Noddle's marsh as a rear guard, swapping volleys with the regulars. "The bullets flew very thick," Corporal Amos Farnsworth of Groton reported. "The balls sung like bees round our heads." From the *Cerberus* quarterdeck, marines manhandled a pair of 3-pounders ashore and from a sandy embankment shelled the ferry landing.

Spattered with fire from both flanks, Lieutenant Graves decided that *Diana* had gone far enough. But as he sought to come about, the wind died. Longboats nosed alongside with hawsers to tow her down Chelsea Creek. Bullets smacked the water. Oarsmen bent low at the gunwales as the schooner inched back toward the wider harbor.

At twilight three hundred militia reinforcements rushed into the skirmish line with their own pair of 3-pounders, the first use of American field artillery in the war. In command was a stubby, rough-hewn brawler with a shock of white hair. Brigadier General Israel Putnam—"Old Put" to his men—was described by the *Middlesex Journal* as "very strongly made, no fat, all bones and muscles; he has a lisp in his speech and is now upwards of sixty years of age." A wool merchant and farmer from Connecticut, barely literate, Putnam "dared to lead where any dared to follow," one admirer observed; another called him "totally unfit for everything but fighting." Stories had been told of him for decades in New England, most involving peril and great courage: how he once tracked down a wolf preying on his sheep, crawled headfirst into its den with a birch-bark torch to shoot it, then dragged the carcass out by the ears; how in the French war when a fire ignited a barracks, he organized a bucket brigade to save three hundred barrels of gunpowder, tossing pails of water onto the burning rafters from a ladder while wearing soaked mittens cut from a blanket; how he had been captured, starved, and tortured by Iroquois in 1758, and only the timely intervention of a French officer kept him from burning at the stake; how, after being shipwrecked on the Cuban coast during the Anglo-American expedition against Havana in 1762, he saved all hands by building rafts from spars and planks; how he had fought rebellious Indians near Detroit in Pontiac's War of 1764, and later explored the Mississippi River valley; how he had left his plow upon hearing news of Lexington to ride a hundred miles in twenty-four hours to Cambridge. Now, wearing his scars and scorches like valor ribbons, he was ready to destroy *Diana*.

She was poised for destruction. After finally coming abreast of Winnisimet ferry just after ten p.m., the schooner was caught in a falling tide, her hull scraping bottom. The rebel fusillade from shore intensified, the gunners firing blindly at shadows on a moonless night, but vicious enough to kill two sailors, wound others, and cause the longboats to cast off their tow ropes. Lieutenant Graves tried to rig a kedge anchor and windlass to haul *Diana* free, but she stuck fast sixty yards from the beach, then heeled over onto her beam ends. The armed sloop *Britannia* eased close to pluck the crew from the canted deck as rebel 3-pounders boomed and Putnam, said to be wading waist-deep across the mudflats, shouted insults and blandishments in the dark. Swarming militiamen stripped the schooner of cannons, a dozen swivel guns, rigging, and sails, then piled hay under her bow and set it ablaze. At three a.m. flames reached the magazine, and *Diana* exploded in a fine rain of splintered oak.

Admiral of the White Graves buried his dead and ordered *Somerset* at dawn to fire long-range on the jubilant crowd capering along the Chelsea shore. Gage was disgusted by the schooner's loss. "The general," an aide wrote, "by no means approved of the admiral's scheme, supposed it to be a trap, which it proved to be." American raiders would return to the islands over the next two weeks, rustling another two thousand head of livestock while burning corn cribs, barns, and—heaping insult on the injuries—a storehouse that Graves had rented for cordage, lumber, and barrel staves.

"Heaven apparently and most evidently fights for us," one Jonathan exulted. Putnam and his men returned to Cambridge in high feather. *Diana's* mast had been salvaged and soon stood as a seventy-six-foot flag-pole on Prospect Hill. A captured British barge with the sail hoisted was placed in a wagon and paraded around the Roxbury meetinghouse in early June to cheers and cannon salutes. "I wish," Putnam was quoted as saying, "we have something of this kind to do every day."

Gage declared martial law on June 12 with a long, windy denunciation of "the infatuated multitudes." He offered to pardon those who "lay down their arms and return to the duties of peaceable subjects," exclusive of Samuel Adams and John Hancock, "whose offenses are of too flagitious a nature" to forgive. He ended the screed with "God save the King."

The same day, Gage wrote to Lord Barrington, the secretary at war, that "things are now come to that crisis that we must avail ourselves of every resource, even to raise the Negroes in our cause. . . . Hanoverians, Hessians, perhaps Russians may be hired." To Lord Dartmouth he warned that he was critically low on both cash—he could not pay his officers—and forage; ships had been sent to Nova Scotia and Quebec seeking hay and oats. Crushing the rebellion, he estimated, would require more frigates and at least 32,000 soldiers, including 10,000 in New York, 7,000 around Lake Champlain, and 15,000 in New England. Another officer writing from Boston on June 12 advised London—the king himself received a copy—that the rebel blockade "is judicious & strong." As for British operations, "all warlike preparations are wanting. No survey of the adjacent country, no proper boats for landing troops, not a sufficient number of horses for the artillery nor for the regimental baggage." The war chest had "about three or four thousand [pounds] only remaining. . . . The rebellious colonies will supply nothing."

Gage's adjutant complained that "every idle report is carried to headquarters and . . . magnified to such a degree that rebels are seen in the air carrying cannon and mortars on their shoulders." Some regulars longed for a decisive battle; "taking the bull by the horns" became an oft-heard phrase in the regiments. "I wish the Americans may be brought to a sense of their duty," an officer wrote in mid-June. "One good drubbing, which I long to give them . . . might have a good effect." As Captain Evelyn told his cousin in London, "If there is an honor in hard knocks, we are likely to have some share."

The imminent arrival of transports with light dragoons, more marines, and several foot regiments would bring the British garrison to over six thousand troops, not enough to subdue Massachusetts, much less the

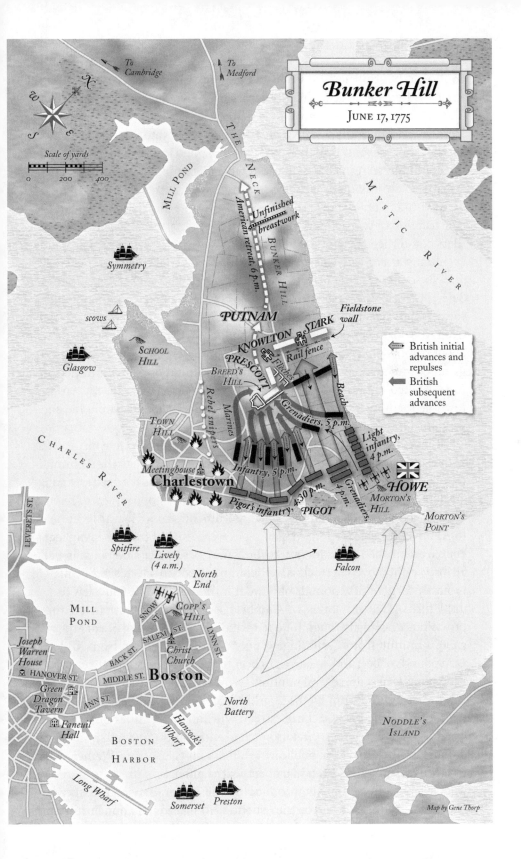

To Cambridge

To Medford

THE NECK

MYSTIC RIVER

Bunker Hill
June 17, 1775

Scale of yards

0   200   400

MILL POND

Symmetry

Unfinished
breastwork

American retreat, 6 p.m.

BUNKER HILL

scows

Fieldstone
wall

PUTNAM

Glasgow

SCHOOL
HILL

KNOWLTON   STARK

PRESCOTT

Rail fence

BREED'S
HILL

Flèche

Beach

British initial
advances and
repulses

British subsequent
advances

Marines

Rebel snipers

TOWN
HILL

Grenadiers, 5 p.m.

Light
infantry,
4 p.m.

CHARLES RIVER

Meetinghouse

Infantry, 5 p.m.

4:30 p.m.

Grenadiers,
4 p.m.

HOWE

Charlestown

Pigot's infantry   PIGOT

MORTON'S
HILL

MORTON'S
POINT

LEVERETT ST.

Spitfire

Lively
(4 a.m.)

North
End

Falcon

MILL
POND

SNOW ST.

COPP'S
HILL

SALEM ST.

LYNN ST.

Joseph
Warren
House

HANOVER ST.

Christ
Church

Green
Dragon
Tavern

BACK ST.

MIDDLE ST.   Boston

ANN ST.

Faneuil
Hall

North
Battery

Hancock's Wharf

BOSTON
HARBOR

NODDLE'S
ISLAND

Long Wharf

Somerset   Preston

Map by Gene Thorp

continent, but sufficient, as Gage told London, to "make an attempt upon some of the rebel posts, which becomes every day more necessary." Two alluring patches of high ground remained unfortified, and Gage knew from an informant that American commanders coveted the same slopes: the elevation beyond Boston Neck known as the Dorchester Heights, and the dominant terrain above Charlestown called Bunker, or Bunker's Hill. A battle plan was made to seize the former on Sunday, June 18, with a bombardment of Roxbury while the rebels were at church, followed by the construction of two artillery redoubts on the heights. If all went well, regulars could then capture the high ground on Charlestown peninsula and eventually attack the American encampment at Cambridge.

No sooner was the plan conceived than it leaked to the Committee of Safety; British officers seemed incapable of keeping their mouths shut in a town full of American spies and eavesdroppers. Intelligence even came from New Hampshire, where a traveler out of Boston told authorities there about rumors of an imminent British sally. Meeting in Hastings House, a gambrel-roofed mansion near the Cambridge Common, the committee on June 15 voted unanimously that "the hill called Bunker's Hill in Charlestown be securely kept and defended." Dorchester Heights would have to wait until more guns and powder could be stockpiled.

The American camps bustled. Arms and ammunition were inspected, with each marching soldier to carry thirty rounds. A note to the Committee of Supply advised that "the army is destitute of shirts & trousers, and if any [are] in store, pray they may be sent." Liquor sales stopped, again. Teamsters carted the books and scientific instruments from Harvard's library to Andover for safekeeping. Organ pipes were yanked from the Anglican church and melted down for musket bullets. An ordnance storehouse issued all forty-eight shovels in stock as well as ammunition to selected regiments— typically forty or fifty pounds of powder, a thousand balls, and a few hundred flints. Commissaries in Cambridge and Roxbury reported that provisions arriving through June 16 included 1,869 loaves of bread and 357 gallons of milk from Cambridge vendors, 60 pairs of shoes from Milton, 1,570 pounds of beef and 40 barrels of beer from Watertown, a ton of candles, 1,500 pounds of soap, several hundred barrels of beans, peas, flour, and salt fish by the quintal, rum by the hogshead, and a few hundred tents, many without poles. All Massachusetts men within twenty miles of the coast were urged to carry their firelocks "to meeting on the Sabbath and other days when they meet for public worship." A sergeant from Wethersfield wrote his wife, "We've been in a great deal of hubbub."

Orders spilled from the headquarters of Major General Ward, who occupied a southeast room on the Hastings House ground floor. Portly and sallow, sporting a powdered wig, boots, and a long coat with silver buttons, Artemas Ward, now forty-seven, had been chosen in February to command the Massachusetts militia on the strength of his long tenure in colonial politics. As a Harvard student, he once helped lead a campaign against "swearing and cursing" at the college; as a justice of the peace in Shrewsbury, he'd levied fines against the profane and could be found in the street reprimanding those who dishonored the Sabbath with unnecessary travel. Massachusetts, he believed, was home to the Chosen People. Ward had never fully recovered his health after the rigors of the French war, from which he'd emerged as a militia lieutenant colonel despite seeing little action. "Attacks of the stone"—kidney stones—still tormented him. Pious, honest, and devoted to the patriot cause, he was also taciturn, torpid, and stubborn. The gambit to hold Bunker Hill in Charlestown that he and the Committee of Safety had concocted was an impulse, not a plan. The rebel force lacked not only sufficient ammunition and field artillery but also combat reserves, a coherent chain of command, and even water. Ward had recently requested from the provincial congress almost sixty guns, fifteen hundred muskets, twenty tons of powder, and a similar quantity of lead; few of those munitions had been forthcoming.

Shortly after six p.m. on Friday, June 16, three Massachusetts regiments drifted through the arching elms and onto the Cambridge Common. They wore the usual homespun linen shirts and breeches tinted with walnut or sumac dye. Most carried a blanket or bedroll, often with a tumpline strap across the forehead to support the weight on their backs. A clergyman's benediction droned over their bowed heads, and with a final amen they replaced their low-crowned hats and turned east down the Charlestown road.

Twilight faded and was gone, and the last birdsong faded with it. The first stars threw down their silver spears. Little rain had fallen in the past month, and dust boiled beneath each step. Candlelight gleamed from the rear of two bull's-eye lanterns carried by sergeants at the head of the column. Officers commanded silence, and only the rattle of carts stacked with entrenching tools broke the quiet. Through parched orchards and across Willis Creek they marched, and past the hulking shadows of Prospect and Winter Hills. As they turned right toward Charlestown, a couple hundred Connecticut troops joined the column, bringing their strength to a thousand men.

General Ward had remained in his Hastings House headquarters, and the column was led by a sinewy, azure-eyed colonel wearing a blue coat with a single row of buttons and a tricorne hat. He carried a linen banyan.

William Prescott of Pepperell, forty-nine and bookish, had fought twice in Canada during wars against the French, earning a reputation for cool self-possession under fire. In this war he reportedly had vowed never to be taken alive. "He was a bold man," one soldier later wrote of him, "and gave his orders like a bold man."

Bold orders this evening would prove to be ill-considered. As the procession crossed Charlestown Neck—barely ten yards wide at high tide—Prescott briefly conferred with the irrepressible Israel Putnam and Colonel Richard Gridley, an artilleryman and engineer who had also fought twice in Canada with distinction. From just below the isthmus, the three officers contemplated the dark contours of Charlestown peninsula, an irregular triangle a mile long and less than half that in width, bracketed by the Mystic and Charles Rivers. Even at night the dominant terrain was obvious: Bunker Hill rose gradually from the Neck for three hundred yards to a rounded crown 110 feet high, commanding not only the single land route off the peninsula, but the approach roads from Cambridge and Medford, as well as the adjacent waters. From the crest a low ridge swept southeast another six hundred yards to the patchwork of pastures, seventy-five feet high and sutured with rail fences, that would be called Breed's Hill. Some fields had been scythed, the grass laid in windrows and cocks; in others it still stood waist-high. Brick kilns and clay pits pocked the steep eastern slope of the Breed's pastures. Gardens and small orchards lay scattered to the west, backing the four hundred houses, shops, and buildings in Charlestown. Most of the three thousand residents had fled inland. The rising moon, three days past full, laved the town in amber light. Beyond the ferry landing and a spiny-masted warship in the Charles lay slumbering Boston.

For reasons never explained and certainly never understood, when the conference ended Prescott ordered the column to continue southeast. Colonel Gridley quickly staked out a redoubt—an imperfect square with sides about 130 feet long—*not* on nearly impregnable Bunker Hill, as the Committee of Safety had specified, but on the southwest slope of Breed's pastureland. Accustomed to pick-and-shovel work, the men grabbed tools from the carts and began hacking at the hillside. Striking clocks in Boston, echoed at higher pitch by a ship's bell, told them it was midnight.

The rhythmic chink of metal on hard ground carried to the *Lively*, another of those leaky vessels in the British squadron, now anchored astride the Charlestown ferryway. As coral light seeped across the eastern horizon at four a.m. on Saturday, June 17, the graveyard watch officer strained to decipher the odd sounds above the groan of the ship's yards and the Charles whispering along her hull. He summoned the captain, whose spyglass soon showed hundreds of tiny dark figures tearing at the distant slope with spade and mattock.

The ship beat to quarters. Sailors tumbled from their hammocks, feet clapping across the deck as they ran to their battle stations. A windlass groaned as the crew winched *Lively* on her cable to align the starboard cannons. A shouted command carried across the gun deck, and tongues of flame burst from the ship in a broadside of 9-pounders. Breeching ropes kept the guns from flying across the deck in recoil; block and tackle ran them forward for the next salvo. Gunners swabbed the smoking barrels, rammed home powder and shot, and another flock of iron balls flew toward Breed's Hill. Other ships eventually joined in—*Glasgow, Symmetry, Falcon, Spitfire*, more than seventy guns all told—along with 24-pounders from the Copp's Hill battery in Boston's North End.

Dawn, that great revealer of predicaments, had fully disclosed Colonel Prescott's. Screaming cannonballs—"tea kettles," in rebel slang—streaked overhead or punched into the hillside, smashing two hogsheads containing the American water supply. "The danger we were in made us think there was treachery, & that we were brought here to be all slain," young Peter Brown would write his mother in Rhode Island. Distance and elevation reduced the bombardment's effect, although Prescott recounted how one militiaman whose head abruptly vanished in a crimson mist "was so near me that my clothes were besmeared with his blood and brains, which I wiped off in some degree with a handful of fresh earth." When other men dropped their tools to gawk at the corpse, Prescott snapped, "Bury him," then strolled off with conspicuous nonchalance, hatless now, waggling his sword and urging the men to dig faster.

The redoubt taking shape was formidable enough, with thick dirt walls six feet high, fire steps for musketmen inside to stand on, and a sally port exit to the north. But no embrasures had been left for cannons; worse yet, Prescott recognized that the British could outflank him on either side. Gage's men would no doubt attack in force across the Charles, seeking to stun the defenders with firepower before closing to complete the slaughter with bayonets. To protect his left flank, Prescott ordered the men to begin building a low breastwork northeast from the sally port to marshy ground at the foot of Breed's Hill.

He also sent an officer to plead for reinforcements, provisions, and water. Artillerymen refused to lend the courier a horse, forcing him to walk four miles to Cambridge, which he found "quiet as the Sabbath." At Hastings House he discovered Dr. Warren, newly appointed as a major general despite his lack of military experience, splayed on an upstairs bed with a crippling headache. General Ward, tormented with another attack of the stone, fretted over the vulnerability of Roxbury, the Dorchester Heights, and his Cambridge supply dumps; British gunfire had been reported at Boston Neck. Not least, Ward worried that only twenty-seven half-barrels of powder remained in his magazines, perhaps enough for forty thousand cartridges. With consent from the Committee of Safety, he reluctantly agreed to send reinforcements to Prescott from the New Hampshire militia camped along the Mystic.

The deep boom of *Lively*'s broadsides had wakened General Gage, as it woke all of Boston. Province House, aglitter in candlelight, soon bustled with red uniforms. Messengers skipped up the broad stone steps from Marlborough Street with news of rebel entrenchments, then skipped back down with orders to find and fetch various commanders. Young officers eager to join the coming attack loitered in the hallway, hoping to be noticed. Sleepy aides fumbled about for decent maps, of which the British still had precious few. Concussion ghosts from the harbor bombardment rattled the windows, and the rap of drums beating assembly carried from the camps.

Several senior officers joined Gage in the council chamber, including Percy, who arrived from his house in nearby Winter Street. But it was three newcomers who drew the eye this morning: Major Generals William Howe, John Burgoyne, and Henry Clinton had reached Boston in late May aboard the *Cerberus*, after a stormy voyage that killed two favorite horses but gave the three men ample time to find common ground for the campaign ahead despite their inevitable rivalry. "The sentiments of Howe, Clinton, and myself have been unanimous from the beginning," Burgoyne declared. The king had personally approved their selection, fearing that without vigorous new leadership in America "we shall only vegetate." They were deemed "the fittest men for the service in the army," as one official in London observed, forming what Burgoyne called "a triumvirate of reputation."

Others were not so sure. Horace Walpole, ever astringent, told his diary that Howe "was reckoned sensible, though so silent that nobody knew whether he was or not," while Burgoyne was "a vain, very ambitious man, with a half understanding that was worse than none." Clinton, he declared, "had not that fault, for he had no sense at all." Their arrival at Long Wharf aboard a frigate named for the mythical three-headed hound guarding the gates of Hades inspired the war's most enduring doggerel: "Behold the *Cerberus*, the Atlantic plough, / Her precious cargo, Burgoyne, Clinton,

Howe, / Bow, wow, wow!" Thereafter known as the three bow-wows, they had wasted little time in undercutting Gage's authority, as in Burgoyne's barbed observation to General Harvey earlier that week that it was "no reflection to say he is unequal to his present station, for few characters in the world would be fit for it. . . . It requires a genius of the very first class."

As the windows trembled and the Old South clock across the street struck the hours, the high command, genius or otherwise, heatedly debated what to do. General Clinton, a dimple-chinned, prickly, and gifted tactician, proposed the boldest course. Early that morning, he had made his own reconnaissance in the dark along the Boston waterfront, listening to the racket from the rebel entrenchment. If Howe and the main British force crossed directly from the North End to Charlestown, Clinton would lead five hundred men ashore in a surprise flanking attack within musket shot of the isthmus, severing the American line of retreat and trapping the enemy on the peninsula.

This scheme found little favor around Gage's council table. Dividing the force would risk defeat in detail of the separate detachments, particularly if thousands of rebel reinforcements stormed the battlefield from Cambridge. Naval support would be tenuous: even shallow-draft vessels had difficulty in the Mystic, which had not been thoroughly sounded, and a milldam west of Charlestown Neck complicated navigation there. No one had forgotten *Diana's* fate in shoal water. Every small boat would be needed to ferry at least fifteen hundred regulars from Boston to Morton's Point on the peninsula. The amphibious assault would have to be made at "full sea"— high tide, close to three p.m.—so that artillery could be manhandled onto dry land rather than through the muddy shallows.

Gage chose a more conventional, direct assault to be led by Howe, the senior major general. As in the march to Concord, most flanker companies— light infantry and grenadiers—had been peeled from their regiments and collected in special battalions. Ten companies of each would muster at Long Wharf, bolstered by several other regiments. The remaining light infantry and grenadiers, backed by additional regiments, would embark at North Battery, with sundry marines and regulars in reserve.

Gage ended the conference with a stark order: "Any man who shall quit his ranks on any pretense, or shall dare to plunder or pillage, will be executed without mercy." With a clatter of boots across the floor, officers hurried down the hall and out the door to prepare their commands for battle.

Admiral Graves, meanwhile, had left his flagship to board the seventy-gun *Somerset*, now anchored in deep water across Boston Harbor. From her gently rocking quarterdeck he could see rebels swarming across the Charlestown hillside around the new earthworks; many were already "entrenched to their chins," as a British officer noted. Men-of-war belched smoke and noise, and tiny black cannonballs traced perfect parabolas against the summer sky, plumping the fields and splintering tree branches without excessive inconvenience to the Jonathans building their forts. To Graves's frustration, the waters lapping Charlestown were too shallow for *Somerset* and other dreadnoughts to warp close; his larger ships would be limited to sending seamen, ammunition, and boats to their smaller sisters.

As the morning ticked by, *Glasgow* and *Symmetry* hammered Charlestown Neck from an anchorage west of the peninsula, supported by a pair of scows, each mounting a 12-pounder. But the ebbing tide kept them from nosing near the milldam, and Graves regretted his failure to build more floating batteries and gun rafts. *Lively*, *Falcon*, and little *Spitfire* glided into the Charlestown channel, popping away while preparing to cover Howe's landing. The roar of the cannonade carried to Cambridge, Roxbury, and other villages; one terrified minister's wife draped blankets over her windows in hopes of deflecting stray bullets.

Shortly before noon, as meridian heat began to build in Boston, long columns of regulars tramped to fife and drum through the town's cobbled streets from the Common to the docks. Each man carried, as ordered, sixty rounds, a day's cooked provisions, and a blanket. The 52nd Foot had been issued gleaming new muskets and bayonets that very morning; they would soon grow filthy with use. By chance, a portion of the 49th Foot had just arrived after a long passage from southern Ireland. Wide-eyed privates, wobbly on their pins after weeks at sea, disembarked on Long Wharf and marched toward the Common with flags flying and drums beating even as the grenadier and light infantry companies from other regiments clambered into the bobbing boats at Long Wharf for the first lift to Charlestown.

At one-thirty p.m., a blue pennant appeared on *Preston*'s signal halyard. Twenty-eight yawls, longboats, cutters, and ketches carrying twelve hundred soldiers pulled away from Long Wharf in a double column, oars winking in syncopation, with a half dozen brass field guns nestled into the lead boats. The cannonade from the ships had ebbed, but now it grew heavier than ever, balls flying, smoke billowing, and the din reverberating like a terrible thunder. Thousands crowded Boston's rooftops and hillsides, perching on tree boughs and clinging to steeples. Among the spectators were regulars left behind and the wives of troops now gliding across the Charles. Loyalists and patriots stood together, aware that sons and fathers and lovers were down there somewhere in harm's way, on the glinting water or the distant hillside.

Here again was an ancient, squalid secret: that war was an enchantment, a sorcery, a seductive spectacle like no other, beguiling the eye and
gorging the senses. They looked because they could not look away. Atop
Bunker Hill, a Connecticut chaplain named David Avery watched the sculling boats approach Morton's Point, then raised both arms to heaven before
asking God's indulgence on "a scene most awful and tremendous."

Astride a lathered white horse, his own halo of tangled white hair
instantly recognizable, General Israel Putnam trotted back and forth across
the American line in a sleeveless waistcoat, smacking shirkers with the flat
of his sword. To an officer pleading with a reluctant militiaman, Putnam
snapped, "Run him through if he won't fight." One captain would later
reflect that Old Put resembled not a field commander so much as the foreman of "a band of sicklemen or ditchers. . . . He might be brave, and had
certainly an honest manliness about him; but it was thought, and perhaps
with reason, that he was not what the time required."

Nine Massachusetts regiments had been ordered to Charlestown from
Cambridge, but at best only five had reached the peninsula; the others were
delayed, misdirected, or misinformed. No one seemed to have a map. Roads
were confusing, the terrain foreign. Troop discipline was "extremely irregular," one officer wrote, "each regiment advancing according to the opinions,
feelings, or caprice of its commander." Putnam had ordered entrenching
tools carried back from the redoubt to belatedly build a fortification on
Bunker Hill; eager volunteers grabbed a shovel or an ax, then retreated
toward the Neck and beyond, never to return. By one count, fewer than 170
men remained with Prescott to hold his redoubt, officers included. "To be
plain," an observer would write Samuel Adams, "it appears to me there
never was more confusion and less command."

Happily for the American cause, some men knew their business. Colonel Prescott continued to improve his imperfect fort and the adjacent
breastwork, positioning men and shouting encouragement. Roughly two
hundred yards behind the breastwork, a tall, enterprising captain from
eastern Connecticut, Thomas Knowlton, recognized the defensive potential of a rail livestock fence that extended northeast for several hundred
yards, from the middle of the peninsula almost to the Mystic. The fence
had been laid on a slight zigzag course and assembled with a method known
as stake-and-rider; a portion of it straddled a two-foot stone wall. Two hundred men helped Captain Knowlton reinforce the southwestern length of
the barrier with additional rails and posts scavenged from other fields. They
then stuffed the gaps with haycocks and sheaves of cut grass to give the

illusion of a solid parapet. Several small field guns hauled by horses from Cambridge were emplaced nearby.

As the British boats beat from Boston, the most critical rebel reinforcements reached Charlestown Neck to the thrum of fife and drum: hundreds of long-striding New Hampshire militiamen, described as a "moving column of uncouth figures clad in homespun." Millers, mariners, and husbandmen, they included the largest regiment in New England, commanded by Colonel John Stark, the lean, beetle-browed son of a Scottish emigrant. Stark's picaresque life had included capture by Indians while hunting in 1752 and his release six weeks later for a hefty ransom. As a Ranger officer in the last French war, he had plodded more than forty miles in snowshoes to fetch help for comrades wounded in an ambush. After surviving the bloody Anglo-American repulse by the French at Fort Carillon in 1758, he and two hundred men subsequently built an eighty-mile road from Crown Point to the Connecticut valley. Upon hearing the news of Lexington, Stark, now forty-six, left his sawmill and his wife, pregnant with their ninth child, and was elected colonel by a unanimous show of hands in a tavern; so many men rallied to him that thirteen companies filled his regiment. At eleven this morning, General Ward's initial order to reinforce Charlestown reached Stark's camp in Medford, four miles up the Mystic. As he would tell the New Hampshire Provincial Congress a few days later, "The battle soon came on."

Stark sent an advance detachment of two hundred men to the peninsula, then tarried long enough at a house converted into an armory for the rest of his force to draw ammunition: fifteen balls, a flint, and a gill cup of powder—five ounces—for each musketman. Crossing the narrow isthmus shortly after two p.m., harassed with round, bar, and chain shot from Royal Navy guns, the Hampshiremen ascended Bunker Hill at a deliberate pace, then descended to the northeast lip of the peninsula. "One fresh man in action," Stark told a captain, "is worth ten fatigued ones." A quick glance disclosed the American peril: despite Knowlton's deft work along the rail fence, and the hasty construction of three small triangular earthworks known as flèches closer to the redoubt, Prescott's position could still be outflanked by redcoats advancing up the Mystic shoreline. To block the narrow, muddy beach, Stark's men scooted down the eight-foot riverbank and quickly stacked fieldstones to build a short, stout wall. Most Hampshiremen took positions behind the fence to extend Knowlton's line, further stuffing it with hay, grass, and stray rails. But sixty musketmen arranged themselves on the beach in a triple row behind the new barricade. There they awaited their enemy.

*　*　*

Thick-featured and taciturn, General Howe in the best of times was said to be afflicted by a "sullen family gloom." He, too, needed but a glance to see his own dilemma. Landing at Morton's Point with the second lift of six hundred infantry and artillery troops from North Battery, Howe climbed a nearby hillock as gunners shouldered their fieldpieces onto dry ground and the empty boats rowed back to Boston. "It was instantly perceived the enemy were very strongly posted," he subsequently told London.

On his far left, rebel gunmen infested rooftops and barns in Charlestown, while up the pasture slopes, five hundred yards from where Howe stood watching with his command group, a large bastion had sprouted from the hillside. The rest of the rebel defenses came into view: the triangular flèches, several guns throwing an occasional ball inaccurately toward the British lines, and the long fence—or was it a wall?—bristling with men stripped to their shirtsleeves. The fields and pastures ended in a short plunge down to the Mystic shoreline. With more rebels clustered atop Bunker Hill and spilling across Charlestown Neck despite the naval gunfire, Howe calculated that he faced "between five and six thousand" Americans—half again their actual number. He sent a courier flying to Province House with a request that Gage send reinforcements immediately; the attack would await their arrival. Redcoats poised to march near Morton's Point broke ranks, grounded their muskets, and sat in the grass to smoke their pipes or gobble a quick dinner of bread and salt meat.

Howe made his plan. The Mystic beach seemed a promising corridor from which to outflank and turn the rebel line. On foot, the general would personally lead the British right wing, including grenadiers assaulting the rail fence while a column of light infantry companies slashed up that river shoreline. The left wing, led by the diminutive, moonfaced Brigadier Robert Pigot, would attack the redoubt to fix the enemy in place and maybe even overrun the parapet once Howe's troops had broken through. Celebrated for his sangfroid against the French at Quebec, the Breton coast, and Havana, Howe was quoted as telling his officers, "I shall not desire one of you to go a step farther than where I go myself at your head." Speed, agility, discipline, and violence would be decisive. Losing Boston, he reminded them, meant moving the entire army onto Graves's ships, "which will be very disagreeable to us all."

Including the reserves soon to arrive, Howe commanded more than twenty-six hundred men. British field guns began popping away at three p.m., "great nasty porridge pots flying through the air & crammed as full of devils as they could hold," as a young militiaman wrote, each ball "whispering along with its blue tail." The bombardment so unnerved the rebel artillery battery up the slope that one American gun captain reportedly "fired a few times, then swung his hat three times round to the enemy and ceased to fire." Regulars tamped out their pipes and shouldered their muskets, bayonets fixed. Junior officers bawled out orders. Ten companies abreast would form a broad assault front on Pigot's wing to the left, followed by ten more, a formation mirrored by Howe's right wing except for the light infantry column along the Mystic, necessarily squeezed into a shoulder-to-shoulder front between river and riverbank.

On order, the great mass of redcoats heaved forward with a clatter of equipment and more bawling commands, the slate-blue Charles behind them and tawny dust clouds churning up with each stride. "Push on!" the troops yelled. "Push on!" Drummers rapped a march cadence, periodically punctuated by the boom of field guns towed forward with drag ropes. Howe marched with the deliberation of a man who had done this before, his eyes on the hillside ahead, trailed by aides, staff officers, and an orderly said to have carried a silver tray with a decanter of wine. Watching from the redoubt as this red tide advanced, Captain Ebenezer Bancroft of Dunstable, Massachusetts, would give voice to every patriot on the battlefield: "It was an awful moment."

The moment grew more awful. For two months, Admiral Graves had longed to rain destruction on rebel heads, and while Howe drafted his plan on Morton's Point, the admiral arrived by barge to note the hazard that enemy snipers in Charlestown posed to Pigot's left flank. Did General Howe wish "to have the place burned?" Graves asked. As a precaution, brick furnaces aboard several warships had prepared all morning to heat cannonballs. General Howe indeed wished it so. A midshipman hurried to relay the order, and fiery balls soon fell on Charlestown like tiny meteors. Worse destruction came from Copp's Hill in the North End, where early Boston settlers had once sought refuge from the "great annoyances of Woolves, Rattle-snakes, and Musketos." British troops had muscled mortars and several mammoth 24-pounders to the edge of the ancient burying ground at Snow and Hill Streets, sixty feet above the Charles. While Generals Clinton and Burgoyne watched, gunners loaded combustible shells known as carcasses, each packed with gunpowder, Swedish pitch, saltpeter, and tallow. The Charlestown meetinghouse, with its slender, towering steeple, provided a conspicuous aiming stake.

The first shell fell short, bursting near the ferry slip. Gunners corrected their elevation, and within minutes "the whole was instantly in flames," Burgoyne would write. Fire loped through Charlestown's streets like a thing alive, igniting buildings at the foot of Chestnut Street and around Mauldin's shipyard. Other structures along the docks followed in quick succession: distilleries, a tannery, warehouses, shipwrights, a cooperage. Fire climbed the pitched roofs—a "grand and melancholy sight," one loyalist observed—then licked through houses away from the waterfront and up to the market-place, incinerating the courthouse and the Three Cranes Tavern. North of the market, on Town Hill, more houses and another distillery caught fire. The light breeze shifted from southwest to east, as it often did on fine summer days, and flames drove lengthwise through Charlestown. Fire ignited more wharves and a ship chandlery. Ebony smoke rose in a column as wide as the town, then "hung like a thunder cloud over the contending armies," an American officer reported. Rebel musketmen scurried from the burning buildings to hide behind stone walls on Breed's Hill and in a nearby barn.

"The church steeples, being made of timber, were great pyramids of fire above the rest," wrote Burgoyne, who had a way with words. "The roar of cannon, mortars, musketry, the crash of churches, ships upon the stocks, the whole streets falling together in ruin, to fill the ear." All in all, the con-flagration was "one of the greatest scenes of war that can be conceived."

Gawkers and gapers now climbed not only Boston rooftops and hill-sides, but "the masts of such ships as were unemployed in the harbor, all crowded with spectators, friends and foes, alike in anxious suspense. It was great, it was high-spirited."

They, too, looked because they could not look away.

The rebels waited, now killing mad. At four p.m., well over two thou-sand regulars ascended the slope in two distinct corps. Swallows swooped above the hills, and the stench of a cremated town filled the nose. Many militiamen had loaded "buck and ball"—a lead bullet and two or three buckshot, known as "Yankee peas." "Fire low," officers told the men. "Aim at their waistbands." Again noting the brighter tint of the British officers' tunics—vibrant from more expensive dyes—they added, "Aim at the hand-some coats. Pick off the commanders." In the redoubt, Prescott angrily waved his sword to rebuke several musketmen who were firing at impos-sible ranges; they were to wait until the enemy was danger close, within six rods or so—a hundred feet. "Aim at their hips," Prescott ordered. "Waste no powder." Five hundred yards to the north, at the far end of the rail fence, Stark told his men to hang fire until they could see the regulars' half-gaiters below their knees. Someone may also have urged waiting till the whites of the enemy's eyes were visible, an order that had been issued to Austrians, Prussians, and possibly other warring armies earlier in the century.

Howe's corps, on the British right, found marching through the thigh-high grass difficult: fence after damnable fence forced the lines to stop and dismantle the rails or climb over them. As planned, light infantrymen angled through a shallow dell that led to the Mystic beach, now screened from the broader battlefield by the riverbank. Eleven companies with more than three hundred men funneled into a tight column, four or five men abreast. Beyond a slight curve in the shoreline stood the newly built field-stone wall, defended by a few dozen rebel musketmen, some kneeling with their gun barrels resting on the stones. Closing at a dog trot to within fifty yards, redcoats from the 23rd Royal Welch Fusiliers in the vanguard of the column lowered their bayonets and prepared to charge.

A stupendous, searing volley ripped into the British ranks, blowing the fusiliers from their feet. Gunsmoke rolled down a beach upholstered with dying regulars as their comrades stepped over them only to also be shot down. With a third of the Welch Fusiliers wounded, mortally or otherwise, the King's Own Light Infantry behind them surged forward; they, too, were slaughtered, followed by the 10th Foot, the 52nd Foot, and other light companies trailing them. "It was like pushing a wax candle against a red-hot plate," the historian Christopher Ward would write. "The head of the column simply melted away." A man five feet, eight inches tall and weighing 168 pounds had an exterior surface of 2,550 square inches, of which a thousand were exposed to gunfire when he was facing an enemy frontally at close range. Rebel musket balls seemed to fill every square inch of that Mystic corridor, blasting enormous entry wounds into enemies panting for the fieldstone wall. Among the British officers shot, "few had less than three or four wounds," a captain later wrote home. Men miraculously unharmed by bullets or buckshot were spattered with wedges of tissue, dislodged teeth, and skull fragments. After a final, futile surge, the regulars turned and ran "in a very great disorder," a witness reported. They left behind ninety-six comrades, dead as mutton.

Howe heard the commotion below the riverbank to his right, but the rail fence just ahead, stiff with hundreds of American gunmen, drew his full attention. As he and the grenadiers took another stride, the top rail erupted in flame and filthy smoke, quickly followed by a volley from the rebel second rank. "The whole line was one blaze," a young Sudbury militiaman named Needham Maynard later recalled. "They fell in heaps, actually in heaps. . . . The bodies lay there very thick." Howe was unhurt, but men on either side of him crumpled. Disemboweled grenadiers, some screaming, some silent, tumbled one atop another. "I discharged my gun three times at the British, taking deliberate aim as if at a squirrel," wrote Simon Fobes, a nineteen-year-old private from Bridgewater. "I had become calm as a clock."

Regulars from two trailing regiments hurried forward to fill gaps in the grenadier line only to be gunned down. A crackle of musketry from the three flèches to Howe's left swept his corps with cross fire. Wounded redcoats dragged themselves through the grass amid shrieks, curses, and plaintive wails for mother. The British return fire tended to fly high: a stand of apple trees behind the American line had few enemy balls embedded in the trunks, but the "branches above were literally cut to pieces," Captain Henry Dearborn reported. A few lightly wounded rebels reloaded muskets for their upright comrades, trimmed lead bullets to fit odd-sized barrels, or acted as spotters: "There. See that officer?"

Howe pulled his men back briefly to regroup—"long enough for us to clean our guns," Maynard, the Sudbury militiaman, noted—then heaved forward again only to be smashed once more. "Their officers were shot down," Maynard added. "There seemed to be nobody to command 'em." The British wounded included Lieutenant Colonel James Abercrombie, the grenadier commander, shot in the thigh by jittery light infantrymen who had joined the rail-fence fight after the carnage on the beach. Before he died, a week later, Abercrombie would tell London that his own army "gave me a plumper"—a volley—"and killed two officers and three privates," while wounding twenty others in fratricidal mayhem. The undisciplined light companies, he suggested, "must be drilled before they are carried to action again." A jeering rebel who recognized the crippled man being helped from the field shouted, "Colonel Abercrombie, are the Yankees cowards?"

A dozen men in Howe's command retinue were now dead or wounded. "For near a minute," an officer observed, "he was quite alone." At last Howe turned and trudged down the hill, unscathed, though his white stockings were slick with British blood. "There was a moment," he subsequently told General Harvey, "that I never felt before."

Brigadier Pigot had suffered few casualties in feinting toward the redoubt—cannonballs from the 24-pounders on Copp's Hill kept defenders crouched beneath their parapet. But now the weight of the British assault necessarily shifted to his corps. Marines, three regiments, and various detached companies pressed toward the crest of Breed's Hill, bedeviled by fences, stone walls, and what Burgoyne called "a thousand impediments." Approaching the redoubt, the line was "stopped by some brick kilns and enclosures, and exposed for some time to the whole of its fire," a British ensign wrote. "And it was here that so many men were lost."

Volley upon volley crashed from the redoubt and the protruding breastwork so that "the enemy fell like grass when mowed," a rebel fifer said. Ebenezer Bancroft, the militia captain from Dunstable, observed, "Our first fire was shockingly fatal." When a well-aimed fusillade ripped into the regulars, a militiaman bellowed, "You have made a furrow through them!" A diarist in the 47th Foot wrote that "for about fifty minutes it resembled rather a continual sheet of lightning and an uninterrupted peal of thunder than the explosion of firearms." Some regulars used dead redcoats to build their own breastworks. An American captain reported that he fired all thirty-five rounds in his ammunition pouch, and then threw stones.

Among the fallen was Major John Pitcairn, the conqueror of Lexington Common, now dying in the grass from at least one ball in the chest. A major in the 52nd Regiment was described by a subordinate as "lying about ten yards from the redoubt in great agony" from five wounds; three dead captains lay near him. "They advanced towards us in order to swallow us up," Private Peter Brown told his mother in Rhode Island, "but they found a choaky mouthful of us." An Irish comrade added, "Diamond cut diamond, and that's the whole story."

Not quite, for diamond would now cut back. Bloody but unbowed, William Howe drew up a new plan. With more than five hundred reserve troops preparing to cross the Charles from Boston, he would renew the attack on the redoubt by shifting two regiments and the surviving grenadiers from his own corps to Pigot's on the left. Companies would advance in tight columns rather than broad assault lines; the regulars would lighten their loads by leaving superfluous kit behind; and they were to attack swiftly, with bayonets only, rather than pausing to shoot and reload. Moreover, eight fieldpieces now on the battlefield would be hauled by drag ropes—each brass 6-pounder weighed a quarter ton—to positions east of the redoubt to batter the defenders. Howe was disgusted to learn that his artillery fire had slackened during the earlier assaults because side boxes on the guns were found to contain 12-pound balls, which were too fat for 6-pound muzzles. He ordered gunners to instead use grapeshot, plum-sized iron balls packed in canvas bags that blew open when fired.

Peering over the parapet from his battered redoubt, Colonel Prescott watched the red tide again creep up the Breed's pastureland. The 150 or so Americans remaining in his small fort—their faces blackened from soot and powder, as if they'd been toiling in a coal yard—had little ammunition left. Militiamen searched pockets for stray cartridges or tapped the final grains from powder horns, tearing strips from their shirttails for wadding. Prescott ordered the last artillery cartridges torn open and the loose powder distributed to his infantry. Except for a single two-gun battery, the four American artillery companies sent into battle had been all but useless this afternoon, beset with cowardice, confusion, and technical ineptitude. Of six guns that reached the peninsula, five now stood silent and the sixth had been hauled away.

The failure of General Ward's headquarters to resupply the redoubt was almost as disheartening as the dearth of reinforcements. Among the few doughty souls to arrive in mid-battle was a familiar if unlikely figure. Dr. Joseph Warren—elegantly dressed in a light coat, a white satin waist-coat with silver lace, and white breeches—strode through the sally port gripping a borrowed gun, his earlier headache gone, or ignored, or mended by the huzzahs that greeted him. Despite the high rank conferred several days earlier by the provincial congress, Warren declined offers of command, insisting that he take post in the line with other musketeers.

Up the peninsula, hundreds of leaderless militiamen "in great confusion" ambled about on Bunker Hill or beyond the Neck, a sergeant reported. A few without muskets brandished pitchforks, shillelaghs, and at least one grain flail. Captain John Chester, who had just arrived with his Connecticut company, found chaos: thirty men cowering behind an apple tree; others behind rocks or haycocks; twenty more escorting a single wounded comrade toward Cambridge "when not more than three or four could touch him to advantage. Others were retreating seemingly without any excuse." One colonel, described as "unwieldy from excessive corpulence," lay sprawled on the ground, proclaiming his exhaustion. British gunners aboard *Glasgow* and *Symmetry* continued to scorch the Neck with iron shot, giving pause to even the lionhearted. "The orders were *press on, press on*," wrote Lieutenant Samuel Blachley Webb, now skittering toward the redoubt with Chester's Connecticut company. "Good God how the balls flew. I freely acknowledge I never had such a tremor come over me before."

The sun had begun to dip in the southwestern sky, dimmed by the black coils of smoke above Charlestown, when Pigot's legions again drew near, high-stepping their dead. British grapeshot spattered the earthworks, driving defenders from the parapet even as American fire wounded a dozen gunners shouldering the fieldpieces into position. "They looked too handsome to be fired at," Corporal Francis Merrifield lamented, "but we had to do it." Prescott told his men to wait until the British vanguard was within thirty yards of the redoubt walls; on command, militiamen hopped up on their fire steps, and a point-blank volley staggered the enemy ranks again. A ball clipped the skull of Captain George Harris, commanding the 5th Foot grenadier company; dragged through the grass by a lieutenant, Harris cried, "For God's sake, let me die in peace." Of four grenadiers who carried him to a nearby copse, three were wounded, one mortally.

But the battle had turned. Regulars pressed close on three sides, leaping across a narrow ditch to hug the berm before scaling the steep ramparts.

American gunshots grew scattered; some Jonathans saved their last round to shoot British officers atop the parapet. "Our firing began to slacken. At last it went out like an old candle," Needham Maynard recalled. More redcoats tumbled into the redoubt, now shooting. "Take their guns away," Prescott yelled, "twitch 'em away." Enemies grappled, grunting and swearing. A brown miasma of smoke and churning dust hung in the air. Americans swung their muskets as clubs, fighting "more like devils than men," a regular reported, and when the walnut stocks shattered, they swung the bent barrels or threw rocks.

Prescott was among the last to escape, "stepping long, with his sword up," parrying bayonet thrusts that snagged his banyan but not his flesh. Peter Brown scrambled over the wall and ran for half a mile; musket balls, he told his mother, "flew like hail stones." Captain Bancroft fought his way out, first with a musket butt, then with his fists, bullets nicking his hat and coat and shearing off his left forefinger. Corporal Farnsworth of Groton would tell his diary, "I received a wound in my right arm, the ball going through a little below my elbow. . . . Another ball struck my back, taking a piece of skin about as big as a penny. . . . I was in great pain."

They were the lucky ones. "Nothing could be more shocking than the carnage that followed the storming of this work," wrote Lieutenant John Waller of the 1st Marines. "We tumbled over the dead to get at the living, who were crowding out of the gorge of the redoubt. . . . 'Twas streaming with blood & strewed with dead and dying men, the soldiers stabbing some and dashing out the brains of others." Thirty American bodies, some mutilated beyond recognition, lay scattered across the shambles. The triumphant, vengeful roar of British regulars could be heard in Boston.

Lieutenant Webb and his Connecticut militia arrived to see the melee spill from the sally port. "I had no other feeling but that of revenge," he wrote. "Four men were shot dead within five feet to me. . . . I escaped with only the graze of a musket ball on my hat." Dr. Warren did not escape: sixty yards from the redoubt, a bullet hit him below the left eye and blew through the back of his head. He toppled without a word.

By five-thirty p.m., rebel forces were in full retreat up the peninsula, bounding from fence to fence, barn to barn, leaving a debris trail of cartridge boxes, tumplines, goatskin knapsacks, even coats and hats shed in the heat of the day. The wounded hobbled, or were carried on backs or in stretchers fashioned from blankets and muskets. On their heels came not only Pigot's regiments but Howe's regular regiments and grenadiers, who had bulled through the breastworks and the three flèches. Also in pursuit was General Clinton, who on his own initiative had crossed the Charles from Copp's Hill, rallied regulars milling in the rear of Pigot's corps, then circled north to give chase. "All was in confusion," he wrote. "I never saw so great a want of order."

Yet for the rebels, disorder brought salvation. The New Hampshire and Connecticut regiments, seeing the redoubt fall, pulled back from the rail fence in an orderly withdrawal to give covering fire for Prescott's fugitives. Some militiamen loitering atop Bunker Hill advanced down the slope to pelt the British pursuers with bullets, a belated but vital contribution to the battle. "The retreat was no flight," Burgoyne would write. "It was even covered with bravery and military skill." Howe had seen enough and suffered enough: when Clinton confronted him north of the redoubt to urge pursuit to the Neck and beyond, Howe "called me back," Clinton wrote later, "I thought a little forcibly."

Americans by the hundreds surged through the gantlet of naval gunfire still scything the only exit from the peninsula. Some died within yards of safety, including Major Andrew McClary, one of Stark's Hampshiremen, hit with a frigate cannonball. "He leaped two or three feet from the ground, pitched forward, and fell dead upon his face," an officer reported. But most straggled unharmed onto the high ground beyond the Neck, exhausted and tormented by thirst. General Putnam followed on his white horse, cradling an armful of salvaged entrenching tools. "I never saw such a carnage of the human race," he would be quoted as saying.

For now the carnage was over, mostly. Rebel snipers in trees and houses across the Neck continued to plink away at enemy pickets, killing a 38th Foot lieutenant with a random shot. The British answered with broadsides from *Glasgow* and salvos from a 12-pounder. Charlestown burned and burned, painting the low clouds bright orange in what one diarist called "a sublime scene of military magnificence and ruin." Marines landed in skiffs to set fire to wooden structures that had escaped the earlier flames. Prescott, ever pugnacious, vowed to retake his lost hill that night if given ammunition, bayonets, and three rested regiments. General Ward sensibly demurred.

"Dearest Friend," Abigail Adams wrote from Braintree to her husband, John, then meeting in Philadelphia with the Continental Congress. "The day, perhaps the decisive day, is come on which the fate of America depends." She continued:

> Charlestown is laid in ashes. . . . Tis expected they will come out over the Neck tonight, and a dreadful battle must ensue. . . . The constant roar of the cannon is so distressing that we cannot eat, drink, or sleep.

Night fell. The British did not come. From Prospect and Winter Hills above the Cambridge road came the excavating sounds of mattock and spade, as militiamen once again stacked their muskets and began to dig the next line of resistance.

British medicos scuffed through the high grass to feel with their feet for the dead and the merely dying, then held their flickering lanterns close to distinguish between the two. Those with a pulse or a glint in the eye were hoisted onto drays and wheeled to barges on the Charles for transport to Boston. "The cries and moans of the dying was shocking," wrote General Clinton, who also picked his way across the battlefield. "I had conversation with many of these poor wretches in their dying moments."

Later studies by the British Army would demonstrate that soldiers wearing conspicuous red uniforms were more than twice as likely to be shot in combat as those in muted blues and grays. The tally at Breed's Hill seemed to anticipate those findings: Gage's army had regained roughly a square mile of rebel territory at a cost exceeding a thousand casualties, or more than a man lost per acre won. Over 40 percent of the attacking force had been killed or wounded, including 226 dead; losses were especially doleful in the elite flanker companies—the light infantry and grenadiers. Nineteen officers also had been killed. Of all the king's officers who would die in battle during the long war against the Americans, more than one out of every eight had perished in four hours on a June afternoon above Charlestown.

Casualties in some units were calamitous. All but four grenadiers from the King's Own were killed or wounded. Of thirty-eight men in the 35th Foot light company, only three escaped rebel bullets; with every officer, sergeant, and corporal hit, the senior private led other surviving privates. After sustaining 123 casualties, British marines were nonplussed to find that their tents in Boston had been plundered during the battle, apparently by regulars not in the field. The Admiralty voiced "astonishment that it could have happened" but declined to pay compensation, because of the precedent such reimbursement would set. Howe, who lost virtually his entire staff to death or injury, admitted to General Harvey that when he studied the casualty lists, "I do it with horror."

Through Saturday night and all day Sunday, as artillery grumbled in the distance, blood-slick wagons, chaises, sedan chairs, wood carts, and barrows hauled broken men from the wharves to makeshift hospitals, barracks, and rooming houses. "The streets were filled with the wounded and the dying, the sight of which, with the lamentations of the women and children over their husbands and fathers, pierced one to the soul," a British official wrote. A woman in Boston told her brother of watching redcoats hobble through town, tormented by flies and pleading for water, "some without noses, some with but one eye, broken legs and arms." Shock and hemorrhage killed many before they reached a surgeon's table; gangrene would kill more. The first coach to the Manufactory House—built two decades earlier for the working poor to make linen and now a general hospital—contained a dying major and three dead captains; the second coach carried four more dead officers. The loyalist judge Peter Oliver encountered a soldier stumbling through town, "his white waistcoat, breeches & stockings being very much dyed by a scarlet hue"; the man told Oliver, "I have three bullets through me," then tottered off. A captain who arrived from England on Sunday wrote his father of finding "wounded and dead officers in every street. Bells tolling, wounded soldiers lying in their tents and crying for assistance to remove some men who had just expired. . . . They remained in this deplorable situation for three days."

Captain George Harris, shot in the head near the redoubt, was saved by trepanning, the boring of a hole in the skull to relieve the pressure from bleeding. Doctors positioned a mirror "so as to give me a sight of my own brain," he later wrote a cousin. "It may convince you and the rest of the world that I have such a thing." Others were less jocular. "I have received two balls, one in my groin and the other near the breast," a wounded soldier wrote his family, according to an account published after the war. "The surgeons inform me that three hours will be the utmost I can survive." Richard Hope, a surgeon in the 52nd Foot, described how the regiment suffered thirty privates killed in action and eighty wounded, "a fourth part of whom will die. . . . It would pierce a heart of stone to hear the daily shrieks and lamentations of the poor widows and fatherless left desolate and friendless three thousand miles from home." The dead included Major Roger Spendlove, who in four decades with the 43rd Foot had survived wounds at Quebec, Martinique, and Havana. Private Clement Nicholson of the 38th Foot had survived a thousand lashes for desertion the previous year, meted out in four ferocious sets of 250, but Bunker Hill would kill him, too.

A physician examining gunshot victims described the "yellowness of the face, paleness of the extremities, a falling of the pulse." Treatment was not far removed from such medieval remedies as pigeon blood for eye wounds or the liberal use of "oil of whelps," an ointment made with earthworms, white wine, and the flesh of dogs boiled alive. Surgeons probed wounded arms and legs with their unwashed fingers, feeling for bone fragments, whose presence indicated a need for immediate amputation. A surgical text recommended that a doctor preparing to lop off a man's limb with a saw "avoid terrifying him with the appearance of the apparatus [and] avoid a useless crowd of spectators." Lucky patients got a grain of opium or a swig of rum, and their ears stuffed with lamb's wool to mask the sound of the sawing. Many were less fortunate. Amputations above the knee took only thirty seconds, but no more than half the patients survived the ordeal or the subsequent sepsis. Orderlies sloshed vinegar across the bloody floor and heaved the next patient onto the plank table. As for those shot in the abdomen, a sniff of a lint probe inserted into the wound would reveal whether gut contamination had set in, in which case, a medical text advised, "we lay the patient quietly in bed, there to take his fate."

"Many of the wounded are daily dying, and many must have both legs amputated," wrote one surgeon, who asserted that rebel gunmen fired nails and iron scrap to inflict maximum damage. Some had also fired pebbles, but only because they had no more bullets. By one tally, only half of the more than eight hundred wounded regulars would ultimately be declared "cured, fit for service." Many in the coming months would also be tormented, sometimes fatally, by "the Yanky"—dysentery, in British slang.

A few miles away, the Yankees also suffered. A New Hampshire surgeon who rushed to Cambridge with a bullet extractor of his own design reported, "I amputated several limbs and extracted many balls the first night." American casualties approached 450, including 138 dead. More than thirty American prisoners, many of them wounded, were dumped at Long Wharf under guard on Saturday night, then jailed the next day; most would be dead by September, foreshadowing the treatment captured Americans could expect in British custody. A surgeon who packed up his instruments in Andover and galloped to Cambridge wrote of the terrible uncertainty besetting a hundred New England towns: "It was not known who were among the slain or living, the wounded or the well." Those who learned the worst soon submitted sad claims for restitution, like Mary Pierce of Pepperell, the widow of a private in Prescott's regiment. She requested compensation of five pounds, twelve shillings for his lost coat, trousers, stockings, shoes, buckles, silk handkerchief, knife, and tobacco box.

To many American fighters, the battle now called Bunker Hill felt like defeat. Ground had been given, the peninsula lost. Many were furious at what a Connecticut captain called a "shameful and scandalous" retreat. Rumors spread of betrayal, of treacherous officers, of gunpowder adulterated with sand, "all of which creates great uneasiness in the camp," a former Boston selectman told his diary. Three artillery companies had performed dismally. Several timid commanders faced court-martial and dismissal from the service. American generalship had been muddled and indecisive, leaving the force "commanded without order and God knows by whom," a senior officer wrote. Although the *Essex Gazette* claimed

Putnam was "inspired by God Almighty with a military genius," Colonel Stark denounced him as "a poltroon." Much blame fell on Artemas Ward, "a general destitute of all military ability," in the opinion of the new president of the provincial congress, James Warren.

The incineration of Charlestown, the first of several American towns to be obliterated during the war, stirred both sorrow and rage. A survey found that 232 houses, 95 barns, 76 shops, 25 warehouses, a dozen mills, 81 miscellaneous buildings, and 17 wharves had burned, with losses exceeding £100,000. Of 450 eventual claims, some came from Bostonians who had moved their household goods to Charlestown for safekeeping, like Sarah Hunstable, who lost nine feather beds, six mahogany chairs, three looking glasses, and more. A church census calculated that two thousand residents had been consigned to "the most aggravated exile."

Yet the battle would soon be seen as a triumph of patriot moxie. "I wish [we] could sell them another hill at the same price," observed a new brigadier general from Rhode Island named Nathanael Greene. The lawyer William Tudor wrote John Adams on June 26, "The ministerial troops gained the hill, but were victorious losers. A few more such victories, and they are undone." Even if Prescott and his comrades were not "supported in a proper manner," wrote Samuel Gray from Roxbury, "this battle has been of infinite service to us—made us more vigilant, watchful, and cautious." Bunker Hill also reinforced the conviction that inflamed citizen soldiers, summoned to battle from field or shop, could hold their own against professional legions, a charming myth that took deep root and would nearly prove the undoing of America. Cheeky rebels soon appropriated a scornful British ditty to serve as a defiant American anthem. "'Yankee Doodle' is now their paean, a favorite of favorites," a British officer said, "esteemed as warlike as 'The Grenadiers' March.'"

For days, Yankees with spyglasses in Roxbury and on Dorchester Heights watched the regulars dig graves. With so many dead men to bury, Gage ordered the mourning bells in Boston silenced. Fallen officers like Major Pitcairn found graves in sanctified ground at Old North or in other churchyards. Their effects were quickly auctioned off in officers' messes or, as in the case of Lieutenant Colonel Abercrombie, at "the large tree in front of the encampment of the 22nd Regiment": swords, pistols, silk waistcoats, fancy hats, mattresses, spurs, all sold to the highest bidder. Page after page of new promotion announcements soon appeared; there was nothing like a bloodletting to advance careers.

Privates were laid in a common pit on the marshy ground between Breed's and Bunker Hills, then dusted with twenty barrels of quicklime. Many who died of their wounds were consigned to trenches on Boston

Common. The American dead on the peninsula were dumped without ceremony into mass graves or hasty bury holes, including Joseph Warren, interred with an anonymous companion in a farmer's frock. Captain Walter Laurie, who had commanded the star-crossed detachment at Concord Bridge, told London that his burial detail had found Warren's body and "stuffed the scoundrel with another rebel into one hole, and there he & his seditious principles may remain." Grave robbing became so pernicious on the peninsula that Howe threatened severe punishment for malefactors. "Added to the meanness of such a practice," he warned, "a pestilence from the infection of the putrefied bodies might reach the camp."

Midsummer gloom pervaded that camp, despite efforts to depict the battle as a triumph. "Another such," Clinton said, "would have ruined us." A cynical officer suggested that the rebels should plan "to lose a battle every week 'til the British army was reduced to nothing." On June 23, Gage ordered an assault on Dorchester Heights, then quickly canceled the attack, convincing himself that he could command the heights with artillery if necessary. Resentments festered among his officers, at the combat shortcomings of their rank and file—"discipline, not to say courage, was wanting," Burgoyne sniffed—and at the high command. "From an absurd and destructive confidence, carelessness, or ignorance, we have lost a thousand of our best men and officers," a seething officer wrote. "We were all wrong at the head."

Gage waited eight days to tell London of Bunker Hill, in a nineteen-sentence dispatch that was spare to the point of duplicity. "This action," he asserted, "has shown the superiority of the king's troops who . . . defeated above three times their own number." An oversized casualty chart with perfectly lined columns contained delicate calligraphic flourishes on the *k*'s and *w*'s that at least gave ornamentation to the killed and wounded. But in a private note to Lord Dartmouth, Gage conceded that casualties were "greater than our force can afford to lose. . . . The rebels are not the despicable rabble too many have supposed them to be. . . . Your Lordship will perceive that the conquest of this country is not easy." In a letter to Barrington on June 26, Gage added, "These people . . . are now spirited up by a rage and enthusiasm as great as ever people were possessed of." He continued:

> You must proceed in earnest or give the business up. The loss we have sustained is greater than we can bear. Small armies can't afford such losses. . . . I wish this cursed place was burned.

The news stunned England. Newspapers promptly published maps of Bunker Hill, which were studied intently by fretful readers. "The ministers now saw America was lost, or not to be recovered but by long time and expense," Walpole told his journal. "Yet, not daring to own their miscarriage, pushed on." Rumors circulated that fratricide had caused half of all British losses, that regulars had thrown down their arms rather than fight, that a disgraced General Gage had returned to England dressed as his wife. In fact, Margaret Kemble Gage came home dressed as herself aboard the three-masted *Charming Nancy*, accompanying sixty widows and orphans, plus 170 badly wounded soldiers. Correspondents who met the ship in Plymouth described "a most shocking spectacle," including "some without legs, and others without arms, and their clothes hanging on them like a loose morning gown." Many were said to be "in a state of complete alcoholic dependence." The Plymouth guildhall collected donations for the widows—sixteen shillings each. One writer, upon viewing this homecoming, concluded that "60,000 men would not be able to bring the Americans under subjection." William Eden wrote Lord North, "If we have eight more such victories, there will be nobody left to bring the news of them."

The king held firm, of course. For months British newspapers would chronicle the presentation of wounded officers at court, as in this announcement: "Yesterday Captain Cockering, who lost his arm at Bunker's Hill, was introduced to His Majesty at St. James's. . . . His Majesty was pleased to present him with a captain's commission in a company of invalids." The king also decided, as Barrington informed Gage, that injury compensation would be paid, retroactive to Lexington. An officer who lost an eye or a limb would receive a year's pay and medical expenses; the widows of officers killed in action would also get a year's pay, plus another third for each child. Those who died of their wounds within six months were "deemed slain in battle." No bonuses were announced for enlisted men.

Another deranged afternoon had come and gone in Massachusetts, and yet that awful Saturday lingered for every man in harm's way. "Some other mode must be adopted than gaining every little hill at the expense of a thousand Englishmen," Glanville Evelyn of the King's Own told his family. Just before midnight on June 17, Evelyn had taken a moment to write his will, philosophically reflecting that those in "the profession of arms hold their lives by a more precarious tenure than any other body of people."

As Captain Evelyn pondered the future, others tried to forget the past. Reverend David Osgood, a New Hampshire regimental chaplain, would recall as an old man how for the remaining eight years of war after Bunker Hill "a burden lay upon my spirits. . . . Visions of horror rose in my imagination, and disturbed my rest." A British officer in the 63rd Regiment of Foot could only agree. "The shocking carnage that day," Major Francis Bushill Sill wrote in a letter home, "never will be erased out of my mind 'till the day of my death."

4.

———◆———

What Shall We Say of Human Nature?

A sultry overcast thickened above the American encampments on Sunday morning, July 2. By order of General Ward, company officers had begun scrutinizing their troops during daily formation for signs of smallpox. Militiamen marched to prayer services for yet another sermon on the evils of profanity. At General Putnam's suggestion, they sometimes shouted *Amen!* loud enough to alarm British sentries.

Even on the Sabbath, British cannons pummeled Roxbury. "The balls came rattling through the houses," a soldier told his diary. "They neither killed nor wounded any of our men, which seems almost impossible." The Yankees answered with a pointless spatter of musketry. Heavy rain began to fall at eleven a.m., sharpening the camp odors of green firewood, animal manure, and human waste. Private Samuel Haws updated his journal: "July 1. Nothing remarkable this day. July 2. Ditto." Private Phineas Ingalls was a bit more descriptive in his Sunday diary entry: "Rained. A new general from Philadelphia."

Possibly not one of the seventeen thousand soldiers now under his command in Massachusetts knew what George Washington of Virginia looked like. Few Americans did. Imaginary portraits that bore no resemblance to him had been sketched and printed in the penny sheets after his unanimous selection by the Continental Congress seventeen days earlier to be "general and commander-in-chief of the American forces," a host to be known as the Continental Army. Now here he was in the flesh, trotting past the sodden pickets just after noon with a small cavalry escort and baggage that included a stack of books on generalship, notably *Military Instructions for Officers Detached in the Field* and a volume with copperplate diagrams on how to build fortifications and otherwise run a war. At Hastings House, a dour Ward handed over his orderly book to the man Private Haws soon called "Lesemo," a perversion of *generalissimo*. No salute was fired; the Lesemo's new army could not spare the powder.

"His personal appearance is truly noble and majestic, being tall and well-proportioned," wrote a doctor in Cambridge. "His dress is a blue coat with buff-colored facings, a rich epaulet on each shoulder, buff underdress, and an elegant small sword, a black cockade in his hat." At age forty-three, he was all that and more: over six feet tall, but so erect he seemed taller; nimble for a large man, as demonstrated on many a dance floor, and so graceful in the saddle that some reckoned him the finest horseman of the age; fair skin that burned easily, lightly spattered with smallpox pits and stretched across high cheekbones beneath wide-set slate-blue eyes; fine hair with a hint of auburn, tied back in a queue. He had first lost teeth in the French and Indian War, symptomatic of the perpetual dental miseries that kept him from smiling much. "His appearance alone gave confidence to the timid and imposed respect on the bold," in one soldier's estimation, or, as a Connecticut congressman observed, "No harum-scarum, ranting, swearing fellow, but sober, steady, and calm." Abigail Adams, who would invite Washington to coffee soon after his arrival, told her husband, John, "Dignity with ease and complacency, the gentleman and soldier look agreeably blended in him. Modesty marks every line and feature of his face." Clearly smitten, she paraphrased the English poet John Dryden: "Mark his majestic fabric! He's a temple / Sacred by birth, and built by hands divine." John Adams, in turn, noted that Washington "possessed the gift of silence," a virtue rarely found in Lawyer Adams.

Washington's other traits, if less visible, would soon become conspicuous enough to those he commanded. Born into Virginia's planter class, he was ambitious and dogged, with a resolve that made him seem tireless. If unquestionably brave, diligent, and sensible, he could also be humorless, aloof, and touchy about his lack of formal education. Those military books in his kit were merely the latest texts of a lifelong autodidact; as a youth he had famously copied 110 maxims from the English translation of a Jesuit etiquette manual, including, "Let your countenance be pleasant but in serious matters somewhat grave.... Do not puff up in the cheeks, loll not out the tongue.... Cleanse not your teeth with the tablecloth." As a twenty-three-year-old colonel commanding Virginia's provincial forces in the last French war, he had been with Braddock—and Thomas Gage—for the disaster on the Monongahela, surviving four bullets through his uniform, another through his hat, and two horses shot dead beneath him, before dragging his mortally wounded commander across the river and riding sixty miles for help in covering the British retreat. That ordeal—more than four hundred British dead, including wounded men scalped or burned alive—gave Washington a tincture of indestructibility while convincing him that "the all-powerful dispensations of Providence" had protected him "beyond all human probability."

He had shed the uniform in 1758, telling his officers, "It really was the greatest honor of my life to command gentlemen who made me happy in their company and easy by their conduct." Over the subsequent seventeen years, he paid little attention to military matters. Yet that experience of observing British commanders, organizing military expeditions, and leading men in battle had served Washington well. He was a talented administrator, with a brain suited to executive action, thanks to a remarkable memory, a knack for incisive thinking and clear writing, and a penchant for detail, learned first as a young officer and then practiced daily as suzerain of his sprawling, complex estate on the Potomac River at Mount Vernon. His fortunes, personal and pecuniary, grew considerably in 1759 when he married Virginia's richest widow, the amiable and attractive Martha Dandridge Custis. Over the years, their convenient business arrangement had become a love match.

Great responsibility would enlarge him. His youthful vainglory—"I heard bullets whistle and believe me there was something charming in the sound," he had written his brother in 1754—had been supplanted by a more mature reflection that those charming bullets meant dead boys and sobbing mothers. War at its core, he acknowledged, was "gloom & horror." Once keen to advance himself and his interests, whether as a land speculator or a young colonel on the make, he now displayed a becoming, if artful, modesty. He was seen as "noble and disinterested," in John Adams's phrase: ecumenical, judicious, formal but not regal, emblematic of republican virtues in sacrificing personal interest to the greater public good, yet elevated above the republican riffraff. As a passionate supporter of the American cause, a well-connected and native-born political figure, and a man "strongly bent to arms," in his phrase, Washington was all but the inevitable choice to become commander in chief. Although he refrained from overtly angling for the post, he had worn his Virginia militia uniform in Congress to remind his fellow delegates of his combat experience. He had declined the offer of a $500 monthly salary, accepting only reimbursement for his expenses. From ferry fares and saddle repairs to grog and Madeira, those would be carefully logged in his account ledgers, beginning with the five horses and the light phaeton he bought before leaving Philadelphia.

Washington professed to be fighting for "all that is dear and valuable in life" against a British regime intent on "despotism to fix the shackles of slavery upon us"—a curious sentiment from someone who owned 135 slaves, including the intrepid Billy Lee, purchased for £61 and now at his side in Cambridge. Clearly he nursed resentments: at the preference given British land speculators, the imperial restrictions on western expansion, and the large debts accumulated with British merchants. Twice he had tried to ascend from the Virginia provincials by securing regular commissions for himself and his officers, and twice he had been snubbed. British tax policies jeopardized his commercial ambitions and offended his moral equilibrium; the royal governor in Virginia had threatened, through a technicality, to annul land grants issued twenty years earlier, which would have stripped Washington of twenty-three thousand wilderness acres.

Yet just as clearly he saw the glory of the American cause: a continental empire to be built upon republican ideals, buttressed with American mettle, ambition, and genius. He also knew that it could all end badly on a Tower Hill scaffold, as it had for the Jacobite rebels of 1745. Thousands had been arrested and at least eighty hanged or beheaded; some of their skulls were still displayed on spikes at Temple Bar in central London. As a precaution, Washington had drafted his will before leaving Philadelphia.

Few would guess that the imposing, confident figure who rode into Cambridge that Sunday afternoon concealed his own anxieties and insecurities. In tears he had told a fellow Virginian, Patrick Henry, "From the day I enter upon the command of the American armies, I date my fall, and the ruin of my reputation." He also lamented leaving Martha alone in Virginia. "It has been a kind of destiny that has thrown me upon this service," he wrote her. "I go fully trusting in the Providence, which has been more bountiful to me than I deserve. . . . I retain an unalterable affection for you, which neither time or distance can change." To his brother he confided, "I am embarked on a wide ocean, boundless in its prospect & from whence, perhaps, no safe harbor is to be found."

Washington would soon move his headquarters into the vacant Vassall House in Cambridge, a gray, three-story Georgian mansion that had been abandoned by its loyalist owner. The orchards, outbuildings, and sweeping vista of the Charles evoked his beloved Mount Vernon, although the house had been used by medicos after Bunker Hill and then as a bivouac by a Marblehead regiment; sanding grease and filth from the floors took more than a week. Washington chose a high-ceilinged, ground-floor room with Delft tile for his bedchamber, parked his new phaeton and saddle horses in the stable, and then set out to fulfill his marching orders from Congress: "take every method in your power, consistent with prudence, to destroy or make prisoners of all persons who are now, or who hereafter shall appear in arms against the good people of the United Colonies." Greene, the young Rhode Island general, would later observe of Washington's arrival, "It seemed as if the spirit of conquest breathed through the whole army."

Washington needed little time to grasp the lay of the land. The former surveyor's mahogany-and-brass spyglass showed two armies barely a mile apart, squinting "at one another like wildcats across a gutter," in one officer's description. The enemy was "strongly entrenched on Bunker's Hill," Washington wrote on July 10 to John Hancock, who as new president of the Continental Congress would be his primary correspondent in Philadelphia. Charlestown Neck had been ditched, palisaded, and fraised to thwart an American attack. White British tents covered the peninsula, and three floating batteries on the Mystic commanded the isthmus. In Roxbury, felled trees and earthen parapets blocked the Neck; many of the buildings that were still standing had been smashed or burned by incessant enemy cannonading. Washington's own "troops of the United Provinces of North America," as he grandly called them, occupied more than 230 buildings from Cambridge to Brookline, two dozen of which were used as hospitals. The enemy's strength was reckoned at 11,500—almost twice the number Gage actually had fit for duty. "Between you and me," Washington wrote a Virginia friend, "I think we are in an exceeding dangerous situation."

Commands cascaded from his headquarters, the first of twelve thousand orders and letters to be issued in his name over the next eight years. Officers of the guard were to stop bantering with British sentries. All strongpoints must be defended; officers were to examine batteries to be sure that American guns were actually pointed toward the enemy. Pikes should be "greased twice a week," and thirteen-foot lances would be made to complement the hundreds of shorter spears already ordered, though chestnut and other brittle wood ought to be avoided. Blacksmiths were authorized to work on Sundays. Because so few Yankees wore uniforms, rank would be color-coded: senior field-grade officers were to wear red or pink cockades in their hats; captains would wear yellow or buff; subalterns, green. A strip of red cloth pinned on the shoulder signified a sergeant; green indicated a corporal. Generals wore chest sashes: purple for major generals, pink for brigadiers, light blue for the commander in chief. Washington agreed to be called "your excellency," despite private grumbling about the imperial implication. "New lords, new laws," the troops told one another.

The Continental Congress had appointed thirteen lesser generals, mostly New Englanders, to serve under His Excellency. The only three who could be considered professional military veterans were former British officers—none had risen above the rank of lieutenant colonel—who had recently thrown in with the rebels. Washington quickly organized his army into three "grand divisions," each commanded by a major general and composed of two brigades, typically with six regiments apiece. Ward led the division on the right wing, around Boston Neck. Putnam commanded the center, at Cambridge. The division on the left wing, overlooking Bunker Hill and ruined Charlestown, was led by Charles Lee, a brusque, vivid eccentric who had spent a quarter century in the king's service before immigrating to America in 1773. Rather than the twenty-five thousand troops he had expected, Washington found—after excruciating efforts to get a reliable tally—that his host had less than fourteen thousand men actually present and fit for duty around Boston.

For every moment when Washington drew his sword or spurred his horse to the sound of the guns, there would be a thousand administrative moments: dictating orders, scribbling letters, convening meetings, hectoring, praising, adjudicating. No sooner had he settled into Vassall House than he recognized that he personally needed to oversee the smallest aspects of the army's operation, from camp kettles to bread quality to the $333 paid an unidentified spy—and logged in his expense book in mid-July—"to go into the town of Boston . . . for the purpose of conveying intelligence of the enemy's movements and designs." He quickly saw that unlike the fantasy army that existed in congressional imaginations—grandly intended, as Washington's commission declared, "for the defense of American liberty and for repelling every hostile invasion thereof"—this army was woefully unskilled; bereft of artillery and engineering expertise, it was led by a very thin officer corps. "We found everything exactly the reverse of what had been represented," General Lee complained. "Not a single man of 'em is [capable] of constructing an oven." Washington also recognized that his own five years as a callow regimental officer had left him, as he wrote, with "the want of experience to move upon a large scale"; like every other American commander, he knew little of cavalry, artillery, the mass movement of armies, or how to command a continental force. Still, service under British officers had deeply imprinted him with European orthodoxy, including strong preferences for offensive warfare, firepower, logistical competence, and rigid discipline. He was no brigand chieftain.

Even as he immersed himself in tactical minutiae, Washington recognized that a commander in chief must be a capable strategist; that brass spyglass had to focus on the horizon as much as on the local battlefield. War, he knew, was a struggle of political wills. Winning a war did not require winning every battle; the French war had proved that. Tactical developments often had little influence on strategic success. And Washington was—instinctively, brilliantly—a political general: in the month following his departure from Philadelphia, he wrote seven letters to Congress, acknowledging its superior authority while maneuvering to get what he needed. He used all the tools of a deft politico: flattery, blandishment, reason, contrition. More letters went to colonial governors. Congress had adopted the

New England militia as a national force, to be augmented with regiments from other colonies, and he was aware that placing a southerner in command of this predominately northern army was a fragile experiment in continental unity.

The coming weeks and months required intimacy with his army, building the mystical bond between leader and led. Who were they? What did they believe? Why did they fight? How long would they fight? Washington would personify the army he commanded, no small irony given the despair and occasional contempt it caused him. That army would become both the fulcrum on which the fate of the nation balanced and the unifying element in the American body politic, a tie that bound together disparate interests of a republic struggling to be born. It was the indispensable institution, led by the indispensable man, and the coupling of a national army with its commander marked the transformation of a rebellion into a revolution. "Confusion and discord reigned in every department," Washington wrote in late July. "However we mend every day, and I flatter myself that in a little time we shall work up these raw materials into good stuff."

Raw indeed. "We were all young," a twenty-one-year-old captain would write, "and in a manner unacquainted with human nature, quite novices in military matters, had everything to learn, and no one to instruct us who knew any better than ourselves." If mostly literate, they were barely educated. "What I had learnt," wrote Stephen Olney, a soldier from Rhode Island, "was mostly rong." The camps were full of Old Testament names: Joshua, Jabez, Ezekiel, Amos, Caleb, Nathan, Nehemiah. Guided by that ancient text, many concluded that Gage was Pharaoh, if not the Antichrist, confronted by a Chosen People who in the past three months had killed or wounded fourteen hundred British Philistines. Some, of course, were here for the six and two-thirds dollars paid each month to privates, more money than a farm laborer might earn. Others were animated by an inchoate patriotism on behalf of a nation that did not yet exist. And more than one sought "to make a man of himself," as was said of seventeen-year-old Jeremiah Greenman, also from Rhode Island.

"Discipline," Washington had written in 1757, "is the soul of an army." Certainly this army was still looking for its soul. American troops, one visitor claimed, were "as dirty a set of mortals as ever disgraced the name of a soldier." Each man lived in "a kennel of his own making." No two companies drilled alike, and together on parade they were described as the finest body of men ever seen out of step. Their infractions were legion: singing on guard duty, voiding "excrement about the fields perniciously," promiscuous shooting for the sake of noise, a tendency by privates to debate their officers, "unnecessary drum beating at night," insolent "murmuring," pilfering thirty bushels of cherries, thirty barrels of apples, and five hundred cabbages from one Chelsea farmer alone. When a small reward was offered for each British cannonball retrieved so that they could be reused, "every ball, as it fell, was surrounded with a great number of men to see who would get it first," a lieutenant in Roxbury reported. Several lost their feet before the bounty was canceled.

The junior officers were not much better, notably those who used soldiers for personal farm labor, or falsified company returns to draw extra provisions, or pointed cocked pistols at their sergeants. Some officers, a Washington aide wrote in mid-August, were "not only ignorant and litigious but scandalously disobedient." Many regiments elected their captains, lieutenants, and even lowly subalterns, often on the basis of civilian friendships, social rank, or political influence; the army was said to suffer from a "nightmare of liberty," inimical to executive power. As for senior officers, few issues plagued Washington more than the endless jockeying for rank. Brigadier generals sulked and bickered all summer over seniority. When one threatened to resign in a snit, Lee wrote him in late July, "For God Almighty's sake . . . for the sake of your country, of mankind, and let me add of your own reputation, discard such sentiments." John Trumbull, a soldier, artist, and the son of Connecticut's governor, wrote while serving in Roxbury, "Officers grumbling about rank and soldiers about pay, everyone thinking himself ill-used and imposed upon."

For hours and days on end, Washington rode from Chelsea to Roxbury and back—inspecting, correcting, fuming—then returned to Vassall House to issue another raft of detailed, exhortatory commands. In the three months following his arrival in Cambridge, the commander in chief on five occasions, in general orders, condemned excessive drinking. Four times he demanded better hygiene. Thirteen times he pleaded for accurate returns from subordinate commanders to gauge the size and health of the army. Company rolls were to be called twice daily, and orders read aloud to ensure comprehension, if not obedience. No man was to appear on sentry duty who was "not perfectly sober and tolerably observing," nor was anyone to appear in formation "without having on his stockings and shoes." Fines were levied: a shilling for swearing, two shillings sixpence for unauthorized gunplay. Courts-martial dealt swift justice to erring officers. More than two dozen would be convicted in Washington's first months of command, for offenses ranging from cowardice or other misbehavior at Bunker Hill— five officers found guilty—to defrauding men of their pay, embezzling provisions, and stabbing a subordinate. Most were cashiered in disgrace.

Washington's conceptions of military justice had been shaped by his years under stern British command. In the spring of 1757 alone, he had approved floggings averaging six hundred lashes each—enough to cripple a man, or even kill him—and presided over courts-martial that imposed more than a dozen death sentences. Such draconian measures were impossible in an army saturated with democratic principles, and Congress stayed his hand by restricting floggings to thirty-nine stripes (soon to be increased to a hundred, at his insistence). If a bit less vindictive, the cat-o'-nine-tails still fell routinely across the backs of convicted men tied to a whipping post known as the "adjutant's daughter." "Saw two men whipt for stealing," a corporal wrote. "O what a pernicious thing it is for a man to steal and cheat his feller nabors, and how provoking to God!" A deserter was not hanged or jailed but sentenced to clean latrines for a week while wearing a sign printed with his offense. A felonious sergeant was drummed from camp with the epithet "MUTINY" on his back.

"My greatest concern is to establish order, regularity & discipline," Washington wrote Hancock. "My difficulties thicken every day." In truth, an immensely wealthy man to the manner born, with scores of slaves to tend his business in his absence, could hardly comprehend the sacrifice made by most of his men in leaving their families, shops, and farms in high season. For that vital link between commander and commanded to be welded imperishably, Washington would have to know in his bones—and the men would have to know that he knew—what was risked and what was lost in serving at his side.

Many small, private tragedies, unseen by his spyglass, would play out over the coming months and years. "News of the death of my child," Lieutenant Benjamin Craft told his journal on August 14. "I hope it will have a sanctifying effect on me and my poor wife. I hope God will enable us to bear all he shall lay upon us." Many were lonely, and fretful for the families they had forsaken. Captain Nathan Peters had recently lost two young children when he left his surviving one-year-old and his pregnant wife, Lois, in Medfield. She was to run their saddlery while he went to war. "Pray write every opportunity, for I live very lonesome," Lois wrote him that summer. "Without some money we cannot carry on the trade any longer, for we have laid out all the money we had for leather. . . . My heart aches for you and all our friends there. . . . Our corn looks well."

Yet Washington complained in August of "an unaccountable kind of stupidity . . . among the officers of the Massachusetts part of the army, who are nearly of the kidney with the privates." New England troops generally "are an exceeding dirty & nasty people," he wrote in confidence to Lund Washington, his cousin and the manager of Mount Vernon. "I need not," he added, "make myself enemies among them by this declaration." In short, His Excellency faced "so many great and capital errors & abuses . . . that my life has been nothing else (since I came here) but one continued round of annoyance & fatigue."

The army surely had far to travel, but so, too, did its commander.

Aggressive and even reckless, Washington longed for a decisive, bloody battle that would cause Britain to lose heart and sue for a political settlement. That appeared unlikely in Boston, where "it is almost impossible for us to get to them," he wrote. Instead, the summer and fall would be limited to skirmishes, raids, and sniping. "Both armies kept squibbing at each other," wrote the loyalist judge Peter Oliver, "but to little purpose."

American whaleboats continued to bedevil Admiral Graves, who warned "all seafaring people" that rebels were trying to lure British ships into shoal water with "false lights." After raiders burned part of the tall stone lighthouse on Little Brewster Island, a rocky speck eight miles east of Boston, Graves sent carpenters guarded by almost three dozen marines to make repairs and relight the beacon. At two a.m. on Monday, July 31, a British sergeant roused the detachment there with a strangled cry, "The whaleboats are coming!" More than three hundred baying Yankees in thirty-three boats, led by Major Benjamin Tupper of Rhode Island, pulled for the shoreline. Marines stumbled to the water's edge, "though not without great confusion," a British midshipman recorded, "many of them in liquor and totally unfit."

Rebel musket balls peppered the wharf and the stone tower, killing a marine lieutenant and several others. A few workmen escaped by swimming toward warships in Lighthouse Channel, but most were captured, along with twenty-four marines. Raiders seized the lantern and lamp oil, then set fire to the outbuildings, the keeper's house, and the tower staircase before rowing to the mainland to receive Washington's praise for their "gallant and soldierlike behavior." One patriot observed that "the once formidable navy of Britain [is] now degraded to a level with the corsairs of Barbary." The British Army tended to agree. "The admiral [is] thought much to blame," Gage's aide reported, while General Burgoyne was even harsher in a letter to London: "It may be asked in England, 'What is the admiral doing?' . . . I can only say what he is *not* doing." Graves seethed, and plotted his revenge against the rebels.

Yet squibbing would not winkle the British from Boston, nor provoke them to give battle. Moreover, Washington could hardly wage a protracted campaign, given that his army was short of virtually everything an army needed: camp kettles, entrenching tools, cartridge boxes, straw, bowls, spoons. "The carpenters will be obliged to stand still for want of nails," a supply officer warned, while another advised in late July, "We are in want of soap for the army." American troops—badly housed, badly clothed, and badly equipped—were at war with the world's greatest commercial and military power, long experienced in expeditionary administration. As an ostensible national government, Congress had begun to improvise the means to fight that war, from printing money and raising regiments to collecting supplies. But the effort thus far seemed disjointed and often half-baked. Although Congress had appointed quartermaster and commissary chiefs, the jobs were neither defined nor supported, and other critical supply posts—notably for ordnance and clothing—would not be created for another eighteen months.

Simply feeding the regiments around Boston had become perilous. Commissary General Joseph Trumbull, a Harvard-educated merchant and another of the Connecticut governor's sons, frantically tried to organize butchers, bakers, storekeepers, and purchasing agents. Coopers were needed to make barrels for preserved meat, and salt—increasingly scarce—was wanted to cure it. Forage, cash, and firewood also grew scarce; an inquiry found that much of the "beef" examined was actually horse. To feed the army through the following spring, Trumbull told Washington, he needed 25,000 barrels of flour, 13,000 barrels of salt beef and pork, 28,000 bushels of peas or beans, 11 tons of fresh beef three times a week, and 22,000 pints of milk, plus 200 barrels of beer or cider, every day, at a total cost of £200,000. By late September, as prices spiraled and supply agents rode to New York to beg for flour, Trumbull worried that by spring the army would face starvation and thus have to disband. "A commissary with twenty thousand gaping mouths open full upon him, and nothing to stop them with," he wrote, "must depend on being devoured himself."

But no shortage was as perilous as that discovered in early August. Washington's staff calculated that an army of twenty thousand men, in thirty-nine regiments with a hundred cannons, required two thousand barrels of gunpowder—a hundred tons. Powder was the *unum necessarium*, as John Adams wrote, the one essential. Each pound contained roughly seven thousand grains, enough for a volley from forty-eight muskets. A big cannon throwing a 32-pound ball required eleven or twelve pounds of powder per shot; an 18-pounder used six or seven pounds. A survey taken soon after Washington's arrival reported 303 barrels in his magazines, or fifteen tons—enough to stave off a British attack, but too little for cannonading. "We are so exceedingly destitute," he told Hancock, "that our artillery will be of little use."

Precisely how destitute became clear from the report laid before the war council that convened at Vassall House on Thursday, August 3. The earlier gunpowder estimate had erroneously included stocks used at Bunker

Hill and in various prodigal skirmishes over the summer. Despite generous shipments to Cambridge from other colonies, the actual supply on hand, including the powder in all New England magazines, totaled 9,937 pounds, less than five tons, or enough for about nine rounds per soldier. Washington was gobsmacked. "The general was so struck that he did not utter a word for half an hour," Brigadier General John Sullivan told the New Hampshire Committee of Safety. "Everyone else was equally surprised." When he finally regained his tongue, Washington told his lieutenants that "our melancholy situation" must "be kept a profound secret." This dire news, he added, was "inconceivable."

More orders fluttered from the headquarters, along with desperate pleas. "Our situation in the article of powder is much more alarming than I had the most distant idea of," Washington wrote Congress on Saturday. "The existence of the army, & the salvation of the country, depends upon something being done for our relief, both speedy and effectual." Every soldier's cartridge box was to be inspected each evening; some regiments levied one-shilling fines for each missing round. Civilians were asked "not to fire a gun at beast, bird, or mark without real necessity." Even the camp reveille gun should be silenced. Desperate raids were contemplated, to Halifax or Bermuda. Pleading "the most distressing want," Massachusetts requested powder from New York, which replied that it, too, was "afflicted and astonished," with less than a hundred pounds for purchase.

A rebel schooner from Santo Domingo, in the West Indies, sailed up the Delaware River in late July under a false French flag with almost seven smuggled tons hidden in the hold beneath molasses barrels. Loaded into a half dozen wagons, the powder was promptly sent north with an armed escort. A second consignment of five tons soon followed, and by late August Washington had enough for twenty-five rounds per soldier, still a paltry amount. War could not be waged with an occasional smuggled windfall, yet not a single American powder mill existed when the rebellion began. Mills operating during the French war had fallen into disrepair or been converted to produce flour or snuff. Of particular concern was the shortage of saltpeter—potassium nitrate, typically collected from human and animal dung, and the only scarce ingredient in gunpowder. Identified as a strategic commodity in the medieval *Book of Fires for the Burning of Enemies*, saltpeter had been imported to Europe from India through Venice for centuries; imperial Britain bought almost two thousand tons a year. The saltpeter was kneaded with small portions of sulfur and charcoal, then pulverized, dusted, glazed, and dried to make gunpowder.

Saltpeter recipes soon appeared in American newspapers and pamphlets for patriots willing to collect the "effluvia of animal bodies" from outhouses, barns, stables, tobacco yards, and pigeon coops, preferably "moistened from time to time with urine." Massachusetts offered £14 per hundred pounds, triple the price paid by Britain for Indian saltpeter. "I am determined never to have saltpeter out of my mind," John Adams declared in October. "It must be had."

Yet it would not be had in sufficient quantities to supply Washington's magazines, which also lacked bayonets, good muskets, cartridge paper, bullet lead, and even shaped flints. In the next two years, at least 90 percent of American gunpowder, or the saltpeter to make it, would somehow have to come from abroad. For now, the shortage required "a very severe economy," as one Washington aide wrote, curtailing tactical operations and imposing a quiescent status quo on the siege of Boston. By early fall, virtually all American cannons had fallen silent but for a single 9-pounder on Prospect Hill, fired occasionally in ornery defiance.

As Washington grappled with his powder problems, another shock jolted the American camp. On Tuesday, October 3, nine generals gathered for a war council with the commander in chief in a large front room at Vassall House. Outside the south windows, autumn colors tinted the elm trees, and the distant Charles glistened with a pewter hue. Wasting no time, Washington informed the council that an anonymous, encrypted "letter in characters," addressed to a British major, had been intercepted in Newport, Rhode Island, and brought to the Cambridge headquarters. The original courier, a woman described by her former husband as "a very lusty woman much pitted with smallpox," had been apprehended and bundled to Cambridge on the rump of a horse for interrogation.

Washington dramatically placed the pages on a table. An unbroken, nonsensical sequence of letters covered the first sheet for twenty-six lines, then spilled onto a second page. After the letter's capture, he said, two copies had been sent for decipherment to trusted men with a knack for puzzles. This code substituted a different letter for each letter in the alphabet; it could be solved by identifying the most frequently used symbols in the cipher and assuming they represented the most common letters in English, starting with *e*, then *t*, then *a*, then *o*, and so forth. Both decryptions had been completed the previous night, and the solutions were identical.

Washington laid one of the translations before his lieutenants. The letter, more than 850 words long, provided details on American strength, artillery in New York, Bunker Hill casualties, troop numbers in Philadelphia, ammunition supplies, and recruiting. "Eighteen thousand brave &

determined with Washington and Lee at their head are no contemptible enemy," the writer had advised. "Remember I never deceived you. . . . A view to independence grows more and more general. . . . Make use of every precaution or I perish."

From clues in the letter and a confession extracted from that lusty, pitted courier the secret author had been identified as Dr. Benjamin Church, recently appointed as the army's surgeon general. He had been arrested, Washington said, and was confined to a room on the second floor of his hospital headquarters, just down the street from Vassall House. A search of his papers had yielded no incriminating evidence.

The next day, Dr. Church—forty-one, florid, and impeccably tailored—appeared under guard before the war council. He seemed an unlikely turncoat. A *Mayflower* descendant, Harvard-educated and medically trained in London, a writer of elegy and satire who could quote Virgil in Latin, he was an expert on smallpox inoculation, a physician for the public almshouse, and a radical firebrand who had performed the postmortem examinations of Boston Massacre victims. As a member of the Committee of Safety, he had supported Benedict Arnold's attack on Ticonderoga and personally escorted Washington into Cambridge three months earlier. True, he had long had a reputation for high living—"much drove for money," it was said—with a fine house in Boston, a country estate, and various mistresses.

Church quickly admitted authorship, but he insisted the letter was a ruse "to influence the enemy to propose immediate terms of accommodation." His intent, if foolish and indiscreet, was to gull "the enemy with a strong idea of our strength" in order to forestall a British attack. Little information had been disclosed that Gage's officers could not read in the newspapers. "I can honestly appeal to heaven for the purity of my intentions," Church insisted. "I have served faithfully. I have never swerved from my duty through fear or temptation." After questioning from each general, he was dismissed and marched back to confinement.

Not a man believed him, least of all Washington. "Good God!" John Adams wrote upon hearing the news. "What shall we say of human nature?" The infamous letter, Adams conceded, "is the oddest thing imaginable. There are so many lies in it, calculated to give the enemy a high idea of our power and importance. . . . Don't let us abandon him for a traitor without certain evidence." But what should be done? British statutes dating to the fourteenth century clearly defined treasonous offenses, including "imagining the death of our lord the king," mounting a rebellion, or seducing the queen. Yet the articles of war recently adopted in Philadelphia failed to address espionage or treason. Uncertain about how best to proceed, Congress sacked Church as surgeon general on October 14 and instructed Massachusetts to decide his fate.

At ten a.m. on Friday, October 27, Church was bundled into a chaise by the county sheriff and escorted by twenty soldiers with fife and drum three miles to the Watertown meetinghouse. Members of the Massachusetts House of Representatives, of which Church was an elected delegate, filled many of the hundred boxes on the ground floor. Spectators packed an upstairs gallery, and armed guards stood at each exit. Summoned by the doorkeeper, Church strode down the aisle to a wooden bar below the pulpit. The Speaker, James Warren, read a dispatch from Washington describing the war council's conclusion that Church was guilty of "holding a criminal correspondence with the enemy." The infamous letter was produced, and the decryption read.

For more than an hour, Church parried the accusations, invoking the Magna Carta, habeas corpus, and his pure heart. He claimed that he had refused a guinea a day to betray the American cause and that he had merely intended to confuse, if not dupe, the British. The letter was "innocently intended, however indiscreetly executed," just a "piece of artifice," ultimately intended for his brother-in-law, a loyalist newspaper publisher. And how, he asked, could he have conducted a criminal correspondence if the letter had not reached the British? General Greene, watching from the gallery, wrote his wife that night, "With art and ingenuity . . . he veiled the villainy of his conduct and by implication transformed vice into virtue." Church "appeared spotless as an angel of light," William Tudor, the judge advocate general, told John Adams.

The assembly broke for a late lunch. After a chicken wing and a mug of flip at Coolidge's Tavern, Church resumed his defense at three-thirty p.m. "Is it criminal, sir, to alarm them with a parade of our strength and preparation?" he asked. "If this is the work of an enemy, where are we to look for a friend?" Invoking his long service to the cause, he added, "Weigh the labors of an active life against the indiscretion of an hour. . . . To your wisdom, gentlemen, to your justice, to your tenderness, I cheerfully submit my fate."

That fate was sealed. The House promptly expelled him for what James Warren called "the wickedness of his heart." Under orders from Congress, Washington sent him with a nine-man prisoner escort to Connecticut, where Church complained of being confined in a "close, dark, and noisome cell"; Congress specifically denied him "the use of pen, ink, and paper." Not for more than 150 years, after scholars sifted through General Gage's private papers, would Church's guilt be irrefutably confirmed: he had been a

British spy at least since early 1775, for cash, and had likely provided information about hidden weapons in Concord, among other rebel secrets.

During Church's lifetime, he was briefly paroled after several physicians reported that asthmatic conditions in the Connecticut dungeon endangered his health. But angry rioters sacked his Boston house and forced him back to jail for his own protection; efforts to exchange him for American prisoners held by the British provoked more riots. His wife and children made their way to London, where the king gave her a £150 pension. In 1778, Church would finally be allowed to go into exile, but the sloop carrying him to Martinique vanished without a trace. He was never heard from again, although his grieving father, a Boston deacon, refused to give up hope to his own dying day. In 1780, he bequeathed £5 and a shelf of books to his son Benjamin, "whether living or dead, God only knows."

All through the fall, bored, mischievous, and gullible American soldiers spread fantastic rumors: that the British had been ordered back to England, that a French fleet had put to sea on America's behalf, that the Spanish had besieged Gibraltar, that eight German generals—or three German princes—would soon arrive with an ammunition ship to help Washington, that Holland had called in debts and forced Britain to declare bankruptcy. It was said on the best authority that a London mob had destroyed the Parliament building and chased Lord North to France.

Autumn sickness crept through the camps, and although the American force exceeded 20,000 by early November, those present and fit for duty remained below 14,000. The officer corps now comprised 60 colonels and lieutenant colonels, 30 majors, 290 captains, 558 lieutenants, and 65 ensigns. Washington's host also included 21 chaplains, 31 surgeons, 1,238 sergeants, and 690 drummers and fifers. All games of chance, including pitch and hustle, which involved a halfpence coin, were forbidden by his order, so to build morale, wrestling matches were staged in late October between the brigades on Winter and Prospect Hills. Men foraged for chestnuts, apples, and turnips; they sang camp songs accompanied by German flutes. Weather forecasters studied the "upper side of the moon" for clues, though no one doubted that winter was coming. The army would need ten thousand cords of firewood in the next few months, and Washington was already fretting over "a most mortifying scarcity" that hindered recruiting and could force his regiments to disperse or risk freezing.

Every day British fire drubbed the bivouacs, sometimes forty or fifty cannonballs for each American shot. "At about 9 a.m. we flung two 18-lb. balls into Boston from the lower fort, just to let them know where to find us, for which the enemy returned 90 shots," a soldier told his diary in October. A comrade wrote of the same incident, "One man had his arm shot off there and two cows killed. Nothing new." Local newspapers carried dozens of reward offers for deserters, including "one Jonathan Hantley, a well-set fellow, about five feet nine inches in height . . . talks with a brogue, pretends to doctor, professes to have great skill in curing cancers"; and Simeon Smith, "about 5 feet 4 inches high, had on a blue coat and black vest . . . his voice in the hermaphrodite fashion"; and "Matthias Smith, a small smart fellow, is apt to say, 'I swear, I swear!' and between his words will spit smart."

For more than twenty years Washington had doubted that amateur citizen soldiers could form what he called "a respectable army," capable of defeating trained, disciplined professionals. Nothing he had seen in Cambridge changed his mind. Militiamen called to arms for a few weeks or months "will never answer your expectations," he had once written. "No dependence is to be placed upon them. They are obstinate and perverse." With most enlistments due to expire in December and January, Washington told Hancock on October 30 that perhaps half of all the junior officers were likely to leave the army and "I fear will communicate the infection" to the enlisted ranks. "I confess," he added, "I have great anxieties upon the subject."

All the more reason to strike the British before winter arrived and his army drifted away. Yet his wish for "a speedy finish of the dispute" found little support among his generals. A proposed amphibious assault on Boston, supported by artillery and a frontal attack at the Neck, was unanimously rejected by his war council for fear that Boston would share Charlestown's charred fate. Washington suggested another plan and it, too, was rejected, to a man, on October 18. "Too great a risk," General Lee advised. "Not practicable under all circumstances," General Greene added.

He had little recourse but to husband his gunpowder, stockpile firewood, and launch an occasional raid or sniping sortie with the ten companies of riflemen Congress had sent from Virginia, Maryland, and Pennsylvania. Unlike muskets, rifle barrels were grooved to spin bullets for greater stability and accuracy. A capable marksman might hit a bull's-eye at two hundred yards, although the weapon was slower to load; the projectile had to be wrapped in a greased linen patch and painstakingly "wanged" down the tighter bore. Moreover, no bayonet had yet been invented that would fit over a rifle muzzle. Riflemen were lethal and exotic, happily demonstrating their sharpshooting prowess while firing from their backs, or while running, or with trusting comrades holding targets between their knees. Many wore fringed hunting shirts, moccasins, and even Indian paint. Throngs of admiring civilians turned out to cheer them as the long-striding companies made their way toward Cambridge. They also proved maddening to their commanders, their boorish or insubordinate behavior sometimes leading to arrests and shackles. "Washington has said he wished they had never come," General Ward told John Adams on October 30. Lee called them "damned riff-raff—dirty, mutinous, and disaffected." Still, a Washington aide reported that rifle fire so unnerved the British "that nothing is to be seen over the breastwork but a hat." A Yankee newspaper warned, "General Gage, take care of your nose."

But General Gage had gone, and he took his nose with him. In late September, *Scarborough* arrived in Boston with orders summoning Gage home, a decision made soon after the news of Bunker Hill reached London. The king had insisted that the general's feelings be spared by pretending that he was being recalled to plan the 1776 campaign. Gage packed his personal papers in white pine boxes and, after a flurry of salutes, sailed aboard the transport *Pallas* at nine p.m. on October 11. He was soon forgotten, both in America and in England, though he continued to draw a salary as the Crown's governor of Massachusetts. Horace Walpole joked that he might be hanged for the errors of his masters.

William Howe moved into Province House as the new "general and commander-in-chief of all His Majesty's forces within the colonies laying on the Atlantic Ocean from Nova Scotia to West Florida inclusive, etc., etc., etc." Major General Howe's sentiments on the occasion could not be discerned, for he remained relentlessly taciturn—"never wastes a monosyllable," Walpole quipped—the better to hide his indecision. Now forty-six and thickset, with bulging eyes and a heavy brow, he bore an uncanny resemblance to his monarch, perhaps because his mother was widely rumored to be the illegitimate daughter of George I. His father, a viscount and the governor of Barbados, had died young in 1735. William Howe's eldest brother, George, deemed "the best officer in the British Army," had also died young, from a French bullet at Fort Carillon in 1758; in gratitude, Massachusetts paid £250 for a monument to his memory in Westminster Abbey. A second brother, Richard, succeeded to the viscount's title and was now an admiral. William emerged belaureled from the French war, not least for his celebrated climb up a St. Lawrence River bluff to reach the Plains of Abraham—"laying hold of stumps and boughs of trees," a witness reported—during Britain's capture of Quebec. Family lore held that he returned to England clad in buckskin and moccasins, to be known thereafter to his siblings as "the Savage."

Elected to Parliament from Nottingham, the Savage advocated restraint in colonial policy and vowed never to take up arms against his American kinsmen—even as he privately advised Lords North and Dartmouth that he was willing to do precisely that. When orders came to report to Boston, he told a constituent that he "could not refuse without incurring the odious name of backwardness to serving my country in a day of distress." He added assurances that "the insurgents are very few in comparison to the whole of the people." Although he rarely spoke, was often wrong when he did, and seemed averse to advice, the manly if morose Howe was a welcome change within the ranks after Old Woman Gage. "He is much beloved by the whole army," a captain wrote. "They feel a confidence in him."

Howe now had some eleven thousand mouths to feed, and little to feed them. "What in God's name are ye all about in England?" an officer wrote in a letter published at home. "Have you forgot us?" Hospitals remained jammed with men suffering from wounds, scurvy, dysentery, and other maladies. "I have eat fresh meat but three times in six weeks," a lieutenant wrote. Rebel whaleboats chased loyalist fishing smacks from coastal waters, severing supplies of cod, haddock, and terrapin. Bad mutton cost a shilling a pound; a skinny goose, twenty shillings. Salt meat was the inevitable staple, though said to be "as hard as wood, as lean as carrion, and as rusty as the devil." General Percy reportedly killed and roasted a foal for his table, while one Winifried McCowen, a camp retainer, took a hundred lashes across her back for stealing and butchering the town bull. A Boston man wrote that he had been "invited by two gentlemen to dine upon rats."

With each passing day, the blockade grew more oppressive. "They are burrowing like rabbits all around us," wrote Captain Glanville Evelyn, now commanding a light infantry company encamped in leaky tents on Bunker Hill. "There's nothing reconciles being shot at . . . so much as being paid for it." General Burgoyne was in high dudgeon. "Our present situation is a consummation of inertness and disgrace," he wrote. "Driven from one hill, you will see the enemy continually retrenched upon the next. . . . Could we at last penetrate ten miles, perhaps we should not attain a single sheep or an ounce of flour, for they remove every article of provisions as they go." By Howe's calculations, to move 32 regiments beyond Boston would require 3,662 horses—plus nearly 50 tons of hay and oats daily to feed them—and 540 wagons. That was almost 3,000 horses and 500 wagons more than he had.

Shifting the army by sea from Boston to New York had been discussed since midsummer. Burgoyne listed eight good reasons to make the move, including the large trove of loyalists there, access to food and forage on Long Island, and control of the Hudson valley corridor to Canada. But permission from London had been late in arriving, as usual, and now the season was too far advanced for a safe passage, given stormy weather, rebel pirates, and the lack of a single secure harbor between Boston and New York. Howe did some more arithmetic: unless five thousand regulars were left to hold Boston, complementing the twelve thousand needed in New York, at least a thousand Crown officials and loyalists would also have to be transported, along with £300,000 in goods, which, Burgoyne urged, "ought on no account to be left to the enemy." Such an exodus would require far more British shipping than was currently available. Inevitably they would have to winter in Boston, as one private wrote, "like birds in a cage."

Badly fed birds, at that. "Starve them out" had been a Yankee rallying cry since April. Britain had never maintained a large army several thousand miles from home without buying local food and fodder; living off the land by plunder was generally impossible for armies in the eighteenth century, even when the land was accessible. To sustain the fleet, in the coming months the Navy and Victualling Boards would hire far more transport tonnage than in the last French war, and that did not include ships needed by the Treasury and Ordnance Board bureaucracies responsible for feeding army troops abroad. As Cardinal Richelieu, the great French statesman during the Thirty Years' War, had warned, "History knows many more armies ruined by want and disorder than by the efforts of their enemies."

British supply contractors were supposed to stockpile at least a six-month food reserve in Boston, yet when Howe took command, the larder held less than a thirty-day supply, including just two dozen bushels of peas. Five storeships from England and Ireland arrived, but most of the 5,200 barrels of flour aboard proved rancid. Regulars composed an impious parody: "Give us each day our daily bread, and forgive us our not eating it."

Strongboxes stuffed with cash were shipped from London to Boston aboard *Centurion, Greyhound*, and other warships; by late fall, more than £300,000 had been requisitioned. But rebels often thwarted British efforts to buy supplies in New York, Baltimore, and elsewhere. Moreover, transaction fees had risen to a staggering 23 percent of the sums spent. Shortages of fodder required slaughtering milk cows in Boston for meat; more than three dozen vessels sailed to Quebec and the Bay of Fundy in search of hay and oats, an unfortunate, if necessary, use of precious shipping. In mid-November, Howe sent London another set of beautiful charts, with exquisite clerical calligraphy and precise double lines drawn in red pencil to separate the columns, all to demonstrate that "there are not provisions for the army in store to serve longer than the beginning of March 1776." Lieutenant William Feilding of the British marines wrote home, "Nothing but a desire of scouring the insolent rebels of our country keeps up the soldiers' spirit."

Alcohol helped, too. American rum was deemed "new and unwholesome," so in September the British government signed an initial contract for 100,000 gallons of West Indies rum to be delivered to the army, complementing 375,000 gallons of porter to help combat scurvy. By spring a half million gallons of rum would be purchased for the Boston garrison at three to five shillings a gallon, the largest single item of expense among government provisions; ten times more was spent on rum than on medicines. The Treasury Board also saw to it that British officials in America received hydrometers—each composed of a glass cylinder, a thermometer, and various weights carefully marked for Jamaica, Grenada, St. Vincent, and other sources of West Indies rum—along with three pages of instructions on how to test each lot to ensure that contractors delivered "the usual and proper proof." Rum had long been a reward for difficult military duty; Howe quietly made it part of the regular ration, issued at a daily rate of a quart for every six men.

Four small British warships and a storeship rounded the Casco Bay headland off Falmouth, Maine, on the mild, breezy morning of Monday, October 16. Nearly two thousand souls lived in remote Falmouth, a hundred miles upcoast from Boston, the men scratching out a living as fishermen, millers, and timberjacks. For more than half a century, Royal Navy agents had routinely come to collect enormous white pines, some of them three feet in diameter and blazed with the king's proprietary broad-arrow insignia. After felling, the great sticks were twitched into the water by twenty yokes of oxen, then lashed into rafts or winched onto ships and hauled across the Atlantic to Portsmouth and other shipyards to be shaped and stepped as the towering masts on the king's biggest men-of-war. To the lament of British shipwrights, that mast trade all but ended with the gunplay at Lexington. Felled timber had been hidden upriver from Falmouth, and after armed rebels twice thwarted British efforts to secure the masts, Royal Navy officers threatened "to beat the town down about their ears."

As the five vessels carefully warped into the harbor the following afternoon, a rumor spread that the intruders simply intended to rustle livestock along the bay. Militiamen hurried off to shoo the flocks and herds to safety. That delusion vanished at four p.m., when a British naval officer with a marine escort rowed to the King Street dock, marched to the crowded town hall in Greele's Lane, and with a flourish delivered a written ultimatum, "full of bad English and worse spelling," one witness complained.

Read aloud twice by a local lawyer who was said to have "a tremor in his voice," the decree warned that in the name of "the best of sovereigns . . . you have been guilty of the most unpardonable rebellion." The flotilla had orders to administer "a just punishment": Falmouth was given two hours to evacuate "the human species out of the said town." "Every heart," a clergyman wrote, "was seized with terror, every countenance changed color, and a profound silence ensued." A three-man delegation rowed out to *Canceaux*, an eight-gun former merchantman, to beg mercy of Lieutenant Henry Mowat, the flotilla commander.

Few sailors knew the upper New England coast better than Mowat, a forty-one-year-old Scot who for more than a decade had surveyed every cove, island, and inlet for Admiralty charts. One senior officer described him as "the most useful person perhaps in America for the service we are engaged in." Mowat held a grudge against Maine militiamen, who had briefly taken him prisoner during a skirmish over the contested masts in Falmouth five months earlier. But his instructions from Admiral Graves went far beyond personal revenge: Graves had been ordered by Lord Sandwich, first lord of the Admiralty, to "show the rebels the weight of an English fleet. . . . You may be blamed for doing little but can never be censured for doing too much." Graves had taken the hint. In early October, he'd told Mowat to "burn, destroy, and lay waste" nine maritime towns northeast of Boston.

So far the chastisement had gone badly. Gales nearly wrecked two of Mowat's ships off Gloucester. Houses in a couple of targeted towns were judged by his gunnery experts to be too scattered to be worth his limited supply of incendiary carcasses. Contrary winds kept the flotilla from reaching Machias, another town two hundred miles up the coast, where a British midshipman and several sailors had been killed in a bloody scrap in June. Falmouth would have to do.

The town "had not the least right to expect any lenity," Mowat told the emissaries. His orders were unequivocal. But because of "the known humanity of the British nation," he would hold his fire if by eight a.m. all small arms, ammunition, and the five carriage guns known to be in Falmouth were surrendered.

All night long the townsfolk debated, fretted, wailed, and debated some more. Horse and ox teams plodded through Queen, Fish, and Middle Streets, hauling away furniture, shop goods, and the infirm. Hothead militiamen vowed to incinerate the town themselves if Falmouth complied with Mowat's demand. A few old muskets were sculled out to the *Canceaux* to buy time, but at dawn the people of Falmouth screwed up their courage and sent another delegation to inform Mowat that they had "resolved by no means to deliver up the cannon and other arms." "Perceiving women and children still in the town," Mowat later told Graves, "I made it forty minutes after nine before the signal was hoisted."

A red flag appeared on *Canceaux*'s main topgallant masthead. Tongues of smoke and flame abruptly licked from the ships' gun decks. "The firing began from all the vessels," a witness later wrote, "a horrible shower of balls from three to nine pounds weight, bombs, carcasses, live shells, grapeshot, and musketballs"—eventually more than three thousand projectiles. The crash of shattered glass and splintered wood echoed along the waterfront, where a dozen merchant coasters also came under bombardment. For three hours fires blazed up only to be swatted out by homeowners and shopkeepers, although some militiamen looted their neighbors while pretending to fight fires. "The oxen, terrified at the smoke and report of the guns, ran with precipitation over the rocks, dashing everything to pieces," another resident wrote.

"At noon," *Canceaux*'s log recorded, "the fire began to be general both in the town and vessels, but being calm the fire did not spread as wished for." Concussion and recoil also fractured several gun carriages on the British ships—the sloop *Spitfire* was "much shattered," Mowat reported—so thirty marines and sailors went ashore to toss torches through windows and doorways. The breeze picked up at two p.m., and by late afternoon Falmouth "presented a broad sheet of flame" from Parsons Lane to Fore Street.

Britain had murdered another Yankee town. The *Essex Gazette* tallied 416 buildings destroyed, including 136 houses, the Episcopal church, various barns, the meetinghouse, the customs house, the library, and the new courthouse. Many of the hundred structures still standing were thoroughly ventilated by balls and shells, and the three-day rain that began at ten p.m. ruined furnishings that had failed to burn. Mowat counted eleven American vessels sunk or burned, four others captured, and a distillery, wharves, and warehouses "all laid into ashes." With his ammunition nearly spent and the flotilla badly in need of repairs, he anchored overnight in ten fathoms, then sailed for Boston. The remaining eight towns on Admiral Graves's chastisement list would be spared.

The admiral claimed to have administered "a severe stroke to the rebels," but he soon took a stroke himself when a letter from London arrived relieving him of command. Graves had done both too little and too much in six months of war; the Admiralty had grown weary of his excuses and the army's complaints. He would be missed by no one except perhaps his nephews. As an act of vengeance, the razing of Falmouth may have brought brief satisfaction, but it made little sense tactically or strategically. While nearly two thousand residents sought shelter at the beginning of a Maine winter, couriers carried the news to the outside world. "It cannot be true," the *Gentleman's Magazine* opined when reports reached London. The French foreign minister called the attack "absurd as well as barbaric." In Cambridge, General Lee denounced "the tragedy acted by these hell hounds of an execrable ministry" and recommended seizing British hostages in New York. "This is savage and barbarous," James Warren wrote John Adams. "What more can we want to justify any step to take, kill, and destroy?"

The wolf had risen in the heart. Enraged and unified, Americans demanded revenge. Coastal towns fortified themselves and organized early warning systems with beacons and express riders. The Yale College library became an armory. Some colonial governments had already authorized privateers—merchantmen converted into warships—to attack enemy shipping, and Congress would soon follow suit. Such patriot marauders collected from a third to the entire value of a captured ship, with severe consequences in the coming years for several thousand British vessels.

Few were angrier than General Washington. He rejected Falmouth's plea for ammunition and men—the commander in chief could hardly disperse his modest army among coastal enclaves—but in a pale fury he denounced British "cruelty and barbarity." More clearly than ever he saw the war as a moral crusade, a death struggle between good and evil. In general orders to the troops he fulminated against "a brutal, savage enemy." Many Americans now agreed with the sentiment published in the *New-England Chronicle* a month after Falmouth's immolation: "We expect soon to break off all kinds of connections with Britain, and form into a grand republic of the American colonies."

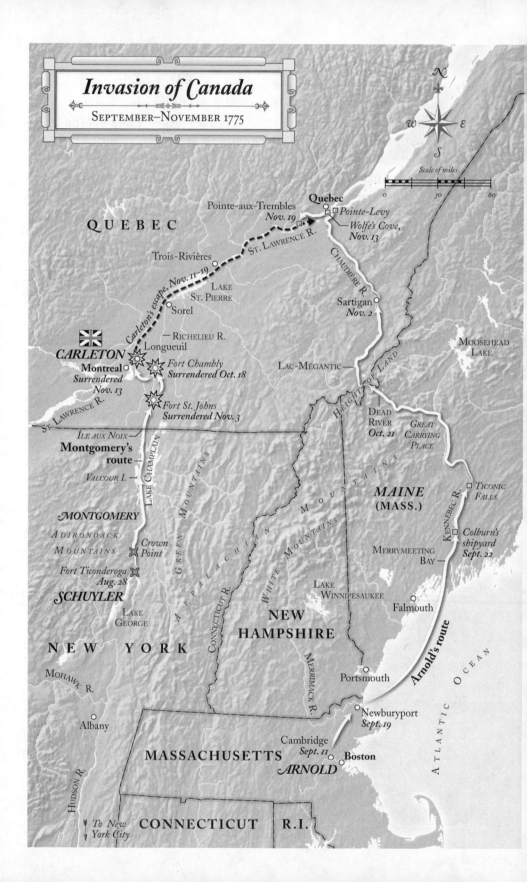

Invasion of Canada
SEPTEMBER–NOVEMBER 1775

Scale of miles
0   30   60

N
W   E
S

QUEBEC

Pointe-aux-Trembles
Nov. 19

Quebec
Pointe-Levy
Wolfe's Cove,
Nov. 13

Trois-Rivières

St. Lawrence R.

Carleton's escape, Nov. 11–19

LAKE
ST. PIERRE

Sorel

CHAUDIÈRE R.

Sartigan
Nov. 2

MOOSEHEAD
LAKE

RICHELIEU R.

Longueuil

CARLETON

Montreal
Surrendered
Nov. 13

Fort Chambly
Surrendered Oct. 18

Lac-Mégantic

St. Lawrence R.

Fort St. Johns
Surrendered Nov. 3

HEIGHT OF LAND

DEAD
RIVER
Oct. 21

GREAT
CARRYING
PLACE

ÎLE AUX NOIX

Montgomery's
route

VALCOUR I.

MONTGOMERY

ADIRONDACK
MOUNTAINS

Crown
Point

Fort Ticonderoga
Aug. 28

SCHUYLER

LAKE
GEORGE

LAKE CHAMPLAIN

GREEN MOUNTAINS

APPALACHIAN

CONNECTICUT R.

WHITE MOUNTAINS

LAKE
WINNIPESAUKEE

MAINE
(MASS.)

KENNEBEC R.

TICONIC
FALLS

Colburn's
shipyard
Sept. 22

MERRYMEETING
BAY

Falmouth

NEW
HAMPSHIRE

NEW   YORK

MOHAWK
R.

Albany

MERRIMACK R.

Portsmouth

Newburyport
Sept. 19

Arnold's route

ATLANTIC OCEAN

HUDSON R.

Cambridge
Sept. 11

MASSACHUSETTS

ARNOLD

Boston

To New
York City

CONNECTICUT   **R.I.**

5.

——

I Shall Try to Retard the Evil Hour

Some 230 miles northwest of Boston, a second siege now threatened Britain's hold on Canada. For almost a month, more than a thousand American troops had surrounded Fort St. Johns, a dank compound twenty miles below Montreal on the swampy western bank of the Richelieu River in what one regular called "the most unhealthy spot in inhabited Canada." A stockade and a dry moat lined with sharpened stakes enclosed a pair of earthen redoubts, two hundred yards apart and connected by a muddy trench. A small stone barracks, a bakery, a powder magazine, and several log buildings chinked with moss stood in the southern redoubt. Thirty cannons crowned the ramparts and poked through sodded embrasures, spitting iron balls whenever the rebels approached or grew too impertinent with their own artillery. By mid-October, seven hundred people were trapped at St. Johns, among them most of the British troops in Canada—drawn from the 26th Foot and the 7th Foot, known as the Royal Fusiliers—as well as most of the Royal Artillery's gunners, eighty women and children, and more than seventy Canadian volunteers. Sentries cried, "Shot!" whenever they spotted smoke and flame from a rebel battery, and hundreds fell on their faces in the mud as the ball whizzed overhead or splatted home, somewhere.

The regulars still wore summer uniforms and suffered from the cold: the first hard frost had set on September 30, followed by eight consecutive days of rain. Some ripped the skirts from their coats to wrap around their feet. The garrison now lived on half-rations and shared a total of twenty blankets, with no bedding or straw for warmth. Only a shallow house cellar in the northern redoubt offered any shelter belowground, and it was crammed with the sick and the groaning wounded. Major Charles Preston, the fort's dimple-chinned commandant, had sent four couriers to plead for help in Montreal. Each slipped from the fort at night and scuttled through the dense Richelieu thickets. But no reply had been heard—"not a syllable," as Preston archly noted—since an order had arrived from the high command in early September to "defend St. Johns to the last extremity."

At one p.m. on Saturday, October 14, many cries of "Shot!" were heard when the rebels opened a new battery with two 12-pounders and two 4-pounders barely three hundred yards away on the river's eastern shore. One cannonball ricocheted from a chimney, demolishing the house and killing a lieutenant; another detonated a barrel of gunpowder in an orange fireball, killing another man and wounding three. Balls battered the fort's gate and clipped its parapet. A 13-inch shell from a rebel mortar called *Old Sow* punched through the barracks roof, blowing out windows while killing two more and wounding five. "The hottest fire this day that hath been done here," an officer told his diary.

The next day was just as hot: 140 rebel rounds bombarded the fort on Sunday, perforating buildings and men. A Canadian cook lost both legs. A twelve-gun British schooner, the *Royal Savage*, was moored between the redoubts along the western riverbank, although the crew fled to the fort after complaining that it was "impossible to sleep on board without being amphibious." Rebel gunners now took aim at *Royal Savage* with heated balls, punching nine holes in the hull and three through the mainmast, then demolishing the sternpost holding the rudder. "The schooner sunk up to her ports . . . and her colors which lay in the hold were scorched," a British lieutenant, John André, wrote in his journal. She soon sank with a gurgle into the Richelieu mud.

Major Preston and most of his men remained defiant, despite the paltry daily ration of roots and salt pork, despite the awful smells seeping from the cellar hospital, despite the rebel riflemen who crept close at dusk for a shot at anyone careless enough to show his silhouette on the rampart. British ammunition stocks dwindled, but gunners still sought out rebel batteries, smashing the hemlocks and the balm of Gilead trees around the American positions north and west of the fort. Yet without prompt relief—whether from Montreal, London, or heaven—few doubted that the last extremity had drawn near. "I am still alive," wrote one of the besieged in late October, "but the will to live diminishes within me."

For nearly a century, Americans had seen Canada as a blood enemy. New Englanders and New Yorkers especially never forgave the atrocities committed by French raiders and their Indian confederates at Deerfield, Schenectady, Fort William Henry, and other frontier settlements. Catholic Quebec was seen as a citadel of popery and tyranny. The French, as a Rhode

Island pastor proclaimed in 1759, were children of the "scarlet whore, the mother of harlots."

Britain's triumph in the Seven Years' War and its acquisition of New France in 1763—known in Quebec as "the Conquest"—gladdened American hearts. Many French Canadians decamped for France. Priests lost the right to collect tithes and the benefit of an established state religion. A small commercial class of English merchants, friendly to American traders, took root. The Canadian population—under a hundred thousand, less than New Jersey—was still largely rural, illiterate, dependent on farming and fur, and essentially feudal. Most were French-Canadian *habitants*, or peasants, now known as "new subjects," since their allegiance to the British Crown was barely a decade old and deeply suspect. Many secretly hoped that France would win back what had been lost or that the "Londoners"—Englishmen— would tire of the weather and go home. Largely descended from Norman colonists sent to the New World by Louis XIV, the *habitants* were described by an eighteenth-century author as "loud, boastful, mendacious, obliging, civil, and honest." A few thousand "old subjects"—Anglo merchants and Crown officials—congregated in Montreal and Quebec City. Nova Scotia and the maritime precincts remained wild, isolated, and sparsely peopled.

As tensions with Britain escalated, many Americans—Benjamin Franklin and Samuel Adams among them—considered Canada a natural component of a united North America. The First Continental Congress in October 1774 sent Canadians an open letter, at once beckoning and sinister: "You have been conquered into liberty. . . . You are a small people, compared to those who with open arms invite you into fellowship." Canadians faced a choice between having "all the rest of North America your unalterable friends, or your inveterate enemies."

The Quebec Act, which took effect in May 1775, infuriated the Americans and altered the political calculus. Canada would be ruled not by an elected assembly, but by a royal governor and his council, a harbinger, in American eyes, of British tyranny across the continent. Even more provocative were the provisions extending Quebec's boundaries south and west, into the rich lands beyond the Appalachians for which American colonists had fought both Indians and the French, and the recognition of the Roman Catholic Church's status in Canada, including the right of Catholics to hold office and citizenship, to again levy parish tithes, to serve in the army, and to retain French civil law. These provisions riled American expansionists— fifty thousand of whom now lived west of the mountains—and revived fears of what one chaplain described as "this vast extended country, which has been for ages the dwelling of Satan." Catholic hordes—likened to a mythical beast found in the Book of Revelation, "drunk with the wine of her fornications"—could well descend on Protestant America. It was said that hundreds of pairs of snowshoes had been readied, should Canadian legions be commanded to march southward.

War in Massachusetts, and the American capture of Ticonderoga and Crown Point, brought matters to a head. Congress dithered, initially proposing to return the two forts rather than end any chance of reconciliation with Britain; then decided to keep them; then dithered some more over whether to preemptively attack Quebec when it became clear that Canada was unlikely to send delegates to Philadelphia despite an invitation to "the oppressed inhabitants" to make common cause as "fellow sufferers." The debate raged for weeks. Even Washington, who had qualms about opening another front, saw utility in capturing Canadian staging grounds before the reinforced British could descend on New York and New England. Others saw a chance to seize the Canadian granary and fur trade, to forestall attacks by Britain's potential Indian allies, and to preclude the need to rebuild Ticonderoga and other frontier defenses. Britain reportedly had fewer than seven hundred regulars scattered across Quebec; two of the four regiments posted there had been sent to Boston in 1774 at Gage's request. Canada conceivably could be captured and converted into the fourteenth American province with fewer than two thousand troops in a quick, cheap campaign. Skeptics argued that an invasion would convert Americans into aggressors, disperse scarce military resources, and alienate both American moderates and British supporters of the colonial cause. Some recalled that during the last war, more than a million British colonists and regulars had needed six years, several of them disastrous, to subdue less than seventy thousand Canadians and their French allies.

In late June, Congress finally ordered Major General Philip Schuyler, a well-born New Yorker, to launch preemptive attacks to prevent Britain from seizing Lake Champlain. He was authorized to "take possession of St. Johns, Montreal, and any other parts of the country" if "practicable" and if the intrusion "will not be disagreeable to the Canadians." Under the guise of promoting continental "peace and security"—Congress promised to "adopt them into our union as a sister colony"—Canada was to be obliterated as a military and political threat. Most Canadians were expected to welcome the incursion, a fantasy not unlike that harbored by Britain about the Americans. This would be the first, but hardly the last, American invasion of another land under the pretext of bettering life for the invaded.

Congress had denounced Catholics for "impiety, bigotry, persecution, murder, and rebellion through every part of the world." Now it found "the

Protestant and Catholic colonies to be strongly linked" by their common antipathy to British oppression. In a gesture of tolerance and perhaps to forestall charges of hypocrisy, Congress also acknowledged that Catholics deserved "liberty of conscience." If nothing else, the Canadian gambit caused Americans to contemplate the practical merits of inclusion, moderation, and religious freedom. The Northern Army, as the invasion host was named, was to be a liberating force, not a vengeful one.

For two months little had gone right in the campaign. The Northern Army comprised twelve hundred ill-trained, ill-equipped, insubordinate troops, many without decent firelocks or gunsmiths at hand to fix them. When General Schuyler reached Ticonderoga at ten p.m. on a July evening, the lone sentinel tried unsuccessfully to waken the watch and the rest of the garrison. "With a penknife only," Schuyler wrote Washington, "I could . . . have set fire to the blockhouse, destroyed the stores, and starved the people here." Three weeks later, having advanced not a step farther north, he reported that he had less than a ton of gunpowder, no carriages to move his field guns, and little food. His men, scattered along the Hudson valley, seemed "much inclined to a seditious and mutinous temper." Carpenters building flat-bottomed bateaux to cross Lake Champlain lacked timber, nails, pitch, and cordage. When Schuyler requested reinforcements, the New York Committee of Safety told him, "Our troops can be of no service to you. They have no arms, clothes, blankets, or ammunition; the officers no commissions; our treasury no money."

Tall, thin, and florid, with kinky hair and a raspy voice, Philip Schuyler was among America's wealthiest and most accomplished men. The scion of émigré Dutch land barons, he owned twenty thousand acres from New York to Detroit, including a brick mansion on a ridge above Albany with a view of the Catskills and hand-painted wallpaper depicting romantic Roman ruins. His country seat on Fish Creek in Saratoga abutted sawmills and a flax plantation that spun linen. He spoke French and Mohawk, understood lumber markets, mathematics, boat-building, slave owning, navigation, hemp cultivation, and, from service in the last war, military logistics. British officers had praised his "zeal, punctuality, and strict honesty." The body of his young friend Lord George Howe, slain by the French at Ticonderoga, lay in the Schuyler family vault for years before permanent burial in a lead casket beneath St. Peter's chancel in Albany. As a delegate to Congress, Schuyler sat with Washington on a committee to collect ammunition and war matériel, then rode north with him from Philadelphia after both received their general's commissions. Among other services rendered the Northern Army, Schuyler helped persuade Iroquois warriors to renounce their traditional allegiance to Britain and to remain neutral, at least for now, in what he described—during pipe-smoking negotiations at Cartwright's Tavern in Albany—as "a family quarrel." To impress the Indians with American strength, he had ordered troops to march in circles through the town, magnifying their numbers.

For all his virtues, Schuyler was wholly unfit to command a field army in the wilderness. His urbane, patrician mien could seem "haughty and overbearing," as one chaplain wrote, especially to New Englanders who habitually disliked the New York Dutch because of border disputes and ethnic frictions. Almost from the start of the campaign, the general was accused of being a secret Tory and of sabotaging the Canadian expedition. Not yet forty-two, he also suffered from "a barbarous complication of disorders," including gout, malaria, and rheumatic afflictions. His clinical bulletins to Washington routinely described "a very severe fit of the ague," or "a copious scorbutic eruption," or "a copious discharge from an internal impostume in my breast." He was not a well man.

Alarming reports in late August of British vessels at St. Johns preparing to sortie onto Lake Champlain forced the Americans into motion. Brigadier General Richard Montgomery set out from Ticonderoga on August 31 with the twelve hundred men and four 12-pounders aboard a schooner, a sloop, and a mismatched flotilla of bateaux, row galleys, and canoes. He urged the ailing Schuyler, his superior, to "follow us in a whaleboat. . . . It will give the men great confidence in your spirit and activity." Despite the "inflexible severity of my disorders," Schuyler subsequently headed north in early September with a stack of proclamations in French to be scattered across Quebec: "We cannot doubt that you are pleased that the Grand Congress have ordered an army into Canada." From Cambridge, Washington wrote, "I trust you will have a feeble enemy to contend with and a whole province on your side."

Wishing did not make it so. Reunited on the upper reaches of Lake Champlain, Schuyler and Montgomery led their men down the Richelieu, which flowed north from the lake for almost eighty miles to the St. Lawrence River. The invaders disembarked on September 6 just short of Fort St. Johns, about a third of the distance to the St. Lawrence, then struggled toward the compound in "a tangled way" for a quarter mile through a swampy woodland, only to be ambushed by Indians and regulars in a confused melee that left nine Americans dead and as many wounded.

For more than a week, the invasion stalled. Priests in Montreal celebrated Canada's deliverance in a thanksgiving mass with a jubilant *Te Deum.* Another American advance on the fort turned to fiasco when strange noises spooked the men, who "ran like sheep," in Montgomery's contemptuous phrase. With difficulty and a threat of bayonets, they were restrained from pushing off in the boats and abandoning their officers on the shoreline. "Such a set of pusillanimous wretches never were collected," Montgomery wrote his wife. "Could I, with decency, leave the army in its present situation, I would not serve an hour longer."

If Montgomery could not abandon the Northern Army, Schuyler could and did. Crippled by rheumatic and perhaps malarial miseries, he reported to Philadelphia that "I am now so low as not to be able to hold the pen." On September 16, soldiers hoisted him into a covered boat and rowed him in the rain back to a Ticonderoga sickbed. "If Job had been a general in my situation," he wrote Congress, "his memory had not been so famous for patience."

Further misfortune befell the invaders when Ethan Allen, the conqueror of Ticonderoga, foolishly decided to storm Montreal with a small band of henchmen rather than enlist Canadian recruits in the countryside, as he had been instructed. Described by one acquaintance as "a singular compound of local barbarisms, scriptural phrases, and oriental wildness," Allen hoped for the glory of a quick victory. But as he approached the city, several dozen regulars and two hundred French and English militiamen sortied through the gates on September 25 to catch him by surprise along the St. Lawrence. "The last I see of Allen," one of his men wrote, "he was surrounded, had hold with both hands the muzzle of a gun, swinging it around." Captured and paraded through Montreal, he would be shipped to England in thirty-pound leg irons and imprisoned in the lower reaches of Pendennis Castle, on the southern coast of Cornwall, a cautionary tale for traitors to the Crown. Allen's "rash and ill-concerted measure," an American chaplain told his journal, "not only served to dishearten the Army and weaken it, but it prejudiced the people against us and both made us enemies and lost us friends." Montgomery added in a dispatch to Schuyler, "I have to lament Mr. Allen's imprudence and ambition."

Despite such misfires and misadventures, Montgomery—tall, bald, and Dublin-born—soon had the whip hand at St. Johns. Reinforcements streamed north across Lake Champlain in October, including Connecticut regiments and a New York artillery detachment with siege guns, bringing American strength to 2,700. Gunners built batteries south of the fort and across the Richelieu to the northeast. More than 350 men slipped ten miles down the river to fire a few cannonballs at the high-walled British fort at Chambly. The 84-man garrison promptly surrendered on October 18, handing over 124 barrels of gunpowder, 233 muskets, 6,600 cartridges in copper-hooped barrels, and ample stocks of flour, pork, and marine supplies.

"We have gotten six tons of powder which, with God's blessing, will finish our business here," Montgomery wrote Schuyler. No less ominous for St. Johns, a putative rescue force from Montreal—some eight hundred *habitants*, Indians, loyal merchants, and regulars—assembled on an island in the St. Lawrence on October 30, then beat across the river toward Longueuil in several dozen bateaux. Three hundred Americans rose up along the south bank to scourge the boats with musketry and grapeshot, killing between a few and a few dozen—depending on the account—without a single Yankee casualty. The bateaux scattered, the *habitants* and loyalists deserted in droves, and St. Johns' last hope for salvation vanished.

Three hundred yards northwest of the beleaguered fort, yet another American battery had been hacked from the swamp and furnished with cannons, mortars, and a chest-high breastworks. Men lugged iron balls from the Richelieu on their shoulders or in slings made from their trousers, while gunners packed the newly acquired powder into cartridges and explosive shells. At ten a.m. on Wednesday, November 1—All Saints' Day—the guns opened in concert with the battery across the river in a stupefying bombardment of a thousand balls and more than fifty shells, which by sunset had "knocked everything in the fort to shatters," an American officer exulted. Montgomery halted the cannonade long enough to send a white flag to the gate, carried by a Canadian prisoner who swore upon the Holy Evangelist that the rescue force from Montreal had indeed been routed, that no more help was forthcoming, and that further resistance would bring "melancholy consequences."

After a fifty-three-day siege, with sixty defenders killed or wounded, his food and powder all but gone, Major Preston had finally had enough. He stalled for a day by trying to squeeze concessions from the Americans. Would the honors of war be observed? Could officers keep their baggage? Sidearms? Why not permit the men to sail for England on parole? "Let me entreat you, sir, to spare the lives of a brave garrison," Montgomery told him. The British would be "treated with brotherly affection" in Connecticut jails. Negotiations briefly broke down when the proposed articles of capitulation suggested that British "fortitude and perseverance" should have been "exerted in a better cause." Preston declared that his men would rather "die with their arms in their hands than submit to the indignity of such a reflection." Montgomery struck the clause but threatened to resume his bombardment "if you do not surrender this day."

At eight a.m. on November 3, a wet, blustery Friday, Montgomery's men shouldered their firelocks in a field south of the fort. A few wore smart uniforms, like the gunners in blue coats with buff facings; more sported drab yeoman togs and slouch hats. To the trill and rap of fife and drum, the defeated garrison marched six abreast with colors flying through the gate, some of them mud-caked, their feet bound in rags. First came the 26th Foot in brick-red coats with pale yellow facings; then the Royal Fusiliers with blue facings; then Royal Artillery troops in dark blue coats and once-white waist-coats, drawing two small guns; and finally sailors in pigtails, Indians in blankets and feathers, a few kilt-clad Scots, carpenters, cooks, servants, and a gaggle of women and fretful children. At least one officer kept a locket portrait of his lover hidden under his tongue in case the Yankees began to pilfer. Major Preston strutted to the front of the American ranks. "The tears run down his cheeks," a Connecticut soldier reported, "and he cried like a child." On Preston's order the troops stacked their muskets—officers kept swords and sidearms—then shuffled into the waiting bateaux for the long journey across Champlain to captivity in New England.

More than three-quarters of the British regulars in Canada had now been captured or killed, along with virtually all of the trained artillerymen. The booty from St. Johns included seventeen fine brass guns, two brass howitzers, twenty-two iron guns, eight hundred stand of small arms, sails, pitch, tar, and precious nails. The cost of the long siege to the American invaders was steep—a hundred combat casualties and another thousand men, including their commanding general, sent back to New York with various ailments. But the front door to Canada had swung open, and thousands of additional Yankees stood ready to march through.

As the last of his captives vanished up the gray Richelieu, Brigadier General Montgomery took a moment to scribble his wife a note. "If I live," he wrote, "you may depend upon it that I will see you this winter."

That Richard Montgomery now prepared to finish conquering Canada for the American cause was no small irony, for as a young regular officer in an earlier life he had helped to conquer it for the British Empire. The youngest son of an Irish baronet, he was commissioned as an ensign after two years of college in Dublin, then devoted sixteen years to the king's service, half of it in North America and the West Indies. Slender and lightly pocked, he blamed "the heat and severity" of combat in Martinique and Cuba in 1762 for the loss of his hair; he blamed a girlfriend for other disorders. "She has clapped me," he wrote a fellow officer in 1769. "The flames of my passion have subsided with those of my urine."

An end to the French war meant an end to promotions, and in 1772, after years as a captain—including wartime service at St. Johns and

Montreal—Montgomery in disgust sold his commission for £1,500. "I have of late conceived a violent passion," he wrote a cousin. "I have cast my eyes on America, where my pride and poverty will be much more at their ease." Packing up his volumes of Hume, Montesquieu, and Franklin's *Experiments*, as well as a new microscope, surveying equipment, and draftsman's tools, he sailed for New York and bought a seventy-acre farm just north of Manhattan. Still only thirty-four, in July 1773 he married well: Janet Livingston was the eldest daughter of a prominent New York patriot judge who owned a thirteen-thousand-acre estate in Albany County. Elected to the New York Provincial Congress when political unrest turned to rebellion, Captain Montgomery abruptly found himself appointed a brigadier general; his "air and manner designated the real soldier," one subordinate wrote. But the honor only deepened his Irish fatalism. He told a former British comrade of a premonition that he would die "by a pistol," and before marching north he wrote his will. "I have been dragged from obscurity much against my inclination and not without some struggle," he told Janet, adding that as soon as he could "slip my neck out of the yoke, I will return to my family and farm."

That yoke still held him, and the ordeal at St. Johns—"half-drowned rats crawling through the swamp," in his description—showed Montgomery how removed the Northern Army was from disciplined proficiency, regardless of its success in capturing the fort. After one contentious conference with his subordinates, he wrote on the minutes, "I can't help observing to how little purpose I am [here]." To his brother-in-law he denounced "the badness of the troops. The New Englanders, I am now convinced, are the worst stuff imaginable for soldiers. . . . The privates are all generals, but not soldiers." New York regiments were "the sweepings of York's streets. . . . 'Tis no uncommon thing to see an officer beastly drunk even on duty." Shortly before Preston's surrender, Montgomery narrowly escaped death when a British cannonball sliced the tail from his uniform coat, knocking him to the ground. Disheartened and depressed, he contemplated resignation. "I have not the talents or temper for such a command," he wrote Schuyler, who was still overseeing the invasion from afar. Generalship, he added, required "acting eternally out of character."

But the command was his until his superiors decided otherwise, and now Montreal beckoned. The Northern Army plodded northwest from St. Johns toward the St. Lawrence, through "mud and mire and scarce a spot of dry ground for miles together," a Connecticut chaplain noted. Baggage carts sank to their axles on roads corduroyed with crumbling logs. Foul weather and a shortage of boats delayed crossing the river, but on November 9 Montgomery sent an ultimatum: unless Montreal unlocked her gates, he would raze the town, leaving eight thousand residents homeless in a Canadian winter.

Built on a ridge parallel to the river's northwestern bank, with eighteen-foot plastered stone walls described as "little more than an egg shell" and a loopholed parapet in bad repair, Montreal was built for commerce and God's glory, not for fighting, except when drunken fur traders grew rowdy. Sometimes called Ville-Marie, the city of Mary, it was founded in the mid-seventeenth century as a shrine to the Virgin, a prayerful place of ecstasies, visions, converted Indians, and beaver pelts. River navigation ended here, and here the boundless western wilderness began. The town had become a "somewhat unsavory assemblage of merchants on the make," a Canadian history observed. "It was no accident that New France never had a printing press." A British officer reported that "the people throw all their dung on the ice in order that it may float away when the winter breaks up."

By Sunday, November 12, when Montgomery reached Récollet, in the southwest suburbs, a delegation of frightened merchants agreed to his capitulation terms. On Monday morning they swung open the Récollet Gate and the Northern Army, led by two wheeled field guns, rambled into Montreal. Some wore British red coats confiscated at Chambly or St. Johns, but most were now so shabby that "a beggar in Europe would be better dressed than they were," one priest said. Down Rue Notre-Dame the column tramped, past seminaries, dingy trapper taverns in the Rue de la Capitale, and a few fine houses of dressed gray limestone with tin roofs and green shutters. The Yankees camped in public storehouses and the citadel barracks at the north end of town. Most took it as a good sign when a marble bust of George III was decapitated by an anonymous vandal and dumped down a well in the Place d'Armes.

Rarely had a fortified town fallen so easily, yet Montgomery took little solace in the triumph. He warned Schuyler on November 13 that his troops were "exceedingly turbulent & indeed mutinous." Only by promising that they could soon go home had he been able "to coax them to Montreal." He was hounded by a "legion of females" pleading for British and Canadian husbands, brothers, and sons captured in the past month, while also battling his own soldiers over their confiscation of those redcoat uniforms. "There was no driving it into their noodles that the clothing was really the property of the [British] soldier, that he had paid for it," Montgomery wrote Janet. To Schuyler he added, "I must go home. . . . I am weary of power." He suggested that Schuyler come to Montreal, or that General Lee take command in Canada, or that Congress send a delegation to oversee the invasion.

None of that was likely with winter descending, and he knew it. Montgomery would have to soldier on alone. One final objective remained before

Canada could be considered an American possession, and that lay 144 miles down the St. Lawrence. "I need not tell you that till Quebec is taken, Canada is unconquered," he wrote his brother-in-law. To Janet he added, "I have courted fortune and found her kind. I have one more favor to solicit, and then I have done."

Forty miles downstream, perhaps the only man able to save Canada for the Crown now pondered how to reverse Montgomery's fortunes. Major General Guy Carleton, governor of the province and commander of the few royal forces still intact, had narrowly escaped capture in Montreal. A few hours before the invaders reached Récollet, Carleton and ninety loyal companions slipped through the shadows to a St. Lawrence wharf, tumbled onto the brig *Gaspé* and ten smaller vessels, then shoved off for Quebec. A witness described the departure as "the saddest funeral." They had reached Sorel—less than halfway to their destination, at the mouth of the Richelieu—when opposing easterly winds and the sudden appearance of American shore batteries forced them to drop anchor to await a dark night and a following breeze before running the gantlet. "I shall try to retard the evil hour," Carleton had written Lord Dartmouth, "though all my hopes of succor now begin to vanish."

Even becalmed in the middle of nowhere, Guy Carleton was a formidable enemy. One acquaintance called him "a man of ten thousand eyes . . . not to be taken unawares." He had showed his contempt for the Americans by refusing to read Montgomery's surrender demand in Montreal, instead ordering the town executioner to ritually tread on the paper before tossing it with tongs into the fireplace. At fifty-one, he was tall and straight, with thinning hair, bushy brows, and cheeks beginning to jowl; a biographer described his "enormous nose mounted like a geological formation in the middle of his rather shapely face." Like Montgomery, he was of Anglo-Irish gentry, and also a third son. Commissioned in 1742, he had been named quartermaster general by his friend James Wolfe for the 1759 expedition that captured Quebec but cost General Wolfe his life. In his will, Wolfe left his books and a thousand pounds to Carleton, who had survived a head wound in that battle and would survive three more wounds in other scraps.

He was quick-tempered, autocratic, humane, and secretive—"everything with him is mystery," a British major observed. Another subordinate called him "one of the most distant, reserved men in the world; he has a rigid strictness in his manner, very unpleasing. . . . In time of danger he possesses a coolness and steadiness." The king himself had praised Carleton, calling him "gallant & sensible" and noting that his "uncorruptness is universally acknowledged." Appointed governor of Canada in 1768, he soon returned to England—in one of his fourteen Atlantic crossings—to advocate the bold, progressive reform that became known as the Quebec Act. During the four years needed to persuade Parliament, Carleton also met and married Maria Howard, an earl's daughter almost thirty years his junior; she had been educated in Versailles, a useful pedigree when they returned to Canada together in late 1774.

He found North America in turmoil, of course, with the fetid spirit of liberty threatening British sovereignty north and south. No sooner had his Quebec Act taken effect than Carleton declared martial law and sent Maria home, the better to battle American interlopers. If the Canadian clergy and affluent French *seigneurs* supported him and his reforms, the *habitants* were wary and the English merchants mostly hostile because of his disdain for democratic niceties. Before fleeing Montreal just ahead of Montgomery, Carleton wrote Dartmouth that his scheme to defend Canada had failed: Lake Champlain lost, the outposts at Chambly and St. Johns overrun, Montreal doomed, and the militia hopelessly inert because of "the stupid baseness of the Canadian peasantry." No longer did Britain have certain military advantages that had helped conquer New France fifteen years earlier, notably logistics bases in New England and New York and thousands of armed American provincials fighting for the Crown; in fact, hundreds of Canadians—the "lower sort"—had now rallied to the rebel cause. When this dispatch reached London, a courtier concluded that Carleton was "one of those men who see affairs in the most unfavorable light."

By Wednesday night, November 15, Carleton saw little reason for optimism on the dark, swirling St. Lawrence. Gunfire from American cannons on both shores, as well as from a floating battery, swept the British vessels "in such a quantity all the soldiers left the deck," a mariner reported. Frightened sailors refused to go aloft to loosen the sails. Pilots turned mutinous, the wind remained contrary, and the master of a British munitions ship carrying several tons of gunpowder vowed to surrender rather than be blown to flinders. A truce flag from Sorel brought another American ultimatum, and this time Carleton had no executioner's fire tongs at hand. Colonel James Easton wrote:

> General Montgomery is in possession of the fortress Montreal. . . . Your own situation is rendered very disagreeable. . . . If you will resign your fleet to me immediately without destroying the effects on board, you and your men shall be used with due civility.

Failure to comply would result in the squadron's annihilation by 32-pounders, the Americans warned, though in truth they had no guns that large.

The moment had arrived for desperate measures. On Thursday night, with help from Jean Baptiste Bouchette—a sloop captain known as the "Wild Pigeon" for his stealth and speed—Carleton disguised himself as a *habitant* in a tasseled wool cap, moccasins, and a blanket coat belted with a *ceinture fléchée*, the traditional peasant sash. Over the *Gaspé*'s rail he climbed, and into a waiting skiff with an orderly, an aide, and several crewmen. At Bouchette's direction, they steered for the river's narrow northern channel, shipping the muffled oars and paddling with cupped hands past American campfires and barking dogs for more than thirty miles to the trading town of Trois-Rivières. There an armed two-masted snow, the *Fell*, would carry him farther downstream.

Behind them, their erstwhile comrades dumped most of the gunpowder and shot into the St. Lawrence, then struck their flags in surrender. Even without the powder, more spoils fell into American hands: 11 rivercraft, 760 barrels of flour, 675 barrels of beef, 8 chests of arms, entrenching tools, additional red coats, 200 pairs of shoes, and more than 100 prisoners, among them Brigadier General Richard Prescott. Carleton had again made good his escape, slipping into Fortress Quebec on November 19. "To the unspeakable joy of the friends of the government, & to the utter dismay of the abettors of sedition and rebellion, Gen. Carleton arrived," a customs officer recorded. "We saw our salvation in his presence."

But as he stripped off his peasant disguise to reemerge as the king's satrap in Canada, Carleton hardly felt like a savior. "We have so many enemies within," he privately wrote Dartmouth from Château St. Louis, the governor's palace. "I think our fate extremely doubtful, to say nothing worse." Of even greater concern were enemies without. As a Quebec merchant had just written, "Intelligence has been received that one Arnold, with 1,500 woodsmen, marched from . . . New England the first of October on an expedition against this place. Their intention must be to enter the city by assault."

That was precisely Colonel Benedict Arnold's intention. The former Connecticut apothecary, who had captured Ticonderoga in cahoots with the star-crossed Ethan Allen, was gathering strength twenty miles west of Quebec City, amid aspen and birch groves in Pointe-aux-Trembles, a riverine hamlet with a church, a nunnery, and a few farmhouses built of flint cobbles. His 675 emaciated men—less than two-thirds the number that had started north with him from Cambridge almost two months earlier—were recuperating from a grueling trek through the Maine wilderness, already lauded by one Canadian admirer as "an undertaking above the race of men in this debauched age." The last miles along the St. Lawrence had been particularly painful. "Most of the soldiers were in constant misery," a Connecticut private wrote, "as they were bare-footed, and the ground frozen and very uneven. We might have been tracked all the way by the blood from our shattered hoofs." At Arnold's request, all shoemakers around Pointe-aux-Trembles were now sewing moccasins for the men from badly tanned hides. *Habitants* brought hampers of roast beef, pork, potatoes, and turnips, despite a recent church edict that barred those disloyal to the Crown from receiving Holy Communion, baptism, or burial in sacred ground. Once his men regained their vigor and were reinforced by Montgomery's troops from Montreal, Arnold planned to "knock up a dust with the garrison at Quebec, who are already panic-struck." His only regret was not capturing the city already. "Had I been ten days sooner," he wrote Washington on November 20, "Quebec must inevitably have fallen into our hands."

Even now, gaunt after his Maine anabasis, Arnold at thirty-four was muscular and graceful, with black hair, a swarthy complexion, and that long, beaky nose. He was adept at fencing, boxing, sailing, shooting, riding, and ice-skating. "There wasn't any waste timber in him," a subordinate observed. Restive and audacious, he was "as brave a man as ever lived," in one comrade's estimation, and as fine a battle captain as America would produce that century, a man born to lead other men in the dark of night. Yet he would forever be an enigma, beset with both a gnawing sense of grievance and the nattering enmity of lesser fellows. His destiny, as the historian James Kirby Martin later wrote, encompassed both "the luminescent hero and the serpentine villain." His Christian name meant "blessed," but that came to be a central irony in his life, for his was an unquiet soul.

His father was a drunk merchant who had started life as a cooper's apprentice, rising high only to tumble low, from the owner of a fine house and a prominent pew in the First Church of Norwich to arrest for public inebriation and debt. Young Benedict was forced to leave school, abandoning the family plan for him to attend Yale. Instead he was apprenticed in 1756 to two brothers who ran a successful pharmacy and trading firm; the boy would later describe himself as a coward until forced to head his household at fifteen. "Be dutiful to superiors, obliging to equals, and affable to inferiors, if any such there be," his mother had told him before her death three years later, adding, "Don't neglect your precious soul, which once lost can never be regained."

His masters were generous and trusting. They sent him on trading voyages to the West Indies and London and, when he turned twenty-one, provided him with a handsome grubstake of £500. He set up his own emporium in the growing seaport of New Haven, selling Bateman's Pectoral Drops, Francis's Female Elixir, and tincture of valerian, an aphrodisiac, as well as earrings, rosewater, surgical instruments, and books ranging from *Paradise Lost* to *Practical Farrier*. His black-and-gold storefront sign proclaimed, SIBI TOTIQUE—for himself and for everyone—and he did not correct customers who called him "Dr. Arnold from London."

His ambitions grew with his business. He bought a forty-ton sloop, the *Fortune*, running her from Montreal to the Bay of Honduras, trading livestock, furs, Spanish gold, cheese, slaves, cotton, and salt. By 1766, at twenty-five, "Captain Arnold" owned three ships and was an adept smuggler of contraband rum and Central American mahogany. More than once he ran afoul of associates, who accused him of jackleg business practices; in that same year he was briefly arrested after failing to pay £1,700 to his London creditors. Even so, as one of New Haven's most prosperous merchants, he married, had three sons, joined the Freemasons to widen his social and business circles, and built a house overlooking the harbor, with a gambrel roof, marble fireplaces, wainscoting, and an orchard with a hundred fruit trees. But British commercial repression pinched him; he grew political, then radical, and in March 1775 was elected captain of a militia company, the Foot Guards, by comrades who saw him as a stalwart, worldly leader.

With the seizure of Ticonderoga and Crown Point, Arnold burst into American history, never to leave. After securing both forts in May 1775, wearing a scarlet militia uniform coat with buff facings and big epaulettes, he led three dozen men on a brief raid across Lake Champlain into Canada to capture thirteen prisoners and a sloop—the *George*, which he renamed *Enterprise*—in what the biographer Willard Sterne Randall would call the first American naval assault as well as the first American attack of a foreign country. In a long letter to the Continental Congress, Arnold was also among the first to urge an invasion of Canada via St. Johns, Chambly, and Montreal, offering to lead the expedition himself "with the smiles of heaven." Congress approved the plan but not the planner, selecting Schuyler and Montgomery instead. A few weeks later, Arnold rode into Cambridge to settle his financial accounts with the provincial congress, which had subsidized the Ticonderoga escapade. He took the opportunity to convince Washington that he was the right man to lead a second invasion force directly to Quebec along a rugged trace used in the past century by Indian raiders, Jesuit missionaries, and French trappers. His proposed route followed the Kennebec and Chaudière Rivers from the coast of the Eastern Country—still part of Massachusetts, but later to become Maine—to the St. Lawrence valley.

The boy in the shop apron had made good. Yet throughout his remarkable ascent he was bedeviled by episodes that suggested a trajectory forever wobbling between shadow and bright light. An accusation in 1770 that he was a drunken whoremonger who had contracted a venereal disease in the West Indies led to a lawsuit, depositions from business colleagues "in regard to my being in perfect health," and a duel. In another incident, Arnold allegedly dragged a sailor from a tavern and administered forty lashes for gossiping about his smuggling activities. Success at Ticonderoga was followed by an ugly quarrel over who was in command—"I took the liberty of breaking his head," Arnold wrote after thrashing another militia colonel—and a brief mutiny during which Arnold was locked in the *Enterprise* cabin. "Col. Arnold has been greatly abused and misrepresented by designing persons," one soldier wrote, but others saw him as headstrong and arrogant. After departing Crown Point in a huff, he learned that his wife had abruptly died, leaving him with three boys under the age of eight. He put them in the care of his faithful sister and headed for Cambridge, telling a friend that "an idle life under my present circumstances would be but a lingering death."

Washington chose to take a chance on him. The commander in chief had contemplated a similar expedition through Canada's back door, and this pugnacious, enterprising, persuasive merchant—this *fighter*—seemed worth a gamble. In early September, he gave Arnold a Continental Army colonel's commission and permission to recruit eleven hundred "active woodsmen" from the regiments in Cambridge for a mission that was "secret though known to everybody," as one officer noted. "Not a moment's time is to be lost," Washington wrote. "The season will be considerably advanced." He believed "that Quebec will fall into our hands a very easy prey."

Few military expeditions would be more heroic or more heartbreaking. "The drums beat and away they go," a rifleman in Cambridge wrote a friend, "to scale the walls of Quebec and spend the winter in joy and festivity among the sweet nuns." The "active woodsmen" were mostly farmers, with a few adventurous oddballs like a wiry nineteen-year-old named Aaron Burr, grandson of the revivalist preacher Jonathan Edwards and son of the former president of the college in Princeton, New Jersey, where young Burr was admitted at age thirteen. Washington also provided three companies of riflemen from Virginia and Pennsylvania, partly to get them out of Cambridge; their acknowledged leader was a deep-chested teamster, sawyer, and "formidable border pugilist" named Daniel Morgan. Captain Morgan, known as "the Old Wagoner," carried a turkey call made out of a conch shell. He also wore scars from a savage British flogging administered after he beat up an insolent regular in 1755 and from an Indian musket ball that perforated his cheek a year later.

After marching forty miles north to Newburyport, Arnold's brigade paraded with flags unfurled near the Merrimack River, listened to a sermon drawn from Exodus in the First Presbyterian Church—"If thy presence go not with me, carry us not up hence"—then clambered onto eleven coasters stinking of fish. "Weighed anchor," the soldier Ebenezer Wild told his journal, "with a pleasant gale, our colors flying, drums beating, fifes playing, and the hills all round covered with pretty girls weeping for their departing swains." The men soon grew seasick—"indifferent whether I lived or died," as one wrote—despite the two hundred pounds of ginger Arnold distributed as an antidote. But by September 22 they had traveled over one hundred miles up the Maine coast, past Honeywell Head and Merrymeeting Bay to Reuben Colburn's shipyard on the banks of the Kennebec.

Here, on Washington's orders, 220 flat-bottomed bateaux were under construction, with flaring sides, tapered ends, and more than 1,300 paddles, oars, and setting poles. One sniff told the men that unseasoned, green pine boards had been used. Not only were the boats cursedly heavy, but they leaked from the moment they touched water, requiring constant bailing. With seams opening faster than they could be caulked, casks of dried peas, salt fish, and beef swelled and spoiled; a hundred tons of provisions— the men ate three thousand pounds of food each day—dwindled at an alarming rate as the armada nosed north. Shallows scraped the bateaux bottoms, forcing men into the frigid river for miles on end, pushing from the stern, pulling by the painters, and cursing the boatbuilders as "infamous villains." "You would have taken the men for amphibious animals," Arnold wrote Washington, "as they were a great part of the time under water." Surveyor John Pierce told his diary, "Every man's teeth chattered in their heads." They chattered more upon waking on the bitter night of September 29 to find wet clothing "frozen a pane of glass thick," as another man wrote, "which proved very disagreeable, being obliged to lie in them." Arnold urged them on with cries of "To Quebec and victory!"

Hemlock and spruce crowded the riverbanks, and autumn colors smeared the hillsides. But soon the land grew poor, with little game to be seen. Ticonic Falls was the first of four cataracts on the Kennebec, and the first of many portages that required lugging bateaux, supplies, and muskets for miles over terrain ever more vertical; from sea level they would climb fourteen hundred feet. "This place," one officer wrote as they rigged ropes and pulleys, "is almost perpendicular." Sickness set in—"a sad plight with the diarrhea," noted Dr. Isaac Senter, the expedition surgeon—followed by the first deaths, from pneumonia, a falling tree, an errant gunshot.

More than 130 miles upriver they left the Kennebec in mid-October and crossed the Great Carrying Place—a thirteen-mile, five-day portage, much of it ascending—to reach the Dead River, a dark, reedy stream that slithered like a black snake toward the Canadian uplands. A terrible storm on October 21, perhaps the tail of an Atlantic hurricane, caused the Dead to rise eight feet in nine hours, sweeping away bedrolls, guns, and food. With "trees tumbling on all quarters," the brigade clung to hilltops and ridgelines. Six inches of snow fell three nights later. More men grew sick, or worse, in what Dr. Senter described as "a direful, howling wilderness." Jemima Warner, among the few women camp followers, tended her sick husband until he died; a comrade recorded that lacking a shovel, "she covered him with leaves, and then took his gun and other implements, and left him with a heavy heart." In late October Arnold learned that his rear battalion, under Lieutenant Colonel Roger Enos, had turned back without permission, taking three hundred troops and much of the expedition's reserve food supply. "Our men made a general prayer," Captain Henry Dearborn wrote in his diary, "that Colonel Enos and all his men might die by the way, or meet with some disaster." Back in Cambridge, Enos would be arrested, court-martialed, and acquitted; those who could testify to his venality were in Canada.

"We are in an absolute danger of starving," a Rhode Island captain wrote. By the time Enos's betrayal was discovered, their food stocks had dwindled to five pints of flour and less than an ounce of salt pork per man. "Dollars were offered for bits of bread as big as the palm of one's hand," Ebenezer Wild recorded. Then even that was gone. A dozen hunters "killed one partridge and divided it into 12 parts," John Pierce wrote on October 29. John Joseph Henry, a sixteen-year-old Pennsylvania rifleman, described how a small duck was shot and carved by his comrades "most fairly into ten shares, each one eyeing the integrity of the division."

Stews were boiled from rawhide thongs, moose-skin breeches, and the rough hides that lined the bateaux floors. Men gnawed on shaving soap, tree sap, birch bark, and lip balm. "This day I roasted my shot pouch and eat it," wrote rifleman George Morison. "It was now four days since I had eat anything save the skin of a squirrel." Young John Henry was offered a greenish broth said to be bear stew, but "this was instantly known to be untrue. It was that of a dog. He was a large black Newfoundland dog" that had belonged to Captain Dearborn, a New Hampshire physician who had fought at Bunker Hill. Men also gobbled down the feet and skin. Jeremiah

Greenman described adding "the head of a squirrel with a parcel of candle-wicks boiled up together, which made a very fine soup without salt. . . . Thinking it was the best that I ever eat."

They trudged on, across a snowy plateau known as the Height of Land, then skirted Lac-Mégantic before starting down the wild, shallow Chaudière—the word meant "boiler"—which tumbled north a hundred miles to the St. Lawrence. More men died, fell behind, or wandered into the trackless forest, never to be seen again. "I must confess that I began to be concerned about our situation," Lieutenant William Humphrey told his journal. "There was no sign of any humane being." By early November, a rifleman wrote, "many of the company were so weak that they could hardly stand. . . . They reeled about like drunken men."

Salvation appeared as a bovine apparition: at midday on Thursday, November 2, forty miles north of Lac-Mégantic, a small herd of horned cattle ambled up the riverbank, driven by several French Canadians. "It was the joyfulest sight that I ever saw," Jeremiah Greenman wrote. "Some could not refrain from crying for joy." Ravenous men slashed open a heifer and threw skin, entrails, "and everything that could be eat" on an open fire. Engorged, they sliced "savage shoes" from the hide for their ruined feet. "Blessed our stars," Dr. Senter noted in his diary.

They also blessed Arnold, for he had saved them—though only after badly miscalculating the distance and duration of their journey. From Colburn's shipyard to Quebec was 270 miles, not 180, as he had told Washington, and the journey would take six weeks, not twenty days. Yet his fortitude and iron will won through. In late October, aware that his men were failing fast, he had lunged ahead with a small vanguard down the Chaudière, racing through the rapids—smashing three bateaux against the rocks and capsizing others—before reaching Sartigan, a hardscrabble settlement of whitewashed houses with thatched roofs and paper windows. Astonished Canadian farmers, he wrote, "received us in the most hospitable manner." Arnold sent the horned cattle upriver, soon followed by mutton, flour, tobacco, and horses to evacuate the lame.

In the coming days his troops straggled into Sartigan, "more like ghosts than men," wrote one rifleman. Filthy, feeble, their clothes torn and their beards matted, they "resembled those animals of New Spain called ourang-outangs," another man wrote. A captain told his family, "We have waded 100 miles." Of the 1,080 who set out from Cambridge in September, about 400 had turned back, or had been sent home as invalids, or had died on the trek, their bones scattered as mileposts across the border uplands. "Our march has been attended with an amazing deal of fatigue," Arnold told Washington, ". . . with a thousand difficulties I never apprehended." The commanding general in reply would praise "your enterprising & persevering spirit," adding, "It is not in the power of any man to command success, but you have done more—you have deserved it."

Ever aggressive, Arnold next resolved to seize Quebec immediately. Over the following week, as the men regained health and weight, he hired carpenters and smiths to make scaling ladders, spears, and grappling hooks. Firelocks were repaired, canoes purchased. Company by company, the men moved north to Pointe-Levy, three miles up the St. Lawrence from Quebec, where locals welcomed them with a country dance featuring bagpipes, fiddle music, and drams of rum. John Pierce wrote of his hosts, "They have their saints placed as big as life which they bow down to and worship as they pass them."

At nine p.m. on November 13, a calm, cold Monday with a late moonrise, the river crossing began in forty canoes. Carefully skirting two British warships that had recently appeared on the St. Lawrence—the *Lizard*, a frigate, and *Hunter*, a sloop—five hundred Americans landed at Wolfe's Cove by four a.m. on Tuesday. They soon climbed the escarpment that nimble William Howe had scaled in 1759 to reach the Plains of Abraham, barely a cannon's shot west of Quebec's massive walls. Later in the day Arnold's men paraded within a few hundred yards of the St. Louis Gate, marching to and fro, while shouting insults in a bootless effort to entice the defenders to fight in the open, just as Wolfe had baited the French sixteen years earlier.

"They huzzahed thrice," a British officer reported. "We answered them with three cheers of defiance, & saluted them with a few cannon loaded with grape & canister shot. They did not wait for a second round." Arnold also dispatched a white flag with a written ultimatum: "If I am obliged to carry the town by storm, you may expect every severity practiced on such occasions." The demand, a Canadian historian later complained, included "the usual mixture of cant, bombast, threats, and bad taste so characteristic of the effusions of this generation of American commanders." British gunners answered with an 18-pound ball fired from the parapet, spattering Arnold's envoy with mud.

Even Colonel Arnold knew when the hour demanded prudence. He had no artillery, few bayonets, little cash, and almost a hundred broken muskets. A tally revealed that his men averaged only five reliable cartridges each. Informants told him the Quebec garrison had nearly nineteen hundred men after reinforcement by the Royal Navy, merchant seamen, and other armed loyalists, more than he'd expected. Although half were "obliged to bear arms against their inclination," as Arnold wrote Montgomery, he calculated that two thousand attackers would be needed "to carry the town."

The informants also warned him that the defenders planned a sudden sally to catch him unawares.

He ordered the men assembled, and at three a.m. on November 19 they staggered west on bloody feet for Pointe-aux-Trembles to await Montgomery. "Very cold morning," Pierce told his diary. "Ground frozen very hard." An armed two-masted snow passed them, heading down the St. Lawrence for Quebec; on deck, they would later learn, stood General Carleton in his *habitant* disguise.

Having survived unspeakable hardship, many men desperately missed their homes and families. "God deliver me from this land of ignorance," Pierce wrote, "and in his own due time return me once more where they can pronounce English." Yet most recognized that more hardship lay ahead. "We have a winter's campaign before us," Captain Samuel Ward, Jr., told his family in Rhode Island. "But I trust we shall have the glory of taking Quebec!"

Good news out of Canada sparked jubilation from Cambridge to Philadelphia and beyond. The invasion gambit had all but succeeded. General Montgomery controlled the Lake Champlain–Richelieu corridor, as well as Montreal and the western St. Lawrence valley. He soon would move east to join forces with Colonel Arnold, now hailed as an American Hannibal for a feat likened to crossing the Alps with elephants in midwinter.

Canadian volunteers flocked to the American standard despite the clergy's threat of eternal damnation. Some publicly acknowledged asking God to help *les Bostonnais*, as they called all Yankees. *Habitants* from sixteen parishes around Quebec City alone would assist the invaders by confiscating British supplies, detaining loyalists and overzealous priests, and ransacking the estates of wealthy *seigneurs* in a spate of score settling. Others provided firewood, built scaling ladders, and stood guard around American camps. "We can expect no assistance from the Canadian peasantry," a Quebec merchant wrote. "They have imbibed a notion that if the rebels get entire possession of the country, they'll be forever exempted from paying taxes."

For the American invaders, the delay in taking St. Johns was nettlesome. A quicker capture of Montreal in early fall might have bagged Carleton and permitted the seizure of defenseless Quebec in a swift coup de main. Aware that Britain would likely dispatch a robust force in the spring to recoup the empire's losses in Canada, both Washington and Schuyler believed that Fortress Quebec must be quickly reduced in the coming weeks, then manned and fortified over the winter to withstand the anticipated assault. Although more than six tons of gunpowder had been sent to the Northern Army, mostly from South Carolina and New York, shortages persisted of everything from food and winter clothing to money and munitions.

Still, with Montgomery and Arnold leading their "famine-proof veterans," victory in the north seemed at hand. A Virginia congressman, Richard Henry Lee, spoke for many when he declared in Philadelphia, "No doubt is entertained here that this Congress will be shortly joined by delegates from Canada, which will then complete the union of fourteen provinces."

6.

— ✦ —

America Is an Ugly Job

By late morning on Thursday, October 26, tens of thousands of high-spirited Londoners filled the streets around Parliament, lured by pleasant fall sunshine and the titillating expectation of trouble. Constables clustered outside the Swan tavern at Westminster Bridge and in St. James's Park, and Foot Guards were issued ten musket cartridges apiece as a precaution. George III was to open a new session of Parliament this afternoon, but an American merchant named Stephen Sayre had been arrested at his Oxford Street house on suspicion of high treason; it was said that Sayre intended to kidnap the king, diverting his hijacked coach to the Tower, where bribed guards would lock the gates behind him and allow seditious rioters to ransack the arsenal. Skeptics declared that if such an outlandish plot existed, the conspirators should be sent to Bedlam asylum rather than to prison. But the authorities took no chances. Sayre himself had been dragged to the Tower, which "raised the curiosity of the public to an extravagant pitch," the London *Public Advertiser* reported. "People imagine something very extraordinary is to happen."

The clock over the main entrance at St. James's Palace touched two p.m. as the king emerged, swaddled in silk and ermine. "The crowd was very great in the courtyard to see His Majesty get into the state coach," a Guards lieutenant wrote. "Everybody agrees that His Majesty never went to the House with such universal shouts of applause." In fact, many hisses could be heard amid the cheers when the royal procession lurched from the palace, led by two horse grenadiers holding drawn swords and three coaches, each pulled by six horses and stuffed with nobles and gentlemen-in-waiting. Behind them followed Horse Guards in red and gold, then trumpeters, Yeomen of the guard, and fourteen liveried footmen in ranks of two. The gilded coach carrying the king was unlike anything in the empire or, perhaps, the world: twenty-four feet long, thirteen feet tall, and weighing four tons, it was drawn—at a glacial pace—by eight Royal Hanoverian Cream horses, each the color of buttermilk and at least fifteen hands high. On the roof, three carved cherubs representing England, Scotland, and Ireland supported a gilt crown, and painted allegorical panels on the doors evoked imperial grandeur. A gilded, fish-tailed sea god sat at each corner above the iron-rimmed wheels to signify Britain's maritime might—appropriately, since the coach's tendency to pitch, yaw, and oscillate made riding in it like "tossing in a rough sea," as a later monarch would complain.

A platoon of constables brought up the rear, scanning the crowd for kidnappers while George settled into his satin-and-velvet cushions. He could hear the hisses as well as the applause, but public disapproval rarely piqued him. He knew that most of his subjects were happy enough that fall. England had never harvested a finer wheat crop, bread prices were down, manufacturing was near full employment, and more money was changing hands in the kingdom "than at any other time since the memory of man," as Lord Barrington put it. Annual deaths still exceeded christenings in London, but the gap had narrowed and Irish immigrants buoyed the population. Violent crime had dropped, and fewer debtors were being jailed. Life for many might still be nasty, brutish, and short, but less so.

The Americans, by contrast, appeared perpetually angry. How long ago it seemed that Harvard College had offered cash prizes for the best poems commemorating George's reign—for the best Latin verse in hexameters, the best Latin ode, the best English long verse. The king tried to ignore things that vexed or displeased him, like the petitions from Bristol and Liverpool urging reconciliation, which he consigned to the "Committee of Oblivion," or the annoying letters from John Wesley, that *Methodist*, who warned that the Americans "will not be frightened. . . . They are as strong as you, they are as valiant as you." In the summer George had refused to receive what the colonials called their Olive Branch Petition, imploring the king to stop the war, repeal the Coercive Acts, and effect "a happy and permanent reconciliation." He would not treat with rebels.

Lord North warned him that the insurrection had "now grown to such a height that it must be treated as a foreign war." Casualty reports from Concord and Bunker Hill certainly bore out the first minister, not to mention the sour rumors from Canada. The king had responded in late August with a "Proclamation of Rebellion," forbidding all commerce with the colonies and requiring every subject to help "in the suppression of such rebellion," on pain of treason. The provincials were "misled by dangerous and ill designing men," the king declared, "forgetting the allegiance which they owe to the power that has protected and supported them." Heralds read the edict at Westminster, Temple Bar, the Royal Exchange, and elsewhere; hisses were heard then, too. He shrugged them off.

British colonial policy, quite simply, sought revenue for the greater good of the empire. But "that damned American war," as North called it, forced the government to confront a displeasing dilemma: either accede to conciliation and forgo income from the colonies or prosecute a war that would cost more money than could ever be squeezed from America. Moreover, success in crushing the rebellion would likely be followed by an expensive, protracted occupation. Even from the lofty vantage of a throne, coherent British war aims were hard to discern.

Yet a king must remain steadfast, and George had thrown himself headlong into the role of captain general—studying military texts, visiting summer encampments, reviewing the Guards regiments. He continued to make his lists and his charts, of "ships building and repairing" at various yards; of guard vessels protecting ports and waterways; of "oak timber in store" (more than fifty-seven thousand loads); of royal ships in ordinary—the reserve fleet—including the number of guns mounted. He made more neat columns: of British garrisons abroad from 1764 to 1775; of the commanders of various cavalry units; of all his regiments, including those in Boston, with the number of officers, musicians, and the rank and file tabulated at the bottom of the page and his arithmetic scratchings in the margins.

Finally he sketched an organizational chart of his army in America, using tiny inked boxes hardly bigger than a pinhead, labeled with regimental numbers. Then he gave his draft to a better artist to convert into a smart diagram with copperplate script, symbols in colored pencils, and tiny cannon silhouettes to represent artillery batteries. It helped him to follow that damned American war.

The state coach clopped to a halt. Welcoming guns saluted the monarch's arrival, rattling windows across Westminster. Horse Guards paraded in Parliament Street to "see that all was quiet," the *Public Advertiser* noted. George strode into the former Queen's Chamber at the southern end of the parliamentary warren, now used by the House of Lords. "Adorned with his crown and regal ornaments," as the official parliamentary account recorded, he took his seat on a straight-backed throne. "He is tall, square over the shoulders," an American loyalist in London wrote. "Shows his teeth too much. His countenance is heavy and lifeless, with white eyebrows." Peers in crimson robes flanked him. On George's command, the usher of the Black Rod summoned several hundred members of the Commons, who soon stood in the back in their coats and boots, shifting from one foot to the other since there were no benches for them. In his precise, regal voice, the king went straight to the American question.

Those who have long too successfully labored to inflame my people in America . . . now openly avow their revolt, hostility, and rebellion. They have raised troops, and are collecting a naval force. They have seized the public revenue, and assumed to themselves legislative, executive, and judicial powers.

Parliament and the Crown had displayed "moderation and forbearance," eager to prevent "the calamities which are inseparable from a state of war." Alas, war had "become more general, and is manifestly carried on for the purpose of establishing an independent empire. I need not dwell upon the fatal effects of the success of such a plan."

The phrase "fatal effects" seemed to hang in the air. Upturned faces ringed the chamber, every peer and commoner in rapt attention.

"To put a speedy end to these disorders by the most decisive exertions," he continued, "I have increased my naval establishment and greatly augmented my land forces." The full fury of the empire would be unleashed on the rebellion. The government also was considering "friendly offers of foreign assistance," with treaties likely. He saw "no probability" that the French or other adversaries would intrude in this family squabble. Finally:

When the unhappy and deluded multitudes, against whom this force will be directed, shall become sensible of their error, I shall be ready to receive the misled with tenderness and mercy.

In twenty minutes he was done and out the door, rumbling back to the palace in his monstrous coach.

A few naysayers disparaged the address. Horace Walpole, for one, counted "three or four gross falsehoods." But the Commons voted with the usual hefty majority to thank His Majesty, noting that "on our firmness or indecision the future fate of the British Empire and of ages yet unborn will depend." An independent America would be "a dangerous rival," in which case "it would have been better for this country that America had never been known than that a great consolidated American empire should exist independent of Britain."

The king could only agree. "Where the cause is just," he would write, "I can never be dismayed."

For George and Queen Charlotte, monarchical rhythms changed little from month to month, or year to year. "They both meet in the breakfast room about a half hour after 8. When she goes to the breakfast, she rings for the children," the king had written in an account of their domestic life. "Every evening after dinner they retire into her apartments to drink coffee, & there they generally spend the remainder of their evening." He fussed with his collections—barometers, clocks, coins, Handel oratorios—or immersed himself in a book and read aloud passages he found especially pithy. Both kept an orchestra and patronized the opera; he played a creditable flute, harpsichord, and violin. Much of their time in the Queen's House—the family residence, later called Buckingham Palace—was spent instructing their growing brood in the ways of royalty, as in Charlotte's letter to George P., the Prince of Wales, read to him by a tutor on his eighth birthday: "Above all things I recommend unto you to fear God.... We are all equal, and become only of consequence by setting good examples to others."

For those with fine houses in the city's fashionable squares—Berkeley, Grosvenor, Cavendish—the seating of Parliament intensified London's social swirl. Parties and dinners were often scheduled for Wednesdays or Saturdays, when the Commons and Lords rarely convened. "Come to London and admire our plumes," one woman wrote a friend in the provinces. "We sweep the skies! A duchess wears six feathers, a lady four, and every milkmaid one at each corner of her cap." Gentlewomen's hair, already piled high, grew higher when Georgiana Spencer, an earl's daughter, created a three-foot coiffure by fastening horsehair pads to her own tresses; sometimes she decorated the tower with stuffed birds, waxed fruit, or tiny wooden trees and sheep. Hair grew so high that women could ride in closed carriages only by sitting on the floor. Young fops known as "Macaroni" pranced through Pall Mall and St. James's Street in tight britches, high heels, and oversized buttons, their hair dyed red one day and blue the next. *Oxford Magazine* defined the Macaroni as "a kind of animal.... It talks without meaning, it smiles without pleasantry ... it wenches without passion."

It also gambled without guilt. If London was "the devil's drawing room," in the phrase of author Tobias Smollett, gaming had become a diabolical national passion despite the monarch's disapproval. Bets could be laid not only on horses, cockfights, and national lottery tickets, but on seemingly any future event, from how long a raindrop took to traverse a windowpane to how long Mr. Jones or Mrs. Smith would live; common wagers involved taking out insurance policies on other people's lives. Walpole described seeing £10,000 on the table at Almack's Club, where players wore eyeshades to conceal their emotions and leather cuffs to preserve their laced ruffles, then turned their coats inside out for luck. Military pensioners in Royal Hospital Chelsea were said to bet on lice races, and workmen repairing a floor in Middle Temple Hall found nearly two hundred dice that over the years had fallen between the cracks. "Play at whist, commerce, backgammon, trictrac, or chess," one society dame advised, "but never at quinze, lou, brag, faro, hazard, or any game of chance." Few heeded her.

London also had more than five hundred coffeehouses, and it was here that politics generally and the American question specifically might be discussed at any hour. Fratricidal war unsettled many Britons, who found it distasteful, if not unnatural. Some feared an endless war, citing published reports—often wildly exaggerated—that the Americans had two hundred thousand armed men, "well trained, ready to march," and that gunsmiths outside Philadelphia were turning out five hundred stand of arms every fortnight. (Pennsylvania craftsmen collectively would make only 806 muskets in 1776.) Those sympathetic to the insurrectionists' cause sometimes donated money to help rebel prisoners. The Duke of Richmond sailed his yacht, reportedly with an American pennant flying, through a British naval squadron.

"I am growing more and more American," James Boswell had written in August. "I see the unreasonableness of taxing them without the consent of their assemblies. I think our ministry are mad in undertaking this desperate war." Others were even more strident, like Lord Mayor John Wilkes, described as "a charming, cross-eyed demagogue" who was elected to Parliament after marriage to an heiress gave him the fortune to bribe enough voters. In answer to the king's Thursday address, Wilkes, whose noisy radicalism made him enormously popular in the colonies, called the war "unjust, felonious, and murderous." The Americans, he warned, "will dispute every inch of territory with you, every narrow pass, every strong defile, every Thermopylae, every Bunker Hill." But opponents of coercion lacked strength and unity. When votes were tallied in the Commons, no faction proved more formidable than the government supporters known as the King's Friends.

Newspaper resistance to colonial policy proved more obdurate, however. Britain now boasted 140 newspapers, including 17 in London. Thirteen million individual news sheets would be printed across the country in 1775, many of them handed round until the print wore off. A reader of the *Gazetteer and New Daily Advertiser* wrote that the "affairs of America engross so much of the attention of the public that every other consideration seems to be laid aside." The king himself insisted that the latest London and American papers be delivered to him as soon as they arrived. A few publications hewed to the ministerial line. The *Royal Gazette*, denounced by competitors as the *Royal Lying Gazette*, promoted the delusions that the colonies would collapse without British trade and that most affluent Americans sought reconciliation. The government encouraged loyalty by paying printers and writers for anti-American screeds, often from the secret service fund and other obscure accounts. Some critics were silenced with cash: the acerbic editor of the *Morning Post* grew milder in exchange for almost £4,000 slipped under the table.

Yet many British "newspapers went straight for the King," the historian George Otto Trevelyan later wrote, depicting him as "a bigoted and vindictive prince, whose administration was odious and corrupt." The war became a cudgel with which political opponents could whack North, Dartmouth, and other government ministers. In early August, the *Stamford Mercury* printed a table showing that more British officers died at Bunker Hill than in the great Battle of Minden in 1759. Other accounts described hardship and poor morale in the British ranks. The radical *Evening Post* denounced the war as "unnatural, unconstitutional, unnecessary, unjust, dangerous, hazardous, and unprofitable."

Biographical profiles of American leaders appeared, their heroic attributes often contrasted to the venality of British politicians, even if the portraits were at times ludicrous. A new article in *Town and Country* told readers how George Washington's daughter had fled to England after the general's men slew her loyalist lover. Of greater consequence were loosened restrictions allowing parliamentary debates to be reported without the six-month delay previously required—or without pretending, as one magazine had, that the published transcript was from the "Senate of Lilliput." The subsequent coverage, as historian Troy O. Bickham would write, "made the American Revolution the first event in which the government's handling of a controversial conflict was aired before an eager national audience."

Irked at the dissent, the government had stepped up covert surveillance and intelligence gathering. Suspected rebel sympathizers in London were ordered "narrowly watched," their neighbors discreetly questioned about irregular activity. The baggage of passengers arriving from North America was searched for rebel correspondence. In a three-room suite off Lombard Street, a growing staff of secret service clerks by mid-September was opening and reading up to a hundred letters a day from the New York mail-bags, with or without warrants, including private correspondence from Royal Navy officers and British officials in America. Additional letters were intercepted from foreign diplomats, European bankers, and political opponents trusting enough to rely on the Royal Mail. Especially intriguing correspondence, such as letters addressed to Dr. Franklin or General Lee, was copied and sent to the king and his senior ministers, while the originals went back to the General Post Office for normal delivery. A superintendent complained of overwork in deciphering coded letters and repairing wax seals so that they appeared unbroken. "I had so much to do," he added in a November memorandum, "that I knew not which way to turn myself." Despite such "difficulty, pains, and trouble," the intelligence collected often was disappointingly thin, little more than gossip. George nevertheless carefully noted the time—to the minute, as usual—he received each batch of pilfered mail.

As October spilled into November, the king immersed himself in tactical details of the American war. George received copies not only of ministry dispatches to and from his generals, but also paymaster and commissary instructions. He reviewed intelligence on possible gunpowder shipments from Lisbon, clandestine activities in Amsterdam and Dunkirk, and river inspectors' reports of suspicious cargoes on the Thames. He was consulted about the choice of commanders, the composition of particular regiments and where they should deploy, and the shipment of salt and candles across the Atlantic. He arranged, at an initial cost of £10,000, for twenty-four hundred German troops to serve at British garrisons in the Mediterranean, freeing regulars there for combat service in North America. He also weighed in on a proposed military assault on the southern colonies; on which widows and orphans of men killed in Boston should receive pensions; and on whether American prisoners should be shipped to India, where the insalubrious British territories were short of white settlers. When Catherine the Great declined to rent him twenty thousand Russian mercenaries—"she had not had the civility to answer in her own hand," George wrote North "at 2 minutes past 8 p.m." on November 3—he insisted that German legions could be hired "at a much cheaper rate, besides more expeditiously than if raised at home." On his orders, the colonel negotiating with various German princelings was told, "Get as many men as you can. . . . The King is extremely anxious."

Broad domestic support for the war eased his anxiety, despite the nattering newspapers and rapscallions like the lord mayor. Solid majorities in both the middle and the upper classes disapproved of colonial impertinence. Edward Gibbon, who was just finishing his first volume on the Roman empire's collapse, wrote in October that the government's "executive power was driven by the national clamor into the most vigorous and repressive measures." Many towns across Britain sent endorsements of ministerial policy to London. "It was the war of the people," North later observed. "It was popular at its commencement, and eagerly embraced by the people and the Parliament."

Without doubt, the disruption of transatlantic trade injured some London merchants, as well as woolen workers in Norwich and linen weavers in Chester. British exports to America plummeted from almost £3 million in 1774 to barely £220,000 this year. But many other businesses thrived. Britain would be at war for more than half of the years between 1695 and 1815, and there was money to be made in those years by traders and vendors, brokers and wholesalers. "The greater number of them begin to snuff . . . a lucrative war," wrote Edmund Burke, the Irish-born political philosopher who represented Bristol in the House of Commons. "War indeed is become a sort of substitute for commerce." Orders poured in from Germany and the Baltics. New markets emerged in Spain, Russia, and Canada. Military contracts boomed, for uniform cloth, munitions, shipping, and provisions of every sort. "We never knew our manufactures, in general, in a more flourishing state," a London firm wrote to a former American customer.

For the king, it was all part of what he called "a great national cause." George "would put heart into the hesitant, stir up the idle, and check the treacherous," the historian Piers Mackesy later observed. "He never wavered from the chosen object of the war." If doubters could be bought, he bought them. To North on November 15, he applauded Generals Howe and Burgoyne for their "unanimity and zeal, the two great ingredients that seem to have been wanting in this campaign." George also sought unanimity and zeal in his ministers, summoning them one by one for audiences in the Royal Closet, his conference room at St. James's, where he talked much and listened little, bounding from subject to subject but always returning to the need for resolve in America. "We have a warm Parliament but an indolent Cabinet," wrote Gibbon, who later told a friend, "The higher people are placed, the more gloomy are their countenances, the more melancholy their language. . . . I fear it arises from their knowledge—a late knowledge—of the difficulty and magnitude of the business."

That surely was the case for Lord Dartmouth, the Psalm Singer and secretary of state for America. Having started a war, Dartmouth had no appetite to wage it; he now often abandoned Whitehall for the solace of his country estate. Franklin had once considered him "truly a good man," but one "who does not seem to have strength equal to his wishes." By early November, the secretary had arranged to leave the American Department by becoming lord privy seal, a pleasant, toothless sinecure. "Lord Dartmouth only stayed long enough," Walpole sniffed, "to prostitute his character and authenticate his hypocrisy."

North also showed weakness in the knees. While affecting a determined ferocity toward the Americans—"we propose to exert ourselves using every species of force to reduce them," he had declared in October—the first minister was weary of relentless opposition attacks, even if they were said to "sink into him like a cannonball into a wool sack." Just hours after the king opened the new Parliament, North's wife wrote that the pressure on her husband was "every day more disagreeable. Indeed it will be impossible for him to bear it much longer." Since hearing of Bunker Hill, he had doubted that Britain could conquer America by force of arms. But when he hinted at resigning, George replied in a note, "You are my sheet anchor." The king would further add, "It has not been my fate in general to be well served. By you I have, and therefore cannot forget it." Loyal North would hold fast and true, even as his countenance grew gloomier, his language more melancholy. He "had neither devised the war nor liked it," Walpole wrote, "but liked his place, whatever he pretended."

Clearly the king needed another champion for his cause, a minister who shared his conviction that battering the colonies into submission was politically tenable, morally justified, and militarily necessary. And he had just the man in mind.

In a silver-tongued brogue that his English colleagues at times had difficulty deciphering, the bespectacled Edmund Burke, for three hours and twenty minutes on Thursday, November 16, implored the House of Commons to abandon the war. As usual during debates on the American problem, the galleries had been cleared of most spectators. Only "four women of quality and a few foreigners" had been admitted, reported the *Morning Chronicle*, perhaps after bribing the doorkeeper.

At Burke's request, the Speaker, in his black gown and full-bottomed wig, ordered peace petitions from clergymen, clothiers, and tradesmen laid on the clerks' table. Burke lamented "the horrors of a civil war . . . [that] may terminate in the dismemberment of our empire, or in a barren and ruinous conquest." He warned that the longer the conflict persisted, the greater the chance "for the interference of the Bourbon powers" in France and Spain. At length he introduced a bill "for composing the present troubles" by suspending any taxes imposed on the Americans unless approved voluntarily by colonial assemblies. As Burke spoke, members squirmed on their benches, murmuring in assent or dissent. Some dozed or wandered out the door to Alice's coffeehouse or to the barbershop.

Sitting next to Lord North on the Treasury bench to the right of the Speaker's chair, a tall, dignified man with sharp eyesight despite his sixty years watched intently as more than a dozen speakers stood in turn to offer their opinions. Years before he had been a prominent general, and though now a bit fleshy he retained his military carriage; one colleague described his "long face, rather strong features, clear blue eyes . . . and a mixture of quickness and a sort of melancholy in his look." Lord George Germain was known in Parliament for urging that Americans be treated with "a Roman severity," and this week he had been appointed American secretary to replace the hapless Dartmouth. After nearly thirty-five years in the Commons, he now stood to deliver his first speech not only as a cabinet member but as a man whose bellicose fervor would make him "chief minister for the civil war," as one British official called him.

He began slowly. Some thought him flustered, though others admired his "pithy, manly sentences." On "this American business," he promised to be "decisive, direct, and firm." Extracting revenue from America was vital. So, too, was parliamentary supremacy. As for the Americans, "they have a right to every liberty which they can enjoy, consistent with the sovereignty and supremacy of this country.

"Let them be happy," Germain added, in the tone of a man who cared not a whit for their happiness. "Nobody can wish them more so than I do." He continued:

> What I have always held, I now stand in office to maintain. To the questions, what force is necessary? What do you mean to send? I answer . . . such forces as are necessary to restore, maintain, and establish the power of this country in America, will not be wanting. . . . If they persist in their appeal to force, the force of the country must be exerted. The spirit of this country will go along with me in that idea, to suppress, to crush such rebellious resistance.

Just before four a.m., after fourteen hours of debate, Burke's proposal was defeated, two to one. "Pity me, encourage me," Germain told a friend, "and I will do my best."

"Some fall so hard, they bound and rise again," the ubiquitous Walpole observed. Such had been the fate of George Germain, born George Sackville, the youngest son of a duke. He was among Britain's most controversial public men of the eighteenth century—esteemed, disgraced, rehabilitated, and raised to high office only to tumble once again. Named for his godfather, George I, and raised in a Kent palace with fifty-two staircases and 365 rooms, he had attended Trinity College in Dublin, said to be "half bear-garden and half brothel," while his father served as lord lieutenant of Ireland. Ambitious and clever, he was an engaging conversationalist who retailed indiscreet stories of the royal family; his fluency in French reputedly put a serrated edge on his English irony. In either language he had a mordant wit, once telling a supplicant, "I find myself debarred the satisfaction of contributing to your happiness and ease." Diligent, capable, and a deft debater, Sackville kept a large library of books he tended not to read, claiming, "I have not genius sufficient for works of mere imagination." Married in 1754—his wife called him "my dearest man"—he proved a good father to five children even as tales circulated of his flagrant homosexuality, both a sin and a capital crime in his day.

He found his calling as a soldier, demonstrating what one admirer called "cannon-proof courage." At the Battle of Fontenoy in 1745, he was so far forward in the fighting that after he was shot in the chest his wounds were dressed in the French king's tent. A year later he pursued Scottish clansmen through the Highlands after their defeat at Culloden, and in 1758, at St. Malo during the Seven Years' War, he was again wounded while fighting the French. "Nobody stood higher," Walpole wrote, "nobody has more ambition or more sense."

Then came the great fall. On August 1, 1759, Lieutenant General Sackville was the senior commander of British forces serving in a coalition army when thirty-seven thousand allied troops battled forty-four thousand Frenchmen near the north German village of Minden. Subordinate to Prince Ferdinand of Brunswick, a man he disliked and distrusted, Sackville failed to move with alacrity when ordered to fling his twenty-four cavalry squadrons against the faltering enemy. The French were defeated anyway, suffering seven thousand casualties in four hours. But they had not been routed. Ferdinand blamed Sackville for the blemished triumph, and a British captain denounced him as a "damned chicken-hearted . . . stinking coward."

Recalled to London, smeared by Grub Street newspapers, Sackville appeared before a court-martial board of fifteen generals to argue that Ferdinand's instructions had been ambiguous and contradictory, that bad terrain had impeded the cavalry, and that only eight minutes had been lost before his reinforcements joined the fight. No matter: he was convicted of disobeying orders and declared "unfit to serve His Majesty in any military capacity whatever." The court fell just short of the two-thirds majority required to execute him. His vindictive monarch, George II, rubbed salt in the wound by ordering the verdict to be written in every regimental orderly book and read out on parade. He was burned in effigy at least once. To his brother-in-law he wrote, "I must live in hopes of better times."

Those times began a few months later when the old king fell dead of a heart attack while sipping morning chocolate on his toilet, to be succeeded by his grandson, George III, who admired Sackville and permitted him to kiss the new monarch's hand. The stain of disgrace proved indelible but not disqualifying. In 1765, Sackville gained readmission to the Privy Council, and in 1769 a widowed, childless cousin left him her fortune and estate in Northamptonshire on the condition that he perpetuate her surname. And so, resurrected, he became Lord George Germain. On Sunday mornings, a friend wrote, "he marched out his whole family in grand cavalcade to his parish church," prepared to upbraid any chorister who sang a false note—"Out of tune, Tom Baker!"—while dispensing sixpence to poor children from his waistcoat pocket. "In punctuality, precision, dispatch, and integrity, he was not to be surpassed," one associate wrote. Another observed simply, "There was no trash in his mind."

He completed his rehabilitation by hewing to Crown policy, particularly in aligning himself with ministry hard-liners on colonial matters. A "riotous rabble" was to blame in America, he had told the Commons a year earlier, people who ought "not trouble themselves with politics and government which they do not understand." He was said by one acolyte to have "all the requisites of a great minister, unless popularity and good luck are to be numbered among them." North was happy enough to have a brawler at his elbow on the Treasury bench. Though neither held the other in affection—Germain privately called North "a trifling supine minister"— they shared the king's conviction that defeat in America spelled the end of empire, as the historian Andrew Jackson O'Shaughnessy later wrote.

The backbiting never ceased, of course. In the tony men's clubs around St. James's he was still "Lord Minden" or the "Minden buggering hero." One witticism held that should the British Army be forced to flee on the battlefield, Germain was the perfect man to lead a retreat. If convivial in private over a glass of claret, in public his mien hardened. Some found him dogmatic, aloof, "quite as cold in his manner as a minister needed be," in a subordinate's estimation. A clergyman described "a reserve and haughtiness in Lord George's manner, which depressed and darkened all that was agreeable and engaging in him." One biographer later posited that it was "his pride, his remoteness, his intransigence, his indifference, his irony, his disdain, his self-command and self-assurance that inflamed mean minds."

Even those who felt no rancor toward Germain greeted his appointment with skepticism. He had been accused of many things over the years, with more epithets to come, but no one had ever charged him with statesmanship. Not least among his ministerial challenges was the fact that more than a few of the men now leading the British Army in North America had served with him in the past, at least peripherally, including Howe, Clinton, and Carleton.

* * *

Despite the expanding war in the colonies, the American Department remained a modest enterprise. Bookcases, dusty cupboards, and desks upholstered with the usual green baize filled four large rooms on the second floor of the Treasury building in Whitehall. Maps of imperial and plantation geography hung on the white plaster walls. The staff comprised two deputies, a half dozen clerks to scribble dispatches and collate enclosures, a charwoman, and a porter whose apparent function was to make petitioners wait for hours before turning them away completely. The office could draw from a government pool of three dozen messengers, but Germain asked that couriers too obese to ride horseback faster than five miles an hour travel instead by coach. As secretary he was paid just under £2,000 annually, although various perquisites nearly tripled the salary, notably the £5 allotment from every fee paid on various documents signed by the king, including military commissions, licenses to sell trees, and appointments at King's College in New York. He also was entitled to £3,000 in secret service funds, plus a thousand ounces of white plate. The £13 paid for an office clock—he was uncommonly punctual—and two books of maps came from his private purse.

Germain believed that hard work could heal most ills, and he threw himself into his new role with vigor: issuing commands, rifling through official papers, scratching missives in his jagged, runic hand, the precise time always affixed on his letters to the king. He had long argued that "natural sloth" impeded British administration, especially in the thicket of bureaucracies and office fiefdoms now entangled with centuries of inertia and bad habits. Good habits could help revive efficiency. An admirer described Germain's executive style as "rapid, yet clear and accurate. . . . There was no obscurity and ambiguity in his compositions." His task would be herculean—to direct the longest, largest expeditionary war Britain had ever fought, concocting an effective counterinsurgency strategy while coordinating troops, shipping, naval escorts, and provisions. The small details alone were bewildering. Might the army in Boston want several dozen Tower wall-pieces that could throw a two-ounce ball five hundred yards with precision? When should six thousand new muskets be shipped to Quebec and Virginia? By what means? Were the lower decks in leased Dutch transport ships properly scuttled to avoid suffocating the horses headed across the Atlantic?

Upon arriving at Whitehall in mid-November, Germain found only bad news from America. Several dozen letters from royal governors in the southern colonies showed that the Crown's efforts to punish Massachusetts had transformed New England grievances into continental resentments. The southern governors believed themselves vulnerable to rude treatment if not assassination, and most had abandoned their capitals for the sanctuary of British warships. "A motley mob . . . inflamed with liquor" had chased Governor Josiah Martin from his palace in North Carolina. In South Carolina, where rebels had amassed "great quantities of warlike stores," Governor William Campbell wrote from the man-of-war *Cherokee*, "I fear it is forgot that His Majesty has any dominions in this part of America." Official dispatches and other royal mail had been stolen in Florida. Virginia's governor, Lord Dunmore, had fled from Williamsburg. "My clerk," he wrote, "is prisoner." Governor James Wright in Georgia seemed especially rattled. "Liberty gentlemen" had pilfered six tons of his gunpowder and snatched his mail. "I begin to think a King's governor has little or no business here," he reported. Rebels in Savannah, he added, included "a parcel of the lowest people, chiefly carpenters, shoemakers, blacksmiths, etc., with a Jew at their head." Wright's dispatches grew increasingly frantic. "No troops, no money, no orders or instructions, and a wild multitude gathering fast," he added. "What can a man do in such a situation?"

Reports from the northern colonies were just as disheartening. A naval captain in Rhode Island wrote of "rebels coming in shoals, armed with muskets, bayonets, sticks and stones," yelling, "Kill the Tories!" Only a Royal Navy threat to put every insurgent to the sword had restored calm. A Connecticut clergyman warned that malice "against the loyalists is so great and implacable that we fear a general massacre." Governor John Wentworth had retreated to Boston after a mob demolished his New Hampshire house. In New York, Governor William Tryon had been chased to the *Duchess of Gordon* in the East River, and the loyal president of King's College had fled all the way to England. When regulars also boarded ships for safety, rebels ransacked their baggage, looted an ordnance magazine, and made off with shore guns from the batteries in lower Manhattan. "The Americans," Tryon warned, "from politicians are now becoming soldiers."

Germain found broad agreement in the government on Britain's strategic objective—to restore the rebellious colonies to their previous imperial subservience—but disagreement on how best to achieve that goal. How to defeat an enemy that lacked a conventional center of gravity, like a capital city, and relied on armed civilians who were said to be "deep into principles"? Should British forces hunt down and destroy rebel forces in the thirteen colonies and Canada? Strangle the colonies with a naval blockade? Divide and conquer by isolating either New England or the southern colonies? Hold New York City while subduing the affluent middle colonies between Virginia and New Jersey?

Lord North and some others in the cabinet now inclined toward a land rather than a naval war in hopes that it would be quicker, cheaper, and less provocative to the French. Such a strategy would also give greater succor to American loyalists, whom most British officials, Germain among them, still believed constituted a colonial majority. Yet doubts persisted. "The Americans may be reduced by the fleet," Secretary at War Barrington had written North, "but never can be by the army." A War Office report warned that fewer than ten thousand regulars in the British Isles could be spared for overseas duty. Given the booming economy, no more than six thousand more were likely to be recruited in time for the 1776 campaign. "Unless it rains men in red coats," a British official wrote, "I know not where we are to get all we shall want." Seventeen recruiting parties in Ireland were enlisting only one or two dozen men per week, combined. "This will never do," wrote General Harvey, the adjutant general. "We are dribletting away the army, & to no purpose."

Germain soon encountered other aggravations. Army recruiters competed with the Royal Navy and the East India Company for men. A dozen departments administered the army and overseas military logistics, with fitful coordination, when not outright rivalry, among them. Shipwrights resisting new efficiency rules had gone on strike, bringing Portsmouth and most other yards to a standstill; almost 130 were fired, hampering ship construction and repair. Too often the king and his men were forced to make crucial decisions in the dark, or at least the dusk. Voyages from England to America usually took ten weeks, though sometimes fifteen or more; return trips with the prevailing winds typically required six weeks. A minister might wait four months for acknowledgment that his instructions had been received, or he might wait forever: forty packet boats carrying the Royal Mail would be captured or founder in storms during the war. Misunderstanding, misinformation, and untimely orders were inevitable, particularly when London relied on such flawed sources of intelligence as loyalists desperate for Crown support and royal governors banished from their own capitals. "America," General Harvey said, "is an ugly job."

Like the man he called "the mildest and best of kings," Germain often invoked the need for "zeal." Sensing that the Americans had advantages of time and space, he vowed to bring "the utmost force of this kingdom to finish the rebellion in one campaign" before other European powers could intervene to aid the rebels. If the insurrection was to be crushed in 1776, half measures would never do.

Zeal could be found in the Prohibitory Act, introduced in the Commons by North on November 20. All vessels found trading with the Americans "shall be forfeited to His Majesty, as if the same were the ships and effects of open enemies." Cargoes taken on the high seas would be considered lawful seizures. Captured American mariners could be pressed into the Royal Navy. American ports were to be blockaded. The act amounted to "a declaration of perpetual war," one British politician observed, although John Adams would call it an "act of independency" that galvanized American resistance. Parliament overwhelmingly approved the measure, and the king gave his assent on December 22. The king also had approved the Admiralty's plan to recall Admiral Graves in hopes that his replacement, Vice Admiral Molyneux Shuldham, a former governor of Newfoundland, would put a spark into the North American squadron.

As for fighting the rebels on land, Germain relied heavily on General Howe's assessment. An unconventional enemy required original tactics, and Howe's experience with light infantry and irregular warfare—fighting from "trees, walls, or hedges"—seemed apposite. The commanding general favored squeezing New England between the blockaded ports and the North River, also known as the Hudson, with an offensive launched into New York from Canada once the American interlopers were expelled from Quebec. Germain agreed: a robust fleet must be dispatched to the St. Lawrence, and another to Boston or New York. He immediately pressed the Admiralty to find sufficient ships not only in Britain, but also in Germany and Holland. More combat troops must also be found, from Scotland, Ireland, and the little German principalities.

Germain also knew that for the past two months, the king had been intimately involved in planning another expedition—to the southern colonies, where Scottish émigrés in North Carolina were "said to be well inclined" to the Crown. Within three days of taking office, Germain had adopted this adventure as his own. On the king's command, seven infantry regiments were to embark in Cork on December 1, with orders "to assist in the suppression of the rebellion." By late November, His Majesty was informed that Howe and the southern governors had been given authority to raise loyalist troops who would receive British arms and be paid as much as regulars. A commodore, the capable Sir Peter Parker, would escort the expedition to the southern colonies with nine warships and fifteen hundred crewmen. The Admiralty ordered *Hawke* to Cape Fear on the North Carolina coast to recruit local pilots—with press warrants, if necessary—and to scout for landing sites.

All this was to be "a profound secret," although, as usual, American agents in London learned of the plan immediately. An assault on the southern colonies would hardly come as a surprise. A recent proposal in the Commons—rejected for the moment—called for sending British regiments to foment slave uprisings, and Governor Dunmore in Virginia had declared that "it is my fixed purpose to arm all my own Negroes and receive all others that will come to me whom I shall declare free."

Zeal, indeed, would be a hallmark of George Germain's ministry. More aggressive than his generals, he intended to send them even more reinforcements than they had requested. Howe, facing a grim winter in Boston, praised "the decisive and masterly strokes . . . effected since your lordship has assumed the conduct of this war." The American secretary's moxie was so striking that even the opposition *Evening Post* predicted he would rise still further in his remarkable rebound to eventually become prime minister. The king was said to be pleased.

Yet amid the green baize desks and the exquisite wall maps in White-hall, certain truths about the American war remained elusive. Neither Germain nor anyone else in government had carefully analyzed whether Britain's troop transports, storeships, men-of-war, and other maritime resources could support an ambitious campaign that now included ancillary assaults in the far south and the far north. Little coordination was imposed on one commander in chief in Canada or another in Boston, or with their naval counterparts. Subordinate generals were permitted, even encouraged, to offer their views directly to policy makers in London. Swayed by loyalist exiles and vindictive Crown officials in the colonies, king and cabinet continued to overestimate the breadth and depth of loyal support. No coherent plan obtained to woo the tens of thousands who straddled the fence in America, or to protect those who rejected insurrection but risked severe retaliation from the rebels.

Finally, Germain, like the best of kings he served, could neither grasp the coherence and appeal of revolutionary ideals, nor comprehend the historical headwinds against which Britain now tacked. The American secretary's lack of "genius sufficient for works of mere imagination" had been acknowledged ironically; that irony would haunt the rest of his days. For now, in a private letter to Howe, he praised the "cordiality & harmony which subsists between you, Clinton, & Burgoyne." He added:

> We want some good news to encourage us to go with the immense expense attending this war. . . . The providing [of] armies at such a distance is a most difficult undertaking. I do the best I can, and then we must trust to Providence for success.

7.

They Fought, Bled, and Died
Like Englishmen

John Murray, the fourth Earl of Dunmore and the royal governor of Virginia, had few rivals as the most detested British official in North America. Now forty-five, he was a short, pugnacious Scot whose father had been arrested for treason in the 1745 Jacobite rising. Young John subsequently chose to serve the English Crown as a soldier and was permitted to inherit the title after his father's death in 1756. His estates in Perthshire provided £3,000 annually, but the fourth earl had accumulated both eleven children and expensive tastes. He hired the eminent artist Joshua Reynolds to paint his portrait, in tam-o'-shanter and highland tartans; he also built a summer house with an enormous stone cupola shaped like a pineapple, later derided as "the most bizarre building in Scotland." Finding himself in financial straits, Dunmore sought to enlarge his fortune abroad. Appointed governor of New York in 1770, he had no sooner arrived than London reassigned him to Virginia, a disappointment that sent him stumbling through Manhattan streets in a drunken rage, roaring, "Damn Virginia . . . I'd asked for New York." One loyalist reflected, "Was there ever such a blockhead?"

Virginians later caricatured Dunmore as an inebriated, arrogant philanderer, but he brought to Williamsburg one of America's largest libraries, an art collection, and assorted musical instruments as evidence of his refinement. He also brought an unquenchable appetite for land, claiming vast tracts between Lake Champlain and what would become Indiana. His popularity surged briefly in 1774 after he launched a punitive military expedition against Shawnee Indians inconvenient to white Virginians who also coveted western acreage. But revolutionary upheaval soon unhorsed him.

Ever since John Rolfe, husband of a young Indian woman named Pocahontas—renamed Rebecca after her conversion to Christianity—learned to cure native tobacco in the early seventeenth century, the crop had dominated Virginia's economy. The thirty-five thousand tons exported annually from the colony by the early 1770s had brought wealth but also more than £1 million in debt, nearly equal to that of the other colonies combined and often incurred by Tidewater planters living beyond their means. Agents for Glasgow and London merchant houses now controlled most of the tobacco yield. Resentment against British imperial constrictions combined with other colonial grievances, and was compounded by anxiety over the loss of local autonomy. Rebel leaders persuaded Virginians that rebellion "would enhance their opportunities and status," the historian Alan Taylor later wrote, while also safeguarding political liberties threatened by an overbearing mother country. Planter aristocrats—like the Washingtons, Lees, and Randolphs—helped lead the uprising, but only by common consent. Moreover, evangelical churches, notably the Baptists and Methodists, were promised elevated standing "by disestablishing the elitist Anglican Church" favored by Crown loyalists.

When, in May 1774, Dunmore dissolved the fractious Virginia assembly, the House of Burgesses, delegates simply moved down the street from the capitol to reconvene in the Apollo Room of the Raleigh Tavern, subsequently forming the Virginia Convention to oversee colonial affairs. Anger deepened; resistance grew general. The colony became a leader in boycotting British goods and in summoning the Continental Congress to Philadelphia. Courts closed. Militia companies drilled. The *Virginia Gazette* published the names of loyalists considered hostile to liberty; some were ordered into western exile or to face the confiscation of their estates. "Lower-class men who did not own property saw the break from Britain as a chance to gain land and become slaveholders," the historian Michael Kranish would write.

Baffled by Virginians' "blind and unreasoning fury," Dunmore brooded in his palace. He peppered London with complaints and with unreliable appraisals of colonial politics, receiving little guidance in return. In April 1775, even before learning of events in Lexington and Concord, he ordered a marine detachment to confiscate gunpowder from the public magazine in Williamsburg on grounds that "the Negroes might have seized upon it." Rebel drums beat and militia "shirtmen"—so named for their distinctive hunting garb—threatened "to seize upon or massacre me," he told Whitehall. After reimbursing the rebels £330 for the powder he had impounded, in early June he fled with his family in the dark of night for refuge first aboard the *Magdalen*, then on the *Fowey*, and eventually on the *Eilbeck*, an unrigged merchant tub he renamed for himself. With his wife and children dispatched to Britain, Dunmore's dominion was reduced to a gaggle of loyalist merchants, clerks, and scrofulous sailors. Still, with just a few hundred more troops, he wrote London in August, "I could reduce the colony to submission."

The *Gazette* would accuse him of "crimes that would even have disgraced the noted pirate Blackbeard." Most of his felonies involved what were derided as "chicken-stealing expeditions" against coastal plantations, although he also impounded a Norfolk printing press from a seditious publisher who dared suggest that Catholic blood ran through Dunmore's veins.

But then the earl decided to become an emancipator.

Roughly five hundred thousand Americans were black, some 20 percent of the population, and nine in ten of those blacks were slaves. In southern colonies, the proportion of blacks to whites was much higher: 40 percent of Virginia's half million people were of African descent—often from cultures with military traditions—and white fear of slave revolts was a prominent reason for keeping colonial militias in fighting trim. Many white masters were reluctant to allow missionaries to convert their chattel for fear that radical Christian notions would make them even less docile. Political turmoil in America gave some slaves hope, and for months runaway blacks had sought protection from the regulars in a belief that British views on slavery differed markedly from those of southern planters.

In truth, although slavery had begun to disappear in England and Wales, Britain's colonial economy was built on a scaffold of bondage. Among many examples, the almost two hundred thousand slaves in Jamaica outnumbered whites fifteen to one, and an uprising in 1760 had been suppressed by shooting several hundred blacks. The slave trade, carried largely in British ships, had never been more prosperous than in the years just before the American rebellion, and Britain would remain the world's foremost slave-trading nation into the nineteenth century.

Dunmore's initial muttering to London in the early summer about emancipation was largely a bluff. He recognized that bound labor was critical to the white commonwealth he governed. The king's government was unenthusiastic about wrecking colonial economies or encouraging slave revolts that might infect the West Indies. But by mid-fall Dunmore was desperate to regain the initiative in Virginia. Reinforced with a few dozen 14th Foot soldiers who'd arrived from St. Augustine, he launched several aggressive Tidewater raids, capturing or destroying seventy-seven rebel guns "without the smallest opposition," as a British captain wrote General Howe on November 1, "which is proof that it would not require a very large force to subdue this colony." Raising the king's standard—unable to find British national colors, Dunmore settled for a regimental banner—he administered loyalty oaths to those who pinned on strips of red cloth as a badge of "true allegiance to his sacred Majesty George III." The price of red fabric rose in Norfolk stores, reflecting demand.

On November 7, using his confiscated printing press, Dunmore declared martial law and issued a proclamation: "I do hereby further declare all indented servants, Negroes, or others (appertaining to rebels) free, that are able and willing to bear arms, they joining His Majesty's troops as soon as may be." Liberation applied only to the able-bodied slaves of his foes. There would be no deliverance for his own fifty-seven slaves—abandoned in Williamsburg when he fled and for whom he would claim compensation from the government—nor would loyalists' chattel be freed. The governor intended to crush a rebellion, not reconfigure the social order.

Still, eager blacks found their way into his ranks. Fitted by the British with linen or sail-canvas shirts, often with the motto "LIBERTY TO SLAVES" across their chests, runaways with names like Sampson, Pompey, and Glasgow were formed into an "Ethiopian Regiment," under white officers. Maryland patriots tried to bar correspondence with Virginia in a futile effort to prevent news of Dunmore's gambit from spreading north. A Philadelphian wrote, "The flame runs like wild fire through the slaves." British sailors in cutters raided riverside plantations in "Negro-catching" forays. On November 14, Dunmore personally led a detachment of Ethiopians, regulars, marines, and twenty Scottish clerks in a rout of Virginia shirtmen at Kemp's Landing, southeast of Norfolk. The Americans loosed a volley or two before fleeing, their leaders reportedly "whipping up their horses" except for those too drunk to ride.

The small victory was good for recruiting both white loyalists—Dunmore boasted that three thousand men had joined him—and black runaways, who, he reported, "are flocking in." The governor triumphantly marched into Norfolk on November 23. Many Tidewater loyalists publicly revealed their sympathies, and some avowed patriots retreated to the safer ground of neutrality. "This pink-cheeked time-server," as the historian Simon Schama called Dunmore, "had become the patriarch of a great black exodus." Thomas Jefferson would later claim that from Virginia alone tens of thousands of slaves escaped servitude during the war, a number likely inflated but suggestive of white anxiety.

"With our little corps I think we have done wonders," Dunmore wrote Howe on November 30. "Had I but a few more men here, I would immediately march to Williamsburg . . . by which I should soon compel the whole colony to submit." Norfolk possessed a fine harbor that "could supply your army and navy with every necessary of life," if properly protected. His senior naval officer added in a dispatch from the *Otter* on December 2 that the Americans, "from their being such cowards and cold weather coming on," were expected to remain quiet through the winter.

That was unlikely. Dunmore had miscalculated: rather than cowing white southerners and pressuring slave owners to remain loyal, he would unify Virginians as never before. An American letter written on December 6 and subsequently published in a London newspaper captured the prevailing sentiment: "Hell itself could not have vomited anything more black than his design of emancipating our slaves."

The proclamation backfired throughout the South, even though many runaways from Georgia to Mount Vernon eventually made their way to coastal waters wherever British men-of-war appeared. Rumors spread that slaves who murdered their masters would be entitled to their estates. The lawyer Patrick Henry, whose recent demand "Give me liberty or give me death" clearly did not countenance "black banditti," circulated copies of Dunmore's announcement in order to inflame white slave owners. For many, a war about political rights now became an existential struggle to prevent the social fabric from unraveling. Even Piedmont yeomen whose slave holdings were limited to renting a field hand or two took offense. Edward Rutledge, a prominent South Carolina politician, wrote in December that arming freed slaves tended "more effectually to work an eternal separation between Great Britain and the colonies than any other expedient which could possibly have been thought of."

The *Virginia Gazette* urged slaves to "obey your masters . . . and expect a better condition in the next world." Another, more sinister article warned, "Whether we suffer or not, if you desert us, you most certainly will." A British official in Annapolis wrote, "This measure of emancipating the Negroes has excited a universal ferment, and will, I apprehend, greatly strengthen the general confederacy." "Devil Dunmore" was vilified as "that ignoramus Negro-thief." Had the British "searched through the world for a person the best fitted to ruin their cause," wrote Richard Henry Lee, "they could not have found a more complete agent than Lord Dunmore."

No slave master was more incensed than General Washington. "That arch traitor to the rights of humanity, Lord Dunmore, should be instantly crushed, if it takes the force of the whole colony to do it," he wrote. In another outburst from Cambridge, Washington told Lee, "Nothing less than depriving him of life or liberty will secure peace in Virginia." Otherwise, the governor "will become the most formidable enemy America has."

A chance to confront the "Negro-thief" soon occurred twelve miles south of Norfolk at Great Bridge, on the rutted road from Carolina. Here

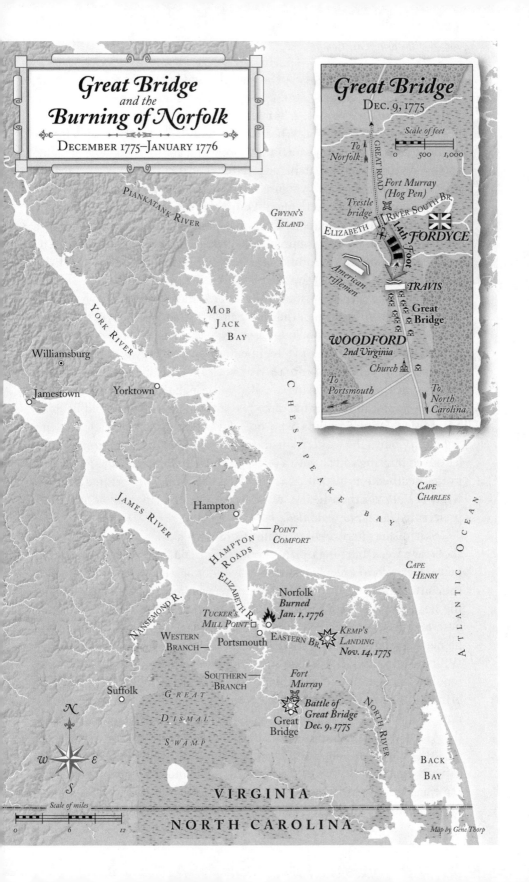

Great Bridge
and the
Burning of Norfolk
DECEMBER 1775–JANUARY 1776

Great Bridge
DEC. 9, 1775

Scale of feet

0   500   1,000

To Norfolk

GREAT ROAD

Fort Murray (Hog Pen)

Trestle bridge

ELIZABETH RIVER SOUTH BR.

14th Foot

FORDYCE

American riflemen

TRAVIS

Great Bridge

WOODFORD
2nd Virginia

Church

To Portsmouth

To North Carolina

PIANKATANK RIVER

GWYNN'S ISLAND

MOB JACK BAY

YORK RIVER

Williamsburg

Jamestown

Yorktown

C H E S A P E A K E   B A Y

CAPE CHARLES

JAMES RIVER

Hampton

POINT COMFORT

HAMPTON ROADS

CAPE HENRY

ELIZABETH R.

A T L A N T I C   O C E A N

NANSEMOND R.

TUCKER'S MILL POINT

Norfolk
Burned Jan. 1, 1776

WESTERN BRANCH

Portsmouth

EASTERN BR.

KEMP'S LANDING
Nov. 14, 1775

SOUTHERN BRANCH

Suffolk

G R E A T

Fort Murray

Battle of Great Bridge
Dec. 9, 1775

Great Bridge

NORTH RIVER

D I S M A L

S W A M P

N

W   E

S

BACK BAY

Scale of miles

0   6   12

VIRGINIA

NORTH CAROLINA

Map by Gene Thorp

two-wheeled carts brought cypress shingles and barreled turpentine from the Great Dismal Swamp, and drovers guided their flocks and herds to Tidewater slaughterhouses. A hamlet of twenty structures dominated by a church stood near the south branch of the Elizabeth River, which was spanned by a trestle bridge forty yards long and approached by long plank causeways through the marshlands. "Nine-tenths of the people are Tories," one Virginian reported, "who are the poorest, miserable wretches I ever saw." Just north of this settlement, Dunmore, exhbiting what a later commentator called "his characteristic unwisdom," had built an earthen fort with two 4-pounders to command the bridge and a wooden stockade to house a garrison of a hundred regulars and Ethiopians. He named the fort for himself, but rebel shirtmen called it the Hog Pen.

By Friday, December 8, more than seven hundred militiamen had gathered a quarter mile south of the Hog Pen. A zigzag breastwork, seven feet high with fire steps and gun loopholes, served as their redoubt. Their numbers included the 2nd Virginia Regiment, commanded by Colonel William Woodford, a French and Indian War veteran. A Culpeper minute company carried a flag displaying a coiled rattlesnake and the motto "DON'T TREAD ON ME"; in their ranks marched a rangy, twenty-year-old lieutenant named John Marshall, who one day would be chief justice of the Supreme Court. The western riflemen typically wore deerskin trousers and leaf-dyed hunting shirts, with a buck's tail affixed to the hat and a scalping knife sheathed on the belt. Many had "*liberty or death*" printed in large white script over their hearts, although one young rifleman admitted to preferring "*liberty or wounded*."

Skirmishers and raiding parties from both sides had exchanged potshots for a week, burning isolated houses to discourage snipers. Some rebel officers wanted to execute captured slaves but agreed to leave their fate to the convention in Williamsburg. Dunmore, who remained aboard his floating headquarters near Norfolk, may have been duped by an American deserter who claimed that the rebels had fewer than three hundred men; he may also have learned, correctly, that more rebels were en route from Williamsburg and North Carolina. The governor dispatched additional regulars to Great Bridge, along with British sailors and loyalist volunteers, bringing the force there to perhaps four hundred. With more impetuous unwisdom, he also ordered the garrison to leave the secure fort and attack the American fortifications before they could be reinforced.

At first light on Saturday, December 9, reveille drums woke the American camp only to be answered with a snicker of musketry from the northern causeway approaching the bridge. The firing at first seemed like "our usual sport—an exchange of a few morning guns," one Virginian wrote.

But moments later Colonel Woodford's adjutant called, "Boys, stand to your arms!" Bullets whistled overhead, and sentries spotted redcoats replacing planks missing from the bridge stringers. British gunners muscled the two 4-pounders from inside the fort and lobbed several rounds toward the American lines. The damp morning thickened with shouts and smoke and the booming cannonade. Lieutenant Edward Travis led an American skirmish line of eighty militiamen to the breastwork, 160 yards below the bridge, while Woodford deployed his main force around the church a quarter mile to the south.

Through smoke and morning haze, grenadiers abruptly appeared on the causeway, six abreast in bearskin caps and red coats with buff facings. With bayonets glinting and two drums beating time, they tramped in parade order across the bridge, shoes clapping the wooden planks. At the head of the column was a tall, homely captain named Charles Fordyce, who had written a friend a week earlier that "a couple of thousand men would settle everything here in the course of this winter." On this morning, at this place, Captain Fordyce had not a couple thousand but 120 regulars, trailed at a safe distance by a scruffy battalion of marines, sailors, volunteers, and liberty-to-slaves Ethiopians. Within fifty yards of the breastwork, Fordyce waved his hat in a gesture of encouragement and was heard to cry, "The day is our own!"

Those were his last coherent words. On order, Travis's men rose up from behind their barricade, took aim, and fired. Lead and flame leaped from the top of the parapet to gall the British column. Fordyce fell with a bullet in the knee. Blotting at the wound with a handkerchief pulled from his cuff, he rose, hobbled forward, and fell again, a few paces from the rebel barrier; fourteen bullets would be counted in his corpse. More gunshots came from the American left, where Culpeper riflemen, Lieutenant Marshall among them, had flanked the bridge along a marsh hummock and now enfiladed the enemy column with cross fire. Volley upon volley blistered the grenadier ranks. "For God's sake," a voice shrieked, "do not murder us!"

The rear guard turned and pelted for the fort. Gunners spiked their 4-pounders by hammering nails into the touchholes; then they ran, too. Grenadiers dragged wounded comrades across the bridge, glancing over their shoulders; shirtmen were said to favor scalping. "We retreated with much fewer brave fellows than we took out," a midshipman from the *Otter* later wrote. Breathless bodies lay scattered before the breastwork like bloody throw rugs. "They fought, bled, and died like Englishmen," reported Captain Richard Kidder Meade of the 2nd Virginia. "Ten and twelve bullets through many. Limbs broke in two or three places. Brains turning out. Good God, what a sight!" The entire action, from reveille to retreat, had lasted half an hour, "an absurd, ridiculous & unnecessary attack," a surviving British officer wrote home.

Thirty-three captured loyalists and reenslaved Ethiopians were handcuffed, black to white, for the march to Williamsburg jail cells. Woodford agreed to return the British dead and wounded under a truce flag. A list recorded the casualties by infirmity: "ball lodged in the leg, no fracture," or "ball lodged in the bowels, judged mortal." One corporal was reportedly still alive despite seventeen wounds. American losses amounted to one man nicked in the finger.

That night at seven p.m., after loading the wounded into wagons and carts, the British garrison crept from the fort and trudged toward Norfolk, five hours north. On Sunday morning, shirtmen found the Hog Pen empty but for a few axes, twenty-nine spades, eleven pairs of shoes, a pair of snuff boxes, and dead grenadiers, now stiff and stripped of their coats and waistcoats. Dunmore's report to London would list seventeen killed and forty-nine wounded, but that excluded blacks and loyalists, who brought the total casualties to more than a hundred.

"His Lordship," one British officer wrote, "has much to answer for."

Norfolk might be a "dirty little borough," in Governor Dunmore's description, but it was Virginia's major port as well as the colony's biggest town, with six thousand residents. Fine houses owned by ship captains and tobacco factors faced the waterfront, and brick warehouses crowded the wharves. Waters converged here: the James and Elizabeth Rivers, the Chesapeake Bay, and, beyond Capes Henry and Charles, the briny deep. Before the war strangled much of the colony's trade, rum, sugar, and European finery—linens, chafing dishes, pewter porringers—were hoisted from the holds of arriving ships, which then were loaded with timber, wheat, salt pork, and countless hogsheads of sweet-scented tobacco. Sailmakers patched canvas shredded in rough crossings, and lighters with bubbling kettles of tar glided through the shallows, carrying carpenters hired to repair leaky merchantmen. An annual fair in Market Square featured bull-baiting and a contest to see who could snatch a gold-laced cap from a greased pole. Fine fiddling might be heard at dances in Masons Hall. The town was despised by many Virginians as a haven for British mercantilists and their Tory collaborators. Yet in better days, Norfolk had flourished.

Those days were gone, and the town's worst days had now arrived. Upon hearing of the defeat at Great Bridge, Dunmore raved incoherently, threatening to hang the boy who brought the news. The bedraggled column of survivors shuffled through Norfolk's cobblestoned streets in the small hours of Sunday morning, December 10. The wounded pleaded for water, and women with pitchers moved among them as the uninjured regulars and Ethiopians marched to the docks to be rowed out to half a dozen ships; Dunmore believed the town indefensible. Some loyalist families soon followed, clutching a few treasured possessions, but much of the population, foreseeing trouble, fled inland or up Tidewater creeks. Men dashed about trying to hire horses and wagons, or at least drays and wheelbarrows. House slaves piled beds, mahogany tables, chairs, and a bit of salt meat onto each conveyance, and off they went, to Portsmouth, or Suffolk, or even the Carolinas, abandoning those handsome homes on Church and Talbot Streets. To bolster their spirits, some could be heard singing as they hurried down Princess Anne Road.

The rebel force, swollen to almost thirteen hundred, had moved toward Norfolk. Woodford yielded command to Colonel Robert Howe, a more senior officer who had brought reinforcements from North Carolina. By Thursday, December 14, the rebels occupied the town, sniping at British vessels and arresting a hundred suspected loyalists for interrogation in Williamsburg. "We have taken up some of the Tories and coupled them to a Negro with handcuffs," one officer reported. "The most stupid kind we discharge."

Dunmore was also reinforced with the arrival, on December 21, of the *Liverpool* after a miserable fourteen-week passage from Britain that had reduced the twenty-eight-gun frigate to a single cask of fetid water. Scurvy plagued the ship and her companion, the ordnance brig *Maria*. But when *Liverpool*'s captain, Henry Bellew, demanded fresh provisions for his crews, rebel riflemen replied with more gunfire. American sentries paraded along the waterfront, yelled taunts from the docks, and seized a brig loaded with salt, the price of which had soared from one shilling per bushel to fifteen. "They have nothing more at heart than the utter destruction of this once most flourishing country," Dunmore wrote London.

By December 31, both the year and British patience had expired. Captain Bellew sent Colonel Howe an odd ultimatum: that "you will cause your sentinels in the town of Norfolk to avoid being seen." American gibes persisted—"every mark of insult," Bellew complained, including insolent sentries walking with "their hats fixed on their bayonets" for sure visibility from his quarterdeck. Bellew moored *Kingfisher*, *Otter*, and *Liverpool*, the three largest men-of-war, with their gun ports broadside to the waterfront. Jack pendants flew from the bowsprits to distinguish these vessels from merchantmen. Dunmore warned civilians loitering in Norfolk to get out.

After a minatory rattle of drums, *Liverpool* fired the first three cannonballs, at three p.m. on Monday, January 1, demolishing a wharf shack used for a guardhouse. Within moments more than a hundred guns lacerated the town, pummeling the warehouses and dockyards in an effort to chivy snipers from their nests. Dirty smoke draped the anchorage as boatloads of British troops rowed ashore to set more fires. Storerooms of pitch and turpentine blazed up, igniting large houses and humble shanties alike. By ten p.m. a crimson glow hung like a halo over the waterfront. "The wind favored their design," Colonels Howe and Woodford wrote in a joint dispatch to authorities in Williamsburg, "and we believe the flames will become general." In a separate note, Howe described "women and children running through a crowd of shot to get out of town. . . . A few have, I hear, been killed. Does it not call for vengeance, both from God and man?" A British midshipman wrote in the early hours of January 2, "The town is still burning, as it will be for three or four days."

That was quite true, for vengeful shirtmen had picked up where British incendiaries left off, burning, looting, and filling their canteens with alcohol pinched from grogshops. "Keep up the jig" became a rallying cry for those determined to punish a Tory town and blame it on the enemy. A witness reported militiamen "drinking rum and crying out, 'Let us make hay while the sun shines.'" Unrestrained by their officers—Howe and Woodford had been disingenuous, if not dishonest, in blaming only the British for the conflagration—they plundered warehouses and residences, selling booty on the streets. A young soldier in Hampton wrote his mother, "At night the fire was so great the clouds above the town appeared as red and bright as they do in an evening at sun setting."

At length the flames subsided. Colonel Howe reported that Norfolk "is in a very ruinous condition." But vengeance had not yet run its course. Paraphrasing the Roman war cry that baneful Carthage must be destroyed, Thomas Jefferson had declared, *"Delenda est Norfolk."* The Virginia Convention agreed and "ordered the remains of Norfolk to be burnt," a major told his wife. "We expect to see the blaze soon." Officers banged on doors, ordering all remaining residents within a mile of the water to evacuate. Shirtmen soon rampaged through the town again, setting blazes to structures still standing on Bermuda, Catherine, and Church Streets.

"The detested town of Norfolk is no more!" a midshipman wrote. The "dirty little borough," now reduced to ash and skeletal chimneys, had suffered greater damage than would befall any town in America during the Revolution. An investigative commission the following year found that of 1,331 structures destroyed in and near Norfolk, the British had demolished 32 before evacuating the town, then burned 19 more during the January 1 bombardment. Militia troops burned 863 in early January, and another 416 in the subsequent razing ordered by the convention. But that accounting remained secret for sixty years and then was buried in a legislative journal that stayed hidden for another century, as the historian John E. Selby would note. Blaming the redcoats for wanton destruction was convenient, and like ruined Falmouth in Maine or Charlestown in Massachusetts, Norfolk became a vivid emblem of British cruelty.

"Never can true reconcilement grow," the *Virginia Gazette* declared, "where wounds of deadly hate have pierced so deep." The war had become both brutal and continental, from Montreal to southern Virginia, and would grow nastier and spread farther. Dunmore's actions drew Virginia into the insurrection full-bore: in mid-January the Virginia Convention enlarged the two existing militia regiments and then created seven more, most of them commanded by officers who had served with Washington during the French war. All nine Virginia regiments would be mustered into the new Continental Army, which Washington was forming into a national force outside Boston, as ordered by Congress. The convention, in an act of independence, also declared Virginia ports open for trade to any nation except Britain, Ireland, and the British West Indies.

Virginians got on with hunting their runaways. A notice in the *Gazette* offered a reward for "a servant boy named Bartholomew Archibald, about 18 years of age, about 5 feet 6 inches high, of a dark complexion, pitted with smallpox, very slim made. . . . I am apt to think he will pass for a free man." Captured "renegadoes" who had served Dunmore were publicly flogged, occasionally after having an ear severed. Some were sold to sugar plantations in the West Indies or sent to work the lead mines in Fincastle County, digging ore for rebel bullets. One account reported that some blacks caught bearing arms for the British had their severed heads impaled on poles at crossroads. Owners were compensated for their losses.

By triggering Norfolk's immolation, Dunmore had ruined his friends and deprived himself of sanctuary. American contempt for the governor only intensified. He was accused in the press of keeping two enslaved girls as "bedmakers," and it was said that he had "barreled up some dead bodies of the smallpox and sent them on shore" to spread disease. Banished from both Williamsburg and Norfolk, he took refuge with a hodgepodge cluster of ninety vessels at Tucker's Mill Point, a malarial spit on the west bank of the Elizabeth River. A six-foot breastwork and a ditch three hundred yards long protected a four-acre encampment where several wells were sunk for fresh water.

But rebel riflemen lurked on the perimeter, and jail fever—typhus— spread through both the Royal Navy crews and the refugees trapped in what was derisively called the "King's Four Acres." Grave mounds began to sprout on the riverbank, first a few, then a few score, and eventually a few hundred, half of them reportedly belonging to freed slaves. Moreover, Dunmore reported, "there was not a ship in the fleet that did not throw one, two, or three or more dead overboard every night." *Otter* became a virtual ghost ship. Dunmore sent armed boats to forage for food along the coast with little success, even as additional runaways slipped into the camp each day. Bread and salt meat supplies began to dwindle, sickness grew epidemic, and soon enough, the governor knew, he would have to lead his wandering tribe elsewhere.

Dunmore poured out his troubles in an endless letter to London. "I wish to God it had been possible to have spared some troops for this colony," he wrote. "I am now morally certain had I had 500 men here six weeks ago . . . [the rebels] would not have been able to raise any number that could possibly have opposed my march to any part of the colony." Instead, the fate befallen the proud royal colony of Virginia "is a mortification."

"God only knows," he added, "what I have suffered."

8.

The Paths of Glory

A lowering sky the color of slag hung over Pointe-aux-Trembles at ten a.m. on Sunday, December 3. Although it was cold enough to split stone, as the *habitants* said, the sight of canvas sails gliding down the St. Lawrence brought Colonel Benedict Arnold and his troops tromping through foot-deep snow from their flint cobble farmhouses to the river's edge. The brig *Gaspé*, the schooner *Mary*, and several smaller vessels—all seized from the British as they'd tried to flee Montreal a fortnight earlier—rounded a point on the north bank, nosing through patches of ice, then hove to and dropped their anchors. Cheers echoed through the aspens as a skiff from the little flotilla scraped onto the beach and Brigadier General Richard Montgomery stepped ashore, ready to complete the conquest of Quebec.

Three hundred soldiers came with him, mostly New Yorkers in captured British uniforms. They brought the combined American invasion force to just under a thousand, half the number Arnold had estimated would be needed to overwhelm Fortress Quebec. Many of Montgomery's New Englanders, including the Green Mountain Boys, had bolted south after Montreal's surrender. "They have such an intemperate desire to return home," General Schuyler told Congress in a note from Ticonderoga, "that nothing can equal it." If short of manpower, Montgomery brought ample munitions and winter garb confiscated from enemy stocks: cannons and mortars; sealskin moccasins, red cloth caps trimmed in fur, and underjackets with corduroy sleeves; full-skirted, hooded white overcoats; and more new uniforms from Britain that had been intended for the 26th and 7th Regiments. Forty more barrels of gunpowder—two tons—would shortly follow from Montreal.

Later that afternoon, Arnold's men paraded before the St. Nicholas chapel, their new moccasins stuffed with hay for extra warmth. Arnold had led them to Canada, but Montgomery would lead them home, eventually, and they took his measure as he took theirs. "He is a gentle, polite man, tall and slender in his make, bald on top of his head," wrote one lieutenant. A rifleman thought him "well-limbed, tall and handsome, though his face was much pockmarked." He "made us a short but energetic and elegant speech," a private added, praising the soldiers' fortitude in the Maine wilderness under the intrepid Arnold, whom Montgomery deemed "active, intelligent, and enterprising." The men offered "a few huzzahs from our freezing bodies" and dispersed to find a blazing hearth. "General Montgomery was born to command," a Pennsylvania rifleman concluded. "His recent successes give us the highest confidence in him."

Arnold had hired a fleet of brightly colored *habitant* sleighs, and on Monday many of the American officers trotted east for twenty miles in a serpentine column, the horses' bells jingling merrily until they reached the snow-entombed Plains of Abraham. Their companies followed on foot or in bateaux with the heavy baggage. Quebec City loomed in the distance, the white-clad spires, battlements, and pitched roofs glistening as though carved from crystal. As planned, Arnold swung north with a vanguard of riflemen to the suburb of St. Roch. His troops occupied buildings that stretched from the sprawling Intendant's Palace—within rifle shot of Quebec's battlements—to a convent and hospital along the St. Charles River, a tributary of the St. Lawrence. Soon after placing his headquarters in Menut's Tavern, a mile west of the city, Arnold scratched out a letter to Washington. He and Montgomery were "making all possible preparations to attack the city, which has a wretched motley garrison of disaffected seamen, marines & inhabitants, the walls in a ruinous situation, & cannot hold out long."

Montgomery had dispersed his New Yorkers across the Plains and placed his own headquarters in Holland House, a high-peaked French château on a hillock two miles southwest of Quebec's St. John Gate. "I wish it were well over with all my heart," he wrote Janet on December 5. "I shan't forget your beaver blanket if I get safe out of this affair, nor your mother's marten skins." In the same sitting he wrote a long dispatch to Schuyler. "The works of Quebec are extremely extensive, and very incapable of being defended," he declared. Yet laying siege to the town hardly seemed feasible, given the small American numbers and the lack of heavy guns; his biggest cannons were 12-pounders, compared to several 32-pounders inside the fortress. Having concluded that a direct assault would be necessary, he envisioned a feint toward the Upper Town around the St. John and St. Louis Gates and a main assault on the Lower Town, fronting the St. Lawrence. Informers had revealed that Governor Carleton, after eluding capture on the river, "is now in town and puts on the show of defense." Montgomery continued:

> I shall be very sorry to be reduced to this mode of attack, because I know the melancholy consequences. But the approaching severe season, and the weakness of the garrison, together with the nature of the works, point it out too strong to be passed by. . . . Fortune often baffles the sanguine expectations of poor mortals. I am not intoxicated with the favors I have received at her hands, but I do think there is a fair prospect of success.

Arnold and his men were impressive, he added. They evinced "a style of discipline among them much superior to what I have been used to seeing this campaign." Still, "I would not wish to see less than ten thousand men ordered here" from the colonies to hold Quebec once the town was captured, since Britain no doubt would send reinforcements in the spring to take it back. In closing he wrote, "The Canadians will be our friends as long as we are able to maintain our ground, but they must not be depended on."

Even as he refined his "storming plan," Montgomery held a wan hope that bombarding Quebec with "fire pills," as his men called their cannonballs, might provoke Carleton into giving battle on open ground outside the walls. In 1759, the illustrious general James Wolfe had considered eight different attack plans here before successfully luring General Louis-Joseph de Montcalm and his French army onto the Plains of Abraham. There, in fifteen minutes on September 13, with what one admiring British historian called "the most perfect volley ever fired on the battlefield," the regulars blew apart Montcalm, his legions, and Versailles's claim to New France.

But Montgomery also knew that Carleton had served in that campaign as Wolfe's quartermaster. The governor was undoubtedly aware that British security this winter lay within Quebec's fortifications, however imperfect. Montcalm had faced starvation in 1759, while Carleton's larders were now full; Wolfe's artillery that summer had wrecked much of the Lower Town with an estimated forty thousand cannonballs, far more than the paltry stock of "fire pills" available to American gunners. Moreover, the French commander had been provoked into attacking because the British were waging a savage war of terror in Quebec against what Wolfe called "Canadian vermin"—razing mills, churches, barns, and an estimated fourteen hundred farmhouses. Their depredations included rape, plunder, scalped *habitants*, and murdered prisoners. "It is war of the worst shape," a British officer had written his wife. Sixteen years later, American invaders could hardly carry out such a campaign and hope to win Canadian fealty. "Wolfe's success was a lucky hit, or rather a series of hits," Montgomery told his father-in-law in a letter. "All sober and scientific calculation was against him."

In an effort to undermine enemy morale, the Americans now allowed peasants to pass into Quebec City with exaggerated reports of a besieging force that exceeded four thousand. *Habitants* also reported that the *Bostonnais* seemed "insensible of cold" and were "musket-proof" because they were wearing armor—the French *toile* (linen) had somehow been perverted to *tôle* (sheet metal). In a direct attempt at intimidation, on Wednesday, December 6, Montgomery sent another lurid American ultimatum to the British garrison. "Should you persist in an unwarrantable defense, the consequences be on your head," he warned. If supplies were destroyed rather than surrendered, "by heavens, there will be no mercy."

The note was carried through the gate by an old woman, only to be tweezed by a drummer with fire tongs and tossed into the hearth, on Carleton's order. Copies tied to rebel arrows and fired over the wall met with similar disdain. A more direct answer came on Friday when Montgomery rode from Holland House to confer with Arnold at Menut's Tavern. Moments after he alighted and walked inside, British cannonballs smashed his parked sleigh and decapitated his horse.

No sooner had the Americans cinched the cordon around Quebec than disgruntlement crept into their ranks. Brutal cold and British cannonading proved dispiriting; the one-dollar bounty Montgomery paid each man hardly bought their sufferance for long. Soldiers afflicted with pleurisy, pneumonia, and other ailments filled the convent hospital on the St. Charles, three-quarters of a mile from the city walls.

"The men begin to be very much beat out and begin to declare that they will go home," the surveyor John Pierce told his diary on December 13. After an incessant barrage the following day and evening, he added, "At night we had one man killed. He belonged to the [artillery] train and was shot through his belly and had one of his arms shot off, and all his inwards lay on the platform." British 9-pounders riddled the cupola of the Intendant's Palace, flushing Arnold's snipers. Seven American soldiers were whipped for theft after plundering Canadian houses of food, heirlooms, cutlery, and mattresses. And, Pierce recorded, the huts used for barracks were infested with "lice, itch, jaundice, crabs, bedbugs, and [an] unknown sight of fleas."

None of these vexations compared to the calamity first noticed in the American regiments on December 6. "The smallpox is all around us," a private wrote, "and there is great danger of its spreading in the army." By December 9, rumors of the disease had even reached British ears inside Quebec. "The smallpox does havoc among them," Thomas Ainslie, a customs collector and militia captain, reported in his diary. "'Tis a deadly infection in Yankee veins."

Deadly indeed. An English writer later described smallpox as "the most terrible of all the ministers of death." Transmitted by human vectors rather than by insects or contaminated water, the variola virus typically caused influenza-like symptoms twelve days after exposure; three or four days later, the first sores erupted, often in the mouth and throat, before spreading to the palms, soles, face, torso, forearms, nostrils, and eyes. By the fourth week, mortality might range from 15 to 60 percent. Survivors—like Washington and Montgomery—were scarred for life and sometimes blinded, though perpetually immune; pocked young men were much prized by military recruiters.

Smallpox ravaged Alexander the Great's army in India in 327 B.C. and eventually became endemic in Europe, killing four hundred thousand Europeans annually by the eighteenth century. In addition to countless low-born victims, royal fatalities included Peter II of Russia, Louis I of Spain, and Louis XV of France. Transmitted by Portuguese and Spanish conquistadors to the New World, "the speckled monster" contributed to the collapse of the Aztec and Inca Empires, while decimating other indigenous tribes. The standard treatments of bleeding and purging were ineffective, as were such exotic regimens as opening the pustules with a golden needle, painting a victim's room red to expel bad humors, and drinking concoctions made from horse manure or jackass fat.

Vaccination using cowpox to tame the disease would not be adopted until the end of the eighteenth century, but inoculation had been practiced for centuries in Asia and Africa, and in 1672 it was introduced to Europe from Persia via Istanbul. Pus swabbed from a smallpox sore was deliberately introduced into an open incision on a healthy patient's arm or thigh. The consequent eruption usually was milder and far less lethal than "natural" infection, although the procedure was risky and could trigger fresh epidemics if those newly inoculated were not isolated. After successful experiments on prisoners and orphans, the British Army inoculated many troops during the Seven Years' War; the disease, if hardly eradicated, rarely became epidemic among the regulars. Frederick the Great likewise inoculated his Prussian legions. First introduced in America during the Boston smallpox epidemic of 1721, the practice of inoculation was legally restricted in New England because of medical uncertainties and a theological conviction, as the historian Elizabeth A. Fenn would write, that it displayed "a distrust of God's overruling care." Few New Englanders had acquired immunity, and colonists elsewhere often could not afford the £3 to £5 cost of inoculation.

Insurrection in America coincided with a smallpox epidemic that would claim more than a hundred thousand lives across the continent from 1775 to 1782. When the disease appeared in the camps outside Quebec, suspicion immediately fell on Carleton. British commanders at Fort Pitt in 1763 had allegedly approved sending blankets from a smallpox hospital to marauding Indians, so urging infected *habitants* to wander into American lines seemed plausible. One Pennsylvanian serving with Arnold would claim that "the smallpox, introduced into our cantonments by the indecorous, yet fascinating arts of the enemy, had already begun its ravages." Upon getting reports from Canada, Jefferson later alleged that "this disorder was sent into our army designedly by the commanding officer in Quebec." Perhaps more likely was the incidental exposure of Arnold's men upon reaching the St. Lawrence in mid-November. The disease was endemic in Montreal and Quebec.

Regardless of the cause, by late December smallpox was spreading among the Americans at an alarming rate. Arnold's surgeon, Isaac Senter, was an inexperienced twenty-two-year-old who had not finished his apprenticeship; his failure to immediately isolate all smallpox patients proved lamentable. Contrary to orders, some men secretly inoculated themselves, often using pus inserted with a pine needle under the fingernail or into a dirty incision hidden beneath sleeves or trousers. Although a smallpox ward was established three miles from the St. Charles hospital, the quarantine was fitfully enforced. Jeremiah Greenman of Rhode Island, still only seventeen, told his diary of the inevitable consequence: "Sum of our company dieth with ye smallpox."

A French writer once observed that "in the new colonies, the Spanish start by building a church, the English a tavern, and the French a fort." When the adventurer Samuel de Champlain dropped anchor on July 3, 1608, seven hundred miles up the St. Lawrence from the Atlantic Ocean at a place known to local Indians as *Kébec*—where the waters narrow—he promptly began fortifying the site to withstand a siege. Only eight of his original twenty-eight colonists remained alive the following spring, but more settlers arrived and a miniature European fortress soon took shape, with a palisade, a ditch, a drawbridge, and bastions mounting cannons.

Over the next 150 years, those defenses were expanded, demolished, allowed to deteriorate, then expanded again. Stone and masonry replaced

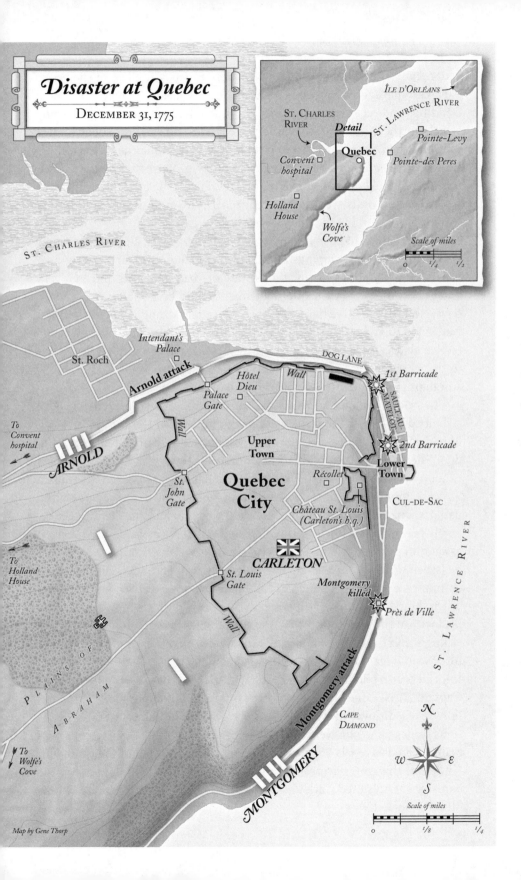

Disaster at Quebec
December 31, 1775

Detail

Île d'Orléans

St. Charles River

St. Lawrence River

Convent hospital

Quebec

Pointe-Levy

Pointe-des Peres

Holland House

Wolfe's Cove

Scale of miles

0 1/4 1/2

St. Charles River

Intendant's Palace

St. Roch

Dog Lane

1st Barricade

Arnold attack

Hôtel Dieu

Wall

Palace Gate

To Convent hospital

ARNOLD

Wall

Sault-au-Matelot

2nd Barricade

Upper Town

Récollet

Lower Town

St. John Gate

Quebec City

Cul-de-Sac

Château St. Louis (Carleton's h.q.)

To Holland House

CARLETON

St. Louis Gate

Montgomery killed

Près de Ville

Wall

St. Lawrence River

Plains of Abraham

Montgomery attack

Cape Diamond

To Wolfe's Cove

MONTGOMERY

N
W   E
S

Scale of miles

0 1/8 1/4

Map by Gene Thorp

cedar and dirt. Redoubts and ramparts were added, as well as an enormous barracks, magazines, and guns with interlocking fields of fire. Government buildings and ecclesiastical compounds lined the squares and meandering streets of the Upper Town, while warehouses, docks, and squat houses crowded the Lower Town, tucked under the cliffs along the river landing. From Cape Diamond—a massive promontory, glittering with quartz crystals, that loomed 330 feet above the St. Lawrence—the fortress revetments, palisades, and walls eventually extended in a two-mile arc around the city to a bluff overlooking the St. Charles.

Few repairs had been made in the past thirty years, and swallows now nested in the crumbling masonry. After the Conquest, a British engineer warned that Quebec's fortifications were of "bad materials and in a very bad condition"; a vigorous bombardment could breach the walls in two days. None of the three main gates was especially strong. Though the outer wall stood thirty to sixty feet high with six bastions, segments lacked a protective glacis and dry moat, permitting attackers to creep close. Ramparts to the west remained vulnerable to enfilading fire because the Plains of Abraham rose higher than even Cape Diamond.

In 1769, Carleton had requested construction of a true citadel to "give stability and permanency to the British dominion over this province." Plans were drafted and redrafted but little was done, despite urgent pleas to London. The defenses continued to deteriorate: gunners test-firing a garrison cannon in October triggered a rock slide that damaged a house in Champlain Street. A month later, the appearance of Arnold's crowbait invaders caused panic when sentries had trouble finding the keys to lock the St. John Gate.

If privately doubtful of the city's ability to withstand an American assault, in public Carleton evinced a calm, determined confidence. By day he issued orders from the copper-roofed Château St. Louis, with its seven chimneys, elegant porte-cochère, and rear balcony overlooking the Lower Town. At night he crossed the street to sleep fully uniformed in a command post within the secure Récollet monastery. Spies and deserters told him of sickness and dissension in enemy ranks; he hoped that much of Arnold's force would leave Canada on January 1, when their enlistments expired. Informers also told him of dissension within the walls—"Grumbletonians," Captain Ainslie called them. In short order, Carleton purged the town of "all useless, disloyal, and treacherous persons," including pacifists and seditious tradesmen, who were ordered to leave by December 1 "under pain of being treated as rebels or spies." A sullen band passed out of the gates with "little else than our necessary clothing," as one exile complained. But the banishment bolstered Carleton's authority. "Cabals then ceased," a British officer reported.

As Montgomery had suspected, the governor had no intention of being lured from his fortress. If the city could hold out for six months, until the ice on the St. Lawrence broke up in May, heavy reinforcements would most likely come from Britain. The town, which included thirty-two hundred women and children, was short of firewood and forage, and no substantial medical supplies had been sent from England in more than a decade. The recently arrived storeship *Elizabeth*, expected to bring artillery munitions, instead proved to be laden with twine and paper. But Quebec's store-rooms held almost 2,000 barrels of flour, 8,000 bushels of wheat, 33 tons of rice, and 406 firkins—11 tons—of butter. Also, in November the frigate *Lizard* had brought firelocks, clothing, and equipment for several thousand men, plus £20,000 in cash.

Carleton's eighteen hundred defenders were barely half the three thousand needed to properly defend Quebec's long walls. They included just over three hundred regulars plus three dozen marines. Hundreds of others remained unreliable, if not treacherous; many showed little martial aptitude despite marching about, as a witness complained, with "a highland piper making a most horrid noise with his bagpipes" by incessantly skirling "Lochaber No More." Recruits just arrived from Newfoundland were described as "Irish fishermen totally unacquainted with the use of arms." Undaunted, Carleton organized four brigades, with daily musket drills and cannoneering lessons from the fortress bombardier. Frenchmen willing to take up arms were offered a shilling and a pint of porter. Several hundred British sailors and merchant seamen agreed to form a Royal Navy battalion after their ships were hauled into Cul-de-Sac, adjacent to the Lower Town, and hove over against King's Wharf for the winter. Each new tar turned private received £3, a greatcoat with red cuffs, and a full landsman's uniform. Sailmakers were put to work sewing sandbags for the crumbling walls, and carpenters hired in the Canadian Maritimes built gun platforms and street barricades.

Perhaps most vital to Quebec's defense was the arrival of a pudding-faced, Hebridean brawler who quickly put starch into both the garrison and Governor Carleton. Lieutenant Colonel Allan Maclean, described by one admiring officer as "beloved, dreaded, and indefatigable," had fought at Culloden in the 1745 Jacobite rising, then fled to Holland until an amnesty allowed his return to Britain. Since then he had served the Crown faithfully on various European and Caribbean battlefields, as well as here, at Wolfe's side, in 1759. The king himself, the previous spring, had approved sending Maclean back to America to raise the Royal Highland Emigrants, a new regiment of loyal Scots, many of them veterans, who had settled in the New World. In November Maclean had slipped into Quebec with 220 of these men wearing scarlet jackets, dark tartan kilts, and raccoon-pelt sporrans, ready to defend Quebec in the fourth siege of the city's history. He, too, slept dressed for action in the Récollet monastery.

With each passing day, the defenses grew stouter. Thousands of spars were stripped from merchant ships or salvaged in lumberyards to build new blockhouses and loopholed palisades. Waterfront windows in the Lower Town were planked up or converted to gunports, and more barriers on Mountain Hill Street blocked access to the Upper Town from the river. Workmen attached lanterns to long poles above the bastions so that "even a dog could be distinguished in the great ditch in the darkest night," as a British engineer later explained. Some 140 cannons now bristled from the battlements, including naval guns hoisted from the *Lizard* and the *Hunter* and manhandled uphill to protect the city's flanks with canister—tin cylinders packed with iron balls—and grapeshot. A few rebel balls smacked the town, toppling the odd chimney. But, as Captain Ainslie noted, "Their shot had no more effect upon our walls than peas would have against a plank."

The cold weather turned colder. "One's senses are benumbed," Ainslie told his diary. "It is employment enough to preserve one's nose." No ungloved hand dared touch metal; an unfortunate sentinel was led to the guardhouse after his eyelids froze shut. Carleton ordered paths shoveled after each snowfall to permit quick movement to the gun platforms. Every man in Quebec, regardless of station, was also required to help clear drifts from the outer walls. The great cathedral bells would ring only in case of attack, summoning defenders to the Grand Parade, where sergeants—wearing distinctive green coats, recently stitched by the town's tailors—would deploy them as needed. Sentries on their rounds at night were to stop calling, "All is well." And under orders issued on December 23, the entire garrison would sleep fully clothed, ready for combat.

General Montgomery had reportedly sworn that he would "dine in Quebec on Christmas or in hell," but instead he spent the holy day inspecting his soldiers and pondering his attack plans. After reviewing Captain Daniel Morgan's assembled riflemen, he reminded them that they stood poised to "rescue a province from the British yoke, win it for our country, and obtain for ourselves immortal honor." The men cheered as usual—the commander's "engaging oratory" was "sensible and concise," Private George Morison observed. Another American wrote, "The fire of patriotism kindled in our breasts, and we resolved to follow wherever he should lead."

Not every man felt that way about Benedict Arnold, and on December 26 Montgomery sat at his writing table in Holland House to tell Schuy-

1. George III inherited his throne in 1760 at age twenty-two, on the eve of Britain's victory in the Seven Years' War, which created the greatest empire the world had known since ancient Rome. As the American rebellion gained strength in the 1770s, he feared that loss of the colonies would lead to Britain's fatal decline. "Blows," he declared, "must decide."

2. The king's four-day review of the British fleet at Portsmouth in June 1773 was the occasion for a grand celebration of national power. Here the royal barge, in the center foreground, passes the stern of the warship *Royal Oak* amid a thunderous salute.

3. A childhood friend of the king, Lord Frederick North became his prime minister in 1770 and would oversee the war against America despite misgivings about the cause. "Upon military matters I speak ignorantly," he once confessed, "and therefore without effect."

4. Known as the "Psalm Singer" for his piety, William Legge, Lord Dartmouth, served as the British colonial secretary in the early months of the American rebellion. Although hardly a warmonger, he believed that prideful insurgents disobeyed both their British masters and their God.

5. "We have troublesome times a-coming for there is a great disturbance abroad in the earth & they say it is tea that caused it," a New Jersey woman wrote in late 1774. Jan Josef Horemans's painting *Tea Time* depicted a European household gentility at odds with the political uproar the commodity caused in America.

6. The largest city in the Western world, London on the march toward war in the mid-1770s was much like London at peace—aggressive, vivid, and alive with animal spirits.

7. Benjamin Franklin's role in the publication of private letters written by a British official regarding colonial affairs led to his appearance in January 1774 before the king's council in the Cockpit, a London amphitheater once used for cock fights. Denounced as a "hoary-headed traitor," Franklin never endured a greater public humiliation.

8. Meeting in what had once been a twelfth-century chapel, the House of Commons retained an ecclesiastical air, even as parliamentarians cracked nuts, peeled oranges, and in the spring of 1774 overwhelmingly approved the government's draconian measures against New England rebels in the aftermath of the Boston Tea Party.

9. Charlotte had been an obscure German princess in 1761 when George chose her sight unseen to be his queen. They wed six hours after her arrival in England; the happy union eventually produced fifteen children, of whom the six eldest appear in this 1770 family portrait.

10. To open the new session of Parliament in October 1775, the king rode from St. James's Palace in this four-ton gilded coach, drawn by eight Royal Hanoverian Cream horses. The vehicle's tendency to pitch, yaw, and oscillate made riding in it like "tossing in a rough sea."

11. In search of a strategy to crush the American rebellion, the king summoned his ministers one by one to St. James's Palace for audiences in the Royal Closet, his conference room. He talked much and listened little, bounding from subject to subject but always returning to the need for iron resolve.

12. As both military commander and royal governor of Massachusetts, Lieutenant General Thomas Gage was Britain's supreme authority in North America. Belatedly seeing that he had underestimated the intensity of the insurgency, he warned London in September 1774, "Conciliating, moderation, reasoning is over. Nothing can be done but by forcible means."

13. Margaret Kemble, daughter of a wealthy New Jersey merchant, married young General Gage in 1758 and eventually bore him eleven children. She would sail to England from Boston in the summer of 1775 on a ship carrying almost two hundred British soldiers badly wounded at Bunker Hill.

14. Born poor and trained as a printer, Benjamin Franklin by age seventy had become world renowned as a scientist, writer, and diplomat. In this 1778 portrait, he wears the marten-fur cap he kept as a souvenir of his star-crossed expedition to Canada two years earlier.

15. An accomplished silversmith and engraver, Paul Revere had served as an equestrian courier since December 1773, when he carried news of the Boston Tea Party to New York and Philadelphia. Sixteen months later he would warn the countryside around Boston of British regulars on the march.

16. The physician Joseph Warren had long been a leader in the Boston resistance movement, rising to the presidency of the Massachusetts Provincial Congress. Commissioned a militia major general on June 14, 1775, he died three days later from a bullet to the head at Bunker Hill.

17. Pious and honest, if stubborn and taciturn, Major General Artemas Ward would command American forces for two months, until superseded by General Washington.

18. A stubby, rough-hewn brawler with a shock of white hair, Brigadier General Israel Putnam was described by one admirer as "totally unfit for everything but fighting."

19. Colonel John Stark of New Hampshire, a veteran of battles against Indians and the French, commanded the largest American regiment in New England, vital in shoring up the rebel line at Bunker Hill.

20. Brigadier Hugh Earl Percy, son of a duke, led a brigade from Boston to reinforce the battered British regulars retreating from Concord. "I had the happiness," he told his father, "of saving them from inevitable destruction."

21. An engraving created less than a year after the war erupted shows British regiments marching into Concord on April 19, 1775. In the foreground, Lieutenant Colonel Francis Smith and Major John Pitcairn scan the countryside for American forces massing outside town.

22. This lithograph depicts British regulars from Boston landing at Morton's Point on June 17, 1775, while others advance toward the American redoubt during the battle of Bunker Hill. Shells from *Somerset* contribute to the incineration of Charlestown.

23. During consultations in Philadelphia with the Continental Congress in the early summer of 1776, General Washington agreed to sit for this portrait—set against the backdrop of liberated Boston—by Charles Willson Peale. Now forty-four years old, he was about to fight his first major battle against the British. "His appearance alone gave confidence to the timid and imposed respect on the bold," one soldier reported.

24. An overweight Boston bookseller who demonstrated a genius for military engineering and gunnery, Henry Knox—shown here in a major general's uniform—soon commanded the Continental artillery. Washington would say of him, "[There was] no one whom I have loved more sincerely."

25. This stately Georgian mansion, abandoned by a loyalist family and later owned by the poet Henry Wadsworth Longfellow, served as Washington's headquarters in Cambridge. The orchards, outbuildings, and vista of the Charles River evoked the commanding general's beloved Mount Vernon in Virginia.

26. Lord George Germain, a former British general who succeeded Dartmouth as the king's American secretary, had been rehabilitated after disgrace on the battlefield in 1759. One biographer concluded that it was "his pride, his remoteness, his intransigence, his indifference, his irony, his disdain, his self-command and self-assurance that inflamed mean minds."

27. John Murray, the fourth earl of Dunmore and the royal governor of Virginia, had few rivals as the most detested British official in North America, particularly after he emancipated slaves owned by his rebel opponents. "That arch traitor to the rights of humanity, Lord Dunmore, should be instantly crushed," Washington declared.

28. Colonel Benedict Arnold of Connecticut was "as brave a man as ever lived," in one comrade's estimation. Born to lead other men in the dark of night, both on land and under sail, he was perhaps the finest battle captain that America would produce in the eighteenth century.

29. Tall, thin, and florid, with kinky hair and erratic health, Major General Philip Schuyler was among America's wealthiest, most accomplished men. He would command the invasion of Canada in 1775.

30. The youngest son of an Irish baronet, Richard Montgomery served sixteen years in the British Army before emigrating to New York in 1772 and accepting an American commission as a brigadier general three years later. "I have been dragged from obscurity much against my inclination," he told his wife.

31. Major General Guy Carleton, the British governor and military commander of Canada, was said by one acquaintance to be "a man of ten thousand eyes . . . not to be taken unawares." Described by George III as "gallant & sensible," Carleton confessed to London that with American invaders approaching Quebec, "I think our fate extremely doubtful."

32. By the end of 1775, the only significant place in Canada not under American control was Fortress Quebec on the St. Lawrence River. Although revetments, palisades, and walls extended in a two-mile arc around the city, the fortifications had fallen into disrepair.

33. With smallpox, frigid weather, and desertion reducing his small force, General Montgomery attacked Quebec during a storm on December 31, 1775. His death, from grapeshot through his thighs and face, was far bloodier than artist John Trumbull's subsequent depiction.

34. A fieldstone mansion on the Rue Notre-Dame in Montreal, the Château Ramezay had once served as headquarters for the fur trade in New France. Benedict Arnold used it for his command post in early 1776 and received Dr. Franklin here on April 29, just as the American occupation of Canada was collapsing.

35. A former British officer who had served capably as Washington's adjutant general, Major General Horatio Gates traveled north in summer 1776 to take command of American troops in Canada only to find that the army had been driven helter-skelter back into New York. The battered force, Gates reported, was in a "deplorable state."

36. After surviving the bloodletting at Bunker Hill, Major General William Howe took command of all British forces in America, overseeing both the evacuation of Boston and the attack on New York. Famously taciturn, he "never wastes a monosyllable," one wit quipped.

37. Major General John Burgoyne, dubbed "General Swagger," was celebrated as much for playwriting in London as for military acumen. His farce *The Blockade of Boston* featured various illiterate Yankee caricatures, including a bumbling rebel general who "can't read but can speechify."

38. The American seizure of commanding ground on Dorchester Heights forced General Howe to abandon Boston for Halifax in mid-March 1776. The evacuation of nine thousand soldiers and more than a thousand loyalists left Britain without a single port on the Atlantic seaboard between Canada and Florida.

ler of his worries. "Three companies of Colonel Arnold's detachment are very averse" to attacking Quebec, he reported. Feuds and personal resentment toward Arnold—the usual enmities of small men that he seemed to accumulate—had festered to the verge of mutiny. "This dangerous party threatens the ruin of our affairs," Montgomery wrote. "I shall, at any rate, be obliged to change my plan of attack, being too weak to put that in execution I had formerly determined on." Many enlistments would expire in less than a week, he noted, and "I must try every means to prevent their departure." Some officers "have offered to stay, provided they may join some other corps. This is resentment against Arnold, and will hurt him so much that I do not think I can consent to it." Montgomery urged Schuyler to "strain every nerve" to send reinforcements when the Lake Champlain ice melted in the spring, or risk losing what had been won. The expedition also needed money: he had barely £500 left. The "Continental dollars" issued by Congress had depreciated and "will not be received by the [Canadian] inhabitants." Finally, he added:

> Having so early reported to you my determination to return home, I take it for granted measures are taken to supply my place. . . . If this business should terminate in a blockade, I shall think myself at liberty to return. However, if possible, I shall first make an effort for the reduction of the town.

Other worries also nagged at him. Sickness and desertion had reduced the American assault force to eight hundred fit men, plus what he called "a few ragamuffin Canadians." (A disaffected priest was willing to give absolution to renegade Catholics in exchange for a sixty-dollar monthly salary and the promise of a bishop's miter.) Defenders would outnumber attackers almost two to one. A trickle of American deserters had bolted into the city—one had been hoisted by rope over the wall so that British sentries did not have to open the gate. They had almost certainly disclosed Montgomery's "storming plan," forcing him to amend his attack again. After considering a combined assault on the Upper Town by scaling the walls near the Cape Diamond bastion, he now reverted to his original scheme of striking the more vulnerable Lower Town, which, though fortified, lay outside the city walls.

Two columns—led by Montgomery and Arnold—would approach from opposite directions on a stormy night. Two smaller diversionary forces would feint toward Cape Diamond and the St. John Gate. If the narrow, heavily defended Mountain Hill Street leading to the Upper Town could not be forced, Montgomery hoped that Carleton—pressured by civilian merchants—would surrender Quebec rather than let the warehouses, dock-yards, and shipping be destroyed. A proposal to seize women, children, and priests in the Lower Town to use as human shields was considered and rejected, according to rifleman John Joseph Henry. Montgomery's appeal to patriotic pride seemed in recent days to have tamped down the mutinous talk; he had also suggested that the sacked city would afford ample plunder. Regardless, the three disgruntled companies finally fell in line, agreeing to attack when the order came. "Amongst our men," John Pierce wrote in his diary, "there is great searchings of heart."

Montgomery tried to remain buoyant. Although he had rebuked Janet in an earlier note—"Write no more of those whining letters . . . I don't want anything to lower my spirits"—now he told her, "I think myself the most fortunate of men." To his brother-in-law he wrote of the impending attack, "'Tis worth the experiment. *Audaces fortuna juvat*"—fortune favors the bold—though he tempted fortune by adding, "Should we fail I don't see any fatal consequences which are likely to attend it."

It was said that in preparing for his own attack on Quebec sixteen years earlier, General Wolfe, who would die in the assault, recited Thomas Gray's "Elegy Written in a Country Churchyard," with its prescient line "The paths of glory lead but to the grave." For his part, General Montcalm wrote an affecting final letter to his wife before riding his black horse onto the Plains of Abraham. "The moment when I shall see you again will be the finest of my life," he told her. "Goodbye, my heart."

Now in the American camps each man prepared for battle in his own fashion. Many settled their debts and washed their clothes; wood smoke from drying racks perfumed shirts and breeches. They finished sharpening pikes and building scaling ladders. "Got all in readiness with our ladders, spears, and so forth, with hearts undaunted," wrote Jeremiah Greenman, the Rhode Islander who had taken up soldiering "to make a man of himself." Because so many wore scavenged British uniforms, each man was to fasten recognition emblems to his hat: a hemlock sprig and a scrap of paper with "*liberty or death*" scribbled on it. Montgomery's twenty-year-old aide-de-camp, Captain John Macpherson, sealed a just-in-case letter to his father in Philadelphia. "If you receive this it will be the last this hand will ever write to you," young Macpherson told him. "Heaven only knows what may be my fate. . . . I experience no reluctance in this cause, to venture a life which I consider is only lent to be used when my country demands it." Captain Jacob Cheeseman, another aide, dressed with meticulous care, then slipped five gold coins into his pocket. That should suffice, he observed, to bury him "with decency."

As for Montgomery, he convened a final conference with his officers at Holland House on Saturday evening, December 30. A vicious storm had begun to blow from the northeast, with heavy snow and frigid winds. Once again they reviewed the plan: two feints, then two converging attacks on the Lower Town. Dr. Senter thought the general seemed "extremely anxious," even despondent, as he paced back and forth, ear cocked to the keening night, which would cover their approaches to Quebec. Montgomery began composing yet another ultimatum for Carleton. "Embrace the opportunity I offer you," he wrote. But at length, in the small hours of Sunday morning as the storm intensified, he concluded that it was time to move out.

Four a.m. had come and gone when an odd flicker of light to the west caught Captain Malcolm Fraser's watchful eye as he trudged between sentry posts along the ramparts. A Royal Highland Emigrant who commanded the Upper Town guard, Fraser squinted through the blowing snow across the Plains of Abraham. Lanterns? Torches? Abruptly two crimson rockets arced into the inky sky above the Cape Diamond bastion, followed by the dull pop of distant gunfire. Skidding on the slick cobbles, Fraser raced to the Récollet monastery, bellowing, "Turn out! Turn out!" Carleton met him at the entrance and ordered a general alarm.

Drums pounded, dogs barked. Five rebel mortars and two small guns began to bombard the town from a battery in St. Roch. The cathedral bells pealed, echoed in a higher pitch by lesser bells from the Jesuit college, the Ursuline convent, and Our Lady of Victory in the Lower Town. Nuns fell to their knees in the vault of the Hôtel Dieu, praying for deliverance. Men with firelocks and torches rushed down St. Louis Street: militia sergeants in green, fusiliers in red coats with blue facings, and emigrants in tartan, their officers brandishing claymores and wicked dirks. Lighted lanterns on long poles were thrust from the battlements, brightening the shadows. Two bands of intruders were spotted, one lurking below the Cape Diamond bastion and the other near the St. John Gate, trying without success to set fire to the heavy doors; both were quickly sniffed out as feints. Cannon fire drove them off while Carleton and Colonel Maclean turned their attention to the Lower Town.

Arnold had assembled almost five hundred cutthroats with scaling ladders near the St. Charles convent in St. Roch. Upon spotting the two rockets that signaled the diversionary attacks on the far side of Quebec, they set off in a lumbering column: Arnold with a thirty-man vanguard, followed by gunners dragging a 6-pounder on a sled, and then Captain Morgan's rifle company leading the rest, their heads bent against the storm, gunlocks wrapped in coat skirts in a vain effort to keep them dry.

As he approached the Palace Gate on Quebec's northern shoulder, Arnold swung into Dog Lane to follow the wall toward the Lower Town. The parapet overhead immediately erupted in muzzle flashes and ferocious musketry, raking the Americans with plunging fire from the Royal Navy Battalion. "We advanced as fast as we could . . . but was obliged to leave our field piece," a gunner later told his journal. The sled and 6-pounder were abandoned in a snowdrift. Hunched men instinctively narrowed their shoulders and hurried forward, unable to see anything above the high gray wall except that fatal winking. Some believed they had been betrayed, and indignant shouts could be heard: "We are sold." An orderly sergeant sprawled flat, leaking blood. "I am a dead man," he murmured. "I wish you would turn me over." A comrade complied, flipping him facedown in the snow to be trampled by the surging column. Captain Jonas Hubbard, who had survived Bunker Hill, would not survive Dog Lane. He too fell, mortally wounded. "March on," he called, "march on."

March on they did, for six hundred yards before the lane bent south into the dim labyrinth of the Lower Town. Ahead loomed the first barrier, a ten-foot wooden wall with musket loopholes. Arnold had no sooner ordered his men to prop ladders against the barricade than he crumpled to the ground: a bullet fragment had sliced through his left leg below the knee, lodging in the calf muscle above his heel. Bleeding badly and in excruciating pain, he shouted encouragement through gritted teeth while hobbling to the rear with help from two men, who carried him the final mile to Dr. Senter's surgery table at the convent hospital.

The column had lost its commander, but Captain Morgan, the gutful former teamster, scrambled up the ladder rungs and peered over the barrier, only to be greeted by a blast of gunfire. One ball pierced his cap; another grazed his cheek. After tumbling to the ground "like a scorched rag," as one chronicler later wrote, his hair and beard singed, Morgan scaled the ladder again and vaulted to the far side. More riflemen followed in a melee of shouts and wild shooting. Confused by the red coats worn by many attackers, the stunned defenders retreated through the street to a nearby house, where their captain, who was said to be "in liquor," soon surrendered with dozens of others. Some threw down their guns, yelling, "*Vive la liberté.*"

Three hundred yards on, a second barricade loomed across an area known as the Sault-au-Matelot—sailor's leap—where a sheer rock face rose on the right, unbroken but for the twisting defile that carried Mountain Hill Street to the Upper Town. The barrier's sally port appeared to be unguarded, but when Morgan urged the attack forward, an impromptu conclave of officers resisted, huddling in the shadows for discussion. The Holland House plan called for Arnold to rendezvous with Montgomery at this spot before advancing uphill. Not only had casualties reduced the column, but as many as two hundred men had lost their way in the snowstorm and were wandering around the docks, sheds, and riverine warehouses. Wet firelocks needed to be dried; prisoners required careful watching.

A strange tranquillity settled over the Lower Town as the order was passed to each company: wait here for General Montgomery and his men. "I was overruled by hard reasoning," Morgan later said. "To these arguments, I sacrificed my own opinion and lost the town."

Two miles southwest, Montgomery led his three hundred New Yorkers along the St. Lawrence shoreline from Wolfe's Cove. The tide had heaved great slabs of ice onto the narrow path, and they picked their way single file around Cape Diamond at six a.m., past the iron cleats used in warmer weather to moor river vessels to the embankment. Squinting through the blinding snow, they spied the first fortification on this side of the Lower Town—a fifteen-foot, unguarded wooden palisade blocking the path. Carpenters with saws and axes quickly hacked a hole large enough for Montgomery to squeeze through, followed by his command staff and soldiers. A hundred yards north, near the King's Wharf and the old forges, another barrier loomed at the edge of the industrial district called Près de Ville. It, too, yielded after a few minutes of violent cutting and gashing. Pushing aside the splintered posts, Montgomery saw a two-story blockhouse fifty yards ahead. He crept forward as others clambered through the gap behind him, including Captains Cheeseman and Macpherson. No light or sound could be heard from what was clearly a stronghold, with musket loopholes and closed firing ports on the second floor. An officer sent forward for a closer look detected no sign of enemies. Perhaps this building, too, had been abandoned. Montgomery drew his sword and advanced.

Captain Adam Barnsfare, master of the merchant ship *Fell*, watched every move of the shadowy intruders through a spyhole in the blockhouse. Three dozen British and Canadian militiamen crowded the ground floor, silent as mice, while nine sailors upstairs held lighted matches next to several small cannons packed with grapeshot. At point-blank range, perhaps no more than twenty yards, Barnsfare gave the command: "Fire!" The ports flew open. Flame spurted from the muzzles and detonations broke the early morning silence, echoing from Cape Diamond's hard flank. "Shrieks and groans followed the discharge," a British witness reported. "When the smoke cleared away there was not a soul to be seen."

At least not a living soul. Grape hit Montgomery in both thighs and, mortally, through the face. He pitched over backward, knees drawn up, the sword flying from his hand. Behind him Cheeseman fell, rose, and fell again for good, the burial gold still in his pocket. Macpherson never moved. Ten other bodies would be found in the snow at Près de Ville. The survivors had plunged back through the barrier opening, dragging the wounded by their collars.

Now the American attack came fully unstitched. As a sullen dawn lightened the eastern sky, scores of British reinforcements swarmed from the Palace Gate. Following the rebel blood trail down Dog Lane, they fell on the rear of Captain Henry Dearborn's company, which had mustered belatedly along the St. Charles before marching into the Lower Town in search of Arnold's column. Facing fire from behind and from the walls above, Dearborn's men scattered among the houses and shops. "We got bewildered," the captain later wrote.

Ahead, in the Sault-au-Matelot, unaware of Montgomery's fate yet sensing that the morning had taken an evil turn, Morgan tried to reorganize an advance toward the Upper Town. Too late: more regulars had manned the second barrier near Mountain Hill Street, bolting the sally port and driving Americans from an adjacent house with their bayonets. When a British lieutenant demanded his surrender, Morgan shot him in the head. But a murderous fire built as enemy soldiers and sailors filled the upper windows along the street. Americans sheltered in doorways, pricking dry powder into their firelock touchholes only to have the wet guns misfire again and again.

Losses mounted among the Yankee officers. A bullet snipped three fingers from Lieutenant Archibald Steele's hand. Captain John Lamb, an artilleryman described by a superior as "a restless genius and of bad temper," took grapeshot in the left cheek, costing him an eye. Lieutenant John Humphreys, a Virginian in Morgan's company, pitched forward in the street with a mortal chest wound. A bullet through the heart killed Captain William Hendricks, a Pennsylvania rifle company commander whose "mild and beautiful countenance" had been much admired by his comrades. "Men groaning with their wounds, women and children screaming and crying," John Pierce would tell his diary. "A terrible scene to behold."

A British 9-pounder, heaved up from Lymeburner's Wharf at nine a.m., convinced even the diehards that the battle was lost. The defiant roar of Morgan's voice in the Sault-au-Matelot faded, along with a few final gunshots. Eyes hollow, faces stained with powder, the Americans tossed their firelocks into the street and stepped out with raised hands. Captain Morgan, weeping in rage, surrendered his sword to a priest.

"A glorious day for us," a British gunner wrote in his journal, "& as complete a little victory as ever was gained."

Nuns with linen bandages bustled about in the chapel of the St. Charles convent, tending to wounded rebels on straw pallets and praying for those beyond nursing. The nunnery occupied an elegant building, dating to the last century and "richly decorated with carved and gilt work," one officer recorded, with "a complete rigged small ship" hanging like a chandelier from the ceiling. Stoves and a great hearth helped revive the half-frozen casualties who continued staggering in on Sunday morning, including Captain Lamb, the gunner, who had been found unconscious and shoeless on a pile of wood shavings in a Lower Town cooper's shop, his left eye gone, his jaw mangled, and his shattered cheek wrapped in a black handkerchief.

Young Dr. Senter moved from pallet to pallet, probing, stitching, and occasionally sighing. With help from the nuns he had plucked the bullet fragment from Arnold's calf, and now the colonel lay flat in his bed with a brace of loaded pistols and a sword at his side, listening for redcoats at the door and denouncing all suggestions of evacuation. On Arnold's order, every bedridden patient still capable of pulling a trigger had been given a firelock. "He was determined," Senter observed, "to kill as many as possible if they came into the room." Upon learning of Montgomery's repulse and death near Cape Diamond, Arnold scribbled a dispatch to Brigadier General David Wooster, now commanding the rear guard in Montreal. "I am exceedingly apprehensive," he wrote. Reports were unclear about whether his own column was still fighting. "They will either carry the Lower Town, be made prisoners, or [be] cut to pieces," he told Wooster. "It is impossible to say what our future operations will be until we know the fate of my detachment."

Sentries outside piled up snow breastworks in hopes of slowing enemy bullets if the British attacked. But Carleton had no intention of risking his victory by chasing rebels through the drifts. There would be cash rewards for the most valiant defenders, and a knighthood for the governor. The bishop ordered a *Te Deum* sung, with hosannas of thanksgiving offered to various guardian angels, protective saints, and the Virgin. A priest denied last rites to a mortally wounded *habitant* who had fought with the Americans until the dying man publicly repented his disloyalty.

In Carleton's irrefutable phrase, the enemy had been "repulsed with slaughter." By the governor's tally, American casualties on December 31 totaled 461, including 30 killed in action, 42 wounded, and 389 captured; more than three dozen prisoners would die of disease or their wounds.

British casualties amounted to 5 dead and 41 wounded; all the defenders who had been captured in the Lower Town were freed.

American prisoners were prodded at bayonet point into the Upper Town, the enlisted men locked in a monastery and their officers consigned to cells in the seminary. "You can have no conception of what kind of men composed their officers," a British major wrote. Interrogations revealed that in civilian life "one major was a blacksmith, another a hatter. Of their captains there was a butcher, a tanner, a shoemaker, a tavern keeper, etc., etc. Yet they all pretended to be gentlemen." With Carleton's indulgence, a half dozen horse-drawn sleds flying a white flag were permitted to bring the prisoners' spare clothing through the Palace Gate.

Yet privation and misery lay ahead. "Fortune was kind enough to save me from either starving or drowning, to bring me to this place to be made a prisoner, which I think to be no great favor," wrote the sardonic Lieutenant William Humphrey. On January 1 he added, "Here I spent a very solitary new year." Some Irish- or English-born privates agreed to join the British Army in exchange for their freedom; most of the prisoners awaited parole arrangements that would take months to secure. Those caught plotting escape were clapped in irons. "Nothing heard or seen but playing at cards, swearing," Private John Melvin told his diary. "Some employ themselves in making wooden spoons." Disease followed them into the cells. "The most of us had the smallpox very hard. Our flesh seemed a mass of corruption," wrote Private Simon Fobes. "At the same time we were almost covered with vermin. . . . Our clothes were stiff with corrupted matter."

Although a crippling attack of gout compounded the pain from his wounded leg, Arnold, now in command, traveled by sleigh ambulance to his new headquarters in Holland House and reimposed a blockade around the city. Quebec remained an "object of the highest importance," he wrote, although a proper siege would require three thousand men, with five thousand needed for a renewed assault. Riflemen resumed their potshots at the battlements and gunners once again lobbed cannonballs over the parapets. What they failed to win by force of arms, the Americans claimed by sheer effrontery: rumors spread that Americans held the Lower Town, the bishop's house, and British powder magazines; that six hundred defenders had been killed; that Montgomery had merely gone to fetch twenty thousand *Bostonnais* reinforcements; and that Carleton had hanged sixty Canadians for treason.

Arnold knew better. To Washington he wrote that "upwards of one hundred officers and soldiers instantly set off for Montreal" after the failed assault; since most enlistments had now expired, "it was with the greatest difficulty I could persuade the rest to make a stand." He was desperate for medical supplies, musket balls, troops, and gunpowder—the American stockpile in Canada was down to four tons. Including his many sick and injured, "our force at this time does not exceed eight hundred men," he wrote Wooster on January 2. "For God's sake, order as many men down as you can possibly spare." To his sister Hannah in Connecticut he added, "That Providence which has carried me through so many dangers is still my protection."

More sleds arrived in the Upper Town, but these bore American dead retrieved from the snow. Stiff as planks, many corpses were "heaped in monstrous piles" in a cold vault known as the Dead House until a spring thaw would allow grave digging to resume. Carleton permitted prisoners to identify dead comrades like Lieutenant Samuel Cooper, who had written his wife shortly before the upcountry march through Maine, "The dangers we are to encounter I know not, but it shall never be said to my children: Your father was a coward." Montgomery's body was found where he fell; a drummer boy scuffing through drifts in Près de Ville also retrieved his sword—a short-bladed hanger with a silver bulldog's head on the ivory handle. A British officer gave the boy seven shillings for the treasure.

Thirteen years earlier, at the siege of Havana, Carleton had served as a colonel in one British regiment when Montgomery was a captain in another. For old times' sake, the governor asked his carpenters to make a "genteel coffin" of fir lined with flannel and draped in a black pall. On Wednesday, January 3, regulars from the 7th Foot, their arms reversed and black scarves knotted on their left elbows, led the cortege past the seminary cell windows where American officers wept. A rocky defile near the St. Louis Gate powder magazine had been used as a Protestant cemetery in Quebec, and here the mortal remains of Richard Montgomery were interred with military honors. He would never know that the previous month, Congress had promoted him to major general. Nor would he know that his puling threats to resign had brought a rebuke from Washington, who on Christmas Eve wrote Schuyler, "When is the time for brave men to exert themselves in the cause of liberty and their country, if this is not?"

A defeated general is always wrong, an eighteenth-century French commander once observed, and a dead one was especially at a loss. Perhaps the best this dead, defeated general could hope for was martyrdom. In that, Montgomery succeeded spectacularly. Poems and songs were composed in his honor, as if "millions of seraphs, clothed in robes of gold" sang his praises, as an ode in the *Virginia Gazette* suggested. Orations, sermons, and theatrical productions followed. The *London Evening Post*, ever keen to embarrass Lord North, eulogized Montgomery on a page bordered with heavy black margins, and the *Scots Magazine* compared him to the immortal Wolfe. Congress rejected a proposal to wear mourning crepe on the grounds that "the general is already embalmed in the heart of every good American." With prodding from Benjamin Franklin, the personal sculptor of Louis XVI agreed to chisel a proper memorial, eventually shipped from Paris to New York in nine packing cases.

Streets, counties, towns, and children would be named for him. Nor did the adulation soon fade. In June 1818, an American delegation arrived in Quebec, located and identified Montgomery's body, and took him home. Three weeks later, Janet, by then seventy-four and still wearing widow's weeds, emerged at midday on the veranda of her estate overlooking the Hudson River below Albany. She watched with a telescope as the steamboat *Richmond* hove to, allowing her to gaze at the new mahogany casket borne on the weather deck. A military band played the "Dead March" from Handel's *Saul*, an honor guard fired a salute, and the boat resumed its journey south. "You may conceive my anguish," Janet wrote a niece. After lying in state in Manhattan's city hall, her husband was interred beside St. Paul's Chapel as harbor guns boomed in tribute.

Montgomery had written his will at Crown Point in August 1775, before marching into Canada; he had divided his estate between Janet and his sister in Ireland. But in a practice common after battles, his effects at Quebec were inventoried at Holland House on January 3, 1776, and his personal kit then auctioned. Several officers, including Captain Aaron Burr, counted out a bag of coins worth £347, including Spanish milled dollars, gold half-joes, English crowns, Connecticut and Massachusetts shillings, and Continental dollars, plus a string of Indian white wampum. His sheets went to the convent hospital, "Dick the Negro boy" got a pair of wool socks, and Montgomery's watch—London-made, with a 22-karat case and a rare ruby cylinder escapement—was saved for Janet after Carleton returned it to the American camp.

The rest was unpacked from a large black trunk and sold off, item by item, to the American officers: two volumes of Polybius, Johnson's *Dictionary of the English Language*, two blankets, a buffalo skin and a clothes brush—bought by Burr—five razors and a strop, spurs, gloves, six muslin cravats, nine pairs of silk stockings, two cotton caps, a tortoiseshell comb. But easily the biggest buyer of Montgomery's wardrobe was Benedict Arnold: three ruffled shirts, six cambric stocks, two Holland waistcoats, a silk neckcloth, a cashmere waistcoat, moccasins, a pair of Indian leggings. Also: a dozen knives and forks, six silver tablespoons, six silver teaspoons, five tablecloths, three linen handkerchiefs, a powder box and muff, an old valise, and a pair of tea tongs purchased in Montreal. The kit guaranteed that General Montgomery would be with Arnold through the hard campaigning still to come.

Arnold learned while recuperating that Congress had promoted him, too. "May heaven protect you that you may long be an ornament to your country," Schuyler wrote the new brigadier general in January, "and sit down in an old age with the comfortable reflection that you have been a good citizen." He had already done the impossible. Now he would be asked to do even more.

"I have no thoughts of leaving this proud town until I first enter it in triumph," Arnold wrote his sister on January 6. "I am in the way of duty, and I know no fear."

Part Two

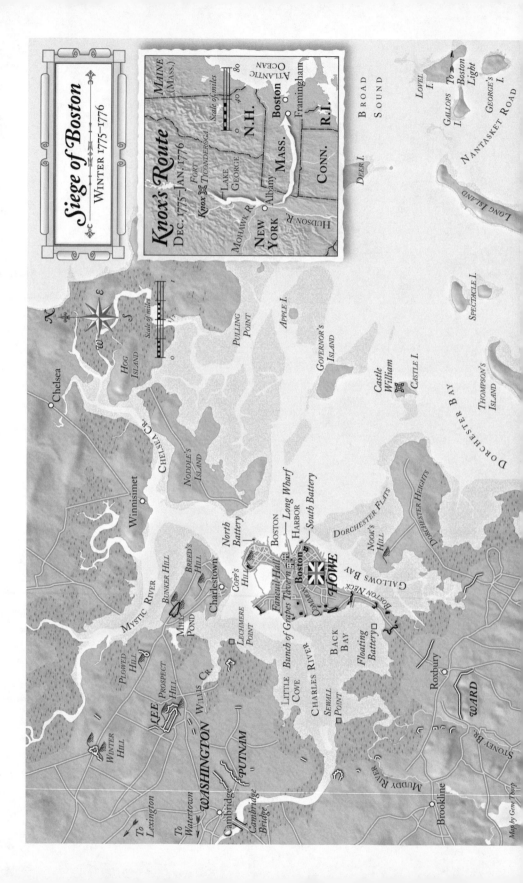

Siege of Boston
WINTER 1775–1776

Knox's Route
DEC. 1775–JAN. 1776

MAINE (MASS.)

N.H.

Boston
Framingham

MASS.
Albany

Knox
Fort
Ticonderoga

LAKE
GEORGE

Mohawk R.

NEW
YORK

Hudson R.

CONN.
R.I.

ATLANTIC
OCEAN

Scale of miles
40   80

BROAD
SOUND

LOVEL I.

GALLOPS I.
GEORGE'S I.

To
Boston
Light

NANTASKET ROAD

LONG ISLAND

DEER I.

SPECTACLE I.

APPLE I.

GOVERNOR'S
ISLAND

PULLING
POINT

Castle
William

CASTLE I.

THOMPSON'S
ISLAND

DORCHESTER BAY

DORCHESTER FLATS

NOOK'S
HILL

DORCHESTER HEIGHTS

Chelsea

Hog
ISLAND

N

Scale of miles

CHELSEA CREEK

NODDLE'S
ISLAND

Winnisimet

MYSTIC RIVER

BUNKER HILL

BREED'S
HILL

Charlestown

Mill
POND

North
Battery

Copp's
Hill

Long Wharf

South Battery

BOSTON

HARBOR

GALLOWS BAY

PLOWED
HILL

WINTER
HILL

LEE

PROSPECT
HILL

WILLIS CR.

LECHMERE
POINT

Faneuil Hall
Bunch of Grapes Tavern

Little
Cove

COMMON

Boston

HOWE

BOSTON NECK

WASHINGTON

PUTNAM

Cambridge

CHARLES RIVER

SEWALL
POINT

BACK
BAY

Floating
Battery

To
Watertown

To
Lexington

Cambridge
Bridge

MUDDY RIVER

STONEY BR.

WARD

Roxbury

Brookline

Map by Gene Thorp

9.

The Ways of Heaven Are Dark and Intricate

The new year brought boredom, sickness, and more misery to occupied Boston. "The cold is so intense that the ink freezes in the pen whilst I write by the fireside," a lieutenant in the 40th Foot wrote to a friend on December 31. "Our little army has suffered severely from the dampness of the season, and from living totally on salt provisions." General Howe warned London that he had only three weeks of fuel left for his garrison. Firewood had grown scarce, and Boston was burning 336 tons of coal a week, with stocks dwindling rapidly. Rebel pirates captured a British collier near Salem, and the Spanish River coal pits in Nova Scotia had flooded. Civilians in Boston were reduced to burning horse dung for heat. The government promised to send three thousand blankets—"coarse, yet strong & well-milled"—plus fifty iron stoves and almost five thousand tons of English coal, despite the outrageous cost of transatlantic shipping.

Howe authorized the garrison to scavenge firewood as necessary. Countless trees had already been reduced to stumps, including a fine row of buttonwoods lining the street near the Old South Meeting House. Each regiment assigned a twenty-man detail with saws, axes, and crowbars to dismantle selected fences, barns, wharves, sailing vessels, warehouses, and a hundred dilapidated houses. The pulpit and pews from Old South were chopped up for kindling—"in a wanton, unprecedented, and impious manner," as church records noted—except for one beautifully carved deacon's box, which was salvaged as a hog sty. With only the sounding board and east galleries spared in Old South, the floor was covered with dirt and used as a riding ring by British dragoons. Books and manuscripts fed British stoves, and many officers agreed with Captain Glanville Evelyn, who told his father he hoped all of Boston burned "that we may be enabled to leave it." The regulars grew so indiscriminate in pulling down houses and fences without permission that Howe ordered an executioner to accompany his provost marshal on patrol "to hang upon the spot the first man he shall detect in the fact, without waiting for further proof by trial."

To bolster morale through this hard winter, masquerade balls were occasionally held at Province House or the Concert Hall on Hanover Street. Lord Percy, now a major general, ordered his band to give serenades. "We have been better amused than could possibly be expected in our situation," one officer wrote. "England seems to have forgot us, and we endeavored to forget ourselves." Officers also organized the Society for Promoting Theatrical Amusements, a *corps dramatique* to raise money for widows and orphans. Boston had long banned all theatricals, including puppet shows, as conducive to "immorality, impiety, and a contempt of religion," but "Howe's Strolling Players"—as they would later be known—delighted in lampooning such sensibilities. Young women were even permitted to play female roles, to the clucking disapproval of Boston matrons. Comedies like *The Citizen* and *The Apprentice* proved enormously popular, and *The Tragedy of Zara*, adapted from a Voltaire drama, was performed several times.

The actors found a fine playhouse in Faneuil Hall, a combined market and meeting hall on Dock Square with a slate roof, eighteen compass-headed windows arranged in two rows across the brick facade, and a thirty-eight-pound grasshopper weathervane crowning the cupola. Long used by rebels as a venue from which to stir trouble—a victim from the Boston Massacre lay in state here—Faneuil Hall was now employed for more refined purposes. The building, Lieutenant William Feilding wrote a friend, "is fitted up very elegantly for a theater." The Strolling Players considered themselves lucky to have a resident dramaturge in General Burgoyne, a companion of the great David Garrick and a habitué of the Green Room at Drury Lane Theatre. Burgoyne's own first play, *The Maid of the Oaks*, written in June 1774, would be performed in London's West End and later as a five-act production at the Theatre Royal. Even the astringent Walpole, who called Burgoyne "General Swagger," would pronounce *The Heiress*, written a decade later, to be "the most genteel comedy in our language." In Boston, the general wrote a rhymed prologue for *Zara*, ridiculing "minds diseased" with Puritan prudery.

Burgoyne had temporarily returned to England in December, but he'd left a parting gift for his comrades: an original farce, titled *The Blockade of Boston*, featuring a bumbling rebel general who "can't read but can speechify" and various illiterate Yankee caricatures, including a tailor turned soldier who stood guard with a measuring tape draped over his shoulders and a large pair of shears protruding from his pocket. The premiere was scheduled for Monday, January 8, and Faneuil Hall was packed to the rafters in anticipation. The evening's first performance—*The Busy Body*, a witty comedy about love and marriage by Susanna Centlivre—ended shortly after eight p.m. to a long ovation. As the audience stood to stretch and chat, sets were changed and actors backstage slipped into new costumes. Then a hush fell over the theater as the curtain rose.

A British orderly sergeant rushed onto the stage, bellowing, "Turn out! Turn out! They're hard at it, hammer and tongs!" Gales of laughter and pounding applause greeted him until he hollered, "If you won't believe me, by Jasus, you need only go to the door." An unmistakable popping noise drifted into the hall. "We heard," one officer reported, "a pretty smart firing of small arms." A shouted order carried from the box seats: "Officers, to your alarm posts!" Men bolted up the aisles for the door, Lieutenant Feilding wrote, "leaving the ladies in the house in a most terrible dilemma."

"A general scene of confusion ensued," according to an account sent to London. "Some skipping over the orchestra, trampling on the fiddles, and in short, everyone making his most speedy retreat. The actors, who were all officers, calling for water to get the paint and smut off their faces." Major Francis Hutcheson described "much fainting among the women. . . . One officer was running to his corps in his petticoats, and another with his face blackened and in a Negro's dress."

A mile to the north, Captain Thomas Knowlton, who six months earlier had fought so valiantly at the rail fence below Bunker Hill, led 130 raiders across the milldam from Cobble Hill to Charlestown. A big moon was sheathed in heavy overcast, and the men hardly cast a shadow as they split into two detachments. Many carried wood chips soaked in brimstone and turpentine. Fourteen houses on Main Street that had escaped the flames of the June 17 bombardment were now used by British patrols, vagrants, and wood scavengers. General Putnam, aware of the festivities scheduled at Faneuil Hall that night, had ordered the raiders to burn the houses and capture the thirty redcoats said to occupy them.

Little went right for Knowlton's men, and even less for the British. Several American firebrands set their blazes too soon, alerting sentinels in the redoubt on the upper slopes of Bunker Hill—known grandly as the Citadel and occupied by six hundred regulars. Alarm shots broke the silence, followed by shouts, men racing about, and a chaotic, sustained fusillade. Gun flashes sparkled across the hillside as British troops fired hundreds of rounds into the Mystic River, at Charlestown Neck, and simply into the air—"a hot and close fire on absolutely nothing at all," in one rebel's estimation. Across the Charles River, officers stampeded from Faneuil Hall, barking orders as the entire garrison scrambled to their gun batteries and alarm posts—much to the amusement of Putnam and his lieutenants, who watched from Cobble Hill "as merry as you please," according to Chaplain

Ebenezer David. Knowlton and his raiders returned on the run "all as hearty as bucks," David added. "I only grieved to hear the foul language." They had killed one regular while capturing a sergeant, several privates, and a woman camp follower. Eight houses burned, and although they "made a great light," by one account, serene airs kept the fire from spreading as planned.

"We all turned out, went to our respective posts, and cursed the Yankees for spoiling our entertainments," Captain Evelyn wrote his cousin on January 15. "They deserve some credit for timing it so well." *The Blockade of Boston*, postponed by the exigencies of war, would premiere to great acclaim later in the month. One of the thespians, Captain Francis Lord Rawdon, wrote home, "I hope we shall soon have done with these scoundrels, for one only dirties one's fingers by meddling with them."

Gossips would claim that General Howe had found his own winter entertainment, and her name was Elizabeth Lloyd Loring. Known to her friends as Betsy, the young Mrs. Loring and her loyalist husband, Joshua, had fled their home in Roxbury for refuge in Boston. He sold provisions to the garrison before later being appointed commissary of prisoners by Howe; scandalmongers alleged that the position encouraged a cuckold's complicity, although little evidence supported this accusation or confirmed Betsy Loring's infidelity in Boston. Even so, it would be asserted that the general and Mrs. Loring shared an enthusiasm for gambling, if not other passions. "Nothing seemed to engage his attention but the faro table, the playhouse, the dancing assembly, and Mrs. Loring," a loyalist New York judge would complain. She came to be known privately to British officers as Delilah, Cleopatra, and, especially, "the Sultana"; behind his back the general was called "the Chevalier." Their alleged liaison later inspired a memorable snatch of balderdash:

Awake, arouse, Sir Billy,
There's forage in the plain,
Ah, leave your little filly,
And open the campaign.

Yet no campaign could be launched in midwinter, particularly given the perils facing the British expeditionary force. In a dispatch to his government on January 16, Howe warned that the rebel army was not "by any means to be despised, having in it many European soldiers & all or most of the young men of spirit in the country. . . . They will not retreat until they have tried their fortune in a battle & are defeated." He dared to wonder whether it might be "better policy to withdraw entirely from the delinquent provinces and leave the colonists to war with each other for sovereignty." British authority in Boston was precarious, even though Howe tried to impose discipline with an iron hand. A marine had been sentenced to eight hundred lashes for striking a lieutenant. A private in the 43rd Foot received a thousand stripes for trading in stolen goods, and his accomplice wife got a hundred, plus three months in jail.

Compounding Howe's worries, smallpox was "spreading universally about the town." The disease killed the master of the *Halifax*, forcing the ship's crew into quarantine. Howe authorized inoculation both for unprotected soldiers and for civilians, despite Boston's historic aversion to the practice. Some residents with symptoms were expelled from the town. Other diseases also raged; a quarter of the rank and file was sick with one malady or another. "Our distresses accumulate every day," a regular wrote. "Our barracks are all hospitals, and so offensive is the stench of the wounds that the very air is infected with the smell." More trenches were dug for the dead on the Common, at times so hastily that "some of the graves are not dug deep enough," Howe complained. By strangling supplies of fresh food, rebel commanders hoped for "a prodigious mortality" to afflict the garrison. Scurvy had in fact grown sufficiently rampant that Howe increased the daily allocation of spruce beer to three pints per man.

No makeshift antiscorbutic would compensate for the dreadful diet fed eleven thousand British mouths and more than six thousand civilians. "The small quantities of provisions in store," Howe wrote London, "fill me with alarms." British suppliers had intended to stockpile enough food by late October to feed the army through the winter. Instead, Howe wrote Germain on January 15, even with his soldiers eating little more than salt meat he had been forced to put them on short rations. A commissary memorandum that day showed barely a month's supply of flour and bread remaining, plus fifty-seven days of salt pork, nine days of butter, no peas, and only enough rice for the sick wards. Howe complained that meat for hospital patients "is frequently purloined." Royal Navy raiders sent to the shores of Long Island Sound brought back sheep, a hundred cows, ducks, geese, and cheese. Howe also sent armed transports to St. Eustatius, in the West Indies, to buy salt meat, and two hundred marines sailed by convoy to load rice in Savannah. But that hardly sufficed. In a plaintive letter, Captain Evelyn asked his father to send "a little beef, butter, or potatoes. Any of them would be extremely acceptable [in] these hard times." He hoped that accounts of privation "may open the eyes of the people at home, and convince them that this is a more serious matter than they apprehended."

To further illustrate these hard times, Howe sent London elaborate charts showing that of thirty-six ships dispatched with provisions from Britain in October and November, fewer than half had reached Boston. Those that arrived tended to be terribly depleted by the journey. For example, of 550 Lincolnshire sheep sent out—after careful deliberation over the "fittest to undergo the voyage"—only 40 came through it alive, despite a bounty of two shillings sixpence offered the ship's masters for each animal delivered safely. The masters concluded that the sheep were "too fat when put on board . . . & the pens too large," so that they were "thrown upon one another by the violent motion of these ships. . . . They crushed one another." Of 290 hogs shipped, a mere 74 survived, despite assurances by the livestock suppliers that "there appears no doubt of these hardy animals getting over in good order." Animal carcasses hoisted through the hatches and heaved over the ships' sides left a sad trail from old England to New England. Howe reported that "the livestock met with worse fate than could have been suspected." A more vivid if hyperbolic account claimed that "the English Channel is white with sheep which have been thrown overboard." Vegetables fared badly, too: of 177 tons of potatoes shipped, nearly all were found to have rotted from excessive heat belowdecks, notwithstanding the shipper's pledge to store "them gently in the hold so as not to bruise them." Hay and beans also were "much damaged" by heat and moisture. Among the provisions to arrive intact were sauerkraut, porter, eleven tons of vinegar, and ample quantities of rum.

Ferocious autumn storms had bedeviled the storeships, driving some back to British ports and forcing others to beat for months in heavy seas across the North Atlantic. "The most severe weather I ever felt," reported Vice Admiral Shuldham, who arrived in Boston on December 30 as Admiral Graves's replacement after a passage that nearly sank the fifty-gun *Chatham*; she would require weeks of repair before going to sea again. No less alarming was the number of ships blown far off course. Another of those fine charts that so disheartened London listed sixteen troop transports and victuallers bound for Massachusetts but forced "by stress of weather" to Antigua, nearly two thousand miles south of Boston. They included the *Brownshall*, which sailed from Spithead with naval supplies on September 24 but would arrive in Antigua five months later with her sails and rigging "tore to pieces" and "only 14 gallons of water on board." *Enterprize*, which sailed from Cork in September with four companies of the 55th Foot, lost her masts in a gale before limping into Antigua. *Argo* left Cork with three companies of the 46th Regiment and eventually beat into Antigua with "her hull, rigging, & sails much damaged."

By early spring, more than two dozen ships bound for Boston could instead be found in the West Indies, among them the *Killingsworth*, carrying seventy tons of flour and salt meat out of Portsmouth; *Felicity*, bearing coal, porter, and livestock from London; and the *Earl of Suffolk*, loaded with coal, sauerkraut, porter, and livestock from the Isle of Wight. Perhaps no voyage better illustrated the harrowing nature of the North Atlantic in winter than that of *Orpheus*, a thirty-two-gun frigate that sailed from Portsmouth in the fall with Admiral Shuldham's convoy. Midshipman Bartholomew James, later an admiral, kept a journal during what was nearly his last ocean crossing.

> The first attack of the wind on the ship carried away our topsail sheets, clew lines, and buntlines. The main clew-garnets, buntlines, and leech lines also broke immediately, and main topmast staysail, jib, and several other sails, with the topsails and courses, blowing in pieces from the masts and yards.

When the storm subsided, Shuldham's *Chatham* and others in the convoy had vanished. Sailors aboard *Orpheus* hoisted a new suit of sails and reeved new rigging just in time for another gale, which "carried away our foremast fifteen or twenty feet above the forecastle"; the main topmast fell "and wounded nine men." Later that morning, the "mainmast also went by the board, crushed down the booms, and stove the long boat and a large cutter all to pieces." Debris from the mizzen topmast knocked out four of the gunner's teeth and broke his right shoulder in two places. "The heavy falls of snow totally prevented erecting jury masts," James wrote. Icy sails grew stiff as tin; crewmen poured boiling water on frozen tackle and sheets and softened the cordage with clubs. The captain swung back to England, fifteen hundred miles away, then turned again toward Boston when the monstrous seas subsided long enough to allow the crew to jury-rig new masts and spars. Nevertheless, James reported, "the season was big with raging winds. . . . Gale followed gale with more severity." A second suit of sails fluttered away in ribbons. Officers defiantly kept Christmas Day, "which we celebrated with dishes and chairs lashed to the table." *Orpheus* "rolled so deep and quick that the guns in the galley drew the ring bolts from the side and broke loose," followed by seventy-four unsecured shot boxes skittering across the deck. By January 25, the daily supply of fresh water was down to half a pint per man, and "all hopes of ever seeing land again had vanished."

But on Wednesday, January 31, the ship—"covered strangely with ice and such a wreck as hardly before ever was seen"—dropped anchor at

Halifax after a ninety-three-day passage that was "distressing beyond all description." Seamanship had won through, barely. Twenty crewmen suffered frostbite, and dozens more were sick or injured. The following Sunday, Midshipman James noted, those who could still walk to church "returned thanks to Almighty God."

Months would pass before *Orpheus* would again be fit for duty, and her travails illuminated the Royal Navy's larger quandary on the North American station as 1776 began. Although the squadron had grown modestly to thirty-eight vessels, carrying almost eight hundred guns, foul weather, crew shortages, and relentless demands from London confounded first Graves and now Shuldham, who would call himself "the football of fortune." In addition to protecting Dunmore in Virginia and the other floating governors along the American seaboard, the navy was to conduct punitive raids; support the army; escort merchantmen; send five ships to protect Nova Scotia, including the vital dockyard at Halifax; aid besieged Quebec; carry dispatches to all compass points; and enforce Parliament's trade ban by stationing men-of-war on approaches to the colonies, from Maine to Florida.

The tasks were too many, the seas too vast, the sails too few. Seventy-two rebel schooners, brigs, and sloops—bearing names like *Molly*, *Deborah*, *Eunice*, and *Rose*—had been captured in the second half of 1775; their impounded cargoes included lumber, whale oil, rum, salt, flour, and slaves (though no gunpowder or other munitions). Yet thousands of others came and went, using remote coves and large harbors, salt creeks and broad rivers. Philadelphia, the biggest American port, would feel little disruption from the Royal Navy through most of 1776.

Worse yet, the Americans had formed their own cockleshell fleet to bedevil British mariners in New England waters. Almost a dozen merchant ships berthed at Marblehead, Plymouth, and Beverly were converted into men-of-war with gun carriages and short-range swivels, as well as topsails and flying jibs for pursuit or flight. Vessels that normally carried a crew of ten or twelve now held fifty, armed with cutlasses, spears, and other boarding weapons; some flew flags depicting a pine tree on a white background with the motto "AN APPEAL TO HEAVEN." Although fitted with ancient cannons "that Noah had in the ark," as one captain joked, and with galley chimneys that leaked so badly "the smoke serves for bedding, victual, drink, and choking," the marauders further complicated Howe's supply woes. By early spring, fifty-five British prizes would be taken, mostly victuallers bound for Boston, like *Unity*, carrying lumber and naval stores, and *Industry*, full of cordwood, turnips, potatoes, butter, and cheese.

The greatest prize, however, was *Nancy*, a lightly armed, 250-ton British ordnance brig that had separated from her convoy during an autumn storm while carrying munitions from Thames armories. For much of November she repeatedly tried to work her way into Boston Harbor against gales and snow squalls, forced each time to claw far to the east for sea room to avoid foundering in shoal water. His Majesty's men-of-war crisscrossed Massachusetts Bay in a frantic search that dragged on for weeks. Twice *Nancy* was found by frigates, first the *Cerberus* and then the *Mercury*, only to be parted during thick weather and darkness within a few leagues of Boston Light. On November 29, tacking in patchy fog twenty miles from the harbor, *Nancy* lay back her sails and hoisted a set of signals for a schooner spied dead ahead and presumed to be a pilot boat sent to guide the brig to safety.

The *Lee* was in fact a converted merchantman, bristling with swivels and 4-pounders, and commanded by John Manley, an English-born veteran of the Royal Navy who had long sailed out of Boston as a commercial skipper. Manley answered the signal flags by sending across a longboat with a boarding party concealed on the thwarts and stern sheets. Not until brigands brandishing pistols and cutlasses scrambled over his gunwales did *Nancy*'s master realize his error. A prize crew took the helm and sailed the brig into nearby Gloucester harbor. For two days stevedores hoisted cargo from *Nancy*'s hold to the deck, and then into wagons backed onto the wharf. An inventory revealed cargo valued at more than £20,000: 2,000 muskets, bayonets, steel ramrods, and cartridge boxes; more than 100,000 flints; 31 tons of musket shot; 10,000 iron balls for 6- and 12-pounders, plus 20,000 1-pound balls; 3,000 case shot; dozens of lanterns and frying pans; 150 camp kettles; over 100,000 nails and 20,000 spikes; 11 gun carriages and 7 ammunition wagons; plus watch coats and harnesses for both horses and men to move field guns. Most impressive was a 13-inch brass mortar, carefully lowered into a wagon bed and driven forty miles southwest to Cambridge. There, before a gleeful crowd, General Putnam used a bottle of rum to christen the mortar "Congress." On the barrel the brass initials "G.R."—George Rex—were amended with a chisel to "G.W."—George Washington. "Congress" was deemed "the noblest piece of ordnance ever landed in America," and rebels crowded close to pat it for good luck. A Boston loyalist lamented in a letter to his sister, "The ways of heaven are dark & intricate."

"Captain Manley's good fortune seems to stick to him," an American officer observed. In the subsequent weeks, sometimes flying a British flag for deception, the captain and his comrades captured eight ships, including *Concord*, carrying coal and dry goods from Scotland; the *Little Hannah*, loaded with rum, cocoa, and oranges from Antigua; and *Betsey*, carrying forage from Virginia. "You no doubt have heard of Captain Manley," one admirer wrote, "because his name is famous, and as many towns contend for the honor of his birth as they did for that of Homer." In January, Washington appointed him commodore "of our little squadron" plying Massachusetts Bay. The commanding general only wished that other skippers would emulate Manley's "great vigilance and industry"; too many, he complained, showed "a fondness to be on shore."

Nancy's capture shocked the king's men in London. Lord Germain complained of the "natural sloth of sea operations." Additional arms shipments to America would be delayed until better security could be adopted, even if that required further burdening the navy. All ordnance vessels would be required to mount at least a dozen carriage guns, with three or more experienced gunners manning each one. "The loss of the ordnance storeship," Lord Sandwich, first lord of the Admiralty, wrote Germain, "is a fatal event."

The winter passed pleasantly enough at Vassall House in Cambridge. Washington's headquarters had been furnished with borrowed Chippendale chairs, yellow tableware, and at least nine chamber pots. Adjutants, orderlies, and couriers came and went from the commanding general's office in the northeast corner on the ground floor, and many convivial meals were served in the adjacent dining room, with its fine view toward the Charles. The Vassall larder benefited from provisions seized on those captured British victuallers, including turtle, loaf sugar, and porter, though Washington rejected a confiscated barrel of tea as politically unpalatable. But the Madeira flowed freely, often ordered in consignments of a hundred bottles or more, and the table fairly groaned with lamb, mutton, veal, and beef, as well as wood ducks, partridges, eels, and smelt.

The house had become even livelier in mid-December with the arrival of Martha Washington in a white coach-and-four adorned with the family crest, accompanied by five slaves wearing scarlet livery. Lady Washington had never been north of Alexandria, Virginia, but would henceforth share her husband's camp life for half of the war's one hundred months. She provided intimacy for a man with few intimates, addressing him privately as "my love." "They are very happy in each other," General Greene reported. In her presence, another observer noted, Washington "throws off the hero and takes on the chatty, agreeable companion." Under five feet tall, with hazel eyes and a lovely smile, she reportedly tugged the general's collar when she wanted his attention, to bring his face to her level. "Patsy," as he called her, was clearly both his match and his mate. He had ordered a curtained, four-poster bed before her arrival—after their marriage sixteen years earlier, his first requisition from a London merchant had included four ounces of Spanish fly, an aphrodisiac made from crushed beetles—and now he arranged to buy her lemons, limes, oranges, and pickles from another captured cargo. "I confess I shudder every time I hear the sound of a gun," she wrote a friend on December 30, "but I endeavor to keep my fears to myself as well as I can."

Lady Washington brought him news from Mount Vernon to supplement the overseer's letters that gave His Excellency such pleasure: the corn crop had been good despite heavy autumn rain; creek-bed stone would be used to finish the chimney tops; the kitchen and storehouse roofs had been painted, and the slave quarters repaired; a new vineyard had been planted; a nasty bull had fatally gored a draft horse. Because of Governor Dunmore's antics, "the common people are most hellishly frightened," but most gentlemen were prepared to defend Mount Vernon and other Potomac plantations as needed.

Across the American encampment, drums beat each morning at first light, and troops manned the lines in force to repel any surprise attack. After sunrise they marched to prayers. Chaplains attended their souls—one sermon sought to prove theologically that Satan was a Tory—while sergeants and junior officers worked on their soldiering skills, from parade drill to fire discipline. British artillery peppered the rebel lines every day, to modest effect; by one tally, enemy guns fired more than two thousand rounds in the six months after the burning of Charlestown but killed only seven Americans in Cambridge and a dozen in Roxbury. Shells arced overhead at night, "moving like stars in the heavens," as a rebel fifer wrote. Mortar shells sometimes struck frozen ground and bounded up again; others plopped into the marshes without detonating, to be dug out by Yankee scavengers eager to extract the powder.

Washington often rode out with his spyglass to Prospect and Cobble Hills, unmistakable in his blue silk moiré sash. Little had changed in six months except for the density of fortifications on both sides. Batteries, parapets, and redoubts extended for twenty miles, with breastworks seventeen feet thick in places. Above Boston Neck, American troops had built a defensive wall along Lamb's Dam, originally constructed to prevent rising tides from flooding the marshes. More than a hundred apple trees had been felled to make an abatis. For their part, the British had emplaced twenty guns at the Neck, plus a mortar battery, six howitzers, a blockhouse, and other defenses.

"I pity our good general who has a greater burden on his shoulders, and more difficulties to struggle with than I think should fall to the share of so good a man," James Warren wrote John Adams in December. "I see he is fatigued and worried." Few knew just how fatigued and how worried.

To Schuyler, Washington alluded to "difficulties and troubles . . . such as I never expected. But they must be borne with." Perhaps only to his aide and confidant Joseph Reed, who had left Cambridge to return to his Philadelphia law practice, did the commanding general reveal his deepest anxieties. "Could I have foreseen what I have, & am likely to experience," he wrote, "no consideration upon earth should have induced me to accept this command." On January 4, he told Reed, "For more than two months past I have scarcely emerged from one difficulty before I have plunged into another. How it will end, God in his great goodness will direct. . . . I distrust everything." Ten days later he added:

> We are now without any money in our treasury, powder in our magazines, arms in our stores. . . . I have often thought how much happier I should have been if, instead of accepting a command under such circumstances, I had taken my musket upon my shoulder & entered the ranks, or . . . retired to the back country, & lived in a wigwam.

For two months Washington had struggled, as he told Hancock, to simultaneously "disband one army and recruit another" within musket range of "twenty-odd British regiments." With thousands of enlistments expiring in December, he personally pleaded with Connecticut regiments to remain in camp at least until the new year, although most had not been paid in weeks. Instead the "vile poltroons," in General Sullivan's phrase, began to abscond even before their terms were up. After ordering one recalcitrant regiment to appear outside his quarters, the unbridled General Lee threatened to have riflemen fire on them, adding, "Men, I do not know what to call you. You are the worst of all creatures."

Officers tried liquor, pleas, shame, and curses to keep the army intact. Nevertheless, by December 10, as Greene wrote, "Connecticut troops are going home in shoals," ignoring jeers from their erstwhile comrades. More departures by other New Englanders followed in what Washington denounced as a "dirty, mercenary spirit." He ordered weapons and ammunition seized from the exiting troops, but scores of muskets disappeared. A Virginia physician noted that revolutionary fervor had faded throughout the colonies. "We were once all fire," he wrote. "Now most of us are become inanimate and indifferent."

As the final enlistments expired with the year, Greene wrote a friend on December 31, "We never have been so weak as we shall be tomorrow when we dismiss the old troops." Of more than three dozen second lieutenants authorized in the Rhode Island and New Hampshire regiments, not one agreed to reenlist. Washington's plan to form a professional army of twenty thousand, capable of confronting British regulars, lay in tatters. But on Monday, January 1, he put on a brave face to applaud soldiers who had agreed to join "the new army, which in every point of view is entirely Continental." A thirteen-gun salute echoed through the Cambridge camp at the raising on a tall staff of a new flag, the precise design of which was not recorded but apparently included thirteen alternating red and white stripes with the superimposed crosses of Saint George and Saint Andrew in the upper left-hand corner. Confused British sentries initially assumed that the flag, which vaguely resembled their own, was a gesture of submission, if not surrender.

Though still drawn largely from New England, this Continental Army was intended to embody national unity, or "at least the illusion of unified purpose, military strength, and political respectability, both at home and abroad," as the historian John Shy would write. An illusion it was: regimental returns on the evening of January 9 showed 8,212 men in the new army, of whom only 5,582 were present and fit for duty. "I find myself weaker than I had any idea of," Washington wrote. He could only guess how many Americans remained in the Northern Army in Canada, and had yet to hear of Montgomery's catastrophe at Quebec. Each regiment now received a numerical designation, starting with riflemen in the 1st Continental Regiment. Greene's three Rhode Island regiments were incorporated into the new 9th and 11th Continentals, but together they mustered only seven hundred men, less than half their authorized strength.

So desperate was Washington for manpower that he reversed an earlier edict prohibiting free blacks from reenlisting, essentially daring skeptical white southerners in Congress to overrule him. They did not, given his convictions that victory could depend on "which side can arm the Negroes faster" and that black volunteers spurned by the American army might join the British. For now, slaves were barred from the ranks. Roughly five thousand African Americans would eventually serve in the Continental Army, a more integrated national force than would exist for nearly two centuries.

Washington also had no choice but to ask New England governors to send five thousand militiamen for extended duty. They arrived in camp sullenly, to be dubbed the "Long-Faced People" by Continental veterans.

After bitter debate, in late December Congress had directed Washington to evict the enemy from Boston "notwithstanding the town and the property in it may thereby be destroyed." Rarely did the aggressive commander in chief need prodding. On Tuesday, January 16, he asked a war council at Vassall House to endorse "the indispensable necessity of making a bold attempt to conquer the ministerial troops in Boston before they can be reinforced in the spring." His generals unanimously agreed to "a vigorous attempt."

But how? Despite the *Nancy* windfall, nearly two thousand soldiers in his feeble army lacked firelocks. Each regiment was given $500 to try to buy muskets in the countryside, though they were cautioned to avoid bidding against one another. A decent Brown Bess with a bayonet could bring $12. Of even greater concern, as Washington told Reed, "our want of powder is inconceivable." In the seventy-five official letters he wrote during the first two months of 1776, Washington mentioned munitions—particularly gunpowder, which he called "the thing"—in half of them, often in obsessive, pleading, fretful terms. Militia regiments arrived with so little gunpowder that fifty barrels were given to them from Continental magazines, leaving barely enough for twenty-four rounds per soldier—less than half the number typically carried by each regular. Washington wanted four hundred barrels—twenty tons—for his infantry alone, plus an ample supply for artillery. But in mid-February he would have no more than five tons in stock, the same paltry amount he had found in Cambridge upon arriving the previous July. More hefty fines were levied for every missing cartridge, and Washington ordered any departing soldier who tried "to carry off a single grain of ammunition" to be "pursued, brought back, and severely punished." But undisciplined shooting persisted, sometimes at redcoats, sometimes at geese. "It is impossible to conceive upon what principle this strange itch for firing originates," Greene wrote.

Other shortages mirrored those plaguing the British. "We have suffered prodigiously for want of wood," Greene added. "We have burnt up all the fences and cut down all the trees for a mile around the camp." The army would burn eight thousand cords in six months, and on particularly cold days, the firewood demand equaled the timber from a four-acre woodlot. Despite efforts by the Committee on Wood in Watertown to organize cutting expeditions, a number of regiments were forced to eat their provisions raw, and many soldiers shivered in their sleep. While 120 barracks were under construction in Cambridge and Roxbury—each man got fourteen square feet of living space—a lumber shortage kept some in tents into January. Hunger in the ranks led to pilfering from nearby farms. "The devil would now and then tell us that it was no harm sometimes to pull a few potatoes and cabbages," one private confessed.

Cheek-by-jowl living led to sickness, regardless of the eight pounds of hard soap allocated weekly to each company. "Autumnal fevers" became winter maladies: typhus, malaria, jaundice, respiratory infections. Men suffering from dysentery were treated with bleeding, purging, and pills of grated pepper, flour, and turpentine, and still they were said to melt away at the bowels. General orders in January required court-martialing soldiers "discovered easing themselves" except in latrine pits, known as "necessaries." Newspapers advertised nostrums and quack cures for various ailments, but legitimate drugs, as well as bandages and tourniquets, quickly ran short in both general and regimental hospitals. In December, the Cambridge pharmacy was down to a single pound of ipecac, used as both a cough syrup and a purgative.

No malady worried Washington more than what some called the "king of terrors." "Smallpox rages all over the town," he wrote Hancock. Howe's expulsion from Boston of more than four hundred civilians suspected of infection, plus claims from British deserters that refugees dumped onto Pulling Point at the harbor entrance were contagious because of recent inoculation, led Washington to condemn "a weapon of defense they are using against us." As in Quebec, no firm evidence existed of British efforts to wage biological warfare, but rumors circulated that they were even using infected counterfeit currency to spread the disease. (A British major publicly proposed a year later, "Dip arrows in . . . smallpox and twang them at the American rebels.") Refugees were quarantined, their effects smoked, and letters from Boston were doused with vinegar. "If we escape the smallpox in this camp & the country round about," Washington wrote Reed, "it will be miraculous."

For now, the camp and the country round about settled into the rhythms of a winter siege and waited for spring. James Gray's store in Medford sold leather breeches, West Indies rum, and barrels of brown sugar. William Thompson in Brookline advertised cocoa by the cask, horsewhips, ink pots, sewing twine, and Tenerife wine. In Cambridge, at the Freemasons' Arms, one J. Keith offered fencing lessons so that "gentlemen of the army may learn the polite accomplishment of the small sword [and] the use of the broad sword, according to the manner of the ancient gladiators of Rome." Mary Gray in Dorchester advertised "a young Negro woman" for sale: "Has had the smallpox."

The usual wild rumors flitted from lip to ear—that a tempest off Newfoundland had drowned four thousand redcoats, and that Washington had given Howe a fortnight to quit Boston before the town would be reduced to ash. The king's bellicose speech to open Parliament was read aloud to shouts and jeers. Riflemen took shots at enemy ramparts—one British officer described them as "the most fatal widow-and-orphan makers in the world." But most American troops stood idle. "We really are tired of inaction," wrote Stephen Moylan, the army's muster master general. He described General Putnam as "still as hard as ever, crying out for powder, powder, ye gods, give us powder."

Inaction, as usual, led some soldiers astray. "There was a man found dead in a room with a woman this morning," Private David How told his diary in February. "It is not known what killed him." The same week Private Obadiah Brown reported, "Two soldiers drank 33 glasses of brandy & gin. One died." If most avoided trouble, few escaped homesickness. "When will the time come that we shall all sit down in our little room and eat a Sunday's dinner together?" Lieutenant Samuel Shaw wrote his family from Prospect Hill. "Perhaps soon. Perhaps never." Shaw added, "A sense of what I owe to my country, my parents, and myself will induce me to behave in a suitable manner."

"You told me that you intended to see me once a month," Sarah Hodgkins, age twenty-four, wrote her husband, Joseph, a cobbler from Lexington who had reenlisted as a lieutenant for another year. "I don't think it is for want of a good will that you don't come home." She admitted missing him in bed "these cold nights" and urged him to write "since that is all the way we have to converse together. It is much to my grief that it is so." Lois Peters told her husband, Captain Nathan Peters, that she had harvested eighty bushels of corn and sold the oxen for £10 to keep their saddlery solvent. "Pray come home as soon as possible. . . . A visit from you at any time would be agreeable." If he sent some cloth, she would sew him a shirt and "take great pleasure in doing it." She signed her letter, "Your loving wife until dead."

Good news, very good news, reached Washington's headquarters on Thursday, January 18, when a bulky, bowlegged man with brilliant gray eyes rode into Cambridge after a two-month absence. Only twenty-five, he habitually wrapped his left hand in a silk handkerchief to conceal the stumps of two fingers amputated after the barrel of his fowling piece exploded in a hunting mishap on Noddle's Island two years earlier. Even as a boy working in a Boston book bindery, he had impressed John Adams with "his pleasing manners and inquisitive turn of mind." He was, the writer Washington Irving would observe, "one of those providential characters which spring up in emergencies as if formed by and for the occasion."

This surely was an emergency, and here was young Henry Knox to announce that against stiff odds he had transported, in midwinter by boat and by sled, fifty-eight fine guns from Fort Ticonderoga and Crown Point—cannons and mortars, brass and iron. Those guns, momentarily parked twenty miles to the west on a muddy roadside in Framingham, were now his, and he was ready and eager to blow the British out of his hometown. But first he had to have a uniform tailored—no simple task for a man who eventually weighed almost three hundred pounds—since he had just learned of his new commission as a colonel in command of all Continental artillery.

In an era of improbable ascents, Henry Knox's rise was among the least likely. At age nine, he had been forced to drop out of Boston Latin Grammar School when his father abandoned the family for the West Indies after his shipbuilding business collapsed. The boy went to work, both in the bindery and as an autodidact, teaching himself passable French and studying *Plutarch's Lives* and *Caesar's Commentaries*. At eighteen he joined a militia artillery company, training on brass 3-pounders under British tutelage and firing salutes for the king's birthday. As a witness to the Boston Massacre, he testified at the subsequent trials and soon after opened his London Book-Store, peddling Bibles, law books, and almanacs in an effort, as he advertised, "to exterminate ignorance and darkness." Knox himself was an attraction. "He was affable without familiarity, dignified without parade, imposing without arrogance," one admirer wrote.

Within three years the shop had become "a fashionable morning lounge" for browsing British officers and well-heeled Bostonians alike, an emporium offering stationery, wallpaper, quills, flutes, Keyser's pills, telescopes, "cordial cephalic snuff," reading glasses, and Hill's "never-failing cure for the bite of a mad dog." And books: twenty volumes of Voltaire, ecclesiastical histories, the eleven-volume *Complete History of England*, treatises on shoeing horses and how to treat venereal disease with mercury, *Tom Jones*, *Tristram Shandy*, and various pirated Irish editions, which were cheaper than books published in England. A few weeks before the British marched to Lexington, Knox offered a shilling pamphlet on "the dispute between Great Britain and the colonies" by a precocious New York college student named Alexander Hamilton.

In June 1774, he married a customer, Lucy Flucker, daughter of the colony's last royal secretary and sister of a British Army lieutenant. A fine chess player and a spirited gambler, she was described by one acquaintance as "a young lady of high intellectual endowments, very fond of books." She would be Knox's equal in patriotic ardor and, almost, in girth. "Her size is enormous," a Boston woman would later write. "I am frightened when I look at her." Knox called her "my charmer"; she called him Harry. Together they had fled the town in late spring, abandoning Boston to the British and the shop to vandals. Knox would be paying off debts to his suppliers until the day he died.

The American camp soon recognized his engineering and artillery skills, as well as his deep reading in military matters. He helped design the entrenchments and fortifications at Roxbury, then trained novice gunners. Though still a volunteer pending approval of his commission by Congress, he sufficiently impressed Washington with the way he shot the guns with his big, maimed hands that he was entrusted with what many considered a fool's errand to Lake Champlain.

Knox had left Cambridge on November 15, traveling first to New York City and then up the Hudson to Albany before reaching Ticonderoga on December 5. In less than two weeks he had selected a "noble train of artillery" weighing sixty tons, lowered the guns from the fortress walls, shipped them thirty miles south across Lake George, then used five hundred fathoms of three-inch rope—more than half a mile—to lash the barrels to forty-two "exceeding strong sleds." He wrote to Washington on December 17, "It is not easy to conceive the difficulties we have had in getting them over the lake, owing to the advanced season of the year and contrary winds." Greater difficulties lay ahead. "Let the touchholes and vents of all the mortars and cannon be turned downwards," he advised his drovers. The heaviest guns required four pairs of horses and an occasional brace of oxen. A timely snowfall permitted the expedition to advance the twenty-six miles to Saratoga, whips cracking, teamsters shouting, the sleds two hundred yards apart and braked on slopes with block and tackle. "The road was dreary, the darkness great," a drover's young son later recalled.

Knox traveled ahead by sleigh and saddle horse to scout the route, hire pull teams, and buy provisions. A blizzard on Christmas as he approached Albany required him to dismount for "a very fatiguing march of about two miles in snow three feet deep"; he was, he admitted, "almost perished with the cold." To Lucy he wrote, "My lovely & dearest friend, those people who love as you and I do never ought to part." The first gun sled reached Albany on January 4. One 18-pounder broke through the ice while crossing the frozen Mohawk River just north of the city and was lost; another broke through the Hudson and was fished out. Teamsters cut holes in the river ice to let water dissolve the snowpack and, upon refreezing, strengthen the ice. Just in case, each sled captain carried an ax to cut the team's traces so sinking guns would not drag the horses to the bottom.

Crowds gathered on the east bank of the Hudson, cheering as each sled came across. The expedition turned south on the post road, then east to follow farm tracks and Indian trails across the Berkshires in Massachusetts. Delays slowed their progress—to wait out a thaw, to fix a broken sled, to fire a noisy 24-pounder called "Old Sow" for delighted townsfolk in Westfield, who toasted the demonstration with whiskey and hard cider. The steeper hills required drag chains, poles shoved under the runners, check ropes wrapped around tree trunks, and lead horses moved to the rear with rope stays and neck yokes to prevent runaway sleds. On January 10, Knox told his diary that they had "climbed mountains from which we might almost have seen all the kingdoms of the earth." A day later he added, "It appeared to me almost a miracle that people with heavy loads should be able to get up & down hills as are here." After crossing the frozen Connecticut River at Springfield, Knox dumped the guns in Framingham for safekeeping, then cantered on to tell Washington what he had done.

Knox had covered more than seven hundred miles since leaving Cambridge, nearly half of it lugging 120,000 pounds of dead metal. The return trip from Ticonderoga had taken forty days, rather than the fifteen he'd anticipated. The journey was a feat of endurance and pluck comparable to Arnold's anabasis through Maine, and his was a hero's welcome at Vassall House. As he prepared for a uniform fitting and to take command of the six hundred gunners in his regiment, he tallied his expedition expenses in an account book: £521, 15 shillings, and a few pence. One day Washington would say of Harry Knox: there was "no one whom I have loved more sincerely."

Knox was at Washington's elbow at ten a.m. on February 11, a frigid Sunday, when they rode to Roxbury for another look at the lay of the land. Major General Ward, commanding the right wing of the Continental Army, greeted them in the colonnaded loyalist mansion he had taken for his headquarters. Silver-studded mahogany doors led to an enormous entry hall with a tessellated floor, according to one description. Large mirrors in ebony frames stood between two grand staircases. Damascus satin upholstered a circular divan, and two cherubs carved from wood fluttered beneath a glass dome, their wings encircling a cut-glass chandelier. After a brief conference, the men left the house with a half dozen other officers, spyglasses in hand, and headed two miles east to the swampy isthmus that led to Dorchester Heights.

"I know the unhappy predicament I stand in," Washington had written the previous day in a long letter to Reed.

> I know that much is expected of me. I know that without men, without arms, without ammunition, without anything fit for the accommodation of a soldier that little is to be done—and which is mortifying. I know that I cannot stand justified to the world without exposing my own weakness & injuring the cause by declaring my wants.

He longed for decisive battle, what he called "the rumpus." With ample guns now available, perhaps a solution to the standoff in Boston could be found on this commanding ground south of town, despite the shortfall of Continental troops, small arms, and powder. Nine houses, most now vacant and ventilated by British fire, stood amid orchards and pastures on the windswept causeway leading to two craggy hills—glacial drumlins—that formed the heights. The summit offered a panoramic view of Boston, the harbor, and the British garrison at Castle William on an island to the east. Gage had intended to seize this high ground in June, but Bunker Hill persuaded him that British naval guns and field artillery could sweep the terrain without the fell cost of occupying it. At Ward's urging, Washington likewise, in the past eight months, had considered shifting troops to Dorchester only to demur for lack of firepower and fear of being trapped by a British landing behind them on the approach to the heights.

The commanding general and his retinue returned on Monday, leaving their horses half a mile from the isthmus to clamber along the rocky crest. This time Washington carried an elaborate artillery chart labeled, "The most important posts and rising ground . . . in the possession of the American and Ministerial Armies, near and in Boston." Distances were calculated between twenty-eight key locations, such as the 490 rods—8,085 feet—from Dorchester Point to Castle William. The author of this chart, Lieutenant Colonel Rufus Putnam, a cousin of the irrepressible general's, had also written Washington a memorandum after his visit the previous day, with a proposal on how to fortify Dorchester Heights despite the ominous British gun batteries at Boston Neck and elsewhere.

A "covered way" could be quickly erected across the isthmus, he urged, protecting engineers and artillerymen as they crossed to the high ground with Colonel Knox's guns. Putnam, a former millwright and self-taught surveyor who had traveled as far west as the Mississippi River, acknowledged that he "had never read a word on the subject of fortification." But a parapet, tall as a man and just over a thousand yards long, would suffice to shield the Dorchester cart path long enough to seize the heights. Because the ground was frozen twenty-eight inches deep, cutting turf to stack as an earthen wall was impossible; "nothing short of timber . . . will answer the purpose," along with hay bales and field stone salvaged from farm walls. He had recently visited a swamp twelve miles distant where almost a hundred tons of timber had already been cut and could be carted to Dorchester for twelve shillings a ton.

Washington was impressed but unconvinced as he trotted back to Cambridge. At ten a.m. on Friday, February 16, he convened another war council with half a dozen generals at Vassall House. A bombardment from the heights "might probably destroy the town without doing much damage to the ministerial troops within it," he argued. Howe could simply order his men onto transport ships in the harbor and wait for the reinforcements from Britain that would arrive in the spring. Powder supplies were still so paltry "that small arms must be our principal reliance." With the Charles finally frozen solid and able to support a Continental attack across the ice into Boston, "a stroke well-aimed at this critical juncture might put a final end to the war." He doubted that Howe had many more than five thousand troops fit for duty. Why not attack them head-on?

He was wrong, even foolish, and his lieutenants saved him from himself. They correctly doubted his estimate of British strength; although sickness ran high in the garrison, Howe in fact had close to nine thousand regulars, plus armed loyalists and the naval squadron. The American force, including a new tranche of militiamen, hardly amounted to thirteen thousand, many still unarmed, far too few for a frontal attack against an entrenched enemy. Greene, who was confined to his sickroom on Prospect Hill with jaundice—"yellow as saffron"—agreed in a letter that a successful attack "would put a finishing stroke to the war," but even with twenty thousand American troops an assault would be "horrible if it succeeded and still more horrible if it failed." Brigadier General Horatio Gates, the adjutant general and a former British officer who, like Washington, had survived the massacre of Braddock's expedition in 1755, worried that Howe's "artillerists . . . are as good as any in Europe." In short, the generals considered Washington's plan "exceedingly doubtful." Better to continue stockpiling powder and prepare "to take possession of Dorchester Hill, with a view of drawing out the enemy."

Washington could hardly conceal his exasperation. The war council "being almost unanimous I must suppose to be right," he wrote Hancock. "Perhaps the irksomeness of my situation . . . might have inclined me to put more to the hazard than was consistent with prudence." Only to Reed did he yield to sarcasm. "Behold! Though we had been waiting all the year for this favorable event, the enterprise was thought too dangerous!" he wrote in a trenchant letter nearly three thousand words long. "The enterprise, if it had been undertaken with resolution, must have succeeded. . . . I am preparing to take post on Dorchester to try if the enemy will be so kind as to come out to us." He positioned extra sentinels around the heights to ensure that the British did not try to seize the high ground before he did. All correspondence into Boston was halted in an effort to avoid alerting the enemy to his plan; a small child permitted to enter the town to join his loyalist parents was first searched for hidden letters.

Heavy sleds from Framingham began to creep toward Roxbury, along with wagons stacked high with swamp timber. "The preparations increase and something great is daily expected," Abigail Adams wrote John on February 21. "Something terrible it will be. I impatiently wait for, yet dread the day."

10.

―――――

The Whipping Snake

War was good for Cork. Convoys bound for North America assembled in the Cove of Kinsale or along the newly extended Navigation Wall in one of Europe's finest harbors. Red sandstone warehouses on the waterfront bulged with flour, peas, and bread from East Anglia, shipped here and earmarked for Canada or Boston or the new battlefront said to be opening soon in the American South. In late fall, eighty thousand bullocks had plodded through the markets north of Blarney Lane and then to the city's abattoirs, where carts day and night hauled away the slaughtered beef for packing in barrels made by sixty master coopers and a thousand journeymen. So much preserved beef came from ox-slaying Cork, much of it intended for the Royal Navy and army regiments abroad, that slaughterhouses used four hundred barrels of salt a day, mostly imported from Portugal. In winter, herds of pigs fattened on potatoes ran through the streets toward a similar fate, and bumboats ferried barreled pork by the ton to the victuallers waiting offshore. Each British soldier deployed to America needed a half ton of food every year to sustain him, and much of it would come through Cork, where the blessed Saint Finbar had built his monastery on the braided river Lee in the sixth century.

The city stank of blood and livestock excrement washed into the same Lee, but to the brokers, shippers, and army contractors who crowded Cork—nearly all of them British Protestants—the smell was of money. They lived on islands in the river, traveling above the squalid streets in sedan chairs led by link boys, and congregating in the evening at the fine new Mansion House on Hammond's Marsh for claret, backgammon, and minuets. For the Irish Catholics—"Saint Patrick's vermin," prohibited from sitting in Parliament, joining trade guilds, holding military commissions, carrying swords, buying land, or practicing law—wartime prosperity was more elusive. Some made their way in the butter trade, packing salted firkins covered with cabbage leaves. Surging demand for wool to make army uniforms helped put idle looms back to work, although to protect the English cloth industry, the Irish could export their wool only to England, and no sheep could be shorn within four miles of the sea to prevent fleeces from being smuggled abroad.

British Army recruiters often appeared in Cork, "beating up" for volunteers with bands and barrels of beer and jingling coin purses. For added firepower in America, London had ordered each regiment expanded to 677 men by adding 10 sergeants, 10 drummers, and 180 privates; Ireland seemed an obvious source of cannon fodder. A regular's pay of eight pence a day, minus deductions for uniforms and provisions, had not increased in a century, but recruiting bounties of more than a guinea were now offered. As announced in mid-December, volunteers no longer had to enlist for life; they could resign at the end of the American war if they had served at least three years. Standards were low: illiteracy in the ranks already ran to two-thirds, and a recruit must only attest that he had "no rupture, nor ever was troubled with fits."

Even so, recruiting remained abysmal. By late winter, Lord Barrington reported to Lord Germain that fewer than a thousand men had been raised in Ireland and Britain together, despite accepting sots, men who spoke only Gaelic, and petty rogues, like the half dozen men from Shrewsbury jail who would be inducted into the 46th Foot. A good Irish potato harvest and lack of enthusiasm for transatlantic travel to a pestilential climate suppressed enlistments in Cork and the other counties. Many Irishmen vowed never to pull trigger on the Americans, "among whom they all have relations," according to an account from Cork. Recruiting had even grown dangerous, with Irish thugs in Dublin and Cork "houghing" regulars at night by severing their Achilles tendons with razors or meat cleavers, the historian Don N. Hagist would write.

"Sad work everywhere in recruiting," General Harvey, the adjutant general, had written in late December. "In these damned times we must exert zeal." Germain, ever zealous, told the king that the "ardor of the nation in this cause has not hitherto arisen to the pitch one could wish." Many British commanders believed that the Irish only brought trouble. Of seventy-one recruits enlisted by the 46th Foot in Ireland between Christmas and early February, fifteen deserted immediately. "They are the very scum of the earth," a recruiting officer complained, "and do their utmost to desert the moment they are clothed." General Howe concurred. The Irish were "certain to desert if put to hard work," he warned, and were "not entitled to the smallest confidence as soldiers."

* * *

Bustling Cork was even busier after being chosen as the launching point for the boldest British gambit of the American war to date, and perhaps the most ill-considered.

Royal governors in the southern colonies had long pleaded for reinforcements to hearten the loyalists—the so-called good Americans—and to splinter the rebellion geographically. Governor Campbell, in South Carolina, believed that two thousand regulars would "set matters right" there and in Georgia. Governor Dunmore, in Virginia, had vowed to "restore order" with "two or three hundred men" before failing miserably. But none was more relentless than Governor Josiah Martin, in North Carolina, a Dublin-born former British Army officer. The colony's population had increased sixfold since 1750, to 275,000, including many émigrés from Scotland deeply loyal to the Crown. But in May 1775, rebels chased the governor from his capital in New Bern to the sanctuary of a British man-of-war on the Cape Fear River below Wilmington. Even then he told London that a small detachment of regulars, plus a generous consignment of arms, would allow him to marshal at least fifteen thousand loyalists in "the back settlements" to reduce both North and South Carolina "to obedience," to "awe the colony of Virginia" into submission, and to prevent rebel regiments from reinforcing New England. Martin's eagerness to avenge his humiliating rout from New Bern had a certain poignancy: over the past three years he had lost three children, most recently his eldest son, to what he called "this most baneful climate."

Before leaving office, Lord Dartmouth had been the first of the king's ministers to be beguiled by the vision of a cheap southern victory. The previous September, he had promised to send ten thousand stand of arms and six fieldpieces to Howe "to enable you to assist [Martin]," while adding, "I must confess, I think he is much too sanguine. . . . There is not much ground to hope anything considerable can be effected there." Yet nothing ventured, nothing gained: Howe was advised "to send one battalion of troops" to North Carolina under an "able & intelligent officer," who would take command of a brigade dispatched to Cape Fear from Cork. "The appearance of a respectable force to the southward," Dartmouth wrote, "will have the effect to restore order and government in those four provinces." After quickly asserting British authority in the South and permitting "the well-affected" to regain control of their colonies, most of the regulars could join Howe in Boston or New York for the spring campaign. "I hope," Dartmouth added, "we are not deceived in the assurances that have been given."

Lord North also embraced this hallucination, certain that a quiescent loyalist majority needed little more than a galvanic spark to rise up. "A small force from home would quickly turn the scale," the first minister had written King George in October, in an eleven-page explanation of the southern strategy that cited "the very important advantages which may be expected." The large slave population and the need for European commodities made the southern colonies vulnerable, North continued. Even if the rebellion was not promptly quashed, "the houses, stores, &c. belonging to the insurgents may be plundered, their provisions may be destroyed." Ringleaders could be arrested, militias disarmed. Referring to himself in the third person, he added:

> Lord North looks upon it, therefore, as certain that a very considerable number of the people in those provinces wish for a speedy accommodation of the disputes with Great Britain. . . . A measure of vigor & éclat will alarm the Americans, & revive the spirits of our friends.

George replied within two hours. "Every means of distressing America," he wrote, "must meet with my concurrence." By the next morning, the king had identified British regiments in Ireland and two artillery companies for the expedition; loyalists in the Carolinas should be offered land grants and army pay to encourage fealty. The Admiralty was ordered to move enough ships to Cork to transport the regiments, along with the sixty tons of baggage, sixty women, and twelve servants each could deploy. Trusted pilots familiar with the North Carolina coast must be hired, while "keeping this matter an impenetrable secret."

With Germain's appointment as American secretary, the expedition grew in size and ambition. Two units intended for Quebec would be diverted south, bringing the force to seven regiments, plus at least twenty field guns. Under Sir Peter Parker's command, men-of-war carrying fifteen hundred crewmen and mounting two hundred guns were assigned to escort the troop transports and storeships. To the king's delight, a favored young general, Charles Earl Cornwallis, a member of the House of Lords, volunteered to join the expedition. Since the North Carolina operation would "probably not be of long duration," Germain wrote, the assault force could also help crush rebels in Virginia or South Carolina, and then perhaps Savannah, before joining Howe "as early in the spring as possible," leaving behind just enough force to "secure the well-affected from danger."

A modest, show-the-flag mission to succor North Carolina loyalists had become an immodest campaign of confused purpose, vaguely intended to subdue a region almost twice the size of the United Kingdom in a couple months by delivering, in the king's words, "a severe blow to the rebels." The confusion could be seen when Barrington arrived at his War Office chambers one morning to find five regiments ordered away from Ireland in December, although "I am not apprized where they are going"; the secretary at war subsequently suggested to the cabinet that "in all military matters not to stir a step without full consultation of able military men." Befuddlement also arose over whether the Cape Fear River was too shallow for British warships, although English seamen had sailed those waters for over a century. Germain's orders to the expedition leaders on December 7 included five paragraphs beginning with "If."

The cardinal principle of concentrating military force had been abandoned by George and his ministers; so, too, had the pursuit of clear strategic goals while avoiding diversionary sideshows. Rebel strength, cohesion, and ruthlessness in the southern colonies were disregarded, loyalist fervor and competence exaggerated. British military resources, already stretched, would be stretched further. Governor Martin's "original, fatal euphoria," in the phrase of the British historian K. G. Davies, carried the day. Curiously, given ample time for reflection while confined to a British frigate on the Cape Fear River, the governor entertained second thoughts. In a whinging, seventeen-paragraph dispatch to London, he conceded that trying to rally loyalists would only inflame the rebels, "sacrifice the friends of government, and disgrace myself." The letter reached Germain in late November, too late to stop an expedition already in motion.

Howe had his own doubts. In a long letter to London on January 16, he questioned whether Governor Martin "is not deceived in his expectations." Would it not have been better to secure New York first before turning south to "designs of less importance"? The rebels, Howe added, certainly knew of the expedition mounting in Cork; the "impenetrable secret" had been penetrated. But, as instructed, he sent an able commander, Major General Henry Clinton, to North Carolina with a small detachment to await the squadron from Ireland. As he sailed south from Boston on January 20, Clinton wrote, "Governors are sanguine, the malady is catching, and ministers [are] sometimes infected."

"Where are we going, how are we going, and what we are going about nobody pretends to conjecture," wrote Captain James Murray of the 57th Foot, among the regiments waiting to sail from Cork. An expedition of only twenty-six hundred men, he told a friend, would "make but little impression on the continent of America." Murray sarcastically proposed "shooting 7 Americans a week, exclusive of women and children, to teach them to defend their liberties."

The southern expedition required impeccable timing, but chaos plagued the mission from the start. December 1, the original sailing date, came and went without the squadron leaving Cork, as did New Year's Day and the queen's birthday in mid-January. Difficulties piled up. Delay followed delay. Ordnance storeships and bomb tenders were not loaded on the Thames until mid-December; then a relentless east wind prevented them from reaching Portsmouth, much less sailing on to Ireland. *Deal Castle* ran aground in Plymouth and had to cut away her masts. *Boreas* was badly hurt after running aground while leaving Spithead. Delays kept Commodore Parker in Portsmouth until December 29, and then an ill wind prevented his arrival in Cork for another week. The *Marquis of Rockingham*, a transport making for Cork's harbor with three companies of the 32nd Foot intended to replace troops bound for America, foundered off the southern coast of Ireland in a gale; the captain, crew, and ninety soldiers drowned. "Misfortunes seldom come alone," Rear Admiral Sir Hugh Palliser, an Admiralty official, wrote Lord Sandwich in early January.

Still more misfortunes followed. Seven transports were found to be incapable of stowing the flat-bottomed boats needed for amphibious landings. A marine lieutenant aboard *Syren* shot dead the frigate's first lieutenant in a duel on January 18. "We are certainly not in luck," General Harvey, the adjutant general, wrote in January, "either in America or in Europe."

Yet luck, that handy scapegoat, was only part of it. The Cork expedition, coupled with difficulties in supplying Boston and preparations for the 1776 campaign season, fully revealed the American quagmire. "Some people begin to be astonished and staggered at the unexpected difficulties we are in," Admiral Palliser wrote Sandwich. "The demands for the small army now in America are so great as to be thought impossible to furnish. . . . What will it be when we have another army there above 20,000 men?" If Howe's host reached 35,000 troops and 4,000 horses later in the year, as anticipated, thirty-seven tons of food and thirty-eight tons of hay and oats would be required *every day*, almost entirely from Britain. Since an army that size would consume some four thousand tons of meat a year, ox-slaying Cork would stay busy.

Already the search for ships to move men and matériel had grown frantic. In early 1776, the Admiralty sought eighty-eight thousand tons of shipping—a typical troop transport might be three hundred tons—but could find only fifty-six thousand. Every harbor in the kingdom was searched. Newspaper ads appealed for ships to lease. Diplomats and agents hired vessels in Amsterdam, Hamburg, and other foreign ports, paying ever higher freight costs. The Admiralty's Navy Board had to compete for tonnage not only with the civilian carrying trade—including slavers—but also with the Ordnance Board, which ran its own fleet. And of course more men-of-war were needed to protect sea routes and additional convoys. In a note penned on January 11, the king had suggested converting colliers into warships. "Every means of obtaining a large force on float ought to be adopted," George wrote. A plea to General Howe urged a quick turnaround of vessels from North America because "this country is so exhausted of ships."

Heavy snow entombed Cork on Wednesday, January 31. "We have been on the point of sailing every day for these three weeks past," Captain Murray wrote on February 1. "Everything is conducted in such a harum-scarum, humble-jumble manner. . . . No situation [is] more abominable than that of waiting from day to day." Seven regiments had been cooped up for nearly a month on more than two dozen transports moored in the harbor. Living on two-thirds rations, each regular received a straw sack mattress, a pillow, a blanket, and a "place of repose" on one of the double-tiered wooden berths, with six soldiers wedged into each tier and sedated with fifty-six gills, or seven quarts, of rum per week, to be shared by the six. Various storeships and men-of-war continued to beat into the Cove of Cork to complete the squadron: the *Pigot* hospital ship, the *Sibella* storeship, the *Levant* victualler, and *Thunder*, a vessel recently used for Arctic exploration but now carrying heavy mortars.

The king grew impatient. In an unusually messy letter to Sandwich— with ink blotches, insertions, and words scratched out—he observed that "every other department had been ready for the southern expedition three weeks sooner than the Navy." Given American obstinacy, "We must show that the English lion when roused has not only his wonted resolution, but has added the swiftness of the race horse." Sandwich replied within hours, filling page after page with excuses and explanations. "Your Majesty has been in some part misinformed," he wrote. "The elements have warred against us most cruelly." Delays had been caused by "contrary winds & accidents, and, I am certain, by nothing that human wisdom could guard against."

On Monday, February 12, Commodore Parker finally ordered signal flags hoisted aloft on his flagship, the *Bristol*. General Cornwallis joined him on the quarterdeck. Tars across the squadron turned their capstans to weigh anchor, topmen unsheeted their sails, and forty-four vessels glided past Dogsnose and Roche's Point before swinging west beyond the Old Head of Kinsale for the open sea. By Parker's count, the expedition numbered five men-of-war, a tender, a storeship, seven army victuallers, three ordnance ships, and twenty-seven transports.

The first storm struck that night, a screaming tempest from the southwest. By first light on Tuesday, nine ships had vanished, mostly blown back to Cork or to refuges in southern England. Gale succeeded gale, for days and then weeks, "the worst weather ever known at sea," one officer asserted. "The wind blew with relentless fury," another witness wrote, "and no man could remain on deck, except he was lashed fast." The victualler *Thetis*, leaking badly, put into Lisbon, while the bomb vessel *Carcass*, minus her mizzenmast, made Plymouth. At least one warship reportedly jettisoned her upper deck guns. *Actaeon's* skipper noted "a prodigious sea" that damaged the frigate's masts and swamped her decks. On March 7, twenty-four days after leaving Cork, Parker reported that he was still off the Iberian coast, with only a third of his squadron intact. Among the ships gone missing were two frigates and twenty transports.

On that same Thursday, Cornwallis laboriously wrote Germain from his cabin on the battered *Bristol*. "Our voyage hitherto has been very unsuccessful," he reported. "The wind has been almost always contrary, and, till the first of this month, constant & most violent gales of wind." Cornwallis added:

> I fear there is no chance of our arrival on the American coast before
> the end of next month at soonest, and the assembling the fleet off Cape
> Fear, where there is no port, may be a work of some time.... Your
> lordship will make allowances for the motion of the ship when you
> are deciphering this scrawl.

Three thousand miles across the Atlantic, Josiah Martin had peered seaward for weeks, seeking a glimpse of the war fleet that would restore him to his stately brick palace in New Bern. Yet from the taffrail of his man-of-war, *Scorpion*, little could be seen except the green water off Cape Fear and an occasional rebel rifleman darting along the shoreline, hoping for a clean shot at the royal governor.

Now thirty-eight, of fitful health and erratic temperament, Martin was one of twenty-three children born to an Anglo-Irish planter whose three hundred slaves provided sugar wealth in Antigua, one of more than a dozen island colonies that remained loyal to the Crown. If "mulish in his temper, and tending much to ye vanity of dress and extravagance," as the elder Martin described young Josiah, the boy grew to be a successful, conscientious man by studying law in London, then joining the army during the last French war to serve in the West Indies and Canada. After resigning as a lieutenant colonel, he married a first cousin in New York and sought a higher calling. Still dependent on his father, Martin called himself "a sinking

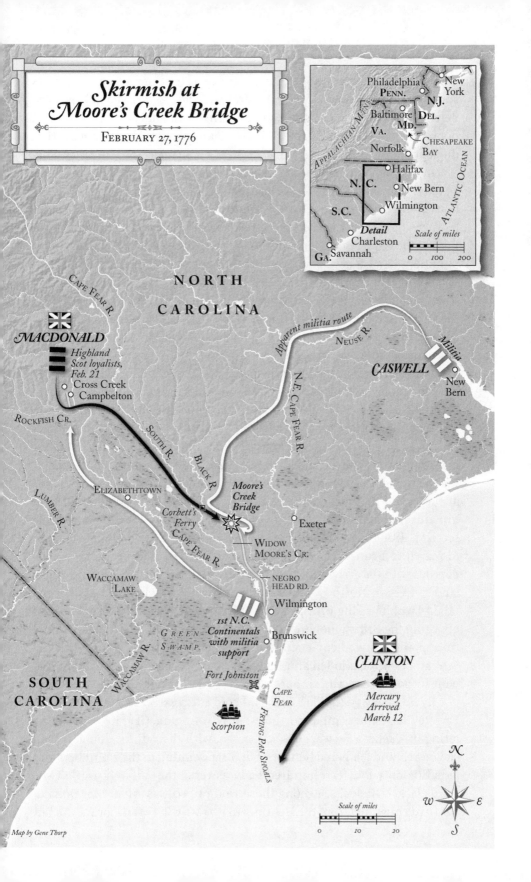

Skirmish at Moore's Creek Bridge

FEBRUARY 27, 1776

Philadelphia
PENN.
New York
N.J.
Baltimore
DEL.
MD.
VA.
CHESAPEAKE BAY
Norfolk
APPALACHIAN MTNS.
Halifax
N. C.
New Bern
ATLANTIC OCEAN
S.C.
Wilmington
Detail
Charleston
GA. Savannah

Scale of miles
0   100   200

NORTH
CAROLINA

CAPE FEAR R.

🇬🇧
MACDONALD
Highland
Scot loyalists,
Feb. 21
Cross Creek
Campbelton

ROCKFISH CR.

Apparent militia route

NEUSE R.

N.E. CAPE FEAR R.

CASWELL

Militia

New
Bern

SOUTH R.

BLACK R.

ELIZABETHTOWN

LUMBER R.

Moore's
Creek
Bridge

Corbett's
Ferry

CAPE FEAR R.

WIDOW
MOORE'S CR.

Exeter

WACCAMAW
LAKE

NEGRO
HEAD RD.

Wilmington

1st N.C.
Continentals
with militia
support

G R E E N
S W A M P

WACCAMAW R.

Brunswick

CLINTON

🇬🇧

Fort Johnston

SOUTH
CAROLINA

CAPE
FEAR

Scorpion

FRYING PAN SHOALS

Mercury
Arrived
March 12

N

W   E

S

Scale of miles
0   10   20

Map by Gene Thorp

man catching at every hope of deliverance." He seemed to rise with his appointment as governor of North Carolina in 1771; he arrived in New Bern determined to bring enlightened government to America's fourth most populous colony, a formidable task for a man considered loyal but unwise, diligent but overbearing.

In the past year, the sinking man had again found himself over his head as insurgency swept across North Carolina. Martin denounced "the seditious in their evil purposes," wrote turgid pleas to London for "a rod of chastisement to correct the rhetoric of revolution," then fled south from New Bern to the Cape Fear River after spiking the palace guns and burying other munitions in a cabbage bed. After briefly barricading himself inside dilapidated Fort Johnston, near the river's mouth, in mid-July he had jumped to what he called the "inglorious captivity" of a British warship; rebels burned the fort behind him. From his tiny ship's cabin, the governor was reduced to fulminating against "the wicked and flagitious" while insurgents organized a provincial congress, chose militia officers, printed money, levied taxes, and routinely intercepted his correspondence with London and Boston.

On January 3, Martin's "despicable and mortifying" fortunes abruptly brightened: an official dispatch from London informed him that an armada gathering at Cork would soon arrive on the coast to join forces with a British general sailing from Boston and those thousands of loyalists the governor had promised to muster in North Carolina. Giddy and impatient, expecting the squadron to loom on the horizon at any moment, Martin on January 10 called on loyal colonists to suppress a "most daring, horrid, and unnatural rebellion" by flocking to the royal standard "with all possible secrecy." Tidewater planters, Piedmont farmers, and other volunteers were to march to Brunswick on the Cape Fear River by mid-February to rendezvous with the arriving expedition. An estimated twelve thousand Highlanders lived in North Carolina, among them many who had fled after the failed Jacobite rising of 1745; having suffered the harsh consequences of opposing the British monarch once, few were inclined to do it again. Martin appointed Brigadier General Donald MacDonald, a sixty-four-year-old veteran of both Culloden and Bunker Hill, to command his loyal militia, with authority to recruit troops by offering land, cash, and tax exemptions.

By February 15, the clans had gathered at Cross Creek—later renamed Fayetteville—ninety miles northwest of Wilmington. Clad in tartan, chattering in Gaelic, they were exotic foemen, with their dirks, double-edged claymores, and feathered bonnets, but disappointing in their numbers and lethality: only fourteen hundred had answered the call and nearly two-thirds lacked firelocks. Among those who rallied was Allan MacDonald, who had emigrated from the Hebrides in 1774 with his wife, Flora, a woman celebrated in song and saga for disguising Bonnie Prince Charlie as an Irish spinning maid and helping the Young Pretender escape to France after his claim to the British throne collapsed at Culloden. Some later insisted that Flora gave a fiery speech from a white charger to inspirit the ranks at Cross Creek, but mainly she seemed to fret. "There are troublous times ahead, I ween," she wrote a friend in February. "God will keep the right."

With British colors improvised from camp equipage, General Mac-Donald began his march to the sea on February 19. Swamps, incessant rain, swollen streams, and desertions impeded the column; two loyalist companies peeled away for home, and other men vanished into the woods after declaring that their "courage was not warproof." The column plod-ded on, ripping down farm fences and bulling through orchards. MacDon-ald offered clemency to rebels who surrendered; when none submitted, he warned, "It is my duty to conquer."

For weeks, North Carolina patriots had feverishly prepared to give battle—collecting weapons, impounding wagons, and putting all river pilots into protective custody. Wheelwrights and blacksmiths repaired gun carriages. Recalcitrant loyalists were arrested or pressed into work gangs to build fortifications. Militia troops and minutemen assembled and, after swearing fidelity to the united colonies, set out to block the enemy's east-ward advance with support from a Continental regiment.

Eighteen miles above Wilmington, eight hundred militiamen from New Bern under Colonel Richard Caswell pitched camp on Monday, Feb-ruary 26, just west of Moore's Creek, a dark, twisting mire forty feet wide and five feet deep. The men had gobbled down bacon and cornmeal and were cleaning their firelocks when a loyalist courier appeared under a truce flag with yet another surrender demand: the Highlanders had drawn within six miles, advancing on Negro Head Point Road. Belatedly realizing that an attack could pin him against the creek, Caswell ordered his men to the east bank; after the troops crossed a timber bridge, a rear guard removed the planks and greased the exposed stringers with tallow and soft soap. Fifty yards beyond the waterline, the men joined another 150 comrades entrenched behind a low mud wall.

They did not have long to wait. Desertion had whittled the loyalist force to perhaps under a thousand, many still without muskets. In a dreary rain on Monday evening, General MacDonald convened a war council, announced that he was too spent to continue, and stumbled off to his tent, so indisposed that he "could not stir from his bed or even give the least advice," a witness reported. His deputy, Lieutenant Colonel Donald McLeod, at one a.m. on Tuesday resumed the march through swampland in a night described as "the darkest that could be seen." Five hours later, stupefied with exhaustion and cold, the marchers came upon dying camp-fires in the abandoned rebel camp west of Moore's Creek. After predictable confusion, the Highlanders drew their blades, shouted, "King George and broadswords!" and with three cheers made for the maimed bridge in the early morning light. Drums beat, pipes skirled. A rebel described the approaching enemy's "banners and plumes waving in the breeze, and all marching in good order but with a quick step."

An assault force of eighty Highlanders surged forward, gripping the sharkskin handles of their claymores and using the points to steady themselves as they shuffled across the slippery stringers. Climbing up the far bank, a few paces from the rebel earthworks, Colonel McLeod waggled his sword and bellowed for his men to follow. A thousand American muskets and rifles answered. The searing blast blew McLeod from his feet and then from this earth; nine bullets and two dozen swan shot would be counted in his corpse. The Highlander front ranks tumbled with him and were quickly blanketed in gray smoke as the roar of rebel fire carried down the creek banks. One American militiaman later said he felt as calm as if "shooting squirrels." Two small Dutch fieldpieces, named "Old Mother Covington" and "Her Daughter," barked and barked again, sweeping the near bank, the far bank, and the bridge, blowing clansmen into the creek below. Dragged under by their heavy kilts, the bodies drifted on the current like tartan water lilies. Highland fire flew high, then grew silent. Hundreds of loyalists turned and scattered into the woods or ran for the supply wagons. Horses slashed loose from their harnesses galloped away, two or three men clinging to each.

The skirmish had lasted three minutes. Two rebels were injured, one mortally. Seventy loyalists were dead or wounded, but hundreds more were soon captured in the swamps. General MacDonald surrendered his sword from his sickbed. Others morosely gave up dirks that had been handed down for generations. From squalid local jails, more than eight hundred loyalist rank and file would be paroled upon swearing not to take up arms again against the united colonies; some thirty officers jammed the tiny cell in Halifax, near the Virginia border, including Allan MacDonald, Flora's husband. Most eventually were marched off to prisons in Pennsylvania and Maryland, their families in some instances forced into hiding while their farms were pillaged. Booty captured at Cross Creek and other strongholds included fifteen hundred firelocks, an arsenal of bladed weapons, thirteen wagons, two large medicine chests, and General MacDonald's muster rolls with the names of all the loyalists he had enlisted. An informant also gave up the loyalist treasury, according to the historian Hugh F. Rankin: £15,000 in gold coins, hidden in a chest under a stable floor.

Civil war had erupted in the American South, but this brief, furious scrap left the rebels ascendant and confident. "Thus has most happily terminated a very dangerous insurrection," wrote Brigadier General James Moore, commander of Continental troops in the colony. "This, we think," the *Pennsylvania Evening Post* added, "will effectually put a stop to Toryism in North Carolina."

Governor Martin remained defiant, if not delusional. He had chosen the precise morning of the Moore's Creek battle to demand "for His Majesty's service" a thousand barrels of flour from Wilmington. A quick rebel reply informed him "it is not in our power to comply," and indelicately noted that loyalist forces to the west were "now surrounded by three armies." Martin denounced "the gasconadings of rebels," but legal proceedings would soon confiscate his ten thousand acres in eastern North Carolina, which were sold at auction along with the carriages, horses, and books—an estate valued at almost £7,000—he had abandoned in New Bern. After checking once again to confirm that no British squadron from Cork could be seen approaching Cape Fear, Martin wrote Germain in March, "I regret this unfortunate delay the more sincerely because it has contravened a plan and purpose of mine." Had reinforcements arrived in early February, "success had most certainly crowned my endeavors."

Even while admitting that he was "a wretched man, *not* of Neptune's element, in the tenth month of confinement on board ship," Martin insisted that London need not feel pessimistic. Blithely he assured Germain, "The little check the loyalists here have received I do not conceive, my lord, will have any extensive ill consequence."

On Tuesday, March 12, the *Mercury*, a sleek, sixth-rate man-of-war, accompanied by the sloop *Falcon* and two transports carrying a pair of light infantry companies, carefully skirted the white breakers on Frying Pan Shoals before dropping anchor in the mouth of the Cape Fear. Major General Clinton, after a gale-battered, seven-week voyage from Boston, was perplexed to find neither an army of Highland loyalists nor a British fleet. As Clinton's secretary wrote, they had come to North Carolina "big with expectation that everything was going swimmingly in our favor." A disheartening shipboard conference with Governor Martin soon revealed otherwise.

As the son and brother-in-law of admirals, Henry Clinton appreciated the uncertainties of expeditionary warfare. Sooner or later, presumably, the squadron from Cork would arrive with the troops he was to command, even though prospects for a successful campaign in North Carolina now seemed dim. Clinton by nature expected the worst, from both people and fate, and as the British general who would serve longer than any other in the American war—including, eventually, four years as commander in chief—he would find his expectations fully realized again and again. Now forty-five, with an ebbing hairline, cleft chin, and large blue eyes, he had known America intimately since the age of thirteen, when his father, after decades of sea duty, became royal governor of New York. Young Henry returned to England from Manhattan at age nineteen to get on with an army career; that profession had now led him back to America and to this place, the Cape Fear River, for his first independent command, even if no one was here to be commanded. The war dismayed him; he blamed Britain as much as America for the fraternal bloodletting. "A most unaccountable madness seems to have seized both countries," he wrote. His task was to help halt the madness, by force of arms.

He would always be an enigma, to his few friends, to his many adversaries, and to history. Fluent in French, an assiduous reader, and a talented violinist with a passion for Haydn, he was often contrarian in his military thinking: in studying Caesar's *Commentaries*, he was drawn not to the Romans but to the barbarians who avoided battle, refusing to be gulled into an uneven fight. In combat he usually sought to turn a flank rather than attack frontally; he had suggested as much before Bunker Hill, to no avail. "There is nothing I dread so much," he said, "as these brave generals." Keenly aware of America's size and the temper of her people, he had advocated a strategy of naval blockade rather than a land war, again to no avail.

Rational, dignified, and brainy, he also could be tetchy, insecure, and obsessive—a "shy bitch," as he called himself. His skills as a planner and as an incisive military thinker were often undercut by his lack of tact— "perhaps I speak too freely," he had mused in December—and by perpetual friction with his equals and superiors. "Furies were at work on his psyche," his biographer William B. Willcox would write. "The man's inadequacy becomes an appreciable force in the working of destiny." Clinton had never completely recovered from wounds sustained while fighting the French in 1762; after walking several miles from the battlefield to a medical tent, he wrote, "I was hacked by an ignorant German surgeon." He suffered an even greater blow a decade later when the young wife he adored died giving birth to their fifth child. That loss left him unbalanced, if not temporarily deranged; two years of depression lifted only after he was sent to observe the Russian army, then fighting Turks in the Balkans. Traveling on the Danube by canoe, revived by a sense of professional purpose, he returned to Britain, placed his children in the care of his dead wife's family, and sailed for Boston to become Howe's deputy upon General Gage's recall.

Frictions soon built between a restless subordinate inclined to give bold advice and a superior inclined to ignore it. Billeted in John Hancock's house, Clinton had supervised the regulars posted on Bunker Hill after the battle, sometimes living with them under canvas. "I like this sort of life best," he wrote. "The society is good, and at night I have a concert at which I am received as a performer!" But, as he wrote Burgoyne, he grew "almost tired of being a subordinate." Howe was plainly relieved to ship him south. Clinton had hardly left Boston when he began brooding over his imprecise instructions and lack of firepower. "This business I feel the weight of," he wrote. "It does not crush me, but [it is] rather too much merely to steady me."

Now there was little to do but wait for the Cork expedition to find its way. Living on oysters, cabbage, and fish, Clinton occasionally slipped ashore to study the local flora and fauna, writing with a naturalist's enthusiasm about magnolia, jasmine, wild honeysuckle, and even "such thunder and such rain." He could be as gullible about mythological southern beasts as royal governors were about loyalist legions. "Among other extraordinary things we have the whipping snake, which meets you in the road and lashes you most unmercifully," he wrote a colleague in Boston. "We are told that two or three of them will kill a horse."

But mostly the long weeks on the Carolina coast allowed him time to ponder how, in his phrase, "to gain the hearts & subdue the minds of America." British affairs in the southern colonies had tumbled, with stinging defeats in Virginia and North Carolina, and fading fortunes in South Carolina and Georgia. Every southern governor was afloat; not one dared set foot in his own capital. Clinton could see that American loyalists were not simply waiting for British regulars to appear, as Germain and others in London believed; on the contrary, they required assurance that a protective force would remain to shield them from rebel retaliation. Shuttling British troops around to put spine in the loyalists "is chimerical, false," Clinton wrote. Even if the Cork brigade arrived intact, it would be so small that "[I] must ever have one foot in my ships."

Clinton stared at the blue horizon, waiting and thinking. How could a civil war be won if the friends of the Crown had already lost in some colonies? How could hearts be gained, minds subdued, and fence straddlers assured that Britain would enforce order and security?

In a dispatch to Germain, he warned that affairs in the South "had lately much changed for the worse." Avenging Moore's Creek would be impossible, given the rebels' strength and the lack of British horses to haul cannons inland. Reports from the South Carolina uplands indicated that the "well-affected there had been defeated & dispersed." Attacking

Charleston "would be very difficult" and would do little to win back the larger province. He believed that a show of force in the Chesapeake before rejoining Howe for a concentrated campaign to secure New York was the wisest course. Further maneuvers in the South at this time would "only serve to inflame minds & sacrifice your friends to the rage and fury of the multitude."

Clinton had heard nothing from Howe: no orders, no advice, no news. Before settling on a course, he would await the arrival of the Cork expedition. He intended to greet the squadron with a large consignment of rum he had purchased in Virginia during his voyage from Boston. Commodore Parker and General Cornwallis undoubtedly had thoughts about what to do next. Together they would decide how to subdue the rage and fury of the multitude. Together they would come up with a plan.

11.

City of Our Solemnities

A t eleven p.m. on Saturday, March 2, twenty American guns intended to distract and distress the British in Boston opened fire from Roxbury, Cobble Hill, and Lechmere Point near Charlestown. "The house this instant shakes with the roar of cannon," Abigail Adams wrote John from Braintree. "No sleep for me tonight." A few shells landed near Faneuil Hall, but the bombardment did little damage; the British answered each shot with two of their own. Hardly had the gunplay begun than four American mortars burst from being overcharged or badly bedded on frozen ground; among the casualties after only three rounds was "Congress," the thirteen-inch brass mortar captured in late November aboard the *Nancy*. Continental troops manned their lines an hour before dawn in hopes that the bombardment would provoke a British sally that never came. The cannonade resumed Sunday night, again with little effect except to further fray civilian nerves. Mrs. Adams described "the rattling of the windows, the jar of the house, the continual roar of 24-pounders." She told John, "I went to bed after 12, but got no rest. The cannon continued firing, and my heart beat pace with them all night."

The seizure of Dorchester Heights was planned for Monday night, and Vassall House bustled with couriers, adjutants, and aides-de-camp swaggering in and out. "Every man's conduct will be marked and rewarded or punished accordingly, and cowardice in a most exemplary manner," Washington told his army in general orders. "One fire well-aimed does more execution than a dozen at long-shot." Each regiment was to send all picks, shovels, and other tools to the quartermaster general in Cambridge for distribution to entrenching gangs. In every redoubt spears were "to be examined, cleaned, and collected in their proper places"; men without muskets would receive lances. Troops were "positively forbid playing of cards and other games of chance at this time of public distress." Hundreds of axmen began clear-cutting orchards, then sharpening branches and tree trunks for abatis and barricades on the high ground.

With two thousand casualties expected, hand barrows were positioned to wheel the wounded from the battlefield. Barracks on Prospect Hill and at Harvard College became hospital wards. Two dozen regimental surgeons met at Brown's Tavern for their assignments; among them they counted only 6 sets of amputation instruments, 2 cases of lancets, 2 more of surgical knives, 859 bandages, 24 tourniquets, and "but few medicines." A front-page advertisement in the *New-England Chronicle* sought nurses for the hospitals in Cambridge and Roxbury, as well as sage, rags, honey, beeswax, thread, and "herbs of all kinds."

Washington's irksome gunpowder reserve was barely adequate, perhaps eight tons. He had borrowed more than four tons from Connecticut, which then sent along two more and a few muskets refurbished with newly straightened barrels. In late February, Rhode Island had risked sending another 3,600 pounds of powder in open carts rather than wait for covered wagons. Lieutenant Colonel Rufus Putnam, the self-taught engineer who'd drafted plans to install a covered way across the isthmus leading to Dorchester Heights, had another brainstorm: fortifications to protect soldiers and gun batteries on the heights could not be excavated in frozen ground, so after consulting a borrowed volume of the *Field Engineer*, a British technical manual, Putnam proposed building "chandeliers," nailed timber frames that could be filled with fascines—bundled sticks—and gabions, wicker baskets packed with stones and gravel. The defenses would at least shield troops from enemy small arms and grapeshot. "We trust," a young Connecticut lieutenant wrote his family on March 4, "that we are fighting the Lord's battle."

A third consecutive evening cannonade erupted on Monday. Henry Knox counted 157 shot and shell fired by American gunners to mask the curious noises in Dorchester. "Our shells raked the houses terribly, and the cries of poor women and children frequently reached our ears," an American lieutenant wrote. British guns answered with heavy counterbattery fire, unwittingly contributing to their own ignorance. "Soon after candlelight, came on a most terrible bombardment & cannonade on both sides," a Boston selectman told his diary, "as if heaven & earth were engaged." Soldiers counted as many as seven projectiles simultaneously tracing red parabolas across the sky. "Sheets of fire seemed to come from our batteries," a British major wrote his father. "Some of the shells crossed one another in the air, and then bursting looked beautiful." An American 18-pound ball fired from Roxbury slammed into a guardhouse manned by the 22nd Foot, wounding four regulars and killing another, "having his legs and thighs broke in a shocking manner," a lieutenant reported.

Under a brilliant full moon, favored by mild airs hinting at spring, eight hundred armed men heaved forward onto the isthmus. Some 280 carts and wagons followed, axles creaking under the weight of entrenching tools, hay bales, and chandeliers. Teamsters whispered into their oxen's ears, keeping their whips silent, as instructed. The men quickly stacked baled hay to assemble Putnam's blind up the ascending lane. Barrels with hoops "well-nailed" also crowded the wagon beds; filled with sand and stones and positioned on the brow of the hill, they would be rolled down the slope to crush, or at least dishearten, any regulars intent on climbing to the crest.

Behind the oxen came another twelve hundred men in a working party commanded by Brigadier General John Thomas. Now fifty-one, "a plain, sociable, sensible, good old man," in one comrade's assessment, Thomas was a Massachusetts physician with more combat experience—including eight campaigns in the French wars—than virtually any American officer. "His merits in the military way have surprised us all," James Warren had told John Adams.

Shoving and hoisting, heaving and grunting, the men positioned the chandeliers—each weighed several hundred pounds—then sent the wagon teams back to Roxbury to haul more timber and hay, gabions and abatis stakes. Dray horses dragged up Knox's guns, which were then muscled onto wooden platforms. "Six works thrown up this night at different places on the hills & high ground," wrote another engineer, Major Jeduthan Baldwin. "A very great work for one night."

At four a.m., on Tuesday, March 5, three thousand additional men climbed the heights to man the fortifications and relieve the fagged, sweating excavators. "The whole procession moved on in solemn silence," an army doctor wrote. Planners had recalled the failure to position rested reinforcements in advance at Bunker Hill. Washington, who was up, down, and around the heights all evening—inspecting, cajoling, encouraging—reminded the men that the Boston Massacre had occurred precisely six years earlier. "Remember the fifth of March," he told them, "and avenge the death of your brethren." The word spread through the ranks, and the men steeled themselves as the sky brightened in the east.

Tickets had sold briskly for the masked ball planned by British officers in the Concert Hall on Monday, March 11. "We hear ten capital cooks are already employed in preparing supper for the masquerade, which is to be the most brilliant thing ever seen in America," a loyalist newspaper noted in late February. Revelers were assured that "by the fifth of March, a number of different masks will be prepared & sold by almost all the milliners and mantua-makers in town."

Alas, there would be no ball, no supper, no brilliant thing. For more than a week, informants had warned Howe of danger afoot, of entrenching tools collected and fascines bundled. "Deserters say they intend to . . . bombard the town from Dorchester," Major Stephen Kemble, the British deputy adjutant general and General Gage's brother-in-law, noted on February 29. "But as yet no sign of their works." Meandering, fretful conversations about possible intervention led to nothing, and by sunrise on Tuesday, March 5, it was too late. British officers clutching their spyglasses pounded up to the rooftops, mouths agape. "A most astonishing night's work," an engineer told his diary with professional admiration. "Must have employed from 15 to 20,000 men." The rebels, another officer wrote, "raised the forts with an expedition equal to that of the genie belonging to Aladdin's wonderful lamp."

Plunging fire could now scour the anchorage, the docks, and the town. Gun ports on the men-of-war flew open and British shore batteries swiveled toward Dorchester. Soon a cannonade unlike any ever known in Boston blistered the hillsides. Balls bounded and rebounded across the terrain; more than seven hundred would be collected by rebel scavengers on Wednesday morning. Some struck home. A Connecticut officer wrote of a young lieutenant in Roxbury hit in the thigh and soon clapped onto a surgeon's table for amputation: "He did not bleed to excess yet his pain was so exquisite, occasioned by the bone being shivered to pieces quite to his hip joint, that he died about 9 o'clock in the morning." Another soldier described a comrade's skull "dashed open by a cannonball. . . . I saw a piece of the skin of his head with the hair on it, which was a light brown, beginning to be sprinkled with white hairs."

But most shots failed to reach the American works, despite British efforts to elevate their barrels by sinking the rear wheels of gun carriages into the ground. "After an unsuccessful fire of about two hours," General Sullivan wrote John Adams, "they grew weary of it and desisted." The works would have to be carried by infantry assault. Warmer temperatures in recent days had cleared ice from the Charles and the harbor. In a quick, snappish conference at Province House, General Percy, who had led the rescue force on Battle Road eleven months earlier, was ordered to attack with twenty-four hundred men.

By midday five regiments had marched across Long Wharf and onto the transports *Success, Venus, Sea Venture, Spy,* and *Good Intent.* Later in the day, light infantry, grenadiers, and two more regiments joined them. Each regular carried a blanket, rum and water in a canteen, and sixty rounds, although they were forbidden to load their muskets; the assault would rely on the bayonet to prevent "confusion among our own men from irregular firing." Howe had not forgotten the fratricidal carnage at Bunker Hill. One eager commander confined to his bed by gout intended to be trundled into battle on a litter borne by six men. A Connecticut soldier watching from the high ground described "dense columns of troops moving down the main street to the wharf, and embarking on board the ships, which moved down the harbor and formed in a kind of crescent." Spectators crowded hilltops and roofs. A British engineer scribbled in his diary, "The fate of this whole army and the town is at stake, not to say the fate of America."

Washington agreed. This was precisely the rumpus he'd yearned for. Anticipating a British lunge toward Dorchester, he had organized a counterstrike. Two floating batteries and forty-five bateaux—each capable of carrying eighty men—were positioned up the Charles River. Under General Putnam, four thousand troops in Cambridge stood ready to make an amphibious assault on Boston while much of Howe's army was beating toward the heights. General Sullivan would land at the powder house on the west edge of town before capturing the batteries around Beacon Hill. General Greene would land at Barton's Point, seize Copp's Hill, and also fling open the gates at Boston Neck to permit Continentals from Roxbury to swarm through. Lookouts were posted on Washington's order with "the best glasses you can procure" to follow enemy movements. A pennant atop Prospect Hill would launch the counterattack.

That signal never came. Delays in loading Percy's troops and artillery at Long Wharf caused Howe to postpone the Dorchester sally until the morning tide on Wednesday, March 6. The transports anchored for the night near Castle William, where a few rebel balls from the Dorchester guns plumped the water without effect. By early Tuesday evening, rain and hail from the south lashed regulars and Continentals alike. Gale winds—"a hurrycane," one diarist insisted—blew down rail fences and sheds, and drove three British transports aground. "What I suffered this night I shall ever bear in mind," wrote Lieutenant Isaac Bangs, a Continental surgeon, after cowering with comrades in an apple orchard. The tempest persisted into Wednesday morning, churning "so great a surf on the shore where the troops must have landed that it was impossible a boat could live," a British officer recorded. The transports tacked back to Long Wharf, to the immense disappointment of Washington, who had imagined that by Wednesday evening Dorchester's slopes would be plastered with dead redcoats. The storm, he wrote, was "the most fortunate circumstance for them, and unfortunate for us."

Howe recognized divine intercession when he saw it. Convening another war council at Province House, he lauded "the honor of the troops" in their willingness to fight, then announced the inevitable: the army would abandon Boston immediately. Rebel possession of Dorchester Heights was simply the last straw. British larders had less than six weeks of food remaining, including only seventeen days of salt pork and ten days of peas. The army was so "very distressed" that the Royal Navy had just loaned Howe a month's supply of provisions; otherwise, Admiral Shuldham told the Admiralty, "the consequence must be fatal."

To carry away nine thousand soldiers, along with their military equipment and twelve hundred dependents, plus more than a thousand loyalists, would require twenty-eight thousand tons of shipping; Shuldham had only twenty-two thousand tons in Boston, some seventy-eight vessels. That meant abandoning all but the most critical kit. "I am justly sensible," Howe told London, "how much more [useful] . . . it would be to His Majesty's service if this army was in a situation to proceed immediately to New York." But food shortages and the danger of meeting a hostile reception required sailing first to the British base at Halifax, a two-week voyage to the northeast. The loyalists could be deposited there, and Howe also intended to retrain and reorganize his force. He would send home officers impaired with "age and infirmities," promote worthy replacements, adapt uniforms and formations to North American combat, and hone the army's light infantry and amphibious tactics.

By Thursday, March 7, news of the imminent departure had filtered through the ranks. No one was pleased by the prospect of months in "Hellifax"—described by Edmund Burke as "that nook of penury and cold"—even though British charities would send tobacco, shoes, and wool caps to the troops, and each officer would get ten gallons of rum as consolation. "Of all the miserable places I ever saw," one captain wrote, "Halifax is the worst." Another officer wrote home, "A cursed, cold, wintry place. . . . Bad times, my friend." Carping grew virulent. "The soldiers think themselves betrayed," one officer wrote. "Fleet and army complain of each other, and both of the people at home."

The empire would soon possess not a single port on the Atlantic seaboard between Canada and Florida. The ignominy of being evicted from Boston stung every man proud of his uniform. Notwithstanding the loan of food, many army officers blamed the navy for their predicament. "O the glory of the British Navy," one major complained bitterly. "Flags flying with all the pomp of war, and the Yankee can spit in their face." Yet others detected a broader culpability. "Hope to God," a colonel wrote, "they will send us some generals worthy the command of a British army."

Evacuation orders issued that Thursday choreographed the withdrawal. Each regiment was to bring its barracks furniture to a warehouse on King Street and collect eighteen butts of porter—an antiscorbutic—at Cowper's Meeting House. All dram shops would be shuttered; Howe was determined "to put a stop to drunkenness in the garrison, which has been too prevalent of late." Arson would be punished by "immediate death" and plunderers "hanged on the spot." To thwart desertion, officers were to sleep in the barracks. The transports received fresh bedding on Friday, but "useless luggage" was to be dumped in the harbor. Each transport would get a month's provisions, including molasses, rice, and flour. Seventeen hundred gallons of brandy were securely stowed. Howe also offered a £50 reward to anyone helping to convict vandals caught defacing portraits of the king and queen.

Long Wharf would serve as the main embarkation pier. Sailors manhandled surplus naval supplies aboard the *Adventure* and the *Francis*, although a great pile of white pine trunks intended as masts for British warships had to be abandoned; later in the war, they would refit a French fleet. Horse transports loaded with mounts and drays fell down to Castle William on March 10 to await the rest of the fleet. Some vessels were scuttled in the harbor for lack of crews: a brigantine, a sloop, a schooner, and two three-hundred-ton ships belonging to John Hancock.

Every hour brought more hard choices about what to take and what to leave, burn, or smash. The commanding general's coach was tipped from the wharf and sank without a trace. The barrack master general's list of abandoned items included 1,107 blankets, 236 stoves, 582 iron pots, and a thousand buckets, as well as 350 tons of hay, 79 horses, and 27 wagons. The commissary general's list included almost 8,000 bushels of wheat, 1,700 gallons of sour wine, and various provisions deemed "unfit for His Majesty's troops to eat," including 32 firkins of rancid butter and half a ton of bad cheese. An artillery clerk's gorgeous script enumerated the ordnance left behind: 29 iron guns, 3,000 cannonballs, 27 gun carriages, and 34 wagons, although most of the wheels were salvaged. A block and tackle collapsed while loading a 13-inch iron mortar and bed weighing almost six tons. That piece and two identical mortars were pitched into the sea. A fourth was spiked and left in the mud.

The British had commandeered 368 houses during their occupation of Boston, and clerks kept careful track of rent to be paid loyalist and neutral landlords, including £120 to the painter John Singleton Copley, who had moved to London in 1774. But as the evacuation gained momentum, indiscipline and panic took root. "All is uproar and confusion," a witness wrote from Boston. "Carts, trucks, wheelbarrows, handbarrows, coaches, chaises are driving as if the very devil is after them." Selectman Timothy Newell told his diary, "Shops, stores, houses plundered, vessels cut to pieces. . . . Sugar and salt thrown into the rivers, which was greatly covered with hogsheads, barrels of flour, house furniture." "A prodigious quantity" of mahogany chairs and tables, some intact and others splintered with axes, littered the streets or bobbed across the harbor. An end-of-days rowdiness took hold. Despite Howe's demand for sobriety, Major Kemble noted in his diary on March 11, "Many of our soldiers this day drunk." A scold with a crier's bell was sent through the town to again forbid inebriation.

Most departing loyalists were tradesmen and rustics—shopkeepers, artisans, mariners, yeomen. Howe also listed some two hundred customs and government officials, along with their families—Henry Knox's in-laws among them—plus eighteen Anglican clergy and kin. The well heeled who chose to leave "that once happy country," as Chief Justice Peter Oliver wrote after boarding the *Pacific*, abandoned elegant houses with carved balustrades and wainscoted drawing rooms, fluted pilasters and tile hearths. Each family spent the week paring a lifetime's accumulated possessions to a cartload or two, then bid against one another to hire draymen for the short trip to the docks. "Nothing but hurry and confusion," a merchant wrote, "every person striving to get out of this place." Marble tables, chimney clocks, Turkey carpets, and damask curtains had to be left behind, of course, but what of the ermine cape and pink silk overdress, the satin waistcoat and blue velvet doublet with slashed sleeves? Which to take: the crimson velvet morning gown or the brown broadcloth coat? The feather bed or the silver tureens?

For these Americans, affluent or otherwise, "the saddest day ever to come to Boston" was at hand, as the author Esther Forbes would write. A final worship service was held at King's Chapel on March 10 before the rector embarked, carrying both the Communion service and the church registry of baptisms, marriages, and burials. Rebels composed taunts as loyalists scuffed onto the docks: "The Tories with their brats and wives, / Have fled to save their wretched lives."

More than twenty regiments were scheduled to board ship on Wednesday evening, March 13, but a pernicious east wind kept the transports pinned within Boston Harbor. For several days, the wind quartered favorably for short spells only to again swing from the east. "Troops were ordered under arms in order to embark," Lieutenant John Barker of the King's Own told his diary on March 15, "but after waiting some time, returned to their quarters, the wind having shifted." Another lieutenant in the same regiment wrote his uncle, "An uncommon bad fate has attended our affairs here from first to last." Delay made them edgy and vandalish. "Our soldiers & sailors committed many irregularities for a day or two before we embarked by breaking into houses and destroying a good deal of valuable furniture," Major Francis Hutcheson would write from the *Adventure*. Armed gangs plundered more warehouses and stores along the waterfront, and rooted through house cellars for liquor. "The inhabitants are greatly terrified," the salt merchant John Rowe informed his diary.

Two regiments of foot with a few iron guns covered the final withdrawal, supported by grenadiers and light infantrymen. On March 15, Howe warned Boston selectmen that he would burn the town if rebels impeded his retreat. To prevent the enemy from rushing their rear guard, British troops barricaded streets with old casks, tree limbs, and hogsheads filled with horse dung. A marine lieutenant scattered crow's feet—four-pointed iron devices designed to impale boots or hooves—outside the gate at Boston Neck. A fair if faint wind finally blew from the west on Sunday, March 17. The army mustered under arms at four a.m. and marched to the wharves an hour later. Boatmen rowed each company to the transports in skiffs and flat-bottoms. "Not a single word was heard from a soldier during the embarkation," wrote Lieutenant William Feilding, a marine adjutant. "Old officers [remarked] that they never saw an army so silent." Many seethed with humiliation, including Feilding. "I hope the rebels will get heartily thrashed," he added. "I would be content to lose a leg & an arm to see them totally defeated and their whole country laid waste."

At eight a.m., a signal recalled the final detachment from Bunker Hill. Two officers pulled shut the obstructions at the foot of Long Wharf and climbed into the last boat. Anchors weighed, the fleet glided with great dignity past Castle William and the harbor entrance. Even now splashes could be heard from barrels and superfluous furniture tossed overboard to make room belowdecks. "We are greatly crowded in the transports," Major Hutcheson wrote. "I believe there never was twenty-three British regiments in such a situation as we are at present." Foot regiments filled two dozen vessels with names like *Baltic Merchant* and *America*; ten more carried dragoons and their horses, while a dozen ordnance ships and fifteen victuallers joined the formation. When Howe and Admiral Shuldham moved to the fore in *Chatham*, her fifty guns answered salutes from the other men-of-war. Hundreds of rebels could be seen silhouetted along the

Dorchester ridgelines, cheering wildly. "We enjoyed the unspeakable sat-isfaction," wrote the American surgeon James Thacher, "of beholding their whole fleet under sail."

But the fleet was not going far, not yet. Abruptly the sails drooped and anchors dropped in the Nantasket Roads channel, just beyond the harbor islands. Before Shuldham would venture into the North Atlantic, there were loads to shift, piles of loose baggage to stow, and water casks to fill. Howe also had unfinished business at Castle William, the eighteen-acre island compound where a British flag had flown since the previous century. At eight-thirty p.m. on March 20, eighty-seven mines began to detonate beneath the corner bastions, batteries, brick breastworks, and outbuildings. Engineers then tossed burning faggots into the barracks and houses. Within minutes a great ruby glow could be seen from Plymouth, more than thirty miles south, where it appeared that all Boston was burning. "The confla-gration was the most pleasingly dreadful that I ever beheld," Judge Oliver wrote from the *Pacific*. "Sometimes it appeared like the eruption of Mount Etna."

With Castle William reduced to "a confused heap of rubbish," nine more companies crowded into the transports. A customs commissioner described sharing a cabin with thirty-six others, "men, women, and children, parents, masters, and mistresses, obliged to pig together on the floor, there being no berths." A loyalist aboard *Centurion* wrote, "No one here is free from the dreadful thought of famine. . . . We have been for this week past put upon two-thirds of allowance."

Howe passed the time on *Chatham* composing a gloomy dispatch to the government from which, he noted, he had received no orders since those dated October 22. "All my struggles to supply the army with provisions" had come to naught, he wrote. "A thousand difficulties arose," and the reb-els forced his hand, "exposing the army to the greatest distresses by remaining in Boston or of withdrawing from it under such straitened cir-cumstances." He added:

> The scene here at present wears a lowering aspect, there not being the least prospect of conciliating this continent until its armies have been roughly dealt with. . . . Such an event will not be readily brought about.

At last they were prepared. A red ensign appeared on *Chatham*'s miz-zen topmast head, with a blue ensign on her starboard mizzen shrouds. Anchors weighed again in the heavy swell. To the sound of billowing can-vas, they crowded on sail and made for the open sea. "It was a magnificent and beautiful sight," John Trumbull, the brigade major in Roxbury, wrote after watching the ships stand out. "We viewed this triumphant and glorious scene with exultation." The king's men would try to put a fine face on the departure by insisting that Howe had only "shifted a position." The army decamped, the *London Gazette* explained, "with the greatest order and regularity, and without the least interruption from the rebels." But that fooled no one. The evacuation "does dishonor to the British nation," the Duke of Manchester told the House of Lords. Walpole believed it "proved the madness of all they were doing. . . . Great abuse fell on Lord George Germain."

For the king's troops—"keen for revenge," as a captain observed—one miserable campaign had ended. But another campaign was certain to follow, with a fresh chance to even the score on a new battlefield. "Expect no more letters from Boston," an officer wrote as the town fell away off the stern. "We have quitted that place." Yet for New Englanders abandoning their homeland, an indelible sadness settled into the dim, dank holds. Few knew where they would go beyond Hellifax, or whether they would ever see America again. John Wentworth, a Harvard classmate of John Adams's who until the recent cataclysm had served for years as the royal governor of New Hampshire, would write, "My destination is quite uncertain. Like an old flapped hat thrown off the top of a house, I am tumbling over and over in the air."

General Washington had not waited for the fleet to disappear over the horizon before claiming his prize. He orchestrated the entry into Boston as meticulously as Howe had organized his exit. The first thousand Continental troops into the town, he decreed, must be smallpox survivors. An informant had told him that the British had "laid several schemes" to infect his army, and so an immune vanguard would look for signs of pestilence. A flurry of orders forbade looting, or "digging after hidden treasures in Charlestown," or using "the odious epithets of 'Tory,' or any other indecent language, it being ungenerous, unmanly, and unsoldier-like." Wary of British perfidy—"something is meditating," Washington warned—he dispatched a dozen agents to interrogate "all such persons as are unknown" along the docks and beaches about whether Howe intended to double back into Boston. "Distrust is the mother of security," an American commander wrote.

Behind beating drums and a junior officer carrying a standard, Colonel Ebenezer Learned and five hundred soldiers proudly wearing their pox scars tiptoed through the crow's feet to force the Roxbury gate late on Sunday morning, March 17. General Putnam, who had crossed the Charles with several regiments to land at Sewall's Point, now proclaimed the town liberated in the "name of the thirteen united colonies of North America." After noting that British sentries on Bunker Hill seemed oddly inert, General Sullivan rode across Charlestown Neck to find uniformed dummies wearing horseshoe gorgets and shirt ruffles made from paper.

After a 333-day siege, Boston once again was a town at peace. "The sun looks brighter," Abigail Adams wrote John, "the birds sing more melodiously." A Connecticut sergeant reported, "Females opened their doors & windows with decanters of wine in their hands to bid us welcome." Patriots who had remained for nearly a year to protect their shops or houses had "become thin, and their flesh wasted, but yet in good spirits," a selectman reported. Loyalists who chose not to flee with Howe, he said, "to their thin visages added looks of guilt."

On Monday morning, Washington rode into Boston for the first time in twenty years. He had last visited in 1756, as a colonel of Virginia provincials petitioning the British for a regular's commission. The conversion of Old South into a riding arena and officers' grogshop especially offended him; seven years of repairs would be needed before the congregation could gather there again. "Strange that the British, who so venerated their own churches, should thus have desecrated ours," he observed. In a letter to Joseph Reed he estimated that the British had abandoned £30,000 worth of goods, including loaded vessels that they failed to scuttle or sail away. He also conceded that "Boston was almost impregnable, every avenue fortified"; it was plain that the frontal assaults he had proposed would likely have ended in disaster. Washington reserved his deepest contempt for Americans who had thrown in with the British. "One or two have done what a great many ought to have done long ago—committed suicide," he told his brother. For those obliged to flee so abruptly from their homeland, "the last trump could not have struck them with greater consternation."

A full accounting of insults to the town would take weeks. "The houses I found to be considerably abused inside, where they had been inhabited by the common soldiery," Dr. John Warren told his diary. "The streets were clean, and upon the whole the town looks much better than I expected." Affluent patriots whose grand homes had been occupied by senior officers typically found their property intact. General Clinton had even replaced a missing backgammon table from John Hancock's mansion overlooking Boston Common, though the stable and coach house showed hard use as hospital wards. ("The family pictures," Washington assured Hancock, "are all left entire and untouched.") John Adams's town house was filthy but undamaged, unlike a neighbor's, where occupiers had reputedly hacked raw meat with cleavers on the mahogany tables. Reverend Samuel Cooper, who had fled Boston soon after the shots at Lexington, informed his diary,

"A melancholy scene. . . . Found all my beds, bedsteads, sheets, blankets, quilts, and coverlids, all my china, glass and crockery ware, &c., &c., plundered." Some were even less fortunate. George Robert Twelves Hewes found that his cobbler's shop had been used first as a British wash house, then burned for firewood. Henry Knox, seeing his London Book-Store for the first time in nearly a year, discovered the windows broken, shelves smashed, and the floor littered with sodden volumes. General Greene ordered that furnishings confiscated from loyalists' and customs officials' homes be distributed in restitution.

Not every vandal escaped. Howe had appointed an Irish-born loyalist lawyer named Crean Brush to handle civilian property during the evacuation; his vessel, *Elizabeth*, carrying £20,000 in woolens, linens, shoes, and other plunder, as well as a dozen regulars from the King's Own, was captured off Cape Ann by the redoubtable Captain John Manley, who in November had seized the *Nancy* munitions ship. Brush would spend eighteen months in a Boston jail before escaping disguised in his wife's clothes.

Washington's troops dragged the harbor near Hancock's Wharf with grappling hooks, fishing out carriage wheels and other debris, according to a Connecticut lieutenant. A search of sixteen wharves found 157 pack saddles, tons of salt and wheat, forty-five vessels in varying degrees of seaworthiness, and "General Gage's coach, a phaeton and harness complete." Enough medications were recovered to stock forty regimental medicine chests and to replenish the Continental Army's hospital department; a loyalist apothecary who owned one of the largest shops in America later claimed that his confiscated inventory "filled from 20 to 25 wagons." Dr. Warren also reported that drugs found in the Alms House, used as a British hospital, had been maliciously spiked with "12 or 14 pounds of arsenic."

Boston's deliverance inspired thanksgiving sermons across the town. One divine drew his text from Second Kings: "Wherefore they arose and fled in the twilight, and left their tents and their horses and their asses, even the camp as it was, and fled for their lives." On Thursday, March 28, Washington and his generals walked in procession with town fathers to the Old Brick Meeting House, led by the sheriff carrying his staff of office. From the pulpit, Reverend Andrew Eliot recounted Boston's travails during the blockade. "Look upon Zion, the city of our solemnities," he said, reciting Isaiah. "Thine eyes shall see Jerusalem a quiet habitation." Following the service, the generals strode to the Bunch of Grapes tavern on King Street for a merry dinner, "after which many proper and pertinent toasts were drunk," according to a newspaper account. "Joy and gratitude sat in every countenance, and smiled in every eye."

Harvard gave Washington an honorary degree, and Congress ordered a gold medal struck showing the goddess Liberty holding a spear and leaning on the commanding general's shoulder as British ships receded in the distance. "Under your directions," Hancock told him, "an undisciplined band of husbandmen in the course of a few months became soldiers." True, he had yet to fight a battle or demonstrate particular martial competence; Boston had been "half a war," as John Adams observed. It remained to be seen how long and how well those husbandmen would fight under Washington's command. Among other small deceptions, he allowed Congress to believe that the Dorchester Heights gambit was his idea, rather than a stratagem imposed by his war council.

Still, the British Army and the Royal Navy had been driven off by a rabblement of farmers and shopkeeps, led by low-born, ascendant men like the plowman Israel Putnam, the anchorsmith Greene, and the book vendor Knox. Washington had displayed persistence and integrity, as well as political agility. This revolutionary hour had passed, to be succeeded by other hours, some of them dreadful. But already the commander in chief was seen as "the embodiment of purpose," in the phrase of his biographer Douglas Southall Freeman. He had showed those skeptics whom he dubbed "chimney-corner heroes" that he knew his business. Always eager for acclaim, he wrote his brother, "I am happy . . . to hear from different quarters that my reputation stands fair."

He also felt an aggressive confidence in America's future. "My countrymen," Washington wrote Reed, ". . . will come reluctantly into the idea of independency. But time, & persecution, brings many wonderful things to pass." As usual he read those countrymen well: they were indeed coming round to similar sentiments. "Great Britain cannot subjugate the colonies," Reverend Eliot declared. "Independence a year ago could not have been publicly mentioned with impunity. Nothing else is now talked of, and I know not what can be done by Great Britain to prevent it."

Precisely what Britain intended was unclear. Reports had circulated for months that German mercenaries were bound for New York, and it seemed likely that Howe would also make his way there eventually. Washington already had sent off his quick-stepping riflemen to defend that town, and they were followed on March 18 by five regiments. Now he prepared to march the rest of his host down through New England on roads miry with spring. Aides and orderlies packed up Vassall House and ordered his campaign equipage from Philadelphia merchants, at a cost to Congress of $434: three walnut camp tables with eighteen stools; a large dining marquee, a baggage tent, and a second marquee with a "chain tent of ticking, arched"; tent pegs and poles, jointed and painted; three iron-banded packing cases with tableware, coffee mugs, tin plates, canisters, and oval dishes; and leather-cased canteens. At Washington's request, Joseph Reed obtained a wagon to haul the general's kit, pulled by "a pair of clever horses, same color."

Soldiers stowed their precious powder horns in hogsheads for safe transport. Fifteen tons of gunpowder awaited the army in New York, with more expected soon. Several hundred wagons, including those abandoned by the British, would haul Knox's guns and military stores, although of the three hundred pull teams expected in Cambridge, only forty had arrived; Massachusetts officials responded by authorizing the impressment of livestock for the army. Moreover, Congress had failed to send cash to pay off the militia for services rendered. "They are gone home much dissatisfied," Washington told Hancock. Most Continental troops received only partial pay for February and March, although several thousand men received "not one farthing."

Clerks hurried from wagon to wagon, recording each teamster's name and his bill of lading. The line of march would carry much of the army through Connecticut to the docks at Norwich, where transports waited to ferry them across Long Island Sound to New York. Bakers had been positioned along the route, although a shortage of bricks to build large bread ovens meant a few house chimneys might have to be demolished.

At sunrise on March 29, General Sullivan set out with the lead brigade, to be followed over several days by the remaining ranks and their commander in chief. Colorful banners inscribed with battle slogans preceded each regiment as the men marched in single file or columns of two. South by southwest they hied, to the sound of creaking wheels and tinkling cow bells and fifers playing "Roslin Castle" or that new battle anthem fairly won from the routed enemy, "Yankee Doodle."

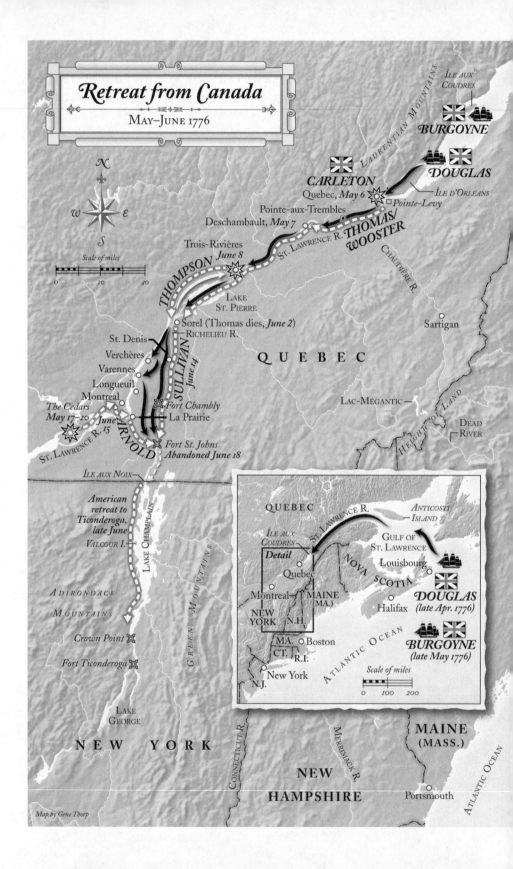

Retreat from Canada
MAY–JUNE 1776

ÎLE AUX COUDRES

BURGOYNE

LAURENTIAN MOUNTAINS

CARLETON

DOUGLAS

Quebec, *May 6*

ÎLE D'ORLÉANS

Pointe-aux-Trembles

Pointe-Levy

Deschambault, *May 7*

THOMAS/ WOOSTER

St. Lawrence R.

CHAUDIÈRE R.

Trois-Rivières *June 8*

THOMPSON

LAKE ST. PIERRE

Sartigan

Sorel (Thomas dies, *June 2*)

St. Denis

RICHELIEU R.

QUEBEC

Verchères

Varennes

SULLIVAN *June 14*

LAC-MÉGANTIC

Longueuil

Montreal

HEIGHT OF LAND

DEAD RIVER

The Cedars *May 17–20*

June 15

ARNOLD

Fort Chambly

La Prairie

ST. LAWRENCE R.

Fort St. Johns *Abandoned June 18*

ÎLE AUX NOIX

American retreat to Ticonderoga, late June

VALCOUR I.

LAKE CHAMPLAIN

GREEN MOUNTAINS

ADIRONDACK MOUNTAINS

Crown Point

Fort Ticonderoga

LAKE GEORGE

NEW YORK

QUEBEC

St. Lawrence R.

ANTICOSTI ISLAND

ÎLE AUX COUDRES

Detail

GULF OF ST. LAWRENCE

Quebec

NOVA SCOTIA

Louisbourg

Montreal

MAINE (MA.)

NEW YORK

N.H.

Halifax

DOUGLAS *(late Apr. 1776)*

MA.

Boston

CT.

R.I.

BURGOYNE *(late May 1776)*

New York

ATLANTIC OCEAN

Scale of miles
0   100   200

N.J.

MAINE (MASS.)

CONNECTICUT R.

MERRIMACK R.

NEW HAMPSHIRE

Portsmouth

ATLANTIC OCEAN

Scale of miles
0   20   40

Map by Gene Thorp

12.

A Strange Reverse of Fortune

A large, expectant crowd gathered along the St. Lawrence at the foot of Montreal's roughcast walls late on Monday afternoon, April 29. They watched a skiff work its way from the south bank across the turbulent spring current, carefully skirting the river shoals. When the boat drew close, a military guard presented arms, and Brigadier General Benedict Arnold stepped forward with a pronounced limp to welcome the burly old man with wispy gray hair now visible in the bow. Cannons crashed out a salute from the stone ramparts. Wind tore dirty smoke from the muzzles after each salvo and carried it downstream. The Canada campaign was saved, at least for the moment: Benjamin Franklin had arrived.

He stepped onto the sandy beach, waving and shaking hands with a vigor that belied both his age—seventy, as of January—and his exhaustion. He had traveled more than a month from Philadelphia to get here: by sloop up the Hudson, by country wagon over washboard lanes from Albany, by squat bateau with a blanket sail—including overland from Lake George to Lake Champlain, pulled on wheels by six yoke of oxen—and by two-wheeled calèche in Canada over roads unworthy of the name. "I begin to apprehend that I have undertaken a fatigue that at my time of life may prove too much for me," he had written a friend "by way of farewell" two weeks earlier. He had rallied, of course, shrugging off the swollen limbs, the vertigo, the faltering eyesight, and the painful boils, to pack up his own bedding—the better to avoid fleas and bedbugs—for another day's journey northward. Last night he had slept at St. Johns, on the floor of a battle-wrecked, pillaged house from which even the door hinges had been filched. All the while he kept his traveling companions amused with tales of a grand life well lived. He also recited a sixteen-stanza ballad of his personal composition titled "The King's Own Regulars," which enumerated various British military mishaps during the past thirty years. Always sardonic toward fools and foes, he had estimated that Britain spent £20,000 for every American rebel killed, even as tens of thousands of American babies were being born. Just try, he said, to "calculate the time and expense necessary to kill us all."

An honor guard led the way through the Vaudreuil Gate into the city, past gawking fur trappers and Indians, scruffy *habitants* and priests in black cassocks with swinging pectoral crosses. The hobbling Arnold chatted amiably with his visitors, showing "good taste and politeness," as one observer wrote, as well as "delicacy, ease, and good breeding." He had arrived in Montreal from Quebec City earlier in the month, exchanging posts with the senior American officer in Canada, General David Wooster, who was now 160 miles downriver directing the tenuous siege of the fortress. Arnold was still recuperating not only from the gunshot below his knee during the failed assault that had killed Montgomery four months earlier, but from a subsequent horseback accident.

Franklin followed the general slowly down the Rue Notre-Dame to the genteel Château Ramezay, from which New France had once run its fur empire. A three-story fieldstone mansion with a river view and high gables to reduce the risk of roof-to-roof fires, the château had formerly been known as La Maison du Castor, Beaver House. Now it served as Arnold's headquarters.

Inside, a throng of local worthies strained for a glimpse of the celebrated Dr. Franklin, who was handed a glass of wine, then ushered into a sitting room for tea. After unleashing his voluble if flawed French to charm a group of attractive young women—pulchritude always revived him—Franklin was led into the dining room for an elaborate supper. Sitting on Arnold's right, weary head propped up with his thumb, he endured one sequined toast after another—to him, to Congress, to the cause—followed by more handsome ladies, this time singing in concert. The recital "proved very agreeable," wrote John Carroll, a Jesuit priest from Maryland traveling with Franklin, "and would have been more so if we had not been so much fatigued with our journey."

After the last brandy had been poured and the last *santé* exchanged, Arnold led his guest a hundred yards down Notre-Dame to what was described as "the best built and perhaps the best furnished house in town," owned by a merchant prince. Here, behind a door that still had hinges, Franklin at last tumbled into the first real bed he had seen in weeks. Important work lay ahead, beginning tomorrow. General Washington himself had recently warned that if Britain managed to keep Canada, the American rebellion "at best will be doubtful, hazardous, and bloody." But first Dr. Franklin needed sleep.

* * *

This mission to Canada was only the latest service Franklin had rendered his country since returning from London the previous spring. A day after the *Pennsylvania Packet* docked at the foot of Market Street in Philadelphia, he had been elected to Congress, eventually serving on thirty-four committees. Some colleagues wondered if his long residence in England made him sympathetic to Britain, if not an agent of the Crown. But most soon agreed with John Adams that he displayed "a disposition entirely American. . . . He does not hesitate at our boldest measures, but rather seems to think us too irresolute and backward." Indeed, Franklin believed that British aggression against Lexington and other injured towns was simply murder. Britain and America, he told a friend, were "on the high road to mutual enmity, hatred, and detestation. A separation will of course be inevitable."

Appointed postmaster general, he donated his £1,000 annual salary to care for wounded soldiers, then organized a system of mail riders every twenty-five to thirty miles from Maine to Savannah, ready to travel day or night. He sketched elaborate motifs for Continental currency to thwart counterfeiters. He designed an infantry pike, organized Delaware River defenses, and urged, unsuccessfully, the use of long bows in combat, since an archer "can discharge four arrows in the time of charging and discharging one bullet." Diligent in attending the various congressional committees to which he was assigned, Franklin immersed himself in the procurement of lead, saltpeter, and gunpowder.

But it was as a diplomat that he was invaluable. Upon joining the Committee of Secret Correspondence in November 1775, he used his vast network of acquaintances abroad—scientific, political, and personal—to seek both intelligence and foreign assistance for the American cause, ever mindful of British counterespionage prowess. (With one Dutch correspondent in The Hague, he used a French cipher with 682 letters numbered consecutively to thwart secret service code crackers.) Nor was he above subterfuge and artful deceit. Meeting a French agent in Philadelphia in December, Franklin purred assurances that the Continental Army grew stronger by the day and that the war was proceeding brilliantly, a message soon passed to Versailles.

And it was as a diplomat that Congress dispatched him to Montreal. Under nineteen paragraphs of instructions signed by Hancock, Franklin's task was nothing less than to restore Canadian faith in America's ideals, innocence, and military commitment after the debacle in Quebec. As leader of a small commission, he was "to settle all disputes between the Canadians and the Continental troops," persuade Canada that "their interests and ours are inseparably united," urge Canadians to join "our union as a sister colony," and pledge "the free and undisturbed exercise of their religion." His delegation included Father Carroll, who was to baptize Canadian children and give absolution to Catholics spurned by "toryfied priests"; the cleric's cousin Charles Carroll, one of the wealthiest men in America, who was both Catholic and fluent in French; and Samuel Chase, a capable if irascible congressman from Maryland known privately as "Bacon Face" for his florid complexion. They were also "to establish a free press . . . of service to the cause of the United Colonies." To that end, Franklin included in his party a French printer living in Philadelphia named Fleury Mesplet, who had wasted no time unpacking his handpress and cases of type in the cellar of the Château Ramezay.

Franklin and his fellow commissioners needed but a few minutes on Tuesday morning to realize how daunting their task had become. Around a large table in the château council chamber, Arnold convened a conference to explain why he had written General Schuyler ten days earlier to tell him that without prompt reinforcement and resupply, "our affairs in this country will be entirely ruined." The American force investing Fortress Quebec now included fewer than two thousand "raw troops, badly clothed and fed, and worse paid, and without discipline." Nearly half were unfit for duty, mostly stricken with smallpox. They faced eighteen hundred defenders and 148 cannons at Quebec under General Carleton and Lieutenant Colonel Maclean. American heavy artillery was "trifling"—a single 18-pounder. The Northern Army had been "disfurnished," in General Washington's delicate term, when all useful ordnance at Ticonderoga was removed to Boston. That hardly mattered, however, since the American magazines at Quebec held only 150 pounds of gunpowder.

The ailing Schuyler had not been with his soldiers in Canada for five months, deepening the contempt many New Englanders harbored toward the Northern Army commander despite his best efforts to keep them supplied from Albany. New troops had begun to arrive once ice on the lakes broke up, but many were badly armed and ill-dressed for Canadian weather—some sported feathers plucked from a New York loyalist's peacock flock. More than a few were "animated with the pleasing thought of plunder," as one officer observed. Schuyler complained that reinforcements "from Pennsylvania are greatly infected with the venereal disease"; soldiers often treated themselves by burning the sores with gunpowder or drinking powder mixed with spring water. Of a thousand stand of arms ordered in New York, only six had been delivered by mid-March. A lack of forage meant a shortage of oxen to pull heavy loads, like guns. The army surgeon reported that most regiments in Canada had no medications or surgical instruments.

Arnold had expected the commissioners to bring hard cash—specie, like pounds sterling or Spanish doubloons—and he was visibly distressed to learn that Franklin had brought nothing. The war chest in Canada contained just $11,000 in paper currency, and the troops were owed three times that in pay. ("A paymaster without money is but a ridiculous animal," the deputy paymaster observed.) Local merchants now shunned depreciated Continental currency as "a burnt child dreads the fire," in Schuyler's phrase. Even the calèche drivers who'd delivered the commissioners from St. Johns to the St. Lawrence on Monday had demanded silver rather than dollars. Washington had directed Arnold "to pay the full value for all provisions," but with what? For two months, the army had been forced to requisition supplies, wagons, and even forced labor, issuing worthless scrip or invalid, often illegible receipts. Firewood was taken at bayonet point.

Morale and discipline had collapsed. Soldiers stole horses and food or ransacked Canadian farms for the gold reputedly hidden in barns and under kitchens. Pilferage, malingering, and desertion were rampant; rumors circulated that supplies shipped north from New York had been diverted to the British. Worse yet, General Wooster—an arrogant, despotic Yale graduate in a large gray periwig—had alienated many Canadians by arresting priests and loyalists, closing Catholic churches, meddling with the fur trade, and telling Montreal citizens, "I regard the whole of you as enemies and rascals." There could be little surprise, one American officer warned, that the Canadian clergy "are unanimous, though privately, against our cause . . . and are now plotting our destruction," or that among both the French and English gentry "seven-eighths are Tories who would wish to see our throats cut." Whatever zeal the *habitants* had once evinced for the American invasion had subsided, not to be roused again; Carleton offered pardons to most seditious Canadians willing to publicly shout, "Long live the king!"

Appalled by Arnold's sorry tale, Franklin and his colleagues took another day for further inquiry and reflection. Clearly they were months too late in coming to Canada. Dithering by Congress had undermined the American venture, perhaps fatally. Despite his cheerless report, Arnold impressed the commissioners. "He will turn out a great man," Charles Carroll predicted. "He has great vivacity, perseverance, resources and intrepidity, and a cool judgment. . . . His lameness does not prevent him from stirring about." But Arnold had been undermined by the scurrilous Wooster, by bad behavior in the ranks, and by lack of support from Philadelphia.

On Wednesday, May 1, the commissioners composed the first of three glum dispatches sent to Hancock over the next week. The American expedition needed at least £20,000 sterling and eight thousand troops, immediately. The force around Quebec had less than ten days' provisions. "It is very difficult to keep soldiers under proper discipline without paying them regularly," they wrote. "This difficulty increases in proportion to the distance the troops are removed from their own country." Most Canadians expected "that we shall be driven out of the province as soon as the king's troops can arrive"; indeed, "we have daily intimations of plots hatching and insurrections intended for expelling us on the first news of the arrival of a British army." It might be necessary "to withdraw our army and fortify the passes on the lakes to prevent the enemy, and the Canadians if they are so inclined, from making eruptions into and depredations on our frontiers." Arnold sent his own simple message to Washington: "Should the enemy receive any considerable reinforcement soon, I make no doubt we shall have our hands full."

Franklin was unsure what more could be done. He understood that a new commander would soon take over at Quebec—John Thomas, the physician-soldier who had performed ably at Dorchester Heights, now promoted to major general. But he also knew, as he wrote Hancock, that "the smallpox is in the army, and General Thomas has unfortunately never had it."

"Your commissioners themselves are in a critical and most irksome situation," he added, "pestered hourly with demands great and small that they cannot answer." Franklin had even given Arnold £343 in gold from his own purse. He felt tired and unwell. His years weighed on him, and he could not help but look south, toward home.

Five thousand souls had spent a secure but tedious winter in Fortress Quebec. Wood grew so scarce that each hearth fire had to warm half a dozen families, even when the temperature outside dropped below minus twenty degrees Fahrenheit. The only mill in town could grind just three bushels of wheat an hour, so most grain was boiled and devoured whole. American gunners had fired nearly eight hundred cannonballs into the town—"Let the shot be well-heated," Arnold advised before leaving for Montreal—and while few casualties resulted, chimneys were decapitated, roofs perforated, and children terrified. Several hundred American prisoners captured on December 31 battled boredom and pestilence: the officers locked up on the seminary's fourth floor and the enlisted men now in Dauphin jail, described as a "dingy, gloomy sepulcher." Scores of British-born American troops had sworn allegiance to the king in exchange for release from jail, but after several deserted while walking sentry duty, Carleton locked them up again. When Captain Daniel Morgan was offered a British commission, he replied, "I hope you will never again insult me."

Lanterns and fire pots still burned along the walls on moonless nights to reveal potential rebel infiltrators, and thorn bushes were heaped on the glacis. A sentry box was hoisted atop a mast thirty feet above the Cape Diamond rampart so lookouts could watch for rebel troops massing. The garrison stayed busy clearing snow from walls and ditches, rearranging guns on the parapets, and walking guard duty. Carleton jailed militiamen who refused duty along the Lower Town wharves for fear of either American riflemen or the ghosts of men slain there on New Year's Eve. The governor was uncertain whether the Yankees had five thousand troops in Canada or twenty-five thousand; all he could do was hold tight and hope for relief from London. The first swallows had been spotted darting above the St. Lawrence on April 21, a good omen.

Deliverance was nearer than he knew. Despite uncertainty over whether Quebec had fallen, Lord Germain worked tirelessly to assemble a rescue expedition of nine regiments that would not only liberate Canada but provide the firepower needed to eventually invade New York down the Lake Champlain–Hudson River corridor. In contrast to the hasty, star-crossed expedition to North Carolina, this mission was mounted deftly. Under Germain's plan, adopted in early January with the king's approval, an advance detachment had sailed from England in March with four men-of-war, three victuallers, and several East Indiamen fitted out as transports to carry the 29th Foot. They would be followed by a larger convoy bearing the remaining regulars, siege artillery, and three thousand German auxiliary troops.

The long passage from the Gulf of St. Lawrence to Quebec could be exceptionally hazardous, with shoals, shifting currents, and treacherous winds; a British war fleet attacking Quebec in 1711 lost eleven ships and nine hundred men to the river. For the current expedition, the Admiralty sought navigation advice from Captain James Cook, the intrepid explorer, who had spent four winters in Canada charting the St. Lawrence, among other waters, and happened to be in London between Pacific voyages. In command of the expedition, aboard the fifty-gun *Isis*, was Captain Charles Douglas, who had assured the Admiralty of his zeal in crushing "this atrocious rebellion in America, the most insolent, the most ungrateful, that ever reared an opprobrious head against an indulgent parent state." Douglas, sent to sea at age twelve, reputedly spoke six languages. He had served at Quebec with Wolfe in 1759, and later in Newfoundland before, as a temporary Russian admiral, helping Catherine the Great reorganize her navy. He had also invented a thermometer capable of measuring water temperature at 260 fathoms and would be credited with designing better systems for aiming, stabilizing, and igniting naval guns. "A very dignified and lovely man," one Hessian wrote of him.

Douglas had often sailed these waters, and he was hardly surprised when *Isis* found herself wedged in pack ice south of Newfoundland on April 13, "the ship receiving many severe shocks," as her log recorded. The ice parted and then closed again, encasing the frigate and her companions, despite their efforts to ram floes ten feet thick. Splinters of sheathing from the hull and the ship's cutwater littered the ice around the prow. "We thought it an enterprise worthy of an English ship-of-the-line in our king and country's sacred cause," Douglas later told the Admiralty. Fog froze on the lines "by which means the ship appeared as if rigged with ropes of crystal near four times their usual diameter," Ensign John Enys on the nearby *Surprize* told his diary. Iron ballast was dropped from the *Isis* bowsprit to crack the ice "but had no effect." The drifting pack carried them backward ten miles on April 15; sailors tossed grapnels from the bow to hook the ice, with the entire crew pulling on hawsers to haul the ship forward. "Unspeakable toil," Douglas wrote, but "all to no purpose." When fresh gales blew from astern, Douglas set studding sails, which carried them only a few boat lengths before they again came to a dead stop. Carpenters nailed three-inch planks to the ships' bows, and attached fenders fashioned from scrap wood and old rope to protect the hulls.

After almost ten days, the ice finally relented. "A breeze getting up broke up the ice," Ensign Enys wrote. "About one o'clock to our great joy we got quite clear." Passing Anticosti Island on April 21, the flotilla entered the mouth of the St. Lawrence in a snowstorm. Light airs and fog caused further delays, but on the evening of May 3, *Isis* anchored off the eastern tip of Île aux Coudres, to be joined a few hours later by *Surprize*, the sloop of war *Martin*, and other ships. Quebec lay sixty miles upstream.

Unaware of his peril, Major General Thomas had arrived at the Quebec camp in early May to find his new command in shambles. Of the thousand Americans fit for duty, three hundred refused to fight since their enlistments had recently expired. Another two hundred had just received smallpox inoculations, against orders, and would be quarantined for weeks. The remainder held a perimeter looping more than twenty miles around the city. There was little food and less powder. "I find there is expected from me more than I think I shall be able to [deliver] unless things were in better order," Thomas had written his wife, Hannah.

Six thousand American reinforcements bound for Canada remained mostly in the Hudson valley or along Lake Champlain. A thief broke into

Thomas's rooms during his second night at Holland House and stole his gold-laced beaver hat; he was reduced to announcing that if the headwear was returned within a day, the thief "shall be entitled to the lace." Even among his stout-hearted troops—and there were still some—a dark fatalism obtained. "If I die you may depend upon it I will die like a good soldier . . . to be a credit to you all," a Pennsylvania sergeant wrote his parents in late April. "Adue! Adue!"

With Fortress Quebec all but impregnable a mile to his east, Thomas agreed to try a desperate measure concocted earlier by Arnold and refined by Wooster, now second-in-command. At seven-thirty p.m. on May 3, as a full moon rose over the St. Lawrence, the brigantine *Peggy* appeared under full sail from behind the Île d'Orléans, three miles downstream of the Lower Town. Lookouts tossed their hats and whooped in exultation. Runners raced uphill to the Château St. Louis to tell General Carleton the breathless news: the first relief ship from Britain was in sight.

Under a northeast breeze the brig glided toward the Cul de Sac anchorage, where sixty vessels were moored along the quays. On Cape Diamond, sentinels hoisted a blue pennant on a flagstaff above the Union Jack and fired five guns—the secret recognition signal. *Peggy* gave no reply, and no one could be seen on her weather deck as she bent toward Queen's Wharf. "Who are you?" a British officer shouted from the waterfront. "Who are you? Answer or we'll sink you."

A light gleamed on the quarterdeck, and someone carrying a lantern sprinted to the forecastle. Abruptly flames licked up the foresail, four guns sprayed grapeshot toward the Lower Town, and *Peggy*'s ports flew open to ventilate the blaze now seen raging belowdecks. Shadowy figures scrambled over the side into three dinghies, then rowed for Pointe-Levy across the St. Lawrence "with amazing speed," a witness reported. Drums beat to arms in the Upper Town. Bells pealed. Defenders rushed to the ramparts, shouting and fumbling with their firelocks. Shells and rockets now began to detonate within *Peggy*. Balls from several shore batteries skipped across the river surface. British tars in the anchorage made ready to fend off the fireship.

But no fending would be necessary. Fifty yards from the wharf, the current and ebbing tide gently nudged the brig back to midstream, a pyre to pale the rising moon. "The tide had the sole command of her & carried her down below the shipping," a British gunner told his journal. The rebel arsonists escaped, although Lieutenant Ephraim Anderson of the 2nd New Jersey Regiment was badly burned and would make his way home swathed in bandages. *Peggy* drifted into the Beauport shallows northeast of the Lower Town. "She afforded a very pretty prospect while she was floating down the river, every now & then sending up sky rockets," the British gunner wrote, "& so continued till she disappeared in the channel. . . . We passed the night in our usual tranquility." A one a.m., the fire winked out with a wet hiss.

No sooner had the excitement subsided than another sail was seen approaching upriver at first light on Monday, May 6. Again soldiers and militia pounded for the walls amid the clamor of drums and bells, and again the recognition flags rose on Cape Diamond. This time the stranger gave a proper reply: a red pennant at the main topgallant masthead, a Union Jack at the mizzen topgallant, and a salute of seven guns spaced out as precisely as clock chimes. The spars and sleek hull of *Surprize* came fully into view, "to the inconceivable joy of all who saw her," Captain Thomas Ainslie told his journal. She would be followed directly by *Isis*, *Martin*, and their sisters. Giddy cheers swept the ramparts. Civilians in robes and nightcaps dashed into the cobbled streets.

"The news soon reached every pillow in town," Ainslie noted. "People half-dressed ran down to the grand battery to feast their eyes with the sight of a ship of war displaying the union flag." *Surprize* dropped her anchors with a splash, and at eight a.m. the 29th Foot began disembarking. Wobbly regulars tried to walk off their sea legs along Près de Ville, where Montgomery had died in the snow.

General Thomas was dismayed, if not surprised. Reports of approaching British ships had reached Holland House the previous day. On Sunday, his war council voted unanimously to evacuate the sick, and Thomas knew that he would soon be forced to abandon the blockade. "In my ideas of war," he wrote Washington, ". . . it would have been highly proper to have made this movement some weeks past." Yet several hours passed on Monday morning after the regulars came ashore before Thomas ordered his men to shoulder arms and begin leaking westward. Now he risked the imminent destruction of the American army in Canada.

At twelve-thirty p.m., lean and immaculate, Carleton emerged from the St. Louis Gate leading three companies of the 29th Foot, followed by marines, Royal Highland Emigrants, sailors, and militiamen. Others spilled from the St. John Gate as more bells clanged, and soon two quickstepping columns of nine hundred troops advanced onto the Plains of Abraham with four horse-drawn field guns. Scarlet-clad grenadiers in bearskin caps held the right flank with emigrants and fusiliers. Marines in red coats with white facings massed on the left, along with British militiamen wearing green and buff. American pickets threw a few wild shots, then ran after their fleeing comrades, chased by a volley of 6-pound balls. Thomas would describe his men as "coming off in good order," but the Continentals fled upriver as if tumbling across a landscape abruptly raised and tilted west. "Look which way soever, one could see men flying and carts driving away with all possible speed," a British diarist wrote. He added:

> We found the roads strewed with rifles and ammunition, while clothes, bread, and pork all lay in heaps in the highway with howitzers and fieldpieces. So great was their panic that they left behind them many papers of consequence to those who wrote them, and to whom they were writ.

Regulars expected the rebels to give battle on the plains, but, a British lieutenant concluded, "It seems they had no stomach for it." Ailing Americans hobbled from their beds into the woods, including many disfigured with new smallpox pustules. Others were too ill to stir. "In the most irregular, helter-skelter manner we raised the siege, leaving everything," wrote Dr. Senter, who for six months had run the hospital in the St. Charles convent. "Most of our sick fell into their hands, with all hospital stores, &c." A few invalids found seats aboard skiffs or bateaux only to be evicted by healthy comrades who dumped them on the beach. "Some of them expired before our parties could get to their relief," Captain Ainslie wrote in his journal.

British soldiers rooting through the American camps found scaling ladders, snowshoes, orderly books, brass guns captured in November at St. Johns, and, on the hearth in Highland House, General Thomas's dinner, still warm and instantly devoured by Maclean's Emigrants. Watching from the *Isis* quarterdeck, Captain Douglas described "a flight perhaps the most precipitate ever heard of." He ordered *Surprize* and *Martin* upriver to scour the shoreline with gunfire "to annoy their retreat"—"the balls made tearing work among the brush," an American private acknowledged—and to capture any loitering rebel rivercraft. Among the prizes seized was a bateau that had just arrived from Ticonderoga with two tons of gunpowder and five hundred muskets. The rebels, Douglas reported, were "now for the first time exposed to their very buckles."

By Tuesday, May 7, most fugitives who'd escaped had reached the riverine settlement of Deschambault, forty miles upstream. Oarsmen in the bateaux chanted, "Row the boat, row," flinching whenever bow chasers on the pursuing warships tossed a ball their way. "Our men excessively exhausted," wrote Colonel Elisha Porter, who had only two loaves of bread to divide among seventy soldiers. Thomas convened a war council at eleven a.m., then ordered his troops to press on another eighty-five miles to Sorel, at the mouth of the Richelieu River. There they could turn south, toward Lake Champlain.

Chaplains privately debated the reason for God's unsparing judgment. "This is the most terrible day I ever saw. God of armies, help us," Reverend Ammi R. Robbins wrote in his diary on Tuesday. "Distress and anxiety in every countenance. The smallpox thick among us." Unwell himself, Robbins sat in a boat with water to his knees as the retreat resumed. "Troops are in such confusion," he added. "Our days are days of darkness."

The bad news flew swiftly to Montreal, prompting Franklin and his colleagues to write Congress on Friday, May 10, "We are afraid it will not be in our power to render our country any further services in this colony." The next morning at eight a.m. Franklin bolted south with Reverend Carroll after some difficulty in finding a carriage to rent. The arduous journey back to Philadelphia would take three weeks. "The doctor's declining state of health, and the bad prospects of our affairs in Canada, made him take this resolution," Charles Carroll observed. As a souvenir, Franklin wore a soft brown cap of marten fur. Hobbled with gout and disappointment, he wrote bleakly, "I find I grow daily more feeble."

Charles Carroll and Samuel Chase were not far behind. Lingering for a few days to inspect the American encampments along the Richelieu, they "found all things in much confusion, extreme disorder, and negligence." Carleton had reined in his pursuit to await the arrival of more regiments from England, but few doubted that the British would soon advance in full force. Food shortages had grown so dire that some troops were put on half-rations. Not even a dogcart could be hired on credit. Hancock had sent the last hard currency in the American treasury—£1,662, 1 shilling, and 3 pence—along with $300,000 in Continental paper currency, neatly stacked in three strongboxes and virtually worthless. Especially dispiriting was news that a garrison of four hundred New England troops at the Cedars, a stockade forty miles west of Montreal, had been duped into surrendering by a force of regulars and Indians barely half their number; a rescue force dispatched from Montreal was ambushed, and a hundred more men captured and stripped of everything from their hats to their shoe buckles. Arnold hurried toward the Cedars in a white rage with more reinforcements, but then agreed to a negotiated prisoner exchange for fear that Indians were about to massacre his men. "I was torn," he confessed, "by the conflicting passions of revenge and humanity."

Along the Richelieu, so many soldiers had inoculated themselves against smallpox without proper supervision or quarantine, usually with pus poked under the fingernails, that General Thomas made self-inoculation a capital crime. The practice continued anyway. Some men who relied on comrades to do the deed were blindfolded so they could not incriminate their inoculators. Reinforcements arriving in Canada from Lake Champlain were promptly exposed and infected by the hundreds. Troops were also short of tents, shoes, entrenching tools, and firelocks; five Pennsylvania companies had delayed marching north for want of weapons other than "damned tomahawks," as their commander complained. "Men indeed we have," Arnold told Thomas, "but almost every other requisite for war is wanting." In their final dispatch to Hancock, the commissioners wrote, "We cannot find words strong enough to describe our miserable situation." The army was "broken and disheartened . . . soldiers without pay, without discipline, and altogether reduced to live from hand to mouth."

They were also soldiers without a leader. On May 21, Thomas sent Wooster a woeful note: "I am at this critical period unfortunately [stricken] with the small pox . . . I shall be for some time unable to discharge the duties of my office." Few victims of the king of terrors suffered more. Blind and disfigured beyond recognition, Thomas was, by the time of his death at dawn on June 2, so rapidly decomposing "that he was obliged to be interred that day," one of his pallbearers wrote. At age fifty-two, he left a widow, three children, and an army reduced to "a great rabble," as Arnold wrote from Montreal, adding, "I wish with all my heart we were out of the country. We had much better begin anew."

Rumors circulated that Washington himself was coming to save the Northern Army, but instead a new commander arrived at Chambly just as Thomas was lowered into his grave. "No one thing is right," Brigadier General John Sullivan wrote Hancock. "Everything is in the utmost confusion . . . [I] shall do everything in my powers to rectify the disorder."

Sullivan, alas, was hardly the man to conjure order from chaos, or to extract victory from defeat. The ruddy, thirty-six-year-old son of indentured Irish servants who had settled in New Hampshire, he was an opinionated, bombastic lawyer, rabidly anti-Catholic and notorious for suing his debtors. His high rank derived from political influence, of which he had much, rather than soldierly acumen, of which he had little. Washington's assessment, in a note to Hancock, was judicious: "He does not want abilities. . . . But he has his wants, and he has his foibles. The latter are manifested in a little tincture of vanity."

Sullivan instantly misread both his political and his military predicaments. "I found joy in every countenance except some very few Tories," he wrote Washington from Sorel on June 6. "It really was very affecting to see the banks of the [Richelieu] lined with men, women, and children, leaping & clapping their hands for joy to see me arrive." That they might leap and clap just as ardently for Carleton had never occurred to him. Spies assured

Sullivan that only three hundred British troops occupied the strategic post of Trois-Rivières, thirty-five miles down the St. Lawrence. To "put a new face on our affairs here," he told Washington, he had decided to attack. "With the assistance of a kind Providence," he added, the Americans could even threaten Fortress Quebec again.

To pursue this fantasy, Sullivan sent Brigadier General William Thompson with two thousand of his healthiest Continentals across the St. Lawrence in fifty bateaux at two a.m. on Saturday, June 8. Leaving 250 men to guard the boats nine miles above Trois-Rivières, Thompson pressed a Canadian farmer, Antonine Gauthier, into service as a guide and veered inland from the shore road to avoid British naval vessels seen on the river. Through ineptitude or guile, Gauthier—described as a "dirt-brown clodhopper"—led the Americans into what Colonel Anthony Wayne called the "most horrid swamp that ever man set foot in . . . so deep and thick with small timber as to prevent a man's seeing twelve yards to front or rear." When the bespattered, mosquito-mauled column at last stumbled back to the river, alert gunners aboard the sloop of war *Martin* opened fire, again driving them into a primeval bog, "full three miles, over knee-deep nearly at every step," another officer wrote. Some lost their shoes in the muck. The summer sun had fully risen by the time "we got disentangled from this dreadful place," added Colonel William Irvine. "The guide proved faithless." With surprise squandered and the Royal Navy astride the river, a prudent retreat was in order, "but no one would propose it." Thompson ordered the attack forward.

It was General Thompson's additional misfortune that the main contingent of British reinforcements had reached Quebec City in late May and was now approaching Trois-Rivières under Carleton's new deputy commander. General John Burgoyne, who had briefly returned to England after seven months in Boston, again found himself in North America. Burgoyne had left a dying wife at home—"I never was put to so severe a trial as this separation," he wrote his friend General Henry Clinton—but he brought with him eight thousand regulars and German auxiliaries, more than £200,000 in cash, 125,000 gallons of rum, and forty tons of baggage. After disembarking at Quebec on May 29, Burgoyne soon advanced westward in a cabriolet "along the banks of the river over a most romantic wild country," his aide-de-camp wrote. "It is quite Arcadian." Several dozen transports worked up the St. Lawrence, jammed rail to rail with soldiers.

At eight a.m. on Saturday, Colonel Wayne led the American van of two hundred Pennsylvanians across a farm field just west of Trois-Rivières, near a wooden Ursuline convent and high-peaked *habitant* cottages. British light infantrymen gave way as more American regiments hurried past a gristmill in a four-pronged assault that for an instant seemed to gain momentum. Then the attackers abruptly spied several thousand regulars and a pair of 6-pounders entrenched behind breastworks on the edge of the village. More enemy troops poured off newly arrived vessels, and flanking fire battered the Continentals from the left bank of the broad blue St. Lawrence. "We had no covering, no artillery, and no prospect of succeeding," an American officer later wrote.

Eighty yards from the British line, the attackers faltered and fell back, blistered with a cross fire of bullets, field artillery shot, and grape from the ships' guns to the right. Grenadiers and light infantry led by the 6-pounders drove the Americans through the tree line, and gusts of naval gunfire once again cudgeled them away from the river and into the swamp. Chased by twelve hundred British pursuers with Indian guides, and, as a young captain later recalled, "devoured by mosquitoes of a monstrous size and innumerable numbers," the Americans crashed through the marshes for another sleepless night. "Nature perhaps never formed a place better calculated for the destruction of an army," a survivor wrote. "The mantle of heaven was our only covering," another added. "No fire, and bad water our only food."

General Thompson hid in the fens that night and the following day before surrendering. "Generals Carleton and Burgoyne were both there, who treated us very politely," according to an officer captured with him. "They ordered us refreshments immediately. Indeed, General Burgoyne served us himself." Others escaped singly or in furtive squads. Colonel Wayne, a thirty-one-year-old surveyor and commander of the 4th Pennsylvania Regiment, managed to collect seven hundred fugitives and outflank the British pursuit a dozen miles upstream. He and his column straggled back to Sorel on Monday despite being "almost spent with fatigue, hunger, & difficulties," as Wayne told Dr. Franklin in a letter.

"Our army was a great deal cut to pieces," a New Jersey sergeant advised his diary on June 9. American casualties totaled about 400, compared to 17 for the British. Carleton reported capturing 244 Americans, including 18 officers. "Upwards of fifty" American bodies were found at Trois-Rivières and in the bogs. Others simply vanished. "Their attempt upon Three Rivers was founded in rashness and executed with timidity, two principles which compounded make a consummation of preposterous conduct," Burgoyne wrote Clinton with his usual magniloquence.

Still, that assessment was difficult to deny. "Our affairs look dark, matters don't go right, and I don't know how they should," an American engineer lamented. Sullivan, in a long, babbling, and inaccurate letter from Sorel, told Washington on June 8, "I am almost certain that victory has been declared in our favor"; the thunder of sporadic cannon fire drifting upriver "shows that our men are in possession of the ground. . . . This with many other circumstances induces me to believe our troops are victorious." But when a courier carrying a truce flag arrived to collect Thompson's baggage, Sullivan grew maudlin. "I now only think of a glorious death or a victory obtained against superior numbers," he wrote on June 12. Nearly three hundred miles south, in Albany, Schuyler displayed the ignorance incumbent on a commanding general who had not seen his army for more than half a year. "I am extremely happy to find that the chaos & confusion which has reigned so triumphantly in our army . . . are on the point of being expelled," he wrote Sullivan on June 13. "We already owe you much, my dear General."

The only expulsion likely was of the Northern Army from Canada. Early on Friday, June 14, Carleton boarded the transport *Rousseau* at Trois-Rivières and ordered his host westward to crush the American invaders for good. Ten thousand regulars, Canadians, and Indians crowded onto more than sixty vessels or marched along a shoreline bright with summer blossoms and river reeds nodding in the breeze. Gulls and herons wheeled overhead, and emerald woodlands stretched north toward the Laurentian Mountains, "in all appearance as old as the world itself," a lieutenant noted. White canvas sails bellied before the breeze, and the many masts were said to resemble "a moving forest." Ensign John Enys of the 29th Foot wrote, "It was one of the most agreeable prospects I ever saw, the islands and shipping being so interspersed with one another."

At nine p.m., wind spilled from those sails, anchors splashed, and the armada hove to half a mile off Sorel, at the mouth of the Richelieu. With his usual deliberation, Carleton had massed his forces and concocted a clever plan: Burgoyne would disembark here with four thousand men to overrun the rebel camp at Sorel, then angle south along the Richelieu toward Chambly and St. Johns, careful not to chase the Americans too ardently. Carleton would sail another fifty miles up the St. Lawrence with the rest of the army to La Prairie, across from Montreal, then lunge cross-country fifteen miles to St. Johns, cutting off the American retreat. He would provide the anvil for Burgoyne's hammer.

Serenaded by crickets and frogs, Burgoyne and his regulars rowed ashore at four a.m. on Sunday with a half dozen 6-pounders and eighty rounds for each gun. Scouts crept up the sand breastworks, bayonets poised, but found only bonfire embers and wagon tracks leading south, as well as drag marks on the Richelieu beach where bateaux had been shoved into the water. The Americans had decamped eighteen hours earlier. At dawn the British formed three columns and began the pursuit, but the fleet remained in sight behind them: the wind had died, and the clouds of white canvas hardly stirred. Carleton's neat plan was already in peril.

General Sullivan had no plan, neat or otherwise. On Thursday night, his war council had convened at Sorel to remind him of the many reasons to flee Canada immediately. Sorel was vulnerable to attack from both the right flank—defended by only an abatis of aspen saplings—and from the rear. By one tally, of eight thousand Continentals north of the border, more than three thousand were sick, mostly with smallpox, which was killing thirty men a day. Measles, dysentery, and other afflictions also took a toll. Of the twelve tons of salt pork and flour needed to feed the army every day, only a fraction had arrived from New York.

Some colonels were uncertain where parts of their regiments could be found, and some regiments had "not a single man fit for duty," as Sullivan himself conceded. Forty officers had asked to resign their commissions; others simply walked south, in company with enlisted deserters. Instructions from Congress to "contest every foot of the ground" were absurd, impossible. If the army was trapped at the mouth of the Richelieu, Sullivan's senior officers told him, he "alone must answer for it." After a long, tense pause, Sullivan agreed to withdraw to Chambly, fifty miles upstream. Hoisting guns, tents, and the infirm into wagons and rivercraft, the garrison abandoned Sorel at ten a.m. on Friday, every man stealing glances over his shoulder.

No one had been more insistent on retreat than Arnold, who several days earlier had traveled from Montreal to inspect the flimsy defenses at Chambly and St. Johns. All hope for luring Canadians to the American cause was now gone, he wrote Sullivan. "Let us quit them & secure our own country before it is too late. There will be more honor in making a safe retreat than hazarding a battle," he urged. "I am content to be the last man who quits this country, and fall so that my country rise. But let us not fall together." Under orders from Schuyler to bring "away from Montreal all the goods you possibly can," Arnold seized woolens, silks, tinware, flour, molasses, and rum from Montreal merchants in exchange for dubious receipts. Nails were particularly needed at Ticonderoga for boatbuilding, and American troops ransacked Château Ramezay, inflicting almost £1,200 in damage. When residents balked at Arnold's demand for carts and wagons, he threatened to burn down the town.

At seven p.m. on Saturday, Arnold and three hundred Continentals pushed away from Montreal in eleven bateaux, "huddled together like cordwood" and battered by raindrops "the size of large peas," as a fifer recorded. The town had served as the capital of American Canada for six months, but with British troops reportedly only a dozen miles distant, it would be abandoned without a fight. Across the St. Lawrence, Arnold torched his boats, then led his men through mud "half a leg deep" to La Prairie and on toward St. Johns, burning bridges and felling trees across the road behind them as they fled.

Three other corps—two British and one American—were now heaving toward the same destination. The capricious east wind had failed completely on the St. Lawrence, forcing Carleton to abandon his ships at Verchères, only fifteen miles upstream from Sorel. On Sunday, June 16, his army reached Varennes, on the right bank, then pivoted southeast toward St. Johns, at least a day behind schedule and more than a day behind Arnold. Carleton would be harshly criticized for dawdling, at Trois-Rivières and in the subsequent pursuit, but he faced vexing obstacles: most of his troops had not regained their land legs or toughened up their marching feet after the long voyage from England, and many were racked with the flux— diarrhea—from eating green fruit plucked in roadside orchards to supplement the salt-meat diet.

Burgoyne, advancing south along the Richelieu with the other British contingent, was likewise beset. A twenty-mile march to St. Denis on June 15 left his brigade so enervated from the summer heat, flux, and paltry provisions that he was forced to rest for a day before resuming the march at midnight on Monday, June 17, the anniversary of Bunker Hill. With drums rapping and fifes tootling, the regulars finally reached Chambly at nine o'clock the next morning to find the square fort and sawmill in flames, and the rebels gone, again. "We began our chase with might & main," Burgoyne's aide wrote, "but the nimble-heel'd rebels had made too much way for us."

General Sullivan had managed another narrow escape, but the final dozen miles to St. Johns would be exhausting, he remarked, "beyond anything that ever I went through." Upon fleeing Chambly, the Americans rowed a hundred bateaux to Point Despair, where a long stretch of "exceeding bad" rapids tumbled with "a current like that of a mill sluice," in one officer's description. Provisions and munitions were unloaded and portaged on the river road, while men immersed to their armpits shoved the boats upstream or pulled them with painters from the bank, pausing long enough to wolf down a meal of rancid pork and unbaked flour. Others demolished bridges and toppled trees; the sound of axes and crashing timber rang loud. A rumor of approaching redcoats triggered panic and sent some "officers running off leaving their men by the side of the river," Lieutenant Colonel Jeduthan Baldwin told his diary. Another lieutenant colonel wrote his wife in New Jersey, "Everything goes against us here."

On Monday night, still a day ahead of their pursuers, the Americans staggered into St. Johns to be reunited with Arnold's band from Montreal. Barns and sheds were jammed with smallpox victims, most unattended by medicos except, occasionally, to be bled. "Some dead, some dying, others at the point of death, some whistling, some singing & many cursing & swearing," a New England physician, Lewis Beebe, noted in his diary. "Nothing to be heard from morning to night, but 'Doctor, doctor, doctor,' from every side. . . . Add to all this, we have nothing to eat."

Soldiers pried more than two tons of lead from the roof of a large house to melt into musket balls, while on Tuesday morning a war council agreed to abandon St. Johns for Île aux Noix, a small island twelve miles south, near the mouth of Lake Champlain. Every available rivercraft began to shuttle cargo, from cannonballs to moribund men, up the Richelieu. "The boats were loaded as deep as they could swim," a New Englander wrote. Captain Charles Cushing of Massachusetts, whose 24th Continental Regiment provided the rear guard, told his journal that "the confusion the army was in was beyond description." When bateaux crewmen balked at loading more passengers, Cushing added, "I took my gun and told them if they did not put on shore that instant, I would fire on them. They went on shore, damning their eyes, and swearing very much."

Late that afternoon, incendiaries set fire to the boatyard and the twin redoubts. Arnold saddled a horse and rode north on reconnaissance. Barely two miles from St. Johns he spotted three companies of British light infantrymen and Canadian volunteers loping along the river road, trailed by 6-pounders and a thick, sinuous column of Burgoyne's redcoats. Wheeling his mount, he galloped back to St. Johns, stripped off the saddle and bridle, then shot the horse. The stink of arson and badly buried corpses wafted across the water. Smoke curled above the old British compound, captured by Montgomery so long ago. Ordering his rear guard into the final boat, Arnold pushed the vessel into the stream himself before scrambling aboard, "and thus indulged the vanity of being the last man who embarked from the shores of the enemy," his aide, Captain James Wilkinson, later wrote.

Dusk draped the Canadian woods. From the muddy bank near the ruined fortifications, a British scout squinting upriver thought he saw a skiff vanish round a bend through the trees. And then he saw nothing, nothing at all.

Île aux Noix seemed to float like a low green raft in the Richelieu, ten miles above the New York border. A mile long and a quarter mile wide, the island bore traces of both old French and British military entrench-ments, now overrun with morning glories, cattails, and goldenrod. Even in the middle of a river, potable water was at a premium, and the place swarmed with mosquitoes, mice, and snakes. A stand of walnut trees had given Île aux Noix its name—"Island of Nuts"—but soldiers called it Isle of Noise or Isle Annoy.

Thousands of American soldiers in fifteen regiments now jammed this two-hundred-acre malarial hell, perhaps half of them suffering from smallpox—described as "the pestilence that walketh in darkness"—or dys-entery, "the destruction that wasteth at noonday," or some other malady. Day by day, twenty to sixty more fell ill in each regiment. For want of tents, most of the sick lay uncovered on the marshy ground. "The lice and mag-gots seemed to vie with each other, creeping in millions over the victims," wrote Captain John Lacey of Pennsylvania. Dr. Beebe described men unable to "see, speak, or walk. . . . No mortal will ever believe what these suffered unless they were eyewitnesses." Pathetic pleas from dying soldiers, he added, "are as little regarded as the singing of crickets in a summer's eve-ning." Another surgeon, Samuel J. Meyrick, later wrote, "We had nothing to give them. It broke my heart, and I wept till I had not more power to weep."

Two burial pits were dug, one for New England and New York troops bivouacked on the eastern half of the island, the other for New Jersey and Pennsylvania regiments to the west. Four soldiers holding the corners of a blanket hauled each dead comrade to those open graves, rolling the corpse onto other corpses—"with no other covering but the rags in which they died," Captain Lacey observed—then shoveling in a bit of dirt at the end of the day. Nearly all were buried in anonymity, nameless in the orderly books and journals of their commanders, their medicos, their divines.

Some officers drank themselves into a stupor, but Arnold and others tried to impose military discipline on this last, awful outpost in Canada. Quartermasters allocated real estate to each regiment. Baggage from St. Johns was unloaded from the bateaux and placed under guard, except for artillery stores, which would be dispatched quickly to Crown Point, near the south end of the lake, along with the first invalids. Color men—laborers—were to dig vaults, or latrines, "at a proper distance from the encampments," and all troops were to use the vaults "instead of defiling the ground of their encampment." A drummer should accompany each regimental commander at all times, ready to rap out twenty-four various signals with rolls and flams. Among other afflictions, marauding Indians killed or captured almost twenty Continentals around Île aux Noix. On June 22, Pennsylvania soldiers seeking spruce beer at a farmhouse a mile from the island rowed unarmed into an ambush; four were killed and seven captured. Arnold sent a war party to retrieve the bodies. "Such a sight I never beheld with my eyes as to see men scalped," an officer confided to his diary. They, too, were laid uncoffined in a common grave, their epitaph carved on a wooden headboard: "SONS OF AMERICA, REST QUIET HERE."

Sullivan seemed stupefied by the misery he commanded. "By a strange reverse of fortune," he wrote Schuyler in another prolix dispatch, "we are driven to the sad necessity of abandoning Canada." This nightmare seemed more "like the effect of imagination than the history of fact." Men in his "decayed and decaying army," he reflected, "are daily dropping off like the Israelites before the destroying angel."

> Heaven sees at present to frown upon us in this quarter & take off those by pestilence who have escaped the sword. . . . Could my own life have saved a retreat so fatal in all its consequences to my country, I would willingly have resigned it.

Sullivan was as quick to disclaim responsibility as he was to propose self-immolation. "The grand post was lost before my arrival & put beyond my power to regain . . . I am sufficiently mortified & sincerely wish I had never seen this fatal country." Although he recognized, as he wrote Washington, that loitering on the island "will not leave us well men enough to carry off the sick," he resisted authorizing a full retreat down Lake Champlain, except for invalids, without explicit orders. "Farther than this," he told Schuyler, "I could not go."

At last, pressed by his subordinates, Sullivan consented to an evacuation as more empty boats arrived from Ticonderoga. "I find myself under an absolute necessity of quitting this island for a place more healthy," he wrote Washington on June 24. "Otherwise the army will never be able to return."

That was true enough. Some regiments had so few healthy men that oarsmen had to be drafted from other units. Even undiseased men were described as "lousy, itchy, and nasty as hogs." Those with tents struck them at dawn on Tuesday, June 25. A white banner raised from the stern of Sullivan's skiff signaled the embarkation. Then a boat with a blue flag led the procession south from the river into the lake, two vessels abreast, with three squadrons following, identified by yellow, red, and green flags, respectively. Each man received a pint of flour and four ounces of malodorous salt pork for his daily ration, cooked on blackened strips of bark when the boats put in to shore each day at noon. A rear guard of twelve hundred Continentals marched down the rim of the lake. "Worse traveling men never traveled," one of them wrote. "It rains exceeding hard, & night comes on."

Those who died during the hundred-mile journey to Crown Point were buried "in as decent a manner as we could" in unmarked graves on the shoreline, a New England doctor added.

Headwinds would keep some boats on the lake for more than a week before they reached their destination. "I never had an idea of pain equal to that which I felt at the evacuation of Canada," Sullivan wrote Hancock. "I hope Congress will not attribute it to my timidity or want of resolution."

But the general's pain could not have been greater than that felt by the likes of Matthew Patten of Bedford, New Hampshire, an Irish immigrant who served on his local Committee of Safety. Patten told his diary of running errands nearby—delivering twenty-six yards of fustian to be "dyed and dressed" by a clothier, then buying a new ax handle, a snuff bottle, and six bushels of salt—before arriving home to find fatal news from Crown Point. His son, John, who had survived a gunshot wound to the left arm at Bunker Hill, had taken ill in Chambly before being evacuated to Île aux Noix, where, on June 20, he passed over. "I got an account of my John's death of the smallpox at Canada," Patten wrote. "He was 24 years and 31 days old."

So ended a botched campaign of liberation and aggrandizement, laden with miscalculation and marred by mishap. As always in war, contingency played an outsized role, starting with delays the previous summer in marching north and in reducing St. Johns. Carleton's narrow escape from Montreal, the disastrous attack at Quebec, and malady all contributed to the American failure. Even the healthy felt heartsick. "I never had an opportunity to distinguish myself, but have ever done my duty in the most dangerous times," Major Richard Howell, a future governor of New Jersey, wrote his brother upon returning to Ticonderoga. "I am convinced I cannot see a worse campaign than this."

American losses would forever remain imprecise. Since the previous fall, at least twelve thousand troops had marched into Canada, and probably fewer than nine thousand marched back. A rough American estimate in mid-July put battle deaths at a thousand and disease fatalities at another thousand. Several thousand others were at least temporarily unfit for service because of wounds or sickness, and still others had deserted. The only precision came from Carleton, who listed 1,374 prisoners in his custody, including 91 officers.

Vivid accounts described the beaten army returning home. "The boats were leaky and without awnings. The sick being laid upon the bottoms without straw were soon drenched in filthy water," wrote John Trumbull, who had just arrived at Crown Point from Manhattan as a newly promoted colonel. "I did not look into tent or hut in which I did not find either a dead or dying man." A chaplain wrote simply, "Their sorrows take hold of me." Dr. Beebe, also at Crown Point, concluded that "God seems to be greatly angry with us."

Some in the colonies could hardly hide their indignation. "The subject is disgusting to me," Samuel Adams said. "I will dismiss it." But John Adams insisted on an investigation. "For God's sake," he wrote Sullivan, "explain to me the causes." To Abigail he wrote, "Our misfortunes in Canada are enough to melt a heart of stone. . . . The smallpox has done us more harm than British armies, Canadians, Indians, Negroes, Hanoverians, Hessians, and all the rest." His long list of supplemental reasons included "our inability to procure hard money," indifferent generalship, and clumsy, fickle support from Congress. Others noted provincial jealousies, quarreling senior officers, and a misreading of Canadian enthusiasm for being conquered into liberty. Without question, an improvised military expedition had been undermined by an inept political and economic campaign.

The American penchant for subjugating those deemed in need of deliverance was hardly extinguished by the calamity in Canada. As the historian Eliot A. Cohen has observed, that impulse would recur often in the centuries to come, "with mixed motives and uncertain outcomes." Canada proved a foreshadow.

Yet even in the summer of 1776, thin silver linings could be glimpsed. The failure to capture Quebec in December precluded having a large army trapped within the walls by enemy reinforcements in the spring. British plans for a thrust into New York were disrupted, momentarily, and some combat strength had been diverted from Howe's main force farther south. If few American commanders enhanced their reputations—"Canada has been a very unfortunate place for generals," Lieutenant Colonel Joseph Vose noted in his journal—the hard school of war transformed some amateur soldiers into warriors. The likes of Anthony Wayne and Daniel Morgan had shown their mettle. "The Canada struggle was a dress rehearsal for the war," historian Justin Harvey Smith later wrote. "It made plain some things that could be done and some that could not."

Mettle would be needed for the battles still to come on the northern front. News of the rebel rout delighted the king and his ministers in Britain, even as they demanded that the campaign continue until a complete victory had been won. In orders carried from London by Burgoyne, Lord Germain told Carleton that after driving the Americans from Canada, "you will endeavor to pass the lakes as early as possible, and in your future progress to contribute to the success of the army under General Howe." Carleton should not feel sanguine, despite liberating Quebec, reclaiming Montreal, and scattering the rebel invaders. "I am sorry you did not get Arnold," Germain would tell him, "for of all the Americans, he is the most enterprising and dangerous."

Arnold certainly saw the danger ahead. The British, he warned Washington in late June, "will doubtless become masters of the lake unless every nerve on our part is strained to exceed them in a naval armament." Not a moment should be lost in replenishing the Northern Army and assembling carpenters, timberjacks, shipwrights, smiths, sailors, and others needed to build an inland fleet capable of challenging the Royal Navy on Lake Champlain. A back door had swung open, imperiling New York and New England, and threatening the American cause.

13.

———

Surrounded by Enemies,
Open and Concealed

P retty little New York perched on the southern tip of what the Indians
called "Mannahatta," the hilly island. The town now comprised four
thousand wooden and brick buildings within less than a square mile, linked
by cobblestoned lanes and sidewalks of flat stone shaded with beech, locust,
elm, and linden trees. Dutch houses with step gables and red or black glazed
tile fronted the streets, although so many brick town houses with gambrel
roofs and grand doors in the London fashion now intruded that one visitor reported, "Here is found Dutch neatness, combined with English taste
and architecture." Already the narrow island had been widened with artificial land along the riverfronts for wharves and warehouses holding Indian
silk and Irish linen, whale fins and seal skins, turpentine and spermaceti
candles. Sail lofts, rope walks, breweries, a nailery, and foundries that made
stoves and ironware pans could be found, along with coopers turning their
casks and milliners stitching headwear in defiance of the British prohibi-
tion on colonial hatmaking. As early as the 1720s, sixteen distillers had
converted molasses to rum, and the usual taverns, gin mills, and ordinar-
ies now crowded the waterfront, serving sailors in tarred britches and
fearnought jackets. A census in late April counted 268 liquor vendors in
Mannahatta.

The last war had brightened the town's prospects—"New York is growing immensely rich," Benjamin Franklin wrote in 1756—not least because
merchants sold goods to both the British and, surreptitiously, the French.
The metropolis continued to spread north, with new streets and churches—
lovely St. Paul's, Brick Presbyterian, Scotch Presbyterian, and the Lutheran
and Methodist meetinghouses had all been built in the 1760s. Milestones
were purchased for the post roads in 1769, and lamplighters on their rounds
each night illuminated the oil fixtures now hung on every seventh house.
Barges brought more than twenty thousand cords of firewood from New
Jersey and Long Island to the town every year, then hauled away dung and

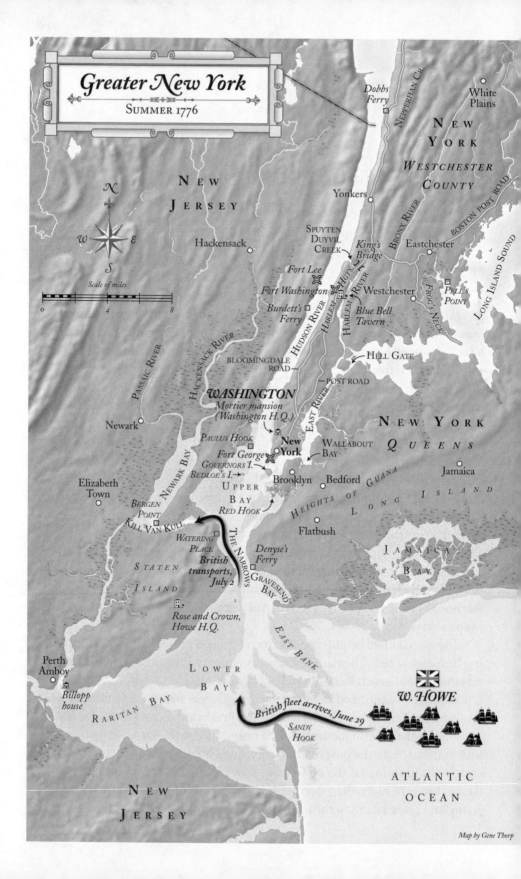

Map by Gene Thorp

human ordure to fertilize farm fields upriver. Demand had increased for perfumers, glovers, cabinet makers, and other harbingers of affluence. The town's well water was so fetid that even horses allegedly refused to drink it, but a new reservoir with pumps and wooden pipes was under construction. In summer, the better sort drove their phaetons or one-horse whiskeys into the country for turtle feasts at the mansions sprouting along the East River. The lower sort still patronized cockfights and bullbaiting. All sorts enjoyed the twenty-four legal holidays celebrated each year.

The current war, however, had defaced New York. "This haughty city is now subjected to all the inconveniences of a garrison town," Lieutenant Colonel William Tudor, the Continental Army's judge advocate, wrote a friend in the spring of 1776. "The fife & drum are continually dinning our ears with Yankee music, & we have few sights more entertaining than the parading & marching of the ill-dressed ragamuffins which compose the army." Hardly a shot had been fired in anger around New York, but perhaps half or more of the twenty-five thousand residents had fled their homes in fear of bloody things to come. "The city looks in some streets as if the plague had been in it, so many houses being shut up," a loyalist pastor told his diary. Those who remained were confined at night by a military curfew. "We all live here like nuns shut up in a nunnery," one letter writer complained.

By early summer, more than twelve thousand soldiers filled tent-and-duckboard cantonments near the Collect Pond, the East River ferry slip, and other camps. Not all the men arriving were disheveled. Delaware troops wore blue coats faced in red, white waistcoats with pewter buttons, black spatterdashes, and blackjacked leather caps, peaked in front. A few regiments could be seen in hunting shirts with matching leggings or in gray surtouts, striped waistcoats, and castor hats with silver buckles. But most still looked like plowmen or barkeeps, their officers distinguished only by the colored cockades on their upturned hat brims. "At least 2,000 are destitute wholly of arms," wrote Colonel Joseph Reed, who had left his law practice in Philadelphia to return to the army as adjutant general after Horatio Gates took a combat command. Nearly as many men carried firelocks in such dysfunction, he added, as "to discourage rather than animate the user."

Since February, soldiers and civilians had toiled shoulder to shoulder with picks, shovels, and axes to fortify the town. Each morning fife and drum summoned work crews from every social class, including leather-aproned artisans and turtle-eating toffs with blistered hands. Slaves delivered by their masters worked every day, whites every other day. All were known as "diggers-in." Under orders from the army high command, streets leading from the waterfront were "traversed and barricadoed. . . . The whole island is to be redoubted." Trenches, breastworks, tree-trunk ramparts, redans, flèches, and sod parapets scarred the town. Orchards were hacked into abatis. Demolished wharves became log barricades, chinked with rocks and broken bottles. By early June, Colonel Henry Knox reported that 19 mortars and 121 cannons—from 3- to 32-pounders, many trundled from Ticonderoga via Boston—had been mounted in more than a dozen batteries as far north as King's Bridge, at the upper nob of the island. Even the royal governor, William Tryon, who since late fall had taken refuge on a British merchantman, was impressed by the rebels' industry. "The streets in the city of New York are barricaded with breastworks," he wrote Germain, "and every headland and commanding spot of ground in its environs are fortified."

The fortifications extended well beyond Manhattan. Across the East River, a defensive line in Brooklyn ran from Wallabout Bay to Gowanus Creek, with a redoubt at Red Hook and an additional line snaking inland for two miles in the direction of Flatbush and Bedford. On a rainy April night, a thousand men with entrenching tools had swarmed onto Governors Island, separated from Brooklyn by narrow Buttermilk Channel; by dawn they had raised breastworks and emplaced ten heavy cannons to keep British ships from ascending the East River. More batteries sprouted at Paulus Hook—later called Jersey City—to block access to New York's other big river, the North, also called the Hudson.

Sparks flew night and day as smiths made musket barrels, bayonets, and ramrods. The upper floor of the Bridewell, a new almshouse and prison on the New York Common, was converted into an armory and a munitions plant. A New Jersey sergeant wrote eighteen diary entries in late March and April, each succinct and identical: "Made cartridges." A rifle regiment took post at Denyse's Ferry on the western end of Long Island, overlooking the Narrows, which linked New York's Upper Bay with the Lower Bay and the open sea. A half dozen horsemen served as a "corps of observation" on high ground along the coast to watch for enemy ships.

Rebel cannons and gunmen had forced Governor Tryon aboard the *Duchess of Gordon* to move beyond range outside the Narrows, along with *Asia, Phoenix, Mercury, Lively,* and several transports. Rebels used hatchets to chop holes in loyalist boats suspected of smuggling provisions to British crews. "May God increase their wants," a Continental colonel declared. Armed sloops, whaleboats, and schooners patrolled as far south as Egg Harbor, on the New Jersey coast. Two of the governor's servants were nabbed while bringing his laundry ashore for washing. To discomfit British navigators, rebel raiders smashed the beacon atop Sandy Hook Light and carried off the lamp oil. Four hundred raiders also pounced on the British

39. "A pretty man does not make a good portrait," the artist Joshua Reynolds said admiringly of Admiral Richard Howe. Known as "Black Dick" for his swarthy complexion, Howe was already among Britain's most celebrated fighting captains when he arrived in New York to command the Royal Navy in North America.

40. This sketch by a British officer on Staten Island shows part of the king's fleet anchored in the Narrows, across from Long Island on July 12, 1776. Admiral Howe's flagship, *Eagle*, can be seen in the middle distance, approaching from the open sea.

40. Famous for helping Bonnie Prince Charlie escape to France after his defeat at Culloden in 1746, Flora MacDonald subsequently left Scotland for North Carolina. Before American rebels captured her husband in the loyalist drubbing at Moore's Creek in February 1776, she had written, "There are troublous times ahead, I ween."

41. Major General Henry Clinton would serve longer in the American war than any British general. A gifted tactician and a talented violinist with a passion for Haydn, he instinctively expected the worst, from both people and fate. "Furies were at work on his psyche," his biographer later wrote.

42. General Charles Earl Cornwallis, a member of the House of Lords, delighted his king by volunteering to join the British expedition against the American South in early 1776. After the disastrous defeat outside Charleston, Cornwallis commanded with distinction in the battles to seize New York.

43. No more flamboyant figure served the American cause in uniform than Major General Charles Lee, a onetime British officer known for his homely mien, love of dogs, and intemperate aggression. One newspaper deemed Lee among "the greatest military characters of the present age," although John Adams acknowledged, "He is a queer creature."

44. Thickset, ruddy William Moultrie was a South Carolina militia colonel in command of the crude fort on Sullivan's Island, near Charleston Bay. As he calmly puffed his pipe and pointed out targets during the daylong battle in June 1776, his gunners inflicted severe casualties on the attacking British naval squadron.

TO BE SOLD on board the
Ship *Bance Ifland*, on tuefday the 6th
of *May* next, at *Afhley-Ferry*; a choice
cargo of about 250 fine healthy

NEGROES,

juft arrived from the
Windward & Rice Coaft.
—The utmoft care has
already been taken, and
fhall be continued, to keep them free from
the leaft danger of being infected with the
SMALL-POX, no boat having been on
board, and all other communication with
people from *Charles-Town* prevented.

Auftin, Laurens, & Appleby.

N. B. Full one Half of the above Negroes have had the
SMALL-POX in their own Country.

46. By 1776 half of Charlestown's twelve thousand residents were white and free, while the other half were neither and subject to sale. The South Carolina militia had long been designed primarily to suppress slave revolts. "Our negroes have all high notions of their liberty," a white resident complained.

47. St. Michael's church steeple was often the first landmark spotted by mariners approaching Charleston. In early June 1776, some fifty British vessels anchored outside the harbor as their commanders pondered how to attack the most heavily fortified city in America.

48. Despite firing seven thousand cannon rounds on June 27, 1776, the British squadron off Sullivan's Island inflicted little damage. British battle casualties exceeded two hundred. "We never had such a drubbing in our lives," a Royal Navy sailor admitted.

49. Even while denouncing royal despotism and enumerating twenty-seven griev-ances, the Declaration of Independence, approved by Congress on July 4, 1776, used soaring language to proclaim the American cause, beginning with, "We hold these truths to be self-evident, that all men are created equal."

50. Thomas Paine had failed at everything he ever attempted in Britain: shop keeping, teaching, tax collecting, corset making, and marriage. But soon after emigrating to Philadelphia in late 1774, he found fame with *Common Sense*, a bold, brilliant pamphlet that made the case for American independence with, in General Washington's assessment, "unanswerable reasoning."

51. On the night of August 16, 1776, two American vessels crammed with flammables attacked a British flotilla anchored in the Hudson River. The fire ships destroyed an enemy tender, but Royal Navy seamen kept flames from spreading through the sails of the frigate *Phoenix*.

52. This nineteenth-century painting by Alonzo Chappel shows the chaotic flight of American troops toward Gowanus Creek near Brooklyn on August 27, 1776, after being all but encircled by the British. "We were drove with much precipitation and confusion," an American major later acknowledged.

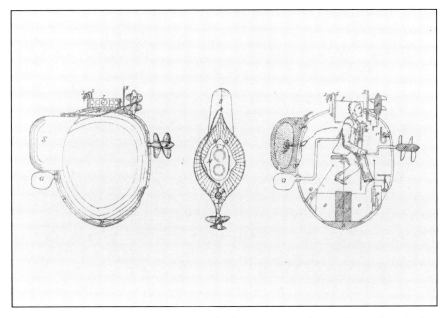

53. Designed and built by David Bushnell of Connecticut, the *Turtle* was described as "a machine altogether different from anything hitherto devised by the art of man." Just before midnight on September 6, 1776, the submersible "water machine" was launched from Manhattan's southern tip to destroy the *Eagle*, Admiral Howe's flagship.

54. Determined to control the Hudson, a trio of British warships accompanied by tenders sailed upriver in early October 1776. Despite underwater obstructions and heavy fire from American batteries, the flotilla managed to pass Fort Washington on Manhattan to the right and Fort Lee in New Jersey to the left. The river was actually much wider than depicted here.

55. On September 15, 1776, five British men-of-war on the East River bombarded American entrenchments along Kip's Bay, a shallow indentation on the Manhattan shoreline. At the same time, several thousand British and German troops crossed the river on flatboats and soon sent the rebels fleeing.

56. A day after the debacle at Kip's Bay, the American commander in chief lured unwary redcoats into a bloody ambush near Harlem Heights along the Hudson. "If this was a scheme of Washington's," a British officer admitted, "it certainly was well-concerted."

57. "I was educated a Quaker, amongst the most superstitious sort," wrote Nathanael Greene, son of a Rhode Island anchorsmith. The youngest Continental general, he soon became a Washington favorite for his decisive mind and rigorous discipline, notwithstanding a catastrophic error in judgment at Fort Washington in November 1776.

58. This loyalist's mansion served as Washington's headquarters for five weeks in northern Manhattan before the Americans finally retreated north into Westchester County. Court-martial boards sometimes convened in the octagonal parlor in the rear of the house.

59. Colonel John Glover commanded the brigade that confronted four thousand enemy troops at Pell's Point in mid-October 1776. Glover wrote, "Oh, the anxiety of mind I was then in for the fate of the day."

60. For more than two years, Captain Glanville Evelyn of the King's Own Regiment had been eager "to scourge the rebellion with rods of iron." He survived heavy combat at Concord, Bunker Hill, and Sullivan's Island, but his luck betrayed him at Pell's Point.

61. On November 20, 1776, General Cornwallis led British regulars and Hessians across the Hudson before climbing a narrow path up the Steep Rocks, which rose more than four hundred feet above the river. From there they pounced on the American redoubt at Fort Lee.

62. Pierre-Augustin Caron, better known as Beaumarchais, took up the American cause as a gunrunner and financier with a passion he normally reserved for the stage and French politics. The author of *The Barber of Seville* and *The Marriage of Figaro* conceded, "My life is a combat."

63. Paris, seen here from the Pont Neuf in 1763, was a town of fads and fashions that rose and fell, came and went. Sophisticates debated whether wine darkened the skin as well as the national mood.

64. Sent to Paris by Congress in mid-1776, the Connecticut politician Silas Deane posed as a Bermuda merchant while arranging for secret munitions shipments to America. He also ran a recruiting office for hundreds of European soldiers of fortune avid to join the rebel cause.

65. Louis XVI, whose self-described ambition was "to be loved," had ascended the French throne in 1774 at the age of nineteen. Aiding America against the British, he concluded, would help restore France to greatness.

66. Charles Gravier, the Comte de Vergennes and France's foreign minister, deplored American revolutionary ideals. But he believed that a protracted, bloody struggle between Britain and America could badly weaken London as France rearmed for the next war against her hereditary enemy.

67. "Every particle of my blood is electrified with revenge," the Philadelphia physician Benjamin Rush admitted after the British captured his father-in-law. Medically educated in Edinburgh and London, Rush attended troops from both sides who were wounded in the fighting across central New Jersey in the winter of 1776–77.

68. The American predicament "wears so unfavorable an aspect," Washington lamented in December 1776, that a desperate gamble was justified. He chose to cross the icy Delaware River on Christmas night, as seen in this 1819 painting by Thomas Sully, in order to surprise the Hessian garrison at Trenton.

69. Major General John Sullivan was a bombastic New Hampshire lawyer, notorious for suing his debtors. He helped redeem unimpressive military performances in Canada and on Long Island by leading the right wing of Washington's attack on Trenton.

70. The Philadelphia lawyer Joseph Reed, who served as Washington's aide and adjutant general, was the commanding general's closest confidant until the discovery in late November 1776 of his disloyal correspondence with General Lee. Reed later provided useful intelligence after leading a cavalry troop to capture British dragoons near Princeton.

71. John Trumbull's painting of the Hessian defeat at Trenton depicts, with dramatic artistic liberty, a mortally wounded Colonel Johann Rall surrendering to Washington. Later caricatured as a drunken fool, Rall was in fact respected as a combat commander.

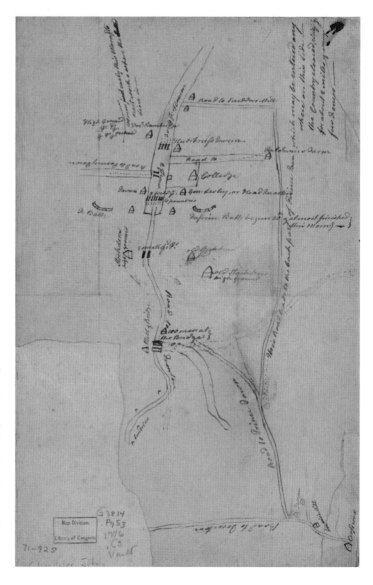

72. A map drawn by a spy in Princeton and given to Washington showed unguarded back roads into the village, as well as British defensive dispositions, headquarters, and other important landmarks useful in planning the surprise attack on January 3, 1777.

73. Major General James Grant, who had led the British left wing at Long Island, commanded royal forces in New Jersey after General Howe's return to New York in mid-December 1776. A stout, gouty former governor of East Florida, Grant was described as "a gamester, a glutton, and an epicure."

74. Brigadier General Hugh Mercer, a Scottish-born physician, had fled to America after supporting the losing side at Culloden in 1746. He led a brigade of Maryland and New England troops both at Trenton and in the flanking attack on Princeton.

75. This sketch by John Trumbull captures the brutality of the bayonet. General Mercer, surprised by a British counterattack near Princeton, spills to the ground after his horse is shot in the foreleg. Despite multiple stab wounds, he would live for more than a week.

76. James Peale's scene, painted at the end of the war, shows superior American firepower overwhelming the weak British garrison in Princeton. Only an hour after capturing the village, Washington led his troops north toward the New Jersey highlands where they would go into winter quarters.

compound at Bedloe's Island—later home to the Statue of Liberty. They burned a hospital and, Tryon complained, "killed a number of poultry I had reserved for General Howe's expected arrival."

That Howe was coming from Halifax, perhaps soon, no one doubted. Every report of approaching sails—a recent sighting proved to be a fogbank—sent more frightened New Yorkers fleeing in carts and coaches piled high with baggage. New York was considered the least disloyal of the thirteen colonies, and those well-affected to the Crown lay low and waited for their hour to come round. At noon on Tuesday, June 4, Tryon's small squadron fired a protracted salute to honor the king's birthday. Loyalist churches lighted candles that evening to pray for His Majesty's good health and continued wisdom. For now, however, allegiance was best whispered; those heard singing "God Save the King" were marched to jail.

Meanwhile, more rebel trenches were dug, more ramparts built, more cannons pointed. Precisely how the mighty Royal Navy was to be defeated, along with General Howe's army and whatever other legions were en route from Britain, remained uncertain. "Great numbers of angels," a Connecticut preacher assured his flock, "no doubt are encamping round our coast for our defense and protection."

His Excellency General Washington had no intention of relying solely on angels. At one p.m. on Thursday, June 6, he returned to New York after more than a fortnight's absence in Philadelphia. To welcome him back, a New England brigade paraded down Broadway in passable military step. Four regiments marched under the double row of trees around the Bowling Green at the foot of the town, then circled the oversized equestrian statue of George III, depicted as a bare-legged, bug-eyed Marcus Aurelius, in a Roman tunic with a laurel crown. Cast in lead, brilliantly gilded, and enclosed by a black iron fence, the statue had been raised on its marble pedestal six years earlier as a now-lamented tribute to the king for repealing the Stamp Act.

Striding back up the avenue past St. Paul's Chapel, the troops filed onto the Common before the Bridewell and arranged themselves in regimental ranks for inspection. Washington strolled across the head of the formation, swapping salutes with his officers. In Philadelphia he had been persuaded by Hancock to sit for the artist Charles Willson Peale, who depicted the commanding general, left hand thrust into his partially unbuttoned waistcoat, against a background of liberated Boston. The portrait showed a stiff, middle-aged man with a paunch, a walking stick, and a double chin. But here in the flesh, ever impressive in his epauletted uniform, Washington was animated, graceful, and trim. He was pleased to find the town "all in a state of peace & quiet," as he would write John Hancock. Many of these troops had believed a Tory rumor that he had gone to Philadelphia to resign his command. In fact, he passed his days discussing grand strategy with Congress. Always careful to pay obeisance to his political masters, he had consulted delegates individually, in committee, and with the entire assembled body in the Pennsylvania State House. The news from Canada was disquieting, of course. Also, an enterprising American rifleman captured at Quebec and shipped in chains to England had just escaped and then made his way home with documents hidden in his waistband that confirmed reports of Britain hiring thousands of German mercenaries to fight in America this summer.

But all in all, Washington had reason to consider his trip to Philadelphia a success. Congress had lauded his achievement in Massachusetts and affirmed his plan for defending New York. He intended to further strengthen fortifications in Brooklyn and secure the East River while building fire rafts and row galleys to safeguard the Hudson. On the assumption that Britain would fling 10,000 men against Ticonderoga and 12,500 at New York, American commanders would be reinforced to provide a two-to-one advantage—20,000 men for the Northern Army and 25,000 for Washington's force. The colonies were to provide another 30,000 militiamen, a third of whom would form a strategic reserve called the Flying Camp—the term derived from the French *camp volant*—that would also help defend the New Jersey coast.

Congress also seemed to be moving toward a proclamation of independence. That would give Washington a clear strategic objective, an American definition of victory: formal separation from Britain and the creation of a new nation. Such clarity in war was invaluable. If the country was asked to sacrifice, the purpose would now be evident. If men were asked to die, they would know why.

The sun had begun to dip over New Jersey when Washington rode more than a mile north through Lispenard's Meadows to the Abraham Mortier mansion, previously owned by the British deputy paymaster general. The Washingtons had lived here since shortly after their arrival in Manhattan, almost two months earlier, and now the commanding general had decided to shift his headquarters into the mansion from a town house on Broadway. Built on rising ground amid baronial oaks, the twenty-six-acre estate stood a few hundred yards from the Hudson and offered the sort of river vista that seemed to soothe Washington.

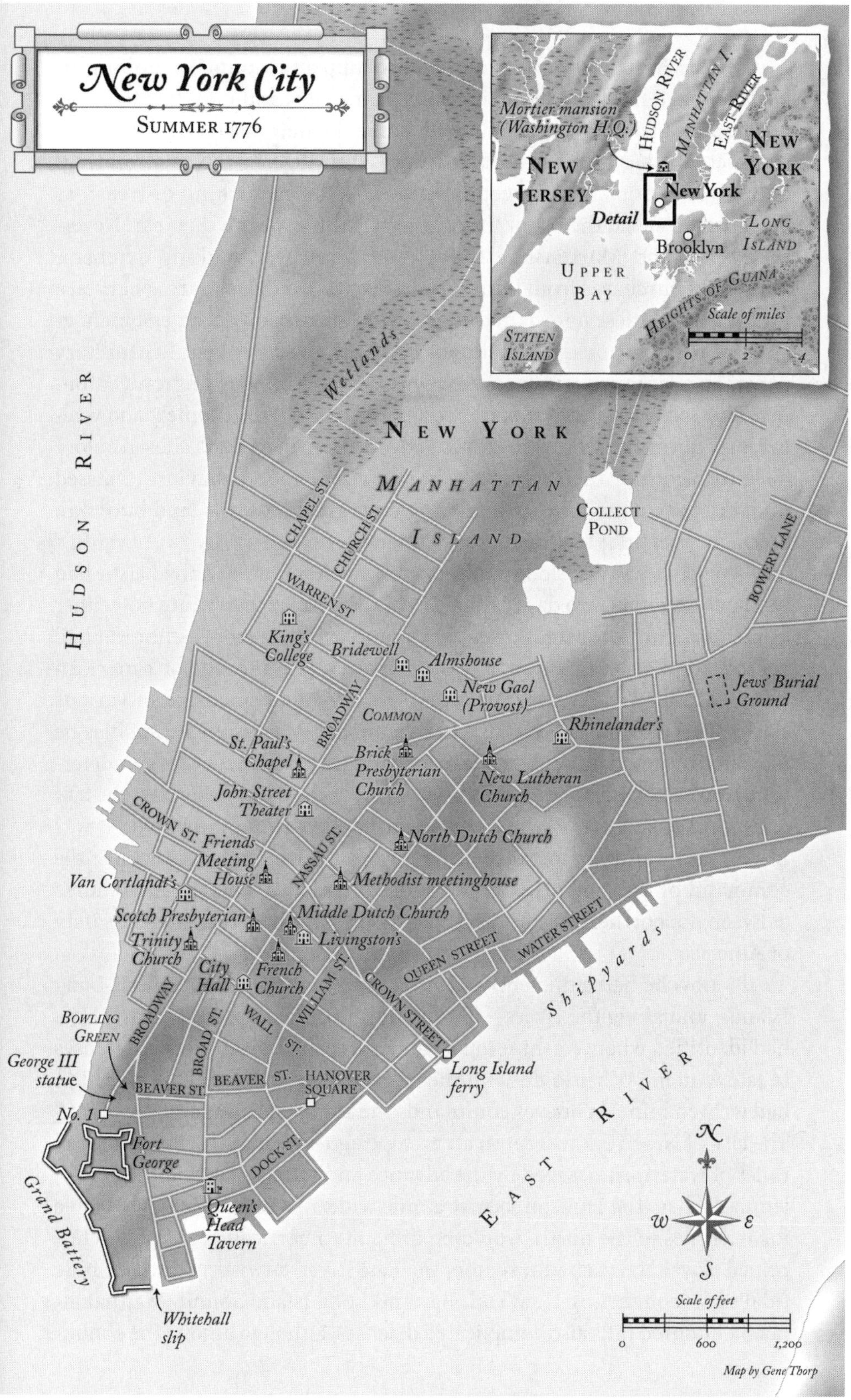
New York City
Summer 1776
Mortier mansion
(Washington H.Q.)
Hudson River
Manhattan I.
East River
New
York
New
Jersey
New York
Detail
Long
Island
Brooklyn
Upper
Bay
Heights of Guana
Scale of miles
0
2
4
Staten
Island
Wetlands
Hudson River
New York
Manhattan
Island
Collect
Pond
Chapel St.
Church St.
Warren St
Bowery Lane
King's
College
Bridewell
Almshouse
New Gaol
(Provost)
Jews' Burial
Ground
Broadway
Common
Rhinelander's
St. Paul's
Chapel
Brick
Presbyterian
Church
New Lutheran
Church
John Street
Theater
Crown St.
Friends
Meeting
House
Nassau St.
North Dutch Church
Van Cortlandt's
Methodist meetinghouse
Scotch Presbyterian
Middle Dutch Church
Livingston's
Trinity
Church
Water Street
Queen Street
Shipyards
City
Hall
French
Church
William St.
Crown Street
Bowling
Green
Broadway
Broad St.
Wall
St.
George III
statue
Beaver St.
Beaver St.
Hanover
Square
Long Island
ferry
East River
No. 1
Fort
George
Dock St.
Grand Battery
Queen's
Head
Tavern
Whitehall
slip
N
W
E
S
Scale of feet
0
600
1,200
Map by Gene Thorp

Yet the Mortier house could hardly supplant Mount Vernon in his heart. He had not been home in more than a year, and only through correspondence with his overseer could he see the new master bedroom and study, completed after his departure for Cambridge, or the new plantings of dogwood, poplar, and weeping willow—"the clever kind of trees," as Washington called them—or the northern addition begun this year. Nevertheless, he and Martha had tried to settle in here, making extensive household purchases from local merchants of china, glassware, a carpet, a featherbed, Chinese porcelain teaware, wine glasses and decanters, mahogany knife cases, and a damask tablecloth. The general kept his military papers in a large red trunk covered with a bearskin. Washington's entourage now included a "Life Guard," composed of fifty "handsomely and well-made" soldiers, five feet, eight inches to five feet, ten inches tall, chosen before he left Boston for their "sobriety, honesty, and good behavior." Dressed in dark blue coats with buff trim, single-breasted red vests, and buckskin breeches, they adopted the motto "Conquer or Die."

"We expect a very bloody summer of it at New York & Canada," he had written his brother two days earlier. "I am sorry to say that we are not, either in men or arms, prepared for it." The grand army under Washington had yet to fight a general action, but in the past year hundreds of American troops had died of disease, misadventure, or wounds incurred in various skirmishes, plus the thousands lost in Canada. What would casualties be like once the fighting began in earnest? Congress had made clear its determination to defend New York to the death; John Adams described the city as "a kind of key to the whole continent," and Washington agreed it was "a post of infinite importance." Should the British "get that town & the command of the North River," he added, "they can stop the intercourse between the northern & southern colonies, upon which depends the safety of America."

By now he had sufficiently scouted the terrain—on Staten and Long Islands, and along the rivers—to confirm the difficulties that Charles Lee had identified when Washington sent him to oversee New York's defenses in late winter. "What to do with the city, I own puzzles me," General Lee had written him. "Whoever commands the sea must command the town." The city of New York was set in an archipelago with almost eight hundred miles of waterfront, carved by the advance and retreat of glaciers fifty millennia earlier. The Hudson, nearly a mile wide at New York and navigable for 150 miles to the north, would be difficult to barricade against a determined Royal Navy assault; so, too, the East River, a twisting, sixteen-mile tidal strait connecting New York Bay and Long Island Sound. Mannahatta's six hundred hills also complicated defenses, although among the conundrums Washington faced was the fact that Brooklyn's high ground loomed above lower Manhattan. Should British gunners seize those slopes, they would have the same advantage the Americans had enjoyed on Dorchester Heights in the struggle for Boston. In war, as in farming, topography was fate.

Washington still yearned for decisive battle. Bleeding the enemy in New York would dampen support for the war in Britain, while emboldening France and other potential American allies. But where to find favorable ground here? Britain's maritime mobility allowed Howe to keep the initiative, landing where and when he chose. Washington also knew that New York's defenses still lacked depth. Many of Knox's heavy guns were obsolete, honeycombed, and badly undermanned. The Continental Army was raw at best, led by callow commanders: the twenty-one American generals who would serve the cause in New York averaged two years of military service apiece, compared to thirty years for their British counterparts.

Still, if the troops fought with brio, the enemy "will have to wade through much blood & slaughter before they can carry any part of our works," Washington told Hancock. To his brother he suggested a further advantage: "If our cause is just, as I do most religiously believe it to be, the same providence which has in many instances appeared for us, will still go on to afford its aid." And if angels with flaming swords descended to protect the coast, so much the better.

Washington's time in Philadelphia gave him a sharper view of the logistical difficulties in waging a continental war. "We resolve to raise regiments," Congressman Joseph Hewes of North Carolina had written in May, ". . . but it is a melancholy fact that near half our men, cannon, muskets, powder, clothes, etc., is to be found nowhere but on paper." The national fathers in Congress displayed a gift for debate and committee work but only a modest aptitude for organized warmaking. A fifteen-thousand-man force required a hundred thousand barrels of flour and ten thousand tons of meat annually, by Washington's calculations. Where that would come from, and how it should be purchased, transported, and distributed, was unclear. The same held true for a hundred other vital commodities, from flints and wagons to shoes and blankets.

Congress had sensibly, if belatedly, acknowledged that the 1774 policy of restricting imports and exports was a failure, hurting the American cause far more than the British economy. Overseas trade had plummeted to less than 40 percent of prewar levels. Prices on many goods would jump

25 percent this year over last; in the coming year they would more than double. In April, American ports were opened to all nations except Britain and her dominions. Congress authorized both its Secret Committee and colonial governments to export goods, except for staves and empty casks, in exchange for imports, except for slaves and East India tea. A brisk trade had resumed. Gunrunners carried rice, flour, fish, candles, indigo, beeswax, and tobacco to France, the Iberian Peninsula, and the West Indies, eager to swap for what British intelligence called "warlike stores."

Gunpowder, that *unum necessarium*, had become relatively abundant by the summer of 1776. Virginia sent at least seven vessels on powder cruises. Massachusetts sent thirty-two. Many were given French names and phony papers. Every few days a ship managed to elude, outrun, or outwit Royal Navy pursuers to bring powder into American ports: five tons into Charleston from St. Eustatius, in the Caribbean; eleven tons into Newburyport from Bordeaux; seven tons into Philadelphia from Le Havre aboard the *Morris*, along with five thousand pigs of lead, a hundred bolts of tent canvas, and twenty chests of arms. Raiders aboard the *Lady Catherine* and *Savannah Pacquet* sailed to Bermuda, waited until the British governor and his fourteen children were asleep, then lowered a confederate through a roof vent into the magazine, so that he could unlock the door from within. The men rolled a ton of powder in barrels down the lawn to their waiting boats without even waking the watchdogs.

In a three-week period in the spring, over sixty tons of powder arrived in the colonies. In early summer it was reported that more than a hundred additional tons could be had in Martinique and St. Eustatius, where the supply was ample enough to push down prices. British agents concluded that French bottoms carried Dutch powder from Amsterdam to Nantes and Bordeaux for transfer to American merchantmen; powder was also leaking through Bilbao, in Spain, and Ostend, in Belgium. Inevitably, some ships were lost—four of eight vessels loaded with cargo for France by the Philadelphia merchant Robert Morris were captured. The *Dickinson*, bulging with flour to trade for gunpowder in Nantes, instead surrendered to the Royal Navy in Bristol on April 8 after the loyalist crew mutinied.

Most smugglers got through, although few voyages would be as dramatic as that of the American brigantine *Nancy*. Returning in June from the Virgin Islands with rum, sugar, and 386 barrels of gunpowder for the Pennsylvania Committee of Safety, she was sighted through the haze off the New Jersey coast by the British thirty-two-gun frigate *Orpheus* and the fourteen-gun sloop *Kingfisher*. Chased onto a shoal in Turtle Gut Inlet, seven miles north of Cape May, *Nancy*'s eleven-man crew, aided by rebel sailors from several nearby vessels, manhandled all but a hundred barrels into the dunes while enemy gunfire tore *Nancy*'s sails to rags, riddled her hull, and sheared off the mainmast. Seamen dumped the remaining powder in the hold and fashioned a fuse from a spare sail and a hot coal. Just as British tars in a longboat pulled up to take possession of the brig, *Nancy* detonated with a blast reportedly heard in Philadelphia. "The pieces of the vessel was falling all round for some time," a midshipman on *Orpheus* recorded, "and the air was totally darkened with the explosion." Seven British sailors died, and the shower of debris included "two laced hats and a leg with a garter."

Particularly devastating to the British was the loss of another ordnance ship, the four-hundred-ton *Hope*. Sailing from Cork, she parted company from her convoy in bad weather and was captured off Boston by the armed schooner *Franklin*. Her cargo, worth at least £40,000, included sixteen hundred muskets, two thousand entrenching tools, thirty thousand nails, and fifteen hundred copper-hooped barrels of powder—seventy-five tons. The king, furious again, decreed that every ordnance ship henceforth must carry at least a dozen carriage guns, with ample cannoneers and naval officers aboard.

Domestic powder production in America also increased, if fitfully. Newspapers printed formulas from the *New Chymical Dictionary* for making powder and saltpeter; learned debates raged over whether the best charcoal was made from pine or other woods. Pennsylvania expanded from one powder mill to ten. "We are better supplied with powder than formerly," Robert Morris wrote. "Our mills make it fast and some colonies have had great success in making saltpeter." Even so, about 90 percent of the twelve hundred tons of powder acquired by late 1777 would be sent from overseas or made with imported saltpeter.

A midsummer tally of Washington's ordnance stores showed that he had 10,353 round shot, 30,000 flints, and 114,000 musket cartridges. "Twelve months ago we were distressed, to a degree that posterity will scarcely credit, for powder. This is now over," John Adams wrote, prematurely, in late June. Yet other critical wants plagued the war effort. Colonel Knox calculated that the army needed at least 250 more field guns of various calibers. Despite collecting church bells and brass door knockers for scrap, American foundries lacked the high-temperature air furnaces needed to cast strong bronze cannons; there were also too few pattern and charcoal makers, woodcutters, limestone miners, banksmen, smiths, brickmakers, and masons to operate both brass and iron furnaces effectively. In May, of nearly two hundred new guns test-fired at two Pennsylvania foundries—typically by loading them with double charges—not one "stood proof" as battle ready. Of another twenty-four tested in New Jersey, eight burst on firing. Of forty-two naval 12-pounders cast in one furnace, eighteen failed. Philadelphia furnaces proved so deficient that a report in the fall would warn "there is not guns in this city for one ship." Building a navy without guns would be difficult.

Making bullets was hard without lead, which by early June had grown "so scarce that no pains should be spared to procure it," Congress warned. Virginia's governor was given authority to retain as many miners, slave or free, as needed to work the lead pits in that colony. In New York, more than a hundred tons of weights from fishing nets, clocks, and window sash cords were collected, along with lead from downspouts, glass cames (often pried from stained glass), and pewter dishes. New York's finest homes yielded thousands of bullets: 1,658 pounds of lead was collected just from Robert Livingston's houses, for which he was paid £62.

In warfare, salt was almost as much a *unum necessarium* as gunpowder. Without the preservative, armies and navies could not stockpile meat and fish. Two bushels of salt—more than a hundred pounds—were needed to cure a thousand pounds of pork. Beef required even more. Salt also was used to tan leather, fix the dyes in military uniforms, churn butter, and supplement livestock feed. Before the war, Americans had imported 1.5 million bushels annually, half from the West Indies and half from Britain or southern Europe. The British trade embargo strangled two-thirds of those imports. Profiteers and hoarders drove up the price, from two shillings a bushel to fourteen by late summer; it would soar as high as seventy-five shillings by July 1777. Salt bandits were reported in Virginia. "This article is exceedingly scarce," a diarist wrote. "If none comes in, the people will revolt."

Pamphlets gave instructions for making salt. To encourage saltworks along the coast, in late May Congress authorized a third of a dollar for each bushel. "All the old women and children are gone down to the Jersey shore to make salt," John Adams wrote. "Salt water is boiling all around the coast, and I hope it will increase." But four hundred gallons of seawater were needed to boil off a bushel of salt, requiring great stacks of firewood. New York offered four dollars a bushel to the Iroquois nations, admired for their saltworks. Virginia spent more than £6,000 to build evaporation ponds along the Chesapeake Bay but collected only fifty bushels, perhaps the most expensive salt in the world. Although smugglers ran cargoes from Bermuda and the Turks Islands, severe shortages would lead to rationing and price-fixing.

For each shortage momentarily slaked, others appeared. Officials in New York begged farmers to raise hemp for rope and flax for linen. Spinners were exempt from militia service, though Connecticut ran short of barrels because so many coopers marched off to fight. Shoemakers were offered eighteen shillings a pair. Wool was so critical that those who ate lambs or ewes were denounced as public enemies. Congress pleaded for bolts of various durable fabrics—ticklenburgs, osnabrigs, Hamburg dowlas. Paper, made from rags and critical for currency and cartridges, grew so desperately short that paper makers were also excused from army service.

Washington often complained that "artificial scarcity" had inflated prices of firewood and forage. Now it seemed evident that "avaricious, ill designing men" were manipulating supplies of salt, wheat, and other vital commodities. The commanding general also battled the cheats who preyed on every army—cobblers using green shoe leather, millers short-weighting their flour, teamsters who lightened their wagon loads by draining the brine from salt pork, spoiling the meat. So much thievery plagued the army in New York that Washington on Tuesday, June 18, ordered the quartermaster general to stamp every tool with "c xiii," denoting the thirteen colonies. That proprietary brand would soon be amended to "United States," and subsequently shortened to "U.S."

That same Tuesday afternoon, Washington rode to the Queen's Head Tavern, a former warehouse at Pearl and Broad Streets. His staff and regimental commanders joined him in the Long Room, the town's most spacious public hall, for a banquet arranged by the New York Convention— the provincial congress—in gratitude for defense of the colony. Accompanied by fife and drum, the officers belted out campaign songs, though everyone was sorry when General Putnam fell ill and retired to his quarters before leading them in "Maggie Lauder," his favorite ballad. Innkeeper Samuel Fraunces kept the libations flowing into the night. He would bill New York £91 for seventy-eight bottles of Madeira and thirty bottles of port, as well as cider, beer, and punch; he also charged sixteen shillings for "wine glasses broken." Thirty-one toasts were raised, starting with the Continental Congress and the American army. On and on they went, to "the colony of New York" (number four), to "the patriotic citizens of London" (number ten), and to "the memory of the brave Montgomery" (number thirty).

The final toast was drunk to "civil and religious liberty to all mankind"— all mankind, that is, except Tories. Civil liberty for loyalists had become another rare commodity. Throughout the colonies, partisan belligerence increased as the insurgency metastasized into a civil war. Congress had resolved that anyone in America who professed allegiance to King George was "guilty of treason." Rhode Island required males over sixteen suspected of "being inimical to the united American colonies" to swear an oath of allegiance; those who resisted could be fined and disenfranchised. Connecticut law now punished "inimicals" who defamed Congress with fines and imprisonment. Loyalists could be barred from traveling, running a tavern, or operating a ferry; their property could be taxed at double normal rates. Loyalist teachers, lawyers, doctors, and apothecaries had trouble keeping their jobs or their clients. Blacksmiths in Massachusetts refused to shoe the horses of suspected inimicals. Some were tarred and feathered, and in one case a loyalist's horse got the same treatment for good measure. For a brief period in June 1776, mail to or from anyone in Albany whose last name began with "Mc" was examined, apparently on the theory that the Scots and Irish were especially suspect. A mob threw rocks at loyalist women on Cape Cod; Rhode Island outlawed prayers for the king. One New Yorker wrote that for those still true to the Crown or simply indifferent to rebellion, "taciturnity is the greatest safety we have and we are obliged to observe it." John Adams, never taciturn, later would be quoted as saying, "I would have hanged my own brother had he taken part with our enemy in the contest."

Few were hanged, at least not yet; incivility rarely turned to bestiality. But no one could say how brutal the war would become. Conformity, censorship, and zealotry now flourished. Even small sins, such as "speaking diminutively of the country congress," might be punished with forced public apologies, boycotts, ostracism, or property confiscation. A mild word of praise for the British government—or simply being suspected of thinking loyal thoughts—could provoke a beating. Militias served as a political constabulary, bolstered by the Continental Army. When Queens County, a loyalist stronghold on Long Island, voted 788 to 221 against sending representatives to the provincial congress, the names of those in the majority were published in the newspaper; they were forbidden to travel, hire a lawyer, or practice a trade. More than a thousand militiamen and Continentals then swept through Queens, arresting opposition leaders, seizing weapons, and extracting allegiance oaths—except from the 250 obdurate men who fled into the swamps to await General Howe's arrival.

Such measures spread. In mid-March, the Continental Congress had authorized the disarmament of "notoriously disaffected" Americans. Confiscated firelocks went to the army. In New York, where hundreds had been arrested, those who refused to attest that all of their weapons had been surrendered were fined five shillings a day. Washington had long favored seizing Tories who might be "active against us." To him that seemed a sensible expedient. "Why," he asked, "should persons who are preying upon the vitals of their country be suffered to stalk at large?" Several dozen recalcitrant loyalists were sent to the abandoned Simsbury copper mine in Connecticut, previously used to jail robbers and counterfeiters but now known as the "Catacomb of Loyalty." Inmates were lowered by windlass seventy feet belowground to rock-walled cells in sections L and M, also called "Hell." Simsbury, described as the first national penitentiary, was said to be a place where "the light of the sun and the light of the gospel are alike shut out." Scores of other loyalists and Quakers who refused to swear allegiance to the rebel cause would be confined to the "Fleet prison"—several scows anchored on the Hudson below Albany and later described as "fetid cesspools of disease, suffering, and privation."

"I can tell a Tory by his looks," Lewis Howell, a surgeon with the 2nd New Jersey Regiment, wrote his father in late June. The good doctor evidently had remarkable diagnostic powers, given the physical resemblance of loyalists and revolutionaries. Both breeds were drawn from all strata of their society, high, low, and middling. The war, as the historian Edmund S. Morgan wrote, "cut sharply across nearly all previous divisions, whether regional, ethnic, religious, or class." Moreover, loyalty was a fluid concept, ebbing and flowing with circumstances and convictions. "No man knows his nearest friends' real sentiments," observed William Smith, the loyalist chief judge in New York. Many good men were divided in their own hearts, but ambivalence in a civil war was a limited virtue. Political moderates confronted a harsh internecine calculus: those not with us are against us.

Perhaps half a million Americans remained committed to the Crown. One scholarly computation asserted that loyalists made up 16 percent of the total population—or about 20 percent of white colonials. Of roughly 3.2 million Americans alive from 1775 to 1783, 513,000 demonstrated loyalty by supporting the British cause, fighting with one of two hundred loyalist units, or eventually going into exile. Other estimates posited that as many as a third of all Americans remained loyal. Although that was probably an exaggeration, their numbers without doubt ran high in certain belts and pockets: along the frontier from the western Carolinas through western New York, for instance, and along the coast of the middle colonies from the lower Chesapeake to Long Island, as well as in the Hudson valley. Loyalists often had shallow roots in America; many were recent immigrants rather than native-born. Others had ties that bound them to the mother country, as placemen or merchants trading with London or Glasgow. "The height of my ambition," a New Yorker wrote, "was and is to live and die a British subject." Anglican churchgoers tended toward loyalism where they were a minority, as in New England, but not where they were dominant, as in South Carolina. (All Anglican clerics were ordained in Britain and swore allegiance to the king.) Families could be sundered just as painfully as communities or colonies, like the Eastchester, New York, clan of Judge Jonathan Fowler, who personally immigrated to Nova Scotia but left behind three sons serving in the American army. Another loyalist, who migrated to Pennsylvania from his native Connecticut in search of greater tolerance, described feeling "like a saint of old, as a pilgrim and stranger in the earth, having no abiding city."

Loyalists typically abhorred both civil disobedience—once begun, where would it end?—and mob violence, including rogue committees of safety formed by "half a dozen fools in your neighborhood," as one man put it, with the arbitrary authority to wreck the lives of their political opponents. "Which is better," the Boston clergyman Mather Byles asked, "to be ruled by one tyrant three thousand miles away or by three thousand tyrants not a mile away?" Most loyalists believed in law, stability, and beneficent British rule, "against which a deluded and hysterical mass, led by demagogues, threw themselves in a frenzy," as the historian Bernard Bailyn wrote. Yet with each passing month, loyalist weaknesses became more evident, including the absence of national leaders and an inability to match the rebels in organization, propaganda, or emotional pitch. By the summer of 1776, it had become clear that only massive British support could prop up the loyal cause.

New York would now become the central battleground, politically and militarily. Determined to purge "Tory Town" of residual loyalists, radical mobs had rampaged through the city and its outer precincts, breaking windows, rustling livestock, and smashing a loyalist printing press before carrying off the type to melt into bullets. During a violent spasm in the second week of June, some accused loyalists were jailed until they pledged allegiance to the American cause. Others were singed with candle flames. "We had some grand Tory rides in this city this week & particular yesterday," a letter writer reported on June 13. "Some of them were handled very roughly, being carried through the streets on rails, their clothes tore from their backs. . . . There is hardly a Tory face to be seen this morning."

Two days later, a committee appointed by the provincial congress convened at noon in the city hall assembly chamber on Wall Street to begin rooting out conspirators against American liberty. Led by the lawyer John Jay, a future Supreme Court chief justice, the tribunal held daily hearings to interrogate the "disaffected" and those suspected of "equivocal character." Over the next several years, similar inquisitions examined hundreds of New Yorkers accused of inimical habits. Presumed guilty, they usually were given a chance to prove their innocence, although, at least in Albany, without calling witnesses or retaining legal counsel. Most were paroled after posting bond; some were exiled or incarcerated in places like the Kingston courthouse, whose jail cells were so insalubrious that officials in meeting rooms upstairs were permitted to smoke to mask the "nauseous and disagreeable effluvia" rising from below.

Hardly had Jay's committee begun work than a grand conspiracy came to light, undone by a loquacious counterfeiter.

Counterfeiting was a cottage industry in the eighteenth century. Up to half of the copper coins circulating in England in 1753 were believed to be dross slugs, sometimes fried in a pan to provide a dark patina of authenticity. Some convicted counterfeiters were banished from Britain to the American colonies, where they resumed their art by making phony Spanish and Portuguese gold or silver coins, despite legal penalties that ranged from the loss of a right thumb to death.

The proliferation of paper currency in the colonies provided new opportunities for "shoving the queer"—passing counterfeit bills of credit. In recent months, the British government had also seized on the chance to undermine the rebel economy by using forged plates. Beginning in January, a printing press aboard *Phoenix* in New York Harbor was suspected of turning out phony bills in a campaign to depreciate American currency that would persist for years. But ordinary criminal gangs posed the more immediate threat. A public notice in a New York newspaper in April warned of counterfeit forty-shilling notes, adding, "They are, upon the whole, a good imitation of the true bills."

Before turning to crime, the English-born engraver Henry Dawkins had made a fair living in Philadelphia turning out bookplates, maps, and even an elaborate astronomical plate to illustrate the transit of Venus across the sun in 1769. Apparently, the lure of printing money rather than earning it proved irresistible; Dawkins and several cronies installed a rolling press in the attic of a house in Huntington, Long Island. To obtain good paper—often the most difficult obstacle to counterfeiting—a confederate named Isaac Ketchum made enough indiscreet inquiries among Philadelphia stationers to arouse suspicion. Ketchum was arrested and interrogated, and at two a.m. on May 12, an army patrol raided the Huntington house. A secret stairway to the garret revealed the press, a bogus twenty-shilling Connecticut note, and other incriminating evidence. Ketchum, Dawkins, and their cronies found themselves confined by leg irons in New York's city hall.

Incarceration in a cellblock known as the Dark Hole showed Ketchum the folly of shoving the queer. On June 9, in a petition to the provincial congress, he confessed his "shame and confusion," noted that he had six children to feed, and then revealed that he "hath something to observe . . . entirely on another subject"—a bit of jailhouse gossip. Released long enough to spill his story to investigators, Ketchum returned to the Dark Hole to collect more information as a secret informant.

Arrests soon followed. By June 20, John Jay's conspiracy committee was conducting a full docket of interrogations about a plot against General Washington. Those implicated—"rough men, but with a very pale countenance," one guard noted—included farmers, tavern keepers, a shoemaker, a tanner "living in the swamp," a schoolteacher, a "pensioner with one arm," a former constable, "a fat man with a blue coat," and a man described only as "a damned rascal." Gunsmith Gilbert Forbes—"a short, thick man with a white coat," whose shop stood on Broadway across from Hull's Tavern— was jailed in fetters. After being threatened with summary execution, Forbes confessed to sending rifles and muskets to Governor Tryon on the *Duchess of Gordon*. The loyalist mayor of New York, David Matthews, was arrested at one a.m. on June 21 at his Long Island summer house in Flatbush; he acknowledged passing £114 in cash from Tryon to Forbes, supposedly for guns and to enlist pro-British agents within the city. "The town is in a good deal of uproar and confusion this morning," a Continental officer wrote his father on June 22. Forty "designing children of the devil" were in custody, as one lieutenant called them, with many more arrests expected. Two hundred soldiers now guarded the cellblocks at city hall. Extra sentries were placed on gun batteries and at Knox's artillery park.

Precisely what these conspirators intended remained murky. Rebel hysteria undoubtedly inflated their designs. Lieutenant Colonel Tudor, the judge advocate, wrote on June 23 of a plot "to assassinate the commander-in-chief, murder all the general officers, blow up the principal magazine, & spike up the cannon," bloody measures to help the British seize New York. It was said that a drummer planned to stab Washington and that a housekeeper aimed to feed him poisoned Long Island peas, a plot discovered only when the pods were instead fed to chickens, which died clucking in agony. It was said that arsonists would set fire to the city in nine places; that plans existed for capturing Red Hook and the Long Island ferry slip to permit British men-of-war to sail up the East River; that Tory battalions waited under arms in woodlands outside the city; that saboteurs planned to destroy the bridge leading from northern Manhattan to Westchester County. Whatever the particulars, a newspaper assured its readers that the plot was "most barbarous and infernal." A Maryland rifleman told his journal that "the soldiery now can scarcely be kept off from murdering those prisoners."

One prisoner aroused particular indignation. Thomas Hickey had been arrested on June 15 and charged—yet another one—with passing counterfeit bills. Stocky and dark-complected, Hickey described himself as an "old countryman," born in England; it was said that he had deserted from the

British Army before settling in Connecticut and joining the Continental Army. Sobriety and good behavior led to his selection in Boston for Washington's Life Guard. But locked in a city hall cell, he had "talked Tory," according to Isaac Ketchum and other informants, claiming to be among almost seven hundred turncoats in New York secretly ready to fight for the British, including eight life guardsmen. As a soldier, Hickey was subject to court-martial, and on Wednesday, June 26, thirteen officers convened in a large room at No. 1 Broadway to mete out justice.

Four witnesses appeared against him. "He informed me that the Army was become damnably corrupted," Ketchum, his former cellmate, reported, "that the [British] fleet was soon expected, and that he and a number of others were in a choir to turn against the American Army when the king's troops should arrive." Hickey had supposedly received two shillings to secretly enlist in the Crown's service. A William Welch testified that the defendant met him in a grogshop in early June, swore him to secrecy on a Bible, then offered a dollar "by way of encouragement" if Welch would sign up to help the British.

Hickey defended himself and proved to be both a poor lawyer and a hapless witness. He told the court that he had "engaged in the scheme at first for the sake of cheating the Tories and getting some money from them." The court deliberated briefly before unanimously finding him guilty of sedition, mutiny, and "holding a treacherous correspondence for the most horrid and detestable purposes." He was sentenced to be "hanged by the neck till he is dead." Washington's war council confirmed the sentence at his headquarters the next day, and the commanding general promptly signed the death warrant.

"There was a vast concourse of people to see ye poor fellow hanged," a doctor wrote his brother. By one estimate, the sportive crowd grew to twenty thousand, packed around the gallows erected early Friday morning with great hammering in a field off Bowery Lane. Four brigades assembled as instructed at ten a.m., then marched in formation to bear witness below the scaffold. Thirteen other conspirators would be sent to prisons in Connecticut and Westchester County, but most of those arrested were released without trial for lack of evidence. Only Hickey would pay with his life.

Eighty Continentals "with good arms and bayonets" escorted the prisoner from his cell. Offered the comfort of clergy, Hickey at first snarled that "they were all cutthroats," then consented to have a chaplain accompany him on his final walk. "He seemed much more penitent than before," Samuel Blachley Webb, Washington's aide, noted in his diary. A blindfold was knotted over his eyes, and the noose tightened under his ear. Death by hanging in the eighteenth century rarely came from a broken neck;

strangulation was more likely. Because the condemned could expect to dangle in agony for half an hour, sometimes his friends would tug on his feet to hasten the end. Hickey had no friends, but perhaps he was fortunate anyway. He "suddenly sank down," a witness reported, "and expired instantly."

The body was hardly cold before Washington's general orders for the day sought to draw a moral lesson from Thomas Hickey's short, sad life. Soldiers were urged "to avoid lewd women, who, by the dying confession of this poor criminal, first led him into practices which ended in an untimely and ignominious death." Whether that advice was heeded, the tawdry, venal details of the so-called Hickey plot—often exaggerated in retelling—"blackened the reputation of the loyalists throughout the country," the historian Carl Van Doren later wrote.

The affair put Washington on edge. "We are indeed, sir, surrounded by enemies, open and concealed," he wrote a friend. "It is next to impossible to know how deep the plot is laid." But with his usual bluff confidence he added, "The all-wise dispenser of events will shield me from such diabolical designs."

For several days, British deserters had warned that the fleet from Halifax was expected hourly. But it still came as a shock at nine a.m. on June 29—a sultry, overcast Saturday—when lookouts watching the sea from a Staten Island hilltop hoisted three red-and-white striped flags, the signal for an approaching fleet of at least twenty ships.

Warning guns barked from the Grand Battery, on the southern tip of Manhattan. American sloops, schooners, and fishing smacks skittered across the Upper Bay to seek refuge up the Hudson. Panicky civilians who had lingered in New York tarried no longer, but crowded the ferries to New Jersey—often still called "the Jerseys," since the colony had once been divided in two—or hurried north by wagon, horseback, or on foot. Henry Knox, who boasted that any British ships within range of his batteries could expect the "finest fight that ever was seen," was enjoying Saturday breakfast with his wife, Lucy, in a window alcove on the second floor of No. 1 Broadway when the tumult began. "You can scarcely conceive of the distress and anxiety," he later told his brother. "The city in an uproar, the alarm guns firing, the troops repairing to their posts. . . . My God, may I never experience the like feelings again!" Lucy hurried off to pack and flee—"I scolded like a fury at her for not having gone before," Knox wrote—along with other officers' wives, including Martha Washington, who had just returned from Philadelphia after successfully undergoing smallpox inoculation.

A Maryland soldier recorded in his diary on Saturday, "As I was upstairs in an outhouse I spied, as I peeped out the bay, something resembling a wood of pine trees trimmed. . . . In about ten minutes the whole bay was as full of shipping as ever it could be. I do declare that I thought all London was afloat." At two p.m. a messenger arrived at the American headquarters in Mortier's mansion to report that more than a hundred square-rigged vessels had now congregated off Sandy Hook. With each subsequent dispatch, the number crept up, eventually exceeding 130. Samuel Webb, Washington's aide, told his diary, "A warm and bloody campaign is the least we may expect."

That was General Howe's expectation as well. Standing on the quarterdeck of *Greyhound*, he watched more troopships with inapt names like *Felicity*, *Good Intent*, and *Friendship* clew up their courses and drop anchor Saturday afternoon. Each vessel was crowded with regulars keen to get ashore and avenge the insults to king and country. Pugnacious frigates tacked around the anchorage, breasting an indigo sea spangled with summer sunlight. Every transport flew signals to identify its purpose or passengers: a pennant with a blue ball from the main topsail for artillery vessels, a broad yellow vane from the fore topmast for hospital ships, a red ball and two white balls for the 10th Regiment of Foot. A detachment of marines and sailors pattered onto the beach at Sandy Hook with a new lantern and casks of oil to revive the seven-story lighthouse.

Howe had slipped unnoticed into the Lower Bay on June 25 with a small naval vanguard, and while awaiting the rest of the fleet he spent several days scrutinizing the American coastline with his spyglass while questioning Governor Tryon and other loyalists about Washington's troop strength, fortifications, and river defenses. The British commander was as eager as any grenadier to launch the offensive that would smash the insurrection. Hoping for a full campaign season in New York, he had wanted to arrive sooner. But the delayed arrival of British victuallers at Halifax and the need for extensive naval repairs following the helter-skelter flight from Boston had "made an earlier removal impracticable," he wrote Germain. The time in Nova Scotia had been spent profitably in training for North American combat: reorganizing regiments, shortening coats and otherwise tailoring uniforms for woodland battlefields, and even ensuring that each soldier had two new flints "of a better sort."

Shortages persisted: shoes, camp kettles, canteens, woolens. And Howe, a voracious reader of American newspapers, found appalling tidings from New England. Despite frantic efforts in London to warn westbound ships that "General Howe with the army have quitted Boston," hapless transport captains carrying troop reinforcements kept blundering into rebel ambushes. On June 8, after a long stern chase, American schooners captured *Anne* and over a hundred soldiers from the 71st Highlanders, a new, two-battalion regiment in bonnets and kilts raised especially to fight the Americans. Also, the rebel armed brig *Andrew Doria* bagged more than two hundred Highlanders aboard the *Oxford* and the *Crawford* without firing a shot. Other marauders seized a Highlander grenadier company on the *Lord Howe*.

Worse yet, the *George* and the *Annabella* fought off rebel attackers on June 16 only to run aground outside Boston Harbor. After a brisk cannonade killed a Highland major and seven privates, both ships struck their colors. Another two hundred Highlanders were captured, including Lieutenant Colonel Archibald Campbell; though he would one day be counted among Britain's greatest generals, with a tomb in the south transept of Westminster Abbey, Campbell would first spend part of the American war in a Massachusetts jail. Over the course of a few weeks in American waters off Boston, British losses included six vessels and crews, plus nearly six hundred soldiers with full kit, including bagpipers. "This is a capital blunder," an outraged Briton wrote, "the result of the most impenetrable stupidity."

Howe could only sigh. He had intended to land his force promptly at Gravesend Bay, on the southwestern rim of Long Island, but reports that rebels infested the ridgeline above the landing beaches caused him to reconsider. Being drawn prematurely into battle would be a mistake; he intended to wait for the arrival—soon, he hoped—of the British and German reinforcements now crossing the Atlantic with the armada commanded by Admiral Lord Richard Howe, his brother. He also expected to be joined before long by General Clinton with the force dispatched to Cape Fear earlier in the year, although precisely what had happened to them was unclear to General Howe. The assembly of these legions in New York would give him more than thirty thousand soldiers and an immense fleet, the greatest expeditionary force Britain had ever dispatched. Simply the sight of this host would no doubt intimidate the enemy and draw thousands of loyalists to the Union Jack. "But I am still of opinion," Howe wrote Germain, "that peace will not be restored in America until the rebel army is defeated."

At eight a.m. on Tuesday, July 2, the first three men-of-war—*Phoenix*, *Rose*, and *Greyhound*—eased from the Lower Bay through the Narrows, carefully skirting the East Bank sandbar that made this channel so treacherous, along with the tides, the currents, and the fickle winds. A few random shots from rebel riflemen whizzed above the spars or into the water.

Lumbering transports followed, *Felicity* and her sisters, each requiring three hours to make the short passage into the Upper Bay. A few rebel 9-pounders finally banged away from Denyse's Ferry, but the gunners, baffled by moving targets, fired wildly, and a snarling broadside from *Asia* soon hushed them.

One by one, the transports swung toward Kill Van Kull, along the upper edge of Staten Island, where Howe knew he would find spring water, summer produce, and citizens well affected to the Crown. With sails brailed and furled, tars hauled out the flat-bottoms brought from Halifax and, helped by twenty local hay boats, shuttled the army to shore in a soaking rain. They were welcomed by gleeful loyalists and fugitive slaves who offered to serve as guides, teamsters, orderlies, and harbor pilots; more than five hundred Staten Islanders, nearly all of the adult male population, would swear allegiance in oaths administered by Governor Tryon. Grenadiers and light infantrymen set up an encampment around a lush oasis called the Watering Place. White tents sprouted in neat rows, and sergeants doled out a generous rum ration.

"We are in the most beautiful island that nature could form or art improve," Major Charles Stuart cheerfully wrote his father. "We have everything we want." The British Army had reclaimed the first corner of New York for the empire.

General Nathanael Greene, commanding the American defenses on Long Island, had closely watched these developments. With information extracted from four careless British prisoners captured at the Narrows, he sent Washington a remarkably accurate intelligence report, including a list of the five British generals now camped on Staten Island.

> The fleet sailed from Halifax the 10th of June and arrived the 29th. The fleet consists of 120 sail of topsail vessels.... They have on board 10,000 troops received at Halifax, besides some of the Scotch brigade.... Four days before the fleet sailed from Halifax, a packet arrived from England that brought an account of Admiral Howe's sailing with a fleet of 150 sail, on board of which was 20,000 troops.... They are expected in here every day.

A cascade of orders in Washington's name spilled from the Mortier house. Fire rafts were to be built. All surplus sandbags and empty hogsheads should be sent to General Putnam for use in fortifications. Small craft, including rowboats, would assemble at docks along the Hudson. Troops should rehearse moving from their bivouacs to their alarm posts by routes that "are least exposed" to naval gunfire. "The General expects all soldiers . . . to load for their first fire with one musket ball and four or eight buckshot. . . . If the enemy is received with such a fire at not more than twenty or thirty yards distance, he has no doubt of their being repulsed."

In truth, the general had many doubts. "We are to oppose 30,000 experienced veterans with about one-third the number," Washington would later write Governor Trumbull in Connecticut. Fearful of being caught in a cross fire, the population of New York had dwindled to perhaps five thousand civilians, an uncertain number of whom hoped to be liberated by the British. Frightened towns along the coast flooded his headquarters with pathetic pleas for help, like the desperate message just received from Newark: "As the king's troops are in possession of Staten Island . . . our wives & children [are] unprotected either from the enemy without, or the Tories & Negroes in the midst of us."

Some American commanders favored an immediate attack on Staten Island, or at least spoiling the British water supply, perhaps with stove black. Neither proposal seemed practical. Washington was beginning to understand the merits of strategic defense—outlasting the enemy's will to wage war even if that meant giving battle only on the most favorable terms. Personally aggressive, convinced of the need to keep the British off-balance, he would watch for chances to turn on his foe with great violence. But he also had begun to grasp the agility and initiative provided Howe by his navy. As he subsequently wrote Hancock, "The amazing advantage the enemy derive from their ships and the command of the water keeps us in a state of constant perplexity and the most anxious conjecture."

For now he would draw strength from the determined men around him, like the Presbyterian chaplain who, while staring from Brooklyn at the enemy fleet, wrote in his journal, "We fear not Tory George & his war-torn army. We fear them not." To his overseer at Mount Vernon, Washington declared, "They are in possession of an island only. . . . This is but a small step towards the conquest of this continent." Still, he quietly sent off his official papers in "a large box nailed up" for safekeeping in Philadelphia.

More orders flew into the field. Sentries were to watch for deserters. The works at King's Bridge, on Manhattan's northern tip, needed to be strengthened. New Jersey militiamen were told to reinforce Greene's brigade on Long Island.

And, in this unsettled hour, Washington offered his men a glimpse inside his heart:

The time is now near at hand which must probably determine whether Americans are to be freemen or slaves. . . . The fate of unborn millions will now depend, under God, on the courage and conduct of this army. . . . Let us therefore animate and encourage each other, and show the whole world, that a freeman contending for liberty on his own ground is superior to any slavish mercenary on earth.

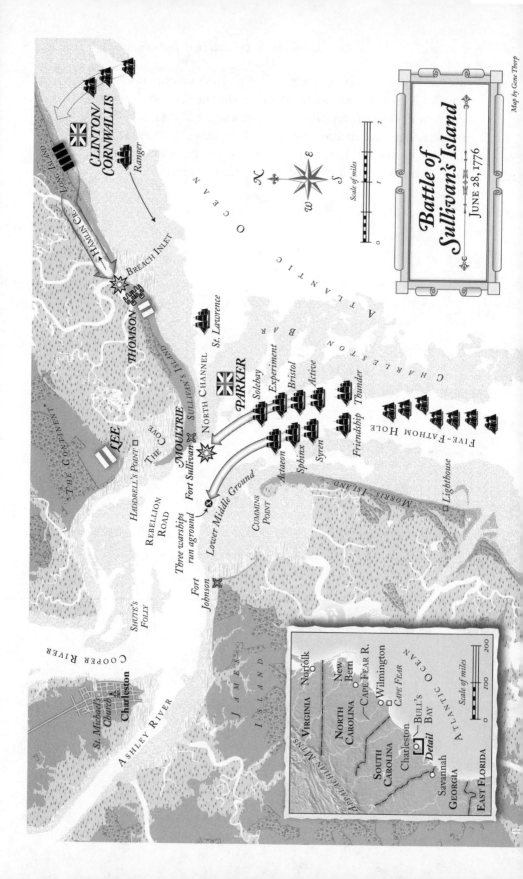

Battle of Sullivan's Island
June 28, 1776

Map by Gene Thorp

Scale of miles
0   1   2

N
E
S
W

ATLANTIC OCEAN

CHARLESTON BAR

CLINTON/ CORNWALLIS

Ranger

LONG ISLAND

HAMLIN CR.

BREACH INLET

THOMSON

SULLIVAN'S ISLAND

St. Lawrence

MOULTRIE
Fort Sullivan

NORTH CHANNEL

PARKER

Solebay
Experiment
Bristol
Active
Thunder

Friendship

Actaeon
Sphinx
Syren

FIVE-FATHOM HOLE

Lighthouse

MORRIS ISLAND

CUMMINS POINT

Lower Middle Ground

Three warships run aground

Fort Johnson

REBELLION ROAD

The Cove

HADDRELL'S POINT

LEE

"THE CONTINENT"

SHUTE'S FOLLY

COOPER RIVER

Charleston
St. Michael's Church

ASHLEY RIVER

JAMES ISLAND

Detail inset

VIRGINIA
Norfolk

NORTH CAROLINA
New Bern
CAPE FEAR R.
Wilmington
CAPE FEAR

SOUTH CAROLINA
Charleston
Detail
Bull's Bay

GEORGIA
Savannah

EAST FLORIDA

APPALACHIAN MTNS.

ATLANTIC OCEAN

Scale of miles
0   100   200

14.

A Dog in a Dancing School

Charleston claimed to be the "London of the Low Country," the richest, most sophisticated town in North America's richest colony. Eight of the ten wealthiest men in America were said to be South Carolinians, and Charleston's collective worth was supposedly sixfold that of Philadelphia. "Every tradesman is a merchant, every merchant is a gentleman, and every gentleman one of the noblesse," a local newspaper boasted. Three thousand broad-wheeled wagons a year rolled into the port with rice, indigo, and other exports. Its master shipwrights had long built sloops, schooners, and brigs for merchant houses in Europe and America. By the early summer of 1776, the town had grown to twelve thousand residents—half white and free, half neither. Every farthing of Charleston's affluence derived from slavery, as plain as the blue-stained palms of the indigo pickers sold on the Custom House auction block, or the ships packed with shackled Gambians and Angolans at Fitzsimmons' Wharf, or the pillory near So Be It Lane for "negroes, mulattoes, and mestizos, who are apt to be riotous and disorderly," according to a town ordinance. In recent years, rumors of war and then war itself had brought "cucumber times"—hardship and disquiet—to noblesse and chattel alike, but the town maintained a cosmopolitan swank. Three theaters produced the likes of *King Lear* and John Dryden's *All for Love*, music societies sponsored frequent concerts, and specialty shops sold toothpick cases, scented pomatum, gilt wallpaper, and Poland hair powder in violet, musk, or civet.

Although plagued with malaria, yellow fever, and an infamous climate—"in the spring a paradise, in the summer a hell, and in the autumn a hospital"—Charleston countered with grace notes. Georgian brick homes wore iron balconies angled to catch the sea breeze, and the new Exchange on the waterfront—among the handsomest public buildings in the colonies—featured Palladian windows, beveled Portland stone, and an octagonal cupola. The town's most singular landmark, St. Michael's Church, had taken eleven years to build, with Dutch tile in the vestibule, a Snetzler organ, and six thousand cypress shingles lapped across the roof. Eight bells hung on oak frames in the loft; cast in London and weighing up to a ton each, they bore names like Seraphim, Gabriel, and Cherubim. The white steeple, soaring 186 feet above Meeting Street, was capped with a gilded vane emblematic of the archangel's sword. It was the first thing mariners saw as they beat for Charleston Harbor.

That steeple and a glint from the vane was the first thing General Henry Clinton saw at noon on Tuesday, June 4, when the British squadron from North Carolina hove to at Charleston Bar, six miles southeast of the waterfront. Fighting the nausea that always distressed him at sea, Clinton stood at the taffrail of the transport *Sovereign*, admiring the emerald shoreline rimming the oblong bay. Fifty vessels flying the king's colors now filled the anchorage after a final, eight-furlong run this morning down the coast from Bull's Bay. Together they brandished nearly three hundred guns and bore twenty-five hundred soldiers and marines, plus a couple thousand seamen. From Long Island, far to the right, to Lawford's Channel, on Clinton's left, sailors in tenders and yawls from *Delegate, St. Lawrence, Ranger,* and the twenty-gun *Sphinx* were busy sounding various shoals and laying buoys to mark the gaps. The fifty-gun flagship, *Bristol*, swung at anchor a few cable lengths away; she carried not only the squadron's naval commander, Sir Peter Parker, but also General Charles Earl Cornwallis—"my friend Lord Cornwallis," Clinton called him—and three floating governors, each driven by rebels from his terrestrial domain: Josiah Martin of North Carolina, William Campbell of South Carolina, and James Wright of Georgia.

The southern expedition, ill-conceived and star-crossed from its inception, now hoped to find coherence and good fortune in American waters. Clinton had waited through much of the spring at Cape Fear, slurping oysters, watching for whipping snakes, and sawing away on his precious fiddle. With North Carolina beyond redemption after the rebel victory at Moore's Creek, there was little he could do but fret about the "unhealthy season approaching us with hasty strides." On April 18, the first British transport from Cork appeared, just as "we had given up all expectations of ever hearing from England or seeing anybody that came from that country," in the exasperated words of Clinton's secretary. In early May, six months after they were initially scheduled to leave Ireland, Parker and Cornwallis arrived with most of the battered squadron—victuallers, ordnance ships, men-of-war, and more than a dozen transports—after a ghastly crossing that left his passengers "very sickly" and required quarantining half a dozen foot companies with various fevers. While the men recuperated, and scouts tacked around Frying Pan Shoals to search for ships still missing, Clinton, Parker, and Cornwallis debated what to do next.

As the senior commander, Clinton advocated abandoning the South in favor of a quick foray up the Chesapeake Bay before consolidating forces with Howe. No pinprick attacks in the Carolinas were likely to gain hearts and subdue minds. But after four months of silence from Howe, a dispatch from Halifax carried by the courier *Nautilus* brought little coherent guidance from the commander in chief. Howe wrote that he intended to make for New York, though he disclosed no timetable and implied no urgency in Clinton's return north. He did mention that Charleston was "an object of importance to His Majesty's service," and Commodore Parker agreed. Two men-of-war sent 150 miles down the coast to scout the South Carolina shoreline returned on May 26 to describe Charleston's defenses "in an imperfect and unfinished state."

Uncharacteristically tractable, Clinton had agreed to venture farther south, writing Howe that he intended only to put his "troops on shore for a few days." As the squadron sortied from Cape Fear on a fair wind in late May, another belated dispatch arrived, this one from Lord Germain, who ordered the expedition to avoid "great loss" and to "proceed immediately" to New York if "nothing could be soon effected that would be of great and essential service." Already under sail, beguiled by the hope of a cheap victory just over the horizon, Clinton, Parker, and Cornwallis concluded that pouncing on Charleston was precisely that "great and essential service." They sailed on.

Now, with Charleston sprawled before them in the distance, confusion, indecision, and tempestuous weather—hallmarks of the southern expedition—again returned. As they drew near the town, Parker suggested quickly flinging troops onto the north end of Sullivan's Island, a four-mile-long barrier spit outside the port; three small warships would provide covering fire while his frigates made diversionary noises farther south. Clinton bridled immediately, decrying such a hasty move as "rash and absurd" and insisting that for any assault "the fleet must give their great assistance" in full measure. Clinton told Cornwallis that the army ought "not attempt anything blindfolded. . . . I must reconnoiter the object before I attempt it." Shifting winds and heaving seas complicated both reconnaissance and the timing of the landings. The expedition's objective also remained inchoate. Capture Charleston? Blockade it? Burn it? Could South Carolina loyalists be inspirited without then leaving them in the lurch? Clinton would later assert that "it never was my intention" to attack the town "without a moral certainty of rapid success," but certainty, moral or otherwise, seemed to recede with each passing hour.

On Tuesday afternoon, Commodore Parker climbed down a ladder from *Bristol*'s rocking deck and stepped into his barge. Now fifty-five, his face carved by a thousand gales, he had fought at sea in various scraps against the Spanish and French with enough swashbuckling panache over nearly four decades to be knighted. This assault, on a feebly defended provincial town at the edge of the world, did not faze him. Bargemen leaned into their oars, sculling through the anchorage, and in a few minutes Parker stood in Clinton's cabin aboard *Sovereign*. The Royal Navy was prepared to "give every assistance," the commodore assured him, but there were several complications that required finesse. One of his two bomb ketches had been dismasted in the Bay of Biscay after leaving Cork, reducing by half the mortar firepower needed for a high-trajectory bombardment. Six submerged passes traversed the Charleston Bar, yet only two could accommodate—barely—deep-draft vessels. *Bristol*, for instance, drew seventeen feet, six inches; even lightened with her guns temporarily removed, her keel would scrape sand. But Parker wanted those fifty cannons to reduce the enemy defenses.

Neither the commodore nor his officers knew the South Carolina seaboard intimately. (A British map labeled the landmass beyond the coastal islands as simply "The Continent.") Only three local pilots were willing to guide his frigates over the bar, and they disagreed about how to do so. Moreover, his ship masters were still uncertain, once across, how many vessels the crucial anchorage at Five-Fathom Hole would accommodate or whether inland waters were deep enough for his largest gunships to range rebel fortifications.

These nautical puzzles could be solved. But it would take time, particularly given heavy seas or a deviant wind. Parker, this afternoon, would signal his captains that the men-of-war should prepare to cross the bar in a couple of days, weather permitting, and "make such attacks as may be necessary to possess themselves of the harbor." In the meantime, would General Clinton consider moving to a cabin on the flagship for easier collaboration? Much of the planning—and bickering—to date had been by messenger and signal flag; candid tête-à-tête exchanges would be simpler, surer. *Bristol* was crowded with governors, but a comfortable berth could certainly be found for the commanding general.

Clinton politely declined, citing his chronic seasickness. "My exceeding bad state of health at sea," he told Parker, "would make it inconvenient for me at this time to move." While waiting for the navy to position itself, he would further ponder a flanking attack from Long Island across Breach Inlet to Sullivan's Island, striking the American rear. He would also compose a proclamation, stern but merciful, to be carried ashore by small boat

under a white flag, advising "the deluded people of the miseries ever atten-
dant upon civil war. I do most earnestly entreat and exhort them ... to
return to their duty to our common sovereign."

No British gasconade was likely to cow Charleston, although the town
had surely been stunned when a lookout cried, "A fleet! A fleet, ho!" The
enemy squadron beyond the bar resembled "a wilderness of ships," one
South Carolinian wrote, "hanging like snow-white clouds from the northeast sky." For several days the "wildest confusion" prevailed. Men sprinted
about in search of horses, carriages, boats. Dispatch riders galloped upcountry to summon militiamen, who collided with women and children fleeing toward Goose Creek in their drays and jolt-wagons. Public records were
carted for safekeeping to Dorchester, twenty miles distant, and printing
presses dismantled for reassembly inland. Bullet smelters pried a few more
pounds of lead from sash cords and church windowpanes. Guards stood
post on every road to discourage deserters; a recent law empowered any
"free white person" to detain any soldier without a pass and to claim a
reward.

Charleston had long been the most heavily fortified city in America.
The town sat on a peninsula formed by the confluence of two rivers, the
Ashley and the Cooper, which provided natural moats on either flank. Millions of bricks had been laid in defensive works since the early eighteenth
century, reinforced with tabby, a mortar made from crushed oyster shells,
lime, sand, ash, and water; a brick "wharf wall" extended for half a mile
along the waterfront, with several redans. In the past year, rumors of a British
southern expedition, and the obliteration of coastal towns like Falmouth
and Norfolk, had inspired more defenses, mostly constructed by slave
gangs. Warehouses on the wharves were leveled for better fields of fire. Traverses and flèches sprouted in the streets. Heavy cannons were mounted
along South Bay, East Bay, and James Island. A plan to obstruct two channels leading to the docks was scrapped when engineers concluded that more
than thirty hulks would have to be sunk to blockade the harbor; instead,
channel markers were obliterated and more guns positioned. Thousands
of palm trees—*Sabal palmetto*—were felled. Palmettos had long been used
against sea erosion, but no one was certain if the spongy trunks could stop
a 32-pound cannonball. Building log barricades of *Sabal palmetto* was an
act of faith, if not desperation.

Two sand cays a mile and a half apart bracketed the harbor entrance,
Sullivan's Island to the northeast and Morris Island to the southeast.
Because of the Lower Middle Ground—a wide, obstructive shoal where one

day Fort Sumter would be built—ships making for the Charleston water-front had to tack close to Sullivan's Island, and here, for months, the Americans had been raising their most ambitious works. An arcadian preserve of pelicans and porpoises, Sullivan's had also served as the reception station for nearly a hundred thousand slaves after the passage from Africa. Now some of those slaves and their descendants were toiling on rustic Fort Sullivan, ferrying thousands of palmetto logs from the mainland, then stacking them into two parallel walls along each face of the square fort, secured with yellow pine dovetails. Sand filled the sixteen-foot gaps between the rampart walls, which rose seven feet and were crowned by a parapet of two-inch oak planks with sniper loopholes and platforms on brick pillars. The works were sturdy enough to support thirty-one cannons—confiscated British 18-pounders and French 26-pounders taken from a captured ship in the last war. A blue flag with a white crescent and the word "LIBERTY" flew above the southeast bastion.

Gorgeous, detailed maps later printed and sold in England depicted Fort Sullivan as a great crenellated fortress, like Windsor Castle or the Tower of London, rather than the homely palmetto pen, roughly an acre in size, that remained unfinished when the British squadron assembled at Charleston Bar. Though large enough to hold a thousand defenders, the garrison numbered less than half that and was commanded by a militia colonel, William Moultrie. A planter-politician who had fought Cherokees on the western frontier, Moultrie at forty-five was thickset and ruddy, with high cheekbones and a receding gray hairline. When the enemy "shall come within the reach of your guns," he told subordinates, "you are to distress them in every shape to the utmost of your powers." To hold the vulnerable northern end of Sullivan's Island against possible British flankers, eight hundred defenders dug in with two cannons—although few of the gunners had ever fired a weapon larger than a rifle—under Colonel William Thomson, another Cherokee-fighting planter, whose nickname was "Old Danger." Colonel Thomson, considered the best shot in South Carolina, arranged his men among the dunes and myrtles overlooking Breach Inlet and, a mile distant, Long Island.

Like their two colonels, many South Carolina militiamen had been blooded in brutal combat against the Indians. Some had also fought in a recent campaign against backcountry loyalists, who'd been forced to disarm and sign loyalty pledges or flee to British refuges in Florida. But for decades South Carolina's militia had been designed primarily to suppress slave revolts. After the bloody Stono Uprising of 1739 left scores of blacks and whites dead, white men were required to carry weapons to church on Sunday and plantations had to employ at least one white for every ten blacks in servitude. Slaves now outnumbered whites in South Carolina, 104,000 to 70,000, despite efforts to curb chattel imports, and the vast majority lived in the low country along the Atlantic seaboard.

British encouragement of slave defections and the emancipatory antics of Governor Dunmore in Virginia had sparked hysteria in South Carolina. It was said that King George had promised every slave who murdered a master the right to keep his plantation. When a new royal governor arrived in Charleston in the summer of 1775, it was also said that he brought fourteen thousand guns to distribute among slaves and Indians; in fact, Lord William Campbell's baggage included nothing more lethal than two mahogany four-poster beds, a harpsichord, and thirty-five volumes of Voltaire. Still, Henry Laurens, who would succeed Hancock as president of the Continental Congress and whose career as a merchant prince in South Carolina included handling the sale of more than ten thousand plantation slaves, insisted that a bondsmen revolt was among Britain's "dark hellish plots for subjugating the colonies."

"We cannot be too watchful," another Charleston resident wrote. "Our negroes have all high notions of their liberty." Two recent episodes in particular revealed the town's febrile state. Shortly after Campbell's arrival, a harbor pilot named Thomas "Jerry" Jeremiah, among the few free blacks in Charleston, was unjustly convicted of treason and hanged outside the Work House. "Jerry was a forward fellow, puffed up by prosperity," Laurens explained, ". . . grown to an amazing pitch of vanity & ambition & withal a very silly coxcomb." Governor Campbell, a former naval officer, had a different view—"The man was murdered. I can call it nothing else"— and fled in the night to sanctuary on a Royal Navy sloop rather than risk a similar end.

The second incident had occurred in mid-December after several hundred fugitive slaves sheltered on Sullivan's Island in hopes of gaining passage aboard British vessels. South Carolina militiamen attacked with Catawba Indian allies, killing an estimated fifty blacks, capturing others, and scattering the rest. South Carolina law now made it a capital crime for slaves to seek sanctuary with the enemy. Anyone encouraging chattel to abscond would also be executed "without the benefit of clergy."

On Saturday, June 8, as several British warships eased across the bar and reconvened in Five-Fathom Hole, Major General Charles Lee cantered into Charleston with a pack of yapping dogs at his heels and two thousand Continental soldiers from Virginia and North Carolina close behind. Sent by Congress as commander of the newly created Southern Department,

Lee, now forty-four, was deemed "the first officer in military knowledge and experience," in Washington's recent assessment, although "rather fickle and violent, I fear, in his temper." Lee intended to prove the commander in chief correct, on all counts.

No more flamboyant figure ever served the American cause in uniform, whether he was wearing his hussar's black dress garnished with a fox pelt and gold-inlaid steel pistols, or his green sherryvallies with leather stripes and buttoned seams, or his Polish general's costume—bone white, faced in blue, and adorned with the red ribbon and enameled star of the Order of Saint Stanislaus. So slender that he seemed to lack shoulders, he had a receding chin, high forehead, tiny hands, and small, deep-set eyes; to call Lee homely was to insult homely men. "His nose is so large," a German officer wrote, "that its shadow darkens the other half of his face." Despite the fancy uniforms, he was habitually unkempt and reputedly owned but three shirts, each in such disrepair that he'd named them Rag, Tag, and Bobtail. The dogs trailed him everywhere, including a favorite Pomeranian called Spada— Italian for "sword"—who sometimes sat with him at table, where they communed in what he called "the language of doggism." "He is a queer creature," John Adams had written of Lee. "But you must love his dogs if you love him, and forgive a thousand whims for the sake of the scholar and soldier." When this letter was published after interception by the British, Lee assured Adams that he considered "the reputation of being whimsical and eccentric rather as a panegyric. . . . And my love of dogs passes with me as a still higher compliment." Besides, he added, "I must have some object to embrace."

He could be a lively if garrulous conversationalist, schooled in Shakespeare and languages and given to vivid invective, as in his description of one former commander as a "blockhead . . . so far sunk in idiotism as to be obliged to wear a bib and bells." His habit of carrying Thucydides in the original Greek burnished his image as a military thinker. If "learned, judicious, and penetrating," as a Boston admirer asserted, he was also restless, impulsive, and something of a poseur. One early biographer called him "a radical free thinker of the unripe, acrid sort," while another wrote that he "took all the liberties of an insolent servant . . . eager, fickle, and violent in spirit." Without question he bore prejudices—against Irishmen, Baptists, Presbyterians, and George III—and he relished his image as an astringent misanthrope. "The strongest proof of a good heart," he said, "is to love dogs and dislike mankind." Lee was the sort who accumulated nicknames and epithets, from Indians ("Boiling Water"), from loyalists ("Liberty Boy"), and from former comrades in the British officer corps ("Rebel Lee"). He was also "Mad Lee," a "querulous clown," a "furious upstart hero," and, most unkindly, "Naso." General Burgoyne told Lord North, with some insight,

"The foundation of his apostasy I believe to be resentment." All in all, Lee was said to be a man who "thunders, lightnings, opens graves, and roars."

That such a boiling, rebellious, beaky grave opener had become Washington's most senior lieutenant reflected both Lee's credentials and the fluidity of high command in the young American army. The son of a British colonel, Lee was commissioned in his father's regiment at age fourteen, sailed to America to fight the French, survived a gunshot to the chest that shattered two ribs at Fort Carillon, and found time to take a Mohawk wife, a chief's daughter who bore him twin sons. He never saw that family again after his unit left New York, and he never married conventionally. Lee later served in Portugal under Burgoyne, winning plaudits for an intrepid raid across the Tagus River to strike his Spanish foes from the rear. But the peace that followed the Seven Years' War left him bored and jaded; reduced by his army to half-pay purgatory, he spent most of the next eight years as an itinerant soldier of fortune in Europe—a "vagabond," in his description—frequenting spas in Hungary, Italy, and Switzerland between campaigns and earning enough gratitude from the king of Poland to become a Polish army major general, sporting that Stanislaus star.

Bouncing about, in late 1773 he bounced to America. He toured the colonies for months, extolling what he called "the last asylum of liberty." The circle of admirers grew ever wider for this witty, unorthodox warrior who quoted Locke and Rousseau, reputedly "sat his horse as if he had often ridden at fox hunts in England," and spoke with authority about redans, redoubts, ravelins, and counterscarps. One newspaper declared him to be among "the greatest military characters of the present age." He built a literary name by publishing a widely read rebuttal to a Tory pamphlet, telling Americans what they longed to hear: that the empire was not invincible, that colonial militias contained "excellent materials," and that yeomen protecting their homes and their liberty could outfight British regulars. Lee more than most could see the American clay grown tall. With his lacerating wit and intemperate opinions—he would call the king a "damned perfidious tyrant" who "should be dethroned if not beheaded"—he explained himself by claiming to be "extremely democratical." John Adams and other radicals adored him, and when war flared in New England, Congress offered him a major generalship and subsequently agreed to indemnify him for losses up to £11,000 if the Crown confiscated his estates. Lee resigned his British commission, renounced his half-pay "in the most public and solemn manner," then rode to Cambridge at Washington's elbow.

His tactical and engineering experience proved valuable during the siege of Boston. General Greene praised his "genius and learning." Two weeks older than Washington, Lee presumed a familiarity that other senior officers avoided, calling him "my dear general" rather than "Your Excellency." For his erstwhile British comrades, he was a marked man. "There is not a soldier or officer in the garrison, and especially [in] his old regiment, but would be happy to get a shot at him," one regular officer had written from Boston. Dispatched to New York in February 1776 to "put that city in the best posture of defense," he was so crippled by gout that he had to be carried into the city on a litter—"a most ridiculous figure," by his own admission. (The wine cellar Lee left behind in Cambridge was sold to settle the debts he also left.) Two weeks later, Congress told him to take command of the faltering expedition in Canada—"I am the only general officer on the Continent who can speak and think in French," he told Washington—then abruptly rescinded the directive and ordered him south instead.

South he skittered in his whirlwind fashion, first to Baltimore, then to Virginia for six weeks with his dogs, his gaudy sherryvallies, and his draconian military philosophy. He had proposed arresting "every governor, government man, placeman, Tory, and enemy to liberty on the continent," asking, "Are we at war or are we not? Are we not at war with the king?" When told of a shortage of horses to reposition field guns, he reportedly snapped, "Chain twenty damned Tories to each gun." In Virginia he jailed unrepentant loyalists, confiscated their livestock and slaves, burned a few houses "in hopes of intimidating the neighborhood," and proposed seizing women and children "as hostages for the good behavior of the husbands and fathers." His methods, he conceded, were "not quite consistent with the regular mode of proceeding."

For all his scorched-earth swagger, British naval mobility confounded him, as it was confounding Washington in New York. An enemy fleet could pounce on Virginia, then shift to the Carolinas or the Chesapeake, and just as quickly return to Virginia. Perhaps inevitably he used a canine metaphor in writing to the commander in chief:

> I am like a dog in a dancing school. I know not where to turn myself, where to fix myself. . . . The uncertainty of the enemy's designs and motions, who can fly in an instant to any spot they choose with their canvas wings, throw me, or would throw Julius Caesar, into this inevitable dilemma. . . . I can only act from surmise and have a very good chance of surmising wrong.

He closed with an apology: "You will excuse, my dear General, the blots and scratches of this letter."

* * *

Now he was squinting at those canvas wings, fifty sets of them, in Five-Fathom Hole and the adjacent anchorages. With the help of accurate intelligence, including intercepted dispatches from Germain, he had surmised correctly: General Clinton and his comrades intended malice against Charleston.

To save the town, the colony, and perhaps the South, Lee had sixty-five hundred troops, about half of them Continentals. Wearing a blue sash as his badge of rank, and given command over Colonels Moultrie, Thomson, and their militias, he dashed about by boat and on horseback with three aides-de-camp, a secretary, and Spada. He personally drafted the schedule for sentries making their rounds five times each night in Charleston and inspected every gun position, including one designed by the colony's senior judge. ("He may be a very good chief justice," Lee sniffed, "but he is a damn bad engineer.") He reinforced fortifications behind Sullivan's Island by positioning fifteen hundred Continentals on the mainland at Haddrell's Point; condemned his riflemen for their "childish, vicious, and scandalous practice" of taking potshots "at a most preposterous distance"; moved Thomson's guns back from the water's edge for greater security; and, given acute gunpowder shortages, imposed "an eternal rule" that no cannons were to be fired at ranges greater than four hundred yards. He knew General Clinton to be "a damned fool," he assured his men, and would challenge him to a duel if the British did not attack soon.

His demand that white men do manual labor usually consigned to slaves offended some in Charleston, and his caustic manner ruffled others. Lee might be "a strange animal," one South Carolina officer concluded, but "we must put up with ten thousand oddities in him on account of his abilities and his attachment to the rights of humanity." Nothing worried Lee more than the vulnerability of Fort Sullivan, which he considered a flimsy palmetto "slaughter pen" for its defenders. "I never could . . . understand on what principle Sullivan's Island was first taken possession of and fortified," he told John Rutledge, the newly elected president of South Carolina. He ordered construction of screens, breastworks, traverses, and an escape bridge built of empty hogsheads across the Cove, an inlet that separated the island from the mainland. "Sir, when those ships come to lay alongside of your fort," he warned Moultrie, "they will knock it down in half an hour." He also had doubts about Moultrie himself. "For heaven's sake, sir," Lee told him, "everybody is well persuaded of your spirit and zeal, but they accuse you of being too easy in command. . . . There is not a greater vice."

Privately Rutledge advised Moultrie, "General Lee wishes you to evacuate the fort. You will not without an order from me. I will sooner cut off my hand than write one." Unaware of this secret directive, Lee apologized for his incessant nattering and "didacktick stile," then nattered some more. Moultrie took no offense. "His coming among us was equal to a reinforcement of 1,000 men," he later wrote of Lee. "He taught us to think lightly of the enemy, and gave a spur to all our actions."

If the Americans faced mortal peril in Charleston, the British encountered their own hazards. Getting the ships across the bar and into position was difficult enough, requiring calm seas and precise navigation. Commodore Parker nudged his frigates and transports over one by one—each to cheers from the squadron—but the victualler *Prince of Piedmont* grounded, bilged, and broke into flinders on North Breaker. Treacherous winds also pushed a schooner aground near the Charleston Light, where rebel buccaneers promptly made her their own. Eighty pigs of iron ballast were shifted into the forward hold of the man-of-war *Active* to even her keel for the short passage into Five-Fathom Hole, but the largest vessels required even greater pains. Sailors took several days to hoist the fifty guns from *Bristol* with block and tackle, lighter them inshore, then reassemble the frigate after she squeezed across the sandy bar during high water. More cheers followed.

As Parker struggled with his ships, five hundred regulars landed on the northeast shoulder of Long Island, pitching camp and ferrying supplies ashore through the thundering surf. This, Clinton had concluded, was "the properest place" to stage his attack on Sullivan's Island. It had been "confidently reported by the pilots," he wrote, that at ebb tide the two islands were "joined by a ford passable on foot" across Breach Inlet. Once the rebel defenses at Fort Sullivan were overrun, Charleston would be exposed to assault. On June 14, Clinton and Cornwallis joined the Long Island camp, followed the next day by soldiers from five troop transports. Three more days would be needed, until nightfall on June 18, to land nearly three thousand men with ten guns through squalls and a high swell from the Atlantic fetch. "There is nothing that grows upon this island," a regular wrote his brother, "it being a mere sand-bank and a few bushes, which harbor millions of musketoes, a greater plague than there can be in hell itself." Troops killed a nine-foot alligator after it attacked a comrade. An officer told his sister, "Broiled salt pork for breakfast, boiled salt pork for dinner, cold salt pork for supper. Even salt beef is now become an object of luxury."

And then, calamity. A closer inspection of Breach Inlet revealed a channel that even at low water was a hundred yards wide and seven feet deep, *not* the eighteen inches Clinton expected. Officers waded up to their nostrils, scuffing for a ford that was not there: easterly winds had piled up the tide, making the inlet deeper than usual and compounding apparent errors in charting the watercourse. "So much was the General prepossessed with the idea of this infernal ford," wrote Captain James Murray of the 57th Foot, a baronet and future general, "that several days and nights were spent in search of it." Pilot boats sounded adjacent creeks and salt marshes with lead lines as rebel rifle fire cracked overhead. Clinton himself spent at least three nights "reconnoitering those infernal bogs," as he put it, returning to camp each dawn, "wet and miry."

To his "unspeakable mortification and disappointment," he sent word to *Bristol*: the army could do little more than conduct a demonstration against Sullivan's Island in hopes of distracting rebel defenders. No landing on the mainland was feasible because of impenetrable swamps, and while the inlet was too deep to wade, it was too shallow for any man-of-war to provide gunfire support. The squadron had brought fifteen flat-bottomed assault boats, but they could transport less than a quarter of Clinton's force at one time to Sullivan's Island and would then land through treacherous surf "in face of an entrenchment well lined with musketry." Such a fragmented attack, without adequate firepower, would easily be defeated in detail. Clinton believed that Colonel Thomson might have several thousand men at the north end of the island, and a brigade of Continentals also waited to counterattack from Haddrell's Point. "Time is precious," he added. "I heartily wish our business was done and we were on our way to the north." To Germain he also explained that no amphibious assault would be possible "without a manifest sacrifice."

If astonished and dismayed by this news, Parker was reluctant to concede defeat. The honor of the Royal Navy was at stake, even if the army had been neutralized. He believed that the rebels would crumple under a bombardment unlike anything ever imagined in these precincts. No doubt Clinton was correct that there was no time to lose: navy crews had lived on two-thirds rations for a month and had not eaten fresh meat since North Carolina. Some sailors were already too weak to man their battle stations; volunteers from the transports were recruited for duty aboard the men-of-war. Bad water and the broiling sun made conditions even worse on Long Island. Not only was "the suffocating heat the most insufferable I ever felt," a surgeon told his diary, but the cay was infested with "spiders, their bodies as large as my coat button."

Confusion between the army and navy grew day by day, aggravated by the lack of personal contact between commanders. Parker notified Clinton of his intent to attack on June 21 and subsequently sent a convoluted list of signals to be hoisted from *Bristol*'s fore topgallant masthead: red-and-white flags; blue flags pierced with white; flags striped red, white, and blue; Union Jacks. The army requested a delay. Clinton then proposed Sunday, June 23; Parker agreed, writing that he looked forward to "the honor of taking you by the hand on Sullivan's Island and congratulating you on the success of His Majesty's armies by land and sea." The attack was fixed for one p.m., but by eleven on Sunday morning the "flattering wind" needed to position the bombardment vessels adjacent to Fort Sullivan had failed. Another postponement followed.

Neither commander was certain of the other's intentions. "I am not master of the extent of your plan," Parker wrote Clinton on June 25, "or informed of the intelligence you have had and the observations you have made." Clinton began to pencil an answer on the back of the commodore's note—"not having candle, pen, ink, or paper"—then gave the courier an oral reply instead: he and Cornwallis hoped to attack Haddrell's Point. Covering fire from the frigates would be welcome. He had little intelligence, since no American deserter had absconded in three weeks. But without doubt the rebels were "everywhere entrenching themselves in the strongest manner."

Rumors circulated within the squadron that no quarter would be afforded the Americans once the attack commenced and that a £5,000 reward was offered for General Lee's head. Such sanguinary threats might once have unsettled the defenders, but not now. "The longer we are kept in the face of the enemy," a militia major wrote, "the less we dread fighting them."

On Friday morning, June 28, Colonel Moultrie rode northeast under a molten sun through the myrtles and live oaks to inspect Old Danger Thomson's entrenchments at Breach Inlet. Stiff with gout, sweat beading across his florid face, Moultrie wore a blue coat trimmed in scarlet, white breeches, and a black feather in his cap. In recent days, General Lee had again chided him about discipline, about the rickety, unfinished bridge across the Cove, about promiscuous shooting, about this, about that. Moultrie had taken the censure in stride; staying busy helped fend off the grief he felt over his wife's death the previous winter. But he shared Lee's worries about ammunition shortages. With barely two tons of powder in his magazine, Moultrie calculated that his guns could fire no more than twenty-six rounds apiece, with enough pinches left to make twenty firelock cartridges for each defender.

As his horse trotted up to the inlet at nine-thirty, Moultrie spied a small flotilla of boats carrying redcoats down Hamlin Creek, between the western shore of Long Island and the mainland. No sooner had he asked Old

Danger his opinion of this apparition than a shrill cry from a lookout in the dunes warned that British men-of-war in Five-Fathom Hole had loosened their topsails and were inbound on the rising tide. Moultrie yanked his mount around and pounded the three miles back to Fort Sullivan, shouting for his drummer to beat the long roll, summoning the garrison to their battle posts.

The bomb ketch *Thunder* was the first to fire, from twenty-six hundred yards southwest of the fort. A 13-inch mortar shell traced a perfect arc across the summer sky before falling short with a frothy splash. More shells followed, again plumping the sea or bursting in midair in a brilliant spray of orange sparks. Gunners added powder and soon ranged the fort, but a shell that squarely struck the American magazine failed to detonate; others were smothered by the soft sand. The only reported rebel casualties from mortar fragments included one man lightly wounded and three ducks, two geese, and a turkey slain. After sixty booming rounds, *Thunder* fell silent; the concussion had opened her seams, and crewmen would spend the afternoon bailing and caulking.

Under Commodore Parker's battle plan, four frigates were to deliver the main bombardment—*Bristol* and *Experiment*, mounting fifty guns apiece, and *Active* and *Solebay*, each with twenty-eight. As instructed, the men-of-war glided into position at precise points opposite the fort's long curtain and the east and west bastions. Local pilots had assured Parker that his ships could close to within seventy yards of the parapets, near enough to rake the defenders with grapeshot and for marine marksmen firing from his tops to drive rebel cannoneers off their guns. But to Parker's incredulity, pilots now studying the riffles and water tints refused to move the larger men-of-war closer than five hundred yards, even at flood tide, and would nudge the smaller vessels only slightly nearer; whether immobilized by fear, ignorance, or duplicity was never certain. After snarled threats and abject pleas, the commodore reluctantly signaled for each ship to drop anchor. Sailors bounded across the decks, fixing spring lines to the cables for slewing the guns into position, then opened fire.

"The fleet was an eternal sheet of fire and smoke," Captain Murray of the 57th Foot wrote from Long Island. "When for four hours the fire grew every moment hotter and hotter, we were lost in wonder and astonishment." Nimble jack-tars sponged, loaded, and ran their pieces forward, fingers plugging ears as a shouted command brought another monstrous roar and more flame spurting from the muzzles. Concussion ghosts rippled trouser legs across the gun decks. The weight of metal from each broadside was fearsome. Swarming balls flew in black flocks across the beach, smacking the merlons and bastions with enough thudding violence to make the palmetto walls tremble. Three rebel gunners serving an 18-pounder near the flagstaff died with little more than a strangled gasp of astonishment when a British ball blew through an embrasure; a splinter from the hand-spike wounded a lieutenant in the cheek. Elsewhere on the battlements, the corpse of Corporal Samuel Yarbury, newly slain, was rolled into the sand and out of the way. A mortally wounded sergeant murmured, "I'm just expiring," and as he was dragged from the blood-slick gun platform, a comrade yelled, "Revenge this brave man's death!"

General Lee had spent the morning in Charleston, where news of the British sortie brought thousands flocking to the rooftops and church steeples, craning their necks for a glimpse of the enemy canvas far down the harbor. Lee galloped to Haddrell's Point, gaping offshore at "the most furious fire I ever saw or heard." Commandeering a jolly boat, he made for Sullivan's Island, but tide and wind confronted him: the boat went nowhere. Forced to direct his defenses from the mainland, Lee sent an aide by canoe to tell Moultrie that should he run out of ammunition, "spike your guns and retreat with all order possible."

Moultrie had no intention of spiking his guns, retreating, or losing the battle. *Sabal palmetto* trunks embedded in deep sand proved pliable and sturdy enough, absorbing iron balls like a sponge. Rebel gun crews had opened their own deliberate fire even before the frigates finished setting their springs. "The fort fired very brisk whilst we were placing the ship," *Bristol*'s log recorded. Shouted orders carried down the bastions—"Mind the commodore! Mind the two 50-gun ships!"—along with a gratifying sound few Americans had ever heard: the crash of rebel cannonballs splintering English oak.

Gray gun smoke draped the fort. Moultrie puffed his pipe, pointing out targets and demanding that every shot hit home. Stripped to their shirtsleeves, faces begrimed with powder, the men passed fire buckets of grog from hand to hand along the platforms. They drank and drew aim, more confident with each shot that the day was going their way, that brave men now dead would indeed be revenged.

General Clinton soon recognized that the day, like the month and the season, was not going his way. As part of his promised diversion for Parker, he had launched the flat-bottomed flotilla seen by Moultrie that morning on Hamlin Creek. Led by a sloop and an armed schooner, the *Lady Williams*, the boats drew close enough to Sullivan's Island to pepper Thomson's breastworks with gunfire as cheering regulars on the southern tip of Long Island pressed toward Breach Inlet. But the rising tide forced

Clinton to retract gun crews shooting across the inlet from an exposed oyster bank redoubt, and scorching fire from Thomson's riflemen and an 18-pounder firing grapeshot soon swept the decks of *Lady Williams* and her sloop consort.

"Every ball took fatal effect," a South Carolina militiaman boasted. "Their numbers diminished very fast." The two larger vessels briefly ran aground in shoal water, then scraped free and fled back up Hamlin Creek "faster than they advanced," a witness recorded. The flatboats trailed close behind like anxious ducklings. "It is impossible to conceive with what eagerness and satisfaction every soldier [had] stepped into the boats," Captain Murray wrote, "equaled by nothing but the marks of vexation and disappointment which appeared upon our return to the camp." Clinton tried several more sorties during the afternoon, to no avail. Lee sent seven hundred Virginia Continentals to reinforce Thomson, doubling his firepower. "The fire taught the enemy to lie closer behind their bank of oyster shells," observed Morgan Brown, a young North Carolinian.

The unstitching of the British assault continued at the other end of Sullivan's Island. Parker had ordered three frigates—*Actaeon*, *Sphinx*, and *Syren*—to swing toward Rebellion Road, the anchorage within Charleston Harbor. They were to enfilade the rebel fort with cross fire, protect the bombardment force from fire rafts, disrupt Moultrie's retreat over the Cove to the Continent, and support any of Clinton's regulars who ventured toward Haddrell's Point. But pilots on the warships, again through error or cozenage, held course too far west, and all three abruptly stuck fast on the Lower Middle Ground, the Sumter shoal. *Sphinx* and *Syren* wrenched loose by midafternoon, the former without her bowsprit and some rigging, the latter missing a kedge anchor and two hawsers. But the 28-gun *Actaeon*, among the Royal Navy's newest, prettiest men-of-war, was wedged tight in the sand despite heroic efforts by the crew to warp free. Her captain, Christopher Atkins, had vowed upon leaving England to "give those fantastic scoundrels a good banging who have dared to treat the mother country with impunity and ingratitude." Now Captain Atkins faced his own banging.

At three p.m., Moultrie ordered his guns silenced after hearing that Clinton had landed between Fort Sullivan and Thomson's outpost; for ninety minutes, until the report was disproved, all powder was reserved for the infantry to contest an enemy beachhead. Scores of frigate balls smacked the palmetto curtain and bastions, unanswered, including one that snapped the flagstaff and brought down the garrison colors. "The Yankees have done fighting," a British sailor bellowed.

Not yet. Sergeant William Jasper cut the blue flag from the broken pole, lashed the banner to a gunner's sponge staff, and planted it in the sand with a wave of his hat. At four-thirty p.m., the American guns erupted again, at a slower tempo but with better effect since the clearing smoke allowed a sharper view of the targets. Good shooting, and luck, parted the cables on both *Bristol* and *Active*, causing the frigates' sterns to swing toward the fort. A renewed cry—"Fire at the commodore!"—echoed along the parapet. "The enemy raked us very much," *Bristol*'s log noted. "The enemy's shot went through and through us." The flagship was struck "fore and aft," a British surgeon added. "Twice the quarterdeck was cleared of every person except Sir Peter." The crack of splintering English oak again carried across the water, along with the screeching of wounded sailors.

Lee finally arrived at Fort Sullivan late in the afternoon to find the defenders "determined and cool to the last degree." Moultrie and his officers politely laid aside their pipes, answered his questions, requested more powder, and returned to the battle. "Colonel," Lee told Moultrie, "I see you are doing very well here, and you have no occasion for me." Describing the garrison in a note to Washington, Lee wrote, "Upon the whole they acted like Romans in the third century." Seven hundred pounds of extra powder were lightered across the Cove with a note to Moultrie from John Rutledge: "Do not make too free with your cannon. Cool and do mischief."

Mischief was done, as no man could attest better than Commodore Parker. Although he would describe the battle as "by far the grandest sight I ever beheld," by early evening all hope for a British victory had vanished. His frigates would fire some 7,000 rounds and burn more than 12 tons of powder—220 barrels between *Bristol* and *Experiment* alone—compared to 960 shot and 4,766 pounds for the Americans. Yet overwhelmingly the damage had fallen hardest on the king's ships. *Experiment* was so riddled that several gunports had merged into one jagged hole. Her log noted: topsails "shot to pieces," main topsail yard "much wounded," courses "shot to pieces." Twenty-three men were dead and fifty-six wounded, including the captain, who lost his left arm. Sailors washed blood and brains from the lower decks.

Bristol, struck seventy times, suffered worse yet. Three rebel balls were embedded in her mainmast, and more in the mizzenmast; the former was shortened twenty-two feet by carpenters, the latter cut away completely. "We are in a shattered condition," an officer wrote. "No slaughterhouse could present so bad a sight, with blood and entrails lying about, as our ship did." Every man serving on the quarterdeck was killed or wounded, among the 111 casualties throughout the ship, 40 of them dead. When a young officer urged Parker to take cover, he answered from the poop ladder, "You want to get rid of me, do you?" He would acknowledge to the Admiralty suffering "several contusions at different times"; in fact, an exploding shell wounded him in the knee and thigh, blew away his britches, and left him able to walk only with support from two sailors. Governor Campbell, who volunteered to fight on the lower gun deck as if he were again a midshipman, took a painful splinter in the left side that would contribute to his death in England two years later at age forty-eight. *Bristol*'s captain, John Morris, was wounded four times but left his post only when chain shot mangled his right forearm; helped belowdecks for amputation above the elbow, he was on the surgeon's table when a cannonball smashed into the cockpit, killing two medicos and wounding the purser. Morris had himself carried back to the quarterdeck only to be hit again, mortally, in the torso. "A prodigious effusion of blood followed," a witness reported. In one of those dying epigrams for which British sea dogs were justly acclaimed, Morris said of his family, "I leave them to the providence of God and the generosity of my country."

At nine p.m., with June's long light fading, his ammunition dwindling, the tide ebbing, and fragments of his ships floating into Charleston Harbor for retrieval by rebel souvenir hunters, Parker signaled for the squadron to withdraw to their earlier moorings in Five-Fathom Hole. *Actaeon*, marooned and canting on her sandbar, was beyond salvage. Captain Atkins received permission from Parker to abandon ship, climbed into his yawl with the crew early Saturday morning, and set the frigate ablaze, her colors still flying.

Watching this humiliation was Lieutenant Jacob Milligan, a rebel naval officer, who led three longboats out to the burning frigate in time to fire several of her guns at *Bristol* as she hobbled into the Five-Fathom anchorage. Milligan and his men then snatched *Actaeon*'s bell and spare sails before sculling back to Sullivan's Island with the captured ensign flying upside down from the prow of the lead American boat. Half an hour later, *Actaeon* exploded in a cascade of oak planks and charred cordage. She burned to the waterline, and the rising pillar of smoke was said by some imaginative South Carolinians to resemble a palmetto tree.

"We never had such a drubbing in our lives," a Royal Navy sailor wrote. British battle casualties exceeded 200, including men wrecked beyond repair. "Numbers die daily of their wounds," a regular wrote his brother in July. Damage to British morale was also devastating. "The miscarriage," one of Clinton's officers conceded, "has greatly disheartened our troops."

For the Americans, losses from the ten-hour bombardment totaled 26 wounded and 12 killed. The dead included a lieutenant's slave boy. Triumphant defenders at Fort Sullivan could be seen "strutting like crows in a gutter," Lee reported. He sent Moultrie's men a hogshead of Antiguan rum as a congratulatory token and was effusive in his praise of South Carolina's militia even as he strutted a bit himself. "It would take a volume to tell you how many clever things were said of you," the physician and congressman Benjamin Rush would write Lee from Philadelphia. "It has given a wonderful turn to our affairs." "Glorious news from So. Carolina," a headline in the *Virginia Gazette* proclaimed. "Huzza!" Victory at Sullivan's Island was a welcome antidote to the disconsolate news from Canada. It further diminished the loyalists, proved the Royal Navy vulnerable, thwarted British ambitions in the South, and boldly punctuated the new assertions of independence emanating from Philadelphia. Reports of Parker's shredded britches provoked a savage snatch of doggerel: "If honor in the breach is lodged / It may from thence be fairly judged, / Sir Peter's honor's gone."

One brief battle would hardly defeat the Royal Navy or deflect the empire's determination to remain intact. It was "proverbial in war," Lee warned the garrison, "that we are never in so great danger as when success makes us confident." To General Clinton he sent hampers of fruit and fresh vegetables, "which perhaps in your situation are not easily procured." Clinton reciprocated with English cheese and a cask of porter, addressed to "Charles Lee, Esq., major general in the service of his Polish majesty."

Lee believed, as he wrote Washington, that "the dilatoriness and stupidity of the enemy saved us." Had shoal water not snagged the three flanking frigates, Fort Sullivan would surely have come in for a dreadful battering. British officers grappled for their own explanations. Captain Lord Rawdon, the deputy adjutant general, concluded that "a long train of little accidents has entirely frustrated every purpose of this expedition." Many were convinced, as Captain Murray wrote, that misreading the depth of Breach Inlet was "the fatal source of all our misfortunes." Yet even had the shallow ford existed, regulars would have been forced to wade across a broad swath of exposed water against entrenched defenders. Miscalculation and misjudgment marred the expedition from conception to conclusion, including Clinton's docile agreement at Cape Fear to swing toward Charleston, against his better instincts.

"This will not be believed when it is first reported in England," one observer in South Carolina predicted. Both Parker and Clinton hurriedly wrote their respective dispatches, the better to influence what London might believe. The commodore's account to the Admiralty evinced equanimity while omitting Clinton's offer of a diversionary attack and other salient details. "If the troops would have cooperated on this attack . . . His Majesty would have been in possession of Sullivan's Island," he wrote, but

"I was satisfied that the landing was impracticable" and would have resulted in "the destruction of many brave men without the least probability of success."

Clinton's version went on for eight pages in his tidy, nearly indecipherable hand, the runic words canting to the right as if into a headwind. He blamed Howe, Parker, and the gods of fortune and misfortune. His private secretary carried the narrative to Lords North and Germain, and thence no doubt to the king, who concluded that the assault on Charleston "has by no means proved dishonorable, [although] perhaps I should have been as well pleased if it had not been attempted."

Ever willing to castigate others to avoid self-reproach, Clinton would hold grudges against both Parker, for "wanton injustice," and Germain, whose brief statement in the official *Gazette* implied a lack of initiative by the army at Breach Inlet. An inveterate brooder, Clinton now had more to brood about. "It is your fate, my dear friend," Captain Sir John Jervis, a future first lord of the Admiralty, advised him, "to have your conduct left to the misapprobation of the public."

Meanwhile, Clinton urged Parker to "lose no time in conveying the troops under my command to . . . William Howe." High summer was upon them, "the devil's own climate," as a navy letter writer observed. "The scurvy begins to make havoc among our little fleet and army." Contrary winds made havoc too, and difficulty in filling water casks, and delays in reembarking the troops. *Bristol* and *Experiment* were so injured that only deft seamanship coaxed them over the bar again and into open water. One final indignity befell the expedition when the *Glasgow Packet* ran aground and began leaking badly. American marauders aboard a ten-gun row galley attacked with a fusillade of grape and round shot. The British tossed their small arms overboard and surrendered—thirty officers and men from the ship's company, plus fifty Highland regulars. Rebels burned the boat.

"In what a chaos are we embarked," Horace Walpole would write after learning details of the Charleston fiasco. Three weeks passed before the expedition collected itself. Then, at first light on July 21, the squadron stood out to sea, steering north by northeast. Many comrades remained behind in watery graves, sewn into canvas shrouds deadweighted with iron shot. The Americans had demonstrated that they "were trained to stratagem and enterprise," Clinton grudgingly acknowledged. "They knew every trick of chicane." Yet the expedition sailed off with several convictions oddly intact, including the certainty that a faithful multitude of southern loyalists still awaited liberation and that defeat at Sullivan's Island—"one of the most singular events that has yet conspired to degrade the name of the British nation," in Captain Murray's sour assessment—had resulted from bad luck and tactical blunders rather than faulty intelligence and strategic misapprehension.

Like their commanding general, many of the king's men had grievances to nurse and scores to settle. Like Clinton, they would be back. It might take years, but they would be back.

Two postscripts would complete Britain's rout in the southern colonies, strengthening the rebellion and guaranteeing a huge rebel sanctuary of more than a quarter million square miles, from the Chesapeake to Florida.

In the first episode, disaffected Cherokee warriors, angry at white encroachment and swindles by villainous land speculators, slathered themselves in black paint before attacking white frontier settlements from Georgia to Virginia in July. More raids followed in the South Carolina backcountry. With the British threat on the coast conveniently dispelled, militia and Continental regiments counterattacked in four expeditions, razing villages and killing some two thousand Indians. "I have now burnt down every town and destroyed all the corn," Colonel Andrew Williamson, the South Carolina commander, reported. Captured Indians were declared "the slave and property of the taker." The failed uprising eviscerated the Cherokees, stripping away an additional five million acres from their nation; it also gave pause to Creeks, Choctaws, and other tribes contemplating armed resistance against the colonists, even as British and American emissaries sought alliances with native chieftains to the north. Southern rebels blamed frontier barbarism on the British, who had generally urged restraint by the Indians although some agents had provided munitions, war paint, and rum. The Cherokee threat unified southern whites and discredited loyalists, some of whom had even fought with the Indians. Britain's influence waned still further.

The second incident occurred at the last British toehold on the southern littoral. Lord Dunmore, the deposed governor of Virginia, had spent three months at Tucker's Mill Point, the noisome, four-acre promontory on the Elizabeth River where he had retreated following the incineration of Norfolk. Smallpox and other maladies tormented his garrison—three hundred grave mounds eventually stippled those four acres. But runaway slaves continued to find Devil Dunmore and to replenish his depleted Ethiopian Regiment. A small naval detachment under a capable captain, Andrew Snape Hamond, had also arrived with a hundred marines, giving the garrison about 200 regulars and 450 militia volunteers, black and white. Only when Charles Lee swept through southern Virginia on his way to Charleston did Tucker's Mill Point become wholly untenable: Lee evicted loyalists from nearby Portsmouth, burned their stores and houses, further cut off British supplies, and harassed the asylum with cannon fire. On May 26, Dunmore and Captain Hamond herded the refugees onto a rickety flotilla of ninety vessels, set fire to the shantytown, and sailed fifty miles up the Chesapeake to a new, final purgatory.

Gwynn's Island spread for two thousand marshy acres across the mouth of the Piankatank River, and here Lord Dunmore planted his flag to again proclaim the king's sovereignty. Sailors cleaned their ships' hulls, varnished the lower masts, tallowed the rigging, and fired a twenty-one-gun salute on the king's birthday. They were joined by yet another floating governor, Robert Eden, who had fled his capital in Annapolis. A few volleys of Royal Navy grape and round shot scattered Virginia militiamen skulking several hundred yards across Milford Haven, on the mainland shore. But the outpost at Gwynn's was doomed. Springs soon began to run dry, and navy longboats sent out for fresh water filled only six casks in four days. Some blacks were inoculated against smallpox, but the disease continued to kill, abetted by fleet fever—typhus—and other maladies. "Lord Dunmore still remains on Gwynn's Island where, caterpillar-like, we hear he has devoured everything in that place," a Virginian wrote Charles Lee on July 6.

At eight a.m. on Tuesday, July 9, ten rebel militia companies from Williamsburg massed along the shoreline with half a dozen guns. Their commander, General Andrew Lewis, personally touched the first match to an 18-pounder; the ball slammed into the hull of the *Dunmore*, the governor's flagship, moored five hundred yards away. More screaming balls followed across Milford Haven, killing a boatswain's mate, smashing china in the master cabin, and lacerating Dunmore's legs with wood splinters. "Good God," he roared, "that ever I should come to this!" The flagship briefly returned fire, then slipped her cables to be towed out of range by navy longboats, the oarsmen bent low as shot flew overhead. Four rebel 9-pounders bombarded the British encampments, flattening tents and scattering the garrison. Panicky cries rose from behind the breastworks: "The shirtmen are coming!" That night Dunmore ordered the island evacuated, abandoning guns, baggage, three tenders, and hundreds of dead or dying refugees. After his flotilla tacked deeper into the Chesapeake, Hamond wrote, "Impossible to describe the distress and confusion."

Three hundred rebels crossed Milford Haven in canoes the next morning. A Virginia shirtman described finding a "number of dead bodies in a state of putrefaction, strewed all the way from their battery to Cherry Point, about two miles in length, without a shovelful of earth upon them." Others, dying, pleaded for help from the water's edge, "beckoning to us." A child was found sucking at the breast of its dead mother. One officer counted 130 graves, "many of them large enough to hold a corporal's guard." Rebel troops terrified of smallpox torched brush shanties on the island, reportedly burning alive those too sick to crawl from the flames. Captain Thomas Posey of the 7th Virginia Regiment later estimated that altogether "at least four or five hundred Negroes lost their lives" on Gwynn's Island, mostly from sickness, along with 150 whites.

Dunmore and his fugitives spent three more weeks wandering around the Chesapeake and up the Potomac River, seeking recruits, stealing cattle, and pillaging rebel homesteads. "We landed, did what mischief we could, and reembarked," Dunmore wrote Germain on July 31. "We have nowhere to go." Another two hundred people died aboard "his floating town," as Hamond called it, to be tossed over the sides at night. Finding the shoreline cobbled with corpses, a Maryland militia officer reported, "We are poisoned with the stench."

In early August, Dunmore divided the floating town into three detachments. The *Otter* would escort most surviving loyalists to St. Augustine, where Britain's hold on Florida remained secure. The *Fowey* and seven ships sailed for England with Governor Eden. Aboard the forty-four-gun *Roebuck*, Dunmore, Hamond, and barely a hundred fit-for-duty regulars, marines, and volunteer troops, white and black, prepared to join British forces in New York. Dunmore was intent on telling his story to General Howe and the high command. Several dozen abandoned vessels—schooners, sloops, snows, scows—were left burning in the bay.

Of the fifteen hundred runaway slaves who had reached British sanctuary since the previous fall, roughly a thousand had perished. Dunmore ordered some black defectors returned to owners who swore loyalty oaths, a betrayal useful to rebel propagandists. The Ethiopian Regiment, nearly obliterated by pox, war, and dreams of freedom, would soon be formally disbanded. Little had come of the Crown's adventurism in the American South. The diversion of Royal Navy ships to Virginia, Cape Fear, and South Carolina had hindered efforts to blockade the Delaware and Chesapeake Bays, allowing American gunrunners virtually unimpeded passage for months. Rebels completely controlled four colonies that now called themselves states—Virginia, Georgia, and the two Carolinas—and for the most part they would be left in peace for the next several years. Virginia loyalists, shattered and dispersed, never again formed a potent force. Thousands of rebel troops, now free to reinforce the Continental Army, tramped off to help General Washington.

As *Roebuck* bent eastward between Cape Charles and Cape Henry, then swept north toward New York, Captain Hamond took time to write a friend. "Our whole exploits have amounted to nothing," he conceded. But, Hamond added, "These little miscarriages I trust will have a good effect in the end. Englishmen always rally when things are at the worst."

15.

A Fight Among Wolves

The fateful news traveled swiftly on the post road from Philadelphia, covering more than ninety miles and crossing five rivers in just a couple of days. Precise copies were then made of the thirteen-hundred-word broadside, titled "A Declaration," that arrived at the Mortier mansion headquarters, and by Tuesday, July 9, General Washington was ready for every soldier in his command to hear what Congress had to say. In his orders that morning, after affirming thirty-nine lashes for two convicted deserters, he instructed the army to assemble at six p.m. on various parade grounds, from Governors Island to King's Bridge. Each brigade major would then read— "with an audible voice"—the proclamation intended to transform a squalid family brawl into a cause as ambitious and righteous as any in human history.

That evening the commander in chief himself appeared on horseback at the Common with a suite of staff officers, not far from where Sergeant Hickey had tumbled from the scaffold two weeks earlier. Erect and somber, Washington rode into the middle of a hollow square formed by New York and Connecticut regiments while a chirpy throng of civilians ringed the greensward. A uniformed aide spurred his horse forward; the crowd hushed as he unfolded his script and began to read: "In Congress, July 4, 1776." Even the most unlettered private recognized that something majestic was in the air.

> We hold these truths to be self-evident, that all men are created equal, that they are endowed by their Creator with certain unalienable rights, that among these are life, liberty, and the pursuit of happiness. That to secure these rights, governments are instituted among men, deriving their just powers from the consent of the governed.

On and on it went, describing the "long train of abuses and usurpations," then denouncing royal despotism, then enumerating twenty-seven grievances. Those shifting from foot to foot as the reader droned through a condemnation of "our British brethren" would have been relieved to know that Congress had pruned the original draft by a quarter for the sake of concision and restraint. The primary author—a lanky, ginger-haired Virginia planter named Thomas Jefferson—was widely acknowledged even at age thirty-three to have "a happy talent of composition," as John Adams conceded. Perched in a swiveling Windsor chair on the second floor of rented rooms at Seventh and High Streets in Philadelphia, a compact, custom-built writing desk in his lap, Jefferson had sought, as he later explained, "to place before mankind the common sense of the subject, in terms so plain and firm as to command their assent. . . . It was intended to be an expression of the American mind."

Just so, despite what he considered the "mutilations" imposed by his congressional colleagues, sitting at tables covered in green baize in the Pennsylvania State House, lashing at horseflies with their handkerchiefs while scratching up his draft with their quills. The leaner, edited result remained a stirring manifesto of republicanism, a radical assertion that power derived not from God or through bloodlines but from the people, and should benefit the many, not just the affluent or well-born. Of the ninety or more declarations and petitions drafted by the colonies in recent months, as counted by the historian Pauline Maier, none surpassed this document in elegance, clarity, or breathtaking vision. That at least a third of the delegates who would sign the Declaration were slave owners— Jefferson alone had two hundred—was a moral catastrophe that could never be reconciled with the avowed principles of equality and "unalienable rights," at least not in the eighteenth century. But as Edmund S. Morgan would write, "The creed of equality did not give men equality, but invited them to claim it, invited them, not to know their place and keep it, but to seek and demand a better place."

The reader finished his oration, a bit hoarse now, by proclaiming all political ties with Britain "to be totally dissolved" and the colonies to be "free and independent states." To this declaration the disputatious men in Philadelphia had pledged "our lives, our fortunes, and our sacred honor." A chaplain recited Psalm 80—"Turn us again, O God of hosts, and cause thy face to shine, and we shall be saved." Loud cheers washed over the Common, and Thomas Mifflin, the adjutant general, reportedly climbed onto a cannon and shouted, "My lads, the Rubicon is crossed!"

Washington trotted back to his headquarters, but the rambunctious crowd meandered south on Broadway. Here George III, identified that very evening in the Declaration as a tyrant "unfit to be the ruler of a free people," sat atop his gilt horse on Bowling Green. Whooping vandals broke through the iron fence surrounding the statue, clambered onto the marble pedestal, and lassoed the equestrian figure. Scores of soldiers and civilians tugged on the ropes until the two-ton statue capsized with a tremendous crash—"leveled with ye dust," a witness reported. The baying crowd decapitated the king, whacked off his nose, and clipped the laurels from his brow. Someone fired a musket ball into the head, and more balls punctured the torso. Others scraped away the ten ounces of gold leaf that covered rider and mount. With fife and drums playing "The Rogue's March," the severed head was first wheeled in a barrow to the Mortier house, then impaled on a spike outside the Blue Bell Tavern. To one spectator the scene evoked the fallen angel Lucifer, as described by poet John Milton: "O, how fallen! How changed!"

The head would be recovered by British Army engineer John Montresor and shipped to England to further illustrate the "disposition of the ungrateful people." The headless rider and horse were carted in fragments to a Connecticut foundry, where patriot women melted the lead, ladled it into molds, and soon sent the army 42,088 bullets. "It is hoped," the surgeon Isaac Bangs told his journal, "that the emanations of the leaden George will make as deep impressions in the bodies of some of his red-coated and Tory subjects."

Exuberant demonstrations erupted throughout the thirteen new states as word of the Declaration spread. Salutes and toasts followed publication of the document in the same issue of the *Virginia Gazette* that listed bounties for runaway slaves. Savannah held a sham burial of King George, accompanied by muffled drums. Other towns staged mock trials and executions. A Long Island village fashioned an effigy of the king with a wooden crown and feathers, wrapped it in a Union Jack packed with gunpowder, then blew it up on a gallows. In Dover, Delaware, rebels tossed George's portrait into a bonfire. "Thus," they announced, "we destroy even the shadow of that king who refused to reign over a free people." In New Hampshire, mobs smashed tavern signs depicting a crown or the king's arms; some merchants refused coins with the king's likeness. Other protesters settled for turning the monarch's image to the wall or hanging it upside down. Delaware troops marched from Wilmington to New Castle, tearing down the royal coat of arms and other "baubles of royalty," which were then stacked before the courthouse and burned to ash. Abigail Adams wrote John of listening as the Declaration was read from a balcony in Boston. Cheers rent the welkin, she reported. Bells rang, shore batteries boomed, and soldiers fired by platoons in celebration. "Every face appeared joyful," she wrote. "Thus ends the royal authority in this state, and all the people shall say amen."

* * *

General Howe had an answer to the Declaration of Independence, and he sent it on Friday afternoon, July 12. Shortly after three p.m., British sailors on five warships weighed anchor off Staten Island, loosened and sheeted home their sails, yanked the tampions from their gun muzzles, and sailed across the Upper Bay in brilliant sunshine, canvas clapping before a brisk southwest breeze. Led by the frigates *Phoenix* and *Rose*, with sixty-four guns between them, the squadron curled along the lower lip of Manhattan and opened fire at 4:05 p.m. "The balls and bullets went through several houses," a pastor wrote, ". . . and the air was filled with the smell of powder." Continental soldiers struck their tents to make the encampments less conspicuous. Terrified civilians nipped into cellars or fled down bystreets toward the Bowery. "The shrieks & cries of these poor creatures running every which way with their children was truly distressing," Washington later wrote.

American gunners returned fire from the Star Redoubt and the Grenadier Battery, from Whitehall Battery and the Oyster Battery near Trinity Church, and, as the enemy vessels heeled up the Hudson, from Paulus Hook in New Jersey. Flame stabbed through the gouts of smoke blanketing the river and its banks. A few of the 196 American balls hit home; most fell short or flew wide. Some cannoneers reportedly were drunk or had failed to join their gun teams when the alarm sounded. Disaster struck at the Grand Battery, below old Fort George, when a new cartridge was rammed down the smoking barrel before it had been properly sponged. Sparks ignited the powder, first tearing off the rammer's arm, then detonating with such violence that six men "were blown all to pieces by imprudence," a passing mariner named Christopher Prince reported. "Their legs, arms, and bodies were all separated, so much so we put them all on two handbarrows and carried them up to Bowling Green, and dug a hole and put their remains in it and covered them over." "This affair," Henry Knox wrote Lucy, "will be of service to my people. It will teach them to moderate their fiery courage."

By four-thirty p.m., the ships had run a gantlet of eleven American batteries and were reduced to popping at scattered farmsteads north of the city. Aboard *Rose*, officers had opened a celebratory claret when a final rebel ball smashed the frigate's pinnace and the captain's unoccupied cot. Still, the damage was light, both ashore and on the ships. Carpenters extracted a few balls out of the hull timbers. *Phoenix* had her sails and rigging perforated; *Rose* also took an 18-pound shot in the foremast. Colonel Knox drew precisely the wrong lesson from the encounter. "It rained balls around them," he told Lucy, "and proves to me beyond a doubt that their ships cannot lay before our batteries."

In fact, the enemy had breezed unhindered up the Hudson past defenses many months in the making and were now anchored in seven fathoms at Tappan Zee, thirty miles into the American rear. Families fled from the river valley. Militia companies blocked defiles leading to the Hudson Highlands and shored up defenses in Poughkeepsie, fifty miles north, where American shipwrights were building two frigates of their own. British marines raided rebel gardens for what one man called "a handkerchief full of salad," while snatching up an occasional hog or calf. Sailors rigged tarpaulins across their decks for shade against the pitiless sun and launched barges to sound the channel. And when snipers plinked away from the shoreline with their fowling pieces, British gunners answered with scalding cannon fire to show that the Hudson, for now, was a British river.

William Howe had moved into the Rose and Crown, a tavern built by Staten Island Huguenots more than a century earlier. Three miles from the Narrows, on a rise off New Dorp Lane, the rambling headquarters overlooked meadows now covered with rows of white tents that stretched toward the earthworks raised by British soldiers along the island's southern shore. Beyond lay the crooked finger of Sandy Hook and the azure Lower Bay, which soon, Howe hoped, would be jammed with the greatest war fleet Britain had ever launched, carrying the largest expeditionary army the Crown had ever assembled.

Until those reinforcements arrived, Howe was under orders from Lord Germain to delay his grand attack in order "that your force may be so increased as to render your success more certain." Yet each day that passed without the arrival of Clinton and Cornwallis from the south, and the German and British host dispatched from England, was another day lost in the campaign season. Germain had hoped the decisive battle would commence "in the month of May or beginning of June." Now late August seemed more likely. Howe had been skeptical of the southern expedition, but he was careful not to cross Germain. "I am amazed," he had recently written the American secretary in an obsequious dispatch, "at decisive and masterly strokes effected since you assumed conduct of war."

Howe's army would eventually include forty-four British battalions—thirty thousand soldiers, if fully manned—plus thirty battalions of "foreign auxiliaries," including almost nine thousand troops in the first wave. He would also have an artillery train of more than two hundred field guns and forty-six mortars. To move and supply these legions, the Navy Board now had more than four hundred transports and victuallers in service, triple the number from six months earlier and triple the tonnage employed

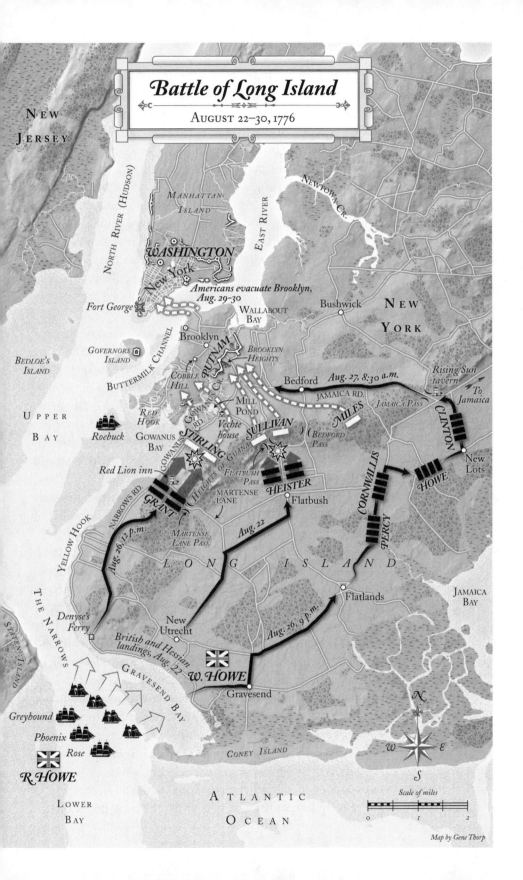

Battle of Long Island

AUGUST 22–30, 1776

NEW JERSEY

MANHATTAN ISLAND

NORTH RIVER (HUDSON)

EAST RIVER

NEWTOWN CR.

WASHINGTON

New York

Americans evacuate Brooklyn, Aug. 29–30

Fort George

WALLABOUT BAY

Bushwick

NEW YORK

BEDLOE'S ISLAND

GOVERNORS ISLAND

Brooklyn

PUTNAM

Brooklyn Heights

Bedford

Aug. 27, 8:30 a.m.

JAMAICA RD.

Rising Sun tavern

To Jamaica

BUTTERMILK CHANNEL

COBBLE HILL

GOWANUS CR.

Mill Pond

JAMAICA PASS

CLINTON

UPPER BAY

RED HOOK

Roebuck

Red Hook

GOWANUS BAY

STIRLING

GOWANUS RD.

Vechte house

SULLIVAN

MILES

BEDFORD PASS

New Lots

Red Lion inn

HEIGHTS OF GUANA

Flatbush Pass

HEISTER

CORNWALLIS

HOWE

GRANT

MARTENSE LANE

Flatbush

PERCY

Aug. 26, 12 p.m.

NARROWS RD.

MARTENSE LANE PASS

Aug. 22

L O N G   I S L A N D

JAMAICA BAY

THE NARROWS

Denyse's Ferry

New Utrecht

Flatlands

STATEN ISLAND

British and Hessian landings, Aug. 22

Aug. 26, 9 p.m.

⊞ *W. HOWE*

Gravesend

N

GRAVESEND BAY

Greyhound

Phoenix

Rose

W   E

S

⊞ *R. HOWE*

CONEY ISLAND

LOWER BAY

A T L A N T I C   O C E A N

Scale of miles

0   1   2

Map by Gene Thorp

at the peak of the Seven Years' War. But the campaign in Massachusetts had revealed too well how the caprices of shipping could impinge on battle plans: only eight of forty transports dispatched from home the previous winter had reached Boston. Difficulties in Cork and Halifax had already chewed into Howe's timetable this spring, and to save a little money, the Treasury had also delayed hiring some storeships.

Seven major contractors in England were to feed the expedition. More than a thousand tons of food a month would be needed, exclusive of the maritime forces. The government hoped that after the 1776 campaign, if the rebels had not surrendered, Howe could "obtain supplies from America itself." Yet he knew better than anyone in London the complexity and expense of his logistical needs, which already were costing him more than £10,000 a week. (In the past year, the government had shipped £560,000 in cash to America.) The enormous stocks of bread he required each month often arrived from Cork moldy, underweight, and, most recently, plagued with Irish rats, which now infested his storehouses on Staten Island. Among other necessities, his assembled force would require 48,000 blankets, 3,400 watch coats, almost 1,500 scythes with whetstones, and scores of carpenters, bricklayers, and wagon masters. The daily rum allowance of a gill for each soldier—about a gallon a month—cost both money and shipping space. Tons of medical supplies would be sent, including two straitjackets. It was hardly too early to consider winter requirements, which would include 64,000 cords of firewood and 70 tons of candles. And many of those tents now neatly arrayed below New Dorp Lane were found to be useless in the rain. Complaints had even reached the king, who was appalled to learn that English tentage stocks had not been inspected since 1759.

Few issues would flummox the British more than how to move inland: waging war away from the coast and navigable rivers required transport for artillery, baggage, and supplies. Otherwise, the rebels could simply dance out of reach, stripping the land of provisions and leaving the regulars like "a cow catching a hare," as a London newspaper indelicately observed. A brass 12-pounder and carriage weighing more than a ton and a half might require six horses to move down a country lane. Howe calculated that his grand army would need almost 4,000 horses and 277 wagons. The unfortunate loss of many drays in Boston had been compounded by delays this spring in shipping more than two hundred five-ton wagons stored in the Tower of London and at Portsmouth. Hiring American teamsters was erratic and expensive—typically fifteen shillings a day for each wagon, team, and driver.

Forage was another enormous problem. Four thousand horses would devour twenty thousand tons of hay and oats a year. Because living off the hostile land was uncertain, two horses typically were needed to pull the fodder eaten by three other horses on campaign. British supply officers also estimated that Howe needed twenty thousand horseshoes, eleven hundred harnesses, and a squad of farriers.

Simply getting horses to New York was proving to be an ordeal. At Howe's request, twenty-one equestrian transports had been leased, some of them Dutch vessels with scuttled decks to allow greater air circulation. Each ship typically carried several dozen animals in narrow stalls, their legs sometimes padded with straw trusses, their hooves hobbled, and their bodies guyed to overhead hooks to prevent toppling when the transport rolled. Of 950 horses shipped to Howe this summer, 412 would die in transit, the carcasses hoisted with slings from the stinking holds and pitched into the sea. Scores more were so enfeebled by the crossing that they died soon after arrival. Some transports proved particularly lethal, like the *Jonge Pieter*, which had embarked seventy-two horses—typically costing sixteen guineas each—and delivered just sixteen alive. The French ambassador in London, who carefully tracked Britain's war exertions, calculated that these equestrian shipping costs alone exceeded £10,000. "This ruinous and mad war," he wrote in a secret dispatch to Versailles, "is the reverse of the philosopher's stone for England."

Howe soldiered on, waiting for reinforcements and plotting campaign strategy in the Rose and Crown. He was cheered by the arrival, shortly after *Phoenix* and *Rose* sortied up the Hudson, of the sixty-four-gun *Eagle*, carrying Vice Admiral Lord Richard Howe, his older brother, who would take command of Royal Navy operations in North America. The promised legions were on the high seas, Admiral Howe assured him; moreover, seventy warships and twelve thousand sailors—more than 40 percent of the entire navy—would soon be in these waters. Lord North sent his own reassurance from England in a message written on June 25, albeit with a slightly desperate undertone. "War and peace, the honor and happiness of Great Britain and of British America, are entrusted to Lord Howe and to you," the first minister told him. "If tranquility is restored to America, it will be in such a manner as to do credit to all those who are concerned in it."

On August 6, the New York Convention lent Washington the fine telescope from King's College with the hope that it would be useful to His Excellency in "discovering the arrangements and operations of the enemy." Certainly there was much to see from a rooftop at the foot of Broadway: the 130 topsail vessels that had arrived from Halifax in June with William Howe; the 150 additional sails that accompanied Richard Howe in July; the battered squadron of 45 vessels led by *Bristol* that arrived on August 1, reportedly carrying General Clinton from Charleston ("as unexpected to us as if he had dropped from the clouds," admitted Colonel Reed, the adjutant general); and the 22-sail convoy that appeared on August 4 after a four-month voyage from the river Clyde carrying three thousand Highlanders, including the 42nd Regiment of Foot in feathered bonnets and the dark tartan kilts that had inspired the regimental nickname, "the Black Watch."

On the late afternoon of August 12, yet another 107 ships slipped through the Narrows to be greeted with British cannon salutes. Aboard were a thousand guardsmen drawn from elite foot regiments often used to protect the monarch. (In reviewing the departing Guards troops at Wimbledon Common, the king had reportedly removed his hat as a gesture of respect.) Also aboard were more than 8,600 German troops—known collectively as Hessians, since most came from landlocked, impoverished Hesse-Kassel. They stood at the rails with their black mustaches and tallowed hair, overjoyed to see land after fourteen weeks at sea. Hundreds suffered from scurvy and diarrhea despite treatment with seawater cocktails, chewing tobacco, and other transatlantic nostrums. Many required new musket cartridges; rats had gnawed into the munitions casks and devoured them, besides eating tents and uniforms. Some still needed brogans, since the British shoes ordered in Portsmouth had proved to be "fine, thin dancing pumps . . . so small that no use can be made of them." They were capable troops, dutiful if homesick and mostly illiterate, former weavers, cobblers, farmhands, foresters, and lacemakers who had turned to soldiering, "a true pell mell of human souls," in one description. Nearly thirty thousand Hessians would be hired to fight in America, where a quarter of them were destined to die; many more would desert or be captured, and barely half would see their fatherland again. Starting with this tranche, each would swear an oath to the English Crown. To rent that loyalty, Britain would pay over £4 million, to them and to their princes.

Despite the spectacle that swam into view through the telescope eyepiece, Washington had no idea what the Howe brothers intended. His only substantive intelligence came from deserters and escaped American prisoners, whose accounts often conflicted. (Congress offered a $4 bounty to every deserter, plus $10 if he brought his firelock.) Already it was clear that the enemy force in New York would be far larger than the 12,500 men assumed by Congress in late spring. Would the British continue to push up the Hudson, perhaps in hopes of joining Carleton's force from Canada? Or would they thread the East River to Long Island Sound, landing behind American fortifications in New York? Or launch amphibious landings on both Manhattan and Long Island? Alerts from the Mortier headquarters, rarely informed by good intelligence, warned of possible attacks up the rivers, or on Long Island, or against Bergen, Elizabeth Town, and Perth Amboy in New Jersey. In a broadside distributed in New York, Washington cautioned that an enemy assault "may be hourly expected," and he urged "women, children, and infirm persons . . . to remove with all expedition." A depleted, skittish town grew emptier and more skittish.

Washington now commanded just over twenty thousand men around New York, in regiments from ten states. Fewer than half were Continentals. "It was a crude, unmilitary host," the nineteenth-century historian Henry P. Johnston would write. "The great mass knew nothing of war." Outrage over the arrival of German mercenaries helped further unify them. "O Britons," a Rhode Island officer wrote, "how art you fallen that you hire foreigners to cut your children's throats?" Although Britain had leased foreign troops in every war this century, Americans saw the practice as additional evidence of the king's depravity. "We, for our ally, have the great God, who requires no subsidy," a surgeon wrote his father in mid-August. Officers and rank-and-file alike steeled themselves for a death struggle. Colonel Edward Hand, an Irish-born physician whose Pennsylvania riflemen were posted at the tip of Long Island above the Narrows, wrote his wife, Kitty, on August 12, "We are well prepared to receive them here. . . . Kiss my dear little daughter for me."

Every day, Washington tried to make his host a bit less crude and a bit more military. He envisioned a disciplined army that would help bind the nation together and provide the American cause with moral fiber. To "preserve the liberty of our country ought to be our only emulation," his general orders declared in early August, "and he will be the best soldier and the best patriot who contributes most to this glorious work, whatever his station, or from whatever part of the continent he may come." Toward that end, commands, pronouncements, and reprimands poured from Mortier mansion: against "the foolish and wicked practice of profane cursing and swearing," against rivalries between New Englanders and southerners, against soldiers "constantly rambling about," against promiscuous shooting, which had again grown so flagrant that only sentries would be permitted to keep their firelocks loaded. Militia captains were ordered to inspect every musket to confirm that "the cartridges fit the bore of the gun"; each musketeer was permitted to carry just six rounds, with a reserve of eighteen kept in a small bundle labeled with his name, to be issued upon alarm. Reward offers for shirkers again appeared in local newspapers, as in the *New York Gazette*'s description of a missing New Jersey soldier: "Had on when he deserted an old wool hat bound with yellow binding, a coarse blue coat. . . . His shirt was very dirty." Soldiers were ordered to keep their canteens filled, with three days of cooked rations at hand. "We must resolve," Washington declared, "to conquer or die."

Some died even before the battle was joined, for summer diseases had lacerated the army. "I am extremely sorry to inform Congress our troops are very sickly," Washington wrote Hancock in early August. Of his 17,225 privates, only 10,514 were present and fit for duty; many were unfit, as an ensign informed his diary, because "a dysentery prevails considerable in the army at this time." Typhoid and typhus also prevailed; the diseases, respectively spread by fecal contamination and by lice, would not be distinguishable until the next century. Malaria grew common, too. "The air of the whole city seems infected," an American doctor wrote. "In almost every street there is a horrid smell." Camp filth and fetid water—some ponds were used for both drinking and washing—contributed to a third of the army falling sick in the summer of 1776. General William Heath observed that "in almost every barn, stable, shed, and even under the fences and bushes, were the sick to be seen."

Some regiments could hardly muster a shadow of themselves. The 17th Continental, mostly drawn from eastern Connecticut, was reduced in August to 214 present-and-fit soldiers of the 728 men authorized. Malaria then laid low their colonel. Disease often was misdiagnosed—even the simple stethoscope would not be invented for another four decades—and treatment frequently was limited to bleeding eight to forty ounces from a sick man, regardless of his symptoms. Medical officers found too few nurses willing to work for the fifty cents a week offered by Congress, and for every caring doctor another seemed to be accused of negligence, incompetence, peculation, or selling medical exemptions to healthy troops. In a fit of pique, Washington would condemn his regimental surgeons as "very great rascals."

Washington's disposition hardly improved upon receiving an alarming note on August 15 from Nathanael Greene, newly promoted to major general and the commander of American defenses on Long Island. "I am confined to my bed with a raging fever," Greene wrote. Evacuated to a private home on Broadway in Manhattan, he would lie dangerously ill for two weeks while the commander in chief scrambled to find a replacement who knew something about how the army's left wing planned to fight.

Sensing their mortality, some soldiers drafted wills and otherwise prepared for the worst. "Don't grieve after me, as I am satisfied in my own mind that the cause I am engaged in is a righteous one," Captain Joseph Howell, Jr., wrote his father in Pennsylvania on August 14. "It is my will that all I have in this world be equally divided between my four sisters."

* * *

Washington also recognized the threat to his right wing from the British sortie up the Hudson, and for weeks he had sought a remedy to this fluvial vulnerability.

New fortifications were ordered at Fort Washington, on Manhattan's northwest rim, as well as on the opposite Jersey shore above Burdett's Ferry, a redoubt soon named Fort Lee to honor the hero of Charleston. Armed row galleys were to be transferred from New England, joining others built in New York. A thousand fire arrows were fashioned to ignite British sails. "Hasten the sinking of vessels and other obstructions in the river at Fort Washington, as fast as possible," the commanding general wrote on August 11. Mimicking contraptions sunk in the Delaware River below Philadelphia, engineers began building enormous timber frames, ballasted with tons of stone and fitted with iron spikes called "pricks" to disembowel enemy ships passing overhead. Known as chevaux-de-frise, these devices were originally intended to impede enemy cavalry; the name was variously mispronounced as "shevrord fres," "chevux de' free," "navy de frize," and "shiver de freeses." One lieutenant preferred simply "our contrivance with a hard name." Several old hulks also were chained together and sunk in the Hudson, though one officer advised Washington that positioning the obstructions involved "the most abstruse problem in hydraulics."

While these preparations advanced, a more direct attack was launched against the Royal Navy on the moonless Friday night of August 16. A hundred-ton sloop named *Polly* and a smaller schooner, each crewed by ten army volunteers, crept from Spuyten Duyvil Creek near Fort Washington; they were towed by row galleys eight miles up the Hudson on a rising tide toward the *Phoenix*, *Rose*, and three tenders, now anchored in a line under the Jersey Palisades across from Yonkers. Both American vessels were crammed with flammables: birch faggots dipped in rosin, bundled straw, wood shavings, barrels of pitch, and canvas strips soaked in boiled turpentine and draped on the rigging. Gunpowder lined the gutters belowdecks, and grappling irons were lashed to the tips of the yards and booms. Small doors had been cut in each stern to allow the incendiaries to escape into trailing whaleboats. John Adams, who took a keen interest in fireship design, had acknowledged that "there seems to be something infernal in this art. But . . . when it is to combat evil, 'tis lawful to employ the devil."

With visibility barely fifty yards, the attackers almost passed the enemy unseen until the clang of a ship's bell at eleven p.m. and a sentry's "All's well" brought them about. The galleys cast off and the fireships swung hard to port, the British spars now silhouetted ahead against the dark mass of the Palisades. The tension, one rebel wrote, was enough "to awaken a panic in the stoutest heart." The American schooner under Ensign John Thomas of New London, Connecticut, made for the *Phoenix* but instead grappled the *Charlotta*, a tender anchored in the way. Thomas fired his gunpowder gutters, fore and aft. Flames leaped into the schooner's rigging and sails before jumping to the tender in an inferno bright enough to be seen on Staten Island, twenty-two miles south. Several singed American crewmen scrambled into the whaleboat to escape, but Thomas and three others dove into the Hudson and vanished.

Gunners aboard *Phoenix* fired on the burning schooner from two hundred yards, then abruptly spied *Polly* bearing down on the frigate's stern. As cannon and musket shot raked *Polly*'s hull and masts, Ensign Thomas Updike Fosdick ignited the powder train and sprang into the whaleboat with his crew. Flame engulfed the cabin and loped across the deck. *Polly* smacked *Phoenix* on the starboard bow, her jib boom thrusting across the frigate's upper deck. Grapples tangled in the British rigging. For twenty minutes Royal Navy seamen on the yardarms battled flames in the fore topsail and headsails, cutting away both the grappling irons and her own anchor cables until the frigate finally wrenched free. *Charlotta* burned to the waterline—American scavengers later salvaged four guns, ten swivels, and a few cutlasses from the charred hulk—but the only other British casualty was a sailor with a singed hand.

The American fireship survivors returned to camp as heroes Saturday morning. At ten a.m., Washington himself arrived to applaud their valor and to give each a $40 reward, plus an extra $10 to "those who stayed last and were somewhat burnt." He lamented the men lost, especially the valiant Ensign Thomas. "His bravery," Washington declared, "entitled him to a better fate."

Phoenix, *Rose*, and the two surviving tenders hoisted sail at five o'clock on Sunday morning. Riding the current and an ebbing tide, they slid past eleven rebel batteries that barked but had little bite, and by seven-thirty the flotilla was again moored off Staten Island. Both frigate captains would be knighted for demonstrating that the Hudson could be traversed at will, Yankee guns, fireships, and shiver de freeses be damned.

A violent, portentous storm swept across New York on Wednesday, August 21. Thunderheads that "seemed as solid as marble" loomed above the harbor at twilight, wrote Major Abner Benedict, and "there followed a crash louder than a thousand cannon discharged at once." Aboard *Eagle*, where the Howe brothers had gathered with senior commanders for a final planning session, "this evening turned out as bad a one as I ever saw," the frigate's captain told his journal. "Terrible thunder, lightning, and prodigious heavy rain." At a regimental camp near Bull's Head tavern in the Bowery, an American captain and two lieutenants were killed by a single lightning bolt. "The points of their swords melted off, and the coins melted in their pockets," Major Benedict recorded. "Their bodies appeared as if they had been roasted, so black and crisped was the skin." A newspaper account of the storm concluded, "When God speaks, who can but fear?"

By early Thursday morning the weather had faired, and at first light crimson columns of British soldiers marched through the puddles from their tent camps to the Staten Island shoreline below the Watering Place. Many had already moved to staging billets on the warships and transports. In the Guards Brigade, each man carried a blanket, a haversack with an extra shirt, and three days' provisions, including thirteen ounces of cooked pork, "purser's weight, per man, per day." Bawling officers read out the articles of war as sergeants measured two gills of rum into each canteen. Foot regiments assembled, lapels trimmed in buff, black, royal blue, green, and yellow, some men still wearing last year's uniforms because rebel pirates had captured the new ones. Highlanders appeared in short red jackets with belted dirks; they stored their cumbersome broadswords in the transport holds, and would soon swap their kilts for more practical breeches. The Hessians came on in dark blue tunics, or green for the *Jäger* huntsmen; officers had removed their rank insignia in deference to the reputed marksmanship of American riflemen.

Seventy-five flatboats had been assembled—each could carry more than five tons while drawing only two feet—plus eleven large bateaux and two galleys. Every boat had a number slathered on the bow and a flag denoting to which of ten landing divisions it belonged. Field guns, their carriages and limbers painted gray, were wheeled onto boats with long gangplanks or hinged bows that dropped to make a ramp. Britain, more than any other naval power, had honed the skills needed for amphibious warfare; drawing lessons from failures earlier in the century against the Spanish and French, the navy had developed specialized landing craft, combat loading and command procedures, fleet organization, naval gunfire and logistical support, and the reconnaissance of hostile shores. Assaults against Louisbourg, various Caribbean islands, the French coast, and a masterful operation at Quebec in 1759 all helped make Long Island look simple, although the Sullivan's Island debacle was a reminder that much could go wrong between sea and shore.

Dawn, said to break with "tropical brilliancy," revealed men-of-war standing up the bay under easy sail, their open gun ports leering. Two bomb ketches and three frigates—*Greyhound* and the doughty *Phoenix* and *Rose*—warped into Gravesend Bay, where leadsmen took soundings in shoal water off the Long Island beaches. Fleet boats crisscrossed the anchorage carrying couriers with dispatch cases clutched to their chests. Before daybreak, Admiral Howe had shifted his flag from *Eagle* to *Phoenix* to be nearer the action, and at eight a.m. a blue-and-white striped flag appeared at the mizzen topmast head. A signal gun popped, and the invasion began.

A stately procession of flatboats emerged from Staten Island, each packed with fifty soldiers holding their musket muzzles up to prevent the ball from tumbling out. Twenty oarsmen stroked in unison, and a coxswain cradled the tiller. "It seemed like a bridge of men from Staten Island to Long Island," one of the admiral's aides observed. More redcoats in more boats pushed off from ships in the anchorage, and at eight-thirty a.m. a red flag sent the entire first wave sculling toward shore. A grapnel tossed from each stern served as a kedge anchor, sailors jumped into the surf to steady the bow, and light infantry regulars spilled onto the sand, along with Highlanders, Hessian grenadiers, *Jäger*, and more British foot regiments. In ten minutes, some 4,000 soldiers were coursing across the beach. Empty boats pulled off to fetch the next wave of men, and empty transports swung away from the anchorage to clear room for those carrying more troops into battle.

Before noon 15,000 men had disembarked, including 500 gunners with 40 field cannons, 1,500 Germans, and 120 light horse cavalrymen. Howe put his field headquarters a mile inland at Gravesend, and Hessians began leveling a road to move their artillery, peppering the adjacent woodlots with musket fire to discourage snipers. Behind the invaders from the Lower Bay to the Upper floated more than 400 vessels, including 30 men-of-war, "their sails spread open to dry, the sun shining clear upon them," wrote Ambrose Serle, private secretary to Admiral Howe. "The green hills and meadows after the rain, and the calm surface of the water . . . exhibited one of the finest & most picturesque scenes that imagination can fancy or the eye behold." Reports indicated that the British vanguard under General Cornwallis was pushing six miles inland toward Flatbush, "without the smallest opposition."

Colonel Hand's Pennsylvania riflemen in fact threw a few desultory shots near Denyse's Ferry at the Narrows—a "kind of dirty firing," in the opinion of Captain James Murray, who had returned with Clinton from South Carolina. When the invaders replied with artillery, Hand pulled his men back through New Utrecht to the wooded slopes above Flatbush, burning forage and corn as they retreated, and shooting cows to keep the herds from British commissaries. Fifteen thousand sheep, horses, and horned cattle occupied western Long Island, along with uncounted hogs; militia companies herded them eastward, slaughtering the laggards and removing grinding stones from gristmills. Farm families also fled east in wagons and on foot, lugging a few sticks of furniture or, in one instance, a "great Dutch Bible with its huge brass clasps and brass corners."

Smoke from burning haystacks corkscrewed into the summer sky, and a lurid orange glow persisted even after the sunset faded. "Women and children were running hither and thither," an elderly woman later recalled. "Men on horseback were riding about in all directions." Long Island loyalists emerged to greet the British and to serve as guides for the eventual drive on Brooklyn, a small village along the East River.

"The inhabitants received us with the utmost joy," a British captain wrote. "They like our gold and silver better than the Congress paper money." General Howe pushed more troops ashore, occupying an eight-mile crescent from Denyse's Ferry, on the Narrows, to the Jamaica Bay marshes, in the east. They picked apples, raided abandoned wine cellars, and traded gunshots with rebel skulkers. "The soldiers & sailors seemed as merry as in a holiday," Serle wrote.

Two more Hessian brigades—over 4,000 men—soon crossed from Staten Island, giving Howe more than 20,000 troops on Long Island, among a total army and naval force of 34,000 at New York. "I never saw better stuff," crowed Captain Lord Rawdon, "and they are as keen for action as ever men were." Finally the empire's might seemed poised to deliver a mortal blow.

"After a few beatings, the people will begin to return to their senses," another officer predicted, ". . . wearied with disorder and panting after the sweets of peace."

Washington struggled to sort through the breathless, contradictory reports flooding Mortier mansion from Long Island. The commanding general promptly sent six regiments of reinforcements, but he waited a day, until Friday, August 23, before crossing the East River to judge for himself whether the British gambit was an uncaged assault or a feint.

He guessed wrong, telling Hancock that "eight or nine thousand" enemy troops had landed at Gravesend Bay—less than half their actual number. He surmised that a larger force remained on Staten Island, staging for a possible strike at Manhattan. He clung to that assessment after another visit on Saturday, reporting that the opposing lines were three miles apart and reasonably stable, with "the foreigners"—Hessians—still on Staten Island. Washington dispatched four more Continental regiments, but he kept back much of his army to counter a phantom British blow.

Nathanael Greene's desperate illness meant that command on Long Island had fallen to John Sullivan, recently promoted by Congress to major

general despite his "wants and foibles"—in Washington's arch phrase—
which had been amply revealed in the Canadian rout. On Saturday, Washington concluded that Sullivan's wants were indeed disqualifying: the
American ranks appeared "disorderly & unsoldierlike," and given to "a scattering, unmeaning, & wasteful fire . . . contemptible in the eyes of the enemy."
He ordered Israel Putnam, who held no qualification other than seniority, to
take over the battlefront, the third American commander on the island in
five days and the least fit for the task. Sullivan, irked at being superseded,
would continue to oversee the forward outposts as Putnam's deputy.

A constellation of ten American forts and batteries stretched across
western Long Island. Breastworks had been raised, fields of fire cleared,
cannons emplaced, killing ranges marked with brush piles. Five miles
inland from Gravesend Bay, a rugged ridge called the Heights of Guana—a
glacial moraine deposited seventeen thousand years earlier—loomed like
a natural outer works above the dusty plain now bustling with redcoats.
Roughly four miles long and up to 150 feet high, bearded with oak, ash, chestnut, tulip, and gum, the heights were traversed by four narrow passes, each
held by Continentals. Greene had evidently intended to fall back from the
Heights of Guana to stouter fortifications on Brooklyn Heights a couple of
miles to the northwest, but Sullivan and now Putnam shoved more than
three thousand troops into three of the four gaps, which were too isolated
for mutual reinforcement. The Guana line was thin and brittle; if punctured
anywhere, it was vulnerable everywhere.

Washington had only a cursory grasp of the terrain here and little sense
of the risk in fragmenting his defenses. His surveyor's eye failed to take the
measure of the land he intended to defend; nor had he considered how to
fight a major battle on Long Island. He ordered Putnam to hold the wooded
passes "at all hazards" and to put "your best men" there. "Practical instructions on defending Guana Heights came almost as afterthoughts," the historian Edward G. Lengel later wrote. "A careful survey could have shown
him the difficulty of holding the ridge."

Late afternoon shadows had begun to lengthen on Monday, August 26,
when Washington rode with his lieutenants to the heights, squinting
through the pass above Flatbush at the enemy encampment that stretched
to the sea. American riflemen drifted among the trees along the ridge crest,
each man wearing a green sprig in his hat for easier recognition by comrades. An artillery battery popped away at the old Dutch tobacco-and-barley
village, now crawling with Hessians. Axmen had felled an enormous white
oak across the rough track leading from Flatbush to Brooklyn, paring the
branches into an abatis. Far fewer tents could be seen on Staten Island,
and the British fleet had concentrated in the Narrows.

"They mean to land the main body of their army on Long Island and make their grand push there," Washington told Hancock in a quick note. Or would they? This concentration, he added in a subsequent note to General Heath, "may possibly be only a feint." He had dispatched still more reinforcements from Manhattan, including a fine Delaware regiment that was the largest in his army and a Maryland regiment that was among the best equipped, kitted out with both uniforms and bayonets. Both commanders, however, were ordered to remain in New York to serve on a court-martial board.

Neither Putnam nor Sullivan knew precisely how many American troops now defended Long Island—perhaps no more than eight thousand. The American line thinned severely to the east, particularly since militia troops were busy herding livestock. On the far left, only four hundred rough-hewn Pennsylvanians guarded the road from Bedford to Jamaica above the easternmost gap in the heights, which was considered too remote to be a threat. Sullivan had paid fifty dollars from his own pocket—"for which," he complained, "I was never reimbursed"—to encourage five mounted militia officers to keep watch within the pass itself.

Washington took a last look at the teeming plain below. Hundreds of cook fires now spewed orange sparks into the heavens. Supply wagons rolled inland from the beaches. British and Hessian detachments marched and countermarched. Garbled shouts could be heard, and a few random shots echoed along the dense green face of the ridgeline. The commanding general turned his horse and headed back to the Brooklyn ferry. After returning to his headquarters, he would set aside the cares of this day by devoting a few minutes to Mount Vernon. In an eight-paragraph note to his overseer, Washington offered advice on where best to sell flour, when to plant new trees, and how to find nails to renovate the north end of the house. As for his British enemies here in New York, he confessed before closing the letter, "What their real design is, I know not."

Sputtering gunfire could be heard on the American right flank shortly after midnight on Tuesday, August 27. Pickets from a Pennsylvania battalion had fired on British foragers rooting through a watermelon patch near the Red Lion inn, where Martense Lane from Flatbush and the Narrows road from Denyse's Ferry met the Gowanus road. The regulars returned fire, retreated, and came on again in stronger numbers, their muzzle flashes flaring in the darkness as they slapped the pickets aside. Under orders from Putnam at four-thirty a.m., Delaware and Maryland Continentals sortied toward the sound of the guns under Brigadier General William Alexander, a wealthy New Jersey merchant, slave trader, and amateur scientist who preferred to be known as Lord Stirling in deference to his disputed claim to a Scottish earldom.

From the marsh lining Gowanus Bay to the western knob of the Heights of Guana, sixteen hundred Americans formed a horseshoe defense in the morning twilight as enemy ranks pressed through apple orchards and up the roadbed. The sun "rose with a red and angry glare," a witness recorded, revealing a British force swollen to two brigades of four regiments each—more than seven thousand men, including Highlanders and loyalist volunteers. From the Grand Battery in Manhattan, a Connecticut militiaman watching the distant surge of redcoats reported that "the motion of the men's bodies while under march . . . gleamed like sheets of fire."

Gunners above the Gowanus road unlimbered two American fieldpieces to slash the British lines. Enemy cannons answered with round shot and grape from three hundred yards, and *Roebuck* traded iron shot with the American battery at Red Hook, hard by the mouth of the East River.

"The balls and shells flew very fast, now and then taking off a head," a Marylander wrote. A lieutenant colonel from Pennsylvania took a bullet through the skull and reportedly "fell without a groan," much less a parting word for the five children he left behind. Soldiers darted forward to strip the British dead of cartridges until a Connecticut regiment dragging an ammunition cart reinforced the line. Enemy skirmishers probed the flanks. A thin red line of regulars raised up, sprayed another volley at the rebels, then stepped back to reload as a second line rose to fire—"battle in the true English taste," a Continental wrote. Another added, "Our men stood it amazingly well." After two hours the gunfire faded and the British retreated two hundred yards. Lord Stirling nursed the delusion that the Continental Army, in open-field battle for the first time against the British, had repulsed the empire.

General Sullivan, in the American center, was likewise deceived. German cannon fire had erupted from Flatbush at dawn, followed by a surge of five thousand Hessians and Scots. Grenadiers and green-coated *Jäger* advanced in skirmish order toward the Guana wood line, trailed by regiments with flashing bayonets. Bullets chewed at the foliage around the white oak barricade, but here too the enemy tide soon faltered and receded, except for artillery and mortar salvos. Continentals peered south through their abatis and from behind tree trunks, bracing for the next assault.

They were looking in the wrong direction. Since his humiliating return from Charleston in early August, Henry Clinton had badgered General Howe with ideas for destroying Washington's army, preferably by outmaneuvering the Americans. "My zeal may perhaps on these occasions have carried me so far as to be at times thought troublesome," Clinton later conceded. Always eager to study the ground, he undertook something no Continental general had bothered to do: he carefully examined the terrain on western Long Island, including the remote bottomland stretching toward Jamaica. Having spent his boyhood in New York, Clinton found the topography familiar, particularly with the help of fine British maps. His subsequent proposal, made two days before the attack from Staten Island, was as old as warfare: fix the enemy in front with a robust feint, then attack his flank. "That, once possessed, gives you the island," he promised.

Howe and his staff at first demurred, condemning the maneuver scheme as "savoring too much of the German school" and arguing, absurdly, that "as the rebels knew nothing of turning a flank, such a movement would have no effect." But after a day of pondering the Heights of Guana, which bore an unsettling tactical resemblance to Bunker Hill, Howe acquiesced. The British commander in chief "did not expect any good from the move," Clinton later wrote, but he agreed to give his tenacious deputy full authority over ten thousand men.

At nine p.m. on Monday, after the last magenta streaks faded in the western sky, the British and their loyalist guides set off northeast from Flatlands, an old Dutch hamlet just inland from Jamaica Bay. Clinton left his campfires burning and his tents standing. Scattering flankers and skirmishers for security, he posted a regiment north of the road "for the purpose of drowning the noise of our cannon over the stones, masking our march, and preventing the enemy's patrols from discovering it." Even with the ranks closed up, the column stretched for nearly two miles under a rising moon three days from full. Cornwallis trailed Clinton, and was followed in turn by Howe and General Percy. Grenadiers, light infantry, and the 17th Light Dragoons came on, along with forty guns, including 3-pounders on agile new carriages and four 12-pounders with the baggage train in the rear. So silent was their movement as they trudged past drove lanes and stone walls that it was said the army's footfall "could scarcely be heard at ten rods' distance"—fifty-five yards. Crossing a narrow bridge over a salt creek, the column slowed, stopped, started, and stopped again. Captain Murray of the 57th Regiment complained the delays were "just long enough to drop asleep and to be disturbed again in order to proceed twenty yards in the same manner."

At two a.m. on Tuesday, a quarter mile from the Rising Sun tavern, Clinton sent forward a mounted patrol under Captain Glanville Evelyn, whose faithful service in Boston and at Sullivan's Island had been rewarded with a position at the head of the column. Evelyn soon returned with five despondent prisoners: the equestrian officers paid to watch the Heights of Guana's easternmost pass on Sullivan's left flank had been captured without firing a shot after mistaking the British horsemen for Americans. Clinton interrogated them, then rousted the tavern owner and his young son, whom he forced to guide his vanguard up a twisting, wooded bridle path across the ridge. Engineers widened the trail with saws rather than noisy axes, extra horses were hitched to pull gun carriages to the brow of the hill, and the column took three hours to move less than two miles. But by dawn Clinton's lead brigade had crossed the heights to straddle the Bedford road. Howe, reportedly wearing a herringbone cloak over his uniform against the chill, soon rode forward to join the front ranks. "The fortune of the day," Captain Murray wrote, "repaid us for the labors of the night."

Stray shooting belatedly alerted the Americans to trouble on their left. Colonel Samuel Miles, who commanded the Pennsylvania militia rifle regiment above Flatbush, hurried two miles through the woods to the Bedford road. "To my great mortification," he later wrote, "I saw the main body of the enemy in full march between me and our lines." A British force had covered ten miles in the dark to fall on the American rear by "a route we never dreamed of," a rifleman conceded. Fighting a hapless rearguard action from hill to hill and tree to tree, Miles and more than 150 of his men would be captured. Others were shot dead or drowned trying to flee through millponds.

"This plan succeeded even beyond our expectations," General Percy wrote his father, "for we were on their flank & in their rear before they knew what we were about." At eight-thirty a.m., Clinton, Howe, and Cornwallis approached Bedford village, only two miles from the main rebel defenses in Brooklyn. "From this instant," Clinton reported, "the enemy showed no disposition to stand." Thirty minutes later he ordered two guns fired in quick succession to signal British forces on the Gowanus road and at Flatbush that the rebels were almost surrounded. The shots echoed and reechoed, like the sound of doom. The catastrophe had begun.

No sooner had the double shots been heard outside Flatbush than the Hessians and Highlanders surged up the heights, this time in earnest. General Leopold Philip de Heister, commanding all German forces in America, urged his *Jäger* forward in loose order through the thick brush, searching for rebels in "the coverts and lurking places." Blue-coated Hessian regiments followed with their lines dressed and their colors flying, drums and hautboys playing as if the ranks were parading "on the Landgrave's birthday," one witness reported. Several hundred Massachusetts troops buckled and broke, abandoning a damask flag embroidered with the word "LIBERTY."

"When they caught only a glimpse of a blue coat, they surrendered immediately and begged on their knees for their lives," Heister reported. "I am surprised that the British troops have achieved so little against these people." With each surrender, the captors let out a triumphant bellow. A Hessian lieutenant told his diary, "The prisoners who knelt and sought to surrender were beaten." Some were harnessed to gun carriages and forced to pull enemy cannons across the ridge until dray horses could be brought up.

General Sullivan had also heard the signal guns, and the crackle of musketry from Colonel Miles's beleaguered Pennsylvanians in the rear told him that his flank had been turned. Across the heights, hundreds of Americans leaked to the rear to find British dragoons and light infantry across their escape paths. "They lay in ambush for us in cornfields and behind walls and the like places," a Massachusetts captain wrote. Cannoneers tried to wheel three field guns to bear on the British ranks, but guardsmen swarmed over the battery. "The English gave little quarter to the enemy," a Hessian colonel reported, "and encouraged our men to do the same thing." A British officer, in turn, professed to be "greatly shocked by the massacres made by the Hessians and Highlanders after victory was decided."

Caught between Clinton's column on the Bedford road and the Hessian-and-Highlander legions cascading over the heights, the Americans ran, hid, then ran some more, chased by whining bullets and braying foes. In a letter home, a soldier later described Sullivan in retreat: "He was in a corn-field close by our lines, with a pistol in each hand. . . . The enemy had formed a line each side of him, and he was going directly between them." He was not going far. At noon three Hessian grenadiers found Sullivan hiding in a grain patch and took him prisoner.

With the collapse of the American left and center, only General Alexander's right wing remained intact. The moonfaced "Lord Stirling," in combat for the first time, seemed a frail reed upon which to lean rebel hopes. Described by his biographer as an "overweight, rheumatic, vain, pompous, gluttonous inebriate," he had run through several fortunes totaling almost £100,000 with his spendthrift ways and aristocratic pretensions, including expenditures for a heavily mortgaged, thousand-acre New Jersey estate with piazzas, a deer park, painted drawing rooms, a wardrobe holding thirty-one coats and fifty-eight vests, and carriages embossed with the coat of arms he claimed as his patrimony. In an effort to raise cash, he had organized a private lottery—George Washington bought sixty tickets—yet still lost money, and was forced to sell many household goods at public auction. Hounded by creditors, flirting with bankruptcy, he drank his way through the war—or so Aaron Burr claimed—attended by a faithful cupbearer named James Monroe. Nevertheless, he was courageous and devoted to the cause, and on August 27, 1776, as one regimental commander testified, "General Lord Stirling fought like a wolf."

The British horde pounding up the Gowanus road under Major General James Grant had swelled to nine thousand men after marine reinforcements with ammunition tumbrels landed in Bennet's Cove at ten a.m. In the absence of orders from Sullivan or a defensive plan from Putnam, Stirling began a fighting retreat only to realize that enemy grenadiers and Highlanders from the 71st Foot blocked the route to Brooklyn Heights. Hessians soon appeared on the slopes to his left, manning field guns to scorch the rebels with plunging fire. Stirling's command began to disintegrate. The 17th Continental lingered too long on the high ground and found itself surrounded; soldiers bolted down game trails or hid from the Germans in hopes of surrendering to the British, believed to be less cruel. Capitulation shouts of "Pardon! Pardon!" carried through the glens. A Pennsylvania regiment fled northeast—"We were obliged to run for near two miles," one officer reported—drawing Hessian volley fire not far from the Flatbush road. "The poltroons ran in the most broken, disgraceful, and precipitate manner," a regular later complained. Some of the Pennsylvanians hid in thickets or in swamp water to their knees. But by midafternoon most had clubbed their firelocks—lowering the muzzles with the butt held high in surrender—and were herded to British prisoner compounds near Jamaica.

Reduced to less than a thousand men, his command facing annihilation, Stirling quickly detached four hundred Marylanders to fight as a rear guard. The rest—Maryland and Delaware troops whose regimental commanders had missed the battle while on court-martial duty in Manhattan—were to break through the British cordon as best they could. Off they marched with shot-torn colors in a double column, herding two dozen enemy prisoners. Half a mile up the Gowanus road they veered left into a serene landscape of ponds and waving rushes; for more than a century Dutch farmers had dammed the salt creeks to cultivate oyster beds and operate mills that ran every six hours as the changing tides coursed up and down narrow flumes. Wading through neck-deep water—the tide was in—they lost seven unlucky men to drowning, but most escaped, clinging to driftwood or an old canoe, prodding their prisoners and encouraged by covering fire from riflemen on the far bank. "When they came out of the water and mud to us, looking like water rats, it was truly a pitiful sight," Private Joseph Plumb Martin later wrote.

Stirling followed up the road with his rearguard Marylanders, breathing hard in the summer heat and lacerated by cannon and musket fire. Only the wind favored the Americans: a northeast breeze kept Admiral Howe's men-of-war from sailing up the East River, where they could have butchered the rebel flank with broadsides. Rather than crowd into the salt marshes with enemy gunmen on his heels, Stirling kept his men moving on the Gowanus road. "Close up!" officers yelled at stragglers. "Close up!" Redcoats fell back to the Vechte farmhouse, a two-story fieldstone building with brick chimneys poking above the gables. Here the fiercest fighting of the day surged back and forth, as the Americans charged, fell back, and charged again in a maelstrom of smoke and singing lead. On Cornwallis's order, British gunners hurried two fieldpieces forward to check the rebels with canister shot, but again the Marylanders heaved toward the house, forcing the enemy inside. Stirling, another officer reported, "animated our young soldiers with almost invincible resolution."

And then it ended. Cornwallis summoned reinforcements, Hessians and grenadiers pressed the rebel flanks with galling fire, and the unholy din faded to a few random gunshots and the usual pathetic cries from the wounded. Several score Americans scattered through the woods or splashed across Gowanus Creek. "We were drove with much precipitation and confusion," Major Mordecai Gist, the Maryland commander, later wrote. More than 250 others lay dead or were captured, including the lupine Stirling, who surrendered to General Heister. Three of the five Maryland companies fighting in the rear guard had been obliterated, and the other two were dreadfully mauled.

A chaplain watching from a redoubt on Brooklyn Heights told his journal, "O doleful! Doleful! Doleful! Blood! Carnage! Fire!" Lieutenant Enoch Anderson of Delaware, who escaped by wading to his chin past a milldam despite a bullet wound in the neck, wrote simply, "A hard day this."

Washington had watched the final struggle from the crown of Cobble Hill, a conical elevation where a four-gun battery had been emplaced a mile northwest of the Vechte house. "Great God!" he was quoted as muttering. "What must my brave boys suffer today?" On this hard day they had indeed suffered: General Howe would list almost twelve hundred American prisoners taken, including three generals, three colonels, and four lieutenant colonels, plus thirty-two cannons seized. A Hessian commander was astonished to find his enemy's officers to be so low-born. "Among the prisoners are many so-called colonels, lieutenant colonels, majors, and other officers who, however, are nothing but mechanics, tailors, shoemakers, wigmakers, barbers, etc."

Howe estimated the total American casualties, including killed and wounded, at 3,300. That was undoubtedly a considerable exaggeration, perhaps as a propaganda ploy. Battle losses, exclusive of the large number captured, likely amounted to a few hundred. British and Hessian casualties totaled 376, including 61 regulars and 2 Germans killed. The Heights of Guana and the Gowanus road grew ripe in the August sun. "The woods near Brooklyn are so noisome with the stench of the dead bodies of the rebels, whom the Hessians and the Highlanders followed thither & destroyed, that they are quite inaccessible," Ambrose Serle reported. A German chaplain wrote home, "The slaughter was horrible. . . . I went over the battlefield among the dead, who mostly had been hacked and shot all to pieces."

Some American units were all but extinguished. The 17th Continental, already desolated by sickness, recorded 208 killed or missing of some 250 men engaged. "After the battle on Long Island," Private Solomon Ingham later wrote, "our regiment was much scattered and torn." Among Washington's brave boys was Colonel Philip Johnston, a Princeton graduate and the son of a judge, shot dead on his thirty-fifth birthday. Captain Joseph Jewett, a company commander, had been bayoneted in the chest and belly—reportedly after surrendering—and was then taken prisoner. "Captain Jewett decayed gradually through the whole day," a captured American lieutenant named Jabez Fitch wrote. "About 2 in the morning [he] was sensible of his being near his end, often repeating that it was hard work to die." Die he did, at five a.m. on August 29. Comrades buried him in an orchard. In a Bible found in the farmhouse that served as a jail for American officers, Lieutenant Fitch took comfort from an epistle to the Ephesians often attributed to St. Paul: "I therefore, the prisoner of the Lord, beseech you that ye walk worthy of the vocation wherewith ye are called."

Those who lived to fight another day were often astonished at their survival. "My preservation I only attribute to the indulgent providence of God," a Pennsylvania rifleman wrote, "for tho' the bullets went around me in every direction, yet I received not a wound." A Maryland officer spared drowning in a salt creek observed, "My height was of use to me, as I touched almost all the way."

No battle in the eight-year war would be larger in the number of combatants—more than forty thousand, naval forces included—and few would be more lopsided. American prisoners huddled in fields and along the shoreline, Serle wrote, "so many that we are perplexed where to confine them." British commanders on Long Island swaggered and crowed. "If a good bleeding can bring those Bible-faced Yankees to their senses," wrote

General Grant, "the fever of independence should soon abate." A Hessian captain added, "After this day, I think we shall hear no more of the riflemen. They have been exterminated from the face of the earth." When the news reached England a few weeks later, celebratory bells pealed and cannons thundered. A huge bonfire in Leeds made the town "quite luminous," and in Limerick the bishop threw a celebratory dinner for the better sort. English stock prices rose in Amsterdam, and in London the king's ministers and their acolytes congratulated one another on the imminent end of the rebellion.

For the Americans, defeat brought despondency and exhaustion. "My ancient corporeal fabric is almost tottering under the fatigue I have lately undergone," wrote a New Jersey officer. Soldiers doubted their field officers, field officers doubted their generals. Finger-pointing abounded. "Less generalship never was shown in any army since the art of war was understood," a lieutenant colonel charged. Nathanael Greene, barely able to sit up in his sickbed, wept at the reports from Long Island. "Gracious God!" he wrote. "To be confined at such a time!"

Faith in Washington plummeted. "Would to heaven General Lee were here, is the language of officers and men," a Delaware colonel reported. Such doubts were justified. The commanding general had misread the battlefield and botched the battle. Though Congress wanted New York defended, Washington had failed to recognize that holding Long Island—the key to holding New York—would be impossible with a weak, divided, overmatched army that lacked naval power. Once the fight began, he did little more than stand on his fortified hill and wait for the bad news to drift in. Even as darkness descended on Tuesday night, he neglected to realize that the Heights of Guana had been completely lost. In the coming days he would tell Hancock that he could still defend New York "if the men would do their duty," an unseemly affront toward the troops by their leader. In his first true test as a battle captain, Washington was found wanting. "In general," John Adams tartly concluded, "our generals were outgeneraled." Washington's best, most redeeming qualities would have to emerge on another field, on another day.

For the moment, his country and his soldiers tried to regroup and affect a dogged determination. "The panic may seize whom it will," Adams declared, "it shall not seize me." Henry Knox mourned the gunners he had lost. "They fought like heroes," he told Lucy, "and are gone to glory." But he suspected there was more pain and sorrow to come. "We want great men, who when fortune frowns will not be discouraged," Knox added. "It is, as I always said, misfortunes that must raise us to the character of a great people."

*   *   *

After leading the flank attack that unhinged the American outer works, General Clinton had hoped to complete the rout by charging through rebel defenses on Brooklyn Heights to pin the enemy against the East River. But William Howe halted the assault in mid-career. "The troops had for that day done handsomely enough," he declared.

On Tuesday night, British tents sprouted two thousand yards south of the Continental pickets. Howe wanted "a cheap and complete victory," as one subordinate noted, but preferably without a headlong assault. Even now rifle bullets from Yankee snipers on the ramparts "continually whistled over our heads and lodged in the trees above us," a British captain reported. Fouled British muskets needed cleaning, the regulars had not eaten a proper meal since Monday, and the ranks were burdened with more than a thousand enemy prisoners. Howe ordered the rebels reduced "by regular approaches"—a formal siege—and on Wednesday night four hundred sappers began digging the first assault trench less than seven hundred yards from the American works.

Some would accuse Howe of timidity, but, as he later told Parliament, he believed Washington still retained his "main army" on Manhattan Island, available as reinforcements. Scrutinizing the American defenses on Brooklyn Heights with his spyglass, he found that they extended for a mile and a half, with parapets, ditches, and an abatis. The enemy redoubts mounted almost forty cannons, most with greater range and weight than British field guns. The regulars had no scaling ladders or fascines with which to cross the ditches. Howe estimated that a frontal attack would cost a thousand to fifteen hundred British casualties, wastage he deemed "inconsiderate, and even criminal," given how precious combat troops were in transatlantic warfare. Cornwallis and other subordinates urged caution as well. Captain Montresor, an experienced engineer now serving Howe as an aide-de-camp, likened the current tactical disadvantage to the ill-conceived, bloody British assault against entrenched French troops at Fort Carillon in 1758. Howe no doubt also recalled Bunker Hill.

Howe may have assumed that his brother could block the East River, severing the line of retreat from Brooklyn. The admiral had, in fact, ordered Sir Peter Parker—recently returned from Sullivan's Island with his wounds healed and his britches repaired—to position five warships up the tidal strait. But the northeast wind persisted, and none could get closer than *Roebuck*, still trading shots with rebel gunners at Red Hook. Given the treacherous shoals and sluicing tides in the East River, no prudent captain wanted to run aground within range of American batteries; the memory of Charleston was too raw. The fireship attack on the Hudson two weeks earlier also gave them pause. "The rebels have six fireships now in sight lying close under cannon of the town," Captain Sir George Collier told Admiral Howe. A sudden sortie through the British anchorage could cost "half of our transports and merchant ships." The admiral ordered protective booms around his vessels, and ten armed skiffs rowed guard a mile above the fleet.

For the moment, General Howe was content to tighten his grip on western Long Island. Flying columns extracted loyalty oaths and seized livestock. A British declaration threatened to "lay waste the property of the disobedient, as persons unworthy of His Majesty's clemency." Some five thousand Long Islanders fled, many to the wharves at Sag Harbor in hopes of passage to Connecticut. But thousands of loyalists seemed eager to help the king's troops: when Howe requested two hundred wagons to move British baggage, local men sent three hundred. By Thursday morning, despite heavy rain, the initial siege trench, one thousand feet long, was finished; a second sap began that would carry assault troops and guns under the brow of the American defenses, as the historian Barnet Schecter later wrote. All day and into the evening, the ominous sound of picks and shovels carried into the American lines.

For two days and two nights, American pickets had waited for the red line of regulars to surge headlong across Brooklyn's muddy fields. More than a hundred men with strong throwing arms stood along the perimeter, each ready to repel attackers with a half dozen crude grenades. Others held sharp pikes to fend off an enemy cavalry charge. But no charge came.

The steady downpour flooded trenches and kept some sentries in water to their waists. Rain also doused cook fires, forcing the Americans to eat their salt pork raw. Colonel Reed estimated that fewer than half of the men had tents; all had begun "to sink under the fatigues and hardships." Twitchy trigger fingers caused so many bullets to whiz through the bivouac "that it seemed dangerous to walk within our own lines," a chaplain complained. Washington continued shifting regiments from Manhattan, and now almost ten thousand men crowded a Brooklyn camp only three miles across. They had been joined by hundreds of Long Island refugee families driving their flocks and herds away from marauding redcoats. A thousand lowing cows wandered the streets.

Washington was alive to his peril. Reed told him of enemy men-of-war beating toward Red Hook, clearly seeking passage up the East River. Another officer, at Wallabout Bay on the American left, passed word that jittery militia troops were too unreliable to be trusted if fighting resumed. The redoubts in Brooklyn might be strong, Washington knew, but the breastworks between were weak. Some abatis had been built of little more than piled brush, no match against sophisticated British siege works. Hundreds of sick and wounded men had been rowed across the river to Manhattan, then carried in the rain to makeshift hospitals. The army reeked of defeat.

At five p.m. on Thursday, August 29, Washington summoned eight of his generals to Four Chimneys, a commodious house in Brooklyn a few steps from the river. Signalmen on the roof waggled flags at the telegraph station in lower Manhattan, a mile to the west. The commanding general wasted no time in putting the question: whether "under all circumstances it would not be eligible to leave Long Island and its dependencies, and remove the army to New York?" Without dissent, his lieutenants voted to evacuate. Among the eight reasons they offered: "our advanced party had met with a defeat," "great confusion and discouragement among the troops," and the wet weather had "spoiled a great part of the ammunition." Washington sent the minutes of the meeting to Philadelphia so Congress would know that he was following "the unanimous advice of all the general officers."

Orders tumbled out. Officers were to collect "every kind of watercraft . . . that could be kept afloat and had either oars or sails," from Spuyten Duyvil Creek, on the northwest shore of Manhattan, to Hell Gate, up the East River. Within a few hours, more than fifty rowboats, scows, pettiaugers, sloops, and schooners converged along the Brooklyn banks, joined by ten flatboats. To conceal the withdrawal, officers were told that the boats would be used to transport reinforcements from New Jersey to Long Island.

One by one Washington's regiments withdrew from the line on Thursday night and shuffled toward the ferry landing above Four Chimneys. Those able to build campfires in the damp night left them burning. The *chink-chink* of British digging could be heard to the southwest. Passwords and countersigns—"Sullivan" and "Greene"—were exchanged in hoarse whispers. Although sergeants cautioned the men not to talk or even cough, one officer described "a deep murmur in the camp which indicated some movement." Hundreds of fretful soldiers, said to be "infected with ungovernable alarm," crowded the riverbank until sentries pushed them back with bayonets. An officer later reported that Washington himself lifted a huge stone above an overloaded skiff and threatened to "sink it to hell" unless order was restored.

Two web-footed Massachusetts regiments, the 14th and 27th Continentals, now took charge of the evacuation and coaxed order from chaos. Fishermen and sailors from Marblehead, Salem, and other briny precincts, they wore blue jackets, white caps, and canvas trousers tarred to shed water. One admirer described them as "hardy, adroit, and weatherproof." Muffling their oars with rags, they rowed the first boatloads of men through spitting rain toward the Manhattan wharves around Fly Market Slip, where a breastworks built from old spars had been chinked with stones and broken junk bottles. The northeast wind and an ebb tide kept sailing vessels moored until eleven p.m., when the breeze abruptly shifted around from the southwest, smoothing the river chop and allowing sailors to unfurl their canvas. By early Friday, watermen were evacuating a thousand soldiers an hour, each vessel so laden that the gunwales sat just inches above the black water. Back and forth they shuttled, silent but for the odd creak of a tiller or an ungreased oarlock.

At two a.m. a providential fogbank settled over Brooklyn—"the pillar of a cloud," in Lieutenant Enoch Anderson's description. "I could scarcely discern a man at six yards' distance," wrote Lieutenant Benjamin Tallmadge. For the last regiments left in the line, the tension grew excruciating as daylight approached, particularly when confused instructions sent some units hurrying prematurely toward the river only to be ordered back to their parapets. False reports of approaching British cavalry caused one Pennsylvania regiment to halt halfway to the water with their pikemen deployed, listening for hoofbeats. At length, every man bolted for the safety of the riverbank. "We very joyfully bid those trenches a long adieu," Lieutenant Tallmadge recorded. The rear guard was ordered "to choke up the street with wagons and carts to prevent the light horse from rushing down upon us."

Yet as dawn brightened the fog, no enemy dragoons appeared. Just before daybreak, Captain Montresor had tiptoed close enough to the rebel works to realize that American sentinels had abandoned their forward posts. Rushing back to Bedford, he alerted General Howe, then clattered forward with a combat patrol. Together they hacked through the abatis—"I was the first person in the works," Montresor later said—but found the enemy gone except for some entrenching tools, a few cows and horses, and three plundering Yankees who had lingered too long in the camp. The last boats could be dimly seen gliding through the gray mist toward Manhattan. One of them carried General Washington. British horsemen galloped to a hill above the river and fired a few carbine rounds. They hit nothing but fog.

"Since Monday scarce any of us have been out of the lines till our passage across the East River was effected yesterday morning," Washington wrote Hancock on Saturday, "and for forty-eight hours preceding that I had hardly been off my horse and never closed my eyes." Back in the Mortier house, he slept the sleep of the saved, confident that he had rescued his army and redeemed his reputation.

"Never was a greater feat of generalship shown than in this retreat," Lieutenant Colonel James Chambers, a Pennsylvanian in the 1st Continental, told his wife, "to bring off an army of twelve thousand men, within sight of a strong enemy possessed of as strong a fleet as ever floated on our seas, without any loss, and saving all the baggage." If Colonel Chambers slightly exaggerated the number of troops plucked from Long Island, his point was taken. "In the history of warfare," Lieutenant Tallmadge wrote, "I do not recollect a more fortunate retreat." Even the garrison on Governors Island had escaped with its tents and provisions despite a bombardment from the *Roebuck*, although ten heavy guns were abandoned. General Putnam, who had nearly lost an army and perhaps the cause, voiced contempt for his enemy. "General Howe is either our friend or no general," he said. "He had our whole army in his power . . . and yet suffered us to escape without the least disruption."

Captain Collier, commander of the *Rainbow*, was among many abashed British officers. "To my inexpressible astonishment and concern, the rebel army have all escaped," he wrote. "I foresee they will give us trouble enough and protract the war, heaven knows how long." Yet the force that straggled back into Manhattan would give no one trouble in the near future. "The merry tones of drums and fifes had ceased," Pastor Ewald Shewkirk told his diary. "Many looked sickly, emaciated, cast down, etc." A captain described New York as "a scene of tumult and confusion and, it might be added, dismay." Colonel William Douglas told his wife in Connecticut, "I expect we soon [will] have a cannonade from our own battery on Long Island, which I have the mortification to think I helped build. . . . We have reason to lament the frowns of heaven on our army."

Of Washington's sixty-seven infantry regiments, forty-two were militia units, rife with sickness and so much desertion that he ordered a straggler line erected at King's Bridge to stop absconders. "Our situation is truly distressing," he wrote Hancock on September 2.

> The militia . . . are dismayed, intractable, and impatient to return [home]. Great numbers of them have gone off, in some instances almost by whole regiments. Their example has infected another part of the army. . . . Our liberties must of necessity be greatly hazarded, if not entirely lost, if their defense is left to any but a permanent, standing army. . . . It would be criminal to conceal the truth at so critical a juncture.

Long Island was forfeit—for seven years and two months, as it turned out—and the American hold on Manhattan seemed tenuous. A day later, Washington's chief engineer, Colonel Rufus Putnam, warned him, "I have reconnoitered every part about the island of New York and . . . find the enemy have such a variety of places to choose out of, that it's impossible to prevent their landing when they please." Many New Yorkers hardly bothered to conceal their glee at British success. "How long we shall stay here is uncertain," a Massachusetts officer wrote his wife in early September. "Our public enemies are numerous, our private ones not a few."

Whatever contempt General Putnam and others felt for the enemy was fully reciprocated. Redcoats stood on the far bank of the East River and yelled insults at the rebels. "They have shewn the greatest pusillanimity that can be imagined from men who pretend to fight for liberty and independence," Lieutenant Loftus Cliffe of the 46th Foot wrote in a letter home. Fifteen hundred Hessians swept through the abandoned American camp, burning hospitals, bedding straw, and anything else they could not loot. Black shafts of smoke rose over Brooklyn. The Howe brothers and their commanders gathered themselves to deliver a lethal stroke to the rebels, once and for all.

"They will never again stand before us in the field," General Percy assured his father from Long Island. "Things seem to be over with them, & I flatter myself that this campaign will put a total end to the war."

16.

A Sentimental Manner of Making War

O arsmen draped in dark cloaks took their seats on the thwarts of two whaleboats just before midnight on Friday, September 6. Not for another hour would the crescent moon rise, and dim starlight blued the stubby dock jutting from Whitehall Battery, on Manhattan's southern tip. From the stern of each boat a trailing rope had been lashed to a vessel shaped like an upright barrel and described by one rebel soldier as "a machine altogether different from anything hitherto devised by the art of man." A sinewy Connecticut sergeant named Ezra Lee lowered himself into the contraption through a narrow opening and pulled shut the brass hatch. On order, the oarsmen stroked away from the shoreline, towing Sergeant Lee behind them as they headed toward Bedloe's Island, two miles southwest.

Hundreds of silhouetted masts and yardarms could be seen poking the stars in the British anchorage. The clang of ships' bells carried across the Upper Bay. Dead ahead loomed the largest and newest of the enemy men-of-war, the sixty-four-gun *Eagle*, moored just off Bedloe's near the New Jersey shore with a crew of more than six hundred men. After a few final strokes, the rowers shipped their oars, cast off the ropes, and swung back to Manhattan, leaving Sergeant Lee to submerge in his odd vessel—the *Turtle*—with the intent of blowing Admiral Howe's flagship out of the water.

Back on the Whitehall dock, the *Turtle*'s inventor could only pace and wait, an ear cocked expectantly for the sound of 150 pounds of gunpowder detonating under *Eagle*'s keel. David Bushnell, a frail farmer's son from Saybrook, Connecticut, had been toiling on his "water machine" for five years, since entering Yale College to read divinity and mathematics at the unorthodox age of thirty-one. After demonstrating that powder could explode underwater—two pounds in a wooden canister blew a hogshead packed with stones far into the air—Bushnell built his vessel from six-inch oak planks girdled with iron bands, meticulously caulking the seams with cork and tar. Seven hundred pounds of lead bolted to the bottom provided ballast, and six small glass ports in the hatch collar admitted light when the vessel was in surface trim, while also allowing the operator modest visibility. A ventilator drew fresh air through one brass tube while stale air was expelled through a second tube; check valves on both snorkels closed automatically to keep out seawater when submerged. The pilot could dive a few fathoms by using a foot treadle to open a valve that flooded the bilge; to surface, two pumps emptied the water to restore buoyancy. Though skeptical of Bushnell's secret project, Washington had provided a small stipend to help him finish it. The commanding general then ordered the *Turtle*—"an effort of genius," he later admitted—brought to New York by wagon and dinghy. He, too, hoped to hear the sound of a British man-of-war blown to kingdom come.

Two miles from the dock, Sergeant Lee struggled to reach his target. An unexpectedly strong tide had carried him down the bay, and for almost three hours he crept back to the west, turning a crank connected to a twelve-inch propeller while steering with a tiller attached through the hull to a small rudder. The first pale gleams of daylight had streaked the eastern horizon when he finally approached the looming frigate, guided by sailors' voices spilling from her upper deck. Lee pushed his foot treadle, seawater gurgled into the bilge, and *Turtle* settled below the surface, easing under the *Eagle*'s broad stern.

Turtle carried on her back a hollowed oak powder magazine that was attached by a rope to a sharp iron auger; Lee was to screw the auger into the frigate's keel, using a handle above his head near the hatch. He would then set the timing mechanism, made for Bushnell by a watchmaker and connected to a gunlock trigger, to detonate the powder in an hour. After jettisoning the magazine—still tied to the auger embedded in *Eagle*'s hull—he would make his escape.

But there would be no blast, no shattered ship tossed from the sea like a hogshead of rocks. The auger would not bite; by mischance, Lee was trying to drill into a heavy metal bar that held the frigate's rudder hinge to the stern. When he shifted *Turtle* in search of better purchase, she abruptly bobbed to the surface next to the frigate, "like a porpoise." With dawn breaking through his little deadlights, as Lee later reported, "I thought the best generalship was to retreat as fast as I could." Cranking his propeller furiously, he crept back across the bay in a heavy swell, surfacing frequently to check his heading.

Abreast of Governors Island and fully exposed by the morning light, Lee spotted several hundred redcoats crowding the parapet, pointing and gaping at the odd craft zigzagging toward Manhattan. Abruptly a twelve-oared British barge put in and gave chase. When the pursuers had closed within fifty yards, Lee armed his powder charge and cut loose the oak magazine. Suspecting a Yankee trick, the barge sheered away—"to my infinite joy," Lee admitted. An American whaleboat dispatched from the Whitehall Battery towed him to the wharf, where General Putnam and David Bushnell waited to hear his report.

Twenty minutes later, the magazine detonated off Governors Island with a stupendous roar, a witness wrote, lifting "a vast column of water to an amazing height." British ships across the Upper Bay beat to quarters and cut their cables amid fearful speculation about "a bomb, a meteor, a water-spout, or an earthquake," a Connecticut officer recorded. Vice Admiral Howe, unaware that the age of submarine warfare had dawned with this day, stood on *Eagle*'s quarterdeck, scanning the silver bay for enemies. Two miles away, Putnam preened along the water's edge shouting, "God curse 'em! That'll do it for 'em!" Soldiers with block and tackle hoisted *Turtle* onto a sloop for transport up the Hudson to Fort Washington in hopes of better luck on another day.

The narrow escape was only the latest and would not be the last for Richard Howe in a swashbuckling career that spanned six decades and seven seas. Known as "Black Dick" for his swarthy complexion, he was burly, weathered, and heavy-browed—"a pretty man does not make a good portrait," the painter Joshua Reynolds said of him in admiration. At four-teen he had left Eton for the Royal Navy, ascending steadily through the ranks and earning a reputation for courage, seamanship, and progressive ideas, both nautical and political. At sixteen he was aboard the *Burford* when a failed attack in the West Indies left her captain and two dozen ship-mates dead; Howe wept at the memory when testifying during an inquest. Off the Barbary Coast he displayed his diplomatic skills by inviting two hundred Moors aboard *Dolphin* for rum punch, which he called "sherbet." While he was commanding *Dunkirk* off Newfoundland in June 1755, his double-shotted broadside blew through the *Alcide*, forcing the French ship to strike and surrender nine hundred men in a scrap considered the first action of the Seven Years' War.

Many more scraps followed. In attacking shore batteries on the island of Aix, Howe closed within forty yards, hollered through a speaking trum-pet for his men to fall flat on the deck to duck enemy fire, and within half an hour forced the French to abandon their guns. Enemy colors captured in another gallant action, this one at Cherbourg, were displayed in Hyde Park, then paraded to the Tower. Once, when an agitated young lieutenant brought news of fire aboard ship, Howe asked, "How does a man *feel* when he is frightened? I need not ask how he *looks*." In November 1759 aboard *Magnanime*, Howe led a British squadron under Sir Edward Hawke into Quiberon Bay through a rising gale in shoal waters on a dead lee shore. Throwing chicken coops and the ship's launch overboard to lighten his draft, he blasted away at *Formidable*, killing the French captain before capturing that ship and then another. The battle at Quiberon proved to be the greatest English sea victory since Drake's day, a triumph that confirmed Britain as a world power. "Give us Black Dick," his sailors boasted, "and we fear nothing."

Now fifty, three years older than his brother William, he was esteemed as a pioneer in gunnery, amphibious tactics, and naval hygiene, including the careful scrubbing of decks and sailors' togs. Even as a vice admiral he fussed over details—kedge anchors, medicos, spar lengths—and his forty-four-page signal book, embossed in gold and stiff with salt, included twenty-four different warnings for fog. On land he was admired for his constancy as a husband—a virtue prized partly for its rarity—and his devoted service in Parliament, where he advocated better pay for mariners. When not at sea or taking the waters in Bath, he could often be found at his Hertfordshire estate, with its descending lawns, fine prospects north and west, and a library that later replicated the admiral's cabin aboard the hundred-gun *Queen Charlotte*. Walpole wrote that Howe was "undaunted as a rock, and as silent." But his opinions, when voiced, could also be double-shotted: recently, when he'd argued with the king over colonial policy during dinner, George had questioned the propriety of cursing one's monarch within earshot of the servants.

Yet in February the king had extended his hand for the admiral to kiss, confirming his appointment as naval commander in chief of the North American station. The selection provoked some skepticism. It was said in London that "Lord Howe both hates and despises Lord Sandwich," an unpromising enmity between one of the navy's preeminent salts and the Admiralty's first lord. Like his brother, Richard Howe hoped for reconciliation rather than a protracted, sanguinary civil war, and he supposed that most Americans either remained loyal to the Crown or were afflicted with a rebellious "contagion" that could be cured.

Partly as a sop to Britons who still hoped for a negotiated settlement, George in the spring had reluctantly agreed to also appoint the Howe brothers as peace commissioners in a last-ditch attempt to end the war. For months the cabinet had wrangled over how far the Howes could go in conciliation; in the end, it was not far at all. Lord Germain, denouncing "a sentimental manner of making war," insisted that the commissioners be constrained in any negotiations. Twenty-four paragraphs of instructions issued in May directed that no blanket pardons be given or concessions tendered until the rebels dissolved Congress and their state assemblies, disbanded their armies, surrendered all forts, guaranteed compensation to injured loyalists, and agreed not to tax British imports. Virtually all peace measures required ratification by London, as the historian Ira D. Gruber later wrote.

Even so, Black Dick remained hopeful, perhaps because he was "much unacquainted" with America, as one observer noted. An overture to Washington to discuss "the King's benevolent intentions" had been rebuffed in July; among other defects, the invitation was addressed "to George Washington Esqr. &c. &c.," pointedly omitting his military rank. The rout on Long Island provided another opening, and Howe hosted the captured generals, Stirling and Sullivan, for several dinners aboard the *Eagle*. He spoke of his family's gratitude for the compassion shown by New Englanders when, almost two decades earlier, his older brother was killed at Fort Carillon. Sullivan took the bait: released from captivity, he arrived in Philadelphia in early September to assure Congress that the admiral was sympathetic to the cause, opposed British meddling in American affairs, and had broad powers of negotiation. Admiral Howe wanted but "half an hour's conversation" with a few members "in their private capacities."

At two p.m. on Wednesday, September 11, Richard Howe stood on a sandy beach just below the Billopp mansion, a fieldstone manor house built on the southwestern nob of Staten Island almost a century earlier, with massive white oak beams and slave quarters in the garret. To please the nose, fresh moss and flowering sprigs had been scattered that morning on the red oak plank floors in the entrance hall and adjacent parlor. Brother William was busy preparing the army's return to action, so the admiral would handle today's encounter alone. Howe wore a knee-length blue uniform coat with white lapels, the buttonholes edged in gold thread. A dress sword sat on his hip and a black cocked hat on his head.

A quarter mile across Arthur Kill, Howe's barge—trimmed in red and gold—pulled away from Perth Amboy, on the Jersey shore. A white flag snapped from the bow. Between the straining navy bargemen sat three skeptical men sent by Congress to hear the admiral's pitch.

Even at a distance Howe recognized the broad shoulders and domed forehead of the senior American in the trio. He and Dr. Franklin had met half a dozen times in London, introduced by the admiral's attractive widowed sister, Caroline, who had become Franklin's chess partner. In the months before Franklin sailed for home in March 1775, Howe served as an intermediary for the government in fitful discussions to find a diplomatic solution to the American crisis. Nothing had come of the effort. Now the two men would try again.

Franklin stepped from the barge, bowed, and introduced his two companions. The plump, short man with a tangle of graying hair was John Adams, now forty, a member of more than two dozen congressional committees and president of the new Continental Board of War and Ordnance. The other was Edward Rutledge, just twenty-six, a London-trained lawyer from South Carolina whom Adams privately considered "young and zealous, a little unsteady and injudicious"—a reasonable description of Adams himself. Together they had traveled for two days from Philadelphia, Adams on horseback, the other two aboard high-wheeled chaises, trotting past dust-caked columns of American troops marching north. None of the three expected much from the Staten Island conference. Adams considered General Sullivan "a decoy duck whom Lord Howe has sent among us to seduce us into a renunciation of our independence." Franklin had replied with acidity to a recent personal letter from Howe, condemning British "barbarity and cruelty" and urging the admiral to "relinquish so odious a command and return to a more honorable private station."

Howe escorted them into the house between two ranks of Hessian grenadiers with fixed bayonets and tall brass caps, each "looking as fierce as ten furies," Adams later wrote. In the fragrant parlor, the men chatted civilly for half an hour around a large table, nibbling on cold ham, tongue, and mutton washed down with claret. Then Howe ordered the table cleared and opened the discussion.

The "declaration of independency" complicated his task, he said, because he had no authority "to consider the colonies in the light of independent states." Nor could he acknowledge Congress as a legitimate body. Therefore he must negotiate with his guests not as congressmen but "merely as gentlemen of ability and influence" whom he hoped would help "put a stop to the calamities of war."

Franklin agreed that "the conversation might be held as amongst friends." Adams quipped that the admiral could consider him "in any character which would be agreeable to your lordship except that of a British subject." Howe eyed him curiously. "Mr. Adams," he said, "is a decided character."

The king's "most earnest desire [is] to make his American subjects happy," he continued, but that required repudiating independence. If the Americans "return to their allegiance and obedience to the government of Great Britain," it was possible they could control their own legislation and taxes. America might again provide "solid advantages" to the empire, in commerce and manpower.

Franklin chuckled. The explosive American birthrate had long been one of his favorite themes. "Ay, my lord, we have a pretty considerable manufactory of men," he said.

Howe's large brown eyes grew solemn. "If America should fall," he said, "I should feel and lament it like the loss of a brother."

"My lord," Franklin replied, with a nod and a droll smile, "we will do our utmost endeavors to save your lordship that mortification."

The discussion meandered, faltered, and grew repetitive. When Howe urged "a stop to these ruinous extremities," Franklin shot back, "Forces have been sent out and towns have been burnt. We cannot now expect happiness under the domination of Great Britain. All former attachments have been obliterated." Each colony had "gone completely through a revolution," Adams added, stripping authority from the Crown and empowering Congress and local assemblies. There could be no return to the old imperial ways. Rutledge suggested that Britain seek alliances with the independent states "before anything is settled with other foreign powers," a thinly veiled reference to American overtures to France.

Howe shrugged. He regretted that the gentlemen "had the trouble of coming so far to so little purpose." After an awkward pause, Franklin said, "Well, my lord, as America is to expect nothing but upon total, unconditional submission—"

Howe interrupted him. Britain did "*not* require unconditional submission," he said. Dr. Franklin and his colleagues ought "not go away with such an idea." Finding no agreement possible after three hours of palaver, Howe walked his guests back to his barge and watched impassively as they glided through late afternoon shadows toward the far shore.

In a note to Washington a few hours later, Rutledge reported that "our conference with Lord Howe has been attended with no immediate advantage." Adams wrote Abigail that Howe "is a well-bred man but his address is not so irresistible. . . . His head is rather confused, I think."

Franklin, ever the finger-drumming chess player, was thinking of his next move, and the moves after that. "We learn by chess the habit of not being discouraged by present bad appearances in the state of our affairs," he would write in "The Morals of Chess," "the habit of hoping for a favorable change, and that of persevering in the search [for] resources." A close look at the British anchorage in New York persuaded him that a French armada from Brest and Toulon could destroy even the formidable Admiral Howe. "Four hundred sail of ships guarded only by two 64-gun ships, two 50s, and six 40s. The rest are all frigates, etc.," he wrote a week later to an American agent who served as an intermediary with Versailles. "Twenty sail of the line would take their whole fleet with ease, and then we could as easily manage their army."

Howe felt deflated as he returned to the *Eagle*. "The three gentlemen were very explicit in their opinions that the associated colonies would not accede to any peace or alliance but as free and independent states," he wrote Germain from his cabin. "The conversation ended, and the gentlemen returned to Amboy."

His secretary was more succinct. "They met, they talked, they parted," Ambrose Serle told his journal. "And now nothing remains but to fight it out."

With each passing day, New York felt less like a fortress and more like a trap to many American soldiers. They were "cooped up, or are in danger of being so, on this tongue of land where we ought never have been," Colonel Joseph Reed, the adjutant general, told his wife, Esther, in early September. "We cannot stay, and yet we do not know how to go. . . . The motions of the enemy are very dark and mysterious." A third of the army's twenty-four thousand men were still sick. One camp emitted "a complication of stinks," a visitor wrote. "The army here is numerous but ragged, dirty, sickly, and ill-disciplined." General Samuel Holden Parsons observed that regional frictions had grown so pernicious that "Pennsylvania and New England troops would as soon fight each other as the enemy."

For every reinforcement to arrive, two soldiers deserted. Connecticut had mobilized nineteen thousand men, almost half the male population between sixteen and fifty, yet desertion and illness had whittled down the state's militia by three-quarters. "The militia are passing home by hundreds in a drove, affrighted and scared out of their wits," a colonel wrote on September 9. A Connecticut officer convicted of forging his own furlough pass was "dressed in women's clothing . . . a wooden sword by his side," one chaplain recorded, then paraded through camp on a spavined nag to be pelted with "cow dung and almost every kind of excrement." A deserter sentenced to be shot was bound, blindfolded, and pushed to his knees before his assembled comrades. "He groaned. I groaned. My soldiers groaned. We all groaned," wrote a Delaware officer who commanded the twenty-two-man firing squad. Suddenly a courier appeared from Washington's headquarters, with a shouted commutation: "A pardon! A pardon!" The reprieved soldier and his would-be executioners all wept in relief.

From his sickbed in early September, General Greene had urged Washington to abandon Manhattan, noting that they had long agreed that the city "would not be tenable if the enemy got possession of Long Island and Governors Island." Greene continued:

> They are now in possession of both these places. . . . Part of the army already has met with a defeat. The country is struck with a panic. . . . A general and speedy retreat is absolutely necessary.

To deprive the British of winter quarters, he added, "I would burn the city and suburbs."

But two days later, when Washington put the issue to a war council at his Mortier headquarters, a majority resisted evacuation, not least because Congress had just affirmed its hope to retain New York undamaged. Instead they agreed on a tactically dodgy compromise that would scatter the army in three divisions across sixteen miles: five thousand to hold the city under Putnam, nine thousand under General Heath to defend King's Bridge, at the northern tip of Manhattan, and, in between, various militia regiments posting the East River. In a long explanation to Hancock, Washington admitted that "on every side there is a choice of difficulties." For now he intended to shun climactic battles except on the most favorable terms, using maneuver to exhaust and bleed the enemy and to protect strategic, defensible terrain like the Hudson Highlands. He wrote:

> On our side the war should be defensive. . . . We should on all occasions avoid a general action or put anything to the risk unless compelled by a necessity into which we ought never to be drawn. . . . It would be presumption to draw out our young troops into open ground against their superiors both in number and discipline. . . . We are now in a strong post but not an impregnable one.

Greene was appalled. He had been too weak to attend the Mortier council, but now he climbed from his bed to scribble a petition, also signed by half a dozen brigadiers, calling the army's predicament "critical & dangerous" and urging Washington to reconsider. On Thursday, September 12, a day after the Staten Island conference, the commander in chief summoned his generals to McGowan's tavern, just south of Harlem on the road from King's Bridge. This time they voted ten to three to evacuate New York City, retracting the army to Harlem Heights—a rocky plateau protected by a steep escarpment facing south—and packing eight thousand men onto the high ground at Fort Washington along the Hudson.

After further rumination on the difficulty of defending New York, Congress had belatedly agreed to abandon the city, but refused to authorize arson. Instead Washington ordered the town stripped. Bells were lowered from church belfries and public buildings, then ferried to Newark to be melted down by cannon foundries. Teamsters hauled provisions to King's Bridge; war stocks that could not be moved were dumped in the river or burned on the shoreline. Sloops and wagons evacuated the sick to New Jersey or Westchester County.

Half an hour after sunset on Saturday, September 14, Washington left Mortier's for the last time; vandals immediately plundered the house and smashed all the mirrors. He rode eight miles north to a new headquarters in another grand Georgian mansion. But ten thousand men still remained south of Harlem Heights, a third of them in the city with Putnam.

Each hour brought heightened anxieties. "The enemy are evidently intending to encompass us on this island by a grand military exertion," Reed wrote Esther that Saturday. "We lie down with the most anxious fears for the fate of tomorrow."

Before dawn on Sunday, September 15, the ominous rattle of anchor chains could be heard by five hundred Connecticut troops entrenched along Kip's Bay, a shallow indentation on the Manhattan shoreline, five miles up the East River from the Grand Battery. Many of the militiamen had been in the army for just a few weeks. Some carried only pikes or pickaxes, which would be of little use this morning.

Daylight revealed five men-of-war—the ubiquitous *Phoenix* and *Rose* among them—moored bow to stern with their gun ports gaping just three hundred yards from the beach. A hushed, sultry calm persisted until ten a.m., when eighty-four flatboats carrying four thousand British and German troops spilled from Newtown Creek, a twisting inlet across the river. The vivid formation spread along the Long Island shoreline "like a large clover field in bloom," Private Joseph Plumb Martin later wrote. Swaying gently as their boats rocked on the current, the Hessians sang hymns while British regulars marked time "by damning themselves and the enemy indiscriminately with wonderful fervency," wrote Captain Lord Rawdon.

Just past the stroke of eleven, the cannonade began, broadside after broadside ripping from seventy carriage guns. Fieldpieces joined in from the far shore. After almost three weeks of inaction, General Howe's troops bayed their approval. "The ships kept up a constant fire," Captain Hammond of the *Roebuck* observed, ". . . making altogether the finest scene one has ever beheld." Ambrose Serle agreed. "The whole scene was awful & grand—I might say beautiful," he wrote. "The hills, the woods, the river, the town, the ships and pillars of smoke, all heightened by a most clear &

delightful morning." For fifty-nine minutes the barrage continued with an unspeakable din. *Orpheus* alone burned almost three tons of powder. *Carysfort* fired twenty broadsides—round, grape, and double-headed shot—with such fury that several gun tackles snapped and the ship's jib caught fire.

Some salvos flew high, but an American captain wrote that "our slight embankment, being hastily thrown up, was fast tumbling away by the enemy's shot." Benjamin Trumbull, chaplain of a Connecticut regiment, reported that gunfire blew apart the flimsy breastworks "and buried our men . . . under sand and sods of earth, and made such a dust and smoke." Fire from British marines perched in the tops swept the defenders. "The rigging was filled with swivels and men with small arms, which obliged our people to keep constantly covered," an American soldier told his wife.

By noon, when the signal was given for the bombardment to lift and the flatboats to advance in four columns, many rebels had already sidled up the slope to the rear. The scrape of British boat bows on the shingle and the heavy tread of brogans clapping across the beach sent others running westward, flinging away their hats and muskets. "The enemy fled on all sides," a midshipman aboard *Orpheus* reported, "confused and calling for quarter." Colonel William Douglas, who commanded the Connecticut brigade, saw that his left wing—three militia regiments—had disintegrated. By the time he ordered the rest of his men to flee, he later wrote, "I found I had but about ten left with me."

Among the first British officers ashore was Major General Clinton. He had implored General Howe to make a more sweeping envelopment by landing farther north at King's Bridge, trapping the Americans on Manhattan. But the commanding general had declined to risk his expedition in the turbulent waters of Hell Gate or against the nearby rebel nine-gun battery at Horn's Hook. "We live by victory. Are we sure of this day?" Clinton had scribbled nervously as he studied the enemy positions at Kip's Bay that morning. "In short, I like it not." Yet when he ordered a subordinate to run across the beach with a white handkerchief, calling for the defenders to surrender, nearly all had already fled.

British light infantry companies surged to the right through the now-empty Connecticut works, and grenadiers led by Cornwallis made for rising ground in the center beyond the beach. Howe's orders to the assault troops advised "an entire dependence on their bayonets," but only on the left, where green-coated Hessian *Jäger* led blue-coated grenadiers, drums pounding, was there anyone left to stab. A British officer reported that sixty surrendering Americans were bayoneted; that was doubtless an exaggera-

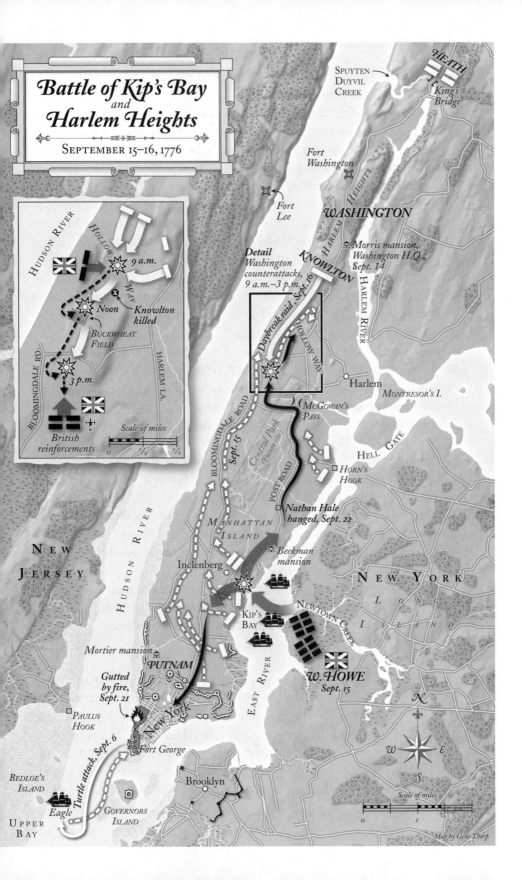

Battle of Kip's Bay
and
Harlem Heights

SEPTEMBER 15–16, 1776

Detail
Washington
counterattacks,
9 a.m.–3 p.m.

9 a.m.

Noon

Knowlton
killed

BUCKWHEAT
FIELD

HOLLOW WAY

HUDSON RIVER

BLOOMINGDALE RD.

HARLEM LA.

3 p.m.

British
reinforcements

Scale of miles

0   ¼   ½

SPUYTEN
DUYVIL
CREEK

HEATH

King's
Bridge

Fort
Washington

HARLEM HEIGHTS

WASHINGTON

Fort
Lee

Morris mansion,
Washington H.Q.,
Sept. 14

KNOWLTON

HARLEM RIVER

Daybreak raid, Sept. 16

HOLLOW WAY

Harlem

MONTRESOR'S I.

McGOWAN'S
PASS

BLOOMINGDALE ROAD

Sept. 15

Central Park
(Future site)

POST ROAD

HELL GATE

HORN'S
HOOK

Nathan Hale
hanged, Sept. 22

MANHATTAN
ISLAND

Inclenberg

Beekman
mansion

NEW YORK

L O N G

NEW
JERSEY

HUDSON RIVER

KIP'S
BAY

NEWTOWN CREEK

I S L A N D

Mortier mansion

PUTNAM

EAST RIVER

W. HOWE
Sept. 15

Gutted
by fire,
Sept. 21

PAULUS
HOOK

New York

N

Fort George

W   E

S

BEDLOE'S
ISLAND

Turtle attack, Sept. 6

Brooklyn

Scale of miles

0   1   2

Eagle

GOVERNORS
ISLAND

UPPER
BAY

Map by Gene Thorp

tion, although some prisoners likely were executed and at least one severed rebel head was seen impaled on a pole.

A thousand yards to the northwest, Washington had raced seven miles from his new headquarters toward the sound of the guns. He now sat his horse on a farm lane edged with stone walls near the post road, conferring with Generals Putnam and Parsons about how to keep the British from pushing north. Hundreds of panting men, with muskets and without, rushed away from the East River. "Take the walls!" Washington shouted at them. "Take the corn field!" Some tried to form a hasty defensive line, but "in a most confused and disordered manner," Parsons acknowledged. Many more scattered inland, glancing over their shoulders. One regimental commander, unable to turn his men, threatened to fire on them, to no avail. "The demons of fear and disorder seemed to take possession of all and everything," Private Martin would write. "The ground was literally covered with arms, knapsacks, staves, coats, hats."

A few hundred yards to the south, a small cluster of redcoats appeared. Washington spurred his mount forward, trying to turn the troops streaming northward ahead of the enemy vanguard. "The General did all in his power to convince them they were in no danger," Lieutenant Colonel Tench Tilghman, a Maryland-born merchant who had become Washington's aide-de-camp a week earlier, wrote his father. "He laid the cane over many of the officers who shewed their men the example of running." Other senior officers asserted that Washington, Putnam, and General Mifflin "caned and whipped" the men, or that the commanding general flung his hat to the ground in exasperation. Greene, who was not on the scene, reported that the enemy had closed within eighty yards before Washington—"so vexed at the infamous conduct of the troops that he sought death rather than life"—could be persuaded to quit the field.

Quit the field he did, regaining his composure as he trotted westward toward the Bloomingdale road. All around him gaggles of soldiers drifted across pastures and down cart paths, away from the enemy.

General Howe came ashore at two p.m. and made his way inland to Inclenberg, a hilltop estate dotted with orchards and soaring hardwoods. Here Clinton had halted his grenadiers after severing the post road. He lacked field guns, and the commanding general's written orders required him to protect the East River bridgehead before advancing. Had the regulars continued another mile or so to the Hudson, bisecting the island, Putnam's division would have been trapped in lower Manhattan. Instead,

Howe spent the next three hours bringing his second lift ashore—over six brigades with another 9,000 soldiers, plus artillery.

That respite was just long enough. An American column of 3,500 men snaked from the city at midafternoon on Sunday for the twelve-mile march along the Hudson toward Harlem Heights. Three British warships—*Renown*, *Repulse*, and *Pearl*—had hurried the evacuation by lobbing a few broadsides into the town. Dressed in a sleeveless waistcoat over a dirty shirt, Putnam rode up and down the line astride a wild-eyed, foaming horse, barking encouragement and urging speed. His new aide, Major Aaron Burr, galloped to a cantonment a mile above the city, persuaded the officers there that the risk of a running battle with the British was less than the risk of being trapped, then guided the men to safety.

Left behind in New York were the entrenchments, redoubts, redans, and ditches built over the past eight months but now useless. Also abandoned was over half of Washington's heavy artillery—sixty-four guns, including fifteen mounted 32-pounders—and twelve thousand round shot, enough to replenish the dwindling British naval ammunition stocks. "They evacuated the city in the utmost precipitation," a British captain wrote, ". . . taking nothing with them but their fears." White flags sprouted from doorways and rooftops as a Hessian brigade swung south on the post road late in the afternoon. Marines came ashore by the Grand Battery, and the 22nd Foot patrolled the Bowery.

On the northern cusp of the island, along the Harlem River, Continental sentries stood with bayonets fixed to keep deserters from bolting for New England. Only women and the very sick were permitted to pass, but "soon however a vast body collected, & the father of confusion himself could not have stirred a greater hubbub," wrote Philip Vickers Fithian, a New Jersey chaplain. "Some swore. Some begged & pleaded. And some, like timorous children, cried." General Mifflin threatened to "discharge the field pieces" into the mob. Rumors spread—that Putnam had been captured, that Washington had lost an arm, that Colonel Knox was missing.

The last was true until the artillery chief appeared on Harlem Heights to great huzzahs late on Sunday. He had seized a boat and escaped up the Hudson, forfeiting to the Hessians a baggage wagon with most of his wardrobe. In a letter to his brother he asked for a bolt of blue twill for a new uniform, or, if necessary, "brown cloth, superfine." Despite the British success, he added defiantly, "I see nothing of the *vast* about them, either in their designs or execution. But good God, if they are little, thou knowest full well we are much less. . . . As the army now stands, it is only a receptacle for ragamuffins."

Teeming rain fell Sunday night. Exhausted, tentless troops "lay upon their arms, covered only by clouds," a Connecticut adjutant wrote. Private Martin added, "We were as wet as water could make us." Many officers felt as heartsick as Knox. "I could wish the transactions of this day blotted out of the annals of America," Colonel William Smallwood of Maryland wrote. "Nothing appeared but fright, disgrace, and confusion." Others, like Chaplain Fithian, saw God's vengeful hand. "We are a sinful nation, O Lord," he acknowledged. "But is it written in thy book concerning us that we must always fly before our enemies?"

Washington had lost another battle, most of another island, and his first city. American casualties in what he called "this disgraceful and dastardly" rout included about 50 killed and, according to a British tally, 371 captured. The prisoners were locked in Dutch and Presbyterian churches converted to jails. Jubilant loyalists sporting red ribbons emerged from New York cellars "like overjoyed Bedlamites," Serle reported, welcoming their liberators with shouts of "God save the king!" It was said that the longer the ribbon, the more intense the loyalty. Captain Henry Duncan of the *Eagle* had his coxswain row him to a dock, where "I was met by a mob who gave me three cheers, took me on their shoulders, carried me to the governor's fort, put me under the English colors now hoisted, and again gave me three cheers." Governor William Tryon also came ashore for the first time in nearly a year to reclaim his colony. He was greeted by "a great concourse of people," one diarist wrote. "Joy and gladness seemed to appear in all countenances."

Hundreds would sign a petition congratulating the Howe brothers. Many also endorsed a "declaration of dependence," affirming their fealty to George III; displayed in Scott's Tavern on Wall Street, it attracted signatures from wealthy landowners, carpenters, bakers, blacksmiths, and barkeeps. British officers strolled through the streets, selecting the finest rebel houses for winter billets. Confiscated property was marked with "G.R." or the king's proprietary broad-arrow insignia. To commemorate the great Sabbath victory, Admiral Howe's personal chaplain reopened St. Paul's Chapel on Broadway. He drew his sermon from the twelfth chapter of Jeremiah: "And it shall come to pass, after I have plucked them out, I will return and have compassion on them."

Monday, September 16, brought the rebels a modest measure of redemption and self-respect. Washington had planned three roughly parallel defensive lines north of the craggy Harlem Heights bluffs, with the new, pentagonal Fort Washington even farther up the island. About ten thousand fit-to-fight men crowded these wooded uplands, hacking at the ground with picks and spades; another six thousand occupied King's Bridge and crossings into Westchester County. Greene's three brigades held the southernmost line, which featured a trio of small redoubts where Manhattan narrowed into its northern panhandle. Two miles away, enemy campfires flickered from glens and meadows near the future Central Park.

Before first light, on Washington's orders, a patrol of 120 men slipped below the lines through the thick forest fronting the Hudson. They were Rangers, a New England troop newly created for scouting and woodland skulking, modeled on a similar unit in the last French war. Lieutenant Colonel Thomas Knowlton, the rangy, thirty-six-year-old Connecticut farmer celebrated for his rail-fence valor at Bunker Hill, led them south.

At daybreak British pickets on the Bloomingdale road spied shadows darting through the trees. Shots flew back and forth. Four hundred regulars scampered up the road to confront the intruders until the Rangers rose from behind a stone wall and threw a scorching volley at fifty yards' range. For half an hour the foes traded gunshots. Thousands of bullets nipped leaves and punctured tree trunks before Knowlton retreated, pressed hard by redcoats. Each side had suffered about ten casualties.

Alerted to the gunfire, Washington rode to the rim of the heights, where shortly after nine a.m. Colonel Reed found him squinting at enemy light infantrymen massing below the Hollow Way, a shallow dale a mile south that angled west toward the Hudson shoreline. As Reed explained the morning's action, the derisive blare of a British hunting horn could be heard above the treetops, sounding the call for a fox under chase. "I never felt such a sensation before," Reed would tell Esther. "It seemed to crown our disgrace."

But Washington had concocted a small, vengeful plan. Serving as decoys, some 150 volunteers from Greene's division scrambled down the bluff to a salt marsh, then fell back a few hundred yards as the eager British rushed forward, firing on the run. Washington fed the rest of the brigade into the brawl—eventually totaling nine hundred men—to keep the enemy transfixed. Meanwhile, Knowlton and his Rangers, joined by Reed and three Virginia rifle companies under Major Andrew Leitch, circled across a rock outcropping to the east, intent on ambushing the British detachment from behind. Yet the flanking force of 230 men had pivoted too soon: they struck the British formation in the side rather than the rear. Redcoats along a rail fence choked with thick brush whirled to their right. A volley riddled Major Leitch with three bullets, one in the hip and two in the gut. Knowlton had turned to urge his men forward when a musket ball slammed into the small of his back. "I mounted him on my horse and brought him off," Reed reported. "Gasping the agonies of death, all his inquiry was if we had driven in the enemy."

The enemy was indeed soon driven. "We had galled them a little," a Virginia captain observed. By noon the British had fallen back a mile to a buckwheat field, dragging their dead and wounded, and pressed by nearly two thousand rebels. The crackle of musketry merged into an unbroken roar. Smoke, reddened by muzzle flashes, rolled across the landscape with each new volley. Howe summoned reinforcements from down the island, including Hessian *Jäger* and the 42nd Highlanders—the Black Watch— with drums pounding and pipes skirling. "We were instantly trotted about three miles without a halt to draw breath," a British grenadier lieutenant wrote. Captain Montresor, Howe's aide, took command of two brass 3-pounders and, when no horse teams could be found, ordered them dragged forward by hand. Each gun fired sixty rounds to keep American flankers along the Hudson from turning the British left wing.

The American line stood four deep in places—firing and loading, firing and loading. Officers cautioned their men not to shoot until they could see the enemy's feet through the smoke. "I could not help feeling an involuntary tremor, as though my knees were giving way," a young lieutenant told his journal. But when the soldier on his right pitched forward, blood spewing from a bullet in the heart, "vengeance was the only feeling."

The British fell back again at three p.m., their ammunition dwindling but with Howe's reserves now piling into the fight. Wary of being outflanked to the east, Washington halted the pursuit and ordered his men to make their way back up the heights. A few final shots rang out, and the battlefield fell silent. The men "gave a hurrah and left the field in good order," wrote Lieutenant Colonel Tilghman, Washington's aide. American casualties were tallied at 60, though they were probably more than twice that, with at least 35 killed. Most of the dead "were drawn to a large hole, which was prepared for the purpose, and buried together," wrote Lieutenant Samuel Richards, who commanded the detail. Knowlton was removed to the shingle-roofed Cross Keys tavern on King's Bridge Road, where he died in the afternoon, leaving a widow and eight children. He "would have been an honor to any country," Washington said. Major Leitch, carried to the Blue Bell Tavern, would linger for two weeks before he passed. He was twenty-six, and comrades buried him in a swale beside the post road.

British casualties exceeded 170, including 14 killed, according to the deputy adjutant general, Major Stephen Kemble, plus 8 Hessians wounded. Ravens hopped stiff-legged around a rocky defile where some of the redcoat dead were interred. "The ungovernable impetuosity of the light troops drew us into the scrap," General Clinton complained. But others saw unwonted mettle in the rebel performance. "If this was a scheme of Washington's," an officer in the 46th Foot wrote, "it certainly was well-concerted."

The small victory in a minor skirmish proved a tonic for the Americans. "Every visage was seen to lighten," one colonel commented. The troops had slugged it out at forty yards' range against British regulars, Highlanders, and Hessians, advancing and withdrawing with reasonable discipline. Captain John Gooch wrote a friend that he had fought the enemy point-blank for precisely "one hour and eight minutes. . . . I'm now ready to give them the second part whenever they have an appetite."

"This affair I am in hopes will be attended with many salutary consequences," Washington wrote Hancock, "as it seems to have greatly inspirited the whole of our troops." Joseph Reed was more exuberant in a letter to Esther. "You can hardly conceive the change it has made in our army," he wrote. "The men have recovered their spirits and feel a confidence which before they had quite lost. I hope the effects will be lasting."

Fear of fire had distressed New York for well over a hundred years. In the mid-seventeenth century, the town bought its first ladders and fire hooks and commissioned cordwainers to make 150 leather water buckets. Officials banned wooden chimneys, thatched roofs, and haystacks. Wardens prohibited blazes in hearths on windy days, and all fires had to be banked or covered in the evening. Watchmen with rattles walked the streets, sniffing for smoke. Two new fire engines were purchased from a London firm in 1731 for £200; twenty men pumped foot treadles on each machine to force water through the leather pipes. Ten fires plagued New York in the spring of 1741, including one in Fort George that spread to the governor's mansion, an army barracks, and a Church of England chapel; confessions of arson—in some cases coerced if not extracted by torture in the "Great Gaol" below city hall—led to hysterical cries of "The Negroes are rising!" The town convicted and executed almost three dozen suspects, burning thirteen black men at the stake and hanging another seventeen blacks and four whites—the supposed ringleaders. Eighty-four slaves were also sold into West Indies bondage, and seven white men were exiled.

Warehouses of pitch, tar, and resin in a maritime town raised the risk of conflagration. After 1766, all new buildings were to be made of brick or stone, and fir and cedar roof shingles were to be replaced by slate or tile, although enforcement remained lax. Ordinances required each household to keep buckets and smother sacks at hand, and to routinely clean chimney flues. New York bought newer engines and by 1772 had expanded its firefighting force to 163 volunteers in eleven companies. Nevertheless, a blaze in December 1773 burned the governor's house to the ground—incinerating £2,000 worth of Lady Tryon's jewelry—and only the snow on adjacent roofs kept the flames from spreading. Fire also destroyed a new general hospital just before it was to open in February 1775. The town resolved to be even more stringent. Construction began on a network of hollow-log water pipes, and in the spring of 1776 fire engines were rigorously tested, including one with an eleven-inch pump that could spray three hundred gallons a minute. "Fire seldom happens," a Scottish visitor observed, "and by the proper disposition of the engines, when it does happen, it is seldom allowed to spread farther than the house it breaks out in."

That thesis would be tested shortly after midnight on Saturday, September 21, when a blaze began in a low groggery called the Fighting Cocks at Whitehall Slip, near the Grand Battery. Some claimed the tavern was occupied by careless tipplers; others said that British soldiers' wives were burning pine boards when a chimney fire ignited. A captured Pennsylvania soldier held aboard *Pearl* in the harbor described seeing flames dance along the waterfront, "a most beautiful and luminous but baleful sight." Driven by a brisk southerly breeze, the fire spread to the north and west, yet no bells clanged in alarm since all had been hauled off to rebel cannon works. A night watchman who smelled smoke along Pearl Street forced open a door to find "the whole interior of the building in flames, from cellar to roof." From Fort Washington, eleven miles north, "the heavens appeared in flames," and a British officer below Harlem claimed the sky grew so bright "we could see a pin on our ground by the blaze." Pastor Shewkirk watched aghast from the Moravian church on Fair Street as flames turned "the whole air red." Hundreds of terrified New Yorkers sought sanctuary on the open greensward of the Common, cowering on the grass as flames licked through the town.

"It is almost impossible to conceive a scene of more horror and distress. The sick, the aged, women and children half-naked, were seen going they knew not where," Captain Frederick Mackenzie told his journal. "The terror was increased by the horrid noise of the burning and falling houses." Admiral Howe sent boatloads of sailors ashore to fight the blaze; his brother ordered two army regiments to join them with a hundred wagons, despite concern that Washington would use the distraction to counterattack. The Guards Brigade marched from their camp on Turtle Bay and spent the night "pulling down houses to impede the progress of the fire," according to one ensign. Flames jumped Broadway near Beaver Street and swept toward the Hudson, following the pretty cobbled streets and burning out one four- or five-story house after another, English and step-gabled Dutch alike. The shallow pitch of the St. Paul's Chapel roof and a balustrade along the eaves allowed a bucket brigade to douse embers before they could ignite. Not so at nearby Trinity Church, the town's tallest structure and an emblem of Anglican gentility. Sparks drifted onto the southern roof, and soon the wooden steeple was engulfed in what Captain Mackenzie called "a lofty pyramid of fire. . . . The whole fell with a great noise," drawing jubilant cheers from rebels watching across the river in New Jersey. Losses at the church totaled £22,000, including a twenty-five-stop organ, leaded glass, paintings, marble monuments, the parsonage, the library, and two charity schools.

An abrupt change in wind direction and a natural firebreak formed by the open terrain at King's College caused the conflagration to subside on Saturday morning. Within a mile-long charred swath, some five hundred houses had been reduced to ash, about a quarter of the city's total. Most docks, warehouses, and commercial buildings were spared, Governor Tryon told Germain, although many small shopkeepers were burned out. Martial law, he added, would remain in force. "Our distresses were great before, but this calamity has increased them tenfold," one New Yorker wrote. "Thousands are reduced to beggary."

The British suspected arson. Reprisals had been meted out even as the fire raged. "Several of the villains have been detected, & have suffered the fate they deserve," wrote Major Francis Hutcheson, a British staff officer. Stories circulated of suspected arsonists summarily executed by vigilantes after being caught with matches or flaming brands. Serle claimed that a grenadier threw one culprit into the flames, while another "found cutting off the handles of the water buckets to prevent their use was the first hung up by the neck till he was dead." A German colonel wrote his prince that "sailors hanged one [suspect] by the heels after his right hand—in which he had held a torch when caught setting fire to a house—had been cut off by a Highlander." During a truce parley with Colonel Reed to discuss a prisoner exchange, Captain Montresor confirmed, as Washington subsequently wrote, that "several of our countrymen had been punished with various deaths . . . some by hanging, others by burning &c."

No persuasive evidence ever emerged that the fires had been set deliberately. Those slain, given no opportunity to defend themselves legally, may have been fighting the blaze or fleeing for their lives. British authorities reportedly detained two hundred other suspects, but all were released despite rewards offered for incriminating testimony. Seven years later, a British commission failed to resolve whether the fire was accidental, deliberate, or a combination of both, although it was generally agreed that no American order led to the city's burning. In September 1776, however, those about to spend the winter in a badly charred town believed the worst of the American high command. "Many circumstances lead to conjecture that Mr. Washington was privy to this villainous act, as he sent all the bells of the churches out of town, under pretense of casting them into cannon," Tryon wrote Germain. General Howe added, "We have reason to suspect there are villains still lurking here, ready to finish the work they have begun."

Washington, for his part, believed the fire was serendipitous. "Had I been left to the dictates of my own judgment, New York should have been laid in ashes before I quitted it. To this end I applied to Congress, but was absolutely forbid," he told his overseer at Mount Vernon. "Providence, or some good honest fellow, has done more for us than we were disposed to do for ourselves."

The gray pall smothering New York on Sunday morning, September 22, was all too visible from the British artillery park near the eastern post road, five miles north of the city. This was Coronation Day—George III had mounted the throne fifteen years earlier—and Royal Artillery gunners prepared to hold forth with the usual earsplitting salute, a rebuke to insolent rebels, who called it "Damnation Day." Gun carriages, limbers, and ammunition wagons stood wheel to wheel in the camp, where sentries challenged approaching strangers with the day's parole ("London") and listened for the countersign ("Great Britain"). Curious regulars surely eyed Captain Montresor's white marquee, where a young American officer captured out of uniform on Long Island now waited for the hangman to summon him to his death.

At age twenty-one, Captain Nathan Hale deserved a longer life and a better fate. "He was calm," Montresor later reported, "and bore himself with gentle dignity." Born and raised in Connecticut, Hale was described by a fellow officer as having "very fair skin, blue eyes, flaxen or very light hair which was always kept short. . . . His bodily agility was remarkable." At Yale, which he entered at fourteen, he was "as active as electric flame," a classmate observed, a student of Hebrew, Greek, Latin, logic, rhetoric, metaphysics, ethics, and more. As a schoolmaster in New London, he taught thirty-two boys for an annual salary of £70. "I love my employment," he wrote in late 1774, "find many friends among strangers, have time for scientific study." The following summer he enlisted in the army, serving at the siege of Boston and marching to New York with his regiment; he had recently joined Knowlton's Rangers as a company commander. When the high command sought a volunteer to spy incognito behind the British lines on Long Island, Hale stepped forward. As Washington later wrote, "Single men in the night will be more likely to ascertain facts than the best glasses in the day."

Dressed in a brown summer suit and pretending to be an itinerant Tory schoolteacher, Hale carried his Yale diploma as a credential. He seemed a poor candidate for espionage. "His nature was too frank and open for deceit and disguise," one classmate said. A subordinate added, "He was too good-looking. . . . He could not deceive. Some scrubby fellow ought to have gone." Precisely what Hale did during his brief career as a clandestine agent after crossing Long Island Sound in mid-September, and how he was unmasked, would remain vague and conjectural. Without doubt, the mission was amateurish and ultimately pointless: the British fully revealed their plans by landing at Kip's Bay and seizing New York as Hale began his perambulations.

Some would claim that he was exposed by a loyalist who recognized him or that he was detained while attempting to slip back across the East River during the great fire. A British officer recorded in his journal that Hale had been caught on Long Island by Lieutenant Colonel Robert Rogers, a renowned woodsman and the most famous colonial fighter in the French war, who had turned against his American brethren by raising a battalion of loyalist rangers for the Howe brothers. Regardless, incriminating notes and sketches were found hidden in Hale's shoes. On Saturday afternoon he had been delivered to General Howe's new headquarters in the James Beekman mansion, a country seat with a Greek pediment and a wide porch overlooking the East River.

In another week, Howe would offer full amnesty to all "deserters from His Majesty's service" despite "the heinousness of their crimes." But with his newly captured city in ashes, he was in no mood to forgive rebel iniquity. He ordered Hale remanded to the provost marshal for execution in the morning; Howe's edict declared him to be "a spy for the enemy, by his own full confession." The prisoner reportedly spent his last night locked in a greenhouse with six large windows next to the Beekman mansion. After daybreak he was bundled to the artillery park a mile north. There the compassionate Montresor offered refuge in his tent while the hangman prepared the rope.

Much would be made of Hale's last words, and admirers later credited him with a line paraphrased from Joseph Addison's *Cato*, revered by republicans: "I only regret that I have but one life to lose for my country." More likely is Captain Mackenzie's contemporary account that "he behaved with great composure and resolution . . . and desired the spectators to be at all times prepared to meet death in whatever shape it might appear." Whether Hale was forced up a ladder and fitted with a noose dangling from a tree limb or hanged by having a cart drawn from under his feet, he departed this earth at eleven o'clock on a bright, hot morning. His corpse was left dangling for several days as a macabre warning, and above him British soldiers suspended the figure of a soldier painted on a board upon which they scribbled, *"George Washington."*

During another truce parley, Montresor would tell an American officer that in his last hour, Hale wrote two farewell letters—neither apparently delivered—and asked the provost marshal for a clergyman and a Bible. Both requests were denied.

Hale died, and the war went on. Today was more brutal than yesterday, and tomorrow would be worse still. Sensible men prepared to meet death in whatever shape it might appear. In a somber letter to a friend in Ireland, Lieutenant Cliffe of the 46th Foot described the fraught week in New York. "The horrors of a civil war are every day before my eyes," he wrote. "I also saw a spy hanging up, a captain of the rebels, a very genteel-looking fellow, and Gen. Washington's effigy hanging over him." Then Cliffe averted his gaze and added: "I never saw a more beautiful country."

Part Three

Battle for Lake Champlain

OCTOBER 1776

To St. Lawrence River

Montreal

— RICHELIEU RIVER

St. Johns

BURGOYNE

— RICHELIEU RIVER

ÎLE AUX NOIX

St. Lawrence R.

QUEBEC

NEW YORK

□ POINT AU FER

CARLETON/PRINGLE

— ÎLE LA MOTTE

POINT AU ROCHE

CUMBERLAND HEAD

Detail

VALCOUR I.

LAKE CHAMPLAIN

Battle, Oct. 11

Arnold, dawn, Oct. 12

SCHUYLER'S ISLAND

FOUR BROTHERS ISLANDS

Washington (row galley) captured, Oct. 13

SPLIT ROCK

British catch Arnold, Oct. 13

BUTTONMOULD BAY
FERRIS BAY

Arnold escapes, Oct. 13

CROWN POINT

British squadron arrives, Oct. 14; return to Canada, late October

ADIRONDACK MOUNTAINS

GREEN MOUNTAINS

Fort Ticonderoga

GATES

RATTLESNAKE HILL (MT. INDEPENDENCE)

Valcour Island

OCTOBER 11

VALCOUR STRAIT

VALCOUR ISLAND

LAKE CHAMPLAIN

ARNOLD

Indian snipers

Indian snipers

Royal Savage

LITTLE ISLAND

Carleton

Maria

Thunderer

Inflexible

American escape, 10 p.m.

CARLETON/PRINGLE

Scale of miles

0   ½   1

N

W   E

S

Scale of miles

0   10   20

Skenesborough

LAKE GEORGE

HUDSON RIVER

WOOD CREEK

Fort George

To Albany

Map by Gene Thorp

17.

———

Master of the Lakes

Autumn colors were well advanced in the Richelieu valley. Brilliant reds, yellows, and oranges lit up the woods around St. Johns, where the percussive sounds of shipbuilding rang along the riverfront. Carpenters and joiners, coopers and caulkers, scavelmen, sawyers, smiths, riggers, spar makers, and oakum boys toiled from first light to last in sheds, sail lofts, and ropewalks. Men sawed, hammered, and chipped away. They swung lipped adzes and caulking mallets and broadaxes wielded with such finesse that a skilled hewer could split timber precisely along a penciled line. "It was no uncommon thing for trees, growing at dawn of day, to form parts of the ship before night," a British lieutenant at St. Johns wrote. General Carleton had informed London that he intended to become "master of the lakes" before ice sealed them shut, but first he must finish building his inland fleet.

The British force in Canada had grown to 13,000 men, and shipyards also bustled in Montreal and Chambly. Any soldier with carpentry skills was put to work on the ways and paid an extra shilling each day for his trouble, or he was sent to the forward camp on Île aux Noix to build warehouses, storerooms, and an ammunition dump. The boggy little island was no less pestiferous than when the Americans had occupied it three months earlier, although dysentery had supplanted smallpox as the dominant affliction. "The misery of this island is indescribable," a German surgeon lamented. On bad days burials occurred hourly, and rebel mass graves were now complemented by a British cemetery, where the epitaphs scratched on headboards included "Do not lament nor me deplore / I am not lost but gone before." By October 1, a vanguard of 5,000 officers and men had assembled around Île aux Noix, plus 500 Canadian loyalists, 800 Indians, and 1,700 Hessians, all preparing to spill down Lake Champlain to attack Crown Point and Fort Ticonderoga.

Guy Carleton had failed to catch the Americans in their graceless flight up the St. Lawrence and the Richelieu in June. A shortage of boats prevented him from pursuing them expeditiously into New York, giving the rebels both time and space to rally. The king and his ministers had now provided Carleton the large force he claimed could "greatly change the face of things on this continent" by joining forces with Howe's army in the Hudson valley and severing New England from the middle colonies. Yet the fighting season had dwindled to just a few weeks, and London was impatient. "Your silence as to your own intended operations . . . is much to be lamented," Lord Germain told him in a recent dispatch.

Carleton replied on September 28, bluntly telling Germain—whom he detested—to revise his expectations. There could be no march to the Hudson until spring, in part because London had been slow in providing the watercraft requested almost a year earlier. "Unfortunately the season is so far advanced that I dare not flatter myself we shall be able to do more this campaign than to draw off their attention and keep back part of their force from General Howe," he wrote. Still, "I expect our fleet will soon sail." His intelligence suggested that the enemy kept 800 men at Crown Point and 10,000 at Ticonderoga.

Carleton's plan was simple enough, although he remained aloof from his lieutenants and secretive as usual, "absorbed within himself, saying little and giving answers to few . . . handling every detail himself," as the British historian Piers Mackesy would write. He intended to seize Lake Champlain this fall and destroy General Arnold or any other rebel foolish enough to challenge his armada. Possession of the American forts at the southern end of the lake would provide a springboard toward New York early next year. Among other preparations, he had enlisted Indian allies at a "congress of savages" in a Jesuit church in Montreal, sitting on a high chair in the nave to treat with warriors slathered in vermilion battle paint; not only were they wearing nose rings, earrings, and a feather for each enemy slain, but, as a British officer recorded, "at the end of the penis the head & neck of some handsome bird is fastened." The chiefs gave Carleton several scalps as an earnest of their fidelity; he reciprocated by ordering £14,000 in "Indian presents" from England. General Burgoyne, who had spent the summer helping to organize the Canada force, complained that "a thousand savages brought into the field cost more than twenty thousand men."

The imminent military expedition and large assemblage of regulars, Canadians, Hessians, Indians, and dependent families required all of Carleton's considerable administrative talents. Supplies from Britain had been late in arriving: most of the twenty-nine victuallers from Cork this summer had not made the St. Lawrence until at least September. Together they carried 2,250 tons of bread and flour, much of it moldy, and 1,300 tons of meat, much of it spoiled because of pickling leaks. London, lacking accurate manpower returns from Quebec, had planned for a ration strength of 12,000 when, in fact, Carleton was feeding 20,000 altogether. Canadian venison and wild pigeons—the dense flocks were said "to darken the air"—supplemented the daily rations, but local food supplies were otherwise so meager that army commissaries warned that no reserves would be available if a protracted siege became necessary at Ticonderoga. The Treasury had just shipped Carleton £100,000 in cash, in addition to the £70,000 sent during the summer, as well as vegetable seeds for garrison gardens, spruce beer, 12,000 pairs of mittens, 22,000 yards of wool cloth for leggings, and 3,000 extra blankets. The Hessians had ample stocks of their beloved zwieback, as well as salt meat and rum.

British expeditions had penetrated the Lake Champlain region in 1690, 1709, 1711, and the 1740s and 1750s, before permanently evicting the French in 1760. The army and navy had extensive experience with bateaux, row galleys, lake sloops, and nasty Adirondacks weather. Over the past nine months, the king's ministers had carefully reviewed the watercraft and other matériel sent up the St. Lawrence in the last war. Modeled on the artillery train Wolfe carried to Canada in 1759, Carleton's suite of brass guns, including some cast just this year, was exceptional. The Admiralty rejected Germain's request for two hundred maritime carpenters as impractical, given the acute needs at Portsmouth and other domestic yards. But twenty shipwrights from Glasgow and ten English house carpenters were dispatched, plus hundreds of veteran sailors to be commanded by the formidable Captain Charles Douglas, who had brought *Isis* through the ice to Quebec in early May. The Admiralty and the Ordnance Board also shipped Carleton three thousand sail needles, fifteen thousand fathoms of rope, a thousand felling axes, eight thousand yards of sail cloth, and three blacksmith forges with bellows and anvils.

Flat-bottomed bateaux had been copied from a French design—thirty-six feet long, six feet wide, and tapered at both ends. Germain wanted at least four hundred sent to Canada. Ten disassembled gunboats also reached the St. Lawrence in July as deck cargo, although the Navy Office complained that the purchase price of more than £4 for each boat was "very unreasonable." Carleton's squadron eventually included twenty-two gunboats with names like *Firebrand*, *Infernal*, *Vesuvius*, and *Aetna*, manned by Royal Artillery and Hessian crews.

As Canadian shipyards assembled the boats brought from England, they also built or refurbished several larger vessels. At St. Johns, much of the hewing and hammering went into the *Thunderer*, a seven-sided, two-masted radeau—a floating gun battery—mounting half a dozen 24-pounders and two howitzers on the lower deck, and six more 12-pounders above. With her ninety-one-foot hull painted orange, like all of Carleton's warships, *Thunderer* carried a brick furnace for heating cannonballs. She was so crowded with guns and three hundred crewmen that personal baggage trailed behind aboard a dozen bateaux.

The squadron also included a flat-bottomed American boat captured on the St. Lawrence and renamed the *Loyal Convert*, as well as two schooners, the twelve-gun *Carleton* and, in honor of the general's wife, the fourteen-gun *Lady Maria*. How to get these deeper-draft vessels past eight miles of Richelieu rapids to St. Johns and then to the lake posed a navigational conundrum. Among several clever young naval officers pondering the problem, none was more ingenious than Lieutenant John Schank, a future admiral known as "Old Purchase" for inventing both an adjustable cot fitted with pulleys and—of perhaps greater utility to the empire—the drop keel, a board that could be raised or lowered through a slot inside a hull to permit sailing in shoal water.

As superintendent of the St. Johns dockyard, Schank helped strip *Maria* of her masts, rigging, and ballast. Over the course of a week she was hoisted from the water near Chambly with block and tackle onto a road parallel to the river that a thousand conscripted *habitants* had just rebuilt. Axmen felled large trees, lopped off the branches, and shoved the logs under *Maria's* keel as rollers. With oxen yoked to the ship's hull and windlasses fixed every twenty yards, whip-cracking teamsters yelling in English and French winched the schooner overland inch by inch in what one naval officer called "terraqueous warfare."

After half a mile, they gave up. The ship was too heavy, the roadbed too soft. The rollers sank into the mud, blocking the supply route to St. Johns. Schank ordered *Maria* dismantled, every plank and frame stripped down to the floor heads by exhausted men said to sing "some melancholy chantey" when they were not cursing. Each component was then hauled to St. Johns for reassembly in the shipyard. Shipwrights similarly undressed the *Carleton* and *Loyal Convert* for transport south, frame by frame.

Carleton's "jigsaw navy" now comprised four men-of-war and scores of gunboats, longboats, bateaux, and birch-bark canoes. Thirty sizable fighting vessels had been built and equipped in just six weeks. But this ensemble was not enough for the cautious commanding general. Spies and scouts told Carleton that rebel shipwrights were likewise building at the far end of the lake. Armed American boats had been spotted in a battle line off Windmill Point, almost at the Richelieu. He ordered Schank to commandeer a Canadian triple-masted, 180-ton frigate under construction on the stocks in Quebec. She, too, was dissected, each piece of wood carefully numbered, then shipped in thirty longboats to Chambly before being carted to the St. Johns yard. Schank and sixteen shipwrights had laid her keel there on September 7. Twenty-seven days later, on October 4—now ninety feet long and renamed *Inflexible*—she slid down a slip coated with tallow and soap, cheered to the echo. The frigate sat at anchor for a week off Île aux Noix while sailors shifted ballast, finished the rigging, raised eighteen 12-pounders to the gun deck, and hoisted a blue ensign above the stern. Lieutenant Schank would command her.

Amassing the extra firepower provided by *Inflexible* had cost Carleton another month of fair weather. But the squadron that now debouched from the Richelieu onto Lake Champlain included several hundred craft, from the smallest canoe to the men-of-war. Seven hundred Royal Navy and merchant transport seamen had shifted from the St. Lawrence to the lake service. General Burgoyne was prepared to lead the army to Crown Point once the enemy vessels had been swept away. As Carleton boarded the *Maria* and prepared to sail south into New York, he was reasonably certain that his jigsaw navy carried double the firepower that any rebel squadron could possibly assemble.

Ninety miles south of Île aux Noix, a sardonic American officer wrote, "What kind of place is Ticonderoga? When God made it (if He ever had a hand in it), it was surely done in the dark. It is one confused jumble of atoms, without order, beauty, or profit. . . . It is one of the most villainous spots under heaven." So many skulls and long bones could still be found from the brutal battle between the French and the British in 1758, he added, "that our people make punchbowls and ladles of them." Thigh bones were found to be handy as tent pegs.

Here the Northern Army had halted after the flight from Canada to lick its wounds and take a stand in hopes of thwarting the merger of Carleton's host with Howe's. "Much depends on the bravery of you who are posted at Ticonderoga," Dr. Franklin had written to Colonel Anthony Wayne at the end of August. "If you prevent the junction of the two armies, their project for this year will be broken." By late summer the American force numbered almost eleven thousand rank and file, although barely half were fit for duty. Batteries mounted more than a hundred guns. Defensive fortifications extended in a long crescent from the old French entrenchments west of Fort Ticonderoga to the aptly named Rattlesnake Hill, east of Lake Champlain, where bitten soldiers were told to drink a quart of olive oil and rub the wound with mercury. General Schuyler sent two hundred cattle on the hoof each week from Albany in hopes that fresh meat would help enervated men regain their vim. Congress emptied warehouses around Philadelphia, ordering up almost four thousand linen shirts and fifteen hundred pairs of shoes to shirtless, shoeless regiments. The large garrison immediately became a magnet for sutlers, hucksters, and mountebanks, "ambitious men of craft and cunning swindlers and deceptive knaves, mean sycophants, toadeaters, & spittle lickers," as a Pennsylvania captain wrote. So much counterfeit money flooded the encampment that all currency was banned except Continental bills. Commanders warned of "various frauds, impositions, and abuses being every day committed by traders."

Smallpox had subsided, but other ailments raged, including "putrid, nervous, bilious, intermitting, & remitting fevers with fluxes," by one doctor's catalog. The Reverend Ebenezer David arrived at Ticonderoga in late August to find his new Massachusetts regiment, the 25th Continental, "in a most sorrowful condition . . . thin in flesh, badly dressed, spirits sunk, &c."; the regimental commander died a week later. Malaria seemed to rise from the lake in a miasma, and brush piles were burned each morning and evening in a futile effort to "purify the air." Smoke discolored the white facings on uniform coats as men huddled over flaming pine knots used as both candles and fumigants. "Everything about this army," an officer wrote Washington, "is infected with the pestilence."

Three thousand patients jammed the hospital at Fort George, thirty miles south of Ticonderoga, where hemlock boughs served for bedding. "In the name of God," one physician pleaded, "what shall we do with them all?" Too often the answer was: bury them. A surgeon estimated that three hundred men had died there in just over a month. When inventories were taken of drug supplies in September, five artillery companies reported, "Medicines—none." Half of the medicinal herbs arriving in wagons that month were described by medicos as "entirely useless" if not toxic. Two ailing Pennsylvania soldiers too weak to crawl during a thunderstorm were found drowned in their hospital tent. On September 14, a Massachusetts regiment reported 40 men fit for duty and 197 unfit; in the larger brigade, every officer but one was sick. "Will you not send for my mother?" a dying boy asked Reverend Ammi Robbins, the brigade chaplain.

> How I wish I could see her. She was opposed to my enlisting. I am now very sorry. Do let her know I am sorry.

Other miseries compounded these miseries. Soldiers robbed civilians, provoking a warning from the high command that "the army is paid to protect, not pilfer the inhabitants." Soldiers also robbed one another. An engineer whose tent was rifled by thieves lost everything except what he was wearing; he wrote, "I am heartily tired of this retreating, ragged, starved, lousy, thievish, pocky army in this unhealthy country." In one week, a court-martial board sentenced various defendants to thirty-nine lashes each for desertion, for threatening to shoot a captain, for threatening to kill a sergeant, for fraudulently enlisting in another regiment to collect the bounty, and for doing so twice. Two officers were drummed from the service for, respectively, knowingly enlisting a deserter and embezzling the company payroll.

Regional enmities grew even more ferocious, including one brawl between Massachusetts troops and Wayne's Pennsylvanians during which several dozen shots were fired. A Pennsylvania officer denounced New Englanders as "low, dirty, griping, cowardly, lying rascals." A scapegoat was needed for the Canadian fiasco, and New Englanders settled on General Schuyler, a New Yorker. He was accused, usually in whispers, of embezzlement, profiteering, Toryism, and treason. "You have many enemies," a friend in Philadelphia warned. When Congress sent auditors to painstakingly scrutinize Northern Army accounts, Schuyler raged, "There never was a man so infamously scandalized and ill-treated as I am."

Schuyler was further insulted by the appearance in Albany of another major general, Horatio Gates, who, after serving capably as Washington's adjutant general, had been promoted and assigned a combat command in Canada only to find that the Canadian campaign had been decisively lost. "I have been deceived and disappointed," Gates wrote John Adams, his patron. Companionable and ambitious—"a strong, clumsy bear," in one comrade's description—Gates sought to nudge Schuyler aside, with encouragement from New Englanders. Schuyler complained of being "barbarously traduced" and vowed to resign. Congress belatedly affirmed Schuyler's seniority—Hancock urged the two generals "to cultivate harmony in all your military operations"—but frictions and factions mottled the Northern Army.

Washington threatened to make things worse. When Schuyler and his lieutenants decided to abandon decrepit, vulnerable Crown Point except for a small screening force, the commander in chief protested with the certitude of a man two hundred miles away and ignorant of the local terrain. "Your relinquishing Crown Point is, in its consequences, a relinquishment of the lakes . . . which is a key to all these colonies," he wrote. Curiously, Washington's meddling pushed Schuyler and Gates to ally in common cause. Gates agreed that the Northern Army's "deplorable state" made concentrating American defenses ten miles south at Ticonderoga tactically necessary. At Crown Point, he wrote Washington, "the ramparts are tumbled down, the casemates are fallen, the barracks burnt, and the whole so perfect a ruin that it would take five times the number of our army, for several summers, to put it in defensible repair."

Acknowledging Gates's "superior military qualifications," Schuyler graciously proposed to give him the field command at Ticonderoga while he returned to Albany to oversee logistical, administrative, and diplomatic matters. An improbable comity seeped into the high command—"the most perfect harmony subsists between us," Schuyler assured Washington—and a wary camaraderie slowly leached through the ranks. The major generals found that they shared two other convictions that would shape their military operations through the fall. The first was that keeping the enemy from quickly attacking Ticonderoga and advancing to the Hudson valley required challenging Carleton's navy on Lake Champlain. The British "will exert themselves in building vessels of force," Schuyler wrote Gates, "yet I think we can outbuild them."

The second conviction was that only one man in the Northern Army could both assemble the American squadron—soon dubbed the Mosquito Fleet—and then lead it into combat as a fighting commodore. "General Arnold, who is perfectly skilled in naval affairs, has most nobly undertaken to command our fleet upon the lake," Gates told Congress. "With infinite satisfaction, I have committed the whole of that department to his care." He added, "Affairs here begin to wear a less gloomy aspect."

In late August, Hannah Arnold, who was raising her brother Benedict's three young sons, had written him from New Haven that she hoped "you may again in peace sit down under your own vine and fig, and none make you afraid. The little boys are well."

There would be no sitting in peace for Brigadier General Arnold, and certainly no one would frighten him. As usual, he was entangled in controversy and fighting a rearguard action against smaller men. In pressing charges against a subordinate for dereliction of duty during the retreat from Canada, Arnold, during the court-martial in Jones's Tavern at Ticonderoga, was in turn accused of looting goods from Montreal. Leaping to his feet in rage, he denounced the court—thirteen senior field-grade officers—for "ungenteel and indecent reflections on a superior officer," then stormed from the room. The presiding colonel issued a warrant for Arnold's arrest on contempt charges, citing his "illegal, illiberal, and disrespectful" conduct. "General Arnold's character has been here traduced lately in the most villainous, assassin-like manner," Captain Wilkinson wrote a friend. Gates promptly intervened, telling Hancock that he felt "obliged to act dictatorially" by dissolving the court. "The warmth of General Arnold's temper might possibly lead him a little farther than is marked by the precise line of decorum," he conceded, but "the United States must not be deprived of that excellent officer's service at this important moment." In a note to Schuyler, Gates admitted that he was "astonished at the calumnies" Arnold seemed to attract. "To be a man of honor, and in an exalted station will ever excite the envy in the mean and undeserving."

Still limping from his Quebec injuries, Arnold now threw himself headlong into the task at hand with his usual rapt intensity. He indeed had "a perfect knowledge in maritime affairs," as Gates assured Washington: Arnold had bought his first trading vessel in 1764, and by the age of twenty-five he owned a commercial squadron that he sometimes sailed himself on expeditions from Connecticut to Canada or the West Indies. He found construction of the Mosquito Fleet already under way, fitfully, in the Skenesborough shipyard on the west bank of Wood Creek, twenty miles below Ticonderoga. Here a loyalist estate built with slave labor a few years earlier included two sawmills, a forge, a foundry, and shops for carpenters, coopers, and farriers. Lumberjacks felled oak and pine, skid horses pulled the timber to the yards—the logs were carefully counted to keep the sawyers honest—and saw gangs worked a long rip blade, usually slicing four planks from each trunk before shaping the boards with augers, chisels, handsaws, and mauls.

Arnold ordered the creek dredged to accelerate the flow of water turning the mill wheels. Stockbridge Indians toiling in the yard were required to wear blue-and-red caps to distinguish them from hostile warriors, and each day more men with tool bags slung over their shoulders arrived from as far away as Philadelphia and Rhode Island to work the ways: carpenters, smiths, riggers, turners, armorers, and craftsmen skilled in making sails, oars, wheels, and ropes. Farriers and other tradesmen were combed from the regiments, including whitesmiths to repair mess kettles, canteens, and tinware. Master shipwrights, lured by food, rum, and thirty-five dollars a month, were organized into work squads of twenty-five men, each assigned to a vessel under construction—framing, planking, and shaping keelsons and knees, setting stem and stern posts, stepping masts, and caulking with the hot pitch that bubbled in kettles between the ways.

Arnold hounded Schuyler and Gates with requests—for oakum, grindstones, bar iron, frying pans, tar brushes, needles, and "about a ton of rum." More than two dozen blacksmiths had reached Skenesborough but with only enough tools for four forges. Until fifteen hundred axes arrived from Albany, some woodsmen chopped down trees with tomahawks. Cordage and sailcloth came from Connecticut. The Salisbury Iron Works sent swivel guns. Hudson River captains provided twenty-six anchors, though "at exorbitant rates." Still Arnold needed more of this and more of that: oars, three dozen lanterns, speaking trumpets, ballast from Rattlesnake Hill, fifty half-hour sandglasses, sixteen hundred fathoms of cordage and hawsers, eight hundred pounds of chalk to whiten stern railings so helmsmen could see one another at night, calfskin for drumheads needed to beat signals across the squadron.

Under Schuyler's earlier direction, four lake gundalows had been built during the summer, and four more were begun. Flat-bottomed, open-decked, pointed at both ends, and fifty-six feet long, painted the same red as local barns, they carried a large rudder and three cannons; lacking keels, with a mast amidships and a single square sail, they were poor sailors with the wind and wretched against it. Keenly aware of the Royal Navy's advantages in manpower and experience, Arnold also wanted vessels that would be both swift under sail and nimble under oars on the narrow lake, which stretched for 120 miles from north to south but was nowhere wider than twelve miles. Shipwrights answered by laying keels for several galleys eighteen feet in the beam and over seventy feet long, with a raised quarterdeck, thirty-six oars, lateen-rigged fore- and mainmasts with triangular sails, and ports for eight or ten guns cut into the bulwarks rather than firing over the gunwales. Arnold had hoped to have thirty boats in his Mosquito Fleet, but by late September he'd mustered only half that. Among them were several vessels commandeered on the lakes or the Richelieu—a sloop and three schooners, including his flagship, the two-masted *Royal Savage*, seized at St. Johns by General Montgomery the previous year.

Congress authorized a bonus of eight shillings a month to any soldier who volunteered for service on "the waters of the Lake Champlain." Arnold's officers sorted them into seamen, gunners, and marines, then tried to teach the rudiments of setting sails, manning the sweeps, fighting from the tops or on a crowded deck, and laying guns to hit a moving target. A detachment poked around Crown Point, excavating British cannons, shot, and seven tons of sheet lead left from the French war. Other guns, rejected by Henry Knox the previous December, were salvaged from Ticonderoga, even though all were inferior cast iron and in some cases dated to the seventeenth century. Except for four 18-pounders, the guns were woefully light for naval combat. The test-firing from gundalows proved disheartening: two mortars fractured immediately and an old cannon burst so catastrophically that a gunner's mate was reportedly "blown into many pieces and scattered on the water." Requests went out to New York forges for swivel, grape, double-headed, and chain shot. Arnold also reported shortages of sponges, rammers, and gun carriages. Powder was so dear that in September, gun crews were permitted a single practice round, shooting at an empty cask bobbing on the lake.

As his squadron made ready, Arnold carefully scouted the lake and its eighty islands. Having dueled with Carleton for much of the past year, he correctly assumed that the chary British commander would wait until he had an overwhelming force before attacking; several menacing reconnaissance sorties by the Americans near the Richelieu were intended to encourage that circumspection. Arnold surmised, with remarkable precision, that the invading force would likely include 10,000 men "landed in Canada from Europe," 26 war vessels carrying more than 100 guns, and 250 bateaux. He positioned lookouts on Île la Motte, in the northern neck of the lake, hired forty Indians to scout the shoreline, and scoured American hospitals for lake pilots healthy enough to guide his boats. He also sent two spies posing as deserters into Canada; their credentials had been sewn inside the soles of their shoes. Gates cautioned Arnold against overextending his force. "It is a defensive war we are carrying on," he wrote. "Therefore, no wanton risk." But, he added, "Should the enemy come up the lake . . . give them reason to repent their temerity."

By mid-September Arnold had found his battleground. Roughly midway between Crown Point and the Richelieu, Valcour Island was a thousand-acre emerald knob, two miles long and separated from the western shore by a strait half a mile wide. Two boats sent to sound the strait reported that it offered "an exceeding fine, secure harbor"—inaccessible from the north because of shoals, and screened from the main channel of the lake by tall trees on the island's crest. On September 23, Arnold moored his squadron in the cove, posting guard boats each night and keeping half the men constantly on deck under arms. "I am positive they will not be able to surprise us," he had written Gates. "I make no doubt of their soon paying us a visit. . . . If they are too many for us, we can retire."

Arnold's bravado concealed misgivings. "When you ask for a frigate, they give you a raft," he reportedly complained. "Ask for sailors, they give you tavern waiters." He had hoped for almost a thousand experienced mariners but got only seventy. Of the five ship's masters in Connecticut to whom he had written offering commands, only one had accepted. He arrived at Ticonderoga in an ox cart, sitting on his sea chest and cradling a sextant in his lap. All told, Arnold was short two hundred crewmen. He wrote Gates:

I must renew my request for more seamen and gunners. . . . The drafts from the regiments at Ticonderoga are a miserable set. Indeed, the men on board the fleet in general are not equal to half their number of good men.

On October 1 he wrote Gates again from Valcour Island, pleading for warm clothing, rum, three hundred pounds of musket balls, and cannon shot—almost two thousand each of grape, chain, and double-headed—plus "100 seamen (no landlubbers)." He asked forgiveness "if with five hundred men half-naked, I should not be able to beat the enemy with seven thousand men, well-clothed, and a naval force, by the best accounts, near equal to ours."

Gates replied on October 3. None of the two hundred mariners promised from New York City had arrived, and "I now give up the hope of seeing them this year." As for munitions and other supplies, he added, "Where it is not to be had, you and the princes of the earth must go unfurnished." Gates sent the squadron twenty barrels of rum in consolation.

By the second week of October, Arnold had begun to doubt whether the man he now called "Carleton the Haughty" would indeed venture south. "The weather is very severe here & gales of wind frequent," he advised Gates. If the enemy failed to appear by mid-month, he intended to pull south and prepare for winter.

He was eager for war news from New York. "I am very anxious for our army & friends below," he added. He also wondered about his own future. Although Gates lauded him as "a most persevering hero," he felt aggrieved and unappreciated. A congressman had warned him, "Your best friends are not your countrymen." "I have some thoughts of going to Congress, & begging leave to resign. Do you think they will make me a major general (*entre nous*)?" he asked Gates. "My character is much injured . . . when I have sacrificed my ease, health, and great part of my private property in the cause of my country." For the moment, he would watch and wait as the autumn weather thickened. "I have received no late intelligence from the northward," he wrote on October 10.

Regardless, he assured Gates, "We are prepared for them at all times."

As sunrise approached just after six o'clock on Friday, October 11, the din of capstans, billowing canvas, and shouted orders carried across the riffling lake below Île la Motte, where British sailors won their anchors and crowded on sail. Deck crews on the orange-hulled schooners hauled the peak and throat halyards. Hessian and Royal Artillery gunners took battle stations, and swarms of gunboats, bateaux, and canoes sorted themselves into an orderly formation that stretched south across waters darker than indigo. A thousand oars and paddles winked in loose syncopation. *Inflexible*'s white sails towered upward for three tiers, fattened by a brisk north wind. Smoke leaked from *Thunderer*'s furnace, where cannonballs glowed like plump cherries.

On the quarterdeck of *Lady Maria* at the head of the battle line, wrapped in wool against the morning chill, stood General Carleton, ever stern, ever impassive. Beside him stood his commodore, Captain Thomas Pringle of the Royal Navy, and Dr. Robert Knox, the senior British Army physician in North America. Past Point au Roche they scudded, then rounded Cumberland Head. An intelligence report had suggested that the rebel Arnold would be found with sixteen ships in Cumberland Bay, along the west shore. But at nine-thirty a.m., "to our great mortification we could discover no ships," Dr. Knox wrote. The flotilla sailed on.

Arnold had been alerted by an alarm gun after a scout boat spotted the approaching enemy seven miles north of Valcour Island. He hoisted a white signal pennant, summoning his senior officers to a war council aboard *Congress*, the galley where he had shifted his flag. In the cramped cabin he reminded his boat captains that General Gates required a "resolute but judicious defense." No doubt their squadron was outgunned and outmanned: the eighty-six guns on fifteen American vessels could throw just over six hundred pounds of metal in one salvo, compared to more than half a ton from the British guns.

Brigadier General David Waterbury, Jr., Arnold's second-in-command and an experienced mariner from Connecticut, urged trying to outsail the British in a fighting retreat to Ticonderoga. Otherwise they would be bottled up in Valcour Bay and bludgeoned to bits. Arnold immediately rejected the suggestion. The callow crews would be no match on the open water for the Royal Navy, as sailors or gunners. Their task, as he saw it, was to delay, disrupt, and confound. With the Mosquito Fleet arrayed in a tight crescent across the mouth of the strait, they could concentrate their fire on enemy ships beating against the north wind. The captains were to drape all of the powder magazines with wet blankets, spread sand on their decks for traction in case of spilled blood, and clear for action. He ended the conference and wished them luck.

Captain Pringle had neglected to dispatch scouts to examine the narrow strait along the western flank of Valcour Island, a blunder explicable only by incompetence alloyed with hubris. Not until his five large sailing vessels had passed the southern tip of the island at eleven a.m. did he realize that the enemy was now behind him with the weather gage advantage.

He also saw four American men-of-war emerging from the strait, their guns popping at the bateaux strung out in the rear of the British formation: Arnold had ordered a sortie to force the action and prevent Carleton from simply blockading the anchorage. *Lady Maria* swung hard to starboard as Pringle hoisted the signal to attack. *Inflexible* skidded on for two miles before topmen could spill enough air from her sails to bring her about for the long, upwind struggle.

Arnold promptly recalled his four decoys. The three row galleys with their weatherly lateen sails easily pirouetted back into position along the crescent. But as *Royal Savage* heeled over in a long reach while tacking clumsily behind her sisters, several enemy rounds clipped her rigging and spars. She abruptly lurched upward, sails drooping and masts splintering: the schooner had run aground on a shallow ledge, twenty feet from Valcour's southern knuckle. Thirty British guns soon sought her range, including 24-pounders. Chain shot shredded the rigging further, and a longboat from the *Loyal Convert* carried a boarding party to the canted deck. American crewmen leaped overboard, splashing for the island.

In a blur of rammers and sponges, British gunners now had the pleasure of aiming *Royal Savage*'s ten cannons and twelve swivels at Arnold's squadron. But the battle soon tipped against them. Four Yankee gundalows darted forward, fired, retreated, reloaded, then darted forward again. American grape and balls killed half the British boarders and drove the others back into their longboat after setting *Royal Savage* ablaze.

"At half past twelve," Arnold recorded, "the engagement became general and very warm." The clamor grew to a roar, of guns and crashing yards, of slatting canvas and blocks rattling and men yelling in pain, fear, or rage. Hundreds of Indians beached their canoes on the island and the mainland, then sniped at the Americans with muskets and arrows, although at such range, Arnold wrote, that they "did little damage." *Inflexible, Thunderer,* and *Maria* struggled against the wind, tacking again and again to creep northward. But British and German gunboats dropped their square lugsails and rowed into the melee, midshipmen counting strokes from each stern, tholes squeaking, bow guns barking. "The cannonade," a Hessian officer reported, "was tremendous."

The schooner *Carleton*, nearest to Arnold's crescent when the brawl began, absorbed a majority of the American fire for an hour and suffered for the attention. "The battle was very hot," one rebel told his journal. "We cut her rigging most all away & bored her through and through." A British officer lost an arm and *Carleton*'s captain fell badly wounded, leaving command to a nineteen-year-old midshipman, Edward Pellew. Pugnacious and fearless, infamous for doing handstands on the yardarms, he was, by his own description, "pockmarked, ugly, uninteresting, and uneducated." Pellew—the future Admiral Viscount Exmouth—rose to the moment, first saving his unconscious captain from being tossed overboard as a corpse, then scrambling onto the bowsprit to pull the luffing jib to windward. With two feet of water in the hold and half the crew dead or wounded, two British gunboats took the schooner in tow and hauled her out of range after Pellew, in a final demonstration of jack-tar moxie, retied a line severed by gunfire.

More battering befell the British, who were, a Royal Navy officer acknowledged, "greatly annoyed by grape shot." An American 12-pound ball punctured the bow of a Hessian boat three inches above the waterline, igniting a powder keg. The blast slew a cannoneer and took off a sailor's leg, and the subsequent fire killed a drummer and helmsman before a nearby gunboat could pluck survivors to safety. Dr. Knox, aboard *Lady Maria*, reported that Carleton "walked the quarterdeck the whole time with the most uncommon complacency of mind and intrepidity." When an 18-pound ball from *Congress* passed close overhead around one p.m., Carleton asked with studied nonchalance, "Well, doctor, how do you like a sea fight?"

In truth, *Maria* had anchored on the outer fringe of the brawl, for which Captain Pringle would be accused of timidity, even cowardice, by several Royal Navy officers. In a bold public letter the following summer, they charged that Pringle "formed no plan nor made any disposition" for battle, despite late intimations that American ambushers might be found behind Valcour Island, and that he was "the only person in the fleet who showed no inclination to fight." The battle was so mismanaged, a Royal Artillery lieutenant added, that barely one-third of the fleet saw sustained action. Pringle would be promoted nonetheless, and die in the next century as a vice admiral.

As the afternoon wore away, the weight of British metal told. *Inflexible* finally drew close enough to fling five searing broadsides. *Philadelphia*, a rebel gundalow fighting with a 12-pounder in the bow, eight swivels, and two seventeenth-century Swedish 9-pounders in the waist, took at least three shots in the hull; she would sink with the setting sun. One of *New York*'s ancient 6-pounders burst into seven fragments upon firing, gouging holes in the boat and tearing apart Lieutenant Thomas Rogers, age twenty-six. His widow, Molly, nine months pregnant, later raised a cenotaph to his memory in Massachusetts, noting that he had died "in the service of his country and in the cause of liberty."

Much of the British fire concentrated on Arnold and his flagship, *Congress*, which took seven balls between wind and water. Two more splintered the mainmast. Bellowing through a speaking trumpet, his face and the gold epaulettes on his uniform black with powder, Arnold seemed so ubiquitous that his foes swore he was bounding from boat to boat during the fight. "We suffered much for want of seamen & gunners," he later told Gates. "I was obliged myself to point most of the guns aboard the *Congress*, which I believe did good execution." With each shuddering salvo fired by his crew, the galley seemed to lift from the lake for an instant.

Shortly before sunset at 5:16 p.m., Arnold ordered the squadron to pull back three hundred yards into the strait. He gobbled down dinner and summoned his boat captains. Twilight had faded as they crowded the stern cabin, bloody and blackened, to give their reports. Three-quarters of their ammunition was gone. Sixty men were dead or wounded. Aboard the sloop *Enterprise*, now serving as a hospital boat, "the doctors cut off great many legs and arms," one Massachusetts militiaman noted. "Seven men threw overboard that died with their wounds while I was aboard." *New York* had lost all of her officers except the captain. *Philadelphia* had gone to the bottom, ten fathoms down. *Washington*, hulled repeatedly, was leaking badly, with her sails shredded, mainmast shot through, lieutenant dead, and captain wounded. Some holes in the *Congress* were large enough for a man to poke his head through.

There was no choice: they would have to make a run for Crown Point, forty-five miles south. Like a rattlesnake, Arnold said, they had struck, venomously, and now must slither away. The British fleet had anchored in a semicircle just outside the mouth of the strait. But having fired well over a thousand rounds, Pringle's gunboats withdrew from the screen line for rearming by *Thunderer* farther out on the lake. Hoisting ammunition from the radeau's hold, lugging it across her deck, and handing it over the side in darkness would take all night. The tiny sliver of a crescent moon had set at dusk; except for the stars, partly dimmed by lake fog, and the dying flames of the *Royal Savage*, now burning to the waterline at the foot of the island, the night would be pitch black.

Arnold's captains returned to their boats and soon hoisted anchor, carefully, quietly, hand over hand, the ropes and blocks slathered with animal grease to prevent squeaking. *Trumbull* led with only enough white sail unfurled for steerage way. A dark lantern gleamed above her tiller, and thick chalk lightened the stern rails for the helmsmen behind. No mariner could cross the shoal water at the north end of the strait in such stygian darkness, so they would swing west to the mainland shore and then south, skirting *Lady Maria* on the left of the British line, where Carleton and Pringle had gone below to dine.

One by one the thirteen surviving boats slid past the enemy, oars muffled with rags, the wounded draped in blankets to smother their moans. British voices could be heard on the water, between the hammer blows of carpenters repairing battle damage. *Washington* and *Congress* brought up the rear. Arnold hardly dared draw breath at the rail, a bright-eyed raven on this raven night.

By Saturday morning they were eight miles up the lake at Schuyler's Island, buffeted by squalls. The gundalow *Spitfire*, no longer seaworthy, was deliberately sunk after transferring the crew to other vessels. *Jersey* was so waterlogged that even a scuttler's torch could not ignite her, and *Washington*'s tattered sails required repair after splitting "from foot to head." Crown Point still lay more than thirty-five miles south, but no enemy sails could be seen on the northern horizon. "On the whole," Arnold told Gates in a hurried note, "I think we have had a very fortunate escape." They pressed on, *Trumbull* in the van leading the surviving vessels past Four Brothers Islands, with *Washington* and *Congress* still as a rear guard. Aboard *Enterprise*, Private Jahiel Stewart would tell his journal, "We thought we was safe."

At dawn, Carleton let his phlegmatic mien drop long enough to indulge in a steaming rage upon seeing that the Americans had fled. Unwilling to believe they had slipped through his pickets, he insisted that Arnold must have led his flotilla north around Valcour Island and across the lake. Some hours were spent in a futile search. *Lady Maria* crossed Champlain's main channel and fired through the morning mist at what appeared to be a raised sail only to discover that the target was a rock whitened with gull guano. The dissident British captains added another indictment against Pringle, blaming the rebel escape not on "the extreme obscurity of the night as you are pleased to say" but on his botched dispositions along the western shore. Even as the recriminations flew, the British squadron wheeled south in pursuit.

Arnold spotted the white specks of enemy canvas at two p.m. Hour by agonizing hour the sails grew larger. The wind had become southerly, rebuffing the cumbrous gundalows, and only by rowing elbow to elbow through another moonless night did the rebels keep any distance from their pursuers. By daybreak on Sunday, the Americans had covered just ten miles from Schuyler's Island, and now the fickle wind played them false, hauling again from the north. *Washington* fell astern, leaking badly, overcrowded, and with one mast shattered. At Split Rock, where the lake narrowed to under a mile, *Lady Maria* opened with her bow chaser at a quarter mile's range; *Inflexible* and *Carleton* soon added broadsides. *Washington* fought back briefly, each recoil from her guns threatening to capsize the galley, then struck her colors. Ahead, *Trumbull*—with oars double-manned and every ounce of ballast pitched overboard—managed to reach Crown Point late in the afternoon, trailed by the sloop *Enterprise*, the schooner *Revenge*, and the battered gundalow *New York*.

That left Arnold. The *Congress*, flanked by four remaining gundalows, skirted the shallows of Buttonmould Bay, along the eastern shore, with seven British vessels bearing down from behind. Two 18-pound stern chasers protruding from the galley's transom heckled the British pursuers, who answered with a ferocious cannonade. From the quarterdeck, Arnold "roared derision at the British when they missed and doffed his battered hat to the enemy in recognition of a fair hit," the historian Harrison Bird later wrote. *Maria* was the first to catch up, raking *Congress* broadside from musket range with grape and round shot while *Carleton* and *Invincible* peppered her under the stern. Through five turns of the sandglass—two and a half hours—forty-four British guns and twenty-two swivels bludgeoned the galley, shredding sails, rigging, hull, and crewmen. The dead were tossed overboard, the injured dragged below, where their shirts and trousers were ripped into tourniquets and a surgeon stuffed gaping wounds with cloth cut from his own coat. Four trailing British gunboats joined the fray, adding their metal and dueling with the gundalows.

From his reconnaissance of Lake Champlain, Arnold knew of Ferris Bay, a small, U-shaped cove just south of Buttonmould. Above the booming guns he shouted his orders before steering the stricken galley through a gap in the encircling British, his men straining at their sweeps. The four gundalows followed. American marines splashed through the shallows and clambered up the steep bank to lay down covering fire while sailors on deck ripped open cartridges and ignited the scattered powder. Dragging their wounded overboard, they scrambled for high ground, chased into the wood line by British grape. Arnold left his colors flying—"a point of honor in a manner almost romantic," an army doctor observed—as flames licked up the spars and tarred rigging. In the fading light, five pyres burned bright on Ferris Bay.

Two hundred men joined Arnold at a house above the lake. "They were so black with the smoke of the powder that they could scarcely be told from Negroes," a farm boy reported, "and their clothes were all blackened with the burnt powder of the guns." Pursued by British troops and Indians, they pressed through the night to cover the nine miles to Crown Point, where Pennsylvania Continentals burned the camp and sawmill before retreating south. Arnold hurried ahead, reaching Ticonderoga at four o'clock on Monday morning, "exceedingly fatigued and unwell, having been without sleep or refreshment for near three days," as he noted in his report.

Gates praised his "gallant behavior and steady good conduct." In a dispatch to Schuyler, he added, "It has pleased providence to preserve General Arnold. Few men ever met with so many hair-breadth escapes in so short a space of time."

Smoke and flame swirled through Crown Point as thirteen British war vessels glided along the shoreline and dropped anchor on Monday, October 14. A few civilians still lingering near the old fort bolted through the forest "in the greatest distress," one witness noted, "leaving all their houses, stuff, clothing &c. to the enemy, or to the flames. A melancholy sight." A British captain rowed ashore under a truce flag, followed by skiffs carrying more than a hundred Yankee prisoners, mostly taken on the *Washington*. General Carleton had plied them with grog and humanity, and now, after they promised not to bear arms against their king until properly exchanged for British prisoners, he set them free. "The rebel fleet upon Lake Champlain has been entirely defeated," he wrote Germain from his cabin on *Lady Maria*. "The season is so far advanced that I cannot yet pretend to inform your lordship whether anything further can be done this year."

Guy Carleton faced the most momentous military decision he would ever make: whether to assault Ticonderoga in hopes of capturing the fortress for winter quarters or return to Canada and wait until spring. He had an intact fleet and substantial artillery, but ferrying the rest of the army to Crown Point would take nearly a week. He had just dispatched a courier to Burgoyne by canoe, carrying both *Washington*'s captured colors, with its thirteen stripes, and orders to immediately load several hundred bateaux at Point au Fer—a few miles below the Richelieu—and sail south. All provisions for the winter would have to come from Canada, and once the lake iced over, return to the north would be impossible. Carleton had already hedged his bets by alerting garrisons in Canada to prepare accommodations for the returning troops; the Germans would bivouac in Trois-Rivières, he advised, "and you will do well to warn the inhabitants."

Ten miles south, few Americans believed that the enemy, having come so far, would turn away. A spy reported that the regulars not only intended to storm Ticonderoga but to spend a comfortable winter in Albany. Gates ordered the prisoners released by the British to be sent south to Skenesborough at once, before they infected his troops with infatuated stories of

Carleton's beneficence. "This stillness," Gates told Schuyler, "will be suc-ceeded immediately by a grand attack."

Each morning, beginning that Monday, the entire garrison stood to, under arms, at four a.m. and again manned the alarm posts each evening before sunset when enemy attacks seemed most likely. Battlements and ramparts bristled with guns and firelocks. Powder supplies had dwindled to less than four thousand pounds, but fifteen additional tons from Schuyler arrived during the week, along with three tons of lead—enough for a hun-dred thousand musket balls—and a thousand bushels of flour. When the attack came, Gates decreed, musketmen were to hold their fire until the enemy was within ten rods—fifty-five yards—and each man received a quarter pound of buckshot to increase the sting. The hospital at Fort George was ordered to "immediately send all the well-men to their regiments." Car-penters and smiths labored to exhaustion building gun carriages as well as a log boom and footbridge across the lake between the fortress and Mount Independence, formerly Rattlesnake Hill. "Our men work with life and spirits this day," Colonel Jeduthan Baldwin wrote on October 16, "which shows a determined resolution to defend the place to the last extreme."

Time was on their side, commanders insisted, as it had been for the defenders of Quebec a year earlier. "General Winter cannot be very far off," one officer said. Still, each passing day brought greater tension. Some men wrote just-in-case letters. "Our situation is critical," William Tennent told his wife, Susanna. "Should I never see you again, I wish you every blessing from the fountain of all goodness & beg you not to grieve for me." Sergeant Timothy Tuttle of the 1st New Jersey Regiment marked time in his diary: "*Oct. 17*: A rainy dull day. The Regulars not come yet. Expect them every day. *Oct. 18*: Rainy day. We expect the Regulars soon. *Oct. 19*: Expect Regulars soon." On Sunday, October 20, a New Jersey chaplain took his sermon from the fourth chapter of Nehemiah: "Be ye not afraid of them. Remember the Lord . . . and fight for your brethren, your sons and daughters, your wives and your houses."

The alarm guns finally sounded on Monday morning, October 28, first from a guard boat below Crown Point, and then in quick succession from a forward battery, from a redoubt along the old French lines, and from bas-tions on Mount Independence. Each boom careered along the rocky slopes and echoed down the lake. Drums pounded. Sergeants hurried among the tents, yelling, "Turn out, turn out!" Every man capable of shouldering a mus-ket stumbled into the lines. The day was crisp and so clear that men posting the high ground could see snow on the Adirondacks thirty miles to the west.

They could also see redcoats spilling from five large gunboats at Three-Mile Point, a half-hour hike from the forward American sentry. Suspecting that the enemy had concentrated on the west side of the lake to attack his left flank, Gates shifted three regiments from Mount Independence. Two enemy scout boats nosed up the eastern shore until a scalding barrage from field guns and the *Trumbull*, moored near the log boom, drove them off with two dead.

And then, like spirits of the lake, the British vanished. For a fortnight Carleton had surveyed Ticonderoga's outer works and pondered his options before deciding that the American fortifications were too strong for a direct assault, and that the late season precluded a siege. Burgoyne agreed, but suggested encircling the defenders—"to have felt their pulse"—in hopes that they would abandon their stronghold in panic. Carleton rejected the proposal as pointless; American deserters had revealed how robust the defenses had become. This last probe on Monday morning, and the sight of over ten thousand defenders glaring from the ramparts, convinced him that no attack could be made without grim losses. The withdrawal to Canada would begin promptly, given "the severity of the approaching season."

Victorious yet morose, the invaders beat north past hardwood stands no longer bright, on choppy waters the color of pig iron: canoes, longboats, gunboats and schooners, the pugnacious *Thunderer* and three-tiered *Inflexible*. Their drums sounded fog warnings as the vessels drifted in and out of thick autumnal banks. A northerly gale forced them ashore one night at Valcour. Here they named the strait Destruction Bay, wishfully perhaps, and fished a few more enemies from the lake. "Some of their dead were then floating on the brink of the water, just as the surf threw them," Lieutenant William Digby of the 53rd Foot told his diary on November 2. "These were ordered to be directly buried." The first snow whitened the lakeshore that night, and in the morning they pressed on for the Richelieu.

At the other end of Lake Champlain, men grateful to have survived another fighting season stood down and breathed deep. "Blessed be God I am alive while others are dead," Archelaus Jay wrote his parents in Massachusetts. Soldier Edmund Munro told his wife:

> Being in great haste I have only time to inform you that I am in good health & high spirits. . . . The nights are cold which puts me in mind of you in your warm bed many times in the night. The enemy have left us.

No sooner had Carleton made himself master of the lakes than the second-guessing began. "Notwithstanding the success on the lake, we terminate the campaign ill," wrote Major General William Phillips, the Royal Artillery chief in Canada. "It is the humor here to suppose that it is no disgrace to retire if it is not done in the face of the enemy." Many feared they had won a tactical victory while frittering away the strategic advantage; the four weeks Carleton spent building *Inflexible* likely cost Britain a year, although Captain Douglas asserted that the vessel had provided the margin of victory in commanding the lake. Lieutenant Colonel Gabriel Christie, hysterical and disloyal toward Carleton, went so far as to write Germain that "confusion and embarrassment appeared everywhere under a commander absorbed within himself. . . . He is totally unfit for such a command, and must ruin His Majesty's affairs and those of England either in a civil or military capacity." Many also felt a grudging admiration for the rebel Arnold, who "behaved like a man of spirit," one general's aide wrote, ". . . and showed himself clever in escaping from Valcour." A British naval historian in the next century would be unstinting in his praise for the Mosquito Fleet: "Never had any force, big or small, lived to better purpose or died more gloriously; for it had saved the lake for that year." Consequences would follow in train.

In a letter to Henry Clinton, Burgoyne worried that the withdrawal northward "puts us in danger . . . of losing the fruits of our summer's labor and autumn victory." His professional dismay was eclipsed by personal anguish: Burgoyne had just received word that his adored wife, Charlotte, a severe asthmatic, had died in England. He told Clinton, another widower, that the news left him "an unconnected cypher. My prospects in the world are closed. Interest, ambition, the animation of life is over." Even before the returning flotilla reached the Richelieu, he bolted for home to find Charlotte interred in the North Cloister of Westminster Abbey, next to their daughter, their only child, who had died at the age of ten a dozen years earlier.

Adding to Burgoyne's miseries, the king initially declined to see him, in apparent pique at "operations conducted without sense or vigor," in Germain's phrase. When finally admitted to the royal presence, Burgoyne "laid himself at His Majesty's feet" and discovered, not without pleasure, that Carleton was in much worse odor than he. He also learned that a letter from Germain in late August had directed Carleton to remain in Quebec while Burgoyne led the field army into New York; that order had miscarried—the courier ship thrice failed to penetrate gales in the Gulf of St. Lawrence before finally returning to England—and a duplicate would not reach Carleton until May 1777. News of the retreat from Crown Point stirred further doubt about the commanding general, and aggravated the mutual enmity he and Germain felt.

For now George chose to pretend that Britain had won a great triumph in Canada. If Carleton was "not so active as might be wished," he could be nudged into a harmless administrative role. Burgoyne, deemed "a more enterprising commander," repaired to Bath to mourn by taking the waters and polishing a seven-page battle plan for the government he titled "Thoughts for Conducting the War from the Side of Canada." Ticonderoga, he told Clinton, "must necessarily fall with small loss & in short time by a regular attack next spring." Once he joined forces with Howe, the rebellion would be all but extinguished. On Christmas Day, Burgoyne wagered the opposition leader Charles James Fox fifty guineas, duly recorded in the betting book at Brooks's, a private upper-class club, "that he will be home victorious from America by Christmas Day 1777." Fox happily took the bet, chortling, "Be not over-sanguine."

Just before the St. Lawrence iced shut, Maria Carleton sailed back to Canada with her three sons and a token for her husband from his king: a knighthood in the Order of the Bath, awarded for liberating Quebec. (Germain had opposed the gesture, churlishly telling General Howe that giving Carleton the red ribbon "made it appear to me of less value.") Carleton joined his family in the Château St. Louis, the enormous Norman tower with a copper roof and a rear balcony overlooking Quebec's Lower Town. As a reunion gift, he gave Maria a new four-seat, single-horse cariole.

Here, on December 31, they commemorated the town's triumphant repulse of the Americans under Montgomery and Arnold precisely a year earlier. The celebration began with a *Te Deum* sung in the cathedral, where every pew was jammed and the walls blazed with candlelight. Militiamen marched through the nave, and at a signal from the bishop a dozen collaborators appeared at the rear door, each with a rope knotted at his neck, to publicly "crave pardon of their God, church, and king." An elaborate supper with sixty covers was served in the château to three hundred diners, who came to their feet at six-thirty p.m. when Sir Guy and Lady Maria entered the Assembly Room. A band struck up "God Save the King," each stanza belted out by a full chorus. A seven p.m. an ode composed for the occasion was delivered with suitable rhetorical flourishes, followed by a grand ball in which guests danced away the old year. "It was universally allowed," the *Quebec Gazette* reported, "to be the completest entertainment of the sort ever known in this province."

By then the king's troops and their German comrades had gone to their winter quarters in a dozen cantonments across Quebec. At St. Johns, the bateaux were hoisted from the water and placed upright on wooden slats to prevent deep snow from crushing the hulls. "Everyone received a pair of long blue cloth overalls, such as boatmen wear, high over the hips and reaching down to the shoes," Captain Georg Pausch, a Hessian artillery-man, wrote from Montreal. Each man also got a blue wool cap, mittens, a white waistcoat, a hooded overcoat cut from wool blankets, and a pair of snowshoes.

Even this garb could not repel the cold, the dark, or the isolation. "I wish with all my heart that we will soon get out of Canada for it can right-fully be called the American Siberia," a surgeon wrote from Trois-Rivières. But most men made do, burrowing into their hutments and warming them-selves with thoughts of the fighting season to come. "Next summer," an officer wrote a friend from St. Johns, "it will be our turn."

This year it had been Benedict Arnold's turn. "No man ever maneu-vered with more dexterity, fought with more bravery, or retreated with more firmness," declared James Thacher, an American army physician. Upon Britain's retraction into Canada—"of as great consequence as if they had been defeated," in Brigadier General Arthur St. Clair's assessment—Arnold promptly headed south with reinforcements for General Washington. When he finally went home to see his sons in Connecticut, he would draw cannon salutes and a hero's welcome in Hartford, Middletown, and New Haven. Once again he had demonstrated that he was the most com-petent battle commander in an American uniform, and perhaps the finest combat officer for either side, able to lead other men through peril, on land or otherwise, with ferocity, prudence, judgment, luck, and an impla-cable will.

Yet, as always, he remained controversial and divisive, his accomplish-ments appreciated more by the British than by many of his compatriots. Richard Henry Lee called him "fiery, hot, and impetuous"—true enough, but Lee's words were uttered in derision rather than admiration. No sooner had the smoke blown free of Champlain than Arnold was accused of sacrificing his squadron without purpose. "General Arnold, our evil genius to the north," a New Jersey colonel charged, ". . . was much the strongest, but he suffered himself to be surrounded." It mattered little to his detrac-tors that he had been grievously wounded and then badly injured at Quebec, lost his wife while serving the cause, helped save the army in Canada, preserved Ticonderoga, and upended British strategy for 1776. More slanders spread, including claims that he had betrayed the sinking *Washington* to save his own skin and then abandoned wounded crew-men to the flames in Ferris Bay. Small wonder that as he made his limping way down the Hudson valley, he carried grievance and resentment within that unquiet soul.

Fewer than three thousand men would stay behind to winter at Ticonderoga under Colonel Wayne. The fortress again become a remote backwater, at least for this fallow season, so forsaken that one soldier complained that a third of the remaining garrison was shoeless. Lean and grizzled, most of the troops collected their paltry belongings and assembled on the parade ground. Regiment upon regiment passed out through the gates with shouldered firelocks, southbound on the long march toward other battles on other fields.

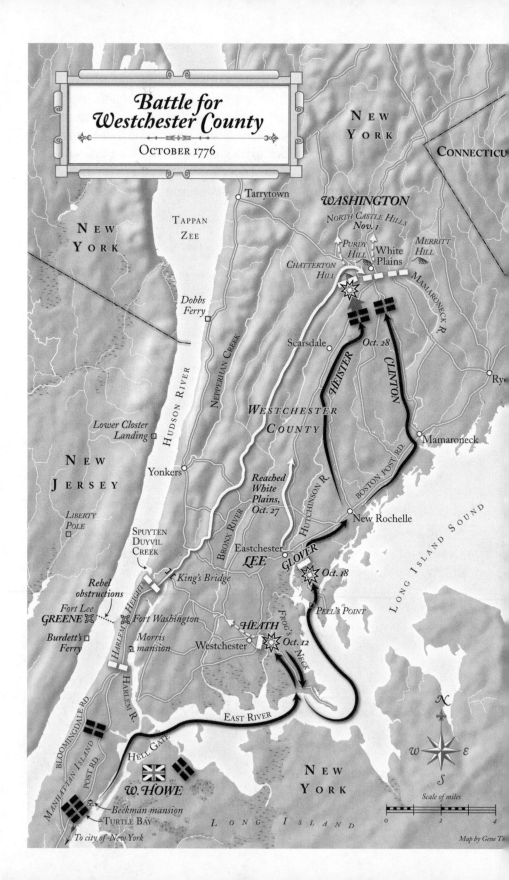

Battle for Westchester County

OCTOBER 1776

NEW YORK

CONNECTICUT

Tarrytown

WASHINGTON

NORTH CASTLE HILLS
Nov. 1

TAPPAN ZEE

Purdy Hill

White Plains

MERRITT HILL

CHATTERTON HILL

NEW YORK

Dobbs Ferry

MAMARONECK R.

Scarsdale

Oct. 28

HEISTER

CLINTON

Rye

Lower Closter Landing

WESTCHESTER COUNTY

Mamaroneck

Yonkers

Reached White Plains, Oct. 27

BOSTON POST RD.

NEW JERSEY

LIBERTY POLE

HUTCHINSON R.

New Rochelle

LONG ISLAND SOUND

SPUYTEN DUYVIL CREEK

Eastchester

LEE

GLOVER

Oct. 18

Rebel obstructions

King's Bridge

Pell's Point

Fort Lee
GREENE

HARLEM HEIGHTS

Fort Washington

HEATH

Oct. 12

Burdett's Ferry

Morris mansion

Westchester

FROG'S NECK

Hell Gate

EAST RIVER

BLOOMINGDALE RD.

MANHATTAN ISLAND

POST RD.

HARLEM R.

W. HOWE

NEW YORK

Beekman mansion

Turtle Bay

To city of New York

L O N G   I S L A N D

Scale of miles

0   2   4

Map by Gene T.

18.

———

The Retrograde Motion of Things

NEW YORK, OCTOBER–NOVEMBER 1776

From the wide portico of his headquarters on Harlem Heights, General Washington could see all too clearly both the ground he had already lost to the British and the terrain now at risk. Built more than a decade earlier on Manhattan's second-highest hill by a loyalist who had since fled to London, the nineteen-room Roger Morris mansion offered a panoramic vista of New York, Brooklyn, and Staten Island far to the south, as well as the Hudson River and New Jersey to the west and, to the north and east, Westchester County and Long Island Sound. American soldiers controlled roughly half of the landscape visible to their commanding general from his high perch, but few doubted that the brothers Howe coveted a larger share before winter set in.

An odd tranquillity had obtained since the New York fire more than a fortnight earlier. "The two armies are as quiet as if they were a thousand miles apart," Washington's aide Lieutenant Colonel Tench Tilghman wrote on October 7. Brigade majors from the American camps at Harlem Heights or King's Bridge tromped across the mansion's yellow pine floors, collected the daily orders and passwords issued by the adjutant general at six p.m., then tromped out again, nodding to sentries in the twin gatehouses flanking the entry drive. Court-martial boards convened either in the large barn down the hill or in the parlor at the back of the mansion, an octagonal chamber more than thirty feet long, with huge sash windows and buckram wall coverings hung from the cornices. Dinner, often with staff officers or commanders, was served at three p.m. in the commodious dining room to the right of the central hallway. The commander in chief's household expense ledger for his five weeks in the Morris mansion showed a hearty appetite for goose, mutton, veal, turkey, pork, and duck; the provisions also included a half dozen six-pound loaves of bread daily, apples, green tea, cider, and 163 bottles of good Madeira. Up the mahogany staircase, Washington slept in a second-floor room on a bed custom-built to accommodate his height, around the corner from the snuggery where his manservant, William Lee, kept his pallet.

The loss of Long Island and then New York had left Washington dejected and waspish. "It is not in the power of words," he wrote his brother John, "to describe the task I have to act. £50,000 should not induce me again to undergo what I have done." To his cousin Lund, the overseer managing Mount Vernon, he added, "If I were to wish the bitterest curse to an enemy on this side of the grave, I should put him in my stead. . . . I never was in such an unhappy, divided state since I was born." He asked that these bleak thoughts remain private, although "if I fall, it may not be amiss that these circumstances be known." The hanging of Nathan Hale left him bloody-minded and ready to retaliate against British agents. "The General is determined if he can bring some of them in his hands under the denomination of spies, to execute them," Tilghman wrote in early October.

"I am wearied to death all day with a variety of perplexing circumstances," Washington told Lund. Nothing was more perplexing than the American army. His force now numbered almost thirty-one thousand, including a large detachment recently shifted into New Jersey under General Greene and the nine fortified positions around King's Bridge, the strongest of which was on the late General Montgomery's estate overlooking both the Albany and Boston post roads. But hardly half the troops were fit for duty. Spring and summer sickness had inevitably been followed by autumn sickness, aggravated by "the shameful inattention in some of the camps to decency and cleanliness," as Washington had complained in his general orders on October 4.

A Delaware surgeon at King's Bridge wrote that "excrementitious matter was scattered indiscriminately throughout the camp. . . . Many died melting as it were, and running off by the bowels." Among those dying from dysentery was Philip Vickers Fithian, the New Jersey militia chaplain. "He has no physician to attend him but an unskillful quack of a surgeon's mate," a fellow divine wrote, then added on October 8, "This morning about 10 o'clock, Mr. Fithian closed his eyes upon the things of time." A single surgeon's mate served five Connecticut regiments; the brigade physicians were all ill. Those sent to hospitals—often no more than a turf hut—lay two to a bed, spreading typhus. Doctors once again pleaded for tents, surgical dressings, drugs, and more doctors. "I beg instruments may be sent us, particularly amputating," a senior medical officer wrote Congress. "The enemy are at hand."

Those who stayed healthy too often behaved badly. Desertion, insubordination, and even mutiny roiled the ranks. Thievery grew so rampant that Washington required regiments to assemble on parade so field officers could inspect knapsacks and tents for plunder. Civilians bolted their doors when American soldiers approached. "Some houses have actually been burnt to cover the theft," Washington told Congress. The troops seemed "infinitely more formidable to the poor farmers & inhabitants" than to the British, he added.

Some believed that the army simply reflected the coarse times. "There is too much corruption, even in this infant age of our republic. Virtue is not in fashion. Vice is not infamous," John Adams wrote Abigail. "I am ashamed of the age I live in." Yet Washington argued more fervently than ever that forging a standing army of soldiers recruited for the duration would remedy many of his ills. In an October 5 letter to Patrick Henry, the recently elected governor of Virginia, he urged that officers selected for new regiments have "a just pretension to the character of a gentleman, a proper sense of honor, & some reputation to lose."

In an anguished, fourteen-paragraph meditation to Hancock, written late at night in the Morris mansion, the commanding general warned that "to place any dependence upon militia is, assuredly, resting upon a broken staff." The "war must be carried on systematically." Since many Continental enlistments would expire at the end of the year, only "by establishing your army upon a permanent footing"—with ample bounties of cash, land, and uniforms to attract good men for a protracted struggle—could the professional British force be checked. A badly paid soldier could not be expected to "ruin himself and his family to serve his country," Washington wrote. "Something is due to the man who puts his life in his hand, hazards his health, & forsakes the sweets of domestic enjoyment." Not only would a disciplined, properly compensated army better serve the nation, Washington argued, but "certain am I that it would be cheaper" than the chaotic practice of flinging militia units willy-nilly into battle.

The chance of a standing army turning into a rogue, despotic force was "remote, and in my judgment . . . not at all to be dreaded," he added. The alternative—adhering to the status quo, with short enlistments, mediocre officers, and reliance on a fickle militia—meant "certain and inevitable ruin." Having made his case with force and coherence, Washington closed by apologizing "for the liberties taken in this letter and for the blots and scratchings therein—not having time to give it more correctly."

The grumble of heavy artillery along the Hudson early on Wednesday morning, October 9, ended the unspoken truce of the past three weeks. Since fleeing downriver after the rebel fireship attack in mid-August, the Royal Navy had been content to position several men-of-war along General

Howe's left flank below Harlem Heights, seven miles upstream from the Grand Battery. Now a trio of vessels—*Phoenix, Roebuck*, and *Tartar*, each with a tender—weighed anchor at seven o'clock on the early tide and swept north, intent on again reclaiming the Hudson for the Crown.

Within twenty minutes, five American batteries above the Manhattan shoreline and two more in New Jersey had found the range. Plunging fire ripped across the Hudson and great splashes leaped up around the ships. "The heights on each side [of] the river produced the noblest effect imaginable," Lieutenant Colonel Tudor, the judge advocate, told a friend. "An echo rebounded from rock to hill, & from hill to rock, & created a sound not unlike distant thunder." Even as he tried to sink the frigates, another colonel admired the British sangfroid. "One gentleman, seemingly in command, walked the second deck as if nothing were the matter," he wrote, "although seven forts kept firing constantly upon the ship." The clang of iron striking oak reverberated on both shores.

Since the first successful British sortie to Tappan Zee on July 12, Washington's engineers had continued their ingenious if quixotic efforts to blockade the river, both with fortifications ashore and with obstructions underwater. A proposal to "shallow the Hudson" by dumping stone in the channel had soon been dismissed as impractical—the river between Forts Lee and Washington was nearly a mile wide—but more spiky chevaux-de-frise were sunk and more vessels readied for scuttling near the hulks already on the bottom. British officers watching with spyglasses had noted this "industry of malevolence," as Ambrose Serle wrote, but could only hope that the majestic river was too broad, too deep, and too swift for such contraptions.

The Hudson was, in fact, vaster than the Americans realized. Two surveyors using a seven-pound lead weight had reported that the waters off Fort Washington were no deeper than seven fathoms, or forty-two feet. They miscalculated: a wide channel along Jeffrey's Hook, where the George Washington Bridge would later stand, was twelve fathoms, an abyss capable of swallowing whatever was dumped into it. In late September, Washington had learned that the obstructions "sunk in the river may not be sufficient for stopping the enemy's ships." New soundings were ordered "with all the secrecy possible."

Too late. At nine a.m. that Wednesday, Captain Hyde Parker swung *Roebuck* into the channel brushing the Manhattan shoreline. A turncoat American who had promised to point out the underwater obstructions stood near the British helmsman, but from either fear or ignorance he remained mute even after Parker laid a brace of pistols on the binnacle and threatened to shoot him. The wind softened, the tide ebbed, and American gunfire raked the six ships, including 32-pound balls from Fort Lee. "Had a hawser been thrown across the river it would have stopped us, so little way had we," a British lieutenant on *Roebuck* wrote. As the cannonade continued, Parker nosed the flotilla within forty yards of the nearest battery where the channel ran deepest, his officers demonstrating a studied nonchalance by, the lieutenant noted, "standing with our arms folded, hearing & seeing the destruction every shot brought with it."

Within an hour the squadron had slipped through the gantlet to fire with bow chasers at rebel rivercraft. A schooner carrying rum and sugar for the Continentals ran aground, followed by two sloops and two row galleys—including the *Independence*, soon renamed *Dependence*. American mariners abandoned ship, wading ashore near Dobbs Ferry and running through the weeds as grapeshot sang after them. Among the day's casualties was the worthy *Turtle*, sent to the bottom when the vessel carrying it capsized. Inventor David Bushnell swam to safety and escaped.

At five p.m., after lashing the riverfront with broadsides, Captain Parker and his squadron anchored in Tappan Zee. Farmers and fishermen fled inland; militiamen peeped through the trees for signs of redcoat regiments disembarking. The British had sailed through the river obstructions "as if they were cobwebs," by one account. "To our surprise and mortification," Colonel Tilghman lamented, "they all ran through without the least difficulty and without receiving any apparent damage from our forts."

The damage was worse than he knew: *Phoenix* had taken four balls through the hull, with various stays, shrouds, and sails shredded, and her mizzenmast shattered. Among the casualties aboard *Roebuck*, a midshipman died after having his leg amputated. "He was most amiable," a shipmate wrote, "and was dearly beloved by all on board." *Tartar* was repeatedly hulled; flying splinters wounded the captain, a marine lieutenant, and a pilot. "The ships had suffered much in their masts and rigging," Admiral Howe would tell the Admiralty. "The loss of men . . . was considerable." The tally included nine dead and twenty-seven wounded. At six p.m., a ship's log noted, the living "committed the bodies of the deceased to the deep."

But once again a hostile British force was in Washington's rear, controlling the Hudson for thirty miles even as General Howe's force inched up the East River toward Long Island Sound. Upper Manhattan, King's Bridge, and Westchester seemed at risk of a double envelopment. Captain Parker and his naval officers passed the time playing *vingt-et-un*—twenty-one—and waiting for orders from the high command. "Nothing can be more alarming than the present situation of our state," the New York Committee of

Safety wrote Washington on October 10 from Fishkill. "The enemy may seize such passes as will cut off all communication between the army and us, and prevent your supplies."

"It would be a joke if it had not too much melancholy in it," Colonel John Haslet, commander of the Delaware regiment, wrote a friend in Philadelphia. "On a few days now seems to hang the fate of the campaign & the American Army. . . . If they succeed, & can draw a line behind us from river to river, we are completely surrounded."

Completely surrounding the Americans would require a military genius beyond William Howe's capacity. Able, sensible, and often plodding, the British commander seemed unsure of his course even though he now had the whip hand in New York. "I look upon the further progress for the campaign to be rather precarious," he had warned Germain in late September. A sally to Rhode Island to secure another winter port might be possible, but he expected no help this year from Carleton's army in Canada; nor were great victories likely from his own legions. Washington's position in Manhattan seemed too strong to attack frontally, and "innumerable difficulties are in our way of turning him on either side"—much less both sides. The battering of Captain Parker's small squadron on the Hudson showed the hazard of audacity, even if it discomfited the enemy.

Howe continued:

> In my situation, I presume I must not risk, as a check at this time would be of infinite detriment to us. . . . I have not the smallest prospect of finishing the contest this campaign, nor until the rebels see preparations in the spring that may preclude all thoughts of further resistance.

He closed by asking for another ten warships in early 1777, plus extra seamen. "We must also have recruits from Europe," he added, "not finding the Americans disposed to serve with arms."

In the weeks since his victories on Long Island and at Kip's Bay, Howe had built redoubts across Manhattan to secure the British encampments. He had also seized Paulus Hook, in New Jersey, to protect the Upper Bay anchorage. But his earlier conviction that destroying the rebel army in decisive battle would be "the most effectual means to terminate this expensive war" had evolved into a more cautious approach of outmaneuvering Washington, occupying rebel territory, then maneuvering again. At his headquarters in the Beekman house, overlooking the East River, Howe spent

October 8 with his generals and his brother, discussing how best to quell the American insurgency. "They did not break up till near 4 o'clock," Captain Frederick Mackenzie told his diary. "The grand point of view is certainly to beat and disperse this, their principal army . . . as they will never be able to assemble another army fit to oppose the King's troops."

Dispersing enemy armies was hardly equivalent to annihilating them. "I must not risk," Howe had told London, and risk he would not. At three p.m. on Friday, October 11, his regiments began to strike their tents, limber their guns, and prepare for a modest flanking move to Frog's Neck, a narrow peninsula jutting southeast into the mouth of Long Island Sound, thirteen miles northeast of the Beekman house. Some 150 gunboats, bateaux, and other watercraft assembled at Turtle Bay, Marston's Wharf, and various embarkation spots on the East River. Staff officers gathered at five p.m. in the Dove Tavern—close to Captain Hale's scaffold—for final orders, and at ten p.m. the sleepy troops marched to their boats with the usual clattering kit and muttered curses. At daybreak on Saturday, the first wave of the assault force pushed off on the morning tide with artillery vessels, horse and troop transports, and men-of-war.

The only real hazard in this short expedition, intended as a shallow envelopment of the American left flank, lay in a tidal raceway three miles above Turtle Bay originally named Hellegat—"Bright Strait"—by a Dutch explorer. The weedy shoreline of what had come to be known as Hell Gate was littered with ancient boat ribs and other detritus from rivercraft upended by a whirlpool vortex said to be among the world's strongest, most treacherous tidal currents. British helmsmen had been warned to hug the starboard channel to avoid enemy guns on the left and the rocky, turbulent middle passage. But as the lead craft approached the churning strait, thick fog "enveloped us with utter darkness," General Clinton reported. Admiral Howe, bolder than his brother, ordered the flotilla to press on despite not being able to see channel buoys or each other. Flatboats collided in the murk, and some deranged transports slid through the passage stern first—a remarkable feat of seamanship—but the only casualties occurred when a hawser from an anchored warship upended an artillery barge, drowning four gunners and sending three 6-pounders to the bottom of Hellegat.

By midday four thousand nauseous soldiers had regained dry land at Frog's Neck, with twice that number bobbing close behind. Reassembled by regiment, the redcoat column soon stepped off toward a causeway that led to the road toward King's Bridge, six miles northwest. Only now did the folly of General Howe's scheme come clear. "Had they pushed their imaginations to discover the worst place," a New Yorker informed Washington's headquarters, "they could not have succeeded better than they have done." At high tide, the two-mile-long peninsula became an island, and rebel troops had torn planks from the causeway bridge. Past the bridge, near a tide mill on the far side of the inlet, twenty-five riflemen under Major William S. Smith crouched behind a tall stack of cordwood.

A blistering first volley sent Howe's vanguard diving for cover. Shots flew back and forth; the regulars built hasty breastworks and searched in vain for an unguarded ford. Stone walls between pastures prevented British gunners from hauling up their artillery and ammunition wagons except on the bullet-swept road. "Our riflemen have directions to attend particularly to taking down their horses," Tench Tilghman wrote. More redcoats poured ashore as rebel reinforcements swarmed toward the cackle of "sentinels popping at each other," a Royal Navy captain noted.

By nightfall eleven thousand British soldiers with sixteen guns were bottled up on the peninsula by eighteen hundred Americans with fewer guns but better ground. The terrain was "as defensible as can be wished," Tilghman declared. Colonel Reed added, "If we cannot fight them here, we cannot do it anywhere." The American commander on the scene, Major General William Heath, wrote Washington on Sunday morning:

> A large number of vessels—ships, brigs, schooners, sloops, lighters, &c.—sailed through Hell Gate yesterday afternoon and came to anchor last night off Frog's Point, where they still remain. During the night, lanterns were lighted and hung out their yardarms, which made a very extraordinary appearance. There has been no movement this morning.

Nor would there be movement for the next five days. This blunder was Howe's third in two months, following the failures to exterminate the Americans on Long Island and to trap the rebel army in New York. Of nine British amphibious landings during a six-month stretch in 1776, this was the clumsiest, excepting Sullivan's Island. It was, in Clinton's exasperated phrase, "a tweedledum business."

Washington had been oblivious to the danger on his left flank until alerted by Heath. By Sunday morning, the size of the British flotilla and reports from deserters persuaded him that this was no feint. "I have reason to believe that the greatest part of their army has moved upwards or is about to do it, pursuing their original plan of getting our rear," he wrote Hancock. In orders to his troops, he asserted that "a brave and gallant behavior for a few days . . . may save our country." Yet while reinforcing the blocking force at Frog's Neck, Washington made no move to evacuate the now vulnerable lines at Harlem Heights, or to counter Howe's gambit by fortifying more high ground in Westchester.

A more discerning battle captain would soon arrive to show the commanding general the error of his ways. "General Lee is hourly expected as if from heaven with a legion of flaming swordsmen," a colonel in New York had written. Like a conquering hero, Lee crossed the Hudson into Westchester County on Monday, October 14, dogs and jubilant soldiers yapping around him. During his march north from Charleston he had been unsparing in chastising Congress for both meddling and for tepid support of the army. "For heaven's sake," he urged Hancock on October 12, "rouse yourselves." To his old British Army comrade Horatio Gates, he wrote, "The Congress seems to stumble every step. I do not mean one or two of the cattle, but the whole stable." Washington should threaten resignation, he added, "unless they refrain from unhinging the army by their absurd interference."

The ranks were thrilled to see him, and word of his arrival aroused "the universal satisfaction of the camp," a New Jersey chaplain wrote. "We expect soon a stroke that will decide the victory of this campaign." Lee promptly recognized that any such stroke likely would come from the enemy: Frog's Neck could not long hold the British lion. He implored Washington to immediately withdraw into Westchester to avoid encirclement. The commander in chief listened attentively, appreciative as usual of Lee's tactical advice. On Wednesday, he and fifteen of his generals gathered at Lee's new headquarters to furiously debate the matter before voting almost unanimously to retreat north. They also agreed—with Lee's concurrence—to retain "as long as possible" a final Manhattan bastion at Fort Washington on the assumption that a couple thousand defenders could hold the high ground indefinitely or, if endangered, escape across the Hudson to New Jersey.

Thirteen thousand American soldiers trudged north out of Manhattan and from around King's Bridge in a slow, sinuous column along the west bank of the Bronx River. A rear guard set fire to abandoned barracks and camp stores. So many wagons and teams had been lost in the past two months that the men pulled much of their baggage and even artillery by hand, or shuttled the kit in tedious relays across farm roads. Herdsmen and militia companies drove hogs, sheep, and branded cattle onto the Westchester tableland. A magazine in Rye, exposed to Royal Navy raiders, was moved to the army's main storehouses at White Plains, fifteen miles north of King's Bridge. Few provisions were to be found in the county except for buckwheat, potatoes, and some corn—soldiers and camp followers continued to plunder without pause—and quartermasters asked New York authorities for thirty thousand bushels of grain, a thousand tons of hay, and as many horses and oxen as possible. Washington also reorganized his army into seven divisions: Lee took command of the largest unit, with the task of anchoring the left wing along Long Island Sound.

At one a.m. on Friday, October 18, Howe moved again, although not far and not gracefully. Four thousand grenadiers, light infantry, and German *Jäger* embarked in two hundred flatboats from the western shore of Frog's Neck, then sailed by moonlight three miles north to Pell's Point. Landing unopposed and apparently undetected, the assault force by midmorning had lumbered more than a mile inland on a country lane with six field guns, relieved to find neither enemy riflemen nor a vandalized bridge impeding the route.

Yet watching through a spyglass from a nearby hilltop was a man who would spoil Howe's day. Colonel John Glover of Marblehead, Massachusetts, a short, burly forty-three-year-old with a high forehead and a jutting jaw, had briefly worked as a cobbler before making his fortune as a liquor retailer, merchant, and shipowner. Now he wore Dutch shirts, a velvet-trimmed coat, and silver shoe buckles, while brandishing a pair of silver pistols, a Scottish broadsword, and a bayonet forged in Genoa. Both the codfish aristocracy in Marblehead and the town's watermen thought enough of Glover to give him command of the local militia, which had become the 14th Continental Regiment. He and his briny men, described by an admirer as "a hardy race, but most extravagantly eccentric & sportful," had been largely responsible for the providential evacuation of Washington's army from Brooklyn two months earlier.

This morning Glover commanded a brigade of four regiments with 750 men, confronting untold thousands of approaching enemies. "Oh, the anxiety of mind I was then in for the fate of the day," Glover admitted in an account written the following week. "My country, my honor, my own life, and everything that was dear, appeared at that critical moment to be at stake. I would have given a thousand worlds to have had General Lee or some other experienced officer present." With not a moment to lose, he sent forward a captain and forty men to pester the British front ranks. A loud, smoky volley from American muskets, fowling pieces, and squirrel rifles was followed by four more volleys before Glover ordered the company to retreat. Enemy infantrymen rushed forward, but at thirty yards' range two hundred Massachusetts troops from the 13th Continental popped up from behind a stone wall on the left side of the lane. As one they fired, and a whizzing swarm of lead shredded the British advance. "The enemy broke," Glover reported.

For ninety minutes Howe's troops collected themselves before surging forward again, this time also pounding the American line with cannon fire. At fifty yards the 13th Continental rose again, and again lacerated the enemy as calmly as though shooting "at a flock of pigeons or ducks," one witness said. After seven volleys, the regiment fell back, shoulders hunched and heads ducked low as they sprinted to the rear. This time when howling British and Hessian soldiers lunged forward, the 3rd Continental, hidden behind a double stone wall on the right, waited until the last instant, then stood and let fly.

Among the intrepid men in red jackets that morning was Captain Glanville Evelyn of the King's Own, now in his eighteenth month of fighting on battlefields that had stretched from the Concord road and Bunker Hill to Sullivan's Island, the Heights of Guana, and Kip's Bay. He remained a fervent believer in the king's cause, contemptuous of his American adversaries and certain that with one more "grand stroke," as he had just written a friend, "the game is up, for they never will assemble again." In a letter three weeks earlier to his mother, now widowed in Ireland, he had enclosed £40 and told her of the fight on Long Island. "I was lucky enough to come off unhurt, but had six of my men killed and wounded," he wrote, adding, "I shall omit no opportunity of writing to you. . . . Your dutiful and affectionate son, W. G. Evelyn."

There would not be another opportunity. Vaulting a wall at the head of his company, intent on closing with the enemy he despised, he was hit by bullets in the left arm, upper thigh, and right leg above the knee. A rebel musketman dashed forward to snatch his hat and canteen before Evelyn's men could drag him out of range. More volleys swept back and forth, seventeen in all from the 3rd Continental before they, too, leapfrogged to the rear.

At noon, Glover spotted British troops under General Cornwallis hastening along the shoreline around the American left flank. The colonel signaled retreat. With a few parting shots, the Continentals swung northwest across Wolf Lane and through Hutchinson Creek, then paused on a hilltop to lob a few iron balls from their three cannons, answered without injury by the Royal Artillery. At dusk the brigade marched on another three miles before posting sentries and tumbling into an exhausted sleep—"the heavens over us and the earth under us," as Glover recorded. He counted eight Americans dead and thirteen wounded in the day's skirmish.

Howe chose not to pursue, and thus forfeited another chance to smash his enemy. A lunge to the west across the shallow, unguarded Bronx River that night might have blocked Washington's shambling retreat from King's Bridge. A lunge to the north would have placed the British Army astride the White Plains uplands before Washington's main force could secure the heights; just three hundred skittish militiamen guarded the supply depot there. But Howe had been hurt worse than he would admit. In a dispatch to London he claimed only three killed and twenty wounded on Friday, although as usual those figures excluded the Hessians, who composed a substantial portion of his force. His total losses were undoubtedly higher, perhaps much higher. British deserters reported eight hundred to a thousand casualties. The historian Joseph J. Ellis, citing a figure of three hundred, would write that "the British lost more men at Pell's Point than they had in the entire Long Island campaign." If the precise number remained uncertain, it was apparently high enough to force the British Army to pause and lick its wounds.

Among those beyond repair was Glanville Evelyn. Carted to New York, he lingered for three weeks, resisting amputation of his morbid right leg until it was too late. He died on November 6, unmarried, without issue, and not yet thirty-five. His will, hurriedly scribbled on that awful night after the bloodbath at Bunker Hill, left five guineas to his servant and the rest of "my worldly substance"—stored in a trunk aboard the victualler *Sovereign*—to Peggie Wright, a family retainer who had followed him from Ireland to Boston, apparently as his lover and companion. She had fled to Halifax in the spring with the British exodus while he was with Clinton at Sullivan's Island but may have been at his bedside when he passed. If Captain Evelyn's rule-Britannia swagger could at times be insufferable, he possessed a devotion to duty and deep human lineaments that even his adversaries could admire. The loss of this "gallant officer," General Howe told Germain, was "much to be regretted." Yet as with so many of his fallen countrymen, zeal for this cause had earned Evelyn little more than an excruciating death and an anonymous grave in a foreign field.

Having missed an opportunity to seize White Plains with a nimble forced march, Howe would now take it with brute force. He later described Westchester as terrain "difficult to be known," with quagmires, thickets, and "devious and dangerous places." Rail fences and stone walls slowed his progress to a close-order crawl on indifferent roads, further impeded by shortages of horses and a gargantuan baggage train. An advance guard of two thousand men crept forward, halting each night on secure ground fortified with artillery. Behind them, hired teamsters in dirty smocks cracked their whips and Royal Navy gunners came ashore to help shoulder the fieldpieces from one ridge to the next. Still the army would need ten days to move seventeen miles; since landing at Staten Island in early July, Howe's battalions had taken more than sixteen weeks to advance thirty-four crow-flying miles.

The invasion force in Westchester had swelled to nineteen thousand with the new arrival of both British reinforcements and another four thousand Germans under General Wilhelm von Knyphausen. After more than three months at sea, this second Hessian division, which included 31 surgeons, 101 drummers, and sundry camp followers, was hardly in fighting trim as it headed to the front from New York, men clutching the hymnals and prayer books donated by their prince. More than fifty Hessians had died during the long passage—along with three hundred horses—and hundreds more arrived sick, mostly with scurvy. "They are in every respect far inferior" to the earlier tranche of Germans, Lieutenant Colonel George Osborn, the British muster master general, wrote Germain. An unsettling number collapsed while on parade in Westchester for General Heister, the German commander. A mile or so from Pell's Point, an unfinished stone church with a dirt floor served as a Hessian hospital, and a mass grave in the sandpit out back awaited more dead men far from home.

Not least among Howe's worries, as Colonel Osborn confided to Germain, was persistent indiscipline in his army. Corporal punishment fell with the usual draconian severity on transgressing regulars—six hundred lashes for two 63rd Foot privates caught robbing a shop, a thousand for thieves from the 22nd Foot who plundered a wine cellar. Another ban on plundering was announced on October 19, even as British soldiers reputedly dug up a farm cemetery in a hunt for silver.

But admonition and reprisal seemed to have little deterrent effect on the Germans. "They were unfortunately led to believe before they left the province of Hesse-Kassel that they were to come to America to establish their private fortunes," Osborn wrote, "and hitherto they have certainly acted with that principle." Ambrose Serle told his diary in October, "They spare nobody, but glean all away like an army of locusts." The avowed British intent to restore order and protect loyal subjects had begun to ring hollow: winning hearts and minds, Howe and his lieutenants knew, was difficult when pockets and larders were pillaged. "The Hessians destroy all the fruits of the earth without regard to Loyalists or rebels," wrote Major Kemble, the deputy adjutant general, "the property of both being equally pretty to them." He added, "No wonder if the country people refuse to join us."

Step by slow step, Howe's avenging force came on. Farmers handed cider and milk to passing redcoats, hoping to curry favor. The British commander placed his headquarters in a tavern on the Boston post road in Eastchester, and on Friday, October 25, two columns began their final approaches toward White Plains: Heister on the left, along the Bronx River past Scarsdale, and Clinton on the right, after advancing from the supply base at New Rochelle on the Mamaroneck road. By Sunday the army had converged on a front stretching several miles from east to west, with enemy high ground ahead. That night the Hessians built enormous campfires from flax stubble to make their strength seem even more formidable. Officers ordered artillery horses driven back and forth dragging chains to suggest the arrival of siege guns.

For more than a week, indulged by Howe's deliberate advance, the Americans had convened at White Plains. The village here consisted of two churches, two taverns, a courthouse, and seventy scattered houses. Grousing over the lack of decent maps, Washington shifted his command post from the Morris mansion to an unpretentious wooden farmhouse near the center of American entrenchments that snaked from Purdy Hill, above the Bronx River in the west, to Merritt Hill, near the Connecticut road on the east.

Not until Sunday morning did the last of Lee's baggage wagons rumble up Village Street, minus some of the general's favorite wines, which the Hessians had purloined in a raid. Just over thirteen thousand fit-for-duty men now held this stony high ground, some wielding iron pikes on long poles in the absence of bayonets. Many regiments also were short of musket cartridges; two hundred thousand had been sent from Philadelphia, but those ammunition convoys remained stalled somewhere in New Jersey. The nights had grown bitter enough for water to freeze in canteens and no one was comfortable, particularly men like the young artillery captain Alexander Hamilton, whose baggage had been abandoned or lost. Sergeant John Smith noted in his diary, "It was very cold lodging on the ground without tents & but very little fires."

Early on Monday, October 28, Washington rode west with Lee for a closer look at his right wing. As they surveyed the terrain, a horseman raced up to announce, "The British are on the camp, sir." The commanding general galloped back to his headquarters, where Reed confirmed that Howe's brigades were barely a mile to the south. *Jäger* and light infantry had swatted aside the American pickets. "Gentlemen," Washington told his officers, "you will repair to your respective posts, and do the best you can."

From Purdy Hill the spectacle was bewitching: thirteen thousand enemy troops emerged from the wood line in impeccable oblong formations of red and blue, brilliantly enameled by the bright sunshine, bayonets gleaming, horses prancing, a hundred banners and pennants barely stirring in the still morning. Two columns divided into eight, and the crash of regimental bands carried across the plain, punctuated by pounding drums and Hessian grenadiers singing some full-throated war ballad. "A bright autumnal sun shed its luster on the polished arms," an American officer wrote, "and the rich array of dress and equipage gave an imposing grandeur." The enemy, Sergeant Smith told his diary, "made a very warlike appearance."

To disrupt this fine parade, Washington ordered Major General Joseph Spencer to push forward with two thousand troops as a blocking force along the muddy Bronx River, forty feet wide and running high. "Now I am going out to the field to be killed," a young soldier mused. General Heister's infantry worked toward Spencer's salient, infiltrating an apple orchard above the riverbed. The Americans fell back from one stone wall to another, and then another. Their muzzle flashes drew enemy artillery fire; smoke from the batteries spiraled up in lazy curls on the light airs. A bold charge by Hessian grenadiers was stopped in mid-career by a New England volley that "scattered them like leaves in a whirlwind," one officer wrote. Several soldiers scampered out to grab abandoned German firelocks and canteens of rum, "which we had time to drink round before they came on again." Come on again they did, menacing the American flanks and pummeling the ranks with gunnery "in a most furious manner." Then light dragoons appeared with their sabers drawn, and the rebel retreat turned into a rout. Flailing men splashed across the river and into the woods beyond. Some tossed away their muskets.

Only this morning, during his aborted reconnaissance ride, had Washington, prodded by Lee, recognized the vulnerability of his right flank. Chatterton Hill, a steep hardwood ridge with a round, cultivated crest, rose almost two hundred feet above the Bronx River, half a mile west of the Continental line. If the British overpowered militia outposts atop this commanding height, their guns could enfilade American entrenchments behind White Plains. Washington ordered the hill reinforced with the Delaware regiment commanded by John Haslet. Tall, wry, and athletic, the Ulster-born Haslet had been educated in Glasgow and ordained as a Presbyterian clergyman before immigrating to America in 1757; after fighting the French in the last war, he had become a physician in Delaware and now commanded the state's Continentals.

No sooner had the colonel and his men gained the Chatterton summit than a Hessian cannonade blistered the hill with what Haslet described as "a continual peal of reiterated thunder." The militia, sheltering behind fieldstone walls and breastworks built of cornstalk clumps, "broke and fled immediately, and were not rallied without much difficulty." More American reinforcements arrived at midday with a brigade of Connecticut, New York, Massachusetts, and Maryland regiments under Brigadier General Alexander McDougall, who now commanded two thousand men on Chatterton's crown.

General Howe sat his horse in a field of wheat stubble along the river, eyeing the hill looming half a mile to the north. He had intended to attack Washington's main line with a thrust up Broadway and a circling movement to the east by Clinton's column. But the bold Hessian lunge toward Chatterton caused him to reconsider. Heister's lead brigade already threatened to turn the rebel line by occupying ground, as Howe observed, "from whence their flank might be galled." Couriers on lathered mounts galloped off with new orders, and just before one p.m. the British attack tilted to the American right. Hessian engineers felled trees and collected fence rails to bridge the river. Two British foot regiments crossed at a ford downstream, then scrambled up the lower slopes only to be slapped back by rebel plunging fire that left the hillside carpeted with dead and wounded redcoats. Two more regular regiments joined the attack. A dozen cannons roared from a meadow just south of Chatterton, and the rumble of Hessian kettledrums carried through the trees.

Howe pushed more reserves into the attack, including dragoons, grenadiers, and another German brigade, bringing the assault force to seven thousand. An insuperable weight of metal now fell on McDougall's lodgment. "The scene was grand and solemn," an American soldier later wrote. "All the adjacent hills smoked as though on fire, and bellowed and trembled with a perpetual cannonade. . . . Fences and walls were knocked down and torn to pieces." Brush fires scorched the soles of Hessian shoes; Heister's troops held their cartridge boxes above the flames as they pressed up the slope. A two-gun American battery—possibly commanded by young Hamilton—threw a few answering rounds until an enemy cannonball struck one carriage "and scattered the shot about, a wad of tow blazing in the middle," Haslet reported. "The artillerymen fled." Private Elisha Bostwick from Connecticut later wrote:

> A cannonball cut down Lt. Young's platoon, which was next to that of mine. The ball first took the head of Smith, a stout, heavy man, & dashed it open; then it took off Chilson's arm . . . then took Taylor across the bowels. It then struck Sergeant Garret of our company on the hip [and] took off the point of the hip bone.

By midafternoon, blue-coated Hessians had emerged from the smoke to form a skirmish line on Chatterton's southwest brow. The rebel militia promptly bolted again, unhinging McDougall's right flank. Now the Continental regiments buckled—retreating, shooting, retreating. The Marylanders fought with notable valor, led by Colonel William Smallwood, a fleshy, prominent planter who had been schooled at Eton, on the Thames. Wounded in the hip and arm, after twenty minutes Smallwood hobbled back with his men toward Purdy Hill, leaving Haslet and three hundred Delaware troops as a rear guard. Then they, too, gave way, fleeing in disorder. The British 2nd Brigade pushed twelve-deep across the crest, yelping in triumph.

Rebel bodies covered the hilltop, including one with his severed head lying between his feet and another with "half his breast shott off," a British corporal recorded. Captain Mackenzie noted that some lacked "shoes or stockings, & several were observed to have only linen drawers on, with a rifle or hunting shirt." After forming in regiments and dressing their lines, the British and Hessians threw up hasty fortifications, then built great barnwood fires to dry their sodden uniforms before lying on their arms for the night. From the plain below, an observer wrote, the campfires "seemed to the eye to mix with the stars."

Washington shortened his lines and braced for the next blow. Howe planned to deliver it on Thursday, October 31, with seven fresh regiments under General Percy, but teeming rains on Wednesday night mired the roads and forced a British postponement. By the time new attack orders went out, the rebels had pivoted back a mile into the rugged upcountry at North Castle. "We encamp in the woods, have no tents," a Pennsylvania sergeant wrote on November 1. "Frost and cold severe." Colonel William Douglas told his wife in Connecticut that his winter coat was missing. "P.S.," he added. "If any opportunity should offer, should be glad of a pair of mittens."

The Westchester campaign sputtered to a close. Many regulars were eager to claim both tactical and moral victories. "Our troops beat them from their strong grounds where they had taken the advantage of fences & stone walls," Lieutenant John Peebles, a 42nd Foot grenadier serving in Clinton's division, told his diary. The Americans "ran off in the greatest confusion . . . and exhibited to our whole army (who were looking on) a recent proof of their inferiority in courage & discipline." But on the night of November 2, American sentries heard the unmistakable clank of departing enemy artillery carriages; within two days the British and Hessians had abandoned their holdings from Chatterton Hill through White Plains. Howe sensibly saw no profit in chasing rebels through broken country without any hope of enticing them into a decisive battle. "I did not think the driving their rear guard further back an object of the least consequence," he told Germain.

The long columns winding toward Dobbs Ferry and King's Bridge, Tench Tilghman wrote, was "the most extraordinary and unexpected [move] that has been made by the enemy in this campaign." What the British intended, Washington told Hancock, was "a matter of much conjecture and speculation." Yet for the first time in weeks, Washington's men breathed easy. "I am delivered from troublesome neighbors," a New York militia officer wrote on November 5, "and have a prospect of sleep tonight." A Massachusetts captain informed his diary, "We washt our shurts."

But other rebels rampaged through White Plains on the pretext of scourging Tories. Stealing livestock, furniture, and even farm implements, they also fashioned burglar's packs from blankets to carry off curtains, mirrors, washtubs, and ladies' hats. Massachusetts troops—said to be "heated with liquor"—burned what they could not carry, including the county courthouse, the Presbyterian church, both taverns, barns full of hay, and most houses on the village green. Their commander, Major Jonathan Williams Austin, a Harvard graduate who had studied law with John Adams, was court-martialed for "wanton, barbarous conduct" and cashiered from the service. Washington condemned him and his accomplices as "cowardly wretches."

Even if Howe had ceded the ground at White Plains, the battle hardly felt like a triumph of American arms. "Our generals showed not equal judgment to that of the enemy," a Maryland lieutenant complained. Yet Washington's generalship had been creditable enough, given his determination to sidestep pitched brawls he was unlikely to win. Though he had again misread the terrain, he made amends, fought hard for a few hours, then slipped away when necessary. Howe would claim that the American casualties amounted to "not less than 250," though they likely were closer to 175. British and Hessian casualties totaled 254, including severe losses in the 35th Foot, which had led the initial charge up Chatterton Hill and counted 17 dead—the regimental commander among them—plus 40 wounded.

As the November days grew shorter and the November nights colder, an unaccountable buoyancy could still be found in rebel ranks despite the perpetual retreat. "The army are no ways disheartened," a young artillery lieutenant named Samuel Shaw wrote his parents near Boston. "We seem pretty generally to believe we shall beat them at last."

Major General Nathanael Greene, who would earn acclaim as one of the finest commanders in American military history, seemed an unlikely great captain. "I was educated a Quaker, amongst the most superstitious

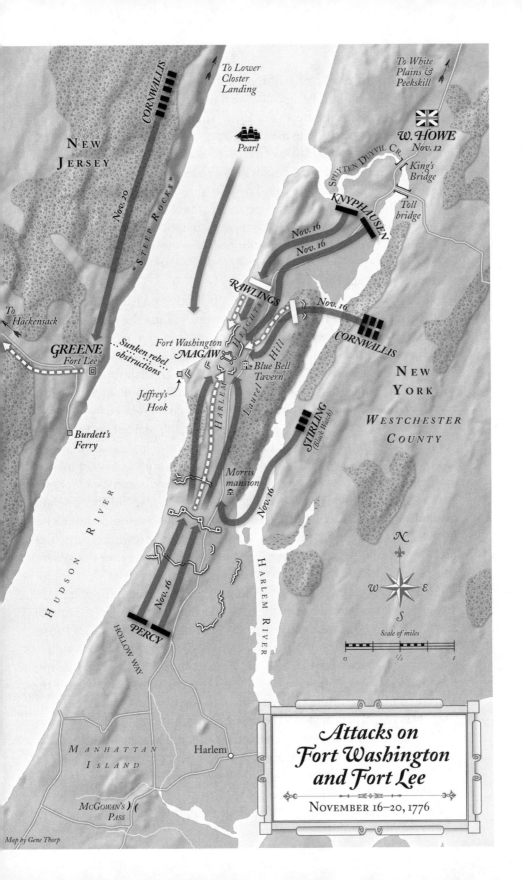

To Lower
Closter
Landing

To White
Plains &
Peekskill

CORNWALLIS

NEW
JERSEY

Pearl

Nov. 20

W. HOWE
Nov. 12

King's
Bridge

SPUYTEN DUYVIL CR.

KNYPHAUSEN

Nov. 16

Nov. 16

Toll
bridge

"STEEP ROCKS"

RAWLINGS

Nov. 16

CORNWALLIS

To
Hackensack

Sunken rebel
obstructions

Fort Washington
MAGAW

HEIGHTS

Blue Bell
Tavern

NEW

GREENE
Fort Lee

Jeffrey's
Hook

Laurel Hill

YORK

WESTCHESTER
COUNTY

Burdett's
Ferry

HARLEM

STIRLING
(Black Watch)

Morris
mansion

Nov. 16

N

HUDSON RIVER

W   E

S

HARLEM RIVER

Scale of miles

Nov. 16

0   ½   1

PERCY

HOLLOW WAY

MANHATTAN
ISLAND

Harlem

Attacks on
Fort Washington
and Fort Lee

NOVEMBER 16–20, 1776

McGOWAN'S
PASS

Map by Gene Thorp

sort," he had written in 1772, a fifth-generation Rhode Islander and the third of eight sons in a black-garbed clan that made anchors and heavy chains. Taught Euclid and a smattering of Latin, young Nathanael otherwise educated himself to dispel "the mist of ignorance," devouring Horace, Swift, Pope, Locke, Blackstone, *Jacob's Law Dictionary*, *Book-keeping Methodized*, and various military treatises, including Frederick the Great's *Instructions for His Generals*. Though he could be thin-skinned and moody, his imitation of the fumbling, pudgy Dr. Slop in *Tristram Shandy* was much praised by his friends for comic verve. A severe asthmatic whose togs smelled of forge smoke, Greene was a double-chinned, blue-eyed bumpkin with a deep chest, brawny shoulders, and heavy palm calluses, which he shaved to make his hands more supple.

The Quakers expelled him in 1773, apparently for visiting an alehouse; that was just as well, for he was called to arms. Joining the Kentish Guards militia, a smart outfit with red jackets trimmed in green, he had failed to win a lieutenancy because of a chronic limp that supposedly disfigured the company's march order. "I feel more mortification than resentment," he wrote. Eight months later, in May 1775, the Rhode Island Assembly promoted Private Greene to General Greene, no doubt influenced by his family and personal connections but perhaps also sensing martial potential. His commission commanded him to "resist, expel, kill, and destroy." He, in turn, vowed to be "neither rash nor timorous, pursuing a conduct marked with manly firmness, but never bordering on phrenzy." Greene had recently married well: his wife was a vivacious, nineteen-year-old Block Island beauty named Catharine Littlefield, called Caty, who would enliven her husband's camps in Cambridge, New York, and elsewhere. "My soul breathes a secret prayer for your happiness amidst these times of general calamity," he had written her in October 1775.

Now thirty-four, Greene was the youngest Continental general and already a Washington favorite for his decisive mind, rigorous discipline, and devotion to both the cause and the commander in chief. His consequential correspondence with His Excellency would exceed six hundred letters. "He is, beyond doubt, a first-rate military genius," Tilghman wrote in early October 1776, "and one in whose opinions the General places the utmost confidence." Henry Knox, who became Greene's intimate friend, later observed, "He came to us the rawest, most untutored being I ever met with, but in less than twelve months he was equal in military knowledge to any general officer in the army, and very superior to most of them."

From his headquarters in a gambrel-roof house above the ferry landing at Fort Lee, Greene had stayed busy through October organizing magazines in New Jersey, grooming roads, building winter huts, and forwarding provisions and munitions across the Hudson to the main army. Upon asking Washington's opinion about retaining the small corner of Manhattan still in rebel hands around Fort Washington, Greene was told in a November 6 reply that the matter would be left "entirely to your discretion"—even though General Putnam ostensibly commanded those defenses. Greene had already increased the garrison there beyond the twelve hundred men originally intended; in coming days he would send more, until the force exceeded three thousand, about half of them Continentals. "I expect General Howe will attempt to possess himself of Mount Washington," Greene told Hancock, "but very much doubt whether he'll succeed." To the garrison commander, Colonel Robert Magaw, he wrote, "The enemy are retreating and it's confidently asserted . . . that they are going into winter quarters."

All of this, including Washington's deference to an inexperienced subordinate, was quite wrongheaded. Looming 265 feet above the Hudson, with steep slopes on three sides, Fort Washington gave the illusion of impregnability. Several outposts and ravelins protected the approaches, and forty-seven cannons had been emplaced, from 3- to 32-pounders; teams of twenty-two oxen pulled the heaviest guns up to the citadel. For months, dust-caked soldiers had wielded axes, shovels, and mattocks to strengthen the pentagonal fort's dirt ramparts, five bastions, and the abatis that enclosed an inner four acres, described by one visitor as "rocky, broken, and disagreeable, but very strong." The citadel had also become a small town. In a field near the Blue Bell Tavern, below the southeast slope, a market swarmed each morning with farmers and peddlers hawking panniers of produce. Off-duty troops and camp followers of every ilk strolled among the stalls, while quartermaster orderlies sniffed about for price gouging.

A British officer called Fort Washington "the strongest post that ever was occupied by an army," but that was balderdash intended to inflate the feat of arms required to capture the place. Built on a granite massif known as Mount Washington, the fortress was impervious to defensive entrenchment: rebel engineers lacked the powder to blast ditches, casemates, magazines, bombproofs, or outworks to keep besiegers at bay. It also had no water and no reservoir; a well started in early summer had been abandoned, and every drop was hauled up in buckets from the Hudson. The guns, if impressive in number, manifestly failed to command the river, which was the raison d'être for the fortress.

Even with recent reinforcements, the long outer perimeter around Fort Washington, which stretched for several miles, required three times more defenders than Greene could spare. "There were intervals in the lines of more than one hundred yards without a man in them," wrote Private John

Adlum, age seventeen. Two Pennsylvania regiments in the garrison, the 3rd and 5th Continentals, were badly weakened by sickness, shrinking from more than a thousand men in June to barely four hundred in mid-November. Even the healthy were enfeebled by months of drudgery, "at once so thankless and preposterous," as Captain Alexander Graydon complained. Still, Colonel Magaw, a lawyer from Carlisle, Pennsylvania, told Greene that if attacked, his garrison could hold out through December—an assertion, Graydon said, that showed "him to have been more miserably deficient in judgment than ever we supposed him to be."

By the mid-eighteenth century, military engineers had developed principles for constructing forts, from the number of men needed to defend each bastion—a thousand or so—to the number of cannons per bastion—a dozen or so—to the need for cavalry sorties and water cisterns. For a typical six-week siege, a hundred tons of powder might be required. When hard-pressed by attackers, a recent British field manual advised, "engines may be contrived to fling heavy stones . . . or to blow dust or sand in their faces," much as besieged Tyre had flung heated sand at Alexander's shock troops, or Hannibal in a sea battle had heaved pots filled with snakes onto enemy ships.

Fort Washington violated virtually all of these precepts and precautions. Worse, the British high command knew with precision the weaknesses of both their opponents and the citadel. Letters from Washington to Congress had been intercepted in late October when a careless courier left his satchel unattended; they revealed poor discipline, inadequate officers—"dreaming, sleepy-headed men"—and other details, "the knowledge of which will be of much service to General Howe," as Captain Mackenzie noted. Moreover, seventeen deserters had absconded from Fort Washington in recent weeks, including William Demont, Magaw's brigade major, who had emigrated from England to Philadelphia a few years earlier and who defected on the night of November 2 with precise information about the thin American defenses, ammunition levels, and faltering morale. He would be rewarded with a sinecure in the British quartermaster department and five shillings a day in blood money from the Crown. Howe, Captain Graydon later reflected, "must have had a perfect knowledge of the ground we occupied."

Washington, by contrast, had little insight into British intentions. "Opinions here are various," Reed wrote Esther on November 6. "A great majority think that . . . they have changed their whole plan and are bending southward, intending to penetrate the Jerseys, and so move on to Philadelphia." A day later, Washington speculated that Howe "must attempt something on account of his reputation, for what has he done as yet with his great army?" What to do with his own army puzzled him, too. After consulting his war council, the commander in chief split the force into four parts: General Heath would post the Hudson Highlands upriver with four thousand men; Lee was to remain in Westchester with seven thousand to block approaches into upstate New York and New England; Greene's detachment in New Jersey would grow to several thousand, scattered at various strong points; and Magaw was left clinging to Manhattan by his dirty fingernails.

At eleven a.m. on Sunday, November 10, Washington cantered northwest from his camp above White Plains to begin a meandering, often frantic journey that would last the rest of the year. By sunset he was in Peekskill to inspect defenses in the Hudson River Gorge below West Point. On Tuesday morning he crossed to the west shore near Haverstraw to ride south into New Jersey with two thousand men. Jumping the Hudson had required a circuitous march of more than sixty miles, because once again the Royal Navy had run the river gantlet and had eyes on the ferry crossings farther south. During the sortie upriver, the frigate *Pearl* and two victuallers had provoked sixty rounds from Magaw's gunners, some of which struck home with the usual perforated sails, splintered oak, and a busted mizzenmast. But now the vessels sat anchored off Dobbs Ferry.

Yet another successful British foray up the Hudson seemed "proof of the inefficacy of all the obstructions we have thrown into it," Washington wrote Greene. Given this failure to blockade the river, it did not seem "prudent to hazard the men and stores" committed to the fort. But, confounded and indecisive, he again deferred to the junior commander: "As you are on the spot, [I] leave it to you to give such orders as to evacuating Mount Washington as you judge best." Although Greene agreed that blockading the river had failed, he assured the commanding general: "I cannot conceive the garrison to be in any great danger. The men can be brought off at any time." Lee agreed, telling Greene, "I begin to think my friend Howe has lost the campaign. . . . May you live long and reap twice a year an abundant crop of laurels."

Late on Wednesday afternoon, Washington arrived at Greene's tidy house beneath a pine tree on the lane leading from Fort Lee to Burdett's Ferry. Here the Jersey Palisades, ancient basalt cliffs known simply as the "Steep Rocks," plunged some three hundred feet to the riverbank. For two days Washington studied the Hudson, the fortifications, and the American positions, swayed by Greene and others despite his own misgivings and several ominous portents, including reports of Hessians massing south of

King's Bridge. "The movements and designs of the enemy are not yet understood," he wrote Hancock on Thursday from Greene's quarters. He still suspected that the enemy intended to lunge through New Jersey toward Philadelphia.

> It seems to be generally believed on all hands that the investing of Fort Washington is one object they have in view. But that can employ but a small part of their force. Whether they intend a southern expedition must be determined by time. To me there appears a probability of it.

Round and round the debate swirled. "His Excellency General Washington has been with me for several days," Greene wrote Knox. "The evacuation or reinforcement of Fort Washington was under consideration, but finally nothing concluded on." Washington later acknowledged a "warfare in my mind, and hesitation."

No hesitation troubled William Howe's mind. The chance to seize several thousand rebels and obliterate their last stronghold on Manhattan was too enticing. After marching with his main army from Dobbs Ferry to King's Bridge on Tuesday, November 12, Howe completed his battle plan: four commands with thirteen thousand men, including twenty Hessian regiments, would converge on Fort Washington like fingers clenching into a fist. On Thursday night, thirty flatboats rowed undetected up the Hudson's east bank, past the citadel and into Spuyten Duyvil Creek to the Harlem River, where they prepared to load seventeen hundred assault troops. A dozen bateaux, also undetected, were positioned in the rushes along a creek bank below the Morris house, ready to transport another eight hundred soldiers. Twenty-one field guns were muscled into batteries along the Harlem River, while General Knyphausen moved two columns north of Fort Washington. General Percy made ready to envelop the fort from the south.

At one p.m. on Friday, November 15, a mounted British officer carrying a white flag trotted from King's Bridge up the steep, dusty ramp to Fort Washington. Lieutenant Colonel James Patterson, Howe's adjutant general, carried a simple ultimatum, which he handed to the American officer sent to intercept him: the rebel garrison was to surrender within two hours or every man would be put to the sword. Magaw, whose headquarters was in the Morris house, scribbled a defiant reply—"Actuated by the most glorious cause that mankind ever fought in, I am determined to defend the post to the very last extremity"—then sent a courier across the Hudson with copies of this correspondence for Greene and a request for advice.

An American soldier named Addison Richardson, now peering over the ramparts, also scratched out a note. "We are here surrounded with Regulars and no way to make our escape but over the North River to the Jerseys," he wrote his wife. "I hope we shall conquer all our enemies through the divine assistance. . . . Love to you and all the children."

Earlier that day, Washington had ridden six miles west of Fort Lee to Hackensack, settling into Judge Peter Zabriskie's three-story house of dressed stone, notable for its Dutch fireplace tiles depicting biblical scenes. The sun had just set when idlers on the village green saw a horseman thunder past, then spring from his mount and rush across the Zabriskie porch, clutching a dispatch from Greene. Moments later Washington strode out the door, waiting impatiently for his own horse to be brought around. At four p.m., Greene had written:

> Enclosed you have a letter from Col. Magaw. The contents will require your Excellency's attention. I have directed Col. Magaw to defend the place until he hears from me. . . . I shall go to the island soon.

The last hint of daylight had long faded by the time the commanding general crossed the Hackensack River and galloped by dim moonlight to the dock below Fort Lee. Stepping into a barge, he ordered the crew to stroke for the far shore, where the stubby black silhouette of the fort could be seen crowning the dark ridgeline a mile to the east. The pungent river smelled of autumn decay. Halfway across the Hudson, a shadow emerged from other shadows, and a westbound skiff carrying Greene and General Putnam pulled alongside. Rowers laid on their oars as the officers conferred in urgent tones above the rhythmic slap of waves against the boats. Magaw seemed in good spirits, Greene reported, and determined to hold out indefinitely. He and Putnam had approved his defensive scheme, then wished him luck. Nothing more could be done until dawn.

The boats returned to Fort Lee. Washington climbed the Steep Rocks above the dock and stared eastward into the ebony night, eyes and ears straining. Finally he found his bed in the gambrel-roofed house and tried to sleep.

He was in the barge again with Greene and Putnam at dawn. As the sun peeped above Manhattan at seven a.m. on this bright, fair Saturday, the first booming could be heard from British cannons on the Harlem River and from the *Pearl*, which had edged down the Hudson to bombard an American redoubt fifteen hundred yards north of the citadel. Putting ashore below Jeffrey's Hook, Washington and his lieutenants stalked toward the Morris mansion "to determine what was best to be done," as Greene would tell Knox. Upon reaching his former headquarters, the commander in chief looked south: mists still lingered in the hollows where Percy's redcoats tacked left and then right near Harlem Heights, probing the American outposts. The cannonade in the north had merged into an unbroken roar. "There we all stood in a very awkward situation," Greene wrote. "We all urged His Excellency to come off." Greene and Putnam offered to stay behind, but Washington insisted they all leave together before the enemy drew closer. Striding back to the Hudson, they climbed into the boat and returned to Fort Lee without seeing Magaw, without issuing any orders, and without influencing the brawl that now unfolded.

Howe's intricate battle scheme had begun badly. A miscalculation of the tides in Spuyten Duyvil Creek kept flatboats from embarking four Guards and light infantry regiments near King's Bridge, delaying the assault and forcing a simultaneous Hessian sally toward the northern outworks of Fort Washington to pull back. But the attack soon regained momentum. The tardy flatboats picked up the passengers and ferried them down the Harlem River to Laurel Hill, a half mile east of the fortress.

Rebel militia lashed the flotilla with gunfire. "The light infantry landed under so heavy a fire of cannon and musketry that the sailors quitted their oars and lay down in the bottom of the boats," Lieutenant Martin Hunter told his journal. "In this situation we must have remained exposed to the enemy's fire had not the soldiers taken the oars and pulled us on shore." A few redcoats fell, but almost two thousand others swarmed ashore, General Howe among them, bulling through the tangled woodland. Grenadiers and a foot regiment reinforced the attack under Cornwallis, bayonets flashing as the outnumbered Americans backed up the slope after their commander was run through with an enemy officer's sword. "The continual thunder of cannons, the drum beat of small arms fire, the screaming of men, and the whinnying of horses completely deafened the participants," one corporal later wrote.

Farther down the Harlem River, two Black Watch battalions—some eight hundred Highlanders—and a foot regiment crossed the river in bateaux, supported by sixteen field guns. Howe had intended only a feint here, but now he ordered a full-blown attack toward the Morris house. Three hundred American gunmen cut down the Highlanders with plunging fire; dozens of bloody tartans and bonnets littered the slope. But by noon the Scots had pushed into the stables and outbuildings. After shooting into the abandoned mansion, they pressed on toward the Hudson, rounding up 170 prisoners along the way.

The day grew dire for Magaw's men. On the American left, General Knyphausen resumed his attack at eleven a.m. with more than four thousand men in two columns, which now split into three. Hessians chopped and wiggled their way through an abatis reportedly two hundred paces deep—Knyphausen himself helped yank the branches apart with his hands—then plodded across boggy ground while *Pearl* barked offshore, lobbing shells, balls, and bar shot at rebel lines on a hillside said to be "rutted up by entrenchments."

Drums pounded, hautboys tootled, and blue-coated Hessians grabbed saplings and laurel bushes to haul themselves up the steep pitch. Rebel grape and rifle bullets whistled all around, riddling the ascending ranks. Dead Germans tumbled down the slope. A chaplain described seeing a green-coated *Jäger* "shot through the head. His brother stood over the body, complaining that he could not be buried. Another Jäger had both eyes shot out. He still lived."

The struggle was particularly vicious around a three-gun battery on the upper tip of the American defenses near Spuyten Duyvil Creek, where Lieutenant Colonel Moses Rawlings and several hundred Maryland and Virginia riflemen fought with what Washington later called "veteran bravery." Enveloped by eight enemy regiments, the rebels darted among the rocks for two hours, targeting enemy officers and inflicting what one American lieutenant called "a great carnage," although "wind blew the smoke full in our faces." Rifle barrels grew scorching hot and so fouled with powder residue that they misfired. Three American officers were killed and three more wounded, Rawlings among them. By two p.m. the redoubt had been overrun. After a fighting withdrawal up the ridgeline—in some cases with fists, rocks, and clubbed firelocks—survivors scuttled over the earthworks and into Fort Washington, relentless Hessians on their heels.

On the far side of the battlefield, in the south, General Percy accompanied by Admiral Howe led 4,200 British and German troops against 800 defenders. After pushing up from Harlem Heights and waiting for Highlanders to sweep past the Morris estate, Percy's wing surged ahead in two columns. Resistance melted away, and soon these enemy ranks also were within musket range of the fortress. Nearly the entire rebel garrison now jammed a few acres behind the ramparts, so crowded they could hardly move, much less fight. "A ball took off a part of two men's heads and wounded another," wrote young Private Adlum, who also noted tears trickling down the cheeks of several officers. Thirst tormented every man. Hungry soldiers broke into food barrels and filled their pockets with biscuits; others tapped the rum casks.

The end came quickly. A courier from Fort Lee, dodging enemy bullets and bayonets as he bounded up the river bluff, brought a message from

Washington urging the garrison to hold out until dark. But around three p.m., as Knyphausen paced and puffed his pipe in a stone barn barely a hundred yards from the fort, a Hessian captain walked forward with a drummer and a white flag. Magaw was soon studying another ultimatum:

> The commander in chief demands an immediate & categorical answer to his second summons of Fort Washington. The garrison must immediately surrender prisoners of war, and give up all their arms, ammunition, & stores of every kind. The general is pleased to allow the garrison to keep possession of their baggage, and the officers to have their swords.

Magaw asked for four hours to deliberate; he was given thirty minutes. The Hessian captain later said of the American colonel, "His fate seemed hard to him." Men wept and cursed and hung out white flags as word of the capitulation spread. "The events of the day had been so unpropitious to our glory," Captain Graydon wrote. "We were both sacrificed and disgraced."

A few men got away, including Lieutenant William Scott, a former New Hampshire shoemaker known as Long Bill who already had escaped by boat from a British jail in Halifax after being captured at Bunker Hill; this time he reportedly swam to safety with a sword tied around his neck and his watch pinned to his hat. Another soldier crossed the Hudson on a raft built from flour casks, with a barrel stave as his paddle. But at four p.m. nearly everyone else marched out through the breastworks toward the post road, stacking their arms between two glowering Hessian regiments. The rebels were "packed together like herring," a German chaplain wrote. "Despite the strictest orders, the prisoners received a number of blows."

"The abuse and plunder commenced," wrote Ensign Isaac Van Horne of Pennsylvania. "Side arms, watches, shoe buckles, and even the clothes on our backs were wrested from us." Sword-wielding Hessian soldiers slashed knapsacks from the prisoners' shoulders. Some rebels were led away by British officers to prevent further debasement, but most regulars were in no mood for clemency. "Young men, ye should never fight against your king," a sergeant told Captain Graydon, and an inflamed British officer bellowed, "What! Taking prisoners! Kill them, kill every man of them!" He calmed down only after the Americans showed abject submission.

Men pleaded for water, for mercy, for treatment of their wounds. Dusk sifted over the forlorn citadel, to be known henceforth as Fort Knyphausen and not to be repossessed by the Americans for more than seven years. Before being marched off to various barns, sties, and coops for the night, the men were segregated into columns of officers and enlisted men. British sergeants with quill pens and paper on their knees took down names and ranks. Then a regular swishing a swagger stick called out, "Come, gentlemen, we are all soldiers. To the right face, *march!*"

Howe's losses on November 16 were substantial: 458 casualties, including 77 killed in action, more than two-thirds of them German. Of the British dead, half belonged to the Black Watch. "It was a pretty little action, neatly designed and very neatly executed," the British historian J. W. Fortescue would write more than a century later, "for Howe at his best was no contemptible commander." For Washington, the losses were frightful: 59 killed, 96 wounded, and 2,830 taken prisoner, including 230 officers. The Americans had also lost 2,800 muskets, 41 guns, and heaps of salt meat, potatoes, and other provisions.

The prisoners would be marched in shuffling columns to New York, heckled by loyalists and soldiers' trulls, who screeched, "Which is Washington? Which is Washington?" American officers who signed paroles were permitted to rent rooms in town or on Long Island; enlisted men were crammed into Dutch churches and unheated sugar houses used as penitentiaries. Redcoat recruiters offered pardons to turncoats willing to enlist in the king's service. Provost marshals also scrutinized the rebel ranks for British deserters, like Thomas Cairns and Edward Crosby, both accused of absconding from the 18th Foot, and Thomas Cox, who had deserted while on guard duty in Boston in April 1775; all three were found guilty of "bearing arms in the rebel service" and condemned to death. Some loyalists believed that everyone captured should be put to the sword. "The most rigid severity at the first would have been the greatest mercy and lenity in the end," wrote Thomas Jones, a former New York supreme court judge and Yale graduate. But Captain Mackenzie told his diary on November 17, "I am of opinion it is right to treat our enemies as if they might one day become our friends."

Few friends would emerge from the ordeal ahead, given the barbaric treatment of American prisoners. Within eighteen months, roughly two-thirds of those captured at Fort Washington would be dead from disease, exposure, or malnutrition. No American defeat in the first five years of war would be more catastrophic, wrenching, or fatal.

Washington had watched the disaster through his telescope from across the Hudson, hearing the pandemonium of battle, then silence, then muffled cheers as the king's colors rose over the ramparts. A soldier at Fort Lee reported that the commanding general "seemed in agony." One of his biographers, Washington Irving, wrote that he wept "with the tenderness of a child." If not, perhaps he should have. "This is a most unfortunate affair and has given me great mortification," Washington wrote his brother John. He claimed that the fort had been held "contrary to my wishes & opinion"—as if someone else were commanding the Continental Army—and that he had not had time to "get round & see the situation of things" before Howe attacked. That was untrue. In his report to Congress, he took responsibility for the calamity while failing to mention his own arrival at Fort Lee three days before the battle, or the confused lines of authority he himself had drawn.

"I feel mad, vexed, sick, and sorry," Greene wrote Henry Knox on November 17. "Never did I need the consoling voice of a friend more than now. . . . This is a most terrible event. Its consequences are justly to be dreaded." Certainly Greene's reputation as a "heaven-born genius" suffered; others now recalled his scant experience and improbable ascent through the ranks. He never acknowledged flaws in his judgment, instead asserting that the garrison had been "struck with a panic . . . and so fell a prey to their own fears." But the disaster aggravated regional enmities. Captain Graydon, like other Pennsylvanians, believed that Greene, the Rhode Islander, would not have exposed three thousand New Englanders to such peril.

Much of the army was stupefied by this latest defeat. "I found myself as unable to preach as they were to hear," a New Jersey chaplain advised his diary. When the news reached General Lee's ear in Westchester, "he was in a towering passion, and said it was a splendid affair for Mr. Howe . . . to have his sores licked by us," an artillery lieutenant reported. To Washington, Lee wrote on November 19, "Oh, General, why would you be over-persuaded by men of inferior judgment to your own? It was a cursed affair." Rumors spread that Washington would be sacked, a prospect not displeasing to Lee, for whom the misfortune of others increasingly served as a whetstone to sharpen his ambition. Concealing his own support for reinforcing Fort Washington, he wrote Benjamin Rush in Philadelphia:

> I foresaw, predicted all that has happened. . . . Let these few lines be thrown into the fire, and in your conversations only acquit me of any share of the misfortune. For my last words to the General were: draw off the garrison, or they will be lost.

The apathy of Congress "amazes me," he continued. "Heaven alone can save you." Or, if not heaven, perhaps Charles Lee could save them. "Had I the powers I could do you much good, might I but dictate one week," he told Rush. "But I am sure you will never give any man the necessary power."

Unaware of this burgeoning disloyalty, Washington tried to regain his balance and revive his army. To his brother he wrote, "I am wearied almost to death with the retrograde motion of things."

*　*　*

General Howe was determined to keep the Americans reeling. At nine p.m. on Tuesday, November 19, Hessian grenadiers, *Jäger*, and five regular brigades struck their tents and marched for the Hudson, the force split between Spuyten Duyvil Creek and Nepperhan Creek in Yonkers. Some dozed in the mud; others boarded rivercraft and waited for a gray, wet dawn. "A very disagreeable night in the flatboats under a thick heavy rain," a British lieutenant told his journal.

At first light, with General Cornwallis in command, several dozen boats pulled across the Hudson to Lower Closter Landing on the New Jersey shore. A rugged path—narrow, slippery, and unguarded—snaked for half a mile up a defile in the Steep Rocks to a farm lane at the rim of the bluff, 440 feet above the river. As a second lift ferried across more troops and eight field guns, including two 6-pounders, a local brewer and two other loyalist guides led the vanguard up what one Hessian lieutenant called a "terrible and impracticable trail." For several hours, grunting soldiers and sailors used drag ropes to haul cannons and caissons to the top. "Fifty men would have sufficed to hold back the entire corps if they had only hurled stones down on us," the Hessian lieutenant wrote. But by one p.m. Cornwallis had assembled five thousand soldiers into two columns before wheeling toward Fort Lee, six miles south. The day faired, and the men moved at quick time down the rutted roads, keen to steal a march on another American garrison.

Greene had been dozing that morning when a galloping messenger arrived with the baleful news of redcoats seemingly levitating from the riverbank. For the past three days, despite a dearth of wagons and boats, he had toiled mightily to evacuate both munitions and winter provisions stockpiled around Fort Lee, including six thousand barrels of pork and flour, ten thousand bushels of grain, and three hundred tons of hay. Now whatever remained must be abandoned. The vulnerable fort was hardly more than an earthen-walled bunker, 250 feet square on ten acres of tableland, with a track leading to the river batteries from several hundred log huts arranged in neat rows outside the bastion. The garrison had dwindled to two thousand troops, many of them militiamen drawn from the Flying Camp reserve.

Shrill cries rang through the redoubt. "Turn out! Turn out! We are all surrounded! Leave everything but your blankets!" Some men pulled on extra clothes rather than carry them in their packs, and in ten minutes the first companies hied west, then north, then west again, skirting the fenny bottomland to reach a crossroads called Liberty Pole.

Here General Washington awaited them. After being alerted by yet another of those galloping, wild-eyed "heralds of calamity," he had dashed five miles from the Zabriskie house to meet Greene and his fugitives. Enemy outriders were said to be within two miles and, an American officer wrote, "determined to push matters." As Washington turned around to lead the column across the New Bridge spanning the Hackensack, Greene rode back to Fort Lee to round up several hundred stragglers before following in trace.

Cornwallis's legions overran the abandoned fort at dusk to find empty tents standing, kettles boiling, and skewered meat roasting by the cook fires. More than a hundred skulking rebels were captured in the nearby woods, many of them dead drunk on pilfered rum. On the right flank a one-eyed Hessian captain named Johann Ewald reported a "flitter of bayonets and a cloud of dust in the distance," evidently the tail of Greene's retreating gaggle. But after a brief skirmish, Cornwallis recalled the pursuit. "Let them go, my dear Ewald, and stay here," he ordered. "We do not want to lose any men. One jäger is worth more than ten rebels."

More booty fell into British hands, including all of the artillery at Fort Lee except a pair of 12-pounders, plus a thousand barrels of flour and eleven pipes of Madeira—almost fourteen hundred gallons, which was soon ladled out to the ranks. "There was a huge magazine of forage, flour, and biscuit," Ewald told his diary. "During the night all the estates in the vicinity were plundered." Redcoats and Hessians would also corral more than two thousand head of cattle. By Howe's reckoning, since landing at Frog's Neck six weeks earlier, his army had seized 148 guns and mortars, almost 12,000 shot and shell, and 400,000 musket cartridges. If some had once questioned Howe's determination to destroy his enemy, no one doubted that he now had the rebels on the run.

The New York campaign had ended, miserably, and New Jersey's miseries had begun. Washington and his generals had nearly lost the war several times in the past three months, through miscalculation, misfortune, imprudence, and deficient military skills. "I am surprised," a congressman from Maryland observed, ". . . that we should be so often surprised in Long Island, York Island, White Plains, Fort Washington, and now Fort Lee." The Continental Army and its militia auxiliaries had been repeatedly overmatched by British regulars and their German auxiliaries. "I firmly believe if heaven had not something very great in store for America, we should ere this have been a ruined people," wrote Lieutenant Shaw, the artilleryman.

Washington spent a glum final night at the Zabriskie house. The rump end of his army straggled into Hackensack in a cold drizzle, shuffling past the courthouse and the sandstone Dutch church, with its stubby white steeple crowned by a brass weathercock. Only the pale candlelight from house windows illuminated the sodden column. "They marched two abreast, looked ragged, some without a shoe to their feet and most of them wrapped in their blankets," one resident wrote. A few deserters slipped away during the night, but most troops found shelter in barns, sheds, or houses between the New Bridge and the Hackensack green. Huge British campfires soon glistened on both sides of the river, and from the east the sounds of Cornwallis's men making merry and plundering local farms could be heard by the weary, beaten rebels in the west.

Early Thursday morning the little American army again assembled in the roadbed before trudging south. Washington scratched out a letter for General Lee, which an express rider carried off to Westchester after Colonel Reed made a fair copy. "The enemy are evidently changing the seat of war to this side of the North River," the commanding general wrote. Although "very much at a loss what now to determine," he had concluded that "the public interest requires your coming over to this side with the Continental troops . . . by the easiest and best passage." In this perilous hour, not a moment should be lost; the British would no doubt soon leap the Hackensack River. Washington added:

> We have not an entrenching tool, & not above 3,000 men, & they much broken & dispirited not only with our ill-success but the loss of their tents & baggage. I have resolved to avoid any attack, though by so doing I must leave a very fine country open to [enemy] ravages.

With that, he rode off in the company of his staff, his Life Guard, and a mounted escort. After stopping at Archibald Campbell's tavern to order wine and water, he fell in with the column as it snaked through the countryside, crossing a shallow creek before turning onto Cow Lane and then angling south by southwest on the old Paramus road. By midday they had reached the Acquackanonk Bridge, a frail log structure twelve feet wide—enough for a single wagon or four men abreast—with timber abutments driven into rock-filled cribs on the muddy bottom. When the last regiment had crossed, a rear guard knocked the span to splinters. The fugitives marched on, another river now between them and their pursuers.

Behind them remained hundreds of dead comrades, thousands more taken prisoner, and tens of thousands of countrymen left to the mercy of an occupying army. Yet for all the misfortune of the recent weeks, for all the heartbreak and exhaustion, a flame still burned in these few as they tramped deeper into New Jersey. Stubborn, resolved, perhaps even undaunted, they somehow kept faith with their cause, with one another, and with those generations yet unborn. "The virtue of the Americans is put to a trial," Greene wrote Caty. "I am hearty and well amidst all the fatigues and hardships. . . . Be of good courage. Don't be distressed. All things will turn out for the best."

Franklin in France

DECEMBER 1776

IRELAND

Dublin

Liverpool

GREAT

BRITAIN

WALES

ENGLAND

Cardiff

London

THAMES

Portsmouth

ENGLISH CHANNEL

Le Havre

NORMANDY

Brest

BRITTANY

Auray

Franklin arrives

Dec. 3

QUIBERON BAY

Reprisal

From Marcus Hook, Penn.

Nantes

Arrives, Dec. 7

Leaves for Paris, Dec. 15

SEINE R.

Paris

Versailles

Arrives, Dec. 21

Chartres

Le Mans

LOIRE R.

LOIRE R.

FRANCE

VIENNE R.

Rochefort

North

Sea

Amsterdam

NETHERLANDS

Ostend

Dunkirk

AUSTRIAN

NETHERLANDS

AUST.

NETH.

Metz

MARNE R.

SEINE R.

Dijon

SAÔNE R.

BAY OF

BISCAY

N

W   E

S

Scale of miles

0   50   100

Bordeaux

DORDOGNE R.

GARONNE R.

RHÔNE R.

Bilbao

SPAIN

Toulon

MEDITERRANEAN

SEA

Map by Gene Thorp.

19.

——◆——

A Quaker in Paris

The old gentleman had gone to sea once again, despite his resolve to remain on dry land for the rest of his days. In late November 1776, Dr. Franklin found himself aboard the heaving *Reprisal*, a triple-masted, hundred-foot-long American warship with a black hull trimmed in white, a splash of yellow across her stern, and the figurehead of a full-busted woman below the bowsprit. From her spanker gaff the vessel flew Continental colors: alternating red and white stripes with three overlapping union crosses in the upper canton. A former merchantman, the *Reprisal* had been built for speed and rebuilt for battle, mounting eighteen carriage guns, twenty swivels, and eight wide-muzzled cohorns. She was not built for a septuagenarian's convenience, and Franklin concurred with Samuel Johnson that ship travel was like being in jail without the comforts of jail. Of the eight Atlantic crossings he would make, this was among the fastest, thanks to fulsome westerlies that kept the canvas billowing and the sea foam scudding. But it was also among the most miserable. Running seas "almost demolished me," he would write, and a salt beef diet aggravated the boils and skin scurf that had plagued him during the Canada expedition the previous spring.

"I am old and good for nothing," he had told Benjamin Rush, his fellow congressman. "As the storekeepers say of their remnants of cloth, I am but a fag end, and you may have me for what you are pleased to give." So it happened that Congress in late October had been pleased to dispatch him to France in hopes of signing "a treaty with his most Christian majesty," King Louis XVI, and to obtain "twenty or thirty thousand muskets and bayonets, and a large supply of ammunition, and brass field pieces to be sent under convoy of France." The instructions tucked into his valise also empowered him to hire "a few good engineers" and to buy or borrow eight ships of the line, "of seventy-four and sixty-four guns, well-manned." Franklin, this fifteenth child of a Boston candlemaker, was to descend on

Versailles like a bolt of the lightning he had so famously tamed, using a diplomat's ploys to persuade the most sophisticated court in Europe to abandon its neutrality in exchange for little more than American gratitude and a chance to further abash perfidious Britain. "It will be proper for you to press for the immediate and explicit declaration of France in our favor," Congress had advised him, and to threaten an American reconciliation with England in the event of any French hesitation. Rarely had a supplicant— a beggar, really—set out with greater presumption, but rarely had Versailles seen anyone like Benjamin Franklin.

He had prepared meticulously, both for the voyage and for his new role. In a vain effort to make himself more comfortable during the passage, Franklin spent £26 on new bedding, linens, and sea stores, packed in three trunks and a great chest along with his books, fine suits, and the soft marten-pelt cap he had picked up in Canada. Then he hired a coach as if to picnic in the countryside and rambled south from Philadelphia to Marcus Hook, on the Delaware River, before secretly boarding the *Reprisal* on October 27. He was greeted by a marine guard and Captain Lambert Wickes, dressed in a high-collared blue uniform with red lapels, slash cuffs, and yellow buttons. Wickes had already earned distinction as a fighting sailor, first in the scrap at Turtle Gut Inlet in June, when the gunrunner *Nancy* blew up in British faces near Cape May; then a few weeks later in capturing three valuable British storeships with more than six hundred hogsheads of sugar and rum; and then, in late July, in a sharp exchange of broadsides with *Shark*, a British armed sloop off the coast of Martinique. As their distinguished passenger settled into his tiny cell belowdecks, Wickes's crewmen hoisted thirty-five casks of indigo into the hold, to be sold in France for £3,000 to underwrite the costs of this diplomatic mission.

Franklin also brought two traveling companions in tow, his grandsons Temple, age sixteen, and Benny, age seven. "If I die," Franklin explained, "I have a child to close my eyes and take care of my remains." Temple, who would serve as his grandfather's secretary, was said by cruel gossips to be a "double-distilled bastard," the illegitimate son of Dr. Franklin's own illegitimate son, William, recently deposed as the royal governor of New Jersey. Nothing in this war would be more agonizing to the old man than his estrangement from William, who as a boy had served as his father's cherished assistant in kite-flying experiments and other scientific pursuits— "the densest happiness I have met with in any part of my life," Benjamin once wrote of the time they spent together. Progressive and capable as a governor, albeit authoritarian and haughty, William adamantly refused to renounce his allegiance to the Crown despite his father's blandishments and reproaches. In July, declared a "virulent enemy to this country" by the

New Jersey assembly, he had been arrested by Continental troops and jailed in Connecticut—"led like a bear . . . to confinement," as he told London, with little more than a straw mat and a slop bucket. Unforgiving and scornful, Benjamin had refused to intervene except to snatch Temple away, insisting, "I have rescued a valuable young man from the danger of being a Tory." Years would pass before he would acknowledge his anguish in a simple declarative sentence: "I have lost my son." Similar estrangements, heartbreaking and brutal, were tearing apart American families from Maine to Georgia.

At noon on November 27, a cry of "Sail, ho!" sounded from the masthead. Captain Wickes studied the horizon through his glass, then went below to Franklin's cabin. Congress had ordered Wickes to sail unswervingly up the Loire River to Nantes, deposit his passengers, then cruise along the English coast for enemy merchantmen, sending any prizes into French ports. "Let old England see how they like to have an active enemy at their own door," the instructions read. But a British merchant vessel headed north had just crossed *Reprisal*'s bow. Franklin authorized the capture, Wickes ran out his six-pounders, and the brig *George* soon lowered her sails in capitulation. An American officer with a prize crew promptly boarded the ship, which had been bound for Cork with barrel staves, turpentine, and three dozen hogsheads of claret. A few hours later *Reprisal* also seized the *LaVigne*, another brig, headed for Hull with cognac and flaxseed.

Franklin was gleeful, assuring Congress that *Reprisal*'s crew was "equal to anything of the kind in the best ships of the king's fleet." Even such small triumphs had been rare for the fledgling Continental Navy, created by Congress a year earlier along with a small Marine Corps. Thirteen American frigates were under construction in Philadelphia, Providence, and other yards, but none had yet seen action for lack of guns, shipwrights, good officers, capable sailors, or opportunity. Commanding some eighty British warships and fifteen thousand seamen—a significant share of the world's greatest navy—Admiral Howe dominated American waters, even if he lacked the means to blockade three thousand miles of coastline or strategic sea-lanes like the Delaware and Chesapeake Bays. Howe's men-of-war would seize 140 American ships in the last nine months of 1776, though very few with munitions and only about one in nine of all the vessels carrying contraband to America from Lisbon, Havana, and seemingly every foreign port in between. Outgunned, outmanned, and outsailed, the Continental Navy provided no real counterweight to Howe's squadron, despite a few pugnacious captains like Wickes and a young, Scottish-born mariner named John Paul Jones, who earlier that month, off Nova Scotia, had seized the British transport *Mellish* and her cargo of sixteen thousand British wool uniforms and thirty thousand pairs of shoes—"the most valuable ship that hath been taken by the American arms," as Captain Jones proudly wrote from his warship, the *Alfred*. Jones had also participated in an earlier raid by a Continental Navy squadron and a couple hundred marines against New Providence in the Bahamas; the raiders captured 2 forts, 88 cannons, and the royal governor, although British merchantmen managed to escape to Florida with 162 barrels of the king's gunpowder.

Yet as Franklin well understood, a belligerent fleet of privateers was greatly aiding the American cause. Exploiting a form of naval warfare used since the thirteenth century, colonial governments in the fall of 1775 had begun issuing letters of marque and reprisal to authorize attacks on enemy vessels by private shipowners. Congress followed suit a few months later. A report to the House of Lords indicated that privateers had taken 733 British merchantmen since the first shots at Lexington; those ships would be among 3,400 captured during the war—a vast flotilla of impounded *Betsys*, *Bettys*, *Hannahs*, *Janes*, *Isabellas*, *Susannahs*, and more than a few *Johns*. About two thousand armed American privateers, carrying eighteen thousand guns and seventy thousand sailors, would prey on enemy shipping on both sides of the Atlantic. Massachusetts alone sent out five *Bunker Hills*, fifteen *Resolutions*, no fewer than twenty-one *Revenges*, and many a *Washington*, *Franklin*, and *General Arnold*. Privateers inevitably competed with the Continental Navy for manpower, munitions, and booty. Discipline was looser on a privateer—naval officers prohibited cursing and required sailors to attend church service twice daily—and the rewards were greater, since those holding private commissions kept the full value of prizes, while Congress now forced naval ships to remit to the public treasury half the value of enemy merchantmen seized. A solicitation in one port beckoned "all gentlemen volunteers who are desirous of making their fortunes in eight weeks." Whalers and fishermen signed on, but also teachers and preachers, according to the historian Helen Augur. "Success . . . in that business," James Warren wrote John Adams, "has been sufficient to make a whole country privateering mad."

The damage to British trade and military victualling was substantial. Insurance premiums on vessels traveling from the West Indies to England at times exceeded 20 percent of the value of the cargo and the ships—higher than during the Seven Years' War—and were still rising. Lloyd's of London estimated that in the first two years of war, rebel privateers would capture several times more merchantmen than the Americans lost in vessels of all sorts. A loyalist trader in Nova Scotia who had five ships taken that fall told his diary, "No protection afforded as yet from government. . . . The people are much engaged in privateering, and very successful." British merchant captains began painting black squares on their hulls in hopes that simulated gun ports would scare away marauders; the *Nelly*, seized while sailing from Honduras to London with a cargo of mahogany and turtles, was found to brandish six real guns and twelve made of wood. An Englishman reported from the Caribbean that in one week fourteen British ships were escorted into Martinique as American prizes, some of them straggling West Indiamen culled from sugar convoys despite protection from Royal Navy escorts. "We go on briskly taking prizes," Abigail Adams told John. "We have a plenty of sugars."

If Franklin could persuade the French to augment this plebeian effort with proper weapons, ships of the line, and other military aid, the American prospects would brighten immeasurably. But a few hours after *Reprisal* seized the two brigs, the westerlies died, then turned contrary. A lookout spotted the southern coast of Brittany on November 28. The loamy scent of land wafted across the quarterdeck, but headwinds kept Wickes forty miles from the mouth of the Loire. After swinging into Quiberon Bay, the ship bobbed about for four days, becalmed, to Franklin's squirming dismay.

On December 3, Wickes hired a fishing smack to row the passengers twenty miles to Auray, a bleak and remote stone village. Franklin tottered ashore with his two grandsons, spent a restive night, then hired a coach for the long overland journey to Nantes. "The carriage was a miserable one," he later wrote, "with tired horses, the evening dark, scarce a traveler but ourselves on the road, and to make it more *comfortable*, the driver stopped near a wood we were to pass through to tell us that a gang of eighteen robbers infested that wood, who but two weeks ago had robbed and murdered some travelers on that very spot."

Curious crowds in Nantes milled about for a glimpse of the famous "Docteur Franklin" as he settled into the Château de la Placelière on December 7. "You can have no conception of the respect with which I am received and treated here by the first people," he wrote his sister. The town fathers hosted a fancy dinner and a celebratory supper, a friendly merchant replenished his purse with a loan of sixteen hundred livres, and Franklin worked on his fractured French in conversations with tradesmen and fellow Masons. But after a week of waiting for *Reprisal* to arrive with his baggage, he left word to have it sent after him, bought a new cabriolet, and on December 15 set off for Paris, 240 miles northeast.

Franklin had revealed nothing publicly about his reasons for traveling. His appearance "has given birth to a thousand conjectures," one diplomat wrote. Some wondered if he had come to take the waters, or retire to Switzerland, or supervise the French publication of his papers. To an American confederate in Paris, he wrote, "I propose to retain my incognito until I ascertain whether the court will receive ministers from the United States."

That a large, balding American, renowned across Europe as a scientist, diplomat, and revolutionary, would remain inconspicuous as he trotted through the French provinces defied probability. Whatever the great man's purpose, Paris was alert and giddy while awaiting his arrival. When word spread in London of Franklin's advance on Paris, British stocks fell. It was also rumored, Horace Walpole wrote, that he "has invented a machine the size of a toothpick case . . . that would reduce St. Paul's to a handful of ashes."

The British ambassador to Versailles, David Murray, known as Lord Stormont, tracked Franklin's progress furlong by furlong and encouraged speculation that he had fled America to avoid the stain of a failed rebellion. "The famous Doctor Franklin is arrived at Nantes with his grandchildren," Stormont told his government. "I look upon him as a dangerous engine, and am sorry that some English frigate did not meet him on the way."

Paris was a clamorous city. Horses' hooves and handcarts rattled across the cobblestones, followed by heavy wine wagons and the four-team Versailles omnibus hauling passengers wedged into a wicker cab. The cries of rummage merchants, brandy vendors, water sellers, and fish peddlers— "Fresh herrings, all a-shiver!"—mingled with pleas for a coin or two from the blind inmates of Quinze-Vingts Hospital, who were turned out each morning in their long robes to beg for a living on the Rue Saint-Honoré. Windmills clattered on Montmartre, violinists sawed away on the avenues, and washerwomen clubbed their linens with wooden batons along the Seine quays. Bells played from fifty parish churches and a hundred monasteries, including a melodious sequence of F, E, D, C from Saint-André-des-Arts; other bells signaled the nightly curfew, rung for at least five centuries. Town criers beat drums to announce orders from the king's council or new death sentences, and for a fee, street singers composed impromptu ballads. In Paris, the dramatist and historian Louis-Sébastien Mercier observed, a man unsung was a man unknown.

No less vivid than the sounds were the smells and sights: roasting meat, baking bread, wheeled cheeses, urine, treacle, cinnamon, ground pepper sold in paper twists, sometimes with a bit of dog dung mixed in to pad the weight. Sidewalks would not appear until the 1780s, and the city streets were fouled with *la boue de Paris*, a black filth from chamber pots and open sewers said to be so caustic that it would eat the hem from a dress in hours. Street valets on the Pont Neuf offered to brush pedestrians' shoes, stockings, and skirts for a few sous. Tossing elms lined the Champs-Élysées, and huge signs hung above the tradesmen's shops—a giant boot, or a glove said to be large enough to conceal a child in each finger. Vendors strolled about with leashed monkeys who wore little soldier uniforms and were trained to doff their caps when someone cried, "Long live the king!" Licensed "bill-stickers" used ladders, brushes, and paste pots each morning to cover city walls with new notices: police orders, bankruptcy sales, quack nostrums, lost dogs, theater advertisements, funeral bulletins. At night some eight thousand lamps suspended from rope pulleys gleamed above the streets. Many now burned tripe oil rather than candles, but lantern boys still loitered outside the theaters, ready to light the way home for patrons wary of footpads.

Paris was also a town of couture, of fads and fashions that rose and fell, came and went. Sophisticates debated whether wine darkened the skin as well as the national mood. By 1776, men's wigs were fading in popularity, and each morning six thousand barbers hastened through the streets with their curling irons, washing out yesterday's pomade and powder from natural hair before applying today's; at noon the barbers turned to surgery. Men and women carried parasols to preserve their facial pallor. For a time the king's pet zebra inspired striped coats and even stockings. Wrist lace concealed dirty cuffs. Women's coiffures included the "porcupine" and the "baby's cap." Skirts were puffed, panniered, and crinolined. A city ordinance required every actress and dancer to wear panties on public stages; wits claimed that they were the only *Parisiennes* who wore underwear.

Miracles and miracle-mongers thrived here, including a child reputedly able to see under the ground and a faith healer who drew enormous crowds to watch him cure the deaf, lame, and blind with his touch—at least until the authorities bundled him out of town. Debtors, madmen, and felons filled the prisons, and so, too, the "good poor"—epileptics, imbeciles, cripples, and paupers. Twice a week the cell blocks fell silent as the most literate inmate read aloud the latest *Gazette de France*, bawling the news through his door grate. In this secular age, the number of holy days had been trimmed to thirty-five, and for many Parisians, Mercier wrote, "pleasure is the chief public preoccupation." The city boasted some three thousand cabarets and fourteen thousand registered prostitutes; unlicensed bordellos tried to avoid police scrutiny by calling themselves dancing schools or charity concert halls. Paris was also full of informants, agents, and operatives—"court spies, town spies, bed, street, and brothel spies, spies upon talkers and wits," a resident claimed. "One servant in every four is a spy."

In the center of this bustling, hustling, watchful metropolis stood a slightly seedy baroque mansion known as the Hôtel des Ambassadeurs de

Hollande, even though the Dutch minister had not lived there for years. Looming above the rue Vieille du Temple, several blocks north of the Seine, the house since late summer had swarmed with clerks, accountants, secretaries, children, kitchen help, a mistress or two, and mysterious men who at all hours rapped on the great wooden door featuring carved gorgons with extended tongues. Interior courtyards and galleries featured bas-relief scenes of Romulus and Remus nursed by their she-wolf, a painted mural of Psyche's marriage to Cupid, and sculpted allegories of Strength, Truth, Peace, and War. The gilded, frescoed salons, with windows modeled after the royal château at Fontainebleau, were littered with theater programs, ledgers, billets-doux, riding whips, musical instruments, and, on occasion, canvas sacks of French and Spanish gold coins. A sign out front indicated that a Spanish commercial house—Roderigue Hortalèz et Cie—occupied the premises, but at least one visitor thought the counting rooms seemed "unbusiness-like."

The firm was, in fact, the government front recently set up for shipping military supplies to America without implicating Versailles or embarrassing Louis XVI. A tall, slender, elegant man said to be the Hortalèz managing director occasionally flitted down the rue Vieille du Temple, but he, too, was not what he seemed, and he never had been. Pierre-Augustin Caron, better known as Beaumarchais, was among the most improbable figures affiliated with the American rebellion; with his celebrated gift for "oozing through keyholes," he was also among the great characters of eighteenth-century France. Now forty-four, born into a family described as *"obscure, mais intéressante,"* he had been apprenticed at age thirteen to his father, a Parisian watchmaker. By twenty he was among the finest horologists in France, a reputation enhanced when he fashioned a tiny watch set in a ring for Madame de Pompadour, the previous king's chief mistress. A gifted musician, he instructed the four daughters of Louis XV in the harp, for which he invented improved foot pedals. He married a rich widow, shed his old name, then married well again after the first wife died.

Minor court positions came to Beaumarchais, including walking in livery with a sword on his hip in the procession that preceded the king's meat course. He made money as an arms dealer in the Seven Years' War, as a lumber merchant, and as an agent for the Crown, including one mission in which he quashed the publication of *Secret Memoirs of a Prostitute*, a salacious pamphlet about a royal courtesan; Beaumarchais bought all the copies from a blackmailer and burned them in a London limekiln. In another recent mission to Britain, he retrieved from a renegade French expatriate an iron safe containing secret war plans drafted in Versailles for an attack on southern England. More government offices came to him, notably lieutenant general of the preserves in the bailiwick, and captain of the warren of the Louvre. Among other adornments, he wore an enormous diamond ring given to him by Empress Maria Theresa of Austria for services rendered, according to the biographer Georges Lemaitre.

He was forever embroiled in spats, duels, lawsuits, indictments, judgments, and misjudgments. "My life," he admitted, "is a combat." During a squabble over a woman in 1773, a sword-wielding duke attacked him in his study, inflicting wounds on the coachman, cook, and footman trying to intervene; Beaumarchais, a witness reported, was "as cheerful and assured as if he had passed the most tranquil day." His bestselling memoir, published in 1774, drew praise from Goethe and Voltaire. In late February 1775, a comedy he had written—much delayed by various disputes, including accusations of insulting French authorities and a stint in jail—finally premiered, to boos, at the Comédie-Française. Beaumarchais radically revised the script overnight to appease what he called the "god of the hissers, spitters, coughers, and disturbers," and *The Barber of Seville* emerged as a sensational European hit, with fifty performances in St. Petersburg alone. Some material trimmed from the original production would eventually appear in his next work, *The Marriage of Figaro.* Mozart and Rossini would make him immortal by bejeweling the plays with music, but his inspired stage character—the versatile, roguish Figaro—embodied what one critic called "the gaiety, the intelligence, the lightness" of the French people. Without doubt he embodied Beaumarchais.

In the past year he had become a rabid enthusiast for the American cause. Intoxicated with republican zeal, he also believed that an ascendant America could tilt the balance of power in Europe and help France avenge her catastrophic defeat in the Seven Years' War. Having lost Canada, India, and other possessions to that "usurping race"—the *Anglais*—the French had been seething at the humiliations imposed under the treaty of 1763, including the requirement that a British official in the French port of Dunkirk approve even slight modifications to seaside piers and fortifications. Intent on revenge when the moment grew ripe, French diplomats and agents tracked every development in the British Empire, notably fleet construction, public debt, and colonial unrest. They even collected maps of the English coast, carefully marked to show prospective invasion beaches.

"All sensible persons are convinced in England that the English colonies are lost to the mother country," Beaumarchais had written during a visit to London in September 1775. "That is also my opinion." He soon had a close confederate in the French foreign minister, Charles Gravier, the comte de Vergennes, an urbane, shrewd public servant who had cut his teeth as a diplomat in Trier, Lisbon, Constantinople, and Stockholm, and whose preeminent ambition was the enfeeblement of Britain and the resurgence of France as a world power. Vergennes deplored the sort of revolutionary folderol proclaimed in the American declaration of independency—at least nine French translations would appear over the next few years—and he knew that infectious democracy imperiled all monarchies. Thomas Jefferson, who admired Vergennes's diplomatic skills, later wrote that "his devotion to the principles of pure despotism renders him unaffectionate to our government."

But, like Beaumarchais, the minister believed that a protracted, bloody struggle between Britain and America—a "long-winded affair," secretly nurtured by Versailles—could badly weaken London even as France rearmed and prepared for the next clash with her hereditary enemy. Vergennes and Beaumarchais often met twice weekly, and their correspondence would exceed a thousand letters in a dozen years.

Converting the new French king to these sentiments would require artful persuasion. Louis XVI had ascended the throne in 1774 at the age of nineteen upon the death of his grandfather, who had been so disfigured by a fatal bout of smallpox that he was not permitted to look in a mirror. "I feel," the new king confessed, "the universe is going to fall on me." Young Louis's profession, it was agreed, was to be a royalist, although his own self-described ambition was "to be loved." He admired George III, but as an absolute monarch and an enthusiast for the divine right of kings, he was unfettered by the sort of constitutional niceties imposed on his British counterpart. Stoop-shouldered and nearsighted—"like a peasant slouching along behind his plow," one observer wrote—he would be widely seen as ineffectual, indolent, immature, and doomed, with a frivolous if beautiful wife, Marie Antoinette, known as "*l'Autrichienne*," the Austrian woman, with stress on *chienne*, or "bitch." That she had not produced an heir six years after their wedding, apparently because the marriage had yet to be consummated, only provoked further eye-rolling in fashionable society.

Though indecisive and a bit dim, Louis was reasonably well disposed toward his subjects. He was also instinctively cautious in foreign affairs. "It is the English, sire, which it concerns you to humiliate and to weaken if you do not wish to be humiliated and weakened yourself," Beaumarchais wrote in one of many urgent epistles that had fluttered into Versailles during the previous winter and spring. If Britain crushed the American rebellion, she would recoup her war costs by "seizing our West India sugar islands," five of which provided two-fifths of all French imports. Should America reconcile with Britain, he told the king, they might join forces to attack France. Unchecked British commercial and maritime strength would dominate Europe for generations. Aiding the Americans, on the other hand, could restore "all that the shameful peace of 1763 deprived us of" by reducing England to "a second-class power."

Vergennes added his own measured, insistent voice. "England is the natural enemy of France," he wrote, "and she is an avid enemy—ambitious, unjust, brimming with bad faith," intent on "the humiliation and ruin of France." The proper strategy was to assure England that the Bourbon regimes—France and Spain—wanted peace while surreptitiously rebuilding the French military and supporting the American insurgents. As if to punctuate the foreign minister's argument, Beaumarchais added, "Engineers and gunpowder!"

Bit by bit the king came round, despite warnings from his finance minister that war would bankrupt France. American élan captured French imaginations and inspired young nobles, who clamored to help the insurgents against British barbarity; even Marie Antoinette was aflutter with enthusiasm for these New World paragons of courage and ingenuous virtue. At Vergennes's direction, a French agent disguised as an Antwerp merchant traveled to Philadelphia and told Congress that France had no interest in reclaiming Canada and that American mariners would be welcome in French ports. "Everyone here is a soldier," the agent reported from Philadelphia with delusional gusto. "The troops are well-clothed, well-paid, and well-commanded. . . . Nothing frightens them."

With Louis's reluctant consent, Beaumarchais at last sprang into action with a scheme worthy of his stagecraft. The first million livres in gold coins—equivalent to nearly £50,000—was transferred from the French treasury to Beaumarchais's carriage, fairly spilling from the sacks. Spain made a similar donation six weeks later, and a third million would come from secret investors in Nantes, Bordeaux, and elsewhere. More coins followed. After setting up the phony Hortalèz commercial house in rue Vieille du Temple, Beaumarchais dashed about to Rochefort and other ports, seeking ships to charter, captains to hire, customs officials to charm or bribe.

He soon accumulated surplus brass field guns and muskets from French armories and arms dealers, arranging for workmen to obliterate the royal coat of arms without weakening the cannon barrels. To the Committee of Secret Correspondence in Philadelphia, he wrote of "my avowed and ardent desire to serve you to the utmost of my power"; he intended nothing less than "to help the brave Americans shake off the yoke of England." In return, he expected American "products of the soil"—at least ten thousand hogsheads of tobacco—which would be sold in France as a means of replenishing his sacks of gold to buy even more munitions. "Beaumarchais is developing his vast schemes for the future," an acquaintance wrote. "He has very large funds at his disposal."

He also had accumulated an American collaborator, a blacksmith's son, Yale graduate, and former congressman from Connecticut named Silas Deane. Sent to Paris by Congress in the early summer of 1776 as a forerunner to the Franklin mission and posing as an overdressed Bermuda merchant named Jones, the monolingual Deane vowed to speak only French, prompting Vergennes to remark after their first meeting, "He must be the most silent man in France, for I defy him to say six consecutive words in French." To further curry Marie Antoinette's favor, Deane urged Congress to ship various items across the Atlantic: a phaeton with two Narragansett bays, apples, an insect collection, walnuts, and an orrery, a contraption illustrating the movement of planets around the sun. His request for other curiosities to pique French interest in America led to discussions in Philadelphia of sending rattlesnakes, woodchucks, flying squirrels, and a moose.

By December, working with Beaumarchais as Vergennes had instructed, Deane had reported shipping 40 tons of saltpeter and 150 tons of gunpowder through Martinique and Amsterdam. Merchants brought samples of uniform cloth and price lists to his rooms in the Hôtel du Grand Villars. He wrote buoyant, windy letters to Versailles pleading for more help and guaranteeing that there would be no separate peace between America and Britain, while trying to explain battlefield setbacks at places like Long Island. He also wrote long, anguished letters to Philadelphia, rebuking Congress for moving slowly, for failing to dispatch ships to pick up contraband, and for ignoring requests for tobacco—he suggested at least twenty thousand hogsheads—to compensate Monsieur Beaumarchais, "a man of wit and genius." To chastise the British, Deane proposed dispatching an American warship to destroy Glasgow.

Deane also found himself running a recruiting office for hundreds of European soldiers of fortune, mountebanks, and genuine freedom fighters avid to join the American cause. "The rage, as I may say, for entering into the American service increases," he had written in November, with many bids for preferment from "persons of the first rank and eminence." Deane issued officer commissions willy-nilly—four hundred by late fall, according to British intelligence—including the rank of "major general in the forces of the United Colonies" to one French artillerist, who also was promised horses, carriages, an adjutant and aides, ten staff officers, and a pension.

Not all were what they seemed. A twenty-two-year-old named Pierre Charles L'Enfant was said to be a lieutenant of engineers, but in fact he had studied art and architecture in Paris, at the Royal Academy of Painting and

Sculpture; one day he would design the new capital of Washington, D.C. Among others presenting himself to Deane was a clean-limbed, nineteen-year-old dragoon captain whose father had been killed fighting the British at Minden in 1759. "His noble lineage, his connections . . . his personal worth, his celebrity, his disinterestedness, and above all his zeal for the liberty of our colonies have alone influenced me," Deane told Congress. Marie-Joseph-Paul-Yves-Roch-Gilbert du Motier—the Marquis de Lafayette—commissioned as a major general on December 7, would sail for America in the spring.

"I am well-nigh harassed to death with applications of officers," Deane wrote the Committee of Secret Correspondence. He added, "Had I ten ships here, I could fill them with passengers to America."

As Dr. Franklin made his way from Nantes to Paris in December, a mysterious "M. Durand" appeared in Le Havre, the rawboned Norman port at the mouth of the Seine. Tall and refined, with a breezy self-confidence, Durand took a keen interest in a large arsenal now being lightered from warehouses along the waterfront to three merchantmen anchored just offshore, *L'Amphitrite*, *La Seine*, and *La Romain*. The cache included 200 brass cannons, brick-red gun carriages, 30,000 stand of shoulder arms, 30 mortars, 4,000 tents, 53 barrels of sulfur, and 200 tons of gunpowder; most had been drawn from surplus stocks in Metz, Dijon, and five other royal arsenals that were now being replenished with new munitions under a French rearmament surge. It was claimed along the docks that the arms were bound for French colonies in the New World. Yet several dozen artillery officers and engineers also milled around the waterfront, waiting to board the three ships. In dramshops and *estaminets*, some of the men, after a libation or two, hinted that their voyage could take them beyond Martinique and Guadeloupe.

By mischance, a provincial production of *Le Barbier de Séville* was in rehearsal in Le Havre. As a local police lieutenant informed Vergennes on December 12, M. Durand abruptly appeared at the theater, appointed himself interim director, and showed even more proprietary interest in the play than in his munitions stockpile. "He made himself known to the whole town by . . . making the actors rehearse, in order that they might play better," an officer wrote Deane. "All this has rendered his precaution he had taken to hide himself under the name of Durand useless."

Informants had advised Lord Stormont, the British ambassador, of suspicious ships fitting out in Normandy, of munitions moving on French roads, and of the Hortalèz facade. Now Stormont learned that the notorious dramaturge Beaumarchais was in Le Havre running guns under a nom de guerre. He protested bitterly to Vergennes, hinting darkly at reprisals from London. Already unsettled by news of another American defeat at White Plains, the French minister and his king took counsel of their fears. Vergennes professed dismay and disavowed all knowledge of skulduggery, and on Monday, December 16, he issued orders prohibiting the departure of any munitions ship.

Sensing trouble of his own making, Beaumarchais had hired more than a hundred stevedores in Le Havre to finish loading his ships on two consecutive nights "amid the wildest confusion," as he acknowledged to Deane. *L'Amphitrite*, reportedly carrying 7,500 knee buckles and 8,500 pairs of stockings as well as munitions, had already slipped from the harbor when the ministry order arrived at ten o'clock Monday night. Undaunted, Beaumarchais ordered the two remaining vessels unloaded, conspicuously, then reloaded by stealth. "I am about to begin by changing the names of the ships, and the rest will be done noiselessly and in the night time," he told Deane, adding, "I have drained to the dregs the cup of duty." Meanwhile, he rushed back to Versailles, and pleaded his case with enough charm and indignation to get the embargo lifted, secretly. "I sincerely thank you," Beaumarchais later wrote Vergennes, "for your goodness in tranquilizing me."

Nothing about this opéra bouffe would be straightforward, of course; nothing ever was with Beaumarchais. Even *L'Amphitrite* would first wander south to Brittany on various diversions before finally steering west for Portsmouth, New Hampshire. Whether the arms she carried were a secret gift from the French government or part of a commercial transaction to be exchanged for tobacco would take years to sort out.

But the ship would reach America in early spring, soon followed by others chartered through Roderigue Hortalèz et Cie. Only *La Seine* fell prey to British cruisers. Many of the surplus muskets and cannons would prove inferior; more than half of the musket locks failed testing and required repair by American gunsmiths. Still, the powder, weapons, and other war cargoes would be useful in coming campaigns, thanks in no small measure to the original Figaro, who, in Deane's estimation, had done more for America than "any other person on this side of the ocean. . . . He has made our affairs entirely his own."

Each morning, rumors circulated that Dr. Franklin had arrived in Paris, and each evening, those rumors were denied, until Saturday, December 21, when at last the report proved true. Deane hurried to meet Franklin's cabriolet in Versailles and escort him into the city, where he and the boys took rooms in the Hôtel d'Entragues on rue de l'Université, near the Pont Royal. Soon a procession of carriages brought sightseers and supplicants keen to meet with "the idol of the day," as one French writer would call him, "that peasant, that septuagenarian philosopher, that learned democrat, that man of the future." Franklin received so many letters that mail was delivered nine times a day. "He was addressed simply as 'Doctor Franklin,'" another Frenchman wrote, "as one would have addressed Plato or Socrates."

Franklin had visited France twice in the 1760s, joking that his tailor and peruke maker "transformed me into a Frenchman. . . . They told me I was become twenty years younger and looked very gallant." Now he was *the* American, a slightly paunchy embodiment of his country, authentic and unpretentious in an inauthentic, pretentious age. Excerpts from the final edition of his *Poor Richard's Almanack*, published in 1758, would be reprinted 145 times before the end of the century, including twenty-eight French translations; reportedly even priests found his aphorisms on prudence, thrift, and diligence to be instructive.

Now Parisians pursued his coach when he traveled through the city, reciting laudatory couplets composed in his honor. The French assumed that as a Pennsylvanian he must be a Quaker, and it was said that a Parisian rake could succeed at seduction just by dressing in black homespun and claiming devotion to America. The powerful, the learned, and the rich were eager to meet this "ornament of the New World"; beautiful women called him *mon cher Papa*, and he ruefully admitted that he was hardpressed to obey the commandment against coveting thy neighbor's wife. A secret police report to the government noted:

> Doctor Franklin . . . is much run after, and fêted. . . . This Quaker wears the full costume of his sect. He has an agreeable physiognomy: spectacles always on his eyes, but little hair. A fur cap is always on his head. He wears no powder, but a neat air. Linen very white. . . . His only defense is a stick in his hand.

As one admirer would observe, he had "just the touch of charlatanism that the sentimentalism of the age demanded." Here, in French eyes, stood Rousseau's natural, uncorrupted man, an antique sage from the American Eden, emblematic of simplicity, austerity, and honesty. Some fashionable women wore wigs that imitated his marten-pelt cap, a style soon called *coiffure à la Franklin*. Others wore Franklin gloves, and fine eateries served chops *à la Franklin*. When he entered a theater, the orchestra rose in its pit and cheered. Engravings of Franklin became a popular New Year's gift, to be displayed on the mantel, and his twinkling image soon appeared on snuff boxes, in countless prints, even on *pots de chambre*. His witticisms were repeated, his silences admired, if not often emulated. As the guest of honor at the luminous Saint-Germain salon of an elderly marquise—only on her deathbed would she repent violating all ten commandments and indulging in all seven mortal sins—Franklin sat by the hearth in his cap and wire-frame spectacles, drawing praise for his "sublime reticence."

On December 23, young Temple rode ten miles to Versailles with his grandfather's written request for an audience. "We flatter ourselves," Franklin told Vergennes, "that the propositions we are instructed to make are such as will not be found unacceptable." Five days later, at a house in Paris, Vergennes welcomed him to France in a clandestine conference also joined by Deane and Arthur Lee of Virginia, who had just arrived in the city as the third member of the American delegation. After mutual exchanges of flattery, Franklin proposed "a treaty of amity and commerce." Congress, he explained, had chosen "to make this offer first to France," which stood to benefit from the American trade that Britain had so wantonly thrown away. Vergennes stressed patience and discretion; French ports would be open to American ships, but under Anglo-French protocols, privateers and prizes could hardly be welcome—at least not yet. The minister professed ignorance about arms shipments from provincial French harbors and barely acknowledged knowing the imprudent M. Beaumarchais.

They parted amicably, having agreed to further talks. Franklin seemed "intelligent but very circumspect," Vergennes wrote in a diplomatic note later that day; he was surprised at how little the Americans seemed to want. The next evening Franklin and his colleagues met the Spanish ambassador, the Count de Aranda, in his majestic villa on the Place Louis XV for another amiable if fruitless conversation. "Franklin speaks very little French, Deane less, and Lee none," Aranda reported. On Sunday, January 5, Franklin penned another, more explicit note to Vergennes, asking for eight fully crewed warships, muskets, field artillery, and ammunition. The request was all the more urgent given the uncertain fate of *L'Amphitrite* and the other vessels carrying the munitions privately obtained by Deane in recent months.

"As other princes of Europe are lending or hiring their troops to Britain against America," he wrote, "it is apprehended that France may, if she thinks fit, afford our independent states the same kind of aid." He and his colleagues cheerfully predicted English ruination: if France, Spain, and America were to unite in a military triumvirate, Britain would "lose all her possessions in the West Indies, much the greatest part of that commerce that has rendered her so opulent, and be reduced to that state of weakness and humiliation she has by her perfidy, her insolence, and her cruelty, both in the east and west, so justly merited." Franklin also brandished the only cudgel he possessed: if the American war effort faltered, he warned, reconciliation with Britain seemed inevitable. America "now offers to France and Spain her amity and commerce," he concluded. "We cannot help suggesting that a considerable delay may be attended with fatal consequences."

Later that Sunday, the three commissioners traveled by coach to Versailles and at six p.m. asked to meet with Vergennes. He declined; the court was too public a venue for such assignations. Instead, his secretary accepted their petition, scribbled a terse acknowledgment, and sent them on their way. The French, Arthur Lee complained, "talk much, do little, and protract everything."

The minister and his king remained skittish, and with good reason. British spies, Deane had warned, "watch every movement of those with whom I am connected." Admiralty agents monitored naval construction in French dockyards, while others tracked suspected contraband bound for America, from linen and drugs to musket balls and bayonets. Some agents communicated with London using a code that assigned a different number to 284 common nouns, proper names, and adjectives: America was 7, ammunition 11, Chesapeake Bay 22, Beaumarchais 26, Versailles 202, General Washington 206, bad 213, good 217. Another spy who had penetrated the American diplomatic staff would send detailed reports on "progress of the treaty with France" and "Franklin's and Deane's correspondence." Lord Stormont was at times misinformed: he reported, erroneously, that Franklin had met Vergennes on December 11, that he had offered France exclusive trading rights in North America, and that French bankers had advanced ten million livres in credit. Even so, Stormont knew a great deal.

Like Lords North and Germain, the British ambassador also recognized that continued peace with France was crucial if America was to be subdued. Bloody fighting in Europe during the Seven Years' War had fatally damaged France's ability to defend her colonial interests; Britain could face a similar dilemma if forced to fight other continental powers when much of the Royal Navy and most of the king's army was in America. For now, London would pretend that Versailles was benign, that King Louis and his court desired only peace, and that occasional rogue arms shipments across the Atlantic hardly mattered.

A long, exquisite dance had begun. Warned by an American living in France that "you are surrounded with spies who watch your every movement," Franklin replied, "I have long observed one rule . . . to be concerned in no affairs that I should blush to have made public, and to do nothing but what spies may see and welcome." That studied nonchalance belied

Franklin's determination to press his cause relentlessly, but with the *discrétion* the French required. Only now was he beginning to see the diplomatic complexities involved: in Europe's balance of power, France was threatened not just by Britain, but also by an ascendant Austria and Russia, and by Portuguese truculence that distracted Bourbon Spain.

Versailles was simply unready for another war. Among other weaknesses, the naval rebuilding program was incomplete, although the French managed to conceal from the Americans, if not the British, how hollow the navy remained. Vergennes could not afford to provoke Britain; in late December, when Stormont had gleefully sent him details about the American drubbing in New York, the minister had replied, "My sincere felicitations upon an event so calculated to contribute to the reestablishment of peace in that part of the globe." Vergennes would practice what he called *"attente expectative,"* watchful waiting.

Franklin faced his own quandary. America could not defeat Britain without substantial French aid, but substantial French aid was unlikely unless America demonstrated that it could defeat Britain. His Most Christian Majesty would hardly give complete support to rebels who were not only Protestant and republican but also militarily inept. Washington and his generals must win on the battlefield.

A bit of good news reached the Americans soon after their frustrating visit to Versailles. The king sent word through a trusted courier that he intended to loan the Americans two million livres, without interest or a repayment date. More clandestine help—*secours secret*—would follow in time. Franklin had impressed the French court. "His conversation is gentle and honest," Vergennes told the French ambassador to London. "He appears to be a man of much talent." But how he planned to enlist the Bourbon regimes as full American allies remained uncertain. "I still don't know what Dr. Franklin has come to accomplish among us," the minister added. "When he first arrived it seemed possible that he had an important mission."

In truth, Franklin had quickly recognized that overbearing demands would gain little. Forbearance, persistence, persuasion, and personal charm would be needed in the coming months to align his country's interests with those of these ancient monarchies. Years later, Silas Deane observed:

> His age and experience, as well as his philosophical temper, led him to prefer a patient perseverance, and to wait events, and to leave the court of France to act from motives of interest only. He used often to say that America was a new and young state, and, like a virgin, ought to wait.

He would listen more than speak, smile more than frown, nod more than implore. "Make haste slowly," Poor Richard had advised. "Diligence is the mother of good luck."

In a dispatch to Congress, Franklin and his colleagues wrote, "The hearts of the French are universally for us, and the cry is strong for immediate war with Britain. . . . But the court has its reasons for postponing it a little longer. In the meantime, preparations for it are making." Still, they added in a postscript, "America should exert herself as if she had no aid to expect but from God and her own valor."

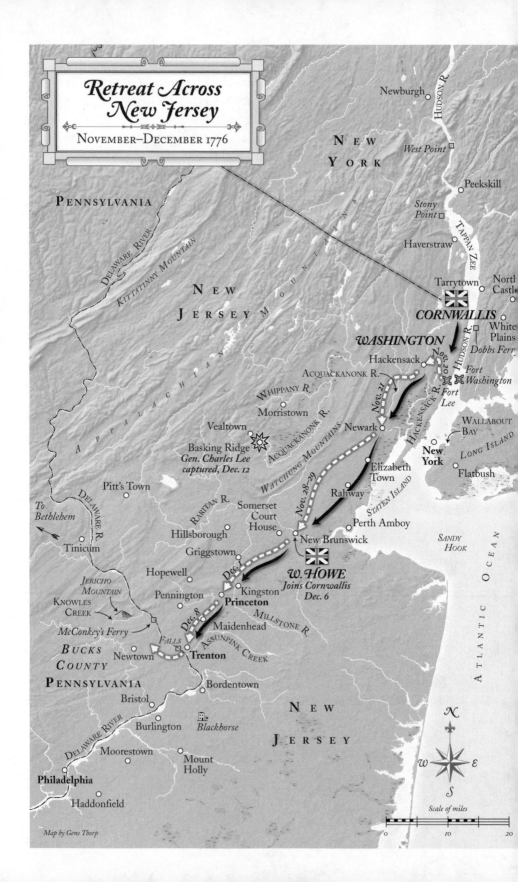

Retreat Across
New Jersey

November–December 1776

NEW YORK

Newburgh

West Point

Peekskill

PENNSYLVANIA

Stony
Point

Haverstraw

Tarrytown   North
Castle

CORNWALLIS   White
Plains

WASHINGTON   Dobbs Ferry

NEW

JERSEY   Hackensack

ACQUACKANONK R.   Fort
Washington

Fort
Lee

Morristown   Newark

Vealtown   WALLABOUT
BAY

Basking Ridge
Gen. Charles Lee
captured, Dec. 12   Elizabeth
Town   NEW
York   LONG ISLAND

Flatbush

Pitt's Town   Rahway   Perth Amboy

To
Bethlehem   Somerset
Court
House   SANDY
HOOK

Tinicum   Hillsborough   New Brunswick

Griggstown   W. HOWE
Joins Cornwallis
Dec. 6

JERICHO
MOUNTAIN   Hopewell

KNOWLES
CREEK   Pennington   Kingston

Princeton

McConkey's Ferry   Maidenhead

BUCKS
COUNTY   FALLS   Trenton

Newtown

PENNSYLVANIA   Bordentown

Bristol   NEW

Burlington   Blackhorse   JERSEY

Moorestown

Mount
Holly   ATLANTIC OCEAN

Philadelphia

Haddonfield

Map by Gene Thorp

Scale of miles

0   10   20

20.

Fire-and-Sword Men

The American army, threadbare and dying, trudged south from Newark in a pelting rain on Thursday, November 28. Muskets, discarded knapsacks, and other spoor littered the miry roads, described by one Maryland ensign as "intolerable bad." The troops numbered 5,410, but desertion thinned the ranks hour by hour, and armed patrols sped ahead to New Jersey crossroads and the Delaware River ferries with orders to seize men who lacked proper papers or a bleeding wound. Night came on, and crowbait soldiers slept in circles with their feet toward the fire, like spokes on a wheel. Most wore rags and rummage, and even those few who owned regulation buff-and-blue uniforms had been reduced by now to "all buff," as one wit observed. "You will wonder what has become of the good army of Americans you were told we had," Captain John Chilton of the 3rd Virginia Regiment wrote his brother. "I really can't tell. They were in some degree imaginary."

At first light on Friday, the column again lurched forward through salt meadows, past stone barns and red sandstone houses with peaked roofs, curved eaves, and double-hung Dutch doors. Mud-spattered refugees also hurried south, glancing sideways at loyalist neighbors who peered back from their parlor windows or loitered on narrow porches, the women in aprons and billowing skirts, the men with faces masked by pipe smoke. Some had already donned green uniforms and pledged allegiance to their king in exchange for amnesty and a guinea or two. Cornwallis and his royal legions were but a few hours behind the rebels, nearly ten thousand strong in two columns angling from Newark toward Elizabeth Town and Rahway. "The church green was covered with Hessians," one townsman had written, "a horrid, frightful sight with their whiskers, brass caps, and kettles or brass drums." Clouds of camp followers, liberated slaves, and whooping loyalists trailed behind, looting abandoned houses, smashing windows, and even prying brass locks from the doors before trundling off with rugs, teapots, and cows.

At midday on Friday, twenty-five miles southwest of Newark, the Americans crossed the Raritan River into New Brunswick, described by one traveler as "a dismal town but pleasantly situated." Storage sheds, three churches, 150 houses, and sundry taverns, including the White Hart and the Sign of the Ship, crowded the waterfront, where in better days sloops and two-masted pettiaugers carried corn, timothy grass, and linseed to New York or the West Indies. "We arrived at Brunswick broken down and fatigued," wrote Lieutenant Enoch Anderson of Delaware, "some without shoes, some had no shirts." Rain fell like birdshot.

Among those retreating with this "wretched remains of a broken army," in Joseph Reed's phrase, was a lanky man just shy of forty with a high forehead, a tippler's red nose, which he often tickled with snuff, and blue eyes described as "full, brilliant, and singularly piercing." His hands had an artisan's hard-knuckle strength, and he was such a graceful skater and swimmer that friends called him "Commodore." English-born, he had immigrated to America just two years earlier, and he had recently spent three months as a Pennsylvania militiaman before becoming General Greene's aide-de-camp at Fort Lee in mid-September.

Thomas Paine had failed at everything he ever attempted in Britain: shopkeeping, teaching, tax collecting (twice), and marriage (also twice). For years he made whalebone corset stays in dreary provincial towns, then worked as an exciseman, chasing Dutch gin and tobacco smugglers along the English coast before being sacked for cause. Forced into bankruptcy— "Trade I do not understand," he admitted—in desperation he sailed for Philadelphia and immediately found work editing the *Pennsylvania Magazine*, printing articles on Voltaire, beavers, suicide, and revolutionary politics. A gifted writer, infused with egalitarian and utopian ideals, he attacked slavery, dueling, animal cruelty, and the oppression of women. On January 10, 1776, a thousand copies of his new pamphlet on the American rebellion had been published anonymously under a simple title suggested by Dr. Benjamin Rush.

Common Sense "burst from the press," Rush reported, and "its effects were sudden and extensive upon the American mind." The pamphlet had sold over 150,000 copies in fifty-six editions, including versions eventually peddled in Edinburgh, Dubrovnik, Moscow, and points in between. "Who is the author of *Common Sense*?" a Rhode Island reader asked. "I can hardly refrain from adoring him." Paine, willing to be adored, soon revealed himself, then repudiated both his copyright claim and his profits, which he donated to the Continental Army for the purchase of mittens. His urgent, muscular prose—"this rude way of writing," in Dr. Franklin's assessment—had "put the torch to combustibles," as another admirer wrote. Paine appealed to the unlettered—farmers, shopmen, mechanics—with an avowed intent "to make those that can scarcely read understand." A Massachusetts reader declared, "Every sentiment has sunk into my well-prepared heart."

Paine's polemic was "a work of genius," the historian Bernard Bailyn would write, "slapdash as it is, rambling as it is, crude as it is." An indictment of the British body politic, blazing with resentment, indignation, and sedition, it attacked hereditary monarchies, class privilege, the colonial system, and loyalism. George III was "the royal brute of Britain," and his government a "detestable junto." One honest citizen had more value "than all the crowned ruffians that ever lived." Reconciliation with the mother country was "a fallacious dream," Paine wrote. "Now is the seed-time of continental union, faith, and honor. . . . We have it in our power to begin the world over again." The nation was destined to become a republic, a lodestar for aspiring peoples everywhere. "The cause of America," he asserted, "is in a great measure the cause of all mankind."

Common Sense had helped nudge Americans toward their declaration of independency, converting fence straddlers into patriots and patriots into radicals. If John Adams was skeptical of both the pamphlet—a "crapulous mass"—and its author, whom he called "a mongrel between pig and puppy," pursuing "a career of mischief," most readers concurred with General Washington, who praised Paine's "sound doctrine and unanswerable reasoning." Yet the dismal events of recent months required another lyrical call for unity, a restatement of transcendent national purpose.

Paine had long greeted acquaintances not with a salutation but with a short bow and an interrogatory: "What news?" Since joining Greene at Fort Lee, he'd found the news to be invariably glum, including defeat in Westchester and the calamity at Fort Washington, which he witnessed from across the Hudson. Paine passed out copies of *Common Sense* to discourage desertion, and he sought to inspirit his new countrymen through newspaper dispatches from the front, written "with a wooden pen on a drumhead" and sent to Philadelphia for publication despite their wild inaccuracies.

During the muddy trudge from Hackensack to Newark and on to New Brunswick, he had scribbled notes for another treatise, one that would be both a plainspoken meditation and an incandescent cry for courage. He envisioned thirteen essays that drew inspiration from this retreat, giving voice to what he called "a passion of patriotism." The first would open with a blunt acknowledgment of distress: "These are the times that try men's souls."

Washington placed his New Brunswick headquarters in Cochrane's Tavern, on the southwest corner of Albany and Neilson Streets. After loitering at Newark for several days in hopes that New Jersey militiamen would rally to him, he had pushed south to avoid being outflanked and to keep his force between the British and Philadelphia, which he assumed was Cornwallis's objective. His call to arms reportedly evoked "nothing but murmuring and desertion."

An eighteen-year-old Virginia officer described seeing the commanding general during the long retreat through northern New Jersey. "A deportment so firm, so dignified, so exalted, but yet so modest and composed, I have never seen in any other person," wrote Lieutenant James Monroe. As usual, Washington's calm mien concealed his anxiety. "No great number of the militia of this state has come in, nor have I reason to expect that any considerable aid will be derived," he privately told Hancock on Saturday, November 30, adding, "The situation of our affairs [is] truly alarming." The New Jersey assembly had fled—from Princeton to Trenton to Burlington to Haddonfield—and would soon dissolve, leaving the state without a government. The College of New Jersey in Princeton had also dispersed, the students scattering and their president fleeing on horseback. "All was confusion and dismay," wrote Lieutenant Benjamin Tallmadge, "and it seemed as if we were on the eve of despair and ruin."

Among other worries, Washington was uncertain where General Lee was or why he had failed to heed repeated entreaties to cross the Hudson from Westchester County and rejoin the main army with five thousand men. Lee's increasingly erratic, bickering behavior had grown nettlesome. "There are times when we must commit treason against the laws of the state for the salvation of the state," he had written to the Massachusetts Council president a week earlier. "The present crisis demands this brave, virtuous kind of treason." Greene advised Washington, "General Lee must be confined within the lines of some general plan, or else his operations will be independent of yours."

In hopes of learning Lee's whereabouts, that Saturday Washington opened a letter from him to Colonel Reed while the adjutant general was traveling on army business to Burlington. The commanding general instantly recognized that Lee, his senior lieutenant, and Reed, his closest confidant, had conducted a disloyal correspondence behind his back. Lee had written:

> I received your most obliging, flattering letter [and] lament with you that fatal indecision of mind which in war is a much greater disqualification than stupidity or even want of personal courage. Accident may put a decisive blunderer in the right, but eternal defeat and miscarriage must attend the man of the best parts if cursed with indecision.

Washington had not seen Reed's preceding letter to Lee, but he could easily surmise the gist. It included these unctuous, unfaithful lines:

> You have decision, a quality often wanting in minds otherwise valuable. . . . I have no doubt had you been here the garrison at Mount Washington would now have composed a part of this army. . . . Oh, General, an indecisive mind is one of the greatest misfortunes that can befall an army. How often I have lamented it this campaign. . . . I think yourself & some others should go to Congress & form the plan of the new army.

Stunned and no doubt saddened, Washington resealed Lee's missive and appended a civil, if icy, note of his own to Reed:

> The enclosed was put into my hands by an express from the White Plains. Having no idea of it being a private letter, much less suspecting the tendency of the correspondence, I opened it. . . . I am, dear sir, your most obedient servant, G. Washington.

Many months would pass before Reed recovered from this deft rebuke, delivered with subtle censure by a great man who had once trusted him with his most private reflections.

An even more grievous injury befell Washington just hours later when almost half of his remaining army walked away. On Sunday, December 1, the enlistments of two brigades from Maryland and New Jersey expired. Despite his personal plea to the assembled ranks, more than two thousand men gathered their kit and made off, unwilling "to stay an hour longer," Washington wrote. Most remaining enlistments would expire in a month. "If those go," he warned, ". . . our force will be reduced to a mere handful." In September, Congress had voted to raise eighty-eight regiments—roughly sixty thousand men—for enlistment terms of three years or the duration of "the present war," but there was little evidence that states would come close to filling their respective quotas. Simply appointing officers for the new Continental units was excruciatingly slow; nary a lieutenant had been chosen by early November. Militia companies came and went—militias from the middle states would be called out twenty-two times in 1776—but now they mostly went, fearful of the approaching enemy and disgruntled at Congress's inability to feed them properly.

If the army remained, by Washington's own description, "a destructive, expensive, disorderly mob," he hardly had time to fret. Scouts reported British dragoons and light infantry sweeping toward New Brunswick; Cornwallis's main legions were just two hours away, their baggage wagons stacked with loot. In a note scribbled to Hancock at one-thirty p.m. on Sunday, he wrote, "The enemy are fast advancing. Some of 'em are now in sight." From a bluff across the Raritan, the cough of British cannon fire shattered the winter quiet. Balls whizzed into town, skipping down cobbled lanes and chewing into storefronts.

Washington ordered his artillery detachment to unlimber long enough to cover the infantry's flight toward Princeton. Some sixty gunners from New York, wearing blue coats, white shoulder belts, and buckskin breeches, swarmed around the five fieldpieces with linstocks, flannel cartridges, and long-handled sponges. Their captain, later described by another officer as "a mere stripling, small, slender, almost delicate . . . with a cocked hat pulled down over his eyes," danced from gun to gun, occasionally patting a barrel "as if it were a favorite horse." Captain Alexander Hamilton, the son of a wandering Scottish wastrel and a sugar islands harlot jailed for adultery, had escaped a dreary St. Croix boyhood when benefactors sent him to New York for an education. "I wish there was a war," Hamilton had written as an ambitious teenager. Now he had his wish. "The enemy fired six to our one" at New Brunswick, a witness recorded. Yet the American guns—complemented by riflemen shooting from houses above the riverbank—galled the enemy enough to hold them at bay until nightfall.

British engineers repaired a sabotaged Raritan bridge two miles upstream, but by the time *Jäger*, grenadiers, and horsemen crossed to the south bank, Washington had slipped away on the Upper Road with Hamilton's artillery train. Only an orange bonfire of a hundred burning tents—too heavy to carry off without wagons—remained behind, along with the Yankee dead and those too sick to move. "When we left Brunswick we had not 3,000 men," Greene wrote a friend, "a very pitiful army to trust the liberties of America upon." Rain further fouled the muddy road. "Every step was above the ankles," a Maryland officer wrote, "and many rose to the knee." At seven-thirty p.m. on Sunday, Washington again wrote Hancock: "It being impossible to oppose them with our present force with the least prospect of success, we shall retreat to the west side of [the] Delaware [River] . . . where it is hoped we shall meet a reinforcement sufficient to check their progress."

For now the British checked themselves, although several days would pass before the Americans realized that their pursuers had stopped at New Brunswick. General Howe had ordered Cornwallis to halt after capturing northeast Jersey. Further pursuit would be "highly blameable," Howe later explained. Crown forces were strung out for more than forty miles along bad roads back to the Hudson, and rebel Lee's corps was lurking behind them, somewhere. "The artillery horses and baggage horses of the army were quite tired," Cornwallis subsequently stated. "I could not have pursued the enemy from Brunswick with any prospect of material advantage, or without greatly distressing the troops under my command."

The halt dismayed many of those troops. "Our army were in great expectation of making Philadelphia their winter quarters, the whole Jerseys seeming to submit to the British government," a Guards lieutenant wrote in his journal on December 2. German officers considered it folly to stop at New Brunswick, although Captain Johann Ewald concluded that Howe's languid pursuit was strategic, in "hopes of ending the war amicably, without shedding the blood of the king's subjects in a needless way." *Jäger* and dragoons consoled themselves with a raid on a nearby rebel estate, where they seized forty-five bottles of Madeira.

Once again the Americans had stolen off, like ghosts at cockcrow. "'Tis almost impossible to catch them," a captain in the 40th Foot complained. "They will neither fight nor totally run away. . . . We seem to be playing at Bo Peep."

Washington kept moving. After leaving a large rear guard in Princeton under General Lord Stirling, who had recently been released from British captivity in a prisoner exchange, the army swung thirteen miles southeast to Trenton, "our officers leading us as if the devil had sent for them," as one sergeant later wrote. Some men who lacked shoes "was obliged to lace on their feet the hide of the cattle we had killed the day before." A Delaware ensign observed that "a thick cloud of darkness and gloom covered the land, and despair was seen in almost every countenance."

On Washington's order, soldiers secured two ferries on the Delaware River below Trenton. They also collected boats, oars, and poles and fashioned rafts from scavenged boards and scantling. Every canoe, barge, and skiff for forty miles was seized or sunk. Large patrols moved upstream to guard fords and other ferry crossings, and to confiscate weapons from those hostile to the cause. The rebel galley *Warren* patrolled the west bank above Philadelphia, and a small flotilla anchored near Trenton to discourage spies and loyalists from crossing into Jersey. Black-and-yellow row galleys helped shuttle the sick and wounded to the Pennsylvania shore, along with many of the two thousand barrels of flour and 250 bushels of salt found in Trenton. Ammunition, barreled pork, and other provisions filled a supply depot at Newtown in Bucks County, five miles west of the river. Troops built huge fires from fence rails, and a Rhode Island sergeant confessed to his diary that his foragers stole "29 fowls that had not got the countersign."

Columns of refugees also staggered toward the Delaware. "They called up the day of judgment," a pastor's daughter reported. "So many frightened people were assembled, with sick and wounded soldiers, all flying for their lives, and with hardly any means of crossing the river." A dispatch from New York authorities to Hancock reported that troops "reduced to the lowest ebb of human wretchedness" were dying for want of blankets, medicine, and physicians. Invalid soldiers began arriving in Pennsylvania by the score and eventually by the hundreds. Many were carted to a three-story stone Moravian monastery in Bethlehem that had been converted into a hospital. "Two died while waiting to be removed from the wagons," according to an account; they were the first of more than sixty to die there in December, "in a large degree due to the effects of exposure." Moravian carpenters built coffins to bury the dead on a bluff above Monocacy Creek. Surviving convalescents would leave scratches across the chapel floor from their steel-tipped crutches.

Puzzled by the enemy's failure to give chase, Washington started back toward central Jersey with twelve hundred men led by Greene on Saturday, December 7. The commanding general had not reached Princeton when a courier from Greene found him on the post road. The king's troops had broken camp in New Brunswick and were driving south, according to Stirling; General Howe had arrived from New York with another brigade and had chosen to resume his offensive with ten thousand men in two columns. "It is beyond a doubt the enemy are advancing, and my Lord Stirling thinks they'll be up here by 12 o'clock," Greene wrote. "I shall make the best disposition I can to oppose them."

Washington sent a message to recall Stirling and Greene rather than risk further combat losses. All Continental forces were to hasten for the Pennsylvania shore. As the last of his troops from Princeton hurried past, the commanding general lingered with a pioneer detachment, "tearing up bridges and cutting down trees to impede the march of the enemy," wrote newly promoted Captain Enoch Anderson, now commanding a Delaware rearguard company. "I was to go no faster than General Washington and his pioneers. It was dusk before we got to Trenton."

Men at the last pitch of exhaustion crowded the river after what one ensign called "a tag-rag race through the Jerseys with General Howe and the English army at our heels." Even with stragglers arriving, the American host now numbered no more than 3,500, plus 2,000 Philadelphia militiamen and a few Pennsylvania Germans. Boats shuttled from shore to shore, laved with light from bonfires on both banks. Reed took a moment at Washington's request to scratch out a dispatch to Hancock on a torn scrap:

> No opposition will be given till we cross the Delaware. Our whole force, if collected, will not exceed six thousand, and they are diminishing every moment by desertion. I can get no other paper than this. You will please excuse it, as well as the hurry of my letter.

Among those waiting to cross that night was a Philadelphia militia lieutenant named Charles Willson Peale, who described himself as "a thin, spare, pale-faced man totally unfit to endure the fatigues of long marches and lying on the cold wet ground." Now thirty-five, Peale had tried his hand at saddlery, clockmaking, and silversmithing before turning to portraiture following two years of study in London under the expatriate master Benjamin West. As a soldier, he painted ivory miniatures of his men, made them false teeth and rawhide moccasins, and prized a firelock with a telescopic sight that he had built with help from the astronomer David Rittenhouse. As the leading portraitist in America, Peale would paint almost twelve hundred faces, including George Washington fourteen times from life. But on this Saturday evening he was just another confused, unfledged officer. "I expected we were to advance toward the enemy, but it was to retreat across the river," he told his journal. He later described how "sick and half-naked veterans of the long retreat streamed past." On the western bank, he added, the army

> made a grand but dreadful appearance. All the shores were lighted up with large fires. The howling of hundreds of men in their difficulties of getting horses and artillery out of the boats made it rather the appearance of hell than any earthly scene.

Washington crossed shortly after dawn on Sunday morning, December 8, followed by Philadelphia cavalry troopers anxiously peering back over their shoulders. At noon the rap of drums and the blare of hautboys drifted across the river from Trenton, where a column of light infantry and three Hessian regiments swaggered into town. Those downed bridges and felled trees had slowed their progress, along with the distraction of plunder in Princeton, but Howe—immaculate in a gold-laced scarlet coat—soon arrived with Cornwallis at his side.

Although the pretty village was mostly deserted, several loyalists "came running toward us, urging us to march through the town in a hurry so we could capture many of the enemy who were just embarking in boats," according to Captain Levin Friedrich Ernst von Münchhausen, Howe's German aide. Surrounded by *Jäger* and infantrymen, the two generals trotted to the sandy floodplain along the Delaware. No rebels could be seen on the broad gray river, but moments later the western shoreline erupted in a scorching bombardment of iron balls and grapeshot, a barrage so intense that Münchhausen believed more than three dozen American guns were shooting. Howe, Cornwallis, and their troops dashed for a ravine leading from the river. "Just as General Howe was about to move back into the town, a ball landed so close to him in soft ground that dirt splattered his body and face," Münchhausen wrote. "A ball took away the hind leg of my horse." The officers scrambled to safety, but Münchhausen reported thirteen soldiers killed or wounded.

Once again, the American fugitives had escaped. "General Howe had a mortgage on the rebel army for some time," a Virginia officer wrote, "but had not yet foreclosed it."

Washington put his headquarters in a brick country house half a mile from the upper Trenton ferry, ready to flee in an instant. New Jersey had been lost. Philadelphia was at risk and, with it, the Congress. The British seemed indomitable. "I am led to think that the enemy are bringing boats with them," the commander in chief wrote Hancock on Monday. "If so, it will be impossible for our small force to give them any considerable opposition in the passage of the river."

Like the rest of their miserable comrades, Captain Anderson and his Delaware rearguard company built lean-tos and scooped out burrows in the Pennsylvania hills. British gunners shouldered their fieldpieces to the wood line outside Trenton and cannonaded the far shore. "We lay amongst the leaves without tents or blankets, laying down with our feet to the fire," Anderson wrote. "We had nothing to cook with but our ramrods, which we run through a piece of meat and roasted it over the fire." He had once read about Charles XII of Sweden, who inured himself to foul weather so that eventually he could lie on the snow in midwinter to nap. "I now often thought of Charles XII," Anderson noted.

Yet for those who had come this far and endured this much, sardonic humor and stubborn defiance would get them through the night, and the next day, and the day following. The British, after all, had to win the war; the Americans only had to avoid losing it. "Never was finer lads at a retreat than we," wrote Lieutenant Colonel Samuel Blachley Webb, a Washington aide-de-camp who had fought valiantly at Bunker Hill and been wounded at White Plains. "No fun for us that I can see. However, I cannot but think we shall drub the dogs."

Fortunately for those camped in the damp woods, Washington had been misinformed: the British carried no boats across New Jersey. Enough materials could be found in Trenton to build a fleet of rivercraft, the historian William S. Stryker later concluded, including forty-eight thousand board feet of lumber, a hardware vendor, and three blacksmith shops. But there would be no amphibious assault into the cannon's mouth across the Delaware. General Howe had intended only to occupy northeast New Jersey during this campaign, with winter cantonments in Newark and New Brunswick. At Cornwallis's urging, he had subsequently marched on to Trenton not only to shoo away the rebels but to secure more billets and additional provisions. The king's troops ate well over a thousand tons of food every month, and their four thousand horses required an even greater weight in forage. The New Jersey granary would help fill those needs. Philadelphia, unlike the rebel army, could not sneak off; the city, now less than thirty miles away, would be there for the taking come spring, if not later in the winter.

Howe had also been encouraged by newly emboldened New Jersey loyalists. Since late November, nearly three thousand men had signed an oath of fidelity—"I will remain in a peaceable obedience to His Majesty"—in exchange for "a full and free pardon of all treasons" and a "protection paper" intended to provide immunity from pillagers. Extending the British occupation to the Delaware would safeguard these faithful subjects, and encourage more to declare themselves.

"The approach of winter putting a stop to any further progress," Howe announced, "the troops will immediately march into quarters." Of 14,000 royalist soldiers in New Jersey, more than 10,000 would bivouac south of the Raritan, including 4,000 in New Brunswick, 3,000 in Princeton, and 3,000 Hessians—nine regiments, with sixteen guns—in Trenton and nearby Bordentown, where the Delaware took a wide bend to the southwest. Rebel skirmishers and row galleys proved such a nuisance along the river that the 42nd Highlanders and a Hessian grenadier regiment moved inland from vulnerable Burlington to Blackhorse, several miles east. But already

Jersey children were learning to say *"Wie geht's?"*—How do you do?—to their German occupiers. Given the heavily armed chain of seventeen posts stretching for seventy miles down the spine of New Jersey, Cornwallis later said, "I apprehended no danger."

Howe would return to New York for the winter and Cornwallis to England. "The chain, I own, is rather too extensive," Howe wrote Lord Germain. "But . . . I conclude the troops will be in perfect security."

To serve as the new British commander in New Jersey, Howe appointed a trusted chum, Major General James Grant, the former governor of East Florida, a stout, gouty Scottish veteran of the French and Indian War, the siege of Boston, and the battle for Long Island. "He was a gamester, a glutton, and an epicure," a British major wrote. "He lived only for himself."

Before sailing for America, Grant had assured Parliament that with five thousand regulars he could march unimpeded through the colonies. An able if tyrannical administrator, he had been consistently wrong about nearly every aspect of American policy, claiming that the rebellion had little support outside New England, that "the business will soon be over without bloodshed," that the Americans "would never dare to face an English army," and that the enemy "in fact does not exist in the Jerseys." Grant's retinue included flocks of ducks and geese—he kept "the best table in the army," an admirer noted—as well as his personal chef, a man named Baptiste who reportedly slept in the same room so he could more easily receive menu suggestions for the next meal.

Howe had hoped that his royal legions would be welcomed in the middle colonies as liberators rather than as conquerors. But the invading force was rife with what one loyalist called "fire-and-sword men." Even before returning to New York, Howe decreed that flour and salt provisions exceeding a family's need should be considered "a rebel store, [to] be seized for the Crown." Confiscation hardly stopped with flour. "They have taken hogs, sheep, horses, and cows, everywhere," Lieutenant Peale told his journal. "Even children have been stripped of their clothes, in which business the Hessian women are the most active."

A German soldier reportedly rode back to Manhattan with a stolen grandfather clock on his horse. In the Raritan valley, 650 houses—the homes of about a third of the families in Middlesex County—would be ransacked or burned, along with mills, churches, and other structures. A Presbyterian pastor wrote that Newark "looked more like a scene of ruin than a pleasant, well-cultivated village. . . . Their plundering is so universal, and their robberies so atrocious, that I cannot fully describe their conduct." The rampage, he added, targeted "fences, barns, stables, and other outhouses, the breaking of chests, drawers, desks, tables, and other furniture." From Elizabeth Town to Burlington, victims carefully listed their losses: silver plate, scarlet cloaks, velvet breeches, swanskin waistcoats, surgical instruments, frying pans, jewelry, bombazine gowns, and a "large mahogany case of wax works." Goose down leaking from feather beds marked the path of spoliation.

Princeton had been insulted by predatory American troops in recent months, but the king's men pillaged with a methodical vengeance, felling apple and pear trees for firewood, burning gristmills, butchering sheep and milk cows, stealing horseshoes from farriers and leather from tanning vats. Nassau Hall at the College of New Jersey was ransacked—the stone cellar became a dungeon—and rare books from Leipzig and Birmingham vanished. "Our army when we lay there spoiled and plundered a good library," a sergeant in the 49th Foot acknowledged. Farmers in nearby villages were beaten and robbed. "Maidenhead and Hopewell are entirely broken up," according to an account published on December 12. "The houses are stripped of every article of furniture, and what is not portable is entirely destroyed." Loyalists suffered as well as patriots, not least because even Hessians who could read the protection papers often ignored them. An outspoken Tory in Newark who cheered the arrival of British soldiers reportedly had "his very shoes taken off his feet, and they threatened to hang him." William Livingston, who had succeeded William Franklin as governor, wrote, "The rapacity of the enemy was boundless, their rapine indiscriminate, and their barbarity unparalleled."

Soon after retreating across the Delaware, Washington also began to get reports of rape by British and Hessian soldiers, especially in a rural area north of Trenton. A magistrate, Jared Sexton, took sworn testimony that proved horrifying: the widow Mary Phillips reported being gang-raped, as did Mary Campbell, five months pregnant, and Elizabeth Cain, age fifteen. Rebekhah Christopher reported being raped by two men. Abigail Palmer, age thirteen, said she was raped by soldiers who threatened to blind her with bayonets if she screamed. Sexton's affidavits were printed in the *Pennsylvania Evening Post* with the victims' names redacted, although they were included in a report subsequently sent to Congress.

Other testimonials accumulated as county justices, clergymen, and the governors of New Jersey and New York investigated further, identifying victims as young as ten and as old as seventy in what the historian David Hackett Fischer described as "an epidemic of rape." "God made these men," a Quaker said of the assailants, "but I am sure the devil governs them." General Greene told the governor of Rhode Island in mid-December that enemy "ravages in the Jerseys exceeds all description. Men slaughtered, women ravished, and houses plundered. Little girls not ten years old ravished. Mothers and daughters ravished in the presence of their husbands and sons."

General Howe would tell the House of Commons that during his command in America only one accusation of rape was brought against a royal soldier, whose prosecution ended when the victim declined to testify. Other allegations, Howe insisted, were American propaganda, although he had tacitly acknowledged disciplinary difficulties in the late fall, when he asked London for additional Guards officers because "it is not in the power of a few officers to keep the men under proper restraint." The historians Leonard Lundin and Sylvia Frey later concluded that most claims of rape were secondhand and lacked corroborative evidence. Yet in late 1776, several British officers encouraged despicable behavior, while others voiced alarm at the resultant atrocities. Captain Francis Lord Rawdon, now commanding a company in the 63rd Foot, wrote in a private letter from New York that "we should, whenever we get further into the country, give free liberty to the soldiers to ravage at will," so that "these infatuated wretches . . . may feel what a calamity war is." He noted that "the fresh meat our men have gotten has made them as riotous as satyrs. A girl cannot step into the bushes to pluck a rose without running the most imminent risk of being ravished."

Major Charles Stuart wrote his father, a former prime minister, that even loyalists were treated like rebels, with "neither their clothing or property spared, but in the most inhuman and barbarous manner torn from them." Soldiers, he added, disregarded repeated orders "against this barbarity." Major Matthew Dixon, the British chief engineer, noted in his orderly book that two soldiers from the 57th Foot had been sentenced to death for rape in New York; "the present licentious behavior of the troops is a disgrace to the country they belong to," he wrote. Major Stephen Kemble, a native of New Brunswick who served as Howe's deputy adjutant, decried "every species of rapine and plunder." Beginning in Westchester County, he had written in his journal of "scandalous behavior" by British troops; the Hessians were "outrageously licentious and . . . threaten with death all such as dare obstruct them in their depredations. Violence to officers frequently used. . . . Shudder for Jersey." Lieutenant John Peebles of the Black Watch made note in his journal of rapes in Rhode Island in December, adding, "There have been other shocking abuses of that nature that have not come to public notice." Joseph Galloway, a Philadelphia lawyer who had served in Congress but would defect to the Howes in New York this month, subsequently denounced "the savage brutality" of the king's troops. "In respect to the rapes," he wrote, "it appears that no less than twenty-three were committed in one neighborhood in New Jersey."

General Grant blamed indiscipline on lax officers, correctly noting that scurrilous behavior could "lose you friends and gain you enemies." Just so: New Jersey militiamen who had been reluctant to join Washington now assailed their oppressors with raids and ambushes. New Jersey, like Westchester County, soon became a dark borderland of uncertain, shifting loyalties and spasmodic violence. Howe's staff estimated that rebel bandits by mid-December had rustled seven hundred oxen and almost a thousand sheep and hogs from British foragers. Patrols were bushwhacked, couriers seized, and eight British baggage wagons captured. Six hundred raiders struck Hackensack while the redcoats were campaigning downstate, seizing fifty Tories.

As Howe prepared to return to New York, Captain Münchhausen wrote, "It is now very unsafe for us to travel in Jersey. The rascal peasants meet our men alone or in small unarmed groups. . . . They shoot them in the head, then quickly hide their rifles and pretend they know nothing."

The approach of fire-and-sword men triggered panic in Philadelphia. Local authorities advised those hoping to avoid the "insults and oppression of a licentious soldier" to flee. "Drums beat," one diarist wrote. "A martial appearance. The shops shut." Armed rebels roamed the town, closing schools and pressing teenage boys into militia companies. Accused loyalists were jailed—witnesses at the Indian Queen Tavern fingered those once heard to sing "God Save the King"—and prisoners were either paroled from the Walnut Street jail or, if unrepentant, sent to cells in Lancaster, York, Carlisle, or Frederick, Maryland. A thousand wagons were assembled to evacuate the city's riches, including half a million musket cartridges, public papers, a gunlock factory, and booty from the prize ship *Sam*, recently captured en route to Liverpool from Barbados with twenty-two thousand silver coins and two and a half tons of ivory. "Numbers of families loading wagons with their furniture, &c.," a Philadelphian wrote on December 10. "Our people in confusion, of all ranks." A note to General Washington reported, "The city is amazingly depopulated."

Congress ordered a day of fasting and prayer, forbidding "all swearing and immorality." On December 12, a day after denouncing a report that they intended to abscond as "false and malicious," several dozen congressmen bolted for Baltimore, giving Washington "full power" to prosecute the war and expunging from the record their earlier denial of flight. Their departure "struck a damp on ye feelings of many," a cavalry captain noted, although some Philadelphians left behind were pleased to hear members complain that Baltimore was a "dirty, infamous, extravagant hole" and the "worst of all terrestrial places."

Continental presses and plates were transported to Baltimore under guard so that Congress could continue printing money. Nearly $25 million had been issued in the past eighteen months, despite a requirement that every bill be numbered and signed by authorized citizens (who received just over a dollar for every thousand bills processed). Promiscuous issuance of paper money without adequate backing in specie or gold inevitably led to depreciation; prices had more than doubled over their prewar average, and they would double again in the coming year as even more bills were printed—the new notes with fancy escutcheons and secret marks intended to thwart counterfeiters. Depreciation "threatens instant and total ruin to the American cause," the Philadelphia financier and congressman Robert Morris wrote the Paris commissioners in December. The day would come when Continental bills were used to light a pipe or a grogshop candle, and fifers would wear jackets made entirely from sheets of worthless American currency.

Before scurrying away, Congress ordered Philadelphia defended "to the last extremity," and Washington sent General Putnam to command the town. Old Put imposed martial law and a ten p.m. curfew, effective December 12. Merchants refusing to accept Continental currency would be arrested and their inventories confiscated. Bell ringers strode through the streets, ordering all able-bodied men to help dig entrenchments or man riverfront defenses that included fire ships, floating batteries, forty chevaux-de-frise, and seven shore guns on Mud Island. Home guard companies of invalids watched bridges on the Schuylkill River and ferry landings on the lower Delaware, where thirteen alarm posts stretched to Cape Henlopen. But when a courier arrived with word that *Roebuck* and several other men-of-war had abruptly appeared in the mouth of Delaware Bay, Putnam ordered combustibles laid along the docks. If the enemy drew closer, he intended to burn four unfinished Continental frigates and a sloop now being built in Philadelphia's yards, and with them, perhaps, the ninety wharves and three miles of waterfront in the New World's busiest port.

By mid-December, one officer wrote, the elegant Chippendale town resembled "a dark and silent wilderness of houses." At least half of Philadelphia's thirty thousand residents had fled, although many Quaker families remained, having no argument with the British. Sick soldiers from the New York and New Jersey campaigns filled the Pennsylvania Hospital at Eighth and Pine and the Bettering House on Spruce Street. Smallpox and camp fever—typhus—swiftly became epidemic, killing fifteen to twenty men a day. "Everything here wears the face of despondency," wrote an army surgeon, despondent himself. Carts piled high with corpses rolled through city streets to a potter's field, where they were laid two deep in pits fifteen to thirty feet square. A gravedigger was quoted as complaining that "they die so fast that he cannot dig graves for them all." Benjamin Rush estimated that at least a thousand soldiers would pass that winter; John Adams put the figure at two thousand.

"Our people knew not the hardships & calamities of war when they so boldly dared Britain to arms," Robert Morris added in his letter to the Paris commissioners. "Dejection of spirits is an epidemical disease, and unless some fortunate event or other gives a turn to the disorder, in time it may prevail." It was rumored, for instance, that unless Charles Lee landed a decisive stroke against Howe's rear, Congress would authorize Washington to accept the best surrender terms he could get from the British.

At last, at long last, General Lee had indeed found his way into New Jersey. With 2,700 Continentals, joined by 1,300 militiamen, he reached Morristown on December 8, lingering there for three days in a vain hope of finding shoes and blankets for his ill-shod, ill-clad legion. On Thursday, December 12, with orders to observe "a most strict silence," the four-mile column plodded south across rolling terrain with a thirty-man advance guard, flankers east and west in single file, and General Sullivan's division in the rear, fifteen paces behind the main body. "I am extremely shocked to hear that your force is so inadequate," Washington told Lee. "I had been taught to think you had been considerably reinforced." As for "the distress of the troops for want of clothes," he wrote, "I feel much, but what can I do?"

None of this pleased Lee, who grumbled about both incompetent officers—"Washington and his puppies" among them—and a country that seemed unaware that "your liberties stand on the verge of perdition," as he told one correspondent. He had planned to harass Howe from behind, "to unnest 'em even in the dead of winter" and force the British garrisons back to New York. Several raids already had been launched—"mud rounds," Lee called them—as part of a grander plan "to reconquer, if I may so express myself, the Jerseys."

"Cannot I do you more service by attacking their rear?" he had asked Washington on December 8. But the commanding general would have none of it. Over the past three weeks, Washington had sent eight increasingly frantic pleas, first suggesting, then entreating, and finally ordering Lee to put on speed. Not only was the army along the Delaware badly outnumbered, but militia regiments simply would not fight without being stiffened by ample Continental troops. Plea number seven, sent on Tuesday,

December 10, directed, "March and join me with all your force.... Do come on." A day later, plea number eight demanded, "Push on with every possible succor you can bring."

On Thursday afternoon, with a weak, watery sun low in the sky, Lee told General Sullivan to bivouac the troops at Vealtown, eight miles south of Morristown. They were to prepare to swing west the next day to eventually cross the Delaware at Tinicum, skirting the large British force in the south. Leaving his personal baggage behind, including his spyglass and pistols, Lee peeled away with an aide, two French volunteer officers, and a squad of fifteen bodyguards; they would spend the night three miles southeast in Basking Ridge at the widow Mary White's tavern, a frame house behind a wooden fence, several hundred yards from the trunk road, where the limbs of an ancient white oak spread above a Presbyterian churchyard. Some would claim that Lee had an assignation with a woman. If so, the tryst hardly improved his sour mood after a day's muddy ride. His favorite mare had been stabled near Princeton during the fall and now likely carried a British rider. Three of his best camp horses had vanished during the march from Westchester, despite his offer of a guinea's reward for each. Worse yet, Spada and his other dogs had been sent to Virginia for safekeeping. Lee was alone.

After peeling off his uniform and donning a nightshirt, he sat at a table and scratched a querulous note to his old friend Horatio Gates, who was headed for Pennsylvania from Ticonderoga with six hundred Northern Army soldiers. After once again complaining about the loss of Fort Washington, Lee turned his pen on the commanding general:

> Entre nous, a certain great man is most damnably deficient. He has thrown me into a situation where I have my choice of difficulties. If I stay in the province, I risk myself and army, and if I do not stay the province is lost forever. I have neither guides, cavalry, medicines, money, shoes, or stockings.... Tories are in my front, rear, and on my flanks. The mass of people is strangely contaminated.... Adieu, my dear friend. God bless you.

As Alexander Hamilton would later observe, Charles Lee had the preposterous notion that *he* was a great man. For two years he had served the patriot cause creditably by demanding discipline in the ranks and lauding the combat prowess of American soldiers against their British enemies. But he was fickle, disloyal, intemperate, and incautious—and now these defects brought him low.

* * *

Alarmed by reports that Lee was somewhere in his rear, on December 12 Cornwallis dispatched thirty-three horsemen from the 16th Light Dragoons to look for him. Flamboyant in their black leather helmets with horsehair plumes and red tunics trimmed in blue, the dragoons cantered north from Pennington toward Morristown, wary of rebel ambushes. "They picked off a good number of us in this shabby method," a British captain later complained. The riders were led by Lieutenant Colonel William Harcourt, the thirty-three-year-old son of an earl and a favorite of Queen Charlotte, whom he had helped escort from Germany to London before her marriage to His Majesty in 1761. Swinging east along the Raritan, the troopers spent the night sleeping on straw in Hillsborough, then rose before dawn on Friday to again tack north on King George Road. The rising sun brought a bright, balmy morning.

A mile from Basking Ridge, perhaps alerted to Lee's presence by loyalist informants, Harcourt sent half a dozen scouts ahead under a young firebrand officer named Banastre Tarleton, the son of a prosperous slave trader who had served as the mayor of Liverpool. Tarleton spotted two rebel sentries, captured them without gunplay, and soon learned that Lee was in a nearby hostelry with paltry security. Colonel Harcourt quickly sketched a plan, and at ten a.m. dragoons edged through the orchard and woodlot bracketing Widow White's tavern.

Inside Lee had dressed, finished his correspondence, and ordered his horse saddled for the short ride to rejoin his corps. Major James Wilkinson, who had arrived in the small hours with dispatches from General Gates, had just eaten a late breakfast when he peered from the window to see redcoats thundering down the front lane. "Here, sir, are the British cavalry!" he yelled. Lee leaped to his feet. "Where? Where is the guard?" he demanded. "Damn the guard, why don't they fire?" Garbled shouts, whinnying horses, and sporadic gunshots could be heard through the walls. Tarleton clattered up to the front entrance—"making all the noise I could," he later reported—then fired into the door, bellowing, "I know General Lee is in the house!" Sixty or seventy British bullets riddled the tavern. Lee paced upstairs, brusquely dismissing a suggestion that he hide in his bed. "If the General does not surrender in five minutes," Tarleton shouted, "I will set fire to the house."

Lee stepped through the front door, bareheaded and disheveled, a blanket coat draped over his dingy white shirt. He was confounded to realize that his captors were from the same dragoon regiment with which he had fought valiantly on the king's behalf in Portugal fourteen years earlier. He expected, a witness heard him say, to be treated "as a gentleman." Regulars hoisted him onto a horse, pinioned his arms, lashed his legs to the stirrups, and galloped south as a bugler let blare a few triumphant notes.

The skirmish had lasted fifteen minutes. Several Continentals in the security detail had fled, but at least two dead rebels lay in the dirt, so badly butchered with sword wounds that "they were put in boxes and interred in the field where they lay," a New Jersey woman reported. Wilkinson and Lee's aide emerged from the tavern as the British hoofbeats faded away, then hurried off to give General Sullivan the news.

"This is a most miraculous event," Tarleton wrote his mother. "It appears like a dream." A regimental band played in Pennington after the dragoons arrived with their prize, having ridden nearly seventy miles that day. Harcourt's men celebrated into the night, toasting the king and getting Lee's horse drunk. "We have captured General Lee," Captain Münchhausen exulted, "the only rebel general whom we had cause to fear." Lee was swiftly shifted to New Brunswick under heavy guard while the British pondered whether to hang him; his letters to General Howe were returned unopened and addressed to "Lieutenant Colonel Lee," his former rank as a British officer.

Bells rang in jubilation when the account reached England; Harcourt, who in the next century would rise to the rank of field marshal, received thanks from both Parliament and his king. A poem in London's *General Evening Post* warned: "Here read thy character, thy peril, Lee, / A traitor's name, a traitor's destiny." British officers flocked to gawk at the famous prisoner in his New Brunswick cell. "So dirty and ungentleman-like a looking general I never saw before," wrote one. "He had on an old blue coat turned up with red, an old cocked hat, and greasy leather breeches." A grenadier lieutenant who met with him several times in December observed, "Though dejected he is very entertaining and communicative. . . . He praises himself much on the affair in Carolina. In a word, he is the most sensible fool I know."

Washington had sent a ninth and final plea to Lee early on Saturday, December 14, unwittingly writing to a man erased from the ranks. "Let me once more request and entreat you to march immediately," the commanding general urged. A few hours later the bad tidings arrived, to general lamentation. "This is a misfortune that cannot be remedied, as we have no officer in the army of equal experience and merit," John Trumbull, the commissary general, told his father. Hancock agreed that "his loss will be severely felt, as he was in a great measure the idol of the officers." Others feared the impact on morale in the ranks. Following Lee's capture, Benjamin Rush wrote a week later, "a distrust has crept in among the troops of the abilities of some of our general officers high in command. They expect nothing now from heaven-taught and book-taught generals."

One of those heaven- and book-taught generals, Nathanael Greene, wrote Caty from Pennsylvania on December 16, "Fortune seems to frown upon the cause of freedom. A combination of evils are pressing in upon us on all sides." Yet upon reflection, Greene told his brother that Lee "undoubtedly is a great general, but all the military knowledge is not confined to him." A Rhode Island soldier agreed that "we could manufacture as good generals out of American stuff."

Washington publicly mourned the loss, but privately he voiced ambivalence about a rival who had become a thorn in his side. "Unhappy man!" he wrote Lund Washington, his Mount Vernon overseer, on December 17. "Taken by his own imprudence, going three or four miles from his own camp to lodge." Later in the month, Washington wrote directly to Lee, enclosing a draft for £116 to ease the discomfort of captivity. "I hope," he added, "you are as happy as a person under your circumstances can possibly be."

Each morning, New York loyalists in their red-ribboned caps gathered outside the charred timbers of Trinity Church to watch the king's troops assemble on parade. An army band played military airs amid canted headstones in the churchyard. Highlanders in tartans or Hessians with tallowed hair and tall brass hats marched left, right, left in a clap of heavy shoes and the rattle of shouldered arms. Civilians cheered when, with a final yawp of shouted commands, the formations peeled apart on the promenade known as the Mall to step off at a steady pace for their guard posts at city hall, Fort George, or the East River docks.

General Howe had returned to the city on December 16, pleased with both this strutting army and with himself. "The whole of the Jerseys, except a very inconsiderable part which we think must of course follow, has submitted," his brother, the admiral, wrote Lord Germain. Much of Rhode Island had also returned to British control earlier this month: with about eighty ships now on the North American station, Admiral Howe had proposed seizing ice-free Narragansett Bay, described by one seafarer as "the best and noblest harbor in America, capable of containing the whole navy of Britain . . . in perfect security."

On December 7, General Henry Clinton and Commodore Sir Peter Parker anchored in Weaver's Cove, six miles north of Newport, despite Clinton's conviction—bluntly avouched, as usual—that the king would be better served by destroying Washington's army or seizing Philadelphia. A day later, in bitter weather but without opposition, seven thousand royal troops stormed ashore in an operation as precise as Sullivan's Island had been discombobulated. At least half the local population fled upstate or into Massachusetts—"they even believe we would eat up the little children," one

Hessian wrote—leaving behind mostly Quakers and loyalists. "The most violent & guilty have gone off," Lieutenant Peebles of the Black Watch told his diary. A rebel clergyman near Providence reflected, "It seems to be our turn now to taste of the heavy calamities of the war. May God deliver us in his own time." Around Narragansett Bay, deliverance would be years in coming.

British newspapers lionized both Howes. The heady accounts of victories at Long Island and Kip's Bay "filled the court with an extravagance of joy," Walpole noted. William Howe was hailed as a new Caesar and commemorated in excruciatingly awful verse, including "He comes, he comes, the hero comes, / Sound, sound your trumpets, beat your drums!" The king was pleased to appoint him one of the Knight Companions of the Most Honourable Order of the Bath, and to receive the Howes' aged mother at court as a mark of royal favor.

Sir William and his battle staff settled into their winter quarters, celebrating the apparent end of the 1776 campaign with what one observer called "ten days of universal jollity." The garrison grew even more jolly with arrival of the *Lord North*, a storeship carrying 8,209 gallons of Antiguan rum. Banquets, gambling, and musical reviews filled most evenings, to the point that Captain Münchhausen grumbled, "We have balls, concerts, and meetings, which I am already weary of. I do not like this frivolous life." Christmas gifts from New York loyalists piled up in Howe's enormous parlor within the mansion at No. 1 Broadway, across from the Bowling Green; in return, he wrote florid thank-you notes in his tidy, sloping hand on stationery with a watermark depicting a powder horn hanging inside a shield, surmounted by a crown. Lord Richard usually remained busy with naval affairs aboard the *Eagle*, but Sir William was often seen at the faro table with his fetching companion from Boston, Betsy Loring, described both as a "flashing blonde" and, less generously, as an "illustrious courtesan." The loyalist judge Thomas Jones claimed that "the Sultana" lost three hundred guineas at a single sitting. It was also whispered that her acquiescent husband, Joshua, now earned a princely £6,000 a year as the Howes' commissary of prisoners, sufficient to turn a blind eye.

Enough refugees and loyalists had returned to New York to nudge the city's population back to twelve thousand; that would almost triple in the next two years. Some lived in "Canvas Town," a foul encampment of hovels thrown up amid burned-out shops and buildings. Others jammed the few houses not claimed by the British with their ubiquitous "G.R." emblem. "Unwholesome smells are occasioned by such a number of people being crowded together in so small a compass, almost like herrings in a barrel, most of them very dirty and not a small number sick of some disease," the traveler Nicholas Cresswell noted in his diary. Stagnant water filled old rebel fortifications and ditches. Street crime by cutpurses, plug-uglies, and drunken redcoats made it "very unsafe in the evenings to be out," a preacher wrote. Also crowding the town were an estimated five thousand British Army "artillery wives" and other camp followers, as well as swarms of escaped slaves and the white men hunting them with posted notices, such as "Rem Cowenhoven offers $15 reward for Jaff, a runaway negro, a pretty forward chap, had on a claret-colored coat and breeches."

Fences and barns were dismembered for firewood—a cord of oak had quadrupled in price to £4. Hessians excavated peat for their stoves from Long Island meadows, to the fury of Dutch farmers, while some regulars burned books pilfered from the King's College library. Fresh meat and vegetable prices doubled and redoubled, although bread was fixed at fourteen coppers for a three-pound loaf. The British military government took on some municipal duties, including street lighting and the appointment of six chimney inspectors to forestall another catastrophic fire. On Long Island, returning farmers repaired their plundered houses and cleared fields of battle detritus; still, travelers complained of "the stink of dead rebels, some of them having lain unburied since last August." Order was enforced by loyalist militias such as the Nassau Blues, also known as both the Nasty Blues and, for their voluble blasphemy, the Holy Ghosters. All wagon cargo to and from New York was searched by redcoats, often with a bayonet. The prudent teamster learned to remove his hat in the presence of regulars, and to tuck that hat under an arm if addressing an officer.

Finally the war seemed to be going Britain's way. General Howe told London in December that supplies shipped on more than sixty victuallers through the fall "have been so wisely planned" that his larders were full. On Christmas Eve, the British commissary reported 2,250 tons of barreled meat on hand—enough to feed 30,000 men for seven months—plus 4,000 tons of wheat and bread, a half million pounds of butter, and more than a year's supply of peas, oatmeal, and rice. Warehouses on Water and Dock Streets swelled with the king's stores, from ammunition and firelocks to pipes of wine and crates of winter clothing.

A brewery near Maiden Lane issued spruce beer to the regiments at four shillings for a thirty-gallon barrel, although any tavern owner serving a soldier or sailor after eight p.m. might have his furniture confiscated by the high command. Merchandise again filled shop shelves: toothbrushes, horsewhips, Lady Molyneux's Italian Paste for the complexion, Moredant's Drops "for curing all disorders," including leprosy. "Bloody news! Bloody news!" penny-sheet hawkers cried from their street corners. "Where are the rebels now?"

A miniaturist set up his easel in William Street to paint regulars and their belles, and officers organized another *corps dramatique*, with productions rehearsed in the John Street Theater under the direction of the British surgeon general, who also played the troupe's "principal low comedian." Handbills sought officers with "histrionic ability" for dramatic roles, while peach-fuzz subalterns and drummer boys in wigs would be transformed into stage queens and femmes fatales. Fourteen Hessian musicians formed the orchestra, and volunteers served as doorkeepers and scene shifters in what was renamed the Theater Royal; the drop curtain featured a painted harlequin holding a wooden sword and the motto "Who would have expected all this *here*?" Stagings of *Richard III*, *The Busy Body*, and *The Beaux' Stratagem* were planned, but the season would open in January with Henry Fielding's *Tom Thumb*, a production benefiting British Army widows and orphans. Tickets could be purchased at the Bible and Crown on Hanover Square.

Where are the rebels now? By Joshua Loring's precise count, at least 4,430 of them occupied vile British jail cells around New York. That number had been captured from Long Island to Fort Lee, with hundreds more bagged in the Jersey chase and other actions. They wore the usual rags, though some had resorted to shawls and skirts made from scavenged curtains or tapestries. "Many of them are such ragamuffins as you never saw in your life," a British officer wrote in December.

New York soon became known as the city of prisons, to the everlasting infamy of the Howes and their empire. By January, several hundred rebel officers would be paroled to Gravesend, Flatbush, and other Long Island villages, paying two dollars a week to room in Dutch farm attics and barns, fending off starvation with oysters and eels, and whiling away their captivity by wrestling, playing fives (a sort of hand tennis), and throwing long bullets (an Irish game that involved tossing heavy stones). "We thus lived in want and perfect idleness for years," an officer captured at Fort Washington later recalled. Among those paroled on Long Island was Ethan Allen, the conqueror of Ticonderoga, who had been shipped back to America after harsh imprisonment in Cornwall. Another officer described him as "a robust, large-framed man, worn down by confinement and hard fare." He would soon be worn down further upon learning that his eleven-year-old son, Joseph, had died of smallpox. "I had promised myself great delight in clasping the charming boy in my arms and in recounting to him my adventures," Allen wrote his brother. "My only son, the darling of my soul."

For enlisted men and other officers remaining in Manhattan, the want and idleness were much worse. At least thirteen jails existed in New York, including the French Church, the First Presbyterian Church, and the Friends Meeting House. About eight hundred inmates crammed the Old North Dutch Church on William Street after the pews were ripped out for fuel and the mahogany pulpit was shipped to London as booty. Perhaps as many were held in the Middle Dutch Church, where, it was whispered, jailers poisoned prisoners to steal their watches and silver buckles. Even more notorious were two of the city's sugar houses, originally built to hold tons of "white gold" from West Indies plantations and now converted into penitentiaries: Van Cortlandt's at the northwest corner of the Trinity churchyard, and Livingston's, a five-story stone structure of dank, tiered cells surrounded by a nine-foot fence on Crown Street (later renamed Liberty).

A New Yorker recounted seeing inmates rotating in groups of a half dozen for ten minutes at a time to crowd each tiny, unglazed window above Crown Street: "Every narrow aperture of those stone walls filled with human heads, face above face, seeking a portion of the external air." Prisoner Samuel Young later described guards slopping food at suppertime "as if to so many hogs—a quantity of old biscuit, broken and in crumbs, mostly molded, and some of it crawling with maggots." Another prisoner wrote, "As soon as the bread fell on the floor it took legs and ran in all directions. So full of life." Some ate undigested bran picked from horse droppings or "damnified pork" soaked in bilgewater during the voyage from England. Inmates sold their breeches or coats to buy scraps or beef bones sold by the guards; others ate insects and rodents. "Cold and famine were now our destiny," a survivor wrote. "Old shoes were bought and eaten with as much relish as a pig or a turkey." One sugar house prisoner reportedly gnawed the flesh from his arms to ward off starvation; another died while trying to eat a brick.

The lucky ones could build a fire every three days. Many cell blocks lacked hearths or wood. Vermin infested the bedding straw. "It was bad in every sense of the word," wrote a surgeon's mate captured in August, "a dirty place, the prisoners wallowing in their own filth." A British captain acknowledged, "If once they are taken sick, they seldom recover." Each morning corpses were pitched from the cells, then hauled off on the dead cart to trenches beyond the Jews' Burial Ground and other grave sites. Prisoners also endured psychological torture. Major Otho Holland Williams of Maryland, badly wounded and captured in mid-November, described being forced to sit on a coffin in a wagon bed with a noose around his neck in a mock execution; others were required to select the rope with which they preferred to be hanged—someday—from several lengths dangled before them. Colónel Robert Magaw, the garrison commander captured at Fort Washington, and six other imprisoned officers wrote to General Howe in mid-December, noting conditions "too melancholy for recital" and requesting proper care for the sick and wounded. By the end of December, according to the historian Edwin G. Burrows, disease and starvation would kill at least half of the Americans captured on Long Island and as many as two-thirds of those taken at Fort Washington—more than two thousand men in all.

Conditions only grew worse. Some rebels who tried to escape were confined in the three-story New Gaol, known as the Provost in homage to William Cunningham, the notorious Dublin-born British provost marshal, who in his younger years reputedly worked as a "scaw-banker," enticing poor Irishmen to emigrate as indentured servants. Immigrating to America himself, he toiled as a horsebreaker before being appointed to supervise the king's jails, first in Boston, then in New York. Cunningham would be accused not only of unwonted cruelty, but of extrajudicial executions and even of destroying Nathan Hale's last letters. A chamber on the Provost's second floor, sardonically called Congress Hall, grew so crowded with officers that while sleeping on the floor they reportedly had to turn over simultaneously on command. One inmate described the Provost as "that engine for breaking hearts."

The transport vessel *Whitby*, anchored in Wallabout Bay, on the East River, foreshadowed greater horrors to come, as many American inmates would be transferred to prison ships in the coming year. Once used to haul livestock and still smeared with dung, the *Whitby* had been dismasted, stripped of her rigging with her portholes barred, and fitted with a ten-foot wall, notched for guards' muskets, between the elevated quarterdeck and the main deck. By year's end, 250 rebels were "crowded promiscuously together," an imprisoned naval lieutenant reported. They lived on sparse salt rations, lacked medical care, were infested with lice, and often went "sixteen hours without a drop of fresh water." The dim, confined purgatory belowdecks reeked of feces, urine, and vomit; once a day excrement tubs were hauled up and dumped over the side. A letter smuggled ashore in December reported, "Our present situation is most wretched. . . . We have no prospect before our eyes but a kind of lingering, inevitable death."

Soon enough, more than two dozen such ships were packed with American soldiers and sailors. Men would die in misery by the thousands, their corpses laid in shallow burial trenches amid bayberry bushes on the mudflats. Other bodies were simply tossed into the East River with a shout of, "There goes another damned Yankee rebel!" For years these remains lay scattered and bleaching along the Brooklyn shoreline, the human spoor of inhumanity, speaking bone to bone about how easy it had become to hate thine enemy.

21.

The Smiles of Providence

C hristmas Eve was joyless in Trenton. Most residents had fled, chased away by fifteen hundred Hessians in blue or green regimental uniforms with yellow waistcoats, white crossbelts, and mustaches darkened with shoeblack. Months of hard campaigning had left the Germans hollow-eyed, jittery, and, as one officer complained, "denuded of small clothes." This drowsy, vacant village seemed like a placid refuge in which to recuperate before the next fighting season. Enemy soldiers from three regiments now filled many of the hundred or so houses in Trenton, including those along King and Queen Streets. Others were billeted in the City and Bull's Head taverns, the jail, the Friends Meeting House, a school, two churches, the post office, the stone barracks built during the French war, and a sentry shed on the arched bridge over Assunpink Creek, just downstream from the three-stone gristmill.

Acrid odors from tanning vats and iron furnaces perfumed the winter air. To the west, ice floes bobbing down the Delaware met the incoming tide at Trenton Falls to pile up in jagged white heaps, five feet deep and fissured with narrow channels of rushing river water. Six brass 3-pounders squatted in a neat row outside a guardhouse in the village center, close to the barn where Hessian artillery horses stood harnessed in their stalls, ready for battle at a moment's notice. As shadows lengthened and the holy night drew near, troops from the duty regiment swung up King Street for the usual changing of the guard at two p.m. A military band circled the brick St. Michael's Anglican Church "like a Roman Catholic procession, wanting only the cross and the banner and the chanting choristers," Lieutenant Andreas Wiederholdt told his diary. The music often lured the garrison commander from his headquarters in the large frame house west of the street. The reedy sound of hautboys particularly charmed him. As Wiederholdt observed, "He never could have enough of them."

Colonel Johann Gottlieb Rall had spent thirty-six of his fifty years in uniform, fighting in Bavaria, on the Rhine, and in Holland. As a soldier of fortune, he had also fought in Turkey and in Russia under Aleksey Grigoryevich Orlov, the reputed killer of Czar Peter III, whose death brought Catherine the Great to the throne. Rall would be caricatured as a drunkard, a martinet, a sybarite, and a military mooncalf, none of which was true. If rough-hewn, he was respected as "a born soldier," in one comrade's estimation, and as a combat leader. His ferocity at White Plains and Fort Washington reportedly earned him the nickname *der Löwe*, the lion. Rall's adjutant, Lieutenant Jakob Piel, described him as "generous, magnanimous, hospitable, and polite to everyone," even if at times "a thought came to him, then another, so that he could not settle on a firm decision." Although Rall spoke neither English nor French, General Howe considered him capable enough to command not only his own regiment but the entire brigade posted at Trenton. Rall's leadership was needed, for the German senior ranks had thinned: one colonel had died of dysentery, another was convalescing from battle wounds, and three generals were hors de combat with various afflictions.

As he settled into his new command at Trenton, Rall alternated between bluster and nervous anxiety. He considered American soldiers "nothing but a lot of farmers." When a major asked him to order shoes from New York for the ranks, he promised to "lead the brigade in bare feet over the ice to Philadelphia." Disquieting reports of rebels massing across the river was just "old woman's talk." "Shit upon shit!" Rall said. "Let them come. We will go at them with the bayonet." Still, he was prudent and meticulous. One regiment remained fully clothed and under arms each night. Sentinels posted the upper roads to Princeton and Pennington, the riverbank, and other approaches into the village. Patrols crisscrossed the countryside to flush ambushers and spies. Before dawn each morning for the past week, seventy men and two field guns had taken positions above a nearby ferry landing to watch for infiltrators.

The rebels had grown bolder. "We have not slept one night in peace since we came to this place," a Hessian subaltern told his journal. Men with blackened faces frequently crossed the river from Pennsylvania to set fires and to snipe at German outposts, killing or capturing the careless. On December 20, Rall sent two dragoons with dispatches to Princeton. An hour later, one wounded rider galloped back to report that his companion had been slain in a rebel ambuscade. Rall sent the letters again, this time with an escort of a hundred men and a 3-pounder.

Rall waved away suggestions that he build earthworks on the high ground south and northeast of Trenton. "I have the enemy in *all* directions," he explained. Some troops reportedly had not removed their cartridge pouches for more than a week. The sick list grew longer day by day. To General Grant in New Brunswick, Rall pleaded for at least two hundred reinforcements at Maidenhead, on the post road between Trenton and Princeton. Grant, who acknowledged looking forward to "a winter of ease and pleasure" with his cook Baptiste and his flocks of dinner fowl, tried to calm his jittery subordinates downstate. Fewer than three hundred rebel gunmen remained in New Jersey, he insisted, adding, "I can hardly believe that Washington would venture at this season of the year to pass the Delaware." No more than "a corporal's guard" was needed to keep the peace in Jersey. Do not, he urged, make "more of the rebels than they deserve." To Rall he wrote:

> I am sorry to hear your brigade has been fatigued or alarmed. You may be assured that the rebel army in Pennsylvania . . . does not exceed eight thousand men who have neither shoes nor stockings, are in fact almost naked, dying of cold, without blankets, and very ill-supplied with provisions.

Moreover, the Trenton garrison was supported by another fifteen hundred Germans in Bordentown, six miles south. Or it had been: on Monday, December 23, Colonel Carl Emil Ulrich von Donop led his brigade on a pointless chase after several hundred rebel raiders near Mount Holly, a dozen miles farther south, determined to "get rid of these troublesome guests." The Americans scattered into the countryside after a desultory skirmish, briefly pursued by *Jäger* and Highlanders. "Almost the whole town was plundered," wrote Captain Johann Ewald, the commander of a *Jäger* company. "And because large stocks of wine were found there, the entire garrison was drunk by evening." Colonel Donop—a tall, ambitious German aristocrat—was instantly enchanted by an attractive young widow, according to Ewald. He sent foraging patrols toward Moorestown and Burlington, but decided to linger with his brigade in Mount Holly through Christmas, eighteen miles from Rall.

From Trenton, patrols sent out on Tuesday exchanged fire with shadowy figures, then returned. "We are insecure both in flank and rear," a Hessian diarist noted. The temperature, which had not risen above freezing all day, fell as the sun set. Stars smeared the sky on this blessed night, but rheumatics could feel in their bones that a winter storm was coming on. To Donop, Rall wrote that his men were "extremely fatigued because of the miserable weather and continuous service." Ludicrous if unsettling rumors spread in the ranks, of impending attacks by "Negroes and yellow dogs."

Shortly before midnight, General Grant again sent a courier to Rall, assuring him that "there are no rebel troops in the Jerseys." But, apparently tipped off by a spy in the American camp, he advised:

> Washington has been informed that our troops have marched into winter quarters and has been told that we are weak at Trenton and Princeton. . . . Lord Stirling expressed a wish to make an attack upon these two places. I don't believe he will attempt it.

Nevertheless, Grant added, "I need not advise you to be upon your guard against an unexpected attack at Trenton."

Twelve miles northwest of Trenton, in a pointed-stone farmhouse tucked against the steep escarpment called Jericho Mountain, Washington had never been busier than on that Tuesday, December 24. More than a week earlier he had moved his headquarters to the two-story William Keith house, three miles from the river. A low stone wall framed the yard. Through the double-fold front door with its big wooden lock, yellow pine brightened the interior walls. Across Knowles Creek and up the four-hundred-foot ridge behind the house, a Continental signal post on the crest waggled flags that could be seen above the bare trees in brigade encampments up and down the Delaware valley.

A steady procession of gallopers rushed up to the house, dismounted, hurried inside, hurried out, remounted, and rode off across Bucks County with orders: move your troops here, or there; be sure every man has cooked rations for three days; "endeavor to magnify your numbers as much as possible," with blazing campfires and theatrical movements to confuse the enemy; "curb the insolence of the disaffected"; guard the river; watch for spies; keep your powder dry. Precisely how many men were fit to fight remained a mystery, as usual. A return two days earlier had tallied 679 officers and 10,744 rank and file, including Lee's corps, but nearly half were sick, furloughed, or otherwise indisposed. That left about 6,100 on duty, less than a quarter of the army's strength in September. Others had arrived since Sunday, including 500 men in Brigadier General Arthur St. Clair's brigade and various militia regiments; others had departed, including General Arnold, sent to Rhode Island as soon as he'd arrived from Ticonderoga, and General Gates, who had ridden off to Baltimore for treatment of his pernicious dysentery—and, less honorably, to be at hand should Congress decide to select a new commander in chief.

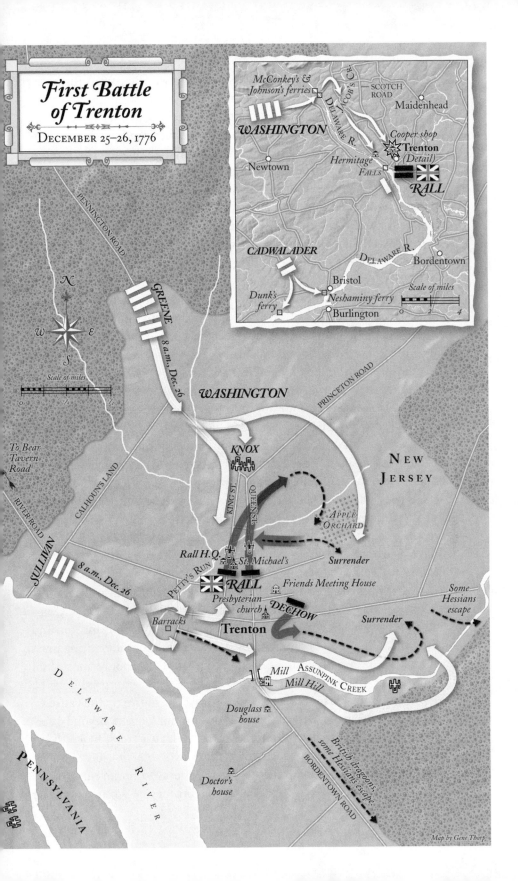

First Battle of Trenton

DECEMBER 25–26, 1776

Inset map (Detail)

McConkey's & Johnson's ferries

SCOTCH ROAD

Maidenhead

WASHINGTON

Cooper shop

Trenton (Detail)

Hermitage

FALLS

Newtown

RALL

CADWALADER

DELAWARE R.

Bordentown

Bristol

Dunk's ferry

Neshaminy ferry

Scale of miles

Burlington

0   2   4

Main map

GREENE

8 a.m., Dec. 26

N
W   E
S

Scale of miles

0   1/4   1/2

To Bear Tavern Road

PENNINGTON ROAD

WASHINGTON

PRINCETON ROAD

RIVER ROAD

CALHOUN'S LAND

KNOX

NEW JERSEY

SULLIVAN

8 a.m., Dec. 26

KING'S ST.

QUEEN ST.

APPLE ORCHARD

Surrender

PETTY'S RUN

Rall H.Q.

St. Michael's

RALL

Friends Meeting House

Some Hessians escape

Barracks

Presbyterian church

DECHOW

Trenton

Surrender

DELAWARE RIVER

Mill

ASSUNPINK CREEK

Mill Hill

Douglass house

British dragoons, some Hessians escape

BORDENTOWN ROAD

PENNSYLVANIA

Doctor's house

Map by Gene Thorp

Among Washington's visitors this morning was Benjamin Rush, the garrulous, animated Philadelphia physician. Rush—a "sprightly, pretty fellow," in John Adams's assessment, but "too much of a talker to be a deep thinker"—had come to tender both medical services and political advice. Medically educated in Edinburgh and London after graduating from college in Princeton at age fourteen, he held progressive views: against slavery, capital punishment, and strong drink; for women's rights, free education, and medical care for the indigent. Given that sickness already had killed far more American soldiers than bullets, he also had opinions on how to keep an army healthy: daily washing of hands and feet; frequent washing of bodies; vigorous scrubbing of cook pots; cropping hair close to the skull to discourage lice; eating mostly vegetables; disinfecting blankets with sunshine. His ardent support for the rebellion had intensified with the recent imprisonment by the British in New Jersey of his father-in-law, Richard Stockton, a fellow signer of the Declaration. "Every particle of my blood," Rush wrote, "is electrified with revenge."

Today he also wanted to take Washington's measure. A year earlier he had praised the general as "one of those illustrious heroes whom providence raises up once in three or four hundred years to save a nation from ruin." Now he was not so sure: ruin seemed at hand. Although he believed Congress should cede Washington "dictatorial power for a few months" until the current crisis abated, he was struck by the commander in chief's glum demeanor and his distracted doodling with pen and ink on slips of paper. "He appeared much depressed," Rush would observe, "and lamented the ragged and dissolving state of his army in affecting terms." As he stood to leave, the doctor picked up a scrap of paper that had fallen to the floor. On it Washington had scribbled the evening's watchwords for his sentries: "Victory or Death."

More visitors came and went, more couriers carried away orders. Writing from Bristol, twenty miles up the Delaware from Philadelphia, Colonel Reed sent a spy's report detailing British dispositions in Princeton and Burlington. "We are all of opinion, my dear General, that something must be attempted," Reed advised, ". . . that even a failure cannot be more fatal than to remain in our present situation. In short, some enterprise must be undertaken in our present circumstances or we must give up the cause."

Washington agreed. In a letter to Lund at Mount Vernon, beyond offering advice on breeding a stallion and planting locust trees, he confided that the American predicament "wears so unfavorable an aspect" that it would be prudent to prepare his personal papers "to remove at a short notice" to safety in western Virginia. To his brother he wrote, "Between you and me, I think our affairs are in a very bad way. . . . If every nerve is not strained to recruit the new army with all possible expedition, I think the game is pretty near up." The prospect of losing the rest of New Jersey to the British particularly galled him. "I am certain that the defection of the people in the lower part of Jersey," he told General Heath, "has been as much owing to the want of an army to look the enemy in the face as to any other cause." The moment had come for an army, his army, to look the enemy in the face.

Late in the afternoon he rode down a byway through frozen fields for four hundred yards to a drafty stone house, twenty feet square with a kitchen appended to the west end. Here Greene kept his headquarters. A dozen others arrived to warm their hands by the fire, including Sullivan, Stirling, St. Clair, Henry Knox, the web-footed John Glover, and Brigadier General Hugh Mercer, a Scottish-born physician who commanded a brigade of New England and Maryland Continentals. To preclude eavesdropping, Greene had sent the house owners to a neighbor's; he had shared sugar from his mess barrel with them, and they were generous in providing turkey, veal, and milk for his table.

For at least ten days, Washington had contemplated a bold lunge into the enemy's flank. "Under the smiles of Providence, we may yet effect an important stroke," he had told his lieutenants, and this evening they intended to review the plan for a final time. Three forces positioned along a twenty-six-mile stretch of the Delaware would cross the river simultaneously before converging on Trenton with five thousand troops. The largest detachment—twenty-four hundred men with eighteen guns—would mass under Washington's direct command on Christmas night eight miles upstream from the village, descending on the Hessian garrison from the north an hour before dawn on Thursday, December 26. "For heaven's sake keep this to yourself, as the discovery of it may prove fatal to us," Washington warned Reed in a confidential letter. Unnerving rumors could already be heard in Philadelphia. Robert Morris had written Washington as early as December 21, "I have been told today that you are preparing to cross into the Jerseys. I hope it may be true."

Each man would carry forty cartridges as well as cooked rations. Informed that some Pennsylvania millers were reluctant to sell wheat and flour to the army, Washington earlier in the week had authorized quartermasters to confiscate any needed supplies, giving Continental vouchers as receipts. The depot in Newtown had purchased more than three hundred heavy blankets from two dozen townships for £678, including the cost of cleaning them at Jenks's fulling mill. A call for volunteers had drawn carpenters, shipwrights, and sailmakers from the Philadelphia boat-yards; sixty sailors organized an artillery company, hauling heavy guns on jury-rigged carriages to Bristol.

The chosen crossing sites were far enough from Trenton to avoid Ger-man patrols but close enough to be within striking distance. At Washing-ton's direction, more than a dozen stout Durham boats would be manned by Glover's Marblehead mariners. Sixty-five feet long, with a curved stem and steep caulked sides, the rivercraft had been used for years to haul iron ore, timber, whiskey, and flour barrels on the Delaware. Fitted with eighteen-foot oars, a thirty-foot curved sweep for steering, and iron-shod setting poles, each Durham could carry fifteen to twenty tons. But even little 3-pounders were too unwieldy for transport by Durham boat; the guns and carriages would be moved, one at a time, by flat ferries. Shipping a hun-dred or more horses across open water—always delicate—would also require great care.

The seven brigades assigned to the assault were understrength, but each had an unusually large ratio of officers and sergeants to the rank and file, in an effort to keep march discipline. Moreover, each brigade included an artillery company to provide firepower when muskets inevitably grew wet, as they had during Montgomery's attack at Quebec. Instead of the two or three field guns per thousand infantrymen typical in eighteenth-century armies, Washington would take nearly nine per thousand—massed artil-lery emboldened foot soldiers. Colonel Knox's epic trek from Ticonderoga a year earlier had persuaded him that guns not only could keep pace with infantry regiments moving cross-country in foul weather but, in fact, could lead them without forfeiting mobility. Powder chests would be wrapped in oilcloth, and charges were encased in starched, tallowed cloth to repel the damp. Knox also designated a small unit to carry spikes and hammers to wreck captured enemy field guns if they could not be carried off. The British had long depended on "the superiority of their artillery," Washington observed, and the Americans would do well to beat them at their own game. As he had told Hancock earlier in the week, "Desperate diseases require desperate measures."

A shiver of excitement ran through the war council. The plan was indeed desperate, but also audacious and calculated. Together they would risk everything, following Washington wherever he led them. Lieutenant Colonel Tudor, the judge advocate, spoke for many in a letter to his future wife written that Christmas Eve: "I cannot desert a man—& it would certainly be a desertion in a court of honor—who has deserted everything to defend his country."

Before Washington dismissed the officers to return to their respective commands, they were reminded of the identifying countersign to be used in the attack: victory or death.

Clouds thickened on Christmas Day, and the wind shifted from west to northeast. Temperatures remained below freezing. "It is fearfully cold and raw," an officer told his diary. "It will be a terrible night for the soldiers who have no shoes." The sun, mostly unseen during the day, set at 4:42 p.m. The moon, a night past full, rose just over an hour later, orange and monstrous behind a shroud of high clouds.

Some men would not see another sunrise, including Captain James Moore, a New Yorker who died of camp fever on Christmas in the millhouse where General Stirling also was quartered. The captain was buried in hard ground at the edge of a timber stand above Pidcock's Creek. He was twenty-four. Others rallied from their sickbeds: young Captain Hamilton dragged himself into the ranks from a Pennsylvania farm where he had convalesced after what he called a "long and severe" illness. His artillery company, reduced to thirty men with two guns, joined Stirling's brigade.

Many historians would subsequently assert that late in the afternoon, officers gathered their men a mile from the river and, at Washington's direction, read aloud from a new pamphlet by the writer known to soldiers as "Common Sense." Little evidence supports such group readings, although Thomas Paine's febrile essay, published a week earlier in Philadelphia and now circulating through the ranks, captured the spirit of the army with which he had recently marched across New Jersey. Paine again condemned both loyalists ("servile, slavish, self-interested") and the king ("a sottish, stupid, stubborn, worthless, brutish man"). Yet *American Crisis No. 1* also reached higher, to "bring reason to your ears" and to claim the high ground for those adhering to the American cause:

> These are the times that try men's souls. The summer soldier and the sunshine patriot will, in this crisis, shrink from the service of their country. But he that stands it *now*, deserves the love and thanks of man and woman. Tyranny, like hell, is not easily conquered; yet we have this consolation with us, that the harder the conflict, the more glorious the triumph.

At dusk, regiments marched in columns toward the ferry crossings. Two New Jersey militiamen joined each brigade as guides. In the attack from the north, three locals in farm garb would serve as scouts, including a Trenton cooper who had just escaped across the river disguised as an old woodcutter. Perched on their walking boards, poling crews eased the Durham boats and other rivercraft from anchorages behind Malta Island and in Knowles Creek to two abutting ferry landings, McConkey's and Johnson's. Here, at the main assault crossing, the river was three hundred yards wide, swift and glistening with cake ice. Troops were reminded that upon reaching the far shore "a profound silence [is] to be enjoined & no man to quit his ranks on pain of death."

Proverbially no plan survives contact with the enemy, but this plan came unstitched even before the first gunshot. Both downstream crossings were thwarted by ice piled high on the rising tide. Below Trenton Falls, eight hundred Pennsylvania militiamen found the river utterly impassable; by midnight, as a nasty snow squall blew in from the north, not a man had set foot in Jersey. Fifteen miles farther south, at Neshaminy Creek near Bristol, Colonel John Cadwalader, a wealthy Philadelphia merchant, discovered similar conditions and ordered his eighteen hundred militiamen to march another six miles south to Dunk's Ferry in search of open water. In this he was disappointed, although five hundred men in the lead regiments embarked at eleven p.m., abandoned their boats in pack ice 150 yards from the left bank, then shuffled over the floes to reach firm ground. "The wind blowing very hard, we had great difficulty," wrote Captain Thomas Rodney of the Delaware militia. Unable to manhandle his artillery, horses, or reserves across, Cadwalader—determined to keep his corps intact—ordered the advance guard back to Pennsylvania. "This greatly irritated the troops," Rodney added, ". . . and they proposed making the attack without both the generals and the artillery." Instead they grudgingly obeyed, returning at four a.m. and then bedding down for a few wretched hours without tents or campfires, spattered with sleet. "We suffered more this night from cold in the snow storm than on any we had yet experienced," one soldier reported. Cadwalader sent a courier to Washington with the dolorous news, adding, "I imagine the badness of the night must have prevented you from passing as intended."

Not so. Above the fall line and beyond the pernicious reach of tidal ice, the main force nosed across the Delaware one wallowing, overloaded boatload at a time. Local river men and Glover's 14th Continentals, in their blue jackets and tarred trousers, handled the craft with skill and brute strength. Knox helped command the crossing, shouting orders, rebukes, and encouragement in his foghorn voice. Greene's advance guard went ashore first to form a perimeter on the far shore. Torches and lanterns—hissing as the snow showers intensified—gilded the ice and brightened the banks at the landing sites. A few men tumbled into the river, including Colonel John Haslet, who had fought with valor in New York; they were fished out, shivering violently, and dried off.

Back and forth the boats shuttled, several dozen troops in each Durham, and one gun or a few wild-eyed horses on each flatboat, the hours slipping past as the storm howled and the temperature eased to just above freezing. "It was as severe a night as ever I saw," one captain wrote. The men, miserable but stoic, "nearly half dead with cold," huddled together above the steep-banked New Jersey riverfront and waited. "It was all the same," a Massachusetts fifer later recalled, "owing to the impossibility of being in a worse situation than their present one."

Washington waited too, eating and drinking in the saddle atop his sorrel mount once he reached Jersey, his broad, ruddy face stung with sleet. "He appeared at that time pensive and solemn in the extreme," one officer noted. When Sullivan, struggling to impose order on the ranks nearby, sent a messenger to report that his wet muskets would likely be useless, Washington replied, "Tell General Sullivan to use the bayonet." Several hours behind schedule, the last lifts disembarked. At four a.m. a command sounded through the ranks—"Shoulder your firelocks!"—and the regiments surged forward. As Knox would write Lucy, "Perseverance accomplished what at first seemed impossible."

The column stretched for more than a mile, first rising east from the river, then turning sharply south onto Bear Tavern Road. As the road angled through dripping copses of hickory and black oak, soldiers draped handkerchiefs, greased rags, coat skirts, and blankets over their musket priming pans, to small effect. Whenever the march stalled momentarily, as night marches inevitably did, men fell asleep on their feet and had to be forcibly roused. Sergeants prodded the sick and lame who lingered by the roadside, but at least two soldiers fell behind and froze to death on the tableland that night.

"Press on. Press on, boys!" Washington urged, trotting along the line and at one point grabbing his horse's mane to avoid being thrown when his mount slipped. "For God's sake, keep by your officers." Knox's artillerymen used drag ropes to ease their guns down a steep defile and across Jacob's Creek, then hauled them up again. Officers tendered advice. "Fire at their legs," a colonel urged. "One man wounded in the leg is better [than] a dead one, for it takes two more to carry him off. . . . Leg them, damn 'em, I say leg them."

A pallid sky in the east foretold a gray, wet Thursday dawn. At Birmingham crossroads, four miles above Trenton, the column stopped briefly. Washington pulled out his timepiece and gave orders that "every officer's watch should be set by his," a Continental captain noted, "and the moment of attack was fixed." Patrols surged ahead to secure the roads and detain early morning travelers heading into or out of Trenton.

Then the army divided. Greene swung left with his division, accompanied by Washington, Knox, and nine fieldpieces, to approach the town from almost due north on Scotch Road. Troops lengthened their stride in what an officer called "a long trot." Sullivan continued onto River Road, also with nine guns, to attack from the northwest along the Delaware.

At precisely eight a.m., a Hessian patrol returned to its outpost in a cramped cooper's shop on Pennington Road, half a mile from the upper village. Lieutenant Wiederholdt listened to his soldiers' report—nothing unusual seen or heard—then stepped outside the guardhouse to see for himself through the freezing rain. At age forty-four, with a quarter century's experience as a soldier, Wiederholdt conceded that at times "my sentinels did not keep a very sharp lookout." He cocked an ear, sniffed the air, and peered into the dim morning. A movement two hundred yards to the north caught his eye. Shadowy figures loped toward him on the road and through the bordering fields.

"*Der Feind! Der Feind! Heraus!*" a sentry shouted. The enemy! Turn out! Seventeen soldiers spilled from the cooperage, fumbling with their firelocks and cartridge boxes as they shook out into a skirmish line. Muzzle flashes winked from the road. Wiederholdt heard the crackle of musketry and the insectile whine of bullets overhead. A second enemy volley was quickly followed by a third before the Hessians returned fire. Now Wiederholdt heard the distant rumble of cannonading along the river to his rear. The gray shapes ahead grew more distinct and more numerous, squeezing both flanks. Wiederholdt ordered a retreat, and his men dashed down Pennington Road, throwing a few answering shots as they bounded from house to house.

Greene's division followed on their heels in three attack columns, heeding orders to "charge the enemy before they had time to form." Washington led in the center. German kettle drums beat to arms, adding to the din of shouts and drumfire. On the northeast edge of the village, where King and Queen Streets converged, Pennsylvania gun crews unlimbered two brass 6-pounders and fired into the town. A pair of howitzers joined the bombardment, along with five New York guns, including Hamilton's pair. Burning fuses on low-velocity shells were plainly visible to enemy soldiers sheltering a few hundred yards ahead. "The hurry, fright, & confusion of the enemy," Knox later wrote, "was [not] unlike that which will be when the last trump shall sound."

The gunfire Wiederholdt heard on River Road announced the timely arrival of Sullivan's division, led by a New Jersey company and a New Hampshire brigade commanded by Colonel John Stark, the stalwart of Bunker Hill. The Americans slammed into a Hessian outpost in the stable master's house behind the Hermitage, a large estate a mile upriver from Trenton. Pickets fired and fled without their knapsacks, attackers surged through fields, gardens, and woodlots, and Yankee cannoneers raking German positions were joined by batteries shooting across the Delaware from Pennsylvania. As Sullivan had predicted, damp firelocks squibbed repeatedly, but superior firepower still sent enemy *Jäger* reeling. One American detachment headed for the old stone barracks while a larger force pressed toward the Assunpink bridge at the foot of Queen Street to block the enemy's retreat route to the south.

Colonel Rall, *der Löwe*, had passed Christmas evening playing checkers in the King Street house where he made his headquarters. The command post was comfortable enough—three sitting rooms with fireplaces on the first floor, a dining room with two hearths, five chambers on the second floor, and a pump by the door. But Rall's quiet game had been interrupted at eight p.m. by rebel raiders—acting without Washington's knowledge—who wounded half a dozen Hessian troopers outside Trenton. When the hubbub subsided, Rall ate supper at a neighbor's, played cards until midnight, and went to bed.

The early morning clamor at both ends of Trenton failed to wake him, and only after a frantic summons from Lieutenant Piel, his adjutant, did Rall appear at a window in his nightshirt. After ducking back inside, he soon reappeared in uniform on King Street to find that the village had become a battlefield. American soldiers rampaged through lanes and gardens, breaking down doors, raking upper windows with musket fire, and trading shots with Hessians crouched behind the gravestones in St. Michael's churchyard. A rebel darted forward, stooped over the body of an enemy officer shot dead in a doorway, then pulled off his boots and scurried away.

Eight horses were led from a nearby stable and hitched to two fieldpieces. On Rall's command, the teams jangled up the street toward the thunder of American cannons shooting from the north. Wheeling their guns into position, eighteen Hessian artillerymen managed to get off a few rounds, including a salvo of grape, before rebel counterbattery fire found them. Balls ripped through the position, disemboweling five horses and stringing bloody intestines across the cobblestones. Rebel snipers from Mercer's brigade infiltrated houses on the German flank, and lacerating small arms fire drove the last gunners from their guns. Within minutes, eight of the eighteen lay dead or wounded. The rest dropped their sponges and handspikes and ran back down the street. "We drove them furiously," a Pennsylvania rifleman told his diary.

Mounting his horse, Rall herded two of his infantry regiments behind St. Michael's to regroup while trying to gauge the size of the American assault. Shouting, "Advance! Advance!" above the clangor, he then led the troops in quickstep across Queen Street to an apple orchard, determined to counterattack Greene's division from the east. This scheme proved bootless. From his vantage at the top of the town, Washington tracked the Hessian movement and ordered a blocking force of riflemen across the Princeton road on the American left flank. Faced with murderous artillery and small arms fire from superior ground, Rall wheeled his brigade back into the center of the village, colors flying. "From their motions," Washington later told Hancock, "they seemed undetermined how to act."

Sleet, rain, and snow seemed to whip simultaneously through streets now banked in white smoke. Hessian musicians pounded drums and tootled a few uncertain bars on their hautboys. As Rall's infantry poured back into King Street, they recovered the two fieldpieces lost earlier, much to Knox's annoyance. On his order, New England gun crews and Virginia infantrymen rushed forward with bayonets and drawn swords. Captain William Washington of the 3rd Virginia Regiment, a former divinity student and a distant cousin of the commander in chief's, pitched to the ground with wounds in both hands; bundled off to a dressing station, he was soon joined by Lieutenant James Monroe, hit in the upper chest and shoulder by a ball that nicked an artery. But their comrades recaptured the Hessian 3-pounders and turned them on the enemy, firing canister. An artillery sergeant reported that the balls made "a terrible squeaking noise" as they swarmed up the street.

Rall tried again to marshal his men. *"Alle, was meine Grenadiers sein, vorwärts!"* he hollered. All who are my grenadiers, forward! But the day was lost. American soldiers flocked through the cross streets to take firing perches in cellars, upper windows, and along the fence at Potts's tanyard by the bark house and stone currying shop. Chipping their flints for a clean surface, picking out touchholes, and drying their priming pans, they fired, reloaded, and fired again, deliberately targeting officers; four Hessian captains fell in short order. The clap of musketry echoed down King Street as hundreds of bullets pinged off walls, cobbles, and headstones. Wounded men dragged themselves into alleys and parlors; others bled to death in the gutter. Rall, still mounted, cocked his head at the pandemonium of gunfire from Sullivan's troops moving up from the river. "Lord," he called, "Lord, what is it?"

Two bullets knocked him from the saddle on the west side of Queen Street. Bleeding badly, gasping for breath, Rall was carried into the Methodist church and laid on a pew. With many officers dead, wounded, or missing, two Hessian regiments again drifted east toward the apple trees. American troops followed only fifty paces behind in a menacing crescent, although some Yankees stooped to snatch up the occasional souvenir. Continentals demanded surrender, shouting in English and German. Fieldpieces were trundled forward to fire point-blank into the orchard. Washington had ordered the gunners to switch from round shot to canister when a battery commander said, "Sir, they have struck."

So they had. Hessian officers lifted their hats on sword points. Color bearers dipped their flags in submission. *Jäger* and grenadiers grounded their muskets or smashed them against the trees, flinging away splintered stocks and bent barrels. Some cut the straps of their cartridge pouches. General Stirling rode forward to collect surrendered swords.

Five hundred yards to the south, the third Hessian regiment had tried to escape across the Assunpink bridge with three hundred men and two guns but found the span blocked by two New England brigades. Angling east up the creek in search of a crossing, the fugitives came under heavy American fire from the rear and both flanks. "The fight became a chase," a Continental officer later wrote. "We stepped off with alacrity, in full cry, and fortunately got into the thickest of them while they were fording a small creek." Some fleeing Germans thrashed through the reeds and waded neck-deep into the icy water only to be swept away. A few dozen escaped. The acting regimental commander, Major Friedrich von Dechow, still recuperating from injuries received at Fort Washington, fell, mortally shot through the hip. When General St. Clair bellowed, "If you do not surrender immediately, I will blow you to pieces," Dechow told his lieutenants, "My dear sirs, do as you like. I am wounded." They, too, capitulated.

A great cheer sounded through the village, echoed in the orchard, on the bridge, and along the Assunpink. Troops tossed their hats in jubilation. From the initial skirmish on Pennington Road, the battle had lasted less than two hours. "Providence," Knox would write, "seemed to have smiled upon every part of this enterprise."

Giddy soldiers donned the tall brass hats filched from dead grenadiers, strutting about with their elbows cocked. Others stacked captured muskets, brass drums, and bayonets in wagons for removal to Pennsylvania or prodded their captives into columns. Some Hessians, having been told that

Yankee rebels ate their prisoners, went glassy-eyed with fear. Washington watched, no doubt with pride and perhaps in amazement. As Rall's sword was collected with the other booty, His Excellency told a subordinate, "This is a glorious day for our country."

In half a morning, Howe had lost almost a thousand of his fourteen thousand men in New Jersey. Casualty estimates would vary, but the king's losses apparently included twenty-two Hessians killed, eighty-three badly wounded, and about nine hundred captured. "Saw a room full of wounded Hessians, one of them with his nose shot off," militia sergeant William Young wrote in his journal. "All of them are in a wretched condition." An American medical officer wrote another physician that five gravely injured enemy soldiers needed shattered limbs removed but "the amputating instruments which you sent for use of the Hessian surgeon . . . were so bad that he could not make use of them." Some men were beyond surgery. Colonel Rall was carried from the Methodist church to his King Street headquarters, which now stood riddled with shot and shell. Washington and Greene briefly visited him to grant parole so that he did not have to be moved again; Rall asked through an interpreter that his men be treated well. He died in agony on Friday evening, "satisfied that it was not necessary for him to outlive his honor," Lieutenant Piel told his diary. "Colonel Rall was truly born to be a soldier, but not a general." He was buried in the Presbyterian yard on Second Street.

Among those who escaped were the only British soldiers in Trenton on Christmas—twenty troopers from the 16th Light Dragoons who had galloped over the Assunpink bridge at the first sound of trouble. Before the bridge was sealed, at least four hundred and perhaps more than six hundred Germans had also eluded capture—musicians, drummers, doctors, camp followers, rank-and-file skedaddlers—who exploited the failure of Colonel Cadwalader and others to seal off the village from the south. Some would be found in various barns and attics, like the two fugitives rousted from a stable by a snarling dog and a farmer's pitchfork. Scouts soon reported that Colonel Donop was so unnerved by the news from Trenton that he abandoned both his comely widow and his casualties in Mount Holly to lead his brigade—including 150 carts and carriages laden with plunder—on a forced march to Princeton. *Jäger* flanked "both sides of the column to prod the drivers on with blows," according to Captain Ewald.

With thousands of enemies less than a day's march away, Washington decided to collect his winnings and return promptly to Pennsylvania. Although his own battle casualties were minor—a dozen killed or wounded—hundreds more suffered from exhaustion, sickness, and cold weather injuries, including frostbite. "I was extremely chilled," a chaplain wrote in his journal, "and came near perishing before I could get to a fire." Many warmed themselves with some of the forty hogsheads of enemy rum discovered in Trenton before Washington could destroy the stocks; other troops reportedly found whiskey and sugar in a cellar, stirred them together with a fence rail in a rain barrel, and used their shoes for tankards. By mid-afternoon on Thursday, ferrymen began shifting the spoils of war west-bound across the Delaware: wagons, brass guns, forty horses, a thousand stand of small arms, a dozen drums, a number of hautboys, and several sets of regimental colors, including a white damask silk square depicting an eagle and the motto *Pro Principe et Patria* stitched in gold.

Hundreds of Hessians were herded into boats, their hair queues "sticking straight back like the handle of an iron skillet," as one Connecticut guard noted. Boatmen ordered all passengers to help dislodge ice sheathing the rivercraft by stamping their feet, "and they all set to jumping at once with their cues flying up & down." Floes piled high along the Delaware banks forced many prisoners to wade through the shallows to reach the Pennsylvania shore before marching to churches, inns, ferry houses, and other makeshift jails. General Stirling invited nineteen junior German officers to dine with him at the Sign of the Red Lion in Newtown, five miles west of Yardley's Ferry. General Putnam would entertain others by displaying the scars on his skull incurred in some ancient Indian fight. "He shook hands with each of us, and we all had to drink a glass of Madeira with him," a Hessian lieutenant wrote. "Nobody but the rebels would have made him a general." Washington dined with four captured field-grade officers at his new headquarters in a small yellow house on Sycamore Street in Newtown. "His countenance is not that of a great hero," one German sniffed. "His eyes have no fire."

At midday on Monday, December 30, a winding column of prisoners snaked into Philadelphia, the officers in farm wagons, the rank and file on foot. Although dirt and battle had dulled their colorful wool uniforms, one witness found them to be "fine, hearty-looking men and well-clad, with knapsacks. . . . On each side in single file were the guards, mostly in light summer dress and some without shoes, but stepping light." Led by a nine-piece Hessian band, they marched two abreast down Front, Market, and Walnut Streets, occasionally pelted with gutter filth by jeering spectators. "The old women howled dreadfully and wanted to throttle us all because we had come to America to rob them of their freedom," a Hessian corporal reported. Writing to Hancock, who had remained in Baltimore with the Congress, Robert Morris remarked that the filthy prisoners looked so benign that "most people seemed very angry they should ever think of running away from such a set of vagabonds." German officers would march on to confinement in western Virginia. The enlisted troops—former weavers, tailors, carpenters, masons, and butchers, according to a prison roster—traveled mostly to Lancaster and other German-speaking precincts of Pennsylvania. Washington had long advocated "a gentleness even to forbearance" toward prisoners, notwithstanding reciprocal British cruelty, and he now reiterated that they "be well-treated." Soon beguiled by this new world, many Hessians eventually chose not to return home.

The search for scapegoats began immediately within the British high command. "This infamous business [is] the most unlucky affair which has happened to us in America," wrote General Grant. "I am quite miserable about it . . . yet I cannot impute any blame to General Howe or myself." Opposition newspapers in England would blame Lord Germain, who blamed Howe, who blamed the Hessians. In dispatches to London, Howe insisted that the two senior German generals—Heister and Knyphausen— "are much too infirm for this war." It was said that when Howe asked how the Hessian brigades in New Jersey could be so outfoxed, Heister replied, "Sir, if you will tell me why you would not make an end of the war at the White Plains, I will then give you an answer." The old war horse was soon recalled to Germany, where he died a month after arriving home.

Colonel Rall, already conveniently dead, drew most of the opprobrium. "Rall's defeat has put us much out of our way. His misconduct is amazing," Howe wrote Germain in late December. Deputy Adjutant General Kemble described Rall as "noisy . . . unacquainted with the language, and a drunkard," thus advancing the calumny that a sober garrison had been inebriated. German officers were hardly less savage. Lieutenant Wiederholdt concluded that there was "more stupidity than courage" in Rall's conduct, even though his most grievous tactical misstep was a failure to bolt for the Assunpink bridge as fast as the British dragoons had. Colonel Donop, hardly heroic, told a Prussian prince that the defeat "is an eternal disgrace to our nation and a clear proof that men are brave only when they are well-led." The landgrave of Hesse would revoke the colors of the regiments humiliated at Trenton until they could "distinguish themselves in the future"; not until an inquiry in 1782 formally blamed the dead—Rall foremost among them—and acquitted the living would the disgraced units receive new standards. "Fabulous Trenton," Wiederholdt observed sourly, "a place I'll remember as long as I live."

"The rebels have taken fresh courage upon this event," Howe warned Germain. That much was certain. "This affair has given new life and spirits to the cause," wrote Reverend Dr. David Griffith, who served the

3rd Virginia Regiment as both chaplain and surgeon. "Things begin to wear a better aspect." Few felt more heartened than Henry Knox, who was promoted to brigadier general in acknowledgment of his steady competence. He wrote Lucy, "my dearly beloved friend," on December 28:

> His Excellency the General has done me the unmerited great honor of thanking me in public orders in terms strong & polite. This I should blush to mention to any other than to you, my dear Lucy, & I am fearful that even my Lucy may think her Harry possessed of a species of little vanity in doing [this] at all. It is an exceeding great satisfaction.

A loyalist in Virginia told his diary, "The minds of the people are much altered. A few days ago they had given up the cause for lost. . . . Now they are all liberty-mad again. . . . Damn them all!" Many in the Continental ranks were liberty-mad enough to favor driving Howe's legions from New Jersey, if not New York. "Never were men in higher spirits than our whole army is," Captain Rodney wrote his brother in late December. "All are determined to extirpate them from the Jerseys."

Washington was determined, too. Victory at Trenton revived his reputation and enhanced his stature. Odes would be penned in his honor, with such immortal couplets as "Washington, though least expected near, / Opened fire upon the Hessians' rear." As Dr. Rush had urged, in late December Congress granted the commanding general autocratic powers for six months to pay enlistment bounties, raise additional regiments, appoint all officers below the rank of general, confiscate provisions, and arrest those who refused Continental currency or "are otherwise disaffected to the American cause." Rodney told his diary, "Gen'l. Washington is dictator." As if reassuring itself, Congress declared that the commander in chief "can safely be entrusted with the most unlimited power."

"The country," one biographer would write, "awakened to the belief that its general was a genius." If that judgment proved premature, victory made a bold, resolute man bolder and even more hell-bent. Washington, a Hessian conceded, was without doubt "a very good rebel."

22.

The Day Is Our Own

The very good rebel arrived back in war-scarred Trenton at noon on Monday, December 30, after crossing the river at McConkey's Ferry with the vanguard of Sullivan's division. He established a new headquarters in a two-story house owned by a loyalist distiller on Queen Street, north of the Assunpink bridge and a few steps from where Rall had been shot down four days earlier. Washington still was uncertain how many men would join him in New Jersey or whether they would remain in the ranks when their enlistments expired the next day. Simply traversing the Delaware from Pennsylvania a second time had proved brutal: several inches of snow had fallen, and the river ice was thick enough to impede boats but too weak to bear the weight of guns and horses. Rowers and ferrymen would struggle for two days to again shuttle brigades to the far shore.

Heartened by his triumph on Christmas night, the commanding general had chosen to stay on the offensive. Several considerations led to his decision. Soon the Delaware would freeze solid, exposing Philadelphia to attack at a time and place of General Howe's choosing. Having finally seized the initiative, Washington was loath to relinquish it. Moreover, he had been surprised to hear from Colonel Cadwalader that his militia brigade had crossed to Burlington on the second attempt early Saturday morning without realizing that Washington had returned to Pennsylvania following the fight in Trenton. Finding the enemy gone except for a few discarded invalids, Cadwalader marched eleven miles north to Bordentown with four guns and nearly two thousand armed dockworkers, artisans, and shopkeepers panting for a fight after Hessian pillagers had thoroughly despoiled the countryside. Along farm lanes and in remote hamlets, red rags recently nailed to front doors as emblems of loyalty to the Crown vanished when the rebel troops reappeared; loyalties were shifting again. The enemy seemed to be unmanned, Cadwalader wrote Washington, and "a pursuit would keep up the panic." He added, "I hope to fall on their rear." Colonel Reed also had returned to his native New Jersey on a scouting expedition; he urged Washington "to cross the river again & pursue the advantages which Providence had presented."

And so here he was, relying once more on his luck, his military intuition, and the fickle god of battle. As each unit traipsed into Trenton, those with expiring enlistments assembled in parade formation "in order to know what force we should have to depend on," Washington told Hancock. Some regiments could muster barely a hundred men; twenty months of hard campaigning had reduced most from a third to a tenth of their original size. Hundreds of men would shamble off in the coming hours, deaf to pleas and blandishments. Sixteen-year-old fifer John Greenwood, a Boston-born veteran of Bunker Hill and Canada, when offered cash and a promotion to remain in uniform for six more weeks, replied, "I would not stay to be a colonel." Sick and infested with vermin—"I had the itch then so bad that my breeches stuck to my thighs, all the skin being off"—he set out for home. Brigadier General Mercer offered three dollars and a pair of shoes for those willing to stay fifteen days; so few accepted that his depleted brigade was combined with another. Even before the Christmas night attack on Trenton, sickness and savage fighting in New York had pared the 1st Delaware Continentals from 750 men to 92. On this bleak Monday, only 6 agreed to fight on, including their colonel, John Haslet, now given command of General Stirling's brigade. His lordship had fallen ill.

But other appeals had greater success. General Thomas Mifflin, a Philadelphia merchant and politician, crossed the Delaware at Bristol with another fifteen hundred militiamen drawn from more than two dozen Pennsylvania units. At Crosswicks, eight miles south of Trenton, he appeared on horseback on Tuesday afternoon before five weary New England regiments whose enlistments were due to expire. Standing in the snow, the Continentals resembled "animated scarecrows," in one observer's description, although shoes, stockings, and breeches had been rushed from Philadelphia several days earlier to outfit them. Wearing an enormous fur hat and a pink blanket coat, Mifflin "made a harangue" about duty and the American cause, Lieutenant Stephen Olney reported; he promised not only a ten-dollar bounty to each man for another six weeks of service, but a share of booty taken from the enemy. "The general required all who agreed to remain to poise their firelocks," wrote Private John Howland of Rhode Island. "The poising commenced by some of each platoon, and was followed by the whole line. . . . We all poised with the rest." Muskets raised, the ranks gave three cheers. Mifflin ordered a gill of rum for each man.

Washington made his own plea to regiments in Trenton the same day. After commending their recent triumph, he spoke with urgency about winning another victory in New Jersey. He, too, promised ten dollars for six weeks of soldiering. Yet when a drum beat for volunteers, not a man stepped forward. Washington touched the flanks of his horse with his spurs and trotted along the line, a thick, imposing figure in his tailored blue uniform and cocked hat. "You have done all I asked you to do, and more than could be reasonably expected," he told them, according to one sergeant's account. "But your country is at stake, your wives, your houses, and all that you hold dear." He acknowledged their "fatigues and hardships," yet stressed that "the present is emphatically the crisis which is to decide our destiny." Again the drum sounded, and this time a few men edged forward, after whispered consultations among themselves. More followed, then many more.

By morning, the army in Trenton would number 3,335 men fit for duty. As additional militia and Continental troops arrived, the number would double to nearly seven thousand, more than half of them Pennsylvanians. "God Almighty inclined their hearts to listen," Greene wrote. "They engaged anew."

Washington had listened, too. He had traveled far since those early months in Cambridge, when he had decried the stupidity of his officers and the unkempt indiscipline of his privates. Together he and the army had been annealed by defeat, death, sorrow, and occasional success. That mystical bond between leader and led had strengthened almost imperceptibly, the consequence of mutual respect and shared faith in a brighter future. He spoke to them affectionately, not as military underlings and social inferiors but as fellow republicans. "Here was a new idea of a gentleman, a moral condition rather than a social rank," the historian David Hackett Fischer would write. "It was also a new idea of honor, which was not defined by rank or status or gender, but by a principle of human dignity and decency."

Now the commanding general just needed cash to make good on his promised bounties. He had already sent one galloper to Robert Morris for hard money to "pay a certain set of people who are of particular use to us"— spies. "Silver would be most convenient," Washington had written. Within hours, Morris sent two canvas bags from Philadelphia filled with 410 Spanish milled dollars, two English crowns, ten shillings, and a French half crown; he also provided a cask of wine, "hearing that you are in want." On New Year's Eve, Washington pleaded for more money. "No time, my dear sir, is to be lost," he warned. At dawn on Wednesday, January 1, Morris scribbled a reply after reportedly borrowing from Quaker businessmen with only his word as security. "I am up very early this morning to dispatch a supply of fifty thousand dollars to your Excellency," he wrote, adding, "The year 1776 is over. I am heartily glad of it & hope you nor America will ever be plagued with such another."

To supplement his spies, Washington sent Colonel Reed with a newly acquired cavalry troop on a reconnaissance mission toward Princeton. A dozen troopers from the Philadelphia Light Horse wore identical chocolate-brown uniforms, faced in white, and round black hats, each festooned with a buck's tail. Not a man among them had seen combat. East by northeast they cantered on chestnut mounts, led by Reed down country lanes and onto Quaker Road. From a wooded knoll almost within view of Princeton's rooftops, they spotted a British soldier strolling between a farmhouse and a nearby barn. Drawing horse pistols from their saddle holsters and sabers from their scabbards, the cavalrymen thundered past the outbuildings, encircled the house, and caught twelve redcoats from the 16th Light Dragoons reportedly "conquering a parcel of mince pies" in the kitchen, beyond reach of their muskets. Only their sergeant escaped, bolting through a back door and into the tree line. In an instant Reed ordered his chagrined captives mounted in pairs before spanking back to Trenton. Interrogated in separate rooms at the Queen Street headquarters, the dragoons revealed that Generals Cornwallis and Grant intended to join forces in Princeton before attacking the rebels with at least eight thousand British regulars and Hessians.

A stiff southerly breeze brought afternoon rain on New Year's Day, miring the roads in mud said to be a "half-leg deep." The temperature climbed above fifty degrees Fahrenheit. The last glint of twilight had faded when Washington summoned his war council to Queen Street. Candles guttered on the tables and sentries ringed the house as men with filthy boots and furrowed brows hunched over a map. Intelligence from Reed's foray and various agents had confirmed that time was precious: a vengeful royal legion would attack within hours. No command decision would be more fateful than the one made now. Should the army retreat south, joining Cadwalader at Crosswicks and Mifflin at Bordentown before escaping into Pennsylvania? Should the forces remain divided, with Cadwalader leading a raid on the British garrison and stores at New Brunswick, perhaps even freeing General Lee? Or should the entire force concentrate in Trenton?

The ubiquitous Dr. Rush, loitering outside the council chamber, was summoned to give his opinion. Although hesitant to offer military advice, Rush assured Washington, as he later wrote, "that all the Philadelphia militia would be very happy in being under his immediate command, and . . . would instantly obey a summons to join his troops at Trenton." Washington nodded, Rush withdrew, and the council immediately agreed to give battle here and now, with all forces massed, Continental and militia. The commander in chief then prescribed how the brigades would deploy. A delaying force of a thousand men had already marched northeast toward

Maidenhead, halfway to Princeton; they would entrench below Five Mile Run, with alarm posts farther northeast at Eight Mile Run. The main American host would hold the high ground above the Assunpink's south bank. General Knox had brought some forty field cannons across the Delaware, including the six brass pieces captured from the Hessians a few days earlier. Many of the guns would defend the bridge from Mill Hill, near the three-stone gristmill; others guarded fords up and down the creek bed. Infantry regiments would shake out for three miles in three extended lines, 250 yards apart and parallel to the Assunpink, with the left wing anchored on the Delaware.

Washington pulled out a piece of foolscap and his sharpened quill. Forgetting that the year had changed, he dated the order "Trenton 9 o'clock p.m. Janry 1st 1776."

> Some pieces of intelligence renders it necessary for you to march your troops immediately to this place. I expect your brigade will be here by five o'clock in the morning without fail. At any rate do not exceed six. . . . Bring your baggage—at least let it follow under a guard.

He recalled Rush and asked him to carry the letter to Cadwalader and Mifflin. Within an hour the doctor was on the muddy road to Crosswicks, escorted through the moonless night by a dragoon from the Philadelphia Light Horse. Washington shifted his headquarters once more, to Jonathan Richmond's tavern south of the Assunpink bridge. The urgent, high-pitched murmur of an army preparing for close combat carried on the wet night. The British were coming, once again.

Stout, double-chinned Charles Cornwallis had ridden fifty hard miles from New York with dragoon outriders to arrive in Princeton late at night on January 1. He had been just hours from sailing for England, his baggage already aboard *Bristol*, when a courier arrived with news of disaster in Trenton and a request from General Howe that he take the field to put things right. Muck-spattered and saddle-sore, he now strode across the wide portico of his new command post at Morven, the baronial brick mansion of Richard Stockton, Dr. Rush's imprisoned father-in-law. Down the post road to the southwest, the glow of British watch fires melted the winter darkness.

British and German staff officers soon gave Cornwallis a fair picture of his new command. Parapets and two batteries had been thrown up around Princeton to forestall surprise attack by the rebels. Since Monday,

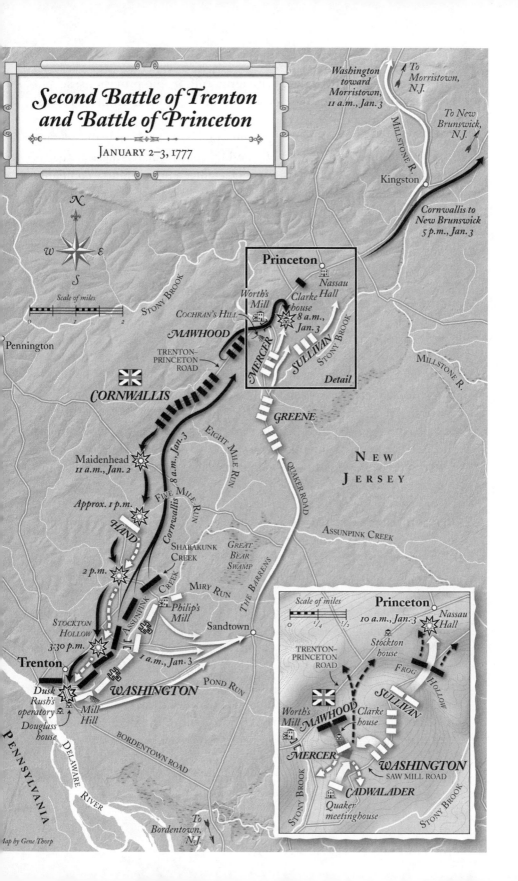

Second Battle of Trenton and Battle of Princeton

JANUARY 2–3, 1777

Washington toward Morristown, 11 a.m., Jan. 3

To Morristown, N.J.

To New Brunswick, N.J.

MILLSTONE R.

Kingston

Cornwallis to New Brunswick 5 p.m., Jan. 3

N
W · E
S

Scale of miles
0 · 1 · 2

STONY BROOK

Princeton

Nassau Hall

Worth's Mill

Clarke house 8 a.m., Jan. 3

COCHRAN'S HILL

MAWHOOD

Pennington

TRENTON-PRINCETON ROAD

MERCER

SULLIVAN

STONY BROOK

MILLSTONE R.

CORNWALLIS

Detail

GREENE

Maidenhead 11 a.m., Jan. 2

EIGHT MILE RUN

Cornwallis 8 a.m., Jan. 3

NEW JERSEY

Approx. 1 p.m.

FIVE MILE RUN

QUAKER ROAD

HAND

SHABAKUNK CREEK

GREAT BEAR SWAMP

ASSUNPINK CREEK

2 p.m.

CREEK

MIRY RUN

THE BARRENS

Philip's Mill

Sandtown

Scale of miles
0 · 1/4 · 1/2

Princeton

10 a.m., Jan. 3

Nassau Hall

STOCKTON HOLLOW 3:30 p.m.

ASSUNPINK CREEK

1 a.m., Jan. 3

POND RUN

Stockton house

TRENTON-PRINCETON ROAD

FROG HOLLOW

Trenton

WASHINGTON

SULLIVAN

Dusk Rush's operatory

Mill Hill

Worth's Mill

MAWHOOD

Clarke house

Douglass house

BORDENTOWN ROAD

MERCER

WASHINGTON SAW MILL ROAD

PENNSYLVANIA

DELAWARE RIVER

CADWALADER

Quaker meetinghouse

STONY BROOK

STONY BROOK

To Bordentown, N.J.

Map by Gene Thorp

forty-two wagons had arrived with ammunition and provisions; surplus baggage and sick troops were evacuated north. Colonel Donop's Hessian brigade had joined the garrison, along with reinforcements from New Brunswick. Major General Grant, who would now be Cornwallis's deputy, had already amassed many of the finest troops in North America: guardsmen, grenadiers, Highlanders, *Jäger*. Of eighteen light infantry companies now in Princeton, seven had led the march to Lexington and eleven fought at Bunker Hill. For them this was a grudge match. Donop, who would have the post of honor in commanding the vanguard, was also bent on avenging the recent humiliation; not only had he issued a no-quarter edict, but any Hessian taking a rebel prisoner would receive fifty lashes.

Several officers had ridden toward Eight Mile Run that day, getting "wet to the skin" from the rain, as one complained, but without seeing any enemy. Yet enemies surely lurked nearby. A dozen heedless dragoons had been captured outside town, and a British captain and his servant were ambushed and killed "by some lurking villains" on the road from New Brunswick. After a skirmish near Stony Brook, a mile west of Princeton, two rebel soldiers were found dead, one shot through the groin and chest, the other through the hip, hand, and face. A mortally wounded regular had been harpooned with an iron musket ramrod under the chin and out through the nose, apparently fired at close range by a gunman who was interrupted while reloading. Donop urged Cornwallis to advance on Trenton in two columns, one down the main road from Princeton and the other swinging wide on the British left flank to turn the American right. But Cornwallis disagreed: he intended to concentrate nine thousand shock troops with twenty-eight guns in a unified, headlong assault.

Drums beat to arms in Princeton well before dawn on Thursday, January 2. Hessians wolfed down a breakfast of biscuits and brandy. By first light the cantonments were extruding a steady parade of regiments onto the post road. Buffeted by gusty winds from the northwest, flankers clumped through the adjacent fields. Although reputedly the best highway in the middle colonies—elms had been planted on the shoulders so that fallen branches could be laid over ruts and mudholes—the road segment toward Trenton was narrow and bisected by streams. Overnight rain, horses' hooves, and wagon traffic soon churned the track into a quagmire. Bands of enemy skirmishers fired on the column from copses and other skulking places. A *Jäger* was shot near Maidenhead, where the vanguard marked time waiting for the trailing brigades to stumble forth from Princeton. Not until noon did the army close up sufficiently for Cornwallis to order a general advance on Trenton. "It was a fine clear day, not a solitary cloud," an eighteen-year-old Virginia ensign wrote. "We could see the glittering of their guns as they marched in column."

American marksmen at Eight Mile and Five Mile Runs had thrown a few harassing shots before dashing back to the main skirmish line beyond Shabakunk Creek, south of Maidenhead. Here rebels demolished the road bridge and concealed themselves by the hundreds in a dense hardwood brake. Colonel Edward Hand's Pennsylvania riflemen lacked bayonets, but a pair of field guns anchored the ranks. As *Jäger* and light infantrymen pushed across the creek bed and up the opposite slope, a searing fusillade of smoke and flame erupted from the trees. Enemy soldiers in red and green slumped to the ground or tumbled backward for cover. The woodland crackled with small arms fire, punctuated with shouts and shrieks. Cornwallis ordered his column to deploy left and right into a battle line. Royal artillerymen muscled their carriages forward, and British cannons lashed the tree line for half an hour. Hand finally ordered his men to fall back to the next position, his right flank covered by Virginia riflemen posted near the meandering Assunpink.

Lengthening shadows stretched across the road as Washington rode to the sound of the guns with Greene and Knox. Colonel Hand had again chosen to defend rising ground, this time overlooking a shallow ravine known as Stockton Hollow. Again the royal troops spread wide. For nearly half an hour gun batteries exchanged salvos, cannonballs shearing away tree branches and careering down the road in both directions. Washington told Hand to "retard the march of the enemy until nightfall" if possible, then hurried back through Trenton.

Shortly before four p.m., in danger of being outflanked, Hand's rear guard whipped a few final shots across the smoke-filled hollow and fell back into the village past the King and Queen Streets junction. The running gunfight had lasted all day and kept the British column crawling at a march pace of one mile per hour.

Galling fire from behind house corners and low earthworks greeted the king's men as they, too, poured into Trenton. No longer confined to the narrow roadbed, British and German regiments fanned out through the village, loping past the taverns, the Quaker meetinghouse, and the serene Presbyterian burial ground, where Colonel Rall lay undreaming in his new grave. To slow the enemy's headlong rush toward the Assunpink, Washington ordered Colonel Daniel Hitchcock's New England brigade across the bridge and into Queen Street.

Muzzle flashes and ricochet sparks grew brighter as daylight faded. A gap opened in Hitchcock's ranks to let Hand's force scurry through, pulling the two field guns behind them. An officer with the retreating Virginia riflemen barked, "Shift for yourselves, boys. Get over the bridge as quick as you can." Men stumbled, fell, then rose up and ran on toward the span, only sixteen feet wide and already "crowded into a dense solid mass," in one description. Although the recent rain had swollen the creek, some troops plunged into the Assunpink and scrambled across a shallow ford just below the bridgehead.

Jäger and light infantry regulars charged down King Street "and fired into our right flank at every space between the houses," wrote Private Howland, the Rhode Island soldier who had poised his firelock to reenlist the previous day. Timely covering fire from Knox's guns on the hillside across the creek flicked the enemy from Hitchcock's flanks and rear as the rebels backed onto the stone bridge. Some failed to escape; among them was John Rosbrugh, a sixty-three-year-old Pennsylvania militia chaplain who found himself stranded in the Blazing Star tavern on King Street after someone stole his horse. Hessian troops seized him near the Assunpink, took his purse and gold watch, then murdered him with their bayonets and sabers. Rosbrugh's naked corpse was found with more than a dozen puncture wounds and slashes across his skull. Leaving behind a widow and five children under the age of ten, he would be buried near Rall in the Presbyterian cemetery.

Across the bridge, Washington sat his horse near the west railing, "firm, composed, and majestic," in Howland's description. As Hitchcock's brigade finally reached the south bank, he ordered the men to take defensive positions in a meadow on the American left, within rifle shot of the Assunpink. Knox's gunnery had for the moment pushed enemy pursuers away from the creek, but thousands of redcoats and Hessians could be heard massing for attack in Trenton's narrow streets. "It appeared to me," Lieutenant Stephen Olney later wrote, "that our army was in the most desperate situation I had ever known it."

Washington was fretful enough about holding the bridge that he summoned part of Mercer's brigade from the far right of the line for reinforcement. The arrival early that morning of Cadwalader and Mifflin with their thirty-six hundred men, mostly Pennsylvanians, meant that the nine American brigades were still outnumbered but not ruinously. Three Virginia regiments defended the southern bridgehead, and when Washington told Lieutenant Colonel Charles Scott to hold the span "to the last extremity," he replied, "Yes, General, so long as there is a man alive." A Virginia captain reportedly added, "We intend to sleep on it." Scott reminded his troops to aim low. "The old boss has put us here to defend the bridge, and by God it must be done," he said. "Whenever you see them fellows first begin to put their feet upon the bridge, do you shin 'em."

In the failing light, Cornwallis, Grant, and other officers studied the American lines with their spyglasses, finding the defenders "exactly in the position Rall should have taken when he was attacked," in the tart assessment of Captain Archibald Robertson, a British engineer. The first lunge by yowling British light infantrymen and *Jäger* swept toward the ford below the bridge; cannon fire from Mill Hill and a thick spray of bullets promptly cuffed them away. "We advanced to the edge of the stream, facing the enemy, who soon found it prudent to fall back under cover of the houses," Private Howland recorded. Moments later a phalanx of grenadiers with four field guns rushed the bridge and had crossed halfway when cannon fire from as close as forty yards pounded the ranks with frightful violence. Rebel riflemen plinked away from revetments and the nearby mill, and the heckle of musketry merged into an unbroken roar. After "about twelve minutes," by one soldier's timekeeping, the redcoats receded, dragging thirty casualties and leaving as many more stunned comrades to be captured. "A very hot fire at ye bridge," a chaplain told his diary.

No sooner had the defenders reloaded than the king's men charged the bridge again. The front of the British column had nosed onto the span once more "when our fire became so destructive that they broke their ranks and fled. . . . Our army raised a shout, and such a shout I never since heard," an American militiaman said. "They shouted as one man." Yet another wave surged down Queen Street, dim forms in the dim light, only to be thrown back for good by canister shot and the hornet whine of bullets. "We shouted after them again," the militiaman added, "but they had had enough of it." Knox's field artillery cannonade was perhaps the heaviest that had ever been fired in the New World. Batteries above the Assunpink "saluted them with great vociferation," he later told Lucy. "Such destruction it made you cannot conceive," wrote Joseph White, an orderly sergeant. "The bridge looked red as blood, with their killed and wounded, and their red coats. The enemy beat a retreat."

Gunners from both sides of the stream swapped salvos until seven p.m., aiming at muzzle flashes five hundred yards away. Washington clattered about on horseback, trailing a cloud of aides and life guardsmen, to confirm that both wings were intact and alert, from the Delaware on his left to the ford at Philip's Mill on the right. Exhilarated men grounded their arms and kindled campfires on the hillsides, roasting skewered salt meat and cleaning their firelocks. "We were ordered to rest," one sergeant scribbled in his diary, and some gathered cedar fence rails to build dry beds.

A Pennsylvanian considered this second battle of Trenton the most "furious engagement that ever was." Captain Ewald, whose *Jäger* had been in the thick of the gunfire, called it "a stubborn outpost fight . . . whereby many men were killed and wounded on both sides."

How many would be forever uncertain. Official British and Hessian tallies minimized losses. American killed, wounded, and missing for the day, from Eight Mile Run to the Assunpink bridge, apparently numbered fifty to a hundred or more. Crown casualties were heavier, perhaps well over three hundred. Whatever the precise butcher's bill, medicos labored through the night, including Benjamin Rush, who toiled in a makeshift operatory near the river, his shirtsleeves bloody from treating twenty wounded soldiers, including a New Englander whose right hand, shattered by a cannonball, hung from his wrist by a scrap of skin. After a brief, exhausted nap in a pile of straw—trying to ignore what he described as "the cries and groans and convulsions" of broken men—Rush and his orderlies loaded the patients into a wagon and headed for Bordentown.

On Thursday evening, as their jaded troops bedded down in the upper village beyond the bite of Knox's guns, Cornwallis and Grant convened a war council. The British quartermaster general, Sir William Erskine, a former dragoon known to intimates as "Woolly," advocated a night attack to catch the rebels unawares. "My lord, if you trust those people tonight," Erskine told Cornwallis, "you will see nothing of them in the morning." The British commander demurred. His brigades were fatigued from slogging through mud all day. Night attacks were notoriously difficult to control, and the rolling Jersey terrain, with its swales and hidden creases, was foreign to him. He suspected that Washington intended to launch another dawn assault, like the sortie against Rall. All regiments would stand to before sunrise, ready to smash any thrust across the creek.

If no attack came, Cornwallis would outflank the enemy to the east—two thousand regulars had already infiltrated the woods near Philip's Mill on the British left wing. Washington, who was sardonically disparaged as "the old fox," had been run to ground. At first light, the king's men would cross for the kill.

The old fox had in fact backed his army across the Assunpink without a clear tactical plan for what to do next. Americans currently owned the high ground, but should Cornwallis force the position, frontally or on the flanks, they faced a helter-skelter rout, if not annihilation against the impassable, ice-choked lower Delaware. Scouts detected an alarming concentration of assault forces on the British left. On Thursday night, desperate for alternatives, Washington convened his own war council of a dozen senior officers at General St. Clair's headquarters in a diminutive frame house owned by army quartermaster Alexander Douglass, six hundred feet south of the creek.

Inspiration is rare enough in the tumult of battle, and genius rarer still. But as Washington listened to his lieutenants discussing their predicament, he abruptly saw with preternatural clarity a stratagem as bold as crossing the Delaware on Christmas night: the army would pivot *east*, looping into Cornwallis's rear at Princeton before marching north toward the British logistics compound at New Brunswick. Reed's recent reconnaissance ride with the Philadelphia Light Horse had confirmed a passable, secluded byroad from Trenton to Princeton, roughly parallel to the post road. A detailed map provided two days earlier by a spy in Princeton showed unguarded back roads into the village from the east, as well as British defensive dispositions.

St. Clair, whose brigade of fourteen hundred men held the American right wing, also saw the beauty of "turning the left of the enemy in the night." So did Greene, Sullivan, Knox, Mercer, Cadwalader, and others. Yes, they agreed, nodding with a glint in their eyes, yes, this might work. With a scrape of chairs and boots on the plank floor, they hurried off to prepare march orders and wake their men.

Heavy baggage and the most awkward guns would be hauled for safekeeping to Burlington on 150 wagons now parked in train on the Bordentown road, more than a mile south of Trenton. At one a.m. on Friday morning, January 3, those first teams departed with what one sergeant called "such a hurry-skurry among all our wagoners." Five hundred men would remain behind through the small hours on Friday to dupe British pickets across the creek: feeding cedar rails into scores of campfires; silhouetting themselves before the flames, "first one and the other to make them believe we were very numerous"; and hacking at the ground with shovels and mattocks to simulate the clang of an army entrenching. Knox also assigned two guns to support the deception and discomfit the British, as he reported, with "a few shells we now & then chucked into town to prevent their enjoying their new quarters securely."

No man spoke above a hoarse whisper as the troops assembled. "We were ordered to move with all the secrecy and stillness imaginable," wrote Major Robert Beale, a Virginian. Artillerymen wrapped their gun carriage wheels in muffling rags and rope. Providentially, as Washington would acknowledge, a cold front had arrived from the west early in the evening, driving the temperature down nearly twenty degrees in a few hours; by Friday morning, thermometers in Philadelphia read twenty-one Fahrenheit.

The muddy ground froze "hard as pavement," Lieutenant Olney recorded—severe on badly shod feet but suitable for moving an artillery train with dispatch. The weather gods had again favored the Americans.

Only the generals knew their destination as more than six thousand soldiers, led by three local guides, crept from their bivouacs, first angling southeast away from Trenton, then east on a country lane. A waning crescent moon rose just before two a.m., dimming the stars but casting little light in the hazy sky. Some horses lacked shoes and slipped on the icy track; handlers steadied them with their shoulders and murmured assurances. Men making yet another night march tripped over the many tree stumps studding the rough trace, then dozed off or slumped to the ground whenever the column halted, soon to be prodded by those behind them. After crossing Miry Run they swung north through the Barrens and past Great Bear Swamp. Thick timber opened onto pasture and farmland, with dormant grain fields and scattered orchards of skeletal apple, peach, and cherry trees. Thorn hedges and six kinds of fencing—two-bar, four-rail, five-rail, split-rail, panel, and pole—kept out intruders.

The first, faint glow of civil twilight was sensed more than seen just before seven a.m. An ocher dawn followed half an hour later. The column, which had covered nine miles in six hours of polar darkness, now halted at a road fork near a fieldstone Quaker meetinghouse, two miles from Princeton. Here Washington divided his army as he had before attacking Trenton the previous week. Sullivan would lead the larger force of five thousand men to the right, up Saw Mill Road, falling on the village from the southern flank. Greene's smaller division of fifteen hundred was to veer north, severing the post road as a blocking force against Cornwallis's inevitable counterattack from Trenton and Maidenhead. Washington believed that the British had left behind in Princeton a single brigade of three regiments to guard the army's stores. The force comprised twelve hundred regulars, including sixty-five German recruits newly integrated into the British ranks despite their ignorance of English, as well as perhaps two hundred other miscellaneous troops.

The sun peeped above the tree line behind the American right flank. "The morning was bright, serene, and extremely cold," Major James Wilkinson would recall, "with a hoar frost which spangled every object." Before the two columns heaved forward on their separate paths, at least one captain passed around a bucket of rum sprinkled with gunpowder. He encouraged his men to each drink half a gill—two ounces. The potion, it was said, gave courage.

* * *

American intelligence had accurately identified the size of the British rear detachment but not its location. A midnight courier from Cornwallis had ordered two of the three regiments in Princeton to join him in Trenton, and as Washington's host crept close to the village early on Friday, more than seven hundred regulars from the 17th Foot and the 55th Foot were marching down the post road with fifty dismounted dragoons, an artillery train, supply wagons, and various convalescents and replacements, including a few Highlanders. They were led by Lieutenant Colonel Charles Mawhood, whose estimable service in uniform had begun in 1752 as a dragoon cornet and included combat in Germany. As usual, Mawhood this morning rode to battle on a high-stepping brown pony with a pair of frisky spaniels cavorting alongside.

The head of the British column had reached Cochran's Hill, almost two miles southwest of Princeton, when mounted scouts descried a formation moving near the Quaker meetinghouse to the east. A cavalry lieutenant sent to investigate soon returned with alarming news: the unidentified troops were not Hessian, as Mawhood originally believed, but rebels, in long columns marching not only toward Princeton on Saw Mill Road but also toward the post road along Stony Brook. They numbered in the thousands.

The British may have been "as much astonished as if an army had dropped perpendicularly upon them," in Knox's subsequent boast to Lucy, but Mawhood acted swiftly. The column would reverse its march order—no easy task on a narrow, slippery track—with the 55th Foot, originally in the rear, moving to high ground east of the road, about halfway back to the village. Most guns would go with them. The wagons would return to Princeton for safety, preceded by an express sent to warn the 40th Foot, still in garrison. Mawhood intended to lead the rest of his command, fewer than four hundred men, cross-country to confront the nearest enemy battalions, now less than half a mile away.

That approaching force under General Greene was bound for a bridge at Worth's Mill, an obvious chokepoint to interdict the post road. Plodding along a rutted track in a glen cut by the meandering Stony Brook, the Americans could neither see nor hear the redcoats ahead. But Washington could. Riding with Sullivan's column, the commanding general was alerted to the apparition of redcoats a half mile or so across the countryside. Whipping out his glass, he studied the distant road cut through the thick trees, concluded he was looking at a modest reconnaissance detachment heading back to Princeton, and sent a galloper to warn Greene. He also ordered General Mercer to peel north off Saw Mill Road to intercept the enemy patrollers before they returned to the village.

Mercer, a burly physician with a compact trunk and long limbs, commanded a brigade of fewer than 350 men. The son of a Scottish clergyman, medically trained in Aberdeen, he had volunteered as a surgeon for Bonnie Prince Charlie and his doomed rebels. Disaster at Culloden in 1746 made Mercer a fugitive, and he eventually found sanctuary in America, first as a frontier doctor, then in Virginia as a respected practitioner with a daughter and four sons. The commander in chief cherished him as a fellow Mason, a fine officer, and a patriot; Mercer's patients included General Washington's mother and Martha Washington's daughter Patsy, an epileptic. Over dinner with Dr. Rush earlier in the week, Mercer had vowed to "cross the mountains and live among the Indians" rather than submit to British authority.

As Mercer spurred his horse to climb toward the post road, for the first time he spied an enemy horseman in the morning glare, "as we view an object when the sun shines directly in our faces," a sergeant later wrote. The general told his riflemen to fire, but the rider wheeled about and vanished before they could pull the trigger. Across the icy slope Mercer rode, veering to the right and keeping below the ridgeline. Twenty skidding Virginians and a hundred Pennsylvania riflemen lumbered after him. In his haste, he deployed no scouts and left most of his command behind to muscle their field guns through the snow and wheat stubble.

Colonel Mawhood had sent his dragoons into the vacant William Clarke farm, several hundred yards below the post road. They were closely trailed by grenadiers, two brass 6-pounders, and 17th Foot troops, who shed their field packs before forming a skirmish line. As Mercer and his lead detachment emerged from a small apple orchard near the Clarke farmhouse, the rebels suddenly confronted their enemy, barely fifty paces away. The dragoons rose as one from behind a split-rail fence and fired with a great clap and a spurt of white smoke. The volley mostly flew high—splintered apple twigs littered the ground behind Mercer's men—although one corporal who fell dead "seemed to bend forward to receive the ball." The Americans returned fire, targeting officers and driving the enemy back more than forty yards. "They retreated eight rods to their packs, which were laid in a line," an American sergeant later wrote. "I advanced to the fence . . . which the enemy had just left, fell on one knee and loaded my musket with ball and buckshot. Our fire was most destructive. Their ranks grew thin." A captain added, "The enemy screamed as if many devils had got hold of them."

Lieutenant William John Hale later told his father that the rebels "gave us a very heavy discharge, which brought down seven of my platoon at once. The rest, being recruits, gave way. I rallied them with some difficulty." Some dragoons also ran, so enraging the foot troops that only an officer's forceful command prevented them from firing at their fleeing comrades.

As the shooting intensified, a grenadier captain toppled over dead. Among others mortally wounded was Captain the Honorable William Leslie of the 17th Foot, an earl's son whose family, in more convivial days, had befriended young Benjamin Rush when he was a medical student in Edinburgh and whose uncle now commanded another of Howe's brigades a few miles down the road. On Christmas Day, young Leslie, age twenty-five, had written his mother in Scotland that the "desolation this unhappy country has suffered must distress every feeling heart," but "the inhabitants deserve it as much as any set of people who ever rebelled against their sovereign." Now those rebellious people had killed him.

The firing grew general. More troops, royal and rebel, charged into the fight. Scarlet stains spread in the snow, and billowing smoke from "the two lines mingled as it rose, and went up in one beautiful cloud," Major Wilkinson observed. Most of Mercer's sharpshooters were riflemen, whose weapons, though accurate, took much longer to reload than muskets and carried no bayonets. As the Yankee rate of fire faltered, on Mawhood's order the British ranks charged across the farmyard with their steel bayonets extended.

The American line crumpled, then disintegrated. "We drove them back through the railings, barns, and orchards," Lieutenant Hale wrote. Captain John Fleming and Lieutenant Bartholomew Yates, both of the 1st Virginia, were clubbed and stabbed repeatedly despite pleas for quarter. Captain Daniel Neil, a New Jersey artilleryman, died at his gun. A bullet struck Mercer's gray horse in the foreleg, spilling him to the ground. The general flailed away with his sword until a regular brained him with a musket butt; others plunged their bayonets into his chest, convinced because of his handsome uniform and fine surtout that they were killing Washington. "I saw him lying on the ground and saw him attempt to rise but fall backward," a militiaman later wrote.

Colonel Haslet pressed forward on foot to take command. Since his dunking in the Delaware during the crossing on Christmas night, he had recently written a friend, "[I] have had the piles and swelled legs. . . . But no matter if we drive them to New York. If I return it will be to salute you. If not, we shall meet in heaven." Heaven it would be. Haslet pitched to the ground with a bullet through the head.

With so many officers bloodied, the troops raced back down the icy slope, wheezing in terror. Colonel Cadwalader's brigade of eleven hundred men had trailed Mercer by two hundred yards, and as the battle uproar intensified ahead, the Philadelphia militia prepared to advance on Greene's order. Then Mercer's men came tearing across the fields, kicking up snow and glancing back over their shoulders as they ran. A menacing crimson formation of regulars appeared behind them with light infantry skirmishers out front, all bayonets aglint. Royal artillerymen fired grape and canister from their own 6-pounders as well as from a captured rebel gun. "The balls," wrote Charles Peale, "whistled their thousand notes around our heads." Ensign Anthony Morris, Jr., a brewer and fighting Quaker from Philadelphia, fell with grape wounds to the knee and chin, as well as a fatal shot to his right temple. Cadwalader's men edged back forty yards in confusion, briefly reformed after much noisy shoving from their officers, then broke again and bolted for the woods.

But the superior rebel numbers soon told. From a knoll on the American left flank, a pair of French-made 4-pounders commanded by Captain Joseph Moulder matched the British guns salvo for salvo and kept the redcoats from mounting another headlong assault. When skirmishers threatened to flank Moulder's guns, Captain Thomas Rodney and fifteen Delaware troops sprinted through gunfire "thick as hail" to provide security behind several nearby haystacks. Bullets nicked the elbow of Rodney's green coat, sliced the sole from his shoe, and clipped his hat, but the British came no closer.

The symphonic gunfire brought Washington galloping on his white charger from the top of Sullivan's column, just south of Princeton. Ordering Hitchcock's New England brigade and Colonel Hand's riflemen to counterattack, he pranced among Cadwalader's militia companies, waving his hat and whooping encouragement. "Parade with us, my brave fellows," a sergeant quoted him as urging. "There is but a handful of the enemy, and we will have them directly." Exposed to fire from both sides, he rode to within thirty yards of British bayonets, by one account, imploring his men to close with the enemy. "I saw him brave all the dangers of the field, and his important life hanging as it were by a single hair with a thousand deaths flying around him," a Philadelphia officer later wrote.

As the militia rallied—"beyond my expectation," Cadwalader admitted—Continental counterattackers surged forward, firing on the march by platoon. "I never saw men looked so furious as they did when running by us," one soldier later wrote. Mawhood's stronghold near William Clarke's orchard was now threatened on three sides, as Mifflin's Pennsylvanians attacked the British right and Hand's rifles fired into the enemy left wing. Additional American gun batteries wheeled up within range to fling more shot and shell at both Mawhood and the 55th Foot, closer to Princeton. Lieutenant Colonel Scott told his Virginians, "Boys, there are two hundred and fifty redcoats on yonder hill and about two hundred and fifty of us. We can beat them." With a mighty shout they hurled forward, but upon reaching the crest the only redcoats to be seen were prone in the snow or scampering toward the post road. "We looked down the hill," an ensign wrote, "and saw them running in confusion." In the field below, Cadwalader cried, "They fly. The day is our own!"

With ten gunners and the artillery horses dead, the British abandoned their 6-pounders after setting the gun carriages ablaze. Ordered by Mawhood to "run away as fast as we could," in a British lieutenant's words, most survivors from the 17th Foot rushed up Stony Brook, then veered left for Maidenhead or plunged ahead toward Pennington. Riflemen and Philadelphia horsemen pursued the fugitives into the woodlands, urged on by Washington. Mawhood could be seen bouncing on his pony across the American front toward Princeton, the two spaniels frolicking alongside. Spotting rebel troops ahead, he wheeled west and escaped through the woods.

The battle shifted into Princeton, a village with sixty houses scattered down a single street and a large stone college building, Nassau Hall, formerly revered as "a seat of learning and politeness" but now a seat of gunplay. A few troops from the 55th Foot, which had bolted from high ground off the post road, joined their 40th Foot comrades behind Frog Hollow, a ravine half a mile due south of town. But when Sullivan's regiments pushed within musket range, killing the captain commanding the position and threatening to envelop both flanks, the regulars fell back to a sturdy breastwork with a sally port near the college yard. Some redcoats barricaded themselves inside Nassau Hall, smashing windows to shoot from the upper floors of their stone stronghold. Others simply ran for their lives, following a baggage-and-artillery train that slipped from the village and headed north as fast as the teams could clop.

A brief delay preceded the final assault while rebel artillery shunted forward, including a battery of 6-pounders commanded by Captain Hamilton. Various accounts held that either one, two, or three shots were fired at the college; a rebel ball may or may not have sailed through a window to demolish an oil portrait of the late George II hanging on the wall. The defenders who had not fled promptly surrendered. An officer stepped from the sally port with a white handkerchief on the point of his sword. "A flag was sent," Charles Peale recorded, "and we huzza'd our victory."

Some two hundred redcoats threw down their arms and capitulated, "a haughty, crabbed set of men," in one American soldier's estimation. An artillery sergeant poking through a college room used by a British officer found tea steeping in a pot, toast on a plate, a gilt-edged Bible, and a new 40th Foot uniform coat lined with white satin, the bright buttons still wrapped in protective paper, "all of which," he reported, "I took." Others snatched up British blankets or loaded flour barrels into wagons. Surplus flour was strewn across the yard, where village women scuttled from their cellars and scooped it into their aprons.

A rebel squad dashed down the post road toward Worth's Mill to demolish the bridge spanning Stony Brook; an axman chopped the sleepers to splinters. On the battlefield around William Clarke's orchard, officers posted sentries to prevent pilfering of the dead and wounded. In the bitter cold, corpses already wore purple masks from blood freezing in capillaries close to the skin. Mercer's men were found "scattered about groaning, dying, and dead," according to a sergeant who had escaped injury except for the tip of a forefinger shot away and bullet holes in his coat skirts. Also groaning was General Mercer himself, still alive although "in a state of entire insensibility, the combined effect of the cold and his wounds." Carried to a farmhouse near Saw Mill Road, he was left in the care of two Quaker women, upon reports of British light horse approaching from Trenton.

A long drum roll sounded assembly in Princeton. Black smoke spiraled into the pale sky from burning British matériel too cumbersome to confiscate. At eleven a.m., just an hour after the village had fallen, Washington gave the command and his army surged northeast, four abreast in a column on the post road. Outriders scouted for trouble, and more than two hundred prisoners shuffled with heads bowed, guarded by riflemen. A hundred lowing cows taken from the British commissary trailed the procession.

In Kingston, four miles from Princeton, Washington halted briefly to confer on horseback with his lieutenants. New Brunswick lay a dozen miles ahead, with supply magazines to plunder and a weak enemy garrison to rout. But his men were near the end of their tether—exhausted, cold, and hungry. Some still lacked shoes. Officers found it difficult to keep them in ranks and to herd stragglers. "The exclamation was general," Wilkinson later wrote. "'O that we had five hundred fresh men to beat up their quarters at Brunswick.'" But Washington knew the difference between a calculated risk and a fool's gamble. "The harassed state of our own troops (many of them having had no rest for two nights & a day) and the danger of losing the advantage we had gained by aiming at too much, induced me by the advice of my officers to relinquish the attempt," he subsequently wrote Hancock.

Instead, the column pivoted northwest, following the east bank of the Millstone River, then crossing to the west bank at Griggstown. Wrecking crews demolished each bridge once the ranks passed. The sun had set when the army reached Somerset Court House, having covered fifteen miles in an afternoon. A thousand stragglers drifted in through the evening. Prisoners were locked up, and the troops crowded lofts and coops, or simply collapsed under wagons and in the open air. Captain Peale's men ignored the risk of vermin, flopping into tavern straw said to have been used by Hessians. "They were glad to lie down," Peale wrote, "and were asleep in a few moments, so that I could not get a single man to go with me in search of provisions."

Sentries posted the approach roads, peering into the night in every direction and wondering what had become of their enemy.

General Cornwallis's disagreeable Friday began with the discovery at dawn that Washington's army had vanished overnight from Trenton. A suspicion that the Americans had fled south to Bordentown was dispelled by "a heavy cannonade in our rear, which surprised everyone," Captain Ewald wrote. Dragoons and light infantry hurried up the road toward Princeton "in a most infernal sweat," as Henry Knox later wrote, "running, puffing & blowing & swearing at being so outwitted."

Cornwallis arrived at Stony Brook to find the demolished bridge sitting in the creek and a pesky pair of rebel stay-behind guns shooting at him from the far side of the gulch. While British 6-pounders drove off the enemy cannons, guardsmen waded waist-deep across a ford eighty yards north of the ruined span. They soon came upon a battlefield littered with bodies frozen in awkward attitudes, like toppled statuary. "The action had been warm," a lieutenant noted in his journal, "but we could not find any of the enemy's parties." Nor would they be found in Princeton. The first British patrol arrived an hour after Washington's departure to discover Nassau Hall empty, the king's magazines burning furiously, and, in Ewald's description, the "vicinity covered with corpses." Not until four p.m. did the rear of the column arrive from Trenton to finish looting the ruined village, which Cornwallis was now determined to abandon. "You would think it had been desolated with the plague and an earthquake," a witness declared, "as well as with the calamities of war."

The British high command initially acknowledged losses for the day of 276 men; as more reports filtered in, the tally eventually grew to 450, or a third of the Princeton garrison. About half had been killed or wounded; the other half were headed to jails in Connecticut or Pennsylvania. American casualties, although imprecisely recorded, likely numbered 60 to 70, about half of them killed. Several dozen dead, British and American, were subsequently buried in a stone quarry. Others were interred, an American major reported, "by hauling them on sleds to great holes and heaping them in." Few went to their graves with the dignity of Colonel Haslet, laid in the yard of the Old Presbyterian Meeting House in Philadelphia with a sixteen-stanza elegy reciting his virtues.

As always, the wounded suffered terribly. A regular shot below the ribs was carried into a house on the post road, beyond treatment but for a cataplasm cloth dipped in vinegar. "He was in very great pain and bled much out of both sides, and often desired to be removed from one place to another, which was done accordingly," an elderly man who lived in the house wrote. "He died about three o'clock in the afternoon." Among American physicians who arrived under a truce flag to care for men from both armies was Benjamin Rush, who rode in from Bordentown to find the battlefield "red in many places with human blood." He was soon red himself after amputating legs from four damaged regulars.

He was surprised to find General Mercer still alive on a blood-soaked mattress. "He is in good spirits, drinks plentifully, sleeps tolerably well, and talks cheerfully on all subjects, as usual," Rush wrote in a note to Richard Henry Lee. He pronounced the patient "out of danger," but Mercer was too good a physician to be deceived. Gesturing to a small, suppurating bayonet puncture under his right arm, he said, "This is a fellow that will very soon do my business." That business was done soon enough: Mercer died in misery on January 12. His corpse was carried across the Delaware for burial with military honors at Christ Church in Philadelphia, another martyr to the cause. "His character was marked with all the traits of one of the heroes of antiquity," Rush wrote, to which Greene added, "He was a fine companion, a sincere friend, a true patriot, and a brave general. May heaven bless his spirit."

At dusk on Friday, Cornwallis led his column onto the road north from Princeton. Fearing that Washington would pillage the New Brunswick cantonment before he could get there, he abandoned some of his sick and wounded, as well as much baggage. With provisions gone, the army battered, and enemies lurking in every glade, New Jersey no longer seemed secure, much less hospitable. The fifteen-mile journey would take sixteen hours, slowed by disheartened men, knackered horses, and the wrecked bridge at Kingston. "I never experienced such a disagreeable night's march in my life," wrote Lieutenant Martin Hunter.

The plodding journey gave officers ample time to ponder what had gone wrong. The loyalist press would dismiss Princeton as a skirmish in which regulars again routed the craven rebels. The 17th Foot was soon lionized on recruiting posters in England as the "Heroes of Prince Town." But those who fought in New Jersey knew better. "This rebellion is most obstinately persisted in," a captain in the 40th Foot told his diary. "By our continual blunders, which the enemy never fail to take advantage of, we seem more to encourage than dishearten them." The engineer Archibald Robinson wrote, "Must hope it will serve as a lesson in future never to despise any enemy too much." Upon hearing the latest news from Trenton and Princeton, General Clinton, in Rhode Island, lambasted Cornwallis's missteps as "the most consummate ignorance I ever heard of [in] any officer above a corporal."

For the Hessians there was at least delicious schadenfreude in hearing that "an English brigade has shared the same fate as the Rall brigade," as General Heister told his prince in Hesse. Captain Ewald observed that the column leaving Princeton seemed "like an army that is thoroughly beaten. . . . Thus the fate of entire kingdoms often depends upon a few blockheads and irresolute men." A German chaplain confessed that "one can no longer lie down to sleep without thinking, this is your last night of freedom."

The column stumbled into New Brunswick before first light on Saturday, January 4, to find the encampment intact and Washington reportedly headed for the secure upcountry twenty miles north, around Morristown. But Cornwallis was taking no chances: the entire garrison would be required to turn to on the perimeter long before daybreak each morning, "to be ready for the scoundrels." Every soldier was to remain armed at all times, and to listen for the three-gun signal that would summon them to their alarm posts. "Our misfortune," one regular wrote, "has been that we have held the enemy too cheap."

The fresh foodstuffs and forage that General Howe had counted on from the New Jersey granary would not be forthcoming this winter. Accounts flooded in of inconstant Jerseymen renouncing the loyalty oaths they had so recently sworn to the Crown. "I am much disappointed with these conquerors of the world," one loyalist wrote. Regulars abandoned their village outposts, including Hackensack on January 5. When troops marched from Elizabeth Town three days later, a rebel brigade fell on their rear, plundering the baggage train and capturing seventy or more Highlanders and Hessians.

Ten thousand of the king's soldiers would spend the remainder of the season wedged into a narrow, ten-mile strip along the Raritan, from Perth Amboy to New Brunswick, protected by the Royal Navy and surviving on salt pork. Nearly all of New Jersey had been forsaken. British horses and boats were positioned on Staten Island to evacuate the remaining enclave if necessary.

"Surely ye force you have now at Brunswick is full sufficient to drive Washington to ye devil, if you could get at him," Howe wrote General Grant in early January. "Washington's wretched behavior . . . plainly indicates ye inability of his ever standing against us when we are in force." But getting at him this winter would prove insuperable, as Howe conceded in a dispatch to Germain. The Americans had chosen "to throw themselves into a strong country" in northern Jersey. Pursuit seemed pointless since "the enemy moves with so much more celerity than we possibly can."

"I do not now see a prospect of terminating the war but by a general action," Howe added, "and I am aware of the difficulties in our way to obtain it."

The American army scuffed into Morristown at sunset on Monday, January 6, three days after leaving Princeton. Captain Peale noted that his men had "feet covered with ice," and other commanders pleaded for mittens, blankets, and shoes. The Philadelphia Council of Safety had instead sent twenty hogsheads of rum. Blacksmiths repaired wagons and shoed horses, armorers fixed dilapidated firelocks, and filthy, smoke-stained men washed themselves and their tattered raiments. For the first time in months, they felt secure enough to breathe deep and sleep well. "Our late success has given our troops great spirits and [they] seem determined to endure every hardship like good soldiers," Captain Nathan Peters wrote his wife, Lois, who was still tending their saddlery in Massachusetts, as she had since Lexington. A chaplain wrote, "How sudden the transition from darkness to light, from grief to joy."

Cornwallis assured Germain on January 8 that Washington "cannot subsist long where he is." Should he bolt for Pennsylvania, "the march alone will destroy his army." Cornwallis was wrong, again; Washington was going nowhere. The army would remain in this rugged stronghold for almost five months, feeding from the Jersey cornucopia. The village of fifty houses occupied a triangular plateau on the Whippany River, protected by the Watchung Mountains and swamps bracketing the approach road from New York, twenty-six miles to the east. The Americans now had an imposing winter line that extended for 150 miles through the Hudson Highlands to Albany, from which they could chivy enemy foragers straying out of New York and New Brunswick. Captain Lord Harris would write a friend in England on January 16, "Washington, to do him justice, has taken advantage of the moment. . . . The whole country is full of their scouting parties whose greatest ambition is to be behind a cover and kill our light dragoons."

Washington moved into a three-story tavern on the northwest face of the Morristown public square, hard by the courthouse and the Baptist church. The winter campaign was over, but he hardly intended to stop fighting. Within a day he was plotting attacks on New York. "If there is a fair opening," he wrote General Heath in Westchester County, "I would have you make the attempt." His army might rest, but he would not, could not. The cares and calamities of the past eighteen months seemed but a prelude to the worries pressing on him now, from resurgent smallpox in the ranks to the sad fact, as he wrote Hancock, that "the treasury has been for some time empty." To his stepson John Parke Custis, he indulged a rare moment of self-pity:

> All our movements have been made with inferior numbers & with a mixed, motley crew who were here today, gone tomorrow. . . . I do not think that any officer since the creation ever had such a variety of difficulties & perplexities to encounter as I have. . . . Providence has heretofore saved us in a remarkable manner, and on this we must principally rely.

No perplexity was more irksome than trying to keep his army intact. The American cause had profited from "two lucky strokes at Trenton and Princeton," as Washington told General Schuyler, but the spring campaign would require more companies, more battalions, more brigades. From the 7,559 effective soldiers under his command in the attack on Princeton, the ranks dwindled every day from desertion or as temporary enlistments expired and men went home. By mid-January, he warned Hancock, his five Virginia regiments had been "reduced to a handful of men." The outstanding regiments of Smallwood and Hand were also enervated. No more than eight hundred New England Continentals remained in camp. "The fluctuating state of an army composed chiefly of militia bids fair to reduce us to the situation in which we were some little time ago, that is, of scarce having an army at all," he wrote. "We are deceiving our enemies with false opinions of our numbers." Congress had resolved four months earlier to raise eighty-eight regiments for the duration. Where were they? Congress, and the country, would have to decide very soon whether to fight on.

Certainly Washington's eighteen months in command had brought bitter lessons: that war was rarely linear, preferring a path of fits and starts, ups and downs, triumphs and cataclysms; that only battle could reveal those with the necessary dark heart for killing, years of killing; that only those with the requisite stamina, aptitude, and luck would be able to see it through; and finally—the hardest of war's hard truths—that for a new nation to live, young men must die, often alone, usually in pain, and sometimes to no obvious purpose. He, more than anyone, would be responsible for ordering those men to their deaths.

For all that, he was determined to remain buoyant, to convey confidence and resolve. "Our affairs here are in a very prosperous train," he wrote Governor Nicholas Cooke of Rhode Island on January 20. "Within a month past, in several engagements with the enemy, we have killed, wounded, and taken prisoners between two and three thousand. . . . If I am properly supported, I hope to close the campaign gloriously for America."

His faith gave others faith; his strength made others strong. "The consequences must be great," Colonel Stephen Moylan wrote from Morristown. "America will—by God, it *must*—be free. . . . I know I never felt so much like one of Homer's deities before. We trod on air." Henry Knox preferred to paraphrase Shakespeare. "There is a tide in the affairs of men such if taken at the flood leads on to victory," he wrote Lucy.

"I look up to heaven and most devoutly thank the great Governor of the Universe for producing this turn in our affairs of America," he added, "& this sentiment, I hope, will so prevail on the hearts of the people as to induce them to be a people chosen of heaven."

Epilogue

A good hanging always drew a festive crowd in England, and by noon on Monday, March 10, 1777, twenty thousand spectators had gathered outside the royal dockyards in Portsmouth to witness justice meted out on the tallest gallows ever erected in the British Isles. From the *Arethusa*, a frigate recently returned to port after chasing American privateers, carpenters had unstepped the sixty-four-foot mizzenmast, hauled it ashore, then raised the great stick above the street just beyond the yard's main gate. A length of rope dangled almost to the ground. At noon, the murmuring mob parted to make way for the sheriff and a creaking tumbrel, upon which a condemned prisoner sat lashed to a chair.

The doomed man, with his ginger hair and tosspot complexion, hardly looked like a threat to an empire on which the sun never set. Yet his crimes had transfixed Britain for weeks, and, after a seven-hour trial, he had been convicted of plotting—with American connivance—to incinerate the king's naval yards in hopes of fatally weakening the Royal Navy. "That he might himself be a witness to the devastation" he had caused, the tumbrel carried the defendant through the charred, noisome ruins of his greatest success as a firebrand: the thousand-foot Great Double Rope House, where strands of hemp had once been woven into the cordage essential for every man-of-war and merchantman in the fleet. He looked and then looked away, and now the cart turned toward the scaffold.

He had been born in Edinburgh twenty-five years earlier as James Aitken, a blacksmith's son, but he often called himself John the Painter after his chosen trade. He was a stammerer, decently educated—arresting constables found a copy of Ovid's *Metamorphoses* in his kit—and he had worked as a journeyman house painter. But crime paid better, and Aitken took up highway robbery, theft, and burglary before immigrating to America in 1773. After two years in the colonies, he returned to Britain, no richer for the experience but an ardent enthusiast for the American insurrection. He joined the British Army in Liverpool to collect the enlistment bonus, then promptly deserted, a ploy he repeated at least twice with different regiments and under various noms de guerre.

During a visit to Portsmouth in 1776 Aitken had conceived his plot, making sketches and taking notes in the vast dock complex, which he found to be indifferently guarded. He hoped to destroy five yards in all—Plymouth, Chatham, Woolwich, and Deptford also made his list—on the fair assumption that without naval stores, repair basins, mast sheds, sail lofts, and seasoned timber, Britain would find it impossible to make war in America. This past fall he had traveled to Paris, shortly before Franklin's arrival, and met twice with the American envoy Silas Deane, who had been intrigued by Aitken's detailed intelligence on British naval facilities, even if he found the Scotsman's eyes "sparkling and wild." By Aitken's account, Deane gave him seventy-two livres—about £4—and a code name—the number 0—and sent him on his way "to burn and destroy the dockyards and shipping belonging to the government."

In Canterbury he paid an artisan to fashion a firebomb of his own design, using a ten-inch canister, a candle, matches, saltpeter, and turpentine. On the afternoon of December 7, Aitken strolled into the Portsmouth rope house, set three fires, and fled. An alarm bell at 4:35 p.m. brought sailors from the anchorage to help workers fight the blaze; they lost the brick building—damage was placed at £20,000—but saved the yard.

Aitken traveled to Plymouth, found the naval base on high alert, and instead made his way to Bristol, where he set more fires in mid-January, burning several warehouses in Quay Lane. The government, now thoroughly annoyed, offered rewards totaling almost £3,000 for capture of the culprit. On January 16, the Admiralty's first lord, the Earl of Sandwich, sent the king investigative reports about "a suspicious person . . . who went by the name of John the Painter" and had been seen lurking around the Portsmouth docks on the day of that fire. On January 27, Aitken was arrested in Hampshire. His tool bag contained tinder, turpentine, and a powder horn.

A parade of witnesses, including the craftsman who made Aitken's incendiary cylinder and a woman who sold him matches, testified at his trial in Winchester's Great Hall. "The jury talked to each other for a second and then pronounced the prisoner guilty," according to a newspaper account, and the judge suggested that the defendant "prepare himself for eternity into which he would be launched in a few days." A day after his conviction, Aitken gave a detailed confession, asserting that Silas Deane had promised to reward his arson if he escaped to Paris. Deane denied everything. The British government demanded Deane's extradition as "a rebellious British subject," but France refused, and the matter was dropped, if not forgotten.

Aitken spent his final fortnight in a drunken haze within the Winchester jail before being carted to the scene of his crime in Portsmouth for a flamboyant state execution. By midday on Monday, the enormous crowd rivaled the one that had gathered for the king's celebrated inspection of the dockyards four years earlier. Shortly before one p.m., Aitken finished his prayers at the foot of the displaced mizzenmast. No clergyman attended him, according to one witness, which "gave many to think him a Roman Catholic." His head hooded and his neck in a noose, with a final sigh he dropped a handkerchief to signal his acquiescence. A team of 350 executioners—ropemakers from the dockyard who had volunteered their services—hoisted him from the ground with pulleys. He died, slowly, by asphyxiation.

The corpse hung from the scaffold for an hour, then was dipped in tar at the Pitch House Jetty and displayed on a gibbet above the beach at Blockhouse Point, near the harbor entrance. It would dangle there for decades. Here curious gawkers could sip gin purchased from a street chapman and contemplate the consequences of sedition. Here, for every American rebel and those who countenanced them, was a cautionary tale.

An early biographer claimed that George III "was never known to sign a death warrant without expressing visible emotions," but the king showed no particular remorse at the fate of John the Painter. Life would hurry on for the busy monarch and his thriving kingdom. There were the usual pleas to sort out, for royal preferment, clemency, and cash. The queen, who continued to produce babies with germinative determination, had also asked for a new home in Windsor, with its great park and lofty perch above the Thames.

Britain was nearing full employment. Stocks held steady, and a second consecutive bumper crop of wheat had brought lower bread prices. War contracts helped compensate for lost trade in America, and the government expected record revenues in 1777. Among other imperial enterprises, the naval captain James Cook set off again on a voyage of discovery, with instructions "to find a northern passage by sea from the Pacific to the Atlantic Ocean," while noting the "genius, temper, disposition, & number of the natives . . . showing them every kind of civility and regard" before claiming their land for the Crown. Edward Gibbon's first volume on the decline and fall of that earlier empire had been published the previous year to acclaim, with subsequent editions "scarcely adequate to the demand," Gibbon exulted. "My book was on every table and almost on every toilet."

The king more than ever was a man of homely pursuits. His library now included *Hints to Gentlemen of Landed Property*, with chapters on improving pastureland, "the great importance of cottages," and "manures considered." He would soon be known as Farmer George. He continued making his lists and, for reasons unclear, copied extracts of letters by David Hume, the Scottish philosopher and essayist, who had died in August. "I live as I please, spend my time according to my fancy, keep a plentiful table for myself and my friends, amuse myself with reading and society," Hume had written. Perhaps the king was envious, but he also copied a sentence Hume wrote shortly before his death: "Though I have reached a considerable age, I shall not live to see any justice done to me."

The war, of course, remained consuming. George had opened the current session of Parliament by announcing that the Americans had not come to their senses, regrettably, although Canada had been recovered and success in New York offered hope for "the most decisive good consequences." He hewed to his eternal theme: that the iniquity of a few American leaders was responsible for mass delusion in the colonies. "If their treason be suffered to take root," he warned, "much mischief must grow from it." He hoped, indeed prayed, that his subjects would reclaim "the blessings of law and liberty . . . which they have fatally and desperately exchanged for all the calamities of war and the arbitrary tyranny of their chiefs." For now, he added, "We must at all events prepare for another campaign."

Benjamin West, the gifted American artist who had lived in London for more than a decade, happened to be painting the king's portrait when a courier brought in a copy of the Declaration of Independence. By West's account, George grew agitated, then silent before finally muttering, "Well, if they cannot be happy under my government, I hope they may not change it for a worse." The cabinet had replied to Congress by hiring an Anglican deacon to write "An Answer to the Declaration," a windy, 132-page treatise of which eight thousand copies were printed and successively labeled as editions two through five "to give the impression of widespread popularity."

More than hack pamphleteering would be needed to assure Parliament and to steady a nation uneasy at the swelling casualty rolls. Returning to London after a long trip, the writer Nathaniel Wraxall this winter found that the American war "had already begun to shed a degree of political gloom over the capital and kingdom." War costs in the past two years totaled £15 million and were escalating rapidly. Partly to save money and partly because of recruiting difficulties, only eleven thousand troops had been raised for the British Army in the year that had ended in September; over the coming year, just half that number would enlist. A sardonic letter from London to America, dated January 1, claimed:

His Majesty intends to open this year's campaign with ninety thousand Hessians, Tories, Negroes, Japanese, Moors, Esquimaux, Persian archers, Laplanders, Feejee Islanders, and light horse. . . . Ye dumbfounded, infatuated, back-bestridden, nose-led-about, priest-ridden, demagogue-beshackled and Congress-becrafted independents, fly, fly, oh fly, for protection to the royal standard, or ye will be swept from the face of the earth.

The dutiful Lord North showed signs of war-weary strain. After breaking an arm in a fall from his horse, the prime minister grew seriously ill in February. The king disapproved of his treatments—bleedings and opiates—and wrote North on February 24, "I strongly recommend abstinence and water as the ablest and safest physicians." Meanwhile, George would serve as his own war minister, obdurate and unwobbling. Beside those horticultural books in his library was a volume bound in red goatskin morocco with marble endpapers entitled *Establishments of His Majesty's Land Forces and Garrisons, 1776*. In delicate, wispy threads of black ink, every regiment was recorded, along with its size, the per diem for officers, and other vital statistics. An "Abstract of the Foreign Troops" projected that British payrolls in 1777 would carry 23,926 hirelings (apparently exclusive of Esquimaux and Persian archers). *A List of Your Majesty's Royal Navy*, also bound in red morocco with small brass clasps, went on for more than a hundred pages to inform the king that he commanded 125 ships of the line—each carrying sixty guns or more—plus 270 frigates and lesser vessels, from sloops and cutters to schooners, yachts, hoys, and even hulks dating to the seventeenth century. Those 395 men-of-war would collectively be manned by 45,000 sailors in 1777. Ships with dimensions written in red ink "are building or under orders to be built."

Who could doubt the ultimate invincibility of such forces? Through the previous fall and into the new year, the tidings from America had been thrilling. Dispatches had reached London in late December with news of victories won, or at least claimed, at Frog's Neck, Pell's Point, White Plains, Fort Washington, and Fort Lee. George had written Sandwich at "30 minutes past 1 p.m." on December 30 that such accounts "are the most agreeable as they exceed the most sanguine expectations." The enemy army seemed to be all but atomized. The poet laureate, William Whitehead, commemorated the new year with an ode asking Americans—"wayward children" and "parricides"—to seek "the blessings of peace." The poem was set to music, and as January passed the king awaited a herald who would surely announce the capture of Philadelphia, if not the rebel surrender.

Instead, in late February the *Bristol* brought what Lord Germain called the "extremely mortifying" news of Trenton and Princeton. Hardly less disturbing was a request from General Howe for another fifteen thousand troops and eight more ships of the line for the spring campaign. Half of the British Army's seventy infantry regiments had already been sent to America. Even if more soldiers were dispatched, it was by no means certain that the fitful, creaky British supply system could sustain them; feeding the force with provisions obtained in America now appeared to be a fantasy. Howe had also fallen out with two of his most experienced generals, Henry Clinton and Hugh Earl Percy. After Howe peevishly criticized his military judgment in the Rhode Island campaign, Percy wrote, "I am so hurt that nothing on earth shall make me stay here to subject myself to such another indignity." Clinton said simply of Howe, "I cannot bear to serve under him." Both men sailed home in vexation.

"You doubtless must have expected ere this that our arms had brought America to obedience," Major Charles Stuart wrote his father, the former prime minister. "I am sorry to inform you that as yet we have effected nothing. . . . Great Britain seems to have been altogether misled with respect to the revolt of this country." Others were coming to the same dour conclusion. "Poor devils as the rebel generals are, they have outgeneraled us more than once," Colonel Allan Maclean, a hero of Quebec, wrote a friend in mid-February. "Washington this whole winter never had more than 7,000 men in the Jerseys, where we had 16,000, and yet we have been tossed and kicked about most amazingly." In a midwinter epiphany, Admiral Howe told his secretary, Ambrose Serle, that "almost all the people of parts and spirit were in the rebellion." Serle confessed, "I almost wish that the colonies had never existed."

Certain shortcomings in Britain's conduct of the war were clear enough even from London, including the ponderous Jersey campaign and the dispersal of forces from Montreal to South Carolina. General Carleton had liberated Canada and cleared Lake Champlain, yet he had failed to expel the Americans from Ticonderoga or to close the gap with British legions farther south. Howe had lost no battle other than the scraps in Trenton and Princeton, yet somehow he occupied only a small cantonment around New York and another in Rhode Island. The rebels controlled every other acre from Albany to Savannah and virtually all of New England. No regular could safely stray more than a furlong from the sea. "It is to be hoped," Germain wrote after learning of the Princeton debacle, "that the dangerous practice of underestimating the enemy may make a lasting impression on the rest of the army."

The Royal Navy's deficiencies also were evident. Despite sailing 148 warships—brandishing 3,298 carriage guns—through American waters over a period of eighteen months, the navy had largely failed to deny sea-lanes to rebel mariners or to blockade the Chesapeake and Delaware Bays. With most vessels needed to support the army, far too few were free to patrol the Atlantic seaboard. Worries that the Bourbon regimes were secretly preparing for another war further complicated naval deployments. Skeptical of purring assurances from Versailles, Lord Sandwich for months had detected signs of a French and Spanish maritime buildup: more ship-yard workers in Brest, intensified fleet repairs at Cadiz, the stockpiling of stores and a surge in bread baking in Toulon. "The accounts of the French armaments multiply so fast," Sandwich wrote, ". . . that every hour is precious, as the French are certainly ahead in their preparations."

At last, in late fall, the cabinet had agreed to act. The navy was instructed to build more warships, including frigates, "without waiting for seasoning" of timber; hire more shipwrights and ropemakers; release guardships from reserve for active service; and, most dramatically, impose a general press in British waters to augment naval manpower. Twenty armed boats seized a thousand swabs along the Thames alone, minus the eight merchant sailors who drowned trying to swim away. A naval arms race had begun: while fighting the rebellion, British strategists would now be required to look in two directions, toward North America and toward the Continent.

Other aspects of the American war remained opaque or unseen. British commanders and their political masters continued to misjudge the American temperament, both in the broad, visionary commitment to a republican future and in the seething resentments that fueled the insurrection. "I trust," Germain wrote the Howes on March 3, "that the unexpected success of the rebels will not so far elate them as to prevent them from seeing the real horrors of their situation." Thomas Paine, who had a shrewd eye for military matters, was closer to the mark in a public letter to Admiral Howe published in early 1777. "In all the wars which you have formerly been concerned in, you had only armies to contend with," Paine observed. "In this case, you have both an army and a country to combat." The Americans, the Scottish economist Adam Smith warned, "feel in themselves at this moment a degree of importance which, perhaps, the greatest subjects in Europe scarce feel. . . . [They] are employed in contriving a new form of government for an extensive empire, which, they flatter themselves will become, and which indeed seems very likely to become, one of the greatest and most formidable that ever was in the world."

The king would soldier on. "We must, at all events, prepare for another campaign," he had told Parliament. The quick, decisive war he desired would not be so quick. Howe would get his men and his warships, or at least some of them. Guns, powder, and six hundred tons of tentage had already been shipped for the battles to come. Parliament also passed a bill introduced by North in February to suspend habeas corpus—the judicial review of forcible detainment—for prisoners seized in America or on the high seas. The suspension of what had been considered a fundamental right under English law would last for six years.

George steeled himself, certain that Britain's imperial policies reflected a divine design. He was but God's instrument. "The tongue of malice may not paint my intentions in those colors she admires," he had written in an undated private meditation. The king continued:

> I do not pretend to any superior abilities, but will give place to no one in meaning to preserve the freedom, happiness, & glory of my dominions & all their inhabitants, and to fulfill the duty to my God. . . . That I have erred is undoubted, otherwise I should not be human. But . . . where I have failed, it has been from the head, not the heart.

In America the long fighting season had finally ended, bringing to a close what John Adams would call "the most critical and dangerous period of the whole Revolutionary War." Except for the occasional raid or affray, the battlefield would remain quiet until spring thawed the ground and heated the blood. In the two years since shots first rang out on Lexington Common, combatants had fought more than 450 military actions and 90 naval skirmishes, according to a tally by the historian Howard H. Peckham. American casualties now approached 9,000, almost a third of them killed or wounded; of the 6,500 Americans captured, an unconscionable number would die in British prisons.

The American army had not been proficient in any conventional sense. Yet an American way of war was emerging, one that stressed hit-and-run celerity, marksmanship, resilience, and sustainment from the broader population; as Washington intended, the army could claim deep emotional and moral ties to the nation it served. Rebels now controlled virtually every government agency, committee, and department in the country. Despite repeated tactical defeats, Continental soldiers had fought the British to at least a strategic draw. "They possess some of the requisites for making good troops, such as extreme cunning, great industry . . . and a spirit of enterprise," Colonel William Harcourt, the dragoon commander who captured Charles Lee, told his father in March 1777. "They are now become a formidable enemy."

The best American soldiers also displayed heroic fortitude, "the courage of endurance by which men at war survive," as the author Samuel Hynes later described it, "a stoic endurance where there is nothing to be done . . . a fine and difficult virtue." Lonely, homesick, bored, and anxious, they nonetheless accepted their peripatetic existence. Major John Cropper, Jr., of the 7th Virginia Regiment, closed a letter to his wife from Philadelphia with, "I am your most affectionate husband, wherever I go."

"I hope the country will not be discouraged at our making some missteps at first," Colonel William Douglas, who commanded a Connecticut regiment, had written his wife in December. "We are new, but shall be old in time." At age thirty-five, Douglas was as old as he would ever be. After two years of fighting in New England, Canada, and New York, he admitted that "my constitution is unsound and broke"; he returned home with a consumptive cough and died in May. Identifying and promoting new combat leaders to replace the likes of Douglas—as well as Montgomery, Thomas, Mercer, Haslet, and other dead commanders—would be a perpetual struggle for this new army as it grew older.

So, too, would be the integration of state militias into a national, professional armed force. Despite Washington's incessant grumbling about militia indiscipline, the local alarm companies had proven an essential constabulary in suppressing loyalists, confronting enemy foragers, gathering intelligence, protecting civilians, and providing combat reserves at crucial moments. "For sudden exertions, the militia certainly do well," Richard Henry Lee wrote Patrick Henry in January 1777. "But they cannot bear the continued discipline of camps and campaigns." That was fair enough, although as General Washington himself acknowledged, they were "more than competent to all the purposes of defensive war." Precisely that sort of war was likely to obtain for the foreseeable future.

Holding together the army and, thus, the cause would inevitably fall to Washington. He had come within a chin whisker of losing the war on several occasions, demonstrating both misjudgment, notably during the defense of Fort Washington, and battlefield shortcomings, such as his failure to read the terrain or enemy intent on Long Island. His lieutenants had saved him from himself more than once, as when they resisted his proposal to launch a frontal assault at Boston. Such misjudgments and shortcomings would persist in coming campaigns.

Yet the commanding general displayed a gift for improvisation and the deft escape, an ability to grab "the occasion by the forelock," as the British historian George Otto Trevelyan noted. He also listened to advice, learned from mistakes, and showed a keen eye for martial talent. As a political general, he would have few equals and no superior in American history; he had adroitly won over both the Congress and his countrymen, including wary New Englanders. "Our late misfortunes have called out the hidden excellences of our commander in chief," wrote Abigail Adams, who then quoted a favorite line from an English poet: "Affliction is the good man's shining time." Affliction revealed Washington's courage, durability, probity, and administrative skill. Since his appointment to lead the new army, he had developed a shrewd understanding of the refractory, independent peoples known collectively as Americans. "A people unused to restraint must be led," he wrote in January 1777, "they will not be drove." He was a leader.

The cause was hardly won. Independence had been proclaimed, not secured. The bloodletting had just begun. "It may be the will of heaven that Americans shall suffer calamities still more wasting and distresses yet more dreadful," John Adams had predicted the previous July. The distress of civil war unleashed by the rebellion would grow only more searing. "Neighbor was against neighbor, father against son and the son against the father," a Connecticut loyalist wrote in 1777, "and he that would not thrust his own blade through his brother's heart was called an infamous felon." As the New York patriot Gouverneur Morris wrote his mother, a loyalist, "Great revolutions of empire are seldom achieved without much human calamity."

Faith would be needed to sustain these revolutionaries—faith in one another and in the America they imagined could emerge from this strife. "I am sure the cause we are engaged in is just, and the call I have to it is clear," the aged Connecticut warrior Seth Pomeroy wrote his son in mid-February, a week before his death. "Who would not go cheerfully, and confront every danger? My love to all the family." In a letter to his son Thomas, age nine, Brigadier General Samuel Holden Parsons wrote, "Remember if I fall in this war, I shall expect you & all my sons to arm in defense of the glorious cause of liberty & lay down your lives in defense of your country, & to avenge my death if necessary."

Yes, more distresses and calamities lay ahead, as Adams foresaw. But he took comfort in believing that the great struggle would remain "an astonishment to vulgar minds all over the world, in this and in future generations." Words evincing a similar sentiment had been scribbled in the orderly book of the 2nd New York Regiment, and they read like lyrics for an anthem sung by a people on the march:

The rising world shall sing of us a thousand years to come
And tell our children's children the wonders we have done.

Author's Note

Given the distracting inconsistency in eighteenth-century punctuation, spelling, capitalization, abbreviation, and grammar, I have corrected some of the more archaic or unorthodox extracts quoted from letters and other written sources. My intent is to improve accessibility and sense for a contemporary reader, while respecting the original meaning, language, and voice.

The abbreviated prefix *HMS*, for "His Majesty's Ship," was not in use until several years after the American Revolution ended. Therefore it does not appear in this account.

Notes

The following abbreviations appear in the endnotes and bibliography. A list of additional unpublished documents, monographs, and websites used in this book appears online at www
.revolutiontrilogy.com.

AA Peter Force, *American Archives* (series, volume, page; e.g., IV: 2, 630)
AFC L. H. Butterfield, ed., *Adams Family Correspondence*
AHR American Historical Review
ANTA Douglas R. Cubbison, *The American Northern Theater Army in 1776*
AP The Adams Papers, Robert J. Taylor et al., eds., FOL
B 1775 Boston 1775 blog, J. L. Bell, www.boston1775.blogspot.com
BA Benedict Arnold
Baldwin Jeduthan Baldwin, *The Revolutionary Journal of Col. Jeduthan Baldwin, 1775–1778*
BARH James Kirby Martin, *Benedict Arnold, Revolutionary Hero*
BC Bancroft Collection, NYPL, Revolutionary Papers
BF Benjamin Franklin
BFTM Bulletin of the Fort Ticonderoga Museum
BNY Barnet Schecter, *The Battle for New York: The City at the Heart of the American Revolution*
BPMP Robert A. Selig et al., "Battle of Princeton Mapping Project: Report of Military Terrain Analysis and Battle Narrative," John Milner Associates, for the Princeton Battlefield Society, Sept. 2010, https://www.mfriends.org/07/library/documents/BATTLEOFPRINCETONMAPPING PROJECT.pdf.
BTP William S. Stryker, *The Battles of Trenton and Princeton*
C 1776 Henry P. Johnston, *The Campaign of 1776 Around New York and Brooklyn*
CFPL Concord Free Public Library
CGW Edward G. Lengel, ed., *A Companion to George Washington*
Chase Ellen Chase, *The Beginnings of the American Revolution*, 3 vols.
CHS Connecticut Historical Society, Hartford
CMSA Commonwealth of Massachusetts State Archives
corr. correspondence
CP Alfred Hoyt Bill, *The Campaign of Princeton, 1776–1777*
Cruikshank Ernest Cruikshank et al., eds., *A History of the Organization, Development and Services of the Military and Naval Forces of Canada*, vol. 2
D&AJA L. H. Butterfield, ed., *Diary and Autobiography of John Adams*
DAR K. G. Davies, ed., *Documents of the American Revolution, 1770–1783*
DCL Allen French, *The Day of Concord and Lexington*
Deary William Paul Deary, "Toward Disaster at Fort Washington, November 1776," Ph.D. diss., George Washington University, 1996
DFM Frederick Mackenzie, *Diary of Frederick Mackenzie*, vol. 1
diss. dissertation
DLAR David Library of the American Revolution, Washington's Crossing, Pennsylvania
DNH Don N. Hagist, *British Soldiers, American Revolution*, www.redcoat76.blogspot.com

ECB Edwin C. Bearrs, "The Battle of Sullivan's Island and the Capture of Fort Moultrie," NPS, June 30, 1968

Evacuation George E. Ellis, *Celebration of the Centennial Anniversary of the Evacuation of Boston*

Evelyn G. D. Scull, ed., *Memoir and Letters of Captain W. Glanville Evelyn, of the 4th Regiment ("King's Own")*

f folio

FL Firestone Library, Princeton University

FOL Founders Online, U.S. National Archives, http://founders.archives.gov/documents/

Fourteenth Mark R. Anderson, *The Battle for the Fourteenth Colony: America's War of Liberation in Canada, 1774–1776*

Freeman Douglas Southall Freeman, *George Washington: A Biography*, vol. 4

Fusilier Frederick Mackenzie, *A British Fusilier in Revolutionary Boston*, ed. Allen French

FYAR Allen French, *The First Year of the American Revolution*

GC Robert Middlekauff, *The Glorious Cause: The American Revolution, 1763–1789*

GCL John Richard Alden, *General Charles Lee: Traitor or Patriot?*

GGW Edward G. Lengel, *General George Washington: A Military Life*

Graves "The Conduct of Vice-Admiral Samuel Graves in North America," 2 vols., manuscript copy, JHU, no pagination

GW George Washington

GWGO George Athan Billias, ed., *George Washington's Generals and Opponents*

GW HQ J. L. Bell, "George Washington's Headquarters and Home," NPS, Feb. 2012

HBAR Ira D. Gruber, *The Howe Brothers and the American Revolution*

HD Harbottle Dorr, Jr., newspaper collection, MHS

HH Henry P. Johnston, *The Battle of Harlem Heights, September 16, 1776*

HL Huntington Library, San Marino, California

HOB Benjamin Franklin Stevens, ed., *General Sir William Howe's Orderly Book*

IMI I. N. Phelps Stokes, *The Iconography of Manhattan Island, 1498–1909*

JAMA *Journal of the American Medical Association*

JAR *Journal of the American Revolution*, www.allthingsliberty.com

JHD John Knox Laughton, ed., "Journals of Henry Duncan, Captain, Royal Navy, 1776–1782," *The Naval Miscellany*, vol. 1, *Publications of the Navy Records Society* 20 (1902)

JHU Johns Hopkins University Library, Baltimore

JMH *Journal of Military History*

Koke Richard J. Koke, "The Struggle for the Hudson," *New-York Historical Society Quarterly* 40, no. 2 (Apr. 1956)

KP *The Kemble Papers: Journals of Lieut.-Col. Stephen Kemble, 1773–1789*, vol. 1, *Collections*, NYHS, 1883, https://archive.org/details/kemblepapers01howegoog

LAC Library and Archives of Canada, Ottawa

LAR Margaret Wheeler Willard, ed., *Letters on the American Revolution, 1774–1776*

LHEP Charles Knowles Bolton, ed., *Letters of Hugh Earl Percy, from Boston and New York, 1774–1776*

Logistics R. Arthur Bowler, *Logistics and the Failure of the British Army in America, 1775–1783*

LP Charles Lee, *The Lee Papers*, NYHS

Lydenberg Harry Miller Lydenberg, ed., "Archibald Robertson: His Diaries and Sketches in America, 1762–1780," *Bulletin of the New York Public Library* 37, no. 11 (Nov. 1933)

Mahan Alfred Thayer Mahan, *The Major Operations of Navies in the War of American Independence*

MCBC Hugh F. Rankin, "The Moore's Creek Bridge Campaign, 1776," *North Carolina Historical Review* 30, no. 1 (Jan. 1953)

MGRM Michael Paul Gabriel, "Major General Richard Montgomery," Ph.D. diss., Pennsylvania State University, 1996

MHQ *Military History Quarterly*

MHS Massachusetts Historical Society, Boston

micro microfilm

MLA Andrew Jackson O'Shaughnessy, *The Men Who Lost America*

MMNHP Minute Man National Historical Park, Massachusetts

MQ Kenneth Roberts, *March to Quebec*

NCCH W. Hugh Moomaw, "The Naval Career of Captain Hamond, 1775–1779," Ph.D. diss., University of Virginia, 1955

n.d. no date

NDAR William Bell Clark et al., eds., *Naval Documents of the American Revolution*

NG Nathanael Greene

n.p. no place

NPS National Park Service

NYHS New-York Historical Society, New York City

NYPL New York Public Library

PBF Leonard W. Labaree et al., eds., *The Papers of Benjamin Franklin*, FOL

PGW W. W. Abbot et al., eds., *The Papers of George Washington*, Revolutionary War Series, University Press of Virginia

PH 18 *The Parliamentary History of England*, vol. 18, 1774–1777

PMHB *Pennsylvania Magazine of History and Biography*

PNG Richard K. Showman et al., eds., *The Papers of General Nathanael Greene*, vol. 1, 1766–1776

PRR David Hackett Fischer, *Paul Revere's Ride*

QMG quartermaster general

RA Royal Archives, Papers of George III, Windsor Castle, England

RI Revolutionary Imprints

RWLLLHK Philip Hamilton, *The Revolutionary War Lives and Letters of Lucy and Henry Knox*

Sabin Douglas P. Sabin, *April 19, 1775: A Historiographical Study*

Salsig Doyen Salsig, ed., *Parole: Quebec; Countersign: Ticonderoga*

Sandwich G. R. Barnes and J. H. Owen, eds., *The Private Papers of John, Earl of Sandwich, First Lord of the Admiralty, 1771–82*

Serle Edward H. Tatum, Jr., ed., *The American Journal of Ambrose Serle*

Shelton Hal T. Shelton, *General Richard Montgomery and the American Revolution: From Redcoat to Rebel*

Siege Richard Frothingham, Jr., *History of the Siege of Boston*

SoC Society of the Cincinnati

s.p. self-published

Spirit '76 Henry Steele Commager and Richard B. Morris, eds., *The Spirit of 'Seventy-Six*

Stevens's Benjamin Franklin Stevens, *B.F. Stevens's Facsimiles of Manuscripts in European Archives*

Stopford-Sackville Historical Manuscripts Commission, *Report on the Manuscripts of Mrs. Stopford-Sackville, of Drayton House, Northamptonshire*

Struggle Justin H. Smith, *Our Struggle for the Fourteenth Colony: Canada and the American Revolution*, 2 vols.

TAR Henry Clinton, *The American Rebellion*

T-P RC Thompson-Pell Research Center, Fort Ticonderoga, New York

ts typescript

UK NA National Archives, Kew, U.K. (formerly Public Record Office)

VBRP Arthur B. Cohn et al., "Valcour Bay Research Project: 1999–2002 Result," Lake Champlain Maritime Museum et al., June 2003

VMHB *Virginia Magazine of History and Biography*

WAI Don Higginbotham, *The War of American Independence: Military Attitudes, Policies, and Practice, 1763–1789*

WC David Hackett Fischer, *Washington's Crossing*

WLC William L. Clements Library, University of Michigan, Ann Arbor

WMQ *William and Mary Quarterly*

WR Christopher Ward, *The War of the Revolution*

PROLOGUE

1 *At three-thirty a.m.:* London Chronicle, June 19, 1773; *General Evening Post*, June 22, 1773; Fortescue, ed., *The Correspondence of King George the Third*, vol. 2, 513 (*"almost impossible"*);

London Evening Post, June 17, 1773 (*"admirals, captains"*); *London Chronicle*, June 19, 1773 (*ten guineas*).

1 *The king himself*: Private Papers, undated, RA GEO/MAIN/#16004–16005; *London Chronicle*, June 19, 1773 (*"three whores"*); Gomme, ed., *The Gentleman's Magazine Library*, 224.

2 *Bells pealed in welcome*: Brooke, *King George III*, 79; author visit, June 2014; *General Evening Post*, June 22, 1773 (*Portsdown Hill*).

2 *Half an hour later*: *General Evening Post*, June 22, 1773 (*White Boys*); author visit, Portsmouth Historic Dockyard, June 2014; "An Account of the Naval Review at Portsmouth," *Annual Register 1773*, 202–07 (*232 guns*); *Morning Chronicle and London Advertiser*, June 30, 1773 (*"will not hurt me"*).

2 *Most of his cabinet ministers*: *Public Advertiser*, June 21, 1773; "An Account of the Naval Review at Portsmouth," *Annual Register 1773*, 202–07 (*"prove victorious"*; *London Evening Post*, June 24, 1773 (*"Wooden Walls"*).

2 *Then it was off*: Marsh, "An Account of the Preparation Made for and the Entertainment of the King at Portsmouth in June 1773," *Colburn's United Service Magazine* (1887), part 1, 433–522; Fortescue, ed., *The Correspondence of King George the Third*, vol. 2, 495 (Fubbs).

3 *Most imposing*: Masefield, *Sea Life in Nelson's Time*, 12; Sandwich account, Portsmouth inspection, UK NA, ADM 7/660, f. 1–27 (Royal Oak); *General Evening Post*, June 24, 1773 (*Spectators lined the walls*).

3 *As he braced himself*: Brooke, *King George III*, 17–18, 79; George to Lord Holderness, Apr. 6, 1774, George III, Private Papers, RA GEO/MAIN/#16009 (*"air, moderate exercise"*); Ayling, *George the Third*, 183; Black, *George III*, 276–77, 406–10; Hibbert, *George III*, 111, 267 (*porphyria*). I am grateful to Dr. Peter C. Agre, a Nobel Prize winner in chemistry at Johns Hopkins University, for his insights on porphyria in October 2017.

3 *Unkind and untrue things*: Plumb, "Our Last King," *American Heritage* 11, no. 4 (June 1960); Brooke, *King George III*, 23; Hibbert, *George III*, 19–20, 73–75, 84 (*"easily abashed"*) and Hibbert, *George III*, 84 (*"wonderful way"*); Namier, "King George III: A Study in Personality," *History Today* 3, no. 1 (Jan. 1953): 610+ (*"sins of his neighbor"*); MLA, 20 (*transit of Venus*); author visit, Royal Library, Windsor Castle, Apr. 14–15, 2016 (*sixty-five thousand books*).

4 *Even his idiosyncrasies*: Ayling, *George the Third*, 175; Private Papers, undated, RA GEO/MAIN/#15659, #15669, #15662, #15676; Huish, *Public and Private Life of His Late Excellent and Most Gracious Majesty, George the Third*, 349 (*"What!"*); William W. Burke and Linnea M. Bass, "Preparing a British Unit for Service in America, the Brigade of Foot Guards, 1776," http://military-historians.org/company/journal/guards/guards.htm (*straps*).

4 *"Born and educated in this country"*: Scott, *British Foreign Policy in the Age of the American Revolution*, 38; Plumb, *England in the Eighteenth Century*, 50–51; Reitan, "The Civil List in Eighteenth-Century British Politics," *Historical Journal* 9, no. 3 (1966): 318+; Fleming, *1776, Year of Illusions*, 81; MLA, 11 (*reforms of the last century*); Ayling, *George the Third*, 179–80 (*"apt to despise"*).

4 *"pertinacity that marks little minds"*: Brougham, *Sketches of Statesmen of the Time of George III*, vol. 3, 9; Pares, *King George III and the Politicians*, 64–65 (*"unforgiving piety"*).

5 *"the wickedest age"*: Hadlow, *A Royal Experiment*, 118; Morris, *The American Revolution Reconsidered*, 32–33.

5 *His obstinacy derived*: Pares, *King George III and the Politicians*, 67–68; Sandwich, vol. 1, xviii; undated documents, "George III Calendar, Sept. 1775–Oct. 1777," RA GEO/MAIN/#2264–#2287 (*endless lists*); Black, *George III*, 118 (*uniform*).

5 *And if his subjects cheered*: Wood, *The American Revolution*, 4–5; Brewer, *The Sinews of Power*, 180, 184 (*European urban growth* and *140,000 retail shops*); Thompson, *The Revolutionary War*, 23; Plumb, *England in the Eighteenth Century*, 82 (*Sheep would double*).

5 *War had played*: Spring, *With Zeal and with Bayonets Only*, 3–4; Coakley and Conn, *The War of the American Revolution*, 13–14; Richard Cavendish, "History Today," 57, no. 3, Mar. 3, 2007, http://www.historytoday.com/richard-cavendish/execution-admiral-byng (*Admiral John Byng*).

5 *The others had indeed*: Syrett, *Shipping and Military Power in the Seven Years War*, 2; Spring, *With Zeal and with Bayonets Only*, 14 (*capturing strongholds*); Brown, *The Good Americans*, 17 ("*Our bells are worn*").

6 *Spoils under the Treaty of Paris*: Wood, *The Radicalism of the American Revolution*, 127; Mackesy, *The War for America*, xiv (*Spain ceded*); Kennedy, *The Rise and Fall of British Naval Mastery*, 105; Gipson, *The Coming of the Revolution*, 6–7; Haas, "The Royal Dockyards: The Earliest Visitations and Reform, 1749–1778," *Historical Journal* 13, no. 2 (1970): 191+ (*nation's largest employer*).

6 "*There shall be*": James, *The British Navy in Adversity*, 19; Countryman, *The American Revolution*, 43; McDougall, *Freedom Just Around the Corner*, 204 ("*completion of happiness*"); Carp, *Defiance of the Patriots*, 22 ("*sun never sets*").

6 *The king had agreed to dine*: "An Account of the Naval Review at Portsmouth," *Annual Register 1773*, 202–07.

6 *More than two thousand mature oaks*: Masefield, *Sea Life in Nelson's Time*, 10–11, 17, 28, 74–75; Volo, *Blue Water Patriots*, 122; Keegan, *The Price of Admiralty*, 1–2 (*wooden world sang*); Rodger, *The Wooden World*, 61 (*sleeping width*).

7 *Thirty dining companions*: Marsh, "An Account of the Preparation Made for and the Entertainment of the King at Portsmouth in June 1773," *Colburn's United Service Magazine* (1887), part 1, 433–522.

7 *At six p.m., the assembled guests*: "An Account of the Naval Review at Portsmouth," *Annual Register 1773*, 202–07; *London Evening Post*, June 24, 1773 (*farthing candles*); *General Evening Post*, June 24, 1773 (*a finer day*).

7 *The king was quartered*: Fortescue, ed., *The Correspondence of King George the Third*, vol. 2, 502; Sandwich account, Portsmouth inspection, UK NA, ADM 7/660, f. 1–27 (*Foot Guards*); Marsh, "An Account of the Preparation Made for and the Entertainment of the King at Portsmouth in June 1773," *Colburn's United Service Magazine* (1887), part 1, 433–522 (*Victory*).

7 *James Boswell might hug*: Brooke, *King George III*, 167; Brebner, *Canada: A Modern History*, 73; Bunker, *An Empire on the Edge*, 107–08 (*thirty separate colonies*); Bailyn, *Voyagers to the West*, 26 (*3 percent*), 40 ("*disease of wandering*"), 57, 59–60 ("*epidemical*" and "*America madness*"); Robson, *The American Revolution, in Its Political and Military Aspects, 1763–1783*, 2–3; Edler, *The Dutch Republic and the American Revolution*, 10–12 (*smoldering resentments*); Tucker and Hendrickson, *The Fall of the First British Empire*, 48; Scott, *British Foreign Policy in the Age of the American Revolution*, 33, 40.

8 *Then there was debt*: Tucker and Hendrickson, *The Fall of the First British Empire*, 86–87; Scott, *British Foreign Policy in the Age of the American Revolution*, 49 (*bankruptcy*). The national debt would reach £245 million by spring 1775. *MLA*, 75–76. Public spending by the British government in 1773 was about £11.3 million. Bunker, *An Empire on the Edge*, 378.

8 *Europe's most heavily taxed citizens*: *MLA*, 13; Brewer, *The Sinews of Power*, 214; *GC*, 61.

8 *The cost of this week's extravaganza*: *Public Advertiser*, June 21, 1773 (*£22,000*). The Royal Navy's expenses exceeded £7,000. Marsh, "An Account of the Preparation Made for and the Entertainment of the King at Portsmouth in June 1773," *Colburn's United Service Magazine* (1887), part 1, 433–522.

8 *paid no more than sixpence*: This is Lord North's calculation in February 1775. *PH* 18, 222; Hibbert, *George III: A Personal History*, 122.

8 *soon exceeded £400,000 a year*: Draper, *A Struggle for Power*, 202, 214n, 299; *WAI*, 29; Wood, *The American Revolution*, 18. Those British regiments were also intended to keep colonists from expanding into the western territories. Ben Baack, "The Economics of the American Revolutionary War," Ohio State University, n.d., https://eh.net/encyclopedia/the-economics-of-the-american-revolutionary-war/.

8 *The Stamp Act, adopted in 1765*: Hibbert, *Redcoats and Rebels*, xix; "The Stamp Act Meets the Bottom Line," *B 1775*, Mar. 18, 2016 (*£45*); *WR*, 8–9; Burrows and Wallace, *Gotham*, 203.

8 *English workers*: Clark, *British Opinion and the American Revolution*, 43–45; *GC*, 112 ("*Where this spirit*"); Hibbert, *Redcoats and Rebels*, 10–11 ("*Champagne Charlie*"); Archer, *As If an*

Enemy's Country, 225; Draper, *A Struggle for Power*, 201; Cometti, ed., *The American Journals of Lt. John Enys*, xviii–xx ("*the Vein Openers*").

9 *An edgy calm returned*: Tucker and Hendrickson, *The Fall of the First British Empire*, 282–83; Buel, *In Irons*, 31 (*economic leverage*); Ketchum, *The Winter Soldiers*, 44 ("*salutary neglect*"); Draper, *A Struggle for Power*, 36 (*fiscal matters*), 113–14 (*hats*), 331 (*cloth*); Plumb, *England in the Eighteenth Century*, 127 ("*no taxation*"); McCullough, *John Adams*, 61.

9 *George had never traveled*: Ayling, *George the Third*, 205; Alden, *The American Revolution*, 8; *GC*, 36 (*doubling every quarter century*); Edmund S. Morgan, "Conflict and Consensus in the American Revolution," in Kurtz and Hutson, eds., *Essays on the American Revolution*, 298 (*European history*); Draper, *A Struggle for Power*, 103 (*fourfold England's rate*); Wood, *The Radicalism of the American Revolution*, 123 (*two-thirds of white colonial men*); May, *The Enlightenment in America*, 35 (*two-thirds were literate*); Wood, *The Americanization of Benjamin Franklin*, 102 (*two-thirds could vote*). The bookshop census extended from 1761 to 1776. Bridenbaugh, *Cities in Revolt*, 380–81.

9 *Also: that eradication*: Gipson, *The Coming of the Revolution*, 215–16; *WAI*, 5 (*crude iron*); Volo, *Blue Water Patriots*, 115; Augur, *The Secret War of Independence*, 41 (*thousand American vessels*).

10 *And: that unlike the Irish*: Shy, "A New Look at Colonial Militia," *WMQ*, 3rd ser., 20, no. 2 (Apr. 1963): 175+.

10 *Sensing its own ignorance*: survey of colonial governors, Henry Strachey Papers, WLC.

10 *seven hours of sleep*: Hibbert, *George III: A Personal History*, 105.

10 *No fool, he was up early*: undated notes, "George III Calendar, Jan. 1774–Aug. 1775," RA GEO/MAIN/#1931; Marsh, "An Account of the Preparation Made for and the Entertainment of the King at Portsmouth in June 1773," *Colburn's United Service Magazine* (1887), part 1, 433–522; "Two Loyal Songs, Proposed to Be Sung Before His Majesty," printed by R. Lee, June 23, 1773, "George III Calendar, July 1772–Dec. 1773, Windsor Castle," RA GEO/MAIN/#1594; "An Account of the Naval Review at Portsmouth," *Annual Register 1773*, 202–07; *Morning Chronicle and London Advertiser*, June 30, 1773.

10 *A half dozen obsolete ships*: Sandwich account, Portsmouth inspection, UK NA, ADM 7/660, f. 1–27.

10 *The Princess Royal*: Black and Woodfine, eds., *The British Navy and the Use of Naval Power in the Eighteenth Century*, 4; Masefield, *Sea Life in Nelson's Time*, 10; Haas, "The Royal Dockyards: The Earliest Visitations and Reform, 1749–1778," *Historical Journal* 13, no. 2 (1970): 191+ (*green timber*).

11 *The urgent naval demands*: Sandwich, vol. 1, 5; Albion, *Forests and Sea Power*, 11–13, 28 (*forty yards long*) ; Graham, *The Royal Navy in the War of Independence*, 4–8; Rodger, *The Command of the Ocean*, 370–71 (*nearing the end*); Knight, "New England Forests and British Seapower: Albion Revised," *American Neptune* 46, no. 4 (Fall 1986): 221+; Knight, "The Building and Maintenance of the British Fleet During the Anglo-French Wars, 1688–1815," *Les Marines de Guerre Européennes*, 38–39 (*two shillings*).

11 *Uneasy lay the head*: Marsh, "An Account of the Preparation Made for and the Entertainment of the King at Portsmouth in June 1773," *Colburn's United Service Magazine* (1887), part 1, 433–522; *London Gazette*, June 26, 1773; Black, *George III*, 98 ("*God Save the King*").

11 *"The king is exceeding"*: Black, *George III*, 98; *General Evening Post*, June 24, 1773; *Lloyds Evening Post*, June 28, 1773.

11 *Later in the year*: Bunker, *An Empire on the Edge*, 191.

12 *"We have troublesome times"*: Gerlach, ed., *New Jersey in the American Revolution*, 134.

12 *Seventeen million pounds*: Carp, *Defiance of the Patriots*, 14, 23 (*opium*); *WR*, 12–13; Labaree, *The Boston Tea Party*, 59; Ferling, *John Adams: A Life*, 90 (*tottered toward bankruptcy*); Murdoch, ed., *Rebellion in America*, 115–16 (*broader British economy*).

12 *Just before the king's excursion*: Labaree, *The Boston Tea Party*, 73, 77; *GC*, 226; Ayling, *George the Third*, 242; Murdoch, ed., *Rebellion in America*, 115–16; *MLA*, 52–53; Morgan, *The Birth of the Republic*, 58; Philbrick, *Bunker Hill*, 8–9 (*more than a third*).

12   *Too clever by half*: Schlesinger, *The Colonial Merchants and the American Revolution*, 592; Christie, *Crisis of the Empire*, 81; Tiedemann et al., *The Other Loyalists*, 8 (*other commodities*); Clark, *British Opinion and the American Revolution*, 73–75; Ketchum, *Divided Loyalties*, 234 (*"weak, effeminate"*); Breen, *The Marketplace of Revolution*, 307 (*"spasms, vapors"*).

12   *"dressed in the Indian manner"*: GC, 232.

13   *three merchant ships*: Labaree, *The Boston Tea Party*, 141–43; Carp, *Defiance of the Patriots*, 129, 139 (*"The devil"*); Parker, *The Power of the Sea*, 31–32 (*brown flakes*); PRR, 299 (*equestrian silversmith*); *Spirit '76*, 3 (*"Rally, Mohawks"*).

13   *"I am much hurt"*: Carp, *Defiance of the Patriots*, 187; Labaree, *The Boston Tea Party*, 179 (*"great wrath"*); "Queries of George Chalmers, with the Answers of General Gage," *Collections*, MHS, vol. 4 (*one witness*); Linebaugh and Rediker, *The Many-Headed Hydra*, 221 (*"metropolis"*); Hibbert, *Redcoats and Rebels*, 24 (*salted ruins*); Fowles, "Craft's Journal of the Siege of Boston," *Historical Collections of the Essex Institute* 3, no. 2 (Apr. 1861): 133+ (*Dictionary Johnson*); Kallich and MacLeish, eds., *The American Revolution Through British Eyes*, 66 (*"race of convicts"*); Donne, ed., *The Correspondence of King George the Third with Lord North*, vol. 2, 8 (*"threatenings and slaughter"*).

13   *What should be done?*: Clark, *British Opinion and the American Revolution*, 84–85; McCusker and Menard, *The Economy of British America*, 43, 284–86 (*20 percent*); Mackesy, *The War for America*, 37 (*Adam Smith*); Hofstadter, ed., *Great Issues in American History*, vol. 2, 46 (*"not an empire"*); Anderson, *The Command of the Howe Brothers During the American Revolution*, 32–41.

14   *"my deluded subjects"*: *The Parliamentary History of England*, vol. 17, 1771–1774, 1407; Draper, *A Struggle for Power*, 415 (*"high treason"*); Robson, *The American Revolution*, 23 (*"anarchy"*).

14   *George's resolve*: Burk, *Old World, New World*, 147; Christie, *Crisis of Empire*, 94–95; Kallich and MacLeish, eds., *The American Revolution Through British Eyes*, 58 (*"insignificance"*).

14   *Here, then, was the crux*: Ellis, *His Excellency: George Washington*, 90; Greene, *Understanding the American Revolution*, 2 (*"Destruction"*); Tucker and Hendrickson, *The Fall of the First British Empire*, 356, 383; Christie, *Crisis of Empire*, 90. Sir Joseph Yorke warned of Europe's scorn. H. M. Scott, *British Foreign Policy in the Age of the American Revolution*, 195.

14   *From late March through June 1774*: McDougall, *Freedom Just Around the Corner*, 227–28; Carp, *Defiance of the Patriots*, 191–93; Bunker, *An Empire on the Edge*, 268; GC, 236–37; Roberts, ed., *Calendar of Home Office Papers of the Reign of George III*, 199 (*British troops*).

15   *With exquisitely bad timing*: Morgan, *The Birth of the Republic*, 60; McDougall, *Freedom Just Around the Corner*, 227–28; Bunker, *An Empire on the Edge*, 276.

15   *"The die"*: Hibbert, *Redcoats and Rebels*, 25.

15   *Despite London's hope of isolating*: Schlesinger, *The Colonial Merchants and the American Revolution*, 307–09; Labaree, *The Boston Tea Party*, 238 (*food, firewood*).

15   *In September, fifty-five delegates*: Wood, *The American Revolution*, 48; Gross, *The Minutemen and Their World*, 58; GC, 253–54, 263–66, 565 (*the Association*); Bushman, *The American Farmer in the Eighteenth Century*, 180 (*publicly shamed*); Breen, *The Marketplace of Revolution*, 298–99, 325–27 (*seven thousand*).

15   *"A most daring spirit"*: PH 18, 33; Ferling, "Myths of the American Revolution," *Smithsonian*, Jan. 2010; Brooke, *King George III*, 171 (*"great lenity"*); Donne, ed., *The Correspondence of King George the Third with Lord North*, vol. 1, 214 (*"Blows must decide"*).

16   *London on the march*: Plumb, *England in the Eighteenth Century*, 12, 89; *Annual Register*, 1775, 83 (*Tyburn gallows*); Porter, *English Society in the Eighteenth Century*, 135 (*two hundred capital crimes*).

16   *The largest city*: Wood, *The Radicalism of the American Revolution*, 59; Chancellor, *The XVIIIth Century in London*, 39; Schwartz, *Daily Life in Johnson's London*, 18, 40; Schama, *Rough Crossings*, 21; Simpson, ed., *The Waiting City*, 224; Schwartz, *Daily Life in Johnson's London*, 161–62 (*Charlies*), 3, 16; Grosely, *A Tour to London*, 45; George, *London Life in the Eighteenth Century*, 85 (*catgut spinners*).

16   *The city had 42 markets*: Conlin, *Tales of Two Cities*, 84; Simpson, ed., *The Waiting City*, 228–29 (*Tobias Smollett*), 45–46 (*Mary Tofts*); Porter, *English Society in the Eighteenth*

Century, 264 (*ten thousand prostitutes*); Arnold, *City of Sin*, 111–15 ("*posture molls*"); Schwartz, *Daily Life in Johnson's London*, 84–85, 103 (*armless man*); George, *London Life in the Eighteenth Century*, 159–62, 204 (*beards stained green*).

17   *For those whose carriages*: Bunker, *An Empire on the Edge*, 351; Plumb, *The First Four Georges*, 101 (*drab German princess*); Brooke, *King George III*, 84 (*six hours after her arrival*); Hadlow, *A Royal Experiment*, 162 (*blue damask*). Charlotte was born in May, but her birthday was officially celebrated on January 18, to avoid crowding the king's birthday in early June.

17   *A peal of bells*: Fitzgerald, *The Good Queen Charlotte*, 70; *Morning Chronicle and London Advertiser*, Jan. 19, 1775; *Middlesex Journal and Evening Advertiser*, Jan. 19–21, 1775; *London Gazette*, Jan. 17–21, 1775.

17   *The evening began badly*: Simpson, ed., *The Waiting City*, 230–31; *Morning Post and Daily Advertiser*, Jan. 20, 1775; *London Chronicle, or Universal Evening Post*, Jan. 17–19, 1775; *Middlesex Journal and Evening Advertiser*, Jan. 19–21, 1775.

17   *Pigmented ceruse*: Schwartz, *Daily Life in Johnson's London* , 128; exhibition signage, Number One, the Royal Crescent, Bath, author visit, Apr. 9, 2016 (*mouse skins*); Quincy, *Memoir of the Life of Josiah Quincy Jun.*, 318 ("*The dresses*"); "George III Calendar, Sept. 1775–Oct. 1777," RA GEO/MAIN/#2501 (*177 peers*); *Gentleman's Magazine*, vol. 45 (1775): 44 (*diamond stomacher*); *Morning Chronicle and London Advertiser*, Jan. 19, 1775 ("*more brilliants*").

18   *The king, regal in a suit*: *St. James Chronicle, or the British Evening Post*, Jan. 17–19, 1775; Bunker, *An Empire on the Edge*, 352–56; Andrews, *Guide to the Materials for American History*, vol. 1, 21; Jensen, *The Founding of a Nation*, 573–74 ("*general plan*"); Ira D. Gruber, "George III Chooses a Commander in Chief," in Hoffman and Albert, eds., *Arms and Independence*, 169.

18   *House of Commons*: St. Stephen's Chapel, www.parliament.uk; Thomas, *The House of Commons in the Eighteenth Century*, 5; Will Monk, "A Brief Guide to the British Government," *JAR*, Sept. 10, 2015, 4.

18   "*papers relating to the disturbances*": PH 18, 74–149; Gipson, *The Triumphant Empire*, 277.

18   *Slouched on the Treasury bench*: Ferling, *Almost a Miracle*, 25; Jesse, *Memoirs of Celebrated Etonians*, vol. 2, 251 ("*prominent eyes*"); Marlow, *Sackville of Drayton*, 2 ("*old hulk*").

19   *In the first decade*: Dull, *A Diplomatic History of the American Revolution*, 26–27; Smith, *The Early Career of Lord North the Prime Minister*, 277; Brooke, *King George III*, 103 (*unsteady handling*); Jesse, *Memoirs of Celebrated Etonians*, vol. 2, 235–36 (*childhood playmate*); George to Lord North, Nov. 5, 1770, Private Papers, undated and 1755–1782, RA GEO/MAIN/#15898 ("*most private and delicate*"), and subsequent exchanges, RA GEO/MAIN/#15899, #15900; *Oxford Dictionary of National Biography*, www.oxforddnb.com/view/article/11669; Tillyard, *A Royal Affair*, 166–81.

19   "*infinite wit*": James, *The British Navy in Adversity*, 25; Hadlow, *A Royal Experiment*, 277 ("*dullness*"); Jesse, *Memoirs of Celebrated Etonians*, vol. 2, 247 ("*free from irascibility*"); Ayling, *George the Third*, 239 ("*without a mask*"); Bunker, *An Empire on the Edge*, 322 (*venison*).

19   *Capable of reciting*: Thomas, *The House of Commons in the Eighteenth Century*, 234.

19   "*fond of indolence*": Lucas, *Lord North*, vol. 2, 3; MLA, 50–51 ("*America must fear you*"); Whiteley, *Lord North*, 144 ("*five frigates*"); Anderson, *The Command of the Howe Brothers During the American Revolution*, 31 ("*no match*"); Rodger, *The Command of the Ocean*, 332 ("*despotism*"); North to William Eden, Aug. 22, 1775, in Ritcheson, *British Politics and the American Revolution*, 198 ("*I speak ignorantly*").

20   *Devoted to George*: Plumb, *The First Four Georges*, 120–22; Morgan, *The Birth of the Republic*, 66 ("*absurd notion*").

20   "*an old Roman senator*": Quincy, *Memoir of the Life of Josiah Quincy Jun.*, 318–19, 321 ("*big with dangers*"), 327 ("*skinned over*"); Plumb, *England in the Eighteenth Century*, 108–09; Plumb, *The First Four Georges*, 126 ("*scarecrow*"); PH 18, 149–56 ("*All attempts*").

20   *The old lion's eloquence*: PH 18, 198, 215; Donne, ed., *The Correspondence of King George the Third with Lord North*, vol. 1, 226–27 ("*madness*").

20   "*enemy in the bowels*": Bunker, *An Empire on the Edge*, 360; Nelson, *General James Grant*, 85–86 (*five thousand British regulars*); *Annual Register*, 1775, 66 ("*pusillanimous*"); PH 18, 226

(*"never dare"*); Thomas, *The House of Commons in the Eighteenth Century,* 241 (*government's cause*). During the Revolution, 176 military officers would sit in the Commons. Ira D. Gruber, "For King and Country," in Denton, ed., *Limits of Loyalty,* 35.

21   *Treasury slush fund*: Namier and Brooke, *The House of Commons,* vol. 1, 77; Donoughue, *British Politics and the American Revolution,* 182; Bunker, *An Empire on the Edge,* 322; LaPrade, ed., *Parliamentary Papers of John Robinson,* 9–11; Van Tyne, *The War of Independence: American Phase,* 143; Porter, *English Society in the Eighteenth Century,* 112–14; Steuart, ed., *The Last Journals of Horace Walpole,* vol. 1, 429 (*"even more corrupt"*).

21   *At 2:30 a.m. on February 7*: PH 18, 265, 292.

21   *Among new members voting*: de Beer, *Gibbon and His World,* 34, 70; Murray, ed., *The Autobiographies of Edward Gibbon,* 309–11; Gibbon, *Autobiography and Correspondence of Edward Gibbon,* 234 (*"We have both the right"*), 235 (*"I sometimes doubt"*); Clark, *British Opinion and the American Revolution,* 279 (*"I took my seat"*).

21   *The king had no doubts*: Fortescue, ed., *The Correspondence of King George the Third,* vol. 3, 171–72.

22   *Shortly before three p.m.*: *Gentleman's Magazine* (weather for Feb. 9, 1775); Grosely, *A Tour to London,* 80; Sheppard, *Memorials of St. James's Palace,* vol. 1, 10–11 (*"irregular pile"*); *London Gazette and New Daily Advertiser,* Feb. 10, 1775 (*"never was known"*).

22   *"We find that a part"*: PH 18, 297–98.

22   *George was nearsighted*: Bunker, *An Empire on the Edge,* 316; PH 18, 298 (*"You may depend"*).

22   *Events now moved*: "George III Calendar, Jan. 1774–Aug. 1775," RA GEO/MAIN/#1954 (*"foreign service"*); PH 18, 298–99 (*fishing grounds*); PH 18, 305–13, 316; John Shy, "Confronting Rebellion," in Peckham, ed., *Sources of American Independence,* vol. 1, 125; George to North, Feb. 11, 1775, "George III Calendar, Jan. 1774–Aug. 1775," RA GEO/MAIN/#1955 (*"so poor"*); Gruber, "George III Chooses a Commander in Chief," in Hoffman and Albert, eds., *Arms and Independence,* 170–74 (*forty-five generals*); Callahan, *Royal Raiders,* 34 (*"frighten me"*).

23   *"Divine Disposer"*: George to North, Feb. 15, 1775, "George III Calendar, Jan. 1774–Aug. 1775," RA GEO/MAIN/#1958.

23   *For more than three centuries*: Wilson, *The Tower of London,* 78–79; Gower, *The Tower of London,* vol. 2, 137; Lepore, *Book of Ages,* 169 (*"Many thousand firearms"*); *An Historical Description of the Tower of London and Its Curiosities,* 33–39, 41–43; ffoulkes, *Inventory and Survey of the Armouries of the Tower of London,* vol. 1, 22–23, 29, 35; Parnell, *The Tower of London, Past and Present,* 7, 47, 57–58, 86.

23   *Gun shops clustered*: Jonathan Ferguson, "Brown Bess: Musket or Mistress?," Royal Armouries website, May 17, 2017, https://blog.royalarmouries.org/2017/05/17/brown-bess-musket-or-mistress/; Blackmore, *British Military Firearms,* 39–49, 57–61, 278; Wilson, *The Tower of London,* 79 (*potency of gunpowder*); Houlding, *Fit for Service,* 144 (*42,000 powder charges*); Willis, *The Struggle for Sea Power,* 40 (*535 barrels*); Ward, *Journal and Letters of the Late Samuel Curwen,* 38 (*"Incredible quantities"*).

24   *"A conquest by land"*: Kennedy, *The Rise and Fall of British Naval Mastery,* 114; Harvey to Irwin, June 30, 1775, UK NA, WO 3/5 (*"as evil an idea"*); Fortescue, *The War of Independence,* 20 (*"impossible"*).

24   *The army's small size*: Stephenson, *Patriot Battles,* 44; Dull, *The French Navy and American Independence,* 16 (*a third the size*); Conway, *The War of American Independence,* 44; Curtis, *The British Army in the American Revolution,* 1–2; Belcher, *The First American Civil War,* vol. 1, 259. At least one scholar has argued that in April 1775 the British Army was down to just over 27,000. Mackesy, *The War for America,* 524–25.

24   *Recruiting was difficult*: Gruber, "For King and Country," in Denton, ed., *Limits of Loyalty,* 26–32; MLA, 4–6; Stephenson, *Patriot Battles,* 44; Conway, "British Army Officers and the American War for Independence," *WMQ,* 3rd ser., 41, no. 2 (Apr. 1984): 265+ (*"great impropriety"*); Donoughue, *British Politics and the American Revolution,* 210 (*"Hessians and Hanoverians"*); Ingrao, *The Hessian Mercenary State,* 136 (*secret negotiations*).

24   *A fateful momentum*: Jesse, *Memoirs of the Life and Reign of King George III,* vol. 1, 584–85 (*"Psalm Singer"*); *The Manuscripts of the Earl of Dartmouth,* vol. 1, iv–v, and vol. 2, v–xvii;

Bunker, *An Empire on the Edge*, 117–22; Bargar, *Lord Dartmouth and the American Revolution*, 10, 161.

25 *And so war stuffs*: William Roy to Barrington, Mar. 15, 1776, UK NA, WO1/890, f. 8; Trevelyan, *The American Revolution*, 199–200 (*"small scale"*).

25 *Troops tramped*: Duane, ed., *Extracts from the Diary of Christopher Marshall*, 16; Don N. Hagist, e-mail to author, Nov. 30, 2015 (*Seven regiments*); Hagist, *British Soldiers, American War*, 53; *DAR*, vol. 9, 9 and 99; Barrington to Germain, Jan. 13, 1776, UK NA CO 5/168, f. 3 (*sixty women*); "Lieutenant Williams' Journal," Buffalo (N.Y.) Public Library, micro, 55 (*Cork grew so crowded*); Boyle, ed., *From Redcoat to Rebel*, 7–13 (*lacked muskets*); Barrington to Germain, Jan. 25, 1776, UK NA CO 5/168, f. 25 (*casks of porter*).

25 *"Our stake is deep"*: Murdoch, ed., *Rebellion in America*, 9; Mackesy, *The War for America*, 38 (*"they will submit"*).

25 *would last 3,059 days*: from April 19, 1775, to the signing of the Treaty of Paris on September 3, 1783.

25 *more than 1,300 actions*: Peckham, ed., *The Toll of Independence*, xii, 130–33; Alden, *The American Revolution*, 9.

26 *Roughly a quarter million*: Spring, *With Zeal and with Bayonets Only*, 28; Peckham, ed., *The Toll of Independence*, 130–33; Wood, *The American Revolution*, 87; Ellis, *Founding Brothers*, 5–6; *WAI*, 1 (*imperial shackles*); Bowen, *John Adams and the American Revolution*, 510 (*silken slippers*). Burrows contends that far more Americans were captured than has usually been estimated—more than 30,000—and that 18,000 of those prisoners may have died in captivity. He also argues that total American deaths during the war numbered "as many as 35,800." *Forgotten Patriots*, xi, 201.

26 *This would not be a war*: Coakley and Conn, *The War of the American Revolution*, 4–5; Martin, "A Contagion of Violence," *Journal of Military Ethics* 14, no. 1 (May 2015): 57+.

26 *Those 3,059 hard days*: Countryman, *The American Revolution*, 7–8; Miller, *Triumph of Freedom*, 3 (*reduction of the empire*); Draper, *A Struggle for Power*, 511 (*£128 million*); Bickham, *Making Headlines*, 7.

27 *An unusual bustle*: author visit, June 9, 2014. David Turnquist argues persuasively that in 1775 the house was No. 27 rather than No. 7, as in some accounts; it later was renumbered as No. 36. He also doubts that Franklin moved back after shifting quarters to No. 1 in 1772. "A Brief History of Benjamin Franklin's Residences on Craven Street, London: 1757–1775," *JAR*, Mar. 23, 2016. The founding director of the Benjamin Franklin House on Craven Street, however, believes "it is likely" that Franklin returned to No. 27 after the spring of 1774. Márcia Balisciano, "Benjamin Franklin and Public History: Restoring Benjamin Franklin House," n.d., www.benjaminfranklinhouse.org, 1–8.

27 *He was famous*: Isaacson, *Benjamin Franklin*, 3; Morgan, *Benjamin Franklin*, 146 (*"universal genius"*); author visit, June 9, 2014; Van Doren, *Benjamin Franklin*, 300–01; www .benjaminfranklinhouse.org (*sun spots*); Márcia Balisciano, "Benjamin Franklin and Public History: Restoring Benjamin Franklin House," n.d., www.benjaminfranklinhouse.org, 4 (*kite-and-key*).

27 *The tall man*: Morgan, *Benjamin Franklin*, 35; BF to Joseph Galloway, Feb. 5–[7], 1775, *PBF* (*"Anxiety"*).

27 *He had chosen to spend*: Lopez, *My Life with Benjamin Franklin*, 148–49; Fleming, ed., *Benjamin Franklin*, 6; Lepore, *Book of Ages*, 83 (*formal schooling*); Wood, *The Americanization of Benjamin Franklin*, 45 (*good causes*), 63 (*new field*); Morgan, *Benjamin Franklin*, 29 (*"died rich"*); Isaacson, *Benjamin Franklin*, 145 (*"Prometheus"*).

28 *He was proud*: Wood, *The Americanization of Benjamin Franklin*, 87, 71–72 (*forty-two different signatures*); Morgan, *Benjamin Franklin*, 174–75 (*"great regard"*).

28 *he had owned slaves*: Lopez, *My Life with Benjamin Franklin*, 197; Wood, *The Americanization of Benjamin Franklin*, 32 (*"intrigues"*); Isaacson, *Benjamin Franklin*, 200 (*coronation*); Morgan, *Benjamin Franklin*, 77–78 (*excluding Germans*), 35; BF, "The Rise and Present State of Our Misunderstanding," *London Chronicle*, Nov. 6–8, 1770, *PBF*; Goodwin, *Benjamin Franklin in London*, 9, 267 (*arrest warrant*).

29 *His good friend Priestley*: Schofield, *The Enlightened Joseph Priestley*, 16–17; Schoenbrun, *Triumph in Paris*, 17; Priestley, *Memoirs of the Rev. Dr. Joseph Priestley*, 20 *(cloth dresser)*, 78–79 *("not live to see")*; Fruchtman, *Atlantic Cousins*, 145–47, 171–72, 180 *(soda water)*; BF to Joseph Galloway, Feb. 5–[7], 1775, *PBF* *("calamities")*; Rutt, *Life and Correspondence of Joseph Priestley*, vol. 1, 211 *("tears trickled")*.

29 *"mutual strength"*: Stourzh, *Benjamin Franklin and American Foreign Policy*, 86; Wood, *The Americanization of Benjamin Franklin*, 129, 147–48 *("palliate")*, 143 *("punctilio")*; Wood, *Revolutionary Characters*, 81 *("insolence")*; Greene, *Understanding the American Revolution*, 40–41 *("foreigners")*.

29 *"Rules by Which a Great Empire"*: Morgan, *Benjamin Franklin*, 35–36; Van Doren, *Benjamin Franklin*, 455.

29 *Then, two years ago*: Wood, *The Americanization of Benjamin Franklin*, 141–44, 147 *("upstart thing")*; Morgan, *Benjamin Franklin*, 199; Brands, *The First American*, 481 *("old snake")*.

30 *On January 29, 1774*: Solomon Lutnick, *The American Revolution and the British Press*, 41–42; Jesse, *Memoirs of the Life and Reign of King George the Third*, vol. 1, 550 *("hoary-headed")*; Isaacson, *Benjamin Franklin*, 277 *(Manchester velvet)*.

30 *In the months since*: BF to W. Franklin, Mar. 22, 1775, *PBF* *("irritated")*; BF to Lord Howe, Dec. 28–31, 1774, *PBF* *(removing British soldiers)*; Greene, *Understanding the American Revolution*, 35 *("letting them alone")*; Clark, *Benjamin Franklin*, 224–25, 253 *("traitor")*; Bunker, *An Empire on the Edge*, 346 *(stock market)*.

30 *"whistling of the winds"*: BF to W. Franklin, Mar. 22, 1775, *PBF*.

30 *"great director"*: Van Doren, *Benjamin Franklin*, 454; Greene, *Understanding the American Revolution*, 259 *("thing out of its place")*; BF to J. Galloway, Feb. 25, 1775, BF to James Bowdoin, Feb. 25, 1775, *PBF* *("rotten state")*.

31 *"a thorough courtier"*: BF to W. Franklin, Sept. 7, 1774, *PBF*; Clark, *Benjamin Franklin*, 265 *(common-law wife)*.

31 *Franklin never went to sea*: Parton, *Life and Times of Benjamin Franklin*, vol. 2, 71; Schoenbrun, *Triumph in Paris*, 3–5 *(Gulf Stream)*; BF to W. Franklin, Mar. 22, 1775, *PBF*; Lepore, *Book of Ages*, 175; Clark, *Benjamin Franklin*, 268–69; Dull, "Franklin the Diplomat: The French Mission," *Transactions of the American Philosophical Society*, new ser., 72, no. 1 (1982): 1+.

31 *The bells of Philadelphia*: Ward, *Journal and Letters of the Late Samuel Curwen*, 26–28; Fruchtman, *Atlantic Cousins*, 327 *("true incendiary")*.

1. GOD HIMSELF OUR CAPTAIN

35 *The mildest winter*: Dexter, *The Literary Diary of Ezra Stiles, D.D., LL.D.*, vol. 1, 529; Gross, *The Minutemen and Their World*, 3 *("warlike preparations")*; Stout, *The Royal Navy in America*, 161–62 *(men-of-war)*; Hulton, *Letters of a Loyalist Lady*, 73 *("very gloomy")*.

35 *Only a bountiful local crop*: corr., William Gordon to "a gentleman in England," *AA*, IV: 2, 625–31; *WR*, 16; Forbes, *Paul Revere and the World He Lived In*, 225; *Boston-Gazette and Country Journal*, Feb. 27, 1775, *HD*; *Spirit '76*, 28 *(tedious detour)*; Bridenbaugh, *Cities in Revolt*, 238, 320–21 *(projects)*; *DCL*, 51; Bunker, *An Empire on the Edge*, 173 *(ninety taverns)*.

35 *Even in better days*: Whitehill, *Boston: A Topographical History*, 38, 46 *(stagnated)*; Scudder, "The Siege of Boston," *Atlantic Monthly* 37 (Apr. 1876): 466+; Bunker, *An Empire on the Edge*, 173 *(single concert hall)*; Scudder, "Life in Boston in the Provincial Period," in Winsor, ed., *The Memorial History of Boston*, vol. 2, 486 *("immorality")*; Bell, *The Road to Concord*, 4 *(as many British soldiers)*; Silverman, *A Cultural History of the American Revolution*, 260 *("warlike red")*.

36 *On Monday morning, March 6*: *Boston-Gazette and Country Journal*, Jan. 6, 1775, *HD*; Fusilier, 37–39 *("immense concourse")*; Betlock et al., *An Architectural History of the Old South Meeting House*, 5–12 *(Flemish-bond)*.

36 *"People's expectations"*: author visit, May 3–6, 2015, signage; Carp, *Defiance of the Patriots*, 100; Forbes, *Paul Revere and the World He Lived In*, 239 *(mass arrests)*; Allan, *John Hancock*, 167 *(draw swords)*; Frothingham, *The Life and Times of Joseph Warren*, 426 *("in our trenches")*; Fusilier, 37–39 *("bludgeon")*.

36 *Samuel Adams was ready*: Ferling, *John Adams: A Life*, 44; *GC*, 165; Bridenbaugh, *Cities in Revolt*, 392; Tourtellot, *Lexington and Concord*, 68; Galloway, *Historical and Political Reflections*, 67 (*"eats little"*); Louis, "Samuel Adams' Tremor," *Neurology* 56, no. 9 (May 8, 2001): 1201+; Bowen, *John Adams and the American Revolution*, 669 (*on his toes*); Philbrick, *Bunker Hill*, 96 (*"no pretense"*).

37 *The crowd hushed*: Later versions depict Warren climbing up a ladder and through a window to reach the pulpit. Contemporary accounts suggest a more conventional entry. Beck, *Igniting the American Revolution*, 382n; Hinderaker, *Boston's Massacre*, 251. The ladder story appears, among other places, in Frothingham, *The Life and Times of Joseph Warren*, 428–29.

37 *He was handsome*: Philbrick, *Bunker Hill*, 46, 68; Davidson, *Propaganda and the American Revolution*, 197 (*"undaunted spirit"*).

37 *Later accounts would depict*: Eric Hinderaker writes that much of the flamboyant description of Warren's appearance was invented in the nineteenth and twentieth centuries. *Boston's Massacre*, 251–52, 335n. Other accounts can be found in Philbrick, *Bunker Hill*, 97; E. Wayne Carp, "The Problem of National Defense in the Early American Republic," in Greene, ed., *The American Revolution*, 22; Wood, *The Idea of America*, 68–70; and Puls, *Samuel Adams*, 168.

37 *"Demosthenian posture"*: Forbes, *Paul Revere and the World He Lived In*, 239; www .drjosephwarren.com (*"Unhappily for us"*).

38 *Several British officers*: Alden, *General Gage in America*, 223. Claims that Warren covered the bullets with his handkerchief may be apocryphal. Hinderaker, *Boston's Massacre*, 252.

38 *"true puritanical whine"*: Philbrick, *Bunker Hill*, 97; Bailyn, *To Begin the World Anew*, 1 (*borderland people*); Morgan, *The Birth of the Republic*, 22–23; Countryman, *The American Revolution*, 63; Wood, *The Idea of America*, 102, 106; Tudor, *The Life of James Otis of Massachusetts*, 464 (*"panting"*).

38 *Reasonably democratic*: Tudor, *The Life of James Otis of Massachusetts*, 447–48; Greenwalt and Orrison, *A Single Blow*, xviii–xix; Morgan, *The Birth of the Republic*, 70 (*elected assemblies*); *GC*, 244–45; Wood, *The Creation of the American Republic, 1776–1787*, 115.

38 *Applause rocked Old South*: *Spirit '76*, 36–37 (*"most seditious"*); Fusilier, 37–39 (*"Fie!"*).

39 *That was but a consonant*: Fusilier, 37–39; *Spirit '76*, 36–37 (*"getting out"*); Forbes, *Paul Revere and the World He Lived In*, 239 (*"like rats"*).

39 *"To be sure"*: Lister, *Concord Fight*, 20.

39 *Across the street*: Fusilier, 37–39.

39 *Thomas Gage was a mild*: *Letters & Papers of John Singleton Copley and Henry Pelham*, 77, 94; *PRR*, 30–36 (*"good and wise"*); Preston, *Braddock's Defeat*, 245 (*Monongahela*); Ketchum, *Divided Loyalties*, 111 (*Fort Carillon*).

40 *"will always keep them quiet"*: Alden, *General Gage in America*, 200–03, 212; Draper, *A Struggle for Power*, 230 (*riven by diverse interests*); Trevelyan, *The American Revolution*, 173 (*shilling pinchers*); Gruber, "The American Revolution as a Conspiracy: The British View," *WMQ*, 3rd ser., 26, no. 3 (July 1969): 360+; *MLA*, 86; *PRR*, 41.

40 *Gage's report*: "Queries of George Chalmers, with the Answers of General Gage," *Collections*, MHS, 4th ser., 4 (1858): 367; Belcher, *The First American Civil War*, vol. 1, 133; *Spirit '76*, 26–27; Dartmouth to Gage, Apr. 9, 1774, *PH* 18, 75–76 (*"quiet the minds"*); Gary Shattuck, "Thomas Gage Reconsidered," *JAR*, Aug. 26, 2015; Belcher, *The First American Civil War*, vol. 1, 144–46.

40 *fifteen hundred insurgents*: Raphael, *The First American Revolution*, 66–67; Ray Raphael, "Blacksmith Timothy Bigelow and the Massachusetts Revolution of 1774," in Young et al., eds., *Revolutionary Founders*, 43; Gross, *The Minutemen and Their World*, 55; French, *The Siege of Boston*, 121–24; *PRR*, 44–48.

42 *"For about fifty miles"*: Breen, *American Insurgents, American Patriots*, 150; "'The Very Time of the Convulsion' in Shrewsbury," *B 1775*, Mar. 21, 2016 (*"at every house"*); Bell, *The Road to Concord*, 38 (*"Powder Alarm"*); Raphael, *The First American Revolution*, 67 (*"Popular rage"*).

42 *Additional episodes followed*: Andrlik et al., eds., *Journal of the American Revolution*, vol. 1, 24; Ray Raphael, "Country Crowds in Revolutionary Massachusetts: Mobs and Militia," *JAR*,

Mar. 16, 2017; *The Journals of Each Provincial Congress of Massachusetts in 1774 and 1775*, i–ii, 7, 16; Allan, *John Hancock*, ix–x (*"empty barrel"*); Bell, *The Road to Concord*, 101 (*only twenty-one*); Greenwalt and Orrison, *A Single Blow*, 20 (*collecting revenue*).

42 *Amassing military supplies*: French, *The Siege of Boston*, 137–39; *MLA*, 115; Breen, *American Insurgents, American Patriots*, 216; *NDAR*, vol. 1, 15, 18–19, 28, 37; Bell, *The Road to Concord*, 112.

42 *Fearing for his own safety*: Shy, *Toward Lexington*, 411–12; Wheildon, *Siege and Evacuation of Boston and Charlestown*, 59; Sumner, *A History of East Boston*, 365; Porter, *Rambles in Old Boston*, 376–77; "Indian Archer Weathervane," MHS, Collections Online, www.masshist .org/database/1769.

43 *"Civil government is near"*: GWGO, 23–24 (*"apply a remedy"*); Carter, ed., *The Correspondence of General Thomas Gage*, vol. 1, 380 (*"phrenzy"*); Bushman, *The American Farmer in the Eighteenth Century*, 172–77 (*closing the Boston port*); Gross, *The Minutemen and Their World*, 60–61; Nevins, *American States During and After the Revolution*, 70–71; Greene, ed., *The American Revolution*, 51–52; Raphael, *A People's History of the American Revolution*, 41–42, 46; Carter, ed., *The Correspondence of General Thomas Gage*, vol. 2, 658–59 (*"blood and treasure"*).

43 *"the acts must and should"*: Donoughue, *British Politics and the American Revolution*, 210.

43 *"lukewarm coward"*: Van Tyne, *The Loyalists in the American Revolution*, 45; French, *The Siege of Boston*, 141 (*"mild general"*); Sargent, ed., *Letters of John Andrews, Esq., of Boston*, 88 (*"Old Woman"*); Nelson, *General James Grant*, 93 (*"his disposition"*); Callahan, *Royal Raiders*, 47 (*effigies*); PRR, 73–74 (*"bung with shoeboys"*); Alden, *General Gage in America*, 237 (*"I pity, dear sir"*).

44 *"Every day, every hour"*: French, *The Siege of Boston*, 146; "Leslie's Retreat," *Essex Institute Historical Collections* 17, no. 2 (Apr. 1880): 190+, and "The Affair at the North Bridge, Salem, February 26, 1775," *Essex Institute Historical Collections* 38, no. 4 (Oct. 1902): 321+; Borneman, *American Spring*, 81–86; PRR, 59–64; *Spirit '76*, 65 (*"Go home"*).

44 *"to keep quiet in the town"*: Peckham, ed., *Sources of American Independence*, 127; Alden, "Why the March to Concord?," *AHR* 49, no. 3 (Apr. 1944): 447; DCL, 57–58; Tourtellot, *Lexington and Concord*, 90.

44 *"on a large scale"*: GWGO, 27.

44 *"dread suspense"*: Gross, *The Minutemen and Their World*, 113.

44 *Yet daily life plodded*: "Henry Knox—Bookseller," *Proceedings*, MHS, 3rd ser., 61 (Oct. 1927–June 1928): 227; *Boston-Gazette and Country Journal*, Jan. 2, Jan. 6, Jan. 23, Feb. 27, Mar. 6, 1775; *Essex Gazette*, Apr. 11, 1775, HD.

45 *Auction houses sold*: *Boston-Gazette and Country Journal*, Apr. 10 and Mar. 13, 1775, HD; Lutnick, *The American Revolution and the British Press*, 40–41 (*Dung Barge*); J. L. Bell, "James Otis, Jr., and Slavery Revisited," *B 1775*, June 8, 2017 (*"servant for life"*); *Boston-Gazette and Country Journal*, Mar. 6, Jan. 2, 1775, HD (*"Walks lame"*); J. L. Bell, "Behaving with Discretion & Calmness," *B 1775*, posted Nov. 25, 2014 (*"take up all Negroes"*).

45 *Freeholders gathered*: *A Report of the Record Commissioners of the City of Boston* (Boston: Rockwell and Churchill, 1887), 222–24 (*"some distance"*); *Boston-Gazette and Country Journal*, Mar. 13 and Apr. 3, 1775, HD.

45 *"once happy town"*: Forbes, *Paul Revere and the World He Lived In*, 225.

45 *"Humbling the Tories"*: Gross, *The Minutemen and Their World*, 54, 56; Wood, *The Radicalism of the American Revolution*, 214 (*smokehouses*); Chase, vol. 3, 128 (*"I sells tea"*); Baldwin, xxxi (*"hemp"*); Van Tyne, *The War of Independence: American Phase*, 25 (*carriage wheels*); Calhoon, *The Loyalists in Revolutionary America*, 257–58 (*"madness"*).

46 *A Calvinist people*: George Tolman, lecture, "Preliminaries of Concord Fight," Concord Antiquarian Society (1901), https://archive.org/stream/preliminariesofcootolm#page/n5/mode /2up: 13; Phillips, *1775*, 307 (*military cargo*); "Biographical Sketch of Col. David Mason of Salem, by His Daughter, Mrs. Susan Smith," *Essex Institute Historical Collections* 48, no. 3 (1912): 204–06 (*powder cartridges*); Shattuck, *A History of the Town of Concord*, 95; "Meagre War Stores of 1775," *Americana* 6 (1911): 102; Griffenhagen, "Drug Supplies in the American Revolution," *Bulletin of the United States National Museum*, 225 (1961): 110+ (*medicine chests*).

46   *Farm carts hauled*: Sargent, ed., *Letters of John Andrews, Esq., of Boston*, 88; Nevins, *American States During and After the Revolution*, 68.

46   *In Concord*: author visit, National Park Service Visitor Center, Concord, Aug. 28, 2015; Concord Museum, author interview with David F. Wood, curator, Aug. 28, 2015; Wheeler, *Concord*, 105–06; Committee of Supply to J. Barrett, Mar. 11, 1775, CMSA, vol. 146, micro (*"faithful men"*); *Journals of Each Provincial Congress of Massachusetts in 1774 and 1775*, 513 (*"shortest notice"*).

46   *The provincial congress also chose*: Tolman, "Preliminaries of Concord Fight," 16; *Spirit '76*, 30 (*"The parson"*); Bell, *The Road to Concord*, 23, 93 (*three times a week*); *WAI*, 47–48; Pickering, *The Life of Timothy Pickering*, vol. 1, 60, 87–88; Clary and Whitehorne, *The Inspectors General of the United States Army, 1777–1903*, 15.

47   *"Behold, God"*: Shattuck, *A History of the Town of Concord*, 93–94.

47   *Boston's natural beauty*: Lushington, *The Life and Services of General Lord Harris*, 43; Williams, *Discord and Civil Wars*, 5–6 (*"too puritanical"*); DNH, Oct. 1, 2010 (*"ready to cut"*); Stout, *The Royal Navy in America*, 168; Moore, *The Diary of the American Revolution*, xxx (*"Jonathan"*).

47   *A Royal Navy officer described*: LAR, 69; Conway, "The Great Mischief Complain'd Of," *WMQ*, 3rd ser., 17, no. 3 (July 1990): 377 (*coarse gestures*); Brown, *The Good Americans*, 118 (*ice-skating*); Wallace, *Appeal to Arms*, 21 (*"Goddams"*); French, *General Gage's Informers*, 50 (*"One active campaign"*).

48   *The British garrison now exceeded*: Don Hagist to author, May 15, 2018. A victualing report put the number of mouths to feed in the Boston garrison in late March 1775 at 4,560. David Chamier to W. Howe, Jan. 17, 1776, UK NA, T 64/108, f. 23–25.

48   *They crowded every corner*: PRR, 308–09 (*thirteen regiments*); Forbes, *Paul Revere and the World He Lived In*, 229; John Montresor, *Map of Boston*, 1775, Royal Collection, RCIN, and anonymous military engineer, *Map of Boston*, 1775, Royal Collection, RCIN, #734011; Frey, *The British Soldier in America*, 98 (*Brattle Square*); Lushington, *The Life and Services of General Lord Harris*, 44 (*throwing stones*); Sargent, ed., *Letters of John Andrews, Esq., of Boston*, 80; Fusilier, 28–29 (*target practice*); Padelford, ed., *Colonial Panorama, 1775*, 43 (*"They run out"*).

48   *Ugly encounters*: Sargent, ed., *Letters of John Andrews, Esq., of Boston*, 87; Moore, *The Diary of the American Revolution*, 13 (*drums and fifes*); Woodbury, *Dorothy Quincy, Wife of John Hancock*, 55 (*vandalized*); Brown, *Beneath Old Roof Trees*, 14–15; *Boston-Gazette and Country Journal*, Mar. 13, 1775, HD; PRR, 70; Fusilier, 39 (*"gave great offense"*).

48   *Anti-Gambling Club*: Frey, *The British Soldier in America*, 65; Barker, *The British in Boston*, 19–20.

48   *Worse still was inebriation*: Kopperman, "'The Cheapest Pay': Alcohol Abuse in the Eighteenth-Century British Army," *JMH* 60, no. 3 (July 1996): 445+; McCusker and Menard, *The Economy of British America*, 190 (*five million gallons*); Miller, *Sea of Glory*, 13; Stout, "Manning the Royal Navy in North America, 1763–1775," *American Neptune* 23, no. 3 (July 1963): 176; PRR, 67 (*five hundred lashes*); Vincent J. R. Kehoe, "A Military Guide: The British Infantry of 1775," Society for the Preservation of Colonial Culture (1974); Sargent, ed., *Letters of John Andrews, Esq., of Boston*, 84; Fusilier, 17–19, 32.

49   *And desert they did*: Forbes, *Paul Revere and the World He Lived In*, 233–34; PRR, 68 (*three hundred acres*).

49   *Estimates of British Army desertions*: Philbrick, *Bunker Hill*, 50. Don N. Hagist places desertions at around 120, and notes that after April 19 they "decreased significantly." DNH, Oct. 1, 2013, and Jan. 13, 2010.

49   *The problem was even worse*: Black and Woodfine, eds., *The British Navy and the Use of Naval Power in the Eighteenth Century*, 130; Brunsman, *The Evil Necessity*, 199. Gardner Weld Allen lists 42,000 naval desertions from 1774 to 1780. *A Naval History of the American Revolution*, vol. 1, 55–56. N.A.M. Rodger notes that the Royal Navy's desertion rate in 1776 exceeded 16 percent, double that in the previous war. *The Command of the Ocean*, 398–99.

49   *Many had been forced into service*: Miller, *Sea of Glory*, 14; Tilley, *The British Navy and the American Revolution*, 14 (*gunports caulked*).

49 *Floggings, and worse*: Hagist, *British Soldiers, American War*, 83–84, 92–97; Barker, *The British in Boston*, 14 (*"remembrance of Christmas"*); DNH, Oct. 1, 2011 (*Vaughan*); *Fusilier*, 41.

49 *By contrast, many young British officers*: Evelyn, 1, 6–8, 12, 28–52; Houlding, *Fit for Service*, 100; Balderston and Syrett, eds., *The Lost War*, 20–22; Gruber, *Books and the British Army in the Age of the American Revolution*, 6 (£3,500); U.K. National Army Museum, http://www.nam.ac.uk/research/famous-units/kings-own-royal-regiment-lancaster (*4th Foot*).

51 *The expected orders arrived*: Alden, *General Gage in America*, 233, 239–44; Bunker, *An Empire on the Edge*, 364.

51 *"The violences committed"*: Dartmouth to Gage, Jan. 27, 1775, *DAR*, vol. 9, 37–41.

52 *orders flew from Province House*: Derek W. Beck, "Dr. Joseph Warrant's Informant," *JAR*, Apr. 3, 2014; Padelford, ed., *Colonial Panorama, 1775*, 55; *LHEP*, 48 (*intended to burn Boston*); Drake, *The Town of Roxbury*, 7; Lockhart, *The Whites of Their Eyes*, 72–73.

52 *Gage had no cavalry*: Gross, *The Minutemen and Their World*, 112: Spring, *With Zeal and with Bayonets Only*, 120; DNH, Apr. 21, 2014 (*five to ten years*). While some accounts state that the British expedition numbered 700 men, Fischer puts the number at "between 800 and 900 Regulars," plus "a few volunteers and Loyalist guides." *PRR*, 114. Beck puts the number at 790, if noncombatant surgeons and musicians are included, plus about 20 mounted patrollers. *Igniting the American Revolution*, 342–44.

52 *"I dare say"*: Barker, *The British in Boston*, 29.

52 *Small, daylong expeditions*: Moore, *The Diary of the American Revolution*, 15; *Fusilier*, 44, 47, 27 (*"taking sketches"*); AA, IV: 1, 1263; "Gage's Instructions," Project Gutenberg, American Antiquarian Society Library.

53 *clandestine espionage network*: French, *General Gage's Informers*, 9–10, 13–15; Philbrick, *Bunker Hill*, 90, 92; Porter, *Rambles in Old Boston*, 97; Shurtleff, *A Topographical and Historical Description of Boston*, 610–17; "Paul Revere's Three Accounts of His Famous Ride," account to Jeremy Belknap, MHS (*on a Bible*); Gage to Dartmouth, Mar. 4 and 28, 1775, UK NA, CO 5/92, f. 115, 123 (*"motions of an army"*); *The Manuscripts of the Earl of Dartmouth*, vol. 2, 278.

53 *That steady gaze of his*: Gross, *The Minutemen and Their World*, 3, 10; Alden, "Why the March to Concord?," *American Historical Review* 49, no. 3 (Apr. 1944): 446+; Bakeless, *Turncoats, Traitors and Heroes*, 29–31; Beck, "Dr. Joseph Warrant's Informant," *JAR*, Apr. 3, 2014.

53 *The Americans, too, had informants*: "Queries of George Chalmers, with the Answers of General Gage," *Collections*, MHS, 4th ser., 4, 367 (*"expeditious intelligence"*); Alden, *General Gage in America*, 242; Beck, "Dr. Joseph Warrant's Informant," *JAR*, Apr. 3, 2014; Sargent, ed., *Letters of John Andrews, Esq., of Boston*, 91 (*"secret expedition"*).

53 *"In want of many men"*: Graves, Apr. 16, 1775; *PRR*, 85–86; Bell, *The Road to Concord*, 151–53 (*rebels had evacuated*).

54 *"You will seize and destroy"*: French, *General Gage's Informers*, 32.

54 *"The war began to redden"*: Adair and Schutz, eds., *Peter Oliver's Origin & Progress of the American Rebellion*, 119, 121.

2. MEN CAME DOWN FROM THE CLOUDS

55 *Shadows scuttled*: Jeremy Belknap, "Journal of My Tour to the Camp," MHS, *Proceedings*, 1st ser., 4 (1858–60): 77+, in RI, "American Accounts of the Siege of Boston," vol. 1.

55 *Not until the moon rose*: the U.S. Naval Observatory, "Sun and Moon Data," puts moonrise in Boston on April 18 at 10:19 p.m. eastern standard time, a waning gibbous phase with 91 percent of the disk illuminated. http://aa.usno.navy.mil/data/docs/RS_OneDay.php. Fischer cites two astronomers who put moonrise at 9:53 p.m., local apparent solar time, or approximately 9:28 p.m. EST. *PRR*, 312.

55 *hundreds of men*: *Fusilier*, 50–51. Back Bay formed the western boundary of the Common in 1775; the marshy shallows had yet to be filled with oyster shells, coal ash, and dirt. Shurtleff, *A Topographical and Historical Description of Boston*, 342.

55 *Moonglow glinted*: Holmes, *Redcoat*, 4, 184, 272–73; Hibbert, *Redcoats and Rebels*, 84.

55 *The navy had collected*: PRR, 115–17; Huston, *The Sinews of War*, 25–26; *Fusilier*, 45; Hagist, ed., *A British Soldier's Story*, xxiii–xxvi; Hagist, *British Soldiers, American War*, 80.

55   *Loading was haphazard*: Galvin, *The Minute Men*, 107; Barker, *The British in Boston*, 31–32.

57   *Few knew their destination*: PRR, 123–27; Joyce Lee Malcom, "The Scene of the Battle, 1775: Historic Grounds Report, MMNHP," NPS, xii–xiv, 45 (*apple and plum orchards*); Smith, *West Cambridge 1775*, 17, 27 ("*flowing river*").

57   "*a good deal agitated*": Fusilier, 50–51.

57   *Joseph Warren may have watched*: "Modern Location of Joseph Warren's North End House," Samuel A. Forman, www.drjosephwarren.com; Sarah Winslow Deming journal, Apr. 18, 1775, "Siege of Boston," MHS, www.masshist.org/online/siege/; Derek W. Beck, "Dr. Joseph Warren's Informant," *JAR*, Apr. 3, 2014; Philbrick, *Bunker Hill*, 118; Tourtellot, *Lexington and Concord*, 51 ("*army of observation*").

57   *The first herald*: Coburn, *The Battle of April 19, 1775*, 21; Holland, *William Dawes and His Ride with Paul Revere*, 20, 23–26 ("*Let thy recreations*"); Tourtellot, *Lexington and Concord*, 93; E. J. Witek, "Major William Dawes, Jr.," www.drbenjaminchurchjr.blogspot.com, Jan. 10, 2011; Drake, *The Town of Roxbury*, 74 ("*slow-jogging horse*").

58   *The second herald*: PRR, 300; Todd Andrlik, "How Paul Revere's Ride Was Published and Censored in 1775," *JAR*, Feb. 3, 2015 (*various newspapers*); PRR, 292–93.

58   *Now forty*: author visit, Revere house, Boston, May 2015; Goss, *The Life of Colonel Paul Revere*, 27–28; PRR, 15 ("*little lambs*").

58   *This was his time*: *Somerset* log, UK NA, ADM 51/906; tidal chart, *Boston-Gazette and Country Journal*, Apr. 17, 1775, HD; "The Wreck of the *HMS Somerset* (III)," NPS, Cape Cod National Seashore, https://www.nps.gov/caco/learn/historyculture/upload/Somersetrack .pdf; Graves, Jan. 8 and Apr. 13, 1775; Graves to Admiralty, Apr. 11, 1775, *DAR*, vol. 9, 94.

58   *In 1775, America*: Davidson, *Propaganda and the American Revolution, 1763–1783*, 83.

58   *Known as Old North*: author visit, Old North Church, May 2015; Tom Dietzel, "The Real Story Behind Thomas Guchy and His Stolen Angels," Old North Foundation, www.oldnorth.com, Feb.–Apr. 2016; Wheildon, *History of Paul Revere's Signal Lanterns*, 22–26; John Lee Watson, "Paul Revere's Signal," MHS, Nov. 9, 1876 ("*a friend*").

59   *lugging two lanterns*: author visit, Concord Museum, Aug. 28, 2015, and e-mail, curator David F. Wood to author, July 21, 2015. The identity of Revere's accomplices was bitterly disputed a century after the event. "Pulling on the Run," *B 1775*, Apr. 17, 2018, and "Shedding Light on the Lanterns Debate," *B 1775*, Apr. 20, 2018.

59   *Two hours later, Revere trotted*: "Paul Revere's Three Accounts of His Famous Ride," MHS; "Come in, Revere; we are not afraid of you," *B 1775*, Apr. 11, 2018 ("*The regulars*"); PRR, 109–10; Tourtellot, *Lexington and Concord*, 34, 58 ("*get up!*"), 75; Jones, *Under Colonial Roofs*, 145–46.

59   *A squad of militiamen*: Clarke, *Opening of the War of the Revolution*, 2–3; Austin, *The Life of Elbridge Gerry*, 68. Another account quotes Hancock as saying, "That is Revere: you need not be afraid of him." *B 1775*, Apr. 11, 2018.

60   *Thirty minutes later*: PRR, 110–12; Tourtellot, *Lexington and Concord*, 111–12.

60   *Now the Lexington bell*: Bailey, *Historical Sketches of Andover*, 307; Brown, *Beside Old Hearth-Stones*, 132; Bolton, *The Private Soldier Under Washington*, 11–12.

60   *Lexington spread across ten thousand*: Tourtellot, *Lexington and Concord*, 30; Phinney, *History of the Battle at Lexington*, 10; PRR, 149–51 ("*great tall man*"); Parker, *Genealogy and Biographical Notes of John Parker of Lexington and His Descendants*, 80–82 (*tuberculosis*).

60   *Massachusetts Bay had been*: Clary and Whitehorne, *The Inspectors General of the United States Army, 1777–1903*, 8; Parkman, *Montcalm and Wolfe*, vol. 2, 85 (*one in four*); DCL, 42–43; Hatch, *The Administration of the American Revolutionary Army*, 1 (*courtship ritual*); Vincent J.-R. Kehoe, "We Were There!," vol. 2, MMNHP, 25 (*two shillings*); PRR, 153, 319.

61   *A scout dispatched*: Clarke, *Opening of the War of the Revolution*, 4; author visit, Lexington, Nov. 16, 2014; Sabin, 33; Douglas P. Sabin, "The New England Tavern: A General Study," MMNHP, 1982, 29 (*warm flip*).

61   *Parker's scout had not ventured*: Lister, *Concord Fight*, 23; Tourtellot, *Lexington and Concord*, 115.

61   *The vanguard making for Concord*: Murdock, *The Nineteenth of April 1775*, 36; Vincent J.-R. Kehoe, "We Were There!," vol. 1, MMNHP, 23; Forbes, *Paul Revere and the World He Lived*

In, 229 (*"Boston legend"*); Conway, *The War of American Independence*, 19–20 (*"chastise-ment"*); PRR, 154–55 (*"banditti"*); Dexter, *The Literary Diary of Ezra Stiles, D.D., LL.D.*, vol. 1, 604–05 (*"a good man"*).

61 *With practiced motions*: lecture, Joseph Seymour, U.S. Army National Guard historian, Society of the Cincinnati, Jan. 16, 2015; e-mail to author, Jan. 21, 2015; Muller, *Attack and Defence of Fortified Places*, 135.

61 *There was nothing precise*: Frey, *The British Soldier in America*, 100; WR, 28–29; N. A. Roberts et al., "A Detailed Study of the Effectiveness and Capabilities of 18th Century Musketry on the Battlefield," in Pollard and Banks, eds., *Bastions and Barbed Wire*, 1–4, 10, 15; Holmes, *Redcoat*, 195 (*"flinty-lipped"*); "Effectiveness of 18th Century Musketry," Old Fort Niagara Association, Jan. 2016, video, https://www.youtube.com/watch?v=8Cw8ktmlF1A&feature=youtu.be; Hugh T. Harrington, "The Inaccuracy of Muskets," *JAR*, July 15, 2013; Hughes, *Firepower*, 10–11.

62 *The fourteen-inch bayonets*: Curtis, *The British Army in the American Revolution*, 16–17.

62 *The British were less than two miles*: Lister, *Concord Fight*, 116; Morgan, *The Birth of the American Republic*, 1; Brown, *Beneath Old Roof Trees*, 33–34 (*powder horns*); Sabin, 33; Gross, *The Minutemen and Their World*, 116–18. Fischer puts the number at "no more than sixty or seventy." PRR, 189 (*"Don't molest them"*).

62 *"There are so few of us"*: GC, 276–77.

62 *Full dawn brought*: Phinney, *History of the Battle at Lexington*, 19; French, *General Gage's Informers*, 53; PRR, 190–91; Philbrick, *Bunker Hill*, 126–27; French, *General Gage's Informers*, 59 (*"Soldiers, don't fire"*); Murdock, *The Nineteenth of April 1775*, 27, 33; John Parker deposition, Apr. 25, 1776, NARA, www.archives.gov/historical-docs/todays-doc/?dod-date=419 (*"Upon their sudden approach"*).

62 *A single gunshot sounded*: Tourtellot, *Lexington and Concord*, 133; James, "Britain's Brown Bess," *Rifle Shooter*, Sept. 23, 2010, www.rifleshootermag.com/rifles/featured_rifles_bess_092407/; Shields, *From Flintlock to M1*, 24; Richard Holmes, *Redcoat*, 195–96. A 2008 study put the Brown Bess muzzle velocity at 1,500 feet per second, while noting great variability in powder quality. N. A. Roberts et al., "A Detailed Study of the Effectiveness and Capabilities of 18th Century Musketry on the Battlefield," in Pollard and Banks, eds., *Bastions and Barbed Wire*, 3, 5, 10.

63 *Billowing smoke grew so dense*: Wheeler, *Voices of 1776*, 21–22; William Sutherland to Henry Clinton, Apr. 26, 1775, in Vincent J.-R. Kehoe, "We Were There!," vol. 1, MMNHP (*spooked mount*).

63 *Few of Parker's men*: Hudson, *History of the Town of Lexington*, vol. 1, 151–52 (*blew off a foot*); Phinney, *History of the Battle at Lexington*, 21; DCL, 143; Coburn, *The Battle of April 19, 1775*, 66–67; Gross, *The Minutemen and Their World*, 116–18 (*slashed at the air*); Barker, *The British in Boston*, 32 (*"men were so wild"*).

63 *Only when Colonel Smith*: William Sutherland to Henry Clinton, Apr. 26, 1775, Vincent J.-R. Kehoe, "We Were There!," vol. 1, MMNHP; PRR, 199–200 (*"I was desirous"*).

63 *The only British casualties*: DCL, 144n; Lister, *Concord Fight*, 24; Sabin, 47 (*bullets in the back*); PRR, 197 (*on his doorstep*).

64 *"Oh, what a glorious morning"*: Lister, *Concord Fight*, 139; Sabin, 30 (*paper cartridges*); Clarke, *Opening of the War of the Revolution*, 9 (*three huzzahs*).

64 *Concord was ready*: "Paul Revere's Three Accounts of His Famous Ride," MHS; Holland, *William Dawes and His Ride with Paul Revere*, 14–15; Chase, vol. 3, 2; PRR, 134–37, 177; Brown, *Beneath Old Roof Trees*, 103 (*"earnestness"*).

64 *Reports of shooting*: Shattuck, *A History of the Town of Concord*, 103–05; Brown, *Beneath Old Roof Trees*, 222.

64 *Militiamen, alone or in clusters*: Chase, vol. 3, 4–5, 7; author visit, Concord Museum, Aug. 28, 2015 (*art form*); Hibbert, *Redcoats and Rebels*, 51–52 (*"cowhide shoes"*); *Proceedings at the Centennial Celebration of the Battle of Lexington* (Boston: Lockwood, Brooks, 1875), 86 (*"Hannah, take good care"*); Sabin, 83.

66 *"It seemed as if men came down"*: PRR, 149; Shattuck, *A History of the Town of Concord*, 103–05; Ferling, *A Leap in the Dark*, 133 (*leather apron*); author visit, Concord Museum, Aug. 28,

2015 (*naval cutlass*); Gross, *The Minutemen and Their World*, 93–94, 105, 107, 190 (*protracted decline*); author visit, Nov. 16, 2014, NPS signage, MMNHP.

66 *Sometime before eight a.m.*: Sabin, 61; Thaddeus Blood account, Vincent J.-R. Kehoe, "We Were There!," vol. 1, MMNHP, 203 (*"The sun shined"*).

66 *They fell back*: Murdock, *The Nineteenth of April 1775*, 58; Amos Barrett, "Concord and Lexington Battle," Apr. 1825, in True, *Journal and Letters of Rev. Henry True*, 31–33; Shattuck, *A History of the Town of Concord*, 105–06 (*"If we die"*); Sabin, 62; PRR, 204–05.

66 *The British brigade wound*: Joyce Lee Malcom, "The Scene of the Battle, 1775: Historic Grounds Report, MMNHP," NPS, 1985, 90–101; Tourtellot, *Lexington and Concord*, 153–54 (*hand-drawn map*).

67 *Gage's late intelligence*: Shattuck, *A History of the Town of Concord*, 99 (*nine other villages*), 105–07; Ripley, *A History of the Fight at Concord on the 19th of April, 1775*, 13; Chase, vol. 3, 16–18; Drake, *History of Middlesex County*, vol. 1, 123.

67 *Since 1654, a bridge had spanned*: Judith Q. Sullivan, "North Bridge Historic Structure Report," MMNHP, NPS, Feb. 2004, 6, 38–40, 50; Joyce Lee Malcom, "The Scene of the Battle, 1775: Historic Grounds Report, MMNHP," NPS, 1985, 110–16.

67 *Seven British companies*: Brown, *Beneath Old Roof Trees*, 86–89; author visit, MMNHP signage, Nov. 16, 2014; Chase, vol. 3, 6–7, 28; Henry De Berniere, "Narrative, &c.," in "Gage's Instructions," Project Gutenberg, American Antiquarian Society Library, reprinted, Arno Press, 1971, "Eyewitness Accounts of the American Revolution," series 3 (*"We did not find"*).

68 *The five Concord militia companies*: Sabin, 70–72, 82; author visit, MMNHP signage, Nov. 16, 2014; French, *General Gage's Informers*, 96–97 (*uneasy British officer*); Wheeler, *Concord*, 128 (*"as solemn"*). Fischer puts the militia number at 500. PRR, 208–09.

68 *"Will you let them burn"*: Gross, *The Minutemen and Their World*, 125.

68 *"I haven't a man who's afraid"*: author visit, MMNHP signage, Nov. 16, 2014; Sabin, 81–84 (*bayonets*); D. Michael Ryan, "White Cockade: A Jacobite Air at the North Bridge?," n.d., https://www2.bc.edu/~hafner/lmm/music-articles/white_cockade_ryan.html; Thaddeus Blood account, Vincent J.-R. Kehoe, "We Were There!," vol. 1, MMNHP, 203 (*"not to fire first"*); PRR, 211; Lister, *Concord Fight*, 25.

68 *Captain Walter Laurie*: French, "The British Expedition to Concord, Massachusetts, in 1775," *Journal of the American Military History Foundation* 1, no. 1 (Spring 1937): 3+.

68 *Without orders, a British soldier fired*: Thaddeus Blood account, Vincent J.-R. Kehoe, "We Were There!," vol. 1, MMNHP, 203; Chase, vol. 3, 44, 37 (*"God damn them"*); Brown, *Beneath Old Roof Trees*, 111 (*"jackknives"*); Joyce Lee Malcom, "The Scene of the Battle, 1775: Historic Grounds Report, MMNHP," NPS, 1985, 122; author visit, MMNHP signage, Nov. 16, 2014.

69 *"A general popping"*: French, *General Gage's Informers*, 96–97; Lister, *Concord Fight*, 27 (*"greatest precipitance"*); Chase, vol. 3, 39 (*"hobbling"*).

69 *Battle smoke draped the river*: *Massachusetts in the American Revolution* (1977): 11, SoC, State Exhibition Series, http://www.societyofthecincinnati.org/scholarship/publications/; *AA*, IV: 2, 630; Sabin, 100–01.

69 *A peculiar quiet descended*: Wheeler, *Concord*, 128; Sabin, 93–97; author visit, John Buttrick house, Nov. 16, 2014; Thaddeus Blood account, Vincent J.-R. Kehoe, "We Were There!," vol. 1, MMNHP, 203 (*"After the fire"*).

69 *Colonel Smith had started*: Lister, *Concord Fight*, 27; Amos Baker affidavit, Vincent J.-R. Kehoe, "We Were There!," vol. 1, MMNHP, 303–04 (*"Now the war"*).

69 *No fifes and drums*: Barker, *The British in Boston*, 34 (*"very fat"*); author visit, Wright Tavern, Nov. 16, 2014; Tourtellot, *Lexington and Concord*, 174–75; PRR, 218.

70 *The first mile*: *DCL*, 218; "Cultural Landscape Report for Battle Road Unit," vol. 1, 2005, MMNHP, 39–44 (*four rods*); final report, "Parker's Revenge Archaeological Project," Friends of the MMNHP, Oct. 2016, 192 (*three hundred yards*); Piers Mackesy, "What the British Army Learned," in Hoffman and Albert, eds., *Arms and Independence*, 201 (*years of combat*); Barker, *The British in Boston*, 35 (*"amazing strong"*).

70 *But the rebels were there*: author visit, Meriam's Corner, Nov. 16, 2014; Rev. William Emerson, diary entry, April 19, 1775, in Emerson, *The Complete Works of Ralph Waldo Emerson*:

Miscellanies, vol. 11, 569; Joyce Lee Malcom, "The Scene of the Battle, 1775: Historic Grounds Report, MMNHP," NPS, 67–68 (*boggy ground*), 75; *Fusilier*, 65–66 ("*ineffectual fire*"); Hudson, *The History of Sudbury, Massachusetts*, 381 (*return volley*); *LAR*, 76–77 ("*barbarity*").

70 *Now the running gun battle*: Chase, vol. 3, 115 ("*monstrous numerous*"); Malcom, "The Scene of the Battle, 1775: Historic Grounds Report, MMNHP," NPS, 72–73, 79–81; Martha Holland, "Documentary Research on the Brooks Tanyard," in Alan T. Synenki, ed., *Archeological Investigations of MMNHP*, 361–62, 377–80; author visit, tannery site, Battle Road signage, Nov. 16, 2014; Brown, *Beneath Old Roof Trees*, 224–25 (*Bloody Curve*). The site often is called, anachronistically, the Bloody Angle.

71 *Plunging fire gashed*: Hudson, *The History of Sudbury, Massachusetts*, 380; Galvin, *The Minute Men*, 176; Chase, vol. 3, 66 ("*like bears*"); Bailey, *Historical Sketches of Andover*, 308 ("*waistcoat*"); Philbrick, *Bunker Hill*, 147–48 ("*wreak vengeance*").

71 *More vengeance lurked*: Sabin, 143; Meg Watters, "Parker's Revenge Narrative Report, Phase I," Feb. 2014, MMNHP; final report, "Parker's Revenge Archaeological Project," Friends of the MMNHP, Oct. 2016, 55, 157–93. By studying more than thirty musket balls found on the site, the authors of this exceptional study inferred the adversaries' tactical positions on the afternoon of April 19, 1775.

71 *The "plaguey fire"*: Trevelyan, *The American Revolution*, 192; Sabin, 147; *PRR*, 230–31; Lister, *Concord Fight*, 29–32, 54 (*right elbow*). Some accounts assert that a pair of handsome Scottish pistols captured by the rebels belonged to Pitcairn, but recent scholarship strongly suggests that they were owned by a grenadier captain from the 38th Foot. E. J. Witek, "The Pitcairn-Putnam Pistols," www.drbenjaminchurchjr.blogspot.com, Dec. 15, 2011.

71 *The combat grew even more*: Sabin, 149–50; NPS signage, MMNHP (*Fiske parlor*).

72 *"Our ammunition began to fail"*: Stephenson, *Patriot Battles*, 126; Holmes, *Redcoat*, 3; Curtis, *The British Army in the American Revolution*, 19; "Narrative, &c.," in "Gage's Instructions," Project Gutenberg, American Antiquarian Society Library, reprinted, Arno Press, 1971, "Eyewitness Accounts of the American Revolution," series 3 ("*if they advanced*").

72 *more than a thousand redcoats*: Beck calculates Percy's force at 1,148, excluding musicians and surgeons. *Igniting the American Revolution*, 346–47.

72 *Smith's beleaguered men*: *Fusilier*, 55; Stedman, *The History of the Origin, Progress, and Termination of the American War*, vol. 1, 118 ("*tongues hanging*"); *LHEP*, 49–51.

72 *Wounded men collapsed*: Douglas P. Sabin, "The New England Tavern: A General Study," MMNHP, 1982, 23; Sabin, 166; Cash, *Medical Men at the Siege of Boston*, 21; Hallahan, *The Day the American Revolution Began*, 11–12; Chase, vol. 3, 94. Sgt. William Munroe, the tavern owner who the previous evening had guarded Reverend Clarke's parsonage, later calculated his losses at £203, 11 shillings. Coburn, *The Battle of April 19, 1775*, 127–28.

72 *To the delight of those rescued*: Chase, vol. 3, 85–88; Hughes, *Firepower*, 16–17; *DCL*, 233, 242–43, 248.

72 *Overseeing this spectacle*: Murdock, *The Nineteenth of April 1775*, 91; Don N. Hagist to author, e-mail, Mar. 2018 (*scarlet, royal blue*); *LHEP*, 15–18, 54 ("*I had the happiness*"); Gruber, *Books and the British Army in the Age of the American Revolution*, 115–16 (*Frederick the Great*); Volo, *Blue Water Patriots*, 137 ("*Cannon lends*").

73 *"This is the most beautiful country"*: *LHEP*, 27, 30–31, 43–44.

73 *Two blunders*: *The Detail and Conduct of the American War*, 9; "The Rev. David McClure's 19th of April," *B 1775*, Apr. 19, 2016 ("*Their countenances*"); *WR*, 47; Kallich and MacLeish, eds., *The American Revolution Through British Eyes*, 50 ("*Yankee Doodle*").

73 *Not until one p.m.*: *LHEP*, 49–51; Duncan, *History of the Royal Regiment of Artillery*, vol. 1, 302 (*140 extra artillery rounds*); Smith, *West Cambridge 1775*, 29–31; Brown, *Beneath Old Roof Trees*, 252–53; Chase, vol. 3, 107–10; Vincent J.-R. Kehoe, "We Were There!," vol. 1, MMNHP, 29; *PRR*, 242–44.

74 *At three-fifteen p.m., Percy ordered*: *Fusilier*, 55; French, "The British Expedition to Concord, Massachusetts, in 1775," *Journal of the American Military History Foundation* 1, no. 1 (Spring 1937): 3+; MMNHP, signage. Sabin estimates that 2,000 rebels pursued from Lexington while another 38 companies with 1,800 men joined the fight in Menotomy. Sabin, 172, 179–80.

74 *Looting began*: Barker, *The British in Boston*, 38–39; Sabin, 174; Chase, vol. 3, 89, 92–94, 169–71 (*beaver hats*); Fusilier, 57–58 (*"enflamed the rebels"*).

74 *"We were attacked"*: Evelyn, 53–54; Sabin, 183; PRR, 256–58; Barker, *The British in Boston*, 35–36 (*"put to death"*).

74 *Over a hundred British bullets*: Murdock, *The Nineteenth of April 1775*, 126–29; Sabin, 177–78, 182 (*"brains dashed"*); Philbrick, *Bunker Hill*, 157; Sanderson, ed., *Lynn in the Revolution*, part 1, RI, 43–44 (*buttons on his waistcoat*); Smith, *West Cambridge 1775*, 38–39; Brown, *Beneath Old Roof Trees*, 255.

75 *"We retired for 15 miles"*: LHEP, 52; Cumming, *British Maps of Colonial America*, 66 (*sketch map*); Winsor, ed., *The Memorial History of Boston*, vol. 3, part 1, 74–75; PRR, 259; French, "The British Expedition to Concord, Massachusetts, in 1775," *Journal of the American Military History Foundation* 1, no. 1 (Spring 1937): 3+ (*"an end that day"*).

75 *The final miles to Charlestown*: "The American Revolution Comes to Cambridge," Cambridge Historical Commission, http://www2.cambridgema.gov/Historic/revolutionarymap.html; LHEP, 27, 30–31, 43–53 (*"to fire at me"*); Lister, *Concord Fight*, 31–32 (*"prudent to dismount"*); Chase, vol. 3, 167 (*"drank like dogs"*); DCL, 259–60 (*"most fatiguing"*).

75 *"filled with women whose husbands"*: "The American Revolution Comes to Cambridge," Cambridge Historical Commission, http://www2.cambridgema.gov/Historic/revolutionary map.html.

76 *Dusk brightened each muzzle flash*: Winsor, ed., *The Memorial History of Boston*, vol. 3, part 1, 74; Heath, *Memoirs of Major-General William Heath*, 8–9; *Siege*, 79–80; Frothingham, "Mr. Frothingham's Remarks," *Proceedings*, MHS, 1875–76: 53+; Frothingham, *The History of Charlestown*, 320 (*"tumult"*); Sabin, 195 (*Edward Barber*); Chase, vol. 3, 192.

76 *The shooting ebbed*: Fusilier, 59; Murdock, *The Nineteenth of April 1775*, 98–99; Brown, *Beside Old Hearth-Stones*, 253 (*"The civil war"*); Chase, vol. 3, 254 (*"nail is driven"*).

76 *A thousand campfires glittered*: Chase, vol. 3, 183; Tomlinson, ed., *The Military Journals of Two Private Soldiers*, 52–53 (*"as much liquor"*); Graves, Apr. 18–19, 1775 (*"laying waste"*); FYAR, 21.

77 *The countryside hardly slept*: Brown, *Beneath Old Roof Trees*, 273; Tourtellot, *Lexington and Concord*, 217–20 (*"great perplexity"*); Chase, vol. 3, 214–15.

77 *Women in Framingham*: George Quintal, Jr., "Patriots of Color," MMNHP report, Feb. 2002, 34 (*"going to kill us"*); Smith, *West Cambridge 1775*, 50; Cash, *Medical Men at the Siege of Boston*, 24 (*Anglican church*); Cutter and Cutter, *History of the Town of Arlington, Massachusetts*, 64; Murdock, *The Nineteenth of April 1775*, 127. Another account put Whittemore's age at seventy-eight in 1775. Katie Turner Getty, "Before the Bayonetting: The Untold Story of Capt. Samuel Whittemore," *JAR*, June 6, 2017.

77 *"Freedom or independence"*: Chase, vol. 3, 142, 147.

77 *In Boston, surgeons toiled*: Lister, *Concord Fight*, 35–37; Fusilier, 61 (*anatomical simplicity*); Chase, vol. 3, 188 (*deliberately scored*); Ganoe, *The History of the United States Army*, 7. Royster writes that "some men split their bullets before loading, causing them to break into four pieces when fired." *A Revolutionary People at War*, 35.

77 *The butcher's bill*: Sabin, 197–98. Various casualty tallies inevitably vary slightly. WR, 50; PRR, 321.

78 *"I saw several dead bodies"*: "The Rev. David McClure's 20th of April," B 1775, May 3, 2016; Brown, *Beneath Old Roof Trees*, 226 (*"a brilliant uniform"*); Joyce Lee Malcom, "The Scene of the Battle, 1775: Historic Grounds Report, Minute Man National Historical Park," NPS, 1985, 56–58.

78 *The fourteen-year-old son*: Murdock, *The Nineteenth of April 1775*, 120; DCL, 183–84 (*"countenance"*); *Proceedings of the Centennial Celebration of the Battle of Lexington*, 87 (*"loving husband"*).

78 *In Danvers, a young girl*: Sabin, 184; Chase, vol. 3, 137; Smith, *West Cambridge 1775*, 52 (*"head to point"*); Tourtellot, *Lexington and Concord*, 141–42; Alexander Cain, "The April 19, 1775, Civilian Evacuation of Lexington," *JAR*, June 27, 2017 (*"a little rainy"*).

78 *The British would never return*: author visit, Concord Museum, Aug. 28, 2015 (*Fifty-eight towns*); Galvin, *The Minute Men*, 3.

78 *tubby, sensible William Heath*: PRR, 246–50. French is generally harsher in his assessment of Heath. *The Day of Concord and Lexington*, 252–54.

79 *attack of kidney stones*: Philbrick, *Bunker Hill*, 164.

79 *The limits of the musket*: WR, 50; DCL, 258; Coakley and Conn, *The War of the American Revolution*, 26. Joseph Seymour, U.S. Army National Guard historian, in an e-mail to the author, Jan. 21, 2015, notes that 29 musket cartridges typically used a pound of gunpowder; at that rate, 75,000 shots would have consumed almost 2,600 pounds.

79 *Fewer than one militiaman*: Fuller, *British Light Infantry in the Eighteenth Century*, 154; Curtis, *The British Army in the American Revolution*, 20; John Bell, "On the Nature and Cure of Gun-Shot Wounds," in *The British Military Library*, vol. 1, 156, 180. American marksmanship on April 19 may have demonstrated that the equation was exaggerated by a factor greater than two: 75,000 ounces of lead, or 4,687 pounds, killed 73 regulars, who, at an average of 150 pounds each, weighed 10,950 pounds collectively. Each British death required about 64 pounds of bullets. This, of course, presumes the bullets weighed exactly an ounce each, that 75,000 were fired, and that no British soldiers died from friendly fire or causes other than rebel gunfire.

79 *"Whoever looks upon them"*: LHEP, 52–53; Fusilier, 74 (*"violent and determined"*).

79 *The British combat performance*: Tourtellot, *Lexington and Concord*, 209; WAI, 63; Fusilier, 73 (*"inattention"*); Harvey to Col. Pigott, and Harvey to Percy, both June 26, 1775, UK NA, WO 3/23, 167–168 (*"unlucky"*).

79 *Like a burning fuse*: PRR, 267; Chase, vol. 3, 287 (*"Gage has fired"*); Stone, *The Life and Recollection of John Howland*, 39 (*"War, war"*); Mott, "The Newspaper Coverage of Lexington and Concord," *New England Quarterly* 17, no. 4 (Dec. 1944): 493–95; Andrlik, *Reporting the Revolutionary War*, 120–22.

79 *In barely three weeks*: Davidson, *Propaganda and the American Revolution, 1763–1783*, 237; PRR, 271; Hibbert, *Redcoats and Rebels*, 37 (*grandfathers shot*); Chase, vol. 3, 203–04 (*pregnant women*); Dexter, *The Literary Diary of Ezra Stiles, D.D., LL.D.*, vol. 1, 538 (*"very affecting"*); Leiby, *The Revolutionary War in the Hackensack Valley*, 25–26; Royster, *A Revolutionary People at War*, 25 (*"the rage militaire"*); Hoock, *Scars of Independence*, 18 (*"looker on"*); Ryden, ed., *Letters to and from Caesar Rodney*, 58–59 (*order drums*); Rossman, *Thomas Mifflin and the Politics of the American Revolution*, 41 (*"thick as bees"*), 35 (*"Broadbrims"*).

80 *Meeting in Concord on April 22*: Sabin, 201; Tourtellot, *Lexington and Concord*, 231–35; J. Warren to BF, Apr. 26, 1775, Feinstone Collection, #2437, DLAR (*"unnatural war"*); David F. Wood, curator, Concord Museum, interview with author, Aug. 28, 2015 (*violated innocence*); Todd Andrlik, "How Paul Revere's Ride Was Published and Censored in 1775," JAR, Feb. 3, 2015.

80 *A swift American schooner*: *Essex Gazette*, Apr. 25, 1775, HD; Rantoul, "The Cruise of the 'Quero': How We Carried the News to the King," *Century Illustrated Monthly Magazine*, Sept. 1899; Bob Ruppert, "A Fast Ship from Salem: Carrying News of War," JAR, Apr. 17, 2015; PRR, 275 (*"profound secret"*); Lutnick, *The American Revolution and the British Press*, 63.

80 *The king's resolve*: Donoughue, *British Politics and the American Revolution*, 275 (*"firmness"*); AA, IV: 2, 870–71 (*"suspension"*); Tourtellot, *Lexington and Concord*, 237–38 (*"looks serious"*).

80 *The news of Concord*: Steuart, ed., *The Last Journals of Horace Walpole*, vol. 1, 465; Philip John Schuyler orderly book, July 21, 1775, HM 663, HL (*guard at St. James's*); *The Manuscripts of the Earl of Dartmouth*, vol. 2, American Papers, 41 (*"All my prejudices"*); Ritcheson, *British Politics and the American Revolution*, 192; Rantoul, "The Cruise of the 'Quero': How We Carried the News to the King," *Century Illustrated Monthly Magazine*, Sept. 1899 (*brig Sukey*); Gage to Dartmouth, Apr. 22, 1775, UK NA, CO 5/92, f. 134, in DAR, vol. 9, 103 (*"threatening an attack"*).

81 *Preparations also continued*: Gross, *The Minutemen and Their World*, 131; Levin, *Abigail Adams*, 505n (*pewter spoons*); Brown, *Beneath Old Roof Trees*, 273 (*pried the shoes*); Chase, vol. 3, 144 (*scarecrow*); PRR, 173 (*Lamentations*).

81 *"the meeting of strong men"*: DCL, 272.

81 *Lieutenant Edward Hull of the 43rd Foot*: "The Rev. David McClure's 20th of April," B 1775, May 3, 2016; Brown, *Beneath Old Roof Trees*, 271–73; Chase, vol. 3, 150–52; "Bevan's Family

Tree Research," http://bevansfamiltytree.blogspot.com/2008_11_01_archive.html; Shurtleff, *A Topographical and Historical Description of Boston*, 446 (*"took heaven"*).

82 *He, at least, would be drummed*: Coburn, *The Battle of April 19, 1775*, 103.

3. I WISH THIS CURSED PLACE WAS BURNED

83 *An army of sorts*: FYAR, 61; Brown, *Beside Old Hearth-Stones*, 132 (*shut the gate*); Ketchum, *Decisive Day*, 54 (*from New Hampshire*); Buel, *Dear Liberty*, 36–37 (*seventy-two towns*); Berthelson, "An Alarm from Lexington," Connecticut Society of the Sons of the American Revolution, www.connecticutsar.org/an-alarm-from-lexington (*"ardor of our people"*); *Spirit '76*, 94–95 (*"only brother"*).

83 *the Grand American Army*: Crane, "The Battle of Bunker Hill," *Lippincott's Monthly*, vol. 65 (Jan.–June 1900): 924+; Murdock, *Bunker Hill: Notes and Queries on a Famous Battle*, 45–46 (*"armed mob"*); Austin, *The Life of Elbridge Gerry*, 78 (*"stripped the seaports"*); Nevins, *American States During and After the Revolution*, 68 (*enlisted fifty-nine others*).

83 *Drums beat reveille*: Ketchum, *Decisive Day*, 87–90; FYAR, 176 (*"clergymen"*); Swett, *History of Bunker Hill Battle*, 10 (*volunteered their services*); orderly book, Moses Fargos, June 14, 1775, *Collections*, CHS, vol. 7, 1879: 11+, in RI, "American Accounts of the Siege of Boston," vol. 1 (*grogshops*); Hamner, *Enduring Battle*, 157; Lockhart, *The Whites of Their Eyes*, 178 (*"took a nap"*); Alden, *General Gage in America*, 256 (*"smallpox"*).

84 *No sooner did the Grand American Army*: Buel, *Dear Liberty*, 36–37; Smith, "The Rise of Artemas Ward, 1727–1777," Ph.D. diss. (University of Colorado, Boulder, 1990), 225 (*"going and coming"*); *Siege*, 107–08 (*feign preponderance*).

84 *"We are in want"*: Reed, ed., *Life and Correspondence of Joseph Reed*, vol. 1, 104; Bell, *The Road to Concord*, 167 (*fieldpieces*); Chidsey, *The Siege of Boston*, 56 (*"tatterdemalions"*); Randall, *Benedict Arnold*, 94–95.

84 *Almost fifty sleepy redcoats*: E. Allen to Jonathan Trumbull, May 12, 1775, T-P RC, #1933; French, *The Taking of Ticonderoga*, 38, 42–53; Stanley, *Canada Invaded*, 22–23.

84 *The captured booty included*: John Brown to Continental Congress, May 20, 1775, *AA*, IV: 2, 623; Smith, *Ethan Allen and the Capture of Fort Ticonderoga*, 85–86; Bascom and Holden, *The Ticonderoga Expedition of 1775*, 54; Holbrook, *Ethan Allen*, 18–19 (*forty-nine gallons*).

84 *Two men led the raid*: BARH, 36, 52, 62–72; Brumwell, *Turncoat*, 25, 29; Belcher, *The First American Civil War*, vol. 1, 167 (*"burglarious"*).

85 *Life in besieged Boston*: AA, IV: 1, 374–76, 747 (*1,778 firelocks*); Samuel Cooper diary, May 6, 1775, HL, CO 271 (*swords*); Sargent, ed., *Letters of John Andrews, Esq., of Boston*, 93–95 (*"parents that are lucky"*).

85 *Loyalists from the countryside*: *Siege*, 95–96; Alexander Cain, "Anxiety and Distress: Civilians Inside the Siege of Boston," *JAR*, Feb. 13, 2017; FYAR, 117–18 (*"distress"*); Lt. Richard Williams, June 12, 1775, display, MMNHP Visitor Center, Concord (*"ruined town"*); William Shirreff to Thomas Williams, May 29, 1775, NDAR, vol. 1, 557–58 (*provender*); Crary, *The Price of Loyalty*, 97 (*"not uncommon"*); Maud M. Hutcheson, "Wiswall, John," *Dictionary of Canadian Biography*, vol. 5, University of Toronto, Université Laval, http://www.biographi.ca/en/bio/wiswall_john_5E.html.

85 *From his Province House headquarters*: Ketchum, *Decisive Day*, 22; orders, July 11, 1775, Frederick Mackenzie papers, vol. C, WLC (*vigil*); Gage to Dartmouth, May 13, 1775, DAR, vol. 7, 325 (*"great multitudes"*); Carter, ed., *The Correspondence of General Thomas Gage*, vol. 1, 399 (*"arming at New York"*); FYAR, 171 (*locked bag*).

86 *Guard boat crews*: *Siege*, 98; Graves, May 13, 1775; Williams, *Discord and Civil Wars*, RI, 3; Evelyn, 55 (*"all in arms"*); LAR, 121 (*"rabble"*); Moore, *Diary of the American Revolution*, xxiv (*"to their graves"*).

86 *There would be ashes*: *Massachusetts Spy*, May 24, 1775; Pierce, *The Diary of John Rowe*, 92; Ford, ed., *Correspondence and Journals of Samuel Blachley Webb*, vol. 1, 58–60 (*"such stupidity"*); "Journal of an Officer of the 47th Regiment of Foot," May 17, 1775, HL, HM 66 (*losses at Dock Square*); *Evacuation*, 130–31 (*Boston's poor*).

86 *Fresh meat for British larders*: Tilley, *The British Navy and the American Revolution*, 4–5; Volo, *Blue Water Patriots*, 150; Deary, 62–63; Willis, *The Struggle for Sea Power*, 37; Beatson, *Naval and Military Memoirs of Great Britain*, vol. 4, 82–87 *(American mariners)*; *WR*, 56; *Evacuation*, 142–43.

87 *On Saturday morning, May 27*: report, Mass. Committee of Safety, n.d., *NDAR*, vol. 1, 545; Brown et al., "The Revolutionary War Battle America Forgot," *New England Quarterly* 86, no. 3 (Sept. 2013): 398+; Green, ed., *Diary Kept by Lieut. Amos Farnsworth*, 10 *(to Hog Island)*; Sumner, *A History of East Boston*, 115, 125 *(Baptist apostates)*; Pierce, *The Diary of John Rowe*, 56–57 *(dueling ground)*.

87 *Aboard the fifty-gun* Preston: *Preston* log, May 27, 1775, *NDAR*, vol. 1, 546; James, *The British Navy in Adversity*, 26; Miller, *Sea of Glory*, 26–27 *(small stroke)*; Barker, *The British in Boston*, 16 *(Pearl Street)*; Tilley, *The British Navy and the American Revolution*, 66 *(venturing out)*; Sandwich, vol. 1, 42 *(thirty vessels)*; *DAR*, vol. 9, 12–13; Graves, Mar. 19, 1775 *("no seizures")*.

87 *Graves badgered the Admiralty*: Graves, Oct. 30, 1774, Jan. 8, 1775; Beatson, *Naval and Military Memoirs of Great Britain*, vol. 4, 82–91; James, *The British Navy in Adversity*, 31 *(ample flint)*; Miller, *Sea of Glory*, 37 *(whom he detested)*; Sandwich, vol. 1, 42 *(nepotism)*; W. Eden to G. Germain, Oct. 3, 1775, *Ninth Report of the Royal Commission on Historical Manuscripts*, part 3 (London: Eyre and Spottiswoode, 1883): 82 *("corrupt admiral")*; *FYAR*, 537 *(mutton)*; Evelyn, 64 *("every man")*.

88 *Graves loathed*: Graves, Feb. 1, 1775; *NDAR*, vol. 1, 546, 554 *(detachment of 170 marines)*; Noddle's Island narrative, n.d., CMSA, #101, vol. 146, "Revolution Military," micro; Brown et al., "The Revolutionary War Battle America Forgot," *New England Quarterly* 86, no. 3 (Sept. 2013): 398+; Green, ed., *Diary Kept by Lieut. Amos Farnsworth*, 10 *("sung like bees")*.

88 *At twilight three hundred militia*: "Journal of an Officer of the 47th Regiment of Foot," HM 66, HL. J. L. Bell, author of *The Road to Concord*, confirms that "that's the first time the provincials fired their cannon in battle." E-mail to author, Jan. 11, 2018.

88 *stubby, rough-hewn brawler*: Moore, *The Diary of the American Revolution*, 182–83; Thacher, *Military Journal*, 405 *("dared to lead")*; *FYAR*, 187 *("totally unfit")*; Cutter, *The Life of Israel Putnam*, 39, 79, 102, 113, 135; Tarbox, *Life of Israel Putnam*, 63, 68; *Connecticut in the American Revolution* (2001): 11, SoC, State Exhibition Series, www.societyofthecincinnati.org /scholarship/publications/; *GC*, 288; GW HQ, 114 *(Pontiac's War)*.

89 *She was poised for destruction*: Brown et al., "The Revolutionary War Battle America Forgot," *New England Quarterly* 86, no. 3 (Sept. 2013): 398+; "A Circumstantial Account of the Late Battle at Chelsea," *New York Journal*, June 8, 1775, *NDAR*, vol. 1, 545; Sumner, *A History of East Boston*, 375.

89 *Admiral of the White* Graves: Sumner, *A History of East Boston*, 375; May 28, 1775, journal entry, KP *("by no means approved")*; *Siege*, 110 *(two thousand head)*; Graves, Jan. 8 and June 7, 1775; Henry Howell Williams to Massachusetts Provincial Congress, June 12, 1775, *AA*, IV: 1, 971; Brown et al., "The Revolutionary War Battle America Forgot," *New England Quarterly* 86, no. 3 (Sept. 2013): 398+.

90 *"Heaven apparently"*: letter, June 1, 1775, *AA*, IV: 1, 874; Avery, "A Chaplain of the American Revolution," *American Monthly*, vol. 17, no. 4 (Oct. 1990): 342+; Green, ed., *Paul Lunt's Diary*, 9 *(flagpole)*; "Diary of Samuel Bixby," *Proceedings*, MHS, vol. 14 (1875–76): 285+ *(British barge)*; Daughan, *If by Sea*, 22 *("every day")*.

90 *Gage declared martial law*: proclamation, June 12, 1775, Frederick Mackenzie papers, vol. D, WLC.

90 *The same day, Gage*: Carter, ed., *The Correspondence of General Thomas Gage*, vol. 2, 684 *("raise the Negroes")*, vol. 1, 402–05 *(hay and oats)*; De Fonblanque, *Political and Military Episodes*, 140–41 *(pay his officers)*; Gage letter, June 12, 1775, "George III Calendar, Jan. 1774–Aug. 1775," RA GEO/MAIN/#2034 *(32,000 soldiers)*; W. Howe to Harvey, June 12, 1775, *Proceedings of the Bunker Hill Monument Association*, June 17, 1907, 109–10; Fortescue, ed., *The Correspondence of King George the Third*, vol. 3, 215 *("all warlike preparations")*.

90 *Gage's adjutant complained*: Willcox, *Portrait of a General*, 45; *Spirit '76*, 135 (*"bull by the horns"*); Lushington, *The Life and Services of General Lord Harris*, 52 (*"good drubbing"*); Evelyn, 58 (*"hard knocks"*).

90 *The imminent arrival of transports*: Knollenberg, "Bunker Hill Re-viewed: A Study in the Conflict of Historical Evidence," *Proceedings*, MHS, 3rd ser., 72 (Oct. 1957–Dec. 1960): 84+; Alden, *General Gage in America*, 265–66. Murdock puts the British force at 6,400. *Bunker Hill*, 6–7.

92 *"make an attempt"*: Gage letter, June 12, 1775, "George III Calendar, Jan. 1774–Aug. 1775," RA GEO/MAIN/#2034; June 17, 1775, KP; French, *General Gage's Informers*, 118–19 (*high ground*); W. Howe to Harvey, and W. Howe to R. Howe, both June 12, 1775, *Proceedings of the Bunker Hill Monument Association*, June 17, 1907, 109–17; W. Howe to Harvey, June 22 and 24, 1775; Fortescue, ed., *The Correspondence of King George the Third*, vol. 3, 220–24; Burgoyne to Stanley, June 25, 1775, *AA*, IV: 2, 1094; Martyn, *The Life of Artemas Ward*, 141n, 115–21; Philbrick, *Bunker Hill*, 191.

92 *No sooner was the plan conceived*: Alden, *General Gage in America*, 266; French, *The Siege of Boston*, 252–53; *AA*, IV: 2, 979 (*from New Hampshire*); letter, Benjamin White, Committee of Safety, June 15, 1775, CMSA, vol. 146, "Revolution Military," micro (*"securely kept"*); Ketchum, *Decisive Day*, 74–75. American commanders recognized the vulnerability of Dorchester Heights. In mid-May, Brig. Gen. John Thomas wrote Ward, "I have thoroughly reconnoitered the ground . . . & much despair of defending it." Thomas to Ward, May 18, 1775, Thomas papers, MHS, micro, reel 3.

92 *The American camps bustled*: minutes, Committee of Safety, June 15, 1775, CMSA, vol. 140, "Revolutionary Miscellaneous, 1775–1778," micro (*thirty rounds*); corr., William Hoskins, June 16, 1775, CMSA, vol. 205, "Revolution Letters, 1775–1783," micro (*"shirts & trousers"*); Smith, "The Rise of Artemas Ward, 1727–1777," Ph.D. diss. (University of Colorado, Boulder, 1990), 234–36 (*Harvard's library*); GW HQ, 227–28; Swett, *History of Bunker Hill Battle*, 18; Winsor, ed., *The Memorial History of Boston*, vol. 3, part 1, 82n; "Sundries Supplies from Ordnance Store, 1775" and "Stores Received from Sundry Persons," PC3/series 2353, folder 1; "Records of Cambridge Store," PS1.05/series 2333X, blotter 4; "Records of Roxbury Store," PS1.05/series 2326X, all CMSA (*provisions arriving*); Provincial Congress, Watertown, June 17, 1775, CMSA, vol. 146, "Revolution Military," micro (*"meeting on the Sabbath"*); Lockhart, *The Whites of Their Eyes*, 184–85 (*"hubbub"*).

92 *Orders spilled from the headquarters*: Paul Lockhart, "Before Washington: The Revolution's First Commander-in-Chief," in Andrlik et al., eds., *Journal of the American Revolution*, vol. 1, 44; Martyn, *The Life of Artemas Ward*, 7–12, 27, 81, 90–91 (*Chosen People*); GW HQ, 101 (*"swearing and cursing"*); WR, 74–75 (*his health*); Lockhart, *The Whites of Their Eyes*, 85–86; "Memoir of Major General Artemas Ward," *New England Historical and Genealogical Register* 5, no. 3 (1851): 271–72; WR, 85–86; *FYAR*, 48–49; Wright, *The Continental Army*, 20 (*coherent chain of command*); Ward to John Thomas, June 3, 1775, Thomas papers, MHS, micro, reel 3 (*almost sixty guns*).

93 *Shortly after six p.m.*: Lockhart, *The Whites of Their Eyes*, 187–88; Brown, *Beside Old Hearth-Stones*, 119–20 (*tumpline*).

93 *Twilight faded*: Chidsey, *The Siege of Boston*, 77; Ketchum, *Decisive Day*, 98–102; W. Prescott to J. Adams, Aug. 25, 1775, FOL (*a thousand men*).

93 *General Ward had remained*: Ellis, *History of the Battle of Bunker's (Breed's) Hill*, 37, 39; Brown, *Beside Old Hearth-Stones*, 8, 23–24, 68; WR, 77; *Siege*, 122, 167 (*twice in Canada*); Philbrick, *Bunker Hill*, 201 (*never to be taken alive*); Temple, *History of Framingham, Massachusetts*, 292 (*"a bold man"*).

94 *Bold orders this evening*: Walker, *Engineers of Independence*, 2–3; Philbrick, *Bunker Hill*, 197; Bernard Bailyn, "The Battle of Bunker Hill," MHS, http://www.masshist.org/bh/index.html (*dominant terrain*); Drake, *History of Middlesex County*, vol. 1, 143; Ellis, *An Oration Delivered*, 30; Ellis, *History of the Battle of Bunker's (Breed's) Hill*, 43; Frothingham, *The Centennial: Battle of Bunker Hill*, 15; "Judge Prescott's Account of the Battle of Bunker Hill" and "Mr. Frothingham's Remarks," *Proceedings*, MHS (1875–76): 68+, 53+. David L. Preston sent me a picture of Gridley's unusual powder horn.

94 *For reasons never explained*: AA, IV: 2, 1373. Accounts vary on the precise shape and size of the redoubt. Beck, *The War Before Independence*, 67; Ketchum, *Decisive Day*, 111; Lockhart, *The Whites of Their Eyes*, 197.

94 *Accustomed to pick-and-shovel work*: Murdock, *Bunker Hill*, 8–9; Ketchum, *Decisive Day*, 111–12; WR, 79.

94 *The rhythmic chink of metal*: S. Graves to P. Stephens, June 16, 1775, DAR, vol. 9, 172; *Lively* journal, June 17, 1775, NDAR 1, 700; Tilley, *The British Navy and the American Revolution*, 36–37; Lockhart, *The Whites of Their Eyes*, 202–03. Dawn was at 4:09 a.m. EST on June 17. "Sun and Moon Data," U.S. Naval Observatory.

95 *The ship beat to quarters*: Standing orders from Graves authorized captains to fire against any threat to their ships. Graves, Apr. 25, 1775 orders, appendix 7.

95 *Sailors tumbled from their hammocks*: Volo, *Blue Water Patriots*, 138; *Somerset* log, June 17–18, 1775, UK NA ADM 51/906; Graves narrative, June 17, 1775, NDAR 1, 704.

95 *Dawn, that great revealer*: Elting, *The Battle of Bunker's Hill*, 25; Dexter, *The Literary Diary of Ezra Stiles, D.D., LL.D.*, vol. 1, 595 (*"danger we were in"*); Wheeler, *Voices of 1776*, 57 (*"besmeared"*); Swett, *History of Bunker Hill*, 22 (*"Bury him"*).

95 *The redoubt taking shape*: Elting, *The Battle of Bunker's Hill*, 24; GGW, 100 (*with bayonets*); "Judge Prescott's Account of the Battle of Bunker Hill" and "Mr. Frothingham's Remarks," *Proceedings*, MHS (1875–76): 68+, 53+; Beck, *The War Before Independence*, 77, 334.

95 *He also sent an officer*: Swett, *History of Bunker Hill*, 24; Martyn, *The Life of Artemas Ward*, 126–29 (*"quiet as the Sabbath"*); Frothingham, *The Life and Times of Joseph Warren*, 512–14 (*headache*); Frothingham, *The Centennial: Battle of Bunker Hill*, 26. Twenty-seven half-barrels would contain about 1,350 pounds of powder, with each pound typically forming 29 musket cartridges. Joseph Seymour, U.S. Army National Guard historian, e-mail to author, Jan. 21, 2015. A British military field manual from 1757 quotes the great French engineer Marquis de Vauban as assuming 30 to 40 musket charges per pound of powder. Muller, *Attack and Defence of Fortified Places*, 135.

96 *With consent from the Committee*: Swett, *History of Bunker Hill*, 25; Ketchum, *Decisive Day*, 127–35.

96 *The deep boom of* Lively's *broadsides*: Murdock, *Earl Percy's Dinner Table*, 10–11, 40–42; Murdock, *Bunker Hill*, 8–9.

96 *Several senior officers*: Elting, *The Battle of Bunker's Hill*, 22; Murdock, *Bunker Hill*, 8–9; Barker, *The British in Boston*, 16n; Mintz, *The Generals of Saratoga*, 62 (*"unanimous from the beginning"*); MLA, 30, 83–84 (*"fittest men"*).

96 *Horace Walpole, ever astringent*: Steuart, ed., *The Last Journals of Horace Walpole*, vol. 1, 433; French, *The Siege of Boston*, 239 (*"Bow, wow, wow!"*); De Fonblanque, *Political and Military Episodes*, 140 (*"no reflection"*).

97 *As the windows trembled*: Willcox, *Portrait of a General*, 46–48; Belcher, *The First American Civil War*, vol. 1, 172.

97 *This scheme found little favor*: Glover, *General Burgoyne in Canada and America*, 84; Elting, *The Battle of Bunker's Hill*, 22; FYAR, 222.

97 *Gage chose a more conventional, direct assault*: W. Howe to R. Howe, June 22, 1775, Stopford-Sackville, vol. 2, 4; Ketchum, *Decisive Day*, 122.

97 *"Any man who shall quit"*: HOB, 1–2; Frothingham, *The Centennial: Battle of Bunker Hill*, 29.

97 *Admiral Graves, meanwhile*: Lister, *Concord Fight*, 49 (*"entrenched"*).

98 *As the morning ticked by*: Graves narrative, June 17, 1775; *Lively, Somerset, Preston, Glasgow, Falcon, Cerberus* journals, all in NDAR, vol. 1, 700–04; Smith, "Dover in the Revolution," *Dedham Historical Register*, vol. 3, 25 (*draped blankets*).

98 *Shortly before noon*: Lockhart, *The Whites of Their Eyes*, 237; HOB, 1–2 (*sixty rounds*); Hunter, *The Journal of Gen. Sir Martin Hunter*, 9–10; Houlding, *Fit for Service*, 141n; Boyle, ed., *From Redcoat to Rebel*, 15, 18 (*49th Foot*).

98 *At one-thirty p.m., a blue pennant*: HOB, 2; W. Howe to R. Howe, June 22, 1775, Stopford-Sackville, vol. 2, 4; Beck, *The War Before Independence*, 84–85, 361; Swett, *History of Bunker Hill Battle*, 26, 29; Ketchum, *Decisive Day*, 136–38, 162.

99   *"most awful and tremendous"*: Kidd, *God of Liberty*, 1–2.

99   *"Run him through"*: Swett, *Notes to His Sketch of Bunker-Hill Battle*, 12; Graydon, *Memoirs of His Own Time*, 179 (*"sicklemen"*).

99   *Nine Massachusetts regiments*: Ketchum, *Decisive Day*, 147; Elting, *The Battle of Bunker's Hill*, 26 (*"extremely irregular"*); Philbrick, *Bunker Hill*, 205; J. L. Bell, "Capt. Ebenezer Bancroft and the Embrasures," *B 1775*, June 14–16, 2014; *FYAR*, 228 (*"To be plain"*).

99   *Roughly two hundred yards behind the breastwork*: HH, 53; Perley, "Colonel Thomas Knowlton," *Historical Collections of the Essex Institute* 58, no. 2 (Apr. 1922): 89+; Philbrick, *Bunker Hill*, 211; Carrington, *Battles of the American Revolution*, 101 (*stake-and-rider*); Ketchum, *Decisive Day*, 143; Swett, *History of Bunker Hill*, 26–27.

100   *"moving column of uncouth figures"*: Moore, *A Life of General John Stark of New Hampshire*, 156–57; Philbrick, *Bunker Hill*, 211–12; Moran, "Major General John Stark of New Hampshire," *Liberty Tree Magazine* (May 2006), www.revolutionarywararchives.org/stark.html; Stark, *Memoir and Official Correspondence of Gen. John Stark*, 17–19, 22–24, 27–29, 112 (*"battle soon came on"*); Coffin, ed., *History of the Battle of Breed's Hill*, 18.

100   *Stark sent an advance detachment*: "Provisions Delivered Various Regiments, 1775," PS1.05/series 2393X, CMSA; Coffin, ed., *History of the Battle of Breed's Hill*, 13, 26 (*"One fresh man"*); Swett, *History of Bunker Hill Battle*, 26; Moore, *A Life of General John Stark of New Hampshire*, 159, 161.

101   *Thick-featured and taciturn*: HOB, vii (*"family gloom"*); W. Howe to R. Howe, June 22, 1775, Stopford-Sackville, vol. 2, 4. Beck's calculations put the second lift, including officers and artillery, at 619. *The War Before Independence*, 362–63.

101   *On his far left*: W. Howe to Harvey, June 22 and 24, 1775, in Fortescue, ed., *The Correspondence of King George the Third*, vol. 3, 220–24; Howe to Gage, June 21, 1775, in Belcher, *The First American Civil War*, vol. 1, 195–98. Beck puts the total number of Americans on the peninsula at 3,500, although barely half were in combat at any one time. *The War Before Independence, 1775–1776*, 370.

101   *Howe made his plan*: Ketchum, *Decisive Day*, 153; MLA, 88–89 (*sangfroid*); Drake, *Bunker Hill*, 43 (*"I shall not desire"* and *"very disagreeable"*); Fuller, *British Light Infantry in the Eighteenth Century*, 125 (*Speed, agility*); Coakley and Conn, *The War of the American Revolution*, 20.

101   *Including the reserves*: W. Howe to Harvey, June 22 and 24, 1775, puts the number at 2,200. Fortescue, ed., *The Correspondence of King George the Third*, vol. 3, 220–24. Beck's tabulation, including officers and artillerymen, sets the figure at 2,635. *The War Before Independence*, 365–66.

101   *British field guns began popping*: log, *Somerset*, June 17–18, 1775, UK NA, ADM 51/906; Ray Raphael, "The Whites of Their Eyes," in Andrlik et al., eds., *Journal of the American Revolution*, vol. 1, 35 (*"blue tail"*); Peter Brown to mother, June 25, 1775, MHS, www.masshist.org/bh/brownp2text.html (*"swung his hat"*); Ellis, *Revolutionary Summer*, 38 (*silver tray*); J. L. Bell, "Capt. Ebenezer Bancroft and the Embrasures," *B 1775*, June 15, 2014 (*"awful moment"*).

102   *"to have the place burned?"*: Graves, Bunker Hill account; Tilley, *The British Navy and the American Revolution*, 38–39; author visit, Copp's Burying Ground, May 2015, signage (*Woolves*); "Instructions Given to the Gentlemen Cadets When They Attend the Royal Laboratory at Woolwich," n.d., Royal Collection, Royal Library, RCIN #1047085 (*carcasses*).

102   *The first shell fell short*: Swett, *History of Bunker Hill Battle*, 38; Burgoyne to Lord Stanley, June 25, 1775, AA, IV: 2, 1094–95 (*"instantly in flames"*); Ketchum, *Decisive Day*, 155 (*"melancholy sight"*); Hunnewell, *A Century of Town Life*, 8–14 (*Three Cranes*); "Three Cranes Tavern," http://www.sec.state.ma.us/mhc/mhcarchexhibitsonline/threecranes.htm; Coffin, *History of the Battle of Breed's Hill*, 21 (*"thunder cloud"*).

103   *"The church steeples"*: Burgoyne to Lord Stanley, June 25, 1775, AA, IV: 2, 1094–95.

103   *Gawkers and gapers*: De Fonblanque, *Political and Military*, 156.

103   *The rebels waited*: Montross, *Rag, Tag and Bobtail*, 33 (*"buck and ball"*); Spring, *With Zeal and with Bayonets Only*, 212–13 (*"Yankee peas"*); Siege, 140 (*"handsome coats"*); Swett, *History of Bunker Hill Battle*, 34 (*angrily waved his sword*); J. L. Bell, "Capt. Ebenezer Bancroft

and the Embrasures," *B 1775*, June 14–16, 2014; Philbrick, *Bunker Hill*, 220 (*"at their hips"*); Brown, *Beside Old Hearth-Stones*, 35 (*"Waste no powder"*); James Wilkinson, "A Rapid Sketch of the Battle of Breed's Hill," in Charles Coffin, ed., *History of the Battle of Breed's Hill*, 13 (*half-gaiters*); Rose, *Men of War*, 30–31; Winsor, ed., *The Memorial History of Boston*, vol. 3, part 1, 85n.

103   *Howe's corps, on the British right*: Moore, *A Life of General John Stark of New Hampshire*, 168.

104   *A stupendous, searing volley*: Rose, *Men of War*, 35, 61 (*"three or four wounds"*); WR, 91 (*"red-hot plate"*); Longmore, *Gunshot Injuries*, 704 (*2,550 square inches*), 31 (*wedges of tissue*); Ketchum, *Decisive Day*, 159 (*"great disorder"*).

104   *They left behind ninety-six comrades*: That count, made by a visitor to the beach the next morning, apparently excluded officers, whose bodies had been removed. Stark, *Memoir and Official Correspondence of Gen. John Stark*, 31; James Wilkinson, "A Rapid Sketch of the Battle of Breed's Hill," in Coffin, ed., *History of the Battle of Breed's Hill*, 13.

104   *Howe heard the commotion*: Temple, *History of Framingham, Massachusetts*, 290 (*"fell in heaps"*); MQ, 578 (*"calm as a clock"*).

104   *Regulars from two trailing regiments*: Ellis, *History of the Battle of Bunker's (Breed's) Hill*, 71; Philbrick, *Bunker Hill*, 222; Moore, *A Life of General John Stark of New Hampshire*, 188 (*odd-sized barrels*); Coffin, ed., *History of the Battle of Breed's Hill*, 23 (*"See that officer?"*).

105   *"Their officers were shot down"*: Temple, *History of Framingham, Massachusetts*, 290; Maj. Francis Hutcheson to Gen. Haldimand, July 24, 1775, Haldimand Papers, LAC, micro H-1431; J. L. Bell, "Reports of Lt. Col. James Abercrombie's Death," *B 1775*, June 23, 2014; Urban, *Fusiliers*, 39.

105   *Before he died, a week later*: Rose, *Men of War*, 37; Hagist, "Shedding Light on Friendly Fire at Bunker Hill," *American Revolution* 1, no. 3 (Oct. 2009): 4+; Don N. Hagist, "James Abercrombie, Much Lamented Victim of Friendly Fire at Bunker Hill," *JAR*, June 14, 2017; AA, IV: 2, 1093 (*"Yankees cowards?"*); LAR, 135.

105   *"For near a minute"*: Philbrick, *Bunker Hill*, 224; HOB, viii (*white stockings*); Ketchum, *Decisive Day*, 162 (*"There was a moment"*).

105   *Brigadier Pigot had suffered*: FYAR, 746; Burgoyne to Lord Stanley, June 25, 1775, AA, IV: 2, 1094–95 (*"thousand impediments"*); Drake, *Bunker Hill*, 26 (*"some brick kilns"*).

105   *Volley upon volley crashed*: Greenwood, ed., *The Revolutionary Services of John Greenwood*, 14 (*"like grass"*); J. L. Bell, "Capt. Ebenezer Bancroft and the Embrasures," *B 1775*, June 15, 2014 (*"shockingly fatal"*); Swett, *History of Bunker Hill Battle*, 14 (*"a furrow"*), 37 (*dead redcoats*); "Journal of an Officer of the 47th Regiment of Foot," June 17, 1775, HM 66, HL (*"sheet of lightning"*); *Siege*, 398 (*threw stones*).

106   *Among the fallen was Major John Pitcairn*: Lt. John Waller, letter to "friend," June 21, 1775, MHS, www.masshist.org/bh/index.html; Maj. Francis Hutcheson to Gen. Haldimand, July 24, 1775, Haldimand Papers, LAC, micro H-1431; J. L. Bell, "Who Killed Major John Pitcairn?," in Andrlik et al., eds., *Journal of the American Revolution*, vol. 1, 42; Peter Brown to mother, June 25, 1775, MHS, www.masshist.org/bh/brownp2text.html (*"choaky mouthful"*); Greenwood, ed., *The Revolutionary Services of John Greenwood*, 14 (*"Diamond cut diamond"*).

106   *Not quite, for diamond would*: WR, 93; Ketchum, *Decisive Day*, 169; WAI, 76; Beck, *The War Before Independence*, 355–57 (*eight fieldpieces*); David McConnell, "British Smooth-Bore Artillery," National Historic Parks and Sites, Canada, 1988, 42.

106   *too fat for 6-pound muzzles*: Duncan, *History of the Royal Regiment of Artillery*, vol. 1, 302–03; *The Detail and Conduct of the American War*, 12–14; Hunter, *The Journal of Gen. Sir Martin Hunter*, 9–10; Murdock, *Bunker Hill*, 27–28; Toll, *Six Frigates*, 8 (*canvas bags*).

106   *Peering over the parapet*: W. Prescott to J. Adams, Aug. 25, 1775, FOL; Cutter, *The Life of Israel Putnam*, 177; Frothingham, *The History of Charlestown*, 83 (*shirttails*), 147–48; GW HQ, 316; J. L. Bell, Benjamin Pierce account, *B 1775*, June 16, 2015; Beck, *The War Before Independence*, 345–48.

107   *The failure of General Ward's headquarters*: Philbrick, *Bunker Hill*, 216–19; Drake, *Bunker Hill*, 50.

107   *Up the peninsula*: Burnham, *Recollections of the Revolutionary War*, 5 (*"great confusion"*); Rose, *Men of War*, 21 (*grain flail*); *Siege*, 391 (*"without any excuse"*); Swett, *History of Bunker*

Hill Battle, 37 (*"corpulence"*); Ford, ed., *Correspondence and Journals of Samuel Blachley Webb*, vol. 1, 64–65 (*"such a tremor"*).

107   *The sun had begun to dip*: Duncan, *History of the Royal Regiment of Artillery*, vol. 1, 302–03; Swett, *History of Bunker Hill Battle*, 43; "Francis Merrifield's Bible," *B 1775*, June 17, 2016 (*"too handsome"*); W. Prescott to J. Adams, Aug. 25, 1775, FOL; "Judge Prescott's Account of the Battle of Bunker Hill," *Proceedings*, MHS (1875–76): 68+ (*staggered the enemy ranks*); Lushington, *The Life and Services of General Lord Harris*, 55–56 (*"let me die"*).

107   *But the battle had turned*: Spring, *With Zeal and with Bayonets Only*, 176; "Judge Prescott's Account of the Battle of Bunker Hill," *Proceedings*, MHS (1875–76): 68+; Temple, *History of Framingham, Massachusetts*, 292 (*"old candle"*); Ferling, *Almost a Miracle*, 58 (*"like devils"*).

108   *Prescott was among the last*: FYAR, 249; "Judge Prescott's Account of the Battle of Bunker Hill," *Proceedings*, MHS (1875–76): 68+; Peter Brown to mother, June 25, 1775, MHS, www .masshist.org/bh/brownp2text.html (*"hail stones"*); J. L. Bell, "Capt. Ebenezer Bancroft and the Embrasures," *B 1775*, June 14–16, 2014 (*forefinger*); Green, ed., *Diary Kept by Lieut. Amos Farnsworth*, 12–13 (*"penny"*).

108   *"Nothing could be more shocking"*: Drake, *Bunker Hill*, 28, 33; Lt. J. Waller to "friend," June 21, 1775, MHS, www.masshist.org/bh/index.html (*"brains"*); Ford, ed., *Correspondence and Journals of Samuel Blachley Webb*, vol. 1, 66; Murdock, *Bunker Hill*, 31. Ellis writes that some wounded Americans were "dispatched with bayonets by British execution squads"; others were taken as prisoners to Boston. *Revolutionary Summer*, 3.

108   *"I had no other feeling"*: Ford, ed., *Correspondence and Journals of Samuel Blachley Webb*, vol. 1, 76; Philbrick, *Bunker Hill*, 229; Forman, *Dr. Joseph Warren*, 358–66; Derek W. Beck, "Founding Martyr: The Life and Death of Dr. Joseph Warren, the American Revolution's Lost Hero," *JAR*, Aug. 20, 2018. Some accounts contend that Warren was shot in the back of the head as he retreated. J. L. Bell, "Dr. Joseph Warren's Body: The photographs?" *B 1775*, Oct. 20, 2007.

108   *By five-thirty p.m.*: Brown, *Beside Old Hearth-Stones*, 119–20; Stephenson, *Patriot Battles*, 153; Cash, *Medical Men at the Siege of Boston*, 56–57 (*stretchers*); Elting, *The Battle of Bunker's Hill*, 36 (*"want of order"*).

109   *"The retreat was no flight"*: De Fonblanque, *Political and Military*, 147. Clinton quoted Howe as saying "that I had saved him, for his left was gone," an unlikely claim given that Pigot's men had just won through. *TAR*, 19.

109   *"He leaped two or three feet"*: Coffin, ed., *History of the Battle of Breed's Hill*, 22; Elting, *The Battle of Bunker's Hill*, 36 (*entrenching tools*); Morse and Elijah Parish, *A Compendious History of New-England*, 281 (*"such a carnage"*).

109   *For now the carnage was over*: June 17, 1775, journal entry, KP; Williams, *Discord and Civil Wars*, 19; Elting, *The Battle of Bunker's Hill*, 36–37; Trumbull, *Reminiscences and Letters of John Trumbull*, 22 (*"sublime scene"*); Beck, *The War Before Independence*, 114; Ketchum, *Decisive Day*, 201–02 (*vowed to retake*).

109   *"Dearest Friend"*: AFC, vol. 1, 222; *Siege*, 210 (*next line of resistance*).

110   *British medicos scuffed*: Ketchum, *Decisive Day*, 185; Willcox, *Portrait of a General*, 50 (*"cries and moans"*).

110   *Later studies*: T. Longmore, *Gunshot Injuries*, 687. The study was conducted a quarter century later.

110   *The tally at Breed's Hill*: *Evacuation*, 59. Casualty figures vary slightly in different accounts. Gage would report 228 killed or died of wounds, and 826 wounded. Knollenberg, "Bunker Hill Re-viewed," *Proceedings*, MHS, 3rd ser., 72 (Oct. 1957–Dec. 1960): 84+. See also *Massachusetts in the American Revolution* (1997): 14, SoC, State Exhibition Series, http://www .societyofthecincinnati.org/scholarship/publications/; Philbrick, *Bunker Hill*, 230; Beck, *The War Before Independence*, 147.

110   *Nineteen officers*: Cash, *Medical Men at the Siege of Boston*, 60; Hoock, *Scars of Independence*, 75 (*one out of every eight*). Lockhart puts the figure at nearly one-quarter of all British Army officer deaths in the war. *The Whites of Their Eyes*, 307.

110   *Casualties in some units: Massachusetts in the American Revolution* (1997): 15, SoC, State Exhibition Series, http://www.societyofthecincinnati.org/scholarship/publications/ (*King's Own*); Rose, *Men of War*, 66–67 (*35th Foot*); Ketchum, *Decisive Day*, 168 (*senior private*); Nicolas, *Historical Record of the Royal Marine Forces*, 86, 90 (*123 casualties*); Admiralty to Maj. Tupper, Aug. 3, 1775, UK NA ADM 2/1168, f. 546 (*tents*); WR, 96 (*virtually his entire staff*); W. Howe to Harvey, June 22 and 24, 1775, in Fortescue, ed., *The Correspondence of King George the Third*, vol. 3, 220–24 (*"with horror"*).

110   *Through Saturday night: Boyne* journal, June 18, 1775, UK NA, ADM 5/129; William Coit to John Thomas, n.d., Thomas papers, MHS, micro, reel 3 (*all day Sunday*); Winsor, ed., *The Memorial History of Boston*, vol. 3, part 1, 89–90.

110   *"The streets were filled"*: Hulton, *Letters of a Loyalist Lady*, 99; "Excerpts from Letters of Isaac Winslow, Loyalist During the Siege of Boston," *New England Historical and Genealogical Register* 56 (1902): 48+ (*hobble*); T. Longmore, *Gunshot Injuries*, 217, 335; Frothingham, *The Centennial: Battle of Bunker Hill*, 109 (*"without noses"*).

111   *Shock and hemorrhage*: Frey, *The British Soldier in America*, 44; author visit, Manufactory House site, May 6, 2015, signage; Cash, *Medical Men at the Siege of Boston*, 61; Frothingham, *The Centennial: Battle of Bunker Hill*, 110 (*dying major*); Adair and Schutz, eds., *Peter Oliver's Origin & Progress of the American Rebellion*, 127 (*"three bullets"*); Stuart-Wortley, *A Prime Minister and His Son*, 70 (*"wounded and dead officers"*).

111   *"It may convince you"*: Lushington, *The Life and Services of General Lord Harris*, 55–57; Ketchum, *Decisive Day*, 187; J. L. Bell, "Hope and Pain on Bunker Hill," *B 1775*, June 30, 2014 (*"heart of stone"*); *New-England Chronicle*, Nov. 30, 1775, HD; "History of the 43rd Regiment of Foot," http://www.243regiment.com/history_43.html (*Roger Spendlove*). Nicholson died of his wounds on August 17, 1775. DNH, Nov. 28, 2009.

111   *A physician examining gunshot victims*: Bell, "On the Nature and Cure of Gun-Shot Wounds," in *The British Military Library*, vol. 1, 218, 308 (*"take his fate"*); author visit, Fort Ticonderoga, Sept. 2015, museum signage (*bone fragments*); Jones, *Plain Concise Practical Remarks on the Treatment of Wounds and Fractures*, 57 (*"terrifying him"*), 364 (*vinegar*); Gillett, *The Army Medical Department*, 18 (*sepsis*).

112   *"Many of the wounded"*: Cash, *Medical Men at the Siege of Boston*, 61; Frey, *The British Soldier in America*, 42 (*"cured, fit"*); corr., L. Cliffe to B. Cliffe, Sept. 21, 1776, Loftus Cliffe papers, WLC (*"Yanky"*).

112   *"I amputated several limbs"*: Estes, "A Disagreeable and Dangerous Employment: Medical Letters from the Siege of Boston, 1775," *Journal of the History of Medicine and Allied Sciences* 31, no. 3 (July 1976): 274. Again, casualty figures vary somewhat. The report to Congress in early July listed 138 Americans killed, 304 wounded, and 7 captured. PGW, vol. 1, 96–97. GW that month put the figures at 138 killed, 36 missing, and 276 wounded. Knollenberg, "Bunker Hill Re-viewed," *Proceedings*, MHS, 3rd ser., 72 (Oct. 1957–Dec. 1960): 84+. See also Murdock, *Bunker Hill*, 76; WR, 96–97.

112   *More than thirty American prisoners*: AFC, vol. 1, 239; Lindsey, "Treatment of American Prisoners of War During the Revolution," *Emporia State Research Studies* 22, no. 1 (Summer 1973): 5+; Bailey, *Historical Sketches of Andover*, 328 (*"It was not known"*).

112   *Those who learned the worst*: also spelled "Peers" and "Peerce." "Revolutionary Miscellany," vol. 139, micro, CMSA; Franek Kiluk, "Bunker Hill Memorial Bench," Pepperell, Mass., www .town.pepperell.ma.us/144/Bunker-Hill-Memorial-Bench.

112   *To many American fighters*: Scheer and Rankin, *Rebels and Redcoats*, 61 (*"shameful"*); "Diary of Ezekiel Price, 1775–6," *Proceedings*, MHS (Nov. 1963): 185+ (*"uneasiness"*); WR, 96–97; Wade and Lively, *This Glorious Cause*, 20 (*"commanded without order"*); Van Tyne, *The War of Independence: American Phase*, 53 (*"military genius"*); Moore, *A Life of General John Stark of New Hampshire*, 197 (*"poltroon"*); Smith, "The Rise of Artemas Ward, 1727–1777," Ph.D. diss. (University of Colorado, Boulder, 1990), 239–41 (*"destitute"*).

113   *The incineration of Charlestown*: Hunnewell, *A Century of Town Life*, 12–14; "Revolutionary Miscellany," CMSA, micro, vol. 139 (*nine feather beds*).

113 *"I wish [we] could sell them"*: author visit, Nov. 16, 2014, Bunker Hill, NPS museum; *Siege*, 394–96 *("infinite service")*; Coakley and Conn, *The War of the American Revolution*, 29; Kallich and MacLeish, eds., *The American Revolution Through British Eyes*, 50 *("favorite of favorites")*.

113 *For days, Yankees with spyglasses*: "Diary of Samuel Bixby," *Proceedings*, MHS, vol. 14 (1975–76): 285+; *AA*, IV: 2, 1651 *(bells)*; Drake, *Bunker Hill*, 48–50; *FYAR*, 323 *("large tree")*; *HOB*, 20 *(promotion announcements)*.

113 *Privates were laid*: Cash, *Medical Men at the Siege of Boston*, 62; Howe, *Boston Common*, 37; Beck, *The War Before Independence*, 155 *("stuffed the scoundrel")*; Cox, *A Proper Sense of Honor*, 184 *("meanness")*.

114 *Midsummer gloom*: Ferling, *Almost a Miracle*, 60 *("ruined us")*; *GC*, 345–46 *("lose a battle")*; Williams, *Discord and Civil Wars*, 20–21; June 22, 1775, journal entry, KP; Alden, *General Gage in America*, 273; De Fonblanque, *Political and Military Episodes*, 147 *("not to say courage")*; *Spirit '76*, 135–36 *("wrong at the head")*. Burgoyne later claimed the Bunker Hill bloodletting had at least affirmed the imperial principle, in doubt after the rout at Concord, "that trained troops are invincible against any numbers or any position of undisciplined rabble." Burgoyne to Germain, Aug. 20, 1775, Sackville-Germain Manuscript, vol. 3, WLC.

114 *Gage waited eight days*: Gage to Dartmouth, June 25, 1775, UK NA CO 5/92, f. 187; Peckham, ed., *Sources of American Independence*, vol. 1, 135 *("You must proceed")*.

114 *The news stunned England*: Black, "A Revolution in Military Cartography? Europe 1650–1815," *JMH* 93, no. 1 (Jan. 2009): 49+; Lutnick, *The American Revolution and the British Press*, 84, 90–91 *(dressed as his wife)*; Steuart, *The Last Journals of Horace Walpole*, vol. 1, 471 *("The ministers now saw")*; Ward, *Journal and Letters of the Late Samuel Curwen*, 33 *(thrown down their arms)*; *FYAR*, 323–24 *("shocking spectacle")*; Conway, "The Great Mischief Complain'd Of," *WMQ*, 3rd ser., 17, no. 3 (July 1990): 370+ *("alcoholic dependence")*; Almon, ed., *The Remembrancer*, vol. 1 (1775), 239 *(sixteen shillings)*; Weintraub, *Iron Tears*, 18 *("under subjection")*; W. Eden to North, Aug. 1775, Stevens's, vol. 5, #456 *("eight more")*.

115 *The king held firm*: *Siege*, 196 *(Captain Cockering)*; Barrington to W. Howe, Aug. 17, 1776, *Calendar of Manuscripts in the Royal Institution, Report on American Manuscripts*, vol. 1, 52 *(injury compensation)*.

115 *"Some other mode"*: Evelyn, 65, 90–91; DNH, Nov. 1, 2013.

115 *"a burden lay upon my spirits"*: Bailey, *Historical Sketches of Andover*, 328.

115 *"The shocking carnage"*: Conway, "To Subdue America," *WMQ*, 3rd ser., 43, no. 3 (July 1986): 381+.

4. WHAT SHALL WE SAY OF HUMAN NATURE?

116 *A sultry overcast*: *PGW*, vol. 1, 58n *(smallpox)*; Patterson, *Knight Errant of Liberty*, 90 *(profanity)*; *Siege*, 226.

116 *Even on the Sabbath*: Heath, *Memoirs of Major-General William Heath*, 17; journal, John Polley, July 2, 1775, LAC, MG 23 B5 *("balls came rattling")*; Tomlinson, ed., *The Military Journals of Two Private Soldiers*, 60 *("Nothing remarkable")*; "Revolutionary War Journal, Kept by Phineas Ingalls," *Essex Institute Historical Collections* 53 (1917): 81+ *("Rained")*.

116 *Possibly not one*: Lengel, *Inventing George Washington*, xi *(Imaginary portraits)*; *PGW*, vol. 3, 229n; *PGW*, vol. 1, 1 *("commander-in-chief")*; *AA*, IV: 2, 1480; *Proceedings*, MHS (1858–60), 60; GW HQ, 77; Ellis, *American Creation*, 31; Anderson, "The Hinge of the Revolution," *Massachusetts Historical Review*, vol. 1 (1999): 20+ *(Hastings House)*; Tomlinson, ed., *The Military Journals of Two Private Soldiers*, 82 *("Lesemo")*; *Proceedings*, MHS (1858–60), 60 *(powder)*.

117 *"His personal appearance"*: Thacher, *Military Journal*, 30; *GGW*, 8–9. Thomas Jefferson called him "the best horseman of his age." Longmore, *The Invention of George Washington*, 182.

117 *fair skin that burned easily*: WC, 7–8; *George Washington's Mount Vernon*, Mount Vernon Ladies' Association, n.d., 157 *(lost teeth)*; Reiss, *Medicine and the American Revolution*, 231 *(dental miseries)*; Ketchum, *The Winter Soldiers*, 33 *("gave confidence")*; Chernow, *Washington: A Life*, 186 *("harum-scarum" and "gift of silence")*; *AFC*, vol. 1, 246 *("Dignity with ease")*. Another version of the congressman's assessment: "no harum Starum ranting Swearing fellow," Rhodehamel, ed., *The American Revolution*, 34.

117 *Washington's other traits*: GGW, 8–10; Burns and Dunn, *George Washington*, 5; Wood, *Revolutionary Characters*, 35–36; Preston, *Braddock's Defeat*, 253–54, 262 (*"dispensations of Providence"*).

118 *He had shed the uniform*: GW to officers of the Virginia Regiment, Jan. 10, 1759, FOL (*"greatest honor"*); "Why Did George Washington Join the Revolution?," Mount Vernon website, https://www.mountvernon.org/george-washington/the-revolutionary-war/why-did-george-washington-join-the-revolution/; William M. Ferraro, "George Washington's Mind," in *CGW*, 548–56 (*talented administrator*); Rakove, *Revolutionaries*, 117; Lengel, *Inventing George Washington*, 58 (*richest widow*); Lengel, *First Entrepreneur*, 39 (*amiable and attractive*).

118 *"I heard bullets whistle"*: Lengel, *First Entrepreneur*, 32 (*"gloom & horror"*); GW to William Fitzhugh, Nov. 15, 1754, FOL (*"strongly bent to arms"*); GGW, 39, 48, 86–87, 90–91 (*account ledgers*); Ferling, *The Ascent of George Washington*, 87–89; McDougall, *Freedom Just Around the Corner*, 250 (*"disinterested"*); Jensen, *The Founding of a Nation*, 611 (*$500*); PGW, vol. 1, 14.

118 *Washington professed to be fighting*: Burns and Dunn, *George Washington*, 11, 21 (*"despotism"* and *regular commissions*); Egerton, *Death or Liberty*, 3, 7 (*135 slaves*); Ray Raphael, "Why Did George Washington Become a Revolutionary?," *JAR*, Feb. 16, 2015 (*resentments*); GGW, 81; Lengel, *First Entrepreneur*, 57, 73; Chernow, *Washington: A Life*, 176–77 (*land grants*); Calloway, *The Indian World of George Washington*, 206, 211 (*twenty-three thousand wilderness acres*).

119 *Yet just as clearly he saw*: Egnal, *A Mighty Empire*, 14, 271; Brooke, *King George III*, 178–79 (*Jacobite rebels*); Hoock, *Scars of Independence*, 78 (*hanged or beheaded*); Porter, *English Society in the Eighteenth Century*, 17 (*Temple Bar*); PGW, vol. 1, 4 (*his will*).

119 *"From the day"*: Chernow, *Washington: A Life*, 199; PGW, vol. 1, 4 (*"kind of destiny"*), 27 (*"unalterable affection"*), 19 (*"embarked"*).

119 *Washington would soon move*: GW HQ, 1–3, 8, 17, 50, 140; author visit, Vassall (Longfellow) House, Cambridge, May 2015; Edward E. Hale, "The Siege of Boston," in Winsor, ed., *The Memorial History of Boston*, vol. 3, part 1, 113; GGW, 95 (*"Take every method"*), 105 (*"spirit of conquest"*).

120 *Washington needed little time*: Chernow, *Washington: A Life*, 207; LAR, 231 (*"wildcats"*); PGW, vol. 1, 85–86 (*"entrenched"*); FYAR, 261–62; Irving, *Life of George Washington*, vol. 2, 5; *Evacuation*, 151–52; GW HQ, 455, 477 (*230 buildings*); PGW, vol. 1, 81n (*11,500*), 99 (*"dangerous situation"*).

120 *Commands cascaded from his headquarters*: J. L. Bell, "George Baylor: Spirited, Willing and Wrong for the Job," *JAR*, Oct. 12, 2015; PGW, vol. 1, 119 (*bantering*), 114–15, 158, 163; J. L. Bell, lecture, "Washington's Artillery," Mar. 15, 2012, Washington's Headquarters National Historic Site (*actually pointed*); AA, IV: 2, 1028, 1425; FYAR, 272; GGW, 107 (*"your excellency"*); *Evacuation*, 145–46 (*"New lords"*).

120 *The Continental Congress had appointed*: WAI, 91; GW to Hancock, Aug. 4, 1775, PGW, vol. 1, 228 (*"grand divisions"*); Wright, *The Continental Army*, 29; Clary and Whitehorne, *The Inspectors General of the United States Army, 1777–1903*, 13 (*twenty-five thousand troops*); PGW, vol. 1, 81n, 231n (*less than fourteen thousand*). Washington's fit-for-duty force through the Revolution would never exceed 24,000. Risch, *Supplying Washington's Army*, 27.

121 *For every moment*: GWGO, 16; Cheryl R. Collins, "Administrator in Chief," in *CGW*, 361; John A. Nagy, "George Washington, Spymaster," in *CGW*, 346 (*"conveying intelligence"*); Edward G. Lengel, "The Revolutionary War," in Blanken et al., eds., *Assessing War*, 67 (*"defense of American liberty"*); Scheer and Rankin, *Rebels and Redcoats*, 77 (*thin officer corps*); LP, vol. 1, 188, 197 (*"exactly the reverse"*); Robson, *The American Revolution*, 171; John W. Hall, "Washington's Irregulars," in *CGW*, 325; Hall, "An Irregular Reconsideration of George Washington and the American Military Tradition," *JMH*, July 2014, 961+.

121 *Even as he immersed himself*: Ferling, *The Ascent of George Washington*, 93; Hatch, *The Administration of the American Revolutionary Army*, 8.

122 *The coming weeks and months*: Ellis, *His Excellency: George Washington*, 73; McDougall, *Freedom Just Around the Corner*, 248; Anderson, *Crucible of War*, xxiii; GW to P. Schuyler, July 28, 1775, PGW, vol. 1, 188–89 (*"Confusion and discord"*).

122 *"We were all young"*: Royster, *A Revolutionary People at War*, 90; Bray and Bushnell, eds., *Diary of a Common Soldier in the American Revolution*, xiv *("mostly rong")*, xv *("man of himself")*; Chidsey, *The Siege of Boston*, 70 *(Chosen People)*; Hatch, *The Administration of the American Revolutionary Army*, 71 *(six and two-thirds dollars)*.

122 *"Discipline," Washington had written*: WC, 15–16; Hibbert, *Redcoats and Rebels*, 70–71 *("as dirty")*; Ganoe, *The History of the United States Army*, 3 *("kennel")*, 10–11 *(out of step)*; PNG, 111, 108; FYAR, 471; Cash, *Medical Men at the Siege of Boston*, 34; Jonathan Green, "Estimate of Damages," May 7, 1776, MHS, www.masshist.org/database/1910 *(thirty bushels)*; Fitch, "A Journal," MHS, *Proceedings* (May 1894): 41+, RI *("every ball")*; Trumbull, *Reminiscences and Letters of John Trumbull*, 19 *(lost their feet)*.

123 *The junior officers*: PGW, vol. 1, 268, 278, 356–57; Griffin, *Stephen Moylan*, 9 *("ignorant and litigious")*; Clary and Whitehorne, *The Inspectors General of the United States Army, 1777–1903*, 13 *(elected their captains)*; Hatch, *The Administration of the American Revolutionary Army*, 19, 36, 38 *(sulked and bickered)*; C. Lee to John Thomas, July 23, 1775, Thomas papers, MHS, micro, reel 3 *("discard such sentiments")*; Silverman, *A Cultural History of the American Revolution*, 288 *("Officers grumbling")*.

123 *Thirteen times he pleaded*: PGW, vol. 1, June through mid-Sept. 1775; PNG, 102 *(Company rolls)*; Wade and Lively, *This Glorious Cause*, 32 *("perfectly sober")*; Greene, *The Life of Nathanael Greene*, vol. 1, 90 *("stockings")*, 112 *(swearing)*; "Journal of Ensign Nathaniel Morgan," *Collections of the Connecticut Historical Society*, vol. 7 (1899): 99+, RI *(two shillings)*; PGW, vols. 1 and 2, July–Dec. 1775 *(more than two dozen)*. Middlekauff writes that "more than fifty officers" faced court-martial by the end of 1775, and "almost all were convicted." *Washington's Revolution*, 89.

123 *Washington's conceptions*: Anderson, "The Hinge of the Revolution," *Massachusetts Historical Review* 1 (1999): 20+. Don N. Hagist notes that surprisingly few men subjected to such brutal beatings appear to have perished. E-mail to author, Mar. 2018.

124 *Such draconian measures*: Maurer, "Military Justice Under General Washington," *Military Affairs* 28, no. 1 (Spring 1964): 8+; Royster, *A Revolutionary People at War*, 78 *("adjutant's daughter")*; Montross, *Rag, Tag and Bobtail*, 44 *("Saw two men")*; FYAR, 478.

124 *"My greatest concern"*: Wallace, *Appeal to Arms*, 55.

124 *"News of the death"*: Fowles, "Craft's Journal of the Siege of Boston," *Historical Collections of the Essex Institute* 3, no. 2 (Apr. 1861): 133+; Guthman, ed., *The Correspondence of Captain Nathan and Lois Peters*, 4, 10–14 *("Pray write")*.

124 *"unaccountable kind of stupidity"*: GW to R. H. Lee, Aug. 29, 1775, PGW, vol. 1, 372–75 *("capital errors")*; PGW, vol. 1, 336 *("dirty & nasty")*.

125 *Aggressive and even reckless*: Chernow, *Washington: A Life*, 208; PGW, vol. 1, 336 *("impossible for us")*; Adair and Schutz, eds., *Peter Oliver's Origin & Progress of the American Rebellion*, 131 *("squibbing")*.

125 *American whaleboats*: Almon, ed., *The Remembrancer*, vol. 1, 151 *("false lights")*; "Historic Light Station Information," Massachusetts, U.S. Coast Guard, www.uscg.mil/history/weblighthouses/LHMA.asp; Jeremy D'Entremont, "History of Boston Light, Massachusetts," www.newenglandlighthouses.net/boston-light-history.html; Dolin, "The Enduring Boston Light," *Boston Globe*, Aug. 30, 2016; Graves, Aug. 17, 1775, letter to Admiralty, and appendix 67 *(Graves sent carpenters)*.

125 *Rebel musket balls peppered*: PGW, vol. 1, 207–08; Tupper to H. Gates, Aug. 3, 1775, AA, IV: 3, 19; W. Tudor to J. Adams, July 31, 1775, AP; Daughan, *If by Sea*, 40; Jeremy D'Entremont, "History of Boston Light, Massachusetts," www.newenglandlighthouses.net/boston-light-history.html; Andrew A. Zellers-Frederick, "Struggle for a Lighthouse: The Raids to Destroy the Boston Light," *JAR*, July 5, 2018; Tilley, *The British Navy and the American Revolution*, 55 *("once formidable navy")*; De Fonblanque, *Political and Military Episodes*, 197 *("It may be asked")*.

125 *"The carpenters will be obliged"*: A. Ward to Committee of Supply, June 21, 1775; June 22, July 1, and July 27 requests to Committee of Supply, all in "Revolution Letters, 1775–1783," vol. 205, micro, CMSA; Huston, *The Sinews of War*, 17; Risch, *Supplying Washington's Army*, 9–10 *(quartermaster and commissary)*.

126 *Simply feeding the regiments*: Johnson, "The Administration of the American Commissariat During the Revolutionary War," Ph.D. diss. (University of Pennsylvania, 1941), 26–32, 38
(*"devoured himself"*), 43–44; Hatch, *The Administration of the American Revolutionary Army*,
88; *PNG*, 95 (*actually horse*); *PGW*, vol. 2, 151 (*Trumbull told Washington*).

126 *But no shortage was as perilous*: Col. Richard Gridley to GW, Oct. 20, 1775, *PGW*, vol. 1, 209–
11; *AA*, IV: 3, 1166. GW would estimate that his infantry alone needed 400 barrels. GW to J.
Hancock, Jan. 30, 1776, *AA*, IV: 4, 891.

126 unum necessarium: J. Adams to J. Warren, Sept. 26, 1775, *AP*.

126 *Each pound contained roughly seven thousand*: Vincent J. R. Kehoe, "A Military Guide: The
British Infantry of 1775"; "Military Pyrotechny," U.S. Military Academy, 1839; Pennsylvania
Committee of Safety, June 14, 1776, *AA*, IV: 6, 1284 (*32-pound ball*); *PGW*, vol. 1, 227, 89
(*"exceedingly destitute"*).

126 *Precisely how destitute*: *PGW*, vol. 1, 227; Reed, ed., *Life and Correspondence of Joseph Reed*, vol.
1, 119; Stephenson, "The Supply of Gunpowder in 1776," *AHR* 30, no. 2 (Jan. 1925): 271+.

127 *"The general was so struck"*: Hammond, *Letters and Papers of Major-General John Sullivan*,
vol. 1, 72; *PGW*, vol. 1, 227 (*"profound secret"*); Nuxoll, "Congress and the Munitions Merchants," Ph.D. diss. (New York University, 1979), 8 (*"inconceivable"*).

127 *"Our situation in the article"*: *PGW*, vol. 1, 219, 227; Greene, *The Life of Nathanael Greene*,
vol. 1, 112 (*one-shilling fines*); *Evacuation*, 74 (*"not to fire"*); *PGW*, vol. 2, 283 (*reveille gun*);
PGW, vol. 1, 216, 221 (*Halifax or Bermuda*); *FYAR*, 182 (*"afflicted and astonished"*).

127 *A rebel schooner from Santo Domingo*: Clark, *Captain Dauntless*, 74–75; J. Adams to J. Warren, July 27, 1775, *AP* (*sent north*); *PGW*, vol. 1, 210n (*second consignment*); *WR*, 108 (*twenty-
five rounds*).

127 *War could not be waged*: York, "Clandestine Aid and the American Revolutionary War
Effort," *Military Affairs* 43, no. 1 (Feb. 1979): 26+. A single mill north of Philadelphia resumed
production but would produce less than a ton in 1775. Salav, "The Production of Gunpowder in Pennsylvania During the American Revolution," *PMHB* 99, no. 4 (Oct. 1975): 422+
(*fallen into disrepair*).

127 *the shortage of saltpeter*: Crocker, *The Gunpowder Industry*, 4, 6, 11–20; Cressy, *Saltpeter*, 1, 155.

127 *Saltpeter recipes*: Forbes, *Paul Revere and the World He Lived In*, 301 (*"effluvia"*); Bartenstein, *New Jersey's Revolutionary War Powder Mill*, 26–27 (*"moistened"*); Cressy, *Saltpeter*,
158–61 (*"I am determined"*).

128 *Yet it would not be had*: Nuxoll, "Congress and the Munitions Merchants," Ph.D. diss. (New
York University, 1979), 8, 15–16; Huston, *The Sinews of War*, 23–25. Carp states that 34.6 percent
of gunpowder in the first two years of the war was made in America. *To Starve the Army at
Pleasure*, 233.

128 *"a very severe economy"*: Reed, ed., *Life and Correspondence of Joseph Reed*, vol. 1, 119;
Stephenson, "The Supply of Gunpowder in 1776," *AHR* 30, no. 2 (Jan. 1925): 271+.

128 *As Washington grappled*: *PGW*, vol. 2, 82–85 (*"letters in characters"*); GW HQ, 421–23 (*"lusty
woman"*); J. Warren to J. Adams, Oct. 1, 1775, *AP*; Greene, *The Life of Nathanael Greene*, vol.
2, 120.

128 *Washington dramatically placed the pages*: GW HQ, 428–29; Nagy, *Dr. Benjamin Church,
Spy*, 111–12.

128 *Washington laid one of the translations*: *PGW*, vol. 2, 103–05.

129 *the secret author*: Church was "chief physician and director-general." The title "surgeon general" in the U.S. Army was created in 1813. French, *General Gage's Informers*, 172.

129 *He had been arrested*: Chase, vol. 3, 209; Austin, *The Life of Elbridge Gerry*, 118; GW HQ, 427.

129 *The next day, Dr. Church*: Cash, *Medical Men at the Siege of Boston*, 117–23; Kiracofe, "Dr. Ben-
jamin Church and the Dilemma of Treason in Revolutionary Massachusetts," *New England
Quarterly* 70, no. 3 (Sept. 1997): 449 (*supported Benedict Arnold's attack*); "Dr. Benjamin
Church, Jr.," *B 1775*, Sept. 21–23, 2017; French, *General Gage's Informers*, 147–51 (*high living*);
GW HQ, 434.

129 *Church quickly admitted*: *PGW*, vol. 2, 83 (*"influence the enemy"*); B. Church to GW, Oct. 3,
1775, *PGW*, vol. 2, 85–87 (*"appeal to heaven"*).

129 *Not a man believed him*: J. Adams to C. Lee, Oct. 13, 1775, and J. Adams to J. Warren, Oct. 18, 1775, *AP*; Bunker, *An Empire on the Edge*, 373–74 (*"imagining the death"*); Maurer, "Military Justice Under General Washington," *Military Affairs* 28, no. 1 (Spring 1964): 8+; GW HQ, 432–34.

130 *At ten a.m. on Friday*: Beck, *The War Before Independence*, 204; "Account of the Examination of Doctor Benjamin Church," Nov. 1775, MHS, Ms. N-2110; *AA*, IV: 3, 1479–90; Whitney, *Historical Sketches of Watertown, Massachusetts*, 334, 388.

130 *For more than an hour*: William Tudor to J. Adams, Oct. 28, 1775, *AP* (*"angel of light"*); Kiracofe, "Dr. Benjamin Church and the Dilemma of Treason in Revolutionary Massachusetts," *New England Quarterly* 70, no. 3 (Sept. 1997): 443+ (*"innocently intended"*); "Dr. Benjamin Church, Jr.," *B 1775*, Sept. 23–24, 2017; *PNG*, 144 (*"art and ingenuity"*).

130 *"Is it criminal, sir"*: "Account of the Examination of Doctor Benjamin Church," Nov. 1775, MHS, Ms. N-2110.

130 *That fate was sealed*: French, *General Gage's Informers*, 192–93 (*"wickedness"*), 196–97 (*irrefutably confirmed*); *PGW*, vol. 2, 380 (*prisoner escort*); Kiracofe, "Dr. Benjamin Church and the Dilemma of Treason in Revolutionary Massachusetts," *New England Quarterly* 70, no. 3 (Sept. 1997): 443+ (*"noisome cell"*).

131 *During Church's lifetime*: Kiracofe, "Dr. Benjamin Church and the Dilemma of Treason in Revolutionary Massachusetts," *New England Quarterly* 70, no. 3 (Sept. 1997): 443+; Cash, *Medical Men at the Siege of Boston*, 124–25; French, *General Gage's Informers*, 158, 198–201 (*"living or dead"*).

131 *All through the fall, bored, mischievous*: Sept. 7, 1775, "Diary of Rev. Benjamin Boardman," *Proceedings*, MHS (May 1892): 400+, RI; Van Tyne, "French Aid Before the Alliance of 1778," *AHR* 31, no. 1 (Oct. 1925): 34 (*French fleet*); Adams, *Revolutionary New England, 1691–1776*, 429 (*chased Lord North*).

131 *Autumn sickness crept through the camps*: *PGW*, vol. 2, 333, 81 (*games of chance*), 291 (*ten thousand cords*), 399 (*"mortifying scarcity"*); Green, ed., *Paul Lunt's Diary*, 15 (*wrestling*); Oct. 27, 1775, "Journal of Simeon Lyman of Sharon," *Collections of the Connecticut Historical Society*, vol. 7 (1899): 113+, RI (*chestnuts*); Oct. 12, 1775, Jabez Fitch, "A Journal," *Proceedings*, MHS (May 1894): 41+, RI (*"upper side"*).

131 *"At about 9 a.m. we flung"*: "Diary of Samuel Bixby," *Proceedings*, MHS, vol. 14 (1875–75): 285+; Fowles, "Craft's Journal of the Siege of Boston," *Historical Collections of the Essex Institute* 3, no. 2 (Apr. 1861): 133+ (*"Nothing new"*); *New-England Chronicle*, July 13 and Nov. 24, 1775, HD (*reward offers*).

132 *For more than twenty years*: Martin and Lender, *A Respectable Army*, 46–47; Fitzpatrick, ed., *The Writings of George Washington*, vol. 2, 97 (*"No dependence"*); *PGW*, vol. 2, 260–61 (*"I confess"*).

132 *All the more reason to strike the British*: *PGW*, vol. 1, 433, 450–51; *GGW*, 115; Chernow, *Washington: A Life*, 207; *PGW*, vol. 2, 184 (*"Too great a risk"*).

132 *He had little recourse but to husband*: Ferling, *Almost a Miracle*, 89; Weigley, *History of the United States Army*, 9, 29; Whelen, *The American Rifle*, 4–5 (*"wanged"*), 15–16, 197.

132 *Riflemen were lethal and exotic*: *PGW*, vol. 1, 445–46, 455; Higginbotham, *Daniel Morgan, Revolutionary Rifleman*, 22–25; Sept. 10, 1775, "Revolutionary Journal of Aaron Wright, 1775," *History Magazine* 6 (July 1862): 208+, RI; GW HQ, 260 (*"Washington has said"*); Lee to B. Rush, Oct. 10, 1775, *LP*, 212 (*"riff-raff"*); Reed, ed., *Life and Correspondence of Joseph Reed*, 117 (*"hat"*); Charles F. Himes, "Colonel Robert Magaw," lecture, Hamilton Library Association, Carlisle, Pa. (1915), 22 (*"your nose"*).

133 *But General Gage had gone*: Gage died in 1787. Alden, *General Gage in America*, 280–86, 293.

133 *William Howe moved into Province House*: "Revolutionary War, British and Hessian Army," box 1, NYHS. Howe's title was formalized in 1776.

133 *"never wastes a monosyllable"*: Glover, *General Burgoyne in Canada and America*, 78; *MLA*, 88 (*uncanny resemblance*); *HOB*, viii (*"laying hold of stumps"*); *WC*, 68–69; *HBAR*, 42n (*"the Savage"*).

134 *Elected to Parliament from Nottingham*: HBAR, 58; *The Detail and Conduct of the American War*, 10–11 (*"insurgents are very few"*); Spring, *With Zeal and with Bayonets Only*, 72 (*"feel a confidence"*).

134 *Howe now had some eleven thousand mouths*: David Chamier to W. Howe, Jan. 17, 1776, Boston, UK NA T 65/108, f. 23–25; *Logistics*, 45; *LAR*, 205 (*"What in God's name"*); *DAR*, vol. 11, 124; Hibbert, *Redcoats and Rebels*, 62; Balderston and Syrett, eds., *The Lost War*, 38–39 (*"fresh meat"*), 53 (*skinny goose*); Evelyn, 67 (*mutton*); Frey, *The British Soldier in America*, 33 (*"hard as wood"*); Hunter, *The Journal of Gen. Sir Martin Hunter*, 13 (*roasted a foal*); HOB, 97 (*town bull*); Timothy Newell, Aug. 1, 1775, signage, NPS Visitor Center, Concord (*"dine upon rats"*).

134 *"They are burrowing like rabbits"*: Evelyn, 67, 69; *FYAR*, 532–33; De Fonblanque, *Political and Military Episodes*, 202–04 (*"inertness"*), 148; W. Howe to Dartmouth, Dec. 2, 1775, including return of livestock, Nov. 27, 1775, other enclosures, UK NA, CO 5/92, f. 342–57.

134 *Shifting the army by sea from Boston*: Belcher, *The First American Civil War*, vol. 1, 201–04 (*"on no account"*); Dartmouth to W. Howe, Sept. 5, 1775, *DAR*, vol. 11, 99; Alden, *General Gage in America*, 274–75; W. Howe to Dartmouth, Oct. 9, 1775, *DAR*, vol. 11, 139–40 (*five thousand regulars*); W. Howe to Dartmouth, Nov. 27, 1775, *DAR*, vol. 10, 140 (*far more British shipping*); *LAR*, 200 (*"birds in a cage"*).

135 *"Starve them out"*: Thacher, *Military Journal*, 17; Rodger, *The Command of the Ocean*, 333 (*Navy and Victualling Boards*); Van Creveld, *Supplying War*, 17 (*"ruined by want"*).

135 *British supply contractors were supposed*: David Chamier to W. Howe, Jan. 17, 1776, Boston, UK NA T 65/108, f. 23–25; "Memorandum of failures on the part of the contractors," Jan. 17, 1776, UK NA, CO 5/93, f 109–13; *Logistics*, 43, 106 (*"our daily bread"*).

135 *Strongboxes stuffed with cash*: requisitions and cash shipments, "George III Calendar, Sept. 1775–Oct. 1777," RA GEO/MAIN/#2396; W. Howe to Robinson, Dec. 31, 1775, UK NA, T 64/108, f 17.

135 *Moreover, transaction fees had risen*: John Robinson to W. Howe, Oct. 1, 1775, "Calendar of Manuscripts in the Royal Institution," *Report on American Manuscripts*, vol. 1, 15; David Chamier to W. Howe, Jan. 17, 1776, Boston, UK NA T 65/108, f. 23–25; *Logistics*, 18; French, *The Siege of Boston*, 341–43 (*milk cows*); Baker, *Government and Contractors*, 206; Curtis, *The British Army in the American Revolution*, 114–16; Syrett, *Shipping and the American War*, 122.

135 *In mid-November, Howe sent London*: W. Howe to Dartmouth, Dec. 2, 1775, UK NA, CO 5/92, f 342–57; Balderston and Syrett, eds., *The Lost War*, 57 (*"Nothing but a desire"*).

136 *Alcohol helped, too*: Baker, *Government and Contractors*, 161–62; Treasury to W. Howe, spring 1776, provision contracts, enclosures, "George III Calendar, Sept. 1775–Oct. 1777," RA GEO/MAIN/#2393–94 (*half million gallons of rum*); Frey, *The British Soldier in America*, 63 (*largest single item*); Baker, *Government and Contractors*, 185 (*ten times more*); Treasury to W. Howe, spring 1776, provision contracts, enclosures, "George III Calendar, Sept. 1775–Oct. 1777," RA GEO/MAIN/#2393–94 (*hydrometers*). The weight sank if the rum was too weak.

136 *Rum had long been a reward*: *Logistics*, 8; Baker, *Government and Contractors*, 162.

136 *Four small British warships*: Willis, *The History of Portland, from 1632 to 1864*, 449–54, 467; Albion, *Forests and Sea Power*, 234–38, 241, 279–80 (*"beat the town down"*); Sandwich, vol. 1, 202.

136 *As the five vessels carefully warped*: Yerxa, *The Burning of Falmouth, 1775*, 134–35 (*"profound silence"*); Goold, *The Burning of Falmouth*, 12 (*"bad English"*); Willis, *The History of Portland, from 1632 to 1864*, 514–21 (*"human species"*).

137 *Few sailors knew the upper New England coast*: Adm. M. Shuldham to Lord Sandwich, Jan. 13, 1776, NCCH, 58n (*"most useful person"*); *AA*, IV: 2, 552–55; Willis, *The History of Portland, from 1632 to 1864*, 510; Sandwich, vol. 1, 66 (*"show the rebels"*); Duncan, *Coastal Maine*, 216; Beck, *The War Before Independence*, 232; Cecere, "A Tale of Two Cities: The Destruction of Falmouth and the Defense of Hampton," *JAR*, Sept. 9, 2015 (*"burn, destroy"*).

137 *So far the chastisement had gone badly*: H. Mowat to S. Graves, Oct. 19, 1775, UK NA, CO 5/123, f 34; Leamon, *Revolution Downeast*, 70; Michael Cecere, "The Village of Machias

Confronts the Royal Navy, June 1775," *JAR*, July 9, 2015; Woodward, "The Revolution's Band of Brothers," *MHQ*, Summer 2010, 80+; *NDAR*, vol. 1, 655; Duncan, *Coastal Maine*, 212.

137 *The town "had not the least right"*: Goold, *The Burning of Falmouth*, 12; H. Mowat to S. Graves, Oct. 19, 1775, UK NA, CO 5/123, f 34 (*"known humanity"*).

137 *All night long the townsfolk debated*: Goold, *The Burning of Falmouth*, 13; H. Mowat to S. Graves, Oct. 19, 1775, UK NA, CO 5/123, f 34 (*"forty minutes after nine"*).

138 *A red flag appeared*: Goold, *The Burning of Falmouth*, 14 (*"shower of balls"*); Hoock, *Scars of Independence*, 88 (*three thousand projectiles*); Leamon, *Revolution Downeast*, 72; *NDAR*, vol. 2, 500 (*"dashing everything"*).

138 *"At noon," Canceaux's log recorded*: H. Mowat to S. Graves, Oct. 19, 1775, UK NA, CO 5/123, f 34; *Canceaux* log, Oct. 18, 1775, *NDAR*, vol. 2, 502 (*thirty marines*); Willis, *The History of Portland, from 1632 to 1864*, 514–21 (*"sheet of flame"*); Yerxa, *The Burning of Falmouth, 1775*, 141.

138 *Britain had murdered another Yankee town*: Willis, *The History of Portland, from 1632 to 1864*, 521; Yerxa, *The Burning of Falmouth, 1775*, 142; H. Mowat to S. Graves, Oct. 19, 1775, UK NA, CO 5/123, f 34; Tilley, *The British Navy and the American Revolution*, 60 (*"all laid into ashes"*).

138 *"a severe stroke to the rebels"*: Duncan, *Coastal Maine*, 218; *DAR*, vol. 9, 14. The town would be rebuilt and renamed Portland.

139 *"It cannot be true"*: Yerxa, *The Burning of Falmouth, 1775*, 147–48; C. Lee to A. McDougall, Oct. 26, 1775, *NDAR*, vol. 2, 607 (*"hell hounds"*); J. Warren to J. Adams, Oct. 20, 1775, *AP*, vol. 3 (*"barbarous"*).

139 *The wolf had risen in the heart*: Gipson, *American Loyalist: Jared Ingersoll*, 340; Allen, *A Naval History of the American Revolution*, vol. 1, 42–47; Morison, *John Paul Jones*, 32–33; Syrett, *Shipping and the American War*, 77.

139 *Few were angrier than General Washington*: *PGW*, vol. 2, 207; Duncan, *Coastal Maine*, 218 (*"cruelty"*); Chernow, *Washington: A Life*, 209 (*moral crusade*); *PGW*, vol. 2, 236 (*"savage enemy"*); Nelson, *George Washington's Secret Navy*, 147 (*"a grand republic"*).

5. I SHALL TRY TO RETARD THE EVIL HOUR

141 *Some 230 miles northwest of Boston*: Hadden, *A Journal Kept in Canada*, 34 (*"unhealthy"*); Fryer, *Battlefields of Canada*, 116; C. Preston, "Plan of St. John's," LAC, MG 23 B10; MGRM, 196–98; *Struggle*, vol. 1, 455 (*"Shot!"*).

141 *The regulars still wore summer uniforms*: C. Preston, narrative, "Papers Relating to the Surrender of Fort St. Johns and Fort Chambly," *Report of the Work of the Public Archives of Canada for the Years 1914 and 1915*, 21 (*twenty blankets* and *"not a syllable"*); corr., Thomas Oakes to family, Oct. 11, 1775, "Documents Relating to the War of 1775," *Report Concerning Canadian Archives for the Year 1904*, appendix 1, 376; *Struggle*, vol. 1, 455 (*ripped the skirts*); corr., Lt. Richardson to unknown, Dec. 7, 1775, "Documents Relating to the War of 1775," *Report Concerning Canadian Archives for the Year 1904*, appendix 1, 378 (*half-rations* and *four couriers*); R. Prescott to C. Preston, "Montreal, Tuesday evening, five o'clock," LAC, MG 23 B10 (*"last extremity"*).

142 *At one p.m. on Saturday, October 14*: Bredenberg, "The *Royal Savage*," *BFTM* 12, no. 2 (Sept. 1966): 128+; C. Preston, narrative, "Papers Relating to the Surrender of Fort St. Johns and Fort Chambly," *Report of the Work of the Public Archives of Canada for the Years 1914 and 1915*, 23; Castonguay, *The Unknown Fort*, 62; Trumbull, "A Concise Journal or Minutes of the Principal Movements Towards St. John's," *Collections of the Connecticut Historical Society*, vol. 7 (1899): 147; Bird, *Attack on Quebec*, 97, 130; Todd, "The March to Montreal and Quebec," *American Historical Register*, Mar. 1895, 641+ (*"hottest fire"*).

142 *The next day was just as hot*: C. Preston, narrative, and W. Hunter to C. Preston, Oct. 17, 1775, "Papers Relating to the Surrender of Fort St. Johns and Fort Chambly," *Report of the Work of the Public Archives of Canada for the Years 1914 and 1915*, 23 (*both legs*), and 11 (*"amphibious"*); *Struggle*, vol. 1, 448 (*sternpost*); "The Royal Fuziliers and the Siege of Ft. St. Jean," https://7thregimentoffoot.weebly.com/siege-of-fort-st-jean.html, 31 (*"scorched"*); Bredenberg, "The *Royal Savage*," *BFTM* 12, no. 2 (Sept. 1966): 128+.

142 *Major Preston and most of his men*: C. Preston, narrative, "Papers Relating to the Surrender of Fort St. Johns and Fort Chambly," *Report of the Work of the Public Archives of Canada for the Years 1914 and 1915*, 23–24; Cruikshank, 8; *Struggle*, vol. 1, 447; Castonguay, *The Unknown Fort*, 63 ("*still alive*").

142 *For nearly a century, Americans*: Cohen, ed., *Canada Preserved*, 1; *WAI*, 9; Anderson, *Crucible of War*, 199; Kidd, *God of Liberty*, 18 ("*scarlet whore*").

143 *Britain's triumph in the Seven Years' War*: Michel Brunet, "French Canada and the Early Decades of British Rule, 1760–1791," Canadian Historical Association, booklet no. 13 (1981), 5–6; *FYAR*, 396 (*state religion*); "Estimated Population of Canada, 1605 to Present," Statistics Canada, http://www.statcan.gc.ca/pub/98-187-x/4151287-eng.htm#27; *Fourteenth*, 17–18; Mayer, "Canada, Congress, and the Continental Army: Strategic Accommodations, 1774–1776," *JAR* 78, no. 2 (Apr. 2014): 503+; *Struggle*, vol. 1, 27–28 ("*boastful, mendacious*").

143 *As tensions with Britain escalated*: Cohen, ed., *Canada Preserved*, 2; Cohen, *Conquered into Liberty*, 134 ("*a small people*").

143 *The Quebec Act, which took effect in May 1775*: Maxime Dagenais, "The Quebec Act," *Canadian Encyclopedia*, http://www.thecanadianencyclopedia.ca/en/article/quebec-act/; Quebec Act, statute, http://founding.com/the-quebec-act/; Creighton, *A History of Canada*, 162–64; Tracy, *The Tercentenary History of Canada*, vol. 2, 583; Brebner, *Canada: A Modern History*, 81; Coupland, *The American Revolution and the British Empire*, 240; *Struggle*, vol. 1, 70–73; McConville, *The King's Three Faces*, 288; Calloway, *The American Revolution in Indian Country*, 19 (*fifty thousand*); Royster, *A Revolutionary People at War*, 99 ("*Satan*"); Kidd, *God of Liberty*, 17, 25, 29, 35, 71–72 ("*her fornications*"); *FYAR*, 399–400; Chittenden, *The Capture of Ticonderoga*, 97 (*snowshoes*).

144 *War in Massachusetts, and the American capture*: *GC*, 286–87; Ferling, *The First of Men*, 122–23. Washington called the Quebec Act "a diabolical scheme." *PGW*, vol. 2, 161.

144 *Others saw a chance to seize the Canadian granary*: *Struggle*, vol. 1, 236; *BARH*, 92; Desjardin, *Through a Howling Wilderness*, 10–11; Reynolds, *Guy Carleton: A Biography*, 55 (*seven hundred regulars*); *WR*, 139; *Struggle*, vol. 1, 237–38; Brebner, *Canada: A Modern History*, 70.

144 *In late June, Congress finally ordered*: *Fourteenth*, 92 ("*take possession*"); Mayer, "Canada, Congress, and the Continental Army: Strategic Accommodations, 1774–1776," *JAR* 78, no. 2 (Apr. 2014): 503+ ("*sister colony*"); Creighton, *A History of Canada*, 162–64 Reynolds, *Guy Carleton*, 76; Dull, *A Diplomatic History of the American Revolution*, 54; Cohen, *Conquered into Liberty*, 135, 146 (*American invasion*).

144 *Congress had denounced Catholics*: *BARH*, 110–11; Mayer, "Canada, Congress, and the Continental Army: Strategic Accommodations, 1774–1776," *JAR* 78, no. 2 (Apr. 2014): 503+ ("*liberty of conscience*"). The Northern Army initially was known as the Separate Army. Berg, *Encyclopedia of Continental Army Units*, 107.

145 *For two months little had gone right*: Bush, *Revolutionary Enigma*, 27; Lossing, *The Life and Times of Philip Schuyler*, vol. 1, 350, 358; *WR*, 146 (*gunsmiths*), 147 ("*mutinous temper*"); *PGW*, vol. 1, 129–30 ("*penknife*"), 202, 256–58 (*no carriages*); P. Schuyler orderly book, Aug. 2, 14, 1775, HM 663, HL; Bush, *Revolutionary Enigma*, 32; *FYAR*, 387 ("*of no service*").

145 *Tall, thin, and florid*: Bush, *Revolutionary Enigma*, 9–10; "Digital Wallpaper at the Schuyler Mansion," *B 1775*, Dec. 26, 2017; Tuckerman, *Life of General Philip Schuyler*, 73, 91; Gerlach, *Proud Patriot*, 52–55, 526n; Lossing, *The Life and Times of Philip Schuyler*, vol. 1, 155 (*lead casket*); *PGW*, vol. 1, 367, 369n; *GWGO*, 60 ("*family quarrel*"); Calloway, *The Indian World of George Washington*, 238–39 (*march in circles*). Schuyler attended conferences with Indian delegates in May and August 1775.

146 *For all his virtues*: Tuckerman, *Life of General Philip Schuyler*, 108; Ketchum, *Saratoga*, 22; Ferling, *Almost a Miracle*, 83 ("*barbarous complication*"); *PGW*, vol. 3, 313, and vol. 4, 56, 380.

146 *Alarming reports in late August of British vessels*: Bush, *Revolutionary Enigma*, 38, 43; *PGW*, vol. 1, 393–94 (*Montgomery set out*), 437 ("*feeble enemy*"); *FYAR*, 393–94 ("*follow us*"); Gerlach, *Proud Patriot*, 59–60 ("*severity*"); Lossing, *The Life and Times of Philip Schuyler*, vol. 1, 400 ("*Grand Congress*").

146 *Wishing did not make it so*: "Journal of Col. Rudolphus Ritzema," *Magazine of American History*, vol. 1 (1877): 99; R. Montgomery to wife, Sept. 5, 1775, in Louise Livingston Hunt, "Biographical Notes Concerning General Richard Montgomery," 1876, NYHS, 12; Lossing, *The Life and Times of Philip Schuyler*, vol. 1, 403 (*"tangled way"*).

146 *For more than a week, the invasion stalled*: "Journal of Col. Rudolphus Ritzema," *Magazine of American History*, vol. 1 (1877), 99–101; Bush, *Revolutionary Enigma*, 45; R. Montgomery to wife, Sept. 12, 1775, in Louise Livingston Hunt, "Biographical Notes Concerning General Richard Montgomery," 1876, NYHS, 11–13 (*"pusillanimous wretches"*).

147 *If Montgomery could not abandon the Northern Army*: Lossing, *The Life and Times of Philip Schuyler*, vol. 1, 406 (*"so low"*), 411 (*"If Job"*); Gerlach, *Proud Patriot*, 65.

147 *Further misfortune befell the invaders*: Cruikshank, 7; Burrows, *Forgotten Patriots*, 193 (*"oriental wildness"*); Ives, "Narrative of Uriah Cross in the Revolutionary War," *New York History* 63, no. 3 (July 1982): 279+ (*"last I see of Allen"*); Atherton, *Montreal, 1535–1914*, vol. 2, 72–73; George Louis Hamilton, commander, Pendennis Castle, to storekeeper, Dec. 21, 1775, UK NA, CO 5/168, f 69; Randall, *Ethan Allen*, 380, 399; Trumbull, "A Concise Journal or Minutes of the Principal Movements Towards St. John's," *Collections of the Connecticut Historical Society*, vol. 7 (1899): 147 (*"ill-concerted"*); Lossing, *The Life and Times of Philip Schuyler*, vol. 1, 424 (*"imprudence"*).

147 *Despite such misfires and misadventures*: Lossing, *The Life and Times of Philip Schuyler*, vol. 1, 414–15, 442; MGRM, 237; Hatch, *Thrust for Canada*, 88–89; Stanley, *Canada Invaded*, 54–55; articles of capitulation, Chambly, Oct. 18, 1775, T-P RC, #2066; "A Return of Captives, Provisions," n.d., T-P RC, FTA Cat. #2003.074.007; Cubbison, *"The Artillery Never Gained More Honour,"* 48.

148 *"We have gotten six tons"*: Shelton, 110–13; Atherton, *Montreal, 1535–1914*, vol. 2, 74; Beck, *The War Before Independence*, 220–21; *Fourteenth*, 135; Lanctôt, *Canada and the American Revolution*, 88–89; Reynolds, *Guy Carleton*, 70.

148 *Three hundred yards northwest*: Shelton, 113; journal, Robert Barwick, Oct. 28, 1775, *NDAR*, vol. 2, appendix F, 1387–1400; Dann, ed., *The Revolution Remembered*, 384 (*slings*); C. Preston, narrative, "Papers Relating to the Surrender of Fort St. Johns and Fort Chambly," *Report of the Work of the Public Archives of Canada for the Years 1914 and 1915*, 25 (*stupefying bombardment*); "Journal of Col. Rudolphus Ritzema," *Magazine of American History*, vol. 1 (1877): 102 (*"shatters"*); corr., B. Trumbull, Nov. 3, 1775, Benjamin Trumbull, "A Concise Journal or Minutes of the Principal Movements Towards St. John's," *Collections of the Connecticut Historical Society*, vol. 7 (1899): 147+; Stanley, *Canada Invaded*, 60 (*"melancholy consequences"*).

148 *After a fifty-three-day siege*: Cruikshank, 9. Stanley puts British casualties at 43, which may exclude artillerymen. *Canada Invaded*, 62.

148 *"Let me entreat you, sir"*: "Papers Relating to the Surrender of Fort St. Johns and Fort Chambly," *Report of the Work of the Public Archives of Canada for the Years 1914 and 1915*, 14; Cruikshank, 9; articles of capitulation, St. Johns, Nov. 2, 1775, T-P RC, #20165.

148 *At eight a.m. on November 3*: Hatch, *Thrust for Canada*, 91–92; *Struggle*, vol. 1, 462–65; WR, 161 (*smart uniforms*); André, *Major André's Journal*, 18–19 (*locket portrait*); Dann, ed., *The Revolution Remembered*, 385 (*"tears run"*); "Papers Relating to the Surrender of Fort St. Johns and Fort Chambly," *Report of the Work of the Public Archives of Canada for the Years 1914 and 1915*, 14–15; Castonguay, *The Unknown Fort*, 68.

149 *More than three-quarters of the British regulars*: Cruikshank, 10; William James, commissary of artillery, return of ordnance from St. Johns, "Journal of the Siege of St. Johns," in "Letters and Reports of the American Campaign," LAC, MG 23 B 8 (*booty from St. Johns*); Manning, *Quebec: The Story of Three Sieges*, 148.

149 *"If I live"*: MGRM, 250.

149 *That Richard Montgomery now prepared*: Shelton, 18–29, 33; R. Montgomery to Perkins Magra, Nov. 27, 1769, WLC, Small Collections, box 38, folder 45 (*"clapped me"*).

149 *An end to the French war*: Louise Livingston Hunt, "Biographical Notes Concerning General Richard Montgomery," 1876, NYHS, 3–4, 14 (*"dragged from obscurity"*); MGRM, 83–89; R. Montgomery to R. R. Livingston, May 20, 1773, Edward Livingston Papers, FL, box 114,

folder 1 (*married well*); Brumwell, *Turncoat*, 48 ("*air and manner*"); R. Montgomery to Perkins Magra, 1774, WLC, Small Collections, box 38, folder 45 ("*by a pistol*"); R. Montgomery will, Aug. 30, 1775, Crown Point, N.Y., Edward Livingston Papers, FL, box 114, folder 1.

150 *That yoke still held him*: Louise Livingston Hunt, "Biographical Notes Concerning General Richard Montgomery," 1876, NYHS, 12–13 ("*half-drowned rats*"); MGRM, 220–21 ("*badness of the troops*"), 229 ("*little purpose*"), 243 ("*not the talents*").

150 *But the command was his*: Montross, *Rag, Tag and Bobtail*, 65 ("*dry ground*"); journal, Robert Barwick, Nov. 7, 1775, NDAR, vol. 2, appendix F, 1387–1400; WR, 161–62; Cruikshank, 12; Shelton, 118.

151 *Built on a ridge parallel*: Fourteenth, 154; author visit, Pointe-à-Callière: Musée d'Archéologie et d'Histoire, Montreal, Aug. 23, 2015, signage; "Following the Trail of Montréal, the 18th-Century Fortified City," http://www.vieux.montreal.qc.ca/fortif/images/depl_a.pdf; *Struggle*, vol. 1, 96–97, 477–78; Brebner, *Canada: A Modern History*, 66 ("*unsavory assemblage*"); Hadden, *A Journal Kept in Canada*, 12 ("*dung on the ice*").

151 *By Sunday, November 12*: Cruikshank, 12; journal, Robert Barwick, Nov. 11, 1775, NDAR, vol. 2, appendix F, 1387–1400 (*wheeled field guns*); Fourteenth, 158 ("*beggar*"), 204 (*marble bust*); Reynolds, *Guy Carleton*, 12; Atherton, *Montreal, 1535–1914*, vol. 2, 76.

151 *Rarely had a fortified town fallen*: PGW, vol. 2, 396–97n ("*coax them*"); Montgomery to wife, Nov. 13, 1775, in Louise Livingston Hunt, "Biographical Notes Concerning General Richard Montgomery," 1876, NYHS, 14 ("*legion of females*"); Shelton, 116–17 ("*no driving it*"); Lossing, *The Life and Times of Philip Schuyler*, vol. 1, 470 ("*weary of power*").

152 *"I need not tell you"*: MGRM, 259, 274–75.

152 *Forty miles downstream*: GWGO, 118; Lanctôt, *Canada and the American Revolution*, 93; Crawford, ed., *The Autobiography of a Yankee Mariner*, 53–54; Fourteenth, 155 ("*saddest funeral*"); Carleton to Dartmouth, Nov. 5, 1775, DAR, vol. 11, 173 ("*try to retard*").

152 *Even becalmed in the middle of nowhere*: MLA, 139–41 ("*ten thousand eyes*"); Fourteenth, 125 (*executioner*); Reynolds, *Guy Carleton*, 6–7, 10–11; *Struggle*, vol. 1, 34 ("*enormous nose*").

152 *He was quick-tempered, autocratic*: *Struggle*, vol. 1, 337 ("*mystery*"); Baxter, ed., *The British Invasion from the North*, 156 ("*distant, reserved*"); G. P. Browne, "Carleton, Guy," *Dictionary of Canadian Biography*, vol. 5, www.biographi.ca/en/bio/carletonguy5E.html ("*gallant*"); Desjardin, *Through Howling Wilderness*, 6 ("*uncorruptness*"); Reynolds, *Guy Carleton*, xii; Bradley, *Sir Guy Carleton (Lord Dorchester)*, 75–77 (*Maria*).

153 *He found North America in turmoil*: Desjardin, *Through a Howling Wilderness*, 126 ("*lower sort*"); Sandwich, vol. 1, 86 ("*unfavorable light*").

153 *By Wednesday night, November 15*: Cruikshank, 127 ("*rendered very disagreeable*"); Crawford, ed., *The Autobiography of a Yankee Mariner*, 55–59 ("*such a quantity*"); GWGO, 118; Stanley, *Canada Invaded*, 67 ("*resign your fleet*").

154 *Failure to comply would result*: Hatch, *Thrust for Canada*, 95–96.

154 *The moment had arrived for desperate measures*: Stanley, *Canada Invaded*, 68–69 ("*Wild Pigeon*"); Reynolds, *Guy Carleton*, 71; Wood, *The Father of British Canada*, 90; Cruikshank, 12; "Critical Adventure of Lord Dorchester in the War of 1775," *United Service Journal*, part 1 (1831): 73–74; Wrong, *Canada and the American Revolution*, 292.

154 *Behind them, their erstwhile comrades*: Beatson, *Naval and Military Memoirs of Great Britain*, vol. 4, 104; Cohen, ed., *Canada Preserved*, 22 ("*unspeakable joy*").

154 *"I think our fate extremely doubtful"*: Carleton to Dartmouth, Nov. 20, 1775, DAR, vol. 11, 186; Hugh Finlay to Anthony Todd, Nov. 1, 1775, in DAR, vol. 11, 170–72 ("*one Arnold*").

154 *That was precisely Colonel Benedict Arnold's*: *Struggle*, vol. 2, 32; Lefkowitz, *Benedict Arnold's Army*, 192–94 ("*undertaking*"); Desjardin, *Through a Howling Wilderness*, 146 ("*constant misery*"), 154, 155 ("*knock up a dust*"); Randall, *Benedict Arnold*, 205; Gabriel, ed., *Quebec During the American Invasion*, xxxvi–xxxvii; Wrong, *Canada and the American Revolution*, 281–82; Ryan, ed., *A Salute to Courage*, 24; Fourteenth, 141–42; PGW, vol. 2, 403–04 ("*ten days sooner*").

155 *Even now, gaunt after his Maine anabasis*: *Struggle*, vol. 1, 524; Randall, *Benedict Arnold*, 24, 33 (*ice-skating*); Bolton, *The Private Soldier Under Washington*, 244 ("*waste timber*"); WR,

66–67 (*"as brave a man"*); BARH, 10 (*"serpentine"*); Brandt, *The Man in the Mirror*, 3 (*"blessed"*).

155 *His father was a drunk merchant*: Brumwell, *Turncoat*, 22, 25 (*cooper's apprentice*); Jacob and Case, *Treacherous Beauty*, 58–59; Randall, *Benedict Arnold*, 24, 27–28; BARH, 26–29; Martin, "The Hero Before the Traitor," *MHQ* 28, no. 3 (Spring 2016): 38+; Brandt, *The Man in the Mirror*, 5 (*"Be dutiful"*); *Struggle*, 117–18 (*"precious soul"*).

156 *His masters were generous*: Wood, *The Radicalism of the American Revolution*, 75; Brandt, *The Man in the Mirror*, 10; Jacob and Case, *Treacherous Beauty*, 58–59.

156 *His ambitions grew with his business*: BARH, 35–37, 48; GWGO, 164–65; Randall, *Benedict Arnold*, 37–38, 41–42, 52, 64–66; Jacob and Case, *Treacherous Beauty*, 61.

156 *With the seizure of Ticonderoga*: Brumwell, *Turncoat*, 37 (*scarlet militia uniform coat*); Randall, *Benedict Arnold*, 103, 124; B. Arnold to Congress, June 13, 1775, AA, IV: 2, 976–77 (*"smiles of heaven"*); Soucier, "Where There Was No Signs of Any Human Being," *JMH* 81, no. 2 (Apr. 2017): 369+; Wilson, *Benedict Arnold*, 42–46.

157 *The boy in the shop apron*: Wilson, *Benedict Arnold*, 38; BARH, 52, 95–96, 101–02; Brumwell, *Turncoat*, 43 (*"breaking his head"*), 46; Brandt, *The Man in the Mirror*, 13–16, 36–37; Palmer, *George Washington and Benedict Arnold*, 105 (*"idle life"*).

157 *Washington chose to take a chance*: Palmer, *George Washington and Benedict Arnold*, 116–18; BARH, 106–07, 114–16; Desjardin, *Through a Howling Wilderness*, 15–16 (*"active woodsmen"*); "Correspondence of the Brothers Joshua and Jedidiah Huntington," *Collections of the Connecticut Historical Society*, vol. 20, 234 (*"secret though known"*); GW to P. Schuyler, Aug. 20, 1775, PGW, vol. 1, 333 (*"Quebec will fall"*).

157 *"The drums beat and away"*: Callahan, *Daniel Morgan*, 65, 80 (*conch shell*); Chernow, *Alexander Hamilton*, 48 (*Burr*); Edwards, "Morgan and His Riflemen," *WMQ* 23, no. 2 (Oct. 1914): 73+ (*"pugilist"*); Higginbotham, *Daniel Morgan, Revolutionary Rifleman*, 4–7 (*scars*).

158 *After marching forty miles north*: Royster, *A Revolutionary People at War*, 24 (*"If thy presence"*); Ebenezer Wild, "A Journal of a March from Cambridge," *Proceedings*, MHS 22, 2nd ser., 2 (Apr. 1886): 265+ (*"Weighed anchor"*). Some scholars believe that Wild's journal was likely a copy of one written by another soldier. Soucier, "Where There Was No Signs of Any Human Being," *JMH* 81, no. 2 (Apr. 2017): 369+.

158 *The men soon grew seasick*: WR, 168 (*"indifferent"*); Brown and Peckham, eds., *Revolutionary War Journals of Henry Dearborn*, 38; Randall, *Benedict Arnold*, 154; Clark, *Following Their Footsteps*, 18–19; *Struggle*, vol. 1, 524.

158 *Here, on Washington's orders*: Clark, *Following Their Footsteps*, 23–24; York, *Patriot on the Kennebec*, 29; Willis, *The Struggle for Sea Power*, 64; Huston, "The Logistics of Arnold's March to Quebec," *Military Affairs* 32, no. 3 (Dec. 1968): 110+ (*seams opening*); Clark, *Following Their Footsteps*, 41 (*"three thousand pounds"*); MQ, 201. In 1938, Kenneth Roberts compiled Arnold's letters and the journals of thirteen expedition members into a remarkably valuable anthology titled *March to Quebec*.

158 *"infamous villains"*: Sept. 30, 1775, "Journal of Captain William Humphrey," LAC, MG 23 B9, CAIN No. 274886; Arnold to GW, Oct. 13, 1775, GW, vol. 2, 155 (*"amphibious animals"*); MQ, 662–63 (*"teeth chattered"*); BARH, 123 (*"To Quebec"*).

158 *Hemlock and spruce crowded*: MQ, 661; Clark, *Following Their Footsteps*, 26, 37; Sept. 30, 1775, "Journal of Captain William Humphrey," LAC, MG 23 B9, CAIN No. 274886 (*"perpendicular"*); Lefkowitz, *Benedict Arnold's Army*, 105; York, *Patriot on the Kennebec*, 60–61 (*"sad plight"*); Bray and Bushnell, eds., *Diary of a Common Soldier in the American Revolution*, 15; Brown and Peckham, eds., *Revolutionary War Journals of Henry Dearborn*, 40.

159 *More than 130 miles upriver*: Clark, *Following Their Footsteps*, 49; author visit, Aug. 2015; MQ, 208 (*"trees tumbling"*), 54–55, 209–10 (*"howling wilderness"*); Huston, "The Logistics of Arnold's March to Quebec," *Military Affairs* 32, no. 3 (Dec. 1968): 110+; Lefkowitz, *Benedict Arnold's Army*, 170–71 (*"heavy heart"*); Brown and Peckham, eds., *Revolutionary War Journals of Henry Dearborn*, 49–50 (*"general prayer"*); Darley, *Voices from a Wilderness Expedition*, 204–05 (*court-martialed*).

159 *"We are in an absolute danger"*: MQ, 258, 214 *(five pints)*, 668–69 *("partridge")*, 319 *("ten shares")*; Wild, "A Journal of a March from Cambridge," *Proceedings*, MHS 22, 2nd ser., 2 (Apr. 1886): 265+ *("bits of bread")*.

159 *Stews were boiled*: MQ, 218–19, 258–59, 528 *("shot pouch")*, 341 *("Newfoundland dog")*; *Struggle*, vol. 1, 592; Codman, *Arnold's Expedition to Quebec*, 101, 107; Nov. 14, 1775, "Journal of Captain William Humphrey," LAC, MG 23 B9, CAIN No. 274886; Desjardin, *Through a Howling Wilderness*, 1; Bray and Bushnell, eds., *Diary of a Common Soldier in the American Revolution*, 18 *("candlewicks")*.

160 *They trudged on*: author visit, Lac-Mégantic and Saint-Georges, Aug. 2015; Oct. 30, 1775, "Journal of Captain William Humphrey," LAC, MG 23 B9, CAIN No. 274886 *("I must confess")*; Smith, *Arnold's March from Cambridge to Quebec*, 276 *("reeled about")*.

160 *Salvation appeared as a bovine*: Brown and Peckham, eds., *Revolutionary War Journals of Henry Dearborn*, 153; Clark, *Following Their Footsteps*, 78; Wild, "A Journal of a March from Cambridge," *Proceedings*, MHS 22, 2nd ser., 2 (Apr. 1886): 265+; Bray and Bushnell, eds., *Diary of a Common Soldier in the American Revolution*, 19 *("joyfulest")*; MQ, 222–23 *("savage shoes")*, 219 *("Blessed our stars")*; "Journal of Matthias Ogden," *Proceedings of the New Jersey Historical Society*, new ser., 13 (1928): 17+.

160 *They also blessed Arnold*: BA to GW, Sept. 25–27, 1775, *PGW*, vol. 2, 41; Lefkowitz, *Benedict Arnold's Army*, 87; Desjardin, *Through a Howling Wilderness*, 110; BA to GW, Nov. 8, 1775, *PGW*, vol. 2, 326–27 *("most hospitable")*; MQ, 59–61; Huston, "The Logistics of Arnold's March to Quebec," *Military Affairs* 32, no. 3 (Dec. 1968): 110+.

160 *In the coming days his troops straggled*: Codman, *Arnold's Expedition to Quebec*, 132; Ward, *A Memoir of Lieut.-Colonel Samuel Ward*, 8 *("waded 100 miles")*; Randall, *Benedict Arnold*, 188; Huston, "The Logistics of Arnold's March to Quebec," *Military Affairs* 32, no. 3 (Dec. 1968): 110+. BA told GW on November 20 that he had "about 650 in the whole" at Pointe-aux-Trembles, including invalids. *PGW*, vol. 2, 403. Different accounts vary on the precise number of Arnold's force, before and after the march.

160 *"Our march has been attended"*: BA to GW, Oct. 28, 1775, *PGW*, vol. 2, 245; GW to BA, Dec. 5, 1775, *PGW*, vol. 2, 493.

161 *Ever aggressive, Arnold next*: Codman, *Arnold's Expedition to Quebec*, 133–38; *Fourteenth*, 149–50; MQ, 674–75 *("saints placed")*.

161 *At nine p.m. on November 13*: MQ, 87; BA to GW, Nov. 20, 1775, *PGW*, vol. 2, 403; "Journal of Matthias Ogden," *Proceedings of the New Jersey Historical Society*, new ser., 13 (1928): 17+; BARH, 146; Codman, *Arnold's Expedition to Quebec*, 145–46; MQ, 677; Nov. 14, 1775, "Journal of Captain William Humphrey," LAC, MG 23 B9, CAIN No. 274886.

161 *"They huzzahed thrice"*: Cohen, ed., *Canada Preserved*, 22; J. M. LeMoine, *The Sword of Brigadier-General Richard Montgomery*, 32; *Struggle*, vol. 2, 28 *("every severity")*; Bradley, *Sir Guy Carleton (Lord Dorchester)*, 111 *("usual mixture")*; "Journal of Matthias Ogden," *Proceedings of the New Jersey Historical Society*, new ser., 13 (1928): 17+ *(18-pound ball)*.

161 *Even Colonel Arnold knew when the hour*: MQ, 91–92; BARH, 149; BA to Montgomery, *AA*, IV: 3, 1696–97 *("obliged to bear arms")*; BA to GW, Nov. 20, 1775, *PGW*, vol. 2, 403 *(five reliable cartridges)*.

162 *He ordered the men assembled*: MQ, 226, 679–80.

162 *"God deliver me from this land"*: MQ, 687–88; Ward, *A Memoir of Lieut.-Colonel Samuel Ward*, 8 *("winter's campaign")*.

162 *Good news out of Canada*: Lefkowitz, *Benedict Arnold's Army*, 192 *(Hannibal)*.

162 *Canadian volunteers flocked*: *Fourteenth*, 141–42; Ryan, ed., *A Salute to Courage*, 24; Mayer, "Canada, Congress, and the Continental Army: Strategic Accommodations, 1774–1776," *JMH* 78, no. 2 (Apr. 2014): 503+ *("les Bostonnais")*; Gabriel, ed., *Quebec During the American Invasion*, xxxvi–xxxvii; Hugh Finlay to Anthony Todd, Sept. 19, 1775, in *DAR*, vol. 11, 119–21 *("expect no assistance")*.

162 *For the American invaders*: *Fourteenth*, 177; "Committee Report on Gunpowder Sent to the Northern Army," Oct. 16, 1775, *AP* *(six tons)*.

163 *Still, with Montgomery and Arnold leading:* Lefkowitz, *Benedict Arnold's Army*, 192 (*"famine-proof"*); *Fourteenth*, 177 (*"fourteen provinces"*).

6. AMERICA IS AN UGLY JOB

164 *By late morning on Thursday, October 26:* London *Public Advertiser*, Oct. 27, 1775, 2–3; Kingsley, "Letters to Lord Polwarth from Sir Francis-Carr Clerke, Aide-de-Camp to General John Burgoyne," *New York History* 79, no. 4 (Oct. 1998): 393+ (*musket cartridges*); Julie Flavell, "The Plot to Kidnap King George III," *BBC History*, Nov. 2006, 12–16 (*hijacked coach*). Sayre was freed on a writ of habeas corpus and £1,000 bail. Nothing came of the charges, and he moved to France in mid-1777.

164 *"raised the curiosity of the public":* London *Public Advertiser*, Oct. 27, 1775, 2–3.

164 *"The crowd was very great in the courtyard":* Kingsley, "Letters to Lord Polwarth from Sir Francis-Carr Clerke, Aide-de-Camp to General John Burgoyne," *New York History* 79, no. 4 (Oct. 1998): 393+; London *Public Advertiser*, Oct. 27, 1775, 2–3; "Royal Hanoverian Creams," *The Regency Redingote: Historical Snippets of Regency England*, https://regencyredingote .wordpress.com/2010/04/30/royal-hanoverian-creams/; "Gold State Coach," Royal Collection Trust, www.royalcollection.org.uk/collection/5000048/gold-state-coach; McCullough, *1776*, 4–5; Ayling, *George the Third*, 206. George IV, a onetime Royal Navy officer, complained of the "rough sea." "Gold Coach a 'Bumpy Ride,'" *BBC News*, June 2, 2002, http://news.bbc.co .uk/2/hi/uk_news/england/1984344.stm.

165 *A platoon of constables brought up the rear:* Peckham, ed., *Sources of American Independence*, vol. 1, 138 (*"memory of man"*); George, *London Life in the Eighteenth Century*, 3, 20, 25, 109.

165 *The Americans, by contrast:* "Gov. Bernard's Book of Poetry," *B 1775*, Mar. 23, 2016; Donne, ed., *The Correspondence of King George the Third with Lord North*, vol. 1, 270n (*"Committee of Oblivion"*); John Wesley to North, June 15, 1775, BC, Bft. vol. 79, 8–9 (*"as valiant"*); Morison, *The Oxford History of the American People*, 218; Wood, *The American Revolution*, 55.

165 *Lord North warned him:* Brooke, *King George III*, 177 (*"foreign war"*); *AA*, IV: 3, 240–41; Kallich and MacLeish, eds., *The American Revolution Through British Eyes*, 79 (*"such rebellion"*); "A Proclamation for Suppressing Rebellion and Sedition," Aug. 23, 1775, https://www.archives .gov/files/historical-docs/doc-content/images/rev-war-king-procl-sedition.pdf; Mackesy, *The War for America*, 29; Donne, ed., *The Correspondence of King George the Third with Lord North*, vol. 1, 264n; Bickham, *Making Headlines*, 84.

166 *"that damned American war":* Callahan, *Royal Raiders*, 33–34; Willcox, *Portrait of a General*, 42.

166 *Yet a king must remain steadfast: MLA*, 29 (*reviewing the Guards*); "George III Calendar, Sept. 1775–Oct. 1777," RA GEO/MAIN/#2269–88 (*"ships building"* and *inked boxes*).

166 *The state coach clopped to a halt:* London *Public Advertiser*, Oct. 27, 1775, 2–3; "History of the Parliamentary Estate," www.parliament.uk; *AA*, VI: 1, 1–3 (*"regal ornaments"*); Nelson, *The American Tory*, 156 (*"tall, square"*); McCullough, *1776*, 10 (*crimson robes*); Thomas, *The House of Commons in the Eighteenth Century*, 4; *PH* 18, 695–99 (*"Those who have long"*).

167 *A few naysayers disparaged:* Steuart, ed., *The Last Journals of Horace Walpole*, vol. 1, 486 (*"falsehoods"*); *PH* 18, 730–32 (*"ages yet unborn"*); Clark, *British Opinion and the American Revolution*, 244 (*"Where the cause is just"*).

167 *For George and Queen Charlotte:* "A Diary of the King & Queen's Private Life," 1769, Private Papers, undated and 1755–1782, RA GEO/MAIN/#15889–93 (*"they retire"*); Ayling, *George the Third*, 200–01, 204–05; Black, *George III*, 171–72, 183; Hibbert, *George III*, 63; Charlotte to H.R.H. George, Aug. 12, 1770, Queen Charlotte, private corr., 1770–1819, RA GEO/ MAIN/#36346, and Charlotte to Charlotte Bruce, Aug. 12, 1770, RA GEO/MAIN/#36348 (*"all equal"*).

168 *For those with fine houses:* Foreman, *The Duchess*, 31–32, 36 (*horsehair*), 56 (*"kind of animal"*); Simpson, ed., *The Waiting City*, 171 (*"plumes"*); Thomas, *John Paul Jones*, 28 (*hair dyed red*).

168 *It also gambled without guilt:* Smollett, *Roderick Random*, 76; Plumb, *The First Four Georges*, 16; Porter, *English Society in the Eighteenth Century*, 238 (*insurance policies*); Timbs, *Clubs and Club Life in London*, 72; Donne, ed., *The Correspondence of King George the Third with*

Lord North, vol. 1, 238n (*coats inside out*); Schwartz, *Daily Life in Johnson's London*, 74–75 (*dice*); Foreman, *The Duchess*, 35 (*"Play at whist"*).

169 *London also had more than five hundred*: Isaacson, *Benjamin Franklin*, 182–83; Almon, ed., *The Remembrancer*, vol. 1, 149 (*"ready to march"*), 100 (*500 stand*); Smith, *Manufacturing Independence*, 12 (*806 muskets*); Brewer, *The Sinews of Power*, 176 (*Duke of Richmond*).

169 *"I am growing more and more American"*: Kallich and MacLeish, eds., *The American Revolution Through British Eyes*, 129; Hibbert, *Redcoats and Rebels*, 76–77 (*Wilkes*); Ian R. Christie, "John Wilkes, British Journalist and Politician," *Encyclopedia Britannica*, 2002, https://www .britannica.com/biography/John-Wilkes; Morison and Commager, *The Growth of the American Republic*, vol. 1, 197 (*"unjust, felonious"*); Ketchum, *The Winter Soldiers*, 78 (*"Thermopylae"*); Christie, "British Politics and the American Revolution," *Albion* 9, no. 3 (Autumn 1977): 205+.

169 *Newspaper resistance to colonial policy*: Bickham, "Sympathizing with Sedition?," *WMQ*, 3rd ser., 59, no. 1 (Jan. 2002): 101+; Bickham, *Making Headlines*, 21, 16 (*"affairs of America"*); Lutnick, *The American Revolution and the British Press*, 12, 16–18 (*the king himself*); Clark, *British Opinion and the American Revolution*, 10 (Royal Lying Gazette); Nagy, *Invisible Ink*, 199 (Morning Post).

170 *Yet many British "newspapers went straight"*: Trevelyan, *The American Revolution*, 217; Bickham, *Making Headlines*, 75, 79; Lutnick, *The American Revolution and the British Press*, 59 (*"unnatural"*).

170 *Biographical profiles of American leaders*: Bickham, "Sympathizing with Sedition?," *WMQ*, 3rd ser., 59, no. 1 (Jan. 2002): 101+.

170 *Irked at the dissent*: John Pownall to Dartmouth, Aug. 5, 1775, *The Manuscripts of the Earl of Dartmouth*, vol. 2, American Papers, 349 (*"narrowly watched"*); *DAR*, vol. 10, 156, 228; Campbell-Smith, *Masters of the Post*, 80 (*three-room suite*); Anthony Todd [Secret Office, General Post Office] to John Pownall, Sept. 13, 1775, Richard Arthur Roberts, ed., *Calendar of Home Office Papers of the Reign of George III*, 420; Hemmeon, *The History of the British Post Office*, 46–47; *The Manuscripts of the Earl of Dartmouth*, vol. 2, American Papers, 301, 330, 357 (*Royal Navy officers*).

170 *Additional letters were intercepted from foreign diplomats*: Campbell-Smith, *Masters of the Post*, 80; Hemmeon, *The History of the British Post Office*, 46–47; Megan Westley, "5 Things You Didn't Know About the Secret Spying Arm of the Post Office," *BBC History Magazine*, Oct. 15, 2014, www.historyextra.com; Dierks, *In My Power*, 208; "From Mr. Todd," *The Manuscripts of the Earl of Dartmouth*, vol. 2, American Papers, 347 (*"to Dr. Franklin"*); Todd to Pownall, Oct. 11, 1775, Roberts, ed., *Calendar of Home Office Papers of the Reign of George III*, 427, 470; Nagy, *Invisible Ink*, 21–22; "From Mr. Todd," *The Manuscripts of the Earl of Dartmouth*, vol. 2, American Papers, 347, 376, 393 (*noted the time*).

171 *As October spilled into November*: Black, *George III*, 228; copies of correspondence and enclosures to George, "George III Calendar, Jan. 1774–Aug. 1775," including Sir Stancier Porter to J. Robinson, July 22, 1775, RA GEO/MAIN/#2082, and subsequent corr., RA GEO/MAIN/ #2095–97, 2105, 2107, 2092, 2102, 2104; North to George, Sept. 9, 1775, "George III Calendar, Sept. 1775–Oct. 1777," RA GEO/MAIN/#2177–78; George to North, Aug. 1, 1775, "George III Calendar, Jan. 1774–Aug. 1775," RA GEO/MAIN/#2061 (*German troops*); George to North, Aug. 9, 1775, "George III Calendar, Jan. 1774–Aug. 1775," RA GEO/MAIN/#2066 (*widows and orphans*); Black, *George III*, 229–30 (*shipped to India*); George to North, Nov. 3, 1775, "George III Calendar, Sept. 1775–Oct. 1777," RA GEO/MAIN/#2211 (*"civility"*); Donne, ed., *The Correspondence of King George the Third with Lord North*, vol. 1, 259, 294 (*"extremely anxious"*).

171 *Broad domestic support for the war*: John Heneage Jesse, *Memoirs of the Life and Reign of King George the Third*, vol. 3, 67; Ketchum, *The Winter Soldiers*, 73 (*"executive power"*), 76–77 (*"war of the people"*); Schlesinger, *The Colonial Merchants and the American Revolution*, 539–40 (*endorsements*).

171 *Without doubt, the disruption of transatlantic trade*: Clark, *British Opinion and the American Revolution*, 95, 99, 105; Breen, *American Insurgents, American Patriots*, 169 (*barely £220,000*); George, *London Life in the Eighteenth Century*, 269 (*money to be made*); Mansfield, *Selected Letters of Edmund Burke*, 234 (*"begin to snuff"*); Schlesinger, *The Colonial Merchants and the*

American Revolution, 539–40; Leathams, Walker & Co. to John Atkinson, Aug. 29, 1775, John Atkinson Papers, WLC (*"flourishing state"*).

172 *For the king, it was all part*: Ketchum, *The Winter Soldiers*, 98–99; Mackesy, *The War for America*, 23 (*"put heart"*); Donne, ed., *The Correspondence of King George the Third with Lord North*, vol. 1, 298 (*"unanimity and zeal"*); Pares, *King George III and the Politicians*, 148–49 (*Royal Closet*); Gruber, "Lord Howe and Lord George Germain: British Politics and the Winning of American Independence," *WMQ*, 3rd ser., 22, no. 2 (Apr. 1965): 225+ (*"warm Parliament"*); Gibbon, *Autobiography and Correspondence of Edward Gibbon*, 239 (*"more gloomy"*).

172 *That surely was the case for Lord Dartmouth*: Bellot, *William Knox*, 140; BF to William Franklin, July 14, 1773, FOL (*"truly a good man"*); Bargar, *Lord Dartmouth and the American Revolution*, 178, 160 (*"prostitute"*).

172 *North also showed weakness*: Anson, ed., *Autobiography and Political Correspondence of Augustus Henry, Third Duke of Grafton, K.G.*, 272; MLA, 58, 74 (*"wool sack"*); Whiteley, *Lord North*, 158 (*"more disagreeable"*); George to North, Nov. 7, 1775, "George III Calendar, Sept. 1775–Oct. 1777," RA GEO/MAIN/#2216 (*"sheet anchor"*); George to North, Mar. 30, 1776, "George III Calendar, Sept. 1775–Oct. 1777," RA GEO/MAIN/#2366 (*"my fate"*); Lucas, *Lord North*, vol. 2, 3 (*"liked his place"*).

173 *In a silver-tongued brogue*: Thomas, *The House of Commons in the Eighteenth Century*, 130–31, 141, 225; Prior, *Memoir of the Life and Character of the Right Hon. Edmund Burke*, vol. 1, 308; Murdoch, ed., *Rebellion in America*, 4; PH 18, 963 (*"women of quality"*).

173 *At Burke's request, the Speaker*: PH 18, 963–82.

173 *Sitting next to Lord North*: Brown, "The Court Martial of Lord George Sackville, Whipping Boy of the Revolutionary War," *WMQ*, 3rd ser., 9, no. 3 (July 1952): 317+ (*"long face"*); Steuart, ed., *The Last Journals of Horace Walpole*, vol. 1, 423–24 (*"Roman severity"*); Spector, *The American Department of the British Government*, 75 (*"chief minister"*).

174 *"pithy, manly sentences"*: Guttridge, "Lord George Germain in Office, 1775–1782," *AHR* 33, no. 1 (Oct. 1927): 23+.

174 *"Let them be happy"*: PH 18, 989–92.

174 *"Pity me, encourage me"*: Guttridge, "Lord George Germain in Office, 1775–1782," *AHR* 33, no. 1 (Oct. 1927): 23+.

174 *"Some fall so hard"*: Guttridge, "Lord George Germain in Office, 1775–1782," *AHR* 33, no. 1 (Oct. 1927): 23+; Weintraub, *Iron Tears*, 31 (*"Kent palace"*); Marlow, *Sackville of Drayton*, 47 (*"bear-garden"*), 20–21 (*"debarred"*), 66 (*"dearest man"*); MLA, 167; Brown, *The American Secretary*, 38–39 (*"I have not genius"*); Mackesy, *The Coward of Minden*, 34–35 (*homosexuality*).

175 *He found his calling as a soldier*: Marlow, *Sackville of Drayton*, 124 (*"cannon-proof"*), 125 (*"Nobody stood higher"*); Brown, "The Court Martial of Lord George Sackville, Whipping Boy of the Revolutionary War," *WMQ*, 3rd ser., 9, no. 3 (July 1952): 317+; MLA, 168.

175 *Then came the great fall*: Mackesy, *The Coward of Minden*, 92–95, 114, 120–24, 132, 141–46; Louis Marlow, *Sackville of Drayton*, 101–04, 108 (*"chicken-hearted"*); Elliott, "The Men That Fought at Minden," *Journal of the American Military Institute* 3, no. 2 (Summer 1939): 80+.

175 *Recalled to London*: Brown, "The Court Martial of Lord George Sackville, Whipping Boy of the Revolutionary War," *WMQ*, 3rd ser., 9, no. 3 (July 1952): 317+; Mackesy, *The War for America*, 48–49; Brown, *The American Secretary*, 11–12; Guttridge, "Lord George Germain in Office, 1775–1782," *AHR* 33, no. 1 (Oct. 1927): 23+ (*burned in effigy*); Marlow, *Sackville of Drayton*, 111 (*"live in hopes"*).

175 *Those times began a few months later*: Mackesy, *The Coward of Minden*, 249–50; Brown, *The American Secretary*, 22–23 (*"Out of tune"*); Cumberland, *Memoirs of Richard Cumberland*, 164 (*"no trash"*).

176 *He completed his rehabilitation*: Brown, *The American Secretary*, 24–25 (*"not trouble themselves"*); Hibbert, *Redcoats and Rebels*, 86–87 (*"all the requisites"*); MLA, 173–75 (*"supine minister"*).

176 *The backbiting never ceased*: Mackesy, *The Coward of Minden*, 251; Bickham, *Making Headlines*, 95 (*"Lord Minden"*); Cumberland, *Memoirs of Richard Cumberland*, 163 (*"quite as cold"*); Marlow, *Sackville of Drayton*, 152–53 (*"his pride"*).

177 *Despite the expanding war*: Bellot, *William Knox*, 108–09.

177 *wait for hours*: Benjamin Franklin complained of waiting three to four hours, and on occasion being turned away. Spector, *The American Department of the British Government*, 41–43, 48–52.

177 *Germain believed that hard work*: Syrett, *Shipping and the American War*, 15 (*centuries of inertia*); Mackesy, *The Coward of Minden*, 252 (*"no obscurity"*); DAR, vol. 10, 32, 29, 319–21 (*Dutch transport ships*).

177 *Upon arriving at Whitehall in mid-November*: DAR, vol. 9, 14–17 (*sanctuary*); 211–12 (*"inflamed with liquor"*); DAR, vol. 10, 31 (*"My clerk"*), 62 (*"warlike stores"*); DAR, vol. 11, 43–44 (*"little or no business"*), 156–57 (*"any dominions"*), 214 (*"the lowest people"*); DAR, vol. 12, 30–31 (*"No troops, no money"*).

178 *Reports from the northern colonies*: DAR, vol. 9, 156 (*Rhode Island*); DAR, vol. 11, 100 (*"becoming soldiers"*), 134 (*mob demolished*), 199 (*"general massacre"*); Brodhead, *Documents Relative to the Colonial History of the State of New York*, vol. 8, 581, 599, 631, 643 (*Governor William Tryon*).

178 *Germain found broad agreement*: Spring, *With Zeal and with Bayonets Only*, 14 (*"deep into principles"*); Palmer, *George Washington's Military Genius*, 40–47.

178 *Lord North and some others*: Conway, "The Politics of British Military and Naval Mobilization, 1775–1783," *English Historical Review* 112, no. 449 (Nov. 1997): 1179+; Dunelm, ed., *The Political Life of William Wildman, Viscount Barrington*, 159 (*"may be reduced"*); Ketchum, *The Winter Soldiers*, 80 (*"men in red coats"*); Harvey to Earl Cornwallis, July 6, 1775, UK NA, WO 3/5 (*"never do"*); Harvey to F. Smith, Nov. 3, 1775, UK NA, WO 3/5 (*"dribletting"*).

179 *Germain soon encountered other aggravations*: MLA, 195–96; Knight, "The Building and Maintenance of the British Fleet During the Anglo-French Wars, 1688–1815," *Les Marines de Guerre Européennes*, 39; Knight, "The Royal Dockyards in England at the Time of the American War of Independence," Ph.D. diss. (University of London, 1972), 116, 121 (*gone on strike*); Ellis, *The Post Office in the Eighteenth Century*, 93; Duncan Campbell-Smith, *Masters of the Post*, 86; Peter Whiteley, *Lord North*, 162–63; HBAR, 357; Marlow, *Sackville of Drayton*, 179–80; Harvey to F. Smith, July 8, 1775, UK NA, WO 3/5 (*"ugly job"*).

179 *Like the man he called*: Germain to W. Howe, Aug. 22, 1776, UK NA, CO 5/93, f. 448 (*"zeal"*); Marlow, *Sackville of Drayton*, 170 (*"utmost force"*).

179 *Zeal could be found*: Bob Ruppert, "Reconciliation No Longer an Option," *JAR*, Nov. 18, 2014; GC, 321; Syrett, *The Royal Navy in European Waters During the American Revolutionary War*, 4; Gipson, *The Triumphant Empire*, 347 (*"perpetual war"*); Jensen, *The Founding of a Nation*, 655 (*"independency"*); John Knox Laughton, "Shuldham, Molyneux," *Dictionary of National Biography*, vol. 52, https://en.wikisource.org/wiki/Shuldham,_Molyneux_(DNB00).

180 *As for fighting the rebels on land*: HBAR, 59; WAI, 150–51; Brown, *The American Secretary*, 48, 52–53, 58.

180 *Germain also knew that for the past two months*: George to North, Oct. 16, 1775, "George III Calendar, Sept. 1775–Oct. 1777," RA GEO/MAIN/#2201 (*"well inclined"*); Germain to Admiralty, Nov. 13, 1775, NDAR, vol. 3, 367 (*"assist in the suppression"*); Admiralty to Germain, Nov. 15, 1775, and précis prepared for the king, NDAR, vol. 3, 368 and 399; Admiralty to Capt. Robert Cooper, Nov. 21, 1775, NDAR, vol. 3, 381 (Hawke).

180 *All this was to be "a profound secret"*: William Lee to overseer in Virginia, Nov. 30, 1775, NDAR, vol. 3, 397 (*American agents*); Piecuch, "Preventing Slave Insurrection in South Carolina and Georgia, 1775–1776," *JAR*, Feb. 21, 2017 (*slave uprisings*); Dunmore to Dartmouth, May 1, 1775, DAR, vol. 9, 109 (*"fixed purpose"*).

181 *Zeal, indeed, would be a hallmark*: MLA, 175–76; HBAR, 85 (*"masterly strokes"*); Gruber, *Books and the British Army in the Age of the American Revolution*, 47; MLA, 175–76.

181 *Yet amid the green baize desks*: Syrett, *Shipping and the American War*, 243–44; Palmer, *George Washington's Military Genius*, 48; FYAR, 552–53.

181 *"cordiality & harmony which subsists"*: private letter, Germain to W. Howe, Jan. 5, 1776, Papers of Lord George Sackville Germain, WLC.

7. THEY FOUGHT, BLED, AND DIED LIKE ENGLISHMEN

182 *John Murray, the fourth Earl of Dunmore*: Selby, *The Revolution in Virginia*, 20, 14 (*Perthshire*); Phillips, *1775*, 477–81; "John Murray, Fourth Earl of Dunmore," *Dictionary of Virginia Biography*, https://www.encyclopediavirginia.org/Dunmore_John_Murray_fourth_earl_of_c_1730-1809; Stevenson, *Exploring Scotland's Heritage*, 83 (*"most bizarre"*); Burrows and Wallace, *Gotham*, 213 (*"Damn Virginia"*); *BNY*, 35 (*"blockhead"*).

182 *Virginians later caricatured Dunmore*: Selby, *The Revolution in Virginia*, 15; Eric Sterner, "Dunmore's War: The Last Colonial Conflict of America's Colonial Era," *JAR*, July 13, 2017 (review of Glenn F. Williams, *Dunmore's War*); Kevin Phillips, *1775*, 477–78; "John Murray, Fourth Earl of Dunmore," *Dictionary of Virginia Biography*, https://www.encyclopediavirginia.org/Dunmore_John_Murray_fourth_earl_of_c_1730-1809.

182 *Shawnee Indians*: Eric Sterner, "Dunmore's War: The Last Colonial Conflict of America's Colonial Era," *JAR*, July 13, 2017 (review of Glenn F. Williams, *Dunmore's War*); Phillips, *1775*, 477–78; "John Murray, Fourth Earl of Dunmore," *Dictionary of Virginia Biography*, https://www.encyclopediavirginia.org/Dunmore_John_Murray_fourth_earl_of_c_1730-1809. The Shawnee had retaliated after white killers slaughtered a chief's family, including a pregnant woman; she was sliced open and her unborn baby impaled on a stake. Calloway, *The Indian World of George Washington*, 206–10.

182 *Ever since John Rolfe*: Wertenbaker, *Norfolk*, 3; "John Rolfe," Jamestown Rediscovery, http://historicjamestowne.org/; Selby, *The Revolution in Virginia*, 26–27; Wood, *The Radicalism of the American Revolution*, 142; Taylor, *The Internal Enemy*, 29–30 (*"opportunities and status"*).

183 *When, in May 1774, Dunmore dissolved*: Kranish, *Flight from Monticello*, 65.

183 *Baffled by Virginians' "blind and unreasoning fury"*: Nevins, *American States During and After the Revolution*, 77; Dunmore to Dartmouth, May 1, 1775, *DAR*, vol. 9, 108 (*"massacre me"*); Dunmore to Dartmouth, May 2, 1775, *DAR*, vol. 9, 133 (*impounded*); Dunmore to Dartmouth, Aug. 2, 1775, *DAR*, vol. 10, 53 (*"reduce the colony"*).

184 *The* Gazette *would accuse him*: Moomaw, "The British Leave Colonial Virginia," *VMHB* 66, no. 2 (Apr. 1958): 147+ (*"Blackbeard"*); Gerald Holland, "The Seizure of the *Virginia Gazette, or Norfolk Intelligencer*," *JAR*, Jan. 20, 2015; Wertenbaker, *Norfolk*, 53–54; Phillips, *1775*, 480.

184 *Roughly five hundred thousand Americans were black*: Ellis, *Revolutionary Summer*, 20; Selby, *The Revolution in Virginia*, 24 (*40 percent*); Frey, *Water from the Rock*, 48–49 (*military traditions*), 25 (*radical Christian*); Shy, *A People Numerous and Armed*, 36–37; Kranish, *Flight from Monticello*, 76; Quarles, *The Negro in the Making of America*, 40; Frey, "Between Slavery and Freedom: Virginia Blacks in the American Revolution," *Journal of Southern History* 49, no. 3 (Aug. 1983): 375+. In 1775, more than 27,000 slaves were still held in bondage in northern colonies. National Museum of African American History and Culture, Washington, D.C., author visit, Mar. 18, 2018.

184 *In truth, although slavery had begun to disappear*: "Britain and the Slave Trade," n.d., National Archives (U.K.), http://www.nationalarchives.gov.uk/slavery/pdf/britain-and-the-trade.pdf; Carrington, *The British West Indies During the American Revolution*, 19 (*15 to 1*), 29 (*never been more prosperous*); Gilbert, *Black Patriots and Loyalists*, 4 (*uprising in 1760*); Frey, *Water from the Rock*, 75 (*foremost slave-trading*).

184 *Dunmore's initial muttering to London*: Taylor, *The Internal Enemy*, 26; Ward, *Charles Scott and the "Spirit of '76,"* 13; Cecere, "A Tale of Two Cities," *JAR*, Sept. 9, 2015; Capt. Samuel Leslie to W. Howe, Nov. 1, 1775, *AA*, IV: 3, 1716 (*"smallest opposition"*); Selby, *The Revolution in Virginia*, 68–69 (*regimental banner*); *AA*, IV: 3, 1671; Wertenbaker, *Norfolk*, 55; Eckenrode, *The Revolution in Virginia*, 68–69 (*red fabric*).

185 *"I do hereby further declare"*: *AA*, IV: 3, 1385; Selby, *The Revolution in Virginia*, 66–67; Egerton, *Death or Liberty*, 73.

185 *Still, eager blacks found their way*: Copeland, "Lord Dunmore's Ethiopian Regiment," *Military Collector & Historian* 58, no. 4 (Winter 2006): 208+; Gilbert, *Black Patriots and Loyalists*, 23 (*bar correspondence*); *LAR*, 233 (*"flame runs"*); Phillips, *1775*, 483 (*"Negro-catching"*);

Capt. Samuel Leslie to W. Howe, Nov. 26, 1775, *AA*, IV: 3, 1717; Wertenbaker, *Norfolk*, 54–55 (*"whipping up"*); Eller, ed., *Chesapeake Bay in the American Revolution*, 81.

185 *The small victory*: Dunmore to W. Howe, Nov. 30, 1775, *AA*, IV: 3, 1713–14; Selby, *The Revolution in Virginia*, 64–69; McDonnell, *The Politics of War*, 152–55; Schama, *Rough Crossings*, 74 (*"time-server"*); Pybus, "Jefferson's Faulty Math: The Question of Slave Defections in the American Revolution," *WMQ*, 3rd ser., 62, no. 2 (Apr. 2005): 243+.

185 *"With our little corps"*: Dunmore to W. Howe, Nov. 30, 1775, *AA*, IV: 3, 1713–14; also, *Virginia Gazette* (Purdie edition), Jan. 26, 1776; Hume, *1775: Another Part of the Field*, 416; Dunmore to W. Howe, Nov. 2, 1775, *AA*, IV: 4, 357; Capt. Matthew Squire to Gage [*sic*], Dec. 2, 1775, in *Virginia Gazette* (Purdie edition), Jan. 26, 1776 (*"such cowards"*).

186 *Dunmore had miscalculated*: Eckenrode, *The Revolution in Virginia*, 73–74; Taylor, *The Internal Enemy*, 23–24; *LAR*, 233 (*"Hell itself"*).

186 *The proclamation backfired throughout the South*: Frey, *Water from the Rock*, 65; "H.M.S. Savage," *Digital Encyclopedia of George Washington*, www.mountvernon.org/digital-encyclopedia /article/hms-savage/; Nash, *The Unknown American Revolution*, 165 (*slaves who murdered*); Gilbert, *Black Patriots and Loyalists*, 17 (*Patrick Henry*); Taylor, *The Internal Enemy*, 29–30; Schama, *Rough Crossings*, 67–68 (*"eternal separation"*).

186 *The* Virginia Gazette *urged slaves*: Mullin, *Flight and Rebellion*, 135; Neimeyer, *America Goes to War*, 69–70 (*"desert us"*); Eddis, *Letters from America*, 251 (*"universal ferment"*); John Morton to Anthony Wayne, Aug. 16, 1776, BC, Bft. vol. 378, 67–69 (*"Devil Dunmore"*); Van Tyne, *The War of Independence: American Phase*, 204 (*"Negro-thief"*); Ballagh, ed., *The Letters of Richard Henry Lee*, vol. 1, 160 (*"best fitted"*).

186 *"That arch traitor to the rights"*: GW to J. Reed, Dec. 15, 1775, *PGW*, vol. 2, 553; GW to R. H. Lee, Dec. 26, 1775, *PGW*, vol. 2, 611 (*"formidable enemy"*).

186 *A chance to confront*: Wertenbaker, *Norfolk*, 34; Wilson, *The Southern Strategy*, 9–11; Smith, *John Marshall*, 45–46; Ward, *Charles Scott and the "Spirit of '76,"* 15 (*"Nine-tenths"*); Eckenrode, *The Revolution in Virginia*, 79 (*"unwisdom"*); Scribner and Tarter, eds., *Revolutionary Virginia*, vol. 5, 5 (*Hog Pen*).

188 *By Friday, December 8*: Scribner and Tarter, eds., *Revolutionary Virginia*, vol. 5, 6; Smith, *John Marshall*, 45–46; Eller, ed., *Chesapeake Bay in the American Revolution*, 77 ("liberty or wounded").

188 *Skirmishers and raiding parties*: Eckenrode, *The Revolution in Virginia*, 81; Bland, *The Bland Papers*, 38 (*American deserter*); Wilson, *The Southern Strategy*, 10–11. Selby puts the number at roughly 300. *The Revolution in Virginia*, 73. Other accounts place the British numbers as high as 672. Scribner and Tarter, eds., *Revolutionary Virginia*, vol. 5, 7.

188 *At first light on Saturday, December 9*: Bland, *The Bland Papers*, 38 (*"usual sport"*); Hume, *1775: Another Part of the Field*, 431 (*"Boys, stand to"*); Selby, *The Revolution in Virginia*, 73.

189 *Through smoke and morning haze*: Scribner and Tarter, eds., *Revolutionary Virginia*, vol. 5, 8–9 (*"day is our own"*); Fordyce to Capt. Urquhart, Dec. 1, 1775, *AA*, IV: 4, 350 (*"settle everything"*); Smith, *John Marshall*, 48.

189 *Those were his last coherent words*: Hume, *1775: Another Part of the Field*, 433–38; Scribner and Tarter, eds., *Revolutionary Virginia*, vol. 5, 9.

189 *The rear guard turned and pelted*: *Virginia Gazette* (Pinkney edition), Dec. 20, 1775, 2; Hume, *1775: Another Part of the Field*, 438; Schama, *Rough Crossings*, 80–81 (*scalping*); *LAR*, 234–35 (*"with much fewer"*); Bland, *The Bland Papers*, 38 (*"like Englishmen"*); Cumming and Rankin, *The Fate of a Nation*, 83 (*"absurd, ridiculous"*).

190 *Thirty-three captured loyalists*: Selby, *The Revolution in Virginia*, 73–74; Hume, *1775: Another Part of the Field*, 440 (*"ball lodged"*); Cumming and Rankin, *The Fate of a Nation*, 84 (*seventeen wounds*).

190 *That night at seven p.m.*: Hume, *1775: Another Part of the Field*, 439–40; Woodford to E. Pendleton, Dec. 10, 1775, in *Virginia Gazette* (Pinkney edition), Dec. 13, 1775, 2; Dunmore to Dartmouth, Feb. 18, 1776, with 32 enclosures, *DAR*, vol. 10, 218–19; Kranish, *Flight from Monticello*, 79 (*excluded blacks*).

190 *"has much to answer for"*: Cumming and Rankin, *The Fate of a Nation*, 85.

190 *Norfolk might be a "dirty little borough"*: Dunmore to Dartmouth, Oct. 5, 1775, *DAR*, vol. 11, 137; Chernow, *Washington: A Life*, 214; Wertenbaker, *Norfolk*, 6, 15–16, 19–21, 32, 42–47.

190 *Those days were gone*: Wertenbaker, *Norfolk*, 59–61; Eller, ed., *Chesapeake Bay in the American Revolution*, 85–87 (*pleaded for water* and *singing*); Forrest, *Historical and Descriptive Sketches of Norfolk and Vicinity*, 87.

191 *The rebel force, swollen to almost thirteen hundred*: Naisawald, "Robert Howe's Operations in Virginia, 1775–1776," *VMHB* 60, no. 3 (July 1952): 437+; Scribner and Tarter, eds., *Revolutionary Virginia*, vol. 5, 12; Eckenrode, *The Revolution in Virginia*, 85 (*interrogation*); Ward, *Charles Scott and the "Spirit of '76*," 18 ("*coupled them to a Negro*").

191 *Dunmore was also reinforced*: H. Bellew to P. Stephens, Jan. 11, 1776, *NDAR*, vol. 3, 737 (*fetid water*); Scribner and Tarter, eds., *Revolutionary Virginia*, vol. 5, 14–15 (*yelled taunts*); Dunmore to Dartmouth [*sic*], Feb. 18, 1776, *DAR*, vol. 12, 60–67 ("*utter destruction*").

191 *By December 31, both the year*: Scribner and Tarter, eds., *Revolutionary Virginia*, vol. 5, 285 ("*sentinels*"); H. Bellew to P. Stephens, Jan. 11, 1776, *NDAR*, vol. 3, 737 ("*every mark*"); Ward, *Charles Scott and the "Spirit of '76*," 17–18.

191 *After a minatory rattle*: Wertenbaker, *Norfolk*, 62; H. Bellew to P. Stephens, Jan. 11, 1776, *NDAR*, vol. 3, 737 (*wharf shack*); Eckenrode, *The Revolution in Virginia*, 86; Ward, *Charles Scott and the "Spirit of '76*," 17–18; *Virginia Gazette* (Purdie edition), Jan. 5, 1776, supplement, 2 ("*wind favored*"); R. Howe to Virginia Convention, Jan. 2, 1776, *AA*, IV: 4, 538 ("*vengeance*"); Scribner and Tarter, eds., *Revolutionary Virginia*, vol. 5, 15 ("*still burning*").

192 *That was quite true*: Selby, *The Revolution in Virginia*, 83 ("*Keep up the jig*" and "*red and bright*"); McDonnell, *The Politics of War*, 169–70 (*disingenuous*); Eckenrode, *The Revolution in Virginia*, 86–87 (*selling booty*).

192 *At length the flames subsided*: Scribner and Tarter, eds., *Revolutionary Virginia*, vol. 5, 355 ("*ruinous*"); T. Jefferson to John Page, Oct. 31, 1775, FOL ("*Delenda*"); Powell, ed., *A Biographical Sketch of Col. Leven Powell*, 15 ("*expect to see*"). The final burning occurred on February 6, 1776. Michael Kranish, *Flight from Monticello*, 82.

192 *"The detested town of Norfolk"*: *AA*, IV: 4, 540; Wertenbaker, *Norfolk*, 64–65 (*investigative commission*); Selby, *The Revolution in Virginia*, 83–84 (*stayed hidden*).

193 *"Never can true reconcilement"*: NCCH, 75; Nevins, *American States During and After the Revolution*, 108–09; Wright, *The Continental Army*, 68–70 (*nine Virginia regiments*); McDonnell, *The Politics of War*, 173 (*open for trade*).

193 *Virginians got on with hunting*: *Virginia Gazette* (Dixon and Hunter edition), Dec. 23, 1775, 3; Frey, "Between Slavery and Freedom: Virginia Blacks in the American Revolution," *Journal of Southern History* 49, no. 3 (Aug. 1983): 375+ ("*renegadoes*"); Taylor, *The Internal Enemy*, 25 (*severed heads*); Pybus, "Jefferson's Faulty Math: The Question of Slave Defections in the American Revolution," *WMQ*, 3rd ser., 62, no. 2 (Apr. 2005): 243+ (*compensated*).

193 *By triggering Norfolk's immolation*: Eckenrode, *The Revolution in Virginia*, 90; Davidson, *Propaganda and the American Revolution, 1763–1783*, 149 ("*barreled up*"); Scribner and Tarter, eds., *Revolutionary Virginia*, vol. 6, 7–8.

193 *But rebel riflemen lurked*: Scribner and Tarter, eds., *Revolutionary Virginia*, vol. 6, 7–8 ("*King's Four Acres*"). An American colonel counted 300 fresh graves after the British departed. Hast, "Loyalism in Revolutionary Virginia: The Norfolk Area and the Eastern Shore," Ph.D. diss. (University of Iowa, 1979), 65. Frey cites 150 dead blacks left along the Elizabeth. Twenty years later, the architect and engineer Benjamin Henry Latrobe reported seeing "many wagonloads of bones of men, women, and children" along the river. "Between Slavery and Freedom: Virginia Blacks in the American Revolution," *Journal of Southern History* 49, no. 3 (Aug. 1983): 375+.

194 *"there was not a ship in the fleet"*: Pybus, "Jefferson's Faulty Math: The Question of Slave Defections in the American Revolution," *WMQ*, 3rd ser., vol. 62, no. 2 (Apr. 2005): 243+; Scribner and Tarter, eds., *Revolutionary Virginia*, vol. 6, 7–8 (*ghost ship*); NCCH, 78.

194 *"I wish to God"*: Dunmore to Dartmouth [*sic*], Feb. 18, 1776, *DAR*, vol. 12, 58–68.

8. THE PATHS OF GLORY

195 *A lowering sky the color*: Several diarists place Montgomery's arrival on December 1 or 2, but Arnold in a letter to GW explicitly cited December 3, with the subsequent move to Quebec the following day. BA to GW, Dec. 5, 1775, *PGW*, vol. 2, 495; *MQ*, 363. Capt. Henry Dearborn, the New Hampshire physician, put Montgomery's arrival at ten a.m. Brown and Peckham, eds., *Revolutionary War Journals of Henry Dearborn*, 60.

195 *it was cold enough to split stone*: Brandt, *The Man in the Mirror*, 71; Codman, *Arnold's Expedition to Quebec*, 180; *Struggle*, 89–90; Ferling, *Almost a Miracle*, 95.

195 *Three hundred soldiers came with him*: Shelton, 122–23, 127 (*"intemperate desire"*); *WR*, 185; Montgomery to Schuyler, Dec. 5, 1775, *AA*, IV: 4, 188–90; MGRM, 276–83; unsigned letter, Dec. 7, 1775, "Documents Relating to the War of 1775," *Report Concerning Canadian Archives for the Year 1904*, appendix 1, LAC, 385 (*Forty more barrels*).

195 *Later that afternoon, Arnold's men*: Codman, *Arnold's Expedition to Quebec*, 180; Brown and Peckham, eds., *Revolutionary War Journals of Henry Dearborn*, 60; "Journal of Captain William Humphrey," LAC, MG 23 B9, CAIN No. 274886, Dec. 2, [sic] 1775 (*"gentle, polite"*); *MQ*, 363 (*"pockmarked"* and *"freezing bodies"*); Shelton, 128 (*"active, intelligent"*); Desjardin, *Through a Howling Wilderness*, 158 (*"born to command"*).

196 *Arnold had hired a fleet*: unsigned letter, Dec. 7, 1775, "Documents Relating to the War of 1775," *Report Concerning Canadian Archives for the Year 1904*, appendix 1, LAC, 385; *Fourteenth*, 182–83; *Struggle*, 99; Walkem, *Summary of the History of the Intendant's Palace*, 1–4; *MQ*, 363; BA to GW, Dec. 5, 1775, *PGW*, vol. 2, 495 (*"all possible preparations"*).

196 *Montgomery had dispersed his New Yorkers*: BARH, 159; *Struggle*, 99; Montgomery to Janet, Dec. 5, 1775, Louise Livingston Hunt, "Biographical Notes Concerning General Richard Montgomery," 1876, NYHS, 16 (*"beaver blanket"*); Montgomery to Schuyler, Dec. 5, 1775, *AA*, IV: 4, 188–90 (*"works of Quebec"*); Shelton, 134.

197 *Even as he refined his "storming plan"*: Ferling, *Almost a Miracle*, 96; MGRM, 276. Sir John Fortescue's "perfect volley" judgment is quoted in Stacey, *Quebec, 1759*, 38, 165.

197 *But Montgomery also knew*: author visit, Battlefields Park, Plains of Abraham, Quebec, signage; Chartrand, *French Fortresses in North America*, 28; James, *The Rise and Fall of the British Empire*, 93 (*"Canadian vermin"*); Stacey, *Quebec, 1759*, 100–03, 106; Anderson, *Crucible of War*, 344 (*"worst shape"*); Hatch, *Thrust for Canada*, 99 (*"sober and scientific"*).

198 *In an effort to undermine enemy morale*: Cohen, ed., *Canada Preserved*, 25 (*"musket-proof"*; Cruikshank, 16 (toile), 138 (*"no mercy"*).

198 *The note was carried*: Shelton, 131 (*fire tongs*); BARH, 163 (*parked sleigh*).

198 *No sooner had the Americans cinched*: Senter, *The Journal of Isaac Senter*, 48.

198 *"The men begin to be very much"*: *Struggle*, 100–01; *MQ*, 692–94 (*"fleas"*), 698 (*whipped for theft*); Hatch, *Thrust for Canada*, 122.

198 *"The smallpox is all around us"*: Desjardin, *Through a Howling Wilderness*, 164; Cohen, ed., *Canada Preserved*, 27 (*"deadly infection"*).

199 *"most terrible of all the ministers"*: Fenn, "Biological Warfare in Eighteenth-Century North America: Beyond Jeffrey Amherst," *Journal of American History* 86, no. 4 (Mar. 2000): 1552+.

199 *Transmitted by human vectors*: Fenn, *Pox Americana*, 6, 16–18; Riedel, "Edward Jenner and the History of Smallpox and Vaccination," *Proceedings*, Baylor University Medical Center, 18, no. 1 (Jan. 2005): 21+; Becker, "Smallpox in Washington's Army," *JMH* 68 (Apr. 2004): 381+; Huston, *The Sinews of War*, 41 (*much prized*).

199 *Smallpox ravaged Alexander*: Riedel, "Edward Jenner and the History of Smallpox and Vaccination," *Proceedings*, Baylor University Medical Center, 18, no. 1 (Jan. 2005): 21+; Reiss, *Medicine and the American Revolution*, 104 (*jackass fat*).

199 *Vaccination using cowpox*: Fenn, *Pox Americana*, 31–33, 41 (*"God's overruling"*); Reiss, *Medicine and the American Revolution*, 106; Riedel, "Edward Jenner and the History of Smallpox and Vaccination," *Proceedings*, Baylor University Medical Center, 18, no. 1 (Jan. 2005): 21; Becker, "Smallpox in Washington's Army," *JMH* 68 (Apr. 2004): 381+; McNeill, *Mosquito Empires*, 200; Cash, *Medical Men at the Siege of Boston*, 11 (*Boston smallpox*).

200 *Insurrection in America coincided*: Fenn, *Pox Americana*, 3, 88; Calloway, *The American Revolution in Indian Country*, 5 (*blankets*); Becker, "Smallpox in Washington's Army," *JMH* 68 (Apr. 2004): 381+ (*"sent into our army"*); Fenn, "Biological Warfare in Eighteenth-Century North America: Beyond Jeffrey Amherst," *Journal of American History* 86, no. 4 (Mar. 2000): 1552+; Cash, "The Canadian Military Campaign of 1775–1776: Medical Problems and Effects of Disease," *JAMA* 236, no. 1 (July 5, 1976): 52+ (*endemic in Montreal*).

200 *Regardless of the cause*: Becker, "Smallpox in Washington's Army," *JMH* 68 (Apr. 2004): 381+; Cash, "The Canadian Military Campaign of 1775–1776: Medical Problems and Effects of Disease," *JAMA* 236, no. 1 (July 5, 1976): 52+; Fenn, *Pox Americana*, 70; Bray and Bushnell, eds., *Diary of a Common Soldier in the American Revolution*, 23 (*"Sum of our company"*).

200 *A French writer once observed*: The quote is attributed to François-René de Chateaubriand. Chartrand, *French Fortresses in North America*, 2.

200 *When the adventurer Samuel de Champlain*: Fischer, *Champlain's Dream*, 244–45, 253, 466.

200 *Over the next 150 years*: author visit, Quebec, Aug. 24–25, 2015, Parcs Canada signage; Bird, *Attack on Quebec*, 25.

202 *Few repairs had been made*: John Marr to Frederick Haldimand, Oct. 1, 1778, "Correspondence with Officers of the Engineers in Canada," LAC, micro, H-1651 (*"bad condition"*); *Struggle*, vol. 2, 78–79; Chartrand, *French Fortresses in North America*, 24.

202 *In 1769, Carleton had requested*: Charbonneau et al., *Quebec: The Fortified City*, 61–62, 155; John Marr to Frederick Haldimand, Oct. 1, 1778, "Correspondence with Officers of the Engineers in Canada," LAC, micro, H-1651; Cruikshank, 85 (*rock slide*); Whiteley, "The British Navy and the Siege of Quebec, 1775–76," *Canadian Historical Review* 61, no. 1 (1980): 3+ (*finding the keys*).

202 *If privately doubtful of the city's ability*: Reynolds, *Guy Carleton*, 13; *GWGO*, 118–19; *Fourteenth*, 191; Stanley, *Canada Invaded*, 81–82 (*"Grumbletonians"*), 86 (*"treated as rebels"*); *Struggle*, vol. 2, 95 (*"useless, disloyal"*); Smith, ed., "Journal Kept in Quebec in 1775 by James Jeffry," *Historical Collections of the Essex Institute* 50, no. 2 (Apr. 1914): 97+ (*"necessary clothing"*); Caldwell, "The Invasion of Canada in 1775," in *Manuscripts Relating to the Early History of Canada*, 7 (*"Cabals"*).

203 *As Montgomery had suspected, the governor*: "Journal of the Siege and Blockade of Quebec," in *Manuscripts Relating to the Early History of Canada*, 116 (*firewood and forage*); Hector Cramahé to Dartmouth, Nov. 19, 1775, *DAR*, vol. 10, 133 (*medical supplies*); *Sandwich*, vol. 1, 82 (*twine and paper*); Cruikshank, 130 (*Quebec's storerooms*), 14; Stanley, *Canada Invaded*, 84–85 (Lizard).

203 *Carleton's eighteen hundred defenders*: *Struggle*, vol. 2, 81; Cruikshank, 18, 14 (*"Irish fishermen"*); Randall, *Benedict Arnold*, 202–03, 207–08; Smith, ed., "Journal Kept in Quebec in 1775 by James Jeffry," *Historical Collections of the Essex Institute* 50, no. 2 (Apr. 1914): 97+ (*"horrid noise"*); Stanley, *Canada Invaded*, 87 (*four brigades*); *Struggle*, vol. 2, 13 (a shilling); Whiteley, "The British Navy and the Siege of Quebec, 1775–76," *Canadian Historical Review* 61, no. 1 (1980): 3+ (*red cuffs*); log, *Lizard*, Nov. 8, 1775, UK NA, ADM 51/550 (*sandbags*).

203 *Perhaps most vital to Quebec's defense*: Morrissey, *Quebec 1775*, 18 (*"beloved, dreaded"*); G.F.G. Stanley, "Allan Maclean," *Dictionary of Canadian Biography*, vol. 4, University of Toronto (2003), http://www.biographi.ca/en/bio/maclean_allan_4E.html; Allen, *Tories*, 100–01; Allen, ed., *The Loyal Americans*, 18; *Struggle*, vol. 2, 20–21; Stanley, *Canada Invaded*, 31, 87.

204 *With each passing day, the defenses*: "General Richard Montgomery—His Sword, Etc.," *BFTM*, vol. 3, no. 1 (1957): 76+ (*"even a dog"*); *Struggle*, 123; *ANTA*, 12; John Danford, "Siege of Quebec by an American Force," Dec. 23, 1775, *LAC*, micro, #A705 (*manhandled uphill*); *Fourteenth*, 187–88; Cohen, ed., *Canada Preserved*, 29 (*"peas"*).

204 *"One's senses are benumbed"*: Würtele, ed., *Blockade of Quebec in 1775–1776*, 25, 27.

204 *No ungloved hand dared*: Codman, *Arnold's Expedition to Quebec*, 208; Reynolds, *Guy Carleton*, 82; *ANTA*, 12; Würtele, ed., *Blockade of Quebec in 1775–1776*, 181–98; John Danford, "Siege of Quebec by an American Force," Dec. 23, 1775, *LAC*, micro, #A705. Another account says two-thirds of the defenders slept on their arms as of December 25. Cruikshank, 18.

Notes to pages 204–209 | 617

204 *General Montgomery had reportedly sworn*: Stanley, *Canada Invaded*, 91 (*"dine in Quebec"*); MQ, 535 (*"sensible and concise"*); Shelton, 137 (*"fire of patriotism"*).

204 *Not every man felt that way*: Struggle, vol. 2, 152.

205 *"Having so early reported"*: Montgomery to Schuyler, AA, IV: 4, 464–65.

205 *Other worries also nagged*: Montgomery to David Wooster, Dec. 16, 1775, AA, IV: 4, 288–89 (*"ragamuffin"*); Lanctôt, *Canada and the American Revolution*, 113–14 (*disaffected priest*); Cruikshank, 17.

205 *Two columns—led by Montgomery and Arnold*: Montgomery told Schuyler of his original focus on the Lower Town in a December 5, 1775, letter. For the subsequent revisions, see *Struggle*, 122–24; Desjardin, *Through a Howling Wilderness*, 168–69; *Fourteenth*, 194; Stanley, *Canada Invaded*, 92; BARH, 164–66.

206 *A proposal to seize women*: MQ, 374 (*human shields*), 701 (*"great searchings"*).

206 *Montgomery tried to remain buoyant*: "General Richard Montgomery," *Harper's New Monthly Magazine* 70, no. 417 (Feb. 1885): 353.

206 *Audaces fortuna juvat*: The last word in the phrase is often spelled *iuvat*. MGRM, 336, 301–02.

206 *"The paths of glory"*: Stacey, *Quebec, 1759*, 136–37, 21–22 (*"my heart"*).

206 *Now in the American camps*: MQ, 702; Bray and Bushnell, eds., *Diary of a Common Soldier in the American Revolution*, 23 (*"all in readiness"*); BARH, 169; D&AJA, vol. 2, 176 (*just-in-case letter*); Hatch, *Thrust for Canada*, 131 (*"If you receive this"*); "Letter from Canada," Feb. 9, 1776, AA, IV: 4, 796 (*"with decency"*).

207 *As for Montgomery, he convened*: *The Journal of Isaac Senter*, 51 (*"anxious"*); *Struggle*, 126 (*"Embrace"*).

207 *Four a.m. had come and gone*: Würtele, ed., *Blockade of Quebec in 1775-1776*, 28; BARH, 169–70; Cruikshank, 18.

207 *Drums pounded, dogs barked*: Beck, *The War Before Independence*, 277; *Struggle*, 127–29; Smith and Kiley, *An Illustrated Encyclopedia of Uniforms from 1775-1783*, 158; WR, 191; Desjardin, *Through a Howling Wilderness*, 171.

207 *Arnold had assembled almost five hundred*: MQ, 189–90; *Struggle*, 130–31.

208 *As he approached the Palace Gate*: Whiteley, "The British Navy and the Siege of Quebec, 1775-6," *Canadian Historical Review* 61, 1 (1980): 3+; Barwick journal, Dec. 31, 1775, NDAR, vol. 2, appendix F, 1387+ (*"obliged to leave"*); MQ, 375–77 (*"We are sold"*); 590–91 (*"turn me over"*).

208 *March on they did*: BARH, 168; *The Journal of Isaac Senter*, 52; Reiss, *Medicine and the American Revolution*, 94; BA to [Hannah Arnold?], Jan. 6, 1776, AA, IV: 4, 589.

208 *The column had lost*: Higginbotham, *Daniel Morgan, Revolutionary Rifleman*, 43–47; Callahan, *Daniel Morgan*, 104; *Struggle*, 33 (*"scorched rag"*); Bradley, *Sir Guy Carleton (Lord Dorchester)*, 130 (*red coats*); John Danford, "Siege of Quebec by an American Force," Dec. 31, 1775, LAC, micro, #A705 (*"in liquor"*); MQ, 275; Hatch, *Thrust for Canada*, 136 ("Vive la liberté"); Caldwell, "The Invasion of Canada in 1775," in *Manuscripts Relating to the Early History of Canada*, 12–13.

208 *Three hundred yards on*: author visit, Quebec, Aug. 24, 2015, signage; "General Daniel Morgan: An Autobiography," *Historical Magazine*, 2nd ser., 9, no. 6 (June 1871): 379–80; Graham, *The Life of General Daniel Morgan*, 98–99; Higginbotham, *Daniel Morgan, Revolutionary Rifleman*, 46.

209 *A strange tranquillity settled*: "General Daniel Morgan: An Autobiography," *Historical Magazine*, 2nd ser., 9, no. 6 (June 1871): 379–80; Callahan, *Daniel Morgan*, 103–05 (*"overruled"*).

209 *Two miles southwest, Montgomery led*: Donald Campbell to David Wooster, Dec. 31, 1775, AA, IV: 4, 480–81; BARH, 167; Codman, *Arnold's Expedition to Quebec*, 154; Caldwell, "The Invasion of Canada in 1775," in *Manuscripts Relating to the Early History of Canada*, 8; Shelton, 148–50; Roche, ed., "Quebec Under Siege, 1775-1776," *Canadian Historical Review* 50 (Mar. 1969): 68+.

209 *Captain Adam Barnsfare, master*: letter, Adam Barnsfare, May 15, 1776, "America: Military Operations in Canada," *Scots Magazine* 38 (1776): 316–17; Cruikshank, 18; John Danford, "Siege of Quebec by an American Force," Dec. 31, 1775, LAC, micro, #A705; Würtele, ed., *Blockade of Quebec in 1775-1776*, 29 (*"Shrieks and groans"*).

210 *At least not a living soul*: Roche, ed., "Quebec Under Siege, 1775–1776," *Canadian Historical Review* 50 (Mar. 1969): 68+; *Struggle*, 143; MGRM, 324; Würtele, ed., *Blockade of Quebec in 1775–1776*, 33.

210 *Now the American attack came fully*: John Danford, "Siege of Quebec by an American Force," Dec. 31, 1775, LAC, micro, #A705; Brown and Peckham, eds., *Revolutionary War Journals of Henry Dearborn*, 67–68 (*"got bewildered"*); Graham, *The Life of General Daniel Morgan*, 102.

210 *soldiers and sailors filled the upper windows*: Higginbotham, *Daniel Morgan, Revolutionary Rifleman*, 47–48; Graham, *The Life of General Daniel Morgan*, 100–02.

210 *Losses mounted among the Yankee*: Hatch, *Thrust for Canada*, 97 (*"restless genius"*), 138; Nichols et al., "Diary of Lieutenant Francis Nichols," *PMHB* 20, no. 4 (1896): 504+; *MQ*, 378–79, 704 (*"terrible scene"*); "Bounty Land Warrant Information Relating to John Humphries, VAS 1670," http://www.revwarapps.org/VAS1670.pdf; Charles F. Himes, "Colonel Robert Magaw: Defender of Fort Washington," lecture, Hamilton Library Association, Carlisle, Pa. (1915): 19 (*"mild and beautiful"*).

210 *A British 9-pounder, heaved up*: Henry Caldwell, "The Invasion of Canada in 1775," in *Manuscripts Relating to the Early History of Canada*, 11; *Struggle*, vol. 2, 139, 146; Higginbotham, *Daniel Morgan, Revolutionary Rifleman*, 49; Würtele, ed., *Blockade of Quebec in 1775–1776*, 19 (*"glorious day for us"*).

211 *Nuns with linen bandages*: Codman, *Arnold's Expedition to Quebec*, 164; *Struggle*, vol. 2, 149; Brown and Peckham, eds., *Revolutionary War Journals of Henry Dearborn*, 65 (*"richly decorated"*); Darley, *Voices from a Wilderness Expedition*, 114 (*"small ship"*); *MQ*, 227–28; Leake, *Memoir of the Life and Times of General John Lamb*, 131–34; Hatch, *Thrust for Canada*, 138; Nichols et al., "Diary of Lieutenant Francis Nichols," *PMHB* 20, no. 4 (1896): 504+.

211 *Young Dr. Senter moved*: *MQ*, 234–35; Arnold to Wooster, Dec. 31, 1775, *AA*, IV: 4, 481–82 (*"apprehensive"*).

211 *Sentries outside piled up snow*: *ANTA*, 27; Shelton, 156–57; Desjardin, *Through a Howling Wilderness*, 204; Hatch, *Thrust for Canada*, 141; *Fourteenth*, 198 (*publicly repented*).

211 *In Carleton's irrefutable phrase*: Shelton, 3; Carleton to Germain, May 14, 1776, *DAR*, vol. 10, 293; Stanley, *Canada Invaded*, 103; MGRM, 332–33 (*British casualties*). By the end of 1776, according to a British tally, 65 American prisoners would die in Quebec. "List of Prisoners Taken in Canada," in Cruikshank, 185.

212 *American prisoners were prodded*: Higginbotham, *Daniel Morgan, Revolutionary Rifleman*, 50–51; Henry Caldwell, "The Invasion of Canada in 1775," in *Manuscripts Relating to the Early History of Canada*, 15 (*"pretended to be gentlemen"*); Reynolds, *Guy Carleton*, 88 (*white flag*).

212 *"Fortune was kind enough"*: "Journal of Captain William Humphrey," LAC, MG 23 B9, CAIN No. 274886, Jan. 1, 1776.

212 *"Nothing heard or seen"*: Melvin, *The Journal of the Expedition to Quebec*, 14; *MQ*, 593 (*"mass of corruption"*).

212 *Although a crippling attack of gout*: Randall, *Benedict Arnold*, 225; *BARH*, 181–82 (*gout* and *"highest importance"*); Lanctôt, *Canada and the American Revolution*, 108, 113.

212 *"upwards of one hundred officers"*: BA to GW, Jan. 14, 1776, *PGW*, vol. 3, 81.

212 *He was desperate for medical supplies*: Donald Campbell to D. Wooster, Jan. 1, 1776, Schoff Revolutionary War Collection, WLC; D. Wooster to GW, *PGW*, vol. 3, 165 (*four tons*); *MQ*, 108–09 (*"our force at this time"*); BA to [Hannah Arnold?], Jan. 6, 1776, *AA*, IV: 4, 589 (*"many dangers"*).

213 *More sleds arrived in the Upper Town*: *MQ*, 389 (*"monstrous piles"*); Royster, *A Revolutionary People at War*, 8 (*"a coward"*); Würtele, *Blockade of Quebec in 1775–1776*, xiii–xiv; Bird, *Attack on Quebec*, 219.

213 *Thirteen years earlier, at the siege of Havana*: Reynolds, *Guy Carleton*, 87; "General Richard Montgomery—His Sword, Etc.," *BFTM* 3, no. 1 (1957): 76+; Baxter, *The British Invasion from the North*, 100n, 134n; author visit, Quebec, signage at St. Louis Gate; GW to Schuyler, Dec. 24, 1775, *PGW*, vol. 2, 599 (*"time for brave men"*).

213 *A defeated general is always wrong*: Stacey, *Quebec, 1759*, 174; MGRM, 348–51; Lutnick, *The American Revolution and the British Press*, 92–93 (*immortal Wolfe*); "Diary of Richard Smith

in the Continental Congress, 1775–1776," part 2, *AHR* 1, no. 3 (Apr. 1896): 493+ ("*embalmed in the heart*"); Shelton, 175 (*memorial*).

214 *Streets, counties, towns*: Shelton, 179–80; Louise Livingston Hunt, "Biographical Notes Concerning General Richard Montgomery," 1876, NYHS, 27–30; "General Richard Montgomery— His Sword, Etc.," *BFTM* 3, no. 1 (1957): 76+; Royster, *A Revolutionary People at War*, 125 ("*Dead March*").

214 *Montgomery had written his will*: Will, R. Montgomery, Aug. 30, 1775, Edward Livingston papers, FL, box 114, folder 11; memo on R. Montgomery's watch, James Seawright, director, Princeton University Visual Arts Program, Aug. 1, 1989, Edward Livingston papers, FL, box 114, folder 1.

214 *The rest was unpacked*: R. Montgomery, inventory of personal effects, Edward Livingston papers, FL, box 114, folder 11; Louise Livingston Hunt, "Biographical Notes Concerning General Richard Montgomery," 1876, NYHS, 19–22.

215 "*May heaven protect you*": P. Schuyler to BA, Jan. 25, 1776, orderly book, HM 663, HL.

215 "*I have no thoughts of leaving*": MQ, 108–09; BA to [Hannah Arnold?], Jan. 6, 1776, *AA*, IV: 4, 589.

9. THE WAYS OF HEAVEN ARE DARK AND INTRICATE

219 *The new year brought boredom*: Carter, *A Genuine Detail of the Several Engagements*, 17–18 ("*ink freezes*"); W. Howe to Dartmouth [*sic*], Dec. 14, 1775, UK NA, CO 5/93, f. 30 (*three weeks of fuel*); Maj. Francis Hutcheson to Maj. Gen. Frederick Haldimand, Dec. 23, 1775, Haldimand Papers, LAC, micro, H-1431. Hutcheson, the brigade major, put weekly coal consumption at 214 chaldrons, with approximately 3,140 pounds in a London chaldron.

219 *Rebel pirates captured a British collier*: Maj. Francis Haldimand to Maj. Gen. Frederick Haldimand, Dec. 23, 1775, Haldimand Papers, LAC, micro, H-1431; Baker, *Government and Contractors*, 190–92 (*Spanish River*); Sargent, ed., *Letters of John Andrews, Esq., of Boston*, 98 (*horse dung*); corr., John Robinson to Gage, July 26, 1775, in unpublished enclosures, "George III Calendar, Jan. 1774–Aug. 1775," RA GEO/MAIN/#2085; also, RA GEO/MAIN/#2109, #2126–2128, all from Robinson (*blankets*).

219 *Howe authorized the garrison*: Scudder, "Life in Boston in the Colonial Period," in Winsor, ed., *The Memorial History of Boston*, vol. 1, 481 (*buttonwoods*); *HOB*, 169; *Siege*, 282; Timothy Newell, "A Journal Kept During the Time Yt [That] Boston Was Shut Up in 1775–6," *Collections*, MHS, 4th ser., 1 (1852): 270–71 (*hog sty*); author visit, Old South, May 2015, signage ("*impious manner*"); Betlock et al., *An Architectural History of the Old South Meeting House*, 17 (*riding ring*); "Topography and Landmarks," in Winsor, ed., *The Memorial History of Boston*, vol. 2, 516–17 (*British stoves*); Evelyn, 73 ("*leave it*"); *HOB*, 160 ("*hang upon the spot*").

220 *To bolster morale*: Scudder, "Life in Boston in the Revolutionary Period," in Winsor, ed., *The Memorial History of Boston*, vol. 3, part 1, 161; *LAR*, 277–78 ("*better amused*"); Scudder, "Life in Boston in the Revolutionary Period," in Winsor, ed., *The Memorial History of Boston*, vol. 3, part 1, 161; J. L. Bell, "A Continental Attack Brings the Curtain Down," *B 1775*, Jan. 8, 2008; *The Tragedy of Zara*, MHS, Mar. 2004 artifact, www.masshist.org ("*immorality, impiety*"); J. D. Lewis, "The American Revolution in South Carolina," http://www.carolana.com/SC /Revolution/british_army_francis_rawdon.html ("*Howe's Strolling Players*"); Evacuation, 168–69; Scudder, "The Siege of Boston," *Atlantic Monthly*, vol. 37 (Apr. 1876): 466+.

220 *The actors found a fine playhouse*: Brown, *Faneuil Hall and Faneuil Hall Market*, 86–88, 96–100, 124–31; Hibbert, *Redcoats and Rebels*, 72 ("*fitted up*"); *MLA*, 129–30 (Maid of the Oaks), 124 ("*General Swagger*"); De Fonblanque, *Political and Military Episodes*, 1–2 ("*most genteel*"); *The Tragedy of Zara*, MHS, Mar. 2004 artifact, www.masshist.org ("*minds diseased*").

220 *Burgoyne had temporarily returned*: Balderston and Syrett, eds., *The Lost War*, 64 ("*can't read*"); J. L. Bell, "On the Lines in Charlestown," *B 1775*, Jan. 9, 2008 (*measuring tape*); J. L. Bell, "A Continental Attack Brings the Curtain Down," *B 1775*, Jan. 8, 2008; Jan. 8, 1776, journal entry, KP (*curtain rose*).

221 "*Turn out! Turn out!*": Hunter, *The Journal of Gen. Sir Martin Hunter*, 14; Lydenberg, 283; J. L. Bell, "A Continental Attack Brings the Curtain Down," *B 1775*, Jan. 8, 2008 ("*smart*

firing"); *Evacuation*, 169–70 ("*alarm posts*"); Balderston and Syrett, eds., *The Lost War*, 58–59 ("*leaving the ladies*").

221 "*A general scene of confusion*": *LAR*, 277–78; Edward E. Hale, "The Siege of Boston," in Winsor, ed., *The Memorial History of Boston*, vol. 3, part 1, 93, 162; Hutcheson to Haldimand, Dec. 23, 1775, Haldimand Papers, LAC, micro, H-1431 ("*face blackened*").

221 *A mile to the north*: GW, among others, noted how dark the night was. GW to Hancock, Jan. 11, 1776, *PGW*, vol. 3, 68–69n; GW to J. Reed, Jan. 14, 1776, and unsigned letter from Cambridge, Jan. 9, 1776, both in *AA*, IV: 4, 612–13, 678.

221 *Many carried wood chips soaked*: Greenwood, ed., *The Revolutionary Services of John Greenwood*, 23–24, 114n; *Siege*, 287–88; Cutter, *The Life of Israel Putnam*, 198. An item in the *New-England Chronicle* on December 21 showed that news of the forthcoming production had reached the Americans. J. L. Bell, "A Continental Attack Brings the Curtain Down," *B 1775*, Jan. 8, 2008.

221 *Little went right for Knowlton's men*: The British outpost rotated every fortnight. *Evelyn*, 74–75; "Archibald Robertson: His Diaries and Sketches in America, 1762–1780," *Bulletin of the NYPL* 37, no. 11 (Nov. 1933): 283.

221 *Alarm shots broke the silence*: GW to Hancock, Jan. 11, 1776, *PGW*, vol. 3, 68–69n; GW to J. Reed, Jan. 14, 1776, and unsigned letter from Cambridge, Jan. 9, 1776, both in *AA*, IV: 4, 678, 612–13; Moore, *The Diary of the American Revolution*, 96–97 ("*hot and close fire*"); Hunter, *The Journal of Gen. Sir Martin Hunter*, 14; Black and Roelker, eds., *A Rhode Island Chaplain in the Revolution*, 7 ("*merry as you please*"); "Remarks by Richard Frothingham," *Proceedings*, MHS, 14 (1875–76): 261+; *Baldwin*, 21 ("*great light*"); diary, John Warren, Jan. 8, 1776, John Collins Warren Papers, MHS, Ms. N-1731, volume 1A (*serene airs*).

222 "*We all turned out*": *Evelyn*, 79–80; Balderston and Syrett, eds., *The Lost War*, 58–59; Spring, *With Zeal and with Bayonets Only*, 128 ("*these scoundrels*").

222 *Gossips would claim*: "Roxbury During the Siege of Boston," NPS, n.d., http://www.nps.gov /bost/learn/education/upload/roxbury.pdf; Wallace, *Appeal to Arms*, 59–60; *BNY*, 97–98 ("*Nothing seemed to engage*"); Sabine, ed., *The New-York Diary of Lieutenant Jabez Fitch*, 37 ("*Sultana*"); Field, *The Battle of Long Island*, 134 ("*Chevalier*"); Ketchum, *Decisive Day*, 35–36 ("*Awake, arouse*"). Don Hagist is skeptical that Howe and Mrs. Loring had an illicit relationship in Boston; most of the evidence of their interactions, including suggestions of an adulterous affair, came later, in New York. DNH to author, May 2018.

222 *Yet no campaign could be launched*: W. Howe to Dartmouth [*sic*], Jan. 16, 1775, UK NA, CO 5/93, f. 64 ("*young men of spirit*"); Maldwyn A. Jones, "Sir William Howe," in *GWGO*, 52 ("*better policy*"); Curtis, *The British Army in the American Revolution*, 28–29.

223 *Compounding Howe's worries*: *HOB*, 148, 156, 218 ("*some of the graves*"); Graves to Admiralty, Nov. 8, 1775, Graves (Halifax); Fenn, *Pox Americana*, 49–50, 89; Cash, *Medical Men at the Siege of Boston*, 113–14 ("*Our distresses*"), 156, 115 (*spruce beer*); N. Greene to Samuel Ward, Sr., Oct. 23, 1775, *PNG*, 140 ("*prodigious mortality*").

223 *No makeshift antiscorbutic*: *HOB*, xviii, 323, lists almost 8,000 rank and file in Boston on January 12, 1776, excluding officers and ancillary personnel. The January 15, 1776, provisions return cites 11,000 men in Boston. "Memorandum of failures on the part of the contractors for victualling His Majesty's Troops at Boston," Jan. 17, 1776, UK NA, CO 5/93, f. 109–13.

223 "*The small quantities of provisions*": Curtis, "The Provisioning of the British Army in the Revolution," *Magazine of History* 18 (Jan.–June 1914): 240+; North to George, Sept. 9, 1775, "George III Calendar, Sept. 1775–Oct. 1777," RA GEO/MAIN/#2177–78 (*British suppliers*); *HOB*, xviii (*short rations*), 155 ("*purloined*"); "Memorandum of failures on the part of the contractors for victualling His Majesty's Troops at Boston," Jan. 17, 1776, UK NA, CO 5/93, f. 109–13 (*flour and bread*); Cash, *Medical Men at the Siege of Boston*, 94–95 (*Royal Navy raiders*); Howe to Dartmouth [*sic*], private letter, Dec. 19, 1775, UK NA, CO 5/93 (*St. Eustatius*); *Evelyn*, 72–76 ("*these hard times*").

224 *To further illustrate these hard times*: Mure, Son & Atkinson to W. Howe, Sept. 25, 1775, "George III Calendar, Jan. 1774–Aug. 1775," RA GEO/MAIN/#2160 ("*fittest*" and "*not to bruise them*"); chart, William Shirreff, deputy QMG, n.d., UK NA, T 64/108, f. 18–19 ("*too fat*" and

"much damaged"); Toll, *Six Frigates*, 13 (*carcasses hoisted*); Howe to Dartmouth [*sic*], private letter, Dec. 19, 1775, UK NA, CO 5/93 ("*worse fate*"); Winsor, ed., *The Memorial History of Boston*, vol. 3, part 1, 81 ("*white with sheep*"); Bowler cites slightly different figures for the surviving livestock. *Logistics*, 53–54.

224 *Ferocious autumn storms*: M. Shuldham to Admiralty, Jan. 15, 1776, Neeser, ed., *The Despatches of Molyneux Shuldham*, 37 ("*most severe*"); Syrett, *The Royal Navy in American Waters*, 23; Laughton, ed., *Journal of Rear-Admiral Bartholomew James*, 17–18; chart, n.d., in W. Howe to Robinson at Treasury, May 8, 1776, UK NA, T 64/108, f. 38 ("*stress of weather*").

225 *By early spring, more than two dozen ships*: B. C. Payne to W. Howe, Feb. 16 and Mar. 1, 1776, with chart, in Howe to Dartmouth [*sic*], Mar. 21, 1776, UK NA, CO 5/93, f. 173, f. 261.

225 *"The first attack of the wind"*: Laughton, ed., *Journal of Rear-Admiral Bartholomew James*, 17–22; Fowler, *Rebels Under Sail*, 35–36.

226 *Months would pass before* Orpheus: squadron disposition, Dec. 3, 1775, *Graves; Sandwich*, vol. 1, 44 ("*football of fortune*"); Syrett, *The Royal Navy in American Waters*, 11.

226 *The tasks were too many*: chart, prizes taken by North American squadron, June 1–Dec. 31, 1775, *Graves; DAR*, vol. 11, 9.

226 *Worse yet, the Americans had formed*: Clark, *George Washington's Navy*, 5, 15n, 27, 29, 36, 40 ("APPEAL TO HEAVEN"), 43–44; Capt. William Coit to S. B. Webb, Nov. 7, 1775, Ford, ed., *Correspondence and Journals of Samuel Blachley Webb*, vol. 1, 116–17 ("*bedding*"); Kenneth J. Hagan, "The Birth of American Naval Strategy," in Stoker et al., eds., *Strategy in the American War of Independence*, 39 (*fifty-five British prizes*); Allen, *A Naval History of the American Revolution*, vol. 1, 62.

226 *The greatest prize, however, was* Nancy: Graves to Admiralty, Nov. 9, Nov. 30, Dec. 4, 1775, and Symons [*Cerberus* captain] to Graves, Nov. 26, 1775, *Graves*.

227 *The* Lee *was in fact*: Allen, *A Naval History of the American Revolution*, vol. 1, 67–69; Miller, *Sea of Glory*, 70–71; Smith, *Fired by Manley Zeal*, 5–7; GW HQ, 370–71 (*boarding party*); Fowler, *Rebels Under Sail*, 30–31; invoice of stores, *Nancy, AA*, IV: 3, 1721–22; Nelson, *George Washington's Secret Navy*, 214–15; Clark, *George Washington's Navy*, 174–75 (*more than £20,000*), 74 ("G.R."); Reed, ed., *Life and Correspondence of Joseph Reed*, vol. 1, 133 (*bottle of rum*); Hulton, *Letters of a Loyalist Lady*, 82 ("*ways of heaven*").

227 *"Captain Manley's good fortune"*: S. Moylan to W. Watson, Dec. 13, 1775, *NDAR*, vol. 3, 81; GW HQ, 370–82; Clark, *George Washington's Navy*, 91–95 ("*Homer*"), 106 ("*vigilance and industry*"); "Lee I (Schooner)," *Dictionary of American Naval Fighting Ships*, Naval History and Heritage Command, www.history.navy.mil/research/histories/ship-histories/danfs/l/lee-i.html; instructions to Capt. Charles Dyar, Jan. 20, 1776, *PGW*, vol. 3, 151 ("*fondness to be on shore*").

228 Nancy's *capture shocked*: Spector, *The American Department of the British Government*, 85–89; *DAR*, vol. 11, 9; Nelson, *George Washington's Secret Navy*, 220 ("*fatal event*").

228 *The winter passed pleasantly enough*: GW HQ, 182–86, 193–94; W. Bartlett to GW, Dec. 14, 1775, *PGW*, vol. 2, 545 (*turtle, loaf sugar*).

228 *The house had become even livelier*: WC, 18; Chernow, *Washington: A Life*, 97, 218; Chadwick, *The General and Mrs. Washington*, 190 (*never been north*); Mary V. Thompson, "As If I Had Been a Very Great Somebody," lecture, Nov. 9, 2002, Mount Vernon, http://catalog.mountvernon.org/cdm/ref/collection/p16829coll4/id/2 ("*throws off the hero*"); GW HQ, 218n, 219 ("*I shudder*"); CGW, xvii; *PGW*, vol. 11, 203 ("*my love*"); Wiencek, *An Imperfect God*, 67–69 (*Spanish fly*); "Family Life for the Washingtons," George Washington's Mount Vernon, http://www.mountvernon.org/george-washington/martha-washington/family-life-for-the-washingtons/ (*tugged his collar*); Griffin, *Stephen Moylan*, 25 (*lemons, limes*).

229 *Lady Washington brought him news*: Lund Washington to GW, Nov. 14 and 24, 1775, *PGW*, vol. 2, 374–75, 421–23.

229 *Across the American encampment*: Samuel Shaw to father, Feb. 5, 1776, Samuel Shaw Papers, MHS; Scudder, "The Siege of Boston," *Atlantic Monthly* 37 (Apr. 1876): 466+ (*Satan was a Tory*); *Siege*, 272; Greenwood, *The Revolutionary Services of John Greenwood*, 21 ("*like stars*").

229 *Washington often rode out*: "Has General Washington's Riband Come Back Around?," *B 1775*, Mar. 13, 2015; *Siege*, 274; *Evacuation*, 12–13; Drake, *The Town of Roxbury*, 76–78, 214.

229 *"I pity our good general"*: James Warren to John Adams, Dec. 3, 1775, *AP*; GW to P. Schuyler, Dec. 5, 1775, *PGW*, vol. 2, 498 (*"must be borne"*); GW to J. Reed, Nov. 28, 1775, *PGW*, vol. 2, 449 (*"Could I have foreseen"*); GW to J. Reed, Jan. 4, 1776, *PGW*, vol. 3, 24–25 (*"scarcely emerged"*); GW to J. Reed, Jan. 14, 1776, *PGW*, vol. 3, 88–89 (*"We are now without any money"*).

230 *For two months Washington had struggled*: GW to J. Hancock, Jan. 4, 1776, *PGW*, vol. 3, 19 (*"disband one army"*); "Correspondence of the Brothers Joshua and Jedidiah Huntington," *Collections of the Connecticut Historical Society*, vol. 20 (1923): 252–53; Hammond, *Letters and Papers of Major-General John Sullivan*, vol. 1, 135 (*"poltroons"*); "Journal of Simeon Lyman of Sharon," *Collections of the Connecticut Historical Society*, vol. 7 (1899), RI: 113+ (*"worst of all creatures"*).

230 *Officers tried liquor, pleas*: "Journal of Simeon Lyman of Sharon," *Collections of the Connecticut Historical Society*, vol. 7 (1899), RI: 113+; *Spirit '76*, 158–59; *PNG*, 160 (*"shoals"*); *GGW*, 116 (*"dirty, mercenary"*); GW to J. Hancock, Dec. 4, 1775, *PGW*, vol. 2, 484; Wright, *The Continental Army*, 55; Raphael, *A People's History of the American Revolution*, 76 (*"once all fire"*).

230 *"We never have been so weak"*: *PNG*, 174; Wright, *The Continental Army*, 51 (*not one agreed*); Weigley, *History of the United States Army*, 33–34; Freeman, 2; *PGW*, vol. 3, 25–26n; McCullough, *1776*, 69. Congress had established a "Union flag," but J. L. Bell notes that there is no evidence that Washington knew this yet. GW HQ, 386.

231 *Though still drawn largely*: Shy, *A People Numerous and Armed*, 221; GW to Massachusetts Council, Jan. 10, 1776, and GW to J. Sullivan, Jan. 10, 1776, *PGW*, vol. 3, 61–62 (*"find myself weaker"*), 65; Lesser, ed., *The Sinews of Independence*, xviii; Wright, *The Continental Army*, 51–54, 110 (*numerical designation*); Tucker, *Rise and Fight Again*, 34 (*less than half*). Confirmation of the disaster at Quebec arrived in Cambridge on January 17. Freeman, 9–10. Another reorganization in 1777 would restore state names to the regimental designations.

231 *So desperate was Washington for manpower*: "Washington's Black Soldiers," *B 1775*, Mar. 2, 9, 11, 2015; Nash, *The Unknown American Revolution*, 228; GW to J. Hancock, Dec. 31, 1775, *PGW*, vol. 2, 623, 625n; Frey, *Water from the Rock*, 78 (*"arm the Negroes"*); Egerton, *Death or Liberty*, 75. An estimated 20,000 blacks fought for the British in loyalist units. Author visit, Mar. 18, 2018, National Museum of African American History and Culture, Washington, D.C.

231 *Washington also had no choice*: GW to New England governments, Dec. 5, 1775, *PGW*, vol. 2, 492; GW to Massachusetts Council, Jan. 10, 1776, *PGW*, vol. 3, 62n; Ferling, *Almost a Miracle*, 80 (*"Long-Faced"*).

231 *After bitter debate, in late December Congress*: *GGW*, 116 (*"notwithstanding the town"*); "Diary of Richard Smith in the Continental Congress, 1775–1776," *AHR* 1, no. 2 (Jan. 1896): 297–98; council of war, Jan. 16, 1776, *PGW*, vol. 3, 103 (*"bold attempt"*).

232 *But how? Despite the Nancy*: GW to J. Hancock, Feb. 9, 1776, *PGW*, vol. 3, 278–79; Risch, *Supplying Washington's Army*, 341–42, 350; general orders, Feb. 24, 1776, *PGW*, vol. 3, 358 (*avoid bidding*); GW to Massachusetts General Court, Feb. 10, 1776, *PGW*, vol. 3, 284–85 (*Brown Bess*); GW to J. Reed, Dec. 25, 1775, *PGW*, vol. 2, 607 (*"inconceivable"*); GW to J. Reed, Feb. 26–Mar. 9, 1776, *PGW*, vol. 3, 370, 376n (*"the thing"*); GW to J. Trumbull, Sr., Feb. 19, 1776, *PGW*, vol. 3, 346; GW to J. Hancock, Jan. 30, 1776, *PGW*, vol. 3, 215–16 (*four hundred barrels*); Stephenson, "The Supply of Gunpowder in 1776," *AHR* 30, no. 2 (Jan. 1925): 271+; Feb. 16, 1776, entry, "Diary of Obadiah Brown," *Quarterly Bulletin of the Westchester County Historical Society* 4, nos. 3 and 4 (July and Oct. 1928), and 5, no. 1 (Jan. 1929) (*hefty fines*); general orders, Jan. 28, 1776, *PGW*, vol. 3, 206 (*"severely punished"*); Greene order, Nov. 10, 1775, *PNG*, 149 (*"strange itch"*).

232 *"We have suffered prodigiously"*: Greene to Samuel Ward, Sr., Dec. 31, 1775, *PNG*, 173; Risch, *Supplying Washington's Army*, 142 (*eight thousand cords*), 140–41 (*fourteen square feet*); Ferling, *The First of Men*, 139; brigade orders, Dec. 24, 1775, "Orderly Book Kept by Jeremiah Fogg," 2nd New Hampshire Regiment, MHS; records, Committee on Wood, Nov. 4 and 22, 1775, CO93/2349X, CMSA; Greene to Samuel Ward, Sr., Dec. 31, 1775, *PNG*, 173 (*provisions raw*); Greene to Samuel Ward, Sr., Dec. 31, 1775, *PNG*, 173; Cash, *Medical Men at the Siege of Boston*, 100; Royster, *A Revolutionary People at War*, 72 (*"The devil"*).

232 *Cheek-by-jowl living*: Cash, *Medical Men at the Siege of Boston*, 81–82, 140; Reiss, *Medicine and the American Revolution*, 15 (*"melt away"*), 180; Hammond, ed., *Diary and Orderly Book*

of Sergeant Jonathan Burton, 14 (*"easing themselves"*); Griffenhagen, "Drug Supplies in the American Revolution," *Bulletin of the United States National Museum* 225 (1961): 110+.

233 *the "king of terrors"*: Duffy, "Public Health in New York City in the Revolution," *JAMA* 236, no. 1 (July 5, 1976): 47+.

233 *"Smallpox rages all over"*: Becker, "Smallpox in Washington's Army," *JMH* 68, no. 2 (Apr. 2004): 381+; Chernow, *Washington: A Life*, 200; GW to J. Hancock, Dec. 4, 11, 14, 1775, *PGW*, vol. 2, 486, 533–34, 548 (*"a weapon of defense"*); John Morgan to GW, Dec. 12, 1775, *PGW*, vol. 2, 541; Joseph Ward to J. Adams, Dec. 3, 1775, *AP*; Estes, "A Disagreeable and Dangerous Employment: Medical Letters from the Siege of Boston, 1775," *Journal of the History of Medicine and Allied Sciences* 31, no. 3 (July 1976): 271+ (*counterfeit currency*); Donkin, *Military Collections and Remarks*, 190–91 (*"Dip arrows"*); William Sever to GW, Dec. 11, 1775, *PGW*, vol. 2, 535; Cash, *Medical Men at the Siege of Boston*, 108–12; Dec. 4, 1775, "Diary of Samuel Bixby," *Proceedings*, MHS, vol. 14 (1875–76): 285+ (*vinegar*); GW to J. Reed, Dec. 15, 1775, *PGW*, vol. 2, 553 (*"If we escape"*).

233 *For now, the camp and the country*: *New-England Chronicle*, Nov. 2 and 30, 1775, and Mar. 6, 1776, HD.

233 *The usual wild rumors*: Dec. 13, 1775, entry, Samuel A. Green, ed., *Diary Kept by Lieut. Amos Farnsworth*, NYHS (*tempest*); "Diary of Ezekiel Price, 1775–6," *Proceedings*, MHS (Nov. 1963): 185+ (*reduced to ash*); *Evacuation*, 155; *WAI*, 103 (*"widow-and-orphan"*); Reed, ed., *Life and Correspondence of Joseph Reed*, vol. 1, 139 (*"tired of inaction"*).

234 *"There was a man found dead"*: Dawson, *Gleanings from the Harvest-Field of American History*, part 4, 6; Feb. 7, 1776, Obadiah Brown diary, MHS, http://nerfc.org/database/viewer .php?item_id=1908&pid=21 (*"33 glasses"*); Quincy, *The Journals of Major Samuel Shaw*, 9 (*"all sit down"*); Samuel Shaw to Francis Shaw, Feb. 24, 1776, Samuel Shaw papers, MHS (*"sense of what I owe"*).

234 *"You told me that you intended"*: Wade and Lively, *This Glorious Cause*, 44, 47–48; Guthman, ed., *The Correspondence of Captain Nathan and Lois Peters*, 24–28 (*"Pray come home"*).

234 *Good news, very good news*: Heath, *Memoirs of Major-General William Heath*, 30; "When Henry Knox Came Back to Cambridge," *B 1775*, Jan. 25, 2017; Callahan, *Henry Knox*, 26 (*fingers amputated*); John Adams autobiography, part 1, "John Adams," through 1776, sheet 52 of 53, *Adams Family Papers: An Electronic Archive*, MHS, http://www.masshist.org/digitaladams/ (*"pleasing manners"*); *GWGO*, 239 (*"providential characters"*); *GC*, 314 (*three hundred pounds*).

235 *In an era of improbable ascents*: Puls, *Henry Knox*, 1–4; Callahan, *Henry Knox*, 19–20; Brooks, *Henry Knox, a Soldier of the Revolution*, 20; "Henry Knox—Bookseller," *Proceedings*, MHS, 3rd ser., 61 (Oct. 1927–June 1928): 227+ (*"exterminate ignorance"*); Drake, *Life and Correspondence of Henry Knox*, 120 (*"affable without familiarity"*).

235 *Within three years the shop*: Drake, *Life and Correspondence of Henry Knox*, 12; "Henry Knox—Bookseller," *Proceedings*, MHS, 3rd ser., 61 (Oct. 1927–June 1928): 227+; Callahan, *Henry Knox*, 20–22; Brooks, *Henry Knox, a Soldier of the Revolution*, 9–10, 17, 19.

235 *In June 1774, he married*: Drake, *Life and Correspondence of Henry Knox*, 17, 125–26; Brooks, *Henry Knox, a Soldier of the Revolution*, 12, 19, 24 (*"intellectual endowments"*); Chernow, *Washington: A Life*, 204–05 (*"Her size"*); Flick, "General Henry Knox's Ticonderoga Expedition," *Quarterly Journal of the New York State Historical Association* 9, no. 2 (Apr. 1928): 119+.

236 *The American camp soon recognized*: *GWGO*, 240; Chernow, *Washington: A Life*, 204–05 (*shot the guns*).

236 *Knox had left Cambridge on November 15*: "Knox's Diary During His Ticonderoga Expedition," *New-England Historical and Genealogical Register* 30 (1876): 321–26; Knox to GW, Dec. 17, 1775, *PGW*, vol. 2, 563–66 (*"noble train"* and *"difficulties we have had"*); Flick, "General Henry Knox's Ticonderoga Expedition," *Quarterly Journal of the New York State Historical Association* 9, no. 2 (Apr. 1928): 119+ (*"touchholes"*); Perry, "Big Guns for Washington," *American Heritage* 6, no. 3 (Apr. 1995), www.americanheritage.com/content/big -guns-washington; Ferling, *Almost a Miracle*, 103; Callahan, *Henry Knox*, 49 (*"road was dreary"*).

236 *Crowds gathered on the east bank*: "Knox's Diary During His Ticonderoga Expedition," *New-England Historical and Genealogical Register*, vol. 30 (1876): 321–26; Puls, *Henry Knox*, 42; Callahan, *Henry Knox*, 52.

237 *Knox had covered more than seven hundred miles*: Puls, *Henry Knox*, 42; "How Many Cannon Did Henry Knox Transport?," *B 1775*, Jan. 26, 2017; Barker, "The Lost Cannon of Crown Point," *Military Collector & Historian* 26, no. 3 (Fall 1974): 159+; Callahan, *Henry Knox*, 56; Chernow, *Washington: A Life*, 204–05 (*"no one whom I have loved"*).

237 *Knox was at Washington's elbow*: R. H. Harrison to A. Ward, Feb. 11, 1776, *PGW*, 298n; Martyn, *The Life of Artemas Ward*, 167–68; Allen, *Tories*, 67 (*colonnaded loyalist mansion*); GW HQ, 563–66 (*swampy isthmus*).

237 *"I know the unhappy predicament"*: GW to J. Reed, Feb. 10, 1776, *PGW*, vol. 3, 286; Freeman, 72–73 (*"rumpus"*); *History of the Town of Dorchester Heights*, 333–36; National Register of Historic Places Registration Form, Dorchester Heights Historic District, NPS, 2001; June 22, 1775, journal entry, KP; Anderson, *The Command of the Howe Brothers During the American Revolution*, 100–02; war council minutes, July 9, 1775, and A. Ward to GW, Aug. 25, 1775, both in *PGW*, vol. 1, 80, 363; Martyn, *The Life of Artemas Ward*, 193.

238 *The commanding general and his retinue*: GW HQ, 567; R. Putnam to GW, Feb. 11, 1776, *PGW*, vol. 3, 295–99 (*artillery chart*).

238 *A "covered way" could be quickly erected*: Buell, ed., *The Memoirs of Rufus Putnam*, 11, 53–55; Baldwin, 25; R. Putnam to GW, Feb. 11, 1776, *PGW*, vol. 3, 295–99 (*"nothing short of timber"*).

238 *Washington was impressed but unconvinced*: minutes, council of war, Feb. 16, 1776, *PGW*, vol. 3, 320–24.

239 *He was wrong, even foolish*: minutes, council of war, Feb. 16, 1776, *PGW*, vol. 3, 320–24. Howe's return for January 12, 1776, lists 7,801 rank and file in Boston, excluding officers and ancillary personnel. About 18 percent of the enlisted strength was sick. *HOB*, xviii, 323; N. Greene to Jacob Greene, Feb. 15, 1776, *PNG*, 194–95 (*"horrible"*).

239 *Washington could hardly conceal*: GW to Hancock, Feb. 18–21, 1776, *PGW*, vol. 3, 335 (*"irksomeness"*); GW to J. Reed, Feb. 26–Mar. 9, 1776, *PGW*, vol. 3, 369 (*"Behold!"*); GW to A. Ward, Feb. 27 and Mar. 1, 1776, *PGW*, vol. 3, 384 and 399n (*extra sentinels* and *small child*).

240 *"The preparations increase"*: A. Adams to J. Adams, Feb. 21, 1776, *AFC*, vol. 1, 350.

10. THE WHIPPING SNAKE

241 *War was good for Cork*: Dickson, *Old World Colony*, 366, 140–41; Crowley et al., eds., *Atlas of Cork City*, 183, 127–30; Jefferies, *Cork: Historical Perspectives*, 152–53, 138; Baker, *Government and Contractors*, 64, 73 (*flour, peas*); Mackesy, *The War for America*, 65–66; Curtis, *The British Army in the American Revolution*, 83; Cusack, *City and County of Cork*, 40 (*Saint Finbar*).

241 *The city stank of blood*: Jefferies, *Cork: Historical Perspectives*, 139–40, 154; Linebaugh and Rediker, *The Many-Headed Hydra*, 187 (*"vermin"*); Marlow, *Sackville of Drayton*, 33–34; Cusack, *City and County of Cork*, 40. Irish Catholics were expelled from the city in 1644 and only gradually readmitted to the English Protestant stronghold. John Crowley et al., eds., *Atlas of Cork City*, 103–27.

241 *Some made their way in the butter trade*: Jefferies, *Cork: Historical Perspectives*, 141, 146 (*idle looms*); Dickson, *Old World Colony*, 377; Plumb, *England in the Eighteenth Century*, 21–22 (*fleeces*).

242 *British Army recruiters often appeared*: Montross, *Rag, Tag and Bobtail*, 71; Hagist, ed., *A British Soldier's Story*, xvii (*added firepower*), 186 (*could resign*); Frey, *The British Soldier in America*, 57 (*eight pence*); Curtis, *The British Army in the American Revolution*, 55 (*a guinea*).

242 *Standards were low*: Frey, *The British Soldier in America*, 68; Curtis, *The British Army in the American Revolution*, 56 (*"no rupture"*). Hagist notes that 50 to 60 percent of discharge papers bore signatures, "consistent with estimates of the rate of male literacy in England." *British Soldiers, American War*, 269.

242 *By late winter, Lord Barrington reported*: Barrington to Germain, Mar. 6, 1776, *DAR*, vol. 10, 234; Montross, *Rag, Tag and Bobtail*, 71; DNH, Feb. 23, 2011 (*Shrewsbury jail*), and Aug. 19,

2013 (*"houghing"*); WR, 208; Spring, *With Zeal and with Bayonets Only*, 29; AA, IV: 3, 168–69 (*"all have relations"*).

242 *"Sad work everywhere"*: Harvey to Lord Gordon, Dec. 28, 1775, UK NA, WO 3/5, f. 109; Brooke, *King George III*, 180 (*"ardor of the nation"*); Conway, "The Politics of British Military and Naval Mobilization, 1775–83," *English Historical Review* 112, no. 449 (Nov. 1997): 1179+ (*fifteen deserted*); Hagist, *British Soldiers, American War*, 247 (*"scum"*); Spring, *With Zeal and with Bayonets Only*, 118 (*"certain to desert"*).

243 *Royal governors in the southern colonies*: The Detail and Conduct of the American War, 108; North to George, Oct. 15, 1775, "George III Calendar, Sept. 1775–Oct. 1777," RA GEO/MAIN/#2196–98 (*"restore order"*); Bailyn, *Faces of Revolution*, 173 (*émigrés from Scotland*); "Expedition to the Southern Colonies," n.d., from "Narrative of Facts Relative to American Affairs," UK NA, CO 5/232, f. 379–430; Smith, *Loyalists and Redcoats*, 18–21; J. Martin to Dartmouth, Jan. 26, 1775, *DAR*, vol. 9, 37 (*"baneful climate"*).

243 *Lord Dartmouth, before leaving office*: Dartmouth to W. Howe, Sept. 15, 1775, *DAR*, vol. 10, 80 (*"enable you"* and *"too sanguine"*); Dartmouth to J. Martin, Sept. 15, 1775, *NDAR*, vol. 2, 718; "Expedition to the Southern Colonies," n.d., from "Narrative of Facts Relative to American Affairs," UK NA, CO 5/232, f. 379–430 (*"able & intelligent"*); Dartmouth to W. Howe, Oct. 22, 1775, *DAR*, vol. 11, 158–61 (*"not deceived in the assurances"*); Robson, "The Expedition to the Southern Colonies, 1775–1776," *English Historical Review* 66, no. 261 (Oct. 1951): 535+.

243 *Lord North also embraced this hallucination*: North to George, Oct. 15, 1775, "George III Calendar, Sept. 1775–Oct. 1777," RA GEO/MAIN/#2196–98.

244 *"Every means of distressing America"*: George to North, Oct. 15, 1775, "George III Calendar, Sept. 1775–Oct. 1777," RA GEO/MAIN/#2199; George to North, Oct. 16, 1775, "George III Calendar, Sept. 1775–Oct. 1777," RA GEO/MAIN/#2201; Robson, "The Expedition to the Southern Colonies, 1775–1776," *English Historical Review* 66, no. 261 (Oct. 1951): 535+ (*"impenetrable secret"*).

244 *With Germain's appointment*: Smith, *Loyalists and Redcoats*, 24; Admiralty to Germain, Nov. 15, 1775, *NDAR*, vol. 3, 368; "Expedition to the Southern Colonies," n.d., from "Narrative of Facts Relative to American Affairs," UK NA, CO 5/232, f. 379–430; Germain to commander of "the Southern Expedition" [H. Clinton], Dec. 7, 1775, UK NA, CO 5/92, f. 375 (*"secure the well-affected"*).

244 *A modest, show-the-flag mission*: *DAR*, vol. 11, 9–13; "Decision at Moore's Creek Bridge," *Cincinnati Fourteen*, Spring 2012, 30+ (*"a severe blow"*); Dunelm, ed., *The Political Life of William Wildman, Viscount Barrington*, 160 (*"not to stir a step"*); Dartmouth to Martin, Nov. 7, 1775, *DAR*, vol. 11, 174; Dartmouth to W. Howe, Nov. 8, 1775, *DAR*, vol. 10, 117; *DAR*, vol. 11, 13; Germain to commander of "the Southern Expedition" [H. Clinton], Dec. 7, 1775, UK NA, CO 5/92, f. 375.

245 *The cardinal principle of concentrating*: Whiteley, *Lord North*, 162; *DAR*, vol. 11, 9–13; Piecuch, *Three Peoples, One King*, 6–7; Bellot, *William Knox*, 140–41; Tilley, *The British Navy and the American Revolution*, 75–79; *DAR*, vol. 12, 12 (*"fatal euphoria"*); Martin to Dartmouth, Aug. 28, 1775, *DAR*, vol. 11, 9, 89 (*"sacrifice the friends"*).

245 *Howe had his own doubts*: Howe to Dartmouth [*sic*], Jan. 16, 1776, UK NA, CO 5/93, f. 64; Willcox, *Portrait of a General*, 68 (*"malady is catching"*).

245 *"Where are we going"*: Murray, *Letters from America*, xv, 17–19.

246 *The southern expedition required*: "Expedition to the Southern Colonies," n.d., from "Narrative of Facts Relative to American Affairs," UK NA, CO 5/232, f. 379–430 (*Parker in Portsmouth*); H. Palliser to Sandwich, Jan. 1 and 3, 1776, *Sandwich*, vol. 1, 93–94 (*cut away her masts*); shipwreck list, eighteenth century, "Shipwrecks of Cork Harbor," http://www.corkshipwrecks.net/ssshipwrecklist18thcent.html (Marquis of Rockingham); Robson, "The Expedition to the Southern Colonies, 1775–1776," *English Historical Review* 66, no. 261 (Oct. 1951): 535+ (*"seldom come alone"*).

246 *Still more misfortunes*: Syrett, *Shipping and the American War*, 48; P. Parker to Admiralty, May 15, 1775, *NDAR*, vol. 5, 111 (*duel*); E. Harvey to [Carleton?], Jan. 3, 1776, UK NA, WO 3/5, f. 110 (*"not in luck"*).

246 *"Some people begin to be astonished"*: H. Palliser to Sandwich, Dec. 27, 1775, *Sandwich*, vol. 1, 88; Cook, *The Long Fuse*, 234 (*"above 20,000 men"*); *Logistics*, 30 (*thirty-seven tons of food*); Baker, *Government and Contractors*, 23 (*four thousand tons of meat*).

246 *Already the search for ships*: DAR, vol. 10, 12; Syrett, *Shipping and the American War*, 10, 81; Syrett, *Shipping and Military Power in the Seven Years War*, 124; Syrett, *The Royal Navy in American Waters*, 40–42; George to Sandwich, Jan. 11, 1776, *Sandwich*, vol. 2, 103 (*"obtaining a large force"*); Curtis, *The British Army in the American Revolution*, 131 (*"so exhausted"*).

247 *Heavy snow entombed Cork*: Crowley et al., eds., *Atlas of Cork City*, 19–20; Murray, *Letters from America*, 21–22 (*"on the point of sailing"*); Syrett, *Shipping and the American War*, 185, 188–89 (*"place of repose"*); P. Parker to P. Stephens, Admiralty, Jan. 6 Jan. 24, 1776, *NDAR*, vol. 3, 484, 533; Winfield, *British Warships in the Age of Sail*, 277 (*Arctic exploration*).

247 *The king grew impatient*: George to Sandwich, Jan. 11, 1776, "George III Calendar, Sept. 1775–Oct. 1777," RA GEO/MAIN/#2329 (*"English lion"*); Sandwich to George, Jan. 11, 1776, "George III Calendar, Sept. 1775–Oct. 1777," RA GEO/MAIN/#2327 (*"warred against us"*); Fortescue, ed., *The Correspondence of King George the Third*, vol. 3, 328.

247 *On Monday, February 12*: P. Parker to P. Stephens, Mar. 7, 1776, *DAR*, vol. 12, 74.

248 *The first storm struck that night*: P. Parker to P. Stephens, Mar. 7, 1776, *DAR*, vol. 12, 74; Admiralty to P. Parker, Mar. 8, 1776, *NDAR*, vol. 4, 953; ECB, 4 (*"worst weather"*); Lipscomb, *The Carolina Lowcountry*, 21 (*"relentless fury"*); P. Parker to P. Stephens, Mar. 7, 1776, *DAR*, vol. 12, 74 (Thetis); *Public Advertiser*, London, Feb. 26, 1776, *NDAR*, vol. 4, 932–33 (*upper deck guns*); Capt. Christopher Atkins, *Actaeon*, to Sandwich, Mar. 13, 1776, *Sandwich*, vol. 2, 121 (*"prodigious sea"*).

248 *"I fear there is no chance"*: Cornwallis to Germain, Mar. 7, 1776, UK NA, CO 5/93, f. 759; Ross, ed., *Correspondence of Charles, First Marquis Cornwallis*, vol. 1, 21.

248 *Now thirty-eight, of fitful health*: Blanks, "The Administration of Governor Josiah Martin in North Carolina," Ph.D. diss. (University of North Carolina, 1948), 1–3; Stumpf, *Josiah Martin*, 33 (*"a sinking man"*); *North Carolina in the American Revolution* (2006): 3, SoC, State Exhibition Series, http://www.societyofthecincinnati.org/scholarship/publications/.

250 *"the seditious in their evil purposes"*: Connor, *Cornelius Harnett*, 94; Stumpf, *Josiah Martin*, 117 (*"rod of chastisement"*), 145 (*"wicked and flagitious"*); MCBC, 23+ (*cabbage bed*); Alden, *The South in the Revolution*, 196–97 (*provincial congress*).

250 *On January 3, Martin's "despicable and mortifying"*: Blanks, "The Administration of Governor Josiah Martin in North Carolina," Ph.D. diss. (University of North Carolina, 1948), 120; Alden, *The South in the Revolution*, 197 (*"daring, horrid"*); Dunkerly, *Redcoats on the River*, 78 (*"possible secrecy"*); "Decision at Moore's Creek Bridge," *Cincinnati Fourteen*, Spring 2012, 30+; Allen, *Tories*, 138; Toffey, *A Woman Nobly Planned*, 122 (*harsh consequences*).

250 *By February 15, the clans had gathered*: MCBC, 23+; Dunkerly, *Redcoats on the River*, 90–91; Toffey, *A Woman Nobly Planned*, 25–29, 121, 124; e-mail, John J. Toffey to author, May 29, 2015 (*his wife, Flora*); MacLean, *Flora MacDonald in America*, 45–48 (*"troublous times"*).

251 *With British colors improvised*: Waddell, *A History of New Hanover County*, vol. 1, 169; MCBC, 23+ (*"not warproof"*); Dunkerly, *Redcoats on the River*, 90–91; D. MacDonald to J. Moore, Feb. 20, 1776, *AA*, IV: 5, 65 (*"duty to conquer"*).

251 *For weeks, North Carolina patriots*: Dunkerly, *Redcoats on the River*, 78, 82–83; MCBC, 23+; Blanks, "The Administration of Governor Josiah Martin in North Carolina," Ph.D. diss. (University of North Carolina, 1948), 126–31.

251 *Eighteen miles above Wilmington*: "Decision at Moore's Creek Bridge," *Cincinnati Fourteen*, Spring 2012, 30+; Hubbard, "Who Commanded at Moore's Creek Bridge?," *North Carolina University Magazine* 7, no. 4 (Nov. 1857): 137+; Dunkerly, *Redcoats on the River*, 94–95; Capps and Davis, "Moore's Creek National Battlefield: An Administrative History," June 1999, NPS, https://www.nps.gov/parkhistory/online_books/mocr/adhi_1.htm.

251 *They did not have long to wait*: Cumming and Rankin, *The Fate of a Nation*, 88; Wilson, *The Southern Strategy*, 30–31; MCBC, 23+; Dunkerly, *Redcoats on the River*, 95 (*"could not stir from his bed"* and *"darkest that could be seen"*); Daniel W. Barefoot, "Moore's Creek Bridge,

Battle of," in William S. Powell, ed., *Encyclopedia of North Carolina* (2006): https://www
.ncpedia.org/moores-creek-bridge-battle; Phillips, *1775*, 528 (*"banners and plumes"*).

252 *An assault force of eighty Highlanders*: Dunkerly, *Redcoats on the River*, 98 (*"shooting squirrels"*); *North Carolina in the American Revolution* (2006): 20, SoC, State Exhibition Series,
http://www.societyofthecincinnati.org/scholarship/publications/ (*sharkskin*); MCBC, 23+
(*nine bullets*).

252 *The skirmish had lasted three minutes*: James M. Clifton, "MacDonald, Donald," in William S. Powell, ed., *Dictionary of North Carolina Biography*, 1991, www.ncpedia.org
/biography/macdonald-donald; Hunt, *Fragments of Revolutionary History*, 102 (*gave up
dirks*); MCBC, 23+ (*fifteen hundred firelocks* and £15,000); DeMond, *The Loyalists in North
Carolina During the Revolution*, 110–12 (*marched off to prisons*); Callahan, *Royal Raiders*, 23
(*muster rolls*).

253 *"Thus has most happily terminated"*: "Decision at Moore's Creek Bridge," *Cincinnati Fourteen*,
Spring 2012, 30+; Moore, *The Diary of the American Revolution*, 101–02 (*"a stop to Toryism"*).

253 *Governor Martin remained defiant*: Waddell, *A History of New Hanover County*, vol. 1, 175–
78 (*"gasconadings"*); Stumpf, *Josiah Martin*, 137 (*sold at auction*); J. Martin to Germain,
Mar. 22, 1776, DAR, vol. 12, 85–90 (*"unfortunate delay"*).

253 *"a wretched man, not of Neptune's"*: Callahan, *Royal Raiders*, 22; J. Martin to Germain,
Mar. 22, 1776, DAR, vol. 12, 85–90 (*"little check"*).

253 *On Tuesday, March 12*, Mercury: "Expedition to the Southern Colonies," n.d., from "Narrative of Facts Relative to American Affairs," UK NA, CO 5/232, f. 379–430; Willcox, *Portrait
of a General*, 77 (*"big with expectation"*).

253 *As the son and brother-in-law of admirals*: O'Shaughnessy, "'To Gain the Hearts and Subdue the Minds of America': General Sir Henry Clinton and the Conduct of the British War
for America," *Proceedings of the American Philosophical Society* 158, no. 3 (Sept. 2014): 199+;
Willcox, *Portrait of a General*, ix, 36–37 (*"madness"*).

254 *He would always be an enigma*: Willcox, *Portrait of a General*, 6, 42–43, 56; MLA, 245; Gruber, *Books and the British Army in the Age of the American Revolution*, 44 (*barbarians*), 77
(*"brave generals"*).

254 *Rational, dignified, and brainy*: MLA, 214 (*"shy bitch"*); TAR, xii–xiii (*"Furies"*), xvi (*died giving birth*), xviii (*"speak too freely"*); Willcox, *Portrait of a General* (*"ignorant German surgeon"*).

255 *"I like this sort of life"*: Willcox, *Portrait of a General*, 61, 67–68 (*"subordinate"*); TAR, xix
(*"feel the weight"*).

255 *Now there was little to do*: FYAR, 645 (*"such thunder"*); Willcox, *Portrait of a General*, 79–80
(*"whipping snake"*).

255 *"gain the hearts & subdue the minds"*: Conway, "To Subdue America," *WMQ*, 3rd ser., 43,
no. 3 (July 1986): 381+; Piecuch, *Three Peoples, One King*, 89; Willcox, *Portrait of a General*,
67–68 (*"one foot in my ships"*), 83 (*"chimerical, false"*), 493.

255 *How could hearts be gained*: Piers Mackesy, "Could the British Have Won the War of Independence?," lecture, Clark University, Worcester, Mass., Sept. 1975.

255 *In a dispatch to Germain, he warned*: "Expedition to the Southern Colonies," n.d., from "Narrative of Facts Relative to American Affairs," UK NA, CO 5/232, f. 379–430 (*"changed for the
worse"* and *"sacrifice your friends"*); Mackesy, *The War for America*, 86.

256 *Clinton had heard nothing from Howe*: P. Parker to Admiralty, May 15, 1776, UK NA, CO
5/125, f. 13 (*rum*).

11. CITY OF OUR SOLEMNITIES

257 *At eleven p.m. on Saturday, March 2*: diary, John Warren, Mar. 2, 1776, MHS, John Collins
Warren Papers, Ms. N-1731, vol. 1A; *GGW*, 123–24; *AFC*, vol. 1, 353 (*"roar of cannon"* and *"rattling of the windows"*); Daniel Hitchcock to William Heath, Mar. [3?], 1776, Heath papers,
MHS, micro, reel P-205 (*near Faneuil Hall*); W. Heath to GW, Mar. 3, 1776, *PGW*, vol. 3, 403,
404n (*two of their own*); Baldwin, 28; Ford, ed., *Correspondence and Journals of Samuel Blachley Webb*, 132–34. Frothingham cites five mortars ruined. *Siege*, 297.

257 *"Every man's conduct will be marked"*: general orders, Mar. 3, 1776, *PGW*, vol. 3, 401–02.

257 *Each regiment was to send all picks*: orderly book, Col. John Robinson, Feb. 26–29, 1776, HL, HM 596 (*"examined, cleaned"* and *"games of chance"*); general orders, Mar. 3, 1776, *PGW*, vol. 3, 402 (*lances*); *GGW*, 124 (*abatis*).

258 *With two thousand casualties expected*: general orders, Mar. 4, 1776, *PGW*, vol. 3, 411 (*Brown's Tavern*); Cash, *Medical Men at the Siege of Boston*, 145 (*"few medicines"*); *New-England Chronicle*, Mar. 6, 1776, HD (*"herbs"*).

258 *Washington's irksome gunpowder reserve*: Freeman, 27; GW HQ, 567; GW to Thomas Mumford, Feb. 13, 1776; Nicholas Cooke to GW, Feb. 16, 1776; J. Trumbull, Sr., to GW, Feb. 16, 1776; GW to J. Trumbull, Sr., Feb. 19 and 22, 1776, all in *PGW*, vol. 3, 304–05n, 325, 328–29, 346, 353–54; Buell, ed., *The Memoirs of Rufus Putnam*, 58 (*"chandeliers"*); Hildreth, *Biographical and Historical Memoirs of the Early Pioneer Settlers of Ohio*, 57–58; Huntington, *Letters Written by Ebenezer Huntington*, 30 (*"the Lord's battle"*).

258 *A third consecutive evening cannonade*: *Siege*, 297–98; Ford, ed., *Correspondence and Journals of Samuel Blachley Webb*, vol. 1, 135 (*"Our shells raked"*); diary, Mar. 4, 1776, Timothy Newell, BC, "Diaries Box 1" (*"Soon after candlelight"*); Freeman, 34 (*seven projectiles*); Stuart-Wortley, *A Prime Minister and His Son*, 78 (*"Sheets of fire"*); Carter, *A Genuine Detail of the Several Engagements*, 25 (*"legs and thighs broke"*); Mar. 4, 1776, journal entry, KP; Balderston and Syrett, eds., *The Lost War*, 70.

259 *Under a brilliant full moon*: Baldwin, 29; Wheildon, *Siege and Evacuation of Boston and Charlestown*, 40; Charles H. Bradford, "Dorchester Heights: Prelude to Independence," n.d., http://www.dorchesteratheneum.org/pdf/Dorchester%20Heights.pdf, 35–38; GW to A. Ward, Mar. 3, 1776, *PGW*, vol. 3, 409 (*"well-nailed"*); Heath, *Memoirs of Major-General William Heath*, 33; Wheildon, *History of Paul Revere's Signal Lanterns*, 60; Thacher, *Military Journal*, 39.

259 *Behind the oxen came another*: William Y. Thompson, *Israel Shreve, Revolutionary War Officer*, 10 (*"sociable, sensible"*); Coffin, ed., *The Life and Services of Major General John Thomas*, 5–7, 9–10; Hatch, *Thrust for Canada*, 180–81; J. Warren to J. Adams, June 27, 1775, *PGW*, vol. 1, 62n (*"His merits"*). Thomas wrote his wife, Hannah, that 3,000 men and 360 ox teams made the ascent at eight p.m. J. Thomas to Hannah Thomas, Mar. 9, 1776, Thomas Papers, MHS, micro, reel 2.

259 *Shoving and hoisting, heaving*: Thacher, *Military Journal*, 38; *GGW*, 123 (*Knox's guns*); Baldwin, 29; GW to John Hancock, Mar. 7–9, 1776, *PGW*, vol. 3, 426–27n.

259 *"The whole procession moved on"*: Thacher, *Military Journal*, 38; Henry Bedinger, "A Rifleman's View of the End of the Siege," *B* 1775, Mar. 17–19, 2017; GW HQ, 579 (*"fifth of March"*).

259 *"We hear ten capital cooks"*: "Remarks by Richard Frothingham," *Proceedings*, MHS, vol. 14 (1875–76): 261+.

260 *Alas, there would be no ball*: Stuart-Wortley, *A Prime Minister and His Son*, 77 (*warned Howe*); Feb. 29, 1776, journal entry, KP (*"bombard the town"*); Powell, "A Connecticut Soldier Under Washington: Elisha Bostwick's Memoirs of the First Years of the Revolution," *WMQ*, 3rd ser., 6, no. 1 (Jan. 1949): 94+ (*up to the rooftops*); Lydenberg, 286 (*"astonishing night's work"*); Smith, "Dover in the Revolution," *Dedham Historical Register* 3 (1892): 25 (*"Aladdin's"*).

260 *Plunging fire could now scour*: GW to Hancock, Mar. 7–9, 1776, *PGW*, vol. 3, 421; Joseph Ward to J. Adams, Mar. 14, 1776, *AP*, vol. 4; Bangs, *Journal of Lieutenant Isaac Bangs*, 12–14 (*more than seven hundred*); "Camp Life in 1776—Siege of Boston," *Historical Magazine and Notes and Queries* 8 (1864): 329 (*"pain was so exquisite"*); Powell, "A Connecticut Soldier Under Washington: Elisha Bostwick's Memoirs of the First Years of the Revolution," *WMQ*, 3rd ser., 6, no. 1 (Jan. 1949): 94+ (*"dashed open"*).

260 *"After an unsuccessful fire"*: J. Sullivan to J. Adams, Mar. 15–19, 1776, *AP*, vol. 4; *Evacuation*, 93–94 (*attack with twenty-four hundred men*).

260 *By midday five regiments had marched*: HOB, 224–25 (*sixty rounds*); corr., George Gillespie to "Dr. Gillespie," Mar. 23, 1776, *NDAR*, vol. 4, 71 (*"irregular firing"*); Hunter, *The Journal of Gen. Sir Martin Hunter*, 15 (*on a litter*); *Diary of Samuel Richards*, 25–26 (*"dense columns"*); Thacher, *Military Journal*, 39 (*hilltops*); Lydenberg, 286 (*"fate of America"*).

261 *Washington agreed*: Siege, 297 (*up the Charles*); plan for attacking Boston, Feb. 18–25, 1776, *PGW*, vol. 3, 332–35.

261 *That signal never came*: Freeman, 37–38; GW to J. Hancock, Mar. 7–9, 1776, *PGW*, vol. 3, 422; *FYAR*, 662 (*"a hurrycane"*); Pierce, *The Diary of John Rowe*, 95; Heath, *Memoirs of Major-General William Heath*, 34; *Evacuation*, 93–94 (*transports aground*); Bangs, *Journal of Lieutenant Isaac Bangs*, 12 (*"What I suffered"*); Carter, *A Genuine Detail of the Several Engagements*, 26 (*"so great a surf"*); GW to C. Lee, Mar. 14, 1776, *PGW*, vol. 3, 467 (*"unfortunate for us"*).

262 *Howe recognized divine intercession*: Lydenberg, 286 (*"honor of the troops"*); Howe to Dartmouth [*sic*], Mar. 21, 1776, UK NA, CO 5/93, f. 173; *Logistics*, 107; Neeser, ed., *The Despatches of Molyneux Shuldham*, xxix, 107 (*"very distressed"*). Lord Sandwich told the king that "the army almost totally subsists on what Mr. Shuldham has been able to spare." Sandwich to George, May 2, 1776, "George III Calendar, Sept. 1775–Oct. 1777," RA GEO/MAIN/#2381.

262 *To carry away nine thousand soldiers*: Syrett, *Shipping and the American War*, 206–07 (*"justly sensible"*); Howe to Treasury, May 8, 1776, UK NA, T 64/108, f. 33–35. Howe listed 1,465 loyalists removed to Halifax by profession or social status, including 213 merchants and "principal inhabitants" of Boston and 924 "farmers, traders, shopkeepers, and mechanics"; he also referred to 200 others whose names he did not have. W. Howe to Germain, May 7, 1776, *DAR*, vol. 10, 287. Most historians put the number closer to a thousand. McCullough, *1776*, 102–05.

262 *But food shortages and the danger of meeting*: Syrett, *Shipping and the American War*, 206–07; Stuart-Wortley, *A Prime Minister and His Son*, 79; "List of Promotions," June 8, 1776, Richard and William Howe Collection, WLC, box 1 (*"age and infirmities"*); *MLA*, 93.

262 *By Thursday, March 7, news*: Abbott, *New York in the American Revolution*, 172 (*"nook of penury"*).

262 *British charities would send tobacco, shoes*: British merchants also sent 100 pipes of Madeira—more than 10,000 imperial gallons—to be divided among the officers. "Bamford's Diary: The Revolutionary Diary of a British Officer," *Maryland Historical Magazine* 27, no. 3 (Sept. 1932): 258.

262 *"Of all the miserable places"*: Balderston and Syrett, eds., *The Lost War*, 75; Eaton, "Chapters in the History of Halifax, Nova Scotia," *Americana* 10 (1915): 773 (*"cursed, cold"*); *Evacuation*, 179 (*"betrayed"*).

262 *The empire would soon possess*: HBAR, 82; F. Hutcheson to Haldimand, Jan. 25, 1776, Haldimand Papers, LAC, micro, H-1431 (*"pomp of war"*); Mackesy, *The War for America*, 77 (*"send us some generals"*).

263 *Evacuation orders issued that Thursday*: HOB, 228–33 (*"drunkenness"* and *"useless luggage"*), 237 (*defacing portraits*); H. Gates to J. Adams, Mar. 8, 1776, in Knollenberg, "The Correspondence of John Adams and Horatio Gates," *Proceedings*, MHS, 3rd ser., 67 (Oct. 1941–May 1944): 138 (*fresh bedding*); *FYAR*, 672 (*month's provisions*); provisions aboard victuallers, Mar. 22, 1776, Shuldham journal, UK NA, ADM 1/484, f. 482 (*brandy*).

263 *Long Wharf would serve*: Neeser, ed., *The Despatches of Molyneux Shuldham*, 137; Albion, *Forests and Sea Power*, 290 (*white pine trunks*); Siege, 307 (*Horse transports*); *Evacuation*, 96 (*vessels were scuttled*).

263 *Every hour brought more hard choices*: Evacuation, 96 (*coach was tipped*); James Robinson, barrack master general, return, May 12, 1776, and livestock abandoned, UK NA, CO 5/93, f. 341, f. 369; commissary general return, May 7, 1776, UK NA, CO 5/93, f. 337; Curtis, *The British Army in the American Revolution*, 95–96; "Return of Ordnance and Stores Destroyed and Left at Boston," Mar. 12, 1776, WLC, George Wray papers, vol. 3; Duncan, *History of the Royal Regiment of Artillery*, vol. 1, 306 (*13-inch iron mortar*); "Return of Ordnance and Stores Destroyed and Left at Boston," May 7, 1776, UK NA, CO 5/93, f. 341; Ketchum, *Decisive Day*, 218–19. Knox and his gunners concluded that more than half of the abandoned ordnance was useless. Return of British ordnance stores, Mar. 22, 1776, *PGW*, vol. 3, 550.

263 *The British had commandeered 368 houses*: W. Howe to Robinson (Treasury), June 4, 1776, UK NA, T 64/108, f. 51–54; Van Tyne, *The Loyalists in the American Revolution*, 57 (*"uproar*

and confusion"); diary, Mar. 10 and 13, 1776, Timothy Newell, BC, "Diaries Box 1" (*"cut to pieces"*); unsigned letter from Cambridge, Mar. 21, 1776, *AA*, IV: 5, 424; French, *The Siege of Boston*, 427; Mar. 11, 1776, journal entry, KP (*"this day drunk"*).

264 *Most departing loyalists were tradesmen*: W. Howe to Germain, May 7, 1776, *DAR*, vol. 10, 287; Forbes, *Paul Revere and the World He Lived In*, 309, 311 (*"once happy country"*); Pierce, *The Diary of John Rowe*, 95 (*"hurry and confusion"*); Eaton, "Chapters in the History of Halifax, Nova Scotia," *Americana* 10 (1915): 783. J. S. Copley's portraits capture the affluent of greater Boston: http://www.johnsingletoncopley.org/slideshow.html.

264 *"the saddest day ever"*: Forbes, *Paul Revere and the World He Lived In*, 311; Allen, *Tories*, 114–15 (*"their wretched lives"*).

264 *"Troops were ordered under arms"*: Barker, *The British in Boston*, 71; James, *The Rise and Fall of the British Empire*, 113 (*"uncommon bad fate"*); F. Hutcheson to Haldimand, Mar. 24, 1776, Haldimand Papers, LAC, micro, H-1431 (*"many irregularities"*); Sargent, ed., *Letters of John Andrews, Esq., of Boston*, 96–97 (*Armed gangs*); Pierce, *The Diary of John Rowe*, 95–96 (*"greatly terrified"*).

265 *Two regiments of foot with a few*: Evacuation, 176–77; diary, Mar. 15, 1776, Timothy Newell, BC, "Diaries Box 1"; Huntington, *Letters Written by Ebenezer Huntington*, 32; Ketchum, *Decisive Day*, 220–21 (*crow's feet*); Mar. 17, 1776, journal entry, KP (*faint wind*); *HOB*, 241 (*army mustered*); Balderston and Syrett, eds., *The Lost War*, 77–78 (*"Not a single word"*).

265 *At eight a.m., a signal recalled*: Lydenberg, 481–82; Boyle, ed., *From Redcoat to Rebel*, 37; F. Hutcheson to Haldimand, Mar. 24, 1776, Haldimand Papers, LAC, micro, H-1431 (*"greatly crowded"*); W. Howe to Robinson (Treasury), May 8, 1776, UK NA, T 64/108, f. 33–35 (*Foot regiments*); Mar. 17, 1776, journal entry, KP; Chernow, *Washington: A Life*, 227; Thacher, *Military Journal*, 41 (*"unspeakable satisfaction"*).

266 *Howe also had unfinished business*: Shurtleff, *A Topographical and Historical Description of Boston*, 495; Scull, ed., "The Montresor Journals," *Collections*, NYHS (1881): 121; Padelford, ed., *Colonial Panorama, 1775*, 57; Josiah Quincy to GW, Mar. 21, 1776, *PGW*, vol. 3, 509n; Lydenberg, 483 (*burning faggots*); Clark, *George Washington's Navy*, 128 (*ruby glow*); Adair and Schutz, eds., *Peter Oliver's Origin & Progress of the American Rebellion*, 143n (*"Mount Etna"*).

266 *With Castle William reduced*: Bangs, *Journal of Lieutenant Isaac Bangs*, 18 (*"rubbish"*); Ketchum, *Decisive Day*, 218–19 (*"pig together"*); Rhodehamel, ed., *The American Revolution*, 113 (*"famine"*).

266 *"All my struggles"*: W. Howe to Dartmouth [*sic*], Mar. 21, 1776, UK NA, CO 5/93, f. 173; *Stopford-Sackville*, vol. 2, 30 (*"a lowering aspect"*).

266 *At last they were prepared*: Josiah Quincy to GW, Mar. 25–26, 1776, *PGW*, vol. 3, 535–36 (*red ensign*); Mar. 28, 1776, journal entry, KP (*open sea*); Trumbull, *Reminiscences and Letters of John Trumbull*, 25 (*"beautiful sight"*); *PH* 18, 1345+ (*"shifted a position"*); Lossing, *The Pictorial Field-Book of the Revolution*, vol. 2, 22 (*"greatest order"*); *Siege*, 322–23 (*"does dishonor"*); Steuart, ed., *The Last Journals of Horace Walpole*, vol. 1, 539–40 (*"proved the madness"*).

267 *"Expect no more letters from Boston"*: *Siege*, 312; Trevelyan, *The American Revolution*, 266–67 (*"old flapped hat"*).

267 *General Washington had not waited*: GW to J. Hancock, Mar. 19, 1776, *PGW*, vol. 3, 490; Becker, "Smallpox in Washington's Army," *JMH* 68 (Apr. 2004): 381+; general orders, Mar. 13 and 14, 1776, *PGW*, vol. 3, 458 and 466 (*"several schemes"* and *"hidden treasures"*); orderly book, Col. John Robinson, Mass. militia, Mar. 13, 1776, HL, HM 596 (*immune vanguard*); order, N. Greene, Mar. 27, 1776, *PNG*, vol. 1, 205 (*"odious epithets"*); general orders, Mar. 17, 1776, *PGW*, vol. 3, 483n (*"meditating"*); GW to Josiah Quincy, Mar. 24, 1776, *PGW*, vol. 3, 529 (*"all such persons"*); William Heath order, Mar. 9, 1776, Heath papers, MHS, micro, reel P-205 (*"Distrust"*).

267 *Behind beating drums*: New-England Chronicle, Mar. 21, 1776, HD; *Siege*, 310; Freeman, 53; Ketchum, *Decisive Day*, 220–21 (*horseshoe gorgets*).

268 *"The sun looks brighter"*: A. Adams to J. Adams, Mar. 31, 1776, *AFC*, vol. 1, 370; Ferling, *Almost a Miracle*, 107 (*"Females opened"*); "Diary of Ezekiel Price, 1775–6," *Proceedings*, MHS (Nov. 1963): 185+ (*"flesh wasted"*).

268 *On Monday morning, Washington rode*: Freeman, 54; Betlock et al., *An Architectural History of the Old South Meeting House*, 18 (*"Strange that the British"*); *History of the Old South Church of Boston*, 68–69; GW to J. Reed, Mar. 19, 1776, *PGW*, vol. 3, 493–94 (*"almost impregnable"*); GW to J. A. Washington, Mar. 31, 1776, *PGW*, vol. 3, 568 (*"suicide"*).

268 *"The houses I found to be considerably abused"*: diary, John Warren, Mar. 17, 1776, MHS, John Collins Warren Papers, Ms. N-1731, vol. 1A; *Siege*, 327; Allan, *John Hancock*, 219–20 (*backgammon table*); GW to J. Hancock, Mar. 19, 1776, *PGW*, vol. 3, 490 (*"family pictures"*); Levin, *Abigail Adams*, 81; Cooper, "Diary of Samuel Cooper, 1775–1776," *AHR* 6, no. 2 (Jan. 1901): 301+ (*"melancholy scene"* and *Greene ordered*); Young, "George Robert Twelves Hewes (1742–1840)," *WMQ*, 3rd ser., 38, no. 4 (Oct. 1981): 561+ (*wash house*); Puls, *Henry Knox*, 47.

269 *Not every vandal escaped*: *The Detail and Conduct of the American War*, 117; Duffy and Coyle, "Crean Brush vs. Ethan Allen: A Winner's Tale," *Vermont History* 70 (Summer–Fall 2002): 103+; Winthrop Sargent to GW, Apr. 7, 1776, *PGW*, vol. 4, 47n; *FYAR*, 672–73 (*wife's clothes*).

269 *Washington's troops dragged the harbor*: "Camp Life in 1776—Siege of Boston," *Historical Magazine and Notes and Queries* 8 (1864): 332; *Siege*, 408; Risch, *Supplying Washington's Army*, 396 (*medications*); Griffenhagen, "Drug Supplies in the American Revolution," *Bulletin of the United States National Museum* 225 (1961): 110+ (*"20 to 25 wagons"*); Cash, *Medical Men at the Siege of Boston*, 151–52 (*"arsenic"*); Gillett, *The Army Medical Department*, 56–57.

269 *Boston's deliverance inspired*: Thayer, *Nathanael Greene*, 82–83 (*Second Kings*); GW to J. Trumbull, Sr., Mar. 28, 1776, *PGW*, vol. 3, 558n (*Bunch of Grapes*).

270 *Harvard gave Washington*: J. Adams to GW, *PGW*, vol. 4, 2n. This congressional medal was never made, perhaps in part because Liberty appears to be leering at Washington; a different design was struck and given to him long after the Revolution.

270 *"Under your directions"*: J. Hancock to GW, Apr. 2, 1776, *PGW*, vol. 4, 16; *GC*, 315–17 (*"half a war"*); *GGW*, 126 (*his idea*).

270 *Still, the British Army and the Royal Navy*: *WR*, 130–31; Freeman, 71–73 (*"embodiment"*); GW to John Augustine Washington, Mar. 31, 1776, *PGW*, vol. 3, 569 (*"my reputation"*).

270 *He also felt an aggressive confidence*: GW to J. Reed, Apr. 1, 1776, *PGW*, vol. 4, 11; *Evacuation*, 191 (*"cannot subjugate"*).

270 *Precisely what Britain intended*: Atwood, *The Hessians*, 59; council of war, Mar. 13, 1776, *PGW*, vol. 3, 461n; GW to J. Hancock, Apr. 23, 1776, *PGW*, vol. 4, 114n (*campaign equipage*); J. Reed to GW, Mar. 15, 1776, *PGW*, vol. 3, 475–78 (*camp tables*); GW to J. Reed, Feb. 26, 1776, *PGW*, vol. 3, 372 (*"clever horses"*).

271 *Soldiers stowed their precious powder*: Dawson, *Gleanings from the Harvest-Field of American History*, part 4, 13; W. Heath to GW, Mar. 31, 1776, *PGW*, vol. 3, 564 (*Fifteen tons*); GW to Knox, Apr. 3, 1776, *PGW*, vol. 4, 23–25 (*impressment of livestock*); GW to Hancock, Apr. 4, 1776, *PGW*, vol. 4, 30–32 (*"much dissatisfied"*).

271 *Clerks hurried from wagon to wagon*: Risch, *Supplying Washington's Army*, 66; Johnson, "The Administration of the American Commissariat During the Revolutionary War," Ph.D. diss. (University of Pennsylvania, 1941), 54–55 (*shortage of bricks*).

271 *At sunrise on March 29*: orderly book, Mar. 28, 1776, Col. John Robinson, HL, HM 596; Ganoe, *The History of the United States Army*, 24.

12. A STRANGE REVERSE OF FORTUNE

273 *A large, expectant crowd gathered*: Guilday, *The Life and Times of John Carroll*, vol. 1, 101; *BARH*, 202; Mayer, *Journal of Charles Carroll of Carrollton*, 92; *Fourteenth*, 304; Rowland, *The Life of Charles Carroll of Carrollton*, vol. 1, 151–52.

273 *He stepped onto the sandy beach*: *Struggle*, vol. 2, 329–30; Lossing, *The Life and Times of Philip Schuyler*, vol. 2, 39–42 (*six yoke*); Mayer, *Journal of Charles Carroll of Carrollton*, 91 (*door hinges*); Wrong, *Canada and the American Revolution*, 309–10; BF to Josiah Quincy, Sr., Apr. 15, 1776, *PBF* (*"I begin to apprehend"*); Bigelow, ed., *The Works of Benjamin Franklin*, vol. 7, 334 (*boils*); Brands, *The First American*, 510–11 (*bedding*); "The King's Own Regulars," *Boston Gazette*, Nov. 27, 1775, *PBF*; BF to J. Priestley, Oct. 3, 1775, *PBF* (*"calculate the time"*).

274 *An honor guard led the way*: *Struggle*, vol. 2, 329–30; *BARH*, 203 (*"delicacy, ease"*); *Fourteenth*, 285.

274 *A three-story fieldstone mansion*: author visit, Château Ramezay, Aug. 22, 2015; e-mail, André Delisle, *directeur général et conservateur*, to author, Sept. 2 and 23, 2015; Browne, *The St. Lawrence River*, 312–16.

274 *Inside, a throng of local worthies*: Rowland, *The Life of Charles Carroll of Carrollton*, vol. 1, 153 (*"so much fatigued"*); *Struggle*, vol. 2, 329–32.

274 *After the last brandy*: Rowland, *The Life of Charles Carroll of Carrollton*, vol. 1, 152 (*"the best built"*); Mayer, *Journal of Charles Carroll of Carrollton*, 92; GW to BA, Jan. 27, 1776, *PGW*, vol. 3, 198 (*"doubtful, hazardous"*).

275 *This mission to Canada*: Dull, "Franklin the Diplomat: The French Mission," *Transcriptions of the American Philosophical Society*, new ser., 72, no. 1 (1982): 1+; Jensen, *The Founding of a Nation*, 618; Brands, *The First American*, 497–500 (*"entirely American"*); Morgan, *Benjamin Franklin*, 221; BF to David Hartley, Oct. 3, 1775, *PBF* (*"mutual enmity"*).

275 *Appointed postmaster general*: Isaacson, *Benjamin Franklin*, 301; Konwiser, *Colonial and Revolutionary Posts*, 49, 53; Van Doren, *Benjamin Franklin*, 535–36 (*Delaware River*); BF to Charles Lee, Feb. 11, 1776, *PBF* (*"four arrows"*); contract between Secret Committee and John and Nicholas Brown, Feb. 6, 1776, and with Thomas Mumford, Nov. 28, 1775, *PBF*.

275 *But it was as a diplomat*: Wood, *The Americanization of Benjamin Franklin*, 169; Augur, *The Secret War of Independence*, 76, 77–79.

275 *As leader of a small commission*: "Instructions and Commission from Congress," Mar. 20, 1776, *PBF*; J. Adams to James Warren, Feb. 18, 1776, *AP* (*"toryfied priests"*); Leonard, *Life of Charles Carroll of Carrollton*, 75; Mayer, *Journal of Charles Carroll of Carrollton*, 18; Ketchum, *Saratoga*, 9 (*"Bacon Face"*); Browne, *The St. Lawrence River*, 315–16; Stanley, *Canada Invaded*, 113–15.

276 *Franklin and his fellow commissioners needed*: *BARH*, 199–203 (*"our affairs"*); BA to GW, May 8, 1776, *PGW*, vol. 4, 230 (*"raw troops"*). Gen. John Thomas would report to the commissioners that he found 1,900 troops at Quebec, barely half fit for duty. Thomas to commissioners, May 7, 1776, *NDAR*, vol. 4, 1436.

276 *They faced eighteen hundred defenders*: *WR*, 196; Gerlach, *Proud Patriot*, 92; Thomas to commissioners, May 7, 1776, *NDAR*, vol. 4, 1436 (*150 pounds*). A Canadian account states that a brass 24-pounder began firing on April 27, 1776. Sheldon S. Cohen, ed., *Canada Preserved*, 104.

276 *The ailing Schuyler*: Bush, *Revolutionary Enigma*, 57–58; Gerlach, *Proud Patriot*, 100, 115; Kidder, *A People Harassed and Exhausted*, 85 (*"pleasing thought"*); Schuyler to Hancock, Feb. 10, 1776, *AA*, IV: 4, 990 (*"venereal disease"*); Bell, "On the Nature and Cure of Gun-Shot Wounds," in *The British Military Library*, vol. 1, 218, 308; Applegate, "Remedial Medicine in the American Revolutionary Army," *Military Medicine*, June 1961, 451; Schuyler to GW, Mar. 9 and 27, 1776, *PGW*, vol. 3, 442 and 551; Jones, *History of the Campaign for the Conquest of Canada in 1776*, 26 (*surgeon reported*).

277 *Arnold had expected the commissioners to bring*: commissioners to Hancock, May 1 and 8, 1776, *PBF* (*demanded silver*); Huston, "The Logistics of Arnold's March to Quebec," *Military Affairs* 32, no. 3 (Dec. 1968): 110+; *Struggle*, vol. 2, 421 (*"paymaster"*); Gerlach, *Proud Patriot*, 78 (*"burnt child"*); Stanley, *Canada Invaded*, 112 (*"full value"*); Coffin, *The Province of Quebec and the Early American Revolution*, 517; Gabriel, ed., *Quebec During the American Invasion*, xxxviii; Stanley, *Canada Invaded*, 112; Cruikshank, 22 (*bayonet point*).

277 *Morale and discipline had collapsed*: *Struggle*, vol. 2, 226, 229; Wrong, *Canada and the American Revolution*, 310–11 (*ransacked*); Gerlach, *Proud Patriot*, 138, 144; Hatch, *Thrust for Canada*, 83, 161–62; Salsig, 63; Lanctôt, *Canada and the American Revolution*, 121; Gabriel, ed., *Quebec During the American Invasion*, xxxix.

277 *"I regard the whole of you as enemies"*: Atherton, *Montreal, 1553–1914*, vol. 2, 79–80; Mayer, *Journal of Charles Carroll of Carrollton*, 16–17 (*"plotting"*); Cruikshank, 22 (*"throats cut"*); Coffin, *The Province of Quebec and the Early American Revolution*, 514; Gabriel, ed., *Quebec During the American Invasion*, xlii (*"Long live"*), 14, 66.

277 *"He will turn out a great man"*: *BARH*, 203.

278   *"It is very difficult to keep soldiers"*: commissioners to Hancock, May 1, 6, and 8, 1776, *PBF*; BA to GW, May 8, 1776, *PGW*, vol. 4, 230 (*"Should the enemy"*).

278   *"the smallpox is in the army"*: commissioners to Hancock, May 1, 1776, *PBF*.

278   *"Your commissioners themselves"*: commissioners to Hancock, May 6 and 8, 1776, *PBF*; Smyth, *The Writings of Benjamin Franklin*, vol. 9, 696.

278   *Five thousand souls had spent*: *Struggle*, vol. 2, 247–48 (*devoured whole*), 259, 261–63, 275–93 (*"dingy, gloomy"* and *"never again insult"*); Reynolds, *Guy Carleton*, 89 (*minus twenty*); Cohen, ed., *Canada Preserved*, 104 (*eight hundred cannonballs*).

279   *Lanterns and fire pots*: Cruikshank, 21 (*sentry box*); May 3, 1776, "Journal of the Siege and Blockade of Quebec," *Manuscripts Relating to the Early History of Canada* (*thorn bushes*); Whiteley, "The British Navy and the Siege of Quebec, 1775–6," *Canadian Historical Review* 61, no. 1 (1980): 3+; Capt. Thomas Dorsey to Joseph Howell, Mar. 30, 1776, NYHS, Misc. Mss., Howell, J; Cohen, ed., *Canada Preserved*, 65 (*ghosts*), 81 (*swallows*); GWGO, 121.

279   *Deliverance was nearer*: Germain to Admiralty, Jan. 4, 1776, *DAR*, vol. 12, 32, 6–7; Germain to W. Howe, Feb. 1, 1776, and Germain to Carleton, Feb. 17, 1776, *DAR*, vol. 12, 55–56; Whiteley, "The British Navy and the Siege of Quebec, 1775–6," *Canadian Historical Review* 61, no. 1 (1980): 3+; Cometti, ed., *The American Journals of Lt. John Enys*, xxii.

279   *The long passage from the Gulf*: Donald E. Graves, "Justice to the Admirals," in Stacey, *Quebec, 1759*, appendix G, 242–44 (*lost eleven ships*); PH 18, 933; Glyndwr Williams, "Cook, James," *Dictionary of Canadian Biography*, vol. 4, http://www.biographi.ca/en/bio/cook_james_4E.html; C. Douglas to Sandwich, Jan. 21, 1776, *Sandwich*, vol. 2, 109 (*"atrocious rebellion"*); Whiteley, "The British Navy and the Siege of Quebec, 1775–6," *Canadian Historical Review* 61, no. 1 (1980): 3+ (*six languages*); Willis, *The Struggle for Sea Power*, 71–73; Thomson and Chambers, eds., *A Biographical Dictionary of Eminent Scotsmen*, vol. 1, 453; Valin, *Fortune's Favorite*, 2, 5, 8 (*"very dignified"*), 16–17, 45–49.

280   *Douglas had often sailed*: log, *Isis*, Apr. 11–22, 1776, UK NA, ADM 51/484; C. Douglas to P. Stephens, Admiralty, May 8, 1776, *NDAR*, vol. 4, 1451 (*"an enterprise"*); Cometti, ed., *The American Journals of Lt. John Enys*, 5.

280   *"A breeze getting up"*: Cometti, ed., *The American Journals of Lt. John Enys*, 5; C. Douglas to P. Stephens, Admiralty, May 8, 1776, *NDAR*, vol. 4, 1451.

280   *Unaware of his peril*: Thomas to GW, May 8, 1776, *PGW*, vol. 4, 231–33; J. Thomas to Hannah, Mar. 30, 1776, Thomas papers, MHS, micro, reel 2.

280   *Six thousand American reinforcements*: *Fourteenth*, 311; Salsig, 96 (*"lace"*); Hodgkinson, "Before Quebec, 1776," *PMHB* 10, no. 2 (July 1886): 158+ (*"If I die"*).

281   *With Fortress Quebec all but impregnable*: Salsig, 97; Roche, "Quebec Under Siege, 1775–1776," *Canadian Historical Review* 50 (Mar. 1969): 68+; Cohen, ed., *Canada Preserved*, 88; *Struggle*, vol. 2, 264–65; Würtele, ed., *Blockade of Quebec in 1775–1776*, 49.

281   *Under a northeast breeze*: Salsig, 97; *Struggle*, vol. 2, 265–67, 588 (*"Who are you?"*).

281   *A light gleamed*: John Danford, "Siege of Quebec by an American Force," May 3, 1776, LAC, micro, #A705; Roche, "Quebec Under Siege, 1775–1776," *Canadian Historical Review* 50 (Mar. 1969): 68+; Cohen, ed., *Canada Preserved*, 88 (*"amazing speed"*).

281   *But no fending would be necessary*: Cruikshank, 23; Würtele, ed., *Blockade of Quebec in 1775–1776*, 49–50 (*"sole command"*); Roche, "Quebec Under Siege, 1775–1776," *Canadian Historical Review* 50 (Mar. 1969): 68+.

282   *No sooner had the excitement subsided*: Capt. John Hamilton to London, Nov. 20, 1775, in Cruikshank, 131, https://archive.org/stream/vol1t3historyoforganizo1quebuoft#page/n301; log, *Isis*, May 6, 1776, UK NA, ADM 51/484.

282   *"The news soon reached"*: Cohen, ed., *Canada Preserved*, 88; *ANTA*, 83.

282   *"In my ideas of war"*: Thomas to GW, May 8, 1776, *PGW*, vol. 4, 231–33.

282   *At twelve-thirty p.m., lean and immaculate*: John Danford, "Siege of Quebec by an American Force," May 6, 1776, LAC, micro, #A705; Cohen, ed., *Canada Preserved*, 89; *Struggle*, vol. 2, 319–20; Bradley, *Sir Guy Carleton (Lord Dorchester)*, 138 (*"We found the roads"*).

283   *"It seems they had no stomach"*: *ANTA*, 83; *MQ*, 238–41 (*"helter-skelter manner"*); Cohen, ed., *Canada Preserved*, 91 (*"expired"*).

283 *British soldiers rooting*: May 6, 1776, "Journal of an Officer of the 47th Regiment of Foot," HL, HM 66 (*scaling ladders*); Cometti, ed., *The American Journals of Lt. John Enys*, 13; *Struggle*, vol. 2, 319–22; C. Douglas to P. Stephens, Admiralty, May 8, 1776, *NDAR*, vol. 4, 1452 (*"most precipitate"* and *"their very buckles"*); Wheeler, *Voices of 1776*, 134 (*"tearing work"*); Thomas to GW, May 8, 1776, *PGW*, vol. 4, 233–34 (*arrived from Ticonderoga*).

283 *"Row the boat, row"*: Robbins, *Journal of the Rev. Ammi R. Robbins*, 17–18; Porter, "An Account of the Expedition from Cambridge to Quebec," *BFTM* 10, no. 1 (1957): 34+ (*"exhausted"*); Thomas to GW, May 8, 1776, *PGW*, vol. 4, 232–33 (*to Sorel*).

284 *"This is the most terrible day"*: Robbins, *Journal of the Rev. Ammi R. Robbins*, 17–19.

284 *The bad news flew swiftly: Fourteenth*, 317–18 (*"We are afraid"*); Van Doren, *Benjamin Franklin*, 548–49 (*bolted south*); Jane Mecom [BF's sister] to Catharine Greene, June 1, 1776, *PBF* (*three weeks*); Mayer, *Journal of Charles Carroll of Carrollton*, 93 (*"declining health"*); BF to Charles Carroll and Samuel Chase, May 27, 1776, *PBF*; Isaacson, *Benjamin Franklin*, 306–07 (*"more feeble"*).

284 *Food shortages had grown so dire*: Baldwin, 42, 44; Hancock to Commissioners, May 24, 1776, *PBF* (£1,662); *Struggle*, vol. 2, 390 (*three strongboxes*).

284 *Arnold hurried toward the Cedars*: Congress subsequently repudiated the deal, but after the American prisoners had been released. Congressional report, July 10, 1776, *AA*, V: 1, 159–66, 801; *An Authentic Narrative of Facts Relating to the Exchange of Prisoners Taken at the Cedars*, 7–14, 21–26, 29, 34–37; *ANTA*, 92–99; *Struggle*, vol. 2, 365–80; Lorimier, *At War with the Americans*, 52–54; Hatch, *Thrust for Canada*, 199–207.

284 *"I was torn"*: Jones, *History of the Campaign for the Conquest of Canada in 1776*, 57–64.

284 *Along the Richelieu, so many soldiers*: Dann, ed., *The Revolution Remembered*, 19; Reiss, *Medicine and the American Revolution*, 95; "Journal of Lieutenant-Colonel Joseph Vose," *Publication of the Colonial Society of Massachusetts*, vol. 7 (1900–02): 244+; Stillé, *Major-General Anthony Wayne*, 24–29 (*"damned tomahawks"*); Arnold to Thomas, May 14, 1776, John Thomas papers, MHS, micro, reel 3 (*"Men indeed"*); Mayer, *Journal of Charles Carroll of Carrollton*, 41 (*"miserable situation"*); Rowland, *The Life of Charles Carroll of Carrollton*, vol. 1, 169 (*"broken and disheartened"*). The commissioners advised Thomas of "the propriety of immediately inoculating all our troops," including himself. Charles Carroll and Samuel Chase to Thomas, May 15, 1776, Thomas papers, MHS, micro, reel 3.

285 *"I am at this critical period"*: Thomas to Wooster, May 21, 1776, Thomas papers, MHS, micro, reel 3; *ANTA*, 105; Porter, "An Account of the Expedition from Cambridge to Quebec," *BFTM* 10, no. 1 (1957): 34+ (*"mortified"*); *BARH*, 217 (*"all my heart"*).

285 *"No one thing is right"*: J. Sullivan to Hancock, June 1, 1776, *AA*, IV: 6, 679–80; Hammond, *Letters and Papers of Major-General John Sullivan*, vol. 1, 212.

285 *Sullivan, alas, was hardly the man*: Whittemore, *A General of the Revolution*, 1–4, 9; Amory, *The Military Services and Public Life of Major-General John Sullivan*, 8–10; *GWGO*, 138; *ANTA*, 107.

285 *"He does not want abilities"*: GW to Hancock, June 17, 1776, *PGW*, vol. 5, 20–21.

285 *Sullivan instantly misread*: J. Sullivan to GW, June 6, 1776, *PGW*, vol. 4, 440–41 (*"very affecting"*); *Struggle*, vol. 2, 400 (*"new face"*); J. Sullivan to GW, June 6, 1776, in Hammond, *Letters and Papers of Major-General John Sullivan*, vol. 1, 219 (*"kind Providence"*).

286 *To pursue this fantasy*: J. Sullivan to GW, June 8, 1776, *PGW*, vol. 4, 467n; *Struggle*, vol. 2, 400–03; author visit, Pointe-du-Lac, Lac Saint-Pierre, Aug. 24, 2015, historical signage (*Antonine Gauthier*); *Struggle*, vol. 2, 405 (*"clodhopper"*); Wayne to BF et al., "Account of the Action at Three Rivers," June 13, 1776, Anthony Wayne Papers, BC, Bft. vol. 378, 33–43 (*"horrid swamp"*); St. Clair, *A Narrative*, 237 (*"knee-deep"*); *ANTA*, 115 (*"faithless"*); unsigned letter, Sorel, June 12, 1776, *AA*, IV: 6, 826–28 (*"propose it"*). Sullivan had advised Thompson to abort the attack "if the prospect of success is not much in your favor." J. Sullivan to GW, June 5, 1776, *PGW*, vol. 4, 444n.

286 *It was General Thompson's additional misfortune*: Willcox, *Portrait of a General*, 97 (*"severe a trial"*); Gradish, "The German Mercenaries in North America During the American Revolution: A Case Study," *Canadian Journal of History* (Mar. 1969): 23+; *Struggle*, vol. 2, 409–

11 (*rum*); William Knox, Whitehall, to George Jackson, Feb. 21, 1776, *DAR*, vol. 10, 222 (*forty tons*); Clerke to Polwarth, July 13, 1776, Ronald F. Kingsley, "Letters to Lord Polwarth from Sir Francis-Carr Clerke, Aide-de-Camp to General John Burgoyne," *New York History* 79, no. 4 (Oct. 1998): 411 (*"Arcadian"*).

286 *At eight a.m. on Saturday*: A. Wayne to BF et al., "Account of the Action at Three Rivers," June 13, 1776, Anthony Wayne Papers, BC, Bft. vol. 378, 33–43; Barker and Huey, *The 1776–1777 Northern Campaigns of the American War for Independence and Their Sequel*, 42–43; unsigned letter, Sorel, June 12, 1776, *AA*, IV: 6, 826–28 (*"no covering"*); *Struggle*, vol. 2, 407–11; Maj. Griffith Williams to Germain, June 23, 1776, *NDAR*, vol. 5, 693; Baxter, ed., *The British Invasion from the North*, 106–08.

287 *Eighty yards from the British line*: unsigned letter, Sorel, June 12, 1776, *AA*, IV: 6, 826–28 (*"mantle of heaven"*); A. Wayne to BF et al., "Account of the Action at Three Rivers," June 13, 1776, Anthony Wayne Papers, BC, Bft. vol. 378, 33–43; Maj. Griffith Williams to Germain, June 23, 1776, *NDAR*, vol. 5, 693; journal, unidentified officer [W. Digby], 47th Foot, June 7–8, 1776, MHS, Ms. S-397; Lacey, "Memoirs of Brigadier-General John Lacey, of Pennsylvania," *PMHB* 25–26 (1901–02): 1+ (*"monstrous size"*); *Struggle*, vol. 2, 414 (*"never formed"*).

287 *General Thompson hid in the fens*: Jones, *History of the Campaign for the Conquest of Canada in 1776*, 76 (*"very politely"*); Stillé, *Major-General Anthony Wayne*, 8, 15, 30–31; A. Wayne to BF et al., "Account of the Action at Three Rivers," June 13, 1776, Anthony Wayne Papers, BC, Bft. vol. 378, 33–43 (*"spent with fatigue"*).

287 *"Our army was a great deal cut"*: Wickman, "The Diary of Timothy Tuttle," *New Jersey History* 113, nos. 3–4 (Fall–Winter 1995): 61+; *ANTA*, 118 (*about 400*), 119 (*"rashness"*); Jones, *History of the Campaign for the Conquest of Canada in 1776*, 77 (*compared to 17*); Carleton to Germain, Aug. 10, 1776, *DAR*, vol. 5, 351; "List of Prisoners Taken in Canada," Cruikshank, 185; Baxter, ed., *The British Invasion from the North*, 106–08.

287 *"Our affairs look dark"*: Baldwin, 51; J. Sullivan to GW, *PGW*, vol. 4, 463–64 (*"in our favor"*); Hammond, *Letters and Papers of Major-General John Sullivan*, vol. 1, 234–35 (*"chaos & confusion"*).

288 *The only expulsion likely*: *Struggle*, vol. 2, 431–32; Stanley, *Canada Invaded*, 129; Baxter, ed., *The British Invasion from the North*, 105 (*"old as the world"*); author visit, Pointe-du-Lac, Lac Saint-Pierre, Aug. 24, 2015; journal, unidentified officer [W. Digby], 47th Foot, June 14, 1776, MHS, Ms. S-397 (*"moving forest"*); Cometti, ed., *The American Journals of Lt. John Enys*, 15 (*"most agreeable"*).

288 *At nine p.m., wind spilled*: journal, June 14–15, 1776, in Maj. G. Williams to Germain, June 23, 1776, "George III Calendar, Sept. 1775–Oct. 1777," RA GEO/MAIN/#2442; Carleton to Germain, June 20, 1776, *DAR*, vol. 12, 152–53; *Logistics*, 216–17.

288 *Serenaded by crickets and frogs*: journal, June 14–15, 1776, in Maj. G. Williams to Germain, June 23, 1776, "George III Calendar, Sept. 1775–Oct. 1777," RA GEO/MAIN/#2442; Clerke to Polwarth, July 13, 1776, in Kingsley, "Letters to Lord Polwarth from Sir Francis-Carr Clerke, Aide-de-Camp to General John Burgoyne," *New York History* 79, no. 4 (Oct. 1998): 412; Hagist, ed., *A British Soldier's Story*, 27; Stanley, *Canada Invaded*, 129.

289 *General Sullivan had no plan*: St. Clair, *A Narrative*, 240–41; Schuyler to GW, June 12, 1776, *PGW*, vol. 4, 510n. "Return of the Continental Forces in Canada, June 12th 1776," listed just over 7,000 troops but acknowledged that it was "impossible to make an accurate return." GW to Hancock, June 23, 1776, *PGW*, vol. 5, 80n.

289 *smallpox, which was killing thirty men a day*: Reiss, *Medicine and the American Revolution*, 95–96; St. Clair, *A Narrative*, 240; *Struggle*, vol. 2, 420 (*only a fraction*).

289 *Some colonels were uncertain*: GW to Hancock, June 23, 1776, *PGW*, vol. 5, 80n; J. Sullivan to GW, June 12, 1776, in Hammond, *Letters and Papers of Major-General John Sullivan*, vol. 1, 229 (*"not a single man"*), 240, 250; *Struggle*, vol. 2, 425 (*"contest every foot"*), 434–36; St. Clair, *A Narrative*, 241 (*withdrawal*).

289 *"Let us quit them"*: Hammond, *Letters and Papers of Major-General John Sullivan*, vol. 1, 237; *Spirit '76*, 220 (*"my country rise"*); Salsig, 136–37 (*dubious receipts*); Schuyler to Thomas [*sic*],

June 4, 1776, *AA*, IV: 6, 711 (*boatbuilding*); André Delisle, *directeur général et conservateur*, Château Ramezay, to author, e-mail, Sept. 23, 2015 (*£1,200 in damage*); *ANTA*, 122.

289 *At seven p.m. on Saturday*: BA to J. Sullivan, June 16, 1776, in Hammond, *Letters and Papers of Major-General John Sullivan*, vol. 1, 242; Greenwood, ed., *The Revolutionary Services of John Greenwood*, 34 (*"large peas"*), 35 (*"half a leg"*); BA to GW, June 25, 1776, *PGW*, vol. 3, 96; *Fourteenth*, 329–30; Salsig, 136–37.

290 *Three other corps*: Logistics, 216–18; Carleton to Germain, June 20, 1776, *DAR*, vol. 12, 152–53.

290 *Burgoyne, advancing south*: Baxter, ed., *The British Invasion from the North*, 116–18; journal, unidentified officer [W. Digby], 47th Foot, June 15–18, 1776, MHS, Ms. S-397; Stanley, *Canada Invaded*, 131–32; Clerke to Polwarth, July 13, 1776, in Kingsley, "Letters to Lord Polwarth from Sir Francis-Carr Clerke, Aide-de-Camp to General John Burgoyne," *New York History* 79, no. 4 (Oct. 1998): 412 (*"our chase"*).

290 *"beyond anything that ever I went through"*: Jones, *History of the Campaign for the Conquest of Canada in 1776*, 83.

290 *Upon fleeing Chambly, the Americans*: Lacey, "Memoirs of Brigadier-General John Lacey, of Pennsylvania," *PMHB* 25–26 (1901–02): 1+; "Journal of Lieutenant-Colonel Joseph Vose," *Publication of the Colonial Society of Massachusetts*, vol. 7 (1900–02): 244+ (*"exceeding bad"*); St. Clair, *A Narrative*, 241 (*"mill sluice"*); Salsig, 136–37; Kirkland, *Journal of Lewis Beebe*, 11 (*sound of axes*); Baldwin, 55 (*"leaving their men"*); Thompson, *Israel Shreve, Revolutionary War Officer*, 16 (*"Everything goes"*).

291 *On Monday night, still a day ahead*: Struggle, vol. 2, 440–41; *BARH*, 220; Kirkland, *Journal of Lewis Beebe*, 9 (*"Some dead"*).

291 *Soldiers pried more than two tons*: Moore, *A Life of General John Stark of New Hampshire*, 231–32; Hatch, *Thrust for Canada*, 224; Baldwin, 56; Porter, "An Account of the Expedition from Cambridge to Quebec," *BFTM* 10, no. 1 (1957): 34+; *Spirit '76*, 217; memoir, William Chamberlin, *Proceedings*, MHS, 2nd ser., 10 (1895–96): 490–506 (*"loaded as deep"*); *ANTA*, 123 (*"beyond description"*).

291 *Late that afternoon, incendiaries*: Carleton to Germain, June 20, 1776, *DAR*, vol. 12, 152–53; journal, unidentified officer [W. Digby], 47th Foot, June 16–18, 1776, MHS, Ms. S-397 (*Burgoyne's redcoats*); Wilkinson, *Memoirs of My Own Times*, vol. 1, 54–55 (*"vanity"*).

291 *Île aux Noix seemed to float*: author visit, Île aux Noix, Aug. 19, 2015; Lynn, ed., *An Eyewitness Account of the American Revolution and New England Life*, 31; Charbonneau, *The Fortifications of Île aux Noix*, 19–25, 66; *ANTA*, 126–27; Wickman, "The Diary of Timothy Tuttle," *New Jersey History* 113, nos. 3–4 (Fall–Winter 1995): 61+.

292 *Thousands of American soldiers*: Salsig, 142; "General Orders for Encampment at Isle aux Noix," June 19, 1776, NYHS, Revolutionary War, British and Hessian Army, box 1; Gillett, *The Army Medical Department*, 63 (*perhaps half*); Moore, *A Life of General John Stark of New Hampshire*, 232 (*"walketh"*); J. Sullivan to GW, June 24, 1776, *PGW*, vol. 5, 92; Lacey, "Memoirs of Brigadier-General John Lacey, of Pennsylvania," *PMHB* 25–26 (1901–02): 1+ (*"lice and maggots"*); *ANTA*, 127 (*"see, speak"*); Kirkland, *Journal of Lewis Beebe*, 12 (*"crickets"*); Trumbull, *Reminiscences and Letters of John Trumbull*, 300 (*"broke my heart"*).

292 *Two burial pits were dug*: Lacey, "Memoirs of Brigadier-General John Lacey, of Pennsylvania," *PMHB* 25–26 (1901–02): 1+ (*"rags"*); Cox, *A Proper Sense of Honor*, 170.

292 *Some officers drank themselves*: Struggle, vol. 2, 444; "General Orders for Encampment at Isle aux Noix," June 19, 1776, NYHS, Revolutionary War, British and Hessian Army, box 1; orderly book, William Walker, June 19, 1776, T-P RC (*"defiling the ground"*); Salsig, 145; J. Sullivan to GW, June 24, 1776, *PGW*, vol. 5, 93 (*marauding Indians*); Porter, "An Account of the Expedition from Cambridge to Quebec," *BFTM* 10, no. 1 (1957): 34+ (*rowed unarmed*); "Journal of Lieutenant-Colonel Joseph Vose," *Publication of the Colonial Society of Massachusetts*, vol. 7 (1900–02): 244+ (*"Such a sight"*); "Journal of an Officer of the 47th Regiment of Foot," June 21, 1776, HL, HM 66 (*"sons of america"*).

293 *"By a strange reverse of fortune"*: J. Sullivan to Schuyler, June 19, 1776, in Hammond, *Letters and Papers of Major-General John Sullivan*, vol. 1, 250; Cruikshank, 31 (*"effect of imagination"*); J. Sullivan to Schuyler, June 25, 1776, Schuyler Papers, BC, vol. 347, 35–37 (*"decaying*

army"); J. Sullivan to Schuyler, June 22, 1776, in Hammond, *Letters and Papers of Major-General John Sullivan*, vol. 1, 257 (*"destroying angel"*).

293   *"Heaven sees at present to frown"*: J. Sullivan to Schuyler, June 25, 1776, Schuyler Papers, BC, vol. 347, 35–37.

293   *"The grand post was lost"*: J. Sullivan to Schuyler, June 19, 1776, in Hammond, *Letters and Papers of Major-General John Sullivan*, vol. 1, 251; J. Sullivan to GW, June 24, 1776, *PGW*, vol. 5, 92 (*"well men"*); Schuyler to GW, June 25, 1776, and Arnold to GW, both in *PGW*, vol. 5, 105n (*"could not go"*) and 96.

293   *"I find myself under"*: J. Sullivan to GW, June 24, 1776, *PGW*, vol. 5, 92.

293   *That was true enough*: J. Sullivan to Schuyler, June 22, 1776, in Hammond, *Letters and Papers of Major-General John Sullivan*, vol. 1, 257 (*oarsmen*); Greenwood, ed., *The Revolutionary Services of John Greenwood*, 36 (*"lousy, itchy"*); Salsig, 149 (*blue flag*); "Journal of Lieutenant-Colonel Joseph Vose," *Publication of the Colonial Society of Massachusetts*, vol. 7 (1900–02): 244 (*"Worse traveling"*); Davis, "Medicine in the Canadian Campaign of the Revolutionary War: The Journal of Doctor Samuel Fisk Merrick," *Bulletin of the History of Medicine* 44, no. 5 (Sept.–Oct. 1970) (*"as decent a manner"*).

294   *"I never had an idea of pain"*: J. Sullivan to Hancock, July 2, 1776, in Hammond, *Letters and Papers of Major-General John Sullivan*, vol. 1, 274.

294   *But the general's pain could not*: Patten, *The Diary of Matthew Patten*, 361.

294   *"I never had an opportunity"*: Richard Howell to Lewis Howell, Sept. 26, 1776, Howell letters collection, HL, HM 67370.

294   *American losses would forever remain*: Ferling, *Almost a Miracle*, 111 (*twelve thousand*); Trumbull, *Reminiscences and Letters of John Trumbull*, 302; *Struggle*, vol. 2, 599; Carleton to Germain, Aug. 10, 1776, *DAR*, vol. 5, 351.

294   *"The boats were leaky"*: Trumbull, *Reminiscences and Letters of John Trumbull*, 28; Robbins, *Journal of the Rev. Ammi R. Robbins*, 33 (*"Their sorrows"*); Kirkland, *Journal of Lewis Beebe*, 14 (*"God seems"*).

295   *"The subject is disgusting"*: S. Adams to Joseph Hawley, July 9, 1776, in Stanley, *Canada Invaded*, 133; J. Adams to J. Sullivan, June 23, 1776, AP (*"explain to me"*); *AFC*, vol. 2, 23, 63 (*"Our misfortunes"*); J. Adams to [Samuel Cooper?], June 9, 1776, AP; *Struggle*, vol. 2, 449–51; Freeman, 143; *Fourteenth*, 347–48, 351–52.

295   *"mixed motives and uncertain outcomes"*: Cohen, *Conquered into Liberty*, 163.

295   *"Canada has been a very unfortunate place"*: "Journal of Lieutenant-Colonel Joseph Vose," *Publication of the Colonial Society of Massachusetts*, vol. 7 (1900–02): 244+; *Struggle*, vol. 2, 453 (*"dress rehearsal"*).

295   *"you will endeavor to pass the lakes"*: Cruikshank, 151; Wilson, *Benedict Arnold*, 125 (*"sorry you did not get"*); Randall, *Benedict Arnold*, 237.

296   *"will doubtless become masters"*: BA to GW, June 25, 1776, *PGW*, vol. 5, 96–97.

13. SURROUNDED BY ENEMIES, OPEN AND CONCEALED

297   *Pretty little New York*: *BNY*, 5–6; Still, *Mirror for Gotham*, 17, 19; Wertenbaker, *Father Knickerbocker Rebels*, 14–15; Jaffee, *New York at War*, 79 (*"Dutch neatness"*); Bridenbaugh, *Cities in Revolt*, 271; Burrows and Wallace, *Gotham*, 123–24 (*distillers*); *IMI*, vol. 4, 922 (*liquor vendors*).

297   *"New York is growing"*: Burrows and Wallace, *Gotham*, 168; *IMI*, vol. 1, 331 (*Milestones*); Ketchum, *Divided Loyalties*, 10 (*lamplighters*); Bridenbaugh, *Cities in Revolt*, 233, 241 (*dung*), 365 (*legal holidays*); Fusilier, 16 (*phaetons*). The water project collapsed after the war began. John Duffy, "Public Health in New York City in the Revolutionary Period," *JAMA* 236, no. 1 (July 5, 1976): 47+.

299   *"This haughty city is now"*: W. Tudor to Delia Jarvis, Apr. 16 and 25, 1776, William Tudor Papers, MHS, Ms., N-1684; *BNY*, 63–64 (*"plague"*); *LAR*, 308 (*"nunnery"*).

299   *By early summer, more than twelve thousand soldiers*: The return of late June listed 12,500 officers and men, including artillery troops. GW to Hancock, June 28, 1776, *PGW*, vol. 5, 136n; Bliven, *Under the Guns*, 247.

299 *Delaware troops wore blue coats*: Ward, *The Delaware Continentals*, 9; *WR*, 205; Wertenbaker, *Father Knickerbocker Rebels*, 77; *Centennial Notes, New York City, 1876*, NYHS [extracts from 1776 newspapers published in *New York Evening Mail*]; Gardner, "The Uniforms of the American Army," *Magazine of American History* 1, no. 8 (Aug. 1877): 470–72; J. Reed to Samuel Tucker, June 28, 1776, *PGW*, vol. 5, 137n ("*destitute*").

299 *Since February, soldiers and civilians*: HH, 11–12; BNY, 84; Jaffee, *New York at War*, 77; *C 1776*, 37–38 (*Slaves delivered*), 57; Abbott, *New York in the American Revolution*, 172–73 ("*diggers-in*"); *IMI*, vol. 4, 919 ("*traversed*"); Bliven, *Under the Guns*, 11–12; Knox to GW, June 10, 1776, *PGW*, vol. 5, 491 (*19 mortars*); Tryon to Germain, Apr. 6, 1776, *DAR*, vol. 12, 107 ("*every headland*").

300 *The fortifications extended well beyond*: Cohn, *Fortifications of New York During the Revolutionary War, 1776–1782*; Field, *The Battle of Long Island*, 139–44; Stiles, *A History of the City of Brooklyn*, vol. 1, 246–61; Apr. 8, 1776, entry, Baldwin, 31–33.

300 *Sparks flew night and day*: Wertenbaker, *Father Knickerbocker Rebels*, 59; *C 1776*, 37–38 (*Bridewell*); Wickman, "The Diary of Timothy Tuttle," *New Jersey History* 113, nos. 3–4 (Fall-Winter 1995): 61+ ("*Made cartridges*"); Stiles, *A History of the City of Brooklyn*, vol. 1, 247–54 ("*corps of observation*").

300 *Rebel cannons and gunmen*: GW to John Augustine Washington, Apr. 29, 1776, *PGW*, vol. 4, 172; Field, *The Battle of Long Island*, 62; *C 1776*, 57–58 ("*May God*"), 37–38 (*lamp oil*); Ford, ed., *Correspondence and Journals of Samuel Blachley Webb*, vol. 1, 140; Bliven, *Under the Guns*, 173 (*laundry*); Wertenbaker, *Father Knickerbocker Rebels*, 74–75 (*Bedloe's*); Tryon to Germain, Apr. 6, 1776, *DAR*, vol. 12, 107 ("*poultry*").

301 *That Howe was coming from Halifax*: Thayer, *Nathanael Greene*, 84; *IMI*, vol. 4, 931 (*candles*); Esmond Wright, "The New York Loyalists," in East and Judd, eds., *The Loyalist Americans*, 74.

301 *"Great numbers of angels"*: Byrd, "Was the American Revolution a Holy War?," *Washington Post*, July 5, 2013.

301 *His Excellency General Washington had*: GW to Hancock, June 7, 1776, *PGW*, vol. 4, 452; Ketchum, *Divided Loyalties*, 16; Bangs, *Journal of Lieutenant Isaac Bangs*, 39–40; Wall, "The Equestrian Statue of George III and the Pedestrian Statue of William Pitt," *Quarterly Bulletin*, NYHS, July 1920, 35+; Bob Ruppert, "The Statue of George III," *JAR*, Sept. 8, 2014; Dunlap, "Long-Toppled Statue of King George III to Ride Again, from a Brooklyn Studio," *New York Times*, Oct. 20, 2016.

301 *Striding back up the avenue*: Bangs, *Journal of Lieutenant Isaac Bangs*, 39–40; Ferling, *The First of Men*, 158 (*Peale*); GW to Hancock, June 7, 1776, *PGW*, vol. 4, 452 ("*state of peace*"); John Langdon to GW, May 10, 1776, *PGW*, vol. 4, 256–57n; Hugh T. Harrington, "The Strange Odyssey of George Merchant, Rifleman," in Andrlik et al., eds., *Journal of the American Revolution*, vol. 1, 70–73; Freeman, 94, 98. For months, reports had circulated from England of British interest in hiring German mercenaries. New York Provincial Congress to GW, Oct. 4, 1775, *PGW*, vol. 2, 94n.

302 *He intended to further strengthen fortifications*: "Expense Account of Journey to and from Philadelphia," May–June 1776, *PGW*, vol. 4, 366–67n; Wright, *The Continental Army*, 85–86; GW to Joseph Trumbull, June 9, 1776, *PGW*, vol. 4, 479n; Baker, *"Villainy and Maddness": Washington's Flying Camp*, 9, 13–14.

302 *Congress also seemed to be moving*: Stoker et al., eds., *Strategy in the American War of Independence*, 5.

302 *The sun had begun to dip*: general orders, Apr. 14, 1776, *PGW*, vol. 4, 60n; *Centennial Notes, New York City, 1876*, NYHS [extracts from 1776 newspapers published in *New York Evening Mail*]; Grund, "The Glory That Was Once Richmond Hill's Is Long Since Faded and Forgotten," part 1, *Villager*, Sept. 13, 1945, http://www.getny.com/grundyrichmondhill .shtml.

304 *Yet the Mortier house could*: GW to Lund Washington, Aug. 19, 1776, *PGW*, vol. 6, 84–85, 87n ("*clever kind*"); Greiff, *The Morris-Jumel Mansion*, 127–28; GW to Robert Hanson Harrison, Jan. 10, 1777, *PGW*, vol. 8, 33 (*bearskin*); general orders, Mar. 11, 1776, *PGW*, vol. 3, 449

(*"handsomely and well-made"*); Lossing, "Washington's Life Guard," *Historical Magazine* 2, no. 5 (May 1858): 129+; Ward, *George Washington's Enforcers*, 59–61; *Centennial Notes, New York City, 1876*, NYHS; "Life Guards," *Digital Encyclopedia of George Washington*, http://www.mountvernon.org/digital-encyclopedia/article/life-guards/ (*"Conquer"*).

304 *"We expect a very bloody summer"*: GW to John Augustine Washington, May 31–June 4, 1776, *PGW*, vol. 4, 413.

304 *The grand army under Washington*: Carp put American dead from all causes in Canada at 5,000 from September 1775 to June 1776, higher than most estimates. *To Starve the Army at Pleasure*, 19.

304 *Congress had made clear its determination*: Ellis, *Revolutionary Summer*, 75; J. Adams to GW, Jan. 6, 1776, *PGW*, vol. 3, 37 (*"kind of key"*); GW to J. Trumbull, Sr., Mar. 14, 1776, *PGW*, vol. 3, 471 (*"infinite importance"*); GW to Lord Stirling, Mar. 14, 1776, *PGW*, vol. 3, 470 (*"get that town"*).

304 *By now he had sufficiently scouted*: IMI, vol. 5, 996; C. Lee to GW, Feb. 19, 1776, *PGW*, vol. 3, 339–40 (*"puzzles me"*); Burrows and Wallace, *Gotham*, 4–5; BNY, 5, 76; Kate Diugosz, "Not the Hudson: A Comprehensive Study of the East River," Fordham University, 2011, http://www.eastriverhistory.webs.com/naturalhistory/treacherouswaters.htm; Sanderson, *Mannahatta*, 78 (*six hundred hills*); Mahan, 67–68 (*Brooklyn's high ground*).

305 *Washington still yearned*: GGW, 150; Drake, *Life and Correspondence of Henry Knox*, 28; Knox to GW, June 10, 1776, *PGW*, vol. 4, 491; Ira D. Gruber, "America's First Battle: Long Island, 27 August 1776," in Heller and Stofft, eds., *America's First Battles, 1776–1965*, 2 (*averaged two years*).

305 *"will have to wade"*: GW to Hancock, July 10, 1776, *PGW*, vol. 5, 260; GW to John Augustine Washington, May 31–June 4, 1776, *PGW*, vol. 4, 413 (*"If our cause"*).

305 *"We resolve to raise regiments"*: Carp, *To Starve the Army at Pleasure*, 17; WAI, 304 (*flour*).

305 *Congress had sensibly, if belatedly*: Buel, *In Irons*, 47 (*less than 40 percent*); Bezanson, *Prices and Inflation During the American Revolution*, 322 (*more than double*); Morison and Commager, *The Growth of the American Republic*, vol. 1, 187; Heidler and Heidler, eds., *Daily Lives of Civilians in Wartime Early America*, 50; Jensen, *The Founding of a Nation*, 659; Schlesinger, *The Colonial Merchants and the American Revolution*, 581 (*staves and empty casks*); Kinsman Peverly to Capt. Thomas Peverly, Dec. 28, 1775, *NDAR*, vol. 3, 270; Nuxoll, "Congress and the Munitions Merchants," Ph.D. diss. (New York University, 1979), 72, 134–38; Amherst to Germain, Mar. 16, 1776, *DAR*, vol. 10, 242 (*"warlike stores"*).

306 *Gunpowder, that* unum necessarium: Augur, *The Secret War of Independence*, 60–61, 84–85; Potts, *French Covert Action in the American Revolution*, 31; York, "Clandestine Aid and the American Revolutionary War Effort," *Military Affairs* 43, no. 1 (Feb. 1979): 26+; Josiah Bartlett to "Col. Whipple," Aug. 18, 1776, *AA*, V: 1, 1024 (*five thousand pigs*); Kerr, *Bermuda and the American Revolution*, 46–50 (*waiting boats*).

306 *In a three-week period in the spring*: Reynolds, "Ammunition Supply in Revolutionary Virginia," *VMHB* 73, no. 1 (Jan. 1965): 56+; Robert Parker to New Hampshire Committee of Safety, July 13, 1776, *AA*, V: 1, 266; Samuel Curson, St. Eustatia, to Comfort Sands, July 20, 1776, *AA*, V: 1, 463 (*push down prices*); Van Alstyne, *Empire and Independence*, 85 (*Bilbao*).

306 *four of eight vessels loaded with cargo for France*: two of the four, mistakenly seized by American privateers, were eventually released. Rappleye, *Robert Morris*, 54.

306 *The Dickinson, bulging with flour*: Bayard, Jackson & Co. to Montaudouin Frères, Jan. 18, 1776, and affidavit, John Sands et al., *Dickinson* crew, Apr. 8, 1776, *DAR*, vol. 12, 48 and 107; Nuxoll, "Congress and the Munitions Merchants," Ph.D. diss. (New York University, 1979), 161; "Letter from Bristol," *London Chronicle*, Apr. 13, 1776, *NDAR*, vol. 4, 1032.

306 *Most smugglers got through*: Clark, *Lambert Wickes*, 46–49; Alberts, *The Golden Voyage*, 6–8; Lundin, *Cockpit of the Revolution*, 113; McGrath, *Give Me a Fast Ship*, 80–82; "The Battle of Turtle Gut Inlet," in Donnelly and Diehl, *Pirates of New Jersey*, 105–07.

307 *"The pieces of the vessel was falling"*: Laughton, ed., *Journal of Rear-Admiral Bartholomew James*, 35; log, *Orpheus*, June 28–29, 1776, UK NA, ADM 51/4279 (*Seven British sailors died*); Clark, *Gallant John Barry*, 96–98 (*"two laced hats"*).

307 *Particularly devastating to the British*: Office of Ordnance to Germain, Aug. 20, 1776, UK NA, CO 5/162, f. 259–61, 275, 286; "Affidavit of William Sowerby," Sept. 5, 1776, *DAR*, vol. 12, 221; Clark, *George Washington's Navy*, 144–47 (*£40,000*); Office of Ordnance to Viscount Townshend, Nov. 30, 1775, UK NA, CO 5/161, f. 210; Ward to Hancock, May 17, 1776, and Ward to GW, May 20, 1776, *AA*, IV: 6, 495–96, 532; report, Col. Samuel Cleveland, Royal Artillery, June 6, 1776, UK NA, CO 5/162, f. 259–61; Germain to Viscount Townshend, Aug. 7 and 29, 1776, UK NA, CO 5/162, f. 271, 299 (*furious again*).

307 *Domestic powder production in America*: Charles C. Smith, "The Manufacture of Gunpowder in America," *Proceedings*, MHS, vol. 14 (1875–76): 248+; Reynolds, "Ammunition Supply in Revolutionary Virginia," *VMHB* 73, no. 1 (Jan. 1965): 56+ (*best charcoal*); York, "Clandestine Aid and the American Revolutionary War Effort," *Military Affairs* 43, no. 1 (Feb. 1979): 26+ (*"better supplied"*); Phillips, *1775*, 313; Stephenson, "The Supply of Gunpowder in 1776," *AHR* 30, no. 2 (Jan. 1925): 271+. By one calculation, American mills made more than a third of the powder, if that made with imported saltpeter is counted. Salav, "The Production of Gunpowder in Pennsylvania During the American Revolution," *PMHB* 99, no. 4 (Oct. 1975): 422+.

307 *A midsummer tally of Washington's ordnance*: Ezek. Cheever to GW, July 22, 1776, *AA*, V: 1, 586; J. Adams to Cotton Tufts, June 30, 1776, in *AFC*, vol. 2, 24–25 (*"posterity"*); Puls, *Henry Knox*, 65 (*250 more* and *air furnaces*); Hufeland, *Westchester County During the American Revolution*, 99 (*church bells*); Volo, *Blue Water Patriots*, 141 (*charcoal makers*); Risch, *Supplying Washington's Army*, 359–60 (*"stood proof"*); Soodalter, "Arming the Revolution," *MHQ* 27, no. 2 (Winter 2015): 80+ (*tested in New Jersey*); William Whipple to John Langdon, Nov. 7, 1776, *AA*, V: 3, 554 (*"there is not guns"*).

308 *Making bullets was hard*: Reynolds, "Ammunition Supply in Revolutionary Virginia," *VMHB* 73, no. 1 (Jan. 1965): 56+; Hufeland, *Westchester County During the American Revolution*, 99; *The American Revolution in New York*, 190; Huston, *The Sinews of War*, 45 (*glass cames*); "Certificates and bills relative to the Americans being short of lead [. . .]," 1776, NYHS, 221 Mss. Mis., N.Y.C. Mss., box 12, #11 (*Livingston's houses*).

308 *In warfare, salt was almost*: Kurlansky, *Salt: A World History*, 6, 127; Rick Beard, "The Salt Wars," *Opinionator* (blog), *New York Times*, Dec. 26, 2013, https://opinionator.blogs.nytimes .com/2013/12/26/the-salt-wars/?_r=0; Martin, "American Privateers and the West Indies Trade," *AHR* 39 (July 1934): 700+; Carrington, *The British West Indies During the American Revolution*, 70 (*strangled two-thirds*); Bezanson, *Prices and Inflation During the American Revolution*, 144–47; Risch, *Supplying Washington's Army*, 198–200; Bowman, "The Scarcity of Salt in Virginia During the American Revolution," *VMHB* 77, no. 4 (Oct. 1969): 464+ (*Salt bandits*); Dorson, ed., *America's Rebels: Narratives of the Patriots*, 139 (*"exceedingly scarce"*).

308 *To encourage saltworks along the coast*: Kurlansky, *Salt: A World History*, 221–22; J. Adams to Abigail Adams, Aug. 29, 1777, in *AFC*, vol. 2, 332 (*"Jersey shore"*); *The American Revolution in New York*, 199 (*four dollars a bushel*); Bowman, "The Scarcity of Salt in Virginia During the American Revolution," *VMHB* 77, no. 4 (Oct. 1969): 464+ (*evaporation ponds*); Kerr, *Bermuda and the American Revolution*, 54–55.

308 *For each shortage momentarily slaked*: *The American Revolution in New York*, 184–87 (*spinners* and *public enemies*); Buel, *Dear Liberty*, 83 (*coopers*); Nuxoll, "Congress and the Munitions Merchants," Ph.D. diss. (New York University, 1979), 36 (*durable fabrics*); Leonard, "Paper as a Critical Commodity During the American Revolution," *PMHB* 74, no. 4 (Oct. 1950): 488+.

309 *Washington often complained*: GW to Massachusetts Council, Aug. 29, 1775, *PGW*, vol. 1, 376; May 30, 1776, *Journals of the American Congress*, vol. 1, 360; Risch, *Supplying Washington's Army*, 423; Carp, *To Starve the Army at Pleasure*, 62–63, 67, 109 (*"avaricious"*); general orders, June 18, 1776, *PGW*, vol. 5, 32.

309 *That same Tuesday afternoon*: general orders, Apr. 16, 1776, *PGW*, vol. 4, 74n; Freeman, 110; Wheeler, *Voices of 1776*, 152 (*"Maggie Lauder"*); Drowne, *A Sketch of Fraunces Tavern*, 13–14 (*"glasses broken"*); minutes, New York Provincial Congress, June 20, 1776, *AA*, IV: 6, 1416 (*toasts*).

309 *The final toast was drunk*: Jones, "'The Rage of Tory-Hunting,'" *JMH* 81, no. 3 (July 2017): 719+ (*"guilty of treason"*); *Spirit '76*, 342 (*"being inimical"*); Buel, *Dear Liberty*, 58–59 (*defamed*

Congress); Ranlet, *The New York Loyalists*, 159–60 (*taxed at double*), 141 (*horse got the same*); Brown, *The Good Americans*, 132 (*Blacksmiths*); BNY, 51; McConville, *The King's Three Faces*, 295 (*threw rocks*), 299 (*outlawed prayers*); FYAR, 462 ("*taciturnity*").

310 "*I would have hanged my own brother*": This assertion by Adams was in a 1780 letter intercepted by the British and subsequently published in London. Ryerson, *The Loyalists of America and Their Times*, vol. 2, 127. See also Haight, *Before the Coming of the Loyalists*, 12; Brown, *The Good Americans*, 144; Raphael, *A People's History of the American Revolution*, 191.

310 *Few were hanged*: One study found about fifty executions of loyalists during the war. Crary, *The Price of Loyalty*, 224.

310 *Conformity, censorship, and zealotry*: FYAR, 449–52; McConville, *The King's Three Faces*, 295 (*loyal thoughts*); Breen, *American Insurgents, American Patriots*, 203, 216; Shy, *A People Numerous and Armed*, 237 (*political constabulary*); Luke and Venables, *Long Island in the American Revolution*, 13–15; Onderdonk, *Documents and Letters Intended to Illustrate the Revolutionary Incidents of Queens County*, 42–44; Ranlet, *The New York Loyalists*, 70, 154–55.

310 *Such measures spread*: Jameson, "Equipment of the Militia of the Middle States, 1775–1781," *Journal of the American Military Institute* 3, no. 1 (Spring 1939): 26+ (*Confiscated firelocks*); *The American Revolution in New York*, 211 (*five shillings*); GW to J. Trumbull, Sr., Nov. 15, 1775, PGW, vol. 2, 379 ("*preying upon*"); Phelps, *Newgate of Connecticut*, 26–27, 53; Brown, *The Good Americans*, 141–42; Peters, *General History of Connecticut*, 143; *Connecticut in the American Revolution* (2001): 22, SoC, State Exhibition Series, http://www.societyofthe cincinnati.org/scholarship/publications/; Hoock, *Scars of Independence*, 49; Bob Grigg, "Old Newgate Prison," Colebrook Historical Society (Conn.), n.d., http://colebrookhistorical society.org/OldNewgatePrison.htm (*national penitentiary*); Wayne Lynch, "Tory Stories from the Simsbury Copper Mine," in Todd Andrlik et al., eds., *Journal of the American Revolution*, vol. 1, 78–80 ("*light of the sun*"); Jones, "'The Rage of Tory-Hunting,'" *JMH* 81, no. 3 (July 2017): 719 ("*fetid cesspools*").

311 "*I can tell a Tory*": Lewis Howell to Ebenezer Howell, June 26, 1776, HL, HM 67278; Edmund S. Morgan, "Conflicts and Consensus in the American Revolution," in Kurtz and Hutson, eds., *Essays on the American Revolution*, 291 ("*cut sharply*"); MLA, 191 ("*No man knows*"); Abbott, *New York in the American Revolution*, 182.

311 *Perhaps half a million Americans*: GC, 565; Tiedemann et al., eds., *The Other Loyalists*, 49; Smith, "The American Loyalists: Notes on Their Organization and Numerical Strength," *WMQ*, 3rd ser., 25, no. 2 (Apr. 1968): 259+ (*demonstrated loyalty*); Allen, *Tories*, xvi; Nelson, *The American Tory*, 87 (*belts and pockets*); Taylor, *American Revolutions*, 138 ("*height of my ambition*"); Brown, *The Good Americans*, 45–47, 57–58; Countryman, *A People in Revolution*, 108, 113–17; Hufeland, *Westchester County During the American Revolution*, 86–87 (*Fowler*); Gipson, *American Loyalist: Jared Ingersoll*, 347 ("*saint of old*"). John Adams, on several occasions long after the war, asserted that "about a third of the people of the colonies were against the revolution." Jasanoff, *Liberty's Exiles*, 6, 364–65n.

312 *Loyalists typically abhorred*: Bailyn, *The Ideological Origins of the American Revolution*, 312 ("*fools*"); Brown, *The Good Americans*, 74 ("*three thousand tyrants*"); Bailyn, *Faces of Revolution*, 210 ("*deluded and hysterical*"); Jasanoff, *Liberty's Exiles*, 8–9; Nelson, *The American Tory*, 40, 64, 89–91, 134.

312 *New York would now become the central*: Ranlet, *The New York Loyalists*, 67, 154–55; *The American Revolution in New York*, 216; Hufeland, *Westchester County During the American Revolution*, 95; Gipson, *American Loyalist: Jared Ingersoll*, xv; IMI, vol. 4, 932; Wertenbaker, *Father Knickerbocker Rebels*, 80–81; Peter Eltin to Richard Varick, June 13, 1776, in *New York City During the American Revolution*, 97 ("*Tory rides*").

312 *Two days later, a committee appointed*: "Proceedings in New York in Relation to Disaffected Persons," AA, IV: 6, 1153–83; "Minutes of the Committee," *Proceedings*, NYHS (1924): ix–xii; IMI, vol. 4, 933; Heidler and Heidler, eds., *Daily Lives of Civilians in Wartime Early America*, 36; Burrows and Wallace, *Gotham*, 231; Bliven, *Under the Guns*, 300–01; *The American Revolution in New York*, 213–19; Hufeland, *Westchester County During the American Revolution*, 89–90; Crary, *The Price of Loyalty*, 202 ("*effluvia*").

313 *Counterfeiting was a cottage industry*: Scott, *Counterfeiting in Colonial America*, 5–8; Smoak, "The Weight of Necessity: Counterfeit Coins in the British Atlantic World, circa 1760–1800," *WMQ* 74, no. 3 (July 2017): 467+; Harlow, "Aspects of Revolutionary Finance, 1775–1783," *AHR* 35, no. 1 (Oct. 1929): 46+ (*penalties*).

313 *The proliferation of paper currency*: MQ, 171 (*"shoving"*); Brown, *The Good Americans*, 87–89 (*forged plates*); Scott, *Counterfeiting in Colonial America*, 253, 259–60 (*campaign to depreciate*); *New-York Gazette and the Weekly Mercury*, Apr. 15, 1776, cited in T. A. Schoppel, "The Hickey Plot," master's thesis, Hunter College (1974), NYHS (*"good imitation"*).

313 *Before turning to crime*: Bakeless, *Turncoats, Traitors and Heroes*, 94–97; Scott, *Counterfeiting in Colonial America*, 260–61; *Calendar of Historical Manuscripts Relating to the War of the Revolution*, vol. 1, 295–96; *IMI*, vol. 4, 934–35.

313 *Incarceration in a cellblock*: letter, J. Townsend to father, June 22, 1776, Misc. Mss. Townsend, J., NYHS; *Calendar of Historical Manuscripts Relating to the War of the Revolution*, vol. 1, 295–96, 316, 320, 325; New York Provincial Congress, June 15, 1776, *AA*, IV: 6, 1406, 1410; Bakeless, *Turncoats, Traitors and Heroes*, 101–02.

314 *Arrests soon followed*: "Diary of Ensign Caleb Clap," *Historical Magazine*, 3rd ser., 3, no. 3 (Mar. 1874): 133+ (*"rough men"*); interrogations, *AA*, IV: 6, 1157–58; Nelson, *The American Tory*, 86.

314 *Gunsmith Gilbert Forbes*: unsigned letters, June 24, 1776, *AA*, IV: 6, 1054; GW to Philip Livingston and John Jay, June 29, 1776, *PGW*, vol. 5, 151–52n; Lossing, "Washington's Life Guard," *Historical Magazine* 2, no. 5 (May 1858): 129+; Freeman, 115–19; interrogations, *AA*, IV: 6, 1164 (*acknowledged passing*); letter, J. Townsend to father, June 22, 1776, Misc. Mss. Townsend, J., NYHS (*"uproar"*); Huntington, *Letters Written by Ebenezer Huntington*, 35 (*"designing children"*); "Diary of Ensign Caleb Clap," *Historical Magazine*, 3rd ser., 3, no. 3 (Mar. 1874): 133+ (*cellblocks*); Puls, *Henry Knox*, 52 (*Extra sentries*).

314 *"assassinate the commander-in-chief"*: William Tudor to Delia Jarvis, June 23, 1776, William Tudor Papers, MHS, Ms. N-1684.

314 *It was said that a drummer*: *BNY*, 96; letter, J. Townsend to father, June 22, 1776, Misc. Mss., Townsend, J., NYHS (*nine places*); GW to Philip Livingston and John Jay, June 29, 1776, *PGW*, vol. 5, 151–52n; interrogations, *AA*, IV: 6, 1178, 1411; Freeman, 121 (*northern Manhattan*); *Centennial Notes, New York City, 1876*, NYHS (*"most barbarous"*); Dandridge, *Historic Shepherdstown*, 144 (*"murdering those prisoners"*).

314 *One prisoner aroused particular*: general orders, June 27, 1776, *PGW*, vol. 5, 112–13n; Van Doren, *Secret History of the American Revolution*, 14–15; interrogation, Israel Youngs, June 26, 1776, *Calendar of Historical Manuscripts Relating to the War of the Revolution*, vol. 1, 366; Hickey court-martial, *AA*, IV: 6, 1085; Bliven, *Under the Guns*, 312 (*No. 1 Broadway*).

315 *Four witnesses appeared*: general orders, June 27, 1776, *PGW*, vol. 5, 112–13n.

315 *"hanged by the neck"*: Hickey court-martial, *AA*, IV: 6, 1085; Van Doren, *Secret History of the American Revolution*, 14–15; war council minutes, June 27, 1776, , *AA*, IV: 6, 1109, 1119–20.

315 *"There was a vast concourse"*: Solomon Drowne to William Drowne, July 13, 1776, in *New York City During the Revolution*, 81; *Constitutional Gazette* (N.Y.), June 29, 1776, *PGW*, vol. 5, 130; news item, July 1, 1776, *AA*, IV: 6, 1119–20; Van Doren, *Secret History of the American Revolution*, 14–15 (*released without trial*).

315 *Eighty Continentals "with good arms"*: general orders, June 27, 1776, *PGW*, vol. 5, 112; "Diary of Ensign Caleb Clap," *Historical Magazine*, 3rd ser., 3, no. 3 (Mar. 1874): 133+ (*"cutthroats"*); Ford, ed., *Correspondence and Journals of Samuel Blachley Webb*, vol. 1, 150 (*"more penitent"*); Schwartz, *Daily Life in Johnson's London*, 147–48 (*tug on his feet*); Bakeless, *Turncoats, Traitors and Heroes*, 108 (*"sank down"*).

316 *The body was hardly cold*: general orders, June 28, 1776, *PGW*, vol. 5, 129; Van Doren, *Secret History of the American Revolution*, 14–15 (*"blackened"*).

316 *"We are indeed, sir, surrounded"*: GW to Jabez Huntington, July 15, 1776, author's possession. I am grateful to the Papers of George Washington project at the University of Virginia for sharing this letter, which is not in *PGW*. From the Roger Wolcott autograph collection, provided by MHS.

316 *For several days, British deserters had warned*: IMI, vol. 4, 935; Ford, ed., *Correspondence and Journals of Samuel Blachley Webb*, vol. 1, 151; June 29, 1776, journal entry, KP (*sultry*); Carbone, *Nathanael Greene*, 33 (*striped flags*).

316 *Warning guns barked*: Flexner, *The Young Hamilton*, 100; Callahan, *Henry Knox*, 64 (*"finest fight"*); Drake, *Life and Correspondence of Henry Knox*, 28 (*"scarcely conceive"*).

317 *"As I was upstairs"*: Balch, ed., *Papers Relating Chiefly to the Maryland Line During the Revolutionary War*, 40; Ford, ed., *Correspondence and Journals of Samuel Blachley Webb*, vol. 1, 151 (*"warm and bloody"*); *Centennial Notes, New York City, 1876*, NYHS (*exceeding 130*).

317 *That was General Howe's expectation*: HOB, 291; HH, 15–16; Spring, *With Zeal and with Bayonets Only*, 127; Frederick Mackenzie papers, WLC, box 1, folder 2 (*yellow vane*); Gallagher, *The Battle of Brooklyn, 1776*, 26; Sandy Hook light dimensions, June 22, 1776, Frederick Mackenzie papers, WLC, box 1, folder 2.

317 *Howe had slipped unnoticed*: W. Howe to Germain, July 7, 1776, UK NA, CO 5/93, f. 433; W. Howe to Germain, June 7, 1776, UK NA, CO 5/93, f. 421 (*"earlier removal"*); Urban, *Fusiliers*, 70 (*shortening coats*); HOB, 291 (*"a better sort"*).

317 *Shortages persisted*: W. Howe to Germain, July 7 and Aug. 6, 1776, UK NA, CO 5/93, f. 433 and 461; John Robinson, Treasury, to J. Adams, collector at Milford Haven, and John Robinson to Robert Gordon, Cork commissary, May 2, 1776, "George III Calendar, Sept. 1775–Oct. 1777," RA GEO/MAIN/#2402 (*"quitted Boston"*); John Robinson to W. Howe, May 2, 1776, UK NA, AO 16/10, f. 33; Syrett, *Shipping and the American War*, 202 (*rebel ambushes*).

318 *American schooners captured* Anne: Daughan, *If by Sea*, 77–78; Syrett, "The Disruption of H.M.S. *Flora's* Convoy, 1776," *Mariner's Mirror* 56, no. 4 (1970): 423+; Fortescue, *The War of Independence*, 26; Walcott, *Sir Archibald Campbell of Inverneill*, 9, 21; Clark, *George Washington's Navy*, 154–55, 164; Miller, *Sea of Glory*, 81–82 (Lord Howe).

318 *the rebel armed brig* Andrew Doria: *Oxford's* prize crew was overpowered by the British prisoners, who then unwittingly sailed back into American custody while trying to reach Gov. Dunmore in Virginia. *Crawford* also was briefly recaptured by the Royal Navy before being taken again by a rebel sloop. McGrath, *Give Me a Fast Ship*, 76–78.

318 *Worse yet, the* George *and the* Annabella: J. L. Bell, commentary on "Traditions of the American War of Independence," *B 1775*, July 16–24, 2015; Walcott, *Sir Archibald Campbell of Inverneill*, 13–20; Miller, *Sea of Glory*, 81–82.

318 *Campbell would first spend part*: Robert A. McGeachy, "The American War of Lieutenant Colonel Archibald Campbell," *Early America Review* 5, no. 2 (Summer–Fall 2001), https://www.varsitytutors.com/earlyamerica/early-america-review/volume-5/the-american-war-of-lieutenant-colonel-archibald-campbell; Westminster Abbey website, http://www.westminster-abbey.org/our-history/people/sir-archibald-and-sir-james-campbell; GW to Massachusetts General Court, Sept. 29, 1776, *PGW*, vol. 5, 431n; Syrett, "The Disruption of H.M.S. *Flora's* Convoy, 1776," *Mariner's Mirror* 56, no. 4 (1970): 423+; unsigned letter, Mar. 9, 1777, in *The Detail and Conduct of the American War*, 15 (*"capital blunder"*).

318 *"But I am still of opinion"*: W. Howe to Germain, July 7, 1776, UK NA, CO 5/93, f. 433; Stuart-Wortley, *A Prime Minister and His Son*, 83.

318 *At eight a.m. on Tuesday, July 2*: Tiedemann and Fingerhut, eds., *The Other New York*, 93; Tilley, *The British Navy and the American Revolution*, 84; GGW, 135; Stuart-Wortley, *A Prime Minister and His Son*, 82; Manders, *The Battle of Long Island*, 22.

319 *One by one, the transports swung*: Manders, *The Battle of Long Island*, 22; Tiedemann and Fingerhut, eds., *The Other New York*, 93.

319 *"We are in the most beautiful island"*: Stuart-Wortley, *A Prime Minister and His Son*, 82–83.

319 *"The fleet sailed from Halifax"*: Greene to GW, July 5, 1776, *PGW*, vol. 5, 211–12.

319 *A cascade of orders in Washington's name*: general orders, June 29 and 30, 1776, *PGW*, vol. 5, 142–44, 155.

320 *"We are to oppose 30,000"*: GW to J. Trumbull, Sr., Aug. 7, 1776, *PGW*, vol. 5, 616; Burrows and Wallace, *Gotham*, 227 (*dwindled*); Newark Committee of Correspondence to GW, July 4, 1776, *PGW*, vol. 5, 207 (*"Tories and Negroes"*).

320 *Some American commanders favored*: WC, 84 (*stove black*); GW to Hancock, July 25, 1777, *PGW*, vol. 10, 410–12, FOL ("*amazing advantage*").

320 "*We fear not Tory George*": Albion and Dodson, eds., *Philip Vickers Fithian: Journal, 1775–1776*, 210; GW to Lund Washington, Aug. 19, 1776, *PGW*, vol. 6, 82–83 ("*small step*"); GW to Hancock, Aug. 13, 1776, *PGW*, vol. 6, 4–5 ("*nailed up*").

321 "*The time is now near at hand*": general orders, July 2, 1776, *PGW*, vol. 5, 180.

14. A DOG IN A DANCING SCHOOL

323 "*London of the Low Country*": the town was officially called Charles Town until 1783. Stokeley, *Fort Moultrie, Constant Defender*, 7, 11.

323 *Eight of the ten wealthiest men*: Gordon, *South Carolina and the American Revolution*, 9; Edgar, *Partisans and Redcoats*, xi (*sixfold*); Stokeley, *Fort Moultrie, Constant Defender*, 8 ("*Every tradesman*"); Bridenbaugh, *Cities in Revolt*, 265; Eliza Layne Martin, "Eliza Lucas Pinckney: Indigo in the Atlantic World," n.d., https://cpb-us-e1.wpmucdn.com/sites .ucsc.edu/dist/f/482/files/2017/08/SocialBiog.Martin.pdf; "Old Slave Mart," Charleston, NPS, https://www.nps.gov/places/old-slave-mart.htm. Slave imports had temporarily ceased as part of the colonial nonimportation agreement. Ryan, *The World of Thomas Jeremiah*, 13, 37.

323 *In recent years, rumors of war*: Stokeley, *Fort Moultrie, Constant Defender*, 10; Bridenbaugh, *Cities in Revolt*, 276 (*hair powder*).

323 *Although plagued with malaria*: Harris, *The Hanging of Thomas Jeremiah*, 19 ("*in the spring*"), 7–8 (*Portland stone*); Waring, "Medicine in Charleston at the Time of the Revolution," *JAMA* 236, no. 1 (July 5, 1976): 31+; "The Old Exchange & Provost Dungeon," http://www .oldexchange.org/; Williams, *St. Michael's*, 14, 24, 143–44, 149; author visit, St. Michael's Church, Mar. 14, 2014.

324 *That steeple and a glint*: ECB, 19 (*Charleston Bar*); Gordon, *South Carolina and the American Revolution*, 37; Parker to Admiralty, July 9, 1776, UK NA, CO 5/125, f. 136; Moultrie, *Memoirs of the American Revolution*, vol. 1, 146–47; Willcox, *Portrait of a General*, 86 ("*my friend*"); Montross, *Rag, Tag and Bobtail*, 100; Col. Lachlan McIntosh to GW, Mar. 8, 1776, *PGW*, vol. 3, 439n.

324 *The southern expedition, ill-conceived*: Willcox, *Portrait of a General*, 56, 84 ("*all expectations*"); *TAR*, 26 ("*unhealthy season*"), 28; Parker to Admiralty, May 15, 1776, UK NA, CO 5/125, f. 13 (*battered squadron*); ECB, 9.

325 *As the senior commander, Clinton had*: Mackesy, *The War for America*, 86 (*quick foray*); ECB, 11 ("*imperfect and unfinished*"); Lipscomb, *The Carolina Lowcountry*, 22.

325 *Uncharacteristically tractable*: ECB, 13–14 ("*on shore*"); "Expedition to the Southern Colonies," Narrative of Facts Relative to American Affairs, n.d., UK NA, CO 5/232, f. 379–430; *TAR*, 29–30.

325 *Now, with Charleston sprawled before them*: Parker to Clinton, and Clinton to Parker, both June 2, 1776, *Sandwich*, vol. 2, 131–32 ("*rash and absurd*"); ECB, 14–19; *DAR*, vol. 12, 13 ("*moral certainty*").

326 *On Tuesday afternoon, Commodore Parker*: Parker to Clinton, June 2, 1776, *Sandwich*, vol. 2, 133–34 ("*every assistance*"); "Expedition to the Southern Colonies," Narrative of Facts Relative to American Affairs, n.d., UK NA, CO 5/232, f. 379–430; Lipscomb, *The Carolina Lowcountry*, 26; ECB, 23 ("*seventeen feet, six inches*"), 27.

326 *Neither the commodore nor his officers*: Lipscomb, *The Carolina Lowcountry*, 26; Ryan, *The World of Thomas Jeremiah*, 149; https://en.wikipedia.org/wiki/Battle_of_Sullivan%27s _Island#/media/File:Fort-Sullivan.jpg ("*The Continent*"); *Sandwich*, vol. 2, 134–37 (*local pilots*); ECB, 20–21, 27.

326 "*make such attacks as may be necessary*": ECB, 20.

326 "*My exceeding bad state*": Robson, "The Expedition to the Southern Colonies, 1775–1776," *English Historical Review* 66, no. 261 (Oct. 1951): 535+; Gordon, *South Carolina and the American Revolution*, 39–40; Southern, ed., *Voices of the American Revolution in the Carolinas*, 42 ("*deluded people*"); ECB, 40; Clinton to Parker, June 6, 1776, *Sandwich*, vol. 2, 137.

327 *No British gasconade*: Horry and Weems, *The Life of General Francis Marion*, 37 ("*wilderness of ships*"); ECB, 30 ("*wildest confusion*" and *smelters*); Ryan, *The World of Thomas Jeremiah*, 148; Kepner, ed., "Notes and Documents: A British View of the Siege of Charleston, 1776," *Journal of Southern History* 2, no. 1 (Feb. 1945): 93+ (*discourage deserters*); Cox, *A Proper Sense of Honor*, 19 ("*free white*").

327 *Charleston had long been the most*: Nic Butler, Ph.D., public historian, Charleston County Public Library, presentation to author, Mar. 14, 2014; Nic Butler, "Demilitarizing Urban Charleston, 1783–1789," www.WalledCityTaskForce.org; Drayton, *Memoirs of the American Revolution*, vol. 2, 280–81; Ryan, *The World of Thomas Jeremiah*, 76–80.

327 *Two sand cays a mile and a half*: ECB, 2, 4, 9–10; author visit, Sullivan's Island, Mar. 14, 2014, signage; Gordon, *South Carolina and the American Revolution*, 41–42; Bragg, *Crescent Moon over Carolina*, 79–80; Mahan, 60; Horry and Weems, *The Life of General Francis Marion*, 36–37.

328 *Gorgeous, detailed maps later printed*: Thomas James, *Plan of the Attack on Fort Sulivan* [*sic*], 1776, etching and engraving, Royal Collection, RCIN #734016, and Thomas James, *View of Fort Sullivan*, 1776, etching and engraving, Royal Collection, RCIN #734017.

328 *Though large enough to hold a thousand defenders*: ECB, 9–10, 26; orderly book, June 4–14, 1776, William Moultrie, HL ("*distress them*"); Moultrie, *Memoirs of the American Revolution*, vol. 1, 150–53; McCrady, *The History of South Carolina in the Revolution*, 152; Bragg, *Crescent Moon over Carolina*, 70–71 ("*Old Danger*"); author visit and interview with Doug MacIntyre, Sullivan's Island, Mar. 14, 2014; MacIntyre, "Thomson Park: Revolutionary War Battle Site," https://thomsonpark.wordpress.com/.

328 *Like their two colonels*: Gordon, *South Carolina and the American Revolution*, 13, 31–32; Alden, *The South in the Revolution*, 200–01; Edgar, *Partisans and Redcoats*, 12–13, 30–33; Shy, *A People Numerous and Armed*, 36–37; Shy, "A New Look at Colonial Militia," *WMQ*, 3rd ser., 20, no. 2 (Apr. 1963): 175+ (*slave revolts*); WAI, 4 (*church on Sunday*); Wood, *Black Majority*, 308, 325 (*one white*); Piecuch, *Three Peoples, One King*, 18 (*outnumbered whites*).

329 *British encouragement of slave defections*: Harris, *The Hanging of Thomas Jeremiah*, 87–89, 100–02; Rakove, *Revolutionaries*, 198 (*ten thousand plantation slaves*); Piecuch, *Three Peoples, One King*, 79 ("*hellish plots*").

329 *"We cannot be too watchful"*: Almon, ed., *The Remembrancer*, vol. 1, 156; Raphael, *Founders*, 217–18 ("*forward fellow*"); W. Campbell to Dartmouth, Aug. 31, 1775, *DAR*, vol. 11, 95–96 ("*man was murdered*").

329 *The second incident had occurred*: Piecuch, *Three Peoples, One King*, 82–83; Piecuch, "Preventing Slave Insurrection in South Carolina and Georgia, 1775–1776," *JAR*, Feb. 21, 2017; W. Campbell to Dartmouth, Aug. 31, 1775, *DAR*, vol. 11, 95–96 ("*benefit of clergy*").

329 *On Saturday, June 8*: ECB, 33; Ferling, *Almost a Miracle*, 128; Hancock to GW, *PGW*, vol. 3, 417n; Hancock to GW, *PGW*, vol. 3, 417n (*Southern Department*); GW to John Augustine Washington, Mar. 31, 1776, *PGW*, vol. 3, 570 ("*first officer*").

330 *No more flamboyant figure*: Mazzagetti, *Charles Lee*, 58; Patterson, *Knight Errant of Liberty*, 55, 77, 83; Eckenrode, *The Revolution in Virginia*, 90; Fiske, *Essays, Historical and Literary*, vol. 1, 68; McBurney, *Kidnapping the Enemy*, 3 ("*His nose*"); McDonald, *The McDonald Papers*, part 1, 65 (*Rag, Tag*); Ferling, *Almost a Miracle*, 46 ("*doggism*"); J. Adams to James Warren, July 24, 1775, *AP* ("*queer creature*"); C. Lee to J. Adams, Oct. 5, 1775, *AP* ("*panegyric*").

330 *He could be a lively if garrulous*: John W. Shy, "Charles Lee: The Soldier as Radical," in *GWGO*, 25; Anderson, *Crucible of War*, 247–48 ("*bib and bells*"); BNY, 41 (*Thucydides*); Van Tyne, *The War of Independence: American Phase*, 236 ("*learned, judicious*" and "*opens graves*"); FYAR, 283–84 (*restless, impulsive*); Fiske, *Essays, Historical and Literary*, vol. 1, 64 ("*free thinker*"); Moore, *The Treason of Charles Lee*, 18 ("*insolent servant*"); Royster, *A Revolutionary People at War*, 42 (*prejudices*); C. Lee to B. Rush, Sept. 19, 1775, *LP*, vol. 1, 207 ("*strongest proof*"); C. Lee to Sidney Lee (sister), June 18, 1756, *LP*, vol. 1, 4 ("*Boiling Water*"); LAR, 35 ("*Liberty Boy*"); July 5, 1775, journal entry, KP ("*Rebel Lee*"); McBurney, *Kidnapping the Enemy*, 4 ("*Mad Lee*"); Patterson, *Knight Errant of Liberty*, 124 ("*querulous clown*"); Griffith,

The War for American Independence, 182 (*"upstart hero"*); *GGW*, 110 (*"Naso"*); *Evacuation*, 147–48 (*"his apostasy"*).

331 *That such a boiling, rebellious, beaky*: C. Lee to Sidney Lee, June 18 and Sept. 16, 1758, Mar. 27, 1771, Mar. 28, 1772, *LP*, vol. 1, 4–5, 11–14, 84–86, 99, 110; John W. Shy, "Charles Lee: The Soldier as Radical," in *GWGO*, 23–25; Papas, *Renegade Revolutionary*, 25, 29, 36–40, 59, 73; Patterson, *Knight Errant of Liberty*, 83; Mazzagetti, *Charles Lee*, 41–43.

331 *Bouncing about, in late 1773*: Papas, *Renegade Revolutionary*, 99–100 (*"last asylum"*); *WAI*, 47 (*Locke*).

331 *"sat his horse as if"*: The description is by Mercy Otis Warren. *BTP*, 58; *WR*, 278 (*redans*, *redoubts*).

331 *"the greatest military characters"*: Papas, *Renegade Revolutionary*, 103.

331 *He built a literary name*: *BNY*, 42–43; John W. Shy, "Charles Lee: The Soldier as Radical," in *GWGO*, 33–34; Papas, *Renegade Revolutionary*, 101–02; C. Lee to Benjamin Rush, Aug. 22, 1775, and Feb. 16, 1776, BC, Bft., vol. 343, 19, 23–25 (*"beheaded"*); Nelson, "Citizen Soldiers or Regulars," *Military Affairs* 43, no. 3 (Oct. 1979): 126+ (*"democratical"*); Fiske, *Essays, Historical and Literary*, vol. 1, 69–72, 78; Patterson, *Knight Errant of Liberty*, 81.

331 *His tactical and engineering experience*: John W. Shy, "Charles Lee: The Soldier as Radical," in *GWGO*, 28 (*"genius"*); Ellis, *His Excellency: George Washington*, 80–81 (*"my dear general"*); "Letter of Harry Farrington Gardner, 1775," *Colonial Society of Massachusetts Publications*, vol. 26 (1927): 292–95 (*"happy to get a shot"*); instructions to C. Lee, Jan. 8, 1776, *PGW*, vol. 3, 53 (*"best posture"*); C. Lee to GW, Feb. 5, 1776, *LP*, vol. 1, 271 (*"ridiculous figure"*); William Palfrey to C. Lee, May 1776, *LP*, vol. 1, 475 (*wine cellar*); C. Lee to GW, Mar. 3, 1776, *PGW*, vol. 3, 404 (*"think in French"*).

332 *South he skittered*: C. Lee to Richard Henry Lee, Dec. 12, 1775, *LP*, vol. 1, 229 (*"every governor"*); C. Lee to Robert Morris, Jan. 23, 1776, *LP*, vol. 1, 255 (*"Are we at war"*); Jones, *History of New York During the Revolutionary War*, vol. 1, 83 (*"Chain twenty"*); Papas, *Renegade Revolutionary*, 160–63; *GCL*, 115; Eckenrode, *The Revolution in Virginia*, 90; C. Lee to Virginia Committee of Safety, Apr. 8 and 11, 1776, *LP*, vol. 1, 393 (*"hostages"*), 411; C. Lee to Edmund Pendleton, May 4, 1776, and reply, May 5, 1776, *LP*, vol. 1, 468–70 (*"in hopes of intimidating"*); Selby, *The Revolution in Virginia*, 93 (*"regular mode"*).

332 *"I am like a dog"*: C. Lee to GW, Apr. 5, 1776, *PGW*, vol. 4, 42–44.

333 *Now he was squinting at those canvas wings*: Papas, *Renegade Revolutionary*, 161, 167.

333 *To save the town, the colony*: McCrady, *The History of South Carolina in the Revolution*, 149–52; *ECB*, 33; *LP*, vol. 2, 70 (*blue sash* and *sentries*), 119 (*aides-de-camp*); Moultrie, *Memoirs of the American Revolution*, vol. 1, 150–51; Stokeley, *Fort Moultrie, Constant Defender*, 18 (*"bad engineer"*).

333 *He reinforced fortifications behind Sullivan's Island*: C. Lee to W. Moultrie and W. Thomson, June 21, 1776, *LP*, vol. 2, 77–79 (*"childish, vicious"*); Moultrie, *Memoirs of the American Revolution*, vol. 1, 158–59 (*"eternal rule"*); *ECB*, 34 (*"damned fool"*).

333 *His demand that white men*: John W. Shy, "Charles Lee: The Soldier as Radical," in *GWGO*, 31; Charles C. Pinckney to mother, June 15, 1776, in Gibbes, *Documentary History of the American Revolution*, 3–4 (*"ten thousand oddities"*); *ECB*, 6–7, 36 (*"slaughter pen"*); C. Lee to J. Rutledge, June 22, 1776, *LP*, vol. 2, 79–82 (*"I never could"*); Stokeley, *Fort Moultrie, Constant Defender*, 19; Fisk, *Anniversary of the Battle at Fort Moultrie*, 9 (*"knock it down"*); Moultrie, *Memoirs of the American Revolution*, vol. 1, 162–63 (*"too easy in command"*).

333 *"General Lee wishes you to evacuate"*: Lipscomb, *The Carolina Lowcountry*, 24; C. Lee to W. Moultrie and W. Thomson, June 21, 1776, *LP*, vol. 2, 77–79 (*"didacktick"*); John W. Shy, "Charles Lee: The Soldier as Radical," in *GWGO*, 31 (*"His coming"*).

334 *If the Americans faced mortal peril*: *TAR*, 377; *NDAR*, vol. 5, 433; *ECB*, 23, 45; log, *Active*, June 7, 1776, *NDAR*, vol. 5, 420 (*Eighty pigs*).

334 *As Parker struggled with his ships*: Stokeley, *Fort Moultrie, Constant Defender*, 18; *TAR*, 30–31 (*"passable on foot"*); *ECB*, 47–48; William Falconer to Anthony Falconer, July 13, 1776, *LP*, vol. 2, 194–95 (*"nothing that grows"*); MacIntyre, "Thomson Park: Revolutionary War Battle

Site," https://thomsonpark.wordpress.com/ (*alligator*); Frey, *The British Soldier in America*, 33 (*"salt pork"*).

334 *And then, calamity*: McCrady, *The History of South Carolina in the Revolution*, 153; Murray, *Letters from America*, 25 (*"infernal ford"*); NDAR, vol. 5, 607–09; TAR, 31n (*"bogs"* and *"wet and miry"*).

335 *"unspeakable mortification and disappointment"*: TAR, 30–31; "Expedition to the Southern Colonies," Narrative of Facts Relative to American Affairs, n.d., UK NA, CO 5/232, f. 379–430; Parker to Clinton, June 20, 1776, *Sandwich*, vol. 2, 139–40; TAR, 30–31 (*"entrenchment"*); Clinton to Brig. Gen. John Vaughan, June 18, 1776, NDAR, vol. 5, 609 (*"Time is precious"*); MacIntyre, "Thomson Park: Revolutionary War Battle Site," https://thomsonpark.wordpress .com/.

335 *If astonished and dismayed by this*: TAR, 33; ECB, 75; Stokeley, *Fort Moultrie, Constant Defender*, 19–21 (*broiling sun*); MacIntyre, "Thomson Park: Revolutionary War Battle Site," https://thomsonpark.wordpress.com/ (*"spiders"*).

335 *Confusion between the army and navy*: TAR, 33 (*signals*); Parker to Clinton, June 22, 1776, NDAR, vol. 5, 689 (*"by the hand"*); "Expedition to the Southern Colonies," Narrative of Facts Relative to American Affairs, n.d., UK NA, CO 5/232, f. 379–430; James, *The British Navy in Adversity*, 43.

336 *"I am not master of the extent"*: Parker to Clinton, June 25, 1776, NDAR, vol. 5, 745–47; Robson, "The Expedition to the Southern Colonies, 1775–1776," *English Historical Review* 66, no. 261 (Oct. 1951): 535+; ECB, 2 (*"entrenching themselves"*).

336 *Rumors circulated*: Gibbes, *Documentary History of the American Revolution*, 12; MacIntyre, "Thomson Park: Revolutionary War Battle Site," https://thomsonpark.wordpress.com/ (*"longer we are kept"*).

336 *On Friday morning, June 28*: "A Return of the Troops in Fort Moultrie," in Gibbes, *Documentary History of the American Revolution*, 5; Bragg, *Crescent Moon over Carolina*, 70–71, 77; Moultrie, *Memoirs of the American Revolution*, vol. 1, 163–65. Moultrie was unaware that Lee intended to replace him as garrison commander that day. ECB, 84.

336 *As his horse trotted up*: Moultrie, *Memoirs of the American Revolution*, vol. 1, 173–81.

337 *The bomb ketch* Thunder: Lipscomb, *The Carolina Lowcountry*, 27–28 (*turkey*); ECB, 77–79 (*opened her seams*).

337 *Under Commodore Parker's battle plan*: NDAR, vol. 5, 784, 797; TAR, 35n; Moultrie, *Memoirs of the American Revolution*, vol. 1, 174–81; ECB, 75–76.

337 *"The fleet was an eternal sheet"*: Murray, *Letters from America*, 26–27; Mahan, 61–62; Drayton, *Memoirs of the American Revolution*, vol. 2, 293–94 (*handspike*); ECB, 81–83, 87; Stokeley, *Fort Moultrie, Constant Defender*, 22–23; Jones, *Sergeant William Jasper*, 21 (*"Revenge"*).

338 *General Lee had spent the morning*: ECB, 84; Montross, *Rag, Tag and Bobtail*, 102; C. Lee to GW, July 1, 1776, LP, vol. 2, 101 (*"most furious"*); C. Lee to Moultrie, June 28, 1776, LP, vol. 2, 91 (*"spike your guns"*).

338 *"The fort fired very brisk"*: journal, *Bristol*, NDAR, vol. 5, 797; Moultrie, *Memoirs of the American Revolution*, vol. 1, 174–78 (*"Mind the commodore"*).

338 *Gray gun smoke draped*: ECB, 87.

338 *General Clinton soon recognized*: ECB, 88–89 (Lady Williams).

339 *"Every ball took fatal effect"*: MacIntyre, "Thomson Park: Revolutionary War Battle Site," https://thomsonpark.wordpress.com/; Lipscomb, *The Carolina Lowcountry*, 39; Gordon, *South Carolina and the American Revolution*, 43; Murray, *Letters from America, 1773–1780*, 28 (*"impossible to conceive"*); Stokeley, *Fort Moultrie, Constant Defender*, 23 (*"taught the enemy"*).

339 *The unstitching of the British assault*: "Expedition to the Southern Colonies," Narrative of Facts Relative to American Affairs, n.d., UK NA, CO 5/232, f. 379–430; journal, *Syren*, June 28, 1776, NDAR, vol. 5, 799; Lipscomb, *The Carolina Lowcountry*, 35–36 (*"fantastic scoundrels"*).

339 *"The Yankees have done fighting"*: ECB, 81.

339 *Sergeant William Jasper cut the blue flag*: Lipscomb, *The Carolina Lowcountry*, 32; Jones, *Sergeant William Jasper*, 19; Bragg, *Crescent Moon over Carolina*, 77; Fisk, *Anniversary of the Battle at Fort Moultrie*, 7 (*"Fire at the commodore!"*); journal, *Bristol*, June 28, 1776, *NDAR*, vol. 5, 797 (*"raked us"*); letter from unnamed surgeon, July 9, 1776, *NDAR*, vol. 5, 1002 (*"Twice the quarterdeck"*).

340 *"I see you are doing very well"*: ECB, 84–85; C. Lee to GW, July 1, 1776, *LP*, vol. 2, 102 (*"like Romans"*); Moultrie, *Memoirs of the American Revolution*, vol. 1, 167 (*"do mischief"*).

340 *"by far the grandest sight"*: Robson, "The Expedition to the Southern Colonies, 1775–1776," *English Historical Review* 66, no. 261 (Oct. 1951): 535+; Volo, *Blue Water Patriots*, 69. Other estimates put the number of British rounds at 12,000. Bragg, *Crescent Moon over Carolina*, 78. Some accounts also put the British powder expenditure at 16 or 17 tons. Stokeley, *Fort Moultrie, Constant Defender*, 26–27; Potts, *French Covert Action in the American Revolution*, 32.

340 *compared to 960 shot*: Bragg, *Crescent Moon over Carolina*, 78; ECB, 96 (4,766 pounds); Lipscomb, *The Carolina Lowcountry*, 33; journal, *Experiment*, July 2–4, 1776, *NDAR*, vol. 5, 929 (*"shot to pieces"*); Parker to Admiralty, July 9, 1776, UK NA, CO 5/125, f. 136 (*lost his arm*).

340 *Bristol, struck seventy times*: ECB, 93; Gibbes, *Documentary History of the American Revolution*, 11; letter from unnamed surgeon, July 9, 1776, *NDAR*, vol. 5, 1002; Parker to Admiralty, July 9, 1776, UK NA, CO 5/125, f. 136; unnamed officer on *Bristol*, July 7, 1776, printed in the *London Chronicle*, Aug. 29, 1776, *NDAR*, vol. 5, 966 (*"shattered condition"*); Mahan, 62 (*"get rid of me"*); C. Lee to Hancock, July 2, 1776, *LP*, vol. 2, 111 (*blew away his britches*).

341 *Governor Campbell, who volunteered to fight*: Harris, *The Hanging of Thomas Jeremiah*, 54–55; Lipscomb, *The Carolina Lowcountry*, 33; Ralfe, *The Naval Biography of Great Britain*, vol. 1, 1 (*"providence of God"*).

341 *At nine p.m., with June's long light fading*: Parker to Admiralty, July 9, 1776, *NDAR*, vol. 5, 998; Charles C. Pinckney to mother, June 29, 1776, Gibbes, *Documentary History of the American Revolution*, 7–9.

341 *Watching this humiliation*: Gibbes, *Documentary History of the American Revolution*, 17; Lipscomb, *The Carolina Lowcountry*, 36 (*palmetto*).

341 *"We never had such a drubbing"*: Clowes, *The Royal Navy*, vol. 3, 379. *Active* and *Solebay* suffered fifteen casualties between them. Casualties to Clinton's force and the rest of the squadron are unknown. *TAR*, 377–79.

341 *"Numbers die daily"*: William Falconer to Anthony Falconer, July 13, 1776, *LP*, vol. 2, 194–95; *LAR*, 324–25 (*"greatly disheartened"*).

341 *For the Americans, losses*: orderly book, June 28 and 30, 1776, William Moultrie, HL (*slave boy* and *Antiguan rum*); GCL, 128 (*"crows"*); B. Rush to C. Lee, July 23, 1776, *LP*, vol. 2, 161 (*"clever things"*); Lipscomb, *The Carolina Lowcountry*, 39 (*"Glorious news"*); DAR, vol. 12, 14; *Constitutional Gazette*, Aug. 7, 1776, *NDAR*, vol. 6, 42 (*"honor in the breach"*).

342 *"we are never in so great danger"*: ECB, 100; C. Lee to Clinton, July 3, 1776, *LP*, vol. 2, 121, 155 (*"not easily procured"*); GCL, 129–30 (*"Polish majesty"*).

342 *"the dilatoriness and stupidity"*: C. Lee to GW, July 1, 1776, *PGW*, vol. 5, 170; Robson, "The Expedition to the Southern Colonies, 1775–1776," *English Historical Review* 66, no. 261 (Oct. 1951): 535+ (*"long train"* and *"fatal source"*).

342 *"This will not be believed"*: Lipscomb, *The Carolina Lowcountry*, 36; Parker to Admiralty, July 9, 1776, UK NA, CO 5/125, f. 136 (*"If the troops"*); *TAR*, 377.

343 *Clinton's version went on*: Clinton to Germain, July 8, 1776, UK NA, CO 5/93, f. 947; Hibbert, *Redcoats and Rebels*, 109; Willcox, *Portrait of a General*, 91; George to Sandwich, Aug. 21, 1776, *Sandwich*, vol. 1, 44 (*"dishonorable"*).

343 *Ever willing to castigate others*: *TAR*, xxii, 36–37; Willcox, *Portrait of a General*, 92; J. Jervis to Clinton, Sept. 16, 1776, in Marie Martel Hatch, ed., "Letters of Captain Sir John Jervis to Sir Henry Clinton, 1774–1782," *American Neptune* 7 (Apr. 1947): 87+.

343 *"lose no time in conveying the troops"*: *TAR*, 37; *LAR*, 340–41 (*"scurvy"*); ECB, 106–07 (*burned the boat*).

343 *"In what a chaos"*: Robson, "The Expedition to the Southern Colonies, 1775–1776," *English Historical Review* 66, no. 261 (Oct. 1951): 535+; James, *The Rise and Fall of the British Empire*, 112 *("chicane")*; Murray, *Letters from America*, 23 *("degrade")*.

344 *In the first episode, disaffected Cherokee*: Piecuch, *Three Peoples, One King*, 28, 68–73; Nash, *The Unknown American Revolution*, 257–59; Karim M. Tiro, "Ambivalent Allies: Strategy and the Native Americans," in Stoker et al., eds., *Strategy in the American War of Independence*, 120–26; Ryan, *The World of Thomas Jeremiah*, 154 *("burnt down")*; Colin G. Calloway, "Declaring Independence and Rebuilding a Nation: Dragging Canoe and the Chickamauga Revolution," in Young et al., eds., *Revolutionary Founders*, 187–91 *("slave and property")*; Calloway, *The American Revolution in Indian Country*, 9, 43, 190–201 *(five million acres)*; John Stuart to Germain, Oct. 26, 1776, *DAR*, vol. 12, 239–42; Edgar, *Partisans and Redcoats*, 36–37.

344 *The second incident occurred*: Wertenbaker, *Norfolk: Historic Southern Port*, 65–66; Fenn, *Pox Americana*, 58 *(grave mounds)*; Pybus, "Jefferson's Faulty Math: The Question of Slave Defections in the American Revolution," *WMQ*, 3rd ser. 62, no. 2 (Apr. 2005): 243+; Selby, *The Revolution in Virginia*, 85, 105; Moomaw, "The British Leave Colonial Virginia," *VMHB* 66, no. 2 (Apr. 1958): 147+.

345 *Gwynn's Island spread for two thousand*: NCCH, 194–95, 205, 225; Cecere, "Battle of Gwynn's Island: Lord Dunmore's Last Stand in Virginia," *JAR*, May 26, 2016; examination of James Cunningham, bookkeeper, *Dolphin* brig, July 18, 1776, *NDAR*, vol. 5, 1135; Schama, *Rough Crossings*, 86–87; Fenn, *Pox Americana*, 59; R. H. Lee to C. Lee, July 6, 1776, *LP*, vol. 2, 124 *("caterpillar-like")*.

345 *At eight a.m. on Tuesday, July 9*: "Particular Account of the Attack and Rout of Lord Dunmore," *AA*, V: 1, 150–51; Selby, *The Revolution in Virginia*, 124; Eckenrode, *The Revolution in Virginia*, 95; *Virginia Gazette*, July 19, 1776, *NDAR*, vol. 5, 1147 *("I should come")*; *AA*, V: 1, 150–51; "Extract of a Letter Dated Williamsburgh [*sic*], Virginia, July 13, 1776," *AA*, V: 1, 151–52; Cecere, "Battle of Gwynn's Island: Lord Dunmore's Last Stand in Virginia," *JAR*, May 26, 2016; Moomaw, "The British Leave Colonial Virginia," *VMHB* 66, no. 2 (Apr. 1958): 147+; Wertenbaker, *Norfolk: Historic Southern Port*, 67 *("shirtmen are coming")*; NCCH, 237 *("distress and confusion")*.

345 *Three hundred rebels crossed*: Powell, ed., *A Biographical Sketch of Col. Leven Powell*, 36; *Virginia Gazette*, July 19, 1776, *NDAR*, vol. 5, 1147; Fenn, *Pox Americana*, 60; Frey, "Between Slavery and Freedom: Virginia Blacks in the American Revolution," *Journal of Southern History* 49, no. 3 (Aug. 1983): 375+ *(found sucking)*; "Particular Account of the Attack and Rout of Lord Dunmore," *AA*, V: 1, 150–51 *("corporal's guard")*; Taylor, *The Internal Enemy*, 26–27; Egerton, *Death or Liberty*, 72; Cecere, "Battle of Gwynn's Island: Lord Dunmore's Last Stand in Virginia," *JAR*, May 26, 2016; Posey, *General Thomas Posey*, 32–33.

346 *"We landed, did what mischief"*: Dunmore to Germain, July 31, 1776, *DAR*, vol. 10; Wertenbaker, *Norfolk: Historic Southern Port*, 67; "List of Ships in Lord Dunmore's Fleet, July 10, 1776," *AA*, V: 1, 152–53; Gilbert, *Black Patriots and Loyalists*, 25 *("poisoned")*.

346 *In early August, Dunmore divided*: A. S. Hamond to Hans Stanley, Aug. 5, 1776, *NDAR*, vol. 6, part 1, 66–70; NCCH, 239–48.

346 *Of the fifteen hundred runaway*: Pybus, "Jefferson's Faulty Math: The Question of Slave Defections in the American Revolution," *WMQ*, 3rd ser., 62, no. 2 (Apr. 2005): 243+; Frey, "Between Slavery and Freedom: Virginia Blacks in the American Revolution," *Journal of Southern History* 49, no. 3 (Aug. 1983): 375+; Copeland, "Lord Dunmore's Ethiopian Regiment," *Military Collector & Historian* 58, no. 4 (Winter 2006): 208+.

346 *Little had come of the Crown's adventurism*: Even in mid-September 1776, no Royal Navy ships blockaded either the Delaware or Chesapeake Bay. Syrett, *Admiral Lord Howe*, 62; Baugh, "The Politics of British Naval Failure, 1775–1777," *American Neptune* 52, no. 4 (Fall 1992): 221+; Alden, *The South in the Revolution*, 206; Harrell, *Loyalism in Virginia*, 62, 65; Cecere, "Battle of Gwynn's Island: Lord Dunmore's Last Stand in Virginia," *JAR*, May 26, 2016.

347 *"Our whole exploits"*: A. S. Hamond to Hans Stanley, Aug. 5, 1776, *NDAR*, vol. 6, part 1, 66–70.

15. A FIGHT AMONG WOLVES

348 *The fateful news traveled*: In the early 1770s, coach travel on the post road between New York and Philadelphia took a day and a half. John P. Snyder, "The Mapping of New Jersey in the American Revolution," New Jersey Historical Commission (1975), 10.

348 *In his orders that morning*: general orders, July 9, 1776, *PGW*, vol. 5, 245–46.

348 *A uniformed aide spurred his horse forward*: *GGW*, 136; Bliven, *Under the Guns*, 345–49.

348 *On and on it went*: Declaration Resources Project, Harvard University, https://declaration .fas.harvard.edu/faq/how-many-grievances-are-declaration-independence. Pauline Maier counted nineteen charges against the king. *American Scripture*, 146–47.

349 *Congress had pruned the original draft*: Maier, *American Scripture*, 143; McDougall, *Freedom Just Around the Corner*, 245; Bailyn, *To Begin the World Anew*, 43 (*"happy talent"*); Ferling, *Independence*, 309; Boudreau, *Independence: A Guide to Historic Philadelphia*, 171–73, 185; Jefferson to H. Lee, May 8, 1825, in *Spirit '76*, 315 (*"American mind"*).

349 *Just so, despite what he considered*: Maier, *American Scripture*, 149 (*"mutilations"*), 48–49 (*ninety or more*); McCullough, *John Adams*, 87, 131; Meacham, *Thomas Jefferson: The Art of Power*, 105 (*horseflies*); *MLA*, 114; Bailyn, *Faces of Revolution*, 102 (*benefit the many*); "Thomas Jefferson, a Brief Biography," https://www.monticello.org/site/jefferson/thomas-jefferson -brief-biography; Freehling, "The Founding Fathers and Slavery," *AHR* 77, no. 1 (Feb. 1972): 81+; Edmund S. Morgan, "Conflict and Consensus in the American Revolution," in Kurtz and Huston, eds., *Essays on the American Revolution*, 307 (*"creed"*).

349 *Loud cheers washed over the Common*: Bliven, *Under the Guns*, 353; *IMI*, vol. 1, 940; Thayer, *Nathaniel Greene*, 93 (*"Rubicon"*).

350 *Scores of soldiers and civilians*: Wertenbaker, *Father Knickerbocker Rebels*, 84; *BNY*, 102; Drowne, *A Sketch of Fraunces Tavern*, 10 (*"ye dust"*); Scull, ed., "The Montresor Journals," *Collections*, NYHS (1881): 123; *GGW*, 136; Bangs, *Journal of Lieutenant Isaac Bangs*, 57 (*gold leaf*); Albion and Dodson, eds., *Philip Vickers Fithian: Journal, 1775–1776*, 190 (*"Rogue's March"*); Burrows and Wallace, *Gotham*, 232.

350 *"O, how fallen!"*: *Paradise Lost*, book 1, line 84; *New York Packet*, July 11, 1776, in *Centennial Notes, New York City, 1876*; Wertenbaker, *Father Knickerbocker Rebels*, 85.

350 *The head would be recovered*: Scull, ed., "The Montresor Journals," *Collections*, NYHS (1881): 123 (*"ungrateful"*); *C 1776*, 59; Bob Ruppert, "The Statue of George III," *JAR*, Sept. 8, 2014; Bangs, *Journal of Lieutenant Isaac Bangs*, 57 (*"emanations"*). More than two centuries later, analysis showed that some musket balls found on the Monmouth battlefield matched the chemical signature of the toppled statue. Dunlap, "Long-Toppled Statue of King George III to Ride Again," *New York Times*, Oct. 22, 2016, A16.

350 *Exuberant demonstrations erupted*: Kranish, *Flight from Monticello*, 90; *AA*, V: 1, 882 (*Savannah*); O'Shaughnessy, "'If Others Will Not Be Active, I Must Drive': George III and the American Revolution," *Early American Studies* 2, no. 1 (Spring 2004): 20 (*mock trials*); Onderdonk, *Revolutionary Incidents of Suffolk and Kings Counties*, 30 (*wooden crown*); *Delaware in the American Revolution* (2002): 7, SoC, State Exhibition Series, https://www .societyofthecincinnati.org/scholarship/publications/ (*"shadow"*); *MLA*, 27–28; McConville, *The King's Three Faces*, 311 (*tavern signs*); *Personal Recollections of Captain Enoch Anderson*, 20 (*"baubles"*); Abigail Adams to J. Adams, July 21, 1776, in *AFC*, vol. 2, 56 (*"joyful"*).

351 *General Howe had an answer*: Lydenberg, 491; Koke, 115+; journal, *Phoenix*, July 12, 1776, *NDAR*, vol. 5, 1037; *C 1776*, 268 (*"balls and bullets"*); Bangs, *Journal of Lieutenant Isaac Bangs*, 59–60 (*tents*); GW to New York Convention, Aug. 17, 1776, *PGW*, vol. 6, 54 (*"shrieks"*).

351 *American gunners returned fire*: Michael Cohn, "Fortification of New York During the Revolutionary War, 1776–1782," New York City Archeological Group (1962); journals, *Phoenix, Rose, Eagle*, July 12, 1776, *NDAR*, vol. 5, 1037–38; Bangs, *Journal of Lieutenant Isaac Bangs*, 59–60; Koke, 115+; Crawford, ed., *The Autobiography of a Yankee Mariner*, 100 (*"imprudence"*); Drake, *Life and Correspondence of Henry Knox*, 28–29 (*"of service"*).

351 *By four-thirty p.m., the ships*: *Sandwich*, vol. 2, 151 (*pinnace*); H. Knox to Lucy, July 15, 1776, in *RWLLLHK*, 43 (*"rained balls"*).

352 *In fact, the enemy had breezed*: Koke, 115+.

352 *William Howe had moved*: Morris, *Morris's Memorial History of Staten Island, New York*, vol. 1, 207–10; Lossing, *The Pictorial Field-Book of the Revolution*, vol. 2, 800n; Mackesy, *The War for America*, 75–76 (*expeditionary army*).

352 *Until those reinforcements arrived*: Germain to W. Howe, May 3, 1776, Papers of Lord George Sackville Germain, WLC (*"your force"*); Germain to W. Howe, Mar. 28, 1776, *DAR*, vol. 12, 95–96 (*"month of May"*); W. Howe to Germain, June 8, 1776, *DAR*, vol. 10, 313 (*"I am amazed"*).

352 *Howe's army would eventually include*: memo to Pownall, Jan. 6, 1776, UK NA, CO 5/162, f. 4–9 (*"auxiliaries"*); Atwood, *The Hessians*, 51 (*nine thousand*); Jeffrey Amherst, ordnance office, to Germain, Jan. 20, 1776, UK NA, CO 5/162, f. 27–29 (*artillery train*); Syrett, *Shipping and the American War*, appendix A, 249; Syrett, *Shipping and Military Power in the Seven Years War*, 32; Robson, *The American Revolution*, 103 (*eight of forty*); *Logistics*, 108, 140–41, 147 (*storeships*).

354 *Seven major contractors*: supply contracts, Apr. 2, 1776, "George III Calendar, Sept. 1775–Oct. 1777," RA GEO/MAIN/#2383. During the war, the British commissary with the main army fed, on average, 35,000 men approximately 37 tons of food daily. *Logistics*, 30.

354 *The government hoped that after the 1776 campaign*: John Robinson to W. Howe, June 24, 1776, "Calendar of Manuscripts in the Royal Institution" [Carleton Papers], *Report on American Manuscripts*, vol. 1, 46 (*"America itself"*); Howe's expenses, Apr. 1 through June 30, 1776, UK NA, T 64/108, f. 64 (*£10,000*); requisitions and cash shipments through June 1776, "George III Calendar, Sept. 1775–Oct. 1777," RA GEO/MAIN/#2396 (*£560,000*); Wright, "Some Notes on the Continental Army," *WMQ*, 2nd ser., 11, no. 2 (Apr. 1931): 81+ (*enormous stocks of bread*); John Robinson, Treasury, to Robert Gordon, commissary general at Cork, July 25, 1776, UK NA, AO 16/10, f. 49 (*moldy*); Robert Gordon to John Robinson, Aug. 20, 1776, UK NA, T 1/125, f. 294; Baker, *Government and Contractors*, 104–05; Howe dispatch, Aug. 6, 1776, UK NA, T 64/108, f. 66 (*rats*).

354 *Among other necessities, his assembled force*: memo to Pownall, Jan. 6, 1776; Whitehall memo, Jan. 7, 1776; Master General of the Ordnance to Whitehall, Jan. 12, 1776, all in UK NA, CO 5/162, f. 4–9, 25; Kopperman, "'The Cheapest Pay': Alcohol Abuse in the Eighteenth-Century British Army," *JMH* 60, no. 3 (July 1996): 447, 454 (*rum*); invoices, medical supplies, Sept. 25, 1776, UK NA, CO 5/168, f. 264–65 (*straitjackets*); "Calculation of Fewel [*sic*] & Candles," Mar. 20, 1777, UK NA, T 64/108, f. 117 (*winter requirements*); *Logistics*, 146 (*tents*); Viscount Weymouth to Master General of the Ordnance, Jan. 23, 1776, UK NA, CO 5/162, f. 37 (*since 1759*).

354 *Few issues would flummox*: Stanley Weintraub, *Iron Tears*, 51 (*"cow"*); Wright, "Some Notes on the Continental Army," *WMQ*, 2nd ser., 11, no. 2 (Apr. 1931): 93; *Logistics*, 55 (*horses*); memo to Pownall, Jan. 6, 1776, UK NA, CO 5/162, f. 4–9 (*277 wagons*); Mackesy, *The War for America*, 80–82; William Roy to Barrington, Mar. 15, 1776, UK NA, WO 1/890, f. 8 (*five-ton wagons*); Huston, *The Sinews of War*, 36 (*American teamsters*).

354 *Forage was another enormous problem*: *Logistics*, 9. A working horse typically ate more than 20 pounds each day. UK NA, T 64/108, f. 40; *Logistics*, 58–59 (*three other horses*); Master General of the Ordnance to Whitehall, Jan. 12, 1776, UK NA, CO 5/162, f. 25 (*horseshoes*).

355 *Simply getting horses*: Lt. Stephen Harris to Whitehall, n.d. [received Dec. 19, 1776], UK NA, CO 5/93, f. 499. Kenneth Roberts vividly describes the perils of shipping horses on the open ocean in his novel *Oliver Wiswell*, 520–21, 523–24.

355 *Of 950 horses shipped to Howe*: Lt. Stephen Harris to Whitehall, n.d. [received Dec. 19, 1776], UK NA, CO 5/93, f. 499; *Logistics*, 24, 60; Garnier to Vergennes, June 4, 1776, *NDAR*, vol. 6, 400 (*"mad war"*).

355 *Howe soldiered on*: Sandwich, vol. 1, 45–46 (*promised legions*); North to W. Howe, June 25, 1776, "Calendar of Manuscripts in the Royal Institution" [Carleton Papers], *Report on American Manuscripts*, vol. 1, 47 (*"War and peace"*).

355 *On August 6, the New York Convention*: Nathaniel Woodhull to GW, Aug. 6, 1776, *PGW*, vol. 590; "Queries," *Magazine of American History* 12 (July–Dec. 1884): 181; Greene to GW, Aug. 2, 1776, *PGW*, vol. 5, 544–45; Reed, ed., *Life and Correspondence of Joseph Reed*, vol. 1, 215 (*"as unexpected"*); Greene to GW, Aug. 4, 1776, *PGW*, vol. 5, 559n; Gruber, ed., *John Peebles'*

American War, 21–23, 53; Bird, "Uniform of the Black Watch in America, 1776–1783," *Journal of the American Military History Foundation* 2, no. 3 (Fall 1938): 171–72; Holmes, *Redcoat*, 187; WC, 46–48; http://www.theblackwatch.co.uk/history-and-research/the-name/.

356 *On the late afternoon of August 12*: Serle, 62; Tucker, ed., "'To My Inexpressible Astonishment,'" *Quarterly*, NYHS, 48, no. 4 (Oct. 1964): 300; Wallace, *Appeal to Arms*, 8; Steuart, ed., *The Last Journals of Horace Walpole*, vol. 1, 511–12 (*Wimbledon*); Atwood, *The Hessians*, 51, 56; Lowell, *The Hessians*, v, 282; David Head, "Hessians," http://www.mountvernon.org/library/digitalhistory/digital-encyclopedia/article/hessians/; Burgoyne, trans., *The Diary of Lieutenant von Bardeleben*, 52; Pfister, *The Voyage of the First Hessian Army from Portsmouth to New York, 1776*, 26–27 (*nostrums*).

356 *Many required new musket cartridges*: Atwood, *The Hessians*, 54; Capt. Edward Foy, Portsmouth, to John Pownall, Apr. 4, 1776, UK NA, CO 5/93, f. 381 (*"dancing pumps"*); Frey, *The British Soldier in America*, 17 (*"pell mell"*); Ewald, *Diary of the American War*, xx; Lowell, *The Hessians*, 291 (*barely half*); Uhlendorf, ed., *Revolution in America*, 10 (*swear an oath*); Crytzer, *Hessians*, xi (*Nearly thirty thousand*), xix–xx (*Britain would pay*).

356 *Despite the spectacle that swam*: WC, 88; GW to William Livingston, July 8, 1776, PGW, vol. 5, 242 (*Congress offered*); Deary, 186–89; Heath, *Memoirs of Major-General William Heath*, 47 (*possible attacks*); proclamation, Aug. 17, 1776, PGW, vol. 5, 45–46 (*"hourly expected"*).

357 *Washington now commanded*: GW to Jonathan Trumbull, Sr., Aug. 7, 1776, PGW, vol. 5, 616; C, 1776, 75 (*"crude"*); Conway, *The War of American Independence*, 51 (*"O Britons"*); Atwood, *The Hessians*, 23 (*every war*); Solomon Drowne to father, Aug. 9, 1776, *New York City During the American Revolution*, 105 (*"no subsidy"*); Edward Hand to Katharine, Aug. 12, 1776, Misc. Mss., Hand, Edward, NYHS (*"well prepared"*).

357 *Every day, Washington tried to make*: general orders, Aug. 1 and 3, 1776, PGW, vol. 5, 534–35 (*"our only emulation"*), 551 (*"foolish and wicked"*); Williams and Appleton, "Elisha Williams' Diary of 1776," *PMHB* 48, no. 4 (1924): 338, 349; general orders, Aug. 23, 1776, PGW, vol. 5, 109 (*issued upon alarm*); Albion and Dodson, eds., *Philip Vickers Fithian: Journal, 1775–1776*, 187n (*"very dirty"*); general orders, Aug. 14, 1776, PGW, vol. 5, 18 (*"conquer or die"*).

358 *"I am extremely sorry to inform"*: GW to Hancock, Aug. 2, 1776, PGW, vol. 5, 547, 616n; "Return of the Army," Aug. 3, 1776, AA, V: 1, 763; "Diary of Ensign Caleb Clap," *Historical Magazine*, 3rd ser., 3, nos. 3 and 4 (Mar. 1874 and Apr. 1875): 133+ and 247+ (*"dysentery"*); Duncan, "Medical Men in the American Revolution: The New York Campaign of 1776," *New York Medical Journal*, Sept.–Oct. 1920, 29 (*"horrid smell"*); Reiss, *Medicine and the American Revolution*, 186–87, 154 (*fetid water*); Heath, *Memoirs of Major-General William Heath*, 44 (*"every barn"*).

358 *Some regiments could hardly muster*: Lewis, *Cut Off*, 61, 70 (*17th Continental*); Gillett, *The Army Medical Department*, 3, 6; Cash, *Medical Men at the Siege of Boston*, 7; Carp, *To Starve the Army at Pleasure*, 31 (*fifty cents*); Applegate, "The Medical Administrators of the American Revolutionary Army," *Military Affairs* 25, no. 1 (Spring 1961): 1+; Williams and Appleton, "Elisha Williams' Diary of 1776," *PMHB* 48, no. 4 (1924): 347; GW to Hancock, Sept. 25, 1776, PGW, vol. 6, 398 (*"rascals"*).

358 *Washington's disposition hardly improved*: Greene, *The Life of Nathanael Greene*, vol. 1, 190; Greene to GW, Aug. 15, 1776, PGW, vol. 6, 30 (*"raging fever"*); Thayer, *Nathanael Greene*, 98–99; Greene to [Jacob Greene?], Aug. 30, 1776, PNG, vol. 1, 291–92. Greene was diagnosed with "a putrid and bilious fever."

358 *Sensing their mortality*: Graydon, *Memoirs of His Own Time*, 166; Ryan, ed., *A Salute to Courage*, 36 (*"Don't grieve"*).

359 *New fortifications were ordered*: Deary, 88–93, 140; Koke, 115+ (*row galleys*); Ruttenber, *Obstructions to the Navigation of Hudson's River*, 21 (*fire arrows*); GW to Rufus Putnam, Aug. 11, 1776, PGW, vol. 5, 669 (*"Hasten the sinking"*); Jackson, *The Pennsylvania Navy*, 353–58, 376 (*Delaware River*); Cutter, *The Life of Israel Putnam*, 226 (*"pricks"*); PGW, vol. 6, 50, 519, 551 (*chevaux-de-frise*); Diamant, *Chaining the Hudson*, 41; Pennsylvania Committee of Safety to Stephen Moylan, June 11, 1776, NDAR, vol. 5, 475 (*"hard name"*); Thomas Mifflin to GW, Aug. 6, 1776, PGW, vol. 5, 580 (*"most abstruse"*); Crawford, ed., *The Autobiography of a Yankee Mariner*, 98–99.

359 *While these preparations advanced, a more direct*: The waxing crescent moon had set before nine p.m. "Sun and Moon Data," U.S. Naval Observatory.

359 *A hundred-ton sloop named* Polly: Koke, 115+; Diamant, *Chaining the Hudson*, 74–76; Calderhead, "British Naval Failure at Long Island," *New York History* 57, no. 3 (July 1976): 321+; J. Adams to David Sewall, June 12, 1776, *AP ("something infernal")*; J. Adams to J. Warren, June 9, 1776, *NDAR*, vol. 5, 437–41.

359 *With visibility barely fifty yards*: Koke, 115+.

360 *Gunners aboard* Phoenix *fired*: journals, *Rose* and *Phoenix*, Aug. 16, 1776, *NDAR*, vol. 6, 206; *Sandwich*, vol. 2, 154; Heath memoir, *NDAR*, vol. 6, 208 *(cutlasses)*.

360 *The American fireship survivors*: general orders, Aug. 18, 1776, *PGW*, vol. 6, 59 *("stayed last")*; Koke, 115+ *("better fate")*.

360 Phoenix, Rose, *and the two surviving tenders*: journals, *Rose* and *Phoenix*, Aug. 18, 1776, *NDAR*, vol. 6, 225–26.

360 *A violent, portentous storm*: Field, *The Battle of Long Island*, 348 *("marble" and "crisped")*, 374; JHD, 111+ *("Terrible thunder")*; Moore, *The Diary of the American Revolution*, 143–44 *("God speaks")*.

361 *By early Thursday morning the weather*: brigade orders, Aug. 19, 1776, Thomas Glyn, "Journal of American Campaign," FL; orderly book, Maj. Matthew Dixon, chief engineer, Aug. 18–20, 1776, HM 615, HL; "Bryan Sweeny, 22nd Regiment," DNH, Aug. 27, 2015 *(last year's uniforms)*; *C 1776*, 83–84; Bird, "Uniform of the Black Watch in America, 1776–1783," *Journal of the American Military History Foundation* 2, no. 3 (Fall 1938): 171–72; Atwood, *The Hessians*, 45; Burgoyne, trans., *The Diary of Lieutenant von Bardeleben*, 52 *(rank insignia)*.

361 *Seventy-five flatboats*: JHD, 111+; R. Howe to Admiralty, Aug. 31, 1776, *AA*, V: 1, 1255; Hugh T. Harrington, "Invading America: The Flatboats That Landed Thousands of British Troops on American Beaches," *JAR*, Mar. 16, 2015; Willis, *The Struggle for Sea Power*, 124–25 *(number slathered)*; Cubbison, *"The Artillery Never Gained More Honour,"* 27 *(painted gray)*; Maj. Francis Hutcheson to Maj. Gen. Frederick Haldimand, Aug. 8, 1776, *NDAR*, vol. 6, 123; *BNY*, 127.

361 *Britain, more than any other naval power*: Rodger, *The Command of the Ocean*, 419–20; Donald E. Graves, "Justice to the Admirals," in Stacey, *Quebec, 1759*, appendix G, 238–40; Syrett, *Shipping and Military Power in the Seven Years War*, 91–96, 100.

361 *Dawn, said to break with "tropical brilliancy"*: Field, *The Battle of Long Island*, 148–49; JHD, 111+; log, *Eagle*, Aug. 21–22, 1776, UK NA, ADM 51/293; Tilley, *The British Navy and the American Revolution*, 88 *(took soundings and shifted his flag)*; Griffith, *The War for American Independence*, 303 *(dispatch cases)*.

362 *"It seemed like a bridge of men"*: Henry Strachey note, Aug. 21 [22], 1776, "Relative to preliminaries to battle of Long Island," in folder with memorandum on Staten Island conference, Sept. 11, 1776, Lord Richard Howe papers, NYPL; "Invading America: The Flatboats That Landed Thousands of British Troops on American Beaches," *JAR*, Mar. 16, 2015 *(kedge anchor)*; Uhlendorf, ed., *Revolution in America*, 33–36; JHD, 111+; R. Howe to Admiralty, Aug. 31, 1776, *AA*, V: 1, 1255.

362 *Before noon 15,000 men*: JHD, 111+; Aug. 21–22, 1776, journal entry, KP *(light horse and "smallest opposition")*; Uhlendorf, ed., *Revolution in America*, 33–36 *(leveling a road)*; HBAR, 101; *BNY*, 4; Serle, 73–74 *("sails spread")*; R. Howe to Germain, Sept. 3, 1776, *AA*, V: 1, 1256.

362 *Colonel Hand's Pennsylvania riflemen*: Murray, *Letters from America*, 31–32; Wertenbaker, *Father Knickerbocker Rebels*, 91; Tiedemann and Fingerhut, eds., *The Other New York*, 27 *("Dutch Bible")*; Field, *The Battle of Long Island*, 336 *(Fifteen thousand)*, 291–93; Sabine, *Suppressed History of General Nathaniel Woodhull*, 27–31, 36; Onderdonk, *Documents and Letters Intended to Illustrate the Revolutionary Incidents of Queens County*, 89; Strong, *History of the Town of Flatbush*, 144 *(fled east)*.

363 *Smoke from burning haystacks*: Field, *The Battle of Long Island*, 152–53; Burrows and Wallace, *Gotham*, 235 *("Women and children")*; Allen, *Tories*, 169.

363 *"The inhabitants received us"*: Hibbert, *Redcoats and Rebels*, 124; *BNY*, 128; Strong, *History of the Town of Flatbush*, 144 *(wine cellars)*; Serle, 71 *("merry")*.

363 *Two more Hessian brigades*: HBAR, 101. Martin puts the total force in New York at "something like 35,000 or more." "A Contagion of Violence," *Journal of Military Ethics* 14, no. 1 (May 2015): 57–73.

363 *"I never saw better stuff"*: Frey, *The British Soldier in America*, 128.

363 *"After a few beatings"*: Spring, *With Zeal and with Bayonets Only*, 20.

363 *He guessed wrong*: GW to Hancock, Aug. 23 and 24, 1776, *PGW*, vol. 6, 111 and 117; *BNY*, 128–29; GW to J. Trumbull, Sr., Aug. 24, 1776, *PGW*, vol. 6, 123–24.

363 *Nathanael Greene's desperate illness*: Congress promoted Sullivan on August 9. Whittemore, *A General of the Revolution*, 32; GW to Hancock, June 17, 1776, *PGW*, vol. 5, 20–21 (*"foibles"*).

364 *On Saturday, Washington concluded*: GW to Israel Putnam, Aug. 25, 1776, *PGW*, vol. 6, 126 (*"disorderly"*); *GGW*, 240–41; Stiles, *A History of the City of Brooklyn*, vol. 1, 259.

364 *A constellation of ten American forts*: "Revolutionary War Forts of New York City," http://www.northamericanforts.com/East/nycity.html#revyork; Gallagher, *The Battle of Brooklyn, 1776*, 79–80, 82; Samuel Holden Parsons to J. Adams, Oct. 8, 1776, *AP*; Barnet Schecter, "George Washington at New York: The Campaign of 1776," in *CGW*, 165–66. The ridge was sometimes called Gowanus Heights; the nomenclature "Heights of Guana" appears on a detailed British map from 1776. https://digitalcollections.nypl.org/items/510d47db-c686-a3d9-e040-e00a18064a99.

364 *Washington had only a cursory grasp*: Thomas A. Rider II, "George Washington: America's First Soldier," in *CGW*, 390; Edward G. Lengel, "The Revolutionary War," in Blanken et al., *Assessing War*, 70–72; GW to I. Putnam, Aug. 25, 1776, *PGW*, vol. 6, 128 (*"best men"*); *GGW*, 141 (*"afterthoughts"*).

364 *Late afternoon shadows had begun*: Baker, "Itinerary of General Washington from June 15, 1775, to December 23, 1783," *PMHB* 14, no. 2 (July 1890): 132; Sullivan orders, Aug. 25, 1776, in *C 1776*, 211 (*green sprig*); Field, *Historic and Antiquarian Scenes in Brooklyn and Its Vicinity*, 29–30; Strong, *History of the Town of Flatbush*, 38; author visit, Dongan Oak site, signage, Aug. 2014.

365 *"They mean to land"*: GW to Hancock, Aug. 26, 1776, and GW to William Heath, Aug. 26, 1776, *PGW*, vol. 6, 129 and 131 (*"only a feint"*).

365 *Neither Putnam nor Sullivan knew*: Stiles, *A History of the City of Brooklyn*, vol. 1, 257n; *GGW*, 141. Schecter puts the number at "8,000 to 9,000," with American defenders on the Heights of Guana outnumbered almost seven to one. *BNY*, 132. Johnston set the number at 7,000. *C 1776*, 97. Fischer estimated the number at 9,450 to 11,000. *WC*, 93.

365 *The American line thinned severely*: *GGW*, 142; Procknow, "Did Generals Mismanage the Battle of Brooklyn?," *JAR*, Apr. 20, 2017; *C 1776*, 120–21 (*"never reimbursed"*); Field, *Historic and Antiquarian Scenes in Brooklyn and Its Vicinity*, 30–31 (*mounted militia*).

365 *Washington took a last look*: Field, *The Battle of Long Island*, 169; *C 1776*, 95–96; GW to Lund Washington, Aug. 26, 1776, *PGW*, vol. 6, 135–36 (*"I know not"*).

365 *Sputtering gunfire could be heard*: *BNY*, 141–43; Gallagher, *The Battle of Brooklyn, 1776*, 110; Nelson, *William Alexander, Lord Stirling*, 36–39, 43, 62; Duer, *The Life of William Alexander, Earl of Stirling*, 11.

366 *From the marsh lining Gowanus Bay*: *C 1776*, 102–06; Burrows, *Forgotten Patriots*, 2; Ward, *The Delaware Continentals*, 30 (*"red and angry"*); Dann, ed., *The Revolution Remembered*, 42 (*"sheets of fire"*).

366 *"The balls and shells flew"*: *C 1776*, 105–06, 122; journal, Col. Samuel J. Atlee, Aug. 27, 1776, *AA*, V: 1, 1251–55; Lewis, *Cut Off*, 103; Ward, *The Delaware Continentals*, 31 (*"English taste"*); *BNY*, 146 (*"amazingly well"*); "Extract of a Letter from a Marylander" [Mordecai Gist], Aug. 30, 1776, *AA*, V: 1, 1232; Stiles, *A History of the City of Brooklyn*, vol. 1, 269–72; Nelson, *William Alexander, Lord Stirling*, 84–85.

366 *General Sullivan, in the American center*: Stiles, *A History of the City of Brooklyn*, vol. 1, 273; Atwood, *The Hessians*, 68; Field, *The Battle of Long Island*, 181–82.

366 *They were looking in the wrong direction*: Procknow, "Did Generals Mismanage the Battle of Brooklyn?," *JAR*, Apr. 20, 2017; *TAR*, 39–41n (*"That, once possessed"*).

367 *Howe and his staff at first*: Willcox, *Portrait of a General*, 105–06 (*"German school"*); TAR, 42n (*"did not expect"*). Burrows puts the British flanking force at "perhaps 14,000 strong." *Forgotten Patriots*, 4.

367 *At nine p.m. on Monday*: Lydenberg, 495; Gallagher, *The Battle of Brooklyn, 1776*, 103; TAR, 41–42 (*"drowning the noise"*); WR, 222–23; "Sun and Moon Data," U.S. Naval Observatory; Duncan, *History of the Royal Regiment of Artillery*, vol. 1, 309; C 1776, 109–10; Stiles, *A History of the City of Brooklyn*, vol. 1, 266n (*"ten rods'"*); Field, *The Battle of Long Island*, 159; Murray, *Letters from America*, 33 (*"drop asleep"*).

367 *At two a.m. on Tuesday*: Inman, "George Inman's Narrative of the American Revolution," *PMHB* 7, no. 3 (1883): 237+; Bradford, ed., "A British Officer's Revolutionary War Journal, 1776–1778," *Maryland Historical Magazine* 56, no. 2 (June 1961): 157; C 1776, 110–11; TAR, 42; Onderdonk, *Revolutionary Incidents of Suffolk and Kings Counties*, 130, 139; Stiles, *A History of the City of Brooklyn*, vol. 1, 266n; historical pamphlet, Evergreens Cemetery, Brooklyn (drawn from John Rousmaniere, *Green Oasis in Brooklyn: The Evergreens Cemetery, 1849–2008*); Field, *Historic and Antiquarian Scenes in Brooklyn and Its Vicinity*, 62–65; Gallagher, *The Battle of Brooklyn, 1776*, 105–06; Murray, *Letters from America*, 33 (*"repaid us"*).

368 *"To my great mortification"*: C 1776, 112–13; *Spirit '76*, 433–35; Gallagher, *The Battle of Brooklyn, 1776*, 113 (*"never dreamed of"*); McMichael, "Diary of Lieutenant James McMichael, of the Pennsylvania Line, 1776–1778," *PMHB* 16, no. 2 (July 1892): 134 (*millponds*).

368 *"This plan succeeded"*: LHEP, 68–69; BNY, 147; TAR, 43 (*"no disposition"*); Lushington, *The Life and Services of General Lord Harris*, 76.

368 *No sooner had the double shots*: Stiles, *A History of the City of Brooklyn*, vol. 1, 273 (*"coverts"*); Ward, *The Delaware Continentals*, 37 (*"Landgrave's birthday"*); Gallagher, *The Battle of Brooklyn, 1776*, 118 (*"LIBERTY"*).

369 *"When they caught only"*: Atwood, *The Hessians*, 68; Dann, ed., *The Revolution Remembered*, 50; Burgoyne, trans., *The Diary of Lieutenant von Bardeleben*, 56 (*"knelt"*); Lowell, *The Hessians*, 63–64 (*harnessed*).

369 *General Sullivan had also heard the signal*: Wade and Lively, *This Glorious Cause*, 78 (*"lay in ambush"*); C 1776, 113–14 (*three field guns*); Von Eelking and Joseph George Rosengarten, *The German Allied Troops in the North American War of Independence*, 24 (*"little quarter"*); Stiles, *A History of the City of Brooklyn*, vol. 1, 274n (*"massacres"*).

369 *"He was in a cornfield"*: Lewis Morris, Jr., to father, Aug. 28, 1776, *Collections*, NYHS (1875): 439; C 1776, 115; Whittemore, *A General of the Revolution*, 39.

369 *With the collapse of the American left*: Nelson, *William Alexander, Lord Stirling*, 84–88 (*"overweight"*), 59–60 (*lottery*); BNY, 82–83 (*spendthrift*); Jones, *History of New York During the Revolutionary War*, vol. 2, 322–23, 587–88; Lundin, *Cockpit of the Revolution*, 22–23, 89–90; Chernow, *Alexander Hamilton*, 45 (*cupbearer*); James Chambers to wife, Sept. 3, 1776, in Ryan, ed., *A Salute to Courage*, 39 (*"like a wolf"*).

370 *The British horde pounding up*: Stiles, *A History of the City of Brooklyn*, vol. 1, 278; Ward, *The Delaware Continentals*, 39–40; C 1776, 116; Field, *The Battle of Long Island*, 193–94 (*slopes to his left*); Lewis, *Cut Off*, 123; Burgoyne, ed., *Enemy Views*, 69–70 (*"Pardon!"*); journal, Col. Samuel J. Atlee, Aug. 27, 1776, *AA*, V: 1, 1251–55 (*"obliged to run"*); Ferling, *Almost a Miracle*, 134 (*"poltroons"*); Nice and Burd, "Extracts from the Diary of Captain John Nice, of the Pennsylvania Line," *PMHB* 16, no. 4 (Jan. 1893): 400–03; Hagist, "'A Token of Surrender' or 'One Mode of Attack': The Firelock Clubb'd," *The Continental Line*, http://www.continentalline .org/articles/article.php?date=9804&article=980401.

370 *Reduced to less than a thousand*: "Extract of a Letter from a Marylander" [Mordecai Gist], Aug. 30, 1776, *AA*, V: 1, 1232; Ward, *The Delaware Continentals*, 39–40; Fraser, *The Stone House at Gowanus*, 78–82; Field, *Historic and Antiquarian Scenes in Brooklyn and Its Vicinity*, 34–37; Col. William Smallwood to Maryland Convention, Oct. 12, 1776, *AA*, V: 2, 1011–14; Field, *The Battle of Long Island*, 194–96; Martin, *A Narrative of a Revolutionary Soldier*, 24 (*"water rats"*).

371 *Stirling followed up the road*: WR, 221; Field, *The Battle of Long Island*, 202 (*"Close up!"*); author visit, Old Stone House, Brooklyn, Aug. 2014; Stirling to GW, Aug. 29, 1776, *PGW*, vol. 6, 160 (*charged, fell back, and charged*); Stiles, *A History of the City of Brooklyn*, vol. 1, 278–79; *C 1776*, 116 (*"invincible resolution"*).

371 *"We were drove with much precipitation"*: "Extract of a Letter from a Marylander" [Mordecai Gist], Aug. 30, 1776, *AA*, V: 1, 1232; Field, *The Battle of Long Island*, 202; Stiles, *A History of the City of Brooklyn*, vol. 1, 279; Tacyn, "To the End: The First Maryland Regiment and the American Revolution," Ph.D. diss. (University of Maryland, College Park, 1999), 59–62 (*obliterated*).

371 *"O doleful!"*: Albion and Dodson, eds., *Philip Vickers Fithian: Journal, 1775–1776*, 218; *Personal Recollections of Captain Enoch Anderson*, 22–23 (*"hard day"*).

371 *Washington had watched*: Field, *The Battle of Long Island*, 202. Another version quoted him as saying, "Good God, what brave fellows I must this day lose." "Archives of Maryland Online," *Maryland Gazette Collection*, http://msa.maryland.gov/megafile/msa/speccol /sc4800/sc4872/001282/html/m1282-1168.html.

371 *General Howe would list almost twelve hundred*: W. Howe to Germain, Sept. 3, 1776, *DAR*, vol. 10, 368; J. Loring, American prisoner tally, Aug. 27, 1776, *AA*, V: 3, 1057. The third general captured, besides Sullivan and Stirling, was Nathaniel Woodhull of New York, who died of his wounds on September 20. *PGW*, vol. 6, 184n; "Ordnance taken from enemy," Aug. 27, 1776, UK NA, CO 5/93, f. 264 (*thirty-two cannons*).

371 *"Among the prisoners are many"*: Lowell, *The Hessians*, 64–68.

372 *Howe estimated the total American casualties*: W. Howe to Germain, with Loring return, Sept. 5, 1776, UK NA, CO 5/93, f. 519, 523. Casualty estimates made by various historians since the eighteenth century vary by a factor of three. *C 1776*, 126–27.

372 *Battle losses, exclusive of those captured*: BNY, 153; WR, 226–27. Burrows estimates that "at least 300" Americans died in the battle. *Forgotten Patriots*, 9.

372 *British and Hessian casualties*: W. Howe to Germain, Sept. 3, 1776, *DAR*, vol. 10, 368; Serle, 91 (*"so noisome"*); Stone, trans., *Letters of Brunswick and Hessian Officers During the American Revolution*, 186 (*"hacked and shot"*).

372 *Some American units were all but extinguished*: Lewis, *Cut Off*, 129–131 (*"scattered and torn"*); *C 1776*, 122 (*thirty-fifth birthday*); Sabine, ed., *The New-York Diary of Lieutenant Jabez Fitch*, 34–37 (*"decayed gradually"*).

372 *"My preservation I only attribute"*: McMichael, "Diary of Lieutenant James McMichael, of the Pennsylvania Line, 1776–1778," *PMHB* 16, no. 2 (July 1892): 135; "Extract of a letter," Aug. 28, 1776, *AA*, V: 1, 1195 (*"My height"*).

372 *No battle in the eight-year war*: BNY, 153; McCullough, *1776*, 178–79; Burrows, *Forgotten Patriots*, 9 (*"we are perplexed"*); GGW, 148 (*"good bleeding"*); Atwood, *The Hessians*, 70 (*"exterminated"*); *C 1776*, 124 (*"quite luminous"*).

373 *"My ancient corporeal fabric"*: Montross, *Rag, Tag and Bobtail*, 114; *C 1776*, 236–37 (*"Less generalship"*); Greene, *The Life of Nathanael Greene*, vol. 1, 204 (*"Gracious God!"*).

373 *Faith in Washington plummeted*: BNY, 154 (*"Would to heaven"*); GGW, 144–45; Lt. Col. Robert Hanson Harrison [GW aide] to Hancock, Aug. 27, 1776, *PGW*, vol. 6, 140–42 (*as darkness descended*); GW to Hancock, Sept. 2, 1776, *PGW*, vol. 6, 200 (*"do their duty"*); J. Adams to Abigail, Oct. 8, 1776, in *AFC*, vol. 2, 140 (*"outgeneraled"*); WR, 226–30.

373 *"The panic may seize"*: J. Adams to Abigail Adams, Sept. 5, 1776, *Adams Family Papers: An Electronic Archive*, MHS, http://www.masshist.org/digitaladams/archive/doc?id=L1776090 5ja&bc=%2Fdigitaladams%2Farchive%2Fbrowse%2Fletters_1774_1777.php; *C 1776*, 123 (*"gone to glory"*). Drake, a Knox biographer, cites slightly different wording. *Life and Correspondence of Henry Knox*, 29.

373 *"We want great men"*: Drake, *Life and Correspondence of Henry Knox*, 30.

374 *After leading the flank attack*: TAR, 43–44; GWGO, 52–53 (*"handsomely enough"*).

374 *On Tuesday night, British tents*: Nelson, *General James Grant*, 100–01 (*"cheap and complete"*); Lushington, *The Life and Services of General Lord Harris*, 77 (*"whistled"*); Gallagher, *The Battle of Brooklyn, 1776*, 138; GGW, 146 (*"regular approaches"*); Lydenberg, 496; TAR, 43–44.

374 *Some would accuse Howe of timidity*: The Narrative of Lieut. Gen. Sir William Howe, 5 (*"even criminal"*), 32, 63; Gallagher, *The Battle of Brooklyn, 1776*, 140–41 (*greater range*); House of Commons inquiry, May 6, 1779, *Parliamentary Register*, vol. 12, 52.

374 *Howe may have assumed that his brother*: R. Howe to Admiralty, Oct. 10, 1776, *AA*, V: 1, 1255–56; John Purdy, *The Columbian Navigator*, vol. 1, 99; Calderhead, "British Naval Failure at Long Island," *New York History* 57, no. 3 (July 1976): 321+ (*"six fireships"*).

375 *For the moment, General Howe was content*: Onderdonk, *Revolutionary Incidents of Suffolk and Kings Counties*, 38, 45 (*"lay waste"*), 48; Luke and Venables, *Long Island in the American Revolution*, 32–33; Gallagher, *The Battle of Brooklyn, 1776*, 158 (*two hundred wagons*); *BNY*, 158 (*second sap*).

375 *For two days and two nights*: Freeman, 168; *BNY*, 156 (*grenades*); Graydon, *Memoirs of His Own Time*, 168 (*pikes*).

375 *The steady downpour flooded trenches*: *C 1776*, 133; Leggett, *The Narrative of Major Abraham Leggett*, 11–12 (*pork raw*); Sedgwick, *A Memoir of the Life of William Livingston*, 203 (*"fatigues"*); Albion and Dodson, eds., *Philip Vickers Fithian: Journal, 1775–1776*, 220 (*"dangerous to walk"*); *WR*, 231; Duncan, "Medical Men in the American Revolution: The New York Campaign of 1776," *New York Medical Journal* (Sept.–Oct. 1920): 27 (*lowing cows*).

375 *Washington was alive*: Reed, ed., *Life and Correspondence of Joseph Reed*, vol. 1, 224–25; *HH*, 22; Duncan, "Medical Men in the American Revolution: The New York Campaign of 1776," *New York Medical Journal* (Sept.–Oct. 1920): 28 (*sick and wounded men*).

376 *At five p.m. on Thursday, August 29*: Stiles, *A History of the City of Brooklyn*, vol. 1, 284n; "Four Chimneys," New York City Parks, https://www.nycgovparks.org/art-and-antiquities /permanent-art-and-monuments/info?monId=545; "Council of War," *PGW*, vol. 6, 153–54 (*"eligible to leave"*); Ferling, *The Ascent of George Washington*, 111; Palmer, *George Washington's Military Genius*, 134 (*"unanimous advice"*).

376 *Orders tumbled out*: Hughes, *Memorial and Documents*, 10, 32–33, 41; Billias, *General John Glover and His Marblehead Mariners*, 100–01; T. Mifflin to W. Heath, Aug. 29, 1776, *AA*, V: 1, 1211 (*transport reinforcements*).

376 *One by one Washington's regiments*: *WR*, 234; *C 1776*, 140–41 (*campfires*), 212 (*Passwords*); Charles F. Himes, "Colonel Robert Magaw: The Defender of Fort Washington," lecture, Hamilton Library Association, Carlisle, Pa. (1915): 33 (*digging*); Martin, *A Narrative of a Revolutionary Soldier*, 26–27 (*not to talk*); Graydon, *Memoirs of His Own Time*, 168 (*"deep murmur"*); Field, *Historic and Antiquarian Scenes in Brooklyn and Its Vicinity*, 92–93 (*"ungovernable alarm"*); *BNY*, 165 (*"sink it to hell"*).

376 *Two web-footed Massachusetts regiments*: Billias, *General John Glover and His Marblehead Mariners*, 69–70, 101; Irving, *Life of George Washington*, vol. 1, 311 (*"hardy, adroit"*); Dunlap, *History of the American Theater*, vol. 1, 71–72; Martin, *A Narrative of a Revolutionary Soldier*, 27; *C 1776*, 140.

377 *At two a.m. a providential fogbank*: *Personal Recollections of Captain Enoch Anderson*, 22; Tallmadge, *Memoir of Col. Benjamin Tallmadge*, 10–11 (*"scarcely discern"*); Graydon, *Memoirs of His Own Time*, 168 (*British cavalry*).

377 *Yet as dawn brightened the fog*: House of Commons inquiry, May 6, 1779, *Parliamentary Register*, vol. 12, 53 (*"I was the first person"*); Scull, ed., "The Montresor Journals," *Collections*, NYHS (1881): 122; GW to Hancock, Aug. 31, 1776, *PGW*, vol. 6, 177; Hughes, *Memorial and Documents*, 40; *BNY*, 166; *WR*, 235; Tallmadge, *Memoir of Col. Benjamin Tallmadge*, 11; Upham, *General John Glover of Marblehead*, 12–13; "The Papers of General Samuel Smith," *Historical Magazine*, 2nd ser., 7 (Feb. 1870): 81 (*carbine rounds*).

377 *"Since Monday scarce any of us"*: GW to Hancock, Aug. 31, 1776, *PGW*, vol. 6, 177.

378 *"Never was a greater feat"*: Ryan, ed., *A Salute to Courage*, 39; "Narrative of Capt. Andrew Snape Hamond," *Roebuck*, Aug. 14–29, 1776, *NDAR*, vol. 6, 353–54; Cohn, "Fortifications of New York During the Revolutionary War, 1776–1782," New York City Archeological Group, 1962; Smith, *Governors Island*, 47–48; *BNY*, 166 (*"history of warfare"* and *"our friend"*).

378 *Captain Collier, commander of Rainbow*: Tucker, ed., "To My Inexpressible Astonishment," *Quarterly*, NYHS, 48, no. 4 (Oct. 1964): 304; *C 1776*, 271 (*"merry tones"*); Graydon, *Memoirs*

of His Own Time, 163 (*"dismay"*); Col. William Douglas to Hannah, Aug. 31, 1776, *Quarterly Bulletin*, NYHS, 13, no. 1 (Apr. 1929) (*"frowns of heaven"*).

378 *Of Washington's sixty-seven infantry regiments*: general orders, Aug. 31, 1776, *PGW*, vol. 6, 173n; GW to Heath, Aug. 30, 1776, *PGW*, vol. 6, 165 (*straggler line*); GW to Hancock, Sept. 2, 1776, *PGW*, vol. 6, 199–200 (*"Our situation"*).

379 *Long Island was forfeit*: Stiles, *A History of the City of Brooklyn*, vol. 1, 290; R. Putnam to GW, Sept. 3, 1776, *PGW*, vol. 6, 210 (*"reconnoitered"*); *C 1776*, 222 (*"public enemies"*).

379 *Whatever contempt General Putnam*: Spring, *With Zeal and with Bayonets Only*, 136; L. Cliffe to "Jack," Sept. 21, 1776, Loftus Cliffe papers, 1769–1784, WLC (*"pusillanimity"*); Boyle, ed., *From Redcoat to Rebel*, 52 (*American camp*).

379 *"They will never again stand"*: Percy to father, Sept. 1, 1776, *LHEP*, 68–69.

16. A SENTIMENTAL MANNER OF MAKING WAR

380 *Oarsmen draped in dark cloaks*: Ezra Lee to David Humphreys, Feb. 20, 1815, *Magazine of American History* 29, no. 1 (Jan. 1893): 263+; Abbot, ed., *The Beginning of Modern Submarine Warfare*, 47–48; Humphreys, *Life and Times of David Humphreys*, vol. 1, 74 (*"altogether different"*); R. Howe to BF, Sept. 10, 1776, "Eagle off Bedlows Island," *PBF* (*Bedloe's*).

380 *Hundreds of silhouetted masts*: Eagle had been commissioned in February 1776. Winfield, *British Warships in the Age of Sail*, 105; Philbrick, *Valiant Ambition*, 22; D. Bushnell to T. Jefferson, Oct. 13, 1787, "The Submarine Turtle: Naval Documents of the Revolutionary War," Naval History and Heritage Command, https://www.history.navy.mil; Brenda Milkofsky, "David Bushnell and His Revolutionary Submarine," https://connecticuthistory .org/david-bushnell-and-his-revolutionary-submarine/.

380 *Back on the Whitehall dock*: Abbot, ed., *The Beginning of Modern Submarine Warfare*, 47–48; Wagner, *Submarine Fighter of the American Revolution*, 18–21, 28–31, 37, 59–60.

381 *Seven hundred pounds of lead*: Ezra Lee to David Humphreys, Feb. 20, 1815, *Magazine of American History* 29, no. 1 (Jan. 1893): 263+; David Bushnell to T. Jefferson, Oct. 13, 1787, *Transactions of the American Philosophical Society* 4 (1799): 303–12; Sanders, "The First American Submarine," *Proceedings*, U.S. Naval Institute, 62, no. 12 (Dec. 1936): 1743+; Thomson, "David Bushnell and the First American Submarine," *Proceedings*, U.S. Naval Institute, 68, no. 2 (Feb. 1942): 176; GW to T. Jefferson, Sept. 26, 1785, "The Submarine Turtle: Naval Documents of the Revolutionary War," Naval History and Heritage Command, https://www .history.navy.mil (*Though skeptical*).

381 *Turtle carried on her back*: "General Principles and Construction of a Sub-Marine Vessel," David Bushnell to T. Jefferson, Oct. 13, 1787, *Transactions of the American Philosophical Society* 4 (1799): 303–12; Wagner, *Submarine Fighter of the American Revolution*, 40–41, 60–62.

381 *But there would be no blast*: Ezra Lee to David Humphreys, Feb. 20, 1815, *Magazine of American History* 29, no. 1 (Jan. 1893): 263+.

381 *Abreast of Governors Island*: Ezra Lee to David Humphreys, Feb. 20, 1815, *Magazine of American History* 29, no. 1 (Jan. 1893): 263+ (*"infinite joy"*); Abbot, ed., *The Beginning of Modern Submarine Warfare*, 47–48, 190 (*whaleboat*).

382 *Twenty minutes later, the magazine*: Humphreys, *Life and Times of David Humphreys*, vol. 1, 74 (*"a bomb, a meteor"*); Wagner, *Submarine Fighter of the American Revolution*, 64–67; Diamant, *Chaining the Hudson*, 33 (*"God curse 'em!"*).

382 *The narrow escape was only the latest*: HBAR, 45 (*"a pretty man"*); Ralfe, *The Naval Biography of Great Britain*, vol. 1, 83–84, 87–88 (*"sherbet"*); James, *The British Navy in Adversity*, 12.

382 *Many more scraps followed*: Ralfe, *The Naval Biography of Great Britain*, vol. 1, 89–90; Jesse, *Memoirs of Celebrated Etonians*, vol. 2, 174 (*"How does a man feel"*); Syrett, *Admiral Lord Howe*, 26–27; Marcus, *Quiberon Bay*, 148–52, 162, 177; HBAR, 49 (*"Give us Black Dick"*).

383 *Now fifty, three years older*: MLA, 89–91; Syrett, *Admiral Lord Howe*, 36, 46; Marcus, *Quiberon Bay*, 188; James, *The British Navy in Adversity*, 45 (*spar lengths*); R. Howe, Signal and Instruction Book, ca. 1776, WLC (*warnings for fog*); HBAR, 51 (*constancy*), 47 (*cursing one's*)

monarch); Ralfe, *The Naval Biography of Great Britain*, vol. 1, 94 (*better pay*); Barrow, *The Life of Richard Earl Howe, K.G.*, 76 (*library*).

383 *Yet in February the king*: Syrett, *Admiral Lord Howe*, 43. Ralfe writes that the hand kiss occurred on March 5. *The Naval Biography of Great Britain*, vol. 1, 94.

383 *It was said in London*: Anderson, *The Command of the Howe Brothers During the American Revolution*, 56 ("*hates and despises*"); HBAR, 53; "A Plan of Accommodation &c.," 1774, Richard and William Howe collection, WLC, Ambrose Serle, 2ADfS; *MLA*, 98–99 ("*contagion*").

383 *Partly as a sop to Britons*: Anderson, *The Command of the Howe Brothers During the American Revolution*, 58, 150–53; Donne, ed., *The Correspondence of King George the Third with Lord North*, vol. 2, 18; Mackesy, *The War for America*, 105 ("*sentimental manner*"); "Instructions to Commissioners for Restoring Peace," May 6, 1776, DAR, vol. 12, 121 (*Twenty-four paragraphs*); DAR, vol. 12, 18; HBAR, 77–78; Ruppert, "Richard Howe: Admiral of the British Fleet in North America and Peace Commissioner," *JAR*, Mar. 7, 2018.

384 *Even so, Black Dick remained hopeful*: HBAR, 79; R. Howe to GW, July 13, 1776, *PGW*, vol. 5, 296; Syrett, *Admiral Lord Howe*, 53; Whittemore, *A General of the Revolution*, 40–42 (*Sullivan took the bait*); J. Adams to Abigail, Sept. 6, 1776, *AFC*, vol. 2, 120 ("*conversation*").

384 *At two p.m. on Wednesday*: log, *Eagle*, Sept. 12, 1776, UK NA, ADM 51/293; author visit, Billopp House, Aug. 2014; "The Historic Billopp House on Staten Island," *Americana* 10 (1915): 965+; Morris, *Morris's Memorial History of Staten Island, New York*, vol. 1, 145–46; D&AJA, vol. 3, 419–20 (*moss*); McCullough, *John Adams*, 155–56 (*dress sword*).

384 *A quarter mile across Arthur Kill*: Schimizzi and Schimizzi, *The Staten Island Peace Conference, September 11, 1776*, 20–21.

384 *Even at a distance*: Caroline Howe to BF, Jan. 3, Jan. 7, Feb. 28, and Mar. 4, 1775, *PBF*; Brands, *The First American*, 485–88; Van Doren, *Benjamin Franklin*, 498–522; BF to William Franklin, Mar. 22, 1775, "Journal of Negotiations," *PBF*.

385 *Franklin stepped from the barge*: D&AJA, vol. 2, 150 ("*young and zealous*"), and vol. 3, 415n, 417–18 ("*decoy duck*"); BF to R. Howe, July 20, 1776, *PBF* ("*barbarity*").

385 *Howe escorted them*: D&AJA, vol. 3, 419–20 ("*ten furies*").

385 *The "declaration of independency"*: Henry Strachey, secretary to the British peace commission, kept a detailed account of the conference. Ford, "Lord Howe's Commission to Pacify the Colonies," *Atlantic Monthly*, June 1896, 758+.

385 *Franklin agreed*: Ford, "Lord Howe's Commission to Pacify the Colonies," *Atlantic Monthly*, June 1896, 758+; D&AJA, vol. 3, 422–23 ("*character*").

385 *The king's "most earnest desire"*: Ford, "Lord Howe's Commission to Pacify the Colonies," *Atlantic Monthly*, June 1896, 758+; D&AJA, vol. 3, 420; Brands, *The First American*, 518.

386 *The discussion meandered, faltered*: D&AJA, vol. 3, 422, 429; Ford, "Lord Howe's Commission to Pacify the Colonies," *Atlantic Monthly*, June 1896, 758; Isaacson, *Benjamin Franklin*, 320.

386 *"our conference with Lord Howe"*: E. Rutledge to GW, Sept. 11, 1776, *PGW*, vol. 6, 286; J. Adams to Abigail, Sept. 14, 1776, *AFC*, vol. 2, 124 ("*not so irresistible*").

386 *"We learn by chess"*: BF, "The Morals of Chess" [before June 28, 1779], FOL; Committee of Secret Correspondence, signed by BF and Robert Morris, to William Bingham, Sept. 21, 1776, *PBF* ("*Four hundred sail*"); Alberts, *The Golden Voyage*, 30–31.

387 *"The three gentlemen"*: R. Howe to Germain, Sept. 20, 1776, UK NA, CO 5/177, f. 75.

387 *"They met, they talked"*: Serle, 101.

387 *With each passing day, New York*: J. Reed to Esther, Sept. 2 and 6, 1776, in Reed, ed., *Life and Correspondence of Joseph Reed*, vol. 1, 230–31 ("*cooped up*"); Duncan, "Medical Men in the American Revolution: The New York Campaign of 1776," *New York Medical Journal* (Sept.–Oct. 1920): 31 (*A third*). GW told Hancock that "at least ¼ of the army" was sick. Sept. 8, 1776, *PGW*, vol. 6, 230.

387 *One camp emitted "a complication"*: Gill and Curtis, eds., *A Man Apart*, 118; Samuel Holden Parsons to J. Adams, Sept. 17, 1776, *AP* ("*fight each other*").

387　*For every reinforcement to arrive*: Buel, *Dear Liberty*, 77, 80 (*half the male population*). GW wrote that "the militia of Connecticut is reduced from 8,000 to less than 2,000 and in a few days will be merely nominal." GW to Hancock, Sept. 8, 1776, *PGW*, vol. 6, 252; *WR*, 239.

387　*"The militia are passing home"*: Daniel Hitchcock to J. Adams, Sept. 9, 1776, *AP*; Sept. 18, 1776, "The Revolutionary War Diary of Chaplain Andrew Hunter," rare book collection, FL, http://www.revwar75.com/library/bob/HunterDiaries.htm (*"women's clothing"*); Cox, *A Proper Sense of Honor*, 112–13 (*"He groaned"*).

388　*"They are now in possession"*: NG to GW, Sept. 5, 1776, *PNG*, vol. 1, 295.

388　*But two days later, when Washington*: Hancock to GW, Sept. 3, 1776, *PGW*, vol. 6, 207; Tench Tilghman to father, Sept. 9, 1776, *Memoir of Lieut. Col. Tench Tilghman*, 135–36; GW to Hancock, Sept. 8, 177, *PGW*, vol. 6, 251 (*scatter the army*); *CGW*, 384–86; Stoker et al., eds., *Strategy in the American War of Independence*, 8, 12–14.

388　*"On our side the war"*: GW to Hancock, Sept. 8, 1776, *PGW*, vol. 6, 249.

388　*Greene was appalled*: "From Certain General Officers" to GW, Sept. 11, 1776, *PGW*, vol. 6, 279.

388　*After further rumination on the difficulty*: Abraham Yates, Jr., to GW, Sept. 5, 1776, and GW to Hugh Mercer, Sept. 11, 1776, *PGW*, vol. 6, 228n and 285–86; *GGW*, 150–52; Duncan, "Medical Men in the American Revolution: The New York Campaign of 1776," *New York Medical Journal* (Sept.–Oct. 1920): 31–32 (*evacuated the sick*); Schwab, *The Revolutionary History of Fort Number Eight*, 17.

389　*Half an hour after sunset on Saturday*: Shelton, *The Jumel Mansion*, 27–28; *IMI*, vol. 5, 1027 (*mirrors*); Bliven, *Battle for Manhattan*, 21 (*remained south*).

389　*"The enemy are evidently intending"*: Reed, *Life and Correspondence of Joseph Reed*, vol. 1, 235.

389　*Before dawn on Sunday*: Col. William Douglas to Hannah Douglas, Sept. 18, 1776, *Quarterly Bulletin*, NYHS, 13, no. 1 (Apr. 1929); journal, *Phoenix*, Sept. 15, 1776, *NDAR*, vol. 6, 839; Bliven, *Battle for Manhattan*, 27, 30.

389　*Daylight revealed five men-of-war*: journals, *Roebuck*, *Orpheus*, and *Rose*, Sept. 15, 1776, *NDAR*, vol. 6, 839–41; Atwood, *The Hessians*, 71; *WR*, 243; Martin, *A Narrative of a Revolutionary Soldier*, 30 (*"clover field"*); orderly book, Maj. Matthew Dixon, Sept. 14, 1776, HL, HM 61; Willcox, *Portrait of a General*, 110–11 (*"damning themselves"*).

389　*Just past the stroke of eleven*: journal, *Eagle*, Sept. 15, 1776, in JHD, 111+; NCCH, 263 (*"finest scene"*); Serle, 104 (*"awful & grand"*); "Journal of Bartholomew James," Sept. 15, 1776, *NDAR*, vol. 6, 841 (*three tons*); journal, *Carysfort*, Sept. 15, 1776, *NDAR*, vol. 6, 849 (*tackles snapped*).

390　*Some salvos flew high*: Hugh T. Harrington, "Invading America: The Flatboats That Landed Thousands of British Troops on American Beaches," Mar. 16, 2015, *JAR* (*"embankment"*); *Spirit '76*, 466 (*flimsy breastworks*); "Letter of Roger Newberry to his wife, Eunice Ely," Sept. 17, 1776, NYHS, A.L.S., AMHC (*"swivels"*).

390　*By noon, when the signal was given*: *DFM*, 47; *WR*, 243; Freeman, 193; "Journal of Bartholomew James," Sept. 15, 1776, *NDAR*, vol. 6, 841 (*"enemy fled"*); Col. William Douglas to Hannah Douglas, Sept. 18, 1776, *Quarterly Bulletin*, NYHS, 13, no. 1 (Apr. 1929); *C 1776*, 241–42 (*"but about ten"*).

390　*Among the first British officers*: Willcox, *Portrait of a General*, 108–09, 111 (*"Are we sure"*); *BNY*, 179–80; Bliven, *Battle for Manhattan*, 19–20; Lydenberg, 499–500 (*already fled*).

390　*British light infantry companies surged*: Thomas Glyn, "Journal of American Campaign," Sept. 15, 1776, FL; *DFM*, 48 (*bayoneted*); Laughton, ed., *Journal of Rear-Admiral Bartholomew James*, 33 (*impaled*). Chernow asserts that dozens of Americans were shot in mass executions. *Washington: A Life*, 252.

392　*A thousand yards to the northwest*: GW to Hancock, Sept. 16, 1776, *PGW*, vol. 6, 313, 315–16n; Shelton, *The Jumel Mansion*, 28–29; Bliven, *Battle for Manhattan*, 45–48. GW sat his horse where the New York Public Library would one day be built. *BNY*, 185.

392　*"Take the walls!"*: testimony, Col. John Tyler court-martial, Oct. 26, 1776, White Plains, N.Y., *AA*, V: 2, 1251–54; Martin, *A Narrative of a Revolutionary Soldier*, 32 (*"arms, knapsacks"*).

392 *A few hundred yards to the south*: Bliven, *Battle for Manhattan*, 49–50; Paltsits, "The Jeopardy of Washington, Sept. 15, 1776," *Quarterly*, NYHS, 32, no. 4 (Oct. 1948): 264–65; Tench Tilghman to father, Sept. 16, 1776, in *Memoir of Lieut. Col. Tench Tilghman*, 137 (*"all in his power"*).

392 *Other senior officers asserted*: Col. William Smallwood to Maryland Convention, Oct. 12, 1776, *AA*, V: 2, 1011–14; Heath, *Memoirs of Major-General William Heath*, 52; *Spirit '76*, 467. "These stories, which apparently were based on 'camp gossip,' cannot be substantiated by eyewitness accounts." *PGW*, vol. 6, 316n.

392 *"so vexed at the infamous conduct"*: N. Greene to Gov. Nicholas Cooke, Sept. 17, 1776, *PNG*, vol. 1, 300.

392 *Quit the field he did*: GW and Putnam conferred again that Sunday afternoon where Times Square later would stand. *BNY*, 188.

392 *General Howe came ashore at two p.m.*: Lydenberg, 499–500; Mackesy, *The War for America*, 89–90; GW to Hancock, Sept. 16, 1776, *PGW*, vol. 6, 315–16n; Bliven, *Battle for Manhattan*, 59–61.

393 *That respite was just long enough*: *BNY*, 188; *IMI*, vol. 5, 1012 (*British warships*); Wertenbaker, *Father Knickerbocker Rebels*, 92 (*waistcoat*); Humphreys, *Life and Times of David Humphreys*, vol. 1, 68; Davis, *Memoirs of Aaron Burr*, vol. 1, 103–06 (*guided the men*).

393 *Left behind in New York*: GW to Hancock, Sept. 16, 1776, *PGW*, vol. 6, 314 (*heavy artillery*); return of ordnance "after the retreat of the rebels, 15 Sept. 1776," UK NA, CO 5/93, f. 277; R. Howe to Philip Stephens, Admiralty, Sept. 18, 1776, UK NA, CO 5/125, f. 339; Balderston and Syrett, eds., *The Lost War*, 101 (*"precipitation"*); *BNY*, 190; *IMI*, vol. 5, 1012; *DFM*, vol. 1, 49.

393 *On the northern cusp of the island*: Sept. 15, 1776, "The Revolutionary War Diary of Chaplain Andrew Hunter," rare book collection, FL, http://www.revwar75.com/library/bob/HunterDiaries.htm; Albion and Dodson, eds., *Philip Vickers Fithian: Journal, 1775–1776*, 232–34 (*"vast body"*); *LAR*, 356; *GWGO*, 244.

393 *The last was true until*: Drake, *Life and Correspondence of Henry Knox*, 30; Samuel Shaw to father, Sept. 18, 1776, Shaw papers, MHS; Callahan, *Henry Knox*, 70 (*"superfine"*); Drake, *Life and Correspondence of Henry Knox*, 31–32 (*"I see nothing"*).

394 *Teeming rain fell Sunday night*: Humphreys, *Life and Times of David Humphreys*, vol. 1, 68 (*"clouds"*); Martin, *A Narrative of a Revolutionary Soldier*, 35 (*"wet"*); W. Smallwood to Maryland Convention, Oct. 12, 1776, *AA*, V: 2, 1013 (*"transactions"*); Albion and Dodson, eds., *Philip Vickers Fithian: Journal, 1775–1776*, 234 (*"sinful nation"*).

394 *Washington had lost another battle*: GW to Hancock, Sept. 16, 1776, *PGW*, vol. 6, 314 (*"disgraceful"*); *GGW*, 154 (*50 killed*). The prisoner tally included the next day's action. J. Loring, prisoner tally, Sept. 15–16, 1776, *AA*, V: 3, 1057.

394 *The prisoners were locked in Dutch*: *C 1776*, 273; Serle, 104 (*"Bedlamites"*); Onderdonk, *Documents and Letters Intended to Illustrate the Revolutionary Incidents of Queens County*, 100 (*longer the ribbon*); journal, *Eagle*, Sept. 15, 1776, in JHD, 111+ (*"three cheers"*); *C 1776*, 273 (*"concourse"*).

394 *Hundreds would sign*: Burrows and Wallace, *Gotham*, 245; Jasanoff, *Liberty's Exiles*, 33 (*"dependence"*); L. Cliffe to "Bat" [Bartholomew Cliffe?], Sept. 21 [*sic*], 1776, Loftus Cliffe papers, WLC; *IMI*, vol. 5, 1026; "A Sermon Preached at St. Paul's, New York, Sept. 22, 1776," NYHS (*Jeremiah*).

394 *Monday, September 16, brought the rebels*: general orders, Sept. 16, 1776, *PGW*, vol. 6, 311–12; *WR*, 241; *HH*, 44.

395 *At daybreak British pickets*: *HH*, 53–55, 58–62; Bliven, *Battle for Manhattan*, 86–87; Diamant, "First Blood for the Infantry, 1776," *Military Affairs* 15, no. 1 (Spring 1951): 16+.

395 *Alerted to the gunfire*: Reed, ed., *Life and Correspondence of Joseph Reed*, vol. 1, 237–38 (*"I never felt"*).

395 *But Washington had concocted*: Bliven, *Battle for Manhattan*, 92–94; *HH*, 69–70; Reed, ed., *Life and Correspondence of Joseph Reed*, vol. 1, 237–38 (*"on my horse"*).

396 *The enemy was indeed soon driven*: Tyler, ed., "The Old Virginia Line in the Middle States During the American Revolution," *Tyler's Quarterly* 12, no. 1 (July 1930): 1+ (*"galled them"*);

Benedict, *The Battle of Harlem Heights*, 2, 44 (*"instantly trotted"*); Scull, ed., "The Montresor Journals," *Collections*, NYHS (1881): 122.

396 *The American line stood*: "An Extract from the Journal of Lieut. David Dimock," *American Monthly* 1 (Oct. 1892): 353–54 (*"tremor"*).

396 *The British fell back again*: Benedict, *The Battle of Harlem Heights*, 44; Tilghman to father, Sept. 19, 1776, *Memoir of Lieut. Col. Tench Tilghman*, 139 (*"good order"*); Bliven, *Battle for Manhattan*, 101–02; GW to Hancock, Sept. 18, 1776, *PGW*, vol. 6, 336; *Diary of Samuel Richards*, 40 (*"large hole"*).

396 *Knowlton was removed to the shingle-roofed*: Smith, *Historical Sketch of Washington's Headquarters*, xi–xii; Perley, "Colonel Thomas Knowlton," *Historical Collections of the Essex Institute* 58, no. 2 (Apr. 1922): 89+; Roger Newberry to wife, Eunice Ely, Sept. 17, 1776, NYHS, ALS; general orders, Sept. 17, 1776, *PGW*, vol. 6, 320 (*"honor to any country"*); Bolton, "Forgotten Things and Places in the City of New York," NYHS, ts., 1918 (*Leitch*).

396 *British casualties exceeded 170*: Sept. 16, 1776, journal entry, KP, 89; HH, 87, 89 (*"impetuosity"*); Tyler, ed., "The Old Virginia Line in the Middle States During the American Revolution," *Tyler's Quarterly* 12, no. 1 (July 1930): 97 (*defile*); L. Cliffe to "Jack," Sept. 21, 1776, Loftus Cliffe papers, WLC (*"well-concerted"*).

397 *"Every visage was seen"*: Benedict, *The Battle of Harlem Heights*, 4; John Gooch to Thomas Fayerweather, Sept. 23, 1776, in Colburn, ed., *American Independence*, 10 (*"second part"*).

397 *"This affair I am in hopes"*: GW to Hancock, Sept. 18, 1776, *PGW*, vol. 6, 333; Reed, ed., *Life and Correspondence of Joseph Reed*, vol. 1, 238 (*"hardly conceive"*).

397 *Fear of fire had distressed New York*: Burrows and Wallace, *Gotham*, 43–45; Lepore, *New York Burning*, xii, xvi, 45, 50, 91–92 (*"Negroes are rising!"*); Linebaugh and Rediker, *The Many-Headed Hydra*, 174–79; Gilbert, *Black Patriots and Loyalists*, 1–2.

397 *Warehouses of pitch, tar*: Burrows and Wallace, *Gotham*, 185–86; Bridenbaugh, *Cities in Revolt*, 292; Still, *Mirror for Gotham*, 29 (*eleven companies*); IMI, vol. 4, 921; Ketchum, *Divided Loyalties*, 248 (*only the snow*); Williams, "Independence and Early American Hospitals, 1751–1812," *JAMA* 236, no. 1 (July 5, 1976): 35+ (*general hospital*).

398 *Construction began on a network*: War brought work on the new water system to a halt. John Duffy, "Public Health in New York City in the Revolutionary Period," *JAMA* 236, no. 1 (July 5, 1976): 47+; IMI, vol. 4, 918 (*eleven-inch pump*); Still, *Mirror for Gotham*, 29 (*"Fire seldom"*).

398 *That thesis would be tested*: Tryon to Germain, Sept. 24, 1776, in John Romeyn Brodhead, *Documents Relative to the Colonial History of the State of New York*, vol. 8, 686; Burrows and Wallace, *Gotham*, 241–42; David Grim, "Fire of 1776," *Collections*, NYHS (1870): 275–76; Lamb and Harrison, *History of the City of New York*, vol. 2, 135–36; Shreve, *Tench Tilghman*, 75; Rose, *Washington's Spies*, 37 (*soldiers' wives*). American prisoners captured at Quebec had just arrived in New York on parole. MQ, 425.

398 *Driven by a brisk southerly breeze*: Obenzinger, *New York on Fire*, 24 (*"whole interior"*); Graydon, *Memoirs of His Own Time*, 178 (*"heavens appeared"*); L. Cliffe to "Jack," Sept. 21, 1776, Loftus Cliffe papers, WLC (*"see a pin"*); Wertenbaker, *Father Knickerbocker Rebels*, 101 (*"air red"*); Burrows and Wallace, *Gotham*, 241–42 (*the Common*). ·

398 *"It is almost impossible to conceive"*: DFM, 60; Thomas Glyn, "Journal of American Campaign," Sept. 21, 1776, FL (*"pulling down houses"*); William W. Burke and Linnea M. Bass, "Brigade of Guards in the American Service," www.brigadeofguards.org/history; Lamb and Harrison, *History of the City of New York*, vol. 2, 135–36.

398 *The shallow pitch of the St. Paul's Chapel*: Wertenbaker, *Father Knickerbocker Rebels*, 101; Grim, "Fire of 1776," *Collections*, NYHS (1870): 275–76; C 1776, 273–74; Burrows and Wallace, *Gotham*, 176, 241–42; BNY, 205; DFM, 60–61 (*"lofty pyramid"*); IMI, vol. 5, 1023 (*twenty-five-stop organ*); Barck, *New York City During the War for Independence*, 81.

399 *An abrupt change in wind direction*: David Grim, "Fire of 1776," *Collections*, NYHS (1870): 275–76; Burrows and Wallace, *Gotham*, 241–42; Tryon to Germain, Sept. 24, 1776, DAR, vol. 12, 230 (*Martial law*); Wertenbaker, *Father Knickerbocker Rebels*, 101 (*"this calamity"*).

399 *The British suspected arson*: HH, 222 (*"villains"*); DFM, 59 (*matches*); Serle, 110 (*"handles"*); Huth et al., "Letters from a Hessian Mercenary," *PMHB* 62, no. 4 (Oct. 1938): 488+ (*"sailors hanged"*); GW to Jonathan Trumbull, Sr., Sept. 23, 1776, *PGW*, vol. 6, 382 (*"various deaths"*).

399 *No persuasive evidence ever emerged*: Wertenbaker, *Father Knickerbocker Rebels*, 102; Barck, *New York City During the War for Independence*, 81; Tryon to Germain, Sept. 24, 1776, in Brodhead, *Documents Relative to the Colonial History of the State of New York*, vol. 8, 686 (*"sent all the bells"*); W. Howe to Germain, Sept. 21, 1776, UK NA, CO 5/93, f. 549 (*"reason to suspect"*).

400 *"Had I been left"*: GW to Lund Washington, Oct. 6, 1776, *PGW*, vol. 6, 494–95.

400 *The gray pall smothering New York*: author visit, Third Ave., New York City, Aug. 2014, historical signage; Bolton, *The Private Soldier Under Washington*, 165 (*"Damnation Day"*); IMI, vol. 5, 1024–25 (*"London"*); Seymour, *Documentary Life of Nathan Hale*, 290–91, 452–53.

400 *"He was calm"*: Seymour, *Documentary Life of Nathan Hale*, 452–53.

400 *Born and raised in Connecticut*: IMI, vol. 5, 1025 (*"fair skin"*); *Connecticut in the American Revolution* (2001): 15, SoC, State Exhibition Series, http://www.societyofthecincinnati.org /scholarship/publications/ (*fourteen*); Wagner, *Submarine Fighter of the American Revolution*, 18 (*"electric flame"*); Rose, *Washington's Spies*, 4, 8–11, 16–17 (*Knowlton's Rangers*); N. Hale to Samuel Hale, Sept. 24, 1774, in Seymour, *Documentary Life of Nathan Hale*, 25 (*£70*); Johnston, *Nathan Hale, 1776*, 137 (*"many friends"*); GW to Anthony Wayne, July 10, 1779, *PGW*, vol. 21, FOL, 432–34 (*"Single men"*).

401 *Dressed in a brown summer suit*: Bass, "Nathan Hale's Mission," *Studies in Intelligence*, Winter 1973, 67+; Seymour, *Documentary Life of Nathan Hale*, 451–53 (*Yale diploma*); BNY, 211 (*"too frank"*); Stuart, *Life of Captain Nathan Hale*, 140 (*"scrubby fellow"*).

401 *Some would claim that he was exposed*: Sept. 22, 1776, diary entry, Capt. William Bamford, in Seymour, *Documentary Life of Nathan Hale*, 445–46; Bakeless, *Turncoats, Traitors and Heroes*, 117–19; Bass, "Nathan Hale's Mission," *Studies in Intelligence*, Winter 1973, 67+; James Hutson, "Nathan Hale Revisited," Library of Congress, *Information Bulletin*, July–Aug. 2003, www.loc.gov/loc/lcib/0307-8/hale.html; Cuneo, *Robert Rogers of the Rangers*, 270; Gara, *The Queen's American Rangers*, 7, 16–17. The Beekman house sat near the current East Fifty-Second Street at First Avenue. Lossing, *The Pictorial Field-Book of the Revolution*, vol. 2, 817.

401 *In another week, Howe*: orders, W. Howe, Sept. 30, 1776, "Headquarters on York Island," Frederick Mackenzie Papers, WLC, vol. D (*"heinousness"*); Seymour, *Documentary Life of Nathan Hale*, 291 (*"full confession"*); Lossing, *The Pictorial Field-Book of the Revolution*, vol. 2, 815n (*greenhouse*).

401 *Much would be made*: Joseph Addison, *Cato: A Tragedy* (1712), act IV, scene 4: "What pity is it / That we can die but once to serve our country." http://oll.libertyfund.org/titles/addison -cato-a-tragedy-and-selected-essays.

401 *"he behaved with great composure"*: DFM, 61–62; Sept. 22, 1776, diary entry, Capt. William Bamford, in Seymour, *Documentary Life of Nathan Hale*, 446, 451; Bakeless, *Turncoats, Traitors and Heroes*, 121; BNY, 214 (*painted on a board*).

402 *During another truce parley, Montresor*: Bass, "Nathan Hale's Mission," *Studies in Intelligence*, Winter 1973, 67+; BNY, 215.

402 *"The horrors of a civil war"*: L. Cliffe to "Bat" [Bartholomew Cliffe?], Sept. 21 [*sic*], 1776, Loftus Cliffe papers, WLC.

17. MASTER OF THE LAKES

405 *Autumn colors were well advanced*: Toll, *Six Frigates*, 12; Knight, *Portsmouth Dockyard Papers*, xxxiii–xxxiv; Willis, *The Struggle for Sea Power*, 144 (*"no uncommon thing"*); Carleton to Robinson (Treasury), Aug. 10, 1776, UK NA, T 1/520 (*"master"*).

405 *The British force in Canada had grown*: BARH, 272 (*13,000 men*); Jones, *History of the Campaign for the Conquest of Canada in 1776*, 116, 161; Charbonneau, *The Fortifications of Île aux Noix*, 69; Lynn, ed., *An Eyewitness Account of the American Revolution and New England Life*, 32 (*"misery"* and *"Do not lament"*); Carleton to Barrington, Oct. 1, 1776, UK NA, CO 5/168, f. 307–08; ANTA, 234.

406 *Guy Carleton had failed to catch*: A. L. Burt, *Guy Carleton, Lord Dorchester, 1724–1808*, Canadian Historical Association Booklets, no. 5 (1968): 8–9 (*"change the face"*); Germain to Carleton, June 21, 1776, *DAR*, vol. 12, 153–55 (*"Your silence"*).

406 *Carleton replied on September 28*: Burt, "The Quarrel Between Germain and Carleton: An Inverted Story," *Canadian Historical Review* 11, no. 3 (1930): 203–12; Carleton to Germain, Sept. 28, 1776, *DAR*, vol. 12, 233 (*"so far advanced"*).

406 *Carleton's plan was simple enough*: Mackesy, *The War for America*, 95 (*"Absorbed within"*); Hadden, *A Journal Kept in Canada*, 13 (*"end of the penis"*), 14 (*"thousand savages"*); Lynn, ed., *An Eyewitness Account of the American Revolution and New England Life*, 24 (*several scalps*); Jones, *History of the Campaign for the Conquest of Canada in 1776*, 156; Baxter, ed., *The British Invasion from the North*, 122; Carleton to French merchants in Montreal, Sept. 26, 1776, and Carleton to Treasury, Nov. 25, 1776, UK NA, T 1/520 (*"Indian presents"*).

406 *The imminent military expedition*: provision ships to Canada, summer 1776, UK NA, T 1/519; Bowler, "Sir Guy Carleton and the Campaign of 1776 in Canada," *Canadian Historical Review* 55, no. 2 (June 1974): 131+; Robinson (Treasury) to Carleton, Sept. 18, 1776, UK NA, AO 16/10, f. 51 (*mittens*); Baxter, ed., *The British Invasion from the North*, 154 (*"darken the air"*); Burgoyne, trans., *Georg Pausch's Journal and Reports of the Campaign in America*, 40 (*zwieback*).

407 *British expeditions had penetrated the Lake Champlain*: VBRP, 7; ordnance memos, Jan. 1776, UK NA, CO 5/162, f. 17–19 (*reviewed the watercraft*); ANTA, 212 (*brass guns*), 233; Navy Office to Philip Stephens, Feb. 2, 1776, UK NA, CO 5/123, f. 187 (*maritime carpenters*); Willis, *The Struggle for Sea Power*, 142 (*house carpenters*); Admiralty and ordnance supplies for Canada, 1776, UK NA, CO 5/162, f. 92 (*sail needles*).

407 *Flat-bottomed bateaux had been copied*: ordnance memos, Jan. 1776, UK NA, CO 5/162, f. 17–19; Admiralty to Germain, Feb. 6, 1776, UK NA, CO 5/123, f. 185; Jones, *History of the Campaign for the Conquest of Canada in 1776*, 161 (*deck cargo*); Navy Office to Philip Stephens, Feb. 29, 1776, UK NA, CO 5/123, f. 360 (*"very unreasonable"*); ANTA, 230–31 (Firebrand).

407 *As Canadian shipyards assembled*: Bellico, *Sails and Steam in the Mountains*, 140–44; ANTA, 232; Randall, *Benedict Arnold*, 301 (*brick furnace*); Bird, *Navies in the Mountains*, 193 (*baggage*).

408 *The squadron also included*: ANTA, 232. Armament estimates reflect those given in VBRP, 22.

408 *How to get these deeper-draft vessels*: W.A.B. Douglas, "Schank, John," *Dictionary of Canadian Biography*, vol. 6, http://www.biographi.ca/en/bio/schank_john_6E.html; Miller, *Sea of Glory*, 169–70.

408 *As superintendent of the St. Johns dockyard*: VBRP, 20; Fowler, *Rebels Under Sail*, 199–200; Bird, *Navies in the Mountains*, 186, 189 (*conscripted* habitants); Nelson, *Benedict Arnold's Navy*, 225–26, 236; Miller, *Sea of Glory*, 169–70; James, *The British Navy in Adversity*, 50–51 (*"terraqueous"*).

408 *After half a mile, they gave up*: Miller, *Sea of Glory*, 170–71 (*dismantled*); Charles Douglas to Philip Stephens (Admiralty), July 23, 1776, *NDAR*, vol. 5, 1184–85; Fowler, *Rebels Under Sail*, 199–200 (*"chantey"*); Mahan, 44–45; Nelson, *Benedict Arnold's Navy*, 226, 236; VBRP, 20.

408 *Carleton's "jigsaw navy"*: Fowler, *Rebels Under Sail*, 200–01; Charles Douglas to Stephens (Admiralty), Oct. 21, 1776, *AA*, V: 2, 1178 (*six weeks* and *laid her keel*); BARH, 273–74 (*American boats*); Charles Douglas to Philip Stephens (Admiralty), July 23, 1776, *NDAR*, vol. 5, 1184–85 (*180-ton frigate*); Lynn, ed., *An Eyewitness Account of the American Revolution and New England Life*, 31 (*tallow*); Bird, *Navies in the Mountains*, 195.

409 *Amassing the extra firepower*: BARH, 273–74; ANTA, 234; Charles Douglas to Stephens (Admiralty), Oct. 21, 1776, *AA*, V: 2, 1178 (*Seven hundred*); Mackesy, *The War for America*, 96 (*double the firepower*).

409 *Ninety miles south of Île aux Noix*: "Lt. Col. Johnston" to Richard Peters, undated, BC, Bft. vol. 378, pp. 79–81 (*"What kind of place"*); "Journal of Lieutenant-Colonel Joseph Vose," *Publication of the Colonial Society of Massachusetts*, vol. 7 (1900–02): 244+.

409 *"Much depends on the bravery"*: BF to Anthony Wayne, Aug. 28, 1776, *PBF*.

409 *By late summer the American force*: Bush, *Revolutionary Enigma*, 66–67; Trumbull, *Reminiscences and Letters of John Trumbull*, 31–32 (*hundred guns*); ANTA, 188–97; Furcron,

"Mount Independence," *BFTM* 9, no. 4 (Winter 1954): 230+; Greenwood, ed., *The Revolutionary Services of John Greenwood*, 37; author visit, Fort Ticonderoga, Aug. 18, 2015, museum signage (*olive oil*); Salsig, 182 (*fresh meat*); Jones, *History of the Campaign for the Conquest of Canada in 1776*, 152; orderly book, 4th Pennsylvania Battalion, July 29, 1776, HL, HM 605 (*shoes*); Lacey, "Memoirs of Brigadier-General John Lacey, of Pennsylvania," *PMHB* 25–26 (1901–02): 1+ (*"swindlers"* and *"various frauds"*); "The Deputy Adjutant General's Orderly Book," *BFTM* 3, no. 2 (July 1933): 88+ (*counterfeit money*).

410 *Smallpox had subsided*: "Letters from Dr. Samuel Kennedy to His Wife in 1776," *PMHB* 8 (1884): 111+ (*"putrid"*); Black and Roelker, eds., *A Rhode Island Chaplain in the Revolution*, 27 (*"thin in flesh"*); Jones, *History of the Campaign for the Conquest of Canada in 1776*, 115; Salsig, 227; *ANTA*, 143; Horatio Gates to GW, July 29, 1776, Gates Papers, NYHS, 3:169 (*"Everything"*).

410 *Three thousand patients jammed*: Gillett, *The Army Medical Department*, 62–64; Horatio Gates to GW, July 29, 1776, Gates Papers, NYHS, 3:169; Griffenhagen, "Drug Supplies in the American Revolution," *Bulletin of the United States National Museum* 225 (1961): 110+; author visit, Fort Ticonderoga, Aug. 18, 2015, museum signage (*drowned*); Robbins, *Journal of the Rev. Ammi R. Robbins*, 39 (*"Will you not send"*).

410 *Other miseries compounded*: Salsig, 214 (*"paid to protect"*), 215–28, 279 (*various defendants*); Baldwin, 60 (*"retreating, ragged"*).

411 *Regional enmities grew even more*: Jones, *History of the Campaign for the Conquest of Canada in 1776*, 122–23 (*brawl*); *ANTA*, 147 (*"low, dirty"*); Asa Douglas, Berkshire County Committees of Safety and Inspection, to GW, June 7, 1776, *PGW*, vol. 4, 449–50 (*scapegoat*); Gerlach, *Proud Patriot*, 182, 195–96 (*"many enemies"*); Gerlach, "Philip Schuyler and 'the Road to Glory': A Question of Loyalty and Competence," *Quarterly*, NYHS, 49, no. 4 (Oct. 1965): 341+ (*"scandalized"*).

411 *Schuyler was further insulted*: Knollenberg, "The Correspondence of John Adams and Horatio Gates," *Proceedings*, MHS, 3rd ser., 67 (Oct. 1941–May 1944): 147 (*"deceived"*); Gerlach, *Proud Patriot*, 161–61 (*"clumsy bear"*), 162–65; Lossing, *The Life and Times of Philip Schuyler*, vol. 2, 97–100, 123 (*"barbarously traduced"*); Schuyler to R. R. Livingston, Oct. 13, 1776, Schuyler Papers, BC, Bft., 75, 347; Tuckerman, *Life of General Philip Schuyler*, 149–51; Gerlach, "Philip Schuyler and 'the Road to Glory': A Question of Loyalty and Competence," *Quarterly*, NYHS, 49, no. 4 (Oct. 1965): 341+; Hancock to Gates, July 8, 1776, Horatio Gates Papers, NYHS, 2:1200 (*"cultivate harmony"*).

411 *"Your relinquishing Crown Point"*: GW to Gates, July 19, 1776, *PGW*, vol. 5, 380–81; Gates to GW, July 29, 1776, *PGW*, vol. 5, 498–501 (*"tumbled down"*).

412 *"the most perfect harmony subsists"*: Schuyler to GW, July 17, 1776, *PGW*, vol. 5, 367–68; Ryan, ed., *A Salute to Courage*, 30–31 (*"outbuild them"*).

412 *The second conviction was that*: Greenwood, ed., *The Revolutionary Services of John Greenwood*, 37; Gates to Hancock, July 29, 1776, *AA*, V: 1, 649 (*"infinite satisfaction"*).

412 *"you may again in peace sit down"*: Hannah Arnold to BA, Aug. 28, 1776, T-P RC. This letter is among BA's personal papers, captured by the British aboard the *Royal Savage* and later deposited at the Musée de la Civilisation in Quebec City. Copies were donated to Fort Ticonderoga in September 2012 by David C. Glenn.

412 *In pressing charges against a subordinate*: orderly book, Adjutant William Walker, July 18, 1776, T-P RC (*Jones's Tavern*); Arnold to court-martial, Aug. 1, 1776, *AA*, V: 1, 1273 (*"ungenteel and indecent"*); "Minute of the Court," *AA*, V: 1, 1273 (*"illegal, illiberal"*); Brumwell, *Turncoat*, 69 (*"traduced lately"*); Brandt, *The Man in the Mirror*, 94–96; Gates to Hancock, Sept. 2, 1776, *AA*, V: 1, 1267 (*"Arnold's temper"*); *BARH*, 242–43 (*"excite the envy"*).

413 *Still limping from his Quebec injuries*: Gates to GW, July 29, 1776, *PGW*, vol. 5, 498–501 (*"perfect knowledge"*); Palmer, *George Washington and Benedict Arnold*, 41–42; *BARH*, 36–37; *Struggle*, vol. 2, 147 (*loyalist estate*); Farmer, "Skenesborough: Continental Navy Shipyard," U.S. Naval Institute, *Proceedings* 90 (Oct. 1964): 160+; *ANTA*, 201; Bird, *Navies in the Mountains*, 170 (*skid horses*); Fowler, *Rebels Under Sail*, 190 (*carefully counted*); Chapelle, *The American Sailing Navy*, 24 (*four planks*).

413   *Arnold ordered the creek dredged*: Arnold to Gates, July 24, 1776, and Capt. J. Wynkoop to
       Gates, July 25, 1776, *AA*, V: 1, 564, 582; "The Deputy Adjutant General's Orderly Book," *BFTM*
       3, no. 2 (July 1933): 88+ (*blue-and-red caps*); Calloway, *The Indian World of George Washing-*
       ton, 220; *ANTA*, 153–54; Fowler, *Rebels Under Sail*, 189–90; Farmer, "Skenesborough: Con-
       tinental Navy Shipyard," U.S. Naval Institute, *Proceedings* 90 (Oct. 1964): 160+; Bird, *Navies*
       in the Mountains, 170.

413   *Arnold hounded Schuyler and Gates*: Richard Varick to Peter Gansevoort, Aug. 2, 1776, to
       GW, Aug. 2, 1776, to Hermanus Schuyler, Aug. 3, 1776, and to Leonard Van Buren, Aug. 3,
       1776, all in *NDAR*, vol. 6, 19, 33–36; Nelson, *Benedict Arnold's Navy*, 243 (*"ton of rum"*), 251
       (*forges*); Bush, *Revolutionary Enigma*, 66 (*tomahawks*); *ANTA*, 205–06 (*swivel guns*); Hagg-
       lund, *A Page from the Past: The Story of the Continental Gundelo* Philadelphia *on Lake*
       Champlain, 1776–1949 (Adirondack Resorts Press, 1949), 7 (*"exorbitant rates"*).

414   *Still Arnold needed more of this*: Arnold to Gates, Aug. 17, 1776, *NDAR*, vol. 6, 216; Richard
       Varick to Leonard Van Buren, Aug. 3, 1776, *NDAR*, vol. 6, 36; Maj. David Rhea, 2nd New
       Jersey Regiment, to "Mr. Conductor, Fort Ticonderoga," July 25, 1776, T-P RC; Bird, *Navies*
       in the Mountains, 169, 181–82.

414   *Under Schuyler's earlier direction*: Some called them gondolas. *ANTA*, 203–04; Morrissey,
       Quebec 1775, 74; Mahan, 43; Nelson, *Benedict Arnold's Navy*, 227–30.

414   *Keenly aware of the Royal Navy's advantages*: Bird, *Navies in the Mountains*, 166–68; Lake
       Champlain Land Trust, http://www.lclt.org/about-lake-champlain/lake-champlain-facts/
       (*twelve miles*); Nelson, *Benedict Arnold's Navy*, 244; Daughan, *If by Sea*, 114; *BARH*, 247–48;
       ANTA, 181.

414   *Congress authorized a bonus*: orderly book, 4th Pennsylvania Battalion, July 23, 1776, HL,
       HM 605; Bird, *Navies in the Mountains*, 172–75 (*sorted them*); Randall, *Benedict Arnold*, 249
       (*seven tons*); *ANTA*, 210–11; *BARH*, 248, 263 (*empty cask*); Baldwin, 64–66 (*"many pieces"*);
       Nelson, *Benedict Arnold's Navy*, 250; Jones, *History of the Campaign for the Conquest of*
       Canada in 1776, 125 (*sponges, rammers*).

415   *As his squadron made ready*: Martin, "The Hero Before the Traitor," *MHQ* 28, no. 3 (Spring
       2016): 38+; "Intelligence Report on the British Forces in Canada and on Lake Champlain,"
       Oct. 1, 1776, *NDAR*, vol. 7, 1081–82 (*"landed in Canada"*); Randall, *Benedict Arnold*, 277–78;
       Salsig, 249; Wickman, ed., "A Most Unsettled Time on Lake Champlain: The October 1776
       Journal of Jahiel Stewart," Vermont Historical Society, *Proceedings* 64, no. 2 (Spring 1996):
       91 (*forty Indians*); Arnold to "Dr. Potts," Aug. 18, 1776, T-P RC, #1941 (*hospitals*); Arnold to
       Gates, Sept. 28, 1776, *NDAR*, vol. 6, 1032 (*soles*); Gates to Arnold, Aug. 7, 1776, NYHS, micro,
       reel 3, plate 527 (*"temerity"*).

415   *By mid-September Arnold had found*: Harrison Bird, *Navies in the Mountains*, 180; Arnold to
       Gates, Sept. 21 and 28, 1776, *NDAR*, vol. 6, 926 (*"fine, secure"*), 1032; Palmer, *History of Lake*
       Champlain, 123–25; Arnold to Gates, Sept. 7 and 18, 1776, *NDAR*, vol. 6, 734, 884 (*"we can retire"*).

415   *"When you ask for a frigate"*: quoted in Randall, *Benedict Arnold*, 258–60; Jonathan Trum-
       bull to Jabez Huntington, Aug. 7, 1776, Feinstone Collection, DLAR, micro, reel 5, no. 2085
       (*five ship's masters*); Miller, *Sea of Glory*, 168 (*ox cart*); "*Trumbull I* (Galley)," Naval History
       and Heritage Command, https://www.history.navy.mil/research/histories/ship-histories/
       danfs/t/trumbull-i.html; Bird, *Navies in the Mountains*, 172–73; Arnold to Gates, Sept. 21,
       1776, NYHS, micro, reel 3, plate 961 (*"miserable set"*).

416   *On October 1 he wrote Gates*: Arnold to Gates, Oct. 1, 1776, *AA*, V: 2, 834–35.

416   *"I now give up the hope of seeing"*: Gates to Arnold, Oct. 3, 1776, Arnold papers from *Royal*
       Savage, T-P RC; Salsig, 251 (*twenty barrels*).

416   *By the second week of October*: Randall, *Benedict Arnold*, 292 (*"Haughty"*); Arnold to Gates,
       Oct. 7, 1776, *NDAR*, vol. 6, 1151–52 (*"very severe"*).

416   *"I am very anxious for our army"*: Arnold to Gates, Oct. 7, 1776, *NDAR*, vol. 6, 1151–52; Palmer,
       George Washington and Benedict Arnold, 164–65 (*"persevering hero"*); Brandt, *The Man in*
       the Mirror, 98 (*"best friends"*); Arnold to Gates, Sept. 2, 1776, *NDAR*, vol. 6, 654 (*"begging*
       leave"); Arnold to Gates, Sept. 7, 1776, *NDAR*, vol. 6, 734 (*"sacrificed my ease"*); Arnold to

Gates, Oct. 10, 1776, *AA*, V: 2, 982 (*"no late intelligence"*); Arnold to Gates, Oct. 7, 1776, *AA*, V: 2, 933 (*"prepared for them"*).

416 *As sunrise approached just after six o'clock:* "Sun and Moon Data," U.S. Naval Observatory; Nelson, *Benedict Arnold's Navy*, 264, 293.

417 *On the quarterdeck of* Lady Maria: Bird, *Navies in the Mountains*, 196–97; J. Robert Maguire, "Dr. Robert Knox's Account of the Battle of Valcour, October 11–13, 1776," *Vermont History* 46, no. 3 (Summer 1978): 3+ (*"mortification"*).

417 *Arnold had been alerted:* Pippenger, "Finding Edward Wigglesworth's Lost Diary," *JAR*, October 11, 2018; Randall, *Benedict Arnold*, 293–94, 299; *BARH*, 267–71 (*"judicious defense"*); Allen, *A Naval History of the American Revolution*, vol. 1, 167–68 (*outgunned*).

417 *Brigadier General David Waterbury, Jr., Arnold's:* Waterbury to Hancock, Oct. 24, 1776, *AA*, V: 2, 1224; *BARH*, 271; Mahan, 47.

417 *Captain Pringle had neglected:* Stanley, *Canada Invaded*, 141–42; Mahan, 52; Bird, *Navies in the Mountains*, 197–98 (*upwind struggle*).

418 *Arnold promptly recalled:* Bird, *Navies in the Mountains*, 199; Palmer, *Battle of Valcour Island on Lake Champlain, October 11th, 1776,* 13.

418 *In a blur of rammers and sponges:* Nelson, *Benedict Arnold's Navy*, 300; Hadden, *A Journal Kept in Canada*, 22.

418 *"At half past twelve":* Arnold to Gates, Oct. 12, 1776, *AA*, V: 2, 1038; Hadden, *A Journal Kept in Canada*, 24; Allen, *A Naval History of the American Revolution*, vol. 1, 170; Hubbard, "Battle at Valcour Island: Benedict Arnold as Hero," *American Heritage* 17, no. 6 (Oct. 1966): https://archive.org/details/american17no6newy; Nelson, *Benedict Arnold's Navy*, 299–300; Bird, *Navies in the Mountains*, 200–01; Mahan, 48–49 (*"cannonade"*).

418 *The schooner* Carleton, *nearest to:* Hadden, *A Journal Kept in Canada*, 22–23; Wickman, ed., "A Most Unsettled Time on Lake Champlain: The October 1776 Journal of Jahiel Stewart," Vermont Historical Society, *Proceedings* 64, no. 2 (Spring 1996): 91 (*"very hot"*); Osler, *The Life of Admiral Viscount Exmouth*, 12, 17–18; Rodger, *The Command of the Ocean*, 385–86 (*"pockmarked"*); Mahan, 48–49; *ANTA*, 238–39.

419 *More battering befell the British:* Miller, *Sea of Glory*, 175 (*"greatly annoyed"*); Burgoyne, ed., *Enemy Views*, 63; Burgoyne, trans., *Georg Pausch's Journal and Reports on the Campaign in America*, 43–44; Bird, *Navies in the Mountains*, 202; Maguire, "Dr. Robert Knox's Account of the Battle of Valcour, October 11–13, 1776," *Vermont History* 46, no. 3 (Summer 1978): 3+ (*"Well, doctor"*).

419 *In truth,* Maria *had anchored:* "An Open Letter to Captain Pringle," June 8, 1777, *BFTM* 1, no. 4 (July 1928): 14+; letter, T-P RC, #1975; Stanley, *Canada Invaded*, 142 (*barely one-third*); Bird, *Navies in the Mountains*, 215.

419 *As the afternoon wore away:* Mahan, 48–49; VBRP, 69, 143–49; Hagglund, *A Page from the Past: The Story of the Continental Gundelo* Philadelphia *on Lake Champlain, 1776–1949* (Adirondack Resorts Press, 1949), 27; Arnold to Gates, Oct. 12, 1776, *AA*, V: 2, 1038. *Philadelphia* later was raised for display in the Smithsonian Institution.

419 *Much of the British fire concentrated:* Arnold to Gates, Oct. 12, 1776, *AA*, V: 2, 1038 (*"suffered much"*); *BARH*, 277 (*black with powder*); Charles Terrot to John Frott, Nov. 13, 1776, T-P RC, #2088 (*ubiquitous*).

420 *Shortly before sunset at 5:16 p.m.:* Bird, *Navies in the Mountains*, 204–05; Arnold to Gates, Oct. 12, 1776, *AA*, V: 2, 1038 (*Sixty men*); Wickman, ed., "A Most Unsettled Time on Lake Champlain: The October 1776 Journal of Jahiel Stewart," Vermont Historical Society, *Proceedings* 64, no. 2 (Spring 1996): 92 (*"doctors cut off"*); Miller, *Sea of Glory*, 175.

420 *There was no choice:* Arnold to Gates, Oct. 12, 1776, *AA*, V: 2, 1038; Bird, *Navies in the Mountains*, 205 (*rattlesnake*); Cometti, ed., *The American Journals of Lt. John Enys*, 20 (*semicircle*); Hadden, *A Journal Kept in Canada*, 24; *ANTA*, 241–42.

420 *Arnold's captains returned to their boats:* Hubbard, "Battle at Valcour Island: Benedict Arnold as Hero," *American Heritage* 17, no. 6 (Oct. 1966): https://archive.org/details/american17no6newy; Bird, *Navies in the Mountains*, 204.

421   *One by one the thirteen*: Miller, *Sea of Glory*, 176.

421   *By Saturday morning they were eight miles*: Pippenger, "Recently Discovered Letters Shed New Light on the Battle of Valcour Island," *JAR*, Oct. 11, 2016; Arnold to Gates, Oct. 12, 1776, and Arnold to Schuyler, Oct. 15, 1776, *AA*, V: 2, 1038 (*"fortunate escape"*), 1080; Palmer, *Battle of Valcour on Lake Champlain, October 11th, 1776*, 18 (*"foot to head"*); Nelson, *Benedict Arnold's Navy*, 310; Wickman, ed., "A Most Unsettled Time on Lake Champlain: The October 1776 Journal of Jahiel Stewart," Vermont Historical Society, *Proceedings* 64, no. 2 (Spring 1996): 92 (*"we was safe"*).

421   *At dawn, Carleton let his phlegmatic mien*: Mahan, 49–50; Bird, *Navies in the Mountains*, 209 (*gull guano*); "An Open Letter to Captain Pringle," June 8, 1777, *BFTM* 1, no. 4 (July 1928): 14+ (*"extreme obscurity"*); Pippenger, "Recently Discovered Letters Shed New Light on the Battle of Valcour Island," *JAR*, Oct. 11, 2016.

421   *Arnold spotted the white specks*: BARH, 281; "An Open Letter to Captain Pringle," June 8, 1777, *BFTM* 1, no. 4 (July 1928): 14+ (*southerly*); Bird, *Navies in the Mountains*, 210; Pippenger, "Recently Discovered Letters Shed New Light on the Battle of Valcour Island," *JAR*, Oct. 11, 2016; Allen, *A Naval History of the American Revolution*, vol. 1, 176; Col. Edward Wigglesworth diary, in Smith, *History of Newburyport*, 358–59 (*oars double-manned*).

422   *That left Arnold*: Bird, *Navies in the Mountains*, 211–12; Arnold to Schuyler, Oct. 15, 1776, *AA*, V: 2, 1080; Nelson, *Benedict Arnold's Navy*, 316–17; Randall, *Benedict Arnold*, 315.

422   *From his reconnaissance of Lake Champlain*: Bird, *Navies in the Mountains*, 212; BARH, 283 (*through a gap*); VBRP, 33 (*high ground*); ANTA, 246–47; Brandt, *The Man in the Mirror*, 109–10 (*"point of honor"*); Nelson, *Benedict Arnold's Navy*, 318–19.

422   *Two hundred men joined Arnold*: Gates to Schuyler, Oct. 15, 1776, *NDAR*, vol. 6, 1277; Barker and Huey, *The 1776–1777 Northern Campaigns for the American War of Independence and Their Sequel*, 94 (*"so black"*); James P. Millard, "The Story of Arnold's Bay," VBRP, http://www.historiclakes.org/Valcour/arnoldsbay.htm; Salsig, 261; Stanley, *Canada Invaded*, 143; Arnold to Schuyler, Oct. 15, 1776, *AA*, V: 2, 1080 (*"fatigued"*).

423   *Gates praised his "gallant behavior"*: Salsig, 261; Gates to Schuyler, Oct. 15, 1776, *NDAR*, vol. 6, 1277 (*"pleased providence"*).

423   *Smoke and flame swirled*: Baldwin, 80–81 (*"greatest distress"*); Trumbull, *Reminiscences and Letters of John Trumbull*, 35–36 (*set them free*); Carleton to Germain, Oct. 14, 1776, *DAR*, vol. 12, 237 (*"entirely defeated"*).

423   *Guy Carleton faced the most momentous*: GWGO, 125; Baxter, ed., *The British Invasion from the North*, 161 (*captured colors*); ANTA, 259; Carleton to M. Tonencour, Oct. 4, 1776, in Cruikshank, 193 (*"warn the inhabitants"*).

423   *Ten miles south, few Americans*: Baldwin, 82 (*Albany*); Trumbull, *Reminiscences and Letters of John Trumbull*, 35–36 (*infected his troops*); BARH, 286 (*"grand attack"*).

424   *Each morning, beginning that Monday*: Robbins, *Journal of the Rev. Ammi R. Robbins*, 44; Jones, *History of the Campaign for the Conquest of Canada in 1776*, 176 (*four thousand tons*); Baldwin, 80–81, 82 (*"life and spirits"*); Salsig, 267; ANTA, 255; Gates to Schuyler, Oct. 15, 1776, *AA*, V: 2, 1080; Lacey, "Memoirs of Brigadier-General John Lacey, of Pennsylvania," *PMHB* 25–26 (1901–02): 1+ (*ten rods*); *Orderly Book of Capt. Ichabod Norton*, 46 (*buckshot*); William Clajon [Gates's secretary] to Dr. Jonathan Potts, Oct. 14, 1776, T-P RC, #1947 (*"well-men"*); Furcron, "Mount Independence," *BFTM* 9, no. 4 (Winter 1954): 230+ (*log boom*).

424   *Time was on their side*: ANTA, 257 (*"General Winter"*); William Tennent to Susanna Tennent, Oct. 15, 1776, photocopy, T-P RC (*"Our situation"*); Wickman, "The Diary of Timothy Tuttle," *New Jersey History* 113, nos. 3–4 (Fall–Winter 1995): 61+; Salsig, 271 (*"Be ye not afraid"*).

424   *The alarm guns finally sounded*: Frazer, "Letter from Ticonderoga, 1776," *BFTM* 10, no. 1 (1962): 450+; Lacey, "Memoirs of Brigadier-General John Lacey, of Pennsylvania," *PMHB* 25–26 (1901–02): 1+ (*"Turn out"*).

424   *They could also see redcoats*: Jones, *History of the Campaign for the Conquest of Canada in 1776*, 187.

425   *And then, like spirits*: GWGO, 125; ANTA, 264 (*"pulse"*), 262 (*"approaching season"*); Glover, *General Burgoyne in Canada and America*, 104; Baxter, ed., *The British Invasion from the*

North, 175. Col. John Trumbull, then Gates's adjutant, put the number of defenders at more than 13,000. *Reminiscences and Letters of John Trumbull*, 36. Other tallies are somewhat lower. Stanley, *Canada Invaded*, 144.

425 *Victorious yet morose*: Baxter, ed., *The British Invasion from the North*, 177 (*"Some of their dead"*).

425 *"Blessed be God I am alive"*: Archer Jay to parents, Oct. 14, 1776, T-P, RC, #2082; Edmund Munro to wife, Oct. 20, 1776, T-P RC, #1966 (*"Being in great haste"*).

425 *No sooner had Carleton made himself*: Cubbison, *"The Artillery Never Gained More Honour,"* 64–65 (*"no disgrace"*); Mackesy, *The War for America*, 96 (*cost Britain a year*); Valin, *Fortune's Favorite*, 35 (*margin of victory*); G. Christie to Germain, Oct. 26, 1776, *Stopford-Sackville*, vol. 2, 45–46 (*"totally unfit"*); Kingsley, "Letters to Lord Polwarth from Sir Francis-Carr Clerke, Aide-de-Camp to General John Burgoyne," *New York History* 79, no. 4 (Oct. 1998): 414 (*"man of spirit"*); Clowes, *The Royal Navy*, vol. 3, 371 (*"saved the lake"*).

426 *In a letter to Henry Clinton*: Nelson, *General Sir Guy Carleton, Lord Dorchester*, 104 (*"fruits"*); Burgoyne to Clinton, Nov. 7, 1776, in Jane Clark, "The Command of the Canadian Army for the Campaign of 1777," *Canadian Historical Review* 10 (June 1929): 132 (*"cypher"*); MLA, 142 (*North Cloister*).

426 *Adding to Burgoyne's miseries*: De Fonblanque, *Political and Military Episodes*, 225 (*"sense or vigor"*), 227 (*"laid himself"*); Cruikshank, 37; A. L. Burt, *Guy Carleton, Lord Dorchester*, Canadian Historical Association Booklets, no. 5 (1968): 10–11; George to North, Dec. 13, 1776, "George the Third Calendar, Sept. 1775–Oct. 1777," RA GEO/MAIN/#2488.

427 *For now George chose to pretend*: De Fonblanque, *Political and Military*, 228–29 (*"Thoughts for Conducting"*); George to North, Dec. 13, 1776, "George the Third Calendar, Sept. 1775–Oct. 1777," RA GEO/MAIN/#2488 (*"not so active"*); ANTA, 264 (*"must necessarily fall"*); Weintraub, *Iron Tears*, 86 (*"home victorious"*).

427 *Just before the St. Lawrence iced*: Nelson, *General Sir Guy Carleton, Lord Dorchester*, 103; Germain to W. Howe, Oct. 18, 1776, *Stopford-Sackville*, vol. 2, 43 (*"less value"*); Reynolds, *Guy Carleton*, 107 (*cariole*).

427 *Here, on December 31*: Hatch, *Thrust for Canada*, 246; Nelson, *General Sir Guy Carleton, Lord Dorchester*, 103 (*"crave pardon"*); *Quebec Gazette*, Jan. 2, 1777, in Cruikshank, 200 (*"completest entertainment"*).

427 *By then the king's troops*: Burgoyne, trans., *Hesse-Hanau Order Books, a Diary and Rosters*, 43–44 (*wooden slats*); Burgoyne, trans., *Georg Pausch's Journal and Reports of the Campaign in America*, 46 (*"Everyone received"*).

428 *Even this garb could not repel*: Lynn, ed., *An Eyewitness Account of the American Revolution and New England Life*, 37 (*"American Siberia"*); Charles Terrot to John Frott, Nov. 13, 1776, T-P RC, #2088 (*"Next summer"*).

428 *This year it had been Benedict Arnold's*: Thacher, *Military Journal*, 65–66 (*"dexterity"*); ANTA, 267 (*"great consequence"*); Randall, *Benedict Arnold*, 323–24.

428 *Yet, as always, he remained controversial*: BARH, 282, 288–89 (*"fiery, hot"*); Sedgwick, *A Memoir of the Life of William Livingston*, 208 (*"evil genius"*); Maguire, "Dr. Robert Knox's Account of the Battle of Valcour, October 11–13, 1776," *Vermont History* 46, no. 3 (Summer 1978): 3+.

429 *Fewer than three thousand men would stay*: ANTA, 268–70; Bolton, *The Private Soldier Under Washington*, 51–52 (*shoeless*).

18. THE RETROGRADE MOTION OF THINGS

431 *From the wide portico*: author visit, Morris-Jumel Mansion, and interview with Emilie Gruchow, director of archives, Aug. 2014; Shelton, *The Jumel Mansion*, 4–5; Smith, "The Roger Morris House, Washington's Headquarters on Harlem Heights, 1776," *Magazine of American History* 6 (1881): 89 A 1765 newspaper advertisement for the property claimed that the vista extended for eighteen miles in all directions. Roger Morris raised the hill another twenty feet. The mansion, still standing, is at West 161st Street. www.morrisjumel.org.

431 *An odd tranquillity had obtained*: Shreve, *Tench Tilghman*, 72 (*"thousand miles"*); Shelton, *The Jumel Mansion*, 36–37, 74, 95; Smith, *Historical Sketch of Washington's Headquarters*,

v–ix; Greiff, *The Morris-Jumel Mansion: A Documentary History*, 126–27; details from Emilie Gruchow, archivist, www.morrisjumel.org (*"William Lee"*).

432 *The loss of Long Island*: GW to John Augustine Washington, Sept. 22, 1776, *PGW*, vol. 6, 374 (*"power of words"*); GW to Lund Washington, Sept. 30, 1776, *PGW*, vol. 6, 4410–42 (*"bitterest curse"*); *IMI*, vol. 5, 1025 (*"execute them"*).

432 *"I am wearied to death"*: general return, Oct. 5, *PGW*, vol. 6, 589n. The numbers exclude more than 6,000 militia troops scattered around New York. In late September, Greene's force totaled more than 5,700. Greene, *The Life of Nathanael Greene*, vol. 1, 216; Shonnard and Spooner, *History of Westchester County*, 352; general orders, Oct. 4, 1776, *PGW*, vol. 6, 462 (*"shameful inattention"*).

432 *A Delaware surgeon at King's Bridge*: Duncan, "Medical Men in the American Revolution: The New York Campaign of 1776," *New York Medical Journal* (Sept.–Oct. 1920): 37–38 (*"melting"*), 3, 9, 17–20 (*"beg instruments"*); Albion and Dodson, eds., *Philip Vickers Fithian: A Journal, 1775-1776*, 239–41 (*"unskillful quack"*); J. Wadsworth to Gov. J. Trumbull, Oct. 11, 1776, *AA*, V: 2, 995 (*single surgeon's mate*).

432 *Those who stayed healthy*: *GGW*, 158–60; general orders, Sept. 22, 1776, *PGW*, vol. 6, 364 (*inspect knapsacks*); GW to Hancock, Sept. 22 and 25, 1776, *PGW*, vol. 6, 368–69, 399–401n (*"Some houses"*).

433 *"There is too much corruption"*: J. Adams to A. Adams, Sept. 22 and Oct. 8, 1776, in *AFC*, vol. 2, 131, 140; GW to Patrick Henry, Oct. 5, 1776, *PGW*, vol. 6, 481–82 (*"just pretension"*).

433 *In an anguished, fourteen-paragraph*: GW to Hancock, Sept. 25, 1776, *PGW*, vol. 6, 393–400.

433 *The grumble of heavy artillery*: Dawson, *Westchester-County, New York, During the American Revolution*, 226–27.

434 *Within twenty minutes, five American batteries*: logs, *Phoenix, Roebuck, Tartar*, Oct. 9, 1776, *NDAR*, vol. 6, 1178–81; W. Tudor to Delia Jarvis, Oct. 9, 1776, MHS, William Tudor Papers, Ms. N-1684 (*"noblest effect"*); McDonald, "British and American Armies in 1776, Before the Battle of White Plains," *The McDonald Papers*, part 1, 8–9 (*"One gentleman"*).

434 *Since the first successful British sortie*: Deary, 140–47, 160–66, 216–18, 237; Charles F. Himes, "Colonel Robert Magaw: The Defender of Fort Washington," paper read to Hamilton Library Association, Carlisle, Pa. (1915): 39 (*"shallow"*); Heusser, *George Washington's Map Maker*, 147–50; Crawford, ed., *The Autobiography of a Yankee Mariner*, 102–05; Walker, *Engineers of Independence*, 119–20; Secret Committee, New York Convention, to GW, Sept. 27, 1776, *PGW*, vol. 6, 414. Various delays kept four ships provided by New York from being sunk before the British squadron passed upriver. GW to John Hancock, Oct. 5, 1776, *PGW*, vol. 6, 478n.

434 *British officers watching with spyglasses*: Serle, 54 (*"malevolence"*). British hydrography intelligence indicated that a navigable channel averaging seven fathoms reached almost to Albany. Deary, 29–30.

434 *The Hudson was, in fact, vaster*: Diamant, *Chaining the Hudson*, 60; Deary, 15, 162–64; Sanderson, *Mannahatta*, 84; William Duer to GW, Sept. 22, 1776, *PGW*, vol. 6, 367 (*"may not be sufficient"*); Ruttenber, *Obstructions to the Navigation of Hudson's River*, 40 (*"secrecy"*).

434 *Too late. At nine a.m. that Wednesday*: Capt. Andrew Snape Hamond narrative, *NDAR*, vol. 6, 1183n; Diamant, *Chaining the Hudson*, 61–62; Deary, 207 (*32-pound balls*); Lt. George Edwards to "Col. Rebow," Nov. 18, 1776, NYHS, Misc. Mss., NYHS (*"hawser"* and *"arms folded"*); NCCH, 273.

435 *Within an hour the squadron*: Bolton, *The Bombardment of New York*, 58–59; Jeremiah Putnam and Nathaniel Cleaves to GW, Oct. 9, 1776, *PGW*, vol. 6, 519–20 (*two sloops*); McDonald, "British and American Armies in 1776, Before the Battle of White Plains," *The McDonald Papers*, part 1, 8–9 (*grapeshot*). Bushnell later salvaged *Turtle*, but she subsequently vanished. Wagner, *Submarine Fighter of the American Revolution*, 73–75.

435 *At five p.m., after lashing the riverfront*: logs, *Phoenix, Roebuck, Tartar*, Oct. 9, 1776, *NDAR*, vol. 6, 1178; Peter R. Livingston to Robert Livingston, Jr., Oct. 10, 1776, NYHS, Donald P. Clark Collection, #92; Bolton, *The Bombardment of New York*, 58–59; Charles F. Himes, "Colonel Robert Magaw: The Defender of Fort Washington," paper read to Hamilton Library

Association, Carlisle, Pa. (1915): 38 (*"cobwebs"*); Tench Tilghman to New York Committee of Correspondence, Oct. 9, 1776, NYHS, Misc. Mss. (*"To our surprise"*).

435 *The damage was worse*: Lt. George Edwards to "Col. Rebow," Nov. 18, 1776, NYHS, Misc. Mss. (*"most amiable"*); Israel Mauduit, *Observations upon the Conduct of Sir William Howe at the White Plains* (*"loss of men"*); logs, *Phoenix, Roebuck, Tartar*, Oct. 9, 1776, *NDAR*, vol. 6, 1178–82 (*"to the deep"*).

435 *But once again a hostile British force*: NCCH, 277 (vingt-et-un); New York Committee of Safety to GW, Oct. 10, 1776, *PGW*, vol. 6, 529 (*"alarming"*).

436 *"It would be a joke"*: Ryden, ed., *Letters to and from Caesar Rodney*, 137–39.

436 *Completely surrounding the Americans*: W. Howe to Germain, Sept. 25, 1776, UK NA, CO 5/93, f. 567 (*"rather precarious"*).

436 *In the weeks since his victories*: HBAR, 104, 121; *DAR*, vol. 12, 5–6; *WAI*, 150–51 (*"most effectual means"*); *DFM*, 74–75 (*"did not break up"*).

437 *Dispersing enemy armies was hardly equivalent*: The peninsula was later called Throgs (or Throggs) Neck. Marston's Wharf was near the current East Eightieth Street. *DFM*, 75–77; Abbatt, *The Battle of Pell's Point*, 4; *TAR*, 49.

437 *The only real hazard*: Gannett, *The Origin of Certain Place Names in the United States*, 154 (*Hellegat*); Burgoyne, ed., *Enemy Views*, 83–88; Diugosz, "Not the Hudson: A Comprehensive Study of the East River," Fordham University (2011), http://www.eastriverhistory.webs .com/naturalhistory/treacherouswaters.htm; *TAR*, 49 (*"utter darkness"*); JHD, 111+ (*channel buoys*); *DFM*, 85–86 (*stern first*); casualty returns, Sept. 17–Oct. 18, 1776, *AA*, V: 3, 1055; Tilley, *The British Navy and the American Revolution*, 92.

437 *By midday four thousand nauseous soldiers*: C 1776, 167, 266n (*"their imaginations"*); Shonnard and Spooner, *History of Westchester County*, 366, 368n; author visit, St. Paul's Church National Historic Site, Mount Vernon, N.Y., and interview with Michael Callahan, NPS, Aug. 2014; Dawson, *Westchester-County, New York, During the American Revolution*, 230–33; McDonald, "British and American Armies in 1776, Before the Battle of White Plains," *The McDonald Papers*, part 1, 5–12. Smith would later become John and Abigail Adams's son-in-law. Hufeland, *Westchester County During the American Revolution*, 111–12.

438 *A blistering first volley*: Tilghman to New York Convention, Oct. 13, 1776, NYHS, Misc. Mss. (*"Our riflemen"*); JHD, 111+ (*"popping"*).

438 *By nightfall eleven thousand British*: Lydenberg, 579; Deary, 248–49; Freeman, 215 (*"If we cannot fight"*); W. Heath to GW, Oct. 13, 1776, *PGW*, vol. 6, 557 (*"A large number of vessels"*).

438 *Nor would there be movement*: Deary, 58; *TAR*, 49n (*"tweedledum"*).

438 *Washington had been oblivious*: Dawson, *Westchester-County, New York, During the American Revolution*, 233; GW to Hancock, Oct. 11–13, 1776, and general orders, Oct. 13, 1776, *PGW*, vol. 6, 535 (*"reason to believe"*), 552–53; BNY, 223.

439 *A more discerning battle captain*: Fort Lee History, 194–95 (*"swordsmen"*); C. Lee to Hancock, Oct. 12, 1776, *LP*, vol. 2, 261 (*"rouse yourselves"*); C. Lee to Gates, Oct. 14, 1776, *LP*, vol. 2, 261 (*"whole stable"*).

439 *The ranks were thrilled*: "The Revolutionary War Diary of Chaplain Andrew Hunter," Oct. 14, 1776, http://www.revwar75.com/library/bob/HunterDiaries.htm (*"universal satisfaction"*); BNY, 224–25; council of war, Oct. 16, 1776, *PGW*, vol. 6, 576.

439 *Thirteen thousand American soldiers trudged*: Shonnard and Spooner, *History of Westchester County*, 383; WR, 256–57, 374 (*magazine in Rye*); Dawson, *Westchester-County, New York, During the American Revolution*, 235, 239n, 248; BNY, 224 (*anchoring the left*).

440 *At one a.m. on Friday, October 18*: Bradford, ed., "A British Officer's Revolutionary War Journal, 1776–1778," *Maryland Historical Magazine* 56, no. 2 (June 1961): 160–61; Billias, "Pelham Bay: A Forgotten Battle," in *Narratives of the Revolution in New York*, 110–11; Hufeland, *Westchester County During the American Revolution*, 116. Pell's Point was later renamed Rodman's Neck.

440 *Yet watching through a spyglass*: Billias, *General John Glover and His Marblehead Mariners*, 6, 18–20, 62–70; GW HQ, 54 (*"hardy race"*).

440 *"Oh, the anxiety of mind"*: John Glover, letter, Oct. 22, 1776, *AA*, V: 2, 1188–89; Abbatt, *The Battle of Pell's Point*, 14 (*four more volleys*).

441 *For ninety minutes Howe's troops*: Billias, "Pelham Bay: A Forgotten Battle," in *Narratives of the Revolution in New York*, 117–18 (*"pigeons"*); Dawson, *Westchester-County, New York, During the American Revolution*, 242–44.

441 *Among the intrepid men*: Evelyn, 9–10, 85–86, 89–90.

441 *There would not be another*: Evelyn, 11; John Glover, letter, Oct. 22, 1776, *AA*, V: 2, 1188–89 (*hat and canteen*).

441 *At noon, Glover spotted*: author visit, interview with Michael Callahan, NPS, St. Paul's Church National Historic Site, Mount Vernon, N.Y., Aug. 2014; Billias, "Pelham Bay: A Forgotten Battle," in *Narratives of the Revolution in New York*, 115–16; John Glover, letter, Oct. 22, 1776, *AA*, V: 2, 1188–89 (*"heavens over us"*).

441 *Howe chose not to pursue*: Billias, "Pelham Bay: A Forgotten Battle," in *Narratives of the Revolution in New York*, 118; Hoffman, *Historic Highlights of Westchester* (White Plains, N.Y.: Battle of White Plains Monument Committee, 1969), n.p. (*skittish militiamen*); W. Howe to Germain, Nov. 30, 1776, *AA*, V: 3, 922; *BNY*, 229; Abbatt, *The Battle of Pell's Point*, 19–20 (*British deserters*); Ellis, *Revolutionary Summer*, 168 (*"lost more men"*).

442 *Among those beyond repair*: Evelyn wrote a memorandum while at Staten Island on August 20, 1776, elaborating on his will. *Evelyn*, 11, 90–95.

442 *If Captain Evelyn's rule-Britannia swagger*: W. Howe to Germain, Nov. 30, 1776, *AA*, V: 3, 921–22 (*"gallant"*).

442 *Having missed an opportunity to seize*: Van Tyne, *The War of Independence: American Phase*, 257 (*"difficult to be known"*); Uhlendorf, ed., *Revolution in America*, 65; letter, "a gentleman in the army," Nov. 1, 1776, *AA*, V: 471 (*halting each night*); Curtis, *The British Army in the American Revolution*, 6–7 (*teamsters*); Boyle, ed., *From Redcoat to Rebel*, 69; *WR*, 261 (*ten days*).

443 *The invasion force in Westchester*: Deary, 266; Ewald, *Diary of the American War*, 5; return of 2nd Hessian division, Admiralty to Germain, June 20, 1776, *DAR*, vol. 5, 322; Eelking and Rosengarten, *The German Allied Troops in the North American War of Independence*, 30 (*prayer books*); convoy report, in Admiralty to Germain, Oct. 26, 1776, *DAR*, vol. 5, 393 (*three hundred horses*); George Osborn to Germain, Oct. 29, 1776, UK NA, CO 5/93, f. 1003 (*"in every respect"*); Atwood, *The Hessians*, 73.

443 *An unsettling number collapsed*: At least one Hessian battalion had been at sea for 142 days. Burgoyne, trans., *Journal of a Hessian Grenadier Battalion*, 48–49 (*on parade*); author visit, St. Paul's Church National Historic Site, Mount Vernon, N.Y., interview with Michael Callahan, NPS, and NPS pamphlets, Aug. 2014 (*mass grave*); *The Story of a Town: 1664–1964* (Eastchester, N.Y., 1964), 9.

443 *Not least among Howe's worries*: courts-martial records, UK NA, WO 71/83, 1–86 (*six hundred lashes*); Oct. 19, 1776, journal entry, KP (*ban on plundering*); Burgoyne, *Enemy Views*, 88 (*farm cemetery*).

443 *"They were unfortunately led to believe"*: George Osborn to Germain, Oct. 29, 1776, UK NA, CO 5/93, f. 1003; Serle, 120 (*"locusts"*); Robert M. Calhoon, "The Reintegration of the Loyalists and the Disaffected," in Greene, ed., *The American Revolution: Its Character and Limits*, 59; Oct. 3 and Nov. 2, 1776, journal entries, KP (*"fruits of the earth"*).

443 *Step by slow step*: Burgoyne, *Enemy Views*, 83 (*cider*); Hoffman, *The Battle of White Plains: October 28, 1776* (White Plains, N.Y.: City of White Plains, 1999), 15 (*in a tavern*); W. Howe to Germain, Nov. 30, 1776, *AA*, V: 3, 922–23; Lydenberg, 583; Eelking and Rosengarten, *The German Allied Troops in the North American War of Independence*, 31 (*campfires*); Burgoyne, trans., "Diary of Private Johannes Reuber, Grenadier Regiment Rall," *The Hessians: Journal of the Johannes Schwalm Historical Association* 5 (2012): 25 (*dragging chains*).

444 *For more than a week, indulged*: Dawson, *Westchester-County, New York, During the American Revolution*, 257; Hoffman, *The Battle of White Plains: October 28, 1776* (White Plains, N.Y.: City of White Plains, 1999), 13; Hildreth, *Biographical and Historical Memoirs of the Early Pioneer Settlers of Ohio*, 61–64 (*maps*); author visit, Jacob Purdy House, Westchester, N.Y., Aug. 2014.

444 *Not until Sunday morning did the last*: Dawson, *Westchester-County, New York, During the American Revolution*, 255–57 (*baggage had been abandoned*); Tallmadge, *Memoir of Col. Benjamin Tallmadge*, 13 (*iron pikes*); Board of War to NG, Oct. 22, 1776, *PNG*, 319–20 (*musket cartridges*); Burgoyne, ed., *Enemy Views*, 80–83 (*water to freeze*); Rau, ed., "Sergeant John Smith's Diary of 1776," *Mississippi Historical Review* 20, no. 2 (Sept. 1933): 258 (*"cold lodging"*).

444 *Early on Monday, October 28*: Heath, *Memoirs of Major-General William Heath*, 68–69 (*"you will repair"*).

444 *From Purdy Hill the spectacle*: Flexner, *The Young Hamilton*, 117; Chernow, *George Washington: A Life*, 258–59; McDonald, *The McDonald Papers*, part 1, 47–49; *WR*, 262 (*"autumnal sun"*); Rau, ed., "Sergeant John Smith's Diary of 1776," *Mississippi Historical Review* 20, no. 2 (Sept. 1933): 258 (*"very warlike"*).

445 *To disrupt this fine parade*: Martin, *A Narrative of a Revolutionary Soldier*, 47 (*"to be killed"*); "Letter from a Gentleman in the Army," Nov. 1, 1776, *AA*, V: 3, 471 (*"leaves in a whirlwind"*); Dawson, *Westchester-County, New York, During the American Revolution*, 260.

445 *Only this morning, during his aborted*: Heath, *Memoirs of Major-General William Heath*, 68–69; *GGW*, 161; McDonald, *The McDonald Papers*, part 1, 31; Hancock to GW, Aug. 10, 1776, *PGW*, vol. 6, 657n; *BTP*, 452–53.

445 *No sooner had the colonel*: J. Haslet to Caesar Rodney, Nov. 12, 1776, *AA*, V: 3, 653 (*"reiterated thunder"* and *"broke and fled"*); Ward, *The Delaware Continentals*, 91 (*cornstalk clumps*); author visit, Battle Hill (Chatterton Hill), White Plains, Aug. 2014, signage; Tacyn, "To the End: The First Maryland Regiment and the American Revolution," Ph.D. diss. (University of Maryland, 1999): 99.

446 *General Howe sat his horse*: W. Howe to Germain, Nov. 30, 1776, *AA*, V: 3, 922–23 (*"galled"*); Hoffman, *Historic Highlights of Westchester* (White Plains, N.Y.: Battle of White Plains Monument Committee, 1969); McDonald, *The McDonald Papers*, part 1, 49, 52 (*kettledrums*); Atwood, *The Hessians*, 74; Hoffman, *The Battle of White Plains: October 28, 1776* (White Plains, N.Y.: City of White Plains, 1999), 17–19.

446 *Howe pushed more reserves*: Ward, *The Delaware Continentals*, 89; author visit, Battle Hill (Chatterton Hill), White Plains, Aug. 2014, historical signage; "Letter from a Gentleman in the Army," Nov. 1, 1776, *AA*, V: 3, 474 (*"grand and solemn"*); Atwood, *The Hessians*, 74–75 (*cartridge boxes*).

446 *A two-gun American battery*: Hamilton's son John claimed that his father fought on Chatterton's Hill, but the evidence is inconclusive. Chernow, *Alexander Hamilton*, 81; J. Haslet to Caesar Rodney, Nov. 12, 1776, *AA*, V: 3, 653 (*"wad of tow"*); Powell, "A Connecticut Soldier Under Washington: Elisha Bostwick's Memoirs of the First Years of the Revolution," *WMQ*, 3rd ser., 6, no. 1 (Jan. 1949): 100–01 (*"A cannonball cut"*).

446 *By midafternoon, blue-coated Hessians*: McDonald, *The McDonald Papers*, part 1, 52–53; Tacyn, "To the End: The First Maryland Regiment and the American Revolution," Ph.D. diss. (University of Maryland, 1999): 12–13 (*Smallwood*); Dawson, *Westchester-County, New York, During the American Revolution*, 267; Hoffman, *The Battle of White Plains: October 28, 1776* (White Plains, N.Y.: City of White Plains, 1999), 23; Boyle, ed., *From Redcoat to Rebel*, 70 (*twelve-deep*).

447 *Rebel bodies covered the hilltop*: Boyle, ed., *From Redcoat to Rebel*, 71 (*"half his breast"*); *DFM*, 98 (*"linen drawers"*); Hufeland, *Westchester County During the American Revolution*, 143–44; Dawson, *Westchester-County, New York, During the American Revolution*, 273–74; Heath, *Memoirs of Major-General William Heath*, 73 (*"the stars"*).

447 *Washington shortened his lines*: *BNY*, 241; W. Howe to Germain, Nov. 30, 1776, *AA*, V: 3, 923; Dawson, *Westchester-County, New York, During the American Revolution*, 274–75; McMichael, "Diary of Lieutenant James McMichael of the Pennsylvania Line, 1776–1778," *PMHB* 16, no. 2 (July 1892): 129+ (*"We encamp"*); Col. William Douglas to Hannah Douglas, Nov. 11, 1776, in *Quarterly Bulletin*, NYHS, 12, no. 1 (Apr. 1928) (*"mittens"*).

447 *The Westchester campaign sputtered*: Gruber, ed., *John Peebles' American War*, 59 (*"Our troops"*); Dawson, *Westchester-County, New York, During the American Revolution*, 277; Anderson, *The Command of the Howe Brothers During the American Revolution*, 197; W. Howe to Germain, Nov. 30, 1776, *AA*, V: 3, 923 (*"least consequence"*).

448 *The long columns winding toward*: Tench Tilghman to Robert R. Livingston, Nov. 6, 1776, *PGW*, vol. 7, 99n (*"extraordinary"*); GW to Hancock, Nov. 6, 1776, *PGW*, vol. 7, 97 (*"conjecture"*); Col. William Malcom to John McKesson, Nov. 5, 1776, *PGW*, vol. 7, 98n (*"troublesome neighbors"*); Coffin, "Diary of Capt. Peter Kimball, 1776," *Granite Monthly* (Mar. 1881): 230+ (*"washt"*).

448 *But other rebels rampaged*: Kim, "The Limits of Politicization in the American Revolution: The Experience of Westchester County, New York," *Journal of American History* 80, no. 3 (Dec. 1993): 878–89; Forster, "Westchester: A House Divided," *New York History* 28, no. 4 (Oct. 1947): 404+; Dawson, *Westchester-County, New York, During the American Revolution*, 277; Hoffman, *Historic Highlights of Westchester* (White Plains, N.Y.: Battle of White Plains Monument Committee, 1969); McDonald, *The McDonald Papers*, part 1, 60 (*"heated"*).

448 *Their commander, Major Jonathan Williams Austin*: Waters, *History of Chelmsford, Massachusetts*, 204; Harvard University, "Index of Harvard Graduates in the Classes of 1642–1772," https://iiif.lib.harvard.edu/manifests/view/drs:46585443$12i; Wroth and Zobel, eds., *Legal Papers of John Adams*, vol. 1, lxxxi; general orders, Nov. 6 and 8, 1776, *PGW*, vol. 7, 91 (*"cowardly wretches"*), 112 (*"barbarous conduct"*); C. Lee to GW, Nov. 12, 1776, *PGW*, vol. 7, 151–52n; GW to Heath, Mar. 30, 1777, *PGW*, vol. 9, 23; Austin court-martial, Nov. 12–13, 1776, *AA*, V: 3, 654; Heitman, *Historical Register of Officers of the Continental Army*, 78.

448 *Even if Howe had ceded the ground*: GGW, 163 (*"Our generals"*); W. Howe to Germain, Nov. 30, 1776, *AA*, V: 3, 923 (*"not less than 250"*); Hufeland, *Westchester County During the American Revolution*, 144; Shonnard and Spooner, *History of Westchester County*, 394; Atkinson, "British Forces in North America, 1774–1781: Their Distribution and Strength," part 2, *Journal of the Society for Army Historical Research* (Autumn 1940): 163+ (*totaled 254*); Trimen, *An Historical Memoir of the 35th Royal Sussex Regiment of Foot*, 55 (*17 dead*).

448 *"The army are no ways disheartened"*: S. Shaw to parents, Oct. 21, 1776, Samuel Shaw papers, MHS. A decade later, Shaw would be the first American consul in Canton.

448 *"I was educated a Quaker"*: NG to Samuel Ward, Jr., Oct. 9, 1772, *PNG*, 47; Greene, *The Life of Nathanael Greene*, vol. 1, 13, 25, 27, 56, 72; *Rhode Island in the American Revolution* (2000): 10, SoC, http://www.societyofthecincinnati.org/scholarship/publications/; NG to William Greene, Aug. 23, 1772, *PNG*, 37 (*asthmatic*); Johnson, *Nathanael Greene*, vol. 1, 13–15 (*calluses*).

450 *The Quakers expelled him*: Golway, *Washington's General*, 39, 44–46 (*"resist, expel"*); NG to Col. James M. Varnum, Oct. 31, 1774, *PNG*, 75–76 (*"mortification"*); NG to Jacob Greene, June 28, 1775, *PNG*, 93 (*"phrenzy"*); Stegeman and Stegeman, *Caty: A Biography of Catharine Littlefield Greene*, 12, 22, 31–32; NG to Caty, Oct. 26, 1775, *PNG*, 65–66, 144 (*"My soul"*).

450 *Now thirty-four, Greene was the youngest*: McCullough, *1776*, 21; *PNG*, xviii, xxix (*six hundred letters*); "Fort Lee, New Jersey: A Sketch of Its Revolutionary History," *Documents of the Assembly of the State of New York*, vol. 42, appendix B (1909), 188; Greene, *The Life of Nathanael Greene*, vol. 1, 216 (*"military genius"*); Thayer, *Nathanael Greene*, 67 (*"rawest"*).

450 *From his headquarters in a gambrel-roof*: Conway, "Fort Lee: The Post at Burdett's Ferry," *Bergen County History: 1775 Annual*, 15, 21; James Renner, "Burdett's Ferry," Edgewater Colony, http://www.edgewatercolonynj.com/about-us; NG to GW, Nov. 5, 1776, *PNG*, 254 (*organizing magazines*); NG to GW, Oct. 31, 1776, and reply from Robert Hanson Harrison (aide), Nov. 5, 1776, *PGW*, vol. 7, 69n (*"your discretion"*); *PNG*, 354 (*Putnam*); GW to Hancock, Nov. 16, 1776, *PGW*, vol. 7, 166n (*increased the garrison*); Deary, 289–91, 374–75 (*half of them Continentals*); NG to Hancock, Nov. 12, 1776, *PNG*, 349 (*"attempt to possess"*); NG to R. Magaw, Nov. 15, 1776, *PNG*, 350 (*"winter quarters"*).

451 *All of this, including Washington's deference*: author visit, Fort Washington, Aug. 2014; Graydon, *Memories of His Own Time*, 186 (*illusion*); de Lancey, "Mount Washington and Its Capture, November 16th, 1776," *Magazine of American History* 1, no. 2, (Feb. 1877): 65+ (*forty-seven cannons*); Bolton, *Fort Washington*, 46 (*3- to 32-pounders*); "The Revolutionary War Diary of Chaplain Andrew Hunter," Sept. 27, 1776, http://www.revwar75.com/library/bob/HunterDiaries.htm (*oxen*); Henry Knox and Rufus Putnam to GW, Oct. 6, 1776, *PGW*, vol.

6, 490–91n; GW to Hancock, Nov. 16, 1776, *PGW*, vol. 7, 166n; *C 1776*, 27 (*"rocky, broken"*); Bolton, *Fort Washington*, 68; Ketchum, *Winter Soldiers*, 128–29 (*price gouging*).

451 *"the strongest post that ever was occupied"*: Schwab, *The Revolutionary History of Fort Number Eight*, 38.

451 *Built on a granite massif*: Graydon, *Memoirs of His Own Time*, 186; *PNG*, 354–55.

451 *Even with recent reinforcements*: Peckham, ed., *Memoirs of the Life of John Adlum in the Revolutionary War*, 50–51 (*"intervals"*); Thayer, *Nathanael Greene*, 120; Deary, 346–47 (*badly weakened*); Graydon, *Memories of His Own Time*, 184 (*"thankless"*), 186 (*"miserably deficient"*); NG to GW, Nov. 9, 1776, *PGW*, vol. 7, 120 (*through December*).

452 *By the mid-eighteenth century, military engineers*: Muller, *Attack and Defence of Fortified Places*, 132–36, 149, 172, 191.

452 *Fort Washington violated virtually all*: Robert Morris to Silas Deane, Dec. 20, 1776, *NDAR*, vol. 7, 528+ (*"dreaming"*); Hancock to GW, Oct. 28, 1776, *PGW*, vol. 7, 42–43n; *DFM*, 96–97 (*"much service"*).

452 *Moreover, seventeen deserters*: Deary, 295–99, 303–04, 314–18. Many years later Demont wrote, "I sacrificed all I was worth in the world to the service of my king and country." De Lancey, "Mount Washington and Its Capture, November 16th, 1776," *Magazine of American History* 1, no. 2 (Feb. 1877): 65+; Ketchum, *Winter Soldiers*, 133–34; Lefkowitz, *The Long Retreat*, 27–28, 32n; Van Doren, *Secret History of the American Revolution*, 17 (*"perfect knowledge"*).

452 *"Opinions here are various"*: *PGW*, vol. 7, 98n; GW to William Livingston, Nov. 7, 1776, *PGW*, vol. 7, 111 (*"attempt something"*); Freeman, 241–42; *GCL*, 145; *BNY*, 245; NG to GW, Nov. 10, 1776, *PGW*, vol. 7, 131.

453 *At eleven a.m. on Sunday, November 10*: Baker, "Itinerary of General Washington from June 15, 1775, to December 23, 1783," *PMHB* 14, no. 2 (July 1890): 111+; GW to John Augustine Washington, Nov. 6–19, 1776, *PGW*, vol. 7, 103 (*circuitous march*); journal, *Pearl*, Nov. 5, 1776, *NDAR*, vol. 7, 48; Deary, 349–50.

453 *Yet another successful British foray*: GW to NG, Nov. 8, 1776, and NG to GW, Nov. 9, 1776, *PGW*, vol. 7, 116 and 120; R. Lee to NG, Nov. 11, 1776, *LP*, vol. 2, 270 (*"my friend Howe"*).

453 *Late on Wednesday afternoon*: Conway, "Fort Lee: The Post at Burdett's Ferry," *Bergen County History, 1775 Annual*, 21; Lefkowitz, *The Long Retreat*, 13n (*"Steep Rocks"*); *Fort Lee History*, 169; Adams, *The Hudson River Guidebook*, 12; Greene, *The Life of Nathanael Greene*, vol. 1, 257 (*Hessians massing*); GW to Hancock, Nov. 14, 1776, *PGW*, vol. 7, 154 (*"movements and designs"*).

454 *Round and round the debate*: NG to Knox, Nov. 17, 1776, *PNG*, 351 (*"under consideration"*); GW to J. Reed, Aug. 22, 1779, cited in *PGW*, vol. 7, 106n (*"hesitation"*).

454 *No hesitation troubled William Howe's*: W. Howe to Germain, Nov. 30, 1776, UK NA, CO 5/93, f. 589. The figure for Howe's force includes support troops. Deary, 358–60, 383.

454 *On Thursday night, thirty flatboats*: Deary, 365–66, 383–91; de Lancey, "Mount Washington and Its Capture, November 16th, 1776," *Magazine of American History* 1, no. 2 (Feb. 1877): 65+.

454 *At one p.m. on Friday*: R. Magaw to NG, *PNG*, 350–51 (*"Actuated"*).

454 *"We are surrounded with Regulars"*: Addison Richardson to wife, Nov. 14, 1776, Feinstone Collection, DLAR, reel 3, #1211.

455 *Earlier that day, Washington had ridden six miles*: Leiby, *The Revolutionary War in the Hackensack Valley*, 7, 57–59 (*dispatch from Greene*); Ketchum, *The Winter Soldiers*, 119; Zabriskie mansion house site, signage, Hackensack; "Washington Mansion House Tavern," historical blueprints, Historical American Buildings Survey, 1936; NG to GW, Nov. 15, 1776, *PNG*, 351 (*"Enclosed you have"*). Sunset was at 4:41 p.m.

455 *The last hint of daylight*: The moon, at less than 20 percent illumination on November 15, set at 8:23 p.m. Leiby, *The Revolutionary War in the Hackensack Valley*, 59 (*to the dock*).

455 *Stepping into a barge, he ordered*: *PNG*, 358n.

455 *The boats returned to Fort Lee*: Greene, *The Life of Nathanael Greene*, vol. 1, 267.

455 *He was in the barge again with Greene*: Sunrise was at 6:49 a.m. on November 16. NG to Knox, Nov. 17, 1776, *PNG*, 352 (*"what was best"*); *WR*, 272; GW to Hancock, Nov. 16, 1776, *PGW*,

vol. 7, 166–67n; Smith, *Historical Sketch of Washington's Headquarters*, x; Bolton, *Fort Washington*, 88.

456 *Howe's intricate battle scheme*: Deary, 391–93.

456 *Rebel militia lashed the flotilla*: Thomas Glyn, "Journal of American Campaign," Nov. 16, 1776, FL; Hunter, *The Journal of Gen. Sir Martin Hunter*, 20 (*"quitted their oars"*); Ketchum, *The Winter Soldiers*, 141–42 (*run through*); Burgoyne, *Enemy Views*, 94 (*"continual thunder"*).

456 *Farther down the Harlem River*: Bolton, *Fort Washington*, 89, 109–10; Ketchum, *The Winter Soldiers*, 145–46; de Lancey, "Mount Washington and Its Capture, November 16th, 1776," *Magazine of American History* 1, no. 2 (Feb. 1877): 65+; Smith, *Historical Sketch of Washington's Headquarters*, x; GW to Hancock, Nov. 16, 1776, *PGW*, vol. 7, 166–67n; W. Howe to Germain, Nov. 30, 1776, *AA*, V: 3, 925.

456 *The day grew dire*: Bolton, *Fort Washington*, 72, 91; Ewald, *Diary of the American War*, 15–16; Uhlendorf, ed., *Revolution in America*, 70; de Lancey, "Mount Washington and Its Capture, November 16th, 1776," *Magazine of American History* 1, no. 2 (Feb. 1877): 65+; Ketchum, *The Winter Soldiers*, 142 (*"rutted up"*).

457 *Drums pounded, hautboys tootled*: Atwood, *The Hessians*, 77–78; Burgoyne, *Enemy Views*, 97 (*"both eyes"*).

457 *The struggle was particularly vicious*: GW to Henry Laurens, Aug. 21, 1778, *PGW*, vol. 16, 345–47 (*"veteran bravery"*); Beakes, *Otho Holland Williams in the American Revolution*, 38; Bolton, *Fort Washington*, 91, 101; Dandridge, *American Prisoners of the Revolution*, 15–16 ("*in our faces*"); Scharf, *History of Maryland*, vol. 2, 265; Dandridge, *Historic Shepherdstown*, 156, 61; Ketchum, *The Winter Soldiers*, 149.

457 *On the far side of the battlefield*: Bolton, *Fort Washington*, 90, 104–06, 110; Peckham, ed., *Memoirs of the Life of John Adlum in the Revolutionary War*, 72 (*"two men's heads"*); Lydenberg, 589 (*rum casks*).

457 *The end came quickly*: Fort Lee History, 212; GW to Hancock, Nov. 16, 1776, *PGW*, vol. 7, 168n; Bolton, *Fort Washington*, 101; Ketchum, *The Winter Soldiers*, 155–56; Serle, 142 ("*immediate & categorical*").

458 *Magaw asked for four hours*: Charles F. Himes, "Colonel Robert Magaw: The Defender of Fort Washington," paper read to Hamilton Library Association, Carlisle, Pa. (1915): 46; Bolton, *Fort Washington*, 101, 117 ("*fate seemed hard*"); Graydon, *Memoirs of His Own Times*, 203, 217 ("*disgraced*").

458 *A few men got away*: Shy, *A People Numerous and Armed*, 168–70 (*Long Bill*); "The Revolutionary War Diary of Chaplain Andrew Hunter," Nov. 17, 1776, http://www.revwar75.com /library/bob/HunterDiaries.htm (*flour casks*); Deary, 398–99; Bolton, *Fort Washington*, 120; Burgoyne, *Enemy Views*, 97 ("*herring*").

458 *"The abuse and plunder"*: Ryan, ed., *A Salute to Courage*, 52; Peckham, ed., *Memoirs of the Life of John Adlum in the Revolutionary War*, 74 (*knapsacks*); Nov. 16, 1776, journal entry, KP (*led away*); Graydon, *Memoirs of His Own Times*, 205 ("*your king*").

458 *Men pleaded for water*: Charles F. Himes, "Colonel Robert Magaw: The Defender of Fort Washington," paper read to Hamilton Library Association, Carlisle, Pa. (1915): 49; Bolton, *Fort Washington*, 112; Graydon, *Memoirs of His Own Times*, 220 ("*Come, gentlemen*").

459 *Howe's losses*: GW to Hancock, Nov. 16, 1776, *PGW*, vol. 7, 169n. As usual, casualty figures vary somewhat among different accounts. The British muster master general told Germain that the Hessians suffered 53 dead and 292 wounded. George Osborne to Germain, Nov. 25, 1776, UK NA, CO 5/93, f. 504. Howe put British losses at 20 dead, 102 wounded, and 6 missing. Howe returns, Sept. 17 to Nov. 16, 1776, *AA*, V: 3, 1055–56.

459 *"It was a pretty little action"*: Fortescue, *A History of the British Army*, vol. 3, 194–95.

459 *For Washington, the losses*: BNY, 255; Deary, 398–99 (*muskets*); Huston, *Logistics of Liberty*, 167 (*salt meat*).

459 *The prisoners would be marched*: Graydon, *Memoirs of His Own Time*, 222–23 ("*Which is Washington?*"); Peckham, ed., *Memoirs of the Life of John Adlum in the Revolutionary War*, 78–79, 86; Ranlet, "British Recruitment of Americans in New York During the American Revolution," *Military Affairs* 48, no. 1 (Jan. 1984): 26; court-martial records, Sept.–Nov. 1776,

UK NA, WO 71/83, 1–86 (*deserters*); Trevelyan, *The American Revolution*, part 2, vol. 1, 347n ("*rigid severity*"); *DFM*, 111 ("*our friends*").

459 *Few friends would emerge from the ordeal*: James McHenry to Benjamin Rush, Nov. 21, 1776, NYHS, Misc. Mss.; *PNG*, 352n–54n (*two-thirds*).

459 *Washington had watched the disaster*: Chernow, *Washington: A Life*, 262; Lefkowitz, *The Long Retreat*, 33 ("*agony*"); Irving, *Life of George Washington*, vol. 2, 424 ("*with the tenderness*"); GW to John Augustine Washington, Nov. 6–19, 1776, *PGW*, vol. 7, 103–04 ("*most unfortunate*"); *PNG*, 354n–55n (*confused lines*).

460 "*I feel mad, vexed*": NG to Knox, Nov. 17, 1776, *PNG*, 352; Deary, 405–06; Thayer, *Nathaniel Greene*, 122–23 ("*fell a prey*" and *New Englanders*).

460 "*I found myself as unable to preach*": "The Revolutionary War Diary of Chaplain Andrew Hunter," Nov. 17, 1776, http://www.revwar75.com/library/bob/HunterDiaries.htm; Quincy, *The Journals of Major Samuel Shaw*, 27 ("*towering passion*"); C. Lee to GW, Nov. 19, 1776, *PGW*, vol. 7, 187 ("*Oh, General*"); *GCL*, 147 (*sacked*).

460 "*I foresaw, predicted all*": C. Lee to B. Rush, Nov. 20, 1776, *LP*, 288.

460 "*I am wearied almost to death*": GW to John Augustine Washington, Nov. 6–19, 1776, *PGW*, vol. 7, 104–05.

461 *General Howe was determined to keep*: Thomas Glyn, "Journal of American Campaign," Nov. 19, 1776, FL; Ewald, *Diary of the American War*, 17, 379n; Hall, *Philipse Manor Hall at Yonkers, N.Y.*, 165–66; Judd, *Fort Lee on the Palisades*, 15–17 (*wet dawn*); Bradford, ed., "A British Officer's Revolutionary War Journal, 1776–1778," *Maryland Historical Magazine* 56, no. 2 (June 1961): 164 ("*disagreeable night*").

461 *At first light, with General Cornwallis*: W. Howe to Germain, Nov. 30, 1776, *AA*, V: 3, 925; Huyler's Landing, "Revolutionary War New Jersey," http://www.revolutionarywarnewjersey .com/new_jersey_revolutionary_war_sites/towns/alpine_nj_revolutionary_war_sites.htm (*rugged path*); Lefkowitz, *The Long Retreat*, 46–48; Bradford, ed., "A British Officer's Revolutionary War Journal, 1776–1778," *Maryland Historical Magazine* 56, no. 2 (June 1961): 164; John Spring, "The Invasion and the Myths Surrounding It," in Karels, ed., *The Revolutionary War in Bergen County*, 26 (*loyalist guides*); Donald M. Londahl-Smidt, "British and Hessian Accounts of the Invasion of 1776," in Karels, ed., *The Revolutionary War in Bergen County*, 23 ("*Fifty men*"); Thomas Glyn, "Journal of American Campaign," Nov. 20, 1776, FL.

461 *Greene had been dozing*: although one history credits a slave girl with tipping off the American camp, the identity of the messenger remains unknown. John Spring, "The Invasion and the Myths Surrounding It," in Karels, ed., *The Revolutionary War in Bergen County*, 25+.

461 *For the past three days*: NG to GW, Nov. 18, 1776, *PNG*, 359–60; Carbone, *Nathanael Greene*, 45; *Fort Lee History*, 214; Leiby, *The Revolutionary War in the Hackensack Valley*, 51–52; Lefkowitz, *The Long Retreat*, 19, 49; Glover, "The Retreat of '76 Across Bergen County," lecture, Bergen County Historical Society, Nov. 20, 1905; "Return of the Forces Encamped on the Jersey Shore, Commanded by Major-General Greene," Nov. 13, 1776, *AA*, V: 3, 663–64.

461 *Shrill cries rang through*: J. White, "The Good Soldier White," *American Heritage* 7, no. 4 (June 1956), https://www.americanheritage.com/content/june-1956 ("*Turn out!*"); Sanderson, ed., *Lynn in the Revolution*, part 1, RI, 155 (*extra clothes*); Glover, "The Retreat of '76 Across Bergen County," lecture, Bergen County Historical Society, Nov. 20, 1905; Lefkowitz, *The Long Retreat*, 49.

461 *Here General Washington awaited*: Freeman, 256–57 ("*heralds of calamity*"); William Grayson (GW aide) to W. Heath, Nov. 20, 1776, *AA*, V: 3, 780; Robert H. Harrison (GW aide) to Schuyler, Nov. 20, 1776, *AA*, V: 3, 781 ("*push matters*"); NG to Nicholas Cooke, Dec. 4, 1776, *PNG*, 362 (*stragglers*).

462 *Cornwallis's legions overran*: Thomas Glyn, "Journal of American Campaign," Nov. 20, 1776, FL; W. Howe to Germain, Nov. 30, 1776, *AA*, V: 3, 925; Donald M. Londahl-Smidt, "British and Hessian Accounts of the Invasion of 1776," in Karels, ed., *The Revolutionary War in Bergen County*, 20–21 (*skulking rebels*); "Journal of a Pennsylvania Soldier, July–December, 1776," *Bulletin of the NYPL* 8 (1904): 549 (*dead drunk*); Ewald, *Diary of the American War*, 17–18 ("*Let them go*").

462 *More booty fell into British hands*: GW to Hancock, Nov. 21, 1776, *PGW*, vol. 7, 182–83; Lt. William John Hale to father, Dec. 19, 1776, "Letters Written During the American War of Independence," in Wylly, ed., *1913 Regimental Annual: The Sherwood Foresters*, 16. In the eighteenth century, a pipe of wine equaled 126 gallons.

462 *"There was a huge magazine"*: Ewald, *Diary of the American War*, 18; Lefkowitz, *The Long Retreat*, 51 (*two thousand head*); captured ordnance return, W. Howe to Germain, Dec. 3, 1776, UK NA, CO 5/93, f. 313 (*148 guns*).

462 *The New York campaign had ended*: *GGW*, 168; Deary, 409 (*"I am surprised"*); Quincy, *The Journals of Major Samuel Shaw*, 26 (*"ruined people"*).

462 *Washington spent a glum final night*: Leiby, *The Revolutionary War in the Hackensack Valley*, 7, 72 (*"two abreast"*); Lefkowitz, *The Long Retreat*, 53 (*campfires*).

463 *"The enemy are evidently changing the seat"*: GW to R. Lee, Nov. 21, 1776, *PGW*, vol. 7, 193–94.

463 *With that, he rode off*: Leiby, *The Revolutionary War in the Hackensack Valley*, 74; Glover, "The Retreat of '76 Across Bergen County," lecture, Bergen County Historical Society, Nov. 20, 1905; Acquackanonk Bridge, Revolutionary War New Jersey, http://www .revolutionarywarnewjersey.com/new_jersey_revolutionary_war_sites/towns/wallington _nj_revolutionary_war_sites.htm. The Acquackanonk became the Passaic River.

463 *"The virtue of the Americans"*: NG to Caty, Dec. 4, 1776, *PNG*, 365.

19. A QUAKER IN PARIS

465 *The old gentleman had gone to sea*: Parton, *Life and Times of Benjamin Franklin*, vol. 2, 71, 205 (*eight Atlantic crossings*); Clark, *Lambert Wickes*, 10 (*heaving* Reprisal); McGrath, *Give Me a Fast Ship*, 106 (*in jail*); Augur, *The Secret War of Independence*, 146; Brands, *The First American*, 527 (*"demolished"*); footnote, BF to Jacques Barbeu-Dubourg, Dec. 4, 1776, *PBF* (*boils*).

465 *"I am old and good for nothing"*: Tomkinson, *Benjamin Franklin*, 107; Isaacson, *Benjamin Franklin*, 321; instructions from the Continental Congress, Sept. 24–Oct. 22, 1776, *PBF* (*"good engineers"*); Schiff, *A Great Improvisation*, 2–3 (*bolt of lightning*); Lopez, *My Life with Benjamin Franklin*, 148–49; Ellis, *Revolutionary Summer*, 98–99.

466 *He had prepared meticulously*: Clark, *Lambert Wickes*, 54–60, 93–94 (*bedding*); Schoenbrun, *Triumph in Paris*, 49–51 (*red lapels* and *indigo*).

466 *Franklin also brought two traveling companions*: BF to Richard Bache, June 2, 1779, *PBF* (*"close my eyes"*); Alberts, *The Golden Voyage*, 42 (*"double-distilled"*); Parton, *Life and Times of Benjamin Franklin*, part 2, 98; BF to Lord Kames, Jan. 3, 1760, *PBF* (*"densest happiness"*). Temple Franklin's papers at the American Philosophical Society indicate that he was born in 1760; his gravestone in Paris indicates 1762, the year his father, William, married.

466 *Progressive and capable as a governor*: W. Franklin to Dartmouth, Apr. 3, 1775, *DAR*, vol. 9; Randall, "William Franklin: The Making of a Conservative," in East and Judd, eds., *The Loyalist Americans*, 64–65; Skemp, *William Franklin*, xi–xii, 218–19; W. Franklin to Germain, Mar. 28, 1776, *DAR*, vol. 12, 97–98; Wood, *The Americanization of Benjamin Franklin*, 161–62; Brands, *The First American*, 525–26 (*"virulent enemy"*); W. Franklin to Dartmouth, Sept. 5, 1775, *DAR*, vol. 10, 74; Louis Arthur Norton, "The Connecticut Captivity of William Franklin, Loyalist," *JAR*, Nov. 1, 2017; Elizabeth Franklin to BF, Aug. 6, 1776, *PBF*; BF to Richard Bache, June 2, 1779, *PBF* (*"I have rescued"*); Randall, *A Little Revenge*, 366 (*"lost my son"*). BF would write to William, "I ought not to blame you for differing in sentiment with me in public affairs. We are men, all subject to errors." Parton, *Life and Times of Benjamin Franklin*, part 2, 98.

467 *At noon on November 27*: Clark, *Lambert Wickes*, 89–92 (*"Let old England"*), 98–99; Lambert Wickes, to Committee of Secret Correspondence, Dec. 13, 1776, *AA*, V: 3, 1197.

467 *Franklin was gleeful*: Augur, *The Secret War of Independence*, 146 (*"equal to anything"*); Miller, *Sea of Glory*, 203–04, 209–10; Brewington, "The Designs of Our First Frigates," *American Neptune* 8 (Jan. 1948): 24–25; Chapelle, *The American Sailing Navy*, 55–56, 61, 71; Toll, *Six Frigates*, 15–16. Congress created the Continental Navy in October 1775, and the Marine Corps a month later.

467 *Commanding some eighty British warships*: unsigned fleet assessment (apparently from Sandwich), June 20, 1776, RA GEO/MAIN/#2439; Allen, *A Naval History of the American Revolution*, vol. 1, 180; NCCH, 285, 296–97; *HBAR*, 81, 103–04; Eddis, *Letters from America*, 345.

467 *Howe's men-of-war would seize 140*: R. Howe to Admiralty, Mar. 31, 1777, *AA*, V: 3, 1523; Syrett, *The Royal Navy in American Waters*, 58–60; Miller, *Sea of Glory*, 194; Baugh, "The Politics of British Naval Failure, 1775–1777," *American Neptune* 52, no. 4 (Fall 1992): 221+.

467 *Outgunned, outmanned, and outsailed*: J. P. Jones to Marine Committee, Nov. 16, 1776, *AA*, V: 3, 738; Barrington to Germain, Jan. 30, 1777, UK NA, CO 5/169, f. 18; journal, Lt. John Trevett, *Providence*, Nov. 1776, *NDAR*, vol. 7, 329; John Bradford to Marine and Secret Committees, Dec. 21, 1776, *NDAR*, vol. 7, 539; *Whitehall Evening Post*, Dec. 25, 1776, *NDAR*, vol. 7, 807; Thomas, *John Paul Jones*, 71; Miller, *Sea of Glory*, 130; Morison, *John Paul Jones*, 78–83; J. P. Jones to Marine Committee, Nov. 12, 1776, and Jan. 12, 1777, *NDAR*, vol. 7, 111 (*"most valuable ship"*), 935.

468 *Jones had also participated*: Gov. Montfort Browne to Germain, Nov. 5, 1776, *NDAR*, vol. 7, 48; McCusker, "The American Invasion of Nassau in the Bahamas," *American Neptune* 25, no. 3 (July 1965): 189+; Smith, *Marines in the Revolution*, 41–57; Lorenz, *John Paul Jones*, 66–67; John Brown to Adm. Clark Gayton, Mar. 22, 1776, *DAR*, vol. 12, 90–92; Beck, ed., *The Correspondence of Esek Hopkins*, 35 (*88 cannons*); Allen, *A Naval History of the American Revolution*, vol. 1, 96–100; author visit, Nassau, Mar. 2018.

468 *Yet as Franklin well understood*: Allen, *Massachusetts Privateers of the Revolution*, 3–4, 9 (*thirteenth century*); Augur, *The Secret War of Independence*, 94–95; vessels taken by American privateers, undated, *AA*, V: 3, 1527; Syrett, *Shipping and the American War*, 77 (*3,400 captured*); Syrett, *Admiral Lord Howe*, 63. Eleven state navies also took enemy prizes. Allen, *A Naval History of the American Revolution*, vol. 1, 38–39, 46–47.

468 *Massachusetts alone sent out five*: Allen, *Massachusetts Privateers of the Revolution*, 65; Augur, *The Secret War of Independence*, 95 (*"gentlemen volunteers"*), 98; Morison, *John Paul Jones*, 32–33; J. Warren to J. Adams, Aug. 15, 1776, *NDAR*, vol. 6, 191 (*"privateering mad"*).

468 *The damage to British trade*: Jameson, *The American Revolution Considered as a Social Movement*, 66; *HBAR*, 140; Brown, "William Bingham, Agent of the Continental Congress in Martinique," *PMHB* 61, no. 1 (Jan. 1937): 54+ (*Seven Years' War*); Albion and Pope, *Sea Lanes in Wartime*, 63 (*still rising*); Augur, *The Secret War of Independence*, 93–94 (*Lloyd's* and *sugar convoys*); Perkins, *The Diary of Simeon Perkins*, xxiii (*"No protection"*); Volo, *Blue Water Patriots*, 79 (*black squares*); Clark, *George Washington's Navy*, 179 (*six real guns*); Abigail Adams to J. Adams, Aug. 17, 1776, in *AFC*, vol. 2, 98 (*"plenty of sugars"*).

469 *If Franklin could persuade*: Clark, *Lambert Wickes*, 99–100 (*Quiberon Bay*).

469 *On December 3, Wickes hired*: BF to Silas Deane, Dec. 7, 1776, *PBF*; Parton, *Life and Times of Benjamin Franklin*, vol. 2, 207.

469 *Curious crowds in Nantes*: BF to Jane Mecom, Dec. 8, 1776, *PBF* (*"no conception"*); Van Doren, *Benjamin Franklin*, 567; Clark, *Lambert Wickes*, 103–04.

469 *Franklin had revealed nothing*: Clark, *Silas Deane*, 93 (*"conjectures"*); Schiff, *A Great Improvisation*, 25; BF to Silas Deane, Dec. 4, 1776, Silas Deane Papers, vol. 1, *Collections*, NYHS (1886): 403 (*"my incognito"*).

470 *When word spread in London*: Schiff, *A Great Improvisation*, 25; H. Walpole to William Mason, Feb. 27, 1777, Peter Cunningham, ed., *The Letters of Horace Walpole*, vol. 6, 417 (*"toothpick"*).

470 *The British ambassador to Versailles*: Schiff, *A Great Improvisation*, 24; Wood, *The Americanization of Benjamin Franklin*, 169–70; Clark, *Benjamin Franklin*, 304 (*"dangerous engine"*).

470 *Paris was a clamorous city*: Garrioch, *The Making of Revolutionary Paris*, 15, 18–19 (*F, E, D, C*); Popkin, ed., *Louis-Sébastien Mercier, Panorama of Paris*, 113–14 (*man unknown*), 133 (*"herrings"*), 165; Hussey, *Paris: The Secret History*, 165; Schiff, *A Great Improvisation*, 45 (*Windmills*).

470 *No less vivid than the sounds*: Simpson, *The Waiting City*, 160 (*dog dung*); Conlin, *Tale of Two Cities*, 73 (*sidewalks*), 183–84; Alsop, *Yankees at the Court*, 66 (*eat the hem*), 68 (*leashed monkeys*); Popkin, ed., *Louis-Sébastien Mercier, Panorama of Paris*, 41, 44, 87, 108–09 (*signs*), 119, 132.

471 *Paris was also a town of couture*: Popkin, ed., *Louis-Sébastien Mercier, Panorama of Paris*, 66, 93, 150 (*underwear*), 175–77, 228 (*darkened the skin*); Alsop, *Yankees at the Court*, 65; Hussey, *Paris: The Secret History*, 190 (*pallor*).

471 *Miracles and miracle-mongers thrived*: Simpson, ed., *The Waiting City*, 44 (*faith healer*), 309 (*bordellos*); Popkin, ed., *Louis-Sébastien Mercier, Panorama of Paris*, 40 ("*court spies*"), 160, 163 (*door grate*), 198 ("*pleasure*"); Garrioch, *The Making of Revolutionary Paris*, 23 (*holy days*); Conlin, *Tale of Two Cities*, 103 (*cabarets*); Schiff, *A Great Improvisation*, 52 (*registered prostitutes*).

471 *In the center of this bustling, hustling*: Lemaitre, *Beaumarchais*, 191; Griffith, *The War for American Independence*, 336–37; David Downie, "Many Lives of Paris' Storied Marais District," http://www.sfgate.com/travel/article/Many-lives-of-Paris-storied-Marais-district-2609974.php (*allegories*); Paul, *Unlikely Allies*, 185 (*Psyche's marriage*); Ferreiro, *Brothers at Arms*, 54–55 (*salons*); Parton, *Life and Times of Benjamin Franklin*, 167–68; Grendel, *Beaumarchais: The Man Who Was Figaro*, 175; Loménie, *Beaumarchais and His Times*, 284, 290.

472 *The firm was, in fact, the government front*: "Attitude of France to the United States," in Wharton, ed., *The Revolutionary Diplomatic Correspondence of the United States*, vol. 1, 365–72; Augur, *The Secret War of Independence*, 114 ("*oozing*"); Hale and Hale, *Franklin in France*, 35 ("*obscure*"); Loménie, *Beaumarchais and His Times*, 60–64; Lemaitre, *Beaumarchais*, 24–26, 44.

472 *Minor court positions came*: S. Kite, *Beaumarchais and the War of American Independence*, vol. 1, 57, 60; Grendel, *Beaumarchais: The Man Who Was Figaro*, 15; Lemaitre, *Beaumarchais*, 85, 134–38, 151–52, 200 (*diamond ring*); Paul, *Unlikely Allies*, 63, 67, 94; Trevelyan, *The American Revolution*, 325; Ferreiro, *Brothers at Arms*, 45–48 (*war plans*); Loménie, *Beaumarchais and His Times*, 83; Trevelyan, *The American Revolution*, 323–24.

473 *He was forever embroiled in spats*: Loménie, *Beaumarchais and His Times*, 249–53, 290 ("*a combat*"); Kite, *Beaumarchais and the War of American Independence*, vol. 1, 187 ("*cheerful and assured*"), 270 ("*the lightness*"), 274–76 ("*hissers, spitters*"); Lemaitre, *Beaumarchais*, 97, 106, 114, 124–29, 159–60 (*a comedy*); Grendel, *Beaumarchais: The Man Who Was Figaro*, 135.

473 *In the past year he had become*: "Attitude of France to the United States," in Wharton, ed., *The Revolutionary Diplomatic Correspondence of the United States*, vol. 1, 365; Van Tyne, "French Aid Before the Alliance of 1778," *AHR* 31, no. 1 (Oct. 1925): 21–22; Tucker and Hendrickson, *The Fall of the First British Empire*, 46–47; Trevelyan, *The American Revolution*, 303–04 (*Dunkirk*); Rodger, *The Command of the Ocean*, 329 (*invasion beaches*); Dull, *The French Navy and American Independence*, 24.

473 *"All sensible persons are convinced"*: Loménie, *Beaumarchais and His Times*, 262; Stourzh, *Benjamin Franklin and American Foreign Policy*, 136–39 (*enfeeblement of Britain*); Bailyn, *To Begin the World Anew*, 134 (*French translations*); Alsop, *Yankees at the Court*, 16 ("*pure despotism*").

474 *But, like Beaumarchais, the minister*: Murphy, *Charles Gravier, Comte de Vergennes*, 235 ("*long-winded*"); James Pritchard, "French Strategy and the American Revolution: A Reappraisal," in Stoker et al., eds., *Strategy in the American War of Independence*, 142–44; Loménie, *Beaumarchais and His Times*, 266; Alsop, *Yankees at the Court*, 60 (*thousand letters*).

474 *Converting the new French king*: Wheatley, ed., *The Historical and Posthumous Memoirs of Sir Nathaniel William Wraxall*, vol. 1, 77 (*smallpox*); Paul, *Unlikely Allies*, 111 ("*the universe*"); Hale and Hale, *Franklin in France*, 75 (*a royalist*); Hussey, *Paris: The Secret History*, 187 ("*to be loved*"); "Attitude of France to the United States," in Wharton, ed., *The Revolutionary Diplomatic Correspondence of the United States*, vol. 1, 332; Alsop, *Yankees at the Court*, 21 ("*peasant slouching*"), 83; Ketchum, *Divided Loyalties*, 257 (*Austrian woman*); Price, *Preserving the Monarchy*, 13, 25.

474 *Though indecisive and a bit dim*: Pritchard, "French Strategy and the American Revolution: A Reappraisal," in Stoker et al., eds., *Strategy in the American War of Independence*, 142–43; Bemis, *The Diplomacy of the American Revolution*, 22 ("*It is the English*"); Hale and Hale, *Franklin in France*, 38–39 ("*sugar islands*"); Dull, *The French Navy and American Independence*, 17 (*two-fifths*); Grendel, *Beaumarchais: The Man Who Was Figaro*, 159–65 ("*shameful peace*").

475 *Vergennes added his own measured*: Isaacson, *Benjamin Franklin*, 337 (*"natural enemy"*); Meng, "A Footnote to Secret Aid in the American Revolution," *AHR* 43, no. 4 (July 1938): 791+; Dull, *The French Navy and American Independence*, 36–37; Lemaitre, *Beaumarchais*, 184 (*"Engineers"*).

475 *Bit by bit the king came round*: Hardman and Price, eds., *Louis XVI and the Comte de Vergennes*, 43–44, 54–55; Bemis, *The Diplomacy of the American Revolution*, 25; Corwin, *French Policy and the American Alliance of 1778*, 73–74, 76–79; "Attitude of France to the United States," in Wharton, ed., *The Revolutionary Diplomatic Correspondence of the United States*, vol. 1, 340 (*American élan*); Lemaitre, *Beaumarchais*, 176–77; Doniol, *Histoire de la Participation de la France à l'Établissement des États-Unis d'Amérique*, vol. 1, 266 (*Antwerp merchant*); Van Tyne, "French Aid Before the Alliance of 1778," *AHR* 31, no. 1 (Oct. 1925): 36–37; Archard de Bonvouloir to Count de Guines, Dec. 28, 1775, *NDAR*, vol. 3, 281 (*"Everyone here"*); Sumner, *The Financier and the Finances of the American Revolution*, 157 (*"Nothing frightens them"*).

475 *With Louis's reluctant consent*: Meng, "A Footnote to Secret Aid in the American Revolution," *AHR* 43, no. 4 (July 1938): 791+.

475 *The first million livres in gold*: Thomas Story report to Committee of Secret Correspondence, Oct. 1, 1776, *PBF*. Eighteen livres was roughly equivalent to £1 sterling, according to Kennedy. *The Rise and Fall of British Naval Mastery*, 111. Ferreiro puts the figure at 23.5 livres to £1. He estimates that the sum was equivalent to $500 million in today's currency. *Brothers at Arms*, 54, 339–40.

475 *More coins followed*: Corwin, *French Policy and the American Alliance of 1778*, 79; Loménie, *Beaumarchais and His Times*, 274–75; Lemaitre, *Beaumarchais*, 190, 198; Kite, *Beaumarchais and the War of American Independence*, vol. 2, 82; Grendel, *Beaumarchais: The Man Who Was Figaro*, 176–80; Ferreiro, *Brothers at Arms*, 54–55.

475 *He soon accumulated surplus brass*: Edward Bancroft narrative, Aug. 14, 1776, *Stevens's*, no. 890, in Silas Deane Papers, *Collections*, NYHS, vol. 1 (1886): 183; Grendel, *Beaumarchais: The Man Who Was Figaro*, 181–82; Lemaitre, *Beaumarchais*, 194 (*"yoke"*), 198 (*"ardent desire"*); Loménie, *Beaumarchais and His Times*, 274 (*"products of the soil"*); James, *Silas Deane*, 18; Sumner, *The Financier and the Finances of the American Revolution*, 163–66; Hale and Hale, *Franklin in France*, 40n (*"vast schemes"*).

476 *He also had accumulated an American collaborator*: James, *Silas Deane*, 1–4; Secret Committee orders, Mar. 3, 1776, Silas Deane papers, *Collections*, NYHS, vol. 1 (1886): 123; Miller, *Sea of Glory*, 189 (*"most silent man"*); Deane to Secret Committee, Nov. 28, 1776, and Deane to Robert Morris, Dec. 13, 1776, Silas Deane papers, *Collections*, NYHS, vol. 1 (1886): 374, 420; Augur, *The Secret War of Independence*, 144; Schiff, *A Great Improvisation*, 9 (*flying squirrels*).

476 *By December, working with Beaumarchais*: York, "Clandestine Aid and the American Revolutionary War Effort," *Military Affairs* 43, no. 1 (Feb. 1979): 28 (*40 tons of saltpeter*); Edward Bancroft narrative, Aug. 14, 1776, *Stevens's*, no. 890, in Silas Deane Papers, *Collections*, NYHS, vol. 1 (1886): 183 (*uniform cloth*); Deane to Secret Committee, Aug. 18, Oct. 1, 8, 17, and 25, 1776, Silas Deane Papers, *Collections*, NYHS, vol. 1 (1886): 196–208, 287–90, 310, 323–25, 337 (*windy letters*); Price, *France and the Chesapeake*, vol. 2, 705; Kite, *Beaumarchais and the War of American Independence*, vol. 2, 92–93 (*"wit and genius"*); Deane to Secret Committee, Dec. 2, 1776, Silas Deane Papers, *Collections*, NYHS, vol. 1 (1886): 340 (*destroy Glasgow*).

476 *Deane also found himself running*: Lemaitre, *Beaumarchais*, 205; Kapp, *The Life of John Kalb, Major-General in the Revolutionary Army*, 85 (*"The rage"*); Van Alstyne, *Empire and Independence*, 100 (*four hundred*); Deane agreement with du Coudray, Sept. 11, 1776, Silas Deane Papers, *Collections*, NYHS, vol. 1 (1886): 230 (*horses, carriages, an adjutant*).

476 *Not all were what they seemed*: Ferreiro, *Brothers at Arms*, 127 (*L'Enfant*); Deane to Secret Committee, Dec. 7, 1776, Silas Deane Papers, *Collections*, NYHS, vol. 1 (1886): 410 (*"noble lineage"*); Kite, *Beaumarchais and the War of American Independence*, vol. 2, 133–34; Kapp, *The Life of John Kalb, Major-General in the Revolutionary Army*, 86.

477 *"I am well-nigh harassed"*: Deane to Committee of Secret Correspondence, Nov. 28, 1776, in Sparks, ed., *The Diplomatic Correspondence of the American Revolution*, 53; Deane to John

Jay, Dec. 3, 1776, in Sparks, ed., *The Diplomatic Correspondence of the American Revolution*, 69 (*"ten ships"*).

477 *As Dr. Franklin made his way*: Lemaitre, *Beaumarchais*, 206–07 (*"M. Durand"*); Deane to John Jay, Dec. 3, 1776, in Sparks, ed., *The Diplomatic Correspondence of the American Revolution*, 68; James, *Silas Deane*, 19; Ferreiro, *Brothers at Arms*, 60; Kapp, *The Life of John Kalb, Major-General in the Revolutionary Army*, 84; Bemis, *The Diplomacy of the American Revolution*, 36–37; Loménie, *Beaumarchais and His Times*, 289–90.

477 *By mischance, a provincial production*: Loménie, *Beaumarchais and His Times*, 291; Baron de Kalb to Deane, Dec. 18, 1776, Silas Deane Papers, *Collections*, NYHS, vol. 1 (1886): 433 (*"He made himself known"*).

477 *Informants had advised Lord Stormont*: North to George III, Dec. 31, 1776, "George III Calendar, Sept. 1775–Oct. 1777," RA GEO/MAIN/#2500; Lemaitre, *Beaumarchais*, 202; Corwin, *French Policy and the American Alliance of 1778*, 88 (*counsel of their fears*); Loménie, *Beaumarchais and His Times*, 294 (*prohibiting the departure*).

478 *Sensing trouble of his own making*: Paul, *Unlikely Allies*, 218–29 (*knee buckles*); Beaumarchais to Deane and De Kalb to Deane, Dec. 17 and 18, 1776, Silas Deane Papers, *Collections*, NYHS, vol. 1 (1886): 424–25 (*"changing the names"*), 426, 433; Kite, *Beaumarchais and the War of American Independence*, vol. 1, 125 (*"tranquilizing me"*).

478 *Nothing about this opéra bouffe*: Deane to Beaumarchais, Jan. 6, 1777; Nicholas Rogers to Deane, Jan. 9, 1777; Deane to Secret Committee, Jan. 10, 1777, Silas Deane Papers, *Collections*, NYHS, vol. 1 (1886): 451–53, 460; Grendel, *Beaumarchais: The Man Who Was Figaro*, 191 (*years to sort out*).

478 *But the ship would reach America*: James, *Silas Deane*, 20; Van Alstyne, *Empire and Independence*, 119–20; York, "Clandestine Aid and the American Revolutionary War Effort," *Military Affairs* 43, no. 1 (Feb. 1979): 29–30.

478 *Many of the surplus muskets and cannons*: William Heath to GW, June 30, 1777, *PGW*, vol. 10, 152–53, FOL. Smith writes that two-thirds of the 41,000 muskets that arrived from France before 1780 needed repairs. *Manufacturing Independence*, x–xii, 9, 216n; Loménie, *Beaumarchais and His Times*, 294–95 (*"our affairs"*).

478 *Each morning, rumors circulated*: Van Doren, *Benjamin Franklin*, 567; "A History of the Official American Presence in France," U.S. State Department, n.d., https://photos.state.gov/libraries/france/45994/irc/uspresenceinfrance.pdf (*Hôtel d'Entragues*); Kite, *Beaumarchais and the War of American Independence*, vol. 1, 119 (*"idol of the day"*); Schiff, *A Great Improvisation*, 29–30 (*nine times*); Nelson, *Thomas Paine*, 104 (*"Plato"*).

479 *Franklin had visited France twice*: Wood, *The Americanization of Benjamin Franklin*, 172 (*"transformed me"*); "Poor Richard Improved, 1758," PBF.

479 *Now Parisians pursued his coach*: Trevelyan, *The American Revolution*, 348–51; Schiff, *A Great Improvisation*, 29–30 (*black homespun*); Morgan, *Benjamin Franklin*, 243, 246–47 (mon cher Papa); Hale and Hale, *Franklin in France*, 90 (*"much run after"*).

479 *"just the touch of charlatanism"*: Corwin, *French Policy and the American Alliance of 1778*, 94.

479 *Here, in French eyes, stood Rousseau's*: Osman, "From Greatest Enemies to Greatest Allies: France and America in the War for Independence," 4th Annual Conference on the American Revolution, Mar. 2015, Williamsburg, Va.; Augur, *The Secret War of Independence*, 148–49; Isaacson, *Benjamin Franklin*, 325 (coiffure); Conway, *Footprints of Famous Americans in Paris*, 10 (*orchestra rose*); Aldridge, *Franklin and His French Contemporaries*, 61 (*on the mantel*); Van Doren, *Benjamin Franklin*, 573; Schiff, *A Great Improvisation*, 39–42 (*"sublime reticence"*).

480 *On December 23, young Temple rode*: commissioners to Vergennes, Dec. 23, 1776, PBF (*"flatter ourselves"*); Arthur Lee to R. H. Lee, Dec. 25, 1776, AA, V: 3, 1415 (*third member*); BF to Committee of Secret Correspondence, Jan. 4, 1777, and Vergennes to commissioners, July 16, 1777, PBF (*"treaty"*).

480 *They parted amicably*: BF to Committee of Secret Correspondence, Jan. 4, 1777, and Vergennes to commissioners, July 16, 1777, PBF.

480 *The next evening Franklin*: Place Louis XV later became the Place de la Concorde. Ferreiro, *Brothers at Arms*, 64; Schiff, *A Great Improvisation*, 33 (*"speaks very little French"*).

480 *"As other princes of Europe"*: commissioners to Vergennes, Jan. 5 and 8, 1777, *PBF*.

481 *Later that Sunday, the three*: Conrad-Alexandre Gérard to commissioners, Jan. 6, 1777, *PBF*; Schiff, *A Great Improvisation*, 47 (*"talk much"*).

481 *The minister and his king remained*: Loménie, *Beaumarchais and His Times*, 288 (*"watched every movement"*); Schaeper, *Edward Bancroft: Scientist, Author, Spy*, 66–67; "Intelligence from Paul Wentworth, received 23 Nov. 1776," *Stevens's*, vol. 2, #131; "Cypher settled with Mr. Wentworth," Dec. 5, 1776, *Stevens's*, vol. 1, #1 (*America was 7*); "Engagement of Dr. Edwards," *Stevens's*, vol. 3, #235 (*"treaty with France"*); Schoenbrun, *Triumph in Paris*, 70 (*erroneously*).

481 *Like Lords North and Germain*: Scott, *British Foreign Policy in the Age of the American Revolution*, 208, 236–39, 242.

481 *A long, exquisite dance*: Juliana Ritchie to BF, Jan. 12, 1777 (*"surrounded"*), and BF to J. Ritchie, Jan. 19, 1777, *PBF* (*"one rule"*).

482 *Versailles was simply unready*: Dull, "Franklin the Diplomat: The French Mission," *Transactions of the American Philosophical Society*, new ser., 72, no. 1 (1982): 1+; Corwin, *French Policy and the American Alliance of 1778*, 86 (*"felicitations"*); Ferreiro, *Brothers at Arms*, 91–92 (*"attente"*).

482 *Franklin faced his own quandary*: Brands, *The First American*, 523 (*French aid*).

482 *A bit of good news*: "The King's Answer to the American Commissioners," Jan. 13, 1777, and American commissioners to Gérard, Jan. 14, 1777, *PBF*; Clark, *Benjamin Franklin*, 306 (*"much talent"*); Schiff, *A Great Improvisation*, 58 (*"important mission"*).

482 *"His age and experience"*: Dull, "Franklin the Diplomat: The French Mission," *Transactions of the American Philosophical Society*, new ser., 72, no. 1 (1982): 1+.

483 *"The hearts of the French"*: commissioners to Committee of Secret Correspondence, Jan. 17–22, 1777, *PBF*.

20. FIRE-AND-SWORD MEN

485 *The American army, threadbare*: GW to William Heath, Nov. 29, 1776, *PGW*, vol. 7, 228n; Dwyer, *The Day Is Ours!*, 35; "Journal of Capt. William Beaty, 1776–1781," *Maryland Historical Magazine* 3, no. 2 (June 1908): 104+ (*"intolerable"*); Continental Army return, Nov. 23, 1776, *AA*, V: 3, 822 (*5,410*); GW to William Livingston, Nov. 30, 1776, *PGW*, vol. 7, 236; *BTP*, 12; Bill, *New Jersey and the Revolutionary War*, 16 (*"all buff"*); Tyler, ed., "The Old Virginia Line in the Middle States During the American Revolution," *Tyler's Quarterly* 12, no. 1 (July 1930): 1+ (*"You will wonder"*).

485 *At first light on Friday*: Bill, *New Jersey and the Revolutionary War*, 2–3; Leiby, *The Revolutionary War in the Hackensack Valley*, 8, 12–13, 33, 77–78, 83–86 (*brass locks*); GW to Hancock, Nov. 30, 1776, *PGW*, vol. 7, 234n; Lefkowitz, *The Long Retreat*, 62 (*"church green"*), 80–81.

486 *At midday on Friday, twenty-five miles*: Lundin, *Cockpit of the Revolution*, 13–14 (*"dismal town"*); Lefkowitz, *The Long Retreat*, 84–85; Leiby, *The Revolutionary War in the Hackensack Valley*, 27; Ward, *The Delaware Continentals*, 98 (*"broken down"*).

486 *Among those retreating*: *WR*, 282 (*"wretched remains"*); Wood, *Revolutionary Characters*, 214–15; Ayer, *Thomas Paine*, 3; Hawke, *Paine*, 14 (*snuff*); Nelson, *Thomas Paine*, 40 (*"full, brilliant"*); Keane, *Tom Paine*, 71 (*"Commodore"*). Only after arriving in America did Thomas Pain add the final *e* to his surname.

486 *Thomas Paine had failed at everything*: Wood, *The American Revolution*, 55; *GC*, 323–24; Nelson, *Thomas Paine*, 17, 38–39; Keane, *Tom Paine*, 30–31, 45, 50–55, 74–78, 94–95 (*beavers, suicide*); Foner, *Tom Paine and Revolutionary America*, 16 (*egalitarian and utopian*); Williamson, *Thomas Paine*, 49, 67–68 (*oppression of women*); Ayer, *Thomas Paine*, 6 (*"Trade I do not"*).

486 Common Sense *"burst from the press"*: Bailyn, *Faces of Revolution*, 67; Wood, *Revolutionary Characters*, 209 (*"effects"*), 220 (*"scarcely read"*); Ayer, *Thomas Paine*, 35; Nelson, *Thomas Paine*, 90 (*mittens*); Keane, *Tom Paine*, 11–12 (*"adoring him"*); Foner, *Tom Paine and Revolutionary America*, 85 (*"rude way"*), 86 (*"well-prepared heart"*); Jensen, *The Founding of a Nation*, 669 (*"combustibles"*); Countryman, *The American Revolution*, 112–13 (*farmers, shopmen*).

487 *"a work of genius"*: Bailyn, *Faces of Revolution*, 67.

487   *An indictment of the British body politic*: Bailyn, *The Ideological Origins of the American Revolution*, 285–86; Nelson, *Thomas Paine*, 80–83; Paine, *"Common Sense," "The Rights of Man," and Other Essential Writings*, 23, 36, 44, 48; *GC*, 324–25.

487   *Common Sense had helped nudge*: Bailyn, *Faces of Revolution*, 71 (*"crapulous"*); Kaminski, ed., *The Founders on the Founders*, xvii (*"career"*). Adams also called Paine a "star of disaster." *D&AJA*, vol. 3, 330. Keane, *Tom Paine*, 111 (*"sound doctrine"*).

487   *Paine had long greeted acquaintances*: Hawke, *Paine*, 58; Keane, *Tom Paine*, 139–40.

487   *During the muddy trudge*: Keane, *Tom Paine*, 142–45 (*"passion"*).

488   *Washington placed his New Brunswick headquarters*: GW to William Heath, Nov. 29, 1776, *PGW*, vol. 7, 228n; "New Brunswick," Revolutionary War New Jersey, http://www.revolutionarywarnewjersey.com/new_jersey_revolutionary_war_sites/towns/new_brunswick_nj_revolutionary_war_sites.htm; GW to Hancock, Dec. 1, 1776, *PGW*, vol. 7, 243 (*pushed south*); Kidder, *A People Harassed and Exhausted*, 168 (*"murmuring"*).

488   *"A deportment so firm, so dignified"*: Brown, ed., *The Autobiography of James Monroe*, 28; GW to Hancock, Nov. 30, 1776, *PGW*, vol. 7, 232–33 (*"No great number"*); Sedgwick, *A Memoir of the Life of William Livingston*, 211 (*soon dissolve*); Bill, *New Jersey and the Revolutionary War*, 16–24; Tallmadge, *Memoir of Col. Benjamin Tallmadge*, 15 (*"confusion and dismay"*).

488   *Among other worries, Washington was*: C. Lee to W. Heath, Nov. 21, 1776, *LP*, vol. 2, 291; GW to C. Lee, Nov. 21, 24, and 27, 1776, and GW to Hancock, Nov. 23, 1776, *PGW*, vol. 7, 194, 196, 208–10, 224; Chernow, *Washington: A Life*, 266–67; *GC*, 362–63.

488   *Lee's increasingly erratic, bickering*: Heath, *Memoirs of Major-General William Heath*, 80–84, 86–87; *GCL*, 151–52; C. Lee to Bowdoin, Nov. 22, 1776, *LP*, vol. 2, 303 (*"treason"*); NG to GW, Dec. 7, 1776, *PNG*, 366 (*"confined"*).

488   *In hopes of learning Lee's whereabouts*: Chernow, *Washington: A Life*, 266–67.

489   *"I received your most obliging"*: Reed to C. Lee, Nov. 21, 1776, *LP*, vol. 2, 293; GW to J. Reed, Nov. 30, 1776, *PGW*, vol. 7, 237–38.

489   *Many months would pass before Reed*: Bancroft, *Joseph Reed: A Historical Essay*, 22.

489   *An even more grievous injury*: Lefkowitz, *The Long Retreat*, 92–93; Continental Army return, Nov. 23, 1776, *AA*, V: 3, 822; NG to N. Cooke, Dec. 4, 1776, *PNG*, 362; GW to Hancock, Dec. 5, 1776, *PGW*, vol. 7, 263 (*"an hour longer"*); GW to Hancock, Nov. 30, 1776, *PGW*, vol. 7, 233 (*"If those go"*).

489   *In September, Congress had voted*: Wright, *The Continental Army*, 91–94; Coakley and Conn, *The War of the American Revolution*, 39; Weigley, *History of the United States Army*, 38 (*nary a lieutenant*); Jameson, "Subsistence for Middle States Militia, 1776–1781," *Military Affairs* 30, no. 3 (Fall 1966): 127.

490   *If the army remained*: GW to Hancock, Dec. 5, 1776, *PGW*, vol. 7, 263 (*"disorderly mob"*); NG to Nicholas Cooke, Dec. 4, 1776, *PNG*, 362; Thayer, *Nathanael Greene*, 130–31; GW to Hancock, Dec. 1, 1776, *PGW*, vol. 7, 244 (*"fast advancing"*).

490   *Washington ordered his artillery*: Chernow, *Alexander Hamilton*, 11–12, 23, 27, 31, 39–40, 72–73; Lefkowitz, *The Long Retreat*, 102 (*"favorite horse"*); A. Hamilton to Edward Stevens, Nov. 11, 1769, Alexander Hamilton Papers: General Correspondence, 1734–1772, LOC; Brookhiser, *Alexander Hamilton, American*, 3, 15–17, 20–21; GW to Hancock, Dec. 1, 1776, *PGW*, vol. 7, 246n (*"six to our one"*).

490   *British engineers repaired*: Münchhausen, *At General Howe's Side*, 6–7; GW to Hancock, Dec. 1, 1776, *PGW*, vol. 7, 246n (*slipped away*); *Personal Recollections of Captain Enoch Anderson*, 27–28 (*burning tents*); Bradford, ed., "A British Officer's Revolutionary War Journal, 1776–1778," *Maryland Historical Magazine* 56, no. 2 (June 1961): 166 (*too sick*); NG to N. Cooke, Dec. 4, 1776, *PNG*, 362 (*"not 3,000"*); "The Papers of General Samuel Smith," *Historical Magazine*, 2nd ser., 7 (Feb. 1870): 81+ (*"Every step"*); GW to Hancock, Dec. 1, 1776, *PGW*, vol. 7, 245 (*"we shall retreat"*).

491   *For now the British checked*: *The Narrative of Lieut. Gen. Sir William Howe*, 7 (*"highly blameable"*); Anderson, *The Command of the Howe Brothers During the American Revolution*, 202 (*"artillery horses"*); Wickwire and Wickwire, *Cornwallis*, 92–94 (*"pursued the enemy"*); Cornwallis, questioned by W. Howe, May 6, 1779, *Parliamentary Register*, vol. 12.

491 *The halt dismayed*: Thomas Glyn, Dec. 2, 1776, "Journal of American Campaign," FL (*"great expectation"*); Atwood, *The Hessians*, 84; Ewald, *Diary of the American War*, 25–27 (*"amicably"*).

491 *"'Tis almost impossible"*: "Bamford's Diary: The Revolutionary Diary of a British Officer," *Maryland Historical Magazine* 27, no. 3 (Sept. 1932): 18.

491 *Washington kept moving*: Louise Rau, ed., "Sergeant John Smith's Diary of 1776," *Mississippi Historical Review* 20, no. 2 (Sept. 1933): 264 (*"as if the devil"*); Ward, *The Delaware Continentals*, 104 (*"darkness and gloom"*).

491 *On Washington's order, soldiers*: GW to Col. Richard Humpton, Dec. 1, 1776, *PGW*, vol. 7, 248–49; Davis, "Washington on the West Bank of the Delaware, 1776," *PMHB* 4, no. 2 (1880): 136; *WC*, 134; Sanderson, ed., *Lynn in the Revolution*, part 1, 156; Kidder, *Crossroads of the Revolution*, 103–05 (*salt*); Ely and Jordan, *History of Bucks County, Pennsylvania*, vol. 2, 119–20; provisions in New Jersey magazines, NG to GW, Oct. 29, 1776, *AA*, V: 2, 1281; Rau, ed., "Sergeant John Smith's Diary of 1776," *Mississippi Historical Review* 20, no. 2 (Sept. 1933): 266–67 (*"29 fowls"*).

492 *Columns of refugees*: Miller, *The Life of Samuel Miller, D.D., LL.D.*, 147 (*"day of judgment"*); N.Y. Convention to Hancock, Dec. 28, 1776, *AA*, V: 3, 1466 (*"lowest ebb"*); Jordan, *The Military Hospitals at Bethlehem and Lititz, Pennsylvania*, 5–9, 18 (*crutches*).

492 *Puzzled by the enemy's failure*: Münchhausen, *At General Howe's Side*, 6–7; *BTP*, 15–17; Lefkowitz, *The Long Retreat*, 114, 118–19; Anderson, *The Command of the Howe Brothers During the American Revolution*, 205; NG to GW, Dec. 7, 1776, *PGW*, vol. 7, 269–70 (*"advancing"*).

492 *Washington sent a message to recall*: NG to GW, Dec. 7, 1776, *PNG*, 367n; Lefkowitz, *The Long Retreat*, 118–19; Cumming and Rankin, *The Fate of a Nation*, 126–27; *Personal Recollections of Captain Enoch Anderson*, 27–28 (*"no faster"*).

493 *Men at the last pitch of exhaustion*: Jacob, *A Biographical Sketch of the Life of the Late Captain Michael Cresap*, 12 (*"tag-rag"*); GW to Hancock, Dec. 8, 1776, *PGW*, vol. 7, 273–75 (*American host*); J. Reed to Hancock, Dec. 7, 1776, *AA*, V: 3, 1107 (*"No opposition"*).

493 *Among those waiting to cross*: Silverman, *A Cultural History of the American Revolution*, 327 (*"thin, spare"*); Sellers, "Charles Willson Peale, Artist-Soldier," *PMHB* 38, no. 3 (1914): 257+; *Charles Willson Peale and His World*, exhibition and brochure, National Portrait Gallery, Washington, D.C., 1982; Thompson, *Washington Along the Delaware*, 5; Harrington, "Charles Willson Peale's 'Riffle with a Tellescope to It,'" *JAR*, July 10, 2013; Lefkowitz, *The Long Retreat*, 120–21 (*"grand but dreadful"*).

493 *Washington crossed shortly after dawn*: Baker, "Itinerary of General Washington from June 15, 1775, to December 23, 1783," *PMHB* 14, no. 2 (July 1890): 140; *History of the First Troop Philadelphia City Cavalry*, 7; *BTP*, 28; GW to Hancock, Dec. 8, 1776, *PGW*, vol. 7, 274n; Kidder, *Crossroads of the Revolution*, 111; Lefkowitz, *The Long Retreat*, 121–22 (*Howe*).

494 *Although the pretty village was mostly*: Münchhausen, *At General Howe's Side*, 6–7. Capt. Johann Ewald put the number of American guns at eighteen and reported only one *Jäger* killed. *Diary of the American War*, 7.

494 *"General Howe had a mortgage"*: *BTP*, 27.

494 *Washington put his headquarters*: GW to Hancock, Dec. 9, 1776, *PGW*, vol. 7, 283–84 (*"bringing boats"*).

494 *"We lay amongst the leaves"*: *Personal Recollections of Captain Enoch Anderson*, 27–29.

495 *Yet for those who had come*: Ellis, *Revolutionary Summer*, 165 (*avoid losing it*).

495 *"Never was finer lads"*: Webb was Silas Deane's stepson. Ford, ed., *Correspondence and Journals of Samuel Blachley Webb*, vol. 1, 175, and vol. 3, 300n; Griffin, "Samuel Blachley Webb: Wethersfield's Ablest Officer," *JAR*, Sept. 19, 2016.

495 *Fortunately for those camped*: *BTP*, 37 (*forty-eight thousand board feet*); *The Narrative of Lieut. Gen. Sir William Howe*, 7; Cornwallis, questioned by W. Howe, May 6, 1779, *Parliamentary Register*, vol. 12; Anderson, *The Command of the Howe Brothers During the American Revolution*, 206; Curtis, *The British Army in the American Revolution*, 116; *Logistics*, 30 (*thousand tons*); Lefkowitz, *The Long Retreat*, 147.

495 *Howe had also been encouraged*: BTP, 324–15 (*"all treasons"*); Bill, *New Jersey and the Revolutionary War*, 24–25 (*"protection paper"*).

495 *"The approach of winter"*: BTP, 48; Smith, *The Battle of Trenton*, 27; *The Narrative of Lieut. Gen. Sir William Howe*, 8–9; Ewald, *Diary of the American War*, 31; WC, 187–88, 394–95; Morris, *Private Journal Kept During a Portion of the Revolutionary War*, 7–11 ("Wie geht's?"); Cornwallis, questioned by W. Howe, May 6, 1779, *Parliamentary Register*, vol. 12 (*"no danger"*).

496 *"The chain, I own"*: W. Howe to Germain, Dec. 20, 1776, DAR, vol. 12, 266.

496 *To serve as the new British commander*: Urban, *Fusiliers*, 80–81; WC, 183–84 (*"gamester"*).

496 *Before sailing for America*: Nelson, *General James Grant*, 85–86, 88 (*"without bloodshed"*), 94–95; Ferling, *Almost a Miracle*, 172; PH 18, 226; James Hutson, "Revolutionary America: The Papers of Gen. James Grant," Library of Congress, *Information Bulletin* 62, no. 4 (Apr. 2003): https://www.loc.gov/loc/lcib/0304/papers.html; Atwood, *The Hessians*, 91; WC, 184.

496 *Howe had hoped that his royal legions*: Conway, "To Subdue America: British Army Officers and the Conduct of the Revolutionary War," WMQ, 3rd ser., 43, no. 3 (July 1986): 392 (*"fire-and-sword"*); BTP, 316–17 (*"rebel store"*); Sellers, "Charles Willson Peale, Artist-Soldier," PMHB 38, no. 3 (1914): 277 (*"hogs, sheep"*).

496 *A German soldier reportedly rode*: Morison, *The Oxford History of the American People*, 243; Vermeule, "Some Revolutionary Incidents in the Raritan Valley," *Proceedings of the New Jersey Historical Society* (Apr. 1921): 73+ (650 houses); Gerlach, ed., *New Jersey in the American Revolution*, 296–97 (*"scene of ruin"*); Lundin, *Cockpit of the Revolution*, 173–74 (losses); Dunlap, *History of the American Theater*, vol. 2, 45–46 (frying pans and feather beds).

497 *Princeton had been insulted*: Calhoon, *The Loyalists in Revolutionary America*, 361–62; Collins, ed., *A Brief Narrative of the Ravages of the British and Hessians at Princeton in 1776–1777*, 4–12, 18 (stealing horseshoes); CP, 24–25, 33 (rare books); Sullivan, "The Battle of Princeton," PMHB 32, no. 1 (1908): 54 (*"a good library"*); "Conduct of the British and Hessian Troops in New Jersey," Dec. 12, 1776, AA, V: 3, 1188 (*"houses are stripped"*); Bill, *New Jersey and the Revolutionary War*, 24–25; Lundin, *Cockpit of the Revolution*, 175; Brown, *The Good Americans*, 118 (*"shoes taken"*); BTP, 24–26 (*"rapacity"*). See also "extract of a letter from an officer of distinction in the American Army," *Pennsylvania Packet*, Dec. 27, 1776, 1.

497 *Soon after retreating*: Kidder, *A People Harassed and Exhausted*, 193–96; WC, 178–79.

497 *Other testimonials accumulated*: WC, 178–79 (*"epidemic"*); Kidder, *A People Harassed and Exhausted*, 193–96; Bill, *New Jersey and the Revolutionary War*, 26; *Maryland Gazette*, Jan. 23, 1777 (*"God made these men"*); BTP, 22; NG to Nicholas Cooke, Dec. 21, 1776, PNG, 374–75 (*"all description"*). A few weeks later, Greene would claim "many hundred women ravished." NG to Nicholas Cooke, Jan. 10, 1777, PNG, vol. 2, 5. See also "Extract of a letter from an officer of distinction in the American Army," *Pennsylvania Packet*, Dec. 27, 1776, 1.

498 *General Howe would tell the House*: Frey, *The British Soldier in America*, 78–79; WC, 178–79; Conway, "'The Great Mischief Complain'd of': Reflections on the Misconduct of British Soldiers in the Revolutionary War," WMQ, 3rd ser., 17, no. 3 (July 1990): 370+ (*"proper restraint"*); Lundin, *Cockpit of the Revolution*, 177. Frey notes that "the majority of reported rape cases were not of civilians but of army wives and children." *The British Soldier in America*, 78–79.

498 *Yet in late 1776, several British officers*: Conway, "To Subdue America: British Army Officers and the Conduct of the Revolutionary War," WMQ, 3rd ser., 43, no. 3 (July 1986): 394–95 (*"free liberty"*); Frey, *The British Soldier in America*, 79 (*"satyrs"*).

498 *Major Charles Stuart wrote his father*: Stuart-Wortley, *A Prime Minister and His Son*, 99 (*"most inhuman"*); orderly book, Matthew Dixon, Sept. 6 and 10, 1776, HL, HM 615 (*"licentious behavior"*); WAI, 165 (*"rapine"*); Nov. 7, 1776, journal entry, KP (*"threaten with death"*); Gruber, ed., *John Peebles' American War*, 74 (*"shocking abuses"*); "Galloway, Joseph," *Biographical Directory of the United States Congress*, http://bioguide.congress.gov/scripts/biodisplay.pl?index=G000026; Sabine, *The American Loyalists*, 21 (*"no less than twenty-three"*).

499 *General Grant blamed indiscipline*: WAI, 165 (*"lose you friends"*); Kwasny, *Washington's Partisan War*, 97 (*ambushes*); Münchhausen, *At General Howe's Side*, 7 (*rebel bandits*); Lundin, *Cockpit of the Revolution*, 184–85 (*baggage wagons*); Leiby, *The Revolutionary War in the Hackensack Valley*, 90–93 (*fifty Tories*).

499 *"It is now very unsafe"*: Münchhausen, *At General Howe's Side*, 7–8.

499 *The approach of fire-and-sword men*: Rossman, *Thomas Mifflin and the Politics of the American Revolution*, 72 (*"insults and oppression"*); Duane, ed., *Extracts from the Diary of Christopher Marshall*, 105 (*"Drums beat"*); Wainwright and Fisher, Dec. 2, 1776, entry, "'A Diary of Trifling Occurrences: Philadelphia, 1776–1778,'" *PMHB* 82, no. 4 (Oct. 1858): 411+ (*closing schools*); Young, "Treason and Its Punishment in Revolutionary Pennsylvania," *PMHB* 90, no. 3 (July 1966): 291–93 (*Indian Queen*); Dorwart, *Invasion and Insurrection*, 120–21, 131; T. Mifflin to GW, Nov. 26, 1776, *PGW*, vol. 7, 220, 222n; *WR*, 286–87 (*"loading wagons"*); Ward, *The Delaware Continentals*, 105 (*"depopulated"*).

499 *Congress ordered a day of fasting*: Rossman, *Thomas Mifflin and the Politics of the American Revolution*, 72 (*"immorality"*); Charles Thomson to GW, Dec. 11, 1776, *PGW*, vol. 7, 302–03n (*"malicious"*); *GGW*, 172 (*"full power"*); *CP*, 12 (*"a damp"*); Ferling, *A Leap in the Dark*, 191 (*"dirty, infamous"*); Griffith, *The War for American Independence*, 333 (*"terrestrial places"*).

500 *Continental presses and plates*: Schuckers, *A Brief Account of the Finances and Paper Money of the Revolutionary War*, 12–16, 20–21; Robinson, *Continental Treasury Administration, 1775–1781*, 19–20, 65–66, 74–75; *The American Revolution in New York*, 112–13, 121; Bullock, *The Finances of the United States from 1775 to 1789*, 123, 126, 132–34; Ferguson, *The Power of the Purse*, 25–32; Bezanson, *Prices and Inflation During the American Revolution*, 12; Bolles, *The Financial History of the United States, from 1774 to 1789*, 53; *AA*, V: 3, 1332–34 (*"total ruin"*); Watson, *Annals of Philadelphia*, 623–24 (*light a pipe*).

500 *Before scurrying away, Congress*: Cutter, *The Life of Israel Putnam*, 274 (*"last extremity"*); Weigley, ed., *Philadelphia: A 300-Year History*, 127–29; Duane, ed., *Extracts from the Diary of Christopher Marshall*, appendix E, 295–97; Rappleye, *Robert Morris*, 90; Wainwright and Fisher, Dec. 12–13, 1776, entries, "'A Diary of Trifling Occurrences: Philadelphia, 1776–1778,'" *PMHB* 82, no. 4 (Oct. 1858): 411+; Dorwart, *Invasion and Insurrection*, 131 (*invalids*); Burdick, *Revolutionary Delaware*, 45 (*thirteen alarm posts*).

500 *But when a courier arrived with word*: Clark, *Captain Dauntless*, 161–65; Daughan, *If by Sea*, 122–23; Bridenbaugh, *Cities in Revolt*, 247 (*busiest port*).

500 *"a dark and silent wilderness"*: Hawke, *Benjamin Rush*, 175.

500 *At least half of Philadelphia's thirty thousand*: Weigley, ed., *Philadelphia: A 300-Year History*, 129; Rappleye, *Robert Morris*, 91 (*Quaker families*); Williams, "Independence and Early American Hospitals, 1751–1812," *JAMA* 236, no. 1 (July 5, 1976): 35+; Gill and Curtis, eds., *A Man Apart*, 116, 125; Powell, ed., *A Biographical Sketch of Col. Leven Powell*, 70 (*"face of despondency"*); Wainwright and Fisher, Dec. 30, 1776, entry, "'A Diary of Trifling Occurrences: Philadelphia, 1776–1778,'" *PMHB* 82, no. 4 (Oct. 1858): 411+ (*"die so fast"*); Lossing, *The Pictorial Field-Book of the Revolution*, vol. 2, 308; Hawke, *Benjamin Rush*, 174 (*a thousand*); J. Adams to Abigail Adams, Apr. 13, 1777, in *AFC*, vol. 2, 209 (*two thousand*).

501 *"Our people knew not"*: Rappleye, *Robert Morris*, 92; Rodney, *Diary of Captain Thomas Rodney*, 13 (*surrender terms*).

501 *At last, at long last, General Lee*: C. Lee to GW, Dec. 11, 1776, *PGW*, vol. 7, 301; *GCL*, 152–54; *LP*, vol. 2, 321 (*"strict silence"*); GW to C. Lee, Dec. 8, 1776, and Nov. 27, 1776, *PGW*, vol. 7, 277 (*"shocked"*), 225.

501 *None of this pleased Lee*: Patterson, *Knight Errant of Liberty*, 152 (*"puppies"*), 159 (*"perdition"*); *GCL*, 151 (*"unrest"*); Papas, *Renegade Revolutionary*, 205–06 (*"mud rounds"*); Heath, *Memoirs of Major-General William Heath*, 90 (*"reconquer"*).

501 *"Cannot I do you more service"*: *LP*, vol. 2, 291, 295, 309, 318, 326, 329, 340, 343; GW to C. Lee, Dec. 10 and 11, 1776, *PGW*, vol. 7, 288 (*"join me"*), 301 (*"Push on"*).

502 *On Thursday afternoon, with a weak, watery sun*: Vealtown was later named Bernardsville. McBurney, *Kidnapping the Enemy*, 28; *GCL*, 155.

502 *Leaving his personal baggage behind*: "Revolutionary War Sites in Basking Ridge, New Jersey," http://www.revolutionarywarnewjersey.com/new_jersey_revolutionary_war_sites/towns/basking_ridge_nj_revolutionary_war_sites.htm; Patterson, *Knight Errant of Liberty*, 163; Chernow, *Washington: A Life*, 267; Lefkowitz, *The Long Retreat*, 131; *LP*, vol. 2, 329–31 (*favorite mare*).

502 *After peeling off his uniform*: Lefkowitz, *The Long Retreat*, 131; C. Lee to Gates, Dec. 12–13, 1776, *LP*, vol. 2, 348 (*"Entre nous"*).

502 *As Alexander Hamilton would later observe*: Robson, *The American Revolution*, 172–73.

503 *Alarmed by reports that Lee*: W. Harcourt to Earl Harcourt, Dec. 17, 1776, Harcourt, ed., *The Harcourt Papers*, vol. 11, 182; McBurney, *Kidnapping the Enemy*, 38–39 (*"They picked off"*), 40–42; *Evelyn*, 104–05. The house where the dragoons slept on December 12 caught fire at one a.m., forcing them to the barn. Tarleton to mother, December 18, 1776, in Bass, *The Green Dragoon*, 21–22.

503 *A mile from Basking Ridge*: Bass, *The Green Dragoon*, 12, 21–22; John Knight, "Top 10 Banastre Tarleton Myths," *JAR*, Aug. 18, 2016; *GCL*, 156.

503 *Inside Lee had dressed*: *C 1776*, 294; Wilkinson, *Memoirs of My Own Times*, vol. 1, 102–05 (*"British cavalry!"* and *"set fire to the house"*); Tarleton to mother, Dec. 18, 1776, in Bass, *The Green Dragoon*, 21–22 (*"all the noise"*).

503 *Lee stepped through the front door*: Wilkinson, *Memoirs of My Own Times*, vol. 1, 106, 111; *C 1776*, 294 (*"a gentleman"*).

504 *The skirmish had lasted fifteen minutes*: Tarleton to mother, Dec. 18, 1776, in Bass, *The Green Dragoon*, 21–22; Papas, *Renegade Revolutionary*, 209; McBurney, *Kidnapping the Enemy*, 51 (*"put in boxes"*); *C 1776*, 294.

504 *"This is a most miraculous event"*: Tarleton to mother, Dec. 18, 1776, in Bass, *The Green Dragoon*, 19–20 (*horse drunk*), 21–22; Harcourt, ed., *The Harcourt Papers*, vol. 11, 204 (*seventy miles*); Münchhausen, *At General Howe's Side*, 7–8 (*"cause to fear"*); Hancock to GW, Jan. 6–7, 1777, *PGW*, vol. 8, 3.

504 *Bells rang in jubilation*: Harcourt, ed., *The Harcourt Papers*, vol. 11, 192–93; McBurney, *Kidnapping the Enemy*, 50 (*"thy peril"*); Hunter, *The Journal of Gen. Sir Martin Hunter*, 23 (*"So dirty"*); Lt. William John Hale to father, Dec. 19, 1776, "Letters Written During the American War of Independence," in Wylly, ed., *1913 Regimental Annual: The Sherwood Foresters*, 15 (*"dejected"*).

504 *"Let me once more request"*: GW to C. Lee, *LP*, vol. 2, 349; Thayer, *Nathanael Greene*, 135 (*"misfortune"*); *GCL*, 160 (*"idol"*); Butterfield, ed., *Letters of Benjamin Rush*, vol. 1, 121 (*"distrust"*).

504 *"Fortune seems to frown"*: NG to Caty, Dec. 16, 1776, *PNG*, 368; NG to Christopher Greene, Jan. 20, 1777, *PNG*, vol. 2, 8 (*"not confined"*); Stone, *The Life and Recollections of John Howland*, 65 (*"American stuff"*).

505 *Washington publicly mourned*: GW to Lund Washington, Dec. 10–17, 1776, *PGW*, vol. 7, 289–90 (*"Unhappy man"*); GW to R. Lee, Dec. 29, 1776, *PGW*, vol. 7, 480 (*"your circumstances"*).

505 *Each morning, New York loyalists*: *CP*, 69–70; Dunlap, *History of the American Theater*, vol. 1, 85–86; Rogers, *The British Army of the Eighteenth Century*, 76.

505 *General Howe had returned*: R. Howe to Germain, Dec. 22, 1776, and Mar. 25, 1777, UK NA, CO 5/177, f. 115, 131; Mahan, 73.

505 *On December 7, General Henry Clinton*: Tilley, *The British Navy and the American Revolution*, 92–94; *DFM*, 123–26; W. Howe to Germain, Dec. 20, 1776, *DAR*, vol. 12, 266; *Rhode Island in the American Revolution* (2000): 8–10, SoC, State Exhibition Series, http://www.societyofthecincinnati.org/scholarship/publications/; Atwood, *The Hessians*, 80 (*"eat up"*); Gruber, ed., *John Peebles' American War*, 71 (*"most violent"*); Dexter, *The Literary Diary of Ezra Stiles, D.D., LL.D.*, vol. 2, 94 (*"calamities"*); Graham, *The Royal Navy in the War of American Independence*, 4; Field, *Esek Hopkins*, 169.

506 *British newspapers lionized both Howes*: Hibbert, *Redcoats and Rebels*, 131; Steuart, ed., *The Last Journals of Horace Walpole*, vol. 1, 574 (*"extravagance"*); Silverman, *A Cultural History of the American Revolution*, 326 (*"He comes"*); Germain to W. Howe, Oct. 18, 1776, UK NA,

CO 5/93, f. 533; Bickham, *Making Headlines*, 93 (*aged mother*). Howe was officially invested with the order by his brother at the queen's birthday celebration in mid-January 1777.

506 *Sir William and his battle staff*: Abbott, *New York in the American Revolution*, 222 (*"jollity"*); W. Howe note, Feb. 2, 1777, "Richard and William Howe Collection," box 1, WLC (*Antiguan rum*); Münchhausen, *At General Howe's Side*, 8–9 (*"balls, concerts"*); Harry Schenawolf, "Washington's New York City Headquarters, No. 1 Broadway," July 9, 2013, "Revolutionary War Journal," http://www.revolutionarywarjournal.com/washingtons-headquarters/; W. Howe to "Mrs. Clarke," Dec. 31, 1776, "Richard and William Howe Collection," box 1, WLC (*thank-you notes*); CP, 68 (*"blonde"*); Wallace, *Appeal to Arms*, 59–60 (*"courtesan"*); BNY, 273–74 (*guineas*); *The Detail and Conduct of the American War*, 17 (£6,000).

506 *Enough refugees and loyalists*: Burrows and Wallace, *Gotham*, 244; BNY, 275 (*"Canvas Town"*); Cresswell, *The Journal of Nicholas Cresswell*, 244 (*"Unwholesome"*); Ranlet, *The New York Loyalists*, 79 (*"very unsafe"*); Frey, *The British Soldier in America*, 61–62 (*"artillery wives"*); Onderdonk, *Revolutionary Incidents of Suffolk and Kings Counties*, 177 (*Jaff*).

507 *Fences and barns were dismembered*: IMI, vol. 5, 1036 (*cord of oak*), 1039, 1044; Stiles, *A History of the City of Brooklyn*, vol. 1, 301–02 (*peat*); Conway, "'The Great Mischief Complain'd of': Reflections on the Misconduct of British Soldiers in the Revolutionary War," WMQ, 3rd ser., 17, no. 3 (July 1990): 370+; Jones, *History of New York During the Revolutionary War*, vol. 1, 136; Barck, *New York City During the War for Independence*, 102, 111–13; Abbott, *New York in the American Revolution*, 215–16; Miller, *Triumph of Freedom*, 124 (*"dead rebels"*); Strong, *History of the Town of Flatbush*, 156 (*Nassau Blues*); Onderdonk, *Documents and Letters Intended to Illustrate the Revolutionary Incidents of Queens County*, 252 (*remove his hat*).

507 *Finally the war seemed to be going*: Logistics, 65; Howe to Treasury, Dec. 2, 1776, UK NA, T 64/108, f. 73–76 (*"wisely planned"*), f. 83–85 (*barreled meat*); Treasury documents, provisions sent to New York, Oct. 2, 1776, UK NA, T 1/519; Wertenbaker, *Father Knickerbocker Rebels*, 105 (*king's stores*).

507 *A brewery near Maiden Lane*: IMI, vol. 5, 1041, 1044; Abbott, *New York in the American Revolution*, 219; "One Hundred and Ten Years Ago," *American Stationer* 32, no. 8 (Aug. 25, 1892): 356; Dunlap, *History of the American Theater*, vol. 1, 94–95 (*"Bloody news!"*).

508 *A miniaturist set up his easel*: IMI, vol. 5, 1042; Dunlap, *History of the American Theater*, vol. 1, 94–95 (*"low comedian"*); Barck, *New York City During the War for Independence*, 171–73 (*"histrionic ability"*); Frey, *The British Soldier in America*, 67–68 (*"Who would have expected"*); Silverman, *A Cultural History of the American Revolution*, 326; CP, 70–71 (*Bible and Crown*).

508 *By Joshua Loring's precise count*: return of American prisoners taken, Aug. 27–Nov. 20, in W. Howe to Germain, Dec. 3, 1776, *DAR*, vol. 10, 417; IMI, vol. 5, 1039 (*"ragamuffins"*).

508 *New York soon became known*: Lindsey, "Treatment of American Prisoners of War During the Revolution," *Emporia State Research Studies* 22, no. 1 (Summer 1973): 5+; Sabine, ed., *The New-York Diary of Lieutenant Jabez Fitch*, 16; Dandridge, *American Prisoners of the Revolution*, 18 (*"We thus lived"*); Bellesiles, *Revolutionary Outlaws*, 128–29 (*"I had promised"*); Jellison, *Ethan Allen: Frontier Rebel*, 170–74 (*"robust"* and *"darling of my soul"*); Randall, *Ethan Allen*, 413–19. Allen later was charged with violating his parole and confined under harsh conditions in the Provost. Burrows, *Forgotten Patriots*, 95.

508 *For enlisted men and other officers*: Bowman, *Captive Americans*, 11–13; Abbott, *New York in the American Revolution*, 208; "Prisons of the Revolution," *Old New York* 1, no. 5 (Dec. 1889): 297+; Onderdonk, *Revolutionary Incidents of Suffolk and Kings Counties*, 207–10; Dandridge, *American Prisoners of the Revolution*, 26, 29; Burrows and Wallace, *Gotham*, 84, 119 (*"white gold"*); Burrows, *Forgotten Patriots*, 23–24, 50.

509 *A New Yorker recounted*: Tacyn, "To the End: The First Maryland Regiment and the American Revolution," Ph.D. diss. (University of Maryland, College Park, 1999), 84–85 (*"narrow aperture"*); Dandridge, *American Prisoners of the Revolution*, 26, 29 (*insects and rodents*); deposition, Samuel Young and William Houston, Dec. 15, 1776, AA, V: 3, 1234 (*"hogs"*); Ranlet, *The New York Loyalists*, 109 (*"took legs"*); Moore, *The Diary of the American Revolution*, 195 (*"damnified pork"*); IMI, vol. 5, 1040; Lindsey, "Treatment of American Prisoners

of War During the Revolution," *Emporia State Research Studies* 22, no. 1 (Summer 1973): 5+; Allen, *Tories*, 198 (*"Old shoes"*); Burrows, *Forgotten Patriots*, 58 (*eat a brick*).

509 *The lucky ones could build*: Sabine, ed., *The New-York Diary of Lieutenant Jabez Fitch*, 64 (*"It was bad"*); Burrows, *Forgotten Patriots*, 26 (*"seldom recover"*), 64 (*two thousand men*); Onderdonk, *Revolutionary Incidents of Suffolk and Kings Counties*, 212 (*corpses*); Beakes, *Otho Holland Williams in the American Revolution*, 46–47 (*mock execution*); Moore, *The Diary of the American Revolution*, 196 (*rope*); Magaw et al. to W. Howe, Dec. 8, 1776, "Calendar of Manuscripts in the Royal Institution," *Report on the American Manuscripts*, vol. 1, 76 (*"too melancholy"*).

510 *Conditions only grew worse*: Dandridge, *American Prisoners of the Revolution*, 35 (*"scaw-banker"*); Onderdonk, *Revolutionary Incidents of Suffolk and Kings Counties*, 207–10; J. L. Bell, "The Myth of Provost William Cunningham," *B 1775*, Oct. 10, 2007; Burrows, *Forgotten Patriots*, 21–22 (*"that engine"*).

510 *The transport vessel* Whitby: Bowman, *Captive Americans*, 41–45; Patton, *Patriot Pirates*, 97 (*"crowded promiscuously"*); affidavit, Lt. Robert Troup, Jan. 17, 1777, in Ryan, ed., *A Salute to Courage*, 67–68; Dzurec, "Prisoners of War and American Self-Image During the American Revolution," *War in History* 20, no. 4 (Nov. 2013): 230+ (*"sixteen hours"*); Timothy Parker et al. aboard *Whitby* to Gov. Jonathan Trumbull, Sr., Dec. 9, 1776, *AA*, V: 3, 1138–39 (*"most wretched"*).

510 *Soon enough, more than two dozen*: Bowman, *Captive Americans*, 42; Greene, *Recollections of the Jersey Prison-Ship*, 58–60; Ramsay, *The History of the American Revolution*, vol. 2, 284–85. Burrows asserts that of the nearly 36,000 American deaths during the Revolution from all causes—a figure somewhat higher than most estimates—roughly half "were in the prisons and prison ships of New York City." *Forgotten Patriots*, 52–55 (*"damned Yankee rebel"*), 201.

21. THE SMILES OF PROVIDENCE

511 *Christmas Eve was joyless*: *CP*, 40; *WC*, appendix M, 404; Wiederhold [*sic*], "Colonel Rall at Trenton," *PMHB* 22, no. 4 (1898): 462+ (*"denuded"*); Lundin, *Cockpit of the Revolution*, 16; *BTP*, 90–98; "Land Use History," Trenton Historical Society, www.trentonhistory.org /Documents/MillHill.History.htm; Kidder, *Crossroads of the Revolution*, 131.

511 *Acrid odors from tanning vats*: Widmer, "The Christmas Campaign: The Ten Days of Trenton and Princeton," New Jersey Historical Commission, 18; Kidder, *A People Harassed and Exhausted*, 19; Lundin, *Cockpit of the Revolution*, 16; *WC*, 254 (*3-pounders*); Smith, *The Battle of Trenton*, 17; Wiederhold [*sic*], "Colonel Rall at Trenton," *PMHB* 22, no. 4 (1898): 462+; *BTP*, 92, 198–99 (*"Catholic procession"* and *"never could"*); Burgoyne, ed., *Enemy Views*, 117; *CP*, 40.

512 *Colonel Johann Gottlieb Rall had spent*: *WC*, 57; *CP*, 38–39; Tucker, *George Washington's Surprise Attack*, 156–58; *BTP*, 199–200 (*"born soldier"*); Ferling, *Almost a Miracle*, 175 (*the lion*); Burgoyne, trans., *Defeat, Disaster and Dedication*, 20 (*"generous, magnanimous"*); Atwood, *The Hessians*, 82, 87, 90.

512 *As he settled into his new command*: *BTP*, 107 (*"farmers"*); Eelking and Rosengarten, *The German Allied Troops in the North American War of Independence*, 43–44 (*"bare feet"*); *CP*, 41–42 (*"woman's talk"*); *WC*, 189 (*"Shit"*); Smith, *The Battle of Trenton*, 13.

512 *"We have not slept one night"*: Lundin, *Cockpit of the Revolution*, 187; Smith, *The Battle of Trenton*, 14; Wiederhold [*sic*], "Colonel Rall at Trenton," *PMHB* 22, no. 4 (1898): 462+.

512 *Rall waved away suggestions*: *WC*, 196 ("all *directions*"); Atwood, *The Hessians*, 89, 91 (*"hardly believe"*); Nelson, *General James Grant*, 108 (*"more of the rebels"*), 109 (*"winter of ease"*); *BTP*, 108 (*"corporal's guard"*); Lundin, *Cockpit of the Revolution*, 188 (*"I am sorry to hear"*).

513 *Moreover, the Trenton garrison*: *WC*, 199–200 (*"troublesome guests"*); Ewald, *Diary of the American War*, xxv–xxvi, 38–42 (*"plundered"*); Lundin, *Cockpit of the Revolution*, 190; Reed, "General Joseph Reed's Narrative of the Movements of the American Army in the Neighborhood of Trenton in the Winter of 1776–77," *PMHB* 8, no. 4 (Dec. 1884): 392.

513 *From Trenton, patrols sent out*: Kidder, *A People Harassed and Exhausted*, 187 (*"insecure"*); *WC*, 205 (*"fatigued"*); Burgoyne, ed., *Enemy Views*, 114 (*"yellow dogs"*); *BTP*, 115–16 (*"no rebel troops"*).

514 *Twelve miles northwest of Trenton*: Davis, "Washington on the West Bank of the Delaware, 1776," *Pennsylvania Magazine of History and Biography* 4, no. 2 (1880): 145–46; Ely and Jordan, *History of Bucks County, Pennsylvania*, vol. 2, 121–23; Thompson, *Washington Along the Delaware*, 17; Smith, *The Battle of Princeton*, 5. Knowles Creek is also known as Jericho Creek.

514 *A steady procession of gallopers*: various orders, e.g., GW to John Cadwalader, Dec. 12 and 24, 1776, *PGW*, vol. 7, 304, 425; GW to Heath, Dec. 16, 1776, *PGW*, vol. 7, 354; general orders, Dec. 25, 1776, *PGW*, vol. 7, 434–36; GW to Hancock, Dec. 24, 1776, *PGW*, vol. 7, 431n (*about 6,100*); *BARH*, 291–92; GW to Gates, Dec. 23, 1776, *PGW*, vol. 7, 418; Nelson, *General Horatio Gates*, 74–77; Wilkinson, *Memoirs of My Own Times*, vol. 1, 126–27; Palmer, *George Washington and Benedict Arnold*, 189.

516 *Among Washington's visitors this morning*: *D&AJA*, vol. 2, 182 (*"sprightly"*); Corner, ed., *The Autobiography of Benjamin Rush*, 125–27; Alexander Leitch, *A Princeton Companion*, 1978, https://etcweb.princeton.edu/CampusWWW/Companion/rush_benjamin.html (*age fourteen*); Hawke, *Benjamin Rush*, 43, 64, 103–06; Fruchtman, *Atlantic Cousins*, 58; Butterfield, ed., *Letters of Benjamin Rush*, 117, 123 (*"Every particle"*); Benjamin Rush, *Directions for Preserving the Health of Soldiers* (1777), in Cutbush, *Observations on the Means of Preserving the Health of Soldiers and Sailors*, appendix, 337.

516 *Today he also wanted to take*: Butterfield, ed., *Letters of Benjamin Rush*, 92 (*"heroes"*); William M. Ferraro, "Standing Against Corruption and Favoritism: Benjamin Rush and George Washington During the Revolutionary and Founding Eras," draft given to author, University of Virginia, 2013; Hawke, *Benjamin Rush*, 176 (*"dictatorial power"*); Corner, ed., *The Autobiography of Benjamin Rush*, 125–27 (*"much depressed"*).

516 *More visitors came and went*: Reed to GW, Dec. 22, 1776, *PGW*, vol. 7, 414–15 (*"We are all"*).

516 *Washington agreed*: GW to Lund Washington, Dec. 10–17, 1776, and GW to Samuel Washington, Dec. 18, 1776, *PGW*, vol. 7, 289–90 (*"aspect"*), 370 (*"our affairs"*); GW to W. Heath, Dec. 18, 1776, *PGW*, vol. 7, 366 (*"defection of the people"*).

517 *Late in the afternoon he rode*: Ely and Jordan, *History of Bucks County, Pennsylvania*, vol. 2, 121–23 (*stone house* and *sugar*); Ward, *Major General Adam Stephen and the Cause of American Liberty*, 150; *BTP*, 112; Golway, *Washington's General*, 107.

517 *For at least ten days*: GW to Gates, Dec. 14, 1776, *PGW*, vol. 7, 333 (*"smiles of Providence"*); Delaware River Basin Commission, river mileage system, http://www.state.nj.us/drbc/basin/river/ (*twenty-six-mile stretch*); *WC*, 208–09, 404; orders, Henry Knox, Dec. 25, 1776, Gilder Lehrman Collection, no. GLC02437.00495; GW to Reed, Dec. 23, 1776, *PGW*, vol. 7, 423 (*"fatal"*); Morris to GW, Dec. 21, 1776, *PGW*, vol. 7, 404 (*"told today"*). I am grateful to Edward G. Lengel for his insights into GW's motivation at this juncture.

517 *Each man would carry*: Risch, *Supplying Washington's Army*, 205; Davis, "Washington on the West Bank of the Delaware, 1776," *Pennsylvania Magazine of History and Biography* 4, no. 2 (1880): 143 (*blankets*).

518 *The chosen crossing sites*: signage and author interviews, boathouse, Washington's Crossing, Pa., Mar. 4, 2014; Brewington, "Washington's Boat at the Delaware Crossing," *American Neptune* 2 (1942): 167+; John U. Rees, "Preliminary Research on River Vessels Used by the Continental Army, 1775–1782," Aug. 1998, DLAR.

518 *The seven brigades assigned*: Wright, *The Continental Army*, 97 (*artillery company*); Weller, "Guns of Destiny," *Military Affairs* 20, no. 1 (Spring 1956): 1+ (*nine per thousand*); *GWGO*, 245–46; Callahan, *Henry Knox*, 83; Cubbison, "The Artillery Never Gained More Honour," 38; orders, Henry Knox, Dec. 25, 1776, Gilder Lehrman Collection, no. GLC02437.00495 (*spikes and hammers*); GW to Hancock, Dec. 20, 1776, *PGW*, vol. 7, 382, 386–87n (*"Desperate diseases"*).

518 *"I cannot desert a man"*: W. Tudor to Delia Jarvis, Dec. 24, 1776, William Tudor Papers, MHS, Ms. N-1684.

519 *Clouds thickened on Christmas*: *WC*, 206, 400–01; *GGW*, 182; William M. Welsch, "Christmas Night 1776: How Did They Cross?," in Andrlik et al., eds., *Journal of the American Revolution*, vol. 1, 104–05. The moon rose at 6:08 p.m., EST. "Sun and Moon Data," U.S. Naval Observatory, Trenton, Dec. 25, 1776.

519 *Some men would not see*: Davis, "Washington on the West Bank of the Delaware, 1776," *Pennsylvania Magazine of History and Biography* 4, no. 2 (1880): 141 (*James Moore*); Chernow, *Alexander Hamilton*, 83–84 ("*long and severe*").

519 *Many historians would subsequently assert*: The pamphlet was published on December 19, before appearing in newspaper form after the battle of Trenton. Conner, "A Brief Publication History of the 'Times That Try Men's Souls,'" *JAR*, Jan. 4, 2016; Chernow, *Washington: A Life*, 271; Foner, *Tom Paine and Revolutionary America*, 139; *WC*, 139.

519 *Little evidence supports*: Jett Conner, "The American Crisis Before Crossing the Delaware," *JAR*, Feb. 25, 2015.

519 *Thomas Paine's febrile essay*: Hawke, *Paine*, 60–61; Keane, *Tom Paine*, 142–45; Nelson, *Thomas Paine*, 107–08.

519 *"These are the times"*: Paine, *"Common Sense," "The Rights of Man," and Other Essential Writings of Thomas Paine*, 75.

519 *At dusk, regiments marched*: Kidder, "Guiding Washington to Trenton," *JAR*, May 6, 2014; Smith, *The Battle of Trenton*, 18; Brewington, "Washington's Boat at the Delaware Crossing," *American Neptune* 2 (1942): 167+; William M. Welsch, "Christmas Night 1776: How Did They Cross?," in Andrlik et al., eds., *Journal of the American Revolution*, vol. 1, 104–05; Oliver Randolph Parry, "Coryell's Ferry in the Revolution," lecture, May 21, 1915; *WC*, 217–18; orders, Henry Knox, Dec. 25, 1776, Gilder Lehrman Collection, no. GLC02437.00495 ("*profound silence*").

520 *Proverbially no plan survives contact*: *WC*, 208–09, 212–14; Baker, *"Villainy and Maddness": Washington's Flying Camp*, 68.

520 *Fifteen miles farther south, at Neshaminy*: Reed, "General Joseph Reed's Narrative of the Movements of the American Army in the Neighborhood of Trenton in the Winter of 1776–1777," *PMHB* 8, no. 4 (Dec. 1884): 393–94; GW to Cadwalader, Dec. 7, 24, and 25, 1776, *PGW*, vol. 7, 269n, 425, 438–39; "Journal of Campaign . . . by a Delaware Captain of Militia," Dec. 25, 1776, diary folder, box 1, Thomas Rodney, NYHS ("*wind blowing*"); Smith, *The Battle of Trenton*, 19; Seymour, *The Pennsylvania Associators*, 165; Rodney, *Diary of Captain Thomas Rodney*, 22–23 ("*greatly irritated*"); Stone, *The Life and Recollections of John Howland*, 69 ("*We suffered*"); Cadwalader to GW, Dec. 26, 1776, *PGW*, vol. 7, 442, 444n ("*the badness*").

520 *Not so. Above the fall line*: Ryden, ed., *Letters to and from Caesar Rodney*, 152–53.

521 *Back and forth the boats shuttled*: William M. Welsch, "Christmas Night 1776: How Did They Cross?," in Andrlik et al., eds., *Journal of the American Revolution*, vol. 1, 104–08; *WC*, 401; *WR*, 294 ("*as severe*"); Greenwood, ed., *The Revolutionary Services of John Greenwood*, 38–42 ("*half dead*"); *GGW*, 181 ("*all the same*").

521 *Washington waited too, eating*: Chernow, *Washington: A Life*, 271 ("*pensive*"); *WR*, 295 ("*bayonet*"); *BTP*, 137–42 ("*Shoulder*"); H. Knox to Lucy, Dec. 28, 1776, *RWLLLHK*, 66 ("*Perseverance*"). Few reliable eyewitness details survive to describe Washington's own crossing of the river; Emanuel Leutze's iconic painting draws heavily from the artist's imagination.

521 *The column stretched for more*: *BTP*, 140–42; *WC*, 230 (*fell behind*).

521 *"Press on"*: Chernow, *Washington: A Life*, 275; Powell, "A Connecticut Soldier Under Washington: Elisha Bostwick's Memoirs of the First Years of the Revolution," *WMQ*, 3rd ser., 6, no. 1 (Jan. 1949): 102, 106 ("*at their legs*").

521 *A pallid sky in the east*: GW to Hancock, Dec. 27, 1776, *PGW*, vol. 7, 457n ("*officer's watch*"). Among those sent ahead was a future president from Virginia, Lt. James Monroe. Brown, ed., *The Autobiography of James Monroe*, 30–31.

522 *Then the army divided*: Powell, ed., *A Biographical Sketch of Col. Leven Powell*, 42–43 ("*long trot*"); *WC*, 228–31.

522 *At precisely eight a.m., a Hessian*: GW to Hancock, Dec. 27, 1776, *PGW*, vol. 7, 454; *BTP*, 147; Atwood, *The Hessians*, 49 (*quarter century's experience*); Wiederhold [sic], "Colonel Rall at Trenton," *PMHB* 22, no. 4 (1898): 462+ ("*lookout*").

522 *"Der Feind!"* *BTP*, 147; Wiederhold [sic], "Colonel Rall at Trenton," *PMHB* 22, no. 4 (1898): 462+; GW to Hancock, Dec. 27, 1776, *PGW*, vol. 7, 454, 456n.

522 *Greene's division followed on their heels*: GW to Hancock, Dec. 27, 1776, *PGW*, vol. 7, 454 (*"charge the enemy"*); *WC*, 230, 244; Seymour, *The Pennsylvania Associators*, 168–69; Weller, "Guns of Destiny," *Military Affairs* 20, no. 1 (Spring 1956): 1+; Knox to Lucy, Dec. 28, 1776, in *RWLLLHK*, 67 (*"hurry, fright"*).

523 *The gunfire Wiederholdt heard*: author visit, Trenton, Mar. 4, 2014, state historical signage; Smith, *The Battle of Trenton*, 22; Kidder, *Crossroads of the Revolution*, 148–49; *WC*, 239; Stark, *Memoir and Official Correspondence of Gen. John Stark*, 39 (*damp firelocks*).

523 *Colonel Rall, der Löwe, had passed*: Stacy Potts house, Trenton, http://www.revolutionary warnewjersey.com/new_jersey_revolutionary_war_sites/towns/trenton_nj_revolutionary _war_sites.htm (*two hearths*). The claim that Rall and his men were inebriated has little historical basis. *CP*, 42–43; *BTP*, 117–25.

523 *The early morning clamor at both ends*: Smith, *The Battle of Trenton*, 22; Eelking and Rosengarten, *The German Allied Troops in the North American War of Independence*, 43; *GGW*, 187; *WR*, 298; Callahan, *Henry Knox*, 87; "The Narrative of Major Thompson Maxwell," *Historical Collections of the Essex Institute* 7, no. 3 (June 1865): 13+ (*pulled off his boots*).

523 *Eight horses were led*: Smith, *The Battle of Trenton*, 22–23; *BTP*, 156–58; *WC*, 244–45; author visit, Trenton, Mar. 4, 2014, state historical signage; McMichael, "Diary of Lieutenant James McMichael, of the Pennsylvania Line, 1776, 1778," *PMHB* 16, no. 2 (July 1892): 140 (*"We drove them"*).

524 *Mounting his horse, Rall herded*: Burgoyne, ed., *Enemy Views*, 120; GW to Hancock, Dec. 27, 1776, *PGW*, vol. 7, 454 (*"From their motions"*), 458n.

524 *Sleet, rain, and snow seemed to whip*: Kidder, *Crossroads of the Revolution*, 158; Brown, ed., *The Autobiography of James Monroe*, 30–31; *WC*, 221, 247; White, *An Narrative of Events . . . in the Revolutionary War*, 15; Stephenson, *Patriot Battles*, 158 (*"squeaking noise"*).

524 *Rall again tried to marshal*: Atwood, *The Hessians*, 93 ("meine Grenadiers"); *BTP*, 156–57, 162–63 (*"Lord, what is it?"*); Kidder, *Crossroads of the Revolution*, 152; *WR*, 300–01; *WC*, 248 (*Hessian captains*).

525 *Two bullets knocked him*: *BTP*, 174; *WC*, 248, 251 (*"they have struck"*), 520n; Smith, *The Battle of Trenton*, 24; Wilkinson, *Memoirs of My Own Times*, vol. 1, 130n.

525 *So they had*: *CP*, 56; *BTP*, 180–82.

525 *Five hundred yards to the south*: *CP*, 56–57; *WC*, 251–52; Powell, ed., *A Biographical Sketch of Col. Leven Powell*, 42–43 (*"fight became a chase"*); *BTP*, 184–85 (*"If you do not"*); Smith, *The Battle of Trenton*, 25 (*"My dear sirs"*).

525 *A great cheer sounded*: *BTP*, 187; H. Knox to Lucy, Dec. 28, 1776, *RWLLLHK*, 67 (*"smiled"*).

525 *Giddy soldiers donned the tall brass*: Greenwood, ed., *The Revolutionary Services of John Greenwood*, 42–43; *CP*, 60 (*ate their prisoners*); Wilkinson, *Memoirs of My Own Times*, vol. 1, 131 (*"glorious day"*).

526 *In half a morning, Howe*: Smith, *The Battle of Trenton*, 6.

526 *Casualty estimates would vary*: *BTP*, 195–96, 408–09; GW to Cadwalader, Dec. 27, 1776, *PGW*, vol. 7, 451n; *WR*, 302; *WC*, 405.

526 *"Saw a room full of wounded"*: Young, "Journal of Sergeant William Young," *PMHB* 8, no. 3 (Oct. 1884): 260–61; Gibson, *Dr. Bodo Otto and the Medical Background of the American Revolution*, 128 (*"amputating"*); *BTP*, 192–93 (*Rall asked* and *Presbyterian yard*); Burgoyne, ed., *Enemy Views*, 116 (*"outlive his honor"*).

526 *Among those who escaped*: *WC*, 254, 261; Smith, *The Battle of Trenton*, 6, 25–26; *CP*, 58–59; Butcher, *The Battle of Trenton*, 37–38 (*pitchfork*); Ewald, *Diary of the American War*, 43 (*"blows"*); Zellers-Frederick, "The Hessians Who Escaped Washington's Trap at Trenton," *JAR*, Apr. 18, 2018.

526 *With thousands of enemies*: Peckham, ed., *The Toll of Independence*, 27. Other tallies show even lower American battle casualties. *WC*, 406.

527 *"I was extremely chilled"*: David Avery, "The Battle of Trenton," *American Monthly* 19, no. 2 (Aug. 1901): 155; Reed, "General Joseph Reed's Narrative of the Movements of the American Army in the Neighborhood of Trenton in the Winter of 1776–1777," *PMHB* 8, no. 4 (Dec. 1884): 391 (*enemy rum*); Callahan, *Henry Knox*, 90 (*shoes*); Jackson, *The Pennsylvania*

Navy, 82 (*ferrymen*); George Clinton to Schuyler, Dec. 29, 1776, Philip Schuyler papers, BC, vol. 347, 111–13 (*forty hogsheads*); *CP*, 5, 58–59 (*Pro Principe*).

527 *Hundreds of Hessians were herded*: Powell, "A Connecticut Soldier Under Washington: Elisha Bostwick's Memoirs of the First Years of the Revolution," *WMQ*, 3rd ser., 6, no. 1 (Jan. 1949): 103 ("*skillet*"); Burgoyne, ed., *Enemy Views*, 122–23; *CP*, 5 (*Red Lion*); Dann, ed., *The Revolution Remembered*, 146 (*Putnam*); Lowell, *The Hessians*, 102 ("*shook hands*"); general orders, Dec. 27, 1776, *PGW*, vol. 7, 449n; Eelking and Rosengarten, *The German Allied Troops in the North American War of Independence*, 48 ("*no fire*").

527 *At midday on Monday, December 30*: *WR*, 304–05 ("*knapsacks*"); Montross, *Rag, Tag and Bobtail*, 170 (*Hessian band*); GW to Pennsylvania Council of Safety, Dec. 29, 1776, *PGW*, vol. 7, 483–84n (*Front, Market* and "*very angry*" and "*forbearance*"); Royster, *A Revolutionary People at War*, 31 ("*howled*"); Burgoyne, trans., *Defeat, Disaster and Dedication*, 79; Krebs, "Useful Enemies: The Treatment of German Prisoners of War During the American War of Independence," *JMH* 77, no. 1 (Jan. 2013): 9+; Eelking and Rosengarten, *The German Allied Troops in the North American War of Independence*, 49 (*German officers*); *BTP*, 196 (*prison roster*); Krebs, *A Generous and Merciful Enemy*, 100–01, 117, 133 (*chose not to return*).

528 *The search for scapegoats*: Nelson, *General James Grant*, 110 ("*infamous business*"); *WC*, 261 (*newspapers*); James, *The British Navy in Adversity*, 49 ("*too infirm*"); *The Detail and Conduct of the American War*, 21 ("*tell me why*"); Atwood, *The Hessians*, 109, 113 (*recalled to Germany*).

528 *Colonel Rall, already conveniently dead*: W. Howe to Germain, Dec. 31, 1776, *Stopford-Sackville*, vol. 2, 53 ("*amazing*"); Dec. 31, 1776, journal entry, KP ("*noisy*"); Burgoyne, ed., *Enemy Views*, 121 ("*stupidity*"); *BTP*, 172–73 (*misstep*); Huth et al., "Letters from a Hessian Mercenary," *PMHB* 62, no. 4 (Oct. 1938): 488+ ("*eternal disgrace*"); Frey, *The British Soldier in America*, 123 ("*distinguish themselves*"); Atwood, *The Hessians*, 114 (*new standards*); *WC*, 188 ("*Fabulous Trenton*").

528 "*The rebels have taken fresh*": W. Howe to Germain, Dec. 31, 1776, *Stopford-Sackville*, vol. 2, 53; Powell, ed., *A Biographical Sketch of Col. Leven Powell*, 73 ("*new life*"); Henry Knox to Lucy, Dec. 28, 1776, in *RWLLLHK*, 68 ("*unmerited*").

529 *A loyalist in Virginia*: Gill and Curtis, eds., *A Man Apart*, 136 ("*much altered*"); Royster, *A Revolutionary People at War*, 119; Ryden, ed., *Letters to and from Caesar Rodney*, 152 ("*Never were men*").

529 *Washington was determined*: Lundin, *Cockpit of the Revolution*, 193 ("*Hessians' rear*").

529 *As Dr. Rush had urged*: The new authority was granted even before Congress heard the Trenton news. Hancock to GW, Dec. 27, 1776, *PGW*, vol. 7, 461–62; *BTP*, 243–44.

529 "*Gen'l Washington is dictator*": Smith, *The Battle of Princeton*, 6; *WR*, 305 ("*awakened*"); *Freeman's Journal* (Portsmouth, N.H.), Jan. 21, 1777, in *PGW*, vol. 8, 13 ("*good rebel*").

22. THE DAY IS OUR OWN

530 *The very good rebel*: Smith, *The Battle of Princeton*, 9; general orders, Dec. 30, 1776, *PGW*, vol. 7, 484n (*headquarters*); *CP*, 78; *WC*, 267.

530 *Heartened by his triumph*: Cadwalader to GW, Dec. 27 and 28, 1776, *PGW*, vol. 7, 451–52 (*crossed to Burlington*), 465 ("*fall on their rear*"); Thomas Rodney, "Journal of Campaign," Dec. 28, 1776, box 1, NYPL; *WC*, 275; Reed, "General Joseph Reed's Narrative of the Movements of the American Army in the Neighborhood of Trenton in the Winter of 1776–77," *PMHB* 8, no. 4 (Dec. 1884): 396–97; Drake, *The Campaign of Trenton*, 96; GW to Reed, Dec. 27, 1776, *PGW*, vol. 7, 464n ("*cross the river*").

531 *And so here he was*: GW to Hancock, Jan. 1, 1777, *PGW*, vol. 7, 504 ("*what force*"); Smith, *The Battle of Princeton*, 10 (*hundred men*); *GGW*, 195 (*hard campaigning*); Greenwood, *The Revolutionary Services of John Greenwood*, 44 ("*a colonel*"); Philemon Baldwin, pension application #S 18 305, in BPMP; Smith, *The Battle of Princeton*, 10; *WC*, 270 (*savage fighting*). A few dozen militiamen also joined the Delaware Continentals. Burdick, *Revolutionary Delaware*, 67.

531 But other appeals had greater success: WC, 275; Stone, *Life and Recollections of John Howland*, 70 (*due to expire* and *"poising"*); Wade and Lively, *This Glorious Cause*, 96–98 (*"scarecrows"*); Williams, *Biography of Revolutionary Heroes*, 162, 192 (*"harangue"*); Rau, ed., "Sergeant John Smith's Diary of 1776," *Mississippi Historical Review* 20, no. 2 (Sept. 1933): 269–70 (*gill of rum*).

531 Washington made his own plea: Sergeant R——, "The Battle of Princeton," *PMHB* 20, no. 4 (1896): 515+ (*"fatigues"*).

532 By morning, the army in Trenton: Smith, *The Battle of Princeton*, 10, 12; WC, 410; Thayer, *Nathanael Greene*, 147 (*"hearts"*).

532 Washington had listened, too: WC, 273 (*"a new idea"*).

532 Now the commanding general just needed cash: GW to R. Morris, Dec. 30, 1776, *PGW*, vol. 7, 489 (*"Silver"*); R. Morris to GW, Dec. 30, 1776, *PGW*, vol. 7, 489–90 (*"you are in want"*); Oberholtzer, *Robert Morris*, 32 (*his word*); R. Morris to GW, Jan. 1, 1776, *PGW*, vol. 7, 508 (*"plagued"*).

533 To supplement his spies: WC, 279–80. Reed later wrote that only six troopers accompanied him. "General Joseph Reed's Narrative of the Movements of the American Army in the Neighborhood of Trenton in the Winter of 1776–77," *PMHB* 8, no. 4 (Dec. 1884): 400; Smith, *The Battle of Princeton*, 11; *History of the First Troop Philadelphia City Cavalry*, 9; Reed, ed., *Life and Correspondence of Joseph Reed*, 283n.

533 A stiff southerly breeze: Smith, *The Battle of Princeton*, 12 (*"half-leg"*); WC, 401 (*fifty degrees*); Cadwalader to GW, Dec. 31, 1776, *PGW*, vol. 7, 491–93 (*sentries ringed*); "General Joseph Reed's Narrative of the Movements of the American Army in the Neighborhood of Trenton in the Winter of 1776–77," *PMHB* 8, no. 4 (Dec. 1884): 400–01.

533 The ubiquitous Dr. Rush: Corner, ed., *The Autobiography of Benjamin Rush*, 125–27 (*"very happy"*); general orders, Dec. 30, 1776, *PGW*, vol. 7, 484; WC, 278, 281; Brooks, *Henry Knox, a Soldier of the Revolution*, 84; Kidder, *Crossroads of the Revolution*, 165, 176; CP, 82.

534 "Some pieces of intelligence": GW to Cadwalader and Mifflin, Jan. 1, 1777, *PGW*, vol. 7, 510–11; CP, 82 (*Richmond's tavern*).

534 Stout, double-chinned: Cornwallis described himself as "rather corpulent." MLA, 249, 253; CP, 84.

534 He had been just hours from sailing: WC, 290; BTP, 248; Morven Museum & Garden, https://morven.org/about-morven/; CP, 84 (*watch fires*).

534 British and German staff officers: Smith, *The Battle of Princeton*, 10; Lydenberg, 595; *PGW*, vol. 7, 494n; WC, 292–93, 310 (*eighteen light infantry companies*); Dwyer, *The Day Is Ours!*, 313.

536 "wet to the skin": Lydenberg, 595.

536 Yet enemies surely lurked: Collins, ed., *A Brief Narrative of the Ravages of the British and Hessians at Princeton in 1776–1777*, 20–21, 23–24; Dwyer, *The Day Is Ours!*, 301–02, 342 (*"lurking villains"*); Ewald, *Diary of the American War*, 50; WC, 291–93; Weller, "Guns of Destiny," *Military Affairs* 20, no. 1 (Spring 1956): 1+. Smith puts the British force at "nearly 10,000." *The Battle of Princeton*, 13. William S. Stryker put the number at "nearly 8,000." BTP, 248.

536 Drums beat to arms: Ewald, *Diary of the American War*, 48 (*brandy*); author visit, Trenton and Princeton battle sites, Mar. 4, 2014, signage; BTP, 258; Smith, *The Battle of Princeton*, 13 (Jäger *was shot*); WC, 295 (*skirmishers*); GGW, 199; Beale, "Revolutionary Experiences of Major Robert Beale," *Northern Neck of Virginia Historical Magazine* 6, no. 1 (Dec. 1956): 500+ (*"clear day"*).

537 American marksmen at Eight Mile: Seymour, *The Pennsylvania Associators*, 171.

537 Shortly before four p.m.: Smith, *The Battle of Princeton*, 13–15; CP, 86 (*march pace*).

537 Galling fire from behind: BTP, 260–61.

538 Muzzle flashes and ricochet sparks: Beale, "Revolutionary Experiences of Major Robert Beale," *Northern Neck of Virginia Historical Magazine* 6, no. 1 (Dec. 1956): 500+ (*"Shift for yourselves"*); BTP, 264; Smith, *The Battle of Princeton*, 16–17 (*"solid mass"*).

538 Jäger and light infantry regulars: Stone, *Life and Recollections of John Howland*, 73 (*"right flank"*); Clyde, *Rosbrugh: A Tale of the Revolution*, 41, 59; First Presbyterian Church Cemetery, http://www.revolutionarywarnewjersey.com/new_jersey_revolutionary_war_sites/towns/trenton_nj_revolutionary_war_sites.htm; BTP, 266–67; WC, 150–51, 300.

538 *Across the bridge, Washington sat*: Stone, *Life and Recollections of John Howland*, 73 (*"firm, composed"*); Williams, *Biography of Revolutionary Heroes*, 193 (*"most desperate"*).

538 *Washington was fretful enough*: CP, 87; GW to Hancock, Jan. 5, 1777, *PGW*, vol. 7, 521; *WC*, 303; Beale, "Revolutionary Experiences of Major Robert Beale," *Northern Neck of Virginia Historical Magazine* 6, no. 1 (Dec. 1956): 500+ (*"last extremity"*); Kidder, *Crossroads of the Revolution*, 178 (*"sleep on it"*); Ward, *Charles Scott and the "Spirit of '76"*, 27 (*"The old boss"*).

539 *In the failing light, Cornwallis*: Lydenberg, 595–97 (*"exactly"*); Stone, *Life and Recollections of John Howland*, 74 (*"We advanced"*); Sellers, "Charles Willson Peale, Artist-Soldier," *PMHB* 38, no. 3 (1914): 279–80; W. Hood, "Relation of the Engagement at Trenton and Princeton on Thursday and Friday the 2nd and 3rd of January 1777," DLAR, micro reel 4, #1907 (*"twelve minutes"*); Smith, *The Battle of Princeton*, 17; *WC*, 305 (*stunned comrades*); Avery, "A Chaplain of the American Revolution," *American Monthly Magazine* 19 (1900–01): 260 (*"hot fire"*).

539 *No sooner had the defenders reloaded*: Dwyer, *The Day Is Ours!*, 323–24 (*"so destructive"*); Weller, "Guns of Destiny," *Military Affairs* 20, no. 1 (Spring 1956): 1+ (*ever been fired*); Drake, *Life and Correspondence of Henry Knox*, 38–40 (*"vociferation"*); J. White, *An Narrative of Events . . . in the Revolutionary War*, 20 (*"red as blood"*).

539 *Gunners from both sides*: Smith, *The Battle of Princeton*, 17; Widmer, "The Christmas Campaign: The Ten Days of Trenton and Princeton," New Jersey Historical Commission (1975): 22; Corner, ed., *The Autobiography of Benjamin Rush*, 127; McMichael, "Diary of Lieutenant James McMichael, of the Pennsylvania Line, 1776–1778," *PMHB* 16, no. 2 (July 1892): 129+ (*"ordered to rest"*); Sellers, "Charles Willson Peale, Artist-Soldier," *PMHB* 38, no. 3 (1914): 279–80; Ferling, *Almost a Miracle*, 183 (*"furious engagement"*); Ewald, *Diary of the American War*, 49 (*"outpost fight"*).

540 *Crown casualties were heavier*: Fischer's analysis of casualties is the most comprehensive. He puts British and German losses for the day at 365, excluding lightly wounded and sick. *WC*, 307, 528–29n. See also Ferling, *Almost a Miracle*, 183; Philbrick, *Valiant Ambition*, 83. Washington guessed that from late December through mid-January, the enemy lost "between two and three thousand." GW to Nicholas Cooke, Jan. 20, 1777, *PGW*, vol. 8, 112.

540 *"cries and groans and convulsions"*: Corner, ed., *The Autobiography of Benjamin Rush*, 129–30.

540 *On Thursday evening, as their jaded troops*: Some sources quote Cornwallis as declaring, "We've got the old fox safe now. We'll go over and bag him in the morning." *WC*, 312–13; Wickwire and Wickwire, *Cornwallis: The American Adventure*, 96. The quote seems perhaps too perfect, even if the sentiment was accurate. *BTP*, 268.

540 *The old fox had in fact*: Ferling, *The First of Men*, 188–89; *BTP*, 269; Alexander Douglass house, http://www.revolutionarywarnewjersey.com/new_jersey_revolutionary_war_sites /towns/trenton_nj_revolutionary_war_sites.htm; Cristina Rojas, "Historic House Being Restored for $300K," July 24, 2017, NJ.com, http://www.nj.com/mercer/index.ssf/2017/07 /historic_house_being_restored_for_1m_yes_george_wa.html.

541 *Inspiration is rare enough*: *WC*, 280–83; Mark Peterson, University of California, Berkeley, "Review of Battle of Princeton Mapping Project," https://www.ias.edu/sites/default/files /media-assets/Peterson-review-Milner-report.pdf, 6–9.

541 *St. Clair, whose brigade*: St. Clair, *A Narrative*, 242. St. Clair's subsequent claim of credit for suggesting the eastward maneuver was supported by some, disputed by others. Wilkinson, *Memoirs of My Own Times*, vol. 1, 140; *PGW*, vol. 7, 526–27n; BPMP, appendix 5.

541 *Heavy baggage and the most awkward*: Smith, *The Battle of Princeton*, 18; Young, "Journal of Sergeant William Young," *PMHB* 8, no. 3 (Oct. 1884): 264 (*"hurry-skurry"*); "Letter from an Officer of Distinction" [Cadwalader], Jan. 5, 1777, in *BTP*, 446; CP, 93; "An Account of the Services of Major Robert Beale of Westmoreland in the War of the Revolution," in BPMP (*"very numerous"*); NG to Nicholas Cooke, Jan. 10, 1777, *PNG*, vol. 2, 4; Ferling, *The First of Men*, 190; H. Knox to Lucy, Jan. 7, 1777, *RWLLLHK*, 69 (*"a few shells"*).

541 *No man spoke above*: "An Account of the Services of Major Robert Beale of Westmoreland in the War of the Revolution," in BPMP (*"secrecy"*); *WR*, 311–12 (*muffling rags*); Smith, *The Battle of Princeton*, 17; *WC*, 316, 401 (*21 Fahrenheit*); Williams, *Biography of Revolutionary Heroes*, 196 (*"pavement"*).

542 *Only the generals knew*: NG to Nicholas Cooke, Jan. 10, 1777, *PNG*, vol. 2, 4; *BTP*, 273; order of battle in BPMP. The moon above Trenton that night was at 33 percent illumination. U.S. Naval Observatory, "Sun and Moon Data," Astronomical Applications Department. Wilkinson described the night as "exceedingly dark, and though calm most severely cold." *Memoirs of My Own Times*, vol. 1, 140.

542 *Some horses lacked shoes*: Stone, *The Life and Recollections of John Howland*, 75; *CP*, 93–94. Split-rail was also known as worm in New Jersey. BPMP, 12–14.

542 *The first, faint glow*: Wilkinson, *Memoirs of My Own Times*, vol. 1, 141; *WC*, 325; Freeman, 349. Some accounts suggest that Washington divided his force into three parts. See Rodney, *Diary of Captain Thomas Rodney*, 33, and BPMP, 23, 45–52.

542 *Washington believed that the British had left*: *BTP*, 278; *WC*, 322–23, 325, 411; BPMP, 45–46, 77. Smith put the British force in Princeton at roughly 850. *The Battle of Princeton*, 19.

542 *The sun peeped above*: Wilkinson, *Memoirs of My Own Times*, vol. 1, 141 (*"hoar frost"*); White, *An Narrative of Events . . . in the Revolutionary War*, 25–26; Smith, *The Battle of Princeton*, 19.

542 *American intelligence had accurately identified*: Inman, "George Inman's Narrative of the American Revolution," *PMHB* 7, no. 3 (1883): 237+; *CP*, 100–01; BPMP, 45–46; *WC*, 327; Civil War Trust, https://www.civilwar.org/learn/biographies/charles-mawhood; *CP*, 99 (*spaniels*).

543 *The head of the British column*: court-martial, Cornet Henry Evatt, 16th Light Dragoons, Oct. 1778, in BPMP, appendix.

543 *The British may have been "as much astonished"*: H. Knox to Lucy, Jan. 7, 1777, *RWLLLHK*, 70; Lt. William John Hale to father, Jan. 15, 1777, "Letters Written During the American War of Independence," in Wylly, ed., *1913 Regimental Annual: The Sherwood Foresters*, 18.

543 *That approaching force under General Greene*: Smith, *The Battle of Princeton*, 20. Some writers assert that Gen. Mercer's brigade led the column toward Worth's Mill. Recent scholarship indicates that Mercer's brigade was still on Saw Mill Road upon being dispatched to confront the British. BPMP, 23, 45–52; Fred Anderson, University of Colorado, review of "The Battle of Princeton Mapping Project," n.d., 4–6, https://www.ias.edu/sites/default/files/media-assets/Anderson-review-Milner-report.pdf.

543 *Riding with Sullivan's column*: BPMP, 50–52, and "Maj. [Apollos] Morris's Account of the Affair at Trenton, 1776," appendix; *WC*, 330.

544 *Mercer, a burly physician*: Waterman, *With Sword and Lancet*, 100–01; BPMP, 45–46, 50–52; Goolrick, *The Life of General Hugh Mercer*, 13–15 (*doomed rebels*); Dacus, "Hugh Mercer: Doctor and Warrior," *JAR*, Jan. 24, 2017; English, *General Hugh Mercer, Forgotten Hero of the American Revolution*, 1–6, 23–25, 37–38, 46, 50–53, 92; "Hugh Mercer," *Americana* 9 (1914): 705+; Corner, ed., *The Autobiography of Benjamin Rush*, 125–27 (*"cross the mountains"*).

544 *As Mercer spurred his horse*: Sergeant R——, "The Battle of Princeton," *PMHB* 20, no. 4 (1896): 515+ (*"sun shines"*); Smith, *The Battle of Princeton*, 20–21; *WC*, 330–31.

544 *Colonel Mawhood had sent*: Sergeant R——, "The Battle of Princeton," *PMHB* 20, no. 4 (1896): 515+; Smith, *The Battle of Princeton*, 21–23; *BTP*, 285 (*"many devils"*).

544 *"gave us a very heavy discharge"*: Lt. William John Hale to father, Jan. 15, 1777, "Letters Written During the American War of Independence," in Wylly, ed., *1913 Regimental Annual: The Sherwood Foresters*, 18; court-martial, Cornet Henry Evatt, 16th Light Dragoons, Oct. 1778, in BPMP, 53–54, appendix (*enraging*).

545 *As the shooting intensified*: Fraser, *The Melvilles, Earls of Melville, and the Leslies, Earls of Leven*, vol. 1, 350–51; *WC*, 311, 331. Leslie would die of his wounds on January 5. The American army buried him with military honors. Conway, "To Subdue America: British Army Officers and the Conduct of the Revolutionary War," *WMQ*, 3rd ser., 43, no. 3 (July 1986): 397 (*"desolation"*).

545 *The firing grew general*: Wilkinson, *Memoirs of My Own Times*, vol. 1, 143 (*"mingled"*).

545 *The American line crumpled*: Lt. William John Hale to father, Jan. 15, 1777, "Letters Written During the American War of Independence," in Wylly, ed., *1913 Regimental Annual: The Sherwood Foresters*, 18 (*"drove them"*); Tyler, ed., "The Old Virginia Line in the Middle States During the American Revolution," *Tyler's Quarterly* 12, no. 1 (July 1930): 1+; *WC*, 333; Smith, *The Battle of Princeton*, 23; *BTP*, 446–48; Wood, *Battles of the Revolutionary War*, 280–82;

English, *General Hugh Mercer, Forgotten Hero of the American Revolution*, 98–99 ("*I saw him*").

545 *Colonel Haslet pressed forward*: Ryden, ed., *Letters to and from Caesar Rodney*, 152–53 ("*meet in heaven*"); Rodney, *Diary of Captain Thomas Rodney*, 34.

545 *With so many officers bloodied*: Smith, *The Battle of Princeton*, 20; Lt. William John Hale to father, Jan. 15, 1777, "Letters Written During the American War of Independence," in Wylly, ed., *1913 Regimental Annual: The Sherwood Foresters*, 18; Sellers, "Charles Willson Peale, Artist-Soldier," *PMHB* 39, no. 3 (1914): 280 ("*thousand notes*"); Potts, "Death of Major [*sic*] Anthony Morris, Jr.," *PMHB* 1, no. 2 (1877): 175+; Robert Gutowski, "Morris Family Breweries in Philadelphia, 1687–c. 1836," https://cms.business-services.upenn.edu/morrisarboretum-blog/320-morris-family-breweries-in-philadelphia-1687-c-1836.html; Stryker, *Documents Relating to the Revolutionary History of the State of New Jersey*, vol. 1, 279; *BTP*, 446–48, 456; Rodney, *Diary of Captain Thomas Rodney*, 34–35; "Letter from an Officer of Distinction" [Cadwalader], Jan. 5, 1777, in *BTP*, 446–48; Smith, *The Battle of Princeton*, 24; Wood, *Battles of the Revolutionary War*, 85–86.

546 *But the superior rebel numbers*: Weller, "Guns of Destiny," *Military Affairs* 20, no. 1 (Spring 1956): 13–14; *CP*, 107; Rodney, *Diary of Captain Thomas Rodney*, 35–36 ("*thick as hail*").

546 *The symphonic gunfire brought*: Sergeant R——, "The Battle of Princeton," *PMHB* 20, no. 4 (1896): 515+ ("*Parade with us*"); letter, James Read to wife, *PMHB* 16 (1892): 466.

546 *As the militia rallied*: "An Account of the Battle of Princeton," Jan. 16, 1777, *Pennsylvania Evening Post*, in *PMHB* 8 (1884): 310 ("*expectation*"); *C 1776*, 303–04; White, *An Narrative of Events . . . in the Revolutionary War*, 25–26 ("*so furious*"); Smith, *The Battle of Princeton*, 24–25; Ryan, ed., *A Salute to Courage*, 57 ("*We can beat them*"); Fred Anderson, University of Colorado, review of "The Battle of Princeton Mapping Project," n.d., 4–6, https://www.ias.edu/sites/default/files/media-assets/Anderson-review-Milner-report.pdf; "Letter from an Officer of Distinction" [Cadwalader], Jan. 5, 1777, in *BTP*, 446 ("*They fly*").

547 *With ten gunners and the artillery horses*: Duncan, *History of the Royal Regiment of Artillery*, vol. 1, 313; GW to Hancock, Jan. 5, 1777, *PGW*, vol. 7, 521; Lt. William John Hale to father, Jan. 15, 1777, "Letters Written During the American War of Independence," in Wylly, ed., *1913 Regimental Annual: The Sherwood Foresters*, 18 ("*run away*"); Wilkinson, *Memoirs of My Own Times*, vol. 1, 144; *WC*, 336; Smith, *The Battle of Princeton*, 25–27; *CP*, 109–10.

547 *The battle shifted into Princeton*: Lundin, *Cockpit of the Revolution*, 15 ("*politeness*"). Capt. Robert Mostyn died at Frog Hollow. BPMP, 73–75; *WC*, 337–39; *BTP*, 289–93; Wilkinson, *Memoirs of My Own Times*, vol. 1, 144.

547 *A brief delay preceded the final assault*: Smith, *The Battle of Princeton*, 27; Chernow, *Alexander Hamilton*, 84–85 (*oil portrait*); Sellers, "Charles Willson Peale, Artist-Soldier," *PMHB* 38, no. 3 (1914): 281 ("*flag was sent*").

547 *Some two hundred redcoats*: *BTP*, 289–90; BPMP, 32–33; Sergeant R——, "The Battle of Princeton," *PMHB* 20, no. 4 (1896): 515+ ("*haughty*"); White, *An Narrative of Events . . . in the Revolutionary War*, 25–26 ("*I took*").

548 *A rebel squad dashed down*: BPMP, 75 (*sleepers*) and William B. Reed account, appendix ("*entire insensibility*"); *WC*, 338 (*prevent pilfering*); Sergeant R——, "The Battle of Princeton," *PMHB* 20, no. 4 (1896): 515+ ("*groaning, dying*"); English, *General Hugh Mercer, Forgotten Hero of the American Revolution*, 100–03; Waterman, *With Sword and Lancet*, 157–58.

548 *A long drum roll sounded*: *WC*, 341.

548 *At eleven a.m., just an hour after*: Smith, *The Battle of Princeton*, 29–30; Doughty, "Washington's March to Morristown, 1777," *Proceedings of the New Jersey Historical Society*, new ser., 5, no. 4 (Oct. 1920); Rodney, *Diary of Captain Thomas Rodney*, 37–41; *CP*, 118.

548 *In Kingston, four miles from Princeton*: Wilkinson, *Memoirs of My Own Times*, vol. 1, 148 ("*exclamation*"); GW to Hancock, Jan. 5, 1777, *PGW*, vol. 7, 523 ("*harassed state*").

548 *Instead, the column pivoted*: St. Clair, *A Narrative*, 244.

548 *The sun had set when the army*: Smith, *The Battle of Princeton*, 30; Rosswurm, *Arms, Country, and Class*, 132; Wilkinson, *Memoirs of My Own Times*, vol. 1, 149; Rodney, *Diary of*

Captain Thomas Rodney, 38; Sellers, "Charles Willson Peale, Artist-Soldier," *PMHB* 38, no. 3 (1914): 282 (*"glad to lie"*).

549 *General Cornwallis's disagreeable Friday*: Lydenberg, 597; Ewald, *Diary of the American War*, 49 (*"heavy cannonade"*); H. Knox to Lucy, Jan. 7, 1777, *RWLLLHK*, 70 (*"infernal sweat"*).

549 *Cornwallis arrived at Stony Brook*: BPMP, 34, 75–76; Thomas Glyn, "Journal of American Campaign," Jan. 3, 1777, FL (*"warm"*); Ewald, *Diary of the American War*, 49 (*"corpses"*); Smith, *The Battle of Princeton*, 29–30 (*"plague"*).

549 *The British high command initially acknowledged*: Fischer, again, has done the most thorough casualty analysis. WC, 413–15; Collins, ed., *A Brief Narrative of the Ravages of the British and Hessians at Princeton in 1776–1777*, 33 (*stone quarry*), 36–37; Capt. John Polhemus memoir, in Ryan, ed., *A Salute to Courage*, 57 (*"great holes"*); Olden House, Revolutionary War New Jersey, http://www.revolutionarywarnewjersey.com/new_jersey_revolutionary _war_sites/towns/princeton_nj_revolutionary_war_sites.htm.

550 *As always, the wounded suffered*: Collins, ed., *A Brief Narrative of the Ravages of the British and Hessians at Princeton in 1776–1777*, 36–37 (*"great pain"*); Olden House, Revolutionary War New Jersey, http://www.revolutionarywarnewjersey.com/new_jersey_revolutionary _war_sites/towns/princeton_nj_revolutionary_war_sites.htm.

550 *Among American physicians who arrived*: Hawke, *Benjamin Rush*, 180–81; Corner, ed., *The Autobiography of Benjamin Rush*, 129–30 (*"human blood"*).

550 *"He is in good spirits"*: Rush to R. H. Lee, Jan. 7, 1777, in Butterfield, ed., *Letters of Benjamin Rush*, vol. 1, 125–26; Waterman, *With Sword and Lancet*, 158 (*"my business"*); Duane, ed., *Extracts from the Diary of Christopher Marshall*, 112 (*military honors*); "Hugh Mercer," George Washington's Mount Vernon, http://www.mountvernon.org/digital-encyclopedia /article/hugh-mercer/ (*"heroes of antiquity"*); Carbone, *Nathanael Greene*, 62–63 (*"fine companion"*).

550 *At dusk on Friday, Cornwallis led*: Thomas Glyn, "Journal of American Campaign," Jan. 3, 1777, FL; *PGW*, vol. 7, 530n; Ewald, *Diary of the American War*, 50; Hunter, *The Journal of Gen. Sir Martin Hunter*, 25 (*"never experienced"*).

550 *The plodding journey gave officers*: Lundin, *Cockpit of the Revolution*, 215; Dwyer, *The Day Is Ours!*, 349 (*"Heroes"*); "Bamford's Diary: The Revolutionary Diary of a British Officer," *Maryland Historical Magazine* 28, no. 1 (Sept. 1932): 24 (*"obstinately persisted"*); Lydenberg, 598 (*"lesson in future"*); Wickwire, *Cornwallis*, 98–99 (*"consummate ignorance"*).

551 *For the Hessians there was*: CP, 125–26 (*"same fate"*); Ewald, *Diary of the American War*, 50 (*"blockheads"*); Lundin, *Cockpit of the Revolution*, 216 (*"last night"*).

551 *The column stumbled into New Brunswick*: Drake, *The Campaign of Trenton*, 111 (*"scoundrels"* and *"Our misfortune"*); Thomas Glyn, "Journal of American Campaign," Jan. 3–9, 1777, FL (*alarm posts*).

551 *The fresh foodstuffs and forage*: Brown, *The Good Americans*, 60 (*"much disappointed"*); Leiby, *The Revolutionary War in the Hackensack Valley*, 102–03; GW to Hancock, Jan. 9, 1777, *PGW*, vol. 8, 24–25 (*rebel brigade*).

551 *Ten thousand of the king's soldiers*: WC, 349–50; Peckham, ed., *Memoirs of the Life of John Adlum in the Revolutionary War*, 108–09 (*evacuate*).

551 *"Surely ye force"*: W. Howe to Grant, Jan. 9, 1777, in BPMP; Ross, ed., *Correspondence of Charles, First Marquis Cornwallis*, vol. 1, 27 (*"strong country"*).

552 *"I do not see a prospect"*: BTP, 482.

552 *The American army scuffed into Morristown*: PGW, vol. 8, 6n; Rosswurm, *Arms, Country, and Class*, 132 (*"feet"*); Wharton to GW, Jan. 3, 1777, *PGW*, vol. 7, 513 (*twenty hogsheads*); Guthman, ed., *The Correspondence of Captain Nathan and Lois Peters*, 50 (*"great spirits"*); Royster, *A Revolutionary People at War*, 119 (*"grief to joy"*).

552 *Cornwallis assured Germain*: Cornwallis to Germain, Jan. 8, 1777, *Stopford-Sackville*, vol. 2, 55; Wilkin, *Some British Soldiers in America*, 192–93 (*"taken advantage"*).

552 *Washington moved into a three-story*: BTP, 303–04; Revolutionary War New Jersey, http:// www.revolutionarywarnewjersey.com/new_jersey_revolutionary_war_sites/towns /morristown_nj_revolutionary_war_sites.htm; GW to Heath, Jan. 7, 1777, *PGW*, vol. 8, 10

(*"fair opening"*); GW to Robert Hanson Harrison, Jan. 20, 1777, and GW to Hancock, Jan. 22, 1777, *PGW*, vol. 8, 117, 127 (*"empty"*); GW to J. P. Custis, Jan. 22, 1777, *PGW*, vol. 8, 123 (*"All our movements"*).

553 *No perplexity was more irksome*: GW to Schuyler, Jan. 18, 1777, *PGW*, vol. 8, 99 (*"lucky strokes"*); Smith, *The Battle of Princeton*, 36; *WC*, 382; GW to Hancock, Jan. 19, 1777, *PGW*, vol. 8, 102–03 (*"false opinions"*); *PGW*, vol. 8, 135n (*eighty-eight regiments*).

554 *"Our affairs here are in"*: GW to Cooke, Jan. 20, 1777, *PGW*, vol. 8, 114.

554 *"The consequences must be great"*: Griffin, *Stephen Moylan*, 47–48.

554 *"I look up to heaven"*: H. Knox to Lucy, Jan. 7, 1777, *RWLLLHK*, 71.

EPILOGUE

555 *A good hanging always drew*: Beatson, *Naval and Military Memoirs of Great Britain*, vol. 4, 124–25; Warner, *John the Painter*, 220.

555 *The doomed man*: letter from Portsmouth, *Pennsylvania Evening Post*, June 3, 1777, *NDAR*, vol. 8, 658; "Jack the Painter," Portsmouth Royal Dockyard Historical Trust, 2015, http://portsmouthdockyard.org.uk/timeline/details/1776-jack-the-painter (*Great Double Rope House*).

555 *He had been born in Edinburgh*: *Public Advertiser* (London), Mar. 8, 1777, *NDAR*, vol. 8, 652–56 (Metamorphoses); Warner, *John the Painter*, 58, 64, 76, 81, 87–89, 90–91, 95; James Aitken, deposition, Mar. 7, 1777, in Fortescue, ed., *The Correspondence of King George the Third*, vol. 3, 423–27; Hedbor, "John the Painter: Terrorist for America," *JAR*, May 1, 2018.

556 *During a visit to Portsmouth*: Warner, *John the Painter*, 103, 107–16, 134.

556 *In Canterbury he paid an artisan*: Warner, *John the Painter*, 117, 127, 137–41.

556 *Aitken traveled to Plymouth*: James Aitken, deposition, Mar. 7, 1777, in Fortescue, ed., *The Correspondence of King George the Third*, vol. 3, 423–27; *Public Advertiser* (London), Jan. 23, 1777, *NDAR*, vol. 8, 541; Warner, *John the Painter*, 165–69 (*offered rewards*); Sandwich to George, Jan. 16, 1777, "George III Calendar, Sept. 1775–Oct. 1777," RA GEO/MAIN/#2507 (*"suspicious person"*); Navy Office memorandum, Jan. 21, 1777, *NDAR*, vol. 8, 542.

556 *A parade of witnesses*: *Public Advertiser* (London), Mar. 8, 1777, *NDAR*, vol. 8, 652–56; James Aitken, deposition, Mar. 7, 1777, in Fortescue, ed., *The Correspondence of King George the Third*, vol. 3, 423–27; "Attitude of France to the United States," in Wharton, ed., *The Revolutionary Diplomatic Correspondence of the United States*, vol. 1, 562 (*"rebellious"*); Warner, *John the Painter*, 213, 231.

557 *Aitken spent his final fortnight*: letter from Portsmouth, *Pennsylvania Evening Post*, June 3, 1777, *NDAR*, vol. 8, 658; "Jack the Painter," Portsmouth Royal Dockyard Historical Trust, 2015, http://portsmouthdockyard.org.uk/timeline/details/1776-jack-the-painter (*350 executioners* and *Pitch House Jetty*); Warner, *John the Painter*, 212, 225, 228–29; Schwartz, *Daily Life in Johnson's London*, 150.

557 *An early biographer claimed*: Holt, *The Public and Domestic Life of . . . George the Third*, vol. 1, 214 (*"never known"*); Ayling, *George the Third*, 254.

557 *Britain was nearing full employment*: secret instructions to Capt. James Cook, July 6, 1776, "George III Calendar, Sept. 1775–Oct. 1777," RA GEO/MAIN/#2449 (*"northern passage"*); Murray, ed., *The Autobiographies of Edward Gibbon*, 309–11.

557 *The king more than ever*: Royal Collection, Royal Library, RCIN #1047499 (*"manures"*); Roberts, *Royal Landscape: The Gardens and Parks of Windsor*, 71–72 (*Farmer George*); extracts of David Hume letters, "George III Calendar, Sept. 1775–Oct. 1777," RA GEO/MAIN/#2435.

558 *The war, of course, remained*: *PH* 18, 1366.

558 *Benjamin West, the gifted American*: Einstein, *Divided Loyalties*, 307 (*"happy"*); Peckham, "Independence: The View from Britain," *Proceedings of the American Antiquarian Society* 85, part 2 (1976): 398–99 (*"widespread popularity"*).

558 *More than hack pamphleteering*: Wheatley, ed., *The Historical and Posthumous Memoirs of Sir Nathaniel William Wraxall*, vol. 1, 98 (*"gloom"*); *FYAR*, appendix 32, 756 (*War costs*); Conway, "British Mobilization in the War of American Independence," *Historical Research* 72, no. 177 (Feb. 1999): 58+ (*half that number*).

559   *"His Majesty intends to open"*: Moore, *The Diary of the American Revolution*, 190.

559   *The dutiful Lord North*: Whiteley, *Lord North*, 164 *(seriously ill)*; George to North, Feb. 24, 1777, "George III Calendar, Sept. 1775–Oct. 1777," RA GEO/MAIN/#2519; medical report, Mar. 1, 1777, RA GEO/MAIN/#2521; Royal Collection, Royal Library, RCIN #1047089 and RCIN #1047165.

559   *Who could doubt the ultimate*: HBAR, 170–71; *Sandwich*, vol. 2, 169 *("most agreeable")*; Weintraub, *Iron Tears*, 89 *("parricides")*.

560   *Instead, in late February the* Bristol: HBAR, 174–75; Gruber, "Lord Howe and Lord George Germain: British Politics and the Winning of American Independence," WMQ, 3rd ser., 22, no. 2 (Apr. 1965): 237–38; Peckham, "Independence: The View from Britain," *Proceedings of the American Antiquarian Society* 85, part 2 (1976): 402–03 *("mortifying")*; Gruber, "For King and Country," in Edgar Denton, ed., *Limits of Loyalty*, 31 *(spring campaign)*; *Logistics*, 240–41.

560   *Howe had also fallen out with two*: Willcox, *Portrait of a General*, 114 *("I cannot bear")*, 127–29 *("I am so hurt")*; LHEP, 79–80; Gruber, *Books and the British Army in the Age of the American Revolution*, 115.

560   *"You doubtless must have expected"*: Stuart-Wortley, *A Prime Minister and His Son*, 91–93; 104–07 *("Poor devils")*; Brown, *The Good Americans*, 64 *("people of parts")*.

560   *Certain shortcomings in Britain's conduct*: CP, 83–84 *("dangerous practice")*.

560   *The Royal Navy's deficiencies*: Black and Woodfine, eds., *The British Navy and the Use of Naval Power in the Eighteenth Century*, 141 *(148 warships)*; Baugh, "The Politics of British Naval Failure, 1775–1777," *American Neptune* 52, no. 4 (Fall 1992): 221+ *(sea-lanes)*; Admiralty memo, cabinet notes, and intelligence notes, June 20, 1776, "George III Calendar, Sept. 1775–Oct. 1777," RA GEO/MAIN/#2439–41 *(detected signs)*; Sandwich to North, Oct. 20, 1776, *Sandwich*, vol. 1, 216 *("French armaments")*.

561   *At last, in late fall, the cabinet*: unsigned memorandum [Sandwich's hand], Oct. 23, 1776, "George III Calendar, Sept. 1775–Oct. 1777," RA GEO/MAIN/#2466; cabinet notes, Nov. 18, 1776, *Sandwich*, vol. 1, 216–18; Syrett, *The Royal Navy in European Waters During the American Revolutionary War*, 14; Scott, *British Foreign Policy in the Age of the American Revolution*, 239–40; Trevelyan, *The American Revolution*, 234 *(thousand swabs)*.

561   *Other aspects of the American war*: Ellis, *Revolutionary Summer*, 171; CP, 137 *("elate them")*; T. Paine, "The American Crisis," Jan. 13, 1777, in Foner, *Tom Paine and Revolutionary America*, 140 *("only armies")*; Smith, *The Wealth of Nations*, vol. 2, 136 *("degree of importance")*.

561   *The king would soldier on*: Stoker et al., eds., *Strategy in the American War of Independence*, 75–76; Barrington to Germain, Dec. 13, 1776, UK NA, CO 5/168, f. 300 *(tentage)*; Halliday, *Habeas Corpus: From England to Empire*, 25–53.

562   *"The tongue of malice"*: undated note, George III, Private Papers, Undated and 1755–1782, RA GEO/MAIN/#15673.

562   *In America the long fighting season*: D&AJA, vol. 3, 437 *("dangerous period")*; Peckham, ed., *The Toll of Independence*, 3–33, 107–14.

562   *The American army had not been proficient*: Shy, *A People Numerous and Armed*, 215–17; Spring, *With Zeal and with Bayonets Only*, 278–79; Harcourt, *The Harcourt Papers*, vol. 9, 207–08 *("requisites")*.

562   *The best American soldiers also displayed*: Hynes, *The Soldiers' Tale*, 58, 114; Ryan, ed., *A Salute to Courage*, 66 *("wherever I go")*.

563   *"I hope the country"*: William Douglas to Hannah Douglas, Oct. 15 and Dec. 5, 1776, *Quarterly Bulletin*, NYHS 13, no. 1 (Apr. 1929).

563   *So, too, would be the integration*: Shy, *A People Numerous and Armed*, 237; CGW, 328–29; Hall, "An Irregular Reconsideration of George Washington and the American Military Tradition," JMH 78 (July 2014): 979–80; E. Wayne Carp, "The Problem of National Defense in the Early American Republic," in Greene, ed., *The American Revolution*, 25; Richard Henry Lee to Patrick Henry, Jan. 9, 1777, *Letters of Delegates to Congress, 1774–1789*, vol. 6 *("sudden exertions")*; GW to Massachusetts General Court, July 9, 1776, PGW, vol. 5, 250 *("competent")*.

563   *Yet the commanding general displayed a gift*: GGW, 168, 365–71; Trevelyan, *The American Revolution*, vol. 3, 124 *("forelock")*; Abigail Adams to Mercy Otis Warren, [Jan.?] 1777, AFC, vol.

2, FOL (*"late misfortunes"*); GW to Stirling, Jan. 19, 1777, *PGW*, vol. 8, 110 (*"unused to restraint"*).

564 *The cause was hardly won*: J. Adams to Abigail, July 3, 1776, *AFC*, vol. 2, FOL (*"will of heaven"*); Morris, *The American Revolution Reconsidered*, 68 (*"Neighbor"*); *Spirit '76*, 346 (*"Great revolutions"*).

564 *Faith would be needed to sustain*: Bailyn, *The Ideological Origins of the American Revolution*, 319; S. Pomeroy to unnamed son, Feb. 11, 1777, in de Forest, ed., *The Journals and Papers of Seth Pomeroy*, 162–67; Ryan, ed., *A Salute to Courage*, 59–60 (*"if I fall"*); J. Adams to James Warren, Mar. 31, 1777, *AP* (*"vulgar minds"*); Royster, *A Revolutionary People at War*, 8 (*"rising world"*).

Sources

BOOKS

Abbatt, William. *The Battle of Pell's Point.* New York: William Abbatt, 1901.

Abbot, W. W., et al., eds. *The Papers of George Washington.* Revolutionary War Series. Vols. 1–8. Charlottesville: University Press of Virginia, 1985–98.

Abbott, Henry L., ed. *The Beginning of Modern Submarine Warfare Under Captain-Lieutenant David Bushnell.* Willets Point, N.Y.: Engineer School of Application, 1881.

Abbott, Wilbur C. *New York in the American Revolution.* New York: Charles Scribner's Sons, 1929.

Adair, Douglass, and John A. Schutz, eds. *Peter Oliver's Origin & Progress of the American Rebellion.* Stanford, Calif.: Stanford University Press, 1961.

Adams, Arthur G. *The Hudson River Guidebook.* 2nd ed. New York: Fordham University Press, 1996.

Adams, James Truslow. *Revolutionary New England, 1691–1776.* Boston: Atlantic Monthly Press, 1923.

Alberts, Robert C. *The Golden Voyage: The Life and Times of William Bingham, 1752–1804.* Boston: Houghton Mifflin, 1969.

Albion, Robert Greenhalgh. *Forests and Sea Power: The Timber Problem of the Royal Navy, 1652–1862.* Cambridge, Mass.: Harvard University Press, 1926.

Albion, Robert Greenhalgh, and Leonidas Dodson, eds. *Philip Vickers Fithian: Journal, 1775–1776.* Princeton, N.J.: Princeton University Press, 1934.

Albion, Robert Greenhalgh, and Jennie Barnes Pope. *Sea Lanes in Wartime: The American Experience, 1775–1942.* New York: W. W. Norton, 1942.

Alden, John R. *The American Revolution, 1775–1783.* New York: Harper Torchbooks, 1963.

———. *General Gage in America.* Baton Rouge: Louisiana State University, 1948.

Alden, John Richard. *General Charles Lee: Traitor or Patriot?* Baton Rouge: Louisiana State University Press, 1951.

———. *The South in the Revolution, 1763–89.* Baton Rouge: Louisiana State University Press, 1957.

Aldridge, Alfred Owen. *Franklin and His French Contemporaries.* New York: New York University Press, 1957.

Allan, Herbert S. *John Hancock: Patriot in Purple.* New York: Macmillan, 1948.

Allen, Gardner Weld. *Massachusetts Privateers of the Revolution.* Cambridge, Mass.: Massachusetts Historical Society, 1927.

———. *A Naval History of the American Revolution.* Vol. 1. Boston: Houghton Mifflin, 1913.

Allen, Robert S. *The Loyal Americans.* Ottawa: National Museums of Canada, 1983.

Allen, Thomas B. *Tories: Fighting for the King in America's First Civil War.* New York: Harper, 2010.

Allison, Robert J. *The American Revolution: A Concise History.* New York: Oxford University Press, 2011.

Almon, J., ed. *The Remembrancer, or Impartial Repository of Public Events.* Vol. 1. London: J. Almon, 1775.

Alsop, Susan Mary. *Yankees at the Court: The First Americans in Paris.* Garden City, N.Y.: Doubleday, 1982.

The American Revolution in New York: Its Political, Social and Economic Significance. Albany: University of the State of New York, 1926.

Amory, Thomas C. *The Military Services and Public Life of Major-General John Sullivan.* Boston: Wiggin and Lunt, 1868.

Anderson, Fred. *Crucible of War: The Seven Years' War and the Fate of Empire in British North America, 1754–1766.* New York: Vintage, 2001.

Anderson, Mark R. *The Battle for the Fourteenth Colony: America's War of Liberation in Canada, 1774–1776.* Hanover, N.H.: University Press of New England, 2013.

Anderson, Troyer Steele. *The Command of the Howe Brothers During the American Revolution.* Cranbury, N.J.: Scholar's Bookshelf, 2005.

André, John. *Major André's Journal.* Tarrytown, N.Y.: William Abbatt, 1930.

Andrews, Charles M. *Guide to the Materials for American History, to 1783, in the Public Record Office of Great Britain.* Vols. 1 and 2. Washington, D.C.: Carnegie Institution, 1912, 1914.

Andrlik, Todd. *Reporting the Revolutionary War.* Naperville, Ill.: Sourcebooks, 2012.

Andrlik, Todd, et al., eds. *Journal of the American Revolution.* Vol. 1. Yellow Springs, Ohio: Ertel Publishing, 2013.

Anson, William R., ed. *Autobiography and Political Correspondence of Augustus Henry, Third Duke of Grafton, K.G.* London: John Murray, 1898.

Archer, Richard. *As If an Enemy's Country: The British Occupation of Boston and the Origins of the American Revolution.* New York: Oxford University Press, 2010.

Arnold, Catharine. *City of Sin: London and Its Vices.* London: Simon & Schuster, 2010.

Atherton, William Henry. *Montreal, 1535–1914.* Vol. 2, *Under British Rule, 1760–1914.* Montreal: S. J. Clarke, 1914.

Atwood, Rodney. *The Hessians.* Cambridge: Cambridge University Press, 1980.

Augur, Helen. *The Secret War of Independence.* New York: Duell, Sloan and Pearce, 1955.

Austin, James T. *The Life of Elbridge Gerry.* Boston: Wells and Lilly, 1828.

Ayer, A. J. *Thomas Paine.* Chicago: University of Chicago Press, 1988.

Ayling, Stanley. *George the Third.* New York: Knopf, 1972.

Bailey, Sarah Loring. *Historical Sketches of Andover.* Boston: Houghton Mifflin, 1880.

Bailyn, Bernard. *Faces of Revolution.* New York: Knopf, 1990.

——. *The Ideological Origins of the American Revolution.* Cambridge, Mass.: Belknap, 1992.

——. *To Begin the World Anew.* New York: Vintage, 2004.

——. *Voyagers to the West.* New York: Vintage, 1988.

Bakeless, John. *Turncoats, Traitors and Heroes.* New York: Da Capo, 1998.

Baker, Norman. *Government and Contractors: The British Treasury and War Supplies, 1775–1983.* London: Athlone, 1971.

Baker, Richard Lee. *"Villainy and Maddness": Washington's Flying Camp.* Baltimore: Clearfield, 2011.

Balch, Thomas, ed. *Papers Relating Chiefly to the Maryland Line During the Revolutionary War.* Philadelphia: Seventy-Six Society, 1857.

Balderston, Marion, and David Syrett, eds. *The Lost War: Letters from British Officers During the American Revolution.* New York: Horizon Press, 1975.

Baldwin, Jeduthan. *The Revolutionary Journal of Col. Jeduthan Baldwin, 1775–1778.* Edited by Thomas Williams Baldwin. Bangor, Me.: s.p., 1906.

Ballagh, James Curtis, ed. *The Letters of Richard Henry Lee.* Vol. 1. New York: Macmillan, 1911.

Bancroft, George. *Joseph Reed: A Historical Essay.* New York: W. J. Widdleton, 1867.

Bangs, Isaac. *Journal of Lieutenant Isaac Bangs, April 1 to July 29, 1776.* Edited by Edward Bangs. Cambridge, Mass.: John Wilson and Son, 1890.

Barck, Oscar. *New York City During the War for Independence.* Port Washington, N.Y.: Ira J. Friedman, 1966.

Bargar, B. D. *Lord Dartmouth and the American Revolution.* Columbia: University of South Carolina Press, 1965.

Barker, John. *The British in Boston: Being the Diary of Lieutenant John Barker of the King's Own Regiment from November 15, 1774, to May 31, 1776.* Cambridge, Mass.: Harvard University Press, 1924.

Barker, Thomas M., and Paul R. Huey. *The 1776–1777 Northern Campaigns of the American War for Independence and Their Sequel.* Fleischmanns, N.Y.: Purple Mountain Press, 2010.

Barnes, G. R., and J. H. Owen, eds. *The Private Papers of John, Earl of Sandwich, First Lord of the Admiralty, 1771–82.* 4 vols. London: Navy Records Society, 1932–38.

Barrow, John. *The Life of Richard Earl Howe, K.G.* London: John Murray, 1838.

Bartenstein, Fred, and Isabel Bartenstein. *New Jersey's Revolutionary War Powder Mill.* Morristown, N.J.: Morris County Historical Society, 1975.

Bascom, Robert O., and James Austin Holden. *The Ticonderoga Expedition of 1775.* New York State Historical Society, 1910.

Bass, Robert D. *The Green Dragoon: The Lives of Banastre Tarleton and Mary Robinson.* Orangeburg, S.C.: Sandlapper, 1973.

Baxter, James Phinney, ed. *The British Invasion from the North.* Albany, N.Y.: Joel Munsell's Sons, 1887.

Beakes, John H., Jr. *Otho Holland Williams in the American Revolution.* Charleston, S.C.: Nautical and Aviation Publishing, 2015.

Beatson, Robert. *Naval and Military Memoirs of Great Britain.* Vol. 4. London: Longman, Hurst, 1804.

Beck, Alverda S. *The Correspondence of Esek Hopkins.* Providence: Rhode Island Historical Society, 1933.

Beck, Derek W. *Igniting the American Revolution, 1773–1775.* Naperville, Ill.: Sourcebooks, 2015.
———. *The War Before Independence, 1775–1776.* Naperville, Ill.: Sourcebooks, 2016.

Belcher, Henry. *The First American Civil War.* Vol. 1. London: Macmillan, 1911.

Bell, J. L. *The Road to Concord.* Yardley, Pa.: Westholme, 2016.

Bellesiles, Michael A. *Revolutionary Outlaws: Ethan Allen and the Struggle for Independence on the Early American Frontier.* Charlottesville: University Press of Virginia, 1993.

Bellico, Russell P. *Sails and Steam in the Mountains.* Fleischmanns, N.Y.: Purple Mountain Press, 2001.

Bellot, Leland J. *William Knox: The Life & Thought of an Eighteenth-Century Imperialist.* Austin: University of Texas Press, 1977.

Bemis, Samuel Flagg. *The Diplomacy of the American Revolution.* Bloomington: Indiana University Press, 1957.

Benedict, Erastus C. *The Battle of Harlem Heights.* New York: A. S. Barnes, 1878.

Berg, Fred Anderson. *Encyclopedia of Continental Army Units.* Harrisburg, Pa.: Stackpole, 1972.

Bergen County History, 1775 Annual. River Edge, N.J.: Bergen County Historical Society, 1975.

Betlock, Lynn, et al. *An Architectural History of the Old South Meeting House.* Boston: Old South Association, 1995.

Bezanson, Anne. *Prices and Inflation During the American Revolution.* Philadelphia: University of Pennsylvania Press, 1951.

Bickham, Troy. *Making Headlines: The American Revolution as Seen Through the British Press.* DeKalb: Northern Illinois University Press, 2009.

Bigelow, John, ed., *The Works of Benjamin Franklin.* Vol. 7. New York: G. P. Putnam's Sons, 1904.

Bill, Alfred Hoyt. *The Campaign of Princeton, 1776–1777.* Princeton, N.J.: Princeton University Press, 1975.
———. *New Jersey and the Revolutionary War.* New Brunswick, N.J.: Rutgers University Press, 1964.

Billias, George Athan. *General John Glover and His Marblehead Mariners.* New York: Henry Holt, 1960.
———, ed. *George Washington's Generals and Opponents.* New York: Da Capo, 1994.

Bird, Harrison. *Attack on Quebec: The American Invasion of Canada, 1775–1776.* New York: Oxford University Press, 1968.
———. *Navies in the Mountains: The Battles on the Waters of Lake Champlain and Lake George, 1609–1814.* New York: Oxford University Press, 1962.

Black, Jeannette D., and William Greene Roelker, eds. *A Rhode Island Chaplain in the Revolution: Letters of Ebenezer David to Nicholas Brown, 1775–1778.* Providence: Rhode Island Society of the Cincinnati, 1949.

Black, Jeremy. *George III, America's Last King.* New Haven, Conn.: Yale University Press, 2008.

Black, Jeremy, and Philip Woodfine, eds. *The British Navy and the Use of Naval Power in the Eighteenth Century.* Leicester, U.K.: Leicester University Press, 1988.

Blackmore, Howard L. *British Military Firearms, 1650–1850.* London: Greenhill, 1994.

Bland, Theodorick, Jr. *The Bland Papers.* Vol. 1, edited by Charles Campbell. Petersburg, Va.: Edmund & Julian C. Ruffin, 1840.

Blanken, Leo J., et al. *Assessing War: The Challenge of Measuring Success and Failure.* Washington, D.C.: Georgetown University Press, 2015.

Bliven, Bruce, Jr. *Battle for Manhattan.* New York: Henry Holt, 1956.

———. *Under the Guns: New York, 1775–1776.* New York: Harper & Row, 1972.

Bolles, Albert S. *The Financial History of the United States, from 1774 to 1789.* New York: D. Appleton, 1892.

Bolton, Charles Knowles, ed. *Letters of Hugh Earl Percy, from Boston and New York, 1774–1776.* Boston: Charles E. Goodspeed, 1902.

———. *The Private Soldier Under Washington.* New York: Charles Scribner's Sons, 1902.

Bolton, Reginald Pelham. *The Bombardment of New York.* New York: s.p., 1915.

———. *Fort Washington.* New York: Empire State Society, 1902.

Borneman, Walter R. *American Spring.* New York: Back Bay Books, 2015.

Boudreau, George W. *Independence: A Guide to Historic Philadelphia.* Yardley, Pa.: Westholme, 2012.

Bowen, Catherine Drinker. *John Adams and the American Revolution.* Boston: Little, Brown, 1950.

Bowler, R. Arthur. *Logistics and the Failure of the British Army in America, 1775–1783.* Princeton, N.J.: Princeton University Press, 1973.

Bowman, Larry G. *Captive Americans: Prisoners During the American Revolution.* Athens: Ohio University Press, 1976.

Boyle, Joseph Lee, ed. *From Redcoat to Rebel: The Thomas Sullivan Journal.* Bowie, Md.: Heritage Books, 1997.

Bradley, A. G. *Sir Guy Carleton (Lord Dorchester).* Toronto: University of Toronto Press, 1966.

Bragg, C. L. *Crescent Moon over Carolina.* Columbia: University of South Carolina Press, 2013.

Brands, H. W. *The First American: The Life and Times of Benjamin Franklin.* New York: Anchor, 2002.

Brandt, Clare. *The Man in the Mirror: A Life of Benedict Arnold.* New York: Random House, 1994.

Bray, Robert C., and Paul E. Bushnell, eds. *Diary of a Common Soldier in the American Revolution, 1775–1783.* DeKalb: Northern Illinois University Press, 1978.

Brebner, J. Bartlet. *Canada: A Modern History.* Ann Arbor: University of Michigan Press, 1960.

Breen, T. H. *American Insurgents, American Patriots: The Revolution of the People.* New York: Hill and Wang, 2010.

———. *The Marketplace of Revolution: How Consumer Politics Shaped American Independence.* New York: Oxford University Press, 2004.

Brewer, John. *The Sinews of Power: War, Money, and the English State, 1688–1783.* Cambridge, Mass.: Harvard University Press, 1990.

Bridenbaugh, Carl. *Cities in Revolt: Urban Life in America, 1743–1776.* London: Oxford University Press, 1971.

Brodhead, John Romeyn. *Documents Relative to the Colonial History of the State of New York.* Vol. 8, edited by E. B. O'Callaghan. Albany, N.Y.: Weed, Parsons, 1857.

Brooke, John. *King George III.* London: Constable, 1985.

Brookhiser, Richard. *Alexander Hamilton, American.* New York: Touchstone, 2000.

Brooks, Noah. *Henry Knox, a Soldier of the Revolution.* New York: G. P. Putnam's Sons, 1900.

Brougham, Henry, Lord. *Sketches of Statesmen of the Time of George III.* Vol. 3. London: Richard Griffin, 1855.

Brown, Abram English. *Beneath Old Roof Trees.* Boston: Lee and Shepard, 1896.

———. *Beside Old Hearth-Stones.* Boston: Lee and Shepard, 1897.

———. *Faneuil Hall and Faneuil Hall Market.* Boston: Lee and Shepard, 1891.

Brown, Gerald Saxon. *The American Secretary: The Colonial Policy of Lord George Germain, 1775–1778*. Ann Arbor: University of Michigan Press, 1963.

Brown, Lloyd A., and Howard H. Peckham, eds. *Revolutionary War Journals of Henry Dearborn, 1775–83*. New York: Da Capo, 1971.

Brown, Stuart Gerry, ed. *The Autobiography of James Monroe*. Syracuse, N.Y.: Syracuse University Press, 2017.

Brown, Wallace. *The Good Americans: The Loyalists in the American Revolution*. New York: William Morrow, 1969.

Browne, George Waldo. *The St. Lawrence River*. New York: G. P. Putnam's Sons, 1905.

Brumwell, Stephen. *Turncoat: Benedict Arnold and the Crisis of American Liberty*. New Haven, Conn.: Yale University Press, 2018.

Brunsman, Denver. *The Evil Necessity: British Naval Impressment in the Eighteenth-Century Atlantic World*. Charlottesville: University of Virginia Press, 2013.

Buel, Richard, Jr. *Dear Liberty: Connecticut's Mobilization for Revolutionary War*. Middletown, Conn.: Wesleyan University Press, 1980.

———. *In Irons: Britain's Naval Supremacy and the American Revolutionary Economy*. New Haven, Conn.: Yale University Press, 1998.

Buell, Rowena, ed. *The Memoirs of Rufus Putnam*. Boston: Houghton Mifflin, 1903.

Bullock, Charles J. *The Finances of the United States from 1775 to 1789*. Madison: University of Wisconsin, 1895.

Bunker, Nick. *An Empire on the Edge: How Britain Came to Fight America*. New York: Vintage, 2015.

Burdick, Kim Rogers. *Revolutionary Delaware: Independence in the First State*. Charleston, S.C.: History Press, 2016.

Burgoyne, Bruce E., trans. *Defeat, Disaster and Dedication*. Bowie, Md.: Heritage Books, 1996.

———, trans. *The Diary of Lieutenant von Bardeleben*. Bowie, Md.: Heritage Books, 1998.

———, ed. *Enemy Views: The American War as Recorded by the Hessian Participants*. Bowie, Md.: Heritage Books, 1996.

———, trans. *Georg Pausch's Journal and Reports of the Campaign in America*. Bowie, Md.: Heritage Books, 1996.

———, trans. *Hesse-Hanau Order Books, a Diary and Rosters*. Westminster, Md.: Heritage Books, 2006.

———, trans. *Journal of a Hessian Grenadier Battalion*. Westminster, Md.: Heritage Books, 2005.

Burk, Kathleen. *Old World, New World: Great Britain and America from the Beginning*. New York: Grove, 2007.

Burnham, John. *Personal Recollections of the Revolutionary War*. Tarrytown, N.Y.: William Abbatt, 1917.

Burns, James MacGregor, and Susan Dunn. *George Washington*. New York: Times Books, 2004.

Burrows, Edwin G. *Forgotten Patriots: The Untold Story of American Prisoners During the Revolutionary War*. New York: Basic Books, 2008.

Burrows, Edwin G., and Mike Wallace. *Gotham: A History of New York City to 1898*. New York: Oxford University Press, 2000.

Bush, Martin H. *Revolutionary Enigma*. Port Washington, N.Y.: Ira J. Friedman, 1969.

Bushman, Richard Lyman. *The American Farmer in the Eighteenth Century: A Social and Cultural History*. New Haven, Conn.: Yale University Press, 2018.

Butcher, H. Borton. *The Battle of Trenton*. Princeton, N.J.: Princeton University Press, 1934.

Butterfield, L. H., ed. *Adams Family Correspondence*. Vols. 1 and 2. New York: Athenaeum, 1965.

———, ed. *Diary and Autobiography of John Adams*. 4 vols. New York: Athenaeum, 1964.

———, ed. *Letters of Benjamin Rush*. Vol. 1. Princeton, N.J.: Princeton University Press, 1951.

Calendar of Historical Manuscripts Relating to the War of the Revolution. Vol. 1. Albany, N.Y.: Weed, Parsons, 1865.

Calhoon, Robert McCluer. *The Loyalists in Revolutionary America, 1760–1781*. New York: Harcourt Brace Jovanovich, 1973.

Callahan, North. *Daniel Morgan: Ranger of the Revolution*. New York: Holt, Rinehart and Winston, 1961.

———. *Henry Knox: General Washington's General*. New York: A. S. Barnes, 1958.

———. *Royal Raiders: The Tories of the American Revolution*. Indianapolis: Bobbs-Merrill, 1963.

Calloway, Colin G. *The American Revolution in Indian Country*. Cambridge: Cambridge University Press, 1996.

———. *The Indian World of George Washington*. New York: Oxford University Press, 2018.

Campbell-Smith, Duncan. *Masters of the Post: The Authorized History of the Royal Mail*. London: Penguin, 2012.

Carbone, Gerald M. *Nathanael Greene: A Biography of the American Revolution*. New York: Palgrave Macmillan, 2010.

Carp, Benjamin L. *Defiance of the Patriots: The Boston Tea Party and the Making of America*. New Haven, Conn.: Yale University Press, 2010.

Carp, E. Wayne. *To Starve the Army at Pleasure: Continental Army Administration and American Political Culture, 1775–1783*. Chapel Hill: University of North Carolina Press, 1984.

Carrington, Henry B. *Battles of the American Revolution, 1775–1781*. New York: Promontory Press, 1974.

Carrington, Selwyn H. H. *The British West Indies During the American Revolution*. Dordrecht, Neth.: Foris Publications, 1988.

Carter, Clarence E., ed. *The Correspondence of General Thomas Gage with the Secretaries of State, and with the War Office and the Treasury, 1763–1775*. 2 vols. Hamden, Conn.: Archon Books, 1969.

Carter, William. *A Genuine Detail of the Several Engagements, Positions, and Movements of the Royal and American Armies, Etc*. London: s.p., 1784.

Cash, Philip. *Medical Men at the Siege of Boston*. Philadelphia: American Philosophical Society, 1973.

Castonguay, Jacques. *The Unknown Fort: Saint-Jean Foils Americans*. Translated by William J. Cozens. Montreal: Les Éditions du Lévier, 1965.

Chadwick, Bruce. *The General and Mrs. Washington*. Naperville, Ill.: Sourcebooks, 2007.

Chancellor, E. Beresford. *The XVIIIth Century in London*. London: B. T. Batsford, 1921.

Chapelle, Howard I. *The American Sailing Navy*. New York: Konecky & Konecky, 1949.

Charbonneau, André. *The Fortifications of Île aux Noix*. Ottawa: Parks Canada, 1994.

Charbonneau, André, Yvon Desloges, and Marc Lafrance. *Quebec, the Fortified City*. Ottawa: Parks Canada, 1982.

Chartrand, René. *French Fortresses in North America, 1535–1763*. Botley, U.K.: Osprey, 2005.

Chase, Ellen. *The Beginnings of the American Revolution*. Vols. 2 and 3. New York: Baker and Taylor, 1910.

Chernow, Ron. *Alexander Hamilton*. New York: Penguin, 2005.

———. *Washington: A Life*. New York: Penguin, 2011.

Chidsey, Donald Barr. *The Siege of Boston*. New York: Crown, 1966.

Chittenden, Lucius E. *The Capture of Ticonderoga*. Rutland, Vt.: Tuttle, 1872.

Christie, I. R. *Crisis of Empire: Great Britain and the American Colonies, 1754–1783*. New York: W. W. Norton, 1967.

Clark, Dora Mae. *British Opinion and the American Revolution*. New York: Russell & Russell, 1966.

Clark, George L. *Silas Deane: A Connecticut Leader in the American Revolution*. New York: G. P. Putnam's Sons, 1913.

Clark, Ronald W. *Benjamin Franklin: A Biography*. New York: Random House, 1983.

Clark, Stephen. *Following Their Footsteps: A Travel Guide . . . of the 1775 Secret Expedition to Capture Quebec*. Scarborough, Me.: s.p., 2012.

Clark, William Bell. *Captain Dauntless: The Story of Nicholas Biddle of the Continental Navy*. Baton Rouge: Louisiana State University Press, 1949.

———. *Gallant John Barry, 1745–1803*. New York: Macmillan, 1938.

———. *George Washington's Navy*. Baton Rouge: Louisiana State University Press, 1960.

———. *Lambert Wickes: Sea Raider and Diplomat.* New Haven, Conn.: Yale University Press, 1932.

Clark, William Bell, et al., eds. *Naval Documents of the American Revolution.* 11 vols. Washington, D.C.: Government Printing Office, 1964–2005.

Clarke, Jonas. *Opening of the War of the Revolution.* Lexington, Mass.: Lexington Historical Society, 1901.

Clary, David A., and Joseph W. A. Whitehorne. *The Inspectors General of the United States Army, 1777–1903.* Washington, D.C.: U.S. Army, 1997.

Clinton, Henry. *The American Rebellion.* Edited by William B. Willcox. New Haven, Conn.: Yale University Press, 1954.

Clowes, William Laird. *The Royal Navy: A History.* Vol. 3. London: Sampson Low, 1898.

Clyde, John C. *Rosbrugh: A Tale of the Revolution.* Easton, Pa.: 1880.

Coakley, Robert W., and Stetson Conn. *The War of the American Revolution.* Washington, D.C.: U.S. Army, 1975.

Coburn, Frank Warren. *The Battle of April 19, 1775.* Lexington, Mass.: Lexington Historical Society, 1922.

Codman, John, 2nd. *Arnold's Expedition to Quebec.* New York: Macmillan, 1901.

Coffin, Charles, ed. *History of the Battle of Breed's Hill.* William J. Condon, 1831.

———, ed. *The Life and Services of Major General John Thomas.* New York: Egbert, Hovey & King, 1844.

Coffin, Victor. *The Province of Quebec and the Early American Revolution.* Madison: University of Wisconsin, 1896.

Cohen, Eliot A. *Conquered into Liberty.* New York: Free Press, 2011.

Cohen, Sheldon S., ed. *Canada Preserved: The Journal of Captain Thomas Ainslie.* New York: New York University Press, 1968.

Cohn, Michael. *Fortifications of New York During the Revolutionary War, 1776–1782.* New York: New York Archeological Group, 1962.

Colburn, Jeremiah, ed. *American Independence.* Boston: D. Clapp & Son, 1876.

Collins, Varnum Lansing, ed. *A Brief Narrative of the Ravages of the British and Hessians at Princeton in 1776–1777.* Princeton, N.J.: University Library, 1906.

Cometti, Elizabeth, ed. *The American Journals of Lt. John Enys.* Syracuse, N.Y.: Syracuse University Press, 1976.

Commager, Henry Steele, and Richard B. Morris, eds. *The Spirit of 'Seventy-Six.* Edison, N.J.: Castle Books, 2002.

Conlin, Jonathan. *Tales of Two Cities: Paris, London, and the Birth of the Modern City.* Berkeley, Calif.: Counterpoint, 2013.

Connor, R.D.W. *Cornelius Hartnett: An Essay in North Carolina History.* Raleigh, N.C.: Edwards & Broughton, 1909.

Conway, John Joseph. *Footprints of Famous Americans in Paris.* New York: John Lane, 1912.

Conway, Stephen. *The War of American Independence, 1775–1783.* London: Edward Arnold, 1995.

Cook, Don. *The Long Fuse: How England Lost the American Colonies, 1760–1785.* New York: Atlantic Monthly Press, 1995.

Corner, George W., ed. *The Autobiography of Benjamin Rush.* Princeton, N.J.: Princeton University Press, 1948.

Corwin, Edward S. *French Policy and the American Alliance of 1778.* Princeton, N.J.: Princeton University Press, 1916.

Countryman, Edward. *The American Revolution.* New York: Hill and Wang, 1994.

———. *A People in Revolution.* New York: W. W. Norton, 1989.

Coupland, R. *The American Revolution and the British Empire.* New York: Russell & Russell, 1965.

Cox, Caroline. *A Proper Sense of Honor: Service and Sacrifice in Washington's Army.* Chapel Hill: University of North Carolina Press, 2004.

Crary, Catherine S. *The Price of Loyalty: Tory Writings from the Revolutionary Era.* New York: McGraw-Hill, 1973.

Crawford, Michael J., ed. *The Autobiography of a Yankee Mariner: Christopher Prince and the American Revolution*. Washington, D.C.: Brassey's, 2002.

Creighton, Donald. *A History of Canada*. Boston: Houghton Mifflin, 1958.

Cresswell, Nicholas. *The Journal of Nicholas Cresswell, 1774–1777*. Carlisle, Mass.: Applewood Books, 1924.

Cressy, David. *Saltpeter: The Mother of Gunpowder*. Oxford: Oxford University Press, 2013.

Crocker, Glenys. *The Gunpowder Industry*. Princes Risborough, U.K.: Shire Publications, 2002.

Crowley, John, et al., eds. *Atlas of Cork City*. Cork, Ire.: Cork University Press, 2005.

Cruikshank, Ernest, et al., eds. *A History of the Organization, Development and Services of the Military and Naval Forces of Canada*. 3 vols. Ottawa: Historical Section, General Staff, 1919.

Crytzer, Brady J. *Hessians*. Yardley, Pa.: Westholme, 2015.

Cubbison, Douglas R. *The American Northern Theater Army in 1776*. Jefferson, N.C.: McFarland, 2010.

———. *"The Artillery Never Gained More Honour": British Artillery in 1776 Valcour Island and 1777 Saratoga Campaigns*. Fleischmanns, N.Y.: Purple Mountain Press, 2007.

Cumberland, Richard. *Memoirs of Richard Cumberland*. Boston: West and Greenleaf, 1806.

Cumming, William P. *British Maps of Colonial America*. Chicago: University of Chicago Press, 1974.

Cumming, William P., and Hugh F. Rankin. *The Fate of a Nation*. London: Phaidon, 1975.

Cuneo, John R. *Robert Rogers of the Rangers*. New York: Oxford University Press, 1959.

Cunningham, Peter, ed. *The Letters of Horace Walpole*. Vol. 6. London: Richard Bentley and Son, 1891.

Currier, John J. *History of Newburyport, Mass., 1764–1905*. Newburyport, Mass.: s.p., 1906.

Curtis, Edward E. *The British Army in the American Revolution*. Gansevoort, N.Y.: Corner House Historical Publications, 1998.

Cusack, M. F. *City and County of Cork*. Dublin: McGlashan and Gill, 1875.

Cutbush, Edward. *Observations on the Means of Preserving the Health of Soldiers and Sailors*. Philadelphia: Thomas Dobson, 1808.

Cutter, Benjamin, and William R. Cutter. *History of the Town of Arlington, Massachusetts*. Boston: David Clapp & Son, 1880.

Cutter, William. *The Life of Israel Putnam*. New York: George F. Cooledge & Brother, 1850.

Dandridge, Danske. *American Prisoners of the Revolution*. Charlottesville, Va.: Michie, 1911.

———. *Historic Shepherdstown*. Charlottesville, Va.: Michie, 1910.

Dann, John C., ed. *The Revolution Remembered*. Chicago: University of Chicago Press, 1980.

Darley, Stephen. *Voices from a Wilderness Expedition*. Bloomington, Ind.: Authorhouse, 2011.

Daughan, George C. *If by Sea: The Forging of the American Navy*. New York: Basic Books, 2008.

Davidson, Philip. *Propaganda and the American Revolution, 1763–1783*. New York: W. W. Norton, 1973.

Davies, K. G., ed. *Documents of the American Revolution, 1770–1783*. 21 vols. Shannon: Irish University Press, 1972–81.

Davis, Matthew L. *Memoirs of Aaron Burr*. Vol. 1. New York: Da Capo, 1971.

Dawson, Henry B. *Gleanings from the Harvest-Field of American History*. Part 4. Morrisania, N.Y.: 1865.

———. *Westchester-County, New York, During the American Revolution*. Morrisania, N.Y.: 1886.

Deane, Silas. *Collections of the New-York Historical Society for the Year 1886*. Vol. 1, *The Deane Papers*. New York: New-York Historical Society, 1887.

de Beer, Gavin. *Gibbon and His World*. New York: Viking, 1968.

De Fonblanque, Edward Barrington. *Political and Military Episodes . . . from the Life and Correspondence of the Right Hon. John Burgoyne*. London: Macmillan, 1876.

de Forest, Louis Effingham, ed. *The Journals and Papers of Seth Pomeroy*. New York: Society of Colonial Wars, 1926.

de Lancey, Edward F. *The Capture of Mount Washington, November 16, 1776, the Result of Treason*. New York: 1877.

DeMond, Robert O. *The Loyalists in North Carolina During the Revolution.* Baltimore: Genealogical Publishing, 1979.

Denton, Edgar, ed. *Limits of Loyalty.* Waterloo, Ont.: Wilfrid Laurier University Press, 1980.

Desjardin, Thomas A. *Through a Howling Wilderness: Benedict Arnold's March to Quebec, 1775.* New York: St. Martin's Griffin, 2006.

The Detail and Conduct of the American War. London: Richardson and Urquhart, 1780.

Dexter, Franklin Bowditch. *The Literary Diary of Ezra Stiles, D.D., LL.D.* Vols. 1 and 2. New York: Charles Scribner's Sons, 1901.

Diamant, Lincoln. *Chaining the Hudson.* New York: Fordham University Press, 2004.

Diary of Samuel Richards, Captain of Connecticut Line War of the Revolution, 1775–1781. Philadelphia: s.p., 1909.

Dickson, David. *Old World Colony: Cork and South Munster, 1630–1830.* Madison: University of Wisconsin Press, 2005.

Dierks, Konstantin. *In My Power: Letter Writing and Communications in Early America.* Philadelphia: University of Pennsylvania Press, 2009.

Doniol, Henri. *Histoire de la Participation de la France à l'Établissement des Étas-Unis d'Amérique.* Vol. 1. Paris: Imprimerie Nationale, 1890.

Donkin, Robert. *Military Collections and Remarks.* New York: H. Gaine, 1777.

Donne, W. Bodham, ed. *The Correspondence of King George the Third with Lord North.* 2 vols. London: John Murray, 1867.

Donnelly, Mark P., and Daniel Diehl. *Pirates of New Jersey.* Mechanicsburg, Pa.: Stackpole, 2010.

Donoughue, Bernard. *British Politics and the American Revolution: The Path to War, 1773–1775.* London: Macmillan, 1964.

Dorson, Richard M., ed. *America's Rebels: Narratives of the Patriots.* Greenwich, Conn.: Fawcett Premier, 1966.

Dorwart, Jeffery M. *Invasion and Insurrection: Security, Defense, and War in the Delaware Valley, 1621–1815.* Newark: University of Delaware Press, 2008.

Drake, Francis S. *Life and Correspondence of Henry Knox.* Boston: Samuel G. Drake, 1873.

———. *The Town of Roxbury: Its Memorable Persons and Places.* Roxbury, Mass.: s.p., 1878.

Drake, Samuel Adams. *Bunker Hill.* Boston: Nichols and Hall, 1875.

———. *The Campaign of Trenton, 1776–1777.* Boston: Lee and Shepard, 1899.

———. *History of Middlesex County, Massachusetts.* Vol. 1. Boston: Estes and Lauriat, 1879.

Draper, Theodore. *A Struggle for Power.* New York: Times Books, 1996.

Drayton, John. *Memoirs of the American Revolution.* 2 vols. Charleston, S.C.: A. E. Miller, 1821.

Drowne, Henry Russell. *A Sketch of Fraunces Tavern.* New York: Fraunces Tavern, 1919.

Duane, William, ed. *Extracts from the Diary of Christopher Marshall.* Albany, N.Y.: Joel Munsell, 1877.

Duer, William Alexander. *The Life of William Alexander, Earl of Stirling.* New York: Wiley & Putnam, 1847.

Dull, Jonathan R. *A Diplomatic History of the American Revolution.* New Haven, Conn.: Yale University Press, 1985.

———. *The French Navy and American Independence.* Princeton, N.J.: Princeton University Press, 1975.

Duncan, Francis. *History of the Royal Regiment of Artillery.* Vol. 1. London: John Murray, 1879.

Duncan, Roger F. *Coastal Maine: A Maritime History.* Woodstock, Vt.: Countryman Press, 2002.

Dunelm, S., ed. *The Political Life of William Wildman, Viscount Barrington.* London: Payne and Foss, 1815.

Dunkerly, Robert M. *Redcoats on the River: Southeastern North Carolina in the Revolutionary War.* Wilmington, N.C.: Dram Tree Books, 2008.

Dunlap, William. *History of the American Theater.* 2 vols. London: Richard Bentley, 1833.

Dwyer, William M. *The Day Is Ours!* New Brunswick, N.J.: Rutgers University Press, 1998.

East, Robert A., and Jacob Judd, eds. *The Loyalist Americans: A Focus on Greater New York.* Tarrytown, N.Y.: Sleepy Hollow Restorations, 1975.

Eckenrode, H. J. *The Revolution in Virginia.* Boston: Houghton Mifflin, 1916.

Eddis, William. *Letters from America*. London: s.p., 1792.

Edgar, Walter. *Partisans and Redcoats: The Southern Conflict That Turned the Tide of the American Revolution*. New York: HarperPerennial, 2003.

Edler, Friedrich. *The Dutch Republic and the American Revolution*. Baltimore: Johns Hopkins Press, 1911.

Eelking, Max von, and Joseph George Rosengarten. *The German Allied Troops in the North American War of Independence*. Driffield, U.K.: Leonaur, 2012.

Egerton, Douglas R. *Death or Liberty: African Americans and Revolutionary America*. New York: Oxford University Press, 2011.

Egnal, Marc. *A Mighty Empire: The Origins of the American Revolution*. Ithaca, N.Y.: Cornell University Press, 1988.

Einstein, Lewis. *Divided Loyalties: Americans in England During the War of Independence*. London: Cobden-Sanderson, 1933.

Eller, Ernest McNeill, ed. *Chesapeake Bay in the American Revolution*. Centreville, Md.: Tidewater, 1981.

Ellis, George E. *Celebration of the Centennial Anniversary of the Evacuation of Boston*. Boston: City Council, 1876.

———. *History of the Battle of Bunker's (Breed's) Hill*. Boston: Lee and Shepard, 1895.

———. *An Oration Delivered*. Boston: William Crosby, 1841.

Ellis, Joseph J. *American Creation*. New York: Knopf, 2007.

———. *Founding Brothers*. New York: Knopf, 2001.

———. *His Excellency: George Washington*. New York: Vintage, 2004.

———. *Revolutionary Summer: The Birth of American Independence*. New York: Knopf, 2013.

Ellis, Kenneth. *The Post Office in the Eighteenth Century*. London: Oxford University Press, 1969.

Elting, John R. *The Battle of Bunker's Hill*. Monmouth Beach, N.J.: Philip Freneau Press, 1975.

Ely, Warren S., and John W. Jordan. *History of Bucks County, Pennsylvania*. Vol. 2. New York: Lewis Publishing, 1905.

Emerson, Ralph Waldo. *The Complete Works of Ralph Waldo Emerson: Miscellanies*. Vol. 11. Boston: Houghton Mifflin, 1903–04.

English, Frederick. *General Hugh Mercer, Forgotten Hero of the American Revolution*. New York: Vantage, 1975.

Ewald, Johann. *Diary of the American War: A Hessian Journal*. Edited and translated by Joseph D. Tustin. New Haven, Conn.: Yale University Press, 1979.

Fenn, Elizabeth A. *Pox Americana*. New York: Hill and Wang, 2002.

Ferguson, E. James. *The Power of the Purse: A History of American Public Finance, 1776–1790*. Chapel Hill: University of North Carolina Press, 1961.

Ferling, John. *Almost a Miracle*. New York: Oxford University Press, 2007.

———. *The Ascent of George Washington*. New York: Bloomsbury, 2009.

———. *The First of Men: A Life of George Washington*. New York: Oxford University Press, 2010.

———. *Independence: The Struggle to Set America Free*. New York: Bloomsbury, 2011.

———. *John Adams: A Life*. New York: Oxford University Press, 2010.

———. *A Leap in the Dark: The Struggle to Create the American Republic*. New York: Oxford University Press, 2005.

Ferreiro, Larrie D. *Brothers at Arms: American Independence and the Men of France and Spain Who Saved It*. New York: Vintage, 2016.

ffoulkes, Charles J. *Inventory and Survey of the Armouries of the Tower of London*. Vol. 1. London: H.M. Stationery Office, 1916.

Field, Edward. *Esek Hopkins: Commander-in-Chief of the Continental Navy During the American Revolution, 1775 to 1778*. Providence: Preston & Rounds, 1898.

Field, T. W. *Historic and Antiquarian Scenes in Brooklyn and Its Vicinity*. Brooklyn: s.p., 1868.

Field, Thomas W. *The Battle of Long Island*. Brooklyn: Long Island Historical Society, 1869.

Fischer, David Hackett. *Champlain's Dream*. New York: Simon & Schuster, 2008.

———. *Paul Revere's Ride*. New York: Oxford University Press, 1995.

———. *Washington's Crossing*. New York: Oxford University Press, 2004.

Fisk, Theophilus. *Anniversary of the Battle at Fort Moultrie*. Charleston, S.C.: Office of the Southern Evangelist, 1836.

Fiske, John. *Essays, Historical and Literary*. Vol. 1. London: Macmillan, 1902.

Fitzgerald, Percy. *The Good Queen Charlotte*. London: Downey, 1899.

Fitzpatrick, John C., ed. *The Writings of George Washington*. Vol. 2. Washington, D.C.: Government Printing Office, 1931.

Fleming, Thomas, ed. *Benjamin Franklin: A Biography in His Own Words*. Vol. 1. New York: Newsweek, 1972.

———. *1776: Year of Illusions*. Edison, N.J.: Castle Books, 1996.

Flexner, James Thomas. *The Young Hamilton*. Boston: Little, Brown, 1978.

Foner, Eric. *Tom Paine and Revolutionary America*. New York: Oxford University Press, 1976.

Forbes, Esther. *Paul Revere and the World He Lived In*. Boston: Houghton Mifflin, 1999.

Force, Peter, ed. *American Archives*. Series 4 and 5. Washington, D.C.: M. St. Clair Clarke and Peter Force, 1837–53.

Ford, Worthington Chauncey, ed. *Correspondence and Journals of Samuel Blachley Webb*. Vol. 1. New York: s.p., 1893.

Foreman, Amanda. *The Duchess*. New York: Random House, 2008.

Forrest, William S. *Historical and Descriptive Sketches of Norfolk and Vicinity*. Philadelphia: Lindsay and Blakiston, 1858.

Fortescue, J. W. *A History of the British Army*. Vol. 3. London: Macmillan, 1911.

Fortescue, John, ed. *The Correspondence of King George the Third*. Vols. 2 and 3. London: Macmillan, 1927–28.

———. *The War of Independence: The British Army in North America, 1775–1783*. London: Greenhill, 1901.

Fort Lee History: Fourteenth Annual Report 1909, of the American Scenic and Historic Preservation Society. Albany, N.Y.: J. B. Lyon, 1909.

Fowler, William M., Jr. *Rebels Under Sail: The American Navy During the Revolution*. New York: Charles Scribner's Sons, 1976.

Fraser, Georgia. *The Stone House at Gowanus*. New York: Witter and Kintner, 1909.

Fraser, William. *The Melvilles, Earls of Melville, and the Leslies, Earls of Leven*. Vol. 1. Edinburgh: 1890.

Freeman, Douglas Southall. *George Washington: A Biography*. Vol. 4. New York: Charles Scribner's Sons, 1951.

French, Allen. *The Day of Concord and Lexington*. Boston: Little, Brown, 1925.

———. *The First Year of the American Revolution*. New York: Octagon, 1968.

———. *General Gage's Informers*. Ann Arbor: University of Michigan Press, 1932.

———. *The Siege of Boston*. New York: Macmillan, 1911.

———. *The Taking of Ticonderoga in 1775: The British Story*. Cambridge, Mass.: Harvard University Press, 1928.

Frey, Sylvia R. *The British Soldier in America*. Austin: University of Texas Press, 1981.

———. *Water from the Rock: Black Resistance in a Revolutionary Age*. Princeton, N.J.: Princeton University Press, 1992.

Frothingham, Richard, Jr. *The History of Charlestown*. Boston: Charles C. Little and James Brown, 1845.

———. *History of the Siege of Boston*. Boston: Charles C. Little and James Brown, 1849.

Frothingham, Richard. *The Centennial: Battle of Bunker Hill*. Boston: Little, Brown, 1875.

———. *The Life and Times of Joseph Warren*. Boston: Little, Brown, 1865.

Fruchtman, Jack, Jr. *Atlantic Cousins: Benjamin Franklin and His Visionary Friends*. New York: Thunder's Mouth Press, 2007.

Fryer, Mary Beacock. *Battlefields of Canada*. Toronto: Dundurn Press, 1986.

Fuller, J.F.C. *British Light Infantry in the Eighteenth Century*. London: Hutchinson, 1925.

Gabriel, Michael P., ed. *Quebec During the American Invasion, 1775–1776: The Journal of François Baby, Gabriel Taschereau, and Jenkin Williams*. Translated by S. Pascale Vergereau-Dewey. East Lansing: Michigan State University Press, 2005.

Gallagher, John J. *The Battle of Brooklyn, 1776*. Edison, N.J.: Castle Books, 2002.

Galloway, Joseph. *Historical and Political Reflections on the Rise and Progress of the American Rebellion*. London: G. Wilkie, 1780.

Galvin, John R. *The Minute Men*. Washington, D.C.: Brassey's, 1996.

Gannett, Henry. *The Origin of Certain Place Names in the United States*. Washington: Government Printing Office, 1905.

Ganoe, William Addleman. *The History of the United States Army*. New York: D. Appleton, 1924.

Gara, Donald J. *The Queen's American Rangers*. Yardley, Pa.: Westholme, 2015.

Garrioch, David. *The Making of Revolutionary Paris*. Berkeley: University of California Press, 2004.

George, M. Dorothy. *London Life in the Eighteenth Century*. New York: Harper & Row, 1964.

Gerlach, Don R. *Proud Patriot: Philip Schuyler and the War of Independence, 1775–1783*. Syracuse, N.Y.: Syracuse University Press, 1987.

Gerlach, Larry R., ed. *New Jersey in the American Revolution, 1763–1783: A Documentary History*. Trenton: New Jersey Historical Commission, 1975.

Gibbes, Robert Wilson. *Documentary History of the American Revolution*. New York: D. Appleton, 1857.

Gibbon, Edward. *Autobiography and Correspondence of Edward Gibbon*. London: Alex. Murray & Son, 1869.

Gibson, James E. *Dr. Bodo Otto and the Medical Background of the American Revolution*. Springfield, Ill.: Charles C. Thomas, 1937.

Gilbert, Alan. *Black Patriots and Loyalists*. Chicago: University of Chicago Press, 2013.

Gill, Harold B., Jr., and George M. Curtis III, eds. *A Man Apart: The Journal of Nicholas Cresswell, 1774–1781*. Lanham, Md.: Lexington Books, 2009.

Gillett, Mary C. *The Army Medical Department, 1775–1818*. Washington, D.C.: U.S. Army, 1981.

Gipson, Lawrence Henry. *American Loyalist: Jared Ingersoll*. New Haven, Conn.: Yale University Press, 1971.

———. *The Coming of the Revolution: 1763–1775*. New York: Harper Torchbooks, 1962.

———. *The Triumphant Empire: Britain Sails into the Storm, 1770–1776*. New York: Knopf, 1967.

Glover, Michael. *General Burgoyne in Canada and America*. London: Gordon & Cremonesi, 1976.

Golway, Terry. *Washington's General: Nathanael Greene and the Triumph of the American Revolution*. New York: Owl, 2006.

Gomme, George Laurence, ed. *The Gentleman's Magazine Library*. London: Elliot Stock, 1883.

Goodwin, George. *Benjamin Franklin in London*. New Haven, Conn.: Yale University Press, 2016.

Goold, William. *The Burning of Falmouth*. Boston: s.p., 1873.

Goolrick, John T. *The Life of General Hugh Mercer*. New York: Neale, 1906.

Gordon, John W. *South Carolina and the American Revolution: A Battlefield History*. Columbia: University of South Carolina Press, 2003.

Goss, Elbridge Henry. *The Life of Colonel Paul Revere*. 2 vols. Boston: Joseph George Cupples, 1891.

Gower, Ronald Sutherland. *The Tower of London*. Vol. 2. London: George Bell & Sons, 1902.

Graham, Gerald S. *The Royal Navy in the American War of Independence*. London: H.M. Stationery Office, 1976.

Graham, James. *The Life of General Daniel Morgan*. New York: Derby & Jackson, 1856.

Grancsay, Stephen C. *American Engraved Powder Horns*. New York: Metropolitan Museum of Art, 1945.

Graydon, Alexander. *Memoirs of His Own Time: With Reminiscences of the Men and Events of the Revolution*. Edited by John Stockton Littell. Philadelphia: Lindsay & Blakiston, 1846.

Green, Samuel A., ed. *Diary Kept by Lieut. Amos Farnsworth of Groton, Mass., During a Part of the Revolutionary War, April, 1775–May, 1779*. Cambridge, Mass.: John Wilson and Son, 1898.

———, ed. *Paul Lunt's Diary, May–December, 1775*. Boston: s.p., 1872.

Greene, Albert. *Recollections of the Jersey Prison-Ship*. Providence: H. H. Brown, 1829.

Greene, George Washington. *The Life of Nathaniel Greene*. Vol. 1. Boston: Houghton Mifflin, 1900.

Greene, Jack P., ed. *The American Revolution: Its Character and Limits*. New York: New York University Press, 1987.

———. *Understanding the American Revolution.* Charlottesville: University Press of Virginia, 1998.

Greenwalt, Phillip S., and Robert Orrison. *A Single Blow: The Battles of Lexington and Concord and the Beginning of the American Revolution, April 19, 1775.* El Dorado Hills, Calif.: Savas Beatie, 2017.

Greenwood, Isaac J., ed. *The Revolutionary Services of John Greenwood.* New York: De Vinne Press, 1922.

Greiff, Constance M. *The Morris-Jumel Mansion: A Documentary History.* Rocky Hill, N.J.: Heritage Studies, 1995.

Grendel, Frédéric. *Beaumarchais: The Man Who Was Figaro.* New York: Thomas Y. Crowell, 1977.

Griffin, Martin I. J. *Stephen Moylan.* Philadelphia: s.p., 1909.

Griffith, Samuel B., II. *The War for American Independence.* Urbana: University of Illinois Press, 2002.

Grosely, Pierre Jean. *A Tour to London.* Vol. 1. London: Lockyer Davis, 1772.

Gross, Robert A. *The Minutemen and Their World.* New York: Hill and Wang, 1992.

Gruber, Ira D. *Books and the British Army in the Age of the American Revolution.* Chapel Hill: University of North Carolina Press, 2010.

———. *The Howe Brothers and the American Revolution.* Chapel Hill: University of North Carolina Press, 1972.

———, ed. *John Peebles' American War, 1776–1782.* Far Thrupp, U.K.: Army Records Society, 1998.

Guilday, Peter. *The Life and Times of James Carroll.* Vol. 1. New York: Encyclopedia Press, 1922.

Guthman, William H., ed. *The Correspondence of Captain Nathan and Lois Peters.* Hartford: Connecticut Historical Society, 1980.

Hadden, James M. *A Journal Kept in Canada and upon Burgoyne's Campaign in 1776 and 1777.* Edited by Horatio Rogers. Albany, N.Y.: Joel Munsell's Sons, 1884.

Hadlow, Janice. *A Royal Experiment: The Private Life of King George III.* New York: Henry Holt, 2014.

Hagist, Don N. *British Soldiers, American War: Voices of the American Revolution.* Yardley, Pa.: Westholme, 2012.

———, ed. *A British Soldier's Story: Roger Lamb's Narrative of the Revolution.* Baraboo, Wis.: Ballindalloch Press, 2004.

Haight, C. *Before the Coming of the Loyalists.* Toronto: Haight, 1897.

Hale, Edward E., and Edward E. Hale, Jr. *Franklin in France.* Boston: Roberts Brothers, 1887.

Hall, Edward Hagaman. *McGown's Pass and Vicinity.* New York: American Scenic and Historic Preservation Society, 1905.

———. *Philipse Manor Hall at Yonkers, N.Y.* New York: American Scenic and Historic Preservation Society, 1912.

Hallahan, William H. *The Day the American Revolution Began.* New York: HarperPerennial, 2001.

Halliday, Paul D. *Habeas Corpus: From England to Empire.* Cambridge, Mass.: Belknap Press, 2012.

Hamilton, Phillip. *The Revolutionary War Lives and Letters of Lucy and Henry Knox.* Baltimore: Johns Hopkins University Press, 2017.

Hammond, Isaac W., ed. *Diary and Orderly Book of Sergeant Jonathan Burton.* Concord, N.H.: Republican Press Association, 1885.

Hammond, Otis G. *Letters and Papers of Major-General John Sullivan.* Vol. 1. Concord: New Hampshire Historical Society, 1930.

Hamner, Christopher H. *Enduring Battle: American Soldiers in Three Wars, 1776–1945.* Lawrence: University Press of Kansas, 2011.

Harcourt, Edward William, ed. *The Harcourt Papers.* 14 vols. Oxford: s.p., 1880–1905.

Hardman, John, and Munro Price, eds. *Louis XVI and the Comte de Vergennes: Correspondence, 1774–1787.* Oxford: Voltaire Foundation, 1998.

Harrell, Isaac Samuel. *Loyalism in Virginia.* New York: AMS Press, 1965.

Harris, J. William. *The Hanging of Thomas Jeremiah.* New Haven, Conn.: Yale University Press, 2009.

Hatch, Charles E., Jr. *The Battle of Moores [sic] Creek Bridge;* Washington, D.C.: National Park Service, 1969.

Hatch, Louis Clinton. *The Administration of the American Revolutionary Army.* New York: Longmans, Green, 1904.

Hatch, Robert McConnell. *Thrust for Canada.* Boston: Houghton Mifflin, 1979.

Hawke, David Freeman. *Benjamin Rush: Revolutionary Gadfly.* Indianapolis: Bobbs-Merrill, 1971.

———. *Paine.* New York: Harper & Row, 1974.

Hayter, Tony, ed. *An Eighteenth-Century Secretary at War: The Papers of William, Viscount Barrington.* London: Bodley Head, 1988.

Heath, William. *Memoirs of Major-General William Heath.* Edited by William Abbatt. New York: William Abbatt, 1901.

Heidler, David S., and Jeanne T. Heidler, eds. *Daily Lives of Civilians in Wartime Early America.* Westport, Conn.: Greenwood, 2007.

Heitman, Francis B. *Historical Register of Officers of the Continental Army During the War of the Revolution.* Baltimore: Genealogical Publishing, 2003.

Heller, Charles E., and William A. Stofft, eds. *America's First Battles, 1776–1965.* Lawrence: University Press of Kansas, 1986.

Hemmeon, J. C. *The History of the British Post Office.* Cambridge, Mass.: Harvard University, 1912.

Heusser, Albert H. *George Washington's Map Maker: A Biography of Robert Erskine.* Edited by Hubert G. Schmidt. New Brunswick, N.J.: Rutgers University Press, 1966.

Hibbert, Christopher. *George III: A Personal History.* New York: Basic Books, 1998.

———. *Redcoats and Rebels.* New York: W. W. Norton, 2002.

Higginbotham, Don. *Daniel Morgan, Revolutionary Rifleman.* Chapel Hill: University of North Carolina Press, 1961.

———. *The War of American Independence: Military Attitudes, Policies, and Practice, 1763–1789.* Boston: Northeastern University Press, 1983.

Hildreth, S. P. *Biographical and Historical Memoirs of the Early Pioneer Settlers of Ohio.* Cincinnati: H. W. Derby, 1852.

Hinderaker, Eric. *Boston's Massacre.* Cambridge, Mass.: Belknap Press, 2017.

An Historical Description of the Tower of London and Its Curiosities. London: J. Newberry, 1753.

Historical Manuscripts Commission. *Report on the Manuscripts of Mrs. Stopford-Sackville, of Drayton House, Northamptonshire.* Vol. 2. London: H.M. Stationery Office, 1910.

History of the First Troop Philadelphia City Cavalry. Philadelphia: Hallowell, 1875.

History of the Town of Dorchester Heights. Boston: Ebenezer Clapp, Jr., 1859.

Hoffman, Ronald, and Peter J. Albert, eds. *Arms and Independence: The Military Character of the American Revolution.* Charlottesville: University Press of Virginia, 1984.

Hofstadter, Richard, ed. *Great Issues in American History.* Vol. 2, *From the Revolution to the Civil War, 1765–1865.* New York: Vintage, 1958.

Holbrook, Stewart H. *Ethan Allen.* Portland, Ore.: Binford & Mort, 1988.

Holland, Henry W. *William Dawes and His Ride with Paul Revere.* Boston: John Wilson and Son, 1878.

Holmes, Richard. *Redcoat: The British Soldier in the Age of the Horse and Musket.* New York: HarperCollins, 2002.

Holt, Edward. *The Public and Domestic Life of His Late Most Gracious Majesty, George the Third.* Vol. 1. London: Sherwood, Neely, and Jones, 1820.

Hoock, Holger. *Scars of Independence: America's Violent Birth.* New York: Crown, 2017.

Horry, P., and M. L. Weems. *The Life of General Francis Marion.* Philadelphia: J. B. Lippincott, 1884.

Houlding, J. A. *Fit for Service: The Training of the British Army, 1715–1795.* Oxford: Clarendon Press, 1981.

Howe, M. A. DeWolfe. *Boston Common: Scenes from Four Centuries.* Boston: Houghton Mifflin, 1921.

Hudson, Alfred Sereno. *The History of Sudbury, Massachusetts.* Sudbury, Mass.: Town of Sudbury, 1889.

Hudson, Charles. *History of the Town of Lexington.* Vol. 1. Boston: Houghton Mifflin, 1913.

Hufeland, Otto. *Westchester County During the American Revolution, 1775–1783.* White Plains, N.Y.: Westchester County Historical Society, 1926.

Hughes, B. P. *Firepower: Weapons Effectiveness on the Battlefield, 1630–1850.* New York: Sarpedon, 1997.

Hughes, Hugh. *Memorial and Documents in the Case of Colonel Hugh Hughes.* Washington, D.C.: s.p., 1802.

Huish, Robert. *Public and Private Life of His Late Excellent and Most Gracious Majesty, George the Third.* London: Thomas Kelly, 1821.

Hulton, Ann. *Letters of a Loyalist Lady.* Cambridge, Mass: Harvard University Press, 1927.

Hume, Ivor Noël. *1775: Another Part of the Field.* London: Eyre & Spottiswoode, 1966.

Humphreys, David. *The Life and Heroic Exploits of Israel Putnam.* New York: Ezra Strong, 1834.

Humphreys, Frank Landon. *Life and Times of David Humphreys.* Vol. 1. New York: G. P. Putnam's Sons, 1917.

Hunnewell, James F. *A Century of Town Life: A History of Charlestown, Massachusetts, 1775–1887.* Boston: Little, Brown, 1888.

Hunt, Gaillard. *Fragments of Revolutionary History.* Brooklyn: Historical Printing Club, 1892.

Hunter, Martin. *The Journal of Gen. Sir Martin Hunter, G.C.M.G., G.C.H.* Edinburgh: Edinburgh Press, 1894.

Huntington, Ebenezer. *Letters Written by Ebenezer Huntington During the American Revolution.* New York: Charles Frederick Heartman, 1914.

Hussey, Andrew. *Paris: The Secret History.* New York: Bloomsbury, 2007.

Huston, James A. *The Logistics of Liberty.* Newark: University of Delaware Press, 1991.

———. *The Sinews of War: Army Logistics, 1775–1953.* Washington, D.C.: U.S. Army, 1988.

Hynes, Samuel. *The Soldiers' Tale: Bearing Witness to Modern War.* New York: Penguin, 1998.

Ingrao, Charles W. *The Hessian Mercenary State: Ideas, Institutions, and Reform Under Frederick II, 1760–1785.* Cambridge: Cambridge University Press, 1987.

Irving, Washington. *Life of George Washington.* Vols. 1 and 2. New York: G. P. Putnam, 1856, 1860.

Isaacson, Walter. *Benjamin Franklin: An American Life.* New York: Simon & Schuster, 2003.

Jackson, John W. *The Pennsylvania Navy, 1775–1781: The Defense of the Delaware.* New Brunswick, N.J.: Rutgers University Press, 1974.

Jacob, John J. *A Biographical Sketch of the Life of the Late Captain Michael Cresap.* Cincinnati: Jonathan F. Uhlhorn, 1866.

Jacob, Mark, and Stephen H. Case. *Treacherous Beauty.* Guilford, Conn.: Lyons Press, 2012.

Jaffe, Steven H. *New York at War.* New York: Basic Books, 2012.

James, Coy Hilton. *Silas Deane, Patriot or Traitor?* East Lansing: Michigan State University Press, 1975.

James, Lawrence. *The Rise and Fall of the British Empire.* New York: St. Martin's Griffin, 1995.

James, W. M. *The British Navy in Adversity: A Study of the War of American Independence.* London: Longmans, Green, 1926.

Jameson, J. Franklin. *The American Revolution Considered as a Social Movement.* Princeton, N.J.: Princeton University Press, 1969.

Jasanoff, Maya. *Liberty's Exiles: The Loss of America and the Remaking of the British Empire.* London: HarperPress, 2011.

Jefferies, Henry Alan. *Cork: Historical Perspectives.* Dublin: Four Courts Press, 2004.

Jellison, Charles A. *Ethan Allen: Frontier Rebel.* Syracuse, N.Y.: Syracuse University Press, 1969.

Jensen, Merrill. *The Founding of a Nation: A History of the American Revolution, 1763–1776.* New York: Oxford University Press, 1968.

Jesse, J. Heneage. *Memoirs of Celebrated Etonians.* Vol. 2. London: Richard Bentley and Son, 1875.

———. *Memoirs of the Life and Reign of King George the Third.* 5 vols. Boston: L. C. Page, 1902.

Johnston, Henry P. *The Battle of Harlem Heights, September 16, 1776.* New York: Macmillan, 1897.

———. *The Campaign of 1776 Around New York and Brooklyn.* Brooklyn: Long Island Historical Society, 1978.

Johnston, Henry Phelps. *Nathan Hale, 1776: Biography and Memorials.* New York: s.p., 1901.

Jones, Alvin Lincoln. *Under Colonial Roofs.* Boston: C. B. Webster, 1894.

Jones, Charles Colcock, Jr. *Sergeant William Jasper.* Savannah: Georgia Historical Society, 1876.

Jones, Charles Henry. *History of the Campaign for the Conquest of Canada in 1776.* Philadelphia: Porter & Coates, 1882.

Jones, John. *Plain Concise Practical Remarks on the Treatment of Wounds and Fractures.* Philadelphia: Robert Bell, 1776.

Jones, Thomas. *History of New York During the Revolutionary War.* 2 vols. Edited by Edward Floyd de Lancey. New York: New-York Historical Society, 1879.

Jordan, John Woolf. *The Military Hospitals at Bethlehem and Lititz, Pennsylvania, During the Revolutionary War.* Wilkes-Barre, Pa.: Wyoming Historical and Geological Society, 1896.

"Journals of Henry Duncan, Captain, Royal Navy, 1776–1782." In *The Naval Miscellany,* edited by John Knox Laughton, vol. 1, Publications of the Navy Records Society, vol. 20. [London]: Navy Records Society, 1902, pp. 111+.

Journals of the American Congress. Vol. 1. Washington, D.C.: Way and Gideon, 1823.

The Journals of Each Provincial Congress of Massachusetts in 1774 and 1775. Boston: Dutton and Wentworth, 1838.

Judd, Jacob. *Fort Lee on the Palisades: The Battle for the Hudson.* Tarrytown, N.Y.: Sleepy Hollow Restorations, 1964.

Kallich, Martin, and Andrew MacLeish, eds. *The American Revolution Through British Eyes.* New York: Harper & Row, 1962.

Kaminski, John P., ed. *The Founders on the Founders.* Charlottesville: University of Virginia Press, 2008.

Kapp, Friedrich. *The Life of John Kalb, Major-General in the Revolutionary Army.* New York: Henry Holt, 1884.

Karels, Carol, ed. *The Revolutionary War in Bergen County.* Charleston, S.C.: History Press, 2007.

Keane, John. *Tom Paine: A Political Life.* New York: Grove Press, 1995.

Keegan, John. *The Price of Admiralty.* New York: Penguin, 1990.

Kemble, Stephen. *The Kemble Papers: Journals of Lieut.-Col. Stephen Kemble, 1773–1789.* Vol. 1. New York: New-York Historical Society, 1883.

Kennedy, Paul M. *The Rise and Fall of British Naval Mastery.* London: Ashfield Press, 1990.

Kerr, Wilfred Brenton. *Bermuda and the American Revolution, 1760–1783.* Archon Books, 1969.

Ketchum, Richard M. *Decisive Day: The Battle for Bunker Hill.* New York: Henry Holt, 1999.

———. *Divided Loyalties.* New York: Henry Holt, 2002.

———. *Saratoga: Turning Point of America's Revolutionary War.* New York: Owl Books, 1999.

———. *The Winter Soldiers: The Battles for Trenton and Princeton.* Garden City, N.Y.: Doubleday, 1973.

Kidd, Thomas S. *God of Liberty: A Religious History of the American Revolution.* New York: Basic Books, 2010.

Kidder, Larry. *Crossroads of the Revolution: Trenton, 1774–1783.* Lawrence Township, N.J.: Knox Press, 2017.

———. *A People Harassed and Exhausted.* S.p., 2013.

Kirkland, Frederic R. *Journal of Lewis Beebe.* Philadelphia: Historical Society of Pennsylvania, 1935.

Kite, Elizabeth S. *Beaumarchais and the War of American Independence.* 2 vols. Boston: Gorham Press, 1918.

Knight, R.J.B. *Portsmouth Dockyard Papers, 1774–1783: The American War.* Portsmouth, U.K.: City of Portsmouth, 1987.

Konwiser, Harry M. *Colonial and Revolutionary Posts: A History of the American Postal Systems.* Richmond, Va.: Dietz Printing, 1931.

Kranish, Michael. *Flight from Monticello: Thomas Jefferson at War.* New York: Oxford University Press, 2010.

Krebs, Daniel. *A Generous and Merciful Enemy: Life for German Prisoners of War During the American Revolution.* Norman: University of Oklahoma Press, 2013.

Kurlansky, Mark. *Salt: A World History.* New York: Penguin, 2003.

Kurtz, Stephen G., and James H. Hutson, eds. *Essays on the American Revolution*. Chapel Hill: University of North Carolina Press, 1973.

Kwasny, Mark V. *Washington's Partisan War, 1775–1783*. Kent, Ohio: Kent State University Press, 1996.

Labaree, Benjamin Woods. *The Boston Tea Party*. Boston: Northeastern University Press, 1979.

Lamb, Martha J., and Mrs. Burton Harrison. *History of the City of New York: Its Origin, Rise, and Progress*. 3 vols. New York: A. S. Barnes, 1877–96.

Lanctôt, Gustave. *Canada and the American Revolution, 1774–1783*. Trans. Margaret M. Cameron. Cambridge, Mass.: Harvard University Press, 1967.

Laprade, William Thomas, ed. *Parliamentary Papers of John Robinson, 1774–1784*. London: Royal Historical Society, 1922.

Laughton, John Knox, ed. *Journal of Rear-Admiral Batholomew James, 1752–1828*. London: Navy Records Society, 1896.

Leake, Isaac Q. *Memoir of the Life and Times of General John Lamb*. Albany, N.Y.: Joel Munsell, 1850.

Leamon, James S. *Revolution Downeast: The War for American Independence in Maine*. Amherst: University of Massachusetts Press, 1993.

Lee, Charles. *The Lee Papers*. 4 vols. New York: New-York Historical Society, 1872–75.

Lefkowitz, Arthur S. *Benedict Arnold's Army: The 1775 American Invasion of Canada During the Revolutionary War*. New York: Savas Beatie, 2008.

———. *The Long Retreat: The Calamitous Defense of New Jersey, 1776*. New Brunswick, N.J.: Rutgers University Press, 1999.

Leggett, Abraham. *The Narrative of Major Abraham Leggett*. New York: s.p., 1865.

Leiby, Adrian C. *The Revolutionary War in the Hackensack Valley*. New Brunswick, N.J.: Rutgers University Press, 1962.

Lemaitre, Georges. *Beaumarchais*. New York: Knopf, 1949.

LeMoine, J. M. *The Sword of Brigadier-General Richard Montgomery*. Quebec: Middleton & Dawson, 1870.

Lengel, Edward G., ed. *A Companion to George Washington*. Chichester, U.K.: Wiley-Blackwell, 2012.

———. *First Entrepreneur: How George Washington Built His—and the Nation's—Prosperity*. Boston: Da Capo, 2016.

———. *General George Washington: A Military Life*. New York: Random House, 2005.

———. *Inventing George Washington*. New York: Harper, 2011.

Leonard, Lewis A. *Life of Charles Carroll of Carrollton*. New York: Moffat, Yard, 1918.

Lepore, Jill. *Book of Ages: The Life and Opinions of Jane Franklin*. New York: Knopf, 2013.

———. *New York Burning*. New York: Vintage, 2006.

Lesser, Charles H., ed. *The Sinews of Independence: Strength Reports of the Continental Army*. Chicago: University of Chicago Press, 1976.

Letters & Papers of John Singleton Copley and Henry Pelham. Boston: Massachusetts Historical Society, 1914.

Levin, Phyllis Lee. *Abigail Adams: A Biography*. New York Thomas Dunne, 2001.

Lewis, Charles H. *Cut Off: Colonel Jedediah Huntington's 17th Continental (Conn.) Regiment at the Battle of Long Island, Aug. 27, 1776*. Westminster, Md.: Heritage Books, 2009.

Linebaugh, Peter, and Marcus Rediker. *The Many-Headed Hydra*. Boston: Beacon Press, 2000.

Lipscomb, Terry W. *The Carolina Lowcountry, April 1775–June 1776, and the Battle of Fort Moultrie*. Columbia: South Carolina Department of Archives and History, 1994.

Lister, Jeremy. *The Concord Fight: Being So Much of the Narrative of Ensign Jeremy Lister of the 10th Regiment of Foot*. Cambridge, Mass.: Harvard University Press, 1931.

Lockhart, Paul. *The Whites of Their Eyes*. New York: Harper, 2011.

Loménie, Louis de. *Beaumarchais and His Times*. Translated by Henry S. Edwards. New York: Harper & Brothers, 1857.

Longmore, Paul K. *The Invention of George Washington*. Charlottesville: University Press of Virginia, 1999.

Longmore, T. *Gunshot Injuries.* London: Longmans, Green, 1895.

———. *A Treatise on Gunshot Wounds.* Philadelphia: J. B. Lippincott, 1862.

Lopez, Claude-Anne. *My Life with Benjamin Franklin.* New Haven, Conn.: Yale University Press, 2000.

Lorenz, Lincoln. *John Paul Jones: Fighter for Freedom and Glory.* Annapolis, Md.: United States Naval Institute, 1943.

Lorimier, Claude de. *At War with the Americans: The Journal of Claude-Nicolas-Guillaume de Lorimier.* Translated by Peter Aichinger. Victoria, B.C.: Press Porcepic, 1981.

Lossing, Benson J. *The Life and Times of Philip Schuyler.* 2 vols. New York: Sheldon, 1860, 1873.

———. *The Pictorial Field-Book of the Revolution.* Vol. 2. New York: Harper & Brothers, 1852.

Lowell, Edward J. *The Hessians.* New York: Harper & Brothers, 1884.

Lucas, Reginald. *Lord North, Second Earl of Guilford, K.G., 1732–1792.* 2 vols. London: Arthur L. Humphreys, 1913.

Luke, Myron H., and Robert W. Venables. *Long Island in the American Revolution.* Albany: New York State American Revolution Bicentennial Commission, 1976.

Lundin, Leonard. *Cockpit of the Revolution: The War for Independence in New Jersey.* Princeton, N.J.: Princeton University Press, 1940.

Lushington, S. R. *The Life and Services of General Lord Harris, G.C.B.* London: John W. Parker, 1840.

Lutnick, Solomon. *The American Revolution and the British Press, 1775–1783.* Columbia: University of Missouri Press, 1976.

Lynn, Mary C., ed. *An Eyewitness Account of the American Revolution and New England Life: The Journal of J. F. Wasmus, German Company Surgeon, 1776–1783.* Translated by Helga Doblin. Westport, Conn.: Greenwood, 1990.

Mackenzie, Frederick. *A British Fusilier in Revolutionary Boston.* Edited by Allen French. Cambridge, Mass.: Harvard University Press, 1926.

———. *Diary of Frederick Mackenzie.* Vol. 1. Cambridge, Mass.: Harvard University Press, 1930.

Mackesy, Piers. *The Coward of Minden.* New York: St. Martin's Press, 1979.

———. *The War for America, 1775–1783.* Lincoln: University of Nebraska Press, 1993.

MacLean, J. P. *Flora MacDonald in America.* Lumberton, N.C.: A. W. McLean, 1909.

Mahan, Alfred Thayer. *The Major Operations of Navies in the War of American Independence.* Hamburg, Ger.: Tredition, 2006.

Maier, Pauline. *American Scripture: Making the Declaration of Independence.* New York: Vintage, 1998.

Manders, Eric I. *The Battle of Long Island.* Monmouth Beach, N.J.: Philip Freneau Press, 1978.

Manning, Stephen. *Quebec: The Story of Three Sieges.* Montreal: McGill–Queen's University Press, 2009.

Mansfield, Harvey C., Jr., ed. *Selected Letters of Edmund Burke.* Chicago: University of Chicago Press, 1984.

Manuscripts of the Earl of Dartmouth. Vols. 1–3. Historical Manuscripts Commission. London: H.M. Stationery Office, 1887.

Manuscripts Relating to the Early History of Canada. Quebec: Dawson, 1875.

Marcus, Geoffrey. *Quiberon Bay.* Barre, Mass.: Barre Publishing, 1963.

Marlow, Louis. *Sackville of Drayton.* Totowa, N.J.: Rowman & Littlefield, 1973.

Martin, James Kirby. *Benedict Arnold, Revolutionary Hero.* New York: New York University Press, 2000.

Martin, James Kirby, and Mark Edward Lender. *A Respectable Army: The Military Origins of the Republic, 1763–1789.* Wheeling, Ill.: Harlan Davidson, 1982.

Martin, James Kirby, and David L. Preston, eds. *Theaters of the American Revolution.* Yardley, Pa.: Westholme, 2017.

Martin, Joseph Plumb. *A Narrative of a Revolutionary Soldier.* New York: Signet Classics, 2010.

Martyn, Charles. *The Life of Artemas Ward.* New York: Artemas Ward, 1921.

Masefield, John. *Sea Life in Nelson's Time.* 1905. Reprint, Annapolis, Md.: Naval Institute Press, 2002.

Mauduit, Israel. *Observations upon the Conduct of Sir William Howe at the White Plains*. Tarrytown, N.Y.: William Abbatt, 1927.

May, Henry F. *The Enlightenment in America*. New York: Oxford University Press, 1976.

Mayer, Brantz. *The Journal of Charles Carroll of Carrollton*. Baltimore: Maryland Historical Society, 1876.

Mazzagetti, Dominick. *Charles Lee: Self Before Country*. New Brunswick, N.J.: Rutgers University Press, 2013.

McBurney, Christian M. *Kidnapping the Enemy: The Special Operations to Capture Generals Charles Lee and Richard Prescott*. Yardley, Pa.: Westholme, 2014.

McConville, Brendan. *The King's Three Faces*. Chapel Hill: University of North Carolina Press, 2006.

McCrady, Edward. *The History of South Carolina in the Revolution, 1775–1780*. New York: Macmillan, 1901.

McCullough, David. *John Adams*. New York: Simon & Schuster, 2001.

———. *1776*. New York: Simon & Schuster, 2005.

McCusker, John J., and Russell R. Menard. *The Economy of British America, 1607–1789*. Chapel Hill: University of North Carolina Press, 1991.

McDonald, John M. *The McDonald Papers*. Part 1. Edited by William S. Hadaway. White Plains, N.Y.: Westchester County Historical Society, 1926.

McDonnell, Michael. *The Politics of War: Race, Class and Conflict in Revolutionary Virginia*. Chapel Hill: University of North Carolina Press, 2007.

McDougall, Walter A. *Freedom Just Around the Corner*. New York: HarperCollins, 2004.

McGrath, Tim. *Give Me a Fast Ship: The Continental Navy and America's Revolution at Sea*. New York: NAL Caliber, 2014.

McNeill, J. R., *Mosquito Empires: Ecology and War in the Greater Caribbean, 1620–1914*. New York: Cambridge University Press, 2010.

Meacham, Jon. *Thomas Jefferson: The Art of Power*. New York: Random House, 2012.

Melvin, James. *The Journal of the Expedition to Quebec*. Philadelphia: Franklin Club, 1864.

Memoir of Lieut. Col. Tench Tilghman. Edited by S. A. Harrison. Albany, N.Y.: J. Munsell, 1876.

Middlekauff, Robert. *The Glorious Cause: The American Revolution, 1763–1789*. New York: Oxford University Press, 2005.

———. *Washington's Revolution*. New York: Vintage, 2016.

Miller, John C. *Triumph of Freedom, 1775–1783*. Boston: Little, Brown, 1948.

Miller, Nathan. *Sea of Glory: A Naval History of the American Revolution*. Charleston, S.C.: Nautical & Aviation Publishing, 1974.

Miller, Samuel. *The Life of Samuel Miller, D.D., LL.D*. Philadelphia: Claxton, Remsen and Haffelfinger, 1869.

Mintz, Max M. *The Generals of Saratoga: John Burgoyne and Horatio Gates*. New Haven, Conn.: Yale University Press, 1990.

Montross, Lynn. *Rag, Tag and Bobtail: The Story of the Continental Army, 1775–1783*. New York: Harper & Brothers, 1952.

Moore, Frank. *The Diary of the American Revolution, 1775–1781*. Edited by John Anthony Scott. New York: Washington Square Press, 1968.

Moore, George H. *The Treason of Charles Lee*. New York: Charles Scribner, 1860.

Moore, Howard Parker. *A Life of General John Stark of New Hampshire*. Boston: Spaulding-Moss, 1949.

Morgan, Edmund S. *Benjamin Franklin*. New Haven, Conn.: Yale University Press, 2002.

———. *The Birth of the Republic, 1763–89*. Chicago: University of Chicago Press, 2013.

Morison, Samuel Eliot. *John Paul Jones: A Sailor's Biography*. New York: Time, 1964.

———. *The Oxford History of the American People*. New York: Oxford University Press, 1965.

Morison, Samuel Eliot, and Henry Steele Commager. *The Growth of the American Republic*. Vol. 1. New York: Oxford University Press, 1965.

Morris, Ira K. *Morris's Memorial History of Staten Island, New York*. Vol. 1. New York: Memorial Publishing, 1898.

Morris, Margaret. *Private Journal Kept During a Portion of the Revolutionary War.* Philadelphia: s.p., 1836.

Morris, Richard B. *The American Revolution Reconsidered.* New York: Harper Torchbooks, 1968.

Morrissey, Brendan. *Quebec 1775: The American Invasion of Canada.* Botley, U.K.: Osprey, 2003.

Morse, Jedidiah, and Elijah Parish. *A Compendious History of New-England.* Charlestown, Mass.: S. Etheridge, 1820.

Moultrie, William. *Memoirs of the American Revolution.* Vol. 1. New York: s.p., 1802.

Muller, John. *The Attac and Defence of Fortified Places.* London: J. Millan, 1757.

Mullin, Gerald W. *Flight and Rebellion: Slave Resistance in Eighteenth Century Virginia.* New York: Oxford University Press, 1974.

Münchhausen, Friedrich Ernst von. *At General Howe's Side, 1776–1778.* Translated by Ernst Kipping and Samuel Stelle Smith. Monmouth Beach, N.J.: Philip Freneau Press, 1974.

Murdoch, David H., ed. *Rebellion in America: A Contemporary British Viewpoint, 1765–1783.* Santa Barbara, Calif.: Clio Books, 1979.

Murdock, Harold. *Bunker Hill: Notes and Queries on a Famous Battle.* Boston: Houghton Mifflin, 1927.

———. *Earl Percy's Dinner Table.* Cambridge, Mass.: Houghton Mifflin, 1907.

———. *The Nineteenth of April 1775.* Boston: Houghton Mifflin, 1923.

Murphy, Orville T. *Charles Gravier, Comte de Vergennes: French Diplomacy in the Age of Revolution, 1719–1787.* Albany: State University of New York Press, 1982.

Murray, James. *Letters from America, 1773–1780.* Edited by Eric Robson. New York: Barnes and Noble, 1950.

Murray, John, ed. *The Autobiographies of Edward Gibbon.* London: John Murray, 1897.

Nagy, John A. *Dr. Benjamin Church: Spy.* Yardley, Pa.: Westholme, 2013.

———. *Invisible Ink: Spycraft of the American Revolution.* Yardley, Pa.: Westholme, 2011.

Namier, Lewis. *England in the Age of the American Revolution.* London: Macmillan, 1974.

Namier, Lewis, and John Brooke. *The House of Commons, 1754–1790.* Vol. 1. London: H.M. Stationery Office, 1964.

The Narrative of Lieut. Gen. Sir William Howe. London: H. Baldwin, 1781.

Narratives of the Revolution in New York. New York: New-York Historical Society, 1975.

Nash, Gary B. *The Unknown American Revolution.* New York: Viking, 2005.

Neeser, Robert Wilden, ed. *The Despatches of Molyneux Shuldham, Vice-Admiral of the Blue.* New York: Naval Historical Society, 1913.

Neimeyer, Charles Patrick. *America Goes to War: A Social History of the Continental Army.* New York: New York University Press, 1996.

Nelson, Craig. *Thomas Paine: Enlightenment, Revolution, and the Birth of Modern Nations.* New York: Viking, 2006.

Nelson, James L. *Benedict Arnold's Navy.* Camden, Me.: McGraw-Hill, 2006.

———. *George Washington's Secret Navy: How the American Revolution Went to Sea.* New York: McGraw-Hill, 2008.

Nelson, Paul David. *General Horatio Gates.* Baton Rouge: Louisiana State University Press, 1976.

———. *General James Grant: Scottish Soldier and Royal Governor of East Florida.* Gainesville: University Press of Florida, 1993.

———. *General Sir Guy Carleton, Lord Dorchester.* Madison, N.J.: Fairleigh Dickinson University Press, 2000.

———. *William Alexander, Lord Stirling.* University: University of Alabama Press, 1987.

Nelson, William H. *The American Tory.* Boston: Beacon Press, 1968.

Nevins, Allan. *The American States During and After the American Revolution, 1775–1789.* New York: Macmillan, 1924.

New England Historical and Genealogical Register. Vol. 5. Boston: Samuel G. Drake, 1851.

New York City During the American Revolution. New York: Mercantile Library Association, 1861.

Nicolas, Paul Harris. *Historical Record of the Royal Marine Forces.* London: Thomas and William Boon, 1845.

Obenzinger, Hilton. *New York on Fire.* Seattle: Real Comet Press, 1989.

Oberholtzer, Ellis Paxson. *Robert Morris: Patriot and Financier.* New York: Macmillan, 1903.

Onderdonk, Henry, Jr. *Documents and Letters Intended to Illustrate the Revolutionary Incidents of Queens County.* New York: Leavitt, Trow, 1846.

———. *Revolutionary Incidents of Suffolk and Kings Counties.* New York: Leavitt, 1849.

Orderly Book of Capt. Ichabod Norton. Fort Edward, N.Y.: Keating & Barnard, 1898.

O'Shaughnessy, Andrew Jackson. *The Men Who Lost America.* New Haven, Conn.: Yale University Press, 2013.

Osler, Edward. *The Life of Admiral Viscount Exmouth.* London: Smith, Elder, 1835.

Padelford, Philip, ed. *Colonial Panorama, 1775: Dr. Robert Honyman's Journal.* San Marino, Calif.: Huntington Library, 1939.

Paine, Thomas. *"Common Sense," "The Rights of Man," and Other Essential Writings.* New York: Meridian, 1984.

Palmer, Dave R. *George Washington and Benedict Arnold.* Washington, D.C.: Regnery, 2006.

———. *George Washington's Military Genius.* Washington, D.C.: Regnery, 2012.

Palmer, Peter S. *History of Lake Champlain, from Its First Exploration by the French in 1609, to the Close of the Year 1814.* Albany, N.Y.: J. Munsell, 1866.

Palmer, Peter Sailly. *Battle of Valcour on Lake Champlain, October 11, 1776.* Plattsburgh, N.Y.: Lake Shore Press, 1876.

Papas, Phillip. *Renegade Revolutionary: The Life of General Charles Lee.* New York: New York University Press, 2014.

Pares, Richard. *King George III and the Politicians.* London: Oxford University Press, 1953.

Parker, Bruce. *The Power of the Sea: Tsunamis, Storm Surges, Rogue Waves, and Our Quest to Predict Disasters.* New York: Palgrave Macmillan, 2010.

Parker, Theodore. *Genealogy and Biographical Notes of John Parker of Lexington and His Descendants.* Worcester, Mass.: Press of Charles Hamilton, 1893.

Parkman, Francis. *Montcalm and Wolfe.* Vol. 2. London: Macmillan, 1885.

The Parliamentary History of England. Vols. 17, 18, and 19. London: T. C. Hansard, 1813–14.

The Parliamentary Register, or History of the Proceedings and Debates of the House of Lords. Vol. 2. London: J. Almon, 1775.

Parnell, Geoffrey. *The Tower of London, Past and Present.* Stroud, U.K.: History Press, 2009.

Parton, James. *Life and Times of Benjamin Franklin.* 2 vols. Boston: Ticknor and Fields, 1867.

Patten, Matthew. *The Diary of Matthew Patten.* Concord, N.H.: Rumford Printing, 1903.

Patterson, Samuel White. *Knight Errant of Liberty: The Triumph and Tragedy of General Charles Lee.* New York: Lantern Press, 1958.

Patton, Robert H. *Patriot Pirates: The Privateer War for Freedom and Fortune in the American Revolution.* New York: Pantheon, 2008.

Paul, Joel Richard. *Unlikely Allies.* New York: Riverhead Books, 2009.

Peckham, Howard H., ed. *Memoirs of the Life of John Adlum in the Revolutionary War.* Chicago: Caxton Club, 1968.

———, ed. *Sources of American Independence.* Vol. 1. Chicago: University of Chicago Press, 1978.

———, ed. *The Toll of Independence.* Chicago: University of Chicago Press, 1974.

Perkins, Simeon. *The Diary of Simeon Perkins.* Toronto: Champlain Society, 1948.

Personal Recollections of Captain Enoch Anderson. Wilmington: Historical Society of Delaware, 1896.

Peters, Samuel. *General History of Connecticut.* New York: D. Appleton, 1877.

Pfister, Albert. *The Voyage of the First Hessian Army from Portsmouth to New York, 1776.* New York: Charles Fred Heartman, 1915.

Phelps, Richard H. *Newgate of Connecticut.* Hartford, Conn.: American Publishing, 1876.

Philbrick, Nathaniel. *Bunker Hill: A City, a Siege, a Revolution.* New York: Penguin, 2013.

———. *Valiant Ambition.* New York: Viking, 2016.

Phillips, Kevin. *1775: A Good Year for Revolution.* New York: Penguin, 2013.

Phinney, Elias. *History of the Battle at Lexington.* Boston: Phelps and Farnham, 1825.

Pickering, Octavius. *The Life of Timothy Pickering.* Vol. 1. Boston: Little, Brown, 1867.

Piecuch, Jim. *Three Peoples, One King: Loyalists, Indians, and Slaves in the Revolutionary South, 1775–1782*. Columbia: University of South Carolina Press, 2008.

Pierce, Edward L. *The Diary of John Rowe: A Boston Merchant, 1764–1779*. Cambridge, Mass.: John Wilson and Son, 1895.

Plumb, J. H. *England in the Eighteenth Century*. London: Penguin, 1950.

——. *The First Four Georges*. Glasgow: Fontana/Collins, 1976.

Pollard, Tony, and Iain Banks, eds. *Bastions and Barbed Wire*. Leiden, Neth.: Brill, 2008.

Popkin, Jeremy D., ed. *Louis-Sébastien Mercier, Panorama of Paris*. University Park: Pennsylvania State University Press, 2003.

Porter, Edward G. *Rambles in Old Boston*. Boston: Cupples and Hurd, 1887.

Porter, Roy. *English Society in the Eighteenth Century*. New York: Penguin, 1990.

Posey, John T. *General Thomas Posey: Son of the American Revolution*. East Lansing: Michigan State University Press, 1992.

Potts, James M. *French Covert Action in the American Revolution*. Lincoln, Neb.: iUniverse, 2005.

Powell, Robert C., ed. *A Biographical Sketch of Col. Leven Powell*. Alexandria, Va.: G. H. Ramey & Son, 1877.

Preston, David L. *Braddock's Defeat: The Battle of the Monongahela and the Road to the Revolution*. New York: Oxford University Press, 2015.

Price, Jacob M. *France and the Chesapeake: A History of the French Tobacco Monopoly, 1674–1791*. 2 vols. Ann Arbor: University of Michigan Press, 1973.

Price, Munro. *Preserving the Monarchy: The Comte de Vergennes, 1774–1787*. Cambridge: Cambridge University Press, 2004.

Priestley, Joseph. *Memoirs of the Rev. Dr. Joseph Priestley*. London: C. Stower, 1809.

Prior, James. *Memoir of the Life and Character of the Right Hon. Edmund Burke*. Vol. 1. London: Baldwin, Cradock, and Joy, 1826.

Proceedings of the Centennial Celebration of the Battle of Lexington. Boston: Lockwood, Brooks, 1875.

Puls, Mark. *Henry Knox: Visionary General of the American Revolution*. New York: Palgrave Macmillan, 2008.

——. *Samuel Adams: Father of the American Revolution*. New York: Palgrave Macmillan, 2009.

Purdy, John. *The Columbian Navigator*. Vol. 1. London: R. H. Laurie, 1839.

Quarles, Benjamin. *The Negro in the Making of America*. New York: Collier Books, 1968.

Quincy, Josiah. *The Journals of Major Samuel Shaw*. Boston: Wm. Crosby and H. P. Nichols, 1847.

——. *Memoir of the Life of Josiah Quincy Jun.* Boston: Cummings, Hilliard, 1825.

Rakove, Jack. *Revolutionaries*. Boston: Houghton Mifflin Harcourt, 2010.

Ralfe, James. *The Naval Biography of Great Britain . . . During the Reign of George III*. Vol. 1. 1828. Reprint, Boston: Gregg Press, 1972.

Ramsay, David. *The History of the American Revolution*. Vol. 2. Philadelphia: R. Aitken, 1789.

Randall, Willard Sterne. *Benedict Arnold: Patriot and Traitor*. New York: William Morrow, 1990.

——. *Ethan Allen: His Life and Times*. New York: W. W. Norton, 2011.

——. *A Little Revenge: Benjamin Franklin and His Son*. Boston: Little, Brown, 1984.

Ranlet, Philip. *The New York Loyalists*. Knoxville: University of Tennessee Press, 1986.

Raphael, Ray. *The First American Revolution*. New York: New Press, 2002.

——. *Founders*. New York: New Press, 2009.

——. *A People's History of the American Revolution*. New York: HarperPerennial, 2002.

Rappleye, Charles. *Robert Morris: Financier of the American Revolution*. New York: Simon & Schuster, 2010.

Reed, William B., ed. *Life and Correspondence of Joseph Reed*. Vol. 1. Philadelphia: Lindsay and Blakiston, 1847.

Reiss, Oscar. *Medicine and the American Revolution*. Jefferson, N.C.: McFarland, 1998.

Reynolds, Paul R. *Guy Carleton: A Biography*. New York: William Morrow, 1980.

Rhodehamel, John, ed. *The American Revolution: Writings from the War of Independence*. New York: Library of America, 2001.

Ripley, Ezra. *A History of the Fight at Concord, on the 19th of April, 1775.* Concord, Mass.: Allen & Atwill, 1827.

Risch, Erna. *Supplying Washington's Army.* Washington, D.C.: U.S. Army, 1986.

Ritcheson, Charles R. *British Politics and the American Revolution.* Norman: University of Oklahoma Press, 1954.

Robbins, Ammi R. *Journal of the Rev. Ammi R. Robbins, a Chaplain in the American Army, in the Northern Campaign of 1776.* New Haven, Conn.: B. L. Hamlen, 1850.

Roberts, Jane. *Royal Landscape: The Gardens and Parks of Windsor.* New Haven, Conn.: Yale University Press, 1997.

Roberts, Kenneth. *March to Quebec.* Garden City, N.Y.: Doubleday, 1947.

Roberts, Richard Arthur, ed. *Calendar of Home Office Papers of the Reign of George III, 1773–1775.* London: H.M. Stationery Office, 1899.

Robinson, Edward Forbes. *Continental Treasury Administration, 1775–1781: A Study in the Financial History of the American Revolution.* Madison: University of Wisconsin, 1969.

Robson, Eric. *The American Revolution, in Its Political and Military Aspects, 1763–1783.* New York: W. W. Norton, 1966.

Rodger, N.A.M. *The Command of the Ocean: A Naval History of Britain, 1649–1815.* London: Penguin, 2006.

———. *The Insatiable Earl: A Life of John Montagu, 4th Earl of Sandwich, 1718–1792.* London: HarperCollins, 1993.

———. *The Wooden World: An Anatomy of the Georgian Navy.* New York: W. W. Norton, 1996.

Rodney, Thomas. *Diary of Captain Thomas Rodney, 1776–1777.* Wilmington: Historical Society of Delaware, 1888.

Rogers, H.C.B. *The British Army of the Eighteenth Century.* Abingdon, U.K.: Routledge, 2015.

Rose, Alexander. *Men of War: The American Soldier in Combat at Bunker Hill, Gettysburg, and Iwo Jima.* New York: Random House, 2015.

———. *Washington's Spies: The Story of America's First Spy Ring.* New York: Bantam, 2007.

Ross, Charles, ed. *The Correspondence of Charles, First Marquis Cornwallis.* Vol. 1. London: John Murray, 1859.

Rossman, Kenneth R. *Thomas Mifflin and the Politics of the American Revolution.* Chapel Hill: University of North Carolina Press, 1952.

Rosswurm, Steven. *Arms, Country, and Class: The Philadelphia Militia and the "Lower Sort" During the American Revolution, 1775–1783.* New Brunswick, N.J.: Rutgers University Press, 1987.

Rowland, Kate Mason. *The Life of Charles Carroll of Carrollton.* Vol. 1. New York: G. P. Putnam, 1898.

Royster, Charles. *A Revolutionary People at War: The Continental Army and American Character, 1775–1783.* Chapel Hill: University of North Carolina Press, 1979.

Rutt, John Towill. *The Life and Correspondence of Joseph Priestley.* Vol. 1. London: R. Hunter, 1831.

Ruttenber, E. M. *Obstructions to the Navigation of Hudson's River.* Albany, N.Y.: J. Munsell, 1860.

Ryan, Dennis P., ed. *A Salute to Courage: The American Revolution as Seen Through Wartime Writings of Officers of the Continental Army and Navy.* New York: Columbia University Press, 1979.

Ryan, William R. *The World of Thomas Jeremiah: Charles Town on the Eve of the American Revolution.* New York: Oxford University Press, 2012.

Ryden, George Herbert, ed. *Letters to and from Caesar Rodney, 1765–1784.* Philadelphia: University of Pennsylvania Press, 1933.

Ryerson, Egerton. *The Loyalists of America and Their Times: From 1620 to 1816.* 2 vols. Toronto: William Briggs, James Campbell & Son, and Willing & Williamson, 1880.

Sabin, Douglas P. *April 19, 1775: A Historiographical Study.* N.p.: Sinclair Street Publishing, 2011.

Sabine, Lorenzo. *The American Loyalists.* Boston: Charles C. Little and James Brown, 1947.

Sabine, W.H.W., ed. *The New-York Diary of Lieutenant Jabez Fitch.* New York: New York Public Library, 1954.

Salsig, Doyen, ed. *Parole: Quebec; Countersign: Ticonderoga.* Cranbury, N.J.: Associated University Presses, 1980.

Sanderson, Eric W. *Mannahatta: A Natural History of New York City*. New York: Abrams, 2009.

Sanderson, Howard Kendall, ed. *Lynn in the Revolution*. Part 1. Boston: W. B. Clarke, 1909.

Sargent, Winthrop, ed. *Letters of John Andrews, Esq., of Boston, 1772–1776*. Cambridge, Mass.: John Wilson and Sons, 1866.

Schaeper, Thomas J. *Edward Bancroft: Scientist, Author, Spy*. New Haven, Conn.: Yale University Press, 2011.

Schama, Simon. *Rough Crossings: Britain, the Slaves and the American Revolution*. New York: HarperCollins, 2007.

Scharf, J. Thomas. *History of Maryland*. Vol. 2. Baltimore: John B. Piet, 1879.

Schecter, Barnet. *The Battle for New York: The City at the Heart of the American Revolution*. London: Pimlico, 2003.

Scheer, George F., and Hugh F. Rankin. *Rebels and Redcoats*. Cleveland: World, 1957.

Schiff, Stacy. *A Great Improvisation: Franklin, France, and the Birth of America*. New York: Henry Holt, 2006.

Schimizzi, Ernest, and Gregory Schimizzi. *The Staten Island Peace Conference, September 11, 1776*. Albany: New York State American Revolution Bicentennial Commission, 1976.

Schlesinger, Arthur M. *The Colonial Merchants and the American Revolution, 1763–1776*. New York: Columbia University, 1918.

Schoenbrun, David. *Triumph in Paris: The Exploits of Benjamin Franklin*. New York: Harper & Row, 1976.

Schofield, Robert E. *The Enlightened Joseph Priestley*. University Park: Pennsylvania State University Press, 2004.

Schuckers, J. W. *A Brief Account of the Finances and Paper Money of the Revolutionary War*. Philadelphia: John Campbell & Son, 1874.

Schwab, John Christopher. *The Revolutionary History of Fort Number Eight*. New Haven, Conn.: s.p., 1897.

Schwartz, Richard B. *Daily Life in Johnson's London*. Madison: University of Wisconsin Press, 1983.

Scott, H. M. *British Foreign Policy in the Age of the American Revolution*. Oxford: Clarendon Press, 1990.

Scott, Kenneth. *Counterfeiting in Colonial America*. Philadelphia: University of Pennsylvania Press, 2000.

Scribner, Robert L., and Brent Tarter, eds. *Revolutionary Virginia: The Road to Independence*. Vol. 5, *The Clash of Arms and the Fourth Convention, 1775–1776*. Charlottesville: University Press of Virginia, 1979.

——, eds. *Revolutionary Virginia: The Road to Independence*. Vol. 6, *The Time for Decision: 1776*. Charlottesville: University Press of Virginia, 1981.

Scull, G. D., ed. *Memoir and Letters of Captain W. Glanville Evelyn, of the 4th Regiment ("King's Own")*. Oxford: James Parker, 1879.

Sedgwick, Theodore. *A Memoir of the Life of William Livingston*. New York: J. & J. Harper, 1833.

Selby, John E. *The Revolution in Virginia, 1775–1783*. Williamsburg, Va.: Colonial Williamsburg Foundation, 2007.

Senter, Isaac. *The Journal of Isaac Senter*. Tarrytown, N.Y.: William Abbatt, 1915.

Seymour, George Dudley. *Documentary Life of Nathan Hale*. New Haven, Conn.: s.p., 1941.

Seymour, Joseph. *The Pennsylvania Associators, 1747–1777*. Yardley, Pa.: Westholme, 2012.

Shattuck, Lemuel. *A History of the Town of Concord*. Boston: Russell, Odiorne, 1835.

Shaw, G. C. *Supply in Modern War*. London: Faber & Faber, 1938.

Shelton, Hal T. *General Richard Montgomery and the American Revolution: From Redcoat to Rebel*. New York: New York University Press, 1994.

Shelton, William Henry. *The Jumel Mansion*. Boston: Houghton Mifflin, 1916.

Sheppard, Edgar. *Memorials of St. James's Palace*. 2 vols. London: Longmans, Green, 1894.

Shields, Joseph W., Jr. *From Flintlock to M1*. New York: Coward-McCann, 1954.

Shonnard, Frederick, and W. W. Spooner. *History of Westchester County*. New York: New York History Co., 1900.

Showman, Richard K., et al. *The Papers of General Nathanael Greene.* 13 vols. Chapel Hill: University of North Carolina Press, 1976–2005.

Shreve, L. G. *Tench Tilghman: The Life and Times of Washington's Aide-de-Camp.* Centreville, Md.: Tidewater, 1982.

Shurtleff, Nathaniel. *A Topographical and Historical Description of Boston.* Boston: City Council 1871.

Shy, John. *A People Numerous and Armed: Reflections on the Military Struggle for American Independence.* Ann Arbor: University of Michigan Press, 2010.

———. *Toward Lexington: The Role of the British Army.* Princeton, N.J.: Princeton University Press, 1965.

Silverman, Kenneth. *A Cultural History of the American Revolution.* New York: Columbia University Press, 1987.

Simpson, Helen, ed. *The Waiting City: Paris, 1782–88.* Philadelphia: J. B. Lippincott, 1933.

Skemp, Sheila L. *William Franklin: Son of a Patriot, Servant of a King.* New York: Oxford University Press, 1990.

Smith, Adam. *An Inquiry into the Nature and Causes of the Wealth of Nations.* 2 vols. London: George Bell & Sons, 1896.

Smith, Charles Daniel. *The Early Career of Lord North the Prime Minister.* London: Athlone Press, 1979.

Smith, Charles R. *Marine in the Revolution.* Washington, D.C.: U.S. Marine Corps, 1975.

Smith, Digby, and Kevin F. Kiley. *An Illustrated History of Uniforms from 1775–1783.* London: Lorenz, 2008.

Smith, E. Vale. *History of Newburyport.* Newburyport, Mass.: s.p., 1854.

Smith, Edmund Banks. *Governors Island: Its Military History Under Three Flags, 1637–1913.* New York: s.p., 1913.

Smith, Emma Adelia Flint. *Historical Sketch of Washington's Headquarters.* New York: Washington Headquarters Association, 1927.

Smith, Frank. *A History of Dover, Massachusetts, as a Precinct, Parish, District, and Town.* Dover, Mass.: Town of Dover, 1897.

Smith, Jean Edward. *John Marshall: Definer of a Nation.* New York: Henry Holt, 1996.

Smith, Justin H. *Arnold's March from Cambridge to Quebec.* New York: G. P. Putnam's Sons, 1903.

———. *Our Struggle for the Fourteenth Colony: Canada and the American Revolution.* 2 vols. New York: G. P. Putnam's Sons, 1907.

Smith, Paul H. *Loyalists and Redcoats: A Study in British Revolutionary Policy.* Chapel Hill: University of North Carolina Press, 1964.

Smith, Philip Chadwick Foster. *Fired by Manley Zeal: A Naval Fiasco of the American Revolution.* Salem, Mass.: Peabody Museum of Salem, 1977.

Smith, Richard B. *Ethan Allen and the Capture of Fort Ticonderoga.* Charleston, S.C.: History Press, 2010.

Smith, Robert F. *Manufacturing Independence: Industrial Innovation in the American Revolution.* Yardley, Pa.: Westholme, 2016.

Smith, Samuel Abbot. *West Cambridge, 1775.* Somerville, Mass.: Arlington Historical Society, 1974.

Smith, Samuel Stelle. *The Battle of Princeton.* Yardley, Pa.: Westholme, 2009.

———. *The Battle of Trenton.* Yardley, Pa.: Westholme, 2009.

Smollett, Tobias. *Roderick Random.* Edited by David Blewett. London: Penguin, 1995.

Smyth, Albert Henry. *The Writings of Benjamin Franklin.* Vol. 9. New York: Macmillan, 1907.

Sohier, Elizabeth Putnam. *History of the Old South Church of Boston.* Boston: Reuben Hildreth, 1876.

Southern, Ed, ed. *Voices of the American Revolution in the Carolinas.* Winston-Salem, N.C.: John F. Blair, 2009.

Sparks, Jared, ed. *The Diplomatic Correspondence of the American Revolution.* Vol. 1. Boston: N. Hale and Gray & Bowen, 1829.

Spector, Margaret Marion. *The American Department of the British Government, 1768–1782.* New York: Columbia University Press, 1940.

Spring, Matthew H. *With Zeal and with Bayonets Only: The British Army on Campaign in North America, 1775–1783*. Norman: University of Oklahoma Press, 2008.

Stacey, C. P. *Quebec, 1759: The Siege and the Battle*. Edited by Donald E. Graves. Montreal: Robin Brass Studio, 2006.

Stanley, George F. G. *Canada Invaded, 1775–1776*. Toronto: A. M. Hakkert, 1973.

Stark, Caleb. *Memoir and Official Correspondence of Gen. John Stark*. Concord, Mass.: Edson C. Eastman, 1877.

St. Clair, Arthur. *A Narrative*. Philadelphia: Jane Aitken, 1812.

Stedman, C. *The History of the Origin, Progress, and Termination of the American War*. 2 vols. London: s.p., 1794.

Stegeman, John F., and Janet A. Stegeman. *Caty: A Biography of Catharine Littlefield Greene*. Athens: University of Georgia Press, 1985.

Stephenson, Michael. *Patriot Battles: How the War of Independence Was Fought*. New York: Harper, 2008.

Steuart, A. Francis, ed. *The Last Journals of Horace Walpole During the Reign of George III from 1771–1783*. Vol. 1. London: John Lane, 1910.

Stevens, Benjamin Franklin. *B. F. Stevens's Facsimiles of Manuscripts in European Archives Relating to America, 1773–1783*. 25 vols. London: Malby & Sons, 1889–98.

———, ed. *General Sir William Howe's Orderly Book*. London: Benjamin Franklin Stevens, 1890.

Stevenson, Jack. *Exploring Scotland's Heritage: Glasgow, Clydesdale and Stirling*. Edinburgh: H.M. Stationery Office, 1995.

Stiles, Henry. *A History of the City of Brooklyn*. Vol. 1. Brooklyn: s.p., 1867.

Still, Bayrd. *Mirror for Gotham: New York as Seen by Contemporaries from Dutch Days to the Present*. New York: Fordham University Press, 1994.

Stillé, Charles J. *Major-General Anthony Wayne and the Pennsylvania Line in the Continental Army*. Philadelphia: J. B. Lippincott, 1893.

Stokeley, Jim. *Fort Moultrie, Constant Defender*. Washington, D.C.: U.S. Department of the Interior, 1985.

Stoker, Donald, et al., eds. *Strategy in the American War of Independence*. London: Routledge, 2011.

Stokes, I. N. Phelps. *The Iconography of Manhattan Island, 1498–1909*. 6 vols. New York: Robert H. Dodd, 1915–28.

Stone, Edwin M. *The Life and Recollections of John Howland*. Providence, R.I.: George H. Whitney, 1857.

Stone, William L., trans. *Letters of Brunswick and Hessian Officers During the American Revolution*. Albany, N.Y.: Joel Munsell's Sons, 1891.

Stourzh, Gerald. *Benjamin Franklin and American Foreign Policy*. Chicago: University of Chicago Press, 1954.

Stout, Neil R. *The Royal Navy in America, 1760–1775: A Study of Enforcement of British Colonial Policy in the Era of the American Revolution*. Annapolis, Md.: Naval Institute Press, 1973.

Strong, Thomas M. *The History of the Town of Flatbush, in Kings County, Long-Island*. New York: Thomas R. Mercein, Jr., 1842.

Stryker, William S. *The Battles of Trenton and Princeton*. Boston: Houghton Mifflin, 1898.

Stuart, I. W. *Life of Captain Nathan Hale: The Martyr-Spy of the American Revolution*. Hartford, Conn.: F. A. Brown, 1856.

Stuart-Wortley, Mrs. E. [Violet], ed. *A Prime Minister and His Son: From the Correspondence of the Third Earl of Bute, and of Lt.-General the Hon. Sir Charles Stuart*. New York: E. P. Dutton, 1925.

Stumpf, Vernon O. *Josiah Martin: The Last Royal Governor of North Carolina*. Durham, N.C.: Carolina Academic Press, 1986.

Sumner, William Graham. *The Financier and the Finances of the American Revolution*. Vol. 1. New York: Dodd, Mead, 1891.

Sumner, William H. *A History of East Boston*. Boston: J. E. Tilton, 1858.

Swett, S. *Notes to His Sketch of Bunker-Hill Battle*. Boston: Munroe and Francis, 1826.

Swett, Samuel. *History of Bunker Hill Battle*. Boston: Munroe and Francis, 1826.

Syrett, David. *Admiral Lord Howe*. Annapolis, Md.: Naval Institute Press, 2006.

———. *The Royal Navy in American Waters, 1775–1783*. Aldershot, U.K.: Scholar Press, 1989.

———. *The Royal Navy in European Waters, 1775–1783*. Aldershot, U.K.: Scholar Press, 1989.

———. *Shipping and the American War, 1775–83: A Study of British Transport Organization*. London: University of London, Athlone Press, 1970.

———. *Shipping and Military Power in the Seven Years War*. Exeter, U.K.: University of Exeter Press, 2008.

Tallmadge, Benjamin. *Memoir of Col. Benjamin Tallmadge*. New York: Thomas Holman, 1858.

Tarbox, Increase N. *Life of Israel Putnam*. Boston: Lockwood, Brooks, 1876.

Tatum, Edward H., Jr., ed. *The American Journal of Ambrose Serle*. San Marino, Calif.: Huntington Library, 1940.

Taylor, Alan. *American Revolutions: A Continental History, 1750–1804*. New York: W. W. Norton, 2016.

———. *The Internal Enemy: Slavery and War in Virginia, 1772–1832*. New York: W. W. Norton, 2014.

Taylor, Robert J., et al., eds. *Papers of John Adams*. 17 vols. Cambridge, Mass.: Harvard University Press, 1977–2014.

Temple, J. H. *History of Framingham, Massachusetts*. Framingham, Mass.: s.p., 1887.

Thacher, James. *Military Journal During the American Revolution, from 1775 to 1783*. Hartford, Conn.: Silas Andrus & Son, 1854.

Thayer, Theodore. *Nathaniel Greene: Strategist of the American Revolution*. New York: Twayne, 1960.

Thomas, Evan. *John Paul Jones: Sailor, Hero, Father of the American Navy*. New York: Simon & Schuster, 2003.

Thomas, P.D.G. *The House of Commons in the Eighteenth Century*. Oxford: Clarendon Press, 1971.

Thomas, Peter D. G. *Lord North*. New York: St. Martin's, 1976.

Thompson, John M. *The Revolutionary War*. Washington, D.C.: National Geographic, 2004.

Thompson, Ray. *Washington Along the Delaware*. Fort Washington, Pa.: Bicentennial Press, 1970.

Thompson, William Y. *Israel Shreve, Revolutionary War Officer*. Ruston, La.: McGinty Trust Fund Publication, 1979.

Thomson, Thomas, and Robert Chambers, eds. *A Biographical Dictionary of Eminent Scotsmen*. Vol. 1. London: Blackie and Son, 1875.

Tiedemann, Joseph S., and Eugene R. Fingerhut., eds. *The Other New York: The American Revolution Beyond New York City, 1763–1787*. Albany: State University of New York Press, 2005.

Tiedemann, Joseph S., Eugene R. Fingerhut, and Robert W. Venables, eds. *The Other Loyalists: Ordinary People, Royalism, and the Revolution in the Middle Colonies, 1763–1787*. Albany: State University of New York Press, 2009.

Tilley, John A. *The British Navy and the American Revolution*. Columbia: University of South Carolina Press, 1987.

Tillyard, Stella. *A Royal Affair: George III and His Troublesome Siblings*. London: Vintage, 2007.

Timbs, John. *Clubs and Club Life in London*. London: John Camden Hotten, 1872.

Toffey, John J. *A Woman Nobly Planned*. Durham, N.C.: Carolina Academic Press, 1997.

Toll, Ian W. *Six Frigates: The Epic History of the Founding of the U.S. Navy*. New York: W. W. Norton, 2008.

Tomkinson, E. M. *Benjamin Franklin*. London: Cassell, 1885.

Tomlinson, Abraham, ed. *The Military Journals of Two Private Soldiers, 1758–1775*. Poughkeepsie, N.Y.: s.p., 1855.

Tourtellot, Arthur B. *Lexington and Concord: The Beginning of the War of the American Revolution*. New York: W. W. Norton, 2000.

Tracy, Frank Basil. *The Tercentenary History of Canada, from Champlain to Laurier*. Vol. 2. New York: P. F. Collier & Son, 1908.

Trevelyan, George Otto. *The American Revolution*. Edited by Richard B. Morris. New York: David McKay, 1964.

Trimen, Richard. *An Historical Memoir of the 35th Royal Sussex Regiment of Foot.* Southampton, U.K.: Southampton Times, 1873.

True, Henry. *Journal and Letters of Rev. Henry True.* Marion, Ohio: Star Press, 1900.

Trumbull, John. *Reminiscences and Letters of John Trumbull.* New York: Wiley and Putnam, 1841.

Tucker, Phillip Thomas. *George Washington's Surprise Attack.* New York: Skyhorse, 2016.

Tucker, Robert W., and David C. Hendrickson. *The Fall of the First British Empire: Origins of the Wars of American Independence.* Baltimore: Johns Hopkins University Press, 1982.

Tucker, Spencer C. *Rise and Fight Again: The Life of Nathanael Greene.* Wilmington, Del.: ISI Books, 2009.

Tuckerman, Bayard. *Life of General Philip Schuyler.* New York: Dodd, Mead, 1904.

Tudor, William. *The Life of James Otis of Massachusetts.* Boston: Wells and Lilly, 1823.

Uhlendorf, Bernard A., ed. and trans. *Revolution in America: Confidential Letters and Journals, 1776–1784, of Adjutant General Major Baurmeister.* New Brunswick, N.J.: Rutgers University Press, 1957.

Upham, William P. *General John Glover of Marblehead.* Salem, Mass.: Essex Institute, 1863.

Urban, Mark. *Fusiliers: The Saga of a British Redcoat Regiment in the American Revolution.* New York: Walker, 2008.

Valin, Christopher J. *Fortune's Favorite: Sir Charles Douglas and the Breaking of the Line.* Tucson, Ariz.: Fireship Press, 2009.

Van Alstyne, Richard W. *Empire and Independence: The International History of the American Revolution.* New York: John Wiley & Sons, 1967.

Van Creveld, Martin. *Supplying War: Logistics from Wallenstein to Patton.* Cambridge: Cambridge University Press, 1997.

Van Doren, Carl. *Benjamin Franklin.* New York: Book-of-the-Month Club, 1980.

———. *Secret History of the American Revolution.* New York: Viking, 1941.

Van Tyne, Claude H. *The War of Independence: American Phase.* Boston: Houghton Mifflin, 1929.

Van Tyne, Claude Halstead. *The Loyalists in the American Revolution.* New York: Macmillan, 1902.

Volo, James M. *Blue Water Patriots: The American Revolution Afloat.* Lanham, Md.: Rowman & Littlefield, 2007.

Waddell, Alfred Moore. *A History of New Hanover County.* Vol. 1. Wilmington, N.C.: n.p., 1910.

Wade, Herbert T., and Robert A. Lively. *This Glorious Cause: The Adventures of Two Company Officers in Washington's Army.* Princeton, N.J.: Princeton University Press, 1958.

Wagner, Frederick. *Submarine Fighter of the American Revolution: The Story of David Bushnell.* New York: Dodd & Mead, 1963.

Walcott, Charles H. *Sir Archibald Campbell of Inverneill.* Boston: Beacon Press, 1898.

Walkem, Charles. *Summary of the History of the Intendant's Palace.* Ottawa: Maclean, Roger, 1880.

Walker, Paul K. *Engineers of Independence: A Documentary History of the Army Engineers in the American Revolution, 1775–1783.* Washington, D.C.: Office of the Chief of Engineers, 2002.

Wallace, Willard M. *Appeal to Arms: A Military History of the American Revolution.* New York: Quadrangle, 1975.

Ward, Christopher L. *The Delaware Continentals, 1776–1783.* Wilmington: Historical Society of Delaware, 1941.

Ward, Christopher. *The War of the Revolution.* Edited by John Richard Alden. 1952. Reprint, New York: Skyhorse, 2011.

Ward, George Atkinson. *Journal and Letters of the Late Samuel Curwen, an American Refugee in England.* New York: C. S. Francis, 1842.

Ward, Harry M. *Charles Scott and the "Spirit of '76."* Charlottesville: University Press of Virginia, 1988.

———. *George Washington's Enforcers: Policing the Continental Army.* Carbondale: Southern Illinois University Press, 2006.

———. *Major General Adam Stephen and the Cause of American Liberty.* Charlottesville: University Press of Virginia, 1989.

Ward, John. *A Memoir of Lieut.-Colonel Samuel Ward, First Rhode Island Regiment.* New York: s.p., 1875.

Warner, Jessica. *John the Painter: Terrorist of the American Revolution*. New York: Thunder's Mouth Press, 2004.

Waterman, Joseph M. *With Sword and Lancet: The Life of General Hugh Mercer*. Richmond, Va.: Garret and Massie, 1941.

Waters, Wilson. *History of Chelmsford, Massachusetts*. Lowell, Mass.: Courier-Citizen, 1917.

Watson, J. Steven. *The Reign of George III, 1760–1815*. Oxford: Clarendon Press, 1976.

Watson, John F. *Annals of Philadelphia*. Philadelphia: E. L. Carey & A. Hart, 1830.

Weigley, Russell F. *History of the United States Army*. Bloomington: Indiana University Press, 1984.

———, ed. *Philadelphia: A 300-Year History*. New York: W. W. Norton, 1982.

Weintraub, Stanley. *Iron Tears: America's Battle for Freedom, Britain's Quagmire*. New York: Free Press, 2005.

Wertenbaker, Thomas J. *Norfolk: Historic Southern Port*. Edited by Marvin W. Schlegel. Durham, N.C.: Duke University Press, 1962.

Wertenbaker, Thomas Jefferson. *Father Knickerbocker Rebels: New York City During the Revolution*. New York: Cooper Square Publishers, 1969.

Wharton, Francis, ed. *The Revolutionary Diplomatic Correspondence of the United States*. Vol. 1. Washington, D.C.: Government Printing Office, 1889.

Wheatley, Henry B., ed. *The Historical and Posthumous Memoirs of Sir Nathaniel William Wraxall*. Vol. 1. London: Bickers & Son, 1884.

Wheeler, Richard. *Voices of 1776*. Greenwich, Conn.: Fawcett, 1973.

Wheeler, Ruth R. *Concord: Climate for Freedom*. Concord, Mass.: Concord Antiquarian Society, 1967.

Wheildon, William W. *History of Paul Revere's Signal Lanterns*. Boston: Lee & Shepard, 1878.

———. *Siege and Evacuation of Boston and Charlestown*. Boston: Lee & Shepard, 1876.

Whelen, Townsend. *The American Rifle*. New York: Century, 1918.

White, J. *An Narrative of Events . . . in the Revolutionary War*. Charlestown, Mass.: n.p., 1833.

Whitehill, Walter Muir. *Boston: A Topographical History*. Cambridge, Mass.: Belknap Press, 1975.

Whiteley, Peter. *Lord North: The Prime Minister Who Lost America*. London: Hambledon Press, 1996.

Whitney, Solon F. *Historical Sketches of Watertown, Massachusetts*. Watertown, Mass.: Historical Society, 1893.

Whittemore, Charles P. *A General of the Revolution: John Sullivan of New Hampshire*. New York: Columbia University Press, 1961.

Wickwire, Franklin, and Mary Wickwire. *Cornwallis: The American Adventure*. Boston: Houghton Mifflin, 1970.

Wiencek, Henry. *An Imperfect God: George Washington, His Slaves, and the Creation of America*. New York: Farrar, Straus and Giroux, 2003.

Wilkin, W. H. *Some British Soldiers in America*. London: Hugh Rees, 1914.

Wilkinson, James. *Memoirs of My Own Times*. Vol. 1. Philadelphia: Abraham Small, 1816.

Willard, Margaret Wheeler, ed. *Letters on the American Revolution, 1774–1776*. Port Washington, N.Y.: Kennikat Press, 1968.

Willcox, William B. ed. *The Papers of Benjamin Franklin*. Vols. 21–23. New Haven, Conn.: Yale University Press, 1978–83.

———. *Portrait of a General: Sir Henry Clinton in the War of Independence*. New York: Knopf, 1964.

Williams, George W. *St. Michael's: Charleston, 1751–1951*. Columbia: University of South Carolina Press, 1951.

Williams, Mrs. [Catherine R.] *Biography of Revolutionary Heroes*. Providence, R.I.: s.p., 1839.

Williams, Richard. *Discord and Civil Wars: Being a Portion of the Journal Kept by Lieutenant Williams*. Buffalo, N.Y.: Easy Hill Press, 1954.

Williamson, Audrey. *Thomas Paine: His Life, Work and Times*. London: George Allen & Unwin, 1973.

Willis, Sam. *The Struggle for Sea Power: A Naval History of American Independence*. London: Atlantic Books, 2015.

Willis, William. *The History of Portland, from 1632 to 1864*. Portland, Me.: Bailey & Noyes, 1865.

Wilson, Barry K. *Benedict Arnold: A Traitor in Our Midst*. Montreal: McGill–Queen's University Press, 2001.

Wilson, David K. *The Southern Strategy: Britain's Conquest of South Carolina and Georgia, 1775–1780*. Columbia: University of South Carolina Press, 2005.

Wilson, Derek. *The Tower of London: A Thousand Years*. London: Allison & Busby, 1998.

Winfield, Rif. *British Warships in the Age of Sail, 1714–1792*. Barnsley, U.K.: Seaforth, 2007.

Winsor, Justin, ed. *The Memorial History of Boston*. 4 vols. Boston: James R. Osgood, 1881–82.

Wood, Gordon S. *The Americanization of Benjamin Franklin*. New York: Penguin, 2005.

———. *The American Revolution*. New York: Modern Library, 2003.

———. *The Creation of the American Republic, 1776–1787*. Chapel Hill: University of North Carolina Press, 1998.

———. *The Idea of America*. New York: Penguin, 2012.

———. *The Radicalism of the American Revolution*. New York: Vintage, 1993.

———. *Revolutionary Characters*. New York: Penguin, 2007.

Wood, Peter H. *Black Majority: Negroes in Colonial South Carolina from 1670 Through the Stono Rebellion*. New York: Norton, 1996.

Wood, W. J. *Battles of the Revolutionary War, 1775–1781*. 1990. Reprint, Cambridge, Mass.: Da Capo, 2003.

Wood, William. *The Father of British Canada: A Chronicle of Carleton*. Toronto: Glasgow Brook, 1920.

Woodbury, Ellen C.D.Q. *Dorothy Quincy, Wife of John Hancock*. Washington, D.C.: Neale, 1901.

Wright, Robert K., Jr. *The Continental Army*. Washington, D.C.: U.S. Army, 1983.

Wrong, George McKinnon. *Canada and the American Revolution*. New York: Macmillan, 1935.

Wroth, L. Kinvin, and Hiller B. Zobel, eds. *Legal Papers of John Adams*. Vol. 1. Cambridge, Mass.: Belknap Press, 1965.

Würtele, Fred C., ed. *Blockade of Quebec in 1775–1776 by the American Revolutionists*. Quebec: Literary and Historical Society of Quebec, 1906.

Wylly, H. C., ed. *1913 Regimental Annual: The Sherwood Foresters*. London: George Allen, 1913.

Yerxa, Donald A. *The Burning of Falmouth, 1775*. Portland, Me.: Maine Historical Society, 1975.

York, Mark A. *Patriot on the Kennebec: Major Reuben Colburn, Benedict Arnold, and the March to Quebec*. Charleston, S.C.: History Press, 2012.

Young, Alfred F., Gary B. Nash, and Ray Raphael, eds. *Revolutionary Founders*. New York: Vintage, 2012.

PERIODICALS

Alden, John Richard. "Why the March to Concord?" *AHR* 49, no. 3 (Apr. 1944): 446+.

"America: Military Operations in Canada." *Scots Magazine* 38 (1776): 316+.

Anderson, Fred W. "The Hinge of the Revolution." *Massachusetts Historical Review* 1 (1999): 20+.

Andreas Wiederhold [*sic*]. "Colonel Rall at Trenton." *PMHB* 22, no. 4 (1898): 462+.

Applegate, Howard Lewis. "The Medical Administrators of the American Revolutionary Army." *Military Affairs* 25, no. 1 (Spring 1961): 1+.

———. "Remedial Medicine in the American Revolutionary Army." *Military Medicine*, June 1961, 451+.

Atkinson, C. T. "British Forces in North America, 1774–1781: Their Distribution and Strength." Part 2. *Journal of the Society for Army Historical Research* (Autumn 1940): 163+.

Baker, William S. "Itinerary of General Washington from June 15, 1775, to December 23, 1783." *PMHB* 14, no. 2 (July 1890): 111+.

"Bamford's Diary: The Revolutionary Diary of a British Officer." *Maryland Historical Magazine* 27, no. 3 (Sept. 1932): 240+.

Barker, E. Eugene. "The Lost Cannon of Crown Point." *Military Collector & Historian* 26, no. 3 (Fall 1974): 159+.

Bass, Streeter. "Nathan Hale's Mission." *Studies in Intelligence* (Winter 1973): 67+.

Baugh, Daniel E. "The Politics of British Naval Failure, 1775–1777." *American Neptune* 52, no. 4 (Fall 1992): 221+.

Beale, Robert. "Revolutionary Experiences of Major Robert Beale." *Northern Neck of Virginia Historical Magazine* 6, no. 1 (Dec. 1956): 500+.

Beard, Rick. "The Salt Wars." *Opinionator* (blog). *New York Times*, Dec. 26, 2013, https://opinionator.blogs.nytimes.com/2013/12/26/the-salt-wars/?_r=0.

Becker, Ann M. "Smallpox in Washington's Army." *JMH* 68 (Apr. 2004): 381+.

Belknap, Jeremy. "Journal of My Tour to the Camp." MHS, *Proceedings*, 1st ser., 4 (1858–60): 77+.

Bickham, Troy O. "Sympathizing with Sedition? George Washington, the British Press, and British Attitudes During the American War of Independence." *WMQ*, 3rd ser., 59, no. 1 (Jan. 2002): 101+.

Bird, Harrison K. "Uniform of the Black Watch in America, 1776–1783." *Journal of the American Military History Foundation* 2, no. 3 (Fall 1938): 171+.

Black, Jeremy. "A Revolution in Military Cartography? Europe, 1650–1815." *JMH* 93, no. 1 (Jan. 2009): 49+.

Bowler, R. Arthur. "Sir Guy Carleton and the Campaign of 1776 in Canada." *Canadian Historical Review* 55, no. 2 (June 1974): 131+.

Bowman, Larry G. "The Scarcity of Salt in Virginia During the American Revolution." *VMHB* 77, no. 4 (Oct. 1969): 464+.

Bradford, S. Sydney, ed. "A British Officer's Revolutionary War Journal, 1776–1778." *Maryland Historical Magazine* 56, no. 2 (June 1961): 150+.

Bredenberg, Oscar R. "The *Royal Savage*." *BFTM* 12, no. 2 (Sept. 1966): 128+.

Brewington, M. V. "The Designs of Our First Frigates." *American Neptune* 8 (Jan. 1948): 10+.

———. "Washington's Boat at the Delaware Crossing." *American Neptune* 2 (1942): 167+.

Brown, Craig J., et al. "The Revolutionary War Battle America Forgot." *New England Quarterly* 86, no. 3 (Sept. 2013): 398+.

Brown, Gerald S. "The Court Martial of Lord George Sackville, Whipping Boy of the Revolutionary War." *WMQ*, 3rd ser., 9, no. 3 (July 1952): 317+.

Brown, Margaret L. "William Bingham, Agent of the Continental Congress in Martinique." *PMHB* 61, no. 1 (Jan. 1937): 54+.

Burgoyne, Bruce E., trans. "Diary of Private Johannes Reuber, Grenadier Regiment Rall." *The Hessians: Journal of the Johannes Schwalm Historical Association* 5 (2012): 25+.

Burt, A. L. "The Quarrel Between Germain and Carleton: An Inverted Story." *Canadian Historical Review* 11, no. 3 (1930): 203+.

Byrd, James P. "Was the American Revolution a Holy War?" *Washington Post*, July 5, 2013.

Calderhead, William L. "British Naval Failure at Long Island." *New York History* 57, no. 3 (July 1976): 321+.

"Camp Life in 1776—Siege of Boston." *Historical Magazine and Notes and Queries* 8 (1864): 332+.

Cash, Philip. "The Canadian Military Campaign of 1775–1776: Medical Problems and Effects of Disease." *JAMA* 236, no. 1 (July 5, 1976): 52+.

Cecere, Michael. "Battle of Gwynn's Island: Lord Dunmore's Last Stand in Virginia." *JAR*, May 26, 2016.

———. "A Tale of Two Cities," *JAR*, Sept. 9, 2015.

Christie, Ian R. "British Politics and the American Revolution." *Albion* 9, no. 3 (Autumn 1977): 205+.

Clark, Jane. "The Command of the Canadian Army for the Campaign of 1777." *Canadian Historical Review*, vol. 10 (June 1929): 129+.

Coffin, Charles Carleton. "Diary of Capt. Peter Kimball, 1776." *Granite Monthly* (Mar. 1881): 230+.

Conner, Jett. "A Brief Publication History of the 'Times That Try Men's Souls.'" *JAR*, Jan. 4, 2016.

Conway, Stephen. "British Army Officers and the American War for Independence." *WMQ*, 3rd ser., 41, no. 2 (Apr. 1984): 265+.

———. "British Mobilization in the War of American Independence." *Historical Research* 72, no. 177 (Feb. 1999): 58+.

———. "The Great Mischief Complain'd Of." *WMQ*, 3rd ser., 17, no. 3 (July 1990): 370+.

———. "The Politics of British Military and Naval Mobilization, 1775–1783." *English Historical Review* 112, no. 449 (Nov. 1997): 1179+.

———. "To Subdue America: British Army Officers and the Conduct of the Revolutionary War." *WMQ*, 3rd ser., 43, no. 3 (July 1986): 381+.

Conway, William F. "Fort Lee: The Post at Burdett's Ferry." *Bergen County History: 1775 Annual*, 1975.

Cooper, Samuel. "Diary of Samuel Cooper, 1775–1776." *AHR* 6, no. 2 (Jan. 1901): 301+.

Copeland, Peter F. "Lord Dunmore's Ethiopian Regiment." *Military Collector & Historian* 58, no. 4 (Winter 2006): 208+.

"Correspondence of the Brothers Joshua and Jedidiah Huntington During the Period of the American Revolution." *Collections of the Connecticut Historical Society* 20 (1923).

Crane, Stephen. "The Battle of Bunker Hill." *Lippincott's Monthly* 65 (Jan.–June 1900): 924+.

"Critical Adventure of Lord Dorchester in the War of 1775." *United Service Journal*, part 1, (1831): 73+.

Curtis, Edward E. "The Provisioning of the British Army in the Revolution." *Magazine of History* 18 (Jan.–June 1914): 240+.

Dacus, Jeff. "Hugh Mercer: Doctor and Warrior." *JAR*, Jan. 24, 2017.

Davis, David B., ed. "Medicine in the Canadian Campaign of the Revolutionary War: The Journal of Doctor Samuel Fisk Merrick." *Bulletin of the History of Medicine* 44, no. 5 (Sept.–Oct. 1970).

Davis, W.H.W. "Washington on the West Bank of the Delaware, 1776." *PMHB* 4, no. 2 (1880): 133+.

"Decision at Moore's Creek Bridge." *Cincinnati Fourteen* (Spring 2012): 30+.

de Lancey, Edward F. "Mount Washington and Its Capture, November 16th, 1776." *Magazine of American History* 1, no. 2 (Feb. 1877): 65+.

"The Deputy Adjutant General's Orderly Book." *BFTM* 3, no. 2 (July 1933): 88+.

Diamant, Lincoln. "First Blood for the Infantry, 1776." *Military Affairs* 15, no. 1 (Spring 1951): 16+.

"Diary of Ensign Caleb Clap." *Historical Magazine*, 3rd ser., 3, nos. 3 and 4 (Mar. 1874 and Apr. 1875): 133+ and 248+.

"Diary of Ezekiel Price, 1775–76." MHS, *Proceedings*, Nov. 1863, 185+.

"Diary of Obadiah Brown." *Quarterly Bulletin of the Westchester County Historical Society* 4, nos. 3 and 4 (July and Oct. 1928), 5, no. 1 (Jan. 1929).

"Diary of Rev. Benjamin Boardman." MHS, *Proceedings* (May 1892): 400+.

"Diary of Richard Smith in the Continental Congress, 1775–1776." Parts 1 and 2. *AHR*, 1, no. 2 and 3 (Jan. and Apr. 1896): 297+ and 493.

"Diary of Samuel Bixby." MHS, *Proceedings* 14 (1875–76): 285+.

Dolin, Eric Jay. "The Enduring Boston Light." *Boston Globe*, Aug. 30, 2016.

Doughty, Joshua, Jr. "Washington's March to Morristown, 1777." *Proceedings of the New Jersey Historical Society*, new ser. 5, no. 4 (Oct. 1920).

Douglas, William. "Letters." *New-York Historical Society Quarterly* 12, no. 1 (Apr. 1928) and 13, no. 1 (Apr. 1929): 150+.

Duffy, John. "Public Health in New York City in the Revolutionary Period." *JAMA* 236, no. 1 (July 5, 1976): 47+.

Duffy, John J., and Eugene A. Coyle. "Crean Brush vs. Ethan Allen: A Winner's Tale." *Vermont History* 70 (Summer–Fall 2002): 103+.

Dull, Jonathan R. "Franklin the Diplomat: The French Mission." *Transactions of the American Philosophical Society*, new ser., 72, no. 1 (1982): 1+.

Duncan, Louis C. "Medical Men in the American Revolution: The New York Campaign of 1776." *New York Medical Journal*, Sept.–Oct. 1920, 1+.

Dunlap, David W. "Long-Toppled Statue of King George III to Ride Again, from a Brooklyn Studio." *New York Times*, Oct. 20, 2016.

Dzurec, David. "Prisoners of War and American Self-Image During the American Revolution." *War in History* 20, no. 4 (Nov. 2013): 230+.

Eaton, Arthur Wentworth Hamilton. "Chapters in the History of Halifax, Nova Scotia." *Americana* 10 (Apr. 1915): 269+.

Edwards, William Waller. "Morgan and His Riflemen." *WMQ* 23, no. 2 (Oct. 1914): 73+.

Elliott, Charles Winslow. "The Men That Fought at Minden." *Journal of the American Military Institute* 3, no. 2 (Summer 1939): 80+.

Estes, J. Worth. "A Disagreeable and Dangerous Employment: Medical Letters from the Siege of Boston, 1775." *Journal of the History of Medicine and Allied Sciences* 31, no. 3 (July 1976): 271+.

"Excerpts from Letters of Isaac Winslow, Loyalist During the Siege of Boston." *New England Historical and Genealogical Register* 56 (1902): 48+.

"An Extract from the Journal of Lieut. David Dimock." *American Monthly* 1 (Oct. 1892): 353+.

Farmer, Edward G. "Skenesborough: Continental Navy Shipyard." U.S. Naval Institute, *Proceedings* 90 (Oct. 1964): 160+.

Fenn, Elizabeth A. "Biological Warfare in Eighteenth-Century North America: Beyond Jeffrey Amherst." *Journal of American History* 86, no. 4 (Mar. 2000): 1552+.

Ferling, John. "Myths of the American Revolution," *Smithsonian*, Jan. 2010, https://www.smithsonianmag.com/history/myths-of-the-american-revolution-10941835/.

Fitch, Jabez, Jr. "A Journal." MHS, *Proceedings*, May 1894, 41+.

Flick, Alexander C. "General Henry Knox's Ticonderoga Expedition." *Quarterly Journal of the New York State Historical Association* 9, no. 2 (Apr. 1928): 119+.

Ford, Paul Leicester. "Lord Howe's Commission to Pacify the Colonies." *Atlantic Monthly*, June 1896, 758+.

Forster, Kent. "Westchester: A House Divided." *New York History* 28, no. 4 (Oct. 1947): 404+.

Fowles, S. P. "Craft's Journal of the Siege of Boston." *Historical Collections of the Essex Institute* 3, no. 2 (Apr. 1861): 133+.

Frazer, Persifer. "Letter from Ticonderoga, 1776." *BFTM* 10, no. 1 (1962): 450+.

Freehling, William W. "The Founding Fathers and Slavery." *AHR* 77, no. 1 (Feb. 1972): 81+.

French, Allen. "The British Expedition to Concord, Massachusetts, in 1775." *Journal of the American Military History Foundation* 1, no. 1 (Spring 1937): 3+.

Frey, Sylvia R. "Between Slavery and Freedom: Virginia Blacks in the American Revolution." *Journal of Southern History* 49, no. 3 (Aug. 1983): 375+.

Frothingham, Richard, Jr. "Mr. Frothingham's Remarks." MHS, *Proceedings* (1875–76): 53+.

Furcron, Thomas B. "Mount Independence." *BFTM* 9, no. 4 (Winter 1954): 230+.

Gardner, Asa Bird. "The Uniforms of the American Army." *Magazine of American History* 1, no. 8 (Aug. 1877): 461+.

"General Daniel Morgan: An Autobiography." *Historical Magazine*, 2nd ser., 9, no. 6 (June 1871): 379+.

"General Principles and Construction of a Sub-Marine Vessel." David Bushnell to Thomas Jefferson, Oct. 13, 1787. *Transactions of the American Philosophical Society*, 4 (1799): 303+.

"General Richard Montgomery." *Harper's New Monthly Magazine*, 70, no. 417 (Feb. 1885): 353+.

"General Richard Montgomery—His Sword, Etc." *BFTM* 3, no. 1 (1957): 76+.

Gerlach, Don R. "Philip Schuyler and 'the Road to Glory': A Question of Loyalty and Competence." *New-York Historical Society Quarterly* 49, no. 4 (Oct. 1965): 341+.

"The Good Soldier White." *American Heritage* 7, no. 4 (June 1956): 74+.

Gradish, Stephen F. "The German Mercenaries in North America During the American Revolution: A Case Study." *Canadian Journal of History* (Mar. 1969): 23+.

Griffenhagen, George B. "Drug Supplies in the American Revolution." *Bulletin of the United States National Museum*, 225 (1961): 110+.

Griffin, Phillip R. "Samuel Blachley Webb: Wethersfield's Ablest Officer." *JAR*, Sept. 19, 2016.

Grim, David. "Fire of 1776." NYHS, *Collections* (1870): 275+.

Gruber, Ira D. "The American Revolution as a Conspiracy: The British View," *WMQ*, 3rd ser., 26, no. 3 (July 1969): 360+.

———. "Lord Howe and Lord George Germain: British Politics and the Winning of American Independence." *WMQ*, 3rd ser., 22, no. 2 (Apr. 1965): 225+.

Guttridge, George H. "Lord George Germain in Office, 1775–1782." *AHR* 33, no. 1 (Oct. 1927): 23+.

Haas, James M. "The Royal Dockyards: The Earliest Visitations and Reform, 1749–1778." *Historical Journal* 13, no. 2 (1970): 191+.

Hagist, Don N. "Shedding Light on Friendly Fire at Bunker Hill." *American Revolution* 1, no. 3 (Oct. 2009): 4+.

Hall, John W. "An Irregular Reconsideration of George Washington and the American Military Tradition." *JMH* 78 (July 2014): 961+.

Harlow, Ralph Volney. "Aspects of Revolutionary Finance, 1775–1783." *AHR* 35, no. 1 (Oct. 1929): 46+.

Harrington, Hugh T. "Charles Willson Peale's 'Riffle with a Tellescope to It.'" *JAR*, July 10, 2013.

Hatch, Marie Martel, ed. "Letters of Captain Sir John Jervis to Sir Henry Clinton, 1774–1782." *American Neptune* 7 (Apr. 1947): 87+.

Hedbor, Lars D. H. "John the Painter: Terrorist for America." *JAR*, May 1, 2018.

"Henry Knox—Bookseller." MHS, *Proceedings*, 3rd ser., 61 (Oct. 1927–June 1928): 227.

"The Historic Billopp House on Staten Island." *Americana* 10 (1915): 965+.

Hodgkinson, Samuel. "Before Quebec, 1776." *PMHB* 10, no. 2 (July 1886): 158+.

Hubbard, F. M. "Who Commanded at Moore's Creek Bridge?" *North Carolina University Magazine* 7, no. 4 (Nov. 1857): 137+.

Hubbard, Timothy William. "Battle at Valcour Island: Benedict Arnold as Hero." *American Heritage* 17, no. 6 (Oct. 1966): https://archive.org/details/american17n06newy.

"Hugh Mercer." *Americana* 9 (1914): 705+.

Huston, James A. "The Logistics of Arnold's March to Quebec." *Military Affairs*, Dec. 1968, 110+.

Huth, Hans, et al. "Letters from a Hessian Mercenary." *PMHB* 62, no. 4 (Oct. 1938): 488+.

Inman, George. "George Inman's Narrative of the American Revolution." *PMHB* 7, no. 3 (1883): 237+.

Ives, Vernon A. "Narrative of Uriah Cross in the Revolutionary War." *New York History* 63, no. 3 (July 1982): 279+.

James, Garry. "Britain's Brown Bess." *Rifle Shooter*, Sept. 23, 2010, www.rifleshootermag.com/rifles/featured_rifles_bess_092407/.

Jameson, Hugh. "Equipment of the Militia of the Middle States, 1775–1781." *Journal of the American Military Institute* 3, no. 1 (Spring 1939): 26+.

———. "Subsistence for Middle States Militia, 1776–1781." *Military Affairs* 30, no. 3 (Fall 1966): 121+.

Henry P. Johnston, ed. "Sergeant Lee's Experience with Bushnell's Submarine Torpedo in 1776." *Magazine of American History* 29, no. 1 (Jan.–June 1893): 263+.

Jones, T. Cole. "'The Rage of Tory-Hunting': Loyalist Prisoners, Civil War, and the Violence of American Independence." *JMH* 81, no. 3 (July 2017): 719+.

"Journal of a Pennsylvania Soldier, July–December, 1776." *Bulletin of the NYPL* 8 (1904): 547+.

"Journal of Capt. William Beaty, 1776–1781," *Maryland Historical Magazine* 3, no. 2 (June 1908): 104+.

"Journal of Col. Rudolphus Ritzema." *Magazine of American History* 1 (1877): 98+.

"Journal of Ensign Nathaniel Morgan." *Collections of the Connecticut Historical Society* 7 (1899): 99+.

"Journal of Lieutenant-Colonel Joseph Vose." *Publication of the Colonial Society of Massachusetts* 7 (1900–02): 244+.

"Journal of Matthias Ogden." New Jersey Historical Society, *Proceedings*, new ser., 13 (1928): 17+.

"Journal of Simeon Lyman of Sharon." *Collections of the Connecticut Historical Society* 7 (1899): 111+.

"Judge Prescott's Account of the Battle of Bunker Hill." MHS, *Proceedings* 14 (1875–76): 68+.

Kepner, Frances Reece, ed. "Notes and Documents: A British View of the Siege of Charleston, 1776." *Journal of Southern History* 2, no. 1 (Feb. 1945): 93+.

Kidder, Larry. "Guiding Washington to Trenton." *JAR*, May 6, 2014.

Kim, Sung Bok. "The Limits of Politicization in the American Revolution: The Experience of Westchester County, New York." *Journal of American History* 80, no. 3 (Dec. 1993): 878+.

Kingsley, Ronald F. "Letters to Lord Polwarth from Sir Francis-Carr Clerke, Aide-de-Camp to General John Burgoyne." *New York History* 79, no. 4 (Oct. 1998): 393+.

Kiracofe, David James. "Dr. Benjamin Church and the Dilemma of Treason in Revolutionary Massachusetts." *New England Quarterly* 70, no. 3 (Sept. 1997): 443+.

Knight, R.J.B. "The Building and Maintenance of the British Fleet During the Anglo-French Wars, 1688–1815." *Les Marines de Guerre Européennes*, 38–39.

———. "New England Forests and British Seapower: Albion Revised." *American Neptune* 46, no. 4 (Fall 1986): 221+.

Knollenberg, Bernhard. "Bunker Hill Re-viewed: A Study in the Conflict of Historical Evidence." MHS, *Proceedings*, 3rd ser., 72 (Oct. 1957–Dec. 1960): 84+.

———. "The Correspondence of John Adams and Horatio Gates." MHS, *Proceedings*, 3rd ser., 67 (Oct. 1941–May 1944): 138+.

"Knox's Diary During His Ticonderoga Expedition." *New-England Historical and Genealogical Register* 30 (1876): 321+.

Koke, Richard J. "The Struggle for the Hudson: The British Naval Expedition Under Captain Hyde Parker and Captain James Wallace, July 12–August 18, 1776." *New-York Historical Society Quarterly* 40, no. 2 (Apr. 1956): 115+.

Kopperman, Paul E. "'The Cheapest Pay': Alcohol Abuse in the Eighteenth-Century British Army." *JMH* 60, no. 3 (July 1996): 445+.

Krebs, Daniel. "Useful Enemies: The Treatment of German Prisoners of War During the American War of Independence." *JMH* 77, no. 1 (Jan. 2013): 9+.

Lacey, John. "Memoirs of Brigadier-General John Lacey, of Pennsylvania." *PMHB*, vols. 25–26 (1901–02): 1+.

Laughton, John Knox, ed. "Journals of Henry Duncan, Captain, Royal Navy, 1776–1782." *The Naval Miscellany*, vol. 1, *Publications of the Navy Records Society* 20 (1902): 111+.

Leonard, Eugenie Andruss. "Paper as a Critical Commodity During the American Revolution." *PMHB* 74, no. 4 (Oct. 1950): 488+.

"Letter of Harry Farrington Gardner, 1775." *Colonial Society of Massachusetts Publications* 26 (1927): 292–95.

"Letters from Dr. Samuel Kennedy to His Wife in 1776." *PMHB* 8 (1884): 111+.

Lindsey, William R. "Treatment of American Prisoners of War During the Revolution." *Emporia State Research Studies* 22, no. 1 (Summer 1973): 5+.

Lossing, Benson J. "Washington's Life Guard." *Historical Magazine* 2, no. 5 (May 1858): 129+.

Louis, Elan D. "Samuel Adams' Tremor." *Neurology* 56, no. 9 (May 8, 2001): 1201+.

Lydenberg, Harry Miller, ed. "Archibald Robertson: His Diaries and Sketches in America, 1762–1780." *Bulletin of the New York Public Library* 37, no. 11 (Nov. 1933): 283+.

Maguire, J. Robert. "Dr. Robert Knox's Account of the Battle of Valcour, October 11–13, 1776." *Vermont History* 46, no. 3 (Summer 1978): 3+.

Marsh, George. "An Account of the Preparation Made for and the Entertainment of the King at Portsmouth in June 1773." Part 1, *Colburn's United Service Magazine* (1887): 433–522.

Martin, Asa E. "American Privateers and the West Indies Trade." *AHR* 39 (July 1934): 700+.

Martin, James Kirby. "A Contagion of Violence." *Journal of Military Ethics* 14, no. 1 (May 2015): 57+.

Maurer, Maurer. "Military Justice Under General Washington." *Military Affairs* 28, no. 1 (Spring 1964): 8+.

Mayer, Holly A. "Canada, Congress, and the Continental Army: Strategic Accommodations, 1774–1776." *JMH* 78, no. 2 (Apr. 2014): 503+.

McCusker, John J., Jr. "The American Invasion of Nassau in the Bahamas." *American Neptune* 25, no. 3 (July 1965): 189+.

McMichael, James. "Diary of Lieutenant James McMichael, of the Pennsylvania Line, 1776–1778." *PMHB* 16, no. 2 (July 1892): 129+.

"Meagre War Stores of 1775." *Americana* 6 (1911): 102.

Meng, John J. "A Footnote to Secret Aid in the American Revolution." *AHR* 43, no. 4 (July 1938): 791+.

Moomaw, W. Hugh. "The British Leave Colonial Virginia." *VMHB* 66, no. 2 (Apr. 1958): 147+.

Moran, Donald N. "Major General John Stark of New Hampshire." *Liberty Tree Magazine*, May 2006, www.revolutionarywararchives.org/stark.html.

Mott, Frank Luther. "The Newspaper Coverage of Lexington and Concord." *New England Quarterly* 17, no. 4 (Dec. 1944): 493+.

Naisawald, Louis VanL. "Robert Howe's Operations in Virginia, 1775–1776." *VMHB* 60, no. 3 (July 1952): 437+.

Namier, Lewis. "King George III: A Study in Personality." *History Today* 3, no. 1 (Jan. 1953): 610+.

"The Narrative of Major Thompson Maxwell." *Historical Collections of the Essex Institute* 7, no. 3 (June 1865): 13+.

Nelson, Paul David. "Citizen Soldiers or Regulars." *Military Affairs* 43, no. 3 (Oct. 1979): 126+.

Newell, Timothy. "A Journal Kept During the Time Yt [That] Boston Was Shut Up in 1775–6." MHS, *Collections*, 4th ser., 1 (1852): 270+.

Nice, John, and Edward Burd. "Extracts from the Diary of Captain John Nice, of the Pennsylvania Line." *PMHB* 16, no. 4 (Jan. 1893): 399+.

Nichols, Francis, et al. "Diary of Lieutenant Francis Nichols." *PMHB* 20, no. 4 (1896): 504+.

"One Hundred and Ten Years Ago." *American Stationer* 32, no. 8 (Aug. 25, 1892): 356+.

"An Open Letter to Captain Pringle." *BFTM* 1, no. 4 (July 1928): 14+.

O'Shaughnessy, Andrew Jackson. "'If Others Will Not Be Active, I Must Drive': George III and the American Revolution." *Early American Studies* 2, no. 1 (Spring 2004): 1+.

———. "'To Gain the Hearts and Subdue the Minds of America': General Sir Henry Clinton and the Conduct of the British War for America." *Proceedings of the American Philosophical Society* 158, no. 3 (Sept. 2014): 199+.

Paltsits, Victor Hugo. "The Jeopardy of Washington, Sept. 15, 1776." *New-York Historical Society Quarterly* 32, no. 4 (Oct. 1948): 253+.

"The Papers of General Samuel Smith." *Historical Magazine* 7, 2nd ser. (Feb. 1870): 81+.

Peckham, Howard H. "Independence: The View from Britain." *Proceedings of the American Antiquarian Society* 85, part 2 (1976): 387+.

Perley, Sidney. "Colonel Thomas Knowlton." *Historical Collections of the Essex Institute* 58, no. 2 (Apr. 1922): 89+.

Perry, Clay. "Big Guns for Washington." *American Heritage* 6, no. 3 (Apr. 1995), www.americanheritage.com/content/big-guns-washington.

Pippenger, C. E. "Finding Edward Wigglesworth's Lost Diary." *JAR*, October 11, 2018.

———. "Recently Discovered Letters Shed New Light on the Battle of Valcour Island." *JAR*, Oct. 11, 2016.

Plumb, J. H. "Our Last King." *American Heritage* 11, no. 4 (June 1960).

Porter, Elisha. "An Account of the Expedition from Cambridge to Quebec." *BFTM* 10, no. 1 (1957): 34+.

Potts, Jonathan. "Death of Major Anthony Morris, Jr., Described in a Letter Written on the Battle-Field near Princeton." *PMHB* 1, no. 2 (1877): 175+.

Powell, William S. "A Connecticut Soldier Under Washington: Elisha Bostwick's Memoirs of the First Years of the Revolution." *WMQ*, 3rd ser., 6, no. 1 (Jan. 1949): 94+.

"Prisons of the Revolution." *Old New York* 1, no. 5 (Dec. 1889): 297+.

Procknow, Gene. "Did Generals Mismanage the Battle of Brooklyn?" *JAR*, Apr. 20, 2017.

Pybus, Cassandra. "Jefferson's Faulty Math: The Question of Slave Defections in the American Revolution." *WMQ*, 3rd ser., 62, no. 2 (Apr. 2005): 243+.

"Queries." *Magazine of American History* 12 (July–Dec. 1884): 181+.

"Queries of George Chalmers, with the Answers of General Gage." *Collections of the Massachusetts Historical Society*, 4th ser., 4 (1858): 367+.

Rankin, Hugh F. "The Moore's Creek Bridge Campaign, 1776." *North Carolina Historical Review* 30, no. 1 (Jan. 1953): 23+.

Ranlet, Philip. "British Recruitment of Americans in New York During the American Revolution." *Military Affairs* 48, no. 1 (Jan. 1984): 26.

Rantoul, Robert S. "The Cruise of the 'Quero': How We Carried the News to the King." *Century Illustrated Monthly Magazine*, Sept. 1899.

Rau, Louise, ed. "Sergeant John Smith's Diary of 1776." *Mississippi Historical Review* 20, no. 2 (Sept. 1933): 247+.

Reed, Joseph. "General Joseph Reed's Narrative of the Movements of the American Army in the Neighborhood of Trenton in the Winter of 1776–1777." *PMHB* 8, no. 4 (Dec. 1884): 391+.

Reitan, E. A. "The Civil List in Eighteenth-Century British Politics." *Historical Journal* 9, no. 3 (1966): 318+.

"Remarks by Richard Frothingham." MHS, *Proceedings* 14 (1875–76): 53+, 261+.

"Revolutionary Journal of Aaron Wright, 1775." *History Magazine* 6 (July 1862): 208+.

"Revolutionary War Journal, Kept by Phineas Ingalls." *Historical Collections of the Essex Institute* 53 (1917): 81+.

Reynolds, Donald E. "Ammunition Supply in Revolutionary Virginia." *VMHB* 73, no. 1 (Jan. 1965): 56+.

Riedel, Stefan. "Edward Jenner and the History of Smallpox and Vaccination." Baylor University Medical Center, *Proceedings* 18, no. 1 (Jan. 2005): 21+.

Robson, Eric. "The Expedition to the Southern Colonies, 1775–1776." *English Historical Review* 66, no. 261 (Oct. 1951): 535+.

Roche, John F., ed. "Quebec Under Siege, 1775–1776." *Canadian Historical Review* 50 (March 1969): 68+.

Ruppert, Bob. "Richard Howe: Admiral of the British Fleet in North America and Peace Commissioner." *JAR*, March 7, 2018.

Salav, David L. "The Production of Gunpowder in Pennsylvania During the American Revolution." *PMHB* 99, no. 4 (Oct. 1975): 422+.

Sanders, Harry. "The First American Submarine." U.S. Naval Institute, *Proceedings* 62, no. 12 (Dec. 1936): 1743+.

Scudder, H. E. "The Siege of Boston." *Atlantic Monthly* 37 (Apr. 1876): 466+.

Scull, G. D., ed. "The Montresor Journals." NYHS, *Collections* (1881): 1+.

Sellers, Horace Wells. "Charles Willson Peale, Artist-Soldier." *PMHB* 38, no. 3 (1914): 257+.

Sergeant R——. "The Battle of Princeton." *PMHB* 20, no. 4 (1896): 515+.

Shy, John W. "A New Look at Colonial Militia." *WMQ*, 3rd ser., 20, no. 2 (Apr. 1963): 175+.

Smith, Frank. "Dover in the Revolution." *Dedham Historical Register* 3 (1892): 25+.

Smith, Paul H. "The American Loyalists: Notes on Their Organization and Numerical Strength." *WMQ*, 3rd ser., 25, no. 2 (Apr. 1968): 259+.

Smith, William, ed. "Journal Kept in Quebec in 1775 by James Jeffry." *Historical Collections of the Essex Institute* 50, no 2 (Apr. 1914): 97+.

Smith, Wilson Cary. "The Roger Morris House, Washington's Headquarters on Harlem Heights, 1776." *Magazine of American History* 6 (1881): 89+.

Smoak, Katherine. "The Weight of Necessity: Counterfeit Coins in the British Atlantic World, Circa 1760–1800." *WMQ* 74, no. 3 (July 2017): 467+.

Soodalter, Ron. "Arming the Revolution." *MHQ* 27, no. 2 (Winter 2015): 80+.

Soucier, Daniel S. "'Where There Was No Signs of Any Human Being': Navigating the Eastern Country Wilderness on Arnold's March to Quebec, 1775." *JMH* 81, no 2 (Apr. 2017): 369+.

Stephenson, Orlando W. "The Supply of Gunpowder in 1776." *AHR* 30, no. 2 (Jan. 1925): 271+.

Stout, Neil R. "Manning the Royal Navy in North America, 1763–1775." *American Neptune* 23, no. 3 (July 1963): 176.

Syrett, David. "The Disruption of H.M.S. *Flora's* Convoy, 1776." *Mariner's Mirror* 56, no. 4 (1970): 423+.

Thomson, David Whittet. "David Bushnell and the First American Submarine." U.S. Naval Institute, *Proceedings* 68, no. 2 (Feb. 1942): 176+.

Todd, Charles Burr. "The March to Montreal and Quebec." *American Historical Register*, March 1895, 641+.

Trumbull, Benjamin. "A Concise Journal or Minutes of the Principal Movements Towards St. John's." *Collections of the Connecticut Historical Society* 7 (1899): 147+.

Tucker, Louis L., ed. "'To My Inexpressible Astonishment': Admiral Sir George Collier's Observations on the Battle of Long Island." *New-York Historical Society Quarterly* 48, no. 4 (Oct. 1964): 293+.

Tyler, Lyon G., ed. "The Old Virginia Line in the Middle States During the American Revolution." *Tyler's Quarterly* 12, no. 1 (July 1930): 1+.

Van Tyne, C. H. "French Aid Before the Alliance of 1778." *AHR* 31, no. 1 (Oct. 1925): 34+.

Vermeule, Cornelius C. "Some Revolutionary Incidents in the Raritan Valley." *Proceedings of the New Jersey Historical Society*, Apr. 1921, 73+.

Wainwright, Nicholas B., and Sarah Logan Fisher. "'A Diary of Trifling Occurrences': Philadelphia, 1776–1778." *PMHB* 82, no. 4 (Oct. 1858): 411+.

Wall, Alexander J. "The Equestrian Statue of George III and the Pedestrian Statue of William Pitt." *New-York Historical Society Quarterly*, July 1920, 35+.

Waring, Joseph I. "Medicine in Charleston at the Time of the Revolution." *JAMA* 236, no. 1 (July 5, 1976): 31+.

Weller, Jac. "Guns of Destiny: Field Artillery in the Trenton-Princeton Campaign." *Military Affairs* 20, no. 1 (Spring 1956): 1+.

Whiteley, W. H. "The British Navy and the Siege of Quebec, 1775–76." *Canadian Historical Review* 61, no. 1 (1980): 3+.

Wickman, Donald. "The Diary of Timothy Tuttle." *New Jersey History* 113, nos. 3–4 (Fall–Winter 1995): 61+.

——, ed. "A Most Unsettled Time on Lake Champlain: The October 1776 Journal of Jahiel Stewart." Vermont Historical Society, *Proceedings* 64, no. 2 (Spring 1996): 89+.

Wild, Ebenezer. "A Journal of a March from Cambridge." MHS, *Proceedings*, 2nd ser., 2 (Apr. 1886): 265+.

Williams, Elisha, and W. Hyde Appleton. "Elisha Williams' Diary of 1776." *PMHB* 48, no. 4 (1924): 334+.

Williams, William H. "Independence and Early American Hospitals, 1751–1812." *JAMA* 236, no. 1 (July 5, 1976): 35+.

Woodward, Colin. "The Revolution's Band of Brothers." *MHQ*, Summer 2010, 80+.

Wright, John W. "Some Notes on the Continental Army." *WMQ*, 2nd ser., 11, no. 2 (Apr. 1931): 81+.

York, Neil L. "Clandestine Aid and the American Revolutionary War Effort: A Re-examination." *Military Affairs* 43, no. 1 (Feb. 1979): 26+.

Young, Alfred F. "George Robert Twelves Hewes (1742–1840)." *WMQ*, 3rd ser., 38, no. 4 (Oct. 1981): 561+.

Young, Henry J. "Treason and Its Punishment in Revolutionary Pennsylvania." *PMHB* 90, no. 3 (July 1966): 287+.

Young, William. "Journal of Sergeant William Young." *PMHB* 8, no. 3 (Oct. 1884): 255+.

Zellers-Frederick, Andrew A. "The Hessians Who Escaped Washington's Trap at Trenton." *JAR*, Apr. 18, 2018.

EIGHTEENTH-CENTURY NEWSPAPERS CITED

British: *Gazetteer and New Daily Advertiser; General Evening Post; Gentleman's Magazine; Lloyd's Evening Post; London Chronicle; London Evening Post; London Gazette and New Daily Advertiser; Middlesex Journal and Evening Advertiser; Morning Chronicle and London Advertiser; Morning Post and Daily Advertiser; Public Advertiser; Scots Magazine; St. James's Chronicle; Whitehall Evening Post*

    American: *Boston Evening-Post; Boston-Gazette and Country Journal; Constitutional Gazette; Essex Gazette; Maryland Gazette; New York Gazette; New-England Chronicle; New-Hampshire Gazette; New York Evening Mail; New York Journal; Pennsylvania Evening Post; Pennsylvania Packet; Virginia Gazette* (various publications under this name)

MANUSCRIPTS, COLLECTIONS, AND ARCHIVES

Bancroft Collection, New York Public Library, New York City
Commonwealth of Massachusetts State Archives, Boston
Concord Free Public Library, Massachusetts
Concord Museum, Massachusetts

David Library of the American Revolution, Pennsylvania
Firestone Library, Princeton University, New Jersey
Founders Online, U.S. National Archives and Records Administration, Washington, D.C.
Georgian Papers, Royal Archives, Windsor Castle, U.K.
Gilder Lehrman Institute of American History, New York City
Huntington Library, San Marino, California
Library and Archives Canada, Ottawa
Library of Congress, Washington, D.C.
Massachusetts Historical Society, Boston
Milton S. Eisenhower Library, Johns Hopkins University, Baltimore
Minute Man National Historical Park, Massachusetts
National Archives, Kew, U.K.
National Museum of African American History and Culture, Washington, D.C.
National Museum of the Royal Navy, Portsmouth, U.K.
New-York Historical Society, New York City
Papers of George Washington, University of Virginia, Charlottesville
Society of the Cincinnati, Washington, D.C.
St. Eustatius Historical Foundation Museum, Oranjestad, St. Eustatius
Thompson-Pell Research Center, Fort Ticonderoga, New York
U.S. Army Military History Institute, Army Heritage and Education Center, Carlisle, Pennsylvania
William L. Clements Library, University of Michigan, Ann Arbor

DOCTORAL DISSERTATIONS

Blanks, Joseph Younger, Jr. "The Administration of Governor Josiah Martin in North Carolina." University of North Carolina, 1948.
Deary, William Paul. "Toward Disaster at Fort Washington, November 1776." George Washington University, 1996.
Gabriel, Michael Paul. "Major General Richard Montgomery." Pennsylvania State University, 1996.
Hast, Adele. "Loyalism in Revolutionary Virginia: The Norfolk Area and the Eastern Shore." University of Iowa, 1979.
Johnson, Victor Leroy. "The Administration of the American Commissariat During the Revolutionary War." University of Pennsylvania, 1941.
Knight, Roger Beckett. "The Royal Dockyards in England at the Time of the American War of Independence." University of London, 1972.
Moomaw, W. Hugh. "The Naval Career of Captain Hamond, 1775–1779." University of Virginia, 1955.
Nuxoll, Elizabeth M. "Congress and the Munitions Merchants." New York University, 1979.
Smith, James Ferrell. "The Rise of Artemas Ward, 1727–1777." University of Colorado, Boulder, 1990.
Tacyn, Mark Andrew. "To the End: The First Maryland Regiment and the American Revolution." University of Maryland, College Park, 1999.

MISCELLANY

"The American Revolution Comes to Cambridge." Cambridge Historical Commission, http://www2.cambridgema.gov/Historic/revolutionarymap.html.
Anderson, Fred. Review, "Battle of Princeton Mapping Project," n.d., University of Colorado, https://www.ias.edu/sites/default/files/media-assets/Anderson-review-Milner-report.pdf.
"Archives of Maryland Online." *Maryland Gazette* Collection, http://msa.maryland.gov/megafile/msa/speccol/sc4800/sc4872/001282/html/m1282-1168.html.
Bailyn, Bernard. "The Battle of Bunker Hill." MHS, http://www.masshist.org/bh/index.html.
Balisciano, Márcia. "Benjamin Franklin and Public History: Restoring Benjamin Franklin House," n.d., www.benjaminfranklinhouse.org.
Barefoot, Daniel W. "Moore's Creek Bridge, Battle of," in William S. Powell, ed., *Encyclopedia of North Carolina* (2006), https://www.ncpedia.org/moores-creek-bridge-battle.

Bearrs, Edwin C. "The Battle of Sullivan's Island and the Capture of Fort Moultrie." NPS, June 30, 1968.

———. "The First Two Fort Moultries: A Structural History." NPS, June 1968.

Bell, J. L. "George Washington's Headquarters and Home." NPS, Feb. 2012.

Bell, John. "On the Nature and Cure of Gun-Shot Wounds." *The British Military Library*. Vol. 1. London: Richard Phillips, 1804.

Berthelson, Robert L. "An Alarm from Lexington." Connecticut Society of the Sons of the American Revolution, www.connecticutsar.org/an-alarm-from-lexington.

Bolton, Reginald Pelham. "Forgotten Things and Places in the City of New York." NYHS, 1918.

Bradford, Charles H. "Dorchester Heights: Prelude to Independence," n.d., http://www.dorchesteratheneum.org/pdf/Dorchester%20Heights.pdf.

Brunet, Michel. *French Canada and the Early Decades of British Rule, 1760–1791*. Canadian Historical Association, booklet no. 13, 1981.

Burke, William W., and Linnea M. Bass. "Brigade of Guards in the American Service," www.brigadeofguards.org/history.

———. "Preparing a British Unit for Service in America: The Brigade of Foot Guards, 1776," http://military-historians.org/company/journal/guards/guards.htm.

Burt, A. L. *Guy Carleton, Lord Dorchester, 1724–1808*. Ottawa: Canadian Historical Association Booklets, no. 5, 1968.

Butler, Nic. "Rediscovering Charleston's Colonial Fortifications: A Weblog for the Mayor's 'Walled City' Task Force, www.WalledCityTaskForce.org.

Capps, Michael A., and Steven A. Davis. "Moore's Creek National Battlefield: An Administrative History," June 1999, NPS, https://www.nps.gov/parkhistory/online_books/mocr/adhi_1.htm.

Charles Willson Peale and His World. Exhibition and brochure, National Portrait Gallery, Washington, D.C., 1982.

Clifton, James M. "MacDonald, Donald," in William S. Powell, ed., *Dictionary of North Carolina Biography*, 1991, www.ncpedia.org/biography/macdonald-donald.

Cohn, Arthur B., et al. "Valcour Bay Research Project: 1999–2002 Result." Lake Champlain Maritime Museum et al., June 2003.

"Complete Sun and Moon Data for One Day." U.S. Naval Observatory, http://aa.usno.navy.mil/data/docs/RS_OneDay.php.

"Cultural Landscape Report for Battle Road Unit." Vol. 1, MMNHP, 2005.

Declaration Resources Project. Harvard University, https://declaration.fas.harvard.edu/faq/how-many-grievances-are-declaration-independence.

Delaware River Basin Commission, river mileage system, http://www.state.nj.us/drbc/basin/river/.

Dietzel, Tom. "The Real Story Behind Thomas Guchy and His Stolen Angels." Old North Foundation, www.oldnorth.com, Feb.–Apr. 2016.

Diugosz, Kate. "Not the Hudson: A Comprehensive Study of the East River." Fordham University, 2011, http://www.eastriverhistory.webs.com/naturalhistory/treacherouswaters.htm.

Douglas, W.A.B. "Schank, John," *Dictionary of Canadian Biography*, vol. 6, http://www.biographi.ca/en/bio/schank_john_6E.html.

"The Effectiveness of 18th Century Musketry." Old Fort Niagara Association, Jan. 2016, video, https://www.youtube.com/watch?v=8Cw8ktmlF1A&feature=youtu.be.

Ferraro, William M. "Standing Against Corruption and Favoritism: Benjamin Rush and George Washington During the Revolutionary and Founding Eras." Draft, University of Virginia, 2013.

"5 Things You Didn't Know About the Secret Spying Arm of the Post Office." *BBC History Magazine*, Oct. 15, 2014, www.historyextra.com.

Flavell, Julie. "The Plot to Kidnap King George III." *BBC History*, Nov. 2006.

"Fort Lee, New Jersey: A Sketch of Its Revolutionary History." *Documents of the Assembly of the State of New York*. Vol. 42, appendix B, 1909.

"Gage's Instructions." Project Gutenberg, American Antiquarian Society Library. Reprint, New York: Arno Press, 1971.

"Galloway, Joseph." *Biographical Directory of the United States Congress*, http://bioguide.congress
.gov/scripts/biodisplay.pl?index=Goooo26.

Glover, T. N. "The Retreat of '76 Across Bergen County." Lecture, Bergen County Historical Society, Nov. 20, 1905, https://archive.org/details/papersproceeding19berg.

"Gold Coach a 'Bumpy Ride." BBC News, June 2, 2002, http://news.bbc.co.uk/2/hi/uk_news
/england/1984344.stm.

"Gold State Coach." Royal Collection Trust, www.royalcollection.org.uk/collection/5000048/gold
-state-coach.

Graves, Samuel. "The Conduct of Vice-Admiral Samuel Graves in North America." 2 vols. Manuscript copy, Johns Hopkins University Library, Baltimore.

Green, Jonathan. "Estimate of Damages," May 7, 1776, MHS, www.masshist.org/database/1910.

Grigg, Bob. "Old Newgate Prison." Colebrook Historical Society (Conn.), n.d., http://
colebrookhistoricalsociety.org/OldNewgatePrison.htm.

Grundy, J. Owen. "The Glory That Was Once Richmond Hill's Is Long Since Faded and Forgotten." Part 1. *Villager*, Sept. 13, 1945, http://www.getny.com/grundyrichmondhill.shtml.

Hagglund, L. F. *A Page from the Past: The Story of the Continental Gundelo* Philadelphia *on Lake
Champlain, 1776–1949*. Adirondack Resorts Press, 1949.

Hagist, Don. "'A Token of Surrender' or 'One Mode of Attack': The Firelock Clubb'd." The Continental Line, http://www.continentalline.org/articles/article.php?date=9804&article=980401.

Himes, Charles F. "Colonel Robert Magaw." Lecture, Hamilton Library Association, Carlisle,
Pa., 1915.

"Historic Light Station Information." U.S. Coast Guard, Massachusetts, www.uscg.mil/history
/weblighthouses/LHMA.asp.

"History of the 43rd Regiment of Foot," http://www.243regiment.com/history_43.html.

"A History of the Official American Presence in France." U.S. State Department, n.d., https://
photos.state.gov/libraries/france/45994/irc/uspresenceinfrance.pdf.

Hoffman, Renoda. *The Battle of White Plains: October 28, 1776*. White Plains, N.Y.: City of White
Plains, 1999.

———. *Historic Highlights of Westchester*. White Plains, N.Y.: Battle of White Plains Monument
Committee, 1969.

Holland, Martha. "Documentary Research on the Brooks Tanyard." In Alan T. Synenki, ed.,
Archeological Investigations of Minute Man National Historic Park (Boston: National Park
Service, 1990).

"Hugh Mercer." George Washington's Mount Vernon, http://www.mountvernon.org/digital
-encyclopedia/article/hugh-mercer/.

Hutson, James. "Nathan Hale Revisited." Library of Congress, "Information Bulletin" (July–
Aug. 2003), www.loc.gov/loc/lcib/0307-8/hale.html.

———. "Revolutionary America: The Papers of Gen. James Grant." Library of Congress, "Information Bulletin," Apr. 2003, https://www.loc.gov/loc/lcib/0304/papers.html.

"Index of Harvard Graduates in the Classes of 1642–1772." Harvard University, https://iiif.lib
.harvard.edu/manifests/view/drs:46585443$12i.

Kehoe, Vincent J.-R. "A Military Guide: The British Infantry of 1775." Society for the Preservation of Colonial Culture, 1974.

———. "We Were There!" Vols. 1 and 2, MMNHP.

"Land Use History." Trenton Historical Society, www.trentonhistory.org/Documents/MillHill
.History.htm.

Leitch, Alexander. *A Princeton Companion*, 1978, https://etcweb.princeton.edu/CampusWWW
/Companion/rush_benjamin.html.

"Life Guards." *Digital Encyclopedia of George Washington*, http://www.mountvernon.org/digital
-encyclopedia/article/life-guards/.

MacIntyre, Doug. "Thomson Park: Revolutionary War Battle Site," https://thomsonpark.wordpress
.com/.

Mackesy, Piers. "Could the British Have Won the War of Independence?" Lecture, Clark University, Worcester, Mass., Sept. 1975.

Malcom, Joyce Lee. "The Scene of the Battle, 1775: Historic Grounds Report, MMNHP." NPS, n.d.

Martin, Eliza Layne. "Eliza Lucas Pinckney: Indigo in the Atlantic World." N.d., http://cwh.ucsc .edu/SocialBiog.Martin.pdf.

McConnell, David. "British Smooth-Bore Artillery." National Historic Parks and Sites, Canada, 1988.

McGeachy, Robert A. "The American War of Lieutenant Colonel Archibald Campbell." *Early America Review*, vol. 5, https://www.varsitytutors.com/earlyamerica/early-america-review /volume-5/the-american-war-of-lieutenant-colonel-archibald-campbell.

Milkofsky, Brenda. "David Bushnell and His Revolutionary Submarine," https://connecticuthistory .org.

Millard, James P. "The Story of Arnold's Bay." Valcour Bay Research Project, http://www .historiclakes.org/Valcour/arnoldsbay.htm.

New York City Revolutionary War Forts, http://www.northamericanforts.com/East/nycity .html#revyork.

"The Old Exchange & Provost Dungeon," http://oldexchange.org/history/.

"Old Slave Mart." Charleston, NPS, https://www.nps.gov/nr/travel/charleston/osm.htm.

Osman, Julia. "From Greatest Enemies to Greatest Allies: France and America in the War for Independence." Lecture, 4th Annual Conference on the American Revolution, March 2015, Williamsburg, Va.

"Parker's Revenge Archaeological Project." Final report, Friends of the Minute Man National Park, Oct. 2016.

Parry, Oliver Randolph. "Coryell's Ferry in the Revolution." Lecture, Fort Washington chapter, Daughters of the American Revolution, May 21, 1915.

Peterson, Mark. "Review of Battle of Princeton Mapping Project." University of California, Berkeley, https://www.ias.edu/sites/default/files/media-assets/Peterson-review-Milner-report.pdf.

Piecuch, Jim. "Preventing Slave Insurrection in South Carolina and Georgia, 1775–1776." *JAR*, Feb. 21, 2017.

"A Plan of the Attack on Fort Sulivan [*sic*]." Print Room, Royal Library, Windsor Castle, n.d., No. 734016-17.

Quintal, George, Jr. "Patriots of Color." MMNHP, Feb. 2002.

Rees, John U. "Preliminary Research on River Vessels Used by the Continental Army, 1775–1782." DLAR, Aug. 1998.

"The Revolutionary War Diary of Chaplain Andrew Hunter," http://www.revwar75.com/library /bob/HunterDiaries.htm.

"Roxbury During the Siege of Boston." NPS, n.d., http://www.nps.gov/bost/learn/education /upload/roxbury.pdf.

Ryan, D. Michael. "White Cockade: A Jacobite Air at the North Bridge?," https://www2.bc.edu /~hafner/lmm/music-articles/white_cockade_ryan.html.

Sabin, Douglas P. "The New England Tavern: A General Study." MMNHP, 1982.

Schenawolf, Harry. "Washington's New York City Headquarters, No. 1 Broadway." "Revolutionary War Journal," July 9, 2013, http://www.revolutionarywarjournal.com/washingtons -headquarters/.

Selig, Robert A., et al. "Battle of Princeton Mapping Project: Report of Military Terrain Analysis and Battle Narrative." John Milner Associates, for Princeton Battlefield Society, Sept. 2010.

Seymour, Joseph. Lecture, U.S. Army National Guard historian. Society of the Cincinnati, Washington, D.C., Jan. 16, 2015.

"Shipwrecks of Cork Harbor," http://www.corkshipwrecks.net/ssshipwrecklist18thcent.html.

Snyder, John P. "The Mapping of New Jersey in the American Revolution." New Jersey Historical Commission, 1975.

State Exhibition Series. Society of the Cincinnati, http://www.societyofthecincinnati.org /scholarship/publications/.

The Story of a Town: 1664–1964. Eastchester, N.Y., 1964.

"The Submarine Turtle: Naval Documents of the Revolutionary War." Naval History and Heritage Command, https://www.history.navy.mil.

Sullivan, Judith Q. "North Bridge Historic Structure Report." MMNHP, Feb. 2004.

Taylor, C. James, ed. *Founding Families: Digital Editions of the Papers of the Winthrops and the Adamses.* MHS, http://www.masshist.org/agde2/.

"Thomas Jefferson, a Brief Biography," https://www.monticello.org/site/jefferson/thomas-jefferson-brief-biography.

Thompson, Mary V. "'As If I Had Been a Very Great Somebody': Martha Washington in the American Revolution." Lecture, Nov. 9, 2002, Mount Vernon, http://catalog.mountvernon.org/cdm/ref/collection/p16829coll4/id/2.

"Washington Mansion House Tavern." Historical blueprints, Historical American Buildings Survey, 1936.

Watters, Meg. "Parker's Revenge Narrative Report, Phase I." MMNHP, Feb. 2014.

Widmer, Kemble. "The Christmas Campaign: The Ten Days of Trenton and Princeton." Trenton: New Jersey Historical Commission, 1975.

"The Wreck of the HMS *Somerset* (III)." NPS, Cape Cod National Seashore, n.d., https://www.nps.gov/caco/learn/historyculture/upload/Somersetrack.pdf.

Acknowledgments

One hundred and two stone steps, and then another twenty-one wooden stairs lead to the garret of the Round Tower in Windsor Castle, twenty miles west of London. Here reside the papers of George III, America's last king. The brassy crash of a military band occasionally drifts up from the courtyard far below, where Coldstream Guards wearing crimson coats and bearskin hats march in perfect step through the Norman Gate. A souvenir shop in the Middle Ward sells castle refrigerator magnets and toy guardsmen, as well as the inevitable corgi key chains, corgi throw pillows, and corgi Christmas ornaments. From the tower battlements can be seen, three miles down the Long Walk to the south, a twenty-five-ton equestrian statue of George, cast from old brass cannons in the decade after his death. He is dressed as Marcus Aurelius, in toga and laurel crown, much like the figure yanked from its pedestal in New York in July 1776 and melted into bullets by regicidal American rebels. Here the king remains mounted atop his plinth, regal and oversized, honored if not revered.

I spent a month with the king's papers in April 2016, as a fellow of the Georgian Papers Programme, climbing to the top of the Round Tower each morning to live in George's world and to better understand why he would wage war against his own subjects for eight years across three thousand miles of ocean. The vast majority of the papers have not been published, and they were only recently opened to scholars as part of an ambitious project by the Royal Archives, Royal Library, and King's College London to catalog and digitize some 350,000 pages.

I acknowledge the permission of Her Majesty, Queen Elizabeth II, for the use of these materials. I'm grateful for assistance from the remarkable professionals at Windsor Castle, particularly Oliver Urquhart Irvine, the librarian and assistant keeper of the Queen's Archives, and Oliver Walton, who serves as the Georgian Papers Programme coordinator and curator, Historical Papers Project. Thanks to Lynnette Beech, Julie Crocker, Allison Derrett, Laura Hobbs, Hannah Litvack, Cherelle Nightingill, and

Emma Stuart. In the Royal Library, I thank Elizabeth Clark Ashby, curator of books and manuscripts, and Megan Gent, conservator. Thanks also to Martin Clayton, head of prints and drawings, and Carly Collier, Print Room assistant. I also thank Christopher Geidt, now Lord Geidt, former private secretary to Queen Elizabeth II.

The Omohundro Institute of Early American History and Culture and the College of William & Mary in Williamsburg, Virginia, are the American partners of the Georgian Papers Programme, and I thank Karin Wulf, the Omohundro director, and her colleagues Martha Howard and Beverly Smith.

Another hundred or more archivists, historians, curators, and librarians at two dozen institutions generously offered expertise and assistance, for which I am indebted.

The William L. Clements Library on the University of Michigan campus in Ann Arbor holds many of the nation's greatest archival treasures from the eighteenth century. I thank Cheney J. Schopieray, the curator of manuscripts; Clayton Lewis, the curator of graphics materials and head of reader services; and Janet Bloom.

At the Papers of George Washington project on the University of Virginia campus in Charlottesville, I received assistance and warm encouragement from Edward G. Lengel, the editor in chief (who subsequently became chief historian at the White House Historical Association), and his colleagues William M. Ferraro and Benjamin Huggins.

In Charleston, South Carolina, I thank Doug MacIntyre for his insights into the action at Breach Inlet near Sullivan's Island; C. J. Cantwell, the tower captain, and Edward Jackson, for an exhilarating tour of the steeple atop St. Michael's Church; Nic Butler, public historian for the Charleston County Public Library, for his expertise on the city's colonial fortifications; and especially David L. Preston, the Westvaco Professor of National Security Studies at the Citadel, for showing me his eighteenth-century town.

At the New-York Historical Society, I thank Joe Festa, Dale Marsha Gregory, Alexander Kassl, Tammy Kiter, and Mariam Touba. Thanks also to Kathie Ludwig at the David Library of the American Revolution in Washington Crossing, Pennsylvania; Matthew Keagle, curator at the Thompson-Pell Research Center at Fort Ticonderoga, New York; David F. Wood, curator at the Concord Museum in Massachusetts; the staff of the Massachusetts Historical Society; the staff of the National Archives in Kew, England; the staff of the Historical Foundation Museum in St. Eustatius; curator David R. Daly and Marissa Cheifetz at the Longfellow House–Washington's Headquarters National Historic Site in Cambridge, Massachusetts; and

Alexandra McEwen and Suzanne Lemaire of the reference services division of the Library and Archives Canada, in Ottawa.

I thank Olga Tsapina, Catherine Wehrey, Jaeda Snow, and Alisa Monheim at the Huntington Library in San Marino, California. At the Society of the Cincinnati in Washington, D.C., where I spent many productive hours, I'm indebted to Jack D. Warren, Jr., executive director; Ellen McCallister Clark, library director; Rachel Jirka, research services librarian; and Hilary Bonn.

Ira D. Gruber, the Harris Masterson, Jr., Professor Emeritus of History at Rice University, in Houston, helped launch me on this literary endeavor with his infectious enthusiasm for the Revolution. At Princeton University, I thank AnnaLee Pauls and John Walako of Rare Books and Special Collections in Firestone Library, and Rossy Mendez, public services project archivist at the Seeley G. Mudd Manuscript Library.

In New York City, thanks to Deborah Woodbridge, caretaker at the Conference House Museum on Staten Island; Tom Trombone at the Harbor Defense Museum and Juan Caez at the Fort Hamilton Visitors' Center; Jeff Richman, historian at Green-Wood Cemetery; Kimberly Maier, executive director of the Old Stone House in Brooklyn; Carol Ward, executive director, and Emilie Gruchow, director of archives, at the Morris-Jumel Mansion, as well as Michael Whitten, marketing coordinator. In Westchester County, New York, I'm grateful to David Osborn, site manager, and Michael Callahan, National Park Service ranger, at St. Paul's Church National Historic Site in Mount Vernon; and to Robert Hoch, president of the White Plains Historical Society, for a tour of the Jacob Purdy House. Particular thanks to my friend Barnet Schecter, who spent two days guiding me across the battle sites of greater New York, from the western tip of Staten Island to the high ground above White Plains.

The distinguished British naval historian Roger J. B. Knight, former deputy director of the National Maritime Museum at Greenwich, offered insight and advice regarding the Royal Navy of the 1770s. Thanks also to Joseph Seymour, the Army National Guard historian at the U.S. Army Center of Military History in Washington, D.C., for helping me understand eighteenth-century munitions. Thanks to Richard Colton, historic weapons supervisor at the Springfield Armory National Historic Site in Massachusetts. At the Château Ramezay, in Montreal, I appreciate the assistance I received from André Delisle, *directeur général et conservateur*, historian Pierre Monette, and Christine Brisson, head of collections and exhibitions.

At Mount Vernon, in Alexandria, Virginia, I thank Douglas Bradburn, the president and CEO, who previously served as founding director of the

Fred W. Smith National Library for the Study of George Washington. Thanks also to Curtis G. Viebranz, the former president, and to Rob Shenk, senior vice president.

At the Commonwealth of Massachusetts State Archives in Boston, I appreciate the assistance of Michael Comeau, executive director; Martha Clark, curator; Jennifer Fauxsmith, reference supervisor; Stephanie Dyson, processing archivist; Caitlin Jones, reference assistant; and Lillian Tiarks, reference intern.

For help in walking the battlefields at Trenton and Princeton, I'm grateful to Ralph Siegel; Roger S. Williams and Kip Cherry of the Princeton Battlefield Society; and Joseph Capone, executive director of Friends of Washington Crossing Park.

For twenty years I have found a port in the storm in Carlisle, Pennsylvania, at the U.S. Army's Military History Institute, part of the Army Heritage and Education Center. There, and at the adjacent U.S. Army War College, I am beholden to Col. (ret.) Charles D. Allen, Tami Davis Biddle, Tom Buffenbarger, Stephen Bye, Conrad C. Crane, Col. Peter D. Crean, Maj. Gen. Anthony A. Cucolo III, Col. Matthew Dawson, Tom Hendrix, Clifton Hyatt, Maj. Gen. John S. Kem, Maj. Gen. William E. Rapp, Shannon Schwaller, Jessica Sheets, and Richard J. Sommers. I particularly appreciate Richard L. Baker's efforts to share his comprehensive research on the Flying Camp.

I appreciate the continued encouragement of the Association of the United States Army, from the past president, Gen. (ret.) Gordon R. Sullivan; his successor, Gen. (ret.) Carter F. Ham; Lt. Gen. (ret.) Thomas G. Rhame; and Lt. Col. (ret.) Roger Cirillo.

Thanks also to Col. Ty Seidule, head of the U.S. Military Academy department of history; Bruce H. Franklin of Westholme Publishing; Alexandra Mosquin, manager of historical services and the archaeology and history branch at Parks Canada; Anthony Page of the University of Tasmania; Bruce and Lynne Venter of America's History, LLC; Gary Mortensen, president of Stoller Family Estate; and Mark French, Matt Jones, Rainey Foster, and Lauren Wolf of Leading Authorities.

I also thank: Peter C. Agre, Liaquat Ahamed, Ed Bearrs, J. L. Bell, Tom Brokaw, James MacGregor Burns, Jonathan R. Dull, David Hackett Fischer, Don N. Hagist, Rachael Hancock, Mark Hilliard, Ellen Himelstein, Allan R. Millett, Wayne R. and Catherine B. Reynolds, Lynn Riedesel, Erica Sagalyn, John J. Toffey, Gregory W. Wendt, Gordon S. Wood, and my fellow scribbler David Maraniss.

In researching this book I had invaluable help from Joseph Balkoski, director of the Maryland Museum of Military History in Baltimore, as well as from my former *Washington Post* colleague Lucy Shackelford, who also tracked down most of the illustrations displayed in these pages. The resourceful Zane Sterling, then a senior at New York University, helped with research at the New York Public Library and the New-York Historical Society. The maps in this volume are the work of master cartographer Gene Thorp, who has been a great partner for five books now.

For twenty years, I have relied on the counsel and friendship of Tim Nenninger, former chief of modern military records at the National Archives and Records Administration in College Park, Maryland. For nearly as long I have benefited from the generosity, hospitality, and companionship of Sir Max Hastings, among the greatest storytelling historians in our language, and his wife, Penny.

I was fortunate to have seven accomplished historians and authors read all or part of the manuscript: Joseph Balkoski, Don N. Hagist, Edward G. Lengel, James Kirby Martin, David L. Preston, Barnet Schecter, and James Scott Wheeler. I am deeply grateful for their expertise and encouragement. Any errors of omission or commission, fact or interpretation, are of course solely my responsibility.

For more than thirty years, I've had the extraordinary benefit of a single editor, John Sterling, and a single literary agent, Rafe Sagalyn, for the seven books we produced together during that span. I thank them publicly and profusely. Thanks, too, to others on the team at Henry Holt and at the publisher's parent company, Macmillan: John Sargent, Don Weisberg, Stephen Rubin, Maggie Richards, Kenn Russell, Meryl Levavi, Kelly Too, Richard Pracher, Jason Liebman, Chuck Thompson, James Meader, Diana Frost, and Caroline Wray. I'm grateful to copy editor Bonnie Thompson for her great diligence and patience, and to publicist extraordinaire Elizabeth Shreve for her unflagging efforts to promote this book.

The solitude of the writerly life is best dispelled by a loving, vivacious family. How lucky I am to have mine: Jane, Rush, Sarah, J.P., and Jessica.

Index

Page numbers in *italics* refer to maps.

Abercrombie, James, 105, 113
"Abstract of the Foreign Troops," 559
Actaeon (British warship), 248, *322*, *339*, *341*
Active (British warship), *322*, *334*, *337*, *340*
Acton minute company, 68, 71–72, 78
Adams, Abigail, 109, 117, 240, 257, 268, 295,
    350, 386, 433, 469, 564
Adams, John, 83, 448
    Army and, 126, 128, 307, 433
    Boston and, 13, 36, 257, 259–60, 267–68
    Bunker Hill and, 109, 113
    on campaign of 1776–77, 562, 564
    Canada and, 295, 411
    Church and, 129–30
    Congress and, 109
    Declaration of Independence and, 349–50
    Falmouth and, 139
    fireships and, 359
    Franklin and, 275
    Hancock and, 42
    Jefferson and, 349
    Knox and, 234
    Lee and, 330–31
    Long Island and, 373
    loyalists and, 310
    New York and, 304
    Paine and, 487
    privateers and, 468–69
    Prohibitory Act and, 180
    Quakers and, 80
    Staten Island Conference and, 385–86
    Warren and, 37, 259
    Washington and, 117–18, 133, 229–30
Adams, John Quincy, 81
Adams, Samuel, 36–39, 53, 57, 59–60, 64, 90,
    99, 143, 295
Adams, Mrs. Samuel, 45
Addison, Joseph, 19, 401
Adlum, John, 451–52, 457
Adventure (British ship), 263, 265

Aetna (British warship), 407
African Americans (blacks), 90, 183–86,
    188–90, 231, 320, 323, 328–29, 346, 397.
    See also slaves and slavery
    Continental Army service by, 231
    population of, 184
Ainslie, Thomas, 199, 202, 204, 282–83
Aitken, James (John the Painter), 555–57
Aix, Battle of, 382
Ajax (British warship), 10
Albany, New York, 146, 236, 276, 312, 412, 423,
    552
Alcide (French ship), 382
Alexander, William, 365. *See* Stirling, Lord
Alexander the Great, 199, 452
Alfred (American warship), 468
Allen, Ethan, 84–85, 147, 154, 508
Allen, Joseph, 508
All for Love (Dryden), 323
America (British transport ship), 265
American Civil War, 26
American colonies
    British ignorance about, 9–10
    impact of war on, 561–63
    news of Concord spreads through, 79–81
    political debate in London on, 14, 169–79
    republic created by, 26–27
    restrictions on western expansion and,
        118
    self governance and, 9
    size of, and difficulty organizing, 7–8
American Crisis (Paine), 488, 519
American prisoners of war, 112, 212, 278–79,
    287, 294, 371–72, 374, 394, 423, 459,
    508–10, 549, 562
American spies, 92, 180–81, 400–402, 516, 533,
    541, 543, 555–56
Amherst, Sir Jeffrey, 24
Anderson, Enoch, 371, 377, 486, 493–95
Anderson, Ephraim, 281

André, John, 142
Andrew Doria (American warship), 318
Andrews, John, 85
Anglican Church, 183, 311
Annabella (British warship), 318
Anne (British transport ship), 318
Anne Boleyn, Queen of England, 22
"Answer to the Declaration, An," 558
Anti-Gambling Club, 48, 52
Antigua, 224, 227, 248, 506
Apprentice, The (comedy), 220
Aranda, Count de, 480
Archibald, Bartholomew, 193
Arethusa (British warship), 555
Argo (British transport ship), 224
Arnold, Benedict
  background of, 155–57, 428
  Canadian retreat and, *272*, 284–85, 289–92,
    296, 428
  grievances of, 412–13, 416, 428–29
  Lake Champlain and, *404*, 406, 412–23,
    426, 428
  Maine route to Quebec and, *140*, 154–62,
    237
  Montgomery's death and, 214–15
  Montreal visit by Franklin and, 273–74,
    276–78
  Quebec and, 161–63, 195–202, *201*, 204–5,
    207–13, 281
  Rhode Island and, 514
  Ticonderoga and, 84–85, 129, 156
  Washington and, 156–58, 160–61
Arnold, Hannah, 213, 215, 412
Asia (British warship), 52, 300, 319
Assunpink Creek, *484*, 511, *515*, 523, 525–26,
  528, 534, 538–40
Atkins, Christopher, 339, 341
Augur, Helen, 468
Austin, Jonathan Williams, 448
Austria, 482
Avery, David, 99
Aztec Empire, 199

Bahamas, 468
Bailyn, Bernard, 312, 487
Baker, John, 39
Baldwin, Jeduthan, 259, 290, 424
"Baleful Influence of Standing Armies, The"
  (Warren), 36
Baltic Merchant (British transport ship),
  265
Baltimore, 35, 136, 332, 499–500, 514, 527
Bancroft, Ebenezer, 102, 105, 108
Bangs, Isaac, 261, 350
Barbados, 133, 499

Barber, Edward, 76
Barber of Seville, The (Beaumarchais),
  473, 477
Barfleur (British warship), 6–7, 10
Barker, John, 52, 57, 63, 70, 74, 264–65
Barnsfare, Adam, 209
Barrett, Amos, 66
Barrett, James, 56, *65*, 66–68
Barrington, Lord William, 24, 43, 90, 114–15,
  165, 179, 242, 244–45
Bartlett, James, 46
Bartlett, W. P., 44
Battle Road, *65*, 70–82, 260
Beale, Robert, 541
Beaumarchais, Pierre-Augustin Caron,
  472–78, 480
Bedford, New Jersey, 68, *298*, 300, *353*, 365,
  368, 377
Bedloe's Island, *298*, 301, *380*, *391*
Beebe, Dr. Lewis, 291–92, 295
Beekman mansion, *430*, 436–37
Beethoven, Ludwig van, 27
Belgium, 306
Bellew, Henry, 191
Benedict, Abner, 360–61
Bermuda, 127, 306, 308
Berwick (British warship), 10
Betsey (merchant ship), 227
Bible
  Ephesians, 372
  Exodus, 158
  Jeremiah, 394
  Nehemiah, 424
  Old Testament, 122
  Psalm 80, 349
  Second Kings, 269
Bickham, Troy O., 170
Bird, Harrison, 422
blacks. *See* African Americans; slaves and
  slavery
Blockade of Boston, The (Burgoyne), 220, 222
Blood, Thaddeus, 66
Blue Bell Tavern, *298*, *350*, *396*, *449*, 451
Book-keeping Methodized, 450
Book of Fires, 127
Bordentown, New Jersey, 495, 513, *515*, 530, 533,
  541, 549–50
Boreas (British ship), 246
Boston, *41*
  British troops in, 9, 14–15, 19–20, 30, 36–42,
    46–52
  Bunker Hill and, 96, 98–99, 102–3, 112–13
  Concord and, 55–58, 70–77, 81
  Declaration of Independence and, 350
  preparations for war in, 35–38, 40–53

siege of, 76–77, 83–92, 113–14, 125, 134–36, 144, 171, 177–81, *218*, 219, 223–25, 231–33, 238–40, 331–32
siege of, broken, 257–71
Boston Committee of Safety, 37, 42, 53, 84, 87, 92–94, 96, 129
Boston Gazette, 45
Boston Harbor, 15, 35, 40, 43, 47, 75–76, *91*, 94–95, 125, 134, *218*, 227
British evacuate, 264–65, 318
British close, 19–24, 40
British enter, 30
rebel raids in, 86–89, 318
Boston Massacre (1770), 9, 36–38, 129, 220, 235, 259
Boston Neck, 52, 58, *65*, 73, 85–86, 96, 120, *218*, 229, 238, 261, 265
Boston News-Letter, 79
Boston Port Bill, 29
Boston Post-Boy, 49
Boston Post Road, *430*, *432*, *443*
Boston Powder Alarm, 40–42
Boston Tea Party, 12–15, 40
Bostwick, Elisha, 446
Boswell, James, 6–7, 13, 169
Bouchette, Jean Baptiste, 154
Bowling Green, *303*, 349, 351
Boyne (British ship), 52
Braddock, Edward, 39, 117, 239
Breach Inlet, *322*, 326, 328, 334, 336, 338, 343
Breed's Hill, 76, *91*, 94–95, 105, 110, 113, *218*
Bridewell armory, 300, *303*
Bristol (British warship), 247, *322*, 324, 326, 334–35, 337–38, 340–41, 343, 356, 534, 560
Bristol, Pennsylvania, *515*, 518
Britannia (British armed sloop), 89
British Admiralty, 1, 47–48, 87–88, 110, 136–39, 180, 228, 244, 246, 262, 279, 280, 340, 342, 407
British Army. *See also* British Army units; *and specific battles; and locations*
American POWs and, 112, 508–10
Boston evacuated by, 270–71
Boston Harbor closed by, 15, 19–24
Boston occupied by, 36–42, 46, 47–52
Boston siege and, 83–92, 131–32
Concord and, 55–82
correspondence surveilled, 170
deserters and, 49, 242, 442, 459
discipline and training and, 114, 317, 443
early preparations for war and, 23–25
George III and, 5, 166, 171
Indian frontier and, 8
Lee hated by, 332

New Jersey winter quarters and, 495–96
New York arrival and, 319
New York winter quarters and, 507
pay and, 115
plunder by, 74, 79, 496–99
preparations for spring of 1777 and, 560–62
rape by, 497–99
recruitment and, 180, 242
reinforcements and, 51–52, 90–92, 181, 318, 558–59
size of, 24–25, 179
smallpox inoculation and, 199
soldier's kit and, 55–57
supplies and logistics and, 90–92, 134–36, 179, 181, 241–42, 246–47, 352–55, 317–18, 507, 560
uniforms and, 110, 317, 361
William Howe replaces Gage as commander-in-chief, 133–35
British Army units, 4
Brigades: 1st 72, 73; 2nd 447
Foot Regiments, 4, 7; 4th (King's Own), 48–50, 63, 70, 74, 104, 110, 115, 264, 269, 441; 5th, 107; 7th (Royal Fusiliers), 141, 149, 195, 213; 10th, 39, 49, 54, 104, 317; 14th, 184, *187*; 17th, 543–45, 547, 550; 18th, 459; 22nd, 113, 258, 393, 443; 23rd (Royal Welch Fusiliers), 47, 49, 74, 104; 26th, 141, 149, 195; 29th, 9, 282, 288; 32nd Foot, 246; 35th, 110, 448; 38th, 47, 63, 109, 111; 40th, 219, 491, 543, 547–48, 551; 42nd (Highlanders Black Watch), 356, 396, 447, *449*, 456, 459, 495, 498, 506; 43rd, 39, 48, 81, 111, 223; 46th, 224, 242, 379, 402; 47th, 48, 105–6; 49th, 98, 497; 52nd, 98, 104, 106, 111; 53rd, 425; 55th, 224, 543, 546–47; 57th, 245, 335, 337, 367, 498; 63rd, 115, 443, 498; 64th, 48; 65th, 86; 71st (Highlanders), 318, 370
Guards Brigade, 361, 398
Highlanders, 318, 343, 356, 361–62, 366, 368, 369, 370, 372, 397, 456, 457, 505, 513, 543
Highland Scot Loyalists, *249*, 250–52
Light Dragoons: 16th, 503, 526, 533; 17th, 367
Marines: 1st, 108
Royal Artillery, 5, 72–74, 102–3, 116, 141, 149, 400, 407, 416–17, 419, 426, 441
Royal Guards, 166
Royal Highland Emigrants, 203, 207, 282, 283
British Cabinet, 177–81
British Navy Board, 135, 246–47, 352, 407
British Ordnance Board, 135, 247, 407

British Parliament, 4, 9, 12, 14–15, 18–23, 38, 73, 134, 153, 164–70, 172–74, 179–81, 226, 374, 383, 496, 504, 558, 561–62
  House of Commons, 14, 18–22, 166–69, 172–73, 176, 179–81, 498
  House of Lords, 20–22, 166, 168, 244, 267, 468
British prisoners of war, 252, 526
British Privy Council, 2, 176
British Royal Closet, 172
British Royal Navy, 2, 5–7, 18. *See also specific battles; locations; and ships*
  American waters commanded by, 467
  Boston and, 22, 24, 47, 86–87, 125, 223, 227, 260, 262, 270, 354
  Boston Tea Party and, 13
  Bunker Hill and, 94–97, 100–102
  Canadian invasion and, 161, 203, 208, 279, 282, 286
  Cape Fear and, 346
  Charleston and, 322, 324–30, 332–38
  Concord and, 55, 57, 76–77
  correspondence surveilled, 170
  counterfeiting and, 313
  deficiencies of, 560–61
  demands on, 226
  desertions and, 49
  Falmouth and, 136–38
  fireship attacks on, 359–60, 374–75
  France and, 481
  Franklin on, 386–87
  George III and, 5–7
  Hudson River and, 453
  Lake Champlain and, 296, 414, 417, 419
  Long Island and, 361–62
  New Jersey and, 551
  New York and, 298, 301, 304, 316–20, 332, 351–55
  preparations for spring 1777 and, 559–62
  privateers and, 469
  recruitment and, 179–80
  Rhode Island and, 178
  Richard Howe takes command of, 355
  ships seized by, 226, 467
  smugglers and, 306–7
  southern expedition and, 244–47, 345–47
  Sullivan's Island and, 336–43
  supplies and, 241
  Virginia and, 193–94, 346
  Westchester County and, 433–35, 438–39, 442
British secret service, 177
British spies, 53, 129–31, 481
British Treasury Board, 19, 21, 135–36, 354, 407
British Victualling Board, 135
British War Office, 179, 244–45
Brooklyn, 298, 300, 302, 305, 320, 431

  American evacuation of, 353, 376–79
  Long Island and, 354, 363, 368, 375–76
Brooklyn Heights, 353, 364, 371, 374
Brooks, Joshua, 68–69, 70
Brown, Abigail, 69
Brown, David, 69
Brown, Morgan, 339
Brown, Obadiah, 234
Brown, Peter, 95, 106, 108
Brown Bess (flintlock musket), 23, 55, 61–62, 232
Brownshall (British transport ship), 224
Brush, Crean, 269
bullets, 308, 312, 327, 350
Bunker Hill, 65, 76, 218, 265, 268
  Battle of, 91, 92–115, 119–21, 126–27, 133–34, 159, 165, 170, 173, 208, 238, 250, 254–55, 259, 261, 294, 374, 441–42, 458, 495, 536
Burbeen, Mary, 66
Burdett's Ferry, 298, 359, 430, 449, 453
Burford (British warship), 382
Burgoyne, Charlotte, 426
Burgoyne, John, 125, 172, 181, 220, 255, 406
  background of, 96–97, 426
  Boston and, 134–35
  Bunker Hill and, 96, 102, 105, 109, 114
  Canada and, 272, 286–91, 295
  Lake Champlain and, 404, 406, 409, 423, 425–27
  Lee and, 330–31
Burke, Edmund, 172–74, 262
Burlington, New Jersey, 495, 497, 515, 516, 530, 541
Burr, Aaron, 157–58, 214, 370, 393
Burrows, Edwin, 510
Bushnell, David, 380–82, 435
Busy Body, The (Centlivre), 220–21, 508
Butterfield, Elizabeth, 81
Butterfield, Samuel, 81
Buttermilk Channel, 300, 353
Buttonmould Bay, 404, 422
Byles, Mather, 312
Byng, John, 5

Cadwalader, John, 515, 520, 526, 530–31, 533–34, 535, 538, 541, 545–47
Caesar's Commentaries, 235, 254
Cain, Elizabeth, 497
Cairns, Thomas, 459
Calvinists, 46
Cambridge, 58, 86, 90, 92, 96, 140, 218, 258
  Arnold's march on Quebec and, 157–59
  Battle Road and, 75–77, 79
  Bunker Hill and, 98, 109–10, 112
  Washington organizes Continental Army in, 116–33, 228–33

Campbell, Archibald, 318, 463
Campbell, Mary, 497
Campbell, William, 178, 324, 329, 341
Canada, 14–15, 40, 134, 172, 332
    British offensive into New York from,
        180–81, 405
    French and Indian War and, 6, 149–50
    population of, 143
Canadian invasion, *140*, 141–63
    Arnold's second route and, *140*, 156–61
    British success in, 558
    as dress rehearsal, 295–96
    Congress orders, 143–45
    Franklin's mission to Montreal and, 273–76
    George III and, 165
    Montgomery and, 148–52
    Montreal captured, 151–52
    Quebec attack and, 195–215, 282–86,
    retreat from, 272, 273–96, 302, 304, 342
    Royal Navy and, 279, 282–83
    Schuyler and, 145–47
    shortages and, 276
    St. Johns and, 148–49
    Sullivan and, 285–86
Canceaux (British warship), 137–38
Caner, Henry, 85
Canterbury, archbishop of, 17
Cape Charles, *187*, 190, 347
Cape Diamond, *201*, 202, 205, 207, 209, 211,
    279, 281–82
Cape Fear, 248, 249,253, 318, 322, 324–25, 342
Cape Fear River, 243, 245, 248–50, *249*
Cape Henry, *187*, 190, 347
Cape May, 306, 466
Carcass (British warship), 248
Caribbean, 6, 14, 361, 469
Carillon, Fort, Battle of, 39–40, 100, 133, 145,
    331, 374, 384. *See also* Ticonderoga
Carleton, Guy, 176, 356, 436
    background of, 152–53
    escapes to Quebec, *140*, 152–54, 162, 294
    knighted, 427
    Lake Champlain and, *404*, 405–9, 412,
        415–21, 423–26, 560
    ousts Americans from Canada, 272,
        276–90, 294–96
    Quebec defended by, 196–98, 200–207, *201*,
        211–14
Carleton (British warship), *404*, 418–19, 422
Carleton, Maria Howard, 153, 427
Carroll, Charles, 276–77, 284
Carroll, Father John, 274, 276, 284
Carysfort (British ship), 390
Castle William, *218*, 238, 261, 263, 265–66
Caswell, Richard, *249*, 251

Catawba Indians, 329
Catherine the Great, Empress of Russia, 171,
    279, 512
Catholic Church, 4, 15, 142–45, 276, 277
Cato (Addison), 19, 401
Centlivre, Susanna, 221
Centurion (British warship), 135, 266
Cerberus (British warship), 88, 96–97, 227
Chambers, James, 378
Chambly, Fort, *140*, 147–48, 151, 153, 156, 272,
    288–90, 294, 408–9
Champlain, Samuel de, 200
Charles II, King of England, 2, 16, 49
Charles River, 75, 83, 87, *218*, 260–61
Charleston, South Carolina, 79, 306, 327, 256
    Sullivan's Island and, 322, 323–29, 333–34,
        338–39, 341–43, 345, 356, 359, 374, 439
    slave revolts and, 329
Charleston Bar, 322, 324, 326, 328
Charlestown, Massachusetts, 58–59, *218*, 221,
    257
    Battle Road and, 75–77
    Bunker Hill and, *91*, 92–95, 97–115
    burning of, 102–3, 109, 113, 193, 221–22,
        229
Charlestown Neck, 59, *65*, 76, 94, 97–98,
    100–101, 107, 109, 120, 221, 268
Charles XII, King of Sweden, 494–95
Charlie, Bonnie Prince, Young Pretender, 251,
    544
Charlotta (British tender), 360
Charlotte, Queen of England, 7, 17–18, 167–68,
    503, 557
Charming Nancy (British ship), 115
Chase, Samuel, 276, 284
Chatham (British warship), 224–25,
    265–67
Chatham, William Pitt, Earl of, 20
Chatterton Hill, *430*, 445–48
Chaudière River, *140*, 156, 160
Cheeseman, Jacob, 206, 209–10
Cherbourg, Battle of, 382
Cherokee (British warship), 178
Cherokee Indians, 328, 344
Chesapeake Bay, *187*, 190, 256, 308, 325,
    345–46, 467, 561
Chester, John, 107
Chilton, John, 485
China, 12
Choctaw Indians, 344
Christie, Gabriel, 426
Christopher, Rebekhah, 497
Church, Benjamin, 129–31
Citizen, The (comedy), 220
Clarke, Rev. Jonas, 59, 64, 72, 78

Clarke, William, farmhouse, firefight at, 535, 544–48
Cleaves, Nathaniel, 77
Cliffe, Loftus, 379, 402
Clinton, Henry, 181, 286, 442, 505
  background of, 96, 176, 253–55
  Boston and, 268
  Bunker Hill and, 96–97, 102, 108–10, 114
  Charleston and, 324–26, 333–35
  Cornwallis and, 551
  Gen. Howe vs., 560
  Kip's Bay and Harlem Heights and, 390, 392, 396–97
  Lake Champlain and, 426, 427
  Long Island and, 353, 362, 366–69, 374
  North Carolina and, 245, 249, 253–56
  New York and, 318, 352, 356
  Sullivan's Island and, 322, 325, 334–36, 338–39, 342–44
  Westchester County and, 430, 438, 444, 446–47
Cobble Hill, 221, 229, 257, 353, 371
Cochran's Hill, 535, 543
Cockering, Captain, 115
Coercive (Intolerable) Acts (1774), 14–15, 20, 30, 37, 40, 43, 66, 73, 165
Cohen, Eliot A, 295
Colburn, Reuben, 140, 158, 160
Collier, Sir George, 375, 378
Committee of Secret Correspondence, 275, 306, 475, 477
committees of safety, 15, 42–43, 294, 312
Common Sense (Paine), 486–87, 519
Complete History of England, 235
Concord, 46–47, 441
  aftermath of, 76–82, 165
  Battle Road retreat from, 65, 69–79
  British march on, 53–59, 56, 61, 64–69
  myth of, 80–81
  news of, spreads, 79–81
  rides of Revere and Dawes and, 58–59
Concord (British merchant ship), 227
Concord militia, 47, 66, 68
Concord River, 54, 61, 66–67, 114. *See also* North Bridge
Condict, Jemima, 12
Congress (American galley), 417, 419–23
Connecticut, 46, 86, 178, 271, 308–12
  loyalists and, 310–12
Connecticut militias and regiments, 43, 83–84, 93, 107–9, 348, 387, 390, 432
Continental Army. *See also* Continental Army regiments; Grand American Army; Northern Army; *and specific battles; and state militias*
  Arnold gains commission in, 157
  artillery and, 300, 305
  assessment of, by 1777, 562–63
  Boston entered by, 267–68
  Boston–New York march by, 270–71
  British expelled from Boston by, 257–58, 261
  Cambridge divisions of, 120–21
  Cambridge winter and, 228–33, 239
  Canadian volunteers and, 162
  Cherokee raids and, 344
  Congress's tepid support of, 126, 305–9, 439
  Crown Point abandoned by, 422–23
  deserters and, 357, 387, 393, 432, 452
  encrypted letter on, 128–29
  free blacks in, 231
  loyalists punished by, 310, 315–16
  medical care and disease in, 232–33, 269, 354, 358, 410, 432, 501, 516 (*see also specific diseases*)
  national unity and, 231
  New York and, 299–302, 305, 357–58, 462
  officers and, 123, 305, 490, 563
  pay problems and, 122, 271
  regional frictions in, 387, 411
  reinforced after Canada, 302
  retreat from Quebec and, 282–83
  retreat into New Jersey and, 463, 464, 485–99
  riflemen from Virginia, Maryland, and Pennsylvania join, 132–33
  Rush on, 516
  shortages of men and supplies and, 120, 125–26, 230, 232, 276–77, 285, 289, 305–9, 489–90, 501, 552–54
  shortages of munitions and, 126–28, 232, 336, 444
  southern militias reinforce, 346
  thievery and, 309, 410–11, 432
  training of, 121–25, 131–33, 357–58, 432–33
  Virginia regiments mustered into, 193
  Washington chosen to command, 116–25, 131–33, 432–33
  Washington on need for standing, 433
  Washington's bond with, 122, 532, 562
  Washington's doubts about, 320, 432–33, 531–32
  winter line of, 552
Continental Army regiments. *See also specific state militias*
  Continentals: 1st, 231, 378; 3rd, 441, 452; 5th, 452; 9th, 231; 11th, 231; 13th, 440–41; 14th, 376, 440, 520; 17th, 358, 370, 372; 24th, 291; 25th, 410; 27th, 376
  Delaware, 299, 365, 370, 436; 1st, 531
  Massachusetts, 368–69

Maryland, 346, 365, 370–72; riflemen, 132, 457

New Jersey, 1st, 424: 2nd, 281, 311

New York, 2nd, 564

North Carolina, 1st, *249*

Pennsylvania, 4th, 287

Rangers, 395, 400

Virginia, 339; 1st, 545; 2nd, *187*, 188–89; 3rd, 485, 524, 529; 7th, 346, 563

Continental Board of War and Ordnance, 385

Continental Congress, First (1774), 15, 18, 20, 42–43, 143

Continental Congress, Second (1775–77), 84, 109

Adm. Howe's overtures to, 384–85

Arnold and, 156, 215, 416

articles of war and, 129–30

British demands and, 384

British evacuation from Boston and, 231–32, 270

Canada and, 144–46, 151, 156, 163, 195, 277–78, 284, 289, 295, 332

Declaration of Independence and, 302, 348–49, 558

deserters and, 356

flees Philadelphia, 494, 499–500

Franklin in Canada and, 275, 277–78, 284

Franklin in France and, 465–67, 475–77, 480, 483

Hancock as president, 120

Knox and, 236

Lake Champlain and, 412, 414

Laurens as president, 329

Lee and, 332, 439, 460

Long Island and, 373, 376

loyalist treason and, 309–11

Montgomery and, 213

New York and, 270, 301–2, 304–6, 309, 356, 358, 388–89, 400

privateers and 139, 468

rapes by British and Hessians and, 497

Rush and, 516

Schuyler and, 145–46, 411

South Carolina and, 329–32

Sullivan and, 363

Ticonderoga and, 144, 410

troops and supplies raised by, 126–27, 132, 271, 305–9, 358, 410, 433, 439, 489–90, 553

Virginia leaders and, 183

Washington and, 116, 118–22, 124, 126–27, 145–46, 231–32, 270, 301–2, 305–6, 373, 376, 433, 452, 460, 489–90, 514, 563

Washington granted autocratic powers by, 529

Continental currency, 205, 277, 284, 500, 529

Continental Marine Corps, 467

Continental Navy, 467–68

Cook, James, 279, 557

Cooke, Nicholas, 554

Cooper, Lt. Samuel, 213

Cooper, Rev. Samuel, 268–69

Copley, John Singleton, 263–64

Copp's Hill battery, 95, 102, 105, 108, *218*, 261

Cork, Ireland, 241–48, 250, 324, 326, 354, 406

Cornwallis, Charles Earl

Charleston and, 324–25, 334

Forts Lee and Washington and, *449*, 456, 461–63

Kip's Bay and, 390

Lee capture and, 503

Long Island and, *353*, 362, 367–68, 371, 374

New Jersey winter quarters and, 496

New York and, 352

Princeton and, 533, 541–43, 549–51

returns to England, 496

southern expedition and, 244, 247–48, 256

Sullivan's Island and, *322*, 324–25, 336

Trenton, Second, and, 534–37, *535*, 539–40, 543, 549, 551

Westchester County and, 441

Washington in Morristown and, 552

Washington's retreat in New Jersey and, *484*, 485, 488, 490–91, 494–95

counterfeiting, 313–15

Craft, Benjamin, 124

Crawford (British transport ship), 318

Creek Indians, 344

Cresswell, Nicholas, 507

Cropper, John, Jr., 563

Crosby, Edward, 459

Cross Creek (*later* Fayetteville), *249*, 250–52

Crown Point, 100, *140*, 214, 272, 292, 294, 295

capture of, 84, 144, 156

Knox carries guns to Boston, 234–35

Lake Champlain battle and, *404*, 405–6, 409, 411–12, 414, 420–26

Cuba, 89, 149

Culloden, Battle of, 39, 175, 203, 250–51, 544

Culpeper minute company, 188–89

Cumberland, Duke of, 19

Cunningham, William, 510

Cushing, Charles, 291

Custis, John Parke, 553

Custis, Patsy, 544

Danvers militia, 74–75, 78

Dartmouth, William Legge, Earl of, 14, 24–25, 43, 51–54, 81, 86, 90, 114, 134, 152–54, 170, 172, 174, 243

David, Ebenezer, 222, 410
Davies, K. G., 245
Davis, Hannah, 66, 78
Davis, Isaac, 66, 68–69, 78
Dawes, William, Jr., *56*, 57–60, 64
Dawkins, Henry, 313
Deal Castle (British warship), 246
Deane, Silas, 476–82, 556
Dearborn, Henry, 105, 159, 210
De Berniere, Henry, 72
Dechow, Friedrich von, *515*, 525
Declaration of Independence, 348–51, 385,
    474, 516, 558
Decline and Fall of the Roman Empire, The
    (Gibbon), 21, 171, 557
Dedham militia, 78
Deerfield massacre, 142
Delaware Bay, 467, 500, 561
Delaware militia, 520
Delaware River, *484*, *485*, 491, 530, 534, 540
    Washington's Christmas crossing to
        Trenton and, *515*, 517–21, 527
    Washington's retreat over, 491–95, 502
Delegate (British ship), 324
Demont, William, 452
Denmark, 12
Denyse's Ferry, *298*, 300, 319, *353*, 362–63, 365
Derby, John, 80
Detroit, Battle of, 89
Diana (British warship), sinking of, 88–90, 97
Dickinson (American ship), 306
Digby, William, 425
Ditson, Thomas, Jr., 48
Dixon, Matthew, 498
Dobbs Ferry, *430*, 435, 448, *449*, 453–54
Dolphin (British ship), 382
Donop, Carl von, 513, 526, 528, 536
Dorchester Heights, 92, 96, 113–14, *218*, 266,
    305
    fortification of, 237–40, 257–63, 270
Dorr, Harbottle, 44
Douglas, Charles, *272*, 279–80, 283, 407,
    426
Douglas, William, 378, 390, 447, 563
Douglass, Alexander, 541
Douglass house, *515*, *535*, 541
Dryden, John, 117, 323
Duchess of Gordon (British warship), 178, 300,
    314
Duckett, Valentine, 49, 55
Duncan, Henry, 394
Dunkirk (British warship), 382
Dunk's ferry, *515*, 520
Dunmore (British merchant ship, *formerly
    Eilbeck*), 183, 345

Dunmore, John Murray, Earl of, 178, 180,
    182–88, 190–91, 193–94, 226, 229, 243, 329,
    344–47
Durand, M., 477
Durant, Keturah, 66
dysentery, 112, 134, 233, 289, 358, 405, 432, 512

Eagle (British warship), 355, 360, 362, 384, 387,
    394, 506
    Turtle attacks, 380–82, *391*
Earl of Suffolk (British transport ship), 225
Eastern Country, Massachusetts. *See* Maine
East India Company, 12, 14, 179, 306
Easton, James, 153
East River, *298*, 299–304, *303*, 314, *353*, 356, 374,
    379, 388, *391*, 392, *430*, 435, 437
Easy Plan of Discipline for a Militia
    (Pickering), 47
Eden, Robert, 345–46
Eden, William, 88, 115
Edwards, Jonathan, 157
Eight Mile Run, 534–36, *535*, 540
"Elegy Written in a Country Churchyard"
    (Gray), 206
Eliot, Rev. Andrew, 269, 270
Elizabeth (British storeship), 203, 269
Elizabeth River, *187*, 188, 190, 193, 344
Elizabeth Town, New Jersey, *484*, *485*, 497, 551
Ellis, Joseph J., 442
Emerson, Rev. William, 44, 47, 66
Enos, Roger, 159
Enterprise (British ship, formerly *George*),
    156–57, 224
Enterprise (American sloop and hospital
    boat), 420–22
Enys, John, 280, 288
Erskine, Sir William "Woolly," 540
Essex Gazette, 80, 83, 112–13, 138
Establishment of His Majesty's Land Forces, 559
Ethiopian Regiment, 185, 188–91, 344, 346
evangelical churches, 24, 183
Evelyn, William Glanville, 49–51, 74, 86, 88,
    90, 115, 134, 219, 222–23, 367–68, 441–42
Everett, Israel, 77
Ewald, Johann, 462, 491, 513, 549, 551
Experiment (British warship), 322, 337, 340,
    343
Experiments and Observations on Electricity
    (Franklin), 28, 150

Falcon (British warship), 51–54, *91*, 95, 98, 253
Falmouth, burning of, 136–39, 193, 327
Faneuil Hall, 40, 44–45, 85, 220–21, 257
Farnsworth, Amos, 88, 108
Feilding, William, 135–36, 220–21, 265

Felicity (British transport ship), 225, 317, 319
Fell (British armed snow), 154
Fell (British merchant ship), 209
Fenn, Elizabeth A., 199
Ferdinand, Prince of Brunswick, 175
Ferguson, William, 49, 55
Ferris Bay, *404*, 422, 428
Field Engineer, 258
Fielding, Henry, 508
Finbar, Saint, 241
Firebrand (British warship), 407
Fischer, David Hackett, 497, 532
Fiske, Ebenezer, 71–72
Fitch, Jabez, 372
Fithian, Philip Vickers, 393–94, 432
Five-Fathom Hole, *322*, 326, 329, 334, 337, 341
Five Mile Run, 534, *535*, 537
Flatbush, *298*, 300, 314, *353*, 362, 364–68, 370
Fleet prison, 311
Fleming, John, 545
Fletcher, Rebecca, 67
Floating Battery, *218*
Florida, 6, 178, 346, 468
Flying Camp reserve, 302, 461
Fobes, Simon, 104, 212
Fontenoy, Battle of, 39, 175
Forbes, Esther, 264
Forbes, Gilbert, 314
Formidable (French ship), 383
Fortescue, J. W., 459
Fortune (merchant sloop), 156
Fosdick, Thomas Updike, 360
Four Brothers Islands, *404*, 421
Fowey (British ship), 183, 346
Fowler, Jonathan, 312
Fox, Charles James, 427
France, 2, 14, 20, 24, 26, 173, 179, 305, 355, 556, 561
    Franklin and, 275, 386, *464*, 465–83
    Seven Years' War and, 1, 5–6, 8–9, 24, 39, 143
    smuggling and, 306
Francis (British ship), 263
Franklin, Benjamin, 143, 150, 287, 297, 409
    background of, 27–31
    Britain and, 27–31, 51, 170
    Dartmouth and, 172
    France and, 386–87, *464*, 465–70, 477–83, 556
    Montgomery and, 214
    Montreal and, 273–78, 284
    Paine and, 487
    son William and, 466–67
    Staten Island Conference and, 384–87
Franklin, Benny, 466

Franklin, Deborah, 31
Franklin, Temple, 466–67, 480
Franklin, William, 28, 31
    arrest of, 466–67
Franklin (American armed schooner), 307
Fraser, Malcolm, 207
Fraunces, Samuel, 309
Frederick the Great, 73, 199, 450
Freeman, Douglas Southall, 270
Freemasons, 156, 233, 469, 544
French, Allen, 81
French and Indian War, 8–9, 24, 39, 60, 64, 66, 89, 93–94, 100, 117, 121, 127, 133, 135, 142–45, 149, 152–53, 188, 193, 197, 248, 254, 259, 297, 331, 395, 401, 407, 409, 414, 445, 496, 511. *See also* Seven Years' War
French Navy, 482
Frey, Sylvia, 498
Friendship (British ship), 317, *322*
Frog Hollow, *535*, 547
Frog's Neck, *430*, 437–40, 559
Frying Pan Shoals, *249*, 253, 325
Fubbs (British royal yacht), 2

Gage, Margaret Kemble, 39–40, 115
Gage, Thomas, 22–23, 120, 122, 144, 238, 254, 260, 269
    background of, 39–41, 117
    Boston siege and, 84–92
    Bunker Hill and, 96–97, 101, 110, 113–15
    Church spies for, 129–31
    Concord and, 53–54, 59, 61, 67, 69, 73, 76–81
    early rebellion and, 40–45, 48–54
    Graves and, 88–89, 125
    Howe replaces, 133–34
    martial law declared by, 90
Galloway, Joseph, 498
Garret, Sargeant, 446
Garrick, David, 11, 220
Gaspé (British warship), 152, 154, 195
Gates, Horatio, 239, 299, 439, 502–3, 514
    Lake Champlain and, *404*, 411–17, 420–21, 423–25
Gauthier, Antonine, 286
Gazette de France, 471
Gazetteer and New Daily Advertiser, 169
Gentleman's Magazine, 139
George I, King of England, 133, 174
George II, King of England, 175
George III, King of England, 73
    Adm. Howe and, 383
    Aitken hanging and, 557
    background and personality of, 3–6, 9, 166–68, 557–58
    Boston siege and, 90

George III, King of England (*cont'd*)
British Army and, 166, 354, 356
British Fleet and, 1–3, 6–7, 10–12, 247
Bunker Hill and, 115, 133
Burgoyne and, 96, 426
Cabinet and, 19, 172–74
Canadian invasion and, 279, 295
Carleton and, 152–53, 406, 426–27
Clinton and, 96
Concord and, 80–81
coronation of, 28, 400
debate on war and, 169–70
Declaration of Independence and, 349–50
early American resistance and, 8–9, 13–16, 18–23, 25
Gage and, 40, 43, 51–52, 133
Gen. Howe and, 96, 506
Germain and, 173–77, 179–81, 242
impact of war on, 557–62
Lee and, 331, 504
Louis XVI and, 474
loyalists and, 181, 309
Maclean and, 203
madness of, 3
mail surveillance and, 170–71
marriage and family and, 17–18, 167–68
New York and, 394
Paine on, 487
Parliament addresses by, 164–67, 233
Prohibitory Act and, 180
reconciliation rejected by, 165–66
slavery and, 329
southern expedition and, 180, 244–45, 247, 343
statues and images of, 301, *303*, 349–50
George, Prince of Wales, 168
George, Fort, *298*, *303*, 351, *353*, 397, *404*, 424, 505
George (British brig), captured off France, 467
George (British ship), captured off Boston, 318
George (Canadian sloop), captured and renamed *Enterprise*, 156
Georgia, 8, 15, 178, 255, 324, 344, 346
Germain, George Sackville, Lord, 481
appointed American secretary, 173–81
Army and, 242
Boston and, 223, 228, 267
Canada and, 279, 295–96
Clinton and, 255–56, 343
Howe brothers and, 383–84, 387
Lake Champlain and, 406–7, 423, 426–27
New Jersey and, 496, 505, 528, 560
New York and, 300, 317–18, 325, 352, 399–400, 443, 436, 442–43

spring 1777 campaign and, 561
southern expedition and, 244–45, 248, 253, 255, 333, 335, 343, 346, 352
German mercenaries, 24, 90, 171, 270, 286, 302, 318, 352, 357, 443, 496. *See also* Hessians
Germany, 172
Gibbon, Edward, 21, 80, 171–72, 557
Gibbs, Will, 49
Gist, Jordecai, 371
Glasgow (British transport ship), 88, *91*, 95, 98, 107, 109
Glasgow Packet (British ship), 343
Glover, John, *430*, 441, 517–18, 520–21
Goethe, J. W. von, 473
Gooch, John, 397
Good Intent (British transport ship), 260, 317
Governors Island, *298*, 300, *354*, 378, 381–82, 388, *391*
Gowanus Road, *353*, 365–66, 368, 370–72
Grand American Army, 83–84, 86
Grand Battery, *303*, 316, 351, 366, 393, 398, 434
Grant, James, *353*, 370, 373, 496, 499, 513–14, 528, 533, 536, 539–40, 551–52
Graves, Samuel, 87–89, 97–98, 101–2, 125, 137–39, 180, 224, 226
Graves, Thomas, 88–89
Gravesend, *298*, 318, *353*, 361–63
Gray, James, 233
Gray, Mary, 233
Gray, Samuel, 113
Gray, Thomas, 206
Graydon, Alexander, 452, 458, 460
Great Bridge, Virginia, Battle of, 186–90, *187*
Great Britain
debate on war in, 165–79, 181
elections of 1774 and, 21
empire and, 1, 5–8, 14
France vs., 473–75, 480–82
impact of war on, 555–62
map of, *32*
monarchy and, 4
Great Carrying Place, *140*, 159
Great Dismal Swamp, *187*, 188
Great War for the Empire, 6, 8
Greene, Nathanael
background of, 448–51
Boston siege and, 132, 230–32, 239, 261, 269–70
Bunker Hill and, 113
Church letter and, 130
Forts Lee and Washington and, *449*, 451–56, 460–63
Harlem Heights and, 395
Lee and, 331, 504–5

New Jersey retreat and, 488, 490, 492–93

New York and, 319–20, 358, 363–64, 373, 387–88, 392

Paine and, 486–87

Princeton and, *535*, 541–43, 545–46

report on British rapes and murders and, 497–98

Trenton, First, and, *515*, 517, 520, 522, 524, 526, 532

Trenton, Second, and, 537, 550

Washington and, 119, 228, 450–51, 453–55, 460

Westchester County and, *430*, 432

Greene, Catharine Littlefield "Caty," 450, 463, 504

Greenman, Jeremiah, 122, 159–60, 200, 206

Green Mountain Boys, 84, 195

Greenwood, John, 531

Greyhound (British warship), 135, 317, 318, *353*, 361

Gridley, Richard, 94

Griffith, Rev. David, 528–29

Gruber, Ira D., 384

Guadeloupe, 477

Guana, Heights of, *353*, 364, 366–68, 372–73, 441

gunpowder, 23–24, 126–28, 145, 163, 171, 178, 183, 232, 258, 275–76, 283, 306–7, 336, 340, 476

gunrunners, 88, 314, 346, 466

habeas corpus, suspended, 562

Hackensack, 455, 462–63, *484*, 487, 551

Haddrell's Point, 322, 333, 335–36, 338–39

Hagist, Don N., 242

Hale, Nathan, *391*, 400–402, 432, 437, 510

Hale, William John, 544, 545

Halifax, 127, 226–27, 262, 301, 316–17, 319, 325, 354, 442

Halifax (British ship), 87, 223

Hamilton, Alexander, 235, 444, 446, 490, 502, 519, 522, 547

Hamlin Creek, 322, 336, 338–39

Hamond, Andrew Snape, 344–47, 389

Hancock, John, 83, 255, 263, 268

army needs and, 433, 439, 553

Arnold and, 413

Boston siege and, 90, 270

Canada and, 284–85, 294

Concord and, 57, 59–60

as Congress president, 120, 329

Forts Lee and Washington and, 454

Franklin in Montreal and, 275, 277–78

Greene and, 451

house vandalized, 48

Lake Champlain and, 411, 413

Lee capture and, 504

Lexington and, 53

Massachusetts Provincial Congress and, 42

New Jersey and, 488, 490–94

New York and, 301–2, 305, 320, 358, 363, 365, 373, 377–79, 388, 397

Princeton and, 548

Trenton and, 518, 524, 527–28, 531

Washington and, 120, 124, 126, 132, 230, 233, 239, 271, 285, 301–2, 305, 320, 358, 363, 365, 373, 377–79, 388, 397, 433, 438–39, 448, 454, 488, 490–94, 518, 524, 527–28, 531, 548, 553

Westchester County and, 438–39, 448

Hand, Edward, 357, 362, *535*, 537–38, 546

Hand, Kitty, 357

Handel, Georg Friedrich, 4, 214

Hannibal, 452

Hantley, Jonathan, 132

Harcourt, William, 503–4, 562

Harlem Heights

evacuation of New York to, *298*, 388–89

Forts Lee and Washington and, *449*, 456–57

Kip's Bay and, *391*, 393–95

Westchester County and, *430*, 431, 434, 439

Harlem River, *391*, 393, *430*, *449*, 454–56

Harrington, Jonathan, 64

Harris, George, 107, 111

Hartwell, Mary, 78

Harvard College, 92–93, 165, 270

Harvey, Edward, 24, 79, 97, 105, 110, 179, 242, 246

Haslet, John, 436, 445–47, 521, 531, 545, 550, 563

Havana, 6, 89, 101, 111, 213, 467

Hawke (British warship), 180

Hawke, Sir Edward, 383

Haws, Samuel, 76, 116

Hawthorne, Nathaniel, 42

Haydn, Joseph, 254

Hayward, James, 71–72

Heath, William, 78, 358, 365, 388, *391*, *430*, 438, 453, 517, 553

Heiress, The (Burgoyne), 220

Heister, Leopold Philip de, *353*, 368–69, 371, *430*, 443–46, 528, 551

Hell Gate, *298*, 376, 390, *391*, *430*, 437–38

Hendricks, William, 210

Henry, John Joseph, 159, 206

Henry, Patrick, 119, 186, 433, 563

Henry VIII, King of England, 18

Hessians, 90, 356, 385, 393, 396–97, 485, 505

Forts Lee and Washington and, 453–54, 456–58, 461–62

Jäger, 361–62, 368, 373, 390, 396, 440, 444, 457, 461, 490–91, 494, 513

Lake Champlain and, 405, 407, 416–19, 428

Hessians (*cont'd*)
Long Island and, *353*, 361–64, 366, 368–72, 379
New York and, 507–8
plunder by, 443–44, 458, 495–98, 530
POWs, 526–28
rape by, 497–98
Trenton and, 511–14, 517, 522, 523–29, 538, 551
Westchester County and, 442–48
Hewes, George Robert Twelves, 269
Hewes, Joseph, 305
Hickey, Thomas, 314–16, 348
Hicks, John, 78
Hints to Gentlemen of Landed Property, 557–58
Hitchcock, Daniel, 537–38, 546
Hodgkins, Joseph, 234
Hodgkins, Sarah, 234
Hog Island, 87–88, *218*
Holland, 8, 12, 46, 306, 512
Holland House, *201*, 282
Holy Ghosters, 507
Honduras, 156
Hope, Richard, 111
Hope (British ordnance ship), capture of, 307
Hope (British warship), 87
Horace, 30, 450
Horn's Hook, 390, *391*
Hortaléz et Cie, 472, 475, 477–78
Hosmer, Abner, 68–69
Hosmer, Joseph, 68
How, David, 234
Howe, Caroline, 384
Howe, George, Viscount, 133, 145
Howe, Richard, Admiral Viscount, 133, 318–19, 380–87, 457, 467, 505–6
Long Island and, 362, 371, 374–75, 379
Narragansett Bay and, 505–6
New York and, 355, 360–61, 394, 398
Paine's letter to, 561
spring 1777 campaign and, 560–61
Staten Island Conference and, 384–87
Westchester County and, 435, 437
Howe, Robert, 191, 192
Howe, William, Major General, *91*, 161, 172, 176, 180, 181, 184, 295, 384, 406
America POWs and, 509–10
appointed commander-in-chief, 133–35
army recruitment and, 242
background and personality of, 96, 133–34, 383–84
Beekman house and, 436–37
Boston evacuated by, 260–62, 264–67, 269

Boston siege and, 133–36, *218*, 219, 222–24, 233, 239
Bunker Hill and, 96–98, 101–6, 108–10, 114
Burgoyne and, 427
Carleton and, 406, 409, 427
Clinton and, 254, 256, 325, 343
Declaration of Independence and, 351
Forts Lee and Washington, *449*, 451–54, 456, 459–62
Germain and, 181
Hale and, 401
Hessians and, 443
Kip's Bay and Harlem Heights and, 389–96, *391*, 506
knighted, 506
Lee and, 501, 504
Long Island and, *353*, 362–63, 366–68, 371–79, 506
New Jersey and, 491–99, 530
New York and, *298*, 301, 305, 310, 317–20, 325, 352–54, 360–61, 398, 400, 496, 498, 501, 506–8, 560
rape and, 498
Rhode Island and, 560
southern expedition and, 184–85, 243, 244–47, 325, 343
spring 1777 campaign and, 560–61
Trenton and Princeton and, 512, 526, 528–29, 534, 551–52
Washington's retreat in New Jersey and, *484*, 491–96
Westchester County and, *430*, 434–48
Howell, Dr. Lewis, 311
Howell, Joseph, Jr., 358
Howell, Richard, 294
Howland, John, 531, 538–39
Hubbard, Jonas, 208
Hudson Highlands, 352, 388, 552
Hudson River (North River), 180, 236, 279, *298*, 300, 302–4, *303*, 320, 351–52, 356, 359, *391*, *404*, *430*, 431, 433–35, *449*, 451, 454–55, 458, 461–63
Hull, Edward, 81–82
Hume, David, 150, 558
Humphrey, William, 212
Humphreys, John, 210
Hundred Years' War, 47
Hunstable, Sarah, 113
Hunter (British warship), 161, 204
Hunter, Martin, 456, 550
Hutcheson, Francis, 221, 265, 399
Hynes, Samuel, 562–63

Île aux Noix, *272*, 291–94, 405, 409
Île la Motte, *404*, 415–16

Inca Empire, 199
Independence (American sloop), 435
India, 6, 12, 14, 127–28, 171, 199
Indians, 8, 10, 15, 40, 100, 144, 149, 199–200,
    284, 287–88, 292, 328–30, *404*, 405–6, 415,
    422. *See also specific tribes*
Industry (British ship), 226
Infernal (British gunboat), 407
Inflexible (British warship), *404*, 408–9,
    417–19, 422, 425–26
Ingalls, Phineas, 116
Ingham, Solomon, 372
Instructions for His Generals (Frederick the
    Great), 450
Invincible (British warship), 422
Ireland, 2, 7, 9–10, 14, 22, 25, 98, 241–42,
    244–46
Iroquois, 89, 146, 308
Irvine, William, 286
Irving, Washington, 234, 459
Isis (British warship), 279–80, 282, 407

Jacobite uprising, 119, 182, 203, 250
Jacob's Law Dictionary, 450
Jamaica, 184
James, Bartholomew, 225–26
James River, *187*, 190
Jasper, William, 339–40
Jay, Archelaus, 425
Jay, John, 312–14
Jefferson, Thomas, 185, 192, 200, 349, 474
Jeremiah, Thomas "Jerry," 329
Jersey (American boat), 421
Jersey Palisades (Steep Rocks), *449*, 453, 455,
    461
Jervis, Sir John, 343
Jewett, Joseph, 372
Johnson, Fort, *322*
Johnson, Samuel, 8, 13, 214, 465
Johnson's ferry, *515*, 520
Johnston, Fort, 249, 250
Johnston, Henry P., 357
Johnston, Philip, 372
Jones, Farwell, 67
Jones, John Paul, 467–68
Jones, Thomas, 459, 506
Jonge Pieter (British equestrian transport), 355

Kant, Immanuel, 28
Keith, J., 233
Keith, William, 514
Kemble, Stephen, 260, 264, 396, 443, 498, 528
Kemp's Landing, rout of, 185, *187*
Kennebec River, *140*, 156, 158–59
Kent (British warship), 3

Ketchum, Isaac, 313–15
Killingsworth (British ship), 225
Kill Van Kull, *298*, 319
Kingfisher (British warship), 191, 306
King Lear (Shakespeare), 323
King's Bridge, *298*, 300, 320, 378, 388, 390, *391*,
    395, *430*, 431–32, 435, 437, 439, 441, 448,
    449, 454, 456
King's College, 177–78, 399, 507
"King's Own Regulars, The" (Franklin), 273
Kingston, New Jersey, *484*, 548, 550
Kipling, Rudyard, 61
Kip's Bay, Battle of, 389–91, *391*, 401, 436, 441,
    506
Knowlton, Thomas, *91*, 99–100, 221–22, *391*,
    395–96, 400
Knox, Henry
    background of, 45, 234–36, 264
    Dorchester Heights and, 238, 258–59,
        269–70
    Greene and, 450, 454–55, 460
    Kip's Bay and Harlem Heights and, 393–94
    Long Island and, 373
    Morristown and, 554
    New York and, 271, 300, 305, 307–8, 314, 316,
        351
    Princeton and, 541, 543, 549
    Ticonderoga guns and, *218*, 234–38, 414
    Trenton, First, and, *515*, 517, 518, 520–25,
        529
    Trenton, Second, and, 534, 537–41
Knox, Lucy Flucker, 235–36, 316, 351, 373, 521,
    529, 539, 543, 554
Knox, Robert, 417, 419
Knyphausen, Wilhelm von, 443, *449*, 454,
    456–58, 528
Kranish, Michael, 183

Lacey, John, 292
Lady Catherine (American powder raider),
    306
Lady Maria (British warship), *404*, 408–9,
    417–23
Lady Williams (British warship), 338–39
Lafayette, Marquis de, 477
Lake Champlain, 84–85, 90, 182, 236, 279, 293
    Battle for, 295–96, *404*, 405–29
    Canadian invasion and, *140*, 144–47, 153,
        156, 162
Lake George, *404*, 236
Lamb, John, 210–11
L'Amphitrite (French merchantman), 477–78,
    480
La Prairie, 272, 288, 290
La Romain (French ship), 477

La Seine (French ship), 477–78
Laurens, Henry, 329
Laurie, Walter, 68–69, 114
LaVigne (British ship), 467
lead, 193, 275, 308, 350
Learned, Ebenezer, 267
Lechmere Point, 58, *218*, 257
Lee, Arthur, 480–81
Lee, Charles, 151, 373
    background and personality of, 121, 330–32,
      502
    Boston siege and, 121, 123, 129, 132–33, *218*,
      230, 331–32
    Canada and, 332
    capture of, *484*, 502–5, 533, 562
    Charleston and, 333–34, 359
    correspondence surveilled, 170
    Falmouth burning and, 139
    Forts Lee and Washington and, 453, 460, 463
    New York and, 304, 332
    New Jersey retreat and, 488–89, 491, 501–4
    Sullivan's Island and, *322*, 329–42
    Virginia and, 345
    Westchester County and, *430*, 439–40,
      444–46
    Washington and, 331–32, 463, 488–89, 502
Lee, Ezra, 380–82
Lee, Richard Henry (VA congressman), 163,
    186, 550, 563
Lee, William "Billy," 118, 432
Lee, Fort, *298*, 359, *391*, *430*, 434, 435, 559
    attack on Fort Washington and, *449*,
      450–51, 453, 455–60, 487
    Howe seizes, 461–63, *484*
Lee (British warship), 227
Leitch, Andrew, 395–96
Lemaitre, Georges, 473
L'Enfant, Pierre Charles, 476–77
Lengel, Edward G., 364
Leslie, William, 545
Levant (British ship), 247
Lewis, Andrew, 345
Lexington, 53
    Battle of, *56*, 62–66, *65*, 71–74, 78, 84, 89,
      100, 106, 275, 536, 562
    rides of Revere and Dawes to, 57–60
Lexington militia, 60–64, *65*, 71
Life Guard, 304, 315, 463
Lincoln militia, 68–69
Lister, Jeremy, 39, 71, 75
List of Your Majesty's Royal Navy, 559
Little Hannah (British transport ship),
    227
Lively (British warship), *91*, 94–96, 98, 300
Liverpool (British warship), 191–92

Livingston, Robert, 308
Livingston, William, 497
Livingston's penitentiary, 509
Lizard (British warship), 161, 203–4
Lloyd's of London, 468
Locke, John, 331, 450
London Chronicle, 2, 28, 30
London Evening Post, 80, 170, 181, 213–14
London Gazette, 22, 267
London *General Evening Post*, 504
London *Morning Chronicle*, 17, 173
London *Morning Post*, 170
London *Public Advertiser*, 164, 166
Long Island, New York, 134, 297, *298*, 300, 304,
    310–11, 314, 318–20, 350
    Battle of, *354*, 361–79, 384, 388, 432, 436,
      440–41, 462, 476, 506–7, 510, 563
Long Island, South Carolina, *322*, 324, 326,
    328, 334, 336, 338
Long Island ferry slip, *303*, 314
Long Island Sound, 271, *298*, 304, 356, *430*, 431,
    435, 437
Long Wharf, 97–98, 112, *218*, 260–61, 263
Lord Howe (British warship), 318
Lord North (British storeship), 506
Loring, Elizabeth Lloyd "Betsy," 222, 506
Loring, Joshua, 222, 506, 508
Louis I, King of Spain, 199
Louis XIV, King of France, 143
Louis XV, King of France, 199, 472
Louis XVI, King of France, 465, 472, 474–75,
    478, 481–82
Louisbourg, Battle of, 60, 361
Lowell, James Russell, 69
Loyal Convert (British flat-bottomed boat),
    408, 418
loyalists, 83, 85–86, 262, 264, 267–69
    British estimates of, 179–81
    militias of, 507
    New Jersey and, 495, 497–98
    New York and, 299–301, 306, 319–20, 506
    number of, 311–12
    punishment of, 178, 309–16, 332
    southern, 180, 183, 191, 243–45, 255, 328,
      343–44, 346
Lundin, Leonard, 498
Lyon (British ship), 10

Macartney, George, 6
MacDonald, Allan, 250–52
MacDonald, Donald, *249*, 250–52
MacDonald, Flora, 250–52
Mackenzie, Frederick, 39, 49, 74, 79, 398–99,
    401, 437, 447, 452, 459
Mackesy, Piers, 172, 406

Maclean, Allan, 203–4, 207, 276, 283, 560
Macpherson, John, 206, 209–10
Magaw, Robert, *449*, 451–58, 509
Magdalen (British ship), 183
Magnanime (British warship), 383
Maidenhead, 497, 513, *515*, 534
    Battle at, *535*, 536–37, 542, 547
Maid of the Oaks, The (Burgoyne), 220
Maier, Pauline, 349
Maine (Eastern Country), 88, *140*, 156–58
Maine militia, 136–37
malaria, 232, 292, 323, 358, 410
Manchester, Duke of, 267
Manhattan, 297, *303*, 304–5, 351, 365, 374, 379,
    387–89, 436, 439. *See also* New York
Manley, John, 227–48, 269
Marcus Aurelius, 8
Marcy, William, 75
Maria, (British warship), 191
Maria Theresa, Empress of Austria, 473
Marie Antoinette, Queen of France, 17, 474–76
Marquis of Rockingham (British warship),
    246
Marriage of Figaro, The (Beaumarchais), 473
Marshall, John, 188–89
Martin (British warship), 280, 282, 286
Martin, James Kirby, 155
Martin, Joseph Plumb, 370, 389, 392, 394
Martin, Josiah, 178, 243, 245, 248–50, 253, 324
Martinique, 111, 149, 306, 466, 469, 476–77
Mary (British schooner), 195
Massachusetts, 14, 144, 306, 354. *See also*
    Boston; Concord; Lexington; *and other
    specific battles and locations*
    loyalists opposed in, 310
    rebellion begun in, 21–22, 40–42, 46–47, 90
Massachusetts Council, 488
Massachusetts House of Representatives, 130
Massachusetts militias, 15, 43, 46–47, 53, 60,
    60–79, *65*, 81, 83–84, 87–89, *91*, 92–96,
    99–110, 112, 116, 127. *See also specific battles*
Massachusetts Provincial Committee of
    Supply, 46, 83, 92
Massachusetts Provincial Congress, 42,
    46–47, 53, 57, 80, 83, 93, 107, 113
Matthews, David, 314
Mawhood, Charles, *535*, 543–47
Maynard, Needham, 104–5, 108
McClary, Andrew, 109
McClure, Rev. David, 78, 81
McConkey's ferry, *484*, *515*, 520, 530
McCowen, Winifried, 134
McDougall, Alexander, 446–47
McLeod, Donald, 251–52
Meade, Richard Kidder, 189

Mellish (British transport ship), 467–68
Melvin, John, 212
Menotomy, *65*, 73–74, 77–79, 81
Mercer, Hugh, 517, 523, 531, *535*, 538, 541,
    543–46, 548, 550, 563
Mercier, Louis-Sébastien, 470–71
Mercury (British warship), 227, *249*, 253, 300
Merrifield, Francis, 107
Mesplet, Fleury, 276
Metamorphoses (Ovid), 555
Methodists, 165, 183
Meyrick, Samuel J., 292
Middlesex Journal, 88
Mifflin, Thomas, 349, 392–93, 531, 533–34, 538,
    546
Miles, Samuel, *353*, 368, 369
*Military Instructions for Officers Detached in
    the Field*, 116
militias. *See specific towns and states*
Milligan, Jacob, 341
Milton, John, 92, 350
Minden, Battle of, 24, 170, 175, 477
Minorca, 5
Minot, George, 67
Minutemen, 43, 53, 66
Mississippi River, 6, 15, 89
Mohawk Indians, 331
Monarch (British ship), 5
Monongahela River, ambush at, 39–40, 117
Monroe, James, 370, 488, 524
Montcalm, Louis-Joseph de, 197, 206
Montesquieu, Baron de, 150
Montgomery, Janet Livingston, 150–52, 196,
    206, 214
Montgomery, Richard, 414, 432, 518, 563
    background of, 149–50, 152
    Canada invasion and, *140*, 146–53, 156
    death of, 210–15, 231, 282
    Quebec and, 155, 161–63, 195–99, *201*, 203–7,
        209–15
    St. Johns and, 147–49
Montreal, 35, 195, 211, 560
    Carleton's escape from, *140*, 152–54, 162, 294
    Franklin's visit to, 273–78, 284
    capture of, *140*, 143–44, 146–47, 150–53, 156,
        162, 200
    retreat from, 272, 284, 288–89
Montresor, John, 350, 374, 377, 396, 399–402
Moore, Capt. James, 519
Moore, Gen. James, 253
Moore's Creek Bridge, skirmish at, *249*,
    251–53, 255, 324
"Morals of Chess, The" (Franklin), 386
Morgan, Daniel, 158, 204, 207–10, 279, 295
Morgan, Edmund S., 311, 349

Morison, George, 159, 204

Morris, Anthony, Jr., 546

Morris, Gouverneur, 564

Morris, John, 341

Morris, Robert, 306, 307, 431, 500–501, 517, 527–28, 532

Morris (American powder ship), 306

Morris mansion, *391, 430,* 431–33, 444, *449,* 454–57

Morristown, New Jersey, *484,* 501, 503, *535,* 551–54

Mortier mansion, *298,* 302, *303,* 304, 317, 319, 348, 350, 356, 363, 378, 389

Morton's Point, *91, 97,* 99, 101–2

Mosquito Fleet, 412–21, 426

Moulder, Joseph, 546

Moultrie, William, *322,* 328, 333–34, 336–42

Mount Vernon, 118–19, 124, 229, 304, 320, 365, 400, 432, 505

Mowat, Henry, 137–39

Moylan, Stephen, 233–34, 554

Mozart, Wolfgang, 27, 473

Münchhausen, Levin F. E. von, 494, 499, 504, 506

munitions, 46, 53, 80–81, 84–88, 92–93, 96, 98, 126–27, 147, 149, 169, 227, 232, 234–37, 263 276, 305–10, 356, 414–16, 424, 444, 462

France and, 465, 475–78, 561

Munro, Edmund, 425

Munroe, John, 63

Munroe, Timothy, 75

Murray, Fort (Hog Pen), *187,* 188–90

Murray, James, 245, 247, 335, 337, 339, 342, 344, 362, 367–68

Nancy (British ordnance brig), capture of, 226–28, 232, 257, 269

Nancy, (American brigantine), smuggling and, 306–7

Nancy (British gunrunner), blown up, 466

Nantes, *464,* 467, 469

Narragansett Bay, 505–6

Narrows, *298,* 300, 318–19, 352, *353,* 356–57, 362–65

Nassau Blues, 507

Nassau Hall, *535,* 547, 549

Nautilus (British ship), 51, 325

Neil, Daniel, 545

Nelly (British merchant ship), 469

Neshaminy ferry, *515*

Newark, 320, *484,* 485, 487–88, 495–97

New Bern, North Carolina, *249,* 243, 248, 250

New Brunswick, New Jersey, *484,* 486–92, 495, 504, 513, 533, *535,* 536, 541, 548, 551

Newburyport, *140,* 158, 306

New Chymical Dictionary, 307

Newell, Timothy, 264

New England, 15, 22, 24, 29–30, 77, 79, 90, 142, 144, 146, 180, 317–18, 560, 563–64. *See also specific battles; states; and towns*

loyalists in, 311

smallpox and, 199–200

New England Chronicle, 139, 258

New England militias, 122, 231

Newfoundland, 233, 279–80, 382

New Gaol (the Provost), 510

New Hampshire, 58, 86, 92, 178, 350

New Hampshire Committee of Safety, 127

New-Hampshire Gazette, 79

New Hampshire militias, 43, 83, 87, 96, 100, 109, 112, 115, 230

New Hampshire Provincial Congress, 100

New Jersey, 31, 178, 297, 302, 306, 308, 316, 431–34, 432, 453, 551–52, 560. *See also* Princeton; Trenton; *and other specific battles and locations*

British pushed out of, 530–54

Grant as British commander in, 496

rapes and killings in, 497–99

Washington's retreat into, 463, *484,* 485–99, 517

New Jersey Assembly, 488

New Jersey militia, 320, 432, 499

Newport, Rhode Island, 505

Newton, Sir Isaac, 28

Newtown, Pennsylvania, 492, *515,* 517, 527

Newtown Creek, *353,* 389, *391*

New York, 8, 15, 40, 58, 86, 90, 127, 134–35, 142, 144, 163, 178, 180, 245, 297–321, 348–79, 416, 553. *See also* Long Island; Ticonderoga; Westchester County *and other specific battles and locations*

British fleet sent to, 180, 256

British plan for thrust from Canada into, 180, 279, 295–96

loyalists in, 311–12

news of Concord reaches, 80

violence vs. loyalists in, 310–16

New York (American gundalow), 419–20

New York Bay, 304

Lower, *298,* 300, 317–18, 352, *353,* 362

Upper, *298,* 300, 316, 319, 351, *353,* 362, 380, 382, 436

New York City, 178, 236, 297–305, 312–13. *See also* Brooklyn; Harlem Heights; Kips' Bay; Long Island; Manhattan; Staten Island; *and other specific battles and locations*

British Navy arrives in, 316–21

British prisons for POWs in, 508–10

burning of, *391*, 397–401
fortification of, 299–300, 351–52
Declaration of Independence and, 348–51
Dunmore flees to, 346–47
maps of, *298*, *303*
Howe's winter quarters in, 76–77, 505–10
Lee and, 332
statue of George III in, 349–50
Washington and defense of, 270–71, 297–321
Washington evacuates, 387–93, 432
New York Committee of Safety, 145, 435–36
New York Convention, 309, 355
New York Dutch, 145–46
New York Gazette, 357
New York militia, 195, 196, 209
New York Provincial Congress, 150, 310, 312
New York regiments, 348
Nicholson, Clement, 111
Noddle's Island, 87–88, *218*, 234
Norfolk, Virginia, 185–88, *187*, 190–93, 327, 344
North, Lord Frederick, 16, 18–25, 30, 40, 50–51, 80–81, 88, 115, 134, 165–66, 170–73, 176, 178–79, 214, 243–44, 330–31, 343, 355, 481, 559, 562
North American Theater, *32*
North Bridge, Battle of, *65*, 66–70, 78, 81
North Carolina, 178, 180, 243–56, *249*, 279, 324, 346
North Carolina militia, *249*, 251–53
Northern Army. *See also* Canadian invasion
composition of, 145
desertion and, 277
discipline problems and, 145, 150–51, 277
frictions in, 411–12
Lake Champlain and, 409–11
Montgomery leads, 146–50
Montreal and, 150–51
Quebec and, 155, 162–63, 276, 278–82
reinforcements and, 145, 147
Schuyler leads, 145–47
shortages of food and supplies and, 145, 147–48, 163, 276–78, 284–89, 296, 409–13
smallpox and, 198–200, 212, 223, 233, 276, 278, 284–85, 289, 291–92, 295
St. Johns and, 147–50
Sullivan leads retreat of, 285–88
Ticonderoga and, 302, 411–12, 429, 502
Northumberland, Duke of, 72
Nova Scotia, 90, 143, 226, 312, 317, 467, 468

Odes (Horace), 30
Old North Church (Christ Church, Boston), 58–59, 76, 113

Old South Meeting House (Boston), 36–39, 44, 48, 219, 268
Olive Branch Petition, 165
Oliver, Peter, 111, 125, 264, 266
Olney, Stephen, 122, 531, 538, 542
Orlov, Aleksey Grigoryevich, 512
Orpheus (British warship), 225–26, 306, 390
Osborn, George, 443
Osgood, Rev. David, 115
O'Shaughnessy, Andrew Jackson, 176
Otter (British warship), 185–86, 189, 191, 194, 346
Ovid, 555
Oxford (British transport ship), 318
Oxford Magazine, 168

Pacific (British ship), 264, 266
Paine, Thomas, 486–88, 519, 561
Pallas (British ship), 133
Palliser, Sir Hugh, 246
Palmer, Abigail, 497
Paris, *464*
Aitken mission to, 556
Franklin mission to, 470–71, 479
Paris, Treaty of (1763), 6, 8, 473
Parker, Hyde, 434–436
Parker, John, *56*, 60–63, 71
Parker, Jonas, 63
Parker, Sir Peter, 180, 244, 246–48, 256, 374, 505
Sullivan's Island and, *322*, 324–26, 334–43
Parkhurst, Noah, 69
Parsons, Lawrence, 67, 69, 71
Parsons, Samuel Holden, 387, 392, 564
Parsons, Thomas, 564
Patten, John, 294
Patten, Matthew, 294
Patterson, James, 454
Paulus Hook (*later* Jersey City), *298*, 300, 351, *391*, 436
Pausch, Georg, 428
Peale, Charles Willson, 493–94, 496, 546–47, 549, 552
portrait of Washington, 301–2
Pearl (British warship), 393, 398, *449*, 453, 455, 457
Peckham, Howard H., 562
Peebles, John, 447, 498, 506
Peggy (warship), 281–82
Pelham, Henry, 85
Pellew, Edward (*later* Viscount Exmouth), 418–19
Pell's Point, *430*, 440–43, 559
Pennsylvania, 169, 307–8
loyalists in, 312
Washington's retreat into, 491–92, 530

Pennsylvania Committee of Safety, 306

Pennsylvania Evening Post, 253, 497

Pennsylvania Hospital, 500

Pennsylvania Magazine, 486

Pennsylvania militias, 80, 285, 286, 365,
    368–70, 372, 520, 531–32

Pennsylvania Packet (American ship), 31, 275

Pennsylvania riflemen, 132, 157, 159, 196, 204,
    210, 357, 362, 537

Percy, Hugh Earl, 65, 72–76, 79, 81, 96, 134,
    220, 260–61, *353*, 367–68, 379, 447, *449*,
    454, 456–57, 560

Peter II, Czar of Russia, 199

Peter III, Czar of Russia, 512

Peters, Lois, 124, 234, 552

Peters, Nathan, 124, 234, 552

Philadelphia, 9, 58, 86, 226, 306, 492, 494,
    499–500
  Congress flees, 499–500
  Continental Congress convenes in, 15, 42, 84
  defense of, 454, 500–501, 530
  Franklin and, 28, 31
  news of Concord reaches, 80, 83
  Washington visits, in June 1776, 301–2,
    305–6

Philadelphia Council of Safety, 552

Philadelphia Light Horse, 533–34, 541

Philadelphia militia, 545

Philadelphia (American gundalow), 419–20

Philip's Mill, *535*, 539, 540

Phillips, Mary, 497

Phillips, William, 426

Phoenix (British warship), 300, 313, 318, 351,
    353, 355, 359–62, 389, 434–35

Pickering, Timothy, 47

Piel, Jakob, 512, 523, 526

Pierce, John, 158–59, 161–62, 198, 210

Pierce, Mary, 112

Pigot (British hospital ship), 247

Pigot, Robert, *91*, 101–2, 105–8

Pitcairn, John, 47–48, *56*, 61–63, 67, 71, 73, 106, 113

Pitt, Fort, 200

Plains of Abraham, 133, 161, 196–97, *201*, 202,
    207, 282

Plutarch's Lives, 235

Pocahontas, 182

Point au Fer, *404*, 423

Point Au Roche, *404*, 417

Pointe-aux-Trembles, 154–55, 162, 195, 272

Pointe-Levy, *140*, 161, *201*, 272, 281

Poland, 331

Polly (American sloop), 359–60

Polybius, 214

Pomeroy, Seth, 564

Pompadour, Madame de, 472

Pontiac's War, 89

Poor Richard's Almanac (Franklin), 28, 479, 483

Pope, Alexander, 450

Porter, Elisha, 283

Portsmouth, England, 1–3, 6–8, 10–12, 555–57

Portugal, 12, 331, 482, 503

Posey, Thomas, 346

Presbyterians, 46, 158, 448

Prescott, Richard, 154

Prescott, William, *91*, 94–96, 99–100, 103,
    106–9, 113

Preston, Charles, 141–42, 148–50

Preston (British warship), 87, *91*, 98

Priestley, Joseph, 27, 29

Prince, Christopher, 351

Prince of Piedmont (British ship), 334

Princess Royal (British warship), 10–11

Princeton, *484*, 488, 490–92, 494–95, 497,
    512–14, 516, 526
  Battle of, 533–34, *535*, 541–51, 553

Princeton College, 157

Pringle, Thomas, *404*, 417–21

prison ships, 510

privateers and pirates, 139, 219, 227–28, 468–69,
    480, 555

"Proclamation of Rebellion" (August 1775), 165

Prohibitory Act (1775), 179–80

Prospect Hill, 128, *218*, 229, 234, 239, 258, 261

Protestantism, 4, 15, 144, 145

Providence, Rhode Island, 79, 506

Prussia, 8

Puritans, 57, 87

Putnam, Israel "Old Put"
  Boston siege and, 116, 120–21, *218*, 221, 234,
    261, 267–68, 270
  Bunker Hill and, *91*, 94, 99, 109, 113
  Diana raid and, 88–90
  Forts Lee and Washington and, 451, 455–56
  Kip's Bay and Harlem Heights and, *391*,
    392–93
  Long Island and, *353*, 364–65, 370, 378–79
  Nancy taken by, 227
  New York and, 309, 319, 388–89
  Philadelphia and, 500
  submarine *Turtle* and, 382
  Trenton, First, and, 527

Putnam, Rufus, 238, 258–59, 379

Quakers, 80, 311, 448, 450, 500, 506

Quebec, 6, 35, 90, 135, 142–44, 177, 244, 427
  Seven Years War and, 24, 60, 101, 111, 133,
    143, 361

Quebec Act (1775), 15, 143, 153

Quebec City, 180, 195–215, *201*
  Arnold's route to, *140*, 154–62

Battle of, *201*, 200–215, 226, 231, 286, 294–95, 302
capture of 1759, 152
Carleton returns to, 427
Northern Army marches on, *140*, 146–52, 161–63
retreat from, *272*, 273–84
Royal Navy dispatched to, 279–80, 282–83
smallpox and, 199–200, 212
Quebec Gazette, 427
Queen Charlotte (British ship), 383
Quero (American schooner), 80
Quiberon Bay, 383, *464*, 469

Rainbow (British warship), 378
Rall, Johann Gottlieb, 512–14, *515*, 523–26, 528, 530, 537–40, 551
Ranger (British warship), 322, 324
Rankin, Hugh F., 252
Raritan River, *484*, 486, 490, 495, 503, 551
Rattlesnake Hill (Mount Independence), *404*, 409, 414, 424–25
Rawdon, Francis Lord, 222, 342, 363, 389, 498
Rawlings, Moses, *449*, 457
Rebellion Road, 322, 339
Récollet, 151–52, *201*, 202, 204, 207
Red Hook, *298*, 300, 314, *353*, 366, 374–75
Reed, Esther, 387, 389, 395, 397, 452
Reed, Joseph
    Cambridge and, 299
    Fort Washington and, 452–53
    New Jersey and, 463, 486, 493, 516–17, 530–31, 533, 541
    New York and, 356, 375, 387, 389, 395–97, 399
    Westchester County and, 438, 444
    Washington and, 230, 232–33, 237, 239, 268, 270–71, 488–89
Renown (British warship), 393
Reprisal (American warship), *464*, 465–67, 469
Repulse (British warship), 393
Revenge (British schooner), 422
Revere, Paul, 13, *56*, 58–59, 64, 79
Revolutionary War
    begun at Concord, 76–80
    British debate over, 165–79, 181
    consequences of, 25–27
    costs of, 273–74
    Franklin on eve of, 27–30
    myths of, 26–27, 80, 113, 144–45
    unique character of, 26–27
Reynolds, Joshua, 182, 382
Rhode Island, 42, 80, 84, 86, 142–43, 178, 258, 309–10, 436

British control of, 505–6, 560
    rape and pilfering in, 498
Rhode Island Assembly, 450
Rhode Island militias, 43, 230
Richard III (Shakespeare), 508
Richards, Samuel, 396
Richardson, Addison, 454–55
Richelieu, Cardinal, 135
Richelieu River, *140*, 141–42, 146, 148, 152, 162, *272*, 283, 284, 288–91, *404*, 406, 408, 415
Richmond, Duke of, 169
Richmond, Jonathan Tavern, 534
Richmond (steamboat), 214
Rittenhouse, David, 493
Robbins, Ammi R., 284, 410
Robertson, Archibald, 539, 551
Rodney, Thomas, 520, 529, 546
Roebuck (British warship), 346–47, *353*, 366, 374, 378, 389, 434–35, 500
Rogers, Molly, 419
Rogers, Robert, 401
Rogers, Thomas, 419
Rolf, John, 182
Rome, ancient, 254, 557
Rosbrugh, John, 538
Rose (British warship), 318, 351, *353*, 355, 359–61, 389
Rose and Crown, *298*, 352, 355
Rossini, Gioachino, 473
Rousseau (British transport ship), 288
Rousseau, Jean-Jacques, 331
Rowe, John, 265
Roxbury, 76, 78, 83–84, 90, 92, 96, 98, 113, 116, 123, 222, 229, 232, 257–61, 266–67
    Knox's guns and, 236–38
Royal Gazette (London), 169
Royal Savage (British warship), sinking of, 142
Royal Savage (American warship), *404*, 414, 418, 420
"Rules by Which a Great Empire May Be Reduced" (Franklin), 29
Rush, Benjamin, 342, 460, 465, 486, 501, 504, 516, 529, 533–34, 540, 544–45, 550
Russell, Jason, 74–75
Russia, 172, 254, 482, 512
Russian mercenaries, 90, 171
Rutledge, Edward, 186, 385–86
Rutledge, John, 333–34, 340

Salem, 40, 42, 44, 46
Salem militia, 65
Salisbury Iron Works, 414
salt, 126, 191, 308
saltpeter, 127–28, 275, 307, 476

Sam (prize ship), 499

Sandwich, John Montagu, 4th Earl of, 137, 228, 246–47, 383, 556, 559, 561

Sandy Hook, *298*, 300, 317, 352

Sartigan, *140*, 160

Savannah, 79, 178, 244, 350

Savannah Pacquet (American powder raider), 306

Saw Mill Road, *535*, 542–43, 548

Sayre, Stephen, 164

Scarborough (British warship), 133

Schama, Simon, 185

Schank, John, 408–9

Schecter, Barnet, 375

School of Good Manners, 57

Schuyler, Philip
  Arnold and, 215, 276, 413
  background of, 145–46
  Canadian invasion and, *140*, 144–48, 150–51, 156, 162, 195–96, 204–5, 213, 276–77, 288–89, 293
  Gates and, 411–12
  Lake Champlain and, 409–10, 411, 414, 423, 424
  Washington and, 230, 553

Schuyler's Island, *404*, 421

Scorpion (British warship), 248, *249*, 253

Scotland, 7, 9, 175

Scots Magazine, 214

Scott, Charles, 538–39, 546–47

Scott, William "Long Bill," 458

scurvy, 134, 136, 191, 223, 343, 356, 443

Sea Venture (British transport ship), 260

Secret Memoirs of a Prostitute, 472

Selby, John E., 193

Senter, Isaac, 159–60, 200, 207–8, 211, 283

Serle, Ambrose, 362–63, 372, 387, 389–90, 394, 434, 443, 560

Seven Years' War, 1, 5–6, 8–9, 11, 20, 24, 26, 143, 175, 199, 331, 354, 382–83, 472–73, 481. *See also* French and Indian War

Sewall Point, *218*, 267–68

Sexton, Jared, 497

Shakespeare, William, 4, 330

Shark (British warship), 466

Shaw, Samuel, 234, 448, 462

Shawnee Indians, 182

Shelburne, Earl of, 29

Shewkirk, Ewald, 378, 398

shipbuilding
  American, 9–10, 136, 296, 352, 408, 413–14, 467, 517–18
  British, 10–11, 136, 166, 179–80, 246–47, 407–9, 561
  France and Spain and, 561

Shuldham, Molyneux, 180, 224–26, 262, 265–66

Shy, John, 231

Sibella (British storeship), 247

Sill, Francis Bushill, 115

Simsbury copper mine, 311

Simsbury Iron Works, 46

Skenesborough, *404*, 413–14, 423

slaves and slavery, 323
  British free, to fight rebels, 180–81, 183–86, 188, 193–94, 329, 344, 346
  Continental Army and, 231
  Declaration of Independence and, 349–50
  Franklin and, 28
  fugitive, 319, 350, 507
  lead mining and, 308
  Massachusetts and, 45, 77, 233
  New York and, 299, 397
  Paine and, 486
  population of, 184, 244, 329
  revolts, 10, 40, 38–29, 180–81, 184, 328–29
  Rush and, 516
  West Indies and, 7
  whites shun labor done by, 333
  Washington and, 118, 231

slave trade, 184, 306, 328–29

smallpox, 37, 45, 116, 198–200, 212, 223, 233, 276, 278, 284–85, 289, 291–92, 295, 344, 410, 500
  inoculation for, 45, 199–200, 223, 233, 284–85, 316

Smallwood, William, 394, 447

Smith, Adam, 13, 561

Smith, Francis, 54, *56*, 61, 63–64, *65*, 67, 69–74

Smith, John, 444–46

Smith, Justin Harvey, 295

Smith, Simeon, 132

Smith, William (judge), 311

Smith, William S. (Major), 438

Smollett, Tobias, 16, 168

smugglers, 12, 87–88, 127, 156–57, 306–8, 467

Society for Promoting Theatrical Amusements (Howe's Strolling Players), 220

Solebay (British ship), 322, 337

Somerset (British warship), 52, 58, *65*, 75, 87–89, *91*, 97–98

Sorel
  capture of, *140*, 152–54
  retreat from, 272, 283, 285, 287–90

South Carolina, 163, 178, 186, 244, 255, 322, 326, 342–43, 346, 560
  Cherokee raids and, 344
  loyalists in, 311, 324
  slave revolts and, 328–29

South Carolina militia, 328–29, 339, 342

Southern Department, created by Congress, 329–32

southern expedition, British, 171, 177–78, 180–81, 255–56, 324–28, 343–47, 352. *See also specific battles and locations*

Sovereign (British ship), 324, 326, 442

Spain, 1, 6, 8–9, 14, 20, 172–73, 306, 475, 480–82, 561

Spencer, Georgiana, 168

Spencer, Joseph, 445

Spenlove, Roger, 111

Sphinx (British warship), 322, 324, 339

Spitfire (British warship), 91, 95, 98, 138

Spitfire (American gundalow), 421

Split Rock, 404, 421–22

Spuyten Duyvil Creek, 298, 359, 376, 391, 430, 449, 454, 456–57, 461

Spy, (British transport ship), 260

Stamford Mercury, 170

Stamp Act (1765), 8, 14, 301

Stark, John, 91, 100, 103, 109, 113, 523

Staten Island, 298, 304, 316, 319–20, 351–52, 354, 360–64, 367, 431, 442

Staten Island Conference, 384–88

St. Augustine, 346

St. Charles River, 196, 198, 201

St. Clair, Arthur, 428, 514, 517, 525, 541

St. Denis, 272, 290

Steele, Archibald, 210

St. Eustatius, 223, 306

Stewart, Jahiel, 421

Stiles, Rev. Ezra, 80

Stirling, William Alexander, Lord, 531
   Forts Lee and Washington and, 449
   Long Island and, 353, 365, 369–71, 384
   New Jersey retreat and, 491–92
   Trenton, First, and, 514, 517, 519, 525, 527

St. Johns, Fort
   Lake Champlain and, 404, 405, 407–9, 427–28
   retreat from Canada and, 272, 273, 283, 288–92, 294
   siege of, 140, 141–42, 144, 146–51, 153, 156, 162, 414

St. Lawrence (British ship), 322, 324

St. Lawrence River, 140, 146, 148, 150, 152, 154–55, 157, 161–62, 180, 195, 200–203, 201, 209, 272, 273, 279–81, 286, 290, 406

St. Malo, Battle of, 175

St. Michael's Church (Charleston), 322, 323–24

St. Michael's Church (Trenton), 515, 523–24

Stockbridge Indians, 413

Stockton, Richard, 516, 534

Stockton Hollow, Battle of, 535, 537

Stono Uprising, 328

Stony Brook, 535, 536, 543, 547–49

Stormont, David Murray, Lord, 470, 477–78, 481

Stow, Olive Jones, 66–67

St. Paul's Chapel (New York), 214, 297, 301, 303, 394, 398–99

St. Roch, 196, 201, 207

Stryker, William S., 495

Stuart, Charles, 319, 498, 560

submarine warfare, first attempt in the *Turtle*, 380–82, 391

Success (British transport ship), 260

Sukey (British warship), 81

Sullivan, Fort, 322, 328, 333–34, 336–37, 339–42

Sullivan, John
   Adm. Howe and, 384–85
   background of, 285
   Boston and, 127, 230, 260–61, 268, 271
   Canadian retreat and, 272, 285–90, 293–95, 364
   Long Island and, 353, 363–66, 368–70
   New Jersey and, 501–2, 504
   Princeton and, 530, 535, 541–43, 546–47
   taken prisoner, 369
   Trenton, First, and, 515, 517, 521–23, 525

Sullivan's Island, Battle of, 322 325–29, 333–44, 361, 374, 438, 441–42

Sumter, Fort, 328, 339

Surprize (British ship), 280, 282

Swift, Jonathan, 450

Symmetry (British warship), 91, 95, 98, 107

Syren (British warship), 246, 322, 339

Tallmadge, Benjamin, 377–78, 488

Tappan Zee, 352, 430, 434–35

Tarleton, Banastre, 503–4

Tarrant, Sarah, 44

Tartar (British warship), 434–35

taxes, 8–9, 12, 38, 119, 169, 173

Taylor, Alan, 183

tea, 9, 12, 306

Tea Act (1773), 12–13

Tennent, Susanna, 424

Tennent, William, 424

Thacher, James, 266, 428

Thetis (British victualler), 248

Thirty Years' War, 135

Thomas, Hannah, 280

Thomas, John (Ensign), 359–60

Thomas, John (General), 259, 272, 278, 280–85, 563

Thompson, William, 233, 272, 286–88

Thomson, William, 322, 328, 333, 335–39

"Thoughts for Conducting the War from the Side of Canada" (Burgoyne), 427

Thucydides, 330
Thunder (British bomb ketch), 247, *322*, 337
Thunderer (British gunboat), *404*, 407, 417–18, 420, 425
Ticonderoga, Fort (*formerly* Fort Carillon), 39
  Allen and Arnold capture, 84–85, 129, 144, 154, 156–57, 508
  Canada invasion and, *140*, 145–47, 195
  Canadian retreat and, *272*, 283, 289, 293–94, 302
  Knox and artillery from, *218*, 234–37, 276, 300, 518
  Lake Champlain and, *404*, 405–7, 409–17, 423–25, 427–29, 502, 560
  Washington and, 302
Ticonic Falls, *140*, 158–59
Tilghman, Tench, 392, 396, 431–32, 435, 438, 448, 450
tobacco, 182–183
Tofts, Mary, 16
Tolman, John, 77
Tom Jones (Fielding), 235
Tom Thumb (Fielding), 508
Town and Country, 170
Townshend Acts (1767), 8–9, 12, 14
trade, 8, 15, 43, 171–72, 179–80, 226, 305–6, 308
Tragedy of Zara, The (Voltaire), 220
Travis, Edward, *187*, 189
Trenton, *484*, 491–92, 494–95, 497
  First Battle of, 511–32, *515*
  Second Battle of, 533–40, *535*, 549–51, 553, 560
Trevelyan, George Otto, 170, 563
Trinity Church, *303*, 351, 399, 505, 509
Tristram Shandy (Sterne), 235, 450
Trois-Rivières, 154, *272*, 286–88, 290, 423, 428
Trumbull, Benjamin, 390
Trumbull, John, 123, 266–67, 294, 504
Trumbull, Jonathan, 320
Trumbull, Joseph, 126
Trumbull (American ship), 420–22, 425
Tryon, Lady, 398
Tryon, William, 178, 300–301, 314, 317, 319, 394, 399–400
Tucker's Mill Point, *187*, 193, 344–45
Tudor, William, 83, 113, 130, 299, 314, 434, 518
Tupper, Benjamin, 125
Turks Islands, 308
Turtle (American submersible), 380–82, *391*, 435
Turtle Bay, 398, *430*, 437
Turtle Gut Inlet, 306, 466
Tuttle, Timothy, 424
typhoid, 358

typhus (camp fever), 193–94, 232, 345, 358, 432, 500, 519

Unity (British victualler), 226
U.S. Supreme Court, 188, 312

*Valcour Island, *404*, 415–19, 421, 425–26
Valiant (British warship), 10
Van Cortlandt's penitentiary, 509
Van Doren, Carl, 316
Van Horne, Isaac, 458
Varennes, *272*, 290
Vassall House, 119, 121, 123, 126–29, 132, 228, 232, 237, 239, 257, 270–71
Vaughan, Robert, 49
Vealtown, New Jersey, *484*, 502
Vechte house, *353*, 371
venereal disease, 276
Venus (British transport ship), 260
Verchères, *272*, 290
Vergennes, Charles Gravier, comte de, 473–78, 480–82
Versailles, 466, 470, 472, 476, 479–82, 561
Vesuvius (British gunboat), 407
Victory (British warship), 7
Virginia, 119, 163, 177–93, *187*, 226, 243–44, 255, 308, 346, 190–93, 327, 344
  Cherokee raids and, 344
  Dunmore's escape and, 344–45
  Dunmore's fight vs. rebels in, 184–86, 193
  gunpowder cruises from, 306
  Lee and, 332
  tobacco exports, 182–83
Virginia Convention, 183, 192–93
Virginia Gazette, 183–84, 186, 193, 213, 342, 350
Virginia House of Burgesses, 183
Virginia militias, 43, 118, 192–93, 345
Virginia riflemen, 132, 157, *187*, 188, 191, 193–94, 395, 457, 537, 538
Virgin Islands, 306
Voltaire, 5, 26, 220, 235, 329, 473, 486
Vose, Joseph, 295
voting rights, 9

Wallabout Bay, *298*, 300, *353*, 375, 510
Waller, John, 108
Walpole, Horace, 21, 25, 80, 96, 115, 133, 167–68, 172–74, 220, 267, 343, 383, 470
Ward, Artemas, 79, 92–94, 96, 100, 107, 109, 113, 116, 120, 133, 237–38
Ward, Christopher, 104
Ward, Samuel, Jr., 162
Warner, Jemima, 159
Warren, James, 113, 130, 139, 229–30, 259, 468
Warren, John, 268–69

Warren, Joseph, 36–39, 42, 44, 46, 53, 57–58,
  80, 84, 95–96, 107–8, 114
Warren (American galley), 492
Washington, Fort, *298,* 359, 388, *391,* 394, 398,
  430, 434, 439
  British capture of, *449,* 451–60, 462, 487,
    502, 510, 512, 559, 563
Washington, George, 116, 183
  Adm. Howe's overtures and, 384, 386
  appearance of, 116–17, 301–2
  appointed commander of Continental
    Army, 116, 118
  army condition and, in early 1777, 563
  army discipline and supply problems and,
    305, 307–9, 432–33, 439, 448, 489–90
  army munitions shortages and, 230, 232, 258
  army training and, in Cambridge, 116–17,
    119–28, 131–33, 230–34, 237–38
  Arnold and, 296, 413, 428
  Arnold's drive to Quebec and, 156–58,
    160–61, 196, 212–13
  autocratic powers and, 529
  background and personality of, 117–19, 121,
    123–24
  Boston entered by, 267–71
  Boston evacuated by British and, 257–59,
    261–62, 563
  Boston siege and, *218,* 228–32, 238–40
  Brooklyn evacuated by, 376–79
  Canadian invasion and, 144–46, 156–57,
    274, 276–77, 282, 285–88, 293, 302, 304
  Charleston and, 340, 342
  Church spying and, 128–31
  colonial governors and, 121
  Congress and, 121–22, 124, 126–27
  Congress and, in New York, 358, 378–79
  Congress and, letters intercepted, 452
  Congress and, Philadelphia visit by, 302,
    305–6
  daughter and, 170
  Declaration of Independence and, 348–51
  Delaware River crossing and, 491–94, *515,*
    517–21, 527
  deserters and, 348, 387
  Dunmore's attempt to free slaves and, 186
  entourage of, 304
  Falmouth burning and, 139
  finances and, 118–19, 230, 532
  Forts Lee and Washington and, 451–57,
    459–63, 563
  French war and, 193
  Greene and, 450–51, 453
  Hale and, 400–402
  Hancock and, 120, 124, 126, 132, 230, 233,
    239, 271, 285, 301–2, 305, 320, 358, 363, 365,

  373, 377–79, 388, 397, 433, 438–39, 448,
    454, 488, 490–94, 518, 524, 527–28, 531,
    548, 553
  Harvard honorary degree and, 270
  Hessian POWS and, 527–28
  Hickey plot vs., in New York, 314–16
  Hudson fireship attack and, 359–60
  Kip's Bay and Harlem Heights and, *391,*
    392–97
  Knox's artillery in Cambridge and, 236–39
  Lake Champlain and, *404,* 410–13
  leadership style of, 121–22, 531–32, 553–54,
    563–64
  Lee and, 330–32, 340, 342
  Lee capture and, 501–2, 504–5
  Lee's criticisms of, 460, 488–89, 502
  Little Brewster Island raid and, 125
  Long Island and, *354,* 363–66, 371–73,
    375–79, 432, 563
  loyalist arrests and, 310, 315–16
  marriage to Martha Custis, 118–19, 228–29
  Massachusetts Bay squadron and, 228
  Montgomery and, 213
  Morris mansion headquarters and, 431–33
  New Jersey retreat and, *484,* 488–93
  New Jersey successes of, 560
  New Jersey winter quarters and, 530–33,
    535, 550–53
  New York army amassed and trained by,
    346, 357–58
  New York arrival by, from Boston, 270–71,
    301–5, 309–10, 315
  New York arrival of Royal Fleet and, 317,
    319–21, 332, 355–57, 359
  New York burning and, 398–400
  New York campaign losses and, 462–63
  New York evacuation and, 387–88, 397, 432
  New York headquarters of, *298,* 302–4
  Paine and, 487
  Peale portraits of, 301–2, 493
  Philadelphia defense and, 499–500
  as political general, 121–22
  Princeton and, *535,* 541–43, 545–48, 550
  Quebec City and, 162–63
  Reed and, 230, 232–33, 237, 239, 268, 270–71,
    488–89
  reports of rape by Hessians and, 497
  Schuyler and, 145–46, 230, 411–12
  smallpox and, 199
  spies and, 432, 533
  spring 1777 preparations and, 562
  standing army urged by, 433
  Stirling and, 369
  strategic and tactical skills of, 121–22, 320
  Sullivan and, 285, 364

Washington, George (*cont'd*)
   telescope and, 355
   Trenton, First, and, 514–29, *515*
   Trenton, Second, and, 533–34, *535*, 537–41
   Turtle submersible and, 381
   Westchester County and, *430*, 431, 434–42,
     444–48
Washington, John (George's brother), 119,
   268, 304–5, 432, 459–60, 516–17
Washington, Lund (George's cousin and
   overseer), 124, 432, 505, 516
Washington, Martha Dandridge Custis
   "Patsy," 118–19, 228–29, 304, 316, 544
Washington, William, 524
Washington (American ship), 420–23, 428
Waterbury, David, Jr., 417
Watertown Committee on Wood, 232
Watson's Corner, *65*, 75, 78
Wayne, Anthony, 286–87, 295, 409, 411, 429
Wealth of Nations, The (Smith), 13–14
Webb, Samuel Blachley, 107–8, 315, 317, 495
Welch, William, 315
Wentworth, John, 178, 267
Wesley, John, 81, 165
West, Benjamin, 493, 558
Westchester County
   Battle for, *430*, 433–48, 487
   rape and plunder in, 498
West Indies, 6–7, 40, 48, 127, 136, 149, 157, 184,
   193, 223–25, 306, 308, 382, 397, 469, 474,
   480
Wheeler, Abner, 66
Whitby (British transport ship), 510
White, Ammi, 69
White, Joseph, 539
White, Mary, 502–3
Whitehall Slip, *303*, 398
Whitehead, William, 559
White Plains, *430*, 439, 442, 444–48, 453, 462,
   478, 495, 512, 528, 559
Whittemore, Samuel, 77

Wickes, Lambert, 466–67, 469
Wiederholdt, Andreas, 511, 522–23, 528
Wild, Ebenezer, 158–59
Wilkes, John, Lord Mayor, 169, 171
Wilkinson, James, 291, 412, 503–4, 542, 545,
   548
Willcox, William B., 254
William Henry, Fort, 142
Williams, Otho Holland, 509
Williamsburg, Virginia, 178, 183
Williamson, Andrew, 344
Wilmington, North Carolina, *249*
Wilson, Isaac, 46
Winthrop, Hannah, 75–76
Wiswall, Rev. John, 85
Woburn Militia, *65*, 78
Wolfe, James, 152, 197–98, 203, 206, 214, 279,
   407
Wolfe's Cove, *140*, 161, *201*, 209
women's rights, 486, 516
Wood, Gordon S., 38
Wood Creek, *404*, 413
Woodford, William, *187*, 188–91
Wooster, David, 211, 213, 272, 274, 277, 281,
   285
Worth's Mill, *535*, 543
Wraxall, Nathaniel, 558
Wren, Christopher, 18
Wright, James, 178, 324
Wright, Peggie, 442

Yale College, 83, 139
"Yankee Doodle," 73, 113, 271
Yarbury, Samuel, 338
Yates, Bartholomew, 545
yellow fever, 323
Yonkers, *298*, 359, 461
Young, Lieutenant, 446
Young, Sgt. William, 526

Zabriskie, Peter, 455, 461–62

About the Author

RICK ATKINSON is the bestselling author of the Liberation Trilogy—*An Army at Dawn*, *The Day of Battle*, and *The Guns at Last Light*—as well as *The Long Gray Line* and other books. His many awards include Pulitzer Prizes for history and journalism. A former staff writer and senior editor at *The Washington Post*, he lives in Washington, D.C.

The British Empire
1775

ARCTIC OCEAN

PACIFIC OCEAN

LABRADOR SEA

NORTH AMERICA

HUDSON BAY

RUPERT'S LAND

QUEBEC

LOUISIANA

INDIAN LANDS

THE THIRTEEN AMERICAN COLONIES

N.Y.

N.H.

MASS.

NOVA SCOTIA

NEWFOUNDLAND

PENN.

VA.

R.I.

CONN.

N.J.

DEL.

MD.

N.C.

S.C.

GA.

W. FL.

E. FL.

GULF OF MEXICO

BERMUDA

BAHAMAS

ATLANTIC

BELIZE

SANTO DOMINGO (FR.)

JAMAICA

MOSQUITO COAST

CARIBBEAN SEA

PACIFIC OCEAN

VIRGIN ISLANDS

ST. EUSTATIUS (DUTCH)

ANGUILLA

BARBUDA

ST. CHRISTOPHER

NEVIS

ANTIGUA

MONTSERRAT

DOMINICA

ST. VINCENT

GRENADA

BARBADOS

TOBAGO

SOUTH AMERICA

Map by Gene Thorp